The German
Churches
under Hitler

The German Churches under Hitler

BACKGROUND, STRUGGLE, AND EPILOGUE

Ernst Christian Helmreich
Bowdoin College

Wayne State University Press
Detroit, 1979

Library of Congress Cataloging in Publication Data

Helmreich, Ernst Christian.
   The German churches under Hitler.

   Bibliography: p.
   Includes index.
   1.   Church and state in Germany—20th century.
2.   Germany—Church history—20th century.   I.   Title.
BR856.H443   261.7′0943   78-17737
ISBN 0-8143-1603-4

To my wife, Louise Roberts Helmreich,
and to our sons, Paul Christian Helmreich
and Jonathan Ernst Helmreich,
both now professors of history

Contents

STRUGGLE

Preface

As the only institutions which did not succumb to Hitler's policy of regimentation (*Gleichschaltung*) the churches during the National Socialist period well deserve careful study and evaluation. Each author writes a book in his own fashion, and some would no doubt organize their volumes differently, or choose to emphasize different themes. To start my account in 1933 when Hitler came to power, or with only a few pages of introduction, seemed to me unwise. To understand "the Church Struggle" (*Kirchenkampf*) one must know something about the history of the German churches. How were they organized and administered in previous periods, how were they financed, what had been the relationship of the churches to the state in the past, and how have these relations changed? What were the major steps in the growth of self-government of the churches? What was the history of church particularism and cooperation before the attempts to reorder church affairs under national socialism? How was the German school system organized, and how did Hitler interfere with the relationship of the churches to the schools? What was the religious pattern of Germany, how did it come about, and what was the basic climate of opinion in regard to religion in twentieth-century Germany? What have been the effects of a gradual but steadily increasing secularization of German society in modern times? These questions and many others seem to require answers if one is to understand the history of the churches under Hitler.

The obvious starting point for such a background history was the Reformation, when the unity of German church life was broken. The complexity of German religious life that developed over the succeeding centuries meant that a narrow approach would not serve. The two great divisions of German Christianity, particularly in their relations to the state, cannot be entirely separated. Yet both the Catholic and the Protestant churches have their own peculiar problems, concerns, and history which should not be blurred by treating them simultaneously. Therefore I decided to deal with them in separate chapters covering definite and easily recognized periods. Although attention is centered on the large Protestant Land churches and the Catholic church, Germany is a country of wide religious diversity. There are numerous Free churches and sects, usually neglected entirely by historians or mentioned in only a few fleeting paragraphs. They are, however, also participants in the interaction of church and state in Germany, and they have gradually obtained greater standing and acceptance. Here they are given recognition by brief references to their history under the Empire and the Weimar Republic, by two chapters devoted to their fate under the Nazis, and by some mention of their present status.

This book is meant to be a contribution to the history of the churches in Germany, particularly in the era of Hitler. It is an attempt to decipher just what went on in German churches during the Kirchenkampf of those years, what actions were taken, for what reasons, and with what effect on the churches themselves. The focus of the study has made it necessary to treat some subjects only in passing. Thus, for example, reference inevitably had to be made to Judaism, but no attempt has been made here to write a history of the Jews or of anti-Semitism in Germany, or of the final terrible events of the Holocaust. This has already been done many times, although there are no doubt new insights and factual data still to be revealed. This book also does not aim to be a history of German theology, although that subject is necessarily touched upon here and there.

Just as it seemed essential to present sufficient background material to the Church Struggle of the Nazi era, so it also seemed advisable to recount the reconstruction of the churches in the postwar period. Some analysis of postwar church institutions and activities is needed to round out and complete the history of the churches under Hitler, for both the churches and the state were affected by the events of the Church Struggle. Whether they have profited by those experiences are matters of present opinion and of future development.

To write a book of this scope necessitates relying on the help of others. In the introductory chapters I have relied considerably on secondary accounts, although here too I have used some primary sources. Throughout I have attempted to use the best monographic literature, and the chapters on the Hitler era, as the footnotes attest, are largely based on primary sources. It seems that I have read countless rolls of microfilms of captured German documents from the National Archives of the United States. I know full well that I have not read all of them, but trust I have not missed many truly important ones. There is some duplication between these films and material found in other archives and document collections, but they contain a massive amount of detail; the Gestapo films especially give ample evidence of what busybodies the police were.

I should especially like to thank Professor Klaus Obermayer of the University of Erlangen for putting at my disposal the excellent library of the Institut für Kirchenrecht und Öffentliches Recht. He was most helpful in my days in Erlangen in 1964, 1968, and 1971, provided me with comfortable places to work, and through his thoughtfulness made life pleasant for my wife and myself. Thanks too should be expressed to Miss Lisa Herziger of the Library of the Westphalian Church in Bielefeld. In this library also are located the Archiv der Evangelischen Kirche in Westfalen and the rich collection of material gathered by the Reverend

Wilhelm Niemöller on the Kirchenkampf. For his and his wife's gracious
reception of wandering scholars I am most appreciative. I also desire to express my thanks to the staffs of the Landeskirchliches Archiv Nürnberg, the Archiv für die Geschichte des Kirchenkampfes an der Kirchlichen Hochschule Berlin-Zehlendorf, the Institut für Zeitgeschichte in Munich, and the Bundesarchiv in Koblenz. I am grateful to Bowdoin College for sabbatical leaves and financial aid, and to its helpful librarians. There are many others, including those who granted me interviews and those who assisted me primarily when I was writing *Religious Education in German Schools* who should be mentioned, but to do so would carry me beyond the realm of practicality. Yet there are three persons whom I must single out for special thanks. Leroy D. Cross, my long-time friend, has again undertaken the typing, having learned with the years to find his way through my longhand copy with its many emendations and insertions. Dr. Sherwyn T. Carr of the Wayne State University Press has edited the volume for publication and has been most helpful and cooperative. My wife, Louise Roberts Helmreich, has not only shared in the pleasure of trips to Europe for research, but has carefully read and helped edit the manuscript. We have shared in the work that has gone into the writing of this volume, and to her I wish to make special acknowledgment of my love and gratitude.

BACKGROUND

The Protestant
Churches
before 1918

The Establishment of State Control

The history of the relationship of the churches and the state in Germany can begin no later than the sixteenth century. The Reformation not only brought great doctrinal changes, but necessitated new methods of church government. When the rights and powers which the bishops had exercised were no longer recognized in the regions which had broken away from the mother church, it became necessary to establish some new authority to carry out at least some of the functions which the bishops had performed. Urged by Luther, the elector of Saxony in 1527 created commissions made up of one ecclesiastic and one layman to conduct a church visitation. Just what the conditions were in the churches had to be determined, and political functions, notably matters relating to marriage and inheritance which had previously been adjudicated in the ecclesiastical courts, had to be provided for. These commissions appointed clergymen as superintendents in the various districts and this office of superintendent may be considered the authority of first instance in the early provisional Protestant church governments.[1]

Consistories
By 1539 a body had been established in Wittenberg which performed duties similar to those undertaken by the consistories that advised and aided the pope or bishops in Catholic church government. The Wittenberg consistory was primarily an ecclesiastical court, while the consistory which was established in Württemberg (1553) had little to do with judicial affairs. The latter was primarily an administrative agency and an instrument of church government.[2]

The Agreement of Passau (1552) and the Peace of Augsburg (1555) suspended the church government of the pre-Reformation bishops in Protestant territories, but did not state who should take over their powers. Actually it was the princes of the various territories who assumed these duties. The princes exercised their powers through consistories, which, following the pattern established in Württemberg and Saxony, were regularly composed of lay and ecclesiastical persons, so as to include men of competence in both state and church affairs. These bodies in turn appointed superintendents to supervise affairs on lower administrative levels and to carry out visitations to the parishes. The competence of these consistories varied according to the state. In some states they remained primarily judicial bodies, administrative duties being vested in other governmental bureaus; in others they became the chief instruments of church administration. The Prussian legal code of 1794 dealt with the matter of competence by stating:

> Among the Protestants the rights and duties of bishops in church matters are as a rule accorded to the consistories.
> The extent of their duties is determined by consistorial and church ordinances, according to the fundamental laws of the various provinces and departments.
> Certain Protestant consistories are under the direction of the proper departments of the state ministry.
> Without the previous knowledge and consent of the consistories no changes in church matters can be undertaken; much less can new church ordinances be adopted.[3]

The consistories always remained state agencies dependent on the government and not on the churches. On the other hand, since important churchmen were always appointed to the consistories, it cannot be said that the church was entirely lay or governmentally controlled and that the church as such had nothing to say in its administration. Very often the consistories protected the rights of the church against the prince.[4] Church and state were not separated; rather secular and ecclesiastical governmental officials cooperated in administering the church. The state through its appointing power, its control over the purse strings, and its power of enacting laws was, however, the dominant power. The Protestant churches sacrificed some of their independence to the state, but without the aid of the princes and ties with the territorial state, it is doubtful if they could have maintained themselves in the struggles of the Counter-Reformation period.

In the Lutheran church, development of church government on the congregational level never took place in this period. In the Reformed congregations, thanks to their inheritance from Zwingli and especially from Calvin, congregational governments with presbyters were established.[5] In some regions, as in the Lower Rhine territory and East Friesia, synods were formed and essentially self-governing free churches were established. However, in many states (Palatinate, Hanau, Anhalt, and Lippe, for example), while congregational presbyters existed, the Reformed churches also came under the control and guidance of the princes.

Summus Episcopus

In actual practice the Protestant princes at the time of the Reformation stepped in when a vacuum was created by the disappearance of the power and authority formerly exercised by church officials. This practice was furthered by the seizure of monastic and other church lands, as it was natural for the prince to consider himself the legal successor of former abbots or bishops. In the early seventeenth century a theoretical justification was elaborated for the position that the prince had assumed in the government of the churches. Johann and Mathew Stephani, writing in the early 1600s, maintained that the prince was the legal successor to the powers of the bishop, powers which the Agreement of Passau and the Peace of Augsburg had cancelled in Protestant lands. The Peace of Westphalia (1648) also provided for the cancellation of the powers of bishops in Protestant territories. The head of the government was the logical heir to these powers; he was not only prince but chief bishop—*summus episcopus*. None of these treaties, however, actually stated who should take over the power of Catholic bishops, and later writers easily demolished the theoretical qualification of the prince as the supreme head of the church. Yet the title and the position of the prince as head of the Protestant Land church (*Landeskirche*) prevailed until the revolution of 1918.[6]

When, during the period of the Napoleonic wars, Catholic princes were granted Protestant lands, they did not hesitate to exercise their rights as summi episcopi of the Protestant churches. In Saxony and Bavaria, where a Catholic dynasty ruled over many Protestant subjects, the king regularly exercised his rights of church government through agencies staffed by Protestants. The rights of the prince stemming from his position as summus episcopus were usually considered personal powers, and legislative bodies had no share in their exercise unless the measures involved the constitution and the state laws. The question of countersignature was not uniformly regulated. In Prussia, for example, the acts of the king as summus episcopus required no signature by a minister in the old provinces, but the countersignature of a minister was required in the new provinces annexed in 1866.

Among the powers accruing to the prince as head of the church were those involving the organization or administration of the church, such as issuing church ordinances, granting privileges and exemptions, establishing church districts, creating church governmental bodies, appointing officials (in many cases even the clergy of a parish), providing for church visitations, exercising authority in disciplinary matters, establishing church holidays, and even, in some cases, determining the norms of worship. The circumscription of his powers was not always easily drawn, but in general he was not supposed to determine matters of faith and doctrine.[7]

Patronage

There was one practice of the medieval church which continued in both the Protestant and Catholic churches after the Reformation, and has not been completely ended to this very day.[8] As far back as the middle of the fifth century, patrons who built a church or granted it lands were awarded certain rights over that church, including the receipt of some church revenues. At first this privilege of patronage was accorded to bishops, but it soon was extended to lay persons. The practice became anchored in canon law, and rights accruing to feudal lords were in due time also permitted to the governing authorities of cities. Patronage rights and duties underwent historical changes. Along with the original donation of land or building of the church, the obligation to keep it in repair was generally recognized. The patron not only came to have the right to name and the obligation to support the priest—to "grant the living," as the phrase goes in English—but he was accorded certain honorific rights, such as to be named in prayers in the church, to have masses said when he or a member of his family died, to be buried within the church or in special graves in the church cemetery, and to occupy certain choice pews. In a country where graves are normally reused every twenty to thirty years, the possibility of lying undisturbed while awaiting Judgment Day no doubt was an honorific right which had its appeal.

Over the centuries these rights and obligations not only were inherited, but became attached to certain lands and territories. Thus the princes finally accumulated many such "livings," although the rights, and particularly the obligations, varied greatly from one section of Germany to another. As the state took over more obligations and control from the churches, it usually permitted old private *Patronate* to remain, for they relieved the state as well as the churches of financial obligations. In fact the state was more concerned with getting the patron to live up to his obligations than with relieving him of his privileges. The rights which the patrons had over appointments no doubt did serve as a conservative influence on the church. In practice there was usually a friendly and close cooperation between the patrons and church authorities; disputes usually involved the money to be paid by the patron for the repairs and upkeep of the parish buildings. Yet the institution of patronage was basically inconsistent with the growing demands of both the Protestant and Catholic church authorities to regulate their own affairs.

Corpus Evangelicorum

At the same time that the Protestant princes were establishing control and administration over the churches in their lands, they were taking steps to protect themselves against attacks by Catholic powers, primarily Emperor Charles V. Their formation of the Torgau League (1526) and of the Schmalkaldic League (1531) led to indecisive armed conflict. They also began to meet as a group during sessions of the Reichstag in order to agree on a common policy for the protection of their interests. The Catholic princes, who could still command a majority in the curia of the Reichstag, wanted all business done in the full meeting, and resisted the Protestant innovation, although they too soon followed suit. The emperor, anxious to obtain the consent of both factions for his special tax levy against the Turks, undertook to mediate between the two groups. He recognized the existence of the Protestants by appointing equal numbers from each confession to various commissions. When Lutheranism received official recognition in the Peace of Augsburg, the problem of building Protestantism into the constitutional structure of the empire became more acute. Gradually the Protestants became a tacitly recognized entity—a *corpus,* as it was called—at meetings of the Reichstag. The Catholic estates, although they long resisted being designated a corpus, nevertheless also held their separate deliberations.

The negotiation of the Peace of Westphalia strengthened this procedure, and the peace treaty provided in rather unspecific terms (Article 52) that when religious matters were being considered in the Reichstag they should not be decided by majority vote but by negotiation between the two confessional groups. The Protestants sought to give a broad interpretation to what constituted religious matters, while the Catholics wanted "religion" restricted to theological and dogmatic questions. Actually the two groups often met separately to determine what stand they would take on all sorts of questions, and each tended to vote as a bloc in the curia meetings. Emperor Charles VI (1711–40) tried unsuccessfully to withdraw the right of Protestants to separate corporative deliberations, but from about 1725 on, the existence of a *Corpus Catholicorum* and a *Corpus Evangelicorum* was universally recognized as part of the constitutional machinery of the empire. The former was under the leadership of the archbishop of Mainz, and the latter under the directorship of the elector of Saxony, who, oddly enough, continued to exercise this office even after the Saxon dynasty converted to Catholicism in 1698.[9]

The two corpora were beset by many divisions—the Protestants by the basic Lutheran-Reformed split, and by the imperial friendship and wavering leadership of the elector of Saxony, and the Catholics by the antagonism between Austria and Bavaria and by the necessity for the emperor to mediate at times between the two confessional parties. The great ecclesiastical princes also often followed diverging policies. Moreover, Protestants and Catholics often had interests which cut across confessional lines, a fact which weakened their respective united fronts, but also smoothed the way for agreement when it came to negotiation as confessional groups.

As a matter of practice the Reichstag continued to meet in three curias—electors, princes, and cities—and also met as two curias—the Corpus Catholicorum and the Corpus Evangelicorum. The existence of a body which spoke with a united voice was very important for German Protestants, although less so for Catholics, who could always look to either the pope or the emperor. The two corpora no doubt contributed to the weakening and eventual disintegration of the empire. On the other hand, they contributed to religious freedom and made it possible for adherents of different confessions to live side by side in a common political association. The disappearance of the Corpus Evangelicorum with the dissolution of the empire in 1806 left the Protestants with no united voice in Germany. Remedying this situation was one of the incentives which led to the formation of the German Evangelical Church Conference (*Deutsche evangelische Kirchenkonferenz*) in 1852.[10]

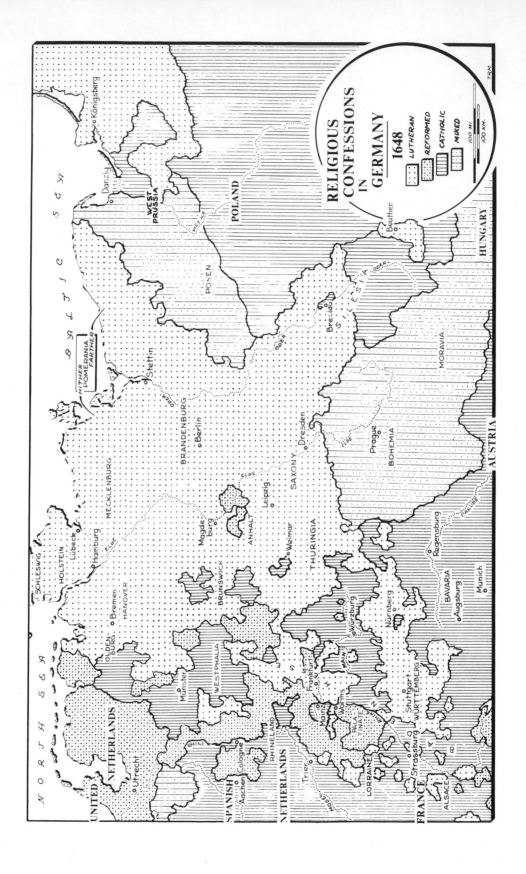

RELIGIOUS CONFESSIONS IN GERMANY 1648

LUTHERAN
REFORMED
CATHOLIC
MIXED

100 MI.
100 KM.

NORTH SEA

BALTIC SEA

UNITED NETHERLANDS

SPANISH NETHERLANDS

NETHERLANDS

FRANCE

LORRAINE

ALSACE

SCHLESWIG

HOLSTEIN

MECKLENBURG

Lübeck

Hamburg

Bremen

HANOVER

OLDEN-BURG

Utrecht

Münster

WESTPHALIA

RHINELAND

Aachen

Cologne

Trier

Mainz

Worms

Frankfurt

PALA-TINATE

Strassburg

WÜRTTEMBERG

Stuttgart

Nürnberg

Würzburg

BAVARIA

Augsburg

Munich

Regensburg

DANUBE

AUSTRIA

HUNGARY

MORAVIA

BOHEMIA

Prague

SILESIA

Breslau

Beuthen

POLAND

POSEN

WEST PRUSSIA

Danzig

Königsberg

VISTULA

ODER

HITHER POMERANIA

FARTHER

Stettin

BRANDENBURG

Berlin

ELBE

Magde-burg

ANHALT

Leipzig

Dresden

SAXONY

Weimar

THURINGIA

BRUNSWICK

ELBE

MAIN

RHINE

MOS.

TRM

This joint government of state and church, along with acceptance of the principle in the Peace of Westphalia (carried over from the Peace of Augsburg) that the prince was to determine the religion of his land, created literally hundreds of Protestant territorial church bodies in seventeenth and eighteenth-century Germany. Doctrinally they were not very different, being either Lutheran or Reformed, yet variations did exist in church practices, in what books were used, what hymns were commonly sung, and what melodies were used, as well as in many other minor matters. The upheaval brought by the French Revolution and Napoleonic period wiped out many of these small states; the German Confederation established in 1815 numbered only thirty-nine states as compared to the three hundred which existed in the days of the Holy Roman Empire. But this territorial consolidation did not mean that there were only thirty-nine Land churches. Rather, when a prince acquired new territories he usually retained, at least for a time, the old territorial church bodies, as for example, the king of Prussia did when he annexed new provinces in 1866. Thus a Lutheran or Reformed prince who previously had one Land church, when he acquired new territories inhabited by subjects of the other Protestant confession, would then have two, a Lutheran and a Reformed Land church. He might also have acquired a significant number of Catholic subjects and henceforth would have a Catholic church within his realm as well.

The Peace of Westphalia had made a gingerly advance toward personal religious toleration. It had provided that if a Lutheran prince should change to Reformed, or vice versa, he could not coerce his subjects to change their religion. This provision also held if a territory was transferred to a prince of the other Protestant confession. The principle of *cuius regio, eius religio* was further restricted in the treaty by the provision that minorities which had peacefully followed their religious cult before 1624 should be tolerated in the future. A subject who, after the conclusion of peace, shifted his religious affiliation from that of his prince could either be tolerated or forced to emigrate, but he was not subject to confiscation of property. Under the treaty a person who was exiled had five years to liquidate his property if he had been of the other religion in 1624, or three years if he changed his religion after the publication of the peace treaties. The treaty also provided that neither Catholic nor Protestant citizens should be discriminated against, but all should have equal opportunities in such matters as guilds, hospitals, and inheritance, and equal right of burial in cemeteries. The Austrian hereditary lands and a part of Silesia, however, were excluded from the Peace of Westphalia, and in these areas the Protestants continued to be restricted.[11]

Nonetheless, the concept of religious toleration continued to gain ground, and Article 16 of the constitution of the German Confederation stated that all adherents of the Christian confessions (meaning Catholic,

Lutheran, and Reformed) in all member states would have equal civil and political rights. The day of the exclusively confessional state in Germany had ended; the day of the religiously neutral state was at hand.[12]

The pietist movement had always tended to stress the practices and beliefs which were common to both Lutheran and Reformed, and to concentrate on the most essential aspects of religious faith. This influence in favor of church unity was strongly supported by another quite different movement, the skepticism, toleration, and rationalism of the Enlightenment. The spirit of nationalism and brotherhood, kindled in the liberation of Germany from the Napoleonic yoke, also worked to this end. Soldiers who fought side by side at Waterloo did not ask who was Catholic, Lutheran, or Reformed. Yet the years following the Napoleonic era brought a general renewal of religious feeling, a movement of awakening (*Erweckungsbewegung*) which stressed a new orthodoxy and conservatism in religion in opposition to the rationalism and liberalism of the Enlightenment.[13] These developments within the churches as well as the need for the governments to reorganize their administration led to four significant movements in the nineteenth century: (1) the unification of the Lutheran and Reformed churches into a United Land church (*Unierte Landeskirche*), primarily in Prussia; (2) the rise of the Free churches and other minor church bodies; (3) the growth of the synodical organizations and their relationship to the church bodies; and (4) the growth of coöperation among the Land churches.

Formation of the United Church

The celebration in 1817 of the three hundredth anniversary of the start of the Reformation served as an impetus to church union. The duke of Nassau had emerged from the Napoleonic settlement ruling over both Reformed and Lutheran territories. On August 5, 1817, he called thirty-eight clergymen representing both denominations to a synod at Idstein. They decided that the differences between the churches had become so much less marked that the two confessions might well join together and form one Evangelical Christian church. There was little opposition to the union, although later a few Lutherans separated themselves from this Land church. But while Nassau was the first, it was Prussia which was most interested in bringing about church union.

The Hohenzollern rulers of Prussia had been Reformed since 1613, although the majority of their subjects were Lutheran. Brandenburg, the very center of their territories, was the first German Land in which both Protestant bodies had equal rights, a tolerance dating from the early seventeenth century. The Great Elector Frederick William, Frederick I, and Frederick William I had all shown their interest in uniting the two confessions, but that was as far as they were able to go. There were actually three consistories in Prussia in the eighteenth century: one for the French Reformed congregations, one for the German Reformed, and one for the Lutheran. In 1808, as a result of the reorganization following Napoleon's victory at Jena, the consistories were abolished and their duties given over to the Ministry of the Interior. This meant that the central supervision of all Protestants was conducted by one authority without special consideration of confessions. This administrative union did not last, and in 1815 the separate consistories were reestablished.[14]

It was Frederick William III (1797–1840) who finally showed some initiative in the matter of unifying the Protestant churches. It seemed senseless that he, as Reformed, and his wife, who came from Mecklenburg and was Lutheran, could not receive the Lord's Supper together.[15] He was also anxious to see church union accomplished for political reasons, as he considered it would be a tie binding his Lutheran eastern provinces with the primarily Reformed provinces along the Rhine. In a memorable declaration of September 27, 1817, he expressed his conviction that the two confessions were one in the basic Christian concepts, and differed only in externals. He called for a union of the two churches, not that the Reformed were to become Lutheran, or the Lutheran were to become Reformed, but rather that they should grow into a new quickened Evangelical Christian church. Personally he no doubt would have liked to have seen a doctrinal unification, a so-called *Consensunion*.[16] Although he issued no decrees or orders, he nevertheless set the example and urged others to follow it by declaring that he would celebrate the Reformation Festival in a united Reformed and Lutheran service at Potsdam. On October 31, the Lord's Supper was celebrated there in a ritual which combined Lutheran and Reformed usages. Common participation in the breaking of bread at the Table of the Lord and a common church government in external matters were to become the hallmarks of the union. Many congregations, especially in the western parts of the monarchy, followed the king's example.

The movement spread to other lands as well. United churches— some merely administrative unions, others with considerable doctrinal uniformity—were established in the Grand Duchy of Hesse (1817–22), in the Bavarian Palatinate and sections of Electoral Hesse (1818), in the Grand Duchy of Baden (1821), and in the principalities of Waldeck (1821), Bernburg (1820), and Dessau (1827). An unsuccessful attempt was made to bring about a union in the Bavarian territories right of the Rhine, although as a result of the negotiations the Protestant church in this section of Bavaria did receive a new constitution which introduced presbyters and synods.

The situation in Prussia was confused in the years following 1817. Some congregations considered themselves Lutheran, some Reformed, and others United. The government appointed men to consistories without reference to their confessions, and in this casual way a measure of unity was achieved. But there was little conformity in church services, for, under the influence of the Enlightenment, pastors for years had ordered their services to their own liking. But Frederick William III loved uniformity and system, and was devoted to old church practices. As early as 1798 he had issued a cabinet order expressing the desirability of having a common Lutheran and Evangelical service book. He now took a personal hand in drawing up such an order of service. Completed at Christmas, 1821, it was adopted for services in the army and at the Berlin cathedral the following year. The king hoped to get it adopted by all congregations of their own free will, and thus achieve a uniform service in the Prussian Land church. However, the pressure to use the new service book aroused a storm of controversy which was termed the "service book quarrel" (*Agendestreit*). Not only was there opposition from theologians to the new book's content and ritual practice, but legalists also raised their voices in protest. Did the king have any right to interfere in matters relating to church doctrine and liturgy? In fact, did he have any rights over the church at all? By May, 1825, out of 7,782 churches in Prussia, 5,243 were using the new service book.[17] The following July the churches were given an alternative. A church could either use the new service book or follow without alteration one that had been approved previously by the authorities and had been used in that particular congregation. Compromise was under way, and with the approval of the king, provisional service books were issued which in parallel formularies took into consideration local customs and practices.

Controversy, however, did not cease, and secessionist movements threatened to make headway. In an effort to forestall them, the king in 1834 issued an explanatory cabinet order.

> The Union does not intend or mean the surrender of a previous confession of belief, and the authority which the confessional statements of the two confessions have hitherto had is not annulled. Through joining the Union, only the spirit of moderation and humility is expressed, which no longer permits the differences in certain teachings of the other confession to furnish an excuse to refuse external church ties. Joining the Union is a matter of free decision, and it is therefore wrong to believe that it is necessary to accept the new service book to join the Union, or that acceptance of the service book means indirectly joining the Union.[18]

Frederick William IV (1840–61) on his accession confirmed the policy expressed in the cabinet order of his predecessor. In 1852 he expressly declared that he was of the opinion that Frederick William III, in inaugurating the union of the churches, never wanted to bring about the change of one confession to the other or to bring about a third confession.

The result of this policy of compromise was (and still is) that in the United church there were congregations which retained their original Reformed or Lutheran character, and there were others in which these confessional differences were merged into a common Evangelical Protestantism.[19] The Prussian government itself treated the churches as united, and the United church was the official Land church of the old provinces. When new territories were added following the successful war of 1866, the Land churches of these new provinces, thanks to Bismarck's wisdom and moderation, were retained, and were treated as separate church bodies by the Prussian government. They were placed directly under the Ministry of Church Affairs and were not subject to the Supreme Church Council (*Oberkirchenrat*), the highest administrative authority of the United church.

While according to the Prussian king the acceptance of the new church union was to be a voluntary matter, in the hands of his bureaucracy it was treated as a governmental order and pressure was actually brought on ministers and congregations to accept it. The three hundredth anniversary of the Confession of Augsburg, June 25, 1830, was considered a proper occasion to push forward the final acceptance of the United church. Cabinet orders of April 4 and 30, 1830, proposed that the anniversary be celebrated by a common celebration of the Lord's Supper by Lutherans and Reformed, and that the Union ritual of the Breaking of Bread be used.

The general superintendent of Silesia, where the Union was not generally accepted, instructed all the clergy under his supervision to celebrate the anniversary by using the common ritual of the United church. Johann Gottfried Scheibel, pastor at Saint Elizabeth's Lutheran Church in Breslau, had long opposed the Union and the new service book. He now protested vigorously, and in a written communication to the king said that for reasons of conscience he could not use the new ritual. The royal reply was curt: "there could be no talk of reasons of conscience; it was his duty as a subject to obey the ordinances of the king."[20] The pastor's plea that members of his congregation should be spared this coercion was also rejected. He undertook to print a protest, whereupon the church superintendent suspended him from his pastorate. A good number of the congregation, including important professors at the university, rallied around the pastor and proclaimed that they would remain true to the faith of their fathers. They formed a congregation and begged the king for legal recognition.

The movement spread and other congregations seceded. Government authorities steadily refused to recognize these churches, suspended and imprisoned their ministers, refused to recognize their ministerial acts, and even used the police and military against them. In 1834 the congregation in Hönigern refused to surrender their church to authorities when their pastor was suspended because he would not use the new service book. For over three months the congregation held the authorities at bay by assembling before the church building. Then on the morning of December 24, 1834, 400 infantry, 50 cuirassiers, and 50 hussars cleared the square before the church and forced open the doors. The church was freed for ministers of the United church to conduct Christmas services, but the congregation remained away.

This incident aroused attention throughout Germany; it caused the crown prince of Prussia tremendous concern. The events of 1834 had led the government to issue the conciliatory statements on the matter of using the new service book. But the government officially refused to recognize the so-called Old Lutheran groups, lest it reflect on the Lutheranism of the many members of the United church. The seceding congregations, however, went their way and soon established ties with like-minded congregations throughout the Prussian kingdom. On September 15, 1841, a general synod, after careful deliberations, drew up a church constitution for this conservative group, known as the Evangelical Lutheran Free Church in Prussia (*Evangelisch-lutherische Freikirche in Preussen*), which continued to serve these congregations through succeeding decades. This was a landmark, for it constituted the first attempt at a synodical constitution of a Lutheran church in Germany. It provided for a supreme church board made up of clerical and lay representatives, and for a general synod representing the congregations which was to meet every four years. The king in 1845 by a general concession granted recognition to these congregations and granted them rights of incorporation. The ministerial acts of their ministers (baptism, marriages, etc.) were now recognized, but they received no financial aid from the state. They were to have their own independent government apart from the regular ecclesiastical authorities. Their meeting places, however, were not accorded the name *Kirche,* a distinction the Old Lutherans sought unsuccessfully to acquire right down to 1918.[21]

The Old Lutheran secessionist movement had established a church body which by 1860 numbered 55,000 members, with congregations scattered throughout the kingdom, and with strongholds in Silesia and Pomerania. But it had even more significance, since in the period when the conflict was most acute a large number of the more stalwart confessionalists emigrated to Australia, where they were instrumental in founding the Australian Lutheran church. Another group, under the leadership of Johann Andreas August Grabau, went to America (1839), and there eventually founded the Buffalo Synod. Emigration was in the air at this time. In the previous year a group of devout Lutherans had left Saxony for the New World, and these eventually formed the strong Missouri Synod. It was this latter body which lent support to a Lutheran group which seceded from the Land church of Saxony in 1871. The example of the Old Lutherans in Prussia was followed in other German states, notably in Hesse, Hanover, Baden, and Hermannsburg-Homburg, where recognized Lutheran Free churches were established. Elsewhere isolated congregations separated themselves from the established churches and struck up ties with the Free church Lutherans in other states. Small Evangelical Reformed Free churches of somewhat different historical background also existed; the Confederation of Reformed Congregations of Lower Saxony, and the Old Reformed church in the province of Hanover.

The religious complexity of Germany, which continues to this day, was thus increased rather than lessened by the attempts at church unity of the early nineteenth century. There were established Lutheran, Reformed, and United Land churches, and of course the Catholic church, all of which were regularly considered public corporations in all states and had special privileges which were not granted to other religious bodies.[22] There were also the Old Lutheran and Old Reformed churches which were usually classed as "Free churches" (*Freikirchen*). Jewish synagogues were regularly tolerated and had corporation status in all states.

In addition to these bodies, there were other small groups scattered about Germany which were usually recognized only as "religious associations" (*Vereine*), although some had the status of public corporations. Among these were the Mennonites and Moravian Brethren, dating back to the sixteenth century, and the Herrnhuter, a small group which, under the influence of pietism, arose in the eighteenth century as an offshoot of the Moravian Brotherhood. Count Nikolaus Ludwig von Zinzendorf (1700–1760) was the guiding spirit of this latter group, which established itself at Herrnhut in Saxony.

The nineteenth century saw a marked increase in sectarianism in Germany; many of these churches were the result of contacts with groups in the United States. Among them were the Baptists and Methodists (1830s), the Swedenborgians (1848), the Irvingians (1848), and the Evangelical Association (*Albrechtsleute*) (1850).[23] In 1840 the church authorities in Prussia took disciplinary action against Pastor Wilhelm F. Sintenis of Magdeburg who had maintained in a newspaper article that prayer to Christ was superstition. A group of rationalists rallied to the support of Sintenis and founded the Association of Protestant Friends, also known as the Friends of Light (*Lichtfreunde*). They formed congregations outside of the established church and were at times subject to excessive police regulations. In 1859 they joined with a small secessionist Catholic group (*Deutschkatholiken*) to form the League of Free Religious Congregations (*Bund freier religiöser Gemeinden*), comprising 53 congregations in 1859, 155 in 1874, and 50 in 1913, with 35,000 members.[24] There were still other smaller groups, such as the Templars, who advocated a return to the Holy Land and established settlements in Palestine (1868),[25] the Plymouth Brethren (Darbyists), Adventists, Nazarenes, the Salvation Army, Christian Scientists, Mormons, and Jehovah's Witnesses (1897).[26]

Regulation and practices varied among the states, but while the Free churches and the sects did not enjoy all the rights and privileges of the Land churches or of the Catholic church, they nevertheless were not persecuted. Their ministerial acts were usually recognized by the state, and they had freedom of worship within their meeting places. They might not always be permitted to use a bell or conduct public processions, restrictions which were prevalent in Prussia, but they had the essential freedoms of propagandizing their faith and making converts. Children from Free church and sectarian families normally attended the Protestant religious classes in the public schools.

The establishment of the Free churches and sects was a product of the liberalism of the nineteenth century, of the renewed interest in religion, and of greater contacts with churches in foreign countries, particularly in the United States and Great Britain. It was also an expression of the growth of the conception of a religiously neutral state which found its roots in the ideas of the Enlightenment. In response to this concept, but also under pressure from church leaders, the state authorities began to share church administration and government with bodies elected by the churches themselves. Everywhere in Germany synodical organizations were established which were associated with the old consistorial bodies, giving rise to a unique synodical-consistorial form of church government.

The Synods and Interchurch Cooperation

Presbyters and synods had always played a more important role in the Reformed than in the Lutheran churches. In Lutheran areas synods were not unknown, but where they existed they were meetings of the clergy and never achieved any power against the governmentally constituted administrative bodies. For many years some church leaders, particularly under pietist influence, sought to quicken the moribund and stodgy Lutheran church government by introducing presbyterial forms at the congregational level. However, no significant progress was made. The changes brought by the Napoleonic upheaval gave impetus to this program of regenerating the administration of the Land churches by the introduction of synodical institutions. It was essential to bring about the participation of individual church members not only in the affairs of the local congregations, but also in the higher echelons of church government.

In 1807 Friedrich Schleiermacher, then the most influential clergyman in Berlin, proposed a new governmental order for the Protestant church in Prussia which would give the church more independence from the state.[27] The latter was to concern itself only with property questions and strictly external matters, leaving the regulation of internal church affairs to the churches. Congregations were to receive presbyters, and synods were to be created to take over general church government. At this time Schleiermacher envisaged synods made up only of clergy, but by 1817 he was advocating synods with both clerical and lay representatives. Yet the attempt in that year to organize synods as part of the governmental structure of the new United church of Prussia met with no success.

Bavaria, however, in 1818 introduced synods of clergy in the Palatinate as well as in its territories right of the Rhine, to which lay delegates were added in 1848. Baden established synods in 1821. After years of difficulties a new church governmental order was adopted in 1835 for the Rhineland-Westphalian districts in Prussia. It was a combination of the old presbyter-synodical order of the Reformed church and the consistorial bodies of the Prussian church government. It became an important precedent in the elaboration of later church constitutions. Frederick William IV came to the throne imbued with a desire to vitalize the Prussian church. In 1846 he called a general synod of notables, but no progress was made. The new Prussian constitution of 1850 provided that the churches of the realm should order their own affairs. It was not, however, until 1873–76 that synodical organizations were established for the United church in the old provinces. Meanwhile synods were established in Württemberg (1854), in Hanover (1864), and in Saxony (1868). Subsequently synodical organizations were inaugurated in the churches of most other states and by World War I had become regular features of church government throughout Germany, except in Mecklenburg and in some smaller Thuringian states.[28]

The synods were always made up of both clerical and lay delegates, elected to the circle synods by the elected governing boards of the local congregations. These local circle synods then elected representatives to the provincial and Land synods. In addition the ruler of the Land usually appointed some delegates to the higher synodical bodies, and there were also delegates from theological faculties of the universities where such existed. The synods always existed alongside the consistorial or other church administrative establishments of the governments. They were meant to be organizations to coordinate and help regulate church affairs, and their competence varied slightly from Land to Land. Their approval was usually required for new church laws, and they also had a part in the administration of church funds. They gradually gained in influence, and exercise by the prince of his rights as summus episcopus increasingly became dependent on the cooperation of the synods. On the other hand, they never became independent institutions of church self-government, for up to 1918 there was no inclination on the part of the civil authorities to remove their controlling hands completely from the church. In makeup and power the German synods were quite different from the synods of Calvin's Switzerland, Knox's Scotland, or of many of the churches in America.

The synods met infrequently—the general synods every four, five, or six years—and were usually dominated by the religious festivities of the occasion rather than by administrative and governmental duties. It was the executive bodies elected by these synods which worked hand in hand with the government authorities in regulating the affairs of the church. Thus in the old provinces of Prussia the administration of the United churches was in the hands of the Evangelical Supreme Church Council (*Evangelischer Oberkirchenrat*), consisting of a president, vice-president, and ten members—some lay, some clerical. These were appointed by the head of the government and were considered members of the civil service. In addition the seven members of the executive body of the Land synod were also special members of the Supreme Church Council and at times were called in to deliberate with that body. Once a year the expanded council met with another eighteen-member board elected by the Land synod, and known as the General Synodical Council (*General-Synodal-Rat*). Here the governmental officials together with the synodical representatives discussed church problems and decided on guiding principles of government and administration. The Land synod also sent representatives to the governmental board that had charge of church educational institutions and seminars.[29]

Interchurch Societies

While the churches were gradually winning a share in the administration of their affairs, they also took steps towards cooperation among themselves. The Land churches naturally concentrated on affairs within their own territories and were not particularly concerned with missions. The German states were not colonial powers, and this incentive to enter the foreign mission field also was lacking. Yet at the very heart of Christianity is the sharing of one another's burden and the preaching of the gospel. Societies were formed to undertake this work which found their support in the church membership at large and in organizations established in individual church congregations. These societies cut across Land church boundaries, for they were as a rule independent of any particular church regime. Nevertheless, the relations between the societies and various church governments were friendly, and in many cases special Sunday collections were authorized to help out the societies.

The foundation of mission societies in all countries dates from the nineteenth century, and there were many such societies formed in Germany.[30] The first of these was the Basel Mission Society, which started as a school for missions in 1815 and relied on German and Swiss support. Other important German organizations were the Leipzig Society (1819), the Berlin Israel Mission (1822), the Berlin Society (1824), the Rhenish Society (1828), the North German Society (1836), and the Berlin Mission for East Africa (1886). The *Gustav-Adolf-Verein* (1832, reorganized 1842), concerned with caring for German Protestants in the diaspora, drew wide support. Yet many of the more orthodox Lutherans did not like this organization, which embraced Lutheran, Reformed, and United Churches, and these formed their own societies, called *Gotteskasten* (1853; since 1922, *Martin-Luther-Bund*), for the care of Lutherans in the diaspora.[31]

Just as organized societies to carry on missions abroad were a development of the nineteenth century, so also were special organizations to carry on various social services at home. The name "inner missions" (*Innere Mission*) was popularized, if not coined, by Johann Hinrich Wichern (1808–81).[32] In 1833, he founded the Rauhe Haus, an institution for wayward children of the city of Hamburg. In 1848, at the Wittenberg Protestant Assembly (*Kirchentag*), Wichern was able to win support for the concept of home missions and from 1849 on there were yearly meetings of the Congress for Inner Missions and of the Central Committee for Inner Missions of the German Evangelical Church. These latter organizations brought together and helped unify the various independent societies devoted to social welfare. More narrowly Lutheran, Pastor Wilhelm Löhe in 1849 founded at Neuendettelsau in Bavaria the Organization for Inner and Foreign Missions in the Spirit of the Lutheran Church. This was combined with a training school for missionaries to Indians and the scattered settlers of the western United States. Following the example of Theodor Fliedner in Kaiserswerth, Löhe also established a hospital and training school for deaconesses.[33] The foundations at Neuendettelsau have maintained themselves as flourishing institutions to this day. Friedrich von Bodelschwingh (1831–1910), another outstanding leader in home mission work, in 1872 undertook the organization of the Bethel Institutions (near Bielefeld) for the care of epileptics.

He also established various workers' colonies where derelicts and tramps might be rehabilitated.[34]

In addition to the organizations for foreign and home missions, there were many other organizations which tended to bring Protestants of various Land churches together. Among the oldest of such organizations were the Bible societies, the Württemberg society dating back to 1812, and the Prussian and Saxon societies to 1814. In the later nineteenth century members of the Community Movement (*Gemeinschaftsbewegung*) were active in the Bible Societies. This movement was an evangelistic effort stemming from pietism, and was influenced by Moody's gospel work in the United States, which was brought to Germany principally by Pearsall Smith. The many groups which were formed—often among students or members of certain professions—stressed conversion, personal holiness, and greater fellowship within the church. They were devoted above all to home missions. In 1888 some of the most influential leaders of the Community Movement met in conference at Pentecost in Gnadau near Magdeburg (*Gnadauer Pfingstkonferenz*). Later conferences, at first biennial, soon became annual affairs. The German Committee for Evangelical Community Care and Evangelization (*Deutsches Komitee für evangelische Gemeinschaftsplege und Evangelisation*), usually referred to as the *Gnadauer Verband*, was formed as a result of the 1894 conference. It was to become a loose central organization (which exists today) for the hundreds of small groups and federations which sprang up in the various Land churches. As one of the early leaders of the movement stated: "In the church, if possible with the church, but not under the church." This meant that the various organizations of the Community Movement were free groups—often organized and supported by pastors—but not under the orders of the various church governments. Fundamentalistic in theology, the members of the movement did strive to put new life into the staid and austere Land churches, an effort which was not always welcomed by the church authorities.[35]

Somewhat akin to the Community Movement was the Evangelical Alliance (*Evangelische Allianz*). It was originated by Thomas Chalmers, who in 1846 called a meeting in London of representatives of several churches. His immediate purpose was to found an organization to counter rising Roman Catholic influence, manifest in England in the Oxford Movement and in Germany in the Cologne Church Conflict (*Kölner Kirchenstreit*) with all its repercussions.[36] The unity and common interests of Evangelical Christians were stressed. The alliance aimed at bringing believing individuals, not churches, together. Representatives of German churches were present and participated in subsequent meetings as well. At the meeting in Berlin in 1857 the Prussian king took an active part. Representatives of the Land churches as well as the Free churches met as individual brothers in Christ. The Evangelical Alliance has maintained itself to the present. One of its activities is sponsoring a week of prayer among its groups throughout the world at the beginning of every year.[37]

Another independent group, the Evangelical Confederation (*Evangelischer Bund*), was perhaps the most vocal Protestant society. It was founded in 1887 to protect German Protestant interests and may be considered a reaction to the resurgence of Catholicism after the end of the struggle between the Catholic church and the government (*Kulturkampf*).[38] In 1914 it had over 500,000 members. In 1882 the first Evangelical Workers' Society was organized, and in 1890 a Union of Evangelical Workers' Societies was formed. By 1912 the union had a membership of 160,000, but it could not begin to match the strength of the socialist labor organizations. Its membership was drawn more from white-collar groups than from factory workers.[39]

The Growth of Church Unity

While the numerous Protestant societies were doing something to break down barriers between the official church bodies, the churches themselves were also drawing together. The desirability of establishing some sort of successor organization to the Corpus Evangelicorum to represent the Protestants of Germany was recognized at various times after 1815. It was, however, not until 1846 that a significant step was taken. The Catholic church was manifesting new vigor after the successful conclusion of the Kölner Kirchenstreit, and the exhibition of the Holy Cloak at Trier (1844) was a tremendous manifestation of resurgent Catholicism. The need to strengthen Protestant forces was one incentive of the new movement towards Protestant unity, but even more important was the general rise of nationalism and desire for political unification which became manifest in Germany in the 1840s. Church unity was to parallel political unification. At the suggestion of the king of Württemberg, a church conference was held in Berlin in 1846 which brought together representatives of twenty-six Land churches. But plans to hold another conference in three years were shattered by the events of the revolution of 1848.[40]

Yet in that very year of revolution two men, Professor Bethmann-Hollweg of Bonn and Professor Friedrich Julius Stahl of Berlin, called a meeting of interested men at Wittenberg. Some 500 prominent persons, mostly theologians and church officials, met at this assembly and discussed the problem of establishing some sort of Protestant union. At subsequent assemblies in Stuttgart (1850) and Eberfeld (1851), bylaws were worked out for periodic conferences, where on the basis of historic confessions there could be a free exchange of opinions on important problems of church life. The possibility was envisioned of furthering cooperation and uniform development without endangering the independence of any Land church. These Kirchentage had taken significant steps toward establishing a future church conference, and they continued to meet, at first yearly, and later every two years, until 1872. In all, sixteen meetings were held, always under the chairmanship of Professor von Bethmann-Hollweg. They remained, as they had started, a meeting of men interested in furthering the work of the Protestant churches. The more conservative Lutherans always absented themselves from these meetings.[41]

The first German Evangelical Church Conference planned at the early Kirchentage met at Eisenach on June 3, 1852, with twenty-four Land church governments represented, among them all the larger church bodies. Subsequently all Land churches participated in these biennial conferences at one time or another. The Supreme Church Council of Vienna continued to participate even after the German Confederation was dissolved in 1866, and delegates from Alsace-Lorraine participated after 1882. The Eisenach Conference, as it came to be called, usually assembled shortly after Pentecost and lasted about eight days. Costs were paid by the Land governments and were divided among them in proportion to the number of church members. The conference was only a consultative body, but gradually with the silent consent of the church authorities it began to appoint commissions and to undertake certain positive programs. Its work took on more and more significance as contacts between Land churches increased, as German unity grew with the establishment of the empire in 1871, as new social and educational problems presented themselves, and as the synodical bodies attained more influence in the various Land churches.

A sample of the topics considered will give some idea of the breadth of discussions and how varied the problems were. The conference dealt with the introduction of Lenten services (1855); the use of choirs in church services (1884); the use of individual cups in communion service (1908); the position of the churches in regard to cremation (1898); church architecture (1861, 1896, 1898); the appointment of nonresident clergy to a Land church (1868); the cooperation of congregations in filling ministerial positions (1859); in-service education of ministers (1896); the churches' relation to the sects (1852, 1855, 1884, 1896); mixed marriages (1853); the position of the Evangelical churches in regard to the introduction of civil marriage laws (1875); the conduct of religious education at the gymnasium (1868); the introduction of an abridged school Bible (1898); religious instruction in the schools (1910); the protection of Sundays and religious holidays (1855); service to emigrants (1855, 1872, 1894); care of the mentally ill (1894); and furtherance of Bible studies in congregations.[42]

The conference did more than discuss, and adopted some positive measures. Most important, it sponsored the *Allgemeines Kirchenblatt für das evangelische Deutschland,* which published ordinances, judicial decisions, and matters of importance which took place in all the Land churches. Its files constitute a mine of information on the German churches. The conference also furthered the gathering and regular publication of church statistics. It appointed commissions which played an important role in the revision (not abandonment) of Luther's translation of the Bible, and established a common text of Luther's Small Catechism which gradually replaced the sixty different editions then in use. The conference sponsored the selection of 150 basic hymns which were to be incorporated in the revision of all song books, as well as a Protestant song and prayer book for use in the army.

The deliberations and work of the conference demonstrated that cooperation could be achieved on many practical matters without touching the independence and government organization of the Land churches or the confessions and ritual to which they adhered. By the end of the century, however, interest in bringing about closer unity was evident. In 1895 the conference discussed the formation of a standing commission to see to carrying out the decisions reached, but no action was taken. The conferences of 1900 and 1902 considered anew the need for a directing body, and decided on the formation of the German Evangelical Church Committee (*Deutsche evangelische Kirchenausschuss*), which held its first meeting on November 10, 1903, the 420th anniversary of Luther's birth. This committee of fifteen members was under the chairmanship of the member from Prussia and was made up of representatives of the consistories of the various Land churches, some of the smaller churches being represented by a joint delegate.[43] The committee was accorded the rights of a public corporation by Prussia in 1905. It was supposed to look after the interests of Protestant churches in relation to other churches at home and abroad, and to care for the spiritual needs of German Protestants in other lands. It could not, however, interfere in any way with the confessional or constitutional status of any of the Land churches. It functioned only when the churches could speak with one voice. Thus in 1904 it drew up a protest over the repeal of the second paragraph of the law banning Jesuits; in 1906 it issued a memorandum on the law in regard to religious toleration as well as a memorandum on the care of German Protestants in foreign lands.[44]

The Eisenach Conference and the German Evangelical Church Committee were the only official ties which existed among the Land churches of Germany. There was no union, not even a church confederation, yet a great deal had been accomplished toward creating more church unity within Protestant Germany. Emperor William II had lent his support to greater cooperation among the Protestant churches. In 1895 he and his wife journeyed to Jerusalem to dedicate the Church of the Redeemer, which was to be an outpost of German Protestantism in the Holy Land. He took care that representatives of all the Protestant Land churches accompanied him on this occasion.

Church Membership and Church Life

The German census of 1910 had permitted each head of a household to select the term which most closely expressed his religious association. In all 526 terms appeared, a totally unmanageable number if meaningful statistics were to be established. Jews alone, for example, used fourteen designations. In the end the summaries listed 39,991,421 Evangelicals (members of Land churches), 23,821,453 Roman Catholics, 283,946 other Christians, 615,021 Jews, and 214,152 "others."[45] The vast majority of Germans were thus members of the various Land

churches or of the Catholic church. These Land churches, and for that
matter the Catholic churches as well, were closely associated with the
governments of the various states, and in addition to their own endowments and gifts were financed by subsidies from the state treasury and
by the imposition of church taxes. These taxes were levied by the
churches under supervision by the government, and in most cases were
collected by the state officials for the churches.

A person was literally born into the church—Protestant or Catholic—received baptism and religious instruction in the schools, and
was confirmed as a matter of course.[46] By a formal procedure, however, persons could withdraw from a church, and in increasing numbers they did so.[47] Yet the total number of withdrawals was small.
Many of those who withdrew from the Land churches joined the Catholic church or the independent Free churches; for others withdrawal
was an expression of atheism or of lack of interest in organized religion.[48] Moreover, if there were withdrawals, there were also additions.
We have fairly reliable figures on Protestant church membership from
1884 on. From 1884 to 1906, except for the years 1891 and 1896, the
number of people joining the Land churches exceeded the number of
withdrawals. However in 1906 the balance shifted, and from then on,
except for the war years 1915–17, withdrawals exceeded additions.
Withdrawals which had numbered 2,090 in 1884 edged upwards to
6,049 in 1905, and then jumped to 17,492 in the following year. But
when the total membership of the Land churches (39,991,421 according to the census of 1910) is considered, this is not an overwhelming
number. The withdrawals were largely the result of organized campaigns by atheistic organizations and by some of the socialist leaders.[49]
Persons who withdrew from the Land churches were denied the privilege of calling on the pastors to baptize, confirm, marry, or bury members of their families. Pastors, however, were instructed to receive
repentent sinners back into the fold on written application, or in case
of crisis, on oral declaration. Such an action meant that an individual
resumed both church membership and the obligations that went with
it. He was committed to the payment of church taxes, to the baptism
and Christian education of his children, and to participation in the life
of the church.

The table of withdrawals and additions on page 38 gives some
indication of the movement in membership in the Land churches.[50]

A person who withdrew formally from a Land church no longer had
to pay church taxes, one of the attractive features of withdrawal. The
levying of these taxes by the churches was largely a development of the
last quarter of the nineteenth century. The old revenues no longer sufficed; therefore some states passed laws permitting both Land churches
and Catholic churches to levy special church taxes under government
supervision. The tax laws varied greatly from state to state. In some
cases they were levied only for local parish purposes, in some for provincial or Land church purposes as well. Usually the tax rate could not
exceed a certain percentage of the state tax rate, and was set by church

Withdrawals from and Additions to Land Churches, 1910–14

Withdrawals:	1910	1911	1912	1913	1914
Without changing to another church	12,296	12,058	15,940	22,996	20,925
Transferring to Catholic church	877	1,011	919	952	692
Transferring to other Christian churches	4,537	4,680	4,869	5,249	3,891
Transferring to Judaism	77	60	77	58	64
Totals	17,787	17,809	21,805	29,255	25,572
Additions:					
Transferring from Catholic church	8,301	8,684	8,488	8,597	7,458
Transferring from other Christian churches	1,117	1,011	919	952	692
Transferring from Judaism	417	466	411	462	439
Totals	9,835	10,161	9,818	10,011	8,589
Net loss: withdrawals less transfers	7,952	7,648	11,987	19,244	16,983

and state officials. It might vary from parish to parish according to how much other income a particular church had from property or endowments. The taxes were principally on income, but in some cases on property, and were usually collected by the state, which received a percentage of the tax as a charge for the work of collecting. In Baden for a time the church collected the taxes itself. Prussia passed a church tax law in 1875, Grand Duchy of Hesse in 1875, Württemberg in 1887, Baden in 1888, and Bavaria in 1892. Other states passed similar measures, and these were all subject to frequent amendment.[51]

Church taxation raised all sorts of complex questions, not the least of which was who was liable. The Prussian law stated simply: "All Evangelicals have to pay the church tax who are residents of the parish." But who was an Evangelical? In general all followers of the German or Swiss reformation were considered Evangelisch. Old Lutherans and Mennonites were expressly given tax exemption by law, but other sects—even the Baptists who had the status of a public corporation—were not.[52] Since many of the members of the so-called sects never made formal application for withdrawal from the Land church, they remained on the tax roll. The laws made detailed provisions for the payment of taxes in cases of mixed marriages, or if a husband withdrew from the church and his wife did not. In the former case half of the husband's liability went to the Protestant church and half to the Catholic church; in the latter the husband had to pay half of the normal tax or persuade his wife also to withdraw. Change of residence and cases of multiple residence also necessitated detailed regulations. To disentangle all the legalities of church tax legislation in the various states would require the patience of Job. Yet the system worked remarkably well and still exists today. The saving grace about the system was that with such a wide tax base individual taxes were not particularly burdensome.

The socialists at times preached withdrawal of church membership, thus cancelling liability for paying church taxes, as a way of bringing the government and churches to heel.[53] Yet this hope was a chimera. A study was made of the financial repercussions of withdrawal from church membership in Berlin for the years 1911–13, and it was found that of those who withdrew just over a third were liable for church taxes, and of those liable more than three-quarters were in the lowest three tax brackets. On paper, the church in Berlin lost 12,367 marks in 1911, 19,988 marks in 1912, and 33,988 marks in 1913. When it is considered that a number of these taxpayers would probably have been delinquent in any case, the total loss to the church was insignificant. Nonpayment of church taxes in Prussia meant that the right to vote in church elections lapsed, no great burden certainly for someone who was indifferent to the church.[54]

In addition to the church taxes, which actually were church revenues collected for the churches by the state, the Land churches received direct subsidies from the state. These grants have a long and varied history, and were in part a recognition of services performed by the churches for the state, or payments in lieu of the secularization of church property and ancient tithes. The money came out of regular state revenues. Since in many of the smaller states there were no special church taxes, the bulk of the expenses of the churches there rested on the state budget. "The financial dependence of the Land churches [on the state]," commented D. J. Schneider, long-time editor of the *Kirchliches Jahrbuch* "exists in very different degrees, but it exists in some fashion everywhere."[55] It is impossible to get any accurate total figures on the contribution by the states to the churches in Germany because church grants were included under different budget headings in the various states: churches, schools, pensions, etc. The direct subsidies paid by Prussia to the Protestant Land churches were between 28 and 29 million marks in 1918 and in 1919. In Baden, where there was a movement (1912–13) led by certain ministers of the independent churches to get parliament to cut the subsidies to the privileged churches, the Protestant Land church was receiving a direct subsidy of 300,000 marks, and the Catholic church 350,000 marks.[56]

Inner Life of the Churches

It is impossible to generalize about the inner life of the church. Everyone complained about lack of church attendance in the years before World War I, although it varied greatly from region to region. On the whole attendance was better in rural than in urban areas, but here also there were so-called dead congregations. It can, however, be said that the areas where church attendance was weakest were greater Berlin, Hamburg, Bremen, Saxony, western Pomerania, Thuringia, part of Brunswick, certain areas of Schleswig-Holstein, and the Mecklenburgs; areas where church attendance was better were Westphalia, Württemberg, Silesia, Bavaria, Hesse and Hesse-Nassau.[57]

While detailed information and exact figures are available on baptisms, marriages, burials, and even attendance at communion, there are no figures on church attendance. An attempt was made in 1913 to tabulate church attendance on three Sundays in the ninety-six churches in Berlin, where membership totaled 2,190,000 souls. Including attendance at children's and youths' services, the average attendance was 4.3 percent. To countercheck on these church figures a socialist-dominated group made a secret count on May 18, 1913, in sixty-eight Berlin churches with a combined seating capacity of 86,116 and a total membership of 1,805,854. They counted 11,252 at the main services. In Baden, on the basis of certain spot checks, they reached a tentative attendance figure of 20 percent. In Alsace-Lorraine a private investigation came up with a 16 percent attendance in Lutheran churches, and 11 percent in Reformed churches, the latter being better represented in the larger cities and industrial areas.[58]

All observers agree that attendance in the big cities was very lax. This was no doubt in part because of the large membership of the individual churches. There were many congregations with a membership of 50,000 to 80,000, and one (Neukölln) with over 200,000 souls. As may well be imagined, communion attendance in these large congregations dropped off; waiting to go to the altar rail can be a taxing experience. The church authorities were doing what they could to split up these large congregations, which were the result of the rapid urbanization and increase of population that occurred in Germany in the late nineteenth century. But the birth rate exceeded the church building rate. In Prussia in 1880 the parish average was 2,185 souls; in 1905, it was 2,575 souls.[59]

On the other hand, church attendance is not necessarily an accurate gauge of Christian affiliation. One should also consider the other evidence of adherence to Christian practices. For example, in 1900 only 2.92 percent of the children born to Evangelical parents were not baptized, and in 1912 only 4.22 percent. If one assumes that not more than half of the children of mixed marriages would be baptized as Protestants, the baptismal figures for these unions in 1900 were 93.36 percent, and in 1912, 103.32 percent. Baptism of illegitimate children born to Protestant mothers dropped from 85.85 percent in 1900 to 81.53 percent in 1912. Few children were withdrawn from classes in religion, a regular subject of instruction in all German schools, and they were regularly confirmed. In 1912 the percentage of Protestant church marriages following civil marriage averaged high in the nineties in most states. Protestant weddings in the case of mixed marriages averaged more than half the total. Attendance at communion declined somewhat in all states in the period 1900–1912, but the statistics on church burials show a rather surprising rise. In Prussia in 1900, for example, 77.59 percent of Protestants received church burial, and in 1912, 85.62 percent. In 1913 there were religious services for 78 percent of the 8,598

Protestants who were cremated.[60] In order properly to evaluate such statistics, one should of course consider similar figures for churches in other countries. But it seems safe to say that the German churches probably fared as well as most others.

On the whole liberal in theology and embracing the results of critical scholarship, the Land churches were nevertheless conservative and patriotic bodies. They upheld the authority and leadership of the state; they tended to side with, rather than against, the government. In accordance with the theory of two estates, the spiritual and the temporal, they were prone to center their interest and attention on church rather than state affairs. Religious liberty was a reality in Germany; the growth of Free churches and numerous religious sects was evidence that the religiously neutral state was willing to grant the churches an increasing measure of self-government. Through the establishment of important synodical and other church bodies, advances had been made on the course which eventually was to remove completely the hand of the state from the churches. As at the time of the Reformation, when the churches failed to find an answer to the demands raised in the Peasants' Revolt, so in the nineteenth century no satisfactory solution was worked out in regard to the rising labor movement.[61] The churches in Germany, like the churches in most countries, were hostile to anything that looked like revolution. They were, however, not unaware of the growing social problems of the day, as is witnessed in their support of inner missions. Yet the broad program of social legislation which came very early in Germany was largely political in origin. The churches followed rather than led in achieving reforms on behalf of the working classes.

Yet if the Protestant churches were conservatively oriented, they were not monolithic. Although law, order, and monarchical feeling have been dominant themes in German history, there is also a liberal tradition that is often overlooked. So it was also in the Protestant churches. Protestant theological students were members of the *Burschenschaften,* the liberal student organizations of their day. Strong Protestant contingents participated in the revolution of 1848 and later did much to combat the increased clericalism of the reinvigorated papacy of the nineteenth century. The Catholics were predominantly behind the Center party; what support the Progressive, the Liberal, and even the Social Democratic parties gained came largely from the ranks of the Protestants, if not from the clergy.

When World War I came the ministers, as did the ministers in other countries, proclaimed from their pulpits the sacredness and holiness of the fatherland's cause and prayed for victory. The parsonages contributed a larger number of sons to the armed forces and suffered proportionally higher casualties than other professional groups. As often happens in periods of crises, more people turned to religion. One thing is certain: at the end of the war most Germans still upheld the values the churches stood for, and when an attempt was made in the first flush of the revolutions of 1918–19 to disparage the position of the churches and of religious education in the schools, the German people insisted on retaining their accustomed institutions and practices.[62] The German church leaders were not complacent about the situation. On the other hand, they were entangled in a web of state and church regulations often centuries old and in practices and customs deeply ingrained in the people, and it was extremely difficult to cast these aside even when some of them were clearly outdated. Hitler and his cohorts were to discover the same truth at a later date.

2.

The Catholic Church before 1918

The Catholic Princes and the Counter-Reformation

The Roman Catholic church through its hierarchical organization was a self-governing institution, but it always had close connections with the state. In fact, the state from the time of the Middle Ages was considered in many ways an arm of the church and was supposed to protect and further its interests, to carry out certain decisions of the ecclesiastical courts, and to help in suppressing heresy. An attempt was made at the time of the Reformation to suppress the new heresies, but it was unsuccessful. The movement was too widespread, and had powerful lay support, and foreign dangers—notably the Turkish invasion—were so great that it was impossible for the emperor to carry out any such policy.

The emperor and other lay princes who remained true to Roman Catholicism were, however, most helpful in stemming the tide of Protestantism. As important as the Jesuits, the Inquisition, the Index, the Council of Trent, the revitalized papacy, and the internal reforms of the church were, without the active cooperation and aid of the Catholic princes the Counter-Reformation would never have been as successful as it was, not only in Germany, but in all of eastern and central Europe. It has been estimated that in 1570 seven-tenths of all the inhabitants of Germany were Protestant.[1] By 1600, Bavaria, largely because of the efforts of Duke Albrecht V, was again entirely Catholic, as was the mark Baden-Baden where he served as regent. The Habsburgs had reconverted Styria, Carinthia, and Carniola, and were pushing this policy elsewhere in their hereditary lands. More important for the Catholic cause was the fact that the big Catholic bishoprics, such as Cologne, Paderborn, Münster, Fulda, Würzburg, and Bamberg, were again firmly under Catholic control, although for a time the threat of their becoming Protestant was very real.

There were many issues involved in the Thirty Years' War (1618–48), and among them was a desire on the part of the emperor to further the policy of recatholization in Germany. Nevertheless, the Lutheran and Reformed churches were of necessity granted recognition at the Peace of Westphalia.[2] Persons practicing minority religions in 1624 were to be tolerated, and while those persons who later chose to convert from their sovereign's religion could be exiled, their property could not be confiscated. The peace treaty also brought recognition of the secularization of some important bishoprics. Bremen (but not the city) and Verden went to Sweden; Kammin, Halberstadt, and Minden went to Brandenburg; Schwerin and Ratzeburg went to Mecklenburg; Metz, Toul, and Verdun went to France. Where these secularized lands came under Protestant princes, the mixed confessional state appeared, a type which henceforth was to multiply. The ecclesiastical states, however, as a rule remained purely Catholic; the regions along the Rhine were dubbed "Priests' Avenue" (*Pfaffen Allee*). Toleration of Protestants in these lands did not come until their secularization in 1803.

State Control of the Church

Following the Peace of Westphalia the Catholic church in Germany remained self-governing with an intact hierarchy. In the Reichstag the Catholic states, lay and ecclesiastical, formed a Corpus Catholicorum under the chairmanship of the archbishop of Mainz, which was the counterpart of the Protestant Corpus Evangelicorum under the chairmanship of the elector of Saxony. Religious questions were decided not by individual votes, but by agreement between these two confessional groups.[3] The purely ecclesiastical states had various administrative organs devoted to the more secular aspects of civil government. But these governmental agencies, even if some lay officials were used, were clerically dominated and controlled. In the Catholic lay states there continued to be close contacts between state officials and the hierarchy through various departments or governmental bureaus. Gradually the influence and activities of the state increased, the Catholic princes often following the example of their Protestant neighbors. This was notably true in the eighteenth century, when under the influence of the Enlightenment the state established a clear predominance over the church. This was the period of state control of the church (*Staatskirchentum*), which is best exemplified by Joseph II's religious policy in Austria, but which found its echo in most German states. The state officials nominated or at least had a deciding voice in the appointment of the hierarchy; they supported the church with subsidies, laid down rules for religious practices on such issues as mixed marriages, limited the jurisdiction of ecclesiastical courts, controlled the correspondence as well as the visitation of bishops and heads of monastic orders, and required governmental approval (*Placet*) for all pronouncements of the hierarchy.

The growing state control of the church was not only a product of the eighteenth-century Enlightenment; it was enhanced by internal conflict within the church and by a marked decline in the status of the papacy. The pope under the prodding of the Jesuits became involved in a long drawn out conflict (seventeenth and eighteenth centuries) over a puritanical reform movement within the church, known from its founder as Jansenism. The Jesuits, expanding their influence, became much too powerful to suit the governments in Portugal (1759), France (1764), and Spain

(1767), and the order was banned from their territories. Largely because of pressure from these governments, the pope dissolved the Jesuit order in 1773. In Prussia, where Frederick II wanted to use the Jesuits in the schools of his newly won provinces of Silesia, and in Russia, where Catherine II wanted to use them in the schools of Poland, the order was permitted to continue. In Prussia it was later dissolved under Frederick William II; in Russia the order was officially reconstituted by the pope in 1801 only to be banned in 1820 by the government.

In addition to the difficulties over the Jesuits, the papacy was beset by another reform movement. In 1763 an auxiliary bishop of Trier, Nikolas von Hontheim (1701–90) under the pseudonym "Justinus Febronius," published a volume on church law entitled *The Status of the Church and the Legitimate Power of the Roman Pontiff* (*De statu ecclesiae et legitima potestate Romani pontifici*). It was an argument for the supremacy of a church council, and in general advocated the curbing of papal power by the extension of episcopal jurisdiction and even that of the lay government. The hierarchy, in Germany as elsewhere at this time, was dominated by clergy drawn from the ranks of the nobility, and they tended to accept Febronian theories, although the book was condemned immediately by the pope. At the request of the Bavarian government the pope in 1785 established a second nuncio at Munich in addition to the one at Cologne. When the new nuncio began to interfere with certain episcopal privileges, the three great Rhenish archbishops—Cologne, Mainz, and Trier—joined with the archbishop of Salzburg in issuing a statement (*Emser Punktation,* 1786) asserting their independence. They came close to advocating a German national church.[4]

By some clever maneuvering the papacy maintained its theoretical position, while in practice seeking the support of Catholic princes against the archbishops. Many bishops also turned to the princes for support against the power of the archbishops. Under these conditions, much of the control of the church in the lay states of Germany passed to the hands of the state, and the clergy looked to their princes rather than to the pope for leadership. It was no longer a question of the church controlling the state; the state now controlled the church. The system of Staatskirchentum reigned supreme in the lay states such as Bavaria, Baden, Württemberg, and Prussia, and in the ecclesiastical states the prince bishops reigned with little reference to papal directives.

The climate of opinion at the end of the eighteenth century laid less stress than heretofore on dogma and on many of the historical practices of the church. The critical spirit of the age evidenced itself in theological writings. At the University of Mainz the Catholic professor of dogmatics published "A Critical History of Papal Infallibility" (1791). Differences between Catholicism and Protestantism were played down, and some Catholic priests and Protestant clergymen began to work together. Catholic theologians busied themselves with bringing out German translations of the Bible, and there was even some cooperation with Protestant Bible societies in distributing the Bible among the populace. In 1805 the head of the theological seminary at Regensburg formed a Catholic Bible society which in ten years distributed over 70,000 New Testaments. This society flourished until 1817, when Pope Pius VII ordered it closed. New songbooks, catechisms, and breviaries appeared, all bearing evidence of the influence of the new ideas of the Enlightenment. Important internal changes in the German Catholic church were taking place, many quite independent of the official policy of the papacy.[5]

The Impact of the French Revolution

The era of the French Revolution brought even more important changes in the organization of the Catholic church in Germany, and cleared the way for the great resurgence of German Catholicism in the nineteenth century. For some time German princes had been looking longingly at the rich territorial possessions of the German ecclesiastical princes. Many similar church possessions had been secularized in the past, and the existence of the remaining ones seemed an anachronism to greedy eyes. The French began the process when they occupied the left bank of the Rhine (1794–95), secularizing important parts of the territories of the archbishops of Cologne, Mainz, and Trier. Many German princelings also lost their lands, and some of the larger German states had to cede small bits of their territories to the French. The Peace of Lunéville (1801) brought further territorial cessions to France, and on August 18, 1802, a French-Russian plan to provide compensation for these princes by secularizing the ecclesiastical states was submitted to the Reichstag at Regensburg. There was much discussion and a good deal of bribery, but the adoption of the proposed plan was a foregone conclusion. In 1803 the *Reichsdeputationshauptschluss* was passed, which secularized all ecclesiastical states to the right of the Rhine except three—the territories held by the archbishop of Mainz, by the Order of Saint John, and by the Teutonic Knights, who maintained their precarious holdings until 1815.[6]

In all, the church lost 1,719 square miles of land, with a population of 3,162,576, and an income of 21,000,000 gulden. The princes all received more territory than they had lost, but some of these gains were only temporary as territorial reshuffling followed the fortunes of battle in the following years. Most of the monastic lands fell into the hands of the princes, which seriously handicapped Catholic education in Germany. The secularization of land and endowments made a church career less attractive to the nobility and broke the traditional hold of the nobility on the higher church positions. The secularization also brought the cession of many Catholic-inhabited territories to Protestant princes. The Reichsdeputationshauptschluss did not require, but did permit, a prince to tolerate citizens of another confession and to grant them full civil status. The day of the single-confession state had ended. The constitution of the German Confederation in 1815 recognized this fact, and provided that members of all Christian confessions should have full civil and political rights in all member states.[7]

These changes necessitated a rearrangement of dioceses. When Napoleon took over the left bank of the Rhine, he created newly arranged bishoprics at Aachen, Mainz, and Trier. The pope recognized these new boundaries when he issued, on November 29, 1801, the bull *Qui Christi Domini vicis,* which reorganized the ecclesiastical provinces on the left bank of the Rhine, allotting some territories to new dioceses and others to already existing French dioceses. For the present the territories on the right bank were to retain their old diocesan boundaries. In some places where definite decisions as to diocesan boundaries were postponed, vicars were appointed to administer these territories. The Reichsdeputationshauptschluss had recognized that new diocesan boundaries were needed and envisaged the conclusion of a concordat with the pope (paragraph 62). The princes all wanted bishops for their own territories. Negotiations for a concordat were begun, but difficulties arose, and the dissolution of the Empire in 1806 ended for the time the possibility of concluding an agreement for all Germany.

Meanwhile some of the states went ahead on their own and issued religious edicts which attempted to regulate church affairs.[8] They expressed the prevailing ideas of the supremacy of civil over ecclesiastical jurisdiction. The establishment of the Confederation of the Rhine (1806) gave Napoleon renewed cause to interfere in German affairs. He made those Protestant princes who joined the confederation promise that henceforth all Catholics in their lands would enjoy the same civil and political rights as Protestants, and that the Catholic church would be granted the same privileges as the Protestant Land churches. Napoleon thus proclaimed himself the protector of Catholics. Yet within a few years he was at war with the pope and annexed the papal states to France in 1809. The pope was in exile, and in the confused situation nothing was accomplished toward the reorganization of the Catholic church in Germany. As existing bishoprics became vacant, no new appointments were made because of the expected regulations of diocesan boundaries, which, however, never materialized. By 1814 there were only five bishops left in Germany, most of them well advanced in years. General vicars (*Generalvikare*) took care of many of the duties in the bishoprics, but they were not permitted to administer the sacraments of ordination or confirmation. Furthermore, many of the parishes remained without priests. There was much to be done when peace returned to Europe in 1815.

While the church had lost much, it had also made some gains. The Enlightenment and the French Revolution had finally brought religious toleration, and this new liberality eventually meant a great deal in Germany, where Catholics were in the minority.[9] Depriving the bishops of their secular territorial jurisdiction in the end gave the church a more independent position. The German bishops were now no longer territorial princes directly involved in small-state rivalry. Control by the governments often proved irksome, and the bishops more than ever before turned to the pope for aid and comfort. They no longer felt inclined to go it alone, but sought strength and help in a policy of ultramontanism.

On the other hand, developments were taking place on the governmental side which also benefited the church. The purely confessional state had vanished from Germany, at first to the regret of the church. Yet in its place had come the state which treated both major Christian confessions equally, and which was to develop into the religiously neutral state where all confessions and denominations would receive impartial treatment. Inextricably bound up with this development was the idea that the churches should on the whole regulate their own affairs. It did not mean an end to the age-old dispute regarding the boundary line between church and state affairs, but it did mean the end of Staatskirchentum as it had developed in the eighteenth century. In the Protestant churches this meant the creation of synodical organizations and the gradual granting of more influence to them by the state; in the Catholic church it meant the establishment of a hierarchy essentially free from state control and imbued with filial loyalty to the pope.

The rebuilding of the church after the chaos of the revolutionary and Napoleonic period did not come overnight, nor did it come without controversy. Between 1815 and 1918, the church received a new diocesan organization; it became involved in certain rather bitter conflicts with the state and developed a strong political party to protect its interests; it expanded its monastic and educational establishments; it built up important lay organizations; and it developed a strong press. In general, it enhanced its status and increased its membership throughout Germany, reflecting the revitalization of the whole Roman Catholic church during the nineteenth century.

The Reorganization of Dioceses

The papacy sent delegates to the Congress of Vienna who were more concerned with bringing about the restoration of the papal states and the settlement of Italian affairs than with dealing with the problems of the German church. A claim was indeed advanced for the return of the secularized lands, to which all the princes turned a deaf ear. A plan was also proposed for the settlement of the affairs of the church throughout Germany in a single agreement with the pope. However, a congress that would have nothing to do with establishing a really united Germany and compromised on a loose German confederation could not bring itself to advocate a unitary settlement of the church problem. It was left for the church to negotiate agreements with each of the states separately.

Instead of a Reich concordat, the papacy was only able to conclude a concordat with Bavaria. This concordat was negotiated in 1817, but it was not published until the following year, when it appeared as an annex to a religious edict which also applied to the Protestant church and granted equal rights to Lutherans and Reformed. There were discrepancies in the wording between the edict and the concordat which led to many disputes. By the concordat, the king of Bavaria was given

the right to nominate bishops as well as a number of the lower clergy,
and he was accorded the right of Placet—that is, all ordinances and
important statements of the church needed his approval before they
could be published in Bavaria. While the concordat thus continued
many of the practices of the Staatskirchentum of the eighteenth century,
it did guarantee to the church all rights according "to divine order and
canon law," and granted Catholic seminaries, clerical supervision of the
public Catholic confessional schools, free communication with the papacy, and the return of some monasteries. A supplementary circumscription bull divided Bavaria into two archbishoprics: Munich-Freising, with
the bishoprics of Passau, Regensburg, and Augsburg; and Bamberg, with
the bishoprics of Würzburg, Eichstätt, and Speyer.[10]

In 1821, the papacy established an Upper Rhine church province,
with an archbishop at Freiburg and five bishoprics—Freiburg for Baden,
Rottenburg for Württemberg, Mainz for Hesse-Darmstadt, Limburg for
Nassau and Frankfurt/Main, and Fulda for Hesse-Kassel. The governments of these territories had been discussing terms of a church settlement among themselves since a meeting at Frankfurt in 1818, and the
negotiations with the papacy were not concluded until 1827. The governments made numerous concessions, but there were many issues left
which led to future disputes. Bishops were to be elected according to
canonical procedures, but the governments were to have the right to
eliminate certain candidates who were unacceptable to them. A similar
arrangement in regard to the election of bishops was part of the settlement which was reached in Hanover (1822–24). Here two bishoprics
were established at Hildesheim and Osnabrück.

The agreement with Prussia was one of the most important, not
only because of Prussia's position in the German Confederation, but
also because Prussia had obtained important additions of Catholic territories in the final territorial settlement of 1815. The government was
most obliging, as it was anxious to conciliate the newly annexed Catholic populations. The famed historian Barthold G. Niebuhr was sent to
Rome to carry on the negotiations, and he gave way on one point after
another. Final settlement was reached in 1821. There were to be two
archbishoprics: Cologne, with the suffragan bishoprics of Trier, Münster,
and Paderborn; and Posen-Gnesen, with the bishopric of Culm (seat at
Pelplin). Breslau and Ermland were to be exempt bishoprics directly
under the pope. Bishops were to be elected by cathedral chapters,
although the government was to have the right to eliminate objectionable candidates from the list before the election. The Prussian government provided liberal subsidies. The Prussian settlement was thus one of
the most favorable that the papacy achieved at this time in all Europe.
So pleased was the pope that, in thanking Frederick William III, he
compared that monarch to Theodosius the Great.[11]

In the other German states, which were predominantly Protestant,
no hierarchies were erected. They were later joined to the Prussian or
Upper Rhine bishoprics, or remained mission territories under apostolic vicars or prefects (*Präfekten*). Among the latter were Saxony,

Mecklenburg-Strelitz, Mecklenburg-Schwerin, Schleswig-Holstein, Schaumburg-Lippe, Reuss-Greiz, Reuss-Schleiz-Gera, Altenburg, Hamburg, Bremen, and Lübeck.

The organization of the church as laid down in this series of agreements remained basic for Germany. In the various state governments there was usually a ministry which supervised church, school, and cultural affairs. At times there were separate Catholic and Protestant sections, but sometimes the same officials administered all church matters. If this were the case, the ministry usually had officials of both confessions, although there were some North German states with such a small Catholic minority that the bureaucracy was likely to be entirely Protestant. In any case, the government officials, whether Catholic or Protestant, were usually more interested in protecting the interests of the state than those of any church body.

Church-State Controversies

The negotiation of the church-state agreements had been difficult, and in every case differences remained. Thus in Bavaria the clergy refused for a time to take an oath to the constitution because they felt the concordat had been significantly shortchanged by the religious edict of 1818. Only after the king made an official statement (*Erklärung von Tegernsee,* September 15, 1821) that the oath applied only to civil duties, and involved nothing that conflicted with divine or church law, were the clergy ready to take the oath. It was a relatively minor conflict, but the church had scored a point against the state.

In the shift of territories Prussia had acquired the city of Bonn with its recently established Catholic university (1786). Prussia lavished money on this institution, and converted it into a Catholic-Protestant university with theological faculties for both confessions. This was done without consulting the pope, with the result that students were withdrawn from the study of Catholic theology there, and the government had to make one concession after another to maintain the university. The smaller states along the upper Rhine also decided to add Catholic theological faculties at their state universities. After completing their work at the universities there, students were to finish their studies at special Catholic seminaries which were to be established. The church did not take kindly to these plans, and long discussions preceded the establishment of Catholic theological faculties at Freiburg for Baden, Tübingen for Württemberg, and Giessen for Hesse-Darmstadt. When Hesse-Nassau established a Catholic theological faculty at Marburg, the bishop of Fulda refused permission for Catholics to study there, and the faculty had to be closed. A similar withdrawal of students ended the Catholic faculty at Giessen in the early 1850s. Behind these controversies was the growing ultramontane influence upon the education of the German priesthood.

Another university squabble eventually became involved in the bitter church-state controversy over mixed marriages (the Kölner Kirchenstreit). In 1819 George Hermes (1775–1831), formerly a professor of Catholic dogmatics at Münster, joined the faculty at Bonn. Although he taught a rational Kantian explanation of revealed religion, his end conclusions in no way overthrew any Catholic doctrines. His classes were very popular, and he had the support of the archbishop of Cologne. Soon, however, a movement set in against Hermes's teachings, for the way he arrived at his conclusions alarmed some people. The new archbishop of Cologne became his bitter opponent, and ordered all students to stay away from the lectures of Hermes's followers. Gregory XVI, in a breve of 1835, condemned Hermes's writings. The cathedral chapter was divided in the controversy and the issue of academic freedom became involved. The opponents of Hermes developed into a group strongly critical of state regulations, and led in opposing the Prussian regulations on mixed marriages.

The question of mixed marriages had caused few difficulties in the predominantly confessional states of the eighteenth century. Where such marriages did occur the education of the children sometimes brought disagreements over the question of whether they should attend the Protestant or the Catholic confessional schools. In 1803 the king of Prussia had issued a regulation that in disputed instances children should be educated in the confession of the father. In 1825 the Prussian edict was extended to the newly acquired western provinces. This solution was not out of line with governmental practices of the time. The Bavarian constitution of 1818 provided that in mixed marriages sons should be brought up in the religion of the father, and daughters in the religion of the mother. Charles VI had as early as 1716 issued similar regulations for Silesia.

In the western Prussian provinces the clergy had recently undertaken before solemnizing a mixed marriage to require, as they were supposed to do under canon law, that children be brought up as Catholics. The practice of the church and the law of the state were now in direct conflict. When the Prussian state could reach no understanding with the Vatican on this matter, it successfully undertook negotiations with the then archbishop of Cologne and with other bishops. An understanding was reached under which the clergy would not insist on Catholic education. When Klemens von Droste-Vischering (1835) became archbishop of Cologne, he not only refused (contrary to earlier assurances) to renew the understanding with the Prussian government, but he publicized the secret agreement. Some Belgian Jesuits got involved in the controversy, and it became a church-wide problem. The papacy, of course, could only side with Droste-Vischering's determination to adhere strictly to canon law. The controversy reached into every Catholic parish in Prussia. Should the priest follow his bishop or the law of the land? In 1837, the Prussian government removed the archbishop from Cologne and interned him at Minden. The arrest caused much popular concern, and anger and resentment among the Catholic populace. The long anticipated persecution of Catholics by Protestant Prussia seemed to be at hand. In Munich, an active Catholic publicist, Johann Joseph Görres (1776–1848), published an inflammatory brochure entitled *Athanasius*. The controversy spread to eastern Prussia. Here the clergy had for years regularly performed mixed marriages without exacting any nuptial agreement. Now the archbishop of Posen-Gnesen decided to enforce the marriage provisions as laid down in canon law. He too was removed from office, and imprisoned in the fortress of Kolberg (1839). The bishop of Breslau resigned his office (1840) when the pope insisted that he enforce the canonical marriage provisions.

The accession of Frederick William IV in 1840 brought a settlement of the Hermesian as well as the mixed marriage controversies, though not without very intricate negotiations. The bishop of Posen was permitted to return, but the king insisted that Droste-Vischering should not be permitted to resume his seat. A coadjutor bishop, Johann von Geissel of Speyer, took over at Cologne with right of succession. The state, after some circumlocution, gave way on the question of mixed marriages, and the clergy in practice were permitted to demand prenuptial agreements. Quietly the state also permitted the church to have more control over the theological faculties at the universities. The king gave up the Placet (1841), and created a separate section for Catholic affairs in the Ministry of Culture.[12]

The Cologne controversy had actually given a great fillip to Catholicism in Germany and strengthened ultramontane influences. The exhibition of the Holy Cloak at Trier in 1844 drew over a million pilgrims within a period of fifty days. This manifestation of Catholic strength aroused much excitement as well as caustic comment among Protestants, and eventually led to the regular Protestant Eisenach conferences.[13] A suspended Catholic priest, Johannes Ronge, denounced the exhibition of the Holy Cloak. He joined with another priest, Johannes Czerski, in calling a meeting of like-minded Catholics, which resulted in the same year in the formation of the so-called German Catholic Church. This secessionist movement (at its height in 1848 it had about 259 congregations and 100,000 members) joined with a small dissident Protestant group in 1859 to form the League of Free Religious Congregations.[14]

In Bavaria, a strongly clerical ministry headed by Karl von Abel (1837–47) made notable concessions to the church. The Placet was retained, but it was modified and, most importantly, not strictly enforced. Ultramontane bishops were installed in many of the bishoprics. In 1838 King Ludwig I happened to read what a good impression a French military contingent made when its members uniformly sank to their knees at the dedication of a church in Algeria. Remembering that Bavarian soldiers had customarily knelt at services until 1803, it struck him that it would be a good idea to reinstitute the practice. He issued an order on August 14, 1838, that the soldiers should kneel at Catholic field masses at the time of consecration and during the benediction, at Corpus Christi processions, and when the sacrament was carried by if they were on guard. The command was to be "Aufs Knie"—"On your knees." In 1803 Bavaria was practically all Catholic, but in 1838 the situation had been changed by the recent territorial additions. When the order was given for the first time at the field service in honor of the king's birthday, two Protestant generals refused to fall on their knees. The Protestant element in the population became aroused. Attempts to temper the order by using only Catholic troops at certain occasions did not quiet the opposition; Protestant representatives raised the issue in the Landtag. The king was not easily moved, but he finally had to give in and the kneeling order was repealed on December 12, 1845. The incident—the so-called *Kniebeug-ungstreit*—did much to discredit the Abel ministry and led to an inner strengthening of the Protestants. In the end it did contribute to the equal treatment of confessions in Bavaria.

The revolution of 1848 brought all religions new freedom to organize. Although the constitution drawn up at the Frankfurt parliament never went into effect, it did indicate the thought of the times, which was slowly to be implemented in the next decades. Article 147 stated:

> Every religious body orders and administers its affairs itself, but remains subject to the general laws of the state. No religious body enjoys through the state precedence over other bodies; a state church henceforth does not exist. New religious bodies can be constituted; a recognition of its confession by the state is not needed.[15]

The new Prussian constitution of 1850 brought a real extension of liberties to the churches. They were henceforth to regulate their own affairs, the state retaining only certain supervisory rights.[16] What these rights were was left to future give-and-take.

In the general conservative reaction of the 1850s, the various state governments tended to see in religion a bulwark against further revolution. Religious education was stressed and the churches in general were accorded more control over the schools.[17] The conclusion of the concordat with Austria in 1855, which wiped out what remained of Joseph II's regulatory legislation, also had its repercussions in Germany. Actually Württemberg (1857) and Baden (1859) concluded new agreements with the pope, which, however, were not accepted by the respective parliaments. There was controversy and at times strife, yet inexorably the remnants of Staatskirchentum gave way.

The dissolution of the German Confederation as the result of Prussia's success in the War of 1866 removed Austria, the strongest Catholic power, from German affairs. Prussia, although as a whole generous and liberal towards the Catholic church, still was looked at askance, and Catholics feared for their status when the German Empire was established in 1871 under Prussian leadership. To protect their interests they organized the Center party, which henceforth became the spokesman for Catholic interests in the various parliamentary bodies of Germany. Bismarck viewed the Center party with alarm. He stated in the Prussian lower chamber on January 30, 1872:

> From my earliest days I have always considered that one of the worst possible political events that could take place was the formation of a confessional party, a party which, if all other confessions accepted the same principle, one would have to oppose by the creation of a united evangelical party. Then we

would always be in an impossible situation, for we would thereby bring theology into the political assemblies and make it a subject of discussion from the tribune. As I returned from France I was able to view this [Center] party in no other light than as a mobilization against the state.[18]

His distaste for the party was increased by the fact that it received strong support from old opposition groups in Hanover, from obstreperous Polish groups in eastern Prussia, and, after 1876, from the newly acquired provinces of Alsace-Lorraine.

The Center party seemed a continuation on German soil of the aggressive action taken by the church under the dynamic leadership of Pius IX (1846–78). Without the support of a council he had proclaimed the dogma of the Immaculate Conception in 1854, and ten years later he issued the Syllabus of Errors, which seemed to condemn all that was liberal or progressive in modern society. At the Vatican Council in 1870, most of the German hierarchy had opposed the dogma of papal infallibility, but once it was adopted they all soon accepted it. A small dissident group of "Old Catholics," who refused to accept the new dogma, established themselves in Germany and sought recognition from the various states. This was granted, much against the wishes of regular Catholic church authorities.

The existence of the Old Catholics raised all sorts of problems. Were they to be permitted to retain their church buildings, or did they have to surrender them to the bishop? Some teachers of Catholic religion in the schools refused to accept papal infallibility, and the hierarchy naturally wanted them removed as instructors. Yet they were state appointees and still taught essentially what they had always taught. The state refused to dismiss them. In 1871, the Prussian government took a step it had been contemplating for some time and abolished the separate Catholic and Protestant sections in the Ministry of Culture. Henceforth Protestant and Catholic affairs would be administered by the same officials. A year later Prussia passed a law which brought all schools under state inspection. Formerly both Protestant and Catholic clergy served as school inspectors as a matter of course, but from 1872 on, they had to receive special appointment. In practice few Catholics received such appointments, especially in the Polish districts. The whole system of Catholic confessional public schools seemed to be threatened.

Prussia and the Catholic church were soon involved in the major church and state struggle known as the Kulturkampf.[19] The name was coined by Dr. Rudolf Virchow, a world-famous pathologist and leader of the Progressive party in the Reichstag. It seemed to him that this "struggle for civilization" was an attempt to achieve the values which the pope had condemned in the Syllabus of Errors, and which the victory of the Ultramontane party at the Vatican Council seemed to endanger. The conflict actually began in some of the South German states, but soon a great part of Germany was involved. In addition to laws in some of the states, especially Prussia, Baden, Hesse, and Bavaria, three laws were passed on the national level. One was an addition to the penal code, the so-called pulpit paragraph of November 28,

1871, which forbade clergy in their official capacity to deal with political matters. A law of June 11, 1872, excluded Jesuits and some related orders (Redemptorists, Lazarists, Priests of the Holy Spirit, Society of the Secret Heart of Jesus) from all Germany. Civil marriage was made obligatory for the whole Empire on February 6, 1875.

The most restrictive laws were those passed in Prussia, which required that state officials be notified of the appointment of clergy, and provided for their education at a German university or approved seminary. In Prussia, out of 4,064 Catholic parishes numbering 8,800,000 souls, 1,103 with 2,085,000 souls came to be without regular pastoral care. As a result of removals (six) and failure to fill vacancies resulting from death (two), the number of bishops actually functioning in office was reduced from twelve to four. In 1875 Prussia dissolved all monastic orders except those caring for the sick, and passed the so-called Breadbasket Law, which stopped subsidies to bishops and priests who refused to obey the laws. The articles of the Prussian constitution which guaranteed self-government to the churches, formerly amended, were now cancelled.

Pius IX reacted to these Prussian measures by declaring them null and void. The conflict, to the distress of both church and state, continued. When Leo XIII succeeded to the papal throne in 1878, he announced his accession to William I in a conciliatory spirit. Vatican officials undertook to moderate the actions of the Center party and get it to support new military legislation. Bismarck in turn modified some of the antichurch measures. In 1885, Bismarck suggested to Spain that Leo XIII be asked to mediate their differences over the Caroline Islands. The pope was pleased with this recognition, and granted Bismarck the highest papal decoration, the Order of Christ. Bismarck repealed more of the antichurch laws, and in 1887 the pope declared the Kulturkampf period ended. Each side had made concessions to the other, but some of the major legislation, such as abolishing the separate Catholic and Protestant sections in the Ministry of Culture, exiling the Jesuits, and requiring civil marriage, remained. On the other hand, the Catholic church and especially the Center party had been strengthened. Catholic orders returned to Prussia in increased numbers. The church profited in the next decades from the general desire to restore religious peace and end state-church conflict. No one wanted a new Kulturkampf.

Monastic Orders and Other Organizations

Monastic institutions in Germany, as elsewhere in Europe, were hard hit by the secularizations of the years following the French Revolution. In 1814, the pope restored the Jesuit order, and the Jesuits soon made their appearance in Germany. It was, however, the revolutionary movements of 1848 that led to the rapid expansion of monasticism in Germany, for these revolutions ended many of the early nineteenth-century police restrictions of the Age of Metternich and brought more freedom of association. This resurgence of monasticism was part and parcel of the great Catholic mid-century revival. Bavaria had 108 monastic settlements in 1840, and 522 in 1869. The figures for Prussia are even more striking; there were 50 settlements in 1849 and 967 in 1872, although the increase in Prussian territory after 1866 should be kept in mind. The Kulturkampf brought the dissolution of most of the monasteries in Prussia and the exile of the Jesuits from all of Germany. Yet by the mid-eighties, monastic orders were again permitted throughout Germany, and the number of institutions increased rapidly. There were 922 in 1883, 2,873 in 1898, and over 7,000 in 1912, with a membership of over 70,000. Many of these were missionary orders active in Germany's newly acquired colonies. In 1904, paragraph two of the anti-Jesuit law of 1872 that regulated the residence of alien and native individual Jesuits in Germany was repealed, but the section of the law which forbade Jesuit institutions or settlements was not repealed until 1917.[20]

The monastic orders were the backbone of the Catholic educational system. Not only did they conduct many private schools, especially higher girls' schools, but they played an important role in the public confessional school system.[21] In many regions their members were employed as regular teachers, and were paid the prescribed salaries which, however, ultimately went to the order and were a most important source of revenue. They often taught other subjects, but religious instruction was their special task. Nonetheless, secular clergy and lay teachers had to help out, for there were simply not enough sisters and brothers for all the things that needed to be done. There were hospitals and various homes for those in need to be staffed. New orders were established, especially devoted to what might be termed social welfare or home mission work. There was also a renewed interest in and support of foreign missions. German monastic orders also had their quota of more mundane callings, such as brewing beer, and the Benedictine monks at Ettal turned out a liqueur which rivaled that of their confreres in France.

The establishment of numerous Catholic lay organizations dates largely from the revolutionary year 1848. In that year, following the examples of France, Ireland, and England, numerous organizations were formed for the protection of religious and church freedom. Many of them were named after Pope Pius. In October, 1848, they held a general meeting and formed the Catholic Association of Germany (*Katholischer Verein Deutschlands*) with the general cooperation of the hierarchy. From that meeting dates the imposing yearly rally of Catholics (*Katholikentag*), which over the years has done much to instill life into many of the Catholic associations.[22]

In 1849 the Boniface Association (*Bonifatiusverein*), named after the great eighth-century apostle to the Germans, was organized to help support work among the Catholic diaspora. By 1907 it had collected over 38,000,000 marks, helped establish over 1,000 parishes, and built over 2,500 churches and mission stations. The Catholic Journeyman's Association was founded in 1846, and this was followed in the 1860s by the Organization of Catholic Labor Unions, which by 1911 had 2,800 locals with a membership of 472,000. The first Catholic student fraternity (*Unitas*) dates back to 1846, and such organizations were soon formed at all universities. Soon after the foundation in France of the Saint Vincent de Paul associations for the care of the needy in local parishes (1833), such associations were established in Germany, and for years were the most important lay social welfare organizations.[23] The Catholic women teachers formed an association in 1885; the men followed suit four years later. Many similar groups were founded for other professions. By 1913 there were 2,656 youth groups with a membership of 254,465. Important general organizations which served to supervise many smaller groups and provide guidance for all sorts of activities were the People's Association for Catholic Germany (*Volksverein für das katholische Deutschland*, 1890), founded by Ludwig Windthorst, the great leader of the Center party; the Charity League for Catholic Germany (*Karitasbund für das katholische Deutschland*, 1897), and the League of Catholic Women (*Katholische Frauenbund*, 1903).[24] It surely took obstinacy and an inordinate desire to go it alone for any German Catholic to escape being a member of one or more of these organizations. The Center party and other regional Catholic political parties also held out the welcome sign. One and all, the organizations did strengthen the church and bring a sense of mutual support. These organizations cut across state and diocesan boundaries, and Catholics were united into a German Catholic church more than ever before. But at the same time, it was a church loyal to Rome and part of the Roman Catholic church universal.[25]

The tremendous growth of Catholic organizations was supported and paralleled by the establishment of a Catholic press. Many parish papers had been founded after 1815, and as a rule they escaped the hands of the censors, for they were hardly radical sheets. The newspapers, however, were usually more outspoken and often came under ban.[26] Papers such as the *Neue Würzburger Zeitung* delighted in attacking things Prussian, and it was excluded from that state. The *Fränkische Courier* received similar treatment in Württemberg. In the period after 1848 and especially after the foundation of the empire, however, the press could circulate freely throughout Germany. *Germania* served as the official organ of the Center party from January 1, 1871, and did not cease publication until December 31, 1938, five years after the party itself had succumbed to Hitler's wiles.

The Catholic papers and journals did yeoman duty during the Kulturkampf and were greatly strengthened by the conflict. In 1878 the *Augustinerverein* was founded to further the Catholic press. Learned Catholic journals had long since appeared in Germany, many supported by religious orders or at the universities. In 1876 the *Görresgesellschaft* was founded for the cultivation of science and learning among Catholics. Its *Philosophisches Jahrbuch* and *Historisches Jahrbuch* have published many scholarly articles and the society has sponsored many other publications.

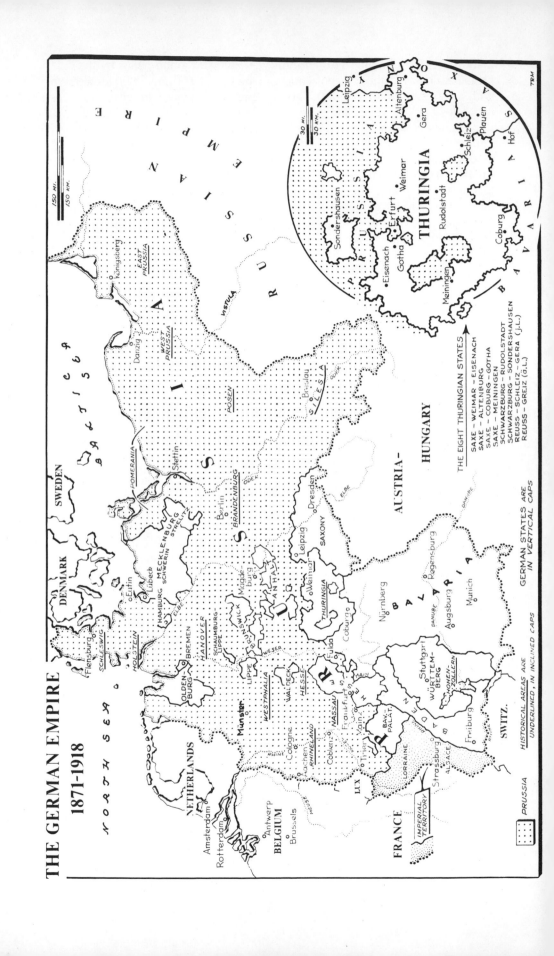

THE GERMAN EMPIRE
1871-1918

RUSSIAN EMPIRE

NORTH SEA

BALTIC SEA

SWEDEN

DENMARK

NETHERLANDS

BELGIUM

FRANCE

SWITZ.

AUSTRIA-HUNGARY

Amsterdam
Rotterdam
Antwerp
Brussels

Flensburg
SCHLESWIG
HOLSTEIN
Eutin
Lübeck
HAMBURG
BREMEN
OLDENBURG
HANOVER
Münster
WESTPHALIA
Cologne
Aachen
RHINELAND
Coblenz
Trier
LUX.
BAV.-PALAT.
LORRAINE
ALSACE
Strassburg
IMPERIAL TERRITORY
Freiburg

Königsberg
EAST PRUSSIA
Danzig
WEST PRUSSIA
POMERANIA
Stettin
ODER
BRANDENBURG
Berlin
MECKLENBURG SCHWERIN
MECKLENBURG STRELITZ
ELBE
SCHAUMBURG LIPPE
BRUNSWICK
WESER
LIPPE
WALDECK
HESSE
NASSAU
Frankfurt
MAIN
Fulda
Coburg

P R U S S I A

SILESIA
Breslau
ODER
POSEN
VISTULA

Magdeburg
ANHALT
Weimar
THURINGIA
Leipzig
SAXONY
Dresden
ELBE

Nürnberg
B A V A R I A
Augsburg
Munich
DANUBE
Regensburg
WÜRTTEMBERG
Stuttgart
HOHENZOLLERN
RHINE

THE EIGHT THURINGIAN STATES

SAXE – WEIMAR – EISENACH
SAXE – ALTENBURG
SAXE – COBURG – GOTHA
SAXE – MEININGEN
SCHWARZBURG – RUDOLSTADT
SCHWARZBURG – SONDERSHAUSEN
REUSS – SCHLEIZ – GERA (j.L.)
REUSS – GREIZ (ö.L.)

GERMAN STATES ARE
IN VERTICAL CAPS

HISTORICAL AREAS ARE
UNDERLINED, IN INCLINED CAPS

PRUSSIA

(inset)

S A X O N Y
Leipzig
Altenburg
Gera
Plauen
Schleiz
Hof
Sondershausen
Eisenach
Gotha
Erfurt
Weimar
THURINGIA
Rudolstadt
Meiningen
Coburg
P R U S S I A
B A V A R I A

30 MI.
30 KM.

150 MI.
150 KM.

TRM

The establishment of a firm organization in the early nineteenth century, the slow but steadfast overthrow of the shackles of Staatskirchentum as it had developed in the eighteenth century, the negotiated adjustments which followed sharp church-state conflicts, the steady expansion of monastic orders, lay organizations, and an articulate press, were not only factors in the development of Catholicism but are also marks of the position the church had achieved in nineteenth-century Germany. On the eve of World War I, Germany had two cardinals and was organized into five archbishoprics (Bamberg, Freiburg, Gnesen-Posen, Cologne, and Munich-Freising), twenty bishoprics, three apostolic vicarates, and two apostolic prefectures. Small portions of Prussian territory were included in the "Austro-Hungarian" bishoprics of Olmütz and Prague. According to the 1910 census, Catholics numbered 23,821,453, and according to the 1915 census, they were served by 18,417 secular clergy. In addition, there were 1,072 regular clergy chiefly concerned with school duties, 891 institutional clergy, and 1,287 holding no church office. There were 335 male monastic establishments, with 1,860 priests, 579 other clergy and scholastics, 3,651 lay brothers, and 274 novices. Female monastic establishments numbered 6,246, with 64,249 members and 4,784 novices.[27]

There are no figures available on church attendance, but at least by European standards German Catholics attended services well. Statistics on the inner life of the church help to indicate the relationship of individuals to the church. In 1915, out of 71,093 civil marriages where both bride and groom were Catholic, 66,670 were later solemnized by the church; out of 32,072 mixed civil marriages, 11,072 were later solemnized by the church. Baptismal figures were high. There were 530,616 live births to Catholic families in 1915 and 531,400 baptisms, which would indicate some carry-over from the previous year. Of 62,749 children born to parents of mixed marriages, only 29,831 received Catholic baptism, a figure which, like the one on mixed marriages, was very disturbing to the church authorities. Of 55,369 illegitimate children born to Catholic mothers, 54,220 were baptized. Of the 418,744 Catholics who died, 399,459 received church burials. There were 224,758,673 communicants, but only 13,893,147 fulfilled their Easter obligation.

The church was free to acquire property and receive gifts and inheritances. It also received direct subsidies—often the continuation of ancient grants of payments resulting from the secularization of land and titles.[28] In some of the states the church could levy church taxes on its members. These were set by the diocesan and state officials, and were usually collected by the state for the church. In many instances the states indirectly assumed a large part of the cost of Catholic education by supporting a confessional school system and by paying teachers of religion in schools which were not divided confessionally. Indeed, the

Catholic church in imperial Germany was satisfactorily situated financially, and it drew heavily on state support. In other ways as well the
Catholic church had made great progress. It had built up a strong and
well-administered church body, amply staffed, with a vast network of
organizations closely related to the daily life of its members. Politically
it was supported by the well-established Center party, and by the widely
diffused confessional and private school system which met the church's
basic educational desires. The old fear that Catholicism was a minority
religion in danger of being overwhelmed by a Protestant majority no
longer haunted the church. It had achieved a standing throughout Germany such as it had not known since the days before the Reformation.

3.

The Constitutional Framework of the Land Churches under the Weimar Republic

The Overthrow of the Princes

The abdication of the princes in November, 1918, closed a four-hundred-year chapter in the history of the Land churches in Germany. As heads of the governments the princes had exercised some powers over the churches, but as summi episcopi of the Protestant churches they had headed the whole church administration. In this latter capacity they acted not as monarchs, but as the principal members of the church. While many of the responsibilities and duties had long since been passed on to church or civil administrative agencies, there were still many things which to the end required the approval of the princes as heads of the churches before they were legal. For example, the princes usually made, or at least confirmed, the appointment of higher church officials, and church law required their approval.[1] But in 1918 the summit was cut off from the whole legal framework of the Protestant churches, and the German churches were very complex legal institutions indeed. If in Germany the state was founded on law, if it was a *Rechtsstaat,* so were the churches.

The first necessity was obviously to place the powers exercised by the rulers in someone else's hands. In most of the Land churches these powers went over to the consistories, which had formerly been appointed by the princes to administer church affairs. The consistories now carried on, but as church rather than as state offices. Ultimately, by civil administrative order or state law, this arrangement was formally recognized.[2] At times the consistories were supplemented by delegates from the synodical bodies. In Prussia, through a law on the temporary organization of state power, the so-called *Notverfassung* of March 20, 1919, the rights formerly exercised by the king over the church were delegated to three Protestant state ministers who soon became known as the "Three Holy Kings." The Prussian consistory, which along with church bodies everywhere asserted the right of the churches to regulate their own affairs, protested this arrangement as a violation of church self-government. However, it was even incorporated into Article 82 of the Prussian constitution (November 30, 1920) with the proviso that the three ministers should exercise their powers only "insofar as the Evangelical churches have not by ecclesiastical laws, approved by state law, transferred such rights to church authorities."[3] This transfer of powers was ultimately done when a church assembly met in Berlin on September 24, 1921. The former powers of the Prussian king as summus episcopus now formally and legally passed into the hands of church authorities. It was a memorable day in the constitutional development of the independent self-government of the Prussian Land churches.[4] Whereas formerly the officials in the higher church affairs were in most states considered state officials, now everywhere they were clearly officers of the church.[5]

The first days of the November Revolution were anxious ones for the church. Although Social Democrats were in control of the national government as well as many of the states, it was primarily proclamations by the state authorities that caused alarm. In Prussia, Saxony, Brunswick, Hamburg, Bremen, and some of the small Thuringian states, radical elements not only demanded complete separation of church and state, but also undertook measures to curtail, if not abolish completely, religious instruction in the schools.[6] The churches were to be shorn—so at least rumor had it—of their rights as public corporations, which would have deprived them of their privilege of raising church taxes and would also have denied them certain special police and legal protections. Church authorities were not long in raising their voices in protest. With elections to the constituent assembly in the offing, none of the leading governing officials wanted to launch a Kulturkampf. The offending decrees, particularly in regard to religious instruction in the schools, were suspended. It was generally agreed that the future status of the churches and of religious instruction would have to be regulated in the new federal constitution, in the state constitutions, and in new church constitutions.

What the burning issues were in those first months of the revolution are indicated in four questions which the church leaders submitted to the political parties in Prussia. They asked how each party stood on the questions of (1) Christian religious instruction in the elementary and higher schools; (2) the retention of chaplains in the army, navy, public hospitals, and prisons; (3) the existing legal position of the churches as public corporations under public law, and especially their rights to tax their members; and (4) the continuation of state subsidies to the churches and the safeguarding of church property. With the exception of the Social Democrats, all the parties expressed themselves in a way agreeable to church authorities on these issues.[7]

The election to the constituent assembly on January 19, 1919, brought the following division of seats: Majority Socialists, 165; Independent Socialists (communists), 22; Democrats, 74; Center party, 89; German People's party, 22; German Nationalists, 42; other small parties, 9. The socialists could muster only 187 votes against 236 of the other parties, all of which were in greater or lesser degree friendly to church interests. It was actually a Social Democrat-Democrat-Center party coali-

tion which dominated the assembly which met at Weimar on February 6,
1919. Early in its deliberations the Weimar Assembly received a petition
from the German Evangelical Church Committee, the executive group of
the German Evangelical Church Conference. The committee spoke for
the Land churches and demanded that the new constitution should recognize: (1) existing Land churches as public corporations; (2) that Sunday and religious holidays as well as church and religious services be
under state protection; (3) that churches be permitted to regulate and
administer their own affairs; (4) that church property be safeguarded, that
state subsidies be stopped only if compensation was arranged in agreement with the churches, and that the churches have the right to tax their
own members; (5) that the Land churches have the right to join together
into a national body with the rights of a public corporation; (6) that the
position of the Land churches be safeguarded in respect to army, navy,
and institutional chaplains, and that the theological faculties be maintained at the universities; and (7) that the Christian character of the elementary schools be maintained.[8]

The status and position of the churches did not cause great difficulties at Weimar, and actually all the points the committee sought found
their way into the constitution, although broadened to apply to all
church bodies, and not only to the Land churches.[9] But the question of
religious education in the schools, in which both Protestants and Catholics were deeply interested, almost disrupted the work of the assembly.
Finally important compromises on the school articles were negotiated
which established not only the interdenominational (*Simultan*) schools,
but permitted confessional schools (where students and teachers are of
one confession) as well. The constitution was approved on July 31, and
went into effect on August 11, 1919. Since the constitution states that
"National law breaks state law" (Article 13), the provisions of the Weimar Constitution laid the guidelines for the provisions of the state and
church constitutions which were to follow.

The Weimar Constitution

Although the old imperial constitution had no provisions in regard
to religion and the churches, these matters being left entirely to the
states, a law of the preceding North German Confederation relating to
religious liberty continued in effect. This Law Relating to the Equality of
Confessions in Civil and Political Matters of July 7, 1869, consisted of
one article which invalidated all existing restrictions of civil and political rights based on differences of religious confessions, and decreed that
the right to take part in communal and state legislative bodies and to
hold public office should not be dependent on any religious qualification. In fact, provisions guaranteeing religious equality already existed in
many of the state constitutions, and the law of 1869 simply gave them
general application in the North German Confederation, and later in the
Empire. This law of 1869 was broader than the old provisions of Article

16 of the Germanic Constitution (1815), which had extended religious freedom to only the three major confessions—Catholic, Lutheran, and Reformed. Since 1869 adherents of non-Christian religions and atheists had not been subject to legal disabilities.[10]

The Weimar Constitution stated that the national government could by legislation establish fundamental principles in regard to the rights and duties of religious associations (Article 10). What the Reich might do under this provision was uncertain. On the other hand, it did provide the possibility of curbing extreme legislation in the states by the enactment of a federal law. The constitution went on specifically to guarantee full religious liberty, and placed the practice of religion under the protection of the state. Religious liberty, however, was to be subject to law. The founding fathers wanted to insure that if certain practices were considered dangerous to the safety of the state or contrary to prevailing moral standards, they could not be continued on the theory that they were religious observances. In short, "state law had precedence over religious commandment."[11] It was clear that the state could require compliance with compulsory vaccination or other similar laws. No one was to be compelled to disclose his religious affiliation unless certain duties depended upon it, or unless it was required for certain statistical purposes. This latter provision made it easier for the churches to collect their taxes, and was essential if the school systems were to be established on a confessional basis. It also was established that if a census taker asked about religious affiliation, he was not trespassing on what the constitution drafters regarded as religious liberty.

The constitution not only guaranteed the religious liberties of the individual, but also the liberties and position of the churches. It stated boldly: "There is no state church" (Article 137). Just what the term "state church" covered was not defined, and it was open to many interpretations. Actually, there had been no one state church in Germany for many years. The constitutional provision no doubt was directed at the close connection which had previously existed between state and church, and was meant to imply what was also expressly stated later, that the churches should regulate their own affairs.

One clause in Article 137 provided that every religious association "shall fill its own offices without assistance from the state or the local authorities." This clause had important implications, for it did away with certain practices which the civil authorities had in some instances adopted in regard to appointment of clergy. These were sometimes referred to as "spurious patronages" (*unechte Patronate*), and were rights to share in the appointment of clergy which did not rest on canon law or on some special service to the church, but were the result of certain sovereign rights over the churches.[12] The old private patronages remained, and since it was often difficult to decide the basis of existing patronage rights, the liquidation of these old obligations and privileges made slow progress. To have abolished the private patronage rights would have relieved the patrons of important financial obligations to repair churches and parsonages. On the other hand, some noble families were interested in maintaining their hereditary position in respect to certain churches.

The churches which had previously been recognized as public corporations were to retain their status. Other religious bodies on application could become public corporations if, as evidenced by their constitution and numbers, they gave promise of being a permanent body. They would thereby gain the right to levy taxes on the basis of civil tax lists, according to the provision of state laws.[13] Should several religious bodies which were public corporations join into an association (*Verband*), this association was also to be considered a public corporation. This provision covered the possible formation of some kind of a confederation or unification of the Land churches. All Germans had the right to form associations and clubs as long as they did not contravene penal laws, and this right extended to the formation of religious associations and clubs as well (Article 24). It should be added that associations formed for the cultivation of a particular philosophy of life (*Weltanschauung*) might achieve the same corporative status as a religious group.

Another important provision for the churches was the safeguarding of their properties and of the subsidies they had been receiving from the state governments (Article 138). All subsidies which by agreement or special legal provision had previously been paid to the churches were to be redeemed with compensation under state law according to norms set up by the national government.[14] This was specifically spelled out again in one of the transitional and concluding articles (Article 173) which stated: "Until the promulgation of a national law provided for by Article 138, existing public grants to religious associations based on law, contract, or special legal title shall remain in force." Since the national government never enacted such legislation, the continued payment of subsidies to the churches was safeguarded. Furthermore, the constitution stated: "The property and other rights of religious associations and religious unions in their cultural, educational, and social welfare institutions, foundations, and other funds shall be guaranteed" (Article 138, section 2).

Sundays and other holidays were to remain as days of rest and were to be protected by law. Members of the armed forces were guaranteed free time sufficient for the fulfillment of their religious duties. Provision was also made, should there be need, for chaplains in the armed services, hospitals, and penal institutions. The articles on schools met in all essentials the demands of the churches. While interdenominational schools were to be the norm, confessional schools at the request of parents and in accordance with state laws were to be permitted. Religious instruction was to be a regular part of the curriculum in all schools except the purely secular (*weltliche*) ones. Theological faculties at the universities were to be continued.[15]

The dismal fears—not entirely unjustified—which prevailed in many circles in the first days of the revolution as to what would happen to religion and the churches were in large part dispelled by the provisions of the Weimar Constitution. No one knew what the future would hold, but certainly the constitution could hardly have gone further in giving status and safety to religion and to religious associations. The churches were assured the right of self-government, financial help, and the continuation of religious instruction in the schools in much the same fashion as before. School inspection by the clergy had been ended in favor of full-time trained lay officials (Article 144), but this change had long been expected. The obligatory union of church and school positions (as when school teachers had to play the organ, for example) was forbidden. The privileged positions held by the Land churches and the Catholic church had given way to the recognition of the equality of other religious denominations. Yet in practice the status and predominance of the large Protestant Land churches and of the Catholic church remained.

The provisions of the federal constitution were so broad and inclusive that there was little left for the state constitutions to add in the way of fundamental rights. In most instances they repeated, unnecessarily, statements on freedom of religion already existing in the Weimar Constitution. Some of the state constitutions were, however, more detailed than the federal constitution, and hence they contained longer statements on the schools, on the regulation of procedures for resigning church memberships, on cemeteries, or on the rights of church patrons. Some of the constitutions, such as those of Thuringia, Hamburg, Anhalt, Lippe, and Schaumburg-Lippe, had nothing at all to say on the position of the churches.

The New Land Church Constitutions

The territorial losses suffered by Germany in World War I and the reduction of the number of federal states through territorial consolidations resulted in a decrease in the number of Land churches and in a reduction in the extent of others. Thus the two Land churches of Alsace-Lorraine disappeared from the list of German churches. When the eight small states of Reuss-Schleiz-Gera, Saxe-Weimar, Saxe-Meiningen, Saxe-Altenburg, Saxe-Gotha, Reuss-Greiz, Schwarzburg-Rudolfstadt, and Schwarzburg-Sondershausen united to form one state of Thuringia, the former Land churches, with the exception of Reuss-Greiz, united to form one Thuringian Land church. In its constitution the Thuringian church went further than the rest in establishing a centralized administration and giving it dominant control over finances.[16] Coburg was joined to Bavaria, and the Coburg Land church was united to the Bavarian Land Church Right of the Rhine. This meant a loss of ten Land churches and the addition of one new one, making a total of twenty-eight Land churches in the German republic. The territory lost by Germany, except for Alsace-Lorraine, had all been in the state of Prussia, and so some of the Prussian Land churches lost areas. The most significant consequent readjustment was the reduction in the number of provincial churches from nine to eight in the Evangelical Church of the Old Prussian Union. Here the remnants of the provinces of Posen and West Prussia were consolidated into one march (*Grenzmark*), Posen-West Prussia.

State boundaries and Land church boundaries, however, were not the same. Thus in Prussia in 1919, there were seven Land churches: (1) the Evangelical Church of the Old Prussian Union, which in turn had eight provincial churches (East Prussia, Brandenburg, Pomerania, Mark Posen-West Prussia, Silesia, Saxony, Westphalia, Rhine Province); (2) Hanover, Lutheran; (3) Hanover, Reformed; (4) Schleswig-Holstein; (5) Hesse-Cassel; (6) Nassau; and (7) Frankfurt. An eighth Land church was added in 1922 when Pyrmont was joined to Prussia (Province of Hanover), and Waldeck was incorporated into Prussia (Province of Nassau) in 1929. While from 1922–29 the civil jurisdiction over these territories changed, the Land church of Waldeck-Pyrmont continued its uninterrupted unity.[17] The Church of the Old Prussian Union also sought to negotiate and maintain tenuous agreements with the churches in the lost territories to the east.[18] Other states besides Prussia had a number of Land churches within their borders, with the result that while the Weimar Republic was a federal union of eighteen states, it included twenty-eight Protestant Land churches. In addition, there were of course the various Free churches and many small sects, as well as the Catholic and Old Catholic churches.

Between 1919 and 1924, twenty-six of these twenty-eight Land churches drew up constitutions, and the churches of Lippe and of Schaumburg-Lippe took steps to update their old fundamental laws, although they did not enact new constitutions.[19] While the formulation of the constitutions was new, and their significance is not to be underestimated, they made no startling innovations. No new churches were established, no new creeds drawn up. Some actually were little more than reformulations of former documents, as for example in Westphalia and the Rhineland, where the Ordinance of 1835, with its basic provisions for a presbyter-synodical church government, was retained.[20] Statements of faith, where they appeared, were largely an affirmation of obvious biblical truths and of the ancient creeds and Reformation confessions. Even these statements tended to arouse controversy, as did the drafting of the preamble of the constitution of the Evangelical Church of the Old Prussian Union, which finally emerged in the following wording:

> True to the inheritance from our fathers, the Evangelical Land church of the older provinces of Prussia stands on the gospel of Jesus Christ, the son of the living God who was crucified for us and arose from the dead, the Lord of the church, as it is given in holy writ, and recognizes the continued validity of its confessions: the apostolic and other ancient church creeds, also the Augsburg Confession, the Apology, the Schmalkaldic Articles and the Lesser and Greater Catechisms of Luther in the Lutheran congregations, and the Heidelberg Catechism in the Reformed as well as other confessions, where such remain in force. The gospel witnessed in the confessions is the untouchable foundation for the teaching, work, and fellowship of the church.[21]

The constitutions were usually very detailed. The one for the Evangelical Church of the Old Prussian Union contained 165 articles and four long annexes, about a hundred compact pages long. In addition there were old laws which remained in effect, and much legislation and many ordinances were necessary to implement the new constitution. Some idea of the legal web surrounding the churches can be ascertained from the fact that Professor Godehard Ebers in 1932 required three stout volumes and a total of 1,968 pages to print the constitutions and relevant laws of the Land churches of Prussia. A fourth volume of commentary contains many additional ordinances and laws.[22] His collection includes only eight of the Land churches, and the material on the others is of a similar nature.

It is not easy to find one's way through this mass of material, and to attempt a church-by-church analysis would not be rewarding. Taken as a whole, the constitutions express an effort to bring the laity more into the affairs of the church. Parish governments were reorganized, expanded, and given more significant powers. More offices were to be filled by direct election of the church members. The old system of indirect election, where lower synods elected representatives to the higher bodies—the Germans dubbed it "the filter system"—practically disappeared. Women received the vote, and so great was the influence of what was happening in the political field that a system of proportional representation was often adopted. The synods, which had made their way slowly in the German churches in the nineteenth century as organs of self-government, now became the dominating sovereign bodies. On the other hand, the old consistories under various names remained as bodies of permanent administrative officials.[23] The German churches thus continued their old synodical-consistorial form of church government, but with the difference that now both bodies were church controlled.

In most instances, the powers which formerly had been exercised by the princes as summi episcopi now went over to special collegial executive committees. These were constituted in various ways but usually stemmed from the highest synodical bodies. There was much disagreement about what the head or chairman of these bodies was to be called. There was a strong movement in many places for the establishment of bishops, an office rarely known in the history of German Protestantism, and which had not existed in the churches before the revolution of 1918. In most places the innovation of the office was rejected. It was felt that the establishment of bishops would inevitably lead to comparisons with those in the Catholic church, and that the Protestant bishops would come off second best. Creating a bishop would also mean that no layman could ever head the church, which would be contrary to the efforts that were being made to bring more lay participation in church government. Some objected because a Protestant bishop would be married, and the title would in German fashion also be associated with his wife. "Frau Bischof" did not sound right to Protestant or Catholic ears. Nevertheless, seven churches established the office of bishop. These included provincial churches within Prussia—the Lutheran Land church in Hanover, the Lutheran Land church in Schleswig-Holstein (one for Schleswig, one for Holstein), and the Evangelical church in Nassau—and the Lutheran Land churches in Saxony, Mecklenburg-Schwerin, Mecklenburg-Strelitz, and Brunswick. Other churches decided to call their chief executive officers by such varied names as general superintendent, church president, and Land president. Whatever the title, their powers were much the same, and bore witness to the realization that church self-government needed rather strong executive leadership as well as a broad parish and synodical organization.[24]

While the church constitutions did organize and establish self-government, they did not attempt to establish complete separation of church and state. It was always realized that the churches as public corporations operated within the framework of the law of the land. Here and there remnants of old state control or supervision of the churches remained, but it was nevertheless on a different basis. For example, in Prussia the state formerly had to give its approval to church laws. Now the state was only to be informed of them. It had a month to file objections to the measures; such objections, however, were permitted only if the measure contravened state law, if it involved the state in carrying out the church law, or if it involved certain property and taxation questions. Should the church authorities feel that the objections of the state were not in order, they could appeal to an administrative court. These particular provisions were repealed in 1931 when the state negotiated an agreement with the Protestant churches. Yet a whole list of reservations remained which the state had originally written into the law of 1924 that recognized and implemented the Prussian church constitutions.[25]

The state was chiefly involved in the financial affairs of the church. As long as the states supplied substantial subsidies to many of the churches and cooperated in the collection of church taxes, they could scarcely avoid involvement. It should be noted that the churches were the ones who were most concerned about maintaining these financial ties with the states; they also wanted the states to enforce sumptuary measures protecting Sundays and church holidays, to provide religious education in the schools, and to maintain theological faculties at the state universities. Their desires were natural, in light of the general German concept that the state was more than a *Polizeistaat,* that it also was a *Kulturstaat,* and as such it had a duty to support religion and the churches along with schools, theaters, orchestras, museums, and other aspects of the cultural life of the nation.

Establishment of the German Evangelical Church Confederation

While nation, states, and churches were busy drawing up their constitutions and reorganizing their governments, a movement to bring about closer union among the Protestant churches was under way. Before the revolution of 1918, the only institutions which represented the Land churches as a whole were the German Evangelical Church Conference (the so-called Eisenach Conference), which had been meeting biennially ever since 1852, and the German Evangelical Church Committee, established in 1903, a sort of standing executive committee made up of delegates from the governing bodies of the Land churches. It was this latter organization which took the initiative.

In early February, 1919, ten members of this committee and five delegates to the Conference of the German Evangelical Workers' Organizations, then meeting in Berlin, held a joint meeting where the calling of a Kirchentag was discussed.[26] D. Bodo Voights, the chairman of the German Evangelical Church Committee, decided that instead of immediately issuing a call for the meeting of a Kirchentag, he would be systematic in order to give the whole procedure a safer legal foundation. With the cooperation of representatives of the Evangelical Workers' Organizations, he issued a call for a preliminary conference to be held at Kassel at the end of the month, to which were invited all previous members of the German Evangelical Church Committee and of the Eisenach Conference, the presidents of the highest synods of each Land, fifty-six representatives of various church organizations, and a number of other interested persons picked by the Evangelical Church Committee. Some 130 of those invited appeared (February 27–28), and it was decided to call a general German Evangelical Kirchentag for the purpose of establishing some sort of permanent organization to bring together all of the Land churches. It was stressed that there was no intention of establishing a United Reich church, and that the independence of each church, particularly in relation to its confessional basis, was to be safeguarded. This Kassel meeting appointed a committee of twenty-one to arrange for the meeting of the Kirchentag and prepare the agenda.[27]

The first postwar German Evangelical Kirchentag assembled in Dresden, September 1–5, 1919. By then the Treaty of Versailles had been signed and the Weimar Constitution adopted. There had been a conscious effort to provide a broad spectrum of membership; representatives from church musical groups, from the theological faculties at the universities, from the teachers of religion in the schools, from the military chaplaincy, and from various other fields were invited. Although there was no direct election of delegates and the appointment procedure tended to be conservative, it was nevertheless the most representative Protestant church body—clerical, lay, men and women—that had ever met in Germany.[28]

The Kirchentag decided to establish a German Evangelical Church Confederation (Deutsche Evangelische Kirchenbund, DEK), "where the German Evangelical Land churches, maintaining their independence on matters of confession and government, could grasp hands."[29] The chief organ of the confederation was to be the German Evangelical Kirchentag. The new confederation was to take over the functions of the German Evangelical Church Conference (Eisenach), and the assembly drafted a statement outlining the original and supervisory powers of the confederation.[30] A committee was appointed to elaborate a draft of a constitution and prepare for the next meeting of the Kirchentag. State-

ments were also adopted on the conduct of synodical elections, the care
of German Protestants in foreign lands, religious education in the
schools, the rights of minority groups in congregations to seek the services of other than the appointed pastors, and on a variety of other
matters. After issuing pronouncements against the proposed trial of William II, and sending greetings to war prisoners, to congregations in
ceded territories, and to various other groups, the Kirchentag adjourned.[31] These latter pronouncements, while natural enough to those
sadly recalling "the good old days," do indicate that the group was not
prepared to turn their backs on the past. Perhaps their strongly patriotic
stand during the war made it difficult for them to accept the realities of a
defeated Germany.

A year later, on September 11–15, 1921, the second Kirchentag
met in Stuttgart. Its chief task was the adoption of the constitution of the
confederation. The preparatory commission had done a careful job, and
the draft was skillfully presented. Debate there was, but no bitter controversy, and the constitution was approved unanimously. The only other
significant question before the Kirchentag was the one of religious education. This was timely, as the Reichstag was considering the enactment
of a national school law. Without decrying the existence of interdenominational schools, the Kirchentag supported the continued existence
of confessional Evangelical schools.

The constitution of the German Evangelical Church Confederation
needed the approval of all Land churches. This was given in the following
months, and on Ascension Day, May 25, 1922, amid great ceremony and
rejoicing in the castle church at Wittenberg, the church where Luther had
preached on so many occasions, the new German Evangelical Church
Confederation was inaugurated. It was not meant to be a united church,
but it did express the genuine desire of the Land churches for more
fellowship, and in the eyes of many it was a step towards a firmer union
which would follow. According to its constitution, the purpose of the
confederation was: (1) to protect and represent the common interests of
the German Evangelical Land churches; (2) to cultivate the common
consciousness of German Protestantism; and (3) to support the religious-
ethical Weltanschauung of the German churches of the Reformation—
"all this while safeguarding the independence of the confederated
churches in respect to their confession, constitution, and administration."[32] The confederation was to have original jurisdiction in representing Protestant interests to foreign countries, to the Reich government, and
to other religious bodies within Germany, and in the care of German
Protestants abroad. Other tasks could be referred to it by member
churches, which, however, needed the approval of the whole confederation before they could be acted upon. It further had the duty of encouraging and soliciting the member churches to support measures relating to
church life as well as to the general social life and welfare of the nation.

The supreme organ of government was the Kirchentag, with a
membership of 210. Of these, 150 were to be elected by the highest

synods of the Land churches in proportion to membership; 60 were to
be appointed by the executive committee of the confederation from
various categories. The Kirchentag was to be elected for a six-year term,
and was to meet at least twice in regular session, although special
sessions could be called. The consent of the Kirchentag was required for
all confederation laws, and it was in every way the highest sovereign
body.

The Church Confederation Council (*Kirchenbundesrat*) constituted
a sort of second chamber, and was made up of representatives of the
church administrations of the member churches, each church having at
least one vote, and the larger churches one representative for every
500,000 souls, although no one church was to have more than two-
fifths of the total vote. It had to approve all confederation church laws
and all administrative measures which involved the confederation's financial obligations.

The Church Committee (*Kirchenausschuss*) was to serve as a collective executive. It was made up of thirty-six members, eighteen elected
by the Kirchentag from its membership, and eighteen delegated by the
Church Confederation Council from its membership. The allotment of
representation to various churches was not unlike the representation in
the old German Evangelical Church Committee established in 1903.
The Church Committee was to be presided over by the head of the
administration of the Church of the Old Prussian Union. It was to represent the confederation before the courts and other governmental bodies,
issue ordinances, and in general carry on the confederation's work.

Article 3 of the constitution provided that a future confederation
law would regulate the conditions under which other Evangelical religious associations could join the confederation. Such a law was enacted
on June 17, 1924, and foresaw the admission of religious associations,
congregations, and clergy outside of Germany to the confederation.
Representatives of such groups were to be invited to the meeting of the
Kirchentag, but were to have only a consultative voice.[33] A member
could withdraw from the confederation at any time (Article 21).

The constitutional framework of the confederation is not unique,
nor did it bring about great innovations; rather, it institutionalized and
advanced the old central church institutions of imperial times. The
leaders did not break with, but continued, the lines along which church
unity had been developing. Wisely too they did not tamper with church
names or confessions. When the National Socialists wanted to regiment
(*gleichschalten*) the Protestant churches, it was not enough to take over
and transform the central governing authorities; they had to take over
each individual Land church with its roots deep in the past—a task
which proved too much for Hitler and his ruthless associates. Had the
historic confessions and Land churches been swept away in 1919–22 in
the interests of church unity, it would have been more difficult to lay a
strong foundation for the Confessing church of the 1930s, the church
which successfully thwarted the policies of the Nazi officials. The religious settlement and the position of the churches established by the

Weimar Constitution are of fundamental significance, for they are the guidelines for all subsequent church-state relations in Germany. The churches were willing to work toward a more centralized church union than they had thus far achieved, but they wanted to do it while retaining their essential freedom. They were not concerned about the Weimar political system, and they failed to realize that political and religious interests were closely entwined. In the end, the basic Weimar constitutional settlement was carried over into the post-World War II era.

4.

Church Life in Protestant Churches during the Weimar Republic

Church Finances and Schools

The enactment of Reich, state, church, and church confederation constitutions in the early post-World War I years by no means settled all legal
questions. The generally bad economic conditions caused great financial distress to the churches. In most cases the states agreed to increase
their subsidies as inflation set in. In Saxony, however, the Land church
had to go to court, where it won a decision obligating the state to pay it
increased subsidies. In other states new laws were enacted which regulated further payments. Both the agreement that Bavaria negotiated with
its two Land churches in November, 1924, and the concordat concluded with the Vatican made provision for payments to the churches,
which were in part based on comparison with the salaries paid certain
state officials. One of the most important clauses of the agreement that
Prussia negotiated with its Protestant Land churches in May, 1931, was
the provision that the state would henceforth pay the churches
4,950,000 marks yearly.[1]

If there were difficulties over the payment of subsidies, the collection of church taxes involved even more church-state problems. The
churches had the right to collect these taxes under provisions of the
federal constitution, but the collection had to be done according to
Land law. Tax laws are always complicated, and the measures relating
to church taxes were no exception. The enactment and constant revision of this legislation went on throughout the 1920s. An additional
complicating factor was that during the Weimar Republic many Jewish
congregations and some of the Free churches which undertook to become corporations under public law were awarded the privilege of
taxing their members.[2]

In the late twenties, as the economic depression cut the revenues of
the churches, another source of revenue was adopted in some of them.
There were many church members, some 40 to 50 percent of the population, who paid no income tax and owned no property, and who
therefore paid no church taxes. Church leaders felt that these people
might also be asked to contribute their mite towards the church, so as to

show no discrimination between the rich and the poor. The states permitted the churches to levy a modest head tax on all members. The age for the imposition of these charges varied; often it was under the age when other tax liabilities began, but there were numerous exemptions, such as for wives or those on public relief. The amounts asked for were not large; in some states it was a uniform levy, in others it was graduated according to income. Under the Prussian law of 1928 which introduced this payment—legally it was a tax—the payments ranged from three to thirty marks. In Baden the fee was two to twelve marks, and in Oldenburg two to four marks. These payments, usually known as "church money" (*Kirchgeld*), were always kept separate from the regular church taxes; they were often collected in a different fashion and assigned to special purposes. In some states they were retained entirely by the local congregations, while in others they were shared, like the regular church taxes, with the provincial or Land church authorities.[3]

The state governments always supervised the levying of Kirchgeld and church taxes; the amount of the levies had to be approved by the governments. In some cases the churches collected the revenues themselves, and at times congregations united to form special church finance offices. The laws, however, permitted the churches to arrange for the state or local fiscal officials to collect the taxes, in which case the civil authorities charged a collection fee averaging 3 to 4 percent. Only state authorities could use coercion to collect unpaid taxes.[4]

The financial legislation alone is evidence that there were many ties left between church and state under the Weimar Republic. Another field of legislation where interests of church and state touched was school affairs. The Reich attempted to pass a national school law several times during the 1920s, but always failed, mainly because no agreement could be reached on whether interdenominational or confessional schools should be established.[5] Both the Protestant churches and the Catholic church were active in furthering their particular aims. The national government was able to enact one important bit of legislation, a law on the religious education of children (July 15, 1921), which settled the thorny problem of which confessional schools children of mixed marriages should attend. Since no other national school laws were passed, schools remained, as before, subject to state legislation. Yet outside of the flurry of protest against religious instruction in the schools which occurred in the first days of the revolution in some states, there was no serious conflict over religious education in the years 1920–1933.

Diverse Movements within the Churches

The cooperation among political parties which had brought about such a favorable settlement for the churches in the Weimar Constitution on the whole continued during the 1920s. This is not to say that there was no controversy, for religion at times played a very important role in politics. Certainly it was Protestant opposition to the election of a Catholic president that helped sweep Hindenburg into office in 1925. The opposition of the Protestant churches to the conclusion of a national concordat also contributed to delaying that agreement until 1933, the era of Hitler, when the Reichstag no longer presented any problems. Religious and ideological differences prevented the enactment of a national school law. But there was no dramatic flare-up of religious antagonisms.

The Center party drew its major support from Catholics, and Protestants tended to vote the other tickets. It has been estimated that 70 to 80 percent of the Protestant clergy were conservative and nationalistic. Their attitude gave rise to a derogatory saying in the 1920s: "The church is politically neutral, but it votes German National."[6] The Social Democrats while still opposing what the party considered the vested interests of the church, had lost their antireligious belligerency. The people had rallied so vigorously to the support of the churches in the first days of the revolution, when some extreme party leaders had tried to inaugurate a radical separation of church and state and of church and schools, that the leaders were convinced that they could gain votes if they adhered to the old party slogan of the Erfurt Program: "Religion is a private matter."[7] They also laid less stress on the other demands of that party program, that no public funds should be used for religious purposes, and that schools should be completely secularized. After all, these points had been conceded when they approved the Weimar Constitution. This tendency of the Social Democrats towards a more moderate antichurch policy was reinforced as the left wing of the party began to go its own way and soon established itself as the Communist party, where the belligerent anticlericals were concentrated. As Social Democratic hostility to communism increased, the party became more willing to soft-pedal its hostility to the churches. A movement within socialism had begun which was to develop to the point that the party after World War II no longer opposed religious instruction in the schools and was not concerned about making the establishment of confessional school systems a critical issue.

Many factors, of course, contributed to this meeting of socialism and religion. The independent self-governing churches could no longer be labelled as tools of the state. The churches, realizing they were losing their influence among the working classes, made conscious efforts to win back their support. While the churches did not change their stripes, they did become less conservative. Their growing concern for the workers was evidenced in their efforts to bring representatives from this group into the governing bodies of the local congregations, and even into the higher echelons of church government. A religious-socialist movement made headway within the church. This movement had existed in some Protestant countries before the war, and was perhaps best represented in Switzerland. It spread to Baden, where in 1919 the People's Church Alliance (*Volkskirchliche Vereinigung*) was formed, which was soon transformed into the People's Church Confederation of Evangelical Socialists (*Volkskirchenbund evangelischer Sozialisten*).[8]

Similar groups were established in other states, and in 1926 it was possible to bring them together into the Confederation of Religious Socialists of Germany (*Bund religiöser Sozialisten Deutschland*). They came to have representatives in the Land synods in Baden and Thuringia, and, after 1930, even one representative in the Kirchentag.[9] There was no set of common policies or beliefs, except perhaps a common emphasis on the basic revolutionary character of Christianity and on the communistic character of the early Christian communities. They supported the establishment of some Christian communistic worker settlements. These groups carried on considerable propaganda and, like the Fabian socialists in England, exercised an influence quite out of proportion to their membership. Clergy who openly professed adherence to socialism were a strange phenomenon in Germany. In 1932 the Brotherhood of Socialist Theologians numbered 200 members, yet the Land churches as a whole tended to put Marxism, socialism, communism, and atheism in one pot; they were all condemned.[10] That the church influence continued to be generally conservative was characteristic not only of German churches, but of churches everywhere.

The socialist Christians not only declaimed against the evils of capitalism, imperialism, and oppression of the masses, but also led in opposing another movement within the churches. This was the attempt to Germanize religion and free it from all "alien racial influence," especially Judaism. The general term "German religious movement" (*Deutschreligöse Bewegung*) applies to all of the Germanizing groups, but they can also be split into two broad divisions. The German Christian Movement (*Deutsch-christliche Bewegung*) sought to maintain ties to Christianity, while the German Faith Movement (*Deutschgläubige Bewegung*) rejected Christianity and returned to early German pagan gods. The similarity in names, and the fact that members of these groups often changed them, does not make it easy to follow their history. In the German Christian Movement, the Confederation for a German Church (*Bund für Deutsche Kirche*), founded by Joachim Kurd Niedlich in 1921, was among the most important.[11] He found his first disciples among his classes at the Arndt-Hochschule in Berlin. This movement sought to use the church to cultivate German nationalism and establish a singular German form of Christianity. It drew heavily on the folk-racial theories of Lagarde, Langbehn, and Houston Stewart Chamberlain, and on the mixture of old Germanic and Christian ideals that Richard Wagner provided in his musical dramas. They sought to cultivate an heroic attitude, spoke a lot about the German soul, German blood, and the alien influences of Judaism. Their purpose was to renew the church, and they urged members to take an active part in German life and to participate in church elections. They were, however, above narrow confessional ties and actively supported the interdenominational schools. Akin to this movement, but more extreme, was the Spiritual Christian Religious Association (*Geist-christliche Religionsgemeinschaft*) founded by Dr. Arthur Dinter in 1927. Dinter was far more racially oriented than Niedlich, and he worked out a racial hierarchy according to which Germans were highest and Jews lowest.

Christ was the godlike Aryan man become incarnate of his own free will in order to help through teaching and example.[12] For a time after 1925 Dinter was the National Socialist leader (*Gauleiter*) in Thuringia, but in 1928, Hitler, in line with his policy of neutrality toward the churches, ordered him dismissed from the party. Dinter had continually tried to impose his religious views on the party, and in spite of his friends' efforts he was never accepted back into the fold.[13]

In Thuringia a somewhat similar movement had developed under the leadership of Pastors Julius Leutheuser and Siegfried Leffler.[14] They had been educated and ordained in the Bavarian church, but becoming uncomfortable within that conservative and orthodox body, departed in 1927 for Thuringia. When the state of Thuringia was created after World War I, seven (later eight) Land churches, previously largely controlled by their state governments, were suddenly forced in the interest of political unity to unite into one self-governing Land church. This could be achieved within the necessary time limits only if eyes were closed to theological differences. Article 3 of the Thuringian church constitution of 1924 stated: "It [the Thuringian Evangelical Church] is by origin and nature a Lutheran church. It wishes to be a home of evangelical freedom and toleration."[15] The result was that the Thuringian church became one of the most liberal and freewheeling in Germany. Here the two young ministers set about trying to awaken their parishioners to a new sort of Christian social consciousness by blending secular and religious ideas as a basis for the regeneration of both church and state. In 1929 they began to call themselves "German Christians" (*Deutsche Christen*), and were soon a small but strident and uncensored group within the Thuringian Land church.[16]

To add to the confusion, there was also a Christian German Movement (*Christlich-deutsche Bewegung*), closely connected with the German National party, which was organized in 1930 primarily in northeastern Germany. It was rightist oriented and directed its attention to combating freethinkers, socialists, communists, and pacifists, and in general supported an ardent nationalism tied closely to the church. The policies and teaching of these various movements were often easy to reconcile with the ideology of the rising National Socialist party. When in May 1932, that party supported the formation of a German Christian Faith Movement (*Glaubensbewegung Deutsche Christen*), some of these groups were soon associated with it, although they did not completely lose their special identities.

The non-Christian German Faith Movement comprised numerous small groups, many of which antedated World War I. Among them were the *Schäfferbund und Deutsche Erneuerungsgemeinde* (1904), the very radical *Germanische Glaubensgemeinschaft* (1908), the *Deutschreligiösen Gemeinschaft* (1911), the *Volkschaft der Nordungen* (1917), the *Tannenbergbund,* founded by General Ludendorff and his wife (1925), and the *Nordische Glaubensgemeinschaft* (1928). In 1931 a number of these Germanic groups joined to form the Nordic Religious Association

(*Nordisch-religiöse Arbeitsgemeinschaft*). Each had its particular empha-sis, but in general these groups turned traditional Christian festivals into commemorative heathen festivals. Christmas became the Birth of the Holy Light or solstice observance; Good Friday became Silent Friday in commemoration of the slaughter of 4,500 martyrs at Verden by Charle-magne; Easter became the Festival of Ostara (a Germanic goddess of spring); Ascension Day became the Return of the Holy Hammer of Donar; and Pentecost became the High May Festival. They developed special rituals for baptisms, weddings, and burials.[17] Many from these groups found support for their views in Alfred Rosenberg's controversial *The Myth of the Twentieth Century* (1930).

Yet another movement in the 1920s should be mentioned. Like the others, it had ties going back to the prewar period, and arose out of the perennial problem of liturgical reform. In 1918 the High Church Alli-ance (*Hochkirchliche Vereinigung*) was formed, which sought a return to certain high church practices of the very early Reformation period. Pastor Heinrich Hansen had called attention to these in his ninety-five theses, drawn up the previous year in observance of the four hundredth anniversary of the beginning of the Reformation. The High Church Alli-ance advocated creating the office of bishop, placing less emphasis on the sermon and more on the sacramental nature of the church, using more candles and vestments, instituting private confession, chanting altar services, employing choir boys and breviaries, and establishing Protestant monasteries. Some persons even foresaw the approach to Catholicism via liturgical reform. The high church movement was influ-ential in that it encouraged liturgical reforms such as the adoption of new service books, many of which revised historic forms and prayers.[18]

The high church movement in a measure ran counter to the prevail-ing effort to bring the laity into the affairs of the church. Protestantism rests on the universal priesthood of all believers, on the assumption that there is no essential difference between the clergy and the laity. At a time when efforts were being made to incorporate these basic ideas into the governmental structure and parish life of the church, the high church movement was stressing the differentiation of the clergy from the laity. It made little headway, however, and the Land churches continued to remain true to Luther's admonition:

> We Christians wish to and must be lords of ceremonies, so that they do not come to dominate as articles of belief, but remain subject to us and serve us when, where, how, and how long we please. For ceremonies have at all times caused heartache, through the devil's cunning and human negligence in converting them into articles of belief—for the masses make no distinction between belief and ceremonies. . . . [19]

Along with these movements a sort of theological renaissance took place. A whole group of younger theologians began writing who were not only to affect German theological thinking but to have worldwide influence. Karl Barth's commentary, *The Epistle to the Romans* (1919, 2d ed. 1921), made him the leader of the new "dialectical theology." He was joined by a group of others: Emil Brunner, Friedrich Gogarten,

Rudolf Bultmann, and Eduard Thurneysen. A more conservative group
was concerned with the study of Luther, and they began to speak of a
"Luther renaissance." Paul Tillich was at the beginning of his tradition-
shattering career. In short, German theological thinking in the first
decades of the twentieth century was breaking new paths, and endeavoring to present a theology attuned to its own day. And, as in other
eras, new theology raised problems for the church as a whole. The
theological thinking of the leaders, of the teachers at the universities,
was on a plane far removed from the orthodox traditional instruction
given in the schools. Germany was not unique in this respect, for the
gap between the theology of the clergy and that of the laity is wide in
most countries. It took a long time for new ideas to filter down from
the university theological schools to the teacher academies, to the lay
teachers of religion, and finally, if ever, to the pupils. Many ideas were
indeed so disguised in theological verbiage and philosophical speculation that they were difficult for the laity to grasp. German theological
writing was theologians' theology—not theology for the common
man.[20]

Inner Life of the Churches

It is difficult to assess the inner life of the church. The increased
secularization of society was a worldwide characteristic of the period
after World War I. Although some of the German churches—Hanover
Lutheran, Württemberg, Baden, Schleswig-Holstein, Thuringia, and
Hesse—had begun to take attendance periodically, there are no adequate figures on church attendance for Germany in the 1920s. It apparently followed much the pattern of the prewar years. It was particularly
bad in the great cities with their too large congregations. If a parish
numbered in the tens of thousands, even a full church, if it seated only a
thousand, did not represent a good percentage of attendance. In general
the baptism, confirmation, marriage, communion, and burial figures
show no great variation from the prewar pattern, although in terms of
percentages there was no doubt a slight decline. This was most notable
in the communion figures, where per hundred of evangelical Protestants
they declined from 30.12 in 1920 to 25.79 in 1930. Church marriages
also declined from 84.17 percent in 1925 to 81.99 percent in 1930; on
the other hand, the percentage of Christian burials rose slightly, from
89.65 in 1920 to 90.87 in 1930. In spite of a good deal of controversy
over the schools in the 1920s, the number of children who were withdrawn from religious education classes was insignificant.[21]

Church withdrawals showed a marked increase, but nevertheless,
considering the total membership and growth of population, it was not
particularly startling. However, no longer did additions to membership
exceed withdrawals as they did in the years before 1906. The year 1919
showed 237,687 withdrawals as compared to 8,724 the previous year.
Between 1919 and 1932, the numbers ranged from a low of 84,169 in

1924 to a high of 243,514 in 1931. In the same period accessions ranged from a low of 11,172 in 1919 to a high of 50,044 in 1932.[22]

Church authorities tended to blame agitation by Marxists (socialists and communists) and by the German Freethinkers' Association (*Deutscher Freidenker-Bund*) for these withdrawals, and there is no doubt that they had a hand in furthering the movement. If, however, the number of withdrawals reflects on the churches, it also indicates the ineffectiveness of the antichurch propaganda. In the September, 1930, elections, the socialist and communist parties received over thirteen million votes. Hermann Mulert, in a careful analysis of the vote, estimates that of these there were probably about three-quarters of a million voters without religious affiliation, and of the remaining some twelve million there were probably about nine million who were Protestant and two to three million who were Catholic.[23] Clearly many Germans did not take the pronouncements of their churches on Marxism seriously; equally clearly they refused to listen to appeals from some party leaders to cut their ties with the churches.

There are other factors which help to account for the withdrawals. In most states the withdrawal procedure was made easier. The bills of rights in the national and state constitutions assured that there should be no discrimination in public employment against anyone who cut his ties with the churches. Public opinion was less harsh on a person who withdrew from the church than during imperial days. Greater liberty in the formation of religious associations, and the new rights accorded such associations under the Weimar Constitution, led to a rapid expansion of the smaller denominations. The Land churches lost members to these bodies in increasing numbers. As these denominations—Methodists, Baptists, and others—obtained the status of public corporations and began to collect church taxes themselves, their members finally took the necessary steps to withdraw from the rolls of the Land churches. The overwhelming reason for the increase in church withdrawals, however, was the more extensive use of church taxes. In Bremen, for example, where few persons ever took the trouble to withdraw from the churches before 1918, the number of withdrawals increased to 6,756 in 1922 and jumped to 22,169 in 1923, after the introduction of church taxes.[24] In the next two years, as the new taxes established themselves, the number dropped back to 170 and 142 respectively. Since the taxes were levied on income and hit the white-collar class the hardest, touching only a few of the laboring class, those who withdrew tended to be middle class. Marxist propaganda to withdraw from churches to escape paying taxes made no great impression on workers if they paid no taxes anyway.

The bad financial situation in the depression years had its repercussions in various fields of church activity. New buildings were desperately needed in order to split up the large congregations, but plans for these were at best temporarily postponed. Small parishes in rural areas were often left without incumbents and turned over to the care of neighboring pastors. At the same time, the number of young men studying theology increased. In 1911 there were 2,663 theological students at

German universities and seminaries; in 1926, there were 2,089; and in 1931, there were 6,791. Yet the normal need for the churches was considered to be 3,600. This yearning for theology might rightly be considered as evidence of interest in religion on the part of youth; on the other hand, it no doubt was partly due to the difficulty of obtaining positions in the other professions and in business. Church leaders worried about what they would do with all these theologians when they finished their studies, a concern which Hitler managed very quickly to dissipate.[25]

The depression struck the church a cruel blow in the field of home missions. In order to help overcome the great housing shortage, the church had sponsored an organization to provide funds for the building of individual homes. Shares were sold and investments made, and for a while all went well. The organization expanded too rapidly, and what a degree of mismanagement had not already brought about was accomplished by the collapse of credit during the depression. Creditors lost, the newspapers harangued, and the inner mission movement of the church was discredited. Yet at the same time, the established church welfare agencies were successfully carrying a bigger load with more limited support.[26] Just one figure should be cited in order to call attention to an institution in the German Protestant churches which parallels, but still is different from the monastic orders of Roman Catholicism. By January, 1931, the number of deaconesses had risen to 26,642, and the number of male deacons to 4,147. These dedicated men and women constituted the backbone of the inner mission work, and many were also active in foreign mission fields.[27]

The loss of German colonies and the restriction placed on German missionary activity in the Treaty of Versailles (Articles 122, 438), together with inflation, disrupted for a time the work of foreign missions. Lutheran churches in other countries took over some of the established mission fields. In 1924 England rescinded the restrictions on German missionary activities in her colonies and mandated territories. This reopening of mission fields coincided with the establishment of sound currency and economic recovery in Germany. India, since it was not under the jurisdiction of the colonial office, was not opened until 1926; Australia, while permitting German missionaries to remain, allowed no new personnel to enter its territories until 1928. France, Belgium, and Portugal, while not always strictly enforcing measures against resident missionaries, continued to restrict the sending of new German appointees to their mandated territories.[28]

With the removal of barriers, the old mission societies soon were back on their feet and carrying on their work. The activity expanded rapidly, and in 1930 twenty-six German Protestant mission societies supported 563 stations and 4,364 substations. There was a missionary staff of 1,435 and a paid native staff of 9,813, and the German public contributed around 7,500,000 marks for this work. The societies also drew substantial gifts from other countries; for example, the old Basel Mission Society was a joint German-Swiss mission. Part of these German funds was raised by the churches in the special Sunday collections which are a regular feature of German church life. The churches were also the agencies which channeled many small gifts made by parishioners to the mission societies.[29]

Along with the surveys on inner missions and foreign missions, the *Kirchliches Jahrbuch* regularly carried a report on "Jews and Jewish Missions."[30] The conversion of Jews was no doubt an aim of the Christian churches from their very beginning in Germany. However, the first mission society for the conversion of Jews dates only from the establishment of the *Berliner Israelmission* (1822). Another important society was established in Cologne (1843); the *Evangelische Lutherische Zentralverein für Mission unter Israel* was established at Leipzig (1871), and its leading spirit, Franz Delitzsch, also established a learned society, the *Institutum Judaicum Delitzschianum* (1880).[31] These societies continued their activity after World War I, and the annual reports not only mention their work but usually give a summary report on Jewry throughout the world. The Land churches supported the Jewish mission. The report written in April, 1932, laments that the general synod of the Church of the Old Prussian Union had cancelled the obligatory church collection on the Tenth Sunday after Trinity which was the main source of funds for the Berlin Association for the Spreading of Christianity among the Jews.[32] This action was no doubt in response to increased anti-Semitism, which had lost its religious orientation and rested instead on a racial basis. It made no difference whether a Jew was a Christian or not. That there was a certain historic antagonism to Jews—as for that matter there was to Catholicism and the "sects"—within the Protestant church is patent. Jews were all too often blamed for the rise of socialism and communism and for what were labelled as the degenerate aspects of modern art and culture. Yet the fact that the church had long supported a Jewish-Christian mission was not without its effect in later years. It was the attempt to introduce the Aryan paragraph into the church, to remove Jewish Christian pastors from their posts, that more than anything else ignited the so-called Church Struggle (*Kirchenkampf*) of the Hitler period, and prevented the total regimentation of the Protestant church.

The economic collapse resulting from the great postwar inflation also had a serious effect on the many Protestant organizations. Some of the old well-established ones, such as the Gustav-Adolf-Verein for work among Protestant Germans in the diaspora, had accumulated large endowments. These were now wiped out.[33] Yet the wide support this society received among the congregations in all Land churches enabled it to continue its work. This was true of the other large church organizations, such as the Evangelical Confederation, which aimed at protecting Protestant interests against Roman Catholicism, the Bible societies, the organizations of pastors, of religious teachers, and similar groups.

The conscious attempt to bring the laity more into the affairs of the church led to a tremendous expansion of various organizations on the parish level. A listing of the church organizations of the various congregations in Breslau, published in 1925, required twenty-three pages. There

were, for example, twelve societies for foreign missions, nine for home
missions, eleven for child care, and two for children's services; there
were twenty-three organizations for men and youths, thirty-four for young
girls, fifty-six Ladies' Aids, twenty-eight groups devoted to strengthening
Protestant life, and seventeen conferences for evangelical social work
and various other specialized groups.[34] The existence of such organizations in a congregation is noteworthy; to evaluate their effectiveness
would be a difficult if not impossible task. But the expansion of congregational organizations does indicate an attempt to socialize the German
churches to some extent, to reach and hold the laity by other means than
the formal church services. The construction of more parish houses was
undertaken, a movement which has accelerated to such an extent that
parish houses are a regular feature in the establishment of new church
congregations in post-World War II Germany.[35]

Among the many organizations there were perhaps none that had
more difficulty than those devoted to youth. The first youth groups
(*Wandervogel*) had been formed in 1901 and they set new norms and
practices for the youth of the country, including the cultivation of folk
songs and dances, the presentation of mystery plays, and night assemblies around bonfires on mountaintops. Postwar Germany was also
swept by a wave of enthusiasm for sport. To some degree all of these
activities found their way into the various youth groups. These groups
had concentrated on Bible study and religious instruction in the past,
but now their activity became more secular. Disillusionment and lack of
employment in the postwar decade added to the difficulties of church
youth work, but also to the need for it. It was hard to avoid permitting
the youth groups to associate themselves with certain political programs, but when that happened, it usually led to a weakening and
disruption of the groups. Hanns Lilje, in an excellent article, "The Evangelical Youth Leadership" (1932), pointed out the danger, insisting that
the youth groups must always be church-centered and above any particular party ties.[36] It was a cry of warning in a period when National
Socialism was infiltrating all kinds of German organizations.

Lilje lists nineteen different Evangelical youth organizations, with a
total membership of 634,003. The two largest were the young men's
Reichsverband der evangelischen Jungmännerbünde Deutschlands, with
a membership of 224,601 drawn largely from among working young
people, and the girls' *Evangelische Verband für die weibliche Jugend,*
with a membership of 241,238. The membership remained rather
steady, with 1931 showing only a slight decrease over 1927, which is
easily accounted for by the low birthrate during the war years. The
youth groups were a tempting morsel for the National Socialists, and in
December, 1934, Reich Bishop Müller did officially permit them to be
absorbed into the Hitler Jugend.[37]

There were also a large number of church magazines of every kind
and description. In 1929, the last year for which statistics in this field are
available before the Nazi era, there were 1,928 independent Protestant
publications, with an edition of 17,090,919. The Evangelical Press Ser-

vice provided material for many of these, and also for the daily secular press. The Land churches published *Sonntagsblätter,* usually eight to twelve pages long, which carried meditations, articles on religious themes, stories, church notices, and news. They were considered the extended pulpit of the church. Editions of 70,000 to 80,000 were not uncommon. Sometimes synods published such a church paper, which often served also as the parish paper, a page being left to be filled in by local congregations. In addition to these papers serving larger church groups, there were also many congregational papers, the average edition numbering around 3,000. Church organizations of various kinds also had their own publications. The one with the widest circulation (500,000) was the *Bote von Bethel,* a quarterly of the famed home mission institutions established by Bodelschwingh. The 1929 statistics showed there were twenty publications with circulations of over 100,000, and ten others which hovered in this range.

"There can be no question," concludes Gerhard E. Stoll, "that the Evangelical magazines in their totality in 1933 represented a very noteworthy instrument of publicity after their aggressive expansion during the years of the Weimar Republic, and that they served in united fashion the evangelical Christians of Germany." With a population of forty million Protestants and a minimum edition of twelve million, every third Protestant received one Protestant magazine. Assuming 3.3 readers to a copy, potentially every Protestant had access to one Protestant publication. However, since it must be assumed that several of the magazines might be taken by one person, while others were entirely uninterested, some duplication no doubt took place in the more religiously conscious circles, and probably many nominal Protestants received none at all.[38] It is clear, however, that there had been tremendous growth in the Protestant press during the Weimar Republic. Potentially, it constituted a strong and significant agency of instruction and propaganda. The National Socialists realized this, and after their first few months in power they began to interfere with it.[39]

The German Evangelical Church Confederation

In accordance with the provisions of the German Evangelical Church Confederation's constitution, an agreement was negotiated with the Moravian Brethren whereby this group was joined to the confederation on June 16, 1924.[40] The Brethren could send a delegate to the Kirchentag, but without having the right to vote. Starting in 1925 with the admission of the Evangelical Reformed congregation in Riga and the German Evangelical congregations in Tientsin and Peking, a whole list of individual German churches throughout the world were affiliated with the confederation.[41] The support of these congregations, which had largely been undertaken by the Church of the Old Prussian Union, was now shifted to the confederation. In October, 1926, the Austrian Lutheran and Reformed churches were admitted in accordance with negotiated agreements. At the Kirchentag in Nürnberg in 1930, the church law was confirmed which affiliated the Confederation of Free Reformed Congregations to the confederation. This union was comprised of the Reformed congregations in Brunswick, Bückeburg, Dresden, Göttingen, Hanau, Leipzig, and Stadthagen. Like the Moravian Brethren, the only other religious association within Germany to join with the Land churches in the confederation, it had only a consultative voice.[42]

The German Evangelical Church Confederation lived up to its goal of presenting a united Protestant front in Germany. The Church Committee spoke for the church by issuing public pronouncements on numerous occasions. It denounced the murder of Foreign Minister Walther Rathenau (1923), stressed the housing shortage and the social work of the church (1925), objected to the "dictated" Treaty of Versailles (1929), and rejected the concept of Germany's sole guilt in World War I (1931). It was active in presenting the views of the Protestant churches on legislation (notably on school matters) before the Reichstag. It proved to be a capable executive body, helping to tide the churches over the difficult inflationary period, establishing closer relations with Protestant churches abroad, and preparing and successfully carrying out the three meetings of the Kirchentag which were held.[43]

On June 14–17, 1924, the first Kirchentag after the inauguration of the confederation met at Bethel-Bielefeld. As befit a meeting held at the site of Bodelschwingh's great home mission center, the Kirchentag discussions centered on social questions. Two of the main addresses were devoted to "Evangelical Marriage and Family Life," and to the "Condition of the Laboring Classes in Germany." Resolutions were passed asking for better legislation on the protection of Sunday as a day of rest, and for a campaign against prostitution and alcoholism.[44]

The Kirchentag assembled again in June, 1927, at Königsberg. Again the theme was the relation of the church to the people and the nation. Two key addresses, "Church and People" and "Church and Fatherland," set a patriotic note. The *Kirchliches Jahrbuch* reported:

> The church stands above parties. It serves its members, regardless of which party they belong to, with equal love, and gives all in its midst the same rights. It has the task of bringing to reality the fundamental principles of God's word. It allows and gives to the state what belongs to the state. The state is an organism established by God with its own important tasks. True to the prescriptions of Holy Writ, the church intercedes for nation, state, and government. Likewise, it surely has the right to make certain moral demands on the state. Especially, it cannot fail to support, in regard to legislation and administration, the eternal standards of moral behavior with independence and candor, and to stand for the demands of a Christian conscience in all public life.[45]

The Kirchentag considered various reports, including one from the Church Committee which was a telling answer to the question "What is the Evangelical Church doing?" The activity of the executive body on matters relating to school and various types of social legislation was detailed in its report, as was its cooperation with the Universal Christian Conference for Life and Work at Stockholm (1925). The matters before the Kirchentag showed clearly that the confederation was a healthy, growing institution.

The last Kirchentag was held in Nürnberg in June, 1930. In commemoration of the four hundredth anniversary of the Confession of Augsburg, it was devoted to the relation of the Reformation to the formation and life of Protestant churches. The Church Committee again made a long report. Forty-seven pages of the report were devoted to relations with foreign churches and to the ecumenical movement. This time it could also state that legislation had finally been passed regulating the hours and presence of young people at taverns. This legislation went a long way towards meeting some of the church demands for protecting youth against the evils of alcoholism. On the other hand, the Kirchentag noted with regret the failure to pass a national school law, and requested the Church Committee to continue its efforts to make religion a regular subject of instruction at the vocational schools. In view of the widespread unemployment, the Kirchentag called upon the government, as well as upon all congregations and their members, to do everything possible to alleviate the need and suffering of the jobless. The Kirchentag again demonstrated that there was a responsible Protestant voice in Germany which was gradually bringing about a greater sense of unity among the Land churches.[46]

Lutheran, Reformed, and United Land churches cooperated in the German Evangelical Church Confederation, but this did not prevent them from continuing old church organizations on confessional lines. The Reformed Confederation for Germany (Reformierter Bund Für Deutschland), founded in 1884, was an organization which brought together congregations, synods, and church members of the Land churches who adhered to Reformed confessional statements, especially the Heidelberg catechism. Its main source of strength was in northwest Germany and in the regions of the Lower Rhine. It had officials and a church paper—Die Reformierte Kirchenzeitung—and it supported the publication of a series of confessional studies. The confederation held a general meeting every two years.[47]

The Lutherans too had their own organization, the General Evangelical Lutheran Conference (Allgemeine Evangelische-Lutherische Konferenz), which dated back to 1868, when the Lutherans in the newly annexed provinces of Prussia feared that the United church would be forced upon them. It had ties particularly with the Lutheran church in Sweden and the other Scandinavian countries. International conferences were held in Lund in 1901 and in Uppsala in 1911. After World War I, the National Lutheran Council in America was responsible for bringing together, at Eisenach in August, 1923, a conference representing Lutheran churches throughout the world. The Lutheran World Council was the result. An executive committee was formed which met yearly, and which led to the second Lutheran World Council meeting in Copenhagen in 1929. Meanwhile, the General Evangelical Lutheran Conference, which had taken a leading part in the formation of the worldwide Lutheran body, continued to act as the main Lutheran confessional group in Germany.[48]

The existence of these Reformed and Lutheran confessional groups
indicates that there was nothing about the German Evangelical Church Confederation which prevented cooperation with other confessional groups outside of Germany. These confessional bodies also served a useful purpose in their support of the World Conference on Faith and Order held in Lausanne in 1927. The officials of the German Evangelical Church Confederation felt that they could not participate in this meeting since the constitution of the confederation definitely reserved all matters touching on confessional matters, church constitutions, and administrations to the respective Land churches. The Church Committee did send General Superintendent William Zöllner of the Church of the Old Prussian Union as a friendly visitor. Churchmen from eleven of the churches which were members of the confederation were in attendance at Lausanne, but not as representatives of it, or as official representatives of the Land churches. In addition, the German Methodists, Baptists, and Evangelical Association sent delegates.[49]

However, the Church Committee played a very important role in the Universal Christian Conference on Life and Work at Stockholm. For the first time the German Protestant churches were represented at an international conference as a united front. The Church Committee had even taken the precaution of including two representatives of the Evangelical Free churches of Germany in the delegation.[50] Archbishop Nathan Söderblom of Sweden, the moving spirit behind this world conference of churches, wrote later that the German delegation was one of the most important of those present and contributed much to the work of the conference. German representatives continued to play an important role in the subsequent meetings of various ecumenical committees.

The regular reports which appear in the *Kirchliches Jahrbuch* from 1927 on attest to the increased interest and participation of the German churches in the ecumenical movement. When they came to power the Nazis did their best to curtail this international cooperation, but their measures were more than counterbalanced by the efforts of the leaders of the Confessing church and the eagerness of foreign churches to maintain contact.

Free Churches and Sects

What constitutes the dividing line between a Free church and a sect has never been clearly defined in Germany. There was, however, never any question but that the Lutheran and Reformed congregations that broke away from the Land churches were Free churches; "to these we may never apply the term 'sects.' "[51] The older religious associations, such as the Mennonites and Moravian Brethren, had only gradually achieved some standing. They had received official recognition, and been recognized as public corporations, but still did not usually rate as Free churches in the supposedly hierarchical scale: Land church, Free church, sect. The Moravian Brethren had, however, achieved a separate listing in the section of the *Kirchliches Jahrbuch* titled "The Church Components of Evangelical Germany."

With the establishment of the Weimar Republic, things began to change. The federal constitution had granted equality to all religious associations. The former sects on application could now obtain the status of public corporations in all the states of Germany, and many of the more important of the independent religious groups did so. On June 19, 1930, Prussia accorded the Old Lutheran congregations the status of a public corporation. By 1931, the Methodists had these rights in nine of the states, the Evangelical Association in five states, and the Baptists in most of the states.[52] The more obstreperous and aggressive groups, such as the Jehovah's Witnesses, the Mormons, the Lorenzianer, and the Weissenberg followers, had not achieved that standing anywhere. The activity of these groups—and there were many others besides—by contrast worked to raise the standing of the old established independent churches such as the Baptists and the Methodists. The status of the latter denominations in the United States and England, and the growing ecumenical movement, no doubt also contributed to raise their standing in Germany.

In 1921 the *Kirchliches Jahrbuch* for the first time added another heading to its list of Protestant churches in Germany. Under the rubric "Other Free Churches" were listed the Mennonites, Episcopal Methodists (*Bischöfliche Methodisten*), Baptists, and the Apostolic congregations. By 1932 the Apostolic groups and the Adventists (which were first listed in 1925) had been dropped from this listing and the Evangelical Association, the Confederation of Evangelical Congregations, and the Salvation Army had been added. While this listing is by no means an official classification, it is nevertheless indicative of the changing status of some of the independent churches.

The Free churches and sects did not join the German Evangelical Church Confederation, with the exception of the Moravian Brethren (1924) and the Confederation of Free Evangelical Reformed Congregations (1930). Yet some of the independent churches also felt the need for more cooperation and fellowship. In 1926 the Baptists, the Methodists, the Evangelical Association, and the Confederation of Free Evangelical Churches united to form an Association of Evangelical Free Churches in Germany.[53] Thus another name was added to the multitude of church groupings in Germany. The name was also somewhat of a misnomer, for it did not include the Old Lutheran and Old Reformed congregations, the historic Free churches of Germany. Yet the new association, with its central authorities and periodic assemblies, did provide a means of giving these particular church groups a more effective voice in German church affairs. Like the confederation which united the Land churches, this association did not meddle with the confessional or governmental basis of any of the member churches.

The Weimar period saw a great expansion in the membership and activity of the independent churches. The official Land churches regarded the growth of these denominations as largely responsible for the growing number of church withdrawals. There were of course also re-admissions to the Land churches from the sects. There apparently was also a noteworthy steady return on the part of children of parents who had withdrawn their membership from the Land churches. This came about naturally, either from marriage with a member of a Land church or from moving to regions where the sects had no congregations. Yet the tide ran steadily against the Land churches. For the years 1920–30, the Land churches lost 106,401 persons to the sects and gained 20,434 from them, a net loss of 85,967.[54]

It was sometimes said "that the growth of the sects was evidence of the sins of the church."[55] An exaggerated statement, no doubt, but still there is a measure of truth in it. Certainly the failure of the Land churches to break up their large congregations, which sometimes num-bered over 50,000, was a factor in turning people to the independent churches. "Our mass congregations are the most fruitful soil for the sects," wrote a church statistician in 1932.[56] People who sought more intimate fellowship, a sense of belonging to a group where their individ-ual work and support was vital, were likely candidates for membership in some of the smaller independent congregations. The fundamentalism of some of the groups and the authority with which they spoke also appealed to many.[57]

There were others who were carried away by the ecstasy and mysti-cism associated with some of the more radical sects. These were not always foreign imports, although the sects were usually considered to be unwelcome gifts from England and the United States to Germany. Two of the more extreme groups, the Lorenzianer and the followers of Joseph Weissenberg, were entirely native to Germany. The former considered Christ as the beginner of salvation, and their prophet, Drechsler Lorenz, as the finisher. Lorenz drew heavily on the book of Revelations and developed a doctrine of the elect. The Weissenberg sect was given to occultism. Mediums claimed to be the mouthpieces of famous men of the past, including Luther, Bismarck, and Goethe, as well as biblical characters. Faith healing was an important part of their worship.[58] The numerous smaller sects, some of which dated well back into the nine-teenth century, increased their activity. Among them were the Catholic-Apostolic congregations, sometimes referred to as Old Apostolic or Ir-vingians, although they rejected the latter name.[59] More aggressive and more popular were the New Apostolic congregations, which split from the parent group around 1860. In 1926 they had approximately 126 congregations in Germany.[60] The Darbyists and Adventists carried on, the latter with particular success. Rudolf Steiner's Anthroposophical movement made rapid gains, and his followers carried forward after his death in 1925.[61] In 1919 the first *Waldorfschule,* which sought to carry out Steiner's ideas on education, was founded at Stuttgart. These schools soon achieved a deserved reputation as excellent and progressive edu-cational institutions.

Jehovah's Witnesses, known in Germany as *Ernste Bibelförscher* until 1931 and then as *Zeugen Jehovas,* were a nettle to both Catholic and Protestant churches. They expanded their activity greatly in the 1920s, and their continued denunciation of the dry institutionalized churches, as well as of policies of the state, put them beyond the pale. In 1928 their freedom from taxation on their buildings and property was cancelled on the ground that they no longer served the common good,[62] yet they continued to flourish and lived to suffer in Hitler's concentration camps. The Mormons also increased their missionary activity in Germany during the Weimar period, but did not create the stir caused by Jehovah's Witnesses.[63]

It is difficult to gauge the growth of the German independent churches. The first time the census tried to get at these figures was in 1910, and then there were so many "religions" reported that it was impossible to group them properly. Subsequently Germany lost important territories, and getting comparative figures was even more difficult. It was not until 1925 that a census was again taken. This time the returns showed 812 religious designations, among them 575 different Christian groups. There were 72 listed under "Evangelical Free Churches," and 167 under "Other Evangelical Religious Organizations." Under the rubric "Other Christian Religious Organizations," which did not include Catholic groups, there were 92 more. Even then some 163,347 Germans gave no religious designation whatever. The only solution for the statisticians was to take the main religious groups and throw the rest together as "others." Hence the significance of the sects can be judged only in comparison to the larger churches; see, for example, the table of figures on all the denominations according to the 1925 census on page 93.[64]

In 1925 Germany was clearly a religiously diverse country. But at the same time, 95.66 percent of the population belonged to the two great groups, the Protestant Land churches and the Roman Catholic church. Another factor should also be borne in mind. While some of the independent denominations withdrew their children from the regular religion classes in the schools and conducted classes of their own, by far the greater number of such children attended the regular Protestant (Evangelical) classes in the schools. There was no attempt to particularize the religious instruction beyond using the Heidelberg catechism in the more pronouncedly Reformed communities, and the Lutheran catechism in the others. A young Methodist, for example, might not become acquainted with many hymns by Wesley, or Moody and Sankey, but he did get to know some of the great historic chorales. That the Protestant religious diversity did not carry over to the schools to any great extent is no doubt due to the overwhelming predominance of the Land churches, and to the tradition and customs to which the independent churches had adapted themselves. Moreover while the religious instruction in the schools was confessional, the more denominational instruction was reserved for confirmation instruction, which children belonging to the sects did not attend.

Protestants	
Evangelical Land churches	39,481,141
Evangelical Lutheran Free churches	178,078
Evangelical Reformed Free churches	9,559
Moravian Brethren (Herrnhuter)	6,445
Mennonites	13,298
Baptists	69,764
Methodists	48,891
Various New Apostolic groups	138,149
Adventists	30,073
Other Evangelical religious organizations	39,279
Total	40,014,677
Other Religious Groups	
Roman Catholics	20,193,334
Greek and Russian Orthodox	18,943
Old Catholics and related groups	33,042
Other Christians	35,595
Jews	564,379
Non-Christian religious groups	2,968
Weltanschauung groups	243,377
Without religion	1,140,957
Without designation	163,347
Total	22,395,942
Total Population of Germany without Saar	62,410,619

The growth of the Free churches and sects is a manifestation of the basic religious liberty which existed under the Weimar Republic. Yet they lived under the shadow of the great Land churches and did not receive equal treatment. For example, they had not received subsidies from the states before the revolution; therefore the provision of the federal constitution that the church subsidies in the churches should be continued did not affect them. They received no regular state gifts. If they had the status of public corporations (and they often had them in one Land and not in another), they could levy their own church taxes, and some did. The overwhelming number, however, continued to raise their funds by freewill offerings. To some people in the Land churches who were eager for a more complete separation of church and state, this was an encouraging example; to a far larger group it was an example of how difficult it would be for the Land churches to continue to function if they gave up their state subsidies and their collections of church taxes. In general, the example of the Free churches only made the Land churches cling to their privileges all the more tenaciously.

Members of some of the Free churches were occasionally handicapped, in spite of constitutional provisions to the contrary, in getting state appointments. Teachers in rural schools were usually required to teach religion along with other subjects, and a Baptist or Methodist, let alone a member of one of the more esoteric sects, would in practice not qualify for this position so far as the appointing authorities were concerned. At public ceremonies it was representatives of the Land churches or the Catholic church who were asked to say the invocations and prayers. When it came to burying their dead, the Free churches and others encountered restrictions not only in the Land church and Catholic cemeteries, but in the public cemeteries as well. The peal of bells or songs at the grave side were often denied them.[65] While the independent churches—call them Free churches or sects— were increasing in status and standing, they still were far from enjoying the recognition which is accorded to churches of all denominations in the United States.

5.

The Catholic Church under the Weimar Republic

The Center Party and the Weimar Constitution

The revolution of November, 1918, which brought the abdication of the princes, did not disrupt the administration of the Catholic church as it did that of the Protestant Land churches of Germany. The rulers had exercised no rights as summi episcopi over the Catholic church. In some instances they did have a definite say in the appointment of the Catholic hierarchy, but these rights accrued to them as state officials and not as church officials. There was no void to be filled; the hierarchy remained and was in a position to act as a powerful spokesman for Catholic interests throughout the first troubled months of revolution. Individually and jointly the bishops issued pastoral letters denouncing the radical secularization of the school systems which was attempted by some socialist leaders in the first flush of revolutionary zeal. There was a certain uneasy "Holy Alliance" with Protestant groups on the issues of the preservation of the "Christian schools" and the rights of the churches. Socialism and bolshevism were the common enemy. The existence of a strong, intact, disciplined organization brought another advantage. The church could carry on effective relief work among its members, thanks in good part to aid which the papacy channeled into Germany. "This the German Catholics will not forget."[1]

Catholicism not only had a strong internal church organization, it also had a strong political ally in the Center party. This party, which in the elections of 1912 had been forced to concede its leading position in the Reichstag (held since 1890) to the Social Democrats, had nevertheless gained in stature during the war years. It had finally achieved a long-sought goal when on April 19, 1917, the last provisions of the anti-Jesuit law of 1872 were repealed. The Jesuits were again free to found establishments in Germany; a hated bit of religious discrimination had at long last been wiped from the statute books. In 1917 Georg von Hertling, the leader of the Center party, became chancellor, and with him the Catholics assumed a more responsible position in the political life of Germany. The Center party was now truly a government party, a position it was to solidify by the part it played in negotiating the Treaty of Versailles and in drawing up the Weimar Constitution.

As a result of the elections to the national assembly, the Social Democrats (164 seats), the Center party (90 seats), and the Democrats (75 plus seats) formed the so-called Weimar Coalition. It was a strange fellowship which bedded down together. Yet it speaks well for the patriotism and the political realism and wisdom of the leaders of all three parties who, in view of the grave situation at home and abroad, were willing to close their eyes to old antagonisms and cooperate for the welfare of Germany. On one extremely important point they were in agreement: they accepted the end of the monarchy and the necessity and desirability of establishing a democratic republic. But this agreement still left many opportunities for basic differences of viewpoint. Compromises were essential as they undertook their three great tasks: governing Germany, negotiating peace with the Allies, and drawing up a new national constitution. Events and decisions in each of these fields of activity influenced decisions reached in other fields. On some points each party held out tenaciously, and in the end the Social Democrats and Center parties alone had to shoulder the onus for signing the Treaty of Versailles.

On no points did the Center party hold out more firmly than on those relating to church and school. Here they benefited from the wise leadership of Professor Dr. Joseph Mansbach, professor of theology at the University of Münster. He was a man of wisdom and understanding, and, what was very important, had stature and position in Catholic church circles. The Catholic church by no means fought the battle for church and school alone; it was in a minority position and needed and received Protestant support. The religious and school provisions of the Weimar Constitution, while not meeting all demands, were on the whole satisfactory to both Catholic and Protestant church authorities.[2]

The conference of archbishops and bishops at Fulda in August, 1919, gladly recognized that the constitutional provisions brought the church greater freedom in many respects, but on some points it felt constrained to protest. Most of these involved possible future actions by the state. For example, fear was expressed as to what the Reich government might do under its power to prescribe fundamental principles in respect to the rights and duties of religious associations. There was also no requirement that the churches must be consulted in establishing state subsidies. "Every religious association [was also] to direct and administer its affairs without interference within the limitations of the law applicable to all." Recollection of the Kulturkampf might well cause uneasiness about "laws applicable to all." The school provisions did not conform completely to canon law; above all the rights of parents to determine the education of their children was not sufficiently protected. The churchmen could not foresee how Hitler at a later date, through coerced parental approval, was to use these very rights of parents in order to bring about the abolition of Catholic and Protestant confessional schools. Yet even in regard to this reservation the bishops were convinced "that a peaceful agreement could be reached without difficulty between responsible state and church officials."[3]

The Position of the Church in the Postwar Era

While the Catholic church did not need to draw up new church constitutions as did the Protestant churches, it did have to adapt itself to the territorial changes in postwar Germany. Even before peace was concluded, French papers began to agitate for the removal of the German bishops from Metz and Strassburg, pointing out that their replacement would afford an excellent opportunity for the pope to show his consideration for French feeling. The bishops, in order to ease the situation, put their dioceses at the disposition of the papacy, and soon French bishops had replaced the Germans.[4]

What to do in the other ceded territories was not so easily or promptly decided. The Vatican had never accepted the demands of modern states that diocesan boundaries should coincide with or be within state boundaries. Thus for years small bits of Prussian territory had remained under the jurisdiction of the bishoprics of Olmütz and Prague. These arrangements continued. The small portions of Prussian territory in the archbishoprics of Gnesen-Posen and Culm, the seats of which were now in Poland, remained (with one exception) in those dioceses, but were given a special administration. The Prussian territories belonging to the *Dekanat Pomesanien* (east of the Polish Corridor) and part of the bishopric of Culm, were transferred on December 25, 1922, to the administration of the German bishopric of Ermland. Memel remained with the bishopric of Ermland; Danzig was made an apostolic administration on April 24, 1922, and became an independent bishopric on December 23, 1925. The ceded territory of North Schleswig remained with the apostolic prefecture of Schleswig-Holstein. Belgium demanded that Eupen-Malmédy be made into a separate bishopric or united with the bishopric of Liège. The archbishop of Cologne, on the other hand, stressed the historic connections of these territories with his diocese. The papacy, in a Solomon-like decision, placed the two small provinces under the spiritual administration of the nuncio to Brussels. However, in 1921 the two districts were separated from the archbishopric of Cologne and made into an independent bishopric. In spite of French demands for change, the two parts of the Saar (Prussian and Bavarian) remained as parts, respectively, of the bishoprics of Trier and Speyer. The only immediate major diocesan reorganization in Germany itself was the reestablishment in 1921 of the historic bishopric of Meissen out of the vicarate of Saxony and the prefecture of Oberlausitz.[5]

The loss of Alsace-Lorraine and the ceded parts of Prussia involved more Catholics than Protestants. According to the census of 1910, there were 4,495,953 Catholics, 1,873,618 Protestants, 76,092 Jews, and 26,368 others in the surrendered territories. These figures do not reflect war deaths or the comparatively small migration of populations which took place in the war years. The wartime confessional changes would no doubt be fairly evenly balanced, with possibly a slightly greater exodus of Protestants to the Reich than Catholics. Numerically Catholics were more of a minority than ever before, constituting slightly less rather than a strong third of the population. On the other hand, they were far more united, for the German Catholic church had lost its Polish and French-speaking members.[6] In times past the attempts to Germanize these "foreign" elements had led to "nationality" struggles which were usually tinged with religious controversy. Now the German Catholic church, except for its connection with the papacy and worldwide Catholicism, was as national as the Protestant churches, with their growing interests in the ecumenical movement.

The shedding of non-German groups did something to bolster the confidence and assertiveness of German Catholicism in the postwar years, and it was also furthered by the new liberties guaranteed by the national and state constitutions. It is a difficult thing to put a finger on, but there was a certain minority complex which had touched many Catholic circles in the past. Some writers spoke of a Catholic ghetto.[7] There was a constant clamor that Catholics did not receive their share of state appointments, especially the most lucrative ones.[8] Politically the Center party had often spent its energies in swimming against the tide; parties out of power are not likely to share the political gravy. For years it was known and often pointed out that the number of Catholic students at secondary schools and the universities was not in proportion to the total Catholic population, while the ratio of Protestants and Jews was disproportionately large. No one, however, ever was able to explain this phenomenon satisfactorily. It was pointed out that the Catholic population was largely rural and was not as interested in higher education as the more urban Protestants and Jews. Economically they were not as well off and could not afford higher schooling. For example, in 1907 they numbered 35.8 percent of the population, and paid only 15 percent of the income tax.[9] Catholics also lacked the influence of the Protestant parsonage which contributed an extraordinarily large number of students to institutions of higher learning. In a country where learning and academic excellence are prized, this Catholic educational disparity was disquieting.

With the Weimar Republic the situation changed. Most of the princes had been Protestant and they had now abdicated. A different political complexion prevailed. The Center party was now a governing party, and it participated in every coalition government during the Weimar Republic. It named four chancellors—Konstantin Fehrenbach, Joseph Wirth, Wilhelm Marx, and Heinrich Bruening—while Wilhelm Cuno and Franz von Papen, although not members of the Center party, were also Catholic. There were many other Catholic ministers and high officials in both the national and state governments. The persistent feeling that Catholics were being discriminated against began to disappear. While the Center party was not able to implement all its church and school policies—the notable failures concerned the conclusion of a concordat with the pope and the enactment of a national school law—it was able to prevent the enactment of legislation in these fields which were inimical to its interests.

The Catholic church also received more official standing in Germany when the Reich in 1920 exchanged diplomatic representatives with the Vatican. Throughout the nineteenth century the apostolic nunciature in Munich had been the sole papal diplomatic mission in non-Austrian Germany. Both William I and William II, although willing to have a Prussian representative in Rome, were opposed to a nunciature in Berlin. After the revolution this policy changed. The national authorities were anxious to have a papal representative at hand. Diego von Bergen, a Protestant who had represented Prussia as minister to the Holy See since 1919, now received the title of German ambassador.[10] In agreeing to this change however, Prussia stipulated that in negotiations concerning Prussian church affairs the Prussian government could negotiate directly with the ambassador.[11] This rather indefinite arrangement was clarified when discussions for a Prussian concordat got under way. The Prussian authorities in 1925 asked that the ambassador also be specifically accredited as Prussian minister to the Holy See. Neither von Bergen nor the Reich government were particularly pleased with this move, but acquiesced. Bergen presented his credentials as Prussian minister to the Vatican on June 15, 1925.[12]

Since May 27, 1917, Monsignor Eugenio Pacelli, who was to become pope in 1939, had served in Munich as nuncio to Bavaria. With the establishment of diplomatic relations with the Reich government in 1920, he was named as the first nuncio to the Reich. Concerned lest the French ambassador, who was scheduled to present his credentials on July 1, 1920, would become the head of the diplomatic corps in Berlin, the Reich authorities urged Pacelli to present his credentials first. He did this on June 30, and was warmly welcomed by President Ebert. In accordance with the Vienna rank arrangements of 1815, Pacelli became doyen of the diplomatic corps.[13] When he was to leave the nunciature in 1929 to become cardinal state secretary in Rome, the problem of who was to be considered doyen again arose. This time the Russian ambassador was the logical candidate, but this was not exactly to the liking of the German authorities or the whole diplomatic corps. Russian Foreign Minister Maksim Litvinov was not disposed to make an issue of it, and agreed to forego the honor if Germany would establish a general rule. This the German government did, and announced that henceforth as a matter of courtesy the papal nuncio would serve as doyen of the diplomatic corps in Berlin, a solution which was acceptable to all the powers.[14] It gave a standing to the nunciature which extended into the period of the Third Reich and to post-World War II West Germany.

Pacelli served as nuncio both to Bavaria and to the Reich until 1925, when after the conclusion of the Bavarian concordat he shifted his residence to Berlin. A new nuncio was named to Munich, and Pacelli, at the express wish of the Prussian authorities, was on June 24, 1925, also accredited to the Prussian government.[15] This double accreditation lasted until 1934, when as a result of the Law on the Reorganization of the Reich (January 30, 1934), the nunciatures of both the Prussian and Bavarian governments, as well as their representation in Rome, were ended.[16] Only the nuncio accredited to the Reich government and the German ambassador to the Vatican with their staffs remained.

In the immediate postwar years the German authorities were most anxious to retain good relations with the Vatican. They valued papal help, notably in maintaining old diocesan boundaries, in the struggle against the further dismemberment of Germany. Above all, they wanted to forestall papal support of the Rhineland separatist movement or the establishment of a Catholic South German state.[17] The Vatican could aid in protecting the rights of German minorities in other countries by supporting the religious privileges of German Catholics. When the curial authorities requested that the German government refrain from publishing the documents on the papal peace negotiations during the war, or in fact any documents dealing directly with the Vatican, the German authorities immediately complied.[18] The Berlin government's desire for good relations with the papacy was also manifest in the negotiations for concordats.

Not only were the political relations between the Vatican and Germany better during Weimar Germany than ever before, but the ties between the Vatican and the German Catholic church were also strengthened in many other ways. The feeling that had prevailed in some circles that Benedict XV (1914–22) was pro-Entente soon vanished in the desperate postwar years when the German church received much succor and support from Rome. German Catholics proved receptive to the wise leadership of the "historian pope," Pius XI (1922–39), and benefited by the general upward surge which Roman Catholicism made in these years.

Pius XI not only had a keen historical sense, thanks to his early training, but he also appreciated the value of propaganda and publicity. He saw to it that a whole series of anniversary dates of Catholic saints and events in church history were celebrated. The years 1925 and 1929, and the period from Easter, 1933, to Easter, 1934, were proclaimed jubilee years. A great number of beatifications and elevations to sainthood were undertaken. He issued a series of significant encyclicals: against laicism, especially of schools (*Quas primas,* 1925); against pan-Christianism and the attempt to bring about church union at great world conferences (*Mortalium animos,* 1928); for union with the Eastern churches (*Rerum Orientalium,* 1928); and perhaps most important of all, *Quadragesimo Anno* (1931) against socialism and in commemoration of the fortieth anniversary of Leo XIII's *Rerum novarum.* The pope was also concerned with bringing the laity more into the service of the church. He was instrumental in establishing new statutes in 1923 for the Catholic Action movement in Italy, and did much to further this movement throughout the church. The pope's interest in German Catholic Action was manifested in a special letter to the archbishop of Breslau on November 13, 1928. Pius XI was also the first pope to use the radio to appeal directly to all Catholics and to the world at large.[19]

All this activity on the part of the church universal had its favorable influence on German Catholicism. It helped to dispel minority complex feelings where they existed. Public manifestations of Catholic strength became more numerous. The annual Catholic assemblies developed into mass gatherings. The festive outdoor mass held at the Dortmund meeting in 1927 reputedly was attended by 80,000 people. Corpus Christi Day processions became more elaborate and were held in many predominantly Protestant cities where they had not been customary. It created a sensation when a Corpus Christi Day procession for the first time moved down Unter den Linden in Berlin, with the chancellor and many other governing officials carrying candles.[20] A certain aggressiveness was also shown in the effort to convert Protestants. Carrying out the provisions of the new code of canon law (1917) led to stricter enforcement of the regulations on mixed marriages. In August, 1920, the Winfried Alliance (Winfried Bund) was formed with the special purpose of seeking converts from Protestantism. A special prayer for "German reunification in faith" was recommended for daily recital by Catholics. Protestants began to speak of the start of a new Counter-Reformation.[21]

The new spirit of Catholicism made itself felt among Catholic authors and artists, and they shared as never before in the intellectual life of the time. Professorships for Catholic Weltanschauung were established at the universities of Frankfurt/Main, Breslau, and Berlin. The Association of Catholic University Graduates (Verband der Vereine der Katholischen Akademiker), which had been founded on the eve of the war, took on new life and soon numbered over 200 local and regional groups with 17,000 members. Its yearly meetings (1921–32) and the many special gatherings of professional groups were recognized religious-educational conferences of high standing. A special papal brief in 1929 paid the association the highest compliments, praising its support of Catholic ideals in relation to the problems of the day.[22] A liturgical reform movement, stressing more participation of the congregation in the service of the mass, drew much attention. Some of the more conservative Catholic leaders became concerned at this innovation, and by the end of the twenties warnings, strictures, and some censorship were in evidence.[23]

Nowhere did the new liberty and freedom for the church manifest itself more than in the growth in monastic foundations and their membership. In 1920 there were 366 monastic establishments for men with 7,030 members and 616 novices; in 1932, there were 640, with 13,206 members and 1,910 novices. The establishments for women had increased from 5,746 with 60,791 members and 5,521 novices in 1920 to 7,147 with 77,525 members and 6,953 novices.[24] Since the 1932 figures do not include Eupen and Malmédy, the actual increase was even greater than these overall figures indicate. Meanwhile the number of secular clergy had increased from 19,369 in 1920 to 21,358 in 1932.[25] The number of Catholic theological students at universities or equivalent institutions dropped from 3,443 in 1920 to 2,648 in 1923, and then began slowly to increase again, until in the summer semester of 1932 they numbered 4,864.[26] The number of Catholics cared for by one active parish priest hovered around 1,250 in the late 1920s.[27] The total number of Catholics in Germany, the figures adjusted to the postwar German territory but including the Saar, according to the census of 1910, was 20,594,816, and in 1933, 21,765,614.[28]

Church Life and Organizations

No data on Catholic church attendance are available, but the figures on participation in sacraments indicate there was little change between 1924 and 1932. They suggest that the loyalty of the laity to the church remained approximately the same despite the increasing secularization of the age.[29] The Catholic church lost members at about the same rate as did the Protestant Land churches. There were also gains by readmissions and by conversions from the Protestant churches.[30] Catholic statistics, while giving total withdrawals, do not break down the figures into how many joined the Land churches or the other Christian sects. According to Protestant figures in 1920, 11,017 Catholics joined the Protestant Land churches, and in 1930, 16,302. The Catholics do give the following numbers of those leaving the Land churches for Roman Catholicism (Protestant figures for the same year are in parentheses): in 1920, 8,570 (1,490); in 1930, 9,190 (1,971).[31] The large discrepancies between the Catholic and Protestant statistics no doubt depended on how members were defined. Protestants did not count children, either for withdrawal or admission, whereas it seems likely that Catholics did. It is clear, however, that in spite of a smaller total membership, the Catholics regularly lost larger numbers to the Protestant Land churches than they won from them.[32] The new canon law code had sharpened the enforcement of strictures in the cases of mixed marriages, which contributed to increased losses to Protestantism.[33] Whatever the intraconfessional exchanges were, they were relatively insignificant compared to the number who withdrew from both Catholic and Land churches and joined no other Christian denomination.

The numerous Catholic organizations which had flourished under the empire suffered in the first postwar years, primarily because of bad economic conditions and the resulting inflation. Yet they were soon on their feet again and more active than ever before. The long tabular list of Catholic organizations which appeared in the 1930–31 *Katholisches Handbuch* gives the number of local groups in each organization and the membership.[34] It also gives founding dates, which indicate a goodly number of new organizations dating from the twenties. Work among Catholic youth was particularly stressed, and new ideas and activities were infused into the youth organizations. The increasing number of public Catholic manifestations—processions, meetings, and festivals—provided many occasions for youth groups to demonstrate their loyalty to the church.

The Catholic press kept pace with the expanding activity of the church and was in good part responsible for it. The daily papers with definite Catholic orientation accounted for around 10–14 percent of the local German daily press circulation, about the same proportion as before 1914. Yet as the Center party increasingly took over the reins of government, the Catholic press gained in significance, and some of the Catholic dailies at times might be classed as government organs. In addition to the daily press, Catholics in 1932 were served by 420 periodicals and other publications. Among these, 29 had editions of over 100,000.[35]

The quality as well as the quantity of Catholic literature increased. Periodicals changed format, new writers appeared, and Catholics played an increasingly significant role in the cultural life of Germany. The big Catholic dailies added Sunday supplements in which they discussed the problems of the time; the staid "scientific supplements" were dropped. The names of these supplements indicate the new spirit which prevailed. The *Germania* had "The New Shore"; the *Kölnische Volkszeitung* had "In Step with the Times"; the *Münstersche Anzeiger* had "On the Path of the Times"; the *Deutsche Volksblatt* in Stuttgart had "Culture and Life"; and the *Essener Volkszeitung* had "From the Intellectual Life of the Present." In 1920, P. Freidrich Muckermann, S.J., undertook the editorship of the literary periodical *Der Gral,* and made it into one of the liveliest cultural magazines of the times. He founded a correspondence bureau and soon was delivering copy to some 400 daily Catholic papers in Germany. He also established a separate news bureau for the church papers. He and his brother founded a *Film-Rundschau* which reviewed films from the Catholic point of view, and which soon exercised a considerable influence on the German film industry. It was not surprising that this influential journalist was one of the first to feel the ire of the Nazis. He fled to exile in Holland, where he gave the Gestapo a hard time trying to stop the papers which he sent across the borders.[36]

The Negotiation of Agreements with the Vatican

The favorable provisions of the federal and state constitutions still left some problems unregulated so far as the churches were concerned. Some of these—notably the school problems and the settling of compensation for prevailing state subsidies to the churches—were to be regulated by law. There was also the provision that the federal government could by legislation establish general principles in regard to the rights and duties of religious associations. It would be an obvious advantage to the Catholic church if it could get some binding agreements which would circumscribe the nature of this legislation. Furthermore, some other matters, such as the regulation of diocesan boundaries and appointment of clergy, went back to agreements concluded in the early nineteenth century, and these needed modernization and new formulation.

The famous concordat of 1801 with Napoleon had ushered in a new era of concordat negotiations, one which was climaxed by the concordat of 1855 with Austria. This agreement was cancelled in 1870 by the Austrian government as a result of the adoption of the dogma of papal infallibility at the Vatican Council. The next decades witnessed a decline in the negotiation of concordats. The first world war, with the resulting creation of new states and the establishment of new democratic governments, made the authorities in Rome anxious to define and guarantee the rights of the church wherever it was possible. This led to a new era of concordat negotiations, and Pius XI was particularly zealous in promoting them.[37]

The Bavarian Concordat

Aside from the agreement with Austria, the papacy in the nineteenth century had been able to conclude only one formal concordat with a German state, the concordat with Bavaria of 1817. It was again with Bavaria that the Vatican negotiated its first German postwar agreement. Even before World War I there had been soundings about revising the concordat of 1817, and as early as September 12, 1919, the Bavarian hierarchy presented the nuncio in Munich with a long memorandum (Denkschrift), "The Situation of the Catholic Church in Bavaria."[38] This memorandum led to a statement of the points which the Holy See thought an agreement with Bavaria should cover. On December 27, 1919, Nuncio Pacelli approached the Bavarian government about negotiating a concordat which would be in accord with the new political situation. The Bavarian cabinet, with the approval of the Landtag, expressed its willingness to negotiate such an agreement.

At the same time discussions were begun with the Reich government, which had also expressed an interest in negotiating a concordat. The first serious discussions between Nuncio Pacelli and Professor Richard Delbrück, councillor for church affairs in the Reich Foreign Office, took place on July 5, 1920.[39] Pacelli, however, decided it would be best to await the conclusion of the Bavarian concordat before trying for a Reich concordat. At this time it was generally thought that a general Reich school law would soon be enacted, and this prospective school legislation forms the backdrop for all the concordat negotiations of the Weimar period.

Prussia also was interested in negotiating with the pope, particularly if Bavaria was to conclude a concordat.[40] It was agreed that under the Weimar Constitution the various states had the right to negotiate their own concordats, but that the Reich could also negotiate one. The exact relationship between a state and a Reich concordat was uncertain, but it was generally held that the former would deal with detailed questions, while the latter would deal with broad principles and would serve as a general covering treaty, a Rahmenkonkordat. Although never completely put aside, the negotiations for a Reich agreement were held in abeyance (from mid-1922 on) while the Bavarian concordat was negotiated.[41]

Although Pacelli was a strong exponent of concluding the Bavarian concordat first because the chances of getting favorable terms from the

church were greatest there, he was troubled by the possibility of later
Reich legislation invalidating the terms of the agreement. This doubt was swept away when he obtained a formal statement from the Reich authorities that they would honor it.⁴² This commitment is important, for it played a part not only in the various concordat negotiations, but in the failure to achieve a national school law.

At this time (1920) Pacelli, although resident in Munich, often discussed matters personally with Reich Foreign Minister Walther Simons and stressed the fact that the negotiations with Bavaria were really designed only to renew the concordat of 1817. This had become necessary because of changes in the Bavarian constitution. As a result of these conversations, Minister Simons on request sent to Pacelli on November 10, 1920, a written memorandum (*Aufzeichnung*) about the Bavarian negotiations. Pacelli was not satisfied with its wording. Availing himself of the help of Prelate Ludwig Kaas, a member of the Reichstag and a man who was to have much to do with the conclusion of the national concordat under Hitler, he informed the German officials of his dissatisfaction. Delbrück of the Foreign Office and Kaas now proposed two revised drafts: the first version stated that the Reich cabinet would have the opportunity of checking whether the provisions of the concordat were in contradiction (*Widerspruch*) with the Reich constitution; the second version stated that the cabinet would have the opportunity to determine whether they were in harmony (*Einklang*) with the constitution. Both versions had a new and most significant final paragraph. Minister Simons chose version two, which was submitted to Pacelli the same day, but contrary to expectations, Pacelli preferred version one. Kaas commented that there was little difference between the versions, and urged accepting the nuncio's choice, since he apparently attached much importance to it. This the Foreign Office officials did, although Ernst von Simson, director of the Vatican section, noted that it was easier for the cabinet to say a provision was not in harmony with the constitution than that it was contrary to the constitution. The government authorities made no difficulties about the final paragraph. The memorandum, as presented to Pacelli on November 13, 1920, stated:

> The Reich government has no objections to the continuance and conclusion of the negotiations for a concordat between the Holy See and the Bavarian government. Presentation of the draft of the concordat to the Reich cabinet before its presentation to the Bavarian Landtag will provide the Reich cabinet with the opportunity to check if the provisions of the concordat are contrary to the Reich constitution.
>
> There is agreement that the concordat which is concluded with Bavaria will not be affected by later Reich laws. (Es herrscht Einverständnis darüber, dass das mit Bayern abgeschlossene Konkordat durch spätere Reichsgesetze nicht berührt wird.)⁴³

The detail about choosing between "*Widerspruch*" and "*Einklang*" indicates with what care Pacelli had conducted the negotiations and what significance he attached to the commitment. Apparently, except for Foreign Minister Simons, Councillor Delbrück, Director von Simson, and State Secretary Edgar von Haniel, no other officers or bureaus of the Foreign Office were consulted. Nor were other Reich ministries consulted, not even the Ministry of the Interior, which had immediate jurisdiction over church affairs. It was not until seven years later that Nuncio Pacelli had cause to appeal to this commitment, and especially to the second part, which was accepted at this time with no discussion.

With the assurance provided by the memorandum, Pacelli felt at ease in pushing negotiations for a concordat, although the Bavarian authorities were hesitant because the Reich had not yet passed the school and teacher preparation measure.[44] These careful Bavarian discussions, often delayed by political events and the unstable financial situation, were finally concluded in the spring of 1924. The draft concordat, after having been approved by the Bavarian cabinet, was sent to the Reich government where it was approved at once. On March 29, 1924, the Bavarian concordat was signed at the Bavarian foreign office.[45]

Parallel agreements still had to be negotiated with the Evangelical Church in Bavaria Right of the Rhine and with the United Protestant Evangelical Christian Church of the Palatinate. The three agreements were then submitted to the Landtag. There was much debate both within and outside the parliament, but the agreements were finally approved.[46] The Bavarian concordat was ratified on January 24, 1925, and the Vatican subsequently awarded decorations to the Bavarian leaders who had been instrumental in bringing the agreement to a successful conclusion.[47]

During these postwar years the German government feared that the papacy might accede to French pressure to detach the Saar territory from the dioceses of Speyer and Trier, but the Bavarian concordat apparently put an end to the possibility. However, the French-dominated Commission for the Government of the Saar Territory immediately notified Foreign Minister Stresemann that it could not be bound by the new Bavarian concordat, but only by the concordat of 1817 and the laws in effect on November 11, 1918. Appointments of clergy by the bishop of Speyer according to procedures of the new concordat afforded a point for the commissioners' protest. This led to various exchanges between the Reich government, Bavaria, and the Vatican. Finally Cardinal Secretary Pietro Gaspari held that the Bavarian concordat was suspended for the Saar, but would apply if the Saar were returned to Germany. This decision was accepted by all concerned, but the French had succeeded in upholding the letter of the law.[48]

The Bavarian concordat guaranteed free exercise of the Catholic religion and recognized the church's right to enact laws within its competence which would bind its members.[49] The church was to be consulted on appointments to Catholic theological faculties at state institutions, and if the church later objected to a professor's teaching or conduct, the state was bound to remove him. At least one professor of history and one of philosophy who had the full approval of church authorities were to be appointed at the universities of Munich and Würzburg. Catholic confessional schools were safeguarded, and instructors in religion were to be approved by the diocesan bishops. Religious instruction was to be continued at least in its existing scope at all middle and higher schools. These educational provisions were no doubt the most significant of the concordat. The financial obligations assumed by the state in the concordat of 1817 were continued, but an increase commensurate with changing economic conditions was granted, and the state undertook a new obligation when it agreed to subsidize seminaries for boys who were destined for the priesthood. The pope had full freedom in the naming of archbishops and bishops. The cathedral chapter was to submit a list of names from which the pope would select the appointee, but before his appointment was officially announced the Bavarian government was to be consulted to see if there were objections of a political nature. Religious orders were to be free to found establishments in Bavaria, the only restriction being that the heads of such houses should have German or Bavarian citizenship.

The Prussian Treaty

With the conclusion of the Bavarian concordat, discussions for a Reich concordat were again begun. They had been permitted to languish since mid-1922, although the best of relations were maintained between the Holy See and the authorities in Berlin. On October 17, 1924, Pacelli approached the chancellor. In a subsequent ministerial conference the chancellor stated that guidelines should be determined for a concordat, and that consideration should be given to the idea of concluding a similar agreement with the German Evangelical Church Confederation.[50] The wheels in the bureaucracy started to turn. Councillor Dr. Hermann Meyer-Rodehüser of the Foreign Office drew up several memoranda on the status of the concordat negotiations.[51] In one he called attention to the fact that as early as 1920 Prussia had declared that if Bavaria concluded a concordat, Prussia would have to do the same. This proved to be the turn events took. On November 27, 1924, the minister president of Prussia, Otto Braun, informed the Reich foreign minister and the Reich minister of the interior that Prussia would now have to conclude a concordat.[52] The final debates over the ratification of the Bavarian concordat, the process of obtaining the special accreditation of Prussian-Vatican diplomatic representatives, the attempt to pass a national school law in 1925, and indeed the general political situation—for this was the period of currency stabilization and the Locarno treaties—delayed these Prussian negotiations. Finally, after some preliminary soundings, negotiations were begun on March 27, 1926, between Nuncio Pacelli and Minister of Religious Affairs Carl H. Becker.[53]

The Reich authorities meanwhile continued to consider the possibility of concluding a Reich concordat. At a July, 1926, meeting of representatives of the Reich Chancellery, the Ministry of the Interior, and the Foreign Office, it was agreed that a national school law must precede the conclusion of a Reich concordat.[54] Representatives of the same ministries met with representatives of the Prussian government in October, and considered the possibility of carrying on Prussian and Reich negotiations simultaneously with the Vatican. Chancellor Wilhelm Marx was anxious to conclude a national concordat, for it would be "a great political achievement for the Reich government," but on the request of Minister President Otto Braun of Prussia he agreed not to press negotiations. Braun in turn promised to keep the Reich government informed on the progress of Prussian negotiations so far as he was permitted by previous assurances of secrecy to the nuncio.[55] Actually the Prussians negotiated very much on their own, and in the end Bergen, as Prussian representative at the Vatican, knew the full text of the Prussian concordat while the Foreign Office in Berlin was still at least officially ignorant of it. He had refused to change his cap to that of Reich ambassador and send the text to the Foreign Office.

The Prussian-Vatican negotiations became involved with the attempt to pass a national school law in 1927. If passage could finally be achieved, one of the most controversial issues in state-church relations would be settled. The history of this proposed legislation is complicated, but there is one episode in it which touches directly on the history of concordats. The draft of a national school law, sponsored by Minister of the Interior Walter von Keudell, favored the interdenominational school. This did not please the Vatican, and there were other provisions in it— notably in regard to the supervision and conduct of religious instruction—which indicated that the law was not in accord with the provisions of the Bavarian concordat.[56] To forestall this legislation Nuncio Pacelli presented a note on October 9, 1927, requesting the Foreign Office to take proper and necessary steps with the government to assure the observance of the commitment of November 13, 1920.[57] This was the first time in seven years that the nuncio had referred to the memorandum. It was quite clear that the Reich officials in 1927 were unaware of the commitment that future Reich legislation would not set aside provisions of the Bavarian concordat, and the councillor for church affairs in the Foreign Office made a study of its origin.[58]

Foreign Minister Stresemann immediately sent Pacelli's note to von Keudell.[59] Von Keudell, taking his time about answering, informed the Foreign Office that he would take a stand on the note when it was clear if and to what extent the Reich law was contrary to the Bavarian concordat.[60] That the papal note did have an effect is clear, for on January 12, 1928, the educational committee of the Reichstag added a subsection to paragraph 16 of the school law which stated that in those territories of the Reich where a cooperation of state and church had been established by law or agreement, this arrangement could continue.[61] This subsection obviously would cover the Bavarian concordat. The addition did not lessen the widespread opposition to the school law in both Protestant and Catholic circles, and especially among teachers. The government, beset by many other problems, decided to drop the school law.[62]

The Vatican, however, had not yet received a reply to its protest of October 9, 1927. Finally in March of 1928, representatives of the Foreign Office, the Chancellery, and the Ministry of the Interior met to consider the draft of a reply worked out by the latter. They proposed ducking the issue at point by stating that since the school law had been dropped, the problem might be considered settled. They did call attention to a reply of June 17, 1925, to an interpellation in the Reichstag by the government then in power, to the effect that "Reich law breaks state law," and this provision of the constitution could not be changed by any agreements that states might conclude with the churches.[63]

To see if an answer along these lines would satisfy the nuncio, Councillor Meyer-Rodehüsser was instructed to visit Pacelli for a private conversation on the matter. The nuncio explained the background of the November 13, 1920, declaration and pointed out that he had submitted the Bavarian concordat directly to the Reich government, which had assured him that there were no differences between the provisions of the concordat and the constitution. Pacelli felt that it was impossible for the government to depart from that declaration now. In his report, the councillor went on to observe:

> The Reich school law is ended. He [Pacelli] does not demand a confirmation of the memorandum of November 13, 1920. If he should receive the reply that the points made in the note were no longer applicable since the Reich school law had failed, the matter would be settled so far as he was concerned; however, if in the answer of the Foreign Office the "said memorandum," particularly its final paragraph, should even be questioned, he would answer very sharply. . . . For the moment he would not press for an answer to his note.[64]

The Foreign Office requested another conference with the Chancellery and Minister of the Interior, which resulted in the final formulation of a note which was sent by Stresemann to the nuncio on April 14, 1928. It pointed out that the problem of whether all the provisions of the school law were in harmony with the Bavarian concordat had reached a new stage (neues Stadium), inasmuch as the Reich government had withdrawn the measure. Under these circumstances the Reich government felt assured of the agreement of the nuncio, if for the time being the government postponed taking a further position on the matter.[65] This note made no reference to the reply to the interpellation in the Reichstag of June, 1925, which had pointed out the supremacy of federal law, a reference the minister of the interior originally wanted included in the answer. In fact the reply was entirely in line with the suggestions made by Pacelli privately to Meyer-Rodehüsser.

In April, 1928, the Reich government was dissolved and the elections brought a swing to the left. A Socialist, Hermann Müller, headed the new Reich cabinet. The elections clarified the political situation for the time being. The chances of the Vatican's achieving either a Reich concordat or a favorable national school law seemed more remote than ever. As the Prussian-Vatican negotiations continued their desultory course, the papacy reluctantly agreed to bypass the school problem in their proposed agreement. By March, 1929, the draft of the Prussian concordat was finished and the Reich government made no objections to its terms. The concordat was ceremoniously signed in the Prussian state ministry on June 14, 1929.[66]

A problem now presented itself. Should the Prussian government present the concordat immediately to the Landtag or, as was done in Bavaria, first draw up a parallel agreement with the Protestant churches? The second course would have delayed things considerably, and in any case, the Prussian government had in a measure regulated its relation with the Protestant churches by the law of April 8, 1924, putting into effect the new Prussian church constitution.

The Protestant authorities had, however, followed the concordat negotiations carefully. When the first general synod of the Prussian Protestant church met in 1925, it was confronted with memorials from most of the church provinces against the proposed Prussian-Vatican concordat. There would have been plenty of votes for a synodical resolution against such an agreement. Deliberation of the issue, however, led to the conclusion that the stand the Protestant church should take would depend on the content and nature of the proposed concordat. Any attempt to deal with the school issues would be sharply opposed, and the Protestant church would also insist on receiving an equivalent—not necessarily similar—agreement with the state. The Protestant church would insist on parity in all matters.[67]

On October 11, 1928, it was announced that the Prussian cabinet had for the first time officially deliberated on the proposed concordat. Since this announcement showed that agreement was very close, the executive bodies of the various Prussian Land churches in letters to the state ministry expressed their view that no concordat should be concluded without a simultaneous agreement with the Protestant churches. From then on this view became the official position of the Protestant church authorities.

The government, on the other hand, took the stand that it would be necessary first of all to complete the concordat in order to know what conclusions should be drawn in respect to an accord with the Protestant church bodies. The government held to this position and submitted the concordat to the Landtag. In July, 1929, the crucial vote was taken, and the concordat was approved by a 243 to 172 vote. The majority was made up of representatives of the Center and Social Democratic parties. The German National party brought in a memorial proposing that the concordat should not go into effect until an agreement with the Protestant churches had been concluded. This motion was defeated, but the governing parties accepted a proposal by the Democratic party that negotiations should be started at once with the Protestant churches for a parallel agreement which would be submitted to the Landtag.

The approval of the concordat by the Landtag led Cardinal Adolf Bertram, as head of the Fulda Bishops' Conference, to send a letter of appreciation and thanks to the Center party delegation in the Landtag. Nuncio Pacelli also presented a note expressing papal satisfaction with the conclusion of the concordat, but lamenting the failure to deal with the school problem. He said that this omission, which was contrary to regular procedure in negotiating concordats, must in no way be considered a precedent. Minister President Braun responded with a reassuring note. A parliamentary majority could simply not be obtained for a concordat

which included school articles. The Prussian government would, however, continue to safeguard the constitutional position of the confessional
schools and of religious instruction. The pope published this exchange of
notes beside the text of the concordat in the *Acta Apostolicae Sedis*. The
curia evidently considered the notes as a sort of explanation of the agreement, and sought to give them official standing.[68]

Ratifications were exchanged in Berlin on August 13, 1929. It was
customary that on conclusion of a concordat the state should make a
gift to the papacy. These gifts, ranging from 15,000 to 50,000 lire, were
used for charitable purposes. When Minister Bergen suggested that a gift
be given the government refused, saying that it was impossible to do so
because of political considerations. It was, however, suggested to the
Prussian episcopacy that they make a payment of 25,000 lire, which
they did.[69]

While not objecting to the terms of the concordat, the Protestant
churches did raise a strong protest against the failure to negotiate an
agreement with them before ratification of the concordat. They announced that they would insist on: (1) a guarantee of equality as to
religious practices, possession of church property, and other church
rights; (2) guarantees as to the independence of the churches, and especially freedom from certain restrictions which were not incumbent on
Catholics; (3) a guarantee of an increase of state subsidy for general
church administrative purposes, including those for the training of
clergy; and on (4) the right of the Supreme Church Council to be consulted on appointments to theological faculties, and on clarification of
the legal relationship of the church to university preachers. It was not
until 1931 that the agreement between the Prussian state and the Protestant church was concluded. The six members of the National Socialist
party in the Prussian diet voted against ratification of this agreement
with the Protestant churches, which only increased the already strained
relations between the church authorities of the Old Prussian Union and
the Nazi party.[70]

The agreement between Prussia and the papal curia of June 14,
1929, actually guaranteed free exercise of the Catholic religion in Prussia and its protection by the state. It superseded the Circumscription Bull
of 1821, and established new diocesan boundaries taking into consideration territorial losses resulting from World War I. Henceforth Prussia
was to have three archbishoprics (Cologne, Breslau, and Paderborn),
and two new bishoprics at Aachen and Berlin were added to the old
Prussian bishoprics of Trier, Limburg, Münster, Osnabrück, Fulda, Hildesheim, and Ermland, with a prelacy, Schneidemühl. Two small bits of
Prussian territory continued to be administered by the bishops of
Olmütz and Prague. The concordat made considerable changes in the
method of appointing bishops, notably restricting the part played by the
cathedral chapter. The cathedral chapter was now to submit a list of
candidates to the pope, who would select three names from the list, and
from these the chapter by secret ballot would choose the bishop. His
name would then be submitted to the Prussian government, and the

papacy was bound not to name the man bishop if there were objections to his appointment on political grounds. A state subsidy of 2,800,000 marks—roughly a million more than it had been receiving—was guaranteed to the church. German bishops, and in general the clergy also, were to be graduates of a German secondary school and to have studied three years of theology and philosophy at a German university, a Catholic seminary, or at the Papal College in Rome. The appropriate bishop was also to be consulted on the appointments to the Catholic theological faculties at the universities.

As has been emphasized earlier, the Prussian concordat, unlike the Bavarian, did not touch on school matters. On the whole it was not a startling document, and was limited to settling the most essential matters; no important changes in the relationship of church and state were involved. Yet within a year the first dispute (*Streitfall*), involving the appointment of a dean in the cathedral chapter at Cologne, arose between Prussia and the Holy See over the interpretation of the concordat. It was a question of the right of the pope to reserve appointments to himself and of whether the curia had duly consulted the cathedral chapters. The controversy dragged on right up to Hitler's accession to power.[71]

The Concordat with Baden

With little prospect of concluding an agreement with the Reich, Pacelli on November 29, 1929, shortly before his recall to Rome to assume the post of cardinal secretary of state, approached the government of Baden in regard to concluding a concordat.[72] The government accepted the offer, asking for a delay until the budget was passed. Starting in October, 1930, negotiations were begun between Cardinal Secretary Pacelli and the Baden authorities. In November, 1932, when the negotiations were practically completed, Baden asked the Foreign Office for a copy of the November 13, 1920, statement about future Reich legislation not controverting the Bavarian concordat. The Foreign Office surmised that Pacelli had informed the Baden leaders of this commitment, and requested the consent of the minister of the interior to give the statement to Baden. The minister had no objections to doing so, providing it was made clear that the Reich government had never officially accepted this statement; that the Ministry of the Interior which had jurisdiction in this field never heard of it until many years later; that Baden be informed of the interpellation in the Reichstag of June 17, 1925, that "Reich law breaks state law"; and that the Reich government did not expect to discuss the validity of the 1920 statement. Meanwhile the Baden Landtag approved the concordat, and the Foreign Office conveniently forgot to answer the request for clarification since Baden never renewed its request for the 1920 statement.[73] It is interesting to note with what tenacity Pacelli held on to the commitment of November 13, 1920, and the reluctance of the Reich government either to accept it or to disavow it. At this time Pacelli not only was behind the Baden inquiry, but as papal secretary in 1933 demanded its recognition as one of the conditions for conclusion of a Reich agreement.[74]

The Baden concordat is brief. A few changes in diocesan boundaries were undertaken, and appointments to bishoprics followed the procedure laid down in the Prussian agreement. It did include some provisions in regard to religious instruction in the schools and to Catholic theological faculty at the University of Freiburg. As they might well have been, the Vatican authorities were pleased with the agreement.[75]

The concordat was approved in the Baden Landtag on December 9, 1932, by a vote of 44-42 with the Socialists, Communists, and National Socialists voting against it. Since a two-thirds vote was necessary to put it into effect immediately, it could only be proclaimed after the customary three months. On March 11, 1933, Nuncio Cesare Orsenigo arrived at Karlsruhe for the ratification ceremonies. Hitler was now in power and Minister President Joseph Schmitt and Minister of Religious Affairs Eugen Baumgartner, who had negotiated the agreement, afraid of being dismissed, had asked the local Catholic authorities to arrange the formal luncheon for the nuncio. Immediately after the signing of the ratification Schmitt indeed was arrested, but when he said he should be allowed to perform the formality of attending the luncheon, he was permitted to do so. Three SS men, one armed, accompanied him and stood guard. Baumgartner soon after was also removed from office. The dean of the archbishopric, Dr. Stumpf, wrote a report on the affair and felt an apology was owed to the nuncio. Fortunately the nuncio did not think an apology necessary, and the incident was closed.[76] The National Socialists, who from the beginning had opposed the concordat, clearly had little respect for it.

The Treaty with Anhalt

While the concordat with Baden was being negotiated, the Vatican had also achieved an agreement on January 4, 1932, with the state of Anhalt. It was a short treaty—not comparable to the concordats with Bavaria, Prussia, or Baden—which regulated the payment by the state of pensions to teachers at certain Catholic schools and subsidies to three Catholic parishes. The sums involved were not great, but the agreement did settle a long-standing dispute which had been complicated by the postwar inflation.[77]

Towards a Reich Concordat

If these state agreements with the Vatican highlighted Catholic-state relations during the Weimar period, the goal of achieving a Reich concordat was never given up by either party. The Reich authorities, on the insistence of Bavaria and Prussia, had desisted from pushing their own negotiations. Nevertheless, they repeatedly studied the problems involved, and particularly the question of what relationship the national concordat should have to the state concordats. While the draft concordat of 1921 had contained detailed provisions in regard to schools, the drafts of 1924 and 1926 carried only minimal statements guaranteeing the continuation of confessional schools where they were established by law. It was generally accepted that the concordat would have to make some reference to schools. On the other hand, there was also general agreement in political circles that a Reich school law was the proper place to settle this vexed issue, and that such a law should be passed before a concordat could be concluded.[78]

Stresemann, for many years foreign minister, much as he wanted good relations with the Vatican, always made clear that he was opposed to a national concordat which would get mixed up with school affairs.[79] The Prussian concordat of 1929 indicated that the Vatican—although reluctantly—might be willing to bypass this issue. When Pacelli, now cardinal and papal state secretary, discussed the matter of a Reich concordat in March, 1930, with the Bavarian representative to the Vatican, he interestingly enough did not even mention the schools. As if foreseeing future events, he stated that he considered a Reich concordat a kind of insurance, if the political development of the Reich into a unitary state should jeopardize the future independent existence of the states.[80] Exactly this development under Hitler was to be used by the Nazis as a reason for claiming that certain provisions of the various state concordats and also the national concordat of 1933 had lost their validity.

Strangely enough, it was the Ministry of Defense which pushed for an agreement. They wanted the well-established Catholic Chaplain Corps to be under the jurisdiction of its own provost (Feldprobst), who would have the standing of a bishop but not be subject to the jurisdiction of the local hierarchy. This had been the practice in the old Prussian army in accordance with a papal breve of May 22, 1868. Under pressure from the German bishops, this arrangement was ended when Feldprobst Dr. Joppen went into retirement in the spring of 1920. The Ministry of Defense had sought ever since to have the old post of military provost reestablished. Under existing arrangements, if a military chaplain wanted to baptize, marry, or bury a dependent of the armed forces, he had to obtain permission from the local bishop or priest.[81]

In April, 1927, the Ministry of Defense submitted a new formulation of the clauses which it would like to see incorporated in the proposed national concordat. There was to be a military provost appointed in agreement between the German president and the Holy See. He was to have jurisdiction over all Catholic soldiers, officers, and civil officials in military employ and their families. He would be exempt from the jurisdiction of the bishops, but the latter were to make candidates for appointment to the chaplaincy corps available.[82] To have one responsible person to deal with, and uniform regulations for the whole Reich instead of varying arrangements in different dioceses, naturally appealed to the military. The German hierarchy, however, always opposed the proposed change and the pope heeded their wishes. Actually the curia was not opposed to the desires of the Ministry of Defense, but treated the matter as a bargaining point to achieve concessions in return.[83]

The Ministry of the Interior took the lead in respect to general concordat matters, but in regard to the military chaplaincy it was decided in February, 1931, that the Foreign Office should have the prime responsibility (federführend).[84] Reich-Vatican discussions led to a papal memorandum of April 23, 1931, which indicated the pope's willingness to accept a military bishop who would be exempt from control or supervision by other bishops, if the Reich in turn would be willing to meet certain requests: (1) abolish the liability to punishment of clergy who out of urgent considerations of conscience performed a marriage before the conclusion of the civil ceremony; (2) undertake not to enact the law foreseen by Article 138 of the constitution in regard to the liquidation of financial payments to the church without prior agreement; and (3) give binding promises, in view of the forthcoming school law under Article 146 of the constitution, of the rights of Catholics in regard to confessional schools and religious instruction.[85]

These demands were politically impossible for a government to meet at that time, and the papacy apparently became more amenable. On July 8, 1931, the state secretary in the Reich Chancellery noted this fact, and undertook to move the negotiations along. He addressed a letter to the minister of finance, to the foreign minister, and to the minister of defense.

> For years the question of the establishment of an exempt field provost for the Catholic members of the Wehrmacht has been unsolved. The Reichswehr understandably lays great worth on an early settlement of this problem, because of military considerations. The negotiations which were conducted by the Foreign Office on this matter with the Vatican have been difficult because the curia made its agreement to the special question dependent on other questions. Mention of these questions is not necessary because, as a result of the most recent negotiations, the curia has given up this position. At present the Vatican is concerned only about a single question, namely, assurances in regard to a Reich law in respect to the settlement (*Ablösung*) of state subsidies. The curia would like to be assured by the Reich chancellor that it would be consulted well before such a law is introduced.[86]

The Reich chancellor was not opposed to giving such an assurance about consultation, since it was normal practice anyway, and the ministers were invited to submit their objections—if any—to the draft of such a letter which the Foreign Office would send to the Vatican.

Chancellor Bruening, soon after, submitted a statement to the nuncio assuring him that the German government would get in touch not only with the papacy but with the German episcopate before introducing a law in regard to the liquidation of state subsidies.[87] Cardinal Secretary Pacelli did not think that the assurances went far enough, and the negotiations languished. On May 2, 1932, the archbishop of Paderborn, Dr. Kaspar Klein, sent a letter to the Ministry of Defense enclosing a draft set of regulations on the Catholic military chaplaincy which rejected completely the post of an exempt military bishop and upheld the jurisdiction of the local bishops. These suggested regulations were politely but firmly rejected by General von Schleicher, who went on to explain the wishes of the military authorities. He expressed a desire to see any statement of the pope in which he approved the position of the German bishops on this matter of jurisdiction, for he had cause to believe that the Holy Father had no fundamental objections to the establishment of an exempt military bishop. It was logical enough that the general's letter should be forwarded to the curia, where it was instrumental in getting the negotiations started again.[88]

Archbishop Klein brought the matter before the Fulda Bishops' Conference, and the delegates agreed to accept the establishment of an exempt military bishop, should the German government and the papacy come to an agreement on the question. The German government was informed of this decision.[89] With the matter cleared by the German bishops, the papal secretary summed up the whole situation in a pro memoria on October 25, 1932. In this carefully drawn document, the Vatican, in line with its previous statements, again expressed its willingness to meet the German requests in regard to a military chaplaincy. However, it considered these negotiations an opportunity to settle various other matters. Among them were the three problems mentioned in the papal memorandum of April, 1931, but now a fourth one was added. The Vatican wanted an express recognition of the commitment which had been made to it back in 1920, and to which it had appealed various times over the past years.

> The Reich government should in agreement with the statement made by the Foreign Minister, II va 515 of November 13, 1920, give the Holy See binding assurances to the effect that any changes in the Constitution or legislation of the Reich will not violate the rights of the church recognized in solemn concordats.[90]

The Vatican thought these were minimal requests, but clearly they were negotiable.

These requests were considered very carefully in Berlin, but no definite text of an answer was reached. It was the general position that the matter of the exempt army bishop should be emphasized, and the Ministry of the Interior did propose refusing to confirm the commitment of 1920.[91] An answer to the pro memoria, however, was never sent because of the new situation created by the beginning of negotiations for a general concordat.[92]

The history of concordat negotiations is in general a confirmation of the excellent status of the Catholic church in the Weimar Republic. It was not that there were no differences, but in general the various governments and the Vatican got along well. The church was eager to get its rights and privileges safeguarded by legal measures, and in this it had the support of the Center party which acted as the watchdog of the church's interests. Party and church each absorbed the strength, but also the weaknesses, of the other. Political opposition to the Center party often led opponents to oppose the church, and made it easy to speak of political Catholicism.

Catholic churchmen were sensitive not only to what they considered the very imminent dangers of socialism and communism, but also to the rising National Socialist movement. The pope protested to the Bavarian minister at the Vatican about the dangers of National Socialist philosophy to Christianity in general, and to the Catholic church in particular.[93] The Hitler putsch of 1923 was castigated as increasing confessional animosity. Yet with the benefit of hindsight it is easy to see

that neither the Vatican nor the hierarchy took sufficient note of the
movement. Few in the 1930s did, and because conditions in Russia were evident to all, communism was the great bugaboo of the day. It was only after the tremendous electoral gains made by the Nazis in the 1930 elections that the bishops gave serious attention to national socialism; up to then it was treated as a relatively minor political aberration.[94]

An intensive campaign of enlightenment following those elections was now attempted, but so divided were the bishops that it was impossible to issue a common declaration against the movement.[95] Various bishops did issue critical statements.[96] In May, 1931, Ambassador Bergen reported on an item published in the *Katholische Vereinigung für nationale Politik* to the effect that the German hierarchy was increasingly directing the activities against the national movement. Such action was not helping to combat bolshevism in western Europe. The *Katholische Vereinigung* had appealed to the pope to restrain the hierarchy from interfering with nationally minded Catholics who were seeking to safeguard the highest values of the nation, and called upon the pope to further the depolitization of the church.[97] This item was supposedly to be sent to the Vatican as indicative of the situation in Germany. It is well to remember there was also, aside from the Center party, a right-wing Catholic political group, strong in old monarchical circles and in some of the monastic orders. Franz von Papen was no doubt the most prominent of these rightist Catholics. They were at heart antidemocratic and authoritarian, and retained the old Catholic resentment of liberalism and socialism. It was easy for many of them to support national socialism. On the other hand, the small Catholic socialist groups under the leadership of Heinrich Mertens and Vitus Heller had little influence and were condemned by the hierarchy.[98]

At this juncture Hermann Göring made a visit to Rome to solicit curial support in dampening the anti-Nazi activity of the German bishops, but he was given the cold shoulder. The bishops, he was told, had to follow their consciences and their religious convictions.[99] On the other hand, it should be noted that the curia never specifically affirmed or recognized the statements made by the bishops against the NSDAP.[100] Policies varied in the different dioceses. In some instances formations clad in party uniform were forbidden to attend church services. In the Cologne diocese, attendance at services by individuals in party uniform or the ostentatious wearing of party symbols was forbidden on October 22, 1932.[101] In places Catholics were forbidden formally to join the Nazi party, on pain of being excluded from the sacraments.[102] Yet many Catholics and even some priests did. Much of the opposition to the Nazis was in the way of rallying support for the Center party. There were no thunderous denunciations of anti-Semitism and National Socialist racial theories in this belated and lukewarm campaign against national socialism. All this is but to say that Catholics and the Catholic church were an integral part of Germany, and like most other Germans, were overwhelmed by the circumstances and events which brought Hitler to power.

STRUGGLE

6.

Early National Socialism and the Churches

The Weimar Heritage

Neither the Protestant nor the Catholic church broke with their heritage from the past during the Weimar Republic. But this is not to say that they remained static. Changes were made which largely continued trends that had already been developing under the Empire. Although the Weimar Constitution boldly proclaimed, "There is no state church," this did not mean that the close relations between the state and church were broken.[1] While the churches became more self-governing, their self-rule was administered under the supervision of the state. The Land churches and the Catholic church, as well as a growing number of the Free churches, were public corporations, and by their very status were subject to some state regulations.

The Protestant churches had, during the Weimar period, given themselves new governing bodies, and laws, orders, and regulations had multiplied, as had the bureaucracy which administered them. It is easy to decry this extensive legalism and emphasize its stultifying effect on church life, but it did mean that the churches on the whole were well run, and that their rights and privileges were founded in law. This legal foundation was very valuable when the Nazis tried arbitrarily to bend the churches to their will. The courts, particularly in the early years of Hitler's rule, decided many appealed cases in favor of churchmen on the basis of law and established procedures. And it was not only the courts which at times stayed Nazi hands. The often maligned bureaucrats, the civil servants who staffed the various state departments and bureaus in charge of religious and cultural affairs, often continued to run things in customary ways to the benefit of the churches. Accustomed to carrying on an orderly procedure, they opposed the irregular innovations of newly installed Nazi officials. The penchant for order and law did not disappear at once in Germany, not even among the Nazis.

But there is more to a church than its organization and the administration of its institutional affairs, important as these matters are in large church bodies. Churches are made up of people; they are a part of society and are beset by all the problems which confront a nation. The Catholic church, through its close ties with the Center party and the

Bavarian People's party, had been forced more than ever to share and bear political responsibilities. A government party throughout most of the days of the republic, the Center party nevertheless had many supporters, especially in the church hierarchy, who looked back to monarchical days with a certain longing.[2] In Protestant church circles many were conservatively inclined and ready to discard existing parliamentary political forms and practices. To point this out is to say nothing more than that the churches were composed of Germans not yet firmly attached to their new form of government. The hardships, the sins of the times, were all too easily blamed on the government which, many Germans felt, needed to be changed and set on new paths.

But if the government needed reform, and there were few Germans no matter what their political allegiance who doubted it, so too did the churches. Within the Catholic church, hierarchically led and true to Rome, the demand for regeneration was not pronounced among the laity, nor could it easily make itself felt. The hierarchy, by no means complacent, were aware that there was much to be done to strengthen the church, and they were all too willing to seek government support in this task. Catholics as a whole were eager to manifest their loyalty to Germany. When the Nazis found increasing acceptance of their claim to be the true repository of patriotism, many rank-and-file Catholics felt their loyalty to state and nation was being jeopardized by the church's continued support of the Catholic parties and their denunciations of national socialism. The patriotic desire not to stand aside while Germany was being rebuilt was probably the factor most influential in bringing about the initial peaceful relations between both Catholic and Protestant churches and national socialism when Hitler became chancellor.

Within the Protestant church, among both clergy and laity, there was wide dissatisfaction with the institutionalism of the church and its loss of contact with individual congregational members. The church no longer seemed to touch the lives of people. Church attendance in large sections of Germany was poor; indifference to religion was widespread. There were organizations within the church which were trying to combat this apathy, notably the various pietistically influenced groups associated in the *Gnadauer Verband*.[3] In the universities an able group of young theologians were bringing new insight to religious problems, and while their work had little effect on the masses, it had stimulated some churchmen and was to bear rich fruit during the church struggle of the Hitler period.

Two historic trends in Protestant church life were accentuated in the Weimar period, and they were particularly important in their effect on later church developments. First was the conviction that the churches should govern themselves. Self-governance might, in fact should, be done with the friendly cooperation of the state, but basically the church and not the state should decide church affairs. The second important trend was towards greater church unity. The German Evangelical Church Confederation was an advance over the Eisenach Conference and the German Evangelical Church Committee of the Empire, but it had not gone far enough. The existence of twenty-eight separate Land churches was generally considered an anachronism, and sharp differences between Reformed and Lutheran had largely disappeared over the years. No one was very sure how a more unified church was to be constituted, but almost everyone desired more unity and cooperation. Few churchmen wanted one centrally controlled church, but many were eager to form a more perfect federal church union to replace the existing confederation. The idea of church unity also carried over into the world ecumenical movement. German church leaders wanted to strengthen worldwide ties and contacts, which was not without importance in the days of bitter church conflict.

The Party and the Churches

In its rise to power the National Socialist party had been careful not to denounce Christianity or the churches. In the "unalterable" twenty-five point program of February 24, 1920, point twenty-four stated:

> We demand the freedom of all religious confessions in the state, insofar as they do not jeopardize its existence or conflict with the manners and moral sentiments of the Germanic race.
> The party as such upholds the point of view of a positive Christianity without tying itself confessionally to any one confession. It combats the Jewish-materialistic spirit at home and abroad and is convinced that a permanent recovery of our Folk can only be achieved from within on the basis of common good before individual good.[4]

It was a masterpiece of political formulation, for it was affirmative rather than negative, and yet it left the central concept undefined. Everyone was free to define "positive Christianity" as he would, and although many ventured an explanation, an official exposition never appeared.[5] Positive Christianity was obviously something which was anti-Marxist and anti-Jewish, and also something above petty interfaith and interdenominational differences. In general it was easier to point out what it was not than what it was. Positive in form, but paradoxically essentially negative in meaning, point twenty-four served the party well.

Hitler, brought up in the Catholic faith and until his death never excommunicated from the church, listing himself to the very end in the party handbook as a Catholic, always paying his church taxes (so far as he paid taxes at all), was particularly careful to mold his image as a supporter of religion, but one who stood above the petty differences of confessions.[6] Fundamentally not a religious man and indifferent to the beliefs and practices of the churches, he nevertheless was well aware of the power and influence of religion. In *Mein Kampf*, aside from the bitter and un-Christian denunciation of the Jews which should have been a warning to all churchmen and laity,[7] he wrote favorably about religion in the few instances where he mentioned it. For example, he stressed the connection between religion and morality and indicated the importance of doctrine and dogma to a church, writing:

> While both denominations keep up missions in Asia and Africa, in order to lead new followers to the doctrine . . . , in Europe proper they lose millions and again millions of adherents of inner homogeneousness, who now face religious life either as strangers, or at least walk ways of their own. These consequences, especially as regards morality, are unfavorable ones.
>
> Remarkable is also the more and more violent fight begun against the dogmatic fundamentals of the various churches, without which, however, the practical existence of a religious faith is unthinkable in this world of man. The great masses of a people do not consist of philosophers, and it is just for them that faith is frequently the sole basis of a moral view of life. The various substitutes have not proved so useful in their success that one would be able to see in them a useful exchange for the former religious creeds. But if religious doctrine and faith are really meant to seize the great masses, then the absolute authority of the contents of this faith is the basis of all effectiveness. . . . The attack upon the dogma in itself resembles, therefore, very strongly also the fight against the general legal fundamentals of the State, and, just as the latter would find its end in a complete anarchy of the State, thus the other, in a worthless religious nihilism.
>
> But for the politician the estimation of the value of a religion must be decided less by the deficiencies which it perhaps shows than by the presence of a visibly better substitute. As long as there is no apparent substitute, that which is present can be demolished only by fools or by criminals.[8]

Hitler was well aware that there was no substitute for religion at hand, and he was not as yet clear if a substitute would be necessary or what its nature would be. One certainly cannot read back into this early period the more pronounced antichurch views of his later years. He did have a concept of a folk state based on blood, race, and soil which would be free of Jewish influence. And with almost prophetic insight he realized that this concept would cause difficulties with the churches. He wrote in the first volume of *Mein Kampf:*

> Thus Protestantism will always interest itself in the promotion of all things German as such, whenever it is a matter of inner purity or increasing national sentiment, the defense of German life, the German language and German liberty, as all this is also rooted firmly in Protestantism; but it will immediately and sharply fight every attempt at saving the nation from the grip of its most deadly enemy, as its attitude towards Judaism is fixed more or less by dogma.[9]

Hitler in this early period was particularly adamant against establishing close ties between church and party, a stance he never really abandoned. In the following passage his spleen was directed particularly against the Catholic church and the Center party. A few paragraphs after stressing the relationship between religion and morality, he wrote:

> But worse than all are the devastations which are brought about by the abuse of religious convictions for political purposes. One can really not proceed too sharply against wretched profiteers who like to see in religion an instrument which may render them political, or rather commercial, services. . . . For one single political job they offer the meaning of an entire faith for sale; for ten parliamentary mandates they ally themselves with the Marxist mortal enemies of all religion—and for one minister's seat they would certainly also marry the Devil, in so far as the latter would not be deterred by a remnant of decency.[10]

Hitler was not averse to some ambiguity. National socialism, he maintained:

> refuses to define its attitude towards questions which either lie outside the frame of its political work, or which are unimportant for it because they are not of fundamental significance. Its task is not that of a religious reformation, but that of a political reorganization of our people. In the two religious denominations it sees two equally valuable pillars for the existence of our people, and for this reason it fights those parties which wish to degrade this foundation of an ethical, religious, and moral prop of our national body to the instrument of their party interests.[11]

Religion and party politics were to be kept separate. "To the political leader the religious doctrines and institutions of his people should always be inviolable, or else he ought not to be a politician but should become a reformer, provided he is made of the right stuff!"[12] Above all, he was opposed to getting involved in a Kulturkampf with the Catholic church, and he rebuked those Germanic leaders, such as Ludendorff, who had launched a campaign against ultramontanism.

> [They] have not crushed Ultramontanism, but they have torn open the folkish movement. I must also protest against any immature head in the ranks of the folkish movement, imagining that he can do what not even a Bismarck was able to to. It will always be the supreme duty of the leadership of the National Socialist movement to offer the keenest opposition to any attempt to put the National Socialist movement at the disposal of such fights, and instantly to drive the propagators of such a scheme from the ranks of the movement. And, in fact, down to the autumn of 1923 this was thoroughly done. *The most believing Protestant* could stand in the ranks of our movement next to *the most believing* Catholic, without ever having to come into the slightest conflict of conscience with his religious convictions. The great common struggle which both carried on against the destroyers of Aryan humanity had, on the contrary, taught them mutual respect and esteem.[13]

The toleration in religious matters that Hitler cultivated was no doubt rooted in indifference, but most people in Germany did not realize this. Catholics and Protestants joined the movement with equal abandon, and some priests and some ministers lent him support. Churchmen, both Protestant and Catholic, spoke of a "Jewish problem" without realizing that the phrase itself was an admission of anti-Semitism.[14] There were few denunciations of anti-Semitism in German pulpits in the 1920s, or for that matter in most pulpits of the Christian world. There were far more condemnations of bolshevism, of increasing secularization, and of the decay of morality and old Christian virtues. These the Nazis also decried. Political allegiances ran strong, and denunciations of National Socialist activity by Protestant and Catholic leaders were more often in the nature of rallying support for other parties than repudiating Nazi ideology. The Catholic hierarchy threw its support to the Center party to the very last, even after Hitler became chancellor, and there were also Protestant leaders who maintained their old political loyalties to the end. It is impossible to measure the extent to which these old political antagonisms contributed to the religious opposition to Hitler in the 1930s.

Shortly before assuming power, the Nazi party gave up the policy of not backing any particular church group. With the Catholic hierarchy still firmly behind the Center party, the only place the Nazis could turn was to the Protestants, and indeed they particularly needed to muster support in some of the predominantly Protestant areas. In the Reichstag elections of 1930, the Christian-Socialist People's Service (*Volksdienst*) had won fourteen seats and the German People's party (*Volkspartei*) four. Both were conservative, yet rather than join with the National Socialists, they sided with the Socialist party in some crucial votes. The National Socialists were also not having much success in some of the Prussian provincial government bodies or in the Prussian diet. Against their wishes and parliamentary opposition, the diet had in May, 1931, approved an agreement with the Prussian Land church which was to parallel the Prussian agreement (concordat) with the Vatican of June 14, 1929. The Nazis denounced the Prussian church authorities for negotiating with the Socialist and Catholic Center parties.[15]

The Church of the Old Prussian Union in particular had expressed its hostility to the Nazi party on various occasions. Certain Nazi party organizations, particularly the Storm Troops (*Sturm Abteilung,* SA), were urging their members to attend church services in uniform and in formation. It was indeed pleasant to see so many faces in church, but was the church after all a place for political demonstrations? On November 10, 1931, the Evangelical Supreme Church Council, the highest administrative authority for the Prussian Land Churches, issued an edict which forbade political organizations in uniform to attend church services. The fact that the customary presentation of flags in church services by church, veterans' and guild organizations on festive occasions was specifically exempted by the decree only heightened Nazi indignation. It was a direct slap at the National Socialists, for, as one of their leaders remarked, "Marxists are not wont to organize group church attendance."[16]

Frustrated, Wilhelm Kube, the head of the National Socialist party group in the Prussian diet, sought to extend the party's influence in Prussia.[17] Church elections were scheduled for November, 1932, in the churches of the Old Prussian Union, and he decided to put the party into these elections. He wrote a sharply worded article advocating this policy (published in the *Völkischer Beobachter,* January 10–11, 1932) which aroused much attention, for it involved a major alteration of Nazi party policy. He actually had been preparing for this change for some time, and had secretly formed a circle of Evangelical National Socialists in Berlin in 1931. With their support, he won the permission of the national party leadership to enter election lists under the name "Evangelical National Socialists" (*Evangelische Nationalsozialisten*). One of the men Kube called to help was the Reverend Joachim Hossenfelder, who had only recently accepted a pastorate at the Berlin Christuskirche.[18] He began to expand the Berlin organization, making contact with groups outside of Prussia. Hitler accepted the new policy, but forced the abandonment of "Evangelical National Socialists" because the name jeopardized the general line of religious neutrality. He proposed a change, and with the blessing of Gregor Strasser, chief of organizational matters, they renamed themselves "German Christians" (*Deutsche Christen*) after the Thuringian group which had coined the name had given their permission.[19]

The German Christian Faith Movement (*Glaubensbewegung Deutsche Christen*) was launched at Berlin in May, and on May 23 Strasser officially placed Hossenfelder in charge of carrying out the electoral campaign for the Prussian church elections. Three days later Hossenfelder issued ten guidelines for the new movement. These guidelines disclaimed any intention of drawing up a confession of faith or of disturbing the confessional bases of the Evangelical church, but called for converting the twenty-eight churches of the German Evangelical Confederation into one Evangelical national church (*Reichskirche*). He avowed that the German Christians did not intend to be a church political party in the customary sense. "The time of parliamentarianism is gone, in the churches as well." The movement stood on a basis of Positive Christianity: a faith as expressed in a German Luther-spirit (*Luther-Geist*) and a heroic piety. German Christians desired to bring an awakened German feeling into the church, to combat Marxism and the political Center party, and to change the Prussian church treaty by the elimination of political clauses. The guidelines proclaimed the importance of racial purity, and declared that faith in Christ does not destroy a race, but deepens and sanctifies it. The Jewish mission is a doorway for foreign blood to enter the body of a nation; marriages between Germans and Jews are especially to be forbidden. The final guideline called for an Evangelical church rooted in the German folk and rejected the spirit of Christian cosmopolitanism, pacifism, internationalism, Free Masonry, etc. A final summary paragraph pointed to the future: "These ten points of the German Christian Faith Movement are a call to gather together, and constitute in broad outlines the directions for a coming Evangelical Reich church, which, under the safeguarding of confessional peace, will develop the strengths of our reformed faith to the best advantage of the German people."[20] In general the German Christians held that "national socialism and Christianity belonged together" so that "Christianity should not lose its connection with the folk and national socialism should not become a movement without faith in God."[21]

By June 6, 1932, the German Christian Faith Movement had an organizational structure similar to that of the National Socialist party; in skeleton form it extended to the whole Reich.[22] Hossenfelder was recognized as Reich leader of the movement and as technical advisor of the party on church questions. In the church elections in the Old Prussian Union, the German Christians gained approximately one-third of the seats, being more successful in the eastern than in the western provinces. More important than this particular electoral achievement was the infiltration of the German Christians into all the Land churches. They were everywhere recognized, if not accepted or endorsed, as a movement within the Protestant churches unfettered by any particular territorial boundaries.

There were those who spoke up against the German Christians, but the real attacks against them were to come later. Of more significance at the time was a collective statement of a group of Protestant pastors, the "Dangers and Disruption of Public Life," a statement which has become known as the "Altona Confession" (*Altonaer Bekenntnis*).[23] It was issued January 11, 1933, and was a well-formulated declaration in the best tradition of German theological scholarship. It showed the influence of Karl Barth and his circle. There were fine sections dealing with the church, the position of man, the state, the duties of the state, and the commandments of God. The memorandum maintained that "no particular state form is the best," and went on to say: "We are called to be obedient to the government. If it should happen that the government acted contrary to the 'best interests of the state,' then each person must decide, when the moment has come, when one must obey God more than man."[24] The ministers concluded: "All that we have stated here is derived from the message of the cross and from God. The words from the cross will be heard with greatest readiness where people are mindful of God's ordained way and remain within the boundaries established by God. The gospels put all of us in the right place, and thereby are also the sole help and complete salvation for our earthly fatherland." The Altona Confession was the forerunner of similar statements drawn up by leaders of the Confessing church in the coming years.

Hitler Becomes Chancellor

When Hitler assumed power on January 30, 1933, he was greeted with enthusiasm by the majority of the German people. Many churchmen were among them, for his carefully guarded image was that of an upholder of religion and the churches and a crusading knight against bolshevism, at once a defender of Germany's honor and the regenerator of the German nation.[25] Pastor Hans Asmussen, one of the important leaders of the Confessing church, characterizes the situation well: "Without doubt there were people in 1933 who already knew what dangers lay in store with national socialism. I did not meet such men in 1933. If I early became an opponent of Hitler, it was by God's grace."[26] Unable to command a clear majority in the Reichstag, Hitler dissolved that body on February 1, and ordered new elections for March 5.

In his first radio address to the German people after coming to power, Hitler announced: "The national government . . . will maintain and defend the foundations on which the power of our nation rests. It will offer strong protection to Christianity as the basis of our collective morality."[27] In a speech at Stuttgart on February 16, 1933, he went even further to assert his devotion to Christianity.

Today Christians and no international atheists stand at the head of Germany. I speak not just of Christianity; no, I also pledge that I never will tie myself to parties who want to destroy Christianity. . . . We want to fill our culture again with the Christian spirit, not just theoretically. No, we want to burn out the rotten developments in literature, in the theater, in the press—in short, burn out this poison which has entered into our whole life and culture during these past fourteen years.[28]

In these days party members were urged to activate their memberships in the church. Those who had contented themselves with civil marriages belatedly sought its blessing. In Frankfurt/Main, the director of the city theater group required every member to belong to a recognized religious body.[29] Fear of losing jobs, and concern about not receiving quick admission to the party or its organizations, were among the chief motives for this return to churches. Some churches instituted a six-month probation period, and many persons never showed up to complete their readmission once the waiting period was over.[30] On February 4, 1933, a desecration or defamation of religious institutions was threatened with civil punishment; at the end of the month steps were taken in Prussia to abolish the 295 secular schools in which religion was not taught, and religion was again made a regular subject of instruction at vocational (*Beruf*) and continuation (*Fortbildung*) schools.[31] Such measures were welcome to church people, who contrasted them with the decrees against religion in the schools enacted in the first revolutionary days of 1918. Jehovah's Witnesses were soon banned, to the delight of most churchmen.[32] The religious formula was again made part of the oath, and the phrase *Gott mit uns* was restored to the official seal of Prussia.[33] Laws and ordinances designed to safeguard Sundays were issued repeatedly.[34]

In order to strengthen his cause in the March, 1933, election, Hitler had the idea of proposing that the government proclaim a day of prayer for "folk and fatherland." He asked Secretary Hans Heinrich Lammers, head of the Reich Chancellery, to consult with Minister of the Interior Wilhelm Frick about the proposal. As the churches were self-governing, such a proclamation would have necessitated consulting the head of the German Evangelical Church Committee, Dr. Hermann Kapler, as well as the presiding officers of the Fulda and Freising-Munich bishops' conferences, Cardinals Adolf Bertram and Michael von Faulhaber. Minister Wilhelm Frick and Dr. Hans Pfundtner, the man in charge of church affairs in the Ministry of the Interior, advised against the proposal. Time would not permit proclaiming such a day of prayer before the election (only one Sunday remained), and besides it was questionable if the negotiations with the churchmen could be carried through easily. It would be better to postpone the matter for the present and consider it calmly and carefully again after the election.[35] The official day of prayer was never held.

The events associated with the Nazi assumption of power and the elections were climaxed by the Reichstag fire of February 27. Few people at that time questioned the official explanation that it was an act of communist terrorism. The next day, in order to "ward off communist acts of violence which endangered the state," President Hindenburg issued an emergency ordinance under Article 48 of the constitution, which suspended the articles of the constitution guaranteeing the liberty of the individual and such rights as freedom of speech, assembly, and communication. As chancellor, Hitler was in charge of implementing the necessary measures, and throughout the Third Reich the ordinance of February 28 was never repealed. It was repeatedly used as the legal basis for arbitrary and restrictive decrees under the pretext of assuring domestic tranquillity and the safety of the state. Hitler was in fact a dictator well before the famous Enabling Act of March 23, which solidified his power and provided additional legal sanctions.[36]

In the March campaign for elections to the Reichstag, the German Christians entered actively into the fray; there were stirring electoral summonses in church papers under their control. A German Christian election proclamation heralded: "The swastika on the breast and the Christian cross in the breast, we will fulfill on the fifth of March our duty to folk and church, and vote List 1 of the Hitler Movement."[37] There were, of course, many factors aside from his appeal to religious feeling which contributed to Hitler's electoral success. The party increased its seats from the 196 won in November, 1932, to 288, but failed to get a clear majority. Its coalition ally, the Kampfront Schwarz-Weiss-Rot, as the former German National People's party now called itself, received 52 mandates. The Catholic Center and Bavarian People's party, with 92, gained two mandates. The Socialists, with 120, lost only one seat, while the Communists, in spite of much coercion, lost only 19 and still commanded 81 seats in the Reichstag.[38] The elections were hardly over when Otto Dibelius, general superintendent of the Land church of Brandenburg, issued a confidential letter to the pastors of his jurisdiction. He criticized some of the views of the German Christians, and admonished his pastors: "In this we must and will be united; that the gospel does not recognize the self-righteous person but the repentant sinner, that it preaches not hate but love, that not folk sentiment but God's kingdom is the substance of its evangelical message."[39] There were other similar passages, and the German Christians who obtained copies of the letter were incensed.

Dibelius did nothing to appease them when he opposed Hitler's plan to open parliament in the old Garnisonkirche in Potsdam, a place hallowed in Prussian history and where Frederick William I and Frederick the Great were buried. The church was in Dibelius's jurisdiction, and he felt that as a matter of principle a parliamentary session did not belong in a church. As a compromise, it was arranged that there should be opening services in local Protestant and Catholic churches for members of the Reichstag, then formal addresses suitable to the ecclesiastical setting by President Hindenburg and Chancellor Hitler in the Garnisonkirche, and finally a parade of the Wehrmacht. Parliament would be opened in Berlin the next day.

Dibelius gave the sermon at the Nikolaikirche, which was attended by Hindenburg, Göring, and other Protestant members of the cabinet and the Reichstag. He made some forthright statements on church-state relations, concluding: "once order has been restored, justice and love must reign once more, so that every man of good will may rejoice in his people." In his autobiography Dibelius comments on the sermon:

> The National Socialists gave me dark looks. They never forgave me those words. Only Göring shook my hand as he escorted the President of the Reich out of the church. "That was the best sermon that I have ever heard," he said. I swallowed the question that was on the tip of my tongue: how many sermons had the Minister President heard in his life?[40]

Hitler and Goebbels did not attend the Catholic service, although they had been expected and a special chair for the chancellor had been placed before the altar. Instead he and Goebbels made a ceremonial visit to the graves of "murdered" SA members in the Luisenstädtischen cemetery in Berlin. Years later he was to remember with pride that he had absented himself from church on this occasion and thus avoided acknowledgment of any aid from the churches.[41]

Hitler and Goebbels were, however, on hand for the ceremony in the Garnisonkirche where the church chimes welcomed the political leaders with the well-known German melody, "Practice always Loyalty and Uprightness" ("*Üb immer Treu und Redlichkeit*"). The Social Democrats boycotted this ceremony, but there were plenty of distinguished guests to take their place, among them Crown Prince Wilhelm and Generalfeldmarschal von Mackensen. Hindenburg spoke first, and then Hitler gave a short address filled with references to German history and ending in an adulatory peroration to Hindenburg. It was well done in the spirit of old Germany, and after Hindenburg had laid wreaths on the graves of the Prussian kings the military review took place.[42]

In his opening address to the Reichstag, Hitler was careful to continue his conciliatory tactics.

> The Government, being resolved to undertake the political and moral purification of our public life, is creating and securing the conditions necessary for a really profound revival of religious life. . . . The National Government regards the two Christian Confessions as the weightiest factor for the maintenance of our nationality. [The Government] will respect agreements concluded between [the churches] and the federal states. The rights [of the churches] are not to be infringed. But the Government hopes and expects that work on the national and moral regeneration of our nation which the authorities have made their task will, on the other hand, be treated with the same respect. They will adopt an attitude of objective justice towards all Confessions. But they cannot permit that the fact of belonging to a certain Confession or a certain race should constitute a release from general legal obligations or even a licence for the commission with impunity or the toleration of crimes. *The National Government will allow and secure to the Christian Confessions the influence which is their due both in the school and in education.* It will be the Government's care to maintain honest cooperation between Church and State; the struggle against materialistic views and for a real national community is just as much in the interest of the German nation as in that of the welfare of our Christian faith. The Government of the Reich, which regards Christianity as the unshakable foundation of the morals and

moral code of the nation, attaches the greatest value to friendly relations with the Holy See and is endeavoring to develop them. . . . The rights of the churches will not be diminished, and their relationship to the State will not be modified.[43]

The address made a profound impression in church circles. The Center party, having earlier received assurances from Hitler in regard to certain demands which he confirmed in his Reichstag address, and its close Catholic associate, the Bavarian People's party, joined with the National Socialists and their German nationalist allies in passing the Enabling Act of March 23, 1933, which gave Hitler power to enact ordinary legislation by decree.[44] The Communists having been excluded from the chamber, the Social Democrats had the distinction of being the only party to vote against the measure. Hitler and the National Socialists were now fully in the saddle, and in a position to push their program ruthlessly for the reorganization of Germany. This policy was termed *Gleichschaltung*, which is variously translated as "coordination" or "regimentation." Its avowed purpose was to bring everything and everyone into line with the theory of national socialism. It meant the introduction of the principle of leadership, the end of democratic election procedures, the suppression of so-called Jewish and Marxist influences; it meant following the leadership of the party and public adulation of the Führer and the Third Reich. Political parties, trade unions, business organizations, professional groups, and even to a great extent the army, succumbed to these Gleichschaltung procedures—but not the churches. The Nazis' attempt to coordinate the churches led to the long, serious, complex conflict which has been aptly named the *Kirchenkampf*.

The Kirchenkampf had many aspects. The struggle to maintain purity of doctrine was more critical in the Protestant than in the Catholic church, for the German Christians, with their acceptance of many of the Nazi racial and folk ideas, threatened to take over the whole Evangelical church. But Nazi racial and eugenic theories also denied basic Catholic doctrinal concepts. The support lent by the state to the German Christians, as well as state policies toward the Christian youth organizations, the church press, the schools, the clergy, and above all the Jews, inevitably brought the churches into varying degrees of conflict with the state and party. While the Kirchenkampf as such was primarily concerned with the freedom of the church within the state and did not challenge Nazism directly as a political system, it was nevertheless a broad channel through which criticism of Nazi policy could and did flow. It was not clear to churchmen at that time that in a totalitarian state all opposition in the end becomes political opposition.

7.

The Establishment of the German Evangelical Church

Plans for a Church Constitution

While the secular authorities were busy remaking Germany, the German Christians felt called upon to strengthen their organization. On April 3–5, 1933, they held their first national assembly in Berlin. Minister President Göring, Minister of the Interior Frick, District Leader Wilhelm Kube, and other prominent party members were honorary members of the directing committee. There were many speeches calling for Gleichschaltung and the introduction of the leadership principle in the Protestant Land churches, and District Leader Kube sharply denounced Dibelius for his critical attitude. The closing resolution stated:

> God has created me a German. Germanism (*Deutschtum*) is a gift of God; God desires that I battle for my Germanism. . . . The believer has the right of revolution against a state that furthers the powers of darkness; he also has these rights against a church governing body that does not recognize without reservation the national regeneration. The church is, for a German, a communion of believers that is duty bound to battle for a Christian Germany. The goal of the German Christian Faith Movement is one Evangelical German church. The state of Adolf Hitler calls for such a church; the church must hear that call.[1]

Meanwhile Dr. Hermann Kapler, chairman of the German Evangelical Church Committee and head of the Supreme Church Council of the Old Prussian Union, had initiated discussions with state as well as church authorities.[2] On April 25, he called a special meeting of the German Evangelical Church Committee, the highest administrative authority of the German Evangelical Church Confederation which had been established in 1922. This body agreed in principle to the establishment of a German Evangelical church on the basis of the existing confessional status, and approved of Kapler's proposal that a committee of Kapler, Bishop Dr. August Marahrens of Hanover (representing the Lutherans), and Dr. Hermann Hesse, director of the seminary at Elberfeld (representing the Reformed), should undertake the task of drawing up a constitution for the new national Evangelical church. This committee enlisted the help of other experts, notably people experienced in church law and administration. Fearful that the committee might permit itself to be pushed into advocating a single united church on the model of the

Church of the Old Prussian Union, Bishop Hans Meiser of Bavaria called a meeting of representatives of all Lutheran Land churches at Würzburg on May 14, 1933.[3] Meiser wanted to unite the Lutherans so that they could influence the new constitution. The resulting directory of six, with Meiser as temporary chairman, was never very effective, yet this Würzburg meeting is significant as an attempt to bring about a closer Lutheran union apart from the Reformed churches.

On April 25, Hitler had named Army District Chaplain Ludwig Müller as his plenipotentiary in matters connected with the Evangelical church, with the special task of furthering all efforts to establish an Evangelical German Reich church.[4] Müller had served as naval chaplain during the war, and in 1926 had become district military chaplain in Königsberg. On a visit there in 1926, Hitler had stayed at Müller's home and afterwards remained in contact with him. In 1930–31 there was tension between the army and the SA in East Prussia, and there were rumors that the government was going to intervene. Hitler asked Müller to intercede with General Werner von Blomberg, the Königsberg commandant, and settle the differences. Müller was successful, and Hitler later showed his gratitude to both men, advancing Blomberg to minister and field marshal, and naming Müller his adviser on church affairs. Müller had become an ardent German Christian, and was the leader of the movement in East Prussia.[5] As a confidant of Hitler he could not well be pushed aside, and he too took part in the constitutional deliberations held at Kloster Loccum in May, 1933. The results of these deliberations were announced on May 26, in the so-called Loccumer Manifest.[6] It was a general statement, not drawn up in constitutional form, and was designed to be laid before a meeting of church leaders for their approval.

While these deliberations had been going on, certain events necessitated Hitler's personal intervention. On April 22, the minister president of Mecklenburg-Schwerin had, without consulting church authorities, appointed a state commissioner for the Evangelical church in that state. The pastors in Mecklenburg denounced the step in a pulpit declaration.[7] Protest telegrams from both churchmen and party members immediately began to reach the government authorities in Berlin. On April 24, Hindenburg forwarded some of them to Hitler for his consideration.[8] Hitler called in Kapler, who had launched an official protest against interference in church affairs, and instructed him to discuss the situation with Minister of the Interior Frick and with Müller, whom he was appointing as his confidant. The upshot was that Frick called Bishop Heinrich Rendtorff of the Mecklenburg-Schwerin church and Minister President Walter Granzow to Berlin, and a settlement was worked out. The commissioner was withdrawn, and a committee was to be appointed by the church which would consult with the state authorities on desirable administrative changes.[9] Bishop Rendtorff, having personally received assurances from Hitler that the church would retain its independence, publicly declared that he was joining the National Socialist party. He later was to see things differently and become one of the leaders of the church opposition.[10]

Under Hossenfelder's leadership, the German Christians announced somewhat radical guidelines for the new church constitution; they included the statement: "The Evangelical church is the church of the German Christians, that is, Christians of Aryan race."[11] In an effort to temper such extremism Müller, with Hitler's approval, took over the protectorship (*Schirmherrschaft*) of the German Christian Faith Movement on May 16. That same day new guidelines for the German Christians were issued which were far more moderate in tone.[12] There was no longer a demand for a pure racial church, and the theses were obviously designed to win acceptance by the Kapler committee on the church constitution.

The Choice of a Reich Bishop

Now able to speak for the German Christians, Müller was in a position to attempt to exert greater influence on the constitutional negotiations. Actually he was intellectually inferior to the others on the committee, and they successfully outmaneuvered him. He was also in a compromising mood, anxious to get a constitution adopted which could be interpreted and manipulated in the future. As the constitutional deliberations were drawing to a close, discussions began as to who was to be the first Reich bishop and head of the new church body. Müller wanted the governmental authorities to have a part in the electoral procedure, but the other committee members were opposed to this. It was finally agreed that the constitution should first be put into effect and agreement reached as to the bishop afterwards. Müller then announced that Hitler would like to receive the church leaders before they had reached a decision on the man. This would be only a formal reception, and Hitler would make no nomination. The committee agreed to this, but while a day was set for the meeting, it had to be cancelled because the chancellor was occupied with pressing foreign affairs.

At this particular juncture, a meeting of district leaders of the German Christians was held in Berlin on May 23. They unanimously nominated Müller as candidate for Reich bishop. Out of loyalty to the Kapler committee, Müller informed them of the action. In spite of his assurances that his candidacy was to be kept secret, the committee doubted if it would be, and announced that they too had agreed on a candidate. When, the next day, they heard that the press agency had informed the newspapers of Müller's candidacy, maintaining that he had the support of the church leaders, Kapler and the others of the committee felt that they must announce the name of their candidate, Pastor Friedrich von Bodelschwingh. The son of the pastor who had founded the great Bethel Inner Mission Center, he was a man respected and venerated by church leaders everywhere. He was a particularly skillful and able preacher, one who could inspire his congregation. He had taken charge of the center after his father's death in 1910.[13] He had never held office in any

church administration, and perhaps for this very reason he was held in
great esteem by both Lutheran and Reformed churches.

On May 26–27, the Council of the German Evangelical Church
Confederation, consisting of delegates of all Land churches, met to consider the work of the Kapler committee. They approved unanimously its
actions and the Loccumer Manifest. All delegates had anticipated that
the council would have to make a statement on the Jewish problem, but
after a three-hour discussion they decided not to do so.[14] It was held that
such a statement would not help the Jews, and would only hurt the
church and further widen the already strained relations between the
church, the state, and the party. The constitution was now ready to be
drafted in final form. The delegates then proceeded to elect the bishop,
although technically the constitution was not yet in force. Müller then
asked for permission to make a statement. Although he esteemed Bodelschwingh highly, he was not the right man; "he was a man for
deaconesses, not for SA men."[15] Not only did he decry Bodelschwingh,
but he had the effrontery to demand that he himself be elected as the
man best suited to bring peace instead of strife in the church.

Dibelius, angered by such an unheard-of appeal for self-advance-
ment, stated that the only possible answer to Müller was the unanimous
election of Bodelschwingh. Others thought differently. Bishop Rendtorff
proposed that Müller be elected, but this was defeated by a vote of
thirteen churches against eleven. A second proposal to offer the position
to Bodelschwingh carried eleven to eight. The next day a final balloting
was held, and Bodelschwingh was elected by a large majority. Only three
Land churches voted in the negative—Württemberg (Bishop Theophil
Wurm), Mecklenburg-Schwerin (Bishop Heinrich Rendtorff) and Hamburg (Head Pastor Simon Schöffel). Later the Bavarian church (Bishop
Hans Meiser) joined the opposition because of the haste with which the
election had been held.[16] After the election Church Councillor Johannes
Kübel of the Frankfurt church spoke with Wurm and expressed his dismay
at his stand: "I, the Frankfurt liberal, am for the Pietist Bodelschwingh,
and you, the Württemberg Pietist, are for Müller." Wurm shrugged his
shoulders: "Yes, right hand, left hand, all mixed up," and turned away.[17]
Bodelschwingh accepted the office, and left Bethel for Berlin to undertake the multitudinous tasks which needed attention.[18]

Things had not been going smoothly among the German Christians,
but Bodelschwingh's election brought the factions together again.
Müller, although he had not done so earlier, challenged the legality of
the election; the opposition maintained that the council had the power
to elect in order to prevent untold harm to the church.[19] Here at least
was an arguable legal point; however, the issue was never settled in the
courts. Moreover, another legal dispute soon arose. Tired from the unusual work load and in poor health, Kapler, president of the Supreme
Church Council of the Old Prussian Union, and as such president of the
German Evangelical Church Confederation, retired on June 21, 1933.
The church authorities were now faced with a problem. Under Article 7
of the agreement between the Evangelical church and the Prussian gov-

ernment (1931), no chairman of any higher church administrative board could be appointed until the Prussian government had been asked whether there were political considerations against his appointment.[20] This clause earlier had been the target of National Socialist opposition, because then it had meant that a Socialist or Catholic Center dominated government would have approval over church officials. Now it was the church officials who did not wish to consult the state officials lest a man be forced upon them who would push the Gleichschaltung of the church. Besides, the new church constitution would be going into effect soon, and it hardly seemed necessary to appoint a new president for such a short term. It was decided to leave the office unfilled, and to charge General Superintendent Ernst Stoltenhoff with carrying on the administration. The Prussian government was informed of this decision of June 22. Later Reich Legal Councillor Wilhelm Flor drew up a study upholding the legality of this procedure, but the Prussian government charged that the agreement of 1931 had been broken and that the church was acting illegally. On June 24, Minister Bernhard Rust dismissed the experienced and able head of the Church Bureau in the Ministry of Culture, Friedrich Trendelenburg, and appointed Provincial Legal Councillor August Jäger state commissioner (*Kommissar*) for all the Evangelical churches in Prussia, with full power to undertake necessary measures.[21]

A more inept appointment could hardly have been made. A son of a rural Evangelical pastor, Jäger became a jurist and was attached to the provincial court in Wiesbaden. When Hitler came to power Jäger went to Berlin, where he entered the Ministry of Culture. Dibelius writes:

> [Jäger] was the very embodiment of the spirit of the National Socialist State. His face, once seen, was not easily forgotten. He had an iron will and such relentless obstinacy that he could maintain, with apparent conviction, that five was an even number, and issue false reports without turning a hair. There was something almost impressive in his sheer malignity and in the energy and singleness of purpose with which he pursued his ends.[22]

Ministerial Councillor Walter Conrad of the Ministry of the Interior states that he never met a man who could rival Jäger in narrowness, presumption, arrogance, and meanness. For Jäger, "life was a juristic matter, and there was nothing that he thought could not be put aside, changed, or established by legal interpretation and administration."[23] Not what was right but what was legal dominated him, and he had a way of making what he wanted legal.

Bodelschwingh, since his election, had been faced with great difficulties. On June 15 the situation had reached such a serious state that he asked Hindenburg for an appointment. The president refused his request, for he was at Neudeck where he had gone for a rest and never received anyone there.[24] Besides, he did not wish to take sides in the disputes and advised Bodelschwingh to meet with the minister of the interior. When Jäger was appointed head of the Prussian churches, Bodelschwingh felt he could not carry out his duties any longer, and on June 24 withdrew from his office as bishop.

Bodelschwingh had failed to win any support in government circles. Hitler was definitely opposed to him, as is clear from a report on a meeting the Führer had with a group of pastors on June 28, 1933. They asked him to prevent division and oppression of the church, to which Hitler replied: "I have nothing to do with church matters and don't want anything to do with them. I am gradually getting fed up with them. (*Sie hängen mir allmählich zum Halse heraus.*) I do not receive my confidant any more. The church must see how to get along by itself." Hitler responded to their approval of Bodelschwingh's election by saying: "Your church took me aback by naming Bodelschwingh as Reich bishop. My will was that the constitution should first be formulated. Then the congregations should decide on it, and then the Reich bishop should be named. They did not do this, but simply named the Reich bishop." When the ministers protested that the nomination was made at this time because it was known the German Christians wanted to proclaim Müller Reich bishop, Hitler continued: "Of this I know nothing, and if it had happened, I would not have approved. The church should not have gone over my head. The church can not confront our times and movement with hostility." The report noted that as various matters were brought up Hitler repeatedly observed: "Of this I know nothing."[25]

It is necessary, but at the same time sad, to recall how deeply ingrained was the feeling among most Germans that if Hitler only knew about certain matters he would set them right. People constantly sought to get their petitions through to the eyes of the Führer. The people in Württemberg repeatedly petitioned their fellow Swabian, Foreign Minister Konstantin von Neurath, to set Hitler "right" on church matters. That he did not know the details and incidents of all conflicts is no doubt true, but the documents concerning church affairs in the Reich Chancellery and in the Foreign Office archives with the official stamp, "Referred to the Führer" (*Der Führer hat Kenntnis*), show clearly that he was kept well informed of the main events in the church struggle. It is likewise clear that at times certain crises were overcome through his personal intervention, and that he was generally disgusted and impatient with the continuing conflict in the church.

But in 1933, as in the immediately succeeding years, Hitler was careful to preserve his image as a religious man interested in the church. On June 22, he agreed to a request to donate an altar Bible to the recently renovated church of Ober-Saulheim in the Palatinate.[26] He repeatedly made minor gifts to small congregations for the purchase of bells, organs, and lights, because these gifts entailed favorable propaganda.[27] Churchmen and fellow party leaders hailed him as the God-sent deliverer of Germany. Minister Rust, in a speech to a mass meeting of German Christians on June 29, 1933, declared: "If anyone can lay claim to God's help, then it is Hitler, for without God's benevolent fatherly hand, without his blessing, the nation would not be where it stands today. It is an unbelievable miracle that God has bestowed on our people."[28] Dibelius reports that in his old pastorate at

Heilsbronnen, his successor "assured the congregation that he had it
on the best authority that Adolf Hitler always carried a copy of the
New Testament in his pocket and that he read Bible verses and stanzas
from a hymnal every morning. This thing was quite generally believed
at the time."[29]

The *Friedensglocke,* an established Methodist church paper published in Zürich, vouched for the authenticity of a touching tale about
Hitler which it had taken from the *Kasseler Sonntagsblatt.*[30] Hitler had
invited a group of deaconesses from the Bethel Institutions into his
home at Obersalzberg:

> The deaconesses entered the chamber and were astonished to see the
> pictures of Frederick the Great, Luther, and Bismarck on the wall. Then Hitler
> said:
> "Those are the three greatest men that God has given the German
> people. From Frederick the Great I have learned bravery, and from Bismarck
> statecraft. The greatest of the three is Dr. Martin Luther, for he made it
> possible to bring unity among the German tribes by giving them a common
> language through his translation of the Bible into German. Ever since I heard
> that Bismarck read the watchwords of the Moravian Brethren every morning,
> I also do it. I can assure you that in all the important decisions which I must
> make, the 'Daily Words' of the Moravian Brethren have been of help."
> One sister could not refrain from saying: "Herr Reichkanzler, from
> where do you get the courage to undertake the great changes in the whole
> Reich?"
> Thereupon Hitler took out of his pocket the New Testament of Dr.
> Martin Luther, which one could see had been used very much, and said
> earnestly: "From God's word."

June 24, 1933, was significant not only for Jäger's appointment as
commissioner of the Prussian Churches and for Bodelschwingh's resignation as bishop, but also as the day that Karl Barth set himself to write
his *Theological Existence Today.* Completed the next day, it was to
become a seminal theological tract for the times. The church is founded
on the word of God, he wrote, and it must find and justify its existence
from that source. It must never waver on this point or it will lose the
very justification for its existence. Was all this so-called church reform
rooted in the word of God, or was it the result of political expediency?
He had little difficulty in showing how political considerations were
affecting the church by quoting the opening words of the Loccumer
Manifest. The tower of church reform, he went on, threatened to collapse because it was hastily constructed and had no firm biblical and
theological foundation. He attacked primarily the establishment of the
office of bishop without first defining the nature of the office. Some
thought they were constituting a more or less honorific office as it
existed in the Scandinavian and English countries, a sort of glorified
general superintendent, but actually they were transferring the principle
of leadership (*Führerprinzip*) from the state to the church. "This leadership principle is sheer nonsense. Who says otherwise, does not know of
what he speaks."[31] If the bishop's office was not to be a powerful one,
why the struggle over whether Bodelschwingh or Müller should hold it?
He went on to say a clear no to the German Christians, and pointed out

how a true Evangelical church could not include them in its membership. This brief summary might make it appear that the essay was largely negative. It was far from that. It was actually a profound positive summons, calling for the churches never to compromise with the word of God. Its basic challenge was to prove an impetus and inspiration in the formation of the Confessing church.

The New Constitution and Church Elections

Placed in charge of the Prussian churches on June 24, Commissioner Jäger lost no time. That same day he dissolved the representative bodies of the various churches of Prussia. He dismissed Professor Dr. August Hinderer, the head of the Evangelical Press Service, and had his offices searched by the SA. The superintendents general of the Provincial churches were replaced by new church commissioners. Everywhere German Christians were put in administrative posts, among the most important appointments being those of Dr. Friedrich Werner as president and Pastor Hossenfelder as vice-president of the Supreme Church Council of Prussia. As Wilhelm Niemöller has commented: "A wild time followed!"[32] One cannot dismiss a man like Dibelius without expecting protests, and they soon followed, not only from the dismissed officials, but from the old church governing bodies, from many pastors, and from members of the congregations.[33] Bodelschwingh, after his resignation, finally was received by Hindenburg at Neudeck.[34] He was able to enlighten the president on the true situation and enlist his support. President Hindenburg then consulted with Hitler on June 29, and the following day wrote a letter asking him to take steps to settle the differences.[35] Hitler was on the spot, for Göring had just made a speech blasting the church leaders and upholding the measures Jäger had initiated.

Yet Hitler's luck held. On his instructions Müller hastily constructed a new constitutional committee.[36] Leading members of the old committee agreed to cooperate, and some other prominent men were added. It was largely a matter of putting the Loccumer Manifest into constitutional form. By July 11 the drafted document was signed by representatives of all the German Land churches. On July 12 Hitler informed Hindenburg that the constitution was completed, that the commissioners would be withdrawn, and that these measures provided assurance that peace would be established in the Evangelical church.[37] Two days later a Reich law confirmed the church constitution, and set July 23 as the date for new elections, according to Land church law, for those church bodies which were to be constituted through direct election of the people.[38] At that time apparently no one raised a serious protest about a national law confirming a church constitution or setting the date for church elections. Later the point was often made that the church elections were not really legal because the state was not qualified to call them.

The preamble of the constitution proclaimed that the German Evangelical church "unites the confessions arising out of the Reformation and co-existing with equal rights in a solemn league."[39] Article 1 had been carefully drawn, and although at a glance it might seem innocuous enough, it later became very significant. It reads: "The inviolable foundation of the German Evangelical church is the gospel of Jesus Christ, as testified to us in the Holy Scriptures and brought to light again in the creeds of the Reformation. The full powers which the church needs for her mission are thereby determined and limited."[40]

Clearly, the new church authorities could do nothing contrary to Holy Writ or to the historic recognized confessions of the church. It came to be a useful base from which opposing forces could attack the actions of the new church authorities. How, for example, could the new central authorities insist on appointing commissioners, let alone bishops, for Reformed churches where the presbyter-synodical form of church government was inextricably part of the confession?

The German Evangelical church (*Deutsche Evangelische Kirche,* DEK) was to be made up of the Land churches which were "to remain independent in confession and worship." The centralized church was to further administrative and legal unity among the member churches. Officials of the Land churches should be appointed only after consultation with the central church authorities. At the head was to be a Lutheran Reich bishop, a provision accepted only reluctantly by the Reformed leaders on the condition that the bishop was to be only the administrator, not the "leader and bearer of the spiritual teaching authority."[41] He was to appoint a Spiritual Ministry consisting of at least three theologians and one jurist. The Spiritual Ministry (Hitler made jibes at the title), under the leadership of the bishop, was to govern the church and legislate for it. There was also to be a national synod of sixty members, two-thirds of whom were chosen by the Land churches from their own synods, and one-third of whom were appointed by the central church. It was to meet once a year, and church laws were to be enacted by it in cooperation with the Spiritual Ministry, or by the latter alone.

In general it can be said that the constitution established a more centralized church than the old German Evangelical Church Confederation; it was not impregnated with parliamentarianism, but rather with the current principles of leadership. It was, however, far from establishing one Protestant Reich church. The various Land churches and the different confessions remained. Later attempts to change this status de facto, if not necessarily de jure, was to cause much anguish, strife, and imprisonment.

With the proclamation of the church constitution, the recently appointed church commissioners were withdrawn and the old officials of the Prussian church were at least temporarily reinstated. In accordance with Article 5 of the constitution, a committee of five was named to carry on the affairs of the national church until the meeting of the synod and the election of the bishop.[42] Attention was now focused on the church elections. An electoral period of only eight days had been allowed, which meant that the German Christians and the National Socialists immediately went into high gear. Anyone could vote who had a baptismal certificate or paid a church tax. Some who had withdrawn from the church hastened to rejoin. In Berlin they had streamers across the street proclaiming: "Every German votes German Christian."[43] Joachim Hossenfelder's declaration—"The German Christians are the SA of Jesus Christ"—became a campaign slogan.[44] A week before the election, the Ministry of Propaganda informed all newspapers that "from the extent of their participation in the editorial campaign for the German Christians, the government will judge what significance individual papers have for the new government."[45] With conditions as they were in the summer of 1933, hardly a single paper dared jeopardize its existence. A few papers were suppressed; others were coerced into supporting the German Christians.

In fact, there was no real opposition party. Single lists were often put up by general agreement, usually allotting about three-fourths of the seats to known German Christians. Since in such cases there were no opposing lists, there was no need for elections. In the whole state of Württemburg and in Schleswig-Holstein, for example, there was no balloting. In Eberfeld, and no doubt elsewhere, no opposition lists were presented because the political leaders held this would indicate opposition to Hitler. In Lippstadt in Westphalia, the local group leader closed the electoral meeting with the summons: "Sieg Heil to the Führer! Sieg Heil to our German Fatherland! Sieg Heil to Jesus Christ!"[46] To be sure, in a few places opposing lists were presented. For example, a group calling itself the "Young Reformation Movement" had been formed during the spring, and on May 9 had issued a manifesto on the reconstruction of the German church in which it boldly rejected the exclusion of non-Aryans from the Christian church.[47] This group, a forerunner of the Confessing church, sponsored an electoral list which they called "Evangelical Church" (*Evangelische Kirche*).[48] The German Christians objected to the name and forced a change on the day before the election to "Gospel and Church" (*Evangelium und Kirche*).[49] There is no question but the party and state authorities exercised undue zeal on behalf of the German Christians. To climax this intervention Hitler, at the urgent solicitation of Bishop Müller, went on the radio on the eve of balloting. He spoke for fifteen minutes of his fight against bolshevism and how national socialism had always affirmed its determination to protect the Christian churches. He touched on the conclusion of the concordat with the Vatican. Denying that he was moved by any questions of faith, dogma, or doctrine, he stated:

> In the interest of the recovery of the German nation, which I regard as indissolubly bound up with the National Socialist Movement, I naturally wish that the new church elections should in their result support our new policy for people and state. For, since the state is ready to guarantee the inner freedom of the religious life, it has the right to hope that in the confessions those forces will be given a hearing which are for their part determined in their resolve to do all in their power for the freedom of the nation. . . . These forces I see primarily marshalled in that part of the Evangelical communion

(*Kirchenvolk*), which in the German Christian Movement has consciously taken its stand on the ground of the National Socialist state—not in an enforced submission but in a living affirmation.[50]

The election on July 23, 1933, resulted in the German Christians winning about two thirds of the seats; the strong Bavarian church was not captured by the German Christians, but the provincial synod of Westphalia was the only synod in the Old Prussian Union where the Gospel and Church list won a majority (80 to 60).[51] The people had spoken. For the moment there was not much criticism, but gradually, as churchmen realized how much external influence there had been and what the results were apt to be, those opposed to the German Christians regularly denounced the elections.

On July 24, a committee of three—Bishop August Marahrens of Hanover, President Heinrich Tilemann of Oldenburg, and Bishop Hans Meiser of Bavaria—had an interview with Hitler at Bayreuth.[52] They were to report personally to the chancellor on the drafting of the constitution, the naming of a committee to head the church temporarily, and on the elections. Hitler stressed the importance of a strong, well-organized Evangelical church which would work in close cooperation with the state. He rejected every interference in matters of doctrine and the preaching of the gospel, and emphasized how much he opposed any revolutionary changes in religious life. He suggested that the state treaty to be drawn up with the Evangelical church would bring restrictions on the political activity of Evangelical clergy similar to those laid upon Catholic clergy in the concordat. His reference to negotiating a treaty with the Protestant church reveals that at least at that time, Hitler conceived of creating one large united Protestant church to stand parallel to the Catholic church. The projected treaty was, however, never considered.

Reorganization in the Land Churches

With the election past, it was time to organize the various governing bodies of the different churches. In Bavaria, Württemberg, and Hanover, the old authorities remained in control. In other Land churches, in district and provincial synods, new men and policies came to the fore. Many churches now began to call their heads "bishops," among them Bavaria, Württemberg, Baden, Thuringia, Hamburg, and Prussia.[53] All told, there was a great strengthening of the powers of the heads of the churches, for the current secular idea of leadership was being carried over into the ecclesiastical field. The number of Land churches lessened when the Land churches of Nassau and Frankfurt/Main united as the Land Church of Nassau-Hesse, and other consolidations also took place. In October, 1933, the churches of Mecklenburg-Schwerin and Mecklenburg-Strelitz voted to unite as of January 1, 1934. In March, 1934, the Church of Reuss-Greiz joined the Thuringian church; in June-July, 1934, the separate Church of

Waldeck-Pyrmont was erased, Waldeck being joined to the Church of Hesse-Kassel, and Pyrmont to the Lutheran Church of Hanover. On August 1, 1934, the Church of Lippe-Detmold was incorporated into the Westphalian provincial church of the Church of the Old Prussian Union.[54]

In many synods delegates appeared in brown shirts, and there was scant resemblance to the traditional tone and spirit of such bodies in the past.[55] Of the seventy-nine elected members of the synod in Schleswig-Holstein, seventy-five were German Christians. The members of the synod entered the church for the opening service between lines of SA and SS men at 11:30 in the morning. There were few addresses, and within several hours the whole church structure was changed. The executive committee was given power to enact measures, even constitutional changes, by decree, and an Aryan paragraph was adopted. At 5:45 p.m., the synod adjourned after a closing prayer, a word of greeting to Hitler, and the singing of "A Mighty Fortress is our God" and the Horst Wessel song.[56] The provincial synod of Westphalia, however, remained true to the old tradition of giving serious consideration to theological and church problems. The Tecklinburg district synod had submitted questions for consideration, and this led to the formulation of theses on the historical confessions, the congregation, church government, the National Socialist state, and the German Christian Faith Movement. The Westphalian synod's resolutions were among the earliest and most significant of the many protest statements that were to be issued during the struggle over the reorganization of the German church.[57]

By far the most important of these synodical meetings, however, was the synod of the Evangelical Church of the Old Prussian Union which was held in Berlin September 5–6, 1933. This synod approved a law which abolished the office of superintendent general and provided for a bishop who would take over the duties of the old church senate. Ludwig Müller was acclaimed to this office. Territorially the church was divided into ten bishoprics, thereby weakening the old provincial church organization. The synod enacted another law, one section of which read:

> Only he may be called as clergyman or official of the general church government who has the prescribed training for his career and who commits himself without reserve to the national government and the German Evangelical Church.
>
> He who is not of Aryan descent or who is married to a person not of Aryan descent may not be called as clergyman or official of the general church government. Clergymen or officials of Aryan descent who marry persons of non-Aryan descent are to be discharged. The determination as to who is to be regarded as a person of non-Aryan descent is made according to the provisions of the law of the Reich.[58]

When it was clear that the Aryan paragraph would be rammed through without proper debate or discussion, the Gospel and Church group (71 out of 227 members) withdrew from the synod. Their withdrawal left the

assembly entirely to the German Christians, who elected a solid delegation of 19 to the national synod. With great enthusiasm and acclaim,
Pastor Hossenfelder was affirmed bishop of Brandenburg.[59] That the
synod would exchange Dibelius for a man of Hossenfelder's caliber
shows the direction it was taking.

The national boycott of Jewish businesses organized by the National Socialist party on April 1, 1933, had brought no public condemnation by church authorities. It was generally regarded as a temporary
manifestation of party exuberance, a one-day protest.[60] At a meeting of
the directors of the Church Confederation on April 26, the following
resolution had been defeated with only one vote cast in its favor, because it was considered to serve no purpose.

> We acknowledge all members of our church without regard to their descent,
> and particularly today those who are fully or partially of Jewish descent. We
> feel with them and will intercede on their behalf as far as it is possible to do
> so. To all public officials we direct the earnest warning that all measures
> undertaken to redress grievances should not overstep the bounds set by the
> commandments of justice and Christian love.[61]

The many inquiries from foreign churchmen and statements in the
world press led President Kapler, at that time still head of the German
Evangelical Church Committee, to circulate a long memorandum, "The
Present Situation in Germany, especially on the Jewish Problem."[62] Fifty
copies were sent to the Foreign Office for its use and distribution. A
copy was sent to the Reich Chancellery, where it was characterized as
"really interesting." To them it no doubt was, for it excused the boycott
and the various measures that the state had taken to decrease Jewish
influence on German life. It enumerated the figures customarily invoked
to show the increase and disproportionate influence of Jews in Germany. There was a reservation or two at the close, stating that the
Jewish problem had not been studied sufficiently in the past and it
should now be considered thoroughly from the theological side. It also
sought to draw a line between "Jews" and "Jewish Christians," a distinction which was dear to churchmen throughout the Hitler period. It
noted the church's obligation to alleviate the suffering Jewish Christians,
and concluded: "It must be emphasized that the legal position of Jewish
Christians in the German Evangelical Land churches has not been affected by the state laws."

The enactment of the Aryan paragraph by the Prussian synod, however, did cause real alarm in church circles. Representatives of three
church districts of the Evangelical Land Church of Hesse-Kassel, who
had assembled for a meeting at Marburg, asked the theological faculties
of the universities of Marburg and Erlangen for an opinion as to whether
the enactment of such Aryan legislation by the church was consistent
with God's word, the historic confessions, and the preamble of the
recently adopted national church constitution. The Marburg faculty gave
a clear-cut negative answer; the racial Jew who had accepted Christianity was a full-fledged member of the Christian church and should not
suffer any discrimination. The Erlangen faculty responded with a very

equivocal statement.[63] The church had always established some requirements as to age and sex for its officials; there was no reason why it
could not add other requirements. If there was to be a true folk church,
if the church was to prosper, the pastor must be one with the congregation. In present-day Germany a Jewish pastor could not be successful.
This did not mean that the few Jewish pastors who were in office should
be dismissed; contrary to the Prussian law, only dismissal, not permission to serve, should require special proofs. Future permission for racial
Jews to enter the Christian ministry would best be left to the bishops. A
statement published independently by Professor Hermann Strathmann,
dean of the Erlangen theological faculty, advanced an even more specious argument.[64] Unmindful of the admonition, "He who is not for me
is against me," the Erlangen professors attempted to carry water on both
shoulders.

The Establishment of the Pastors' Emergency League

The Young Reformation Movement which had sponsored the Gospel and Church electoral list had never been very well-organized. After
the church elections, and particularly after the meeting of the Prussian
synod and its acceptance of the Aryan paragraph, it was clear that if the
opposition was to have any say, or if individuals were to be in any way
protected against arbitrary acts by the new authorities, some firmer organization was needed. It was apparently three rather obscure members
of the Young Reformation Movement—Pastors Eugene Weschke, Günter
Jacob, and Herbert Goltzen of the Mark—who were among the first to
further the formation of a special organization of pastors.[65] They initiated discussions with Berlin colleagues, notably with Pastor Gerhard
Jacobi of the Kaiser-Wilhelm-Gedächtniskirche and Pastor Martin
Niemöller, pastor of a strong congregation in Dahlem. The latter was
also in charge of conducting the affairs of the Young Reformation Movement. Niemöller was enthusiastic about the proposal, and at a meeting
of kindred spirits in Berlin, sixty pastors pledged themselves to support
such an emergency organization. When it was impossible to persuade
Bodelschwingh and Bishop Marahrens to head up the organization,
Niemöller undertook the task himself. The list of addresses used by the
Young Reformation Movement was at hand, and this served as an initial
mailing list for a general invitation issued on September 21 to pastors
throughout Germany to join in the Pastor's Emergency League (*Pfarrer-
notbund*). Niemöller, who was to become the very personification of the
league, had a streak of his mother in him—forthright, strong, uncompro-
mising, fearless.[66] Because of the general disorder and hardship arising
from recent measures, the league was being formed, among other purposes, to succor and support brother pastors who were undergoing persecution and suffering. Each member was asked to sign a four-point
pledge:

1. I pledge myself to fulfill my office as a servant of the Word, bound only by Holy Scripture and by the confessions of the Reformation as the correct exposition of the Holy Scripture.
2. I pledge myself to protest unreservedly against every infringement upon such a confessional position.
3. I realize that I share responsibility to the extent of my powers together with those who are persecuted on account of such a confessional position.
4. In making this pledge I bear witness that the application of the Aryan paragraph in the area of the church of Christ is an infringement upon such a confessional position.[67]

The pledge, it may be noted, was centered on church affairs and the opposition to the Aryan paragraph was limited to applying it in the "area of the church of Christ." It was no summons to political opposition; as the Reichsführer SS in his report on the situation in the Protestant churches of February–March, 1935, put it, if there were examples of Protestant ministers opposing the state, this was not the fault of the Notbund. Its leadership had always repudiated such attacks.[68]

Signatures to the pledge of the Pastors' Emergency League flooded in, and when the first national synod met at Wittenberg on September 27, 1933, the league issued a statement of protest against the ruthless silencing of the minorities in deliberative bodies, and against the adoption of the Aryan paragraph—which was contrary to Holy Writ and historic confessions. The statement demanded that the national synod further the unfettered preaching of the gospel.[69]

The synod had been opened with much pomp. Most of the members were German Christians, and the few others could do no more than issue their protest. Ludwig Müller, already bishop of the Prussian church and holder of various other titles and positions, was elected Reich bishop. He at once appointed, with Hitler's approval, the Spiritual Ministry—consisting of Hossenfelder (to represent the United church), Bishop Schöffel (to represent the Lutherans), and Dr. Otto Weber from Elberfeld (to represent the Reformed). The legal member was to be Dr. Friedrich Werner.[70] There was no attempt at the synod to enact an Aryan paragraph, but there was also no condemnation of the provincial churches which had taken that step. The archbishop of Sweden had declared that he would have to separate his church publicly from the German Evangelical church if the national synod should adopt an Aryan paragraph. The German Foreign Office, in a letter of September 22, advised against its adoption, preferring if necessary to achieve the goals of the paragraph through administrative measures.[71] Theology professor Wilhelm Dibelius later expressed his thanks for the intervention of the Foreign Office.[72] Müller was well aware of international feeling, and, being eager to quiet opposition, was willing to make this concession.

Meanwhile, membership in the Pastors' Emergency League mounted, and by the end of the year had reached about 6,000.[73] In October a small group met in Niemöller's home and decided on some organizational measures. There was to be a directing brotherhood council (Bruderrat) of eight members, and advisory groups of specialists in various fields were to be established. On many questions there were differences of opinion, but there was unanimity in regard to opposing a church Aryan paragraph. There is no doubt this opposition was based on doctrine and principle, for the number of non-Aryan pastors was indeed small. In the whole period from the sixteenth century to the nineteenth, there are records of only 63 non-Aryan pastors; in 1933 there were 37 "full" Jewish pastors living, of whom eight were retired.[74] It is clear that Jews were a very small minority in a total of around 18,000 pastors, but this fact did not lessen the significance of the principles and doctrines involved. Actually, the Aryan paragraph would later be directed against the laity in the churches, where far greater numbers were affected.

Crisis among the German Christians

Elected bishop and with the synod behind him, Müller attempted a policy of reconciliation. On September 26, 1933, Minister of the Interior Frick had issued a statement that it was a matter for regret that many officials had dropped their church memberships. It was to be hoped that the National Socialist victory would bring officials to their better selves, and that they would return to the churches. This, however, must be done freely by individuals, and at the special request of the chancellor he would ask that no pressure be brought on officials to resume church membership.[75] In a proclamation issued on October 11, Müller assured all German pastors that he would never permit anyone to suffer any disadvantage because he did not belong to the German Christians. "The church-political struggle has ended, the struggle for the soul of the folk begins. And so I call to all pastors: put yourself with confidence into this struggle. That is the best way to achieve unity of purpose and action."[76] Two days later Rudolph Hess, the Führer's deputy, decreed in a toleration edict that no National Socialist should suffer because he did not belong to a certain religious party.[77]

In fact, many National Socialists were not pleased with the recent close cooperation between the party and the German Christians, nor for that matter with the conclusion of the concordat with the Vatican. They preferred the original Nazi policy of remaining aloof from church ties. Alfred Rosenberg was one of the first to express his views when he maintained in an article in the *Völkischer Beobachter* of August 16, 1933, that the party should support no church group.[78] He soon forced the dissolution of the German Christian Cultural Office. At about the same time the newspapers were exempted from further active support of the German Christians. The German Christian *Reichsbote* joined in the peace offensive, and warned against the well-meant but erroneous aim of making the great National Socialist movement into a religion and equating the Third Reich with the kingdom of God.[79] Such dangerous tendencies could be avoided only if the separate natures of state and church were recognized and the two kept apart.

It was during this period that Hitler, at the request of the United

States' embassy on October 31, 1933, received the Reverend Charles S.
Macfarland, general secretary emeritus of the Federal Council of Churches of Christ in America.[80] Macfarland, who knew Germany well, was on a fact-finding mission, and before the interview submitted a memorandum to Hitler. He warned that the introduction of the Aryan paragraph into the church constitution would mean a break with the churches of the United States and of the whole world. Hitler assured him that while he wanted one united church, he had absolutely no intention of intervening in its internal organization or influencing its doctrine. Macfarland informed Hitler that he had the impression that the opposition groups, while personally loyal to the Führer, felt that the German Christians had closer contact with him. "Would it not be good," he asked, "to meet with both groups and bring about agreement through his authority?" Hitler was willing to do this, but he would have to be asked, and he authorized Macfarland to make use as he saw fit of his willingness to meet and work out a compromise. Macfarland was duly impressed by Hitler's sincerity, and wrote:

> The fact is Adolf Hitler is the conservative and restraining personal force in Germany today (in contrast to such leaders as Goehring and Goebbels). One can discover many indications of that influence to some extent in his speeches, but still more in his counsels and guidance. And now, even if he may be charged with having laid hands on the church, it is quite possible that he may become its protector from his own original mistaken measures and more particularly those of his overzealous and somewhat delirious followers in the Church.
>
> If the present ground is held, the Church may not only free itself from National Socialism, but also from the state and may do it largely with the help of Adolf Hitler.[81]

The lull in the church conflict is not unassociated with events in foreign policy. On October 14, Hitler withdrew Germany from the Disarmament Conference and the League of Nations. It was a popular move in Germany, and the following day Martin Niemöller joined with others in a telegram to Hitler:

> In this decisive hour for folk and fatherland we greet our Führer. We give thanks for this manly deed and the clear words that safeguard Germany's honor. In the name of 2,500 Evangelical pastors who do not belong to the German Christian Faith movement, we pledge our true support and prayerful thoughts.[82]

Hitler's policy was overwhelmingly endorsed in a plebiscite on November 12, and the next evening some 20,000 German Christians gathered at the Sportspalast in Berlin. The meeting had been arranged by Dr. Reinhold Krause, leader of the Greater Berlin district of the Faith movement, member of the Brandenburg provincial synod and the Prussian Land synod, and holder of other church offices. The meeting was opened with great fanfare and a parade of flags. A brass ensemble intoned "A Mighty Fortress is our God," and there were some short addresses, including one by Hossenfelder.[83] Soon Dr. Krause was launched on the main address of the evening, entitled "The Tasks of a

German Reich Church in the Spirit of Dr. Martin Luther." There was little resemblance to the spirit of Luther in the address except in the forthrightness with which Krause expressed his views. These were repeated in a resolution which the assembly adopted by acclaim. There is dispute if various church leaders who were present voted against them or not, but it matters little, for everybody knew they would be adopted and a no would go unheard. The resolution, consisting of six paragraphs, could not be understood, let alone seriously considered, in an assembly of 20,000. Its full impact came later when it was published. Some of its most significant points were:

> An enduring peace can only be created by the transfer or removal of all pastors who are neither willing or able to cooperate in leading the religious renewal of our people and the fulfillment of the religious reformation in the spirit of National Socialism.
>
> We expect from our nation's church that it will immediately carry through the Aryan paragraph corresponding to the church law passed by the Prussian general synod. Besides this, we expect the church to bring together all Protestant Christians of alien blood in special church congregations and that it undertakes to form a Jewish Christian Church.
>
> We expect that our nation's church as a German People's Church (Volkskirche) should free itself from all things not German in its services and confession, especially from the Old Testament with its Jewish system of quid pro quo morality (jüdischen Lohnmoral).[84]

The speeches and resolutions reverberated through the land. Bishop Wurm compares the reaction to the thrust of a stick in an anthill: "Everything fell apart and into confusion."[85] Protests poured in. The next day Pastor Gerhard Jacobi, Martin Niemöller, and his brother Wilhelm visited Müller and in the name of the Pastors' Emergency League demanded that he discipline the church leaders present at the meeting and resign his office of protector of the German Christians. The utterances indeed had been too much for the bishop, and Krause was immediately removed from all his church positions. On November 15, Müller issued a sharp denunciation, especially of Krause's attack on the Old Testament: "Such views and demands are nothing else but an unbearable attack on the confessions of the church. Such a spirit the administration and leadership of the Evangelical church completely rejects. . . . "[86] As a protest against Müller's statement, on the same day Rosenberg officially withdrew from the Evangelical Lutheran church.[87]

For the past several months a significant number of pastors had withdrawn their allegiance from the German Christians and joined the Pastors' Emergency League. A group withdrawal of 150 members in Württemberg in September had gone a long way towards confirming Bishop Wurm's leadership of that important Land church.[88] Now the disintegration of the German Christian Movement set in. Many individual pastors withdrew and added their names to the ever-lengthening roll of the Pastors' Emergency League. Theological professors who had originally lent prestige to the German Christians now called it quits, among them Karl Fezer, Paul Rückert, Heinrich Bornkamm, Gerhard and Helmut Kittel, Friedrich Gogarten, and Hermann W. Beyer.[89] On the other

hand, Krause did not take his dismissal lying down, but started to recruit
a group of followers. He spoke far and wide, gradually becoming more
and more antichurch, and eventually joining the anti-Christian German
Faith Movement. In Saxony, Bishop Friedrich Coch went so far as to
reject the German Christian guidelines, adopting the new name "Folk
Mission Movement of Saxony, German Christian."[90] Here they drew up
a new program of twenty-eight theses which only added more controversy. The theological faculty of the University of Leipzig, when asked
for an opinion, declared that these theses "in important points conflicted not only in word but in spirit with the historic confessions."[91]

In an effort to bring the movement together again and assert his
leadership, Hossenfelder called a leadership meeting at Weimar for November 23–24. The meeting was a fiasco. Not only did the Bavarian
German Christians withdraw and pledge their continued support to
Bishop Meiser, but Hossenfelder lost control of the Thuringian movement, which declared itself independent of the national leadership, assuming its old name, "German Christian Church Movement" (Kirchenbewegung Deutsche Christen, KDC).[92] It eventually came to challenge
effectively the official German Christian leadership. On returning to
Berlin the evening of the twenty-fourth, Hossenfelder and fifty of his
stalwarts went to see Bishop Müller. They talked until three in the
morning, and Müller again expressed his confidence in Hossenfelder,
instead of dismissing him as many of the churchmen were demanding.
"Hossenfelder and I are inseparable," the bishop declared, although
very shortly he did not disguise his willingness to sacrifice his friend.[93]

As a gesture to Hossenfelder, Müller asked Bishop Schöffel of the
Spiritual Ministry to share the supervision of the Lutheran churches with
Bishop Coch of Saxony. Schöffel refused to do so and resigned, which
evoked an organizational crisis. The church leaders of Baden, Bavaria,
Eutin, Hamburg, Hanover, Oldenburg, Thuringia, and Württemberg
brought pressure on Müller to reconstitute the whole Spiritual Ministry.
The upshot was that the remaining three members of the ministry were
forced to resign, and at the suggestion of the church leaders Müller
named a new Spiritual Ministry consisting of Dr. Hans Lauerer (Lutheran), Dr. Hermann W. Beyer (United), and Pastor Otto Weber (Reformed), with Dr. Friedrich Werner continuing on as the legal representative. This new ministry was a complete failure. Lauerer never took
office, Weber left on December 22, and Beyer left shortly after the new
year. Müller was forced to dismiss Dr. Werner for disciplinary reasons.
The latter fought his dismissal, and at least temporarily received the
support of Minister of the Interior Frick.[94]

One of the measures the new Spiritual Ministry achieved before its
disintegration was a decree of December 4 forbidding all officials of the
Reich church government to belong to church political parties. Bishop
Müller consequently resigned as protector of the German Christian Faith
Movement. Hossenfelder, desiring to circumvent the law, maintained
that the German Christians were not a political party but a faith movement, but such specious arguments did him no good. Under renewed

pressure, Müller finally deprived him of all his church offices, which meant he was no longer bishop of Brandenburg, deputy bishop of Prussia, or a member of the Prussian Evangelical Supreme Church Council. On December 21, Hossenfelder also had to surrender his leadership of the German Christian Faith Movement.[95] He, like Krause, recruited a small group of followers, which further splintered the German Christians. Dr. Christian Kinder, a young Gauleiter of the movement from Schleswig-Holstein and a convinced Lutheran, was given the task of reuniting the German Christians. He had not joined them until after the church elections of 1933, and now was given leave by the church authorities in Kiel to take over his new post. Actually, he had been one of the more active leaders of the opposition within the movement to Hossenfelder's leadership. He began by abandoning the term "Faith Movement" (*Glaubensbewegung*); henceforth the National Socialists of the Evangelical church would carry the name "German Christian Reich Movement" (*Reichsbewegung Deutsche Christen,* RDC). As new guidelines he adopted the twenty-eight theses drawn up by the Church of Saxony.[96] But the German Christians had reached their zenith. Although they continued to play a role in the succeeding years, it was a diminishing one.

The Sportspalast scandal had also had its effect in secular governmental circles. The blunders of the German Christians were recognized, and with the direct authorization of Hitler, Minister of the Interior Frick on November 30 ordered that state authorities should not intervene in church affairs: "The Reich chancellor has made the definite decision that, inasmuch as it is clearly a matter of church concern, there should be no interference from the outside in this conflict of opinions. All police intervention, such as protective custody [and] confiscation of mail, are especially forbidden."[97] Hindenburg summoned Hitler and Frick on the afternoon of November 30 to discuss the church situation. Soon after the president and several cabinet ministers, as well as many of the Lutheran bishops, cancelled their intention of attending Müller's installation service, scheduled for December 3 in the Berlin cathedral. This service was called off at the last minute, an indication of how serious the church disturbances were and of how low Müller's prestige had sunk. The next day Hitler ordered the Reich bishop to be told: "We will go along with this only for a brief time; then we will act and you had better look out!"[98] Matters had reached the point that the Ministry of Propaganda forbade the press to mention the church conflict, which of course only heightened rumors and led to the impression abroad that the church was being suppressed. Undaunted, the national church authorities submitted a long memorandum and a request for 4,750,000 marks so that they could carry on their work. Their request was given short shrift, for as Frick pointed out, a united church administration should bring savings, not greater expense. The government was interested only in a church where peace and order prevailed. If peace were not restored, the state could not put Reich funds at the disposal of the Reich church. This threat to cut off funds, Müller retorted, was unbearable.[99]

It was in this period of complete disorder that Müller, on his own and without authorization from anyone, signed an agreement on December 19 with Baldur von Schirach, the Reich youth leader, incorporating the Evangelical Youth Organization into the Hitler Youth. Negotiations had been going on for some time between Bishop Müller's church officials, party leaders, heads of the Evangelical Youth Organization, and other church leaders.[100] Müller issued a pious declaration to parents, saying he had been forced to take the step because of his responsibility for furthering the religious training of young people. He apparently hoped to transform the Hitler Youth by infiltrating it with religion and getting its members to go en masse to church at least once a month.[101] This measure aroused tremendous concern in church circles. President Hindenburg did not like it, but Müller's action no doubt found favor among certain National Socialists and strengthened his position with Hitler.[102] As the official church paper noted: "It was an impossible situation and a direct affront to Adolph Hitler that the Evangelical Youth Organization considered themselves too good to join with the Hitler Youth.[103]

Bishop Meiser and others protested the incorporation of the Evangelical Youth Organization, and soon steps were taken to form new church youth groups. The existing youth organizations were dissolved and groups known as Evangelical Congregational Youth (*Evangelische Gemeindejugend*) were formed which remained free from Shirach's clutches.[104] In Bavaria, and elsewhere as well, the church created a new office of Land youth minister (*Landesjugendpfarrer*). District youth ministers were soon appointed and began supervising intensified youth activity within the congregations. Retreats and summer camps were instituted. All sport activity was banned at these gatherings, but even Himmler came to rule that the young people could go swimming and engage in some light calisthenics. The Evangelical churches by no means surrendered their youth completely to the Hitler Youth and to the party, although the latter continually followed a policy of harassment.[105]

By the end of 1933, the church situation was critical. Not only were the leaders of important Land churches pressuring Bishop Müller, but so also were government officials. Conrad reports that Minister Rust, head of the Ministry of Culture, after dealing with Bishop Wurm of Württemberg, exclaimed: "Never again will I stick my finger in the church."[106] The Spiritual Ministry was no longer functioning, and without it Müller had no way legally to administer the church or enact church legislation. Yet this did not deter him. On January 4, 1934, he issued a decree optimistically entitled "Ordinance in Respect to Restoring Orderly Conditions in the German Evangelical Church":

> Church services are exclusively for expounding the pure gospel. The misuse of church services for church-political affairs, in whatever form, is to be stopped. Permission to use churches or other church rooms for church-politi-

cal meetings of any kind is forbidden. Any church official who attacks the church government or its actions publicly or by distributing statements, especially flyers, is guilty of violating his pastoral duties.[107]

There were other more technical matters (among them a restoration of the Aryan paragraph in the Prussian church), but the decree was soon labelled the "Muzzle Law" (*Maulkorbgesetz*). The Pastors' Emergency League reacted at once and requested its members to read a declaration from the pulpit on either January 7 or 14. It drew attention to the nonexistence of a Spiritual Ministry, the illegality of the Müller decree, and the attempt to curb the freedom of the pulpit, and ended with a pertinent quotation from the Confession of Augsburg: "Where the bishops teach, maintain, or uphold something contrary to the gospel, we have God's command in such a case not to obey. One should also not follow properly elected bishops when they are in error."[108] Some 3,500 ministers read the declaration, although in Bavaria, Württemberg, and a number of other churches, in response to Müller's plea, the declaration was not read. The leaders of these churches did not necessarily approve the law, but they preferred to await the results of a scheduled meeting of church leaders with the Führer on January 17. Yet their decision aroused hard feelings and threatened a split in the Pastors' Emergency League. Müller meanwhile suspended a number of the pastors who had read the pulpit declaration, and various coercive measures were taken against others.

Amid the turmoil President Hindenburg, having been briefed by Bodelschwingh and Reich Finance Minister Lutz, Count von Schwerin-Krosigk, took a hand.[109] On January 12, 1934, he received Bishop Müller and his general secretary, Bishop Heinrich Oberheid. Hindenburg explained that he was doing this for his personal orientation and out of a desire to aid as an Evangelical Christian. Three things concerned him: (1) the appointments to the Spiritual Ministry; (2) the incorporation of the Evangelical Youth into the Hitler Youth; and (3) the measures taken by the bishop to secure peace in the church. These last had gone too far and were considered a threat to use force. He, like others, was fearful that the opposition groups, if pushed too far, would break away and form a Free church—something which no one actually wanted. Müller answered, but apparently made no great impression, for Hindenburg asked that Hitler be directly informed that he had no special personal confidence in Müller. Hindenburg respected the Reich bishop because of his office and as the confidant of the chancellor on church questions. "Personally," so the report drawn up by Secretary Otto Meissner continues, "the president is of the opinion that the Reich bishop, partly because of health reasons, partly because of lack of authority, is not in a position to improve the present anxiety-arousing troubled conditions in the Evangelical church and to protect its unity."[110]

It was clear something should be done. Hitler not only had Hindenburg and the churchmen to deal with, but he also needed to appease certain radical groups in his own party. He made a gesture to them when, on January 24, he entrusted Alfred Rosenberg with the complete

spiritual and ideological instruction and education of the National Socialist party. The Catholic church took his action as an occasion to
place Rosenberg's *Myth of the Twentieth Century* on the index.[111] Although Hitler was always careful not to express publicly his approval of
the volume, his support of the author was an irritant to Protestant and
Catholic leaders alike.

The meeting Hitler had originally scheduled for January 24 with a
select group of church leaders was postponed until the next day because he wanted to attend the funeral of architect Paul Troost in Munich. The churchmen who had gathered in Berlin thus had time to agree
on a memorandum to be presented to the government.[112] The morning
of January 25, just as Martin Niemöller was about to leave his home to
meet with the other church leaders, he received a telephone call from
Professor Walter Künneth inquiring how things were going. Niemöller,
in a hurry, breakfasting and telephoning at the same time, did not particularly consider his words. He is supposed to have said: "We have
laid our mines; we have sent our memorandum to the president [which
was designed to bring about the fall of the Reich bishop]; we have
prepared the situation well; before our meeting today, the chancellor is
to be received by the president and will receive from him extreme
unction (*letzte Ölung*)."[113] There are various versions of this telephone
conversation, and the rumor soon spread that it had been taken down
on a phonograph record. Such a record has never been found, but a
written notation of the intercepted conversation was found in the files of
the secret police.[114]

When Hitler received the church leaders, Göring, who had added
himself to the interview, opened the proceedings. As chief of police he
had secret information. In dramatic fashion and certainly with some
elaboration, he now read a report on Niemöller's telephone conversation. Hitler reacted sharply, asking if they thought they could in this
fashion drive a wedge between him and the president. "Even if I had
wanted to separate myself from the Reich bishop, I could not do it now,
that you will understand."[115] Niemöller stepped to the fore, explained
carefully the intentions of the group and the situation in the church, and
apparently remained standing in front of his fellows.[116] At times the
exchange became heated, but proper decorum was maintained. In view
of the repercussions from the church conflict on foreign affairs, Hitler
appealed to the church leaders to support Müller and complete the
work of unifying the church. If the church leaders could not agree, he
would withdraw both his protecting hand and state financial support.
Other men expressed their views, and at the close of the audience
Hitler, in customary German fashion, shook hands with everyone.[117]

At the audience it was clear that the majority of the churchmen
were disposed to meet Hitler's request. The next day they sent three
emissaries (Bishop Schöffel of Hamburg, Bishop Marahrens of Hanover,
and President Jakob Kessler of the Church of the Palatinate) to Müller to
arrange for a meeting to see what could be done. On the following day,
January 27, 1934, Müller met with this group of churchmen, and in a

long address further explained his and Hitler's plans.[118] Finally the church leaders, among them the bishops of the large Lutheran churches, agreed again to support Müller, in view of his promises that: (1) in all important questions he would consult the Council of Bishops; (2) he would appoint a new Spiritual Ministry; and (3) in all matters of faith, political force should be excluded.[119]

Niemöller and the leaders of the Pastors' Emergency League had absented themselves from the meeting with Müller and continued their open hostility to him. They decried the capitulation of the Lutheran bishops, particularly those of the larger churches—Meiser of Bavaria, Wurm of Württemberg, and Marahrens of Hanover. These men, struggling to maintain control of their own churches, were at times more willing to compromise on what they considered secondary matters. They wanted to prevent the total disorder and disruption that had occurred in the Prussian church. Their policies often weakened the opposition to official Berlin policy, but on the other hand, had the bulwark which their churches constituted fallen to Berlin domination, the governing authorities could have worked their will with greater dispatch and ruthlessness throughout the nation.

The division among the church leaders following the reception by the chancellor led to a notable decline in the membership of the Pastors' Emergency League. It had reached its high point with 7,036 members in January, 1934; now some 1,200 Bavarian and 350 Hanoverian pastors withdrew without notice. In addition, 250 Württemberg pastors individually resigned, and the Württemberg branch of the league dissolved itself. This left a membership of 5,256, which remained relatively unchanged in the following years.[120]

The cohorts of Bishop Müller continued to press their policies in the various Land churches. One of the most significant individual actions was the pensioning off, on January 30, 1934, of Pastor Hans Asmussen in Schleswig-Holstein because "his actions up to now do not give surety that he will at all times support unreservedly the German Evangelical church."[121] The generalization was no doubt true, but hardly a ground for dismissal, and Asmussen objected to no avail. He was, however, freed to help combat the state's domination of the churches, and he became one of the most active pamphleteers of the Kirchenkampf period, discussing mainly theological issues.[122] After a year in power, the National Socialists had not achieved a Gleichschaltung of the Protestant churches. In fact, they had aroused an effective opposition which was to crystallize in the establishment of the Confessing church.

In order to further the coordination of a unified church policy in line with the Führer's directives, Hess established, on February 27, 1934, the Bureau for Cultural Peace (Abteilung für kulturellen Frieden) within the party structure. It was to be headed by Hermann von Detten, a Catholic, and all political leaders were to consult him before taking action in regard to church affairs. In this way Hess and the party would have an opportunity to influence the inauguration of policies and legislation dealing with the churches.[123]

The First Confessing Synods and the Confessing Church

Bishop Müller's New Policies

The official communiqué on the meeting of the Reich bishop with the church leaders reaffirmed their statement of unconditional loyalty to the Third Reich and its Führer, concluding: "The assembled church leaders place themselves solidly behind the Reich bishop and are willing to carry out his measures and ordinances as he wishes, to oppose church political opposition to these measures, and to strengthen with all the constitutional powers they have the authority of the Reich bishop."[1] Taking this as a vote of confidence, as he might well do, Müller set to work. A flood of coercive measures of all sorts—removal from office, denial of the right to preach, transfer to new posts, forced retirements—was loosed upon members of the Pastors' Emergency League.[2] On February 23, 1934, the bishop appointed a new Spiritual Ministry. Membership was considered an honorary office and the ministry was to be consulted only on important occasions. It was clear that Müller and his office intended to direct the German Evangelical church.[3]

On March 2, a new church law challenged the autonomy of the Church of the Old Prussian Union, and that body was incorporated directly into the German Evangelical church. This policy of incorporation (*Eingliederung*) was pursued until within a few months most of the smaller churches had been made integral parts of the national church. On March 7, administrative changes were introduced in the German Evangelical church, and Bishop Heinrich Oberheid was appointed Müller's chief of staff.[4] The title had military connotations befitting the aggressive policy Müller had undertaken. He also created a church foreign office (*Kirchliches Aussenamt*) and put Senior Consistory Councillor Dr. Theodor Heckel as bishop in charge. "Bishop" was rapidly degenerating into a mere administrative designation. Churches in Brazil, South Africa, and Chile, which had been tied to the churches of the Old Prussian Union, Hanover, and Saxony, respectively, were now placed under the control of this new office. All communications with churches abroad were to be channeled through Bishop Heckel.[5] It was especially significant that he was to have jurisdiction over all ecumenical contacts.

The ministers and church leaders thus disciplined by Bishop Müller did not accept his measures quietly.[6] Innumerable legal processes were started, and in the large majority of cases the court held for the accused ministers. It did not take Bishops Wurm and Meiser long to discover that Müller was keeping none of his promises to them, and that it had been a mistake to pledge their loyalty to him. Through the good offices of Foreign Minister von Neurath, who was greatly concerned about the attention the church conflict was receiving in the foreign press, an interview with Hitler was arranged for the two South German bishops on March 13.[7] Wurm had resolved it was time to tell Hitler the truth. They found the chancellor in a truculent mood. The bishops had been advised that if Hitler yelled they should yell in turn, and for two hours they shouted at each other. Meiser declared that "if Müller did not resign there was nothing left for them to do but to become his majesty's loyal opposition," to which Hitler fired back, "This you are not; you are traitors to the nation and the folk."[8] In the end Hitler said he would act as an honest broker; he would place a Westphalian noble, Captain Franz Pfeffer von Salomon, in charge of negotiations. Von Pfeffer was a former Free Corps leader and a Catholic who had never been entrusted with Protestant church affairs. He evoked no confidence, and what activity he undertook was without results.

The troubled situation in the Protestant German church had led Bishop George Bell of England and Archbishop Erling Eidem of Sweden, as well as Lutheran churches in America, to protest to Reich Bishop Müller, but their pleas had no effect. Churchmen in Germany then suggested that Bell and Eidem appeal directly to Hitler.[9] Bell was reserved, for he feared Hitler might consider it a request for state interference. It was finally decided that Eidem should seek a private interview. Birger Forell, the minister of the Swedish congregation in Berlin, was able to arrange such an interview for May 2, 1934. Eidem had earlier gone over the situation with Dr. Hanns Lilje, a prominent Lutheran pastor, and had carefully prepared a memorandum which he read. He expressed no desire to intervene in German affairs; rather, he wanted to convey the concern of other churches about conditions in the German church. He did criticize Bishop Müller and the present church administration. Hitler then spoke for about forty minutes, went into a tantrum and pounded the table, but failed to answer the points Eidem had raised. He asserted that both the Protestant and Catholic churches would be swept away if he intervened, criticized the leaders of the opposition, and defended Bishop Müller. The result of the interview was that Eidem counselled against any external intervention. It would in his opinion do more harm than good; it would hurt the budding Confessing church, and make it harder to keep in contact with its leaders.[10]

When Wurm and Meiser returned to their churches they did their best to enlighten the people. Wurm preached in many different places in Württemberg; in Bavaria Meiser issued a long statement containing an analysis of the office of bishop in the Protestant church.[11] Müller again began to issue pronouncements supposedly intended to restore peace to the church. He declared that it was necessary to strengthen and extend the external organization of the church.[12] On April 12, he summoned Ministerial Director August Jäger from the Ministry of Science, Culture, and Education, where he was in charge of church affairs (and would continue to hold that office) to become the legal representative in the recently formed Spiritual Ministry. Jäger had once before held church office only to be forced to retire.[13] He now brought with him the blessing of Minister Rust and, as legal protector (*Rechtswalter*) of the church, he immediately began to push the centralization of church government.

Müller and Jäger picked the church of Württemberg as their first target, and on Saturday night and Sunday morning, April 14–15, the radio announced irregularities in the enactment of the church budget in that state, adding that Bishop Wurm could no longer be tolerated as a public personality in the new Germany.[14] Actually his actions were unassailable, and the regularly constituted Württemberg church assembly stood by him. Memoranda from local congregations and many pastors began to pour into the Berlin church office and the Foreign Office, asserting their support of Wurm. The signers appealed to von Neurath as a good Christian Swabian to help them out. He did send a batch of these protest telegrams and letters to Minister of the Interior Frick for his "friendly consideration."[15]

Bishop Wurm was able to maintain control of his church, but the future looked ominous, and he went to Munich to seek counsel and support from Meiser. By long standing invitation, Wurm was to preach in Ulm the following Sunday, April 22, 1934. He and Meiser agreed to use the occasion for a demonstration, and invited representatives of other Confessing churches, as the opposition was now being called, to attend the service. And they did indeed come. Wurm gave his sermon to a mass congregation, and the bishop of Bavaria read a ringing manifesto decrying the attempt of a false church regime to take over regularly constituted church governments.[16] The declaration stated that the delegates there assembled were speaking as the "lawful German Evangelical church," a position which the Confessing church was later always to maintain. The Ulm meeting did much to dispel the estrangement that had arisen among the Confessing church leaders after the January 25 meeting with Hitler. The time was ripe to bring the various islands of resistance together into a national resistance organization.

Free Synods and Plans for a Confessing Church

The disorder in the church and the continuing attack on the doctrinal foundations of the faith by the German Christians impelled groups of pastors to gather for consultation and mutual encouragement.[17] These meetings, called "free synods," were outside of the regular church government, although the old authorities often participated in them. One of the first and most important was the Free Reformed synod which met at Barmen-Gemarke on January 3–4, 1934, largely at the initiative of Pastor Karl Immer, who was to become one of the more intrepid leaders in the Church Struggle.[18] The invitation stated that only those should attend who unreservedly held to the Old and New Testament as God's word and the only source of faith. Some 320 representatives from 167 congregations throughout Germany came to this meeting. It was followed by a Free Evangelical synod of the Rhineland, also held at Barmen on February 18–19, where a significant step forward was made, for the meeting was attended by Lutheran, Reformed, and United representatives from 30 out of the 33 district synods. The synod was truly Evangelical–not Reformed, Lutheran, or United. The leaders of the Pastors' Emergency League, meeting in Hanover at this time, successfully petitioned to be accepted into this synod so that they with their Rhenish brethren could work together towards a Free Evangelical synod for all Germany.

Free synods of varying constituencies were held in other parts of Germany. Under the reorganization measures necessitated by the new Prussian church law of March 2, 1934, the old provincial synods were to be reconstituted. The old synods were to meet and as the only order of business were to select from their membership a smaller group to be the new synod. The decree specifically prohibited any discussion. The provincial Westphalian synod met on March 16, and its venerated and distinguished leader, President Karl Koch, made some opening remarks stressing the importance of the meeting.[19] Bishop Bruno Adler, who had been appointed by Müller to the newly created diocese of Münster, objected, calling attention to the fact that there was to be no discussion. Koch then declared he would have to adjourn the meeting. Bishop Adler reminded them that if they did not elect, he was empowered to appoint the new synodical members. With that he and his German Christian cohorts, who were in a minority, left the meeting. The synod was in the process of hearing another report when two Gestapo officials appeared, dissolved the assembly, and forbade any further meeting. Instead of scattering, that very afternoon the membership met in the parish house of the local congregation and constituted itself the First Westphalian Confessing Synod. Representatives of all 24 district synods attended, as well as guests from other Land churches. This new extralegal synod elected Koch as their head, and constituted a brotherhood council to assist him. Resolutions were passed and the synod was concluded with a communion service in the Reinhold church. It was conducted by Pastor von Bodelschwingh, a Lutheran, and he was assisted by Superintendent Karl Niemann, a Reformed pastor. Reformed, Lutheran, and United gathered together in true evangelical spirit at the Table of the Lord and extended the right hand of fellowship, an unusual ecumenical manifestation for Germany.[20]

The Confessing synod determined to carry its cause to the laity. Two days later, on March 18, 25,000 congregational members met at Dortmund, a remarkable achievement considering the short time for publicity.[21] They were addressed by Koch, Bodelschwingh, and others. Mass meetings, formerly the specialty of the German Christians with their flags and stirring music, now became one of the important methods of expressing support for the Confessing church.

To prepare for a national free synod a group known as the Working Committee of the Confessional Association (*Arbeitsausschuss der Be-* *kenntnisgemeinschaft*) met at Nürnberg on April 11, 1934. This so- called *Nürnberger Ausschuss* took part in a meeting held at Ulm, organ- ized by Bishops Wurm and Meiser to protest actions by the Berlin church authorities. The committee met several times subsequently, and on May 22, thanks to much deliberation and hard work, invitations could be sent out by the brotherhood council of the Pastors' Emergency League to attend a meeting of a Free synod of the German Evangelical church to be held at Barmen. To prevent infiltration by the German Christians, the invitation stated:

> We ask that you send only such men as have the complete confidence of the Confessional congregation both at home and beyond their territorial church. Only such men can be considered as delegates who refuse to subordinate themselves to a heretical and despotic church government or to work with such a regime. The Brotherhood Council must reserve the right to refuse those delegates who, they know, do not meet these specifications.[22]

Before this Free national synod assembled, the First Confessing Synod of the Evangelical Church of the Old Prussian Union met at Barmen for an historic one-day session, May 29, 1934. Here the groundwork was laid for the establishment of the Confessing church. The synod called for gathering all Evangelical Christians within the Church of the Old Prussian Union who, on the basis of Holy Writ and confession, desired to establish a truly Evangelical church. This Confessing church was to be a self-governing body within the Land church. To declare allegiance to it did not involve dropping membership in the Land church; in fact, the synod maintained that the Confessing church was the only legitimate Evangelical Church of the Old Prussian Union, because it alone rested on the confessional basis essential for a constitutional administration.

The synod set forth a preliminary organizational scheme which soon became the pattern for the Confessing churches in those areas where the regularly constituted church authorities were in the hands of men who accepted the leadership of Bishop Müller and the official church headquarters in Berlin. Most of the staff of the official church offices were newly appointed German Christians, although here and there members of the old church bureaucracy did continue to serve, and often did much to ease the path of the Confessing churches.

The Confessing church was to be based on the Confessing congregation, which was to elect a brotherhood council. A written list of congregational members was to be constituted, which was later accomplished by passing out red cards for members to sign.[23] The brotherhood councils of the congregations were to send delegates to the Confessing synod of the church district. Each district was to elect a brotherhood council, and they in turn were to elect delegates to the Confessing synod of the province, which also had its brotherhood council. Delegates of the provincial brotherhood councils were to form the Confessing synod of the Evangelical Church of the Old Prussian Union. Here again a brotherhood council was to be named, and this body in turn was to name five of its members as the Council of the Evangelical Church of the Old Prussian Union. This council was to act as a permanent secretariat of the brotherhood council; it actually became the working executive and directing body of the Confessing church in the Old Prussian Union and furnished the militant leadership for the Confessing church of all Germany.

To aid in the financing of the Confessing church, a matter which involved primarily the administrative officials above the congregational level, the synod asked the congregational members voluntarily to tax themselves 10 percent of their regular church tax payments, which in most places continued to be collected by the state for the regular church offices. In addition, the congregations were asked to raise collections at all services and special meetings for the work of the Confessing church. These funds were to be sent to the Confessing church synod offices of the province, which would then allot the money to all echelons of the Confessing church. In practice this schematic organization could not always be carried out, but it does help to explain and clarify the nature of the Confessing church movement.[24] The action of the Prussian synod smoothed the way for the national synod meeting the next day.

Barmen and the Development of the Confessing Church

One hundred thirty-eight delegates from twenty-six Land and provincial churches appeared for the Reich synod, among them many of the most distinguished churchmen of Germany.[25] Experienced men were in charge, papers had been thoughtfully prepared, and above all a spirit prevailed which would not succumb to obstructive petty confessional differences. The synod proceeded smoothly. It declared loyalty to the German Evangelical church as a confederation of German confessional churches united by the acceptance of the one Lord and the one holy, universal, apostolic church. It attempted no exact creedal formulation, but its six-point statement of Evangelical truths was later often referred to as "the Barmen Confession." It was a masterpiece of drafting. Each point was introduced by appropriate scriptural passages followed by a statement of what the synod affirmed, and then by an equally important statement of what it rejected.[26]

The theological statement was carefully reasoned and concise, and it is difficult to distill it further. It affirmed in Article 1 that "Jesus Christ as he is attested for us in Holy Scripture is the one Word of God which we have to hear and which we have to trust and obey in life and in death." Christ is the revelation of God to man. It is in and through Christ that man achieved freedom, a freedom which is not subject to control by either political or ecclesiastical authoritarianism. As the declaration asserts in regard to the true functions of both state and church:

We reject the false doctrine, as though the state over and beyond its special commission [providing for justice and peace] should become the

single and totalitarian order of human life, thus fulfilling the Church's voca-
tion as well.

 We reject the false doctrine, as though the Church over and beyond its
special commission [proclaiming the Kingdom of God, God's commandment
and righteousness] should and could appropriate the characteristics, the
tasks, and the dignity of the state, thus itself becoming an organ of the state.

As a scholar who has written extensively on the Barmen Confession puts
it: "Barmen was concerned with the freedom of the Word of God and
the church's freedom under that Word as the ground and guarantor of
all psychological, personal, social, economic and political freedoms."[27]
The statement of faith also dealt with the errors of the German Christians. It rejected what they stood for and everything connected with
Bishop Müller and his work.

 The synod not only considered what might be termed doctrinal or
theological questions, but also turned to more practical and no less
urgent matters. It specifically denied to the present authorities of the
German Evangelical church the right to undertake a reform of the
church constitution and demanded the observance of the present document. It established a distinguished brotherhood council to direct affairs
and appoint committees, but insisted that in all important matters the
council must seek the decision of the Confessing synod.[28] This clearly
indicated their intention of holding other such synods with all the implications this held for the future of the German churches. One of the most
important committees that the synod foresaw was to concern itself with
the training and recruitment of young pastors. It also directed special
attention to the need for upholding one another by meeting in smaller
synods, and at long last even the pastor's most loyal helper and confi-
dante received some recognition when it was agreed "that at such
meetings from time to time the pastor's wife should take part."[29]

 The Barmen synod brought to the fore the concept of a national
Confessing church, one which never sought to take itself out of the
national church body, but always maintained that it constituted the true
German Evangelical church. After Barmen, there were, de facto if not de
jure, two German Evangelical churches—the Confessing church and the
regularly constituted church authorities under Reich Bishop Müller and
the Berlin headquarters.

 In certain of the Land churches the old established authorities were
able to retain control, and these authorities always adhered—at times
with varying degrees of ardor—to the Confessing church. These Confessing Land churches came to be known as "intact churches"; the
authorities there continued to administer and supervise, often on a very
laissez-faire basis, the minority of congregations and pastors within their
jurisdictions who went over to the German Christians. The best examples of such intact churches were those of Bavaria and Württemberg,
to which could be added with some reservations Hanover-Lutheran,
Hanover-Reformed, the Reformed Church of Lippe, and the United
Church of Baden. The Provincial Church of Westphalia also retained a
good measure of its old self-government.[30] In the rest, the so-called

disturbed church areas, the administration and governing authorities of the Land churches came largely under the control of German Christians who accepted the policies of the national church administration.

Conflicts were most severe in the disturbed church areas. In some parishes the pastors, the local lay governing boards of the congregation, and the majority of the members of the congregation adhered to the Confessing church. In many other parishes, on the other hand, only a minority of members signed the red membership cards and thus constituted merely a Confessing group within the regular parish.[31] These minority groups often met as Bible study classes or organized their own special meetings. Many no doubt signed red cards more out of political than religious motivation, as an opportunity of registering opposition to the Nazi regime, but no church by its very nature can well reject those who wish to participate in its work. It is clear, however, that the vast majority signed because of religious conviction, and that the signers constituted the core of the Confessing church. They were usually the most active and concerned church people. This did not necessarily mean that nonsigners were German Christians; they might be neutral, indifferent, or too afraid to sign. At times the German Christians circulated their own membership cards, and a rather belligerently split congregation would result. In Bavaria, where the German Christians were very much in the minority, their membership card stated: "I declare herewith my membership in the Faith Movement 'German Christian' whose program I accept and whose leadership I accept. I am of Aryan descent and do not belong to any lodge [Free Masons or other secret order]."[32]

The same pastors, usually several in larger parishes, served the Confessing group and the other parish members as well. The regular church services were open to everyone and pastors administered to all who sought their aid. At times in the same large parish there were pastors who were active in the Confessing church and others who were not. Sometimes the congregations split;[33] at times the local congregational boards were composed of both Confessing church members and German Christians. It is obvious that these divisions could lead to tensions and conflict, but the dualism came to be recognized, and pastors and laity accommodated themselves to it. It was even recognized by the government. Reichminister of Church Affairs Hanns Kerrl wrote to Land Bishop Ernst Dietrich of Frankfurt, a belligerent German Christian, in October, 1935:

> I am concerned, in the interest of quieting many fellow citizens, that all members of an Evangelical congregation who want to hear the gospel preached according to the views of the Confessing group should have a pastor and a church at their disposal. Vice versa, it must be expected of the Confessing group that they make similar arrangements for minorities of another persuasion. It must be left to local authorities to make suitable arrangements in individual cases.[34]

The provision for "religious minorities" always caused difficulties and led to much recrimination.[35]

Under such confused and varying conditions, adherence to the Confessing church led to many problems of conscience. They are well mirrored in the personal account of Johannes Kübel, a Frankfurt pastor who describes the events of the fall of 1934. The Confessing pastors of Frankfurt/Main met in a farewell service for the chairman of their brotherhood council, Pastor Karl Veidt, who was being transferred by Land Bishop Dietrich for insignificant reasons. The churches were closed to them by the legal church authorities, and so the service had to be held in the Hippodrome. It was attended by "thousands." Pastor Kübel comments:

> After the sermon we Confessing pastors of Frankfurt and the surrounding area gathered before the altar and in all our names Veidt rescinded our loyalty to Land Bishop Dietrich and to Reich Bishop Müller and announced that we were taking up the struggle against them. . . . From this day on we neglected every official and personal communication with the Land bishop and the provost. We answered no inquiries, sent in no reports, attended none of the meetings and conferences that they called, and recognized only the brotherhood council as our governing body.
> . . . And so I shepherded the Confessing group in my congregation and took part and served in the meetings and consultations of the brotherhood circle. But the longer they continued, the stronger my reservations became as to the leadership of the brotherhood council. The change of emphasis from a struggle for freedom and right into a struggle over the confession I could accept. But the development of the Confessing church into a formal church body alongside of the regular church authorities and the claim of the Brotherhood Councils to be regular church authorities caused me difficulty. . . . My sense of reality and my sense of orderliness was disturbed by the fact that the brotherhood councils actually had powers and authority only over our vicars. As soon as it came to appointing, transferring and pensioning a pastor, when questions regarding law, of church property of the parish, of church taxes, and other church matters were concerned, the most passionate Confessing pastor was dependent on the service of the regular church authorities. It went against my sense of correctness that we should demand the rights of Land church pastors, but to a great extent refuse to fulfill their duties. According to my convictions it was impossible to reconcile the gospel of the tax penny with the fact that we refused all and every obedience to the church office from which after all we received our salaries.[36]

No doubt many others in the Confessing church felt much the way Pastor Kübel did. They could not accept Müller and his policies; on the other hand, they longed for some reconciliation with an established and recognized order which they could accept. And it was by no means all hostility among the Confessing church authorities, official church administration, and government officials. The Confessing church, for example, was never completely cut off from state funds, although at times subsidies were curbed, and pastors' salaries curtailed or stopped. After all, most of the Confessing pastors had been regularly appointed and installed, were established in their positions, and were legally entitled to salaries which could not be cut off without cause. If they were, recourse could be had to the courts and in a majority of cases, at least in the opening years of the church conflict, the pastors won their cases.

In general the Confessing church pastors and congregations continued to be financed through the customary church taxes, Kirchgeld, income from lands, state subsidies, and church collections. With its claim to be the true German Evangelical church, the Confessing church always maintained its right to historic revenue, particularly from the church taxes which were levied on all German Protestants who had not officially withdrawn from the various Land churches. Difficulties often arose, especially as the state began to tighten its supervision of church finances through the establishment of special finance sections in some of the church administrations. Much depended on the particular bent of officials, but also on tax laws of the various Lands. In Westphalia, for example, the church tax was legally a parish tax and the parish in turn sent a portion of its collections to the district, provincial, and national headquarters. In other Lands, the Land churches or the Land churches along with subsidiary units, such as a union of churches in a city, levied the taxes.[37]

In Westphalia, where the Confessing church was strong, there had been no breakdown of the established church financial system. Suddenly, on December 31, 1936, the Reich minister of finance forbade the finance authorities in the district of Münster to use legal sanctions to force payment of church taxes.[38] A later declaration of January 23, 1937, exempted the Catholic church from this decree. Although approximately 90 percent of the church taxes were voluntarily paid, the various Protestant congregations and church officials objected strenuously against the abolition of legal sanctions. It undermined the whole church tax structure and struck at the position of the church as a corporation under public law. A way out was found when district governmental officials decreed that where it had been customary for communal authorities to undertake sanctions to enforce collection of church taxes this procedure could be continued.[39] Thus the decree of the finance minister was in effect set aside. In Württemberg, where a German Christian in Stuttgart refused to pay his church taxes and his refusal was approved by the police president, the union of churches in Stuttgart brought suit, and the court reversed the decision of the police president.[40] Pastor Hans Asmussen, who had much to do with financing the Confessing church in Prussia, reports that he dealt quite openly with the finance authorities in regard to church tax funds.[41] All told, the finances of the Confessing church were state-related; they were far from being financed by freewill offerings as were the Free churches.

There was considerable give-and-take over the questions of theological training, examination, and appointment, notably in the early years. As the government gradually appointed more German Christian oriented professors to the theological faculties at the universities, the Confessing church was forced to rely on establishing its own institutions.[42] An exceptionally large number of theological students were drawn to the Confessing church, many going to study and be ordained by the intact Land churches. The seminary in Bethel under the direction of Pastor Bodelschwingh attracted many "Confessing" students.[43] The regular church authorities could not well push them all aside, for they would have had no one to fill future vacancies. It was, however, necessary for a vicar or pastor trained, examined, and ordained by the Confessing church to obtain an official legitimation of his status. Only then could he be legally appointed to a parish and paid a salary from regular church funds. Such legal appointments could only be made by the regular church officials. And once he was appointed, who should install him—the customary consistory official or a member of the brotherhood council? Often the local official church superintendents, a step removed from Berlin or the Land and provincial church offices, and anxious to keep the church life of their districts going, would cooperate with the Confessing church. Church patrons also aided in getting young Confessing church pastors appointed to parishes. Usually traditional and orthodox in theology, these patrons were not in most instances interested in the German Christians.[44] Their proposed candidates could be refused appointment by the consistory officials, but if this happened the officials were likely to run into difficulties with the patron about the upkeep of buildings. The official church authorities did not like to challenge the patrons, for they did not have much luck when they resorted to court procedure.

There were occasions when the regular church officials refused to legalize men named by the brotherhood councils to take over certain Confessing congregations. When this happened the Confessing church authorities had to pay their candidates' salaries. There were at times bitter disputes—which seem almost humorous today but which at the time certainly were not—as to who was the "legal" pastor of a congregation. Pastors dressed in their robes opposed one another and claimed the right to conduct services. The necessity of getting an official confirmation to a new appointment also often hindered pastors from moving to another parish, and thus from improving their status.

The Confessing church never had a clear-cut structure. It was unique in its organizational complexity; it had no constitution, no elaborate system of laws and ordinances comparable to the usual German church administration. It always claimed to be the true German Evangelical church, and thereby did not cut itself off from the legalistic maze created by the past. Instead it made use of these laws, customs, and traditions to protect itself. It claimed for itself "rights of necessity" (Notrecht). It was in fact simply a conglomeration of intact churches, of brotherhood councils on various levels, of Free (Confessing) synods, of pastors' brotherhood circles, of individual congregations and groups of such congregations, of small groups within parishes which as a whole were loyal to the official church administrations, and of individual pastors and laymen.[45] It is beyond dispute that the Confessing church suffered persecution of all kinds, and that the hands of state and party officials at times rested heavily upon it. But even some of the German Christians, favored and supported by the government, had their moments of irritation with the Berlin leadership.[46] Many of them too could not accept the ever-increasing religious indifference and the growing paganism of the regime.

The nature and being of the Confessing church is not easily grasped. Pastors may well have been instrumental in its formation and furnished its leadership, but as it developed it was far from being a mere "pastors' church." It was rooted in and supported by the people, the members of the congregation.[47] It is not without significance that in the Confessing church, at least in some areas, it became the practice for the congregation to join the pastor in saying the Lord's Prayer and the Apostles' Creed—not a universal practice in German churches.[48] If the Confessing church never was able to achieve a strong unity, if at times it split into factions over policies to be followed, if the strong intact Lutheran churches seemed to go their own way and seek primarily their own ends,[49] nevertheless there always remained a loyalty to the concept of a Confessing church—a group of Christians and churches who could and would not accept the religious ideas and religious policies of the Nazi rulers, and who sought to preserve the purity of the gospel as stated in the Old and New Testaments and again brought to light in the historic Lutheran and Reformed confessional statements.

9.

Gleichschaltung and Recurrent Crises

Gleichschaltung and Attacks on Church Leaders

The setback Jäger and Müller suffered when they attempted to take over the Church of Württemberg in mid-April did not deter them from continuing the policy of incorporating various Land churches into the national church. The list of incorporations is impressive, but there were protests and countermeasures. The policy could not be characterized as a ringing success even before it met defeat at the hands of the two large South German churches.

The Church of the Old Prussian Union was incorporated on March 2. Others followed: Hesse-Nassau (May 7); Evangelical Lutheran of the Free State of Saxony (May 7); Schleswig-Holstein Evangelical Lutheran (May 7); Thuringian Evangelical (May 14); Hanover Evangelical Lutheran (with reservations, May 16); Hamburg Evangelical Lutheran (May 25); Brunswick Evangelical Lutheran (June 2); Oldenburg Evangelical Lutheran (June 15); Bremen Evangelical (June 15); Palatinate Evangelical (July 3); Lübeck Evangelical Lutheran (July 14); Baden Evangelical (July 14); Electoral Hesse-Waldeck (July 17); Lübeck Lutheran in the Free State of Oldenburg (July 18). In addition some had been absorbed into other churches. The churches of Lippe, Birkenfeld, and Anhalt had been joined to the Church of the Old Prussian Union; the churches of the two Mecklenburgs had been united into one; the church of Reuss-Greiz had been joined to the Thuringian church; Pyrmont had been joined to Hanover; and Waldeck to Electoral Hesse. Bishop Marahrens had indeed been able to retain some authority in the Lutheran Church of Hanover, but the only real prizes which remained beyond Jäger's grasp were the churches of Württemberg and Bavaria.[1]

This outwardly imposing list of achievements had aroused much concern and comment in the foreign press. The government authorities were particularly sensitive to foreign comment because of the Blood Purge of June 30, 1934. Jäger even had the effrontery to claim, in an attempt to intimidate them, that some of the people who opposed his policy were connected with events which had necessitated the purge.[2]

Müller and Jäger laid their further plans carefully. They had attempted to arrange a meeting of the leaders of the Land churches to discuss measures for establishing peace in the church. However, Wurm,

Meiser, and others refused to attend any meeting at which Müller presided. Müller and Jäger thereupon went ahead on their own. On July 7, they issued a law on reconstituting the national synod. Then they obtained an interview with Hitler on July 19, and the press announced that the chancellor was pleased with the progress being made towards the unification and peaceful development of the church.[3] Under their new law Müller and Jäger were able to displace certain members of the synod, so that when the body met on August 8 they had a safe majority at their beck and call.[4] They showed little respect for the memory of President Hindenburg, who had died on August 2, and for whom an official two-week period of national mourning had been proclaimed. Jäger gave a lengthy address in which he praised Hitler as the instrument of God. The synod members meekly did what was expected of them. They approved two new church laws, one of which confirmed and legalized all of Müller and Jäger's recent measures, while the other prepared the way for incorporating the Bavarian and Württemberg churches administratively into the national church.[5] They also called for an oath of loyalty to Hitler, who after the death of Hindenburg was officially both Führer and chancellor of Germany. The Brotherhood Council of the Confessing Synod of the German Evangelical Church answered with a sharp protest, declaring: "Loyalty to Müller's church government is disloyalty to God."[6] Nor were their words less direct when they decried the forthcoming installation of Müller as bishop. This finally took place with great pomp on September 23, 1934, in the Berlin cathedral, but with only German Christian bishops present and with scant participation by political officials.[7]

Müller could not have been a very happy man on the day of his installation, although he had long sought this ecclesiastical blessing, for he was definitely in difficulties.[8] With Jäger he had started to move against the churches in Württemberg and Bavaria. On September 3 an ordinance had been issued incorporating these churches into the national church, and a few days later Consistorial Councillor Paul Walzer of Berlin was made commissioner of the Church of Württemberg.[9] On September 14, Müller placed Bishop Wurm on leave of absence and removed him from all local and national church offices.[10] Protest meetings were held, and petition after petition descended on Stuttgart, Munich, and Berlin, expressing the loyalty of congregations and individuals to their bishops. Foreign papers took up the hue and cry. As if there was not enough to worry about, on September 19 Müller stated in Hanover: "Adolf Hitler is so closely akin to the Evangelical church that he can almost be considered one of its members."[11] The censor was able to suppress this statement, but the concluding passage of the speech was widely quoted at home and abroad. Müller affirmed: "What we want is a Rome-free German church, and the goal for which we struggle is one state, one folk, one church." Catholics were now disturbed too; furthermore, the London embassy reported to Berlin that the address had had a catastrophic effect on opinion in England.[12] That later published versions omitted the reference to a Rome-free church did not satisfy the critics.

Even before this report from London had reached Berlin, Foreign
Minister von Neurath, after consultation with Hitler, had Bishop Müller
on the carpet. On September 20 he informed the bishop that he could
not ignore the repercussions of his actions on the Evangelical churches
abroad, especially in England, America, and Scandinavia. This church
opposition would unite with groups who opposed Germany for other
reasons. Müller's recent actions in Hanover, Württemberg, and Bavaria
had aroused concern, and von Neurath could not permit him to jeopardize the total policy of the Reich and hinder the work of reconstruction. His remark about wanting to create a Rome-free church had
aroused the Catholics and could turn the vote in the Saar against Germany. When Müller said he had been misquoted, von Neurath advised
him that if the news releases of the Ministry of Propaganda did not
please him, he should review them before they were released. Von
Neurath concluded: "I told the Reich bishop that I had been authorized
by the chancellor to tell him the following: If he did not succeed in
bringing about the unity of the Evangelical church through peaceful
means, and if he made another address like the one in Hanover, he
would in the future receive no support from the chancellor, and he
[Hitler] would have seen him for the last time."[13] But von Neurath was
under no illusions that he had accomplished much. He wrote the next
day: "I had opportunity yesterday to inform at length the Reich bishop
personally on the effect his and his deputies' actions were having on
public opinion, not only in South Germany but among Germans abroad.
I regret that I found he had little understanding of the situation."[14]

As von Neurath anticipated, Müller and Jäger were not easily
curbed. With Müller now a duly consecrated bishop, they proceeded to
press the incorporation of the South German churches. It was not a
simple matter. The existing church constitutions had to be altered, and
church governing bodies reconstituted, which involved replacing old
officials.[15] At times offices had to be cleared by force, and finally, on
October 6, Bishop Wurm was arrested. Meiser was dismissed from office by Jäger on October 11, but that evening he preached to an overflowing congregation in Saint Matthew's Church on the text: "Now the
just shall live by faith: but if any man draw back, my soul shall have no
pleasure in him. But we are not of them who draw back into perdition,
but of them that believe to the saving of the soul" (Hebrews 10:38–
39).[16] All the Protestant clergy of Munich that were free from duties had
appeared in ministerial robes and pledged support of their bishop. After
the services there were demonstrations on the street, and the crowds
accompanied the bishop to his residence. The next day Meiser was
accorded the honor of house arrest. His child was forbidden to attend
school, and Meiser was denied the right to walk in his garden. The
bishops came under increased surveillance, and finally two police officers were installed in Bishop Wurm's residence around the clock.

Prayer and intercession services were held far and wide in
Württemberg and Bavarian churches. The Brotherhood Council of the
Confessing church called together the Second Synod of the Confessing

Church of Germany, which met at Berlin-Dahlem on October 19–20, 1934.[17] In addition to important doctrinal statements, the synod issued a sharp protest against the use of force by national church authorities in Württemberg and Bavaria. The theological faculty of the University of Tübingen denounced the actions of Müller and Jäger as unscriptural.[18] People gathered before the residences of their bishops in mass demonstrations of support; petitions with hundreds and thousands of signatures were sent off to Berlin. Delegations claiming to represent 60,000 and 70,000 peasants respectively from different sections of Bavaria appeared before the Bavarian state governor pledging their support to Bishop Meiser and true evangelical doctrine.[19] All the Nazi district governors reported that the large majority of Protestant pastors and laity—up to 95 percent—stood loyally behind their bishop.[20] The news that the Bavarian church was to be divided into two dioceses—Nürnberg and Munich—did nothing to allay aroused emotions. Individuals with special connections sent letters to von Neurath.[21] Many pleaded with von Neurath to tell Hitler the truth. It is clear the feeling was still widespread that if Hitler only knew the true situation, he would set things right.

Suddenly, on October 26, Jäger resigned, Wurm and Meiser were freed, and they, along with Bishop Marahrens of Hanover, were invited to an interview with Hitler on October 30.[22] What had brought this reversal of policy? No doubt it was a combination of various pressures. The arrests of Wurm and Meiser had caused concern throughout Germany, and even Dr. Christian Kinder, the head of the German Christians, insisted repeatedly that Jäger—with whom he also had differences—would have to go.[23] The countless expressions of protest against Müller's action and of loyalty to Wurm and Meiser were also of great importance. Bavarian Minister President Ludwig Siebert and Reichsstatthalter General Franz Ritter von Epp pressed for the restoration of Meiser to his office. Justice Minister Gürtner apparently was able to impress the chancellor with the argument that these actions were contrary to the church constitution of 1933 which Hitler had approved.[24] But the coup de grace and the timing of the capitulation seem to be traceable to the archbishop of Canterbury.

It has long been held that Foreign Minister von Neurath played an important part in checking Müller because he was concerned about the agitation in the foreign press.[25] This is true, but in mid-October news arrived from London which strengthened his hand. On October 12, a very secret dispatch from the London embassy, meant only for von Neurath and State Secretary Hans-Heinrich Dieckhoff, brought word that George K. A. Bell, bishop of Chichester and president of the Universal Christian Council for Life and Work, had sought an interview. Both he and the archbishop of Canterbury were deeply concerned over news of the use of force against German churchmen, and should these accounts prove correct, "an early publicly declared break between all foreign Protestant churches and the German Protestant church led by the Reich Bishop was inevitable."[26] The English bishop placed the most blame on Jäger. Chargé d'affaires Otto von Bismarck added that it was "absolutely essential to have the church conflict settled soon if German-English relations were to be improved." The report was immediately sent on to State Secretary Lammers in the Reich Chancellery with the request that it be communicated to Hitler. This was done.[27]

Four days later, immediately after the return of Ambassador Leopold von Hoesch to London, the archbishop of Canterbury sought an interview. He referred to the bishop of Chichester's conversation, and again stressed that it was unbearable for English churchmen to witness the use of police force against high church officials. On October 24 there would be a meeting of English bishops, and at that time he would have to make a statement on the German situation. The bishop of Uppsala (Erling Eidem) and Pastor Marc Boegner, the head of the French Protestant church, were awaiting his lead, as they also would have to take a stand. He would probably also consult with Cardinal Francis Bourne, Catholic primate in England, in regard to a possible joint pronouncement. As a possible solution, he suggested a repeal of the measures taken against Bishops Wurm and Meiser and Dr. Koch of Westphalia, dismissal of Jäger, the cessation of present coercive measures, and a summons to leading personalities for a free exchange of opinion as to how unity of the German church could be attained. He would wait until October 24, and then do what he had to do.[28]

The archbishop of Canterbury (Rev. Cosmo G. Lang) was considered friendly to the new Germany, and his statements carried weight in Berlin. On October 16 von Neurath had laid before Hitler a memorandum on the reaction of the foreign press to church affairs in Germany.[29] He pointed out that the Administrative Committee of the Stockholm Movement was about to consider the situation of the German churches, and that the Lutheran World Council was scheduled to meet in Munich November 12–19, and the Reformed Churches of the World in Amsterdam the end of November. "One had to consider the possibility of these groups taking decisions which would be uncomfortable not only for the church but for the Reich." He also requested that this new message from London be laid before the Führer as soon as possible.[30] At this time Germany was doing its best to win British friendship, and von Neurath, who had been ambassador at London, was personally very anxious to maintain good relations with England.[31] Hoesch was informed by telephone on October 22 that things were in flux in Germany, and important declarations were expected soon.[32] He was instructed to contact the archbishop of Canterbury and see that he made no irreparable decision on the twenty-fourth. The archbishop was amenable to Hoesch's plea, and ready to postpone his statement if there was a chance for a peaceful solution. A note on a copy of Hoesch's report of this response reads: "The Führer knows of this. He has discussed this matter with the Reich bishop."[33]

As a matter of fact, by October 23 the decision had been reached in Berlin that Jäger would have to go, but there were some party members who felt he should be kept until December.[34] Müller's status no doubt also caused some soul-searching. Bishop Marahrens had let it be known that he felt there would be no peace in the church without his dismissal.[35] On October 25 (originally October 23) Hitler was scheduled to receive the Reich bishop and the other provincial and Land bishops, who were meeting in Berlin, and by a special act of state to confirm the close ties between church and state. Müller was scheduled to take an oath of loyalty to the Führer. This reception was now indefinitely postponed, adding significance to Hitler's request that Wurm, Meiser, and Marahrens should come to Berlin.[36]

In a letter to Ambassador Hoesch on October 27, the archbishop of Canterbury expressed his satisfaction over the relief of tension in the church conflict.[37] He continued to follow events closely, and ten days later he wrote:

> It is very remarkable that the very suggestions which I ventured to make were so soon carried out. Certainly the tensity of the situation has been relieved. There are still many troubles ahead. . . . My only concern was as to the *use of coercive* methods, and *these have been so greatly mitigated for the present and I hope* altogether, I am relieved from the necessity of taking any such public action as that which I mentioned when you were here.[38]

There can be no doubt that von Neurath, concerned over Germany's status abroad, partly in view of the forthcoming Saar plebiscite, was instrumental in bringing Hitler to intervene and quiet the church crisis.[39] The threat of action by the archbishop of Canterbury had brought things to a head in Berlin. Bishop Wurm immediately sent von Neurath a telegram thanking him for his efforts.[40] With Jäger gone, would it be possible to bring about Müller's dismissal? It was generally anticipated that Wurm, Meiser, and Marahrens would raise this issue when they met with the Führer on October 30.

On the very eve of that meeting, Pastor Bodelschwingh, the churchmen's first choice for Reich bishop in 1933, telephoned the Reich Chancellery, pleading that the Führer should not declare to the bishops that "he held unconditionally to Müller. This kind of a declaration would tighten the situation."[41] Bodelschwingh was convinced that Müller would have to remain in office for a long time, but he nevertheless felt it was a mistake for the Führer to express such an idea. Hitler was given the message. Whether he was influenced by Bodelschwingh's advice is uncertain, but at least he seemed to follow it. When, during the October 30 interview, Bishop Marahrens suggested that Müller should sacrifice his office for the sake of restoring peace, Hitler—who had been very self-controlled up to that point—became excited and shouted: "This he can do; who is stopping him? I am not related by blood or marriage to him. I get no subsidies from him. He can do what he wants."[42] Dr. Rudolf Buttmann of the Ministry of the Interior was elated, and felt sure Minister Frick, who was present at the interview, would get Müller to resign. Instead a very chagrined Buttmann had to tell the bishops the next day that Frick had informed Müller that Hitler had not demanded his resignation.[43]

In contrast with the interviews in March, this October meeting was an orderly affair. Hitler wanted to know how the bishops stood in relation to the Reich church. In anticipation of this very question, the bishops had prepared a written statement expressing their support of the constitution of July 11, 1933, but insisting that they must have people at the head of the church in whom they had confidence. Hitler glanced over the paper, and then observed: "We could establish relations between church and state in Germany on an entirely different basis, for example on the pattern of the USA."[44] Frick objected because it departed too much from German tradition. He then observed: "The bishops have a strong weapon in their hands. That is the law. All suits that the Reich bishop inaugurates against Land churches and against individual pastors are being lost, and this is detrimental to the authority of the state." When it came to issuing a communiqué on the meeting, Hitler insisted on a simple announcement: "The Führer and chancellor today received Land Bishops Dr. Marahrens, Dr. Meiser, and Dr. Wurm."[45]

The unsuccessful attempt to incorporate the churches of Württemberg and Bavaria, along with the furor it raised, led to a change in government tactics. Müller continued in office, but he soon lost all power and was completely sidetracked.[46] For the moment at least, the state curtailed its direct intervention in church affairs, although it was far from giving the churches a free hand. The Confessing church, true to its claim to be *the* German Evangelical church, established a new provisional church administrative directory, but this body never received the support of all within the Confessing church, nor did it receive the official backing of the state. Within a few months the state undertook anew to settle the vexed church situation by establishing a separate Ministry of Church Affairs.

The First Provisional Church Directory

It took some weeks for Bishops Wurm and Meiser to clear out the new men who had moved into their church offices, but soon they were administering and preaching as always.[47] To prevent any further coercion, Frick on November 1 ordered: "All interference by state authorities, except for general police measures, is forbidden under any circumstances. Contrary ordinances are rescinded."[48] In line with this hands-off policy, when local police arrested Otto Dibelius because of disturbances occurring in connection with his talk at Neurupping on "The Church Struggle," the Gestapo immediately ordered his release.[49] And when Reichsstatthalter Robert Wagner asked Hitler for directives regarding church developments in Baden, he was informed that Hitler would give no further instructions concerning church difficulties.[50] Wagner was excited because on November 13 Bishop Julius Kühlewein had notified Müller that he had decided to ignore the directives of the Reich church leaders and take the leadership of the Church of Baden into his own hands, since the Reich church leaders no longer had the authority to restore peace and unity.[51] Bishop Otto Zänker took similar action in the

provincial church of Silesia, but later agreed to a compromise with
Müller.[52]

To clarify the situation, on November 20, 1934, Müller issued two
ordinances nullifying the church laws issued in 1934 for the Reich
church (January 26, March 2, August 9), and for the Church of the Old
Prussian Union (January 26, February 5, March 1).[53] With these edicts
the old laws were restored, which only compounded the legalistic confusion in the German churches. It is not easy to sweep aside laws in
effect for some time and undo actions taken under them. What the
return to the old laws meant to Frick was clear in his speech on November 30. Müller had shown his goodwill by returning to the old legal
basis, and now it was up to the other side to do the same. "I demand, as
responsible Reich Minister for Church Affairs, final unification. The
people are fed up with these quarrels among pastors. I will not permit
that these conflicts be financed further and will cut off their financial
subsidies."[54] It was an ominous statement, as future policy would bear
out.

Many churchmen, church organizations, groups of university professors, and brotherhood councils had petitioned Müller to resign for the
good of the church, but he refused.[55] There was nothing for the opposition forces to do but set up their own national church government. The
Dahlem synod in October had attempted to establish an independent
emergency church government. It had resolved that the leadership and
representation of the German Evangelical church should rest in the
Reich Brotherhood Council (Reichsbruderrat), and that from its members
there should be chosen a Council of the German Evangelical Church
(Rat der DEK) to conduct its business. In practice the most ardent confessional leaders came to constitute this council, and their fiery leadership was not always well received by the more moderate members of
the parent council.

On October 29 the Reich Brotherhood Council issued more detailed statements on the relations of the various confessing congregations to the central authorities. These were generally not well received
by the rank and file.[56] Long discussions followed between representatives of the Confessing groups in the disrupted churches (those churches
under the control of German Christians loyal to Müller) and the intact
churches of Hanover, Württemberg, and Bavaria. The result was the
creation on November 22, 1934 by agreement of the intact churches
and the Reich Brotherhood Council, of the Provisional Directory
(Vorläufige Leitung) of five men to direct the affairs of the German
Evangelical church, thus sidetracking to a great extent the Council of the
German Evangelical Church, the executive body of the Brotherhood
Council. Bishop Marahrens of Hanover—a known adept compromiser
and slow to reach decisions—was made chairman, the other members
being President Karl Koch (United), Pastor Paul Humburg (Reformed),
Church Councillor Thomas Breit (Lutheran), and, as the legal expert,
Reich Court Councillor Wilhelm Flor (soon to be replaced by Dr. Eber-
hard Fiedler).[57] The Brotherhood Council was to be increased to not

more than thirty members. Karl Barth, Martin Niemöller, Karl Immer,
and Hermann H. Hesse, to show their displeasure with the turn of events which seemed to weaken the Dahlem synod line, resigned from the Brotherhood Council.

The Provisional Directory had much organizational work to supervise. In all Land churches where Müller had control of the church offices the Confessing church had achieved some sort of organization. Müller, of course, denounced the Provisional Directory, but he could not hinder its going about its work.[58] A Peace of Advent seemed to descend on the church. Pastors inquired if it was still necessary to remit the monthly assessment of five marks to the Pastors' Emergency League for the help of disciplined brethren. A meeting of the brotherhood council of the league met and discovered that in many places salaries were still curbed, pastors were still imprisoned, and fines were still imposed. In November they had paid out 21,480 marks to pastors who had had their salaries cut and for other purposes, and of this amount, 15,124 marks were still owed.[59] Yet compared to the previous months, the closing weeks of 1934 were peaceful. Germany was heading towards the Saar plebiscite to be held on January 13, 1935. It resulted in an overwhelming vote for return to Germany, and Hitler made a victory speech which impressed the archbishop of Canterbury by its conciliatory tone.[60]

The Provisional Directory was faced by two great problems. The resignation from the Brotherhood Council of some of the most prominent leaders of the Confessing church movement was a storm signal which must be heeded. The directory had to strengthen its position among the various local brotherhood councils of the Confessing churches. These councils were as a rule rather radical and did not shudder at the thought of assuming a Free church status. On the other hand, the bishops of the intact churches were struggling to keep their churches together and tended to view problems from this angle.

It also seemed necessary to achieve—if possible—some official state recognition of the Confessing church. Many pastors were in prison, and there was always the danger of a new wave of arrests. If this hostile policy was ever to be stopped and the men freed, some ties with the government were necessary. All still hoped that a truly united German Evangelical church could be established on the basis of the constitution of July 11, 1933. The Provisional Directory sought to replace the Müller regime, and after the cancellation of Jäger's measures there was a feeling that one could start to build anew.

One of the first things the directory did was submit a detailed "Proposal for a New Church Order" to the government.[61] It would have established a new church administrative body drawn from people known to be loyal to the historic confessions, which were, according to the church constitution, to be the basis of the Reich church. Since this provision would in practice have excluded the German Christians, it was not surprising that nothing came of the proposal. Müller would have been eliminated, and he had firm supporters in the higher echelons of the party hierarchy, notably Göring and Hitler.

The Provisional Directory did win some additional support. Aside from the older recognized Confessing churches with their brotherhood councils and the intact churches, other Land churches with an ordered church government, such as Baden, Electoral Hesse-Waldeck, Lippe-Detmold, and Schaumburg-Lippe, formed ties with it. It also had the recognition of intrachurch groups like the large missionary and deaconess organizations, the Gustav-Adolf-Verein, the Confederation of Pastors' Organizations, the Lutheran Council, and the Reformed Confederation of Germany.[62] But this broader support was a mixed blessing, for it threatened the very basis of the Confessing church movement—the theological declarations of the Confessing synods of Barmen and Dahlem. The inner unity of the Confessing church was weakened; instead of the opposition front growing stronger, differences and factions within it increased.

The Provisional Directory was also immediately faced with the problem which had been before the churches for some time, the oath of loyalty to the Führer. It was required of all state officials, which of course included professors and teachers of religion as well as many church officials. The oath read: "I swear: I will be true and obedient to the Führer of the German Reich and nation Adolf Hitler, observe the laws, and conscientiously fulfill my official duties, so help me God."[63] The Provisional Directory asked the theological faculties of the universities for opinions on the question, but the Ministry of the Interior undertook to forestall their submission.[64] However, the directory produced a very effective public statement. It maintained that in all oaths there was a Christian reservation.

> As in an appeal to God, so also in an oath it is intrinsically understood that before God nothing is promised or affirmed, nor can his aid be prayed for, which is contrary to his revealed will. This fundamental Christian conception of an oath makes it unnecessary to make additions, or deletions, or reservations when an oath is taken.[65]

Professor Karl Barth, under fire at the time, declared that in view of this public statement he was willing to take the oath.[66] His dismissal from the Bonn faculty had already been decided upon, however, and he was forced to leave Germany. He returned to his native Switzerland, where he continued by his teaching and writing to support the Confessing church.

The Provisional Directory also found it necessary to issue a statement against the German Faith Movement. At a meeting in Eisenach July 29–30, 1933, the most important Germanic religious organizations had united to form a Working Association of the German Faith Movement (Arbeitsgemeinschaft der deutschen Glaubensbewegung).[67] Two of its most important leaders were Professor Jakob W. Hauer of Tübingen and Count Ernst zu Reventlow. The various groups, however, to a great extent retained their individual identities. A year later a new name was adopted, the German Faith Movement (Die Deutsche Glaubensbewegung). At first the movement received little direct support from the National Socialist party, but gradually party leaders, notably Alfred Rosenberg, began to extend more aid and comfort to the various Germanic

religious movements. The statement by the Provisional Directory on February 21, 1935, condemning the German Faith Movement was followed by an even sharper denunciation drawn up by the Second Confession Synod of the Evangelical Church of the Old Prussian Union which met at Dahlem on March 4–5.[68] Beginning with an affirmation of the First Commandment, it went on to denounce those who were setting up lesser gods of blood, race, folk, honor, and freedom. While the attack was directed at the Faith Movement, it nevertheless had wider implications for the party and the state. Pastors in Prussia were asked to read the declaration from their pulpits on Sunday, March 17.

The minister of the interior undertook to forbid the reading of the declaration, and on the Saturday before, police officials everywhere visited Confessing ministers advising them against doing so. As it happened, universal military service was introduced on March 16, and the churches were expected to offer thanks on Sunday for this restoration of German honor. In spite of widespread pressure and police intimidation, many Prussian pastors read the synod's statement. The reaction of Minister of the Interior Frick was inevitable. Over 500 ministers were arrested. Two days later, Ministerial Director Buttmann submitted a report to the Reich Chancellery confirming that the "rumor of 500 arrests" was true; many of these, however, were only house arrest.[69] Reports of further police action filtered in, and soon the number arrested stood at 715. Clearly Frick had overreached himself. Forced to back down, he invited members of the Provisional Directory to come to see him, and Bishop Marahrens was able to smooth the ruffled feathers by emphasizing that the declaration was only against the new heathen religion. An introductory formula was worked out to the effect that the statement of the Prussian synod was simply an amplification of that earlier issued by the Provisional Directory, and with this explanation it was now proper to read it from pulpits.[70] The arrested ministers were soon released. Yet the episode showed how insecure the church was.

In April, 1935, there was a big meeting of the German Faith Movement in the Berlin Sportspalast. What little centralized leadership the movement had was weakened by factional strife, and it continued to be made up of a bewildering number of small groups, some of which were recognized by the state as public corporations with all their special rights and privileges. In 1935–36, the members of all these groups began to be identified as being "God believing" (*gottgläubig*), and the term received official sanction in November, 1936.[71] Not all those who so designated themselves were members of these groups, but the term did, nevertheless, indicate that they no longer identified themselves with the Evangelical or Catholic churches, even if they had not officially withdrawn. In June, 1940, Jews were no longer permitted to designate themselves "God believing"; if they no longer wanted a religious affiliation and refused to classify themselves as "Godless," they might affirm that they belonged to no religious society.[72]

The Nazi party lent support to these Germanic cults by furthering festivals such as the celebration of the winter solstice and by their everlasting emphasis on ancestry and race. Göring, in a greatly publicized speech on the Hesselberg in Bavaria in June, 1935, acclaimed the recognition of old cult sites and the lighting of solstice fires.[73] Yet the Germanic religious groups always remained a fringe movement; they never won wide acceptance among the people. Most Germans who were indifferent to the Christian churches could not be brought to worship Woden and Thor either. Nonetheless, the increased publicity and favor accorded the German Faith Movement caused concern not only in church circles, but also in party ranks. The Cologne secret police reported: "It is worthy of note that even party members, SA and SS men, ask openly how these government measures can be reconciled with the words of the Führer that Positive Christianity was to be protected."[74]

Not only in Prussia but in other Land churches, the police were harassing pastors of the Confessing church.[75] In April, 1935, Bishop Wurm advised Minister Rust that as a first step toward peace the state would have to dispel the impression that it was backing the German Christians; the state would have to separate itself from Bishop Müller. Rosenberg's position, according to Wurm, was also a difficult problem; he would have to choose between his political duties and attempting to further the ideas advanced in his *Myth of the Twentieth Century*. No church could accept this book. The state should also recognize the Provisional Directory of the German Evangelical Church, for "ties with this body were the only way that led forwards."[76]

Even Minister of Economics Hjalmar Schacht joined in demanding a change in church policy. On May 3, 1935, he sent Hitler a letter in which he listed three things which retarded exports. First, there was the church problem which led to great hostility abroad and affected German trade relations. In spite of the apparent desire to unite the churches, no legal steps had been taken to this end. A Reich bishop had been named who had undertaken illegal measures which aroused clergy of various persuasions to resistance. "Clergy are therefore arrested, dealt with as criminals, their honor and health harmed, all without any legal basis. Overzealous party warriors can defame and injure men of diverse confessions without the state exercising its duties of protection." The excesses against Jews also harmed German exports. The state should determine the rights Jews were to have and protect them within these rights. The activity of the secret police should also be restricted. They were a power unto themselves, mocked the edicts of the minister of the interior, and imprisoned men without giving reasons for their actions.[77]

But in spite of all protests, there was no visible change in policy. In increasing numbers, pastors were denied the right to speak, their houses were searched, they were dismissed, pensioned, and arrested, and some were even placed in concentration camps. Clearly churchmen needed mutual support, and it was decided to hold a third Confessing synod at Augsburg.

On April 4, 1935, President Koch of the Confessing synod met with a small group to discuss the current situation of the Confessing church in respect to the state. They agreed it was advisable to call a synod meeting, and proposed that President Koch should assemble a group of church leaders, including the bishops of the large Lutheran churches, to see if they could reach agreement on a program.[78] This larger group apparently never was called together, and it was the Reich Brotherhood Council that in the end decided to call the synod at Augsburg on May 6–7. Bishop Meiser, who was informed of this by letter on April 26, quite rightly declared that it was impossible to make all necessary preparations on such short notice. He insisted on a later date.[79]

The question of whether or not to call a synod had not been officially discussed by the Provisional Directory (President Koch was, however, a member), nor had there been any discussions about the program with the large intact churches.[80] Since there was to be a theological declaration, which always was likely to raise controversial issues, it did seem that undue haste was being urged. Ever since November, 1934, when the Provisional Directory was appointed, differences between the brotherhood councils, the Provisional Directory, and the intact churches were manifest. One purpose of the synod was to allay these differences, but to accomplish this more joint preliminary discussion and debate was desirable. After two postponements, the date of the synod was finally set as May 22–23.

To overcome various objections raised by Meiser, who as host to the synod felt a responsibility for its success, Koch sent two special emissaries, Wilhelm von Armin-Lützlow and Pastor Heinz Kloppenburg, to Munich to iron out difficulties. In a conference on May 9, general agreement was reached. There would not be an official synodical communion service, but on the final day the Augsburg congregation would hold a communion service according to the rite of the Bavarian church where, as was customary in Augsburg, all might partake, including the Reformed. The Bavarians insisted that the synodical members be carefully grouped according to confessions—Lutheran, Reformed, or United.[81]

The possible presence of Karl Barth at the synod also created difficulties. Barth was again drawing attention in the German press, and the secretariat of the Reich bishop had included a statement on him in its press releases. Barth was quoted as having replied to a question concerning Swiss national defense by saying that the Swiss should take care to make the north frontier against Germany very strong. Although Barth was now teaching in Switzerland, he was still recognized as a synodical delegate by the Rhenish church. It was difficult to challenge his right to attend the Augsburg meeting, and no one really wanted to say him nay. Meiser, however, was fearful of police intervention, and changed his "request that he not be sent" to a condition that he not be present if the synod was to be held in Bavaria. The difficulty was overcome by a personal appeal to Barth that he not attend in order to avoid controversy or police intervention.[82]

The meeting seemed set, although the agenda had not been clarified. But again plans went awry when it was announced that the Reichstag was to be opened on the evening of May 21. It was generally expected that Hitler would say something about the church situation, and if the synod were in session it would obviously have to take note of his pronouncements without due time for consideration. It seemed best to postpone the synod again, and Meiser insisted on this, suggesting that it be held the first part of June.[83]

No one was happy about the postponement, and Koch decided to call a conference of representatives of the brotherhood councils of the disrupted churches to discuss the current church situation. The invitation was issued on May 18, and the conference met at Gohfeld and Bergkirchen, near Bad Oeynhausen, on May 22–26, the days the synod was originally scheduled to meet. Representatives from all the German Lands attended. The agenda began:

> Within the Confessing church of Germany, which the Provisional Directory considers as part of its jurisdiction, there are, side by side, churches with administrations recognized by the state (so-called intact churches) and churches which are under the administration of brotherhood councils.
> Both types have in common their determination to order their affairs according to the word of God as it is confirmed in the confessions of the churches. But their totally different administrations confront each type with special tasks. For special purposes within the Confessing church there already exist special groupings: the Lutheran Council and the Free Reformed Synod. The Lutheran churches of Hanover, Bavaria, and Württemberg have entered into a special agreement. It is now proposed that the churches with nonrecognized church administrations (disrupted churches) form themselves into a confederation. The following tasks make the formation of the confederation necessary:
> 1. Grouping and support of the confessing congregation
> 2. Training of ministers
> 3. Establishing security for confessional preaching and administration of sacraments
> 4. Exercising emergency church governments
> 5. Regulating relations to the intact churches
> 6. Establishing a common position in regard to state actions in churches where the administration has not as yet been recognized by the state.
> The confederation would be formed by the brotherhood councils of the disrupted Land churches, and a committee of six elected by the brotherhood councils would conduct its affairs.[84]

The proposal aroused animated discussion which Koch had difficulty curtailing. It was soon clear that most delegates were against establishing a separate confederation of the disrupted churches. This would increase the disunity within the Confessing church. What was needed was a public word from all the Confessing churches. Such a statement would hearten the twenty Confessing pastors who were then in concentration camps.

All recognized, however, that there were problems facing the disrupted churches which did not affect the intact churches. For example, how far should the brotherhood councils of a Confessing church collaborate with the state-recognized church regimes in their respective Lands? Was it possible strictly to live up to the Dahlem resolution, which asked "all Christian congregations, their pastors and deacons, not to accept any orders of the existing Reich church government and its officials, and to withdraw from cooperation with those who want to continue to obey these authorities."[85] It was generally understood that they could not well forego all cooperation with the state-recognized church authorities, for example, in regard to church taxes, salaries, or renting church property. On the other hand, there were certain matters on which the Confessing church could not yield, such as church collections, training and ordination of pastors, or even the vacations of pastors, which were often only a way of removing a man from his position.

In the end, while the conference refused to establish a separate confederation, it agreed to request the Reich Brotherhood Council to establish a committee consisting of four members of the council and two additional men from disrupted churches which were not represented on the council. This committee would study the special problems of the disrupted churches. Later, for example, the committee drew up a report on how far it was permissible or necessary for Confessing congregations or churches to deal with the state-recognized authorities.[86] No hard and fast lines could be established, but they recommended that such negotiations be conducted through, or at the authorization of, the brotherhood councils. The Confessing church, of course, never gave up its claim to be the legal and regular church administration in all the disrupted Land churches. The decision not to establish a separate confederation was no doubt wise, for it is questionable how strong that confederation could have become, and it would certainly have resulted in increased tension with the intact churches.

With the conference over, attention was directed to calling the national synod into session. In a meeting held in Berlin on May 24 of representatives of the Provisional Directory, the Reich Brotherhood Council, the Confessing Synodical Organization, and the intact churches, it was decided to hold the synod meeting on June 4–6, 1935.[87] The Berlin meeting was followed by a gathering of kindred church leaders in Würzburg on May 27.[88] The result was that when the synod finally met, ideas had been clarified and various differences had been smoothed over.

With all the previous controversy, it is not surprising that when the churchmen met in Augsburg they were chiefly concerned with setting aside differences within their own ranks. The synod of the Confessing church was recognized as the regular synodical authority of the German Evangelical church, and consequently also as the highest authority for the Confessing church, comprising both the intact churches and the Confessing churches in the disrupted Land churches. A reconstituted Brotherhood Council elected by the synod from its own members was to see that the decisions of the synod were carried out, and also act as an advisory body to the Provisional Directory, which was confirmed as the supreme administrative body. The rift that occurred when the Provisional Directory was first named was healed when Martin Niemöller and the other dissenting members, with the exception of Karl Barth who was now in Switzerland, returned to the Brotherhood Council. This restored unity was manifested in the drafting of statements addressed to the pastors and deacons, to the government (which called for the end of arrests and harassment of the clergy), to the pastors who were kept from carrying out their ministerial duties, and to those responsible for the training and examination of pastors.[89] It was on the whole a synod of reconciliation and moderation, especially when contrasted to the synods of Barmen and Dahlem. Even a representative of the Ministry of the Interior took part, and on the eve of its meeting the state freed all pastors held in concentration camps and prisons.[90] Barth, with a touch of sarcasm, referred to it as "a new Peace of Augsburg," and maintained that the ill-defined relationship between Provisional Directory, Brotherhood Council, and synod would not work out.[91] If in the end Barth proved to be right, it was not entirely because of the decisions and actions taken at Augsburg. The synod served the church well at the time.

The Establishment of the Ministry of Church Affairs

The state also inaugurated new policies which profoundly affected the future development of the Confessing church. On February 3, 1935, Supreme Church Councillor Dr. Werner of the Church of the Old Prussian Union had issued an ordinance establishing special financial sections in the various administrative bodies of the church.[92] There is something to be said for the measure, for the orderly administration of finances had been disrupted by the controversy in the church. Each financial section was to be made up of specialists concerned with church taxes, assessments, and the budget, and was to supervise finances in general, particularly the payment of salaries and pensions. This measure aroused no great concern, since after all it was enacted by church authorities and staffed by regular church employees. On March 11, however, with the approval of Hitler and the Reich government, the Prussian state issued a law authorizing such financial sections, but requiring them to be made up of men from the general church administration appointed by the state minister in charge of church affairs. The finance sections were now state rather than church bodies, and with this law "the state undertook by way of controlling the finances directly to intervene in inner church differences in order to end them through coercion."[93] The sections were to supervise and administer the property and finances of the church and were to be responsible to the state for the orderly application of state subsidies. Yet their exact function and relation to the churches were never expressly defined. More importantly, the state minister in charge of church affairs was empowered to issue ordinances necessary to carrying out the law. Although these financial sections were still technically to be staffed by church officials, the Prussian state government had now taken an important step towards dominating the church by controlling its finances. It would not take long or much maneuvering to staff the sections with men willing to do the bidding of the state and who had little loyalty to the church. In the future finance sections were introduced in certain other Land churches, and were increasingly to become an instrument of state control over the church.[94]

One of the great sources of support of the Confessing church were the courts. Countless suits were brought against the actions of the Müller regime and against the police for payment of salaries, for illegal dismissal from office, and for a host of other charges.[95] These suits had been won time and time again, for it was easy to prove the illegality of the Müller regime and of the police measures taken to enforce his edicts, especially when the pre-Hitler judges still presided in the courts. In order to stop these court victories, a special court was established on June 26, 1935, under the Ministry of the Interior—the Court (*Beschlussstelle*) for Legal Matters Affecting the Evangelical Church. If there was a question involving the legality of a church law enacted after May 1, 1933, the suit was to be transferred to this court and there was to be no appeal from its decision. The court's jurisdiction extended to the whole Reich and in effect legalized the Müller regime. The Provisional Directory of the Confessing church was not long in launching a protest. The Third Confessing Synod of the Church of the Old Prussian Union, meeting in Berlin in September, 1935, issued a strong statement, not only against the establishment of this special court but also against the new finance sections in the Prussian church administation. Actually the court was slow in getting under way, yet it did function, particularly from 1937 to 1939. Since the transfer of cases to its jurisdiction took time, it did much to delay and prevent judicial redress of grievances.[96]

It is clear that the government was preparing for a new attempt at solving the church problem. As early as March 3, 1935, the *New York Times* carried a "reliable report" that Hitler was considering the creation of a "Minister of Evangelics" in order "to make the Protestant Church toe the mark."[97] Bernhard Rust, minister of culture, was supposedly under consideration for the position. At the same time the United States' ambassador reported that Hanns Kerrl was also among the candidates for the post.[98] Hitler, according to the *Times*, had discussed the plan with Reich Bishop Müller. The latter had explained that one reason for his failure to unify the Protestant churches was that he had no temporal executive power. This lack was now to be remedied, but not to Müller's benefit. On July 16, 1935, a brief edict was issued transferring all church affairs previously dealt with by the Reich and Prussian Departments of the Interior, and by the Reich and Prussian Departments of Science, Instruction, and Education to a new Ministry of Church Affairs.[99] It was to be headed by the former minister without portfolio, Hanns Kerrl, who was generally held to be a sincere and active member of the Protestant church. He had read widely in church history, although he was neither a trained theologian nor an expert on church administrative affairs. A former adviser of Hindenburg, Count von Schwerin-Krosigk, was to write later: "As a theologian he was attacked by the churches, as a Christian by the Party."[100] Kerrl had been in charge of *Raumordnung,* that is, of supervising resettlements made necessary by the erection of air fields, army camps, and new industries. Berlin wits now referred to him as minister for "space and eternity" (*Raum und Ewigkeit*).[101] All who knew him agree that he was deeply concerned about the church, and apparently confident that he could bring about a reconciliation of the factions and the final establishment of a German Evangelical church which everyone could support. Certainly there is much to be said for the concentration of church affairs, Protestant as well as Catholic, in one new ministry.[102] But this too was more easily said than done. Education still remained under the jurisdiction of Minister Rust in the Department of Science, Instruction, and Education. And it was exactly at this time that the reorganization of the German school system was undertaken.[103] It engendered new state conflicts with the churches, for they were involved in many ways in the educational system. The issues were old, but now they added another complication to the already complex relations between the state and the churches, and among the churches themselves.

It may be noted that Hitler at this time was still claiming close support by the Almighty. In a speech at Rosenheim on August 11, 1935, he stated:

> This I might well say to those who believe they alone have leased the blessing of heaven. Fifteen years ago I had nothing but my faith and will. Today the movement is the movement of all Germany, today the movement has conquered the German nation and constitutes the Reich. Would this have been possible without the blessing of the Almighty? Or do those that at that time ruined Germany want to claim that they had God's blessing? What we are, we did not become against but with the will of God's providence.[104]

Minister of the Interior Frick, in announcing to the state governments on July 22, 1935, that he was turning the administration of church affairs over to Minister Kerrl and the newly created Ministry of Church Affairs, took care to point out that he was still responsible for police matters. He asked them to refer to his office copies of all cases involving arrests of clerics, denying them the right to speak, and other disciplinary matters.[105] Frick thus undercut the authority of Kerrl, who realized that if his pacification efforts were to succeed he must have some control over the police. On September 5, he was able to issue an ordinance stating that in agreement with the minister of the interior, during the period of transition decisions in regard to police matters that affected the churches were to be referred to the church ministry. Until further notice all instances of protective arrest, deportation, denial of right to speak, confiscation of property, or other measures affecting the church were to be submitted to him for approval before they were undertaken.[106]

How effectively Kerrl exercised these powers it is impossible to say.

Certainly he never controlled the police in church matters, although at times he was consulted when important actions were undertaken. He also initiated directives of his own to the police. On October 19, 1935, he rescinded all police measures that had been taken against the clergy and told the authorities of the Land churches that it was desirable that disciplinary measures against the churches should also be cancelled.[107] On November 4, 1935, he ordered for the time being an easing of restrictive measures against the church press.[108] On April 4, 1936, he asked the police to rescind all denials of residence or of speaking that had been imposed on Catholic and Protestant ministers before March 29, 1936. He further requested reports on all imprisoned clerics to see if they could be freed. This amnesty was extended in recognition of the successful plebiscite approving the reoccupation of the Rhineland.[109]

The Evangelical Weeks

It was in this period, when the antichurch policy and the growing antagonism of the party became manifest, that a new program was inaugurated to awaken the laity to the dangers threatening their churches. It developed out of the work of the German Student Association (*Deutsche Christliche Studentenvereinigung*). Large public meetings—"religious emphasis weeks," to borrow a name from American college life—were to be held to discuss religious questions. A Committee on Evangelical Weeks was established under the chairmanship of President Paul Humburg of the Rhineland and Dr. Reinold von Thadden of Pomerania, with Dr. Eberhard Müller as secretary.

The first such mass gathering was held in Hanover, August 26–30, 1935, and attendance exceeded all expectations. There was no attempt to discuss the church conflict directly. The addresses dealt with fundamental religious questions, but if there was a discussion on "The Church According to the Doctrines of the Reformation," the implications for the current situation were surely patent. The themes of this and subsequent gatherings tended to stress the problems of truth (*Wahrheitsfragen*). The leaders of the movement always considered the Evangelical Weeks as missionary events and insisted on the freedom to preach the gospel. Dr. Zöllner, head of the Reich Church Committee constituted in the autumn of 1935, warmly supported the meetings.[110]

Leading personalities of the Confessing church were the popular speakers, and soon the police began to interfere. In the summer and fall of 1936, two speakers were kept from participating. At the end of the year two Evangelical Weeks scheduled for January, 1937, at Nürnberg and Erfurt were forbidden. This led to a sharp protest to Minister Kerrl by Bishop Wurm, who also sent his protest to Foreign Minister von Neurath.[111] The ban against the meeting in Nürnberg was lifted, but not against the one in Erfurt, where the organizers had invited Bishop Meiser, Superintendent Dibelius, and Bishop Wurm to speak, respectively, at Saturday night, Sunday morning, and Sunday afternoon services. After Meiser arrived at Erfurt he was told he could not speak. As no written prohibition was presented, Meiser insisted on going ahead with the service. During the altar liturgy, which was being conducted by the pastor of the church, the sexton approached Meiser and told him he must come at once to see Governor Dr. Weber in the antechamber of the church. When Weber said he would have to intervene by force if Meiser attempted to preach, the bishop promised he would not, but insisted on the right to dismiss the congregation with a benediction. The local pastor informed the congregation of the situation, and after saying the Lord's Prayer together Meiser gave the benediction.[112]

Such interference naturally aroused much concern among the laity and clergy. Yet the practice continued, and between January 1 and August 1, 1937, six planned Evangelical Weeks and three Evangelical Days were banned on various grounds. By instituting the Evangelical Weeks the churches had encouraged their members to gather together in large numbers for worship and to search in common for the understanding of religious truth. The authorities, however, objected to all mass gatherings which were not subject to their control and direction. Finally in 1938, Evangelical Weeks were forbidden completely. They had, however, served a useful purpose and served as precedents for the highly successful German Evangelical Kirchentage and Evangelical academies of the postwar period.[113]

10.

The Era of the Church Committees

Kerrl's Appointment of Church Committees

On assuming office, Minister Kerrl intended to proceed tactfully and carefully. He started by calling a conference of representatives of all Land governments, of the Ministry of the Interior, of the Gestapo, and various other governmental officials. It met in Berlin on August 8, 1935, and reports on the situation of the churches in each Land were made and proposals put forward as to what should be done. In some sections there was little unrest, but in general the situation was very unsatisfactory. A summary of Kerrl's views at the end of the conference says:

> The guidelines according to which the movement and the state would have to conduct church policy had become clear as a result of the discussions. How one would have to proceed tactically about various matters would have to be reserved for decision by the Führer. He agreed that the party must participate in church-political questions. The turmoil that existed presently in the church life of Germany was due to the incorrect church-political measures that the party and state had so far employed. This one must admit. It was indefensible that within the movement there was one official position (Art. 24 of the party program) and also an unofficial position (Rosenberg's view) in regard to Christianity. It was necessary according to his view to eliminate the unofficial position.[1]

On August 21, 1935, Kerrl met with leading personalities who were close to the German Christians, among them Reich Bishop Müller, and discussed with them the situation within the Evangelical church. Two days later he met with leaders of the Confessing church as well as with men who represented more neutral positions, and then some weeks later with Catholic leaders.[2] The members of the Provisional Directory, the bishops of the intact churches, Martin Niemöller as head of the Pastors' Emergency League, and a good representation of other groups attended the meeting of Confessional church leaders, although the Confessing church of the Old Prussian Union might well have been better represented. Kerrl spoke of the need for taking further measures to regulate church finances and disciplinary proceedings on the part of the churches, of appointing a Spiritual Ministry, and of calling together a church council. "I will not," he said, "tolerate quarrels within the church any longer. I will not separate state and church, because I don't want to see everything disintegrate. I want to see state and church continue to be tied together."[3] He denounced the "neopaganism" of the German Faith Movement and promised protection of the Christian confessions. The discussions seemed to proceed smoothly enough, but actually Kerrl was feeling his way and made no concrete proposals.

On September 15, at the Nürnberg party congress, amidst great fanfare the Nürnberg Laws were proclaimed, which defined who was a Jew and laid the basis of all future discriminatory legislation in the Reich.[4] Under these laws and the important supplementary decrees of November 14, Jews were to be denied German citizenship and placed under many restrictions. A Jew was one who was descended from three or four Jewish grandparents, or who was descended from two Jewish grandparents, provided he professed the Jewish faith or was married to a Jew. Persons with two racially full Jewish grandparents were classed as Mischlinge of the first degree, those with one such grandparent as Mischlinge of the second degree. Such "mixed offspring" could with special permission marry Aryans and were at times freed from other restrictions placed on Jews. There were, alas, no ringing denunciations of these measures from the church authorities at the time.[5] They were absorbed with the problems of church organization, administration, and jurisdiction, and apparently paid little attention to growing anti-Semitism, except as it affected Christian racial Jews. The German Christians, particularly the leaders in Saxony, requested the minister for church affairs to establish separate congregations for Christian Jews. This he refused to do, as he considered the time inopportune.[6]

On September 24, 1935, Kerrl undertook his first decisive measure. Before the minister of the interior had surrendered his jurisdiction over church affairs, the ministry had begun to draft a law designed to establish peace in the Protestant church. The minister of the interior was to be given authority to take such steps as were necessary to "restore constitutional conditions" in the German Evangelical church. Kerrl now took over this idea but substituted the word "ordered" for "constitutional," a very significant change. It meant that his decree power would not necessarily be limited by the church constitution of July, 1933; he could "rule and govern as he pleased."[7]

Kerrl apparently first had the idea of making Bishop Marahrens of Hanover Reich church administrator (Reichskirchenverweser), which would have been in line with National Socialist principles of leadership. Obviously such an appointment would have been possible only if Müller resigned, but neither he nor Hitler were so inclined. The result was that Kerrl hit upon the idea of appointing committees (Kirchenausschüsse) to direct the various churches. On October 3, his first directive implementing the law to establish the security of the German Evangelical church announced the establishment of a Reich church committee and one for the Church of the Old Prussian Union, both to be made up of churchmen.[8] The committees seemed to be planned as a transitional arrangement, for they were to exist at the longest only until September 30, 1937. He deliberately refused to name any members of the Confessing church governing bodies to the committees, for, as he put it, if he did this some-

one would want him to appoint Bishop Müller as well, and he did not
contemplate committing such an act of folly.[9] He succeeded in getting an
able group, mostly men of moderate views, to serve on the two committees. Dr. W. Zöllner, former general superintendent of the Provincial
Church of Westphalia and a much respected Lutheran churchman, came
out of retirement to accept the chairmanship of the Reich committee. In a
letter to Hitler on February 9, 1936, Zöllner said he was entering church
service again in order to help, for it was a matter of Holy Writ. He would
try to explain to the people "that church and state, in their struggle to give
new forms to their divine tasks, implement each other."[10] The membership of the committees was made known when they issued a joint
appeal to all Evangelical Christians for help and support in ending the
church conflict. After quoting Article 1 of the church constitution, they
continued:

> Out of these bonds of faith we admonish and ask the Evangelical congrega-
> tions to support with prayer, loyalty and obedience Volk, Reich, and Führer.
> We said yes to the National Socialist creation of a nation on the basis of race,
> blood, and soil. We say yes to the will for freedom, national honor, and
> social sacrifice, even to the surrender of life for the community of the people.
> We recognize in this the God-given reality of our German nation.[11]

That Dr. Zöllner would lend his name to this pronouncement
caused surprise among many who had previously known him.[12] That
Otto Dibelius was not among them seems certain, for a few months later
he was to write to Marahrens:

> I know Zöllner very well from long years of working with him. He is strong in
> words and clear in his perception. But send him up against a foe and he will
> always capitulate. . . . He has never pushed anything through against an
> opponent—no, never. How often have I said before: this lion roars, but he
> does not bite. It will be so again. No, with Zöllner nothing will be accom-
> plished; this can be done only with clear-cut decisions in the country.[13]

On November 14, 1935, Hitler recognized Kerrl's efforts by dissolving
the party Bureau for Cultural Peace (*Abteilung für den kulturellen
Frieden*), as the Ministry of Church Affairs had taken over most of its
tasks. Party officials were again admonished to stand aside from the
church controversy. Hess issued an order: "All leaders of the party, its
member organizations and associated groups, are to avoid intervening
in all church or religious matters; all individual actions are forbidden.
Notice of encroachments of politicizing clerics and so on are to be laid
before me."[14]

The Reaction of the Churches

The Council of the Evangelical Church of the Old Prussian Union
decided that it would establish no connections with either the Reich
Church Committee or the committees which were established in the
various provincial churches.[15] The Reich Brotherhood Council had
reacted against the establishment of the committees even before their

membership had been named, and announced that the already established governing bodies of the Confessing church would continue to
function.[16] Yet it did not reject the Reich committee out of hand, and
asked the Provisional Directory to conduct negotiations with Minister
Kerrl. The disorder in the church was so great that there was widespread
desire to see if Kerrl's efforts would lead to something. The Provisional
Directory decided ''that members of the Confessing church should be
permitted to work with the committees, wherever the committee was
independent from a church regime not in accord with confessional
standards and where the concerns of the Confessing church were fully
protected.''[17] Marahrens believed that the directory should cooperate
with the committees regardless of what the Reich Brotherhood Council
did. This view prevailed, and after numerous and lengthy discussions,
the Provisional Directory reached a consensus on November 6 ''that it
could and should work with the committees as official state organs in all
possible ways.''[18] Yet the problem of cooperation continued to be debated, and eventually led to the resignation of Paul Humburg from the
directory.

The Bavarian and Hanover-Lutheran churches expressed their
readiness, with some reservations, to support the Reich committee.
Many individuals and groups in the Confessing church in the disturbed
church areas also felt it possible and proper to cooperate with the
committees.[19] Pastor Bodelschwingh of Bethel, for example, advocated
such a policy.[20] On the other hand, some (usually the more militant and
ardent) rejected the committees outright. They thought that the committees, being state established, were consequently bound to state and
party. To recognize them meant the acknowledgment of the German
Christian usurpation of the church government. The committees did not
recognize the confessional basis of the church; there were German
Christians among their membership, and this made it impossible to do
away with German Christian influence and bring about a true renewal
of the church.[21] At least at first, the main groups of the German Christians accepted the idea of the committees. Dr. Kinder had resigned his
leadership of the movement in June and returned to his old position in
the church office in Schleswig-Holstein. He was succeeded as head of
the German Christian Reich Movement by Wilhelm Rehm, leader of the
German Christians in Württemberg.[22]

With the establishment of the church committees, Müller was eased
out of his administrative duties. He soon lost his office and his official
automobile; little was left to him except his residence and the right to
preach, but he retained his title and salary until his death.[23] Müller was
not the only one who was sidelined. Since 1933, only party members
had been appointed and reached the higher positions in the official
church administrative bodies. A number of these were now dismissed
and more church oriented persons appointed, which led to the charge
that the Reich Church Committee was favoring the Confessing church.
In fact the committee tried to steer a middle course and bring the
Confessing church and the German Christian groups together. One of its

first steps was to issue regulations in regard to permitting minority groups—whether Confessing church or German Christian—to use the local church building.[24]

The establishment of provincial and Land church committees often encroached on church bodies controlled by German Christians. For example, on November 11, 1935, in a second ordinance, Kerrl created a new church council in Nassau-Hesse, which included the rather rabid German Christian bishop, Dr. Ernst L. Dietrich. This council was to give way to a church committee on January 15, 1936, of which the bishop was not a member. The establishment of a church committee in Saxony, by a third ordinance on November 21, did much to trim the sails of Bishop Coch, one of the leading German Christian bishops. Former superintendent Hugo Hahn and Court Preacher Arndt von Kirbach, as well as other leaders of the Confessing church, cooperated with the Saxon committee, and their return to church service enabled the committee to establish effective ties with Confessing and moderate middle groups in Saxony.[25] A fourth ordinance established a church committee in Electoral Hesse-Waldeck, which curtailed German Christian influence there. In Brunswick and Schleswig-Holstein, the moderate German Christian bishops cooperated, and here the church governments were reorganized; in Brunswick the new setup was called a "church government" (*Kirchenregierung*), whereas in Schleswig-Holstein the new term "Land church committee" (*Landeskirchenausschuss*) was used.[26] In other German Christian controlled churches, where brotherhood councils were not a disrupting influence, church committees were not established, nor were they established in the intact churches of Bavaria, Württemberg, Baden, and Hanover. The Reich Church Committee, and notably the committees which had been established in all Prussian provincial churches (except in Westphalia and Rhineland), did not have clear sailing. All the old church bodies of the pre-Kerrl period continued to function, despite the creation of these new committees.

Kerrl met with the Provisional Directory on November 27, 1935. He wanted the directors to resign and the various brotherhood councils to dissolve themselves, which would have left the church government entirely in the hands of the church committees. The Provisional Directory refused to comply, and insisted that the church-elected bodies must retain the spiritual leadership; the committees might have control over so-called outer matters. Kerrl refused to consider this division of authority. He would give them time to reconsider their decision, but if they did not, he would dissolve the Provisional Directory and the Reich Brotherhood Council at the beginning of December. He emphasized his ultimatum by reminding the churchmen: "Adolf Hitler has again hammered into the heart of the German people the faith and deeds of Jesus. The folk is awakened and is led by us and no one else. True Christianity and National Socialism are identical."[27] As the report of the meeting by a group of Reformed pastors put it: "With this war was declared."

Kerrl was as good as his word, although he proceeded circumspectly. There was no forthright dissolution of the Confessing church bodies, but on December 2 he issued a fifth ordinance in which he forbade any other church organization or group to undertake any church governmental duties in all territories where new church governments had been established under the authority of the law of September 24, 1935. He undertook to spell out such forbidden actions, which included especially "the filling of pastoral positions, the naming of ministerial assistants, the examination and ordination of candidates for the Evangelical Land churches, the visitation of churches, the ordering of pulpit declarations, the levying and administration of church taxes and assessments, the announcement of church offerings and collections in connection with congregational events, as well as the calling of synods." After this enumeration, striking directly at the activities of the Confessing church authorities, it did little good to add: "The freedom of the churches to preach, and the nurture of religious fellowship church organizations and groups is not disturbed."[28]

To have permitted this ordinance to go unchallenged would have meant the end of the Confessing church in the disrupted church areas; it did not apply to the intact churches. The state-appointed committees would be administering what certainly were internal church affairs, and the authorities of the Confessing church in Prussia issued a sharp protest. Otto Dibelius wrote a sensational memorandum, "The State Church is Here," in which he roundly denounced the measures taken by Kerrl and pointed out the dangers to the independence of the church. It was an able and trenchant exposition, which Martin Niemöller published and delivered to all the brotherhood councils.[29]

The dissimilar tactics and attitudes towards the church committees of the various branches of the Confessing church could no longer be overlooked, and led to a stormy discussion in the Reich Brotherhood Council on January 3, 1936. The representatives from the disrupted churches refused to go along with the committees, while the representatives of the intact churches gave qualified approval. The council, by a vote of 17 to 11, declared the Provisional Directory no longer qualified to conduct negotiations for the Confessing church. The Reich Brotherhood Council mistrusted even the limited support which the Provisional Directory had so far accorded the Reich Church Committee, and declared that until the synod met, the council would undertake the leadership of the Confessing church. It appointed a committee to prepare for the synod and direct affairs.[30] The Provisional Directory, meeting the same day, refused to consider itself dismissed, but agreed with the council that a synod should be called. The differences within the directory itself led to the resignation of Dr. Paul Humburg, the Reformed church member, on January 14. He maintained that his withdrawal ended the directory, and that above all it should make no further decisions in regard to the Reich Church Committee, but instead leave them to the future synod. The Provisional Directory, however, continued to carry on as before.[31]

In calling for the convening of a synod, the Reich Brotherhood Council had maintained that it should be made up of the same constituencies as had been represented in the Augsburg synod. According to the decisions of the Augsburg meeting, the national synod was to be reconstituted, which had not yet been accomplished, and would have caused a long delay because various local synods would have to be called first. This was not done, and there were those at that time and since who have questioned whether the Oeynhausen meeting was a true synod. In fact, at eleven o'clock on February 17, 1936, the night before the meeting, the Reich Brotherhood Council was hastily called together to consider the protest of the Hanover Lutheran church on this very point. The Bavarian church also raised procedural questions. Finally, at 2 a.m., the council decided nevertheless to ask President Koch to convene the synod the next morning as planned. Unwilling to risk a conflict in a plenary session, the president undertook further negotiations the next day. Finally they decided to pray over the matter, and they joined in a church service at four o'clock. Thereupon President Koch was petitioned to convene the synod, and he did so at 5:35 p.m.[32]

It was not an auspicious beginning, but it illustrates how divided the Confessing church was, how far it had moved from the unity which had prevailed at Barmen and Dahlem and even at Augsburg. Old confessional differences between Reformed, Lutheran, and United had for some time been coming up again. But the biggest division was between the disrupted churches and the intact churches. The Confessing churches in the disrupted church areas were those affected by Kerrl's church committees and his other measures; the leaders of the intact churches were struggling to keep control of their churches, and as long as Kerrl did not pressure them too much, they were inclined to cooperate with him. It was customary at the synod meetings for various confessional groups (*Konvente*) to meet separately to decide on the stand which they would take—party caucuses, so to speak. The Lutheran group was not well organized, as there was some disagreement about membership. It was finally decided that all who claimed to belong should join the Lutheran Konvent. In spite of the importance of the Lutheran churches of Hanover, Bavaria, and Württemberg, the majority lay with the Lutherans from the United churches and those from other areas. This too led to differences which influenced all the proceedings of the synod.[33]

The synod, originally scheduled for two days, lasted six, February 17–22, 1936. Even so, some of the decisions were rushed. One of the least controversial but nevertheless important resolutions was the one on German schools. It denounced the encouragement of Germanic religious ideas and the general de-Christianization of instruction. An appeal was made to the state, to church congregations, and to parents to combat this trend. The theme of the synod was "Church Administration." Kerrl's church committees, which included representatives of the German Christians, were denounced because it was impossible to recognize a church administration which was not bound to doctrinal truth and did not have the freedom of rejecting false teachings. It was impossible for the Confessing church to dissolve its established administrative authorities as envisaged by Kerrl's ordinance of December 2. The Reich Brotherhood Council was reconstituted so as to consist of nine members from the Old Prussian Union, twelve from the other churches, eight members which the synod elected, a representative of the Reformed faith, and President Koch. This new council was empowered to elect a new Provisional Directory. In spite of long debate and serious differences of opinion—which were to manifest themselves again later—the resolutions on church government were adopted with only three negative votes and one abstention in a synod of 143 members. At 5:53 p.m. on February 22, the synod of Oeynhausen adjourned; it was to be the last Confessing synod of the German Evangelical church.[34]

In spite of the near unanimity with which the resolutions had passed, the differences which appeared at the Reich Brotherhood Council and Provisional Directory meetings on January 3 had not been overcome. The brotherhood councils of the disrupted churches did indeed come closer together. Kerrl had meanwhile put the December 2 decree into effect in the provinces of Westphalia and Rhineland, with the result that the Confessing churches of all Prussia were more united than ever. A Second Provisional Directory, as voted by the Synod, was named, consisting of Pastor Fritz Müller (Berlin-Dahlem, Lutheran), Pastor Otto Fricke (Frankfurt/Main, Lutheran), Superintendent Martin Albertz (Berlin-Spandau, Reformed), Pastor Hans Böhm (Berlin-Zehlendorf, Lutheran), and Pastor Bernard Forck (Hamburg, Lutheran).[35] This Second Provisional Directory, although it in theory headed all the Confessing churches, in practice exercised control only over part of them. There was tension between the men of the new and old directories.[36] Those members of the Reformed churches who held that it was possible to work with the church committees formed a working committee (*Arbeitsausschusses der reformierten Kirchen*) on July 3, 1936.[37] A great number of the pastors and congregations of the Hanover Reformed church, however, rejected the committee and supported the Second Provisional Directory. The result was that the Reformed Confederation for Germany was divided in its policies, which heightened the disunity in the Confessing church. The Second Provisional Directory received the firm support of the Lutherans in the Old Prussian Union, but only nominal recognition from a newly formed organization, the Luther Council.

The Establishment of the Luther Council

It was clear at the Oeynhausen synod that the more radical leaders of the Confessing church—the co-called Dahlem wing—would dominate the new Reich Brotherhood Council as well as the Second Provisional Directory. The Lutheran leaders, particularly those of the intact

churches, were increasingly uncomfortable under this leadership, and
they decided to strengthen their separate Lutheran organization.

At the very beginning of the effort to form a united German Protestant church, General Superintendent William Zöllner of Westphalia,
on April 13, 1933, had issued an appeal to all Lutherans to support the
unification negotiations.[38] He and other influential Lutherans desired to
see that the new church would have a Lutheran character and a Lutheran head. Then and later, they wanted to prevent the extension of
the church organization of the Old Prussian Union to all Germany.
They felt that this union of Reformed and Lutheran into one church,
even if they were to maintain their own separate confessions, nevertheless weakened the confessional unity which was necessary for a true
church. In May, 1933, there had been a conference of Luthern bishops
in Würzburg which led to the forming of a Lutheran directory under
the chairmanship of Bishop Meiser of Bavaria.[39] It never developed
into a strong body, but did serve to further the Lutheran position in the
negotiations which resulted in the church constitution of 1933. After
the synod of Barmen (May, 1934), in which the Confessing church
Lutherans participated, a group of Lutheran Bavarian theologians nevertheless felt called upon to issue the so-called Ansbach Memorandum,
which criticized the Barmen declaration and proclaimed strong support
for the Führer.[40]

The efforts to stress Lutheranism as such gathered momentum as the
leaders of the Lutheran churches held various meetings in the next
months. Partly as a countermove and partly for protection against the
Müller-Jäger policy of incorporating Land churches into the national
church, on August 25, 1934, they formed the Lutheran Council (*Lutherischer Rat*) to consist of the bishops of Hanover, Württemberg, and
Bavaria, and representatives of various theological faculties and Lutheran societies. It had no church governmental or legal authority. To
bring greater cooperation and strengthen the impact of Lutheranism, the
churches of Hanover, Württemberg, and Bavaria, on February 12, 1935,
formed the Lutheran Pact (*Lutherischer Pakt*). They agreed to exchange
theological candidates, and undertook to further work on a common
song book as well as service book. On July 2–5, 1935, a mass rally took
place at Hanover, in which Lutherans of the Confessing church from all
the Land churches participated. It was meant to strengthen the spirit of
Lutheranism, and the new national folk religious movement was condemned in the theses presented to the rally. On the other hand, there
was also a strong expression of loyalty to the state of Adolf Hitler.[41]

In spite of these efforts to maintain and strengthen a separate "Lutheran way," the Lutherans found themselves at Oeynhausen ill prepared to further their particular views; they were themselves divided,
even those who held themselves to be members of the Confessing
church. One particular Lutheran group which served as a watchdog and
voice of conscience was the so-called Church-Theological Society (*Die
kirchliche-theologische Sozietät*) in Württemberg.[42] It was a group, varying in size, of young pastors who began to meet around 1930 to con-

sider various theological questions arising out of the proposed revision of a service book. They had no formal organization, but the directing spirits were Pastors Hermann Diem, Heinrich Pausel, Wolfgang Metzger, and Paul Schempp. They soon came to have differences with the regular church authorities. The Church of Württemberg, however, was one of the more liberal and less centralized German Lutheran churches, where there was little emphasis on historic confessions as such.[43] Above all the church authorities had no thought of exercising church discipline, and the leadership of Bishop Wurm was generally accepted. When the Kirchenkampf came, members of the Church-Theological Society quite naturally became strong upholders of the Confessing church. The society lent its support to the first and second directories, even when the bishops of the Lutheran churches tended to withhold theirs.[44] Then too, the various brotherhood councils in the Lutheran churches where German Christians were in control were likely to hold different views from the bishops of the intact churches who were struggling to keep their churches together. These men sometimes felt it necessary to make concessions in order not to lose everything.

After Oeynhausen, in meetings on March 11 and 18, 1936, the bishops of Hanover, Bavaria and Württemberg, along with the brotherhood councils of Saxony, Mecklenburg, and Thuringia, and later of Brunswick, Schleswig-Holstein, and Lübeck, formed the Council of the Evangelical Lutheran Church of Germany (*Rat der Evangelisch-Lutherischen Kirche Deutschland*).[45] They did this in order to protect the interests of Lutheranism in Germany by establishing a united front, one which would furnish a special Lutheran leadership to cooperate closely with all offices of the Confessing church. The "Luther Council" (*Lutherrat*), as it was commonly called to distinguish it from the earlier Lutheran Council (*Lutherischer Rat*), established its headquarters in Berlin, and set up a permanent secretariat with Senior Church Councillor Thomas Breit of Bavaria as its chairman. It was expressly stated that the Luther Council was "to look after the common spiritual direction of the Lutheran churches and their organizations and that these consider themselves part of the Confessing Church."[46] What the establishment of the Luther Council actually did was to divide the Confessing church into two groups. It naturally aroused much hard feeling among the leaders of the other Confessing churches. The Second Provisional Directory itself, comprised mostly of Lutherans from Prussian churches, challenged the right of the council to speak for the Lutherans of Germany.[47]

The End of the Church Committees

The intact Lutheran churches and the Luther Council were inclined to go along with the Reich Church Committee, although with certain important reservations. The Luther Council, as the spokesman of Lutheranism, steadily refused to recognize the committee as a legitimate church government because it was not confessionally oriented. It maintained that a constitutional church administration as envisioned in the constitution of the German Evangelical church of 1933 did not exist.[48] This negative attitude, along with the more pronounced opposition of the Second Provisional Directory, did not, however, deter the Reich Church Committee from carrying on. It issued numerous decrees designed to prepare a new order for the Evangelical church. It established eight deliberative commissions (Kammer), among them one on theology, one for legal matters, and one for educational affairs, all charged with working out plans for the future. Plans were made to take part in the great ecumenical meetings scheduled for 1937. It sought to bring about the appointment of further state church committees in Mecklenburg, Thuringia, Lübeck, Bremen, and Oldenburg, but without success.[49] It pressured the Bavarian and Württemberg church administrations to undertake negotiations with the German Christians so as to bring about cooperation with them. In some cities church buildings were to be put at the disposal of the German Christians. These efforts had little effect, because there were few German Christians in these areas and their numbers were declining.

The Reich Church Committee also felt called upon to protest against the ever-increasing secularization of society and the disparagement of religion. In a "Word to the Congregations," it raised the problem of Sunday observance and the need to insist on the religious education of youth. "It is wrong when the hours of religious instruction in schools are used for something else than to bring the children in touch with the Bible. Instruction in other subjects must not be permitted to tear down what has been built up in the home and in the religion classes."[50] The committee also issued a memorandum on the excesses of the Thuringian Christians. On the other hand, it reached agreements with the more moderate German Christian groups, but this only led to new denunciations of the committee by the Second Provisional Directory.

The Second Provisional Directory also wrote Hitler a pointedly phrased letter on May 28, 1936, which dealt with (1) the dangers of de–Christianization, (2) the interpretation of positive Christianity currently being made by party leaders, (3) the disruption of church order, (4) the attack against the confessions, (5) the compulsion to accept the National Socialist Weltanschauung with all its anti-Semitism and its insistence on blood, race and soil, (6) the restrictions on religious publications and the insistence on loyalty oaths, and (7) the deification of the National Socialist state. "Only a few years ago the Führer himself disapproved placing his pictures on Evangelical altars. Today his opinions are increasingly accepted as normative not only in political matters, but in matters of morality and law, and he is being surrounded with the religious dignity of a folk priest and hailed as an intercessor between God and the folk."[51] The letter was carefully considered and drawn up; it was a religious, not a political manifesto. Yet the expression of religious convictions and concerns inevitably led to sharp protests against the policy of the state. The Protestant leaders hit at the very core and foundation of Nazi power in their fifth point:

[The National Socialist] Weltanschauung is often held to be a positive re-placement for Christianity when the latter has been overcome. When blood, folk, race, and honor are accorded the place of eternal values (*Ewigkeitswer-ten*) the Evangelical Christian, by the first commandment, is forced to deny this evaluation. When the Aryan person is glorified, God's word testifies to the sinfulness of all men; when within the concepts of National Socialist Weltanschauung an anti-Semitism is forced on Christians which demands hatred of the Jews (*Judenhass*), there stands opposed to this the Christian command of love of your neighbor. It causes a specially severe conflict of consciences for our Evangelical congregation members, when in line with their parental duties, they must combat these anti-Christian ideas in the minds of their children.

The memorandum is replete with rejections of Nazi policies, and it is not surprising that state officials objected to it.

The first draft was the work of Hans Asmussen, and it was gone over in several meetings of the Second Provisional Directory.[52] It had been reviewed at a meeting of the Reich Brotherhood Council in Frank-furt on May 13, 1936, at which representatives of practically all churches belonging to the Luther Council were present. Supposedly only three copies were made of the final version. One was handed in at the Reich Chancellery on June 4, designated for Hitler, a second was given for safe-keeping to Pastor Birger Forell of the Swedish church in Berlin, and a third to Dr. Friedrich Weissler, head of the chancellery office of the Second Provisional Directory. The directory meant the letter to be strictly confidential and had not even informed the various church governments or the brotherhood councils.[53] Weissler, however, gave the memorandum to Ernst Tillich to study for one night, and he copied it. Tillich apparently shared his scoop with Werner Koch, both men having connections with the foreign press.[54]

Actually, from the very first the memorandum was not as secret as the directory wished or as is usually thought to have been the case. On the very day, June 4, 1936, that the letter to Hitler was handed in to the Reich Chancellery, Ferdinand Lathrop Mayer, United States' chargé d'affaires ad interim, submitted a report to the State Department men-tioning the memorandum and describing its contents.[55] Henry L. Hen-riod, of the Universal Christian Council for Life and Work, who was in Berlin, obtained a copy of the memorandum, which he sent to Bishop Bell of Chichester on June 8, only four days after it had been left at the Reich Chancellery by Dr. Wilhelm Jannasch. Bell replied a few days later: "I have read the Confessional address to Hitler—a fine document. Our support of the Confessional Church is all the more necessary."[56] Hermann Kötzschke, a retired minister who claimed good connections with the Ministry of Church Affairs and the German Christians but called himself a member of the Confessing church, and who was then a newspaperman, somehow got hold of the document. In the second week of July, he tried to sell it to different correspondents for 100 marks, but he was successful with only a few Americans, among them the correspondent of the *New York Herald Tribune*. On July 15 he gave it gratis to all agencies and most newspapers, accompanying it with an

anonymous letter explaining that this was the first time the Provisional
Directory had taken a clear stand on public questions. He considered
the document so important that he was furnishing the complete text. It
did have page-long supporting annexes which he did not submit, but as
far as he considered them necesary he mentioned them in annotations.[57]

The first public mention and analysis of the memorandum appeared
in the *New York Herald Tribune* on July 16. Under the dateline of
Berlin, July 20, the paper published an English translation on July 28.
On July 23, the memorandum appeared in the *Basler Nachrichten*. It
was only after the publication of the complete text that the Nazis
launched a bitter press campaign against the Confessing church.

The Provisional Directory and the Reich Brotherhood Council of
the Confessing church answered on August 23, with a strongly worded
pulpit declaration addressed to Evangelical Christendom and to the government in Germany, reiterating much of what had been said in the
letter to Hitler.[58] It was not read in the Hanover, Württemberg, and
Bavarian churches, although the bishops in the latter two states issued
more moderately phrased statements of their own, addressed to their
congregations, some weeks later.[59] The pulpit declaration was printed
and multigraphed, and it is estimated that a million copies were circulated in Germany.

The Provisional Directory's charge that Hitler was being deified
was well taken; there is abundant evidence to support it.[60] For example,
Supreme Group Leader Schultz, speaking at a meeting of the National
Socialist Confederation of Students at the Ordensburg of the NSDAP at
Prössinsee in Pomerania, stated:

> I do not want to blaspheme God, but I ask: Who was greater, Christ or Hitler?
> Christ had at the time of his death twelve apostles, who, however, did not
> even remain true to him. Hitler, however, today has a folk of 70 million
> behind him. We cannot tolerate that another organization is established
> alongside of us that has a different spirit than ours. We must crush it. Na-
> tional Socialism in all earnestness says: I am the Lord thy God, thou shalt
> have no other gods before me. . . . Then ours is the kingdom and the power;
> for we have a strong Wehrmacht, and the glory—for we are again a re-
> spected nation, and may God will, in eternity. Heil Hitler![61]

Bishop Meiser, in an outspoken address in Ansbach on December 13,
1936, in which he defended his attendance at the Committee of the
Lutheran World Conference in New York, posited the danger of national
socialism becoming the religion of the Germans. He quoted a Nazi
official as saying: "Hitler is God, and his book *Mein Kampf* the Bible."[62]

The Reich Church Committee, while it had been able to win the
cooperation of some of the more moderate German Christians, increasingly aroused the ire of the radical groups. They charged those German
Christians who worked along with the committees with committing treason in the interest of the Confessing front. The Thuringian German
Christian Church Movement had grown stronger and won the support of
various splinter groups against the more moderate German Christian
Reich Movement. The party authorities always threw their support to the

Thuringian groups, and the Thuringians began a "missionary" support of isolated German Christian congregations in the intact churches and elsewhere. They sent out preachers to lend aid and comfort to disciplined German Christian ministers, especially in the intact church areas, and gave them financial support if their salaries were curtailed.[63] Dr. Zöllner of the Reich Church Committee resignedly recognized that because of their political support he would be unable to unseat the Thuringian German Christians.[64] On November 6, 1936, he had telegraphed Hitler: "Public contempt for Christian beliefs on the parts of high officials of the state and of the party is unbearable for the whole German Evangelical church. The Reich Church Committee reiterates its request for an audience." A week later he was notified that Hitler was unable to receive the committee.[65] As long as the Thuringian German Christians remained in control of important churches—and they were in charge of the administration in Thuringia, Mecklenburg, and Lübeck—Zöllner would be unable to achieve church unity. To him, as to the Confessing church, the Thuringians were beyond the pale. With outspoken opposition on the part of the Reich Brotherhood Council and of the Second Provisional Directory, with only toleration by the Luther Council, with the increasing hostility of the radical German Christians and of many of the party leaders, the days of the church committees were numbered. Both in the church and in the government, the committees had been unable to overcome the handicap of their status as men of the church appointed by the state. No one was satisfied.[66]

In an effort to strengthen its position and establish a body which would represent the Evangelical church more broadly, the Reich Church Committee called a meeting in Berlin on November 19–20, 1936, of the heads of the church committees and leaders of the provincial churches of the Old Prussian Union, of the Land churches of Saxony, Hanover (Lutheran and Reformed), Württemberg, Nassau-Hesse, Bavaria, Schleswig-Holstein, Hamburg, Electoral Hesse-Waldeck, Baden, Palatinate, Brunswick, Lippe, and Schaumburg-Lippe.[67] Representatives of the Thuringian German Christian dominated churches and of the Confessing church as such were absent. It is also questionable how adequately the provincial church committees of Prussia really represented these churches. Yet it was nevertheless an impressive effort to listen to a large number of official German church administrations. Only the churches of Mecklenburg, Thuringia, Lübeck, Bremen, and a part of Oldenburg were missing. The conference submitted two significant statements to state authorities. While expressing their willingness to support the Führer in the conflict against bolshevism, they decried the ever-increasing propaganda against the Christian religion within Germany. The church leaders supported the Reich Church Committee in its efforts to stop this progressive dechristianization. They also agreed with the committee that no church administration in the hands of men who adhered to the doctrines of the Thuringian German Christians had the right to control a German church. Their statement was directed especially against the administration of the churches of Thuringia and Mecklenburg.[68]

The Reich Church Committee decided to consult the church leaders regularly, and as a result they created the Church Leaders' Conference (*Kirchenführerkonferenz*). At their second meeting on December 10–11, representatives of the brotherhood councils of the churches of Thuringia, Mecklenburg, and Lübeck were also present. This time the situation in the church of Lübeck, where there had long been difficulties, was the center of attention.[69] The bishop and church council had summarily dismissed nine pastors who adhered to the Confessing church. The conference expressed its indignation and instructed the Reich Church Committee to seek their reinstatement. Dr. Zöllner did his best, and finally resolved to visit Lübeck and speak a word of encouragement to the pastors. At the instigation of the Ministry of Church Affairs, he was forbidden by the police to make the journey. This was the last straw. For months the ministry had not actively backed the committee, particularly after Hermann Muhs was appointed as state secretary to the ministry in November, 1936. Now its chairman was denied one of the specific privileges and duties which had been accorded him—the right to preach throughout the Reich. The upshot was that the committee resigned on February 12, 1937.[70]

The committee explained its decision in a covering letter, citing: (1) the failure of the ministry to support its efforts, especially in the churches where the Thuringian German Christians had control; (2) the restriction on publication of the decisions of the committee; (3) the refusal to allow the committee's president to visit Lübeck; (4) the inability of the committee to obtain entrée to the Führer; (5) the continuing unrestricted antichurch propaganda, in spite of pleas that it should be curbed; and (6) the statement by Minister Kerrl that he was contemplating measures which would in effect mean the end of the constitution of the German Evangelical church, a document the Führer himself had confirmed.[71]

The letter advances ample reasons for the failure of the Reich Church Committee. However, it does not mention the deep-seated hostility of the brotherhood councils, which never did give the church committees their full support, and as one friendly critic put it, "did everything they could to undermine their work."[72] From mid-December on, Zöllner and Fritz Müller, as head of the Second Provisional Directory, had been carrying on negotiations. Zöllner wanted official confirmation of his committee by the Confessing church to parallel the recognition he had from the state. This Fritz Müller steadfastly refused because German Christians held positions on certain boards established by the Reich Church Committee. (For example, Dr. Christian Kinder was a member of the board on constitutional matters, and Dr. Werner Petersmann was on the board of theological questions.) Zöllner concluded: "You hold to your old views in regard to the German Christians; I consider them wrong. I want a church with the German Christians (without the Thuringians); you want to build a church without the German Christians."[73] Because of this basic difference, it was impossible for Zöllner and his committee ever to reach an agreement with many of the important Confessional churchmen.

The letter of resignation also fails to make clear that Kerrl and the committees received no support from the party and many state authorities. If Kerrl let the committee down, he was himself let down by his state and party cohorts. He had only reached the post of district leader in the party, and he therefore did not have much prestige in party circles. The party was definitely moving away from the churches. In 1933, it was the thing to do for party members to join the church and participate in its services, but now the thing to do was to withdraw from the church and boycott religious observances. The committee specifically protested against the propaganda for church withdrawals. Kerrl (and this could also be said for members of the committees) had the best intentions and a serious desire to work out a new church order when the committees were appointed in the fall of 1935. They had not succeeded, and what Hitler supposedly said of Kerrl when he heard of his death on December 14, 1941, might, with equal appropriateness, be said of the demise of the Reich Church Committee: "His motives were certainly honorable, but it simply was a hopeless experiment to try to unite national socialism and Christianity."[74]

The resignation had an epilogue. The next day Kerrl spoke to the chairmen of the remaining provincial and Land church committees and vented his spleen:

> Catholic Bishop Galen and the Evangelical General Superintendent Zöllner had tried to convince him what Christianity was: what was essential was the recognition that Jesus was the son of God. This was ridiculous and beside the point. To permit the personality of Jesus to influence you, to live a Christianity of deed—this was all that counted. . . . The clergy say Jesus is a Jew; they speak of the Jew Paul and say salvation comes from the Jews. That can't be permitted.[75]

Such remarks, which soon became known beyond the inner circle, begged for a refutation, and it was not slow in coming. Otto Dibelius wrote an open letter to Kerrl in which he lectured him roundly.[76] For his pains Dibelius had to answer before a special court, but much to the discomfort of the suing minister, he was freed. In his speech Kerrl had also attacked Martin Niemöller, who was not slow in answering him.[77] The era of the church committees, for all intents and purposes, was at an end.

For a time the various provincial church committees hung on. Better relations even developed between the Prussian committee and the brotherhood council of the Old Prussian Union. An agreement was worked out on May 4, 1937, in which the committee recognized the seminaries, ordinations, and appointments of the Confessing church.[78] Yet the Land church committees were also doomed. From August 23 to September 30, 1937, all the provincial and Land church committees were officially dismissed, except the one in Electoral Hesse-Waldeck which continued to function until the end of the war. The dismissal of the committee in Saxony, which had done much constructive work, required coercion and the use of force. Dissension in this strife-torn Land church again increased.[79] The duties of the committees were in general taken over by juridically trained officials in the central offices of the various churches and by heads of the financial sections.[80] In Prussia Dr. Werner, president of the Supreme Council of the old Prussian Union, head of the church chancellery and of its financial section, took charge. Thus, while Minister Kerrl continued to head the Ministry of Church Affairs, Werner, a German Christian, became the most powerful church official not only in the Prussian but in the Reich church as well.

II.

Unrest in the Protestant Churches, 1937–39

The Calling of Church Elections

The resignation of the Reich Church Committee had been undesired and unexpected. Kerrl immediately announced that no church elections were contemplated. "In such a situation as that of the church at present, one can elect nothing."[1] He promised that new measures for the regulation of church affairs would be announced on February 15, 1937. He then left for Berchtesgaden to report to Hitler. What transpired in this interview is not known, but Hitler did exactly what Kerrl had promised would not happen. To the surprise of everyone, he ordered new church elections, through which "in complete freedom and according to their own decisions, the church people of Germany should give themselves a new constitution and thereby establish a new order."[2] It is significant that he spoke of "church people" and not of the German churches. Kerrl was assigned the task of making preparations for the election of this general synod. No date, however, was set for the elections.

When it resigned, the Reich Church Committee had suggested that the Church Leaders' Conference should take over the direction of the German Evangelical church. The suggestion had no firm legal basis, but the conference did take up the proposal on February 12, the very day the committee resigned. It appointed an ad hoc committee (*Gremium*), headed by Pastor Dr. Hanns Lilje, consisting of one Lutheran, one Reformed, and one United church representative, to more or less head up the Church Leaders' Conference. After the announcement of the forthcoming church elections, the Gremium at once called the conference together for a meeting on February 18–19.[3] The conference was willing to cooperate with the Reich Ministry of Church Affairs in preparing for the elections, but insisted that they must be carried out by the churches. The churches as such must be heard, for the church constitution of 1933 provided for a confederation of churches based on their respective confessions. When the Gremium forwarded this communication to Kerrl, he flatly refused to recognize their authority. Instead he addressed himself to Bishop Marahrens as the senior bishop in length of service, pointing out certain conditions which had to be met before he could discuss the elections.[4]

There was nothing the Church Leaders' Conference could do if it were to continue functioning but recast its leadership. It replaced the Gremium with a Church Leaders' Directory under the chairmanship of Bishop Marahrens, the other members being Bishop Wurm, Land Superintendent Dr. Walter Hollweg, and President Richard Zimmerman.[5] It was a strong directorate, and although the Church Leaders' Conference never became a powerful governing organization, it was able to maintain itself until the end of the Reich. It had, to be sure, close and interlocking relations with the Luther Council. Its relations with the Second Provincial Directory however, were tenuous, for that body always claimed that it was the true head of the German Evangelical church, and steadily refused to recognize the various provincial church committees which at that time were still members of the Church Leaders' Conference. One thing which gave the conference standing and lent weight to its pronouncements was that there were men associated with it like Marahrens, Wurm, and Meiser, who had standing in the ecumenical movement and were well known outside of Germany.

Kerrl, however, never did negotiate with the Church Leaders' Directory or any other group in regard to regulations for carrying out the elections. But the churches could not afford to wait, and immediately began to prepare for them. They were determined that there should be no repetition of the 1933 procedures. Above all, there would be no one list of candidates for all Germany, nor would every technical member of the church (those who were baptized and paid church taxes) vote. According to old practice, only those who actively took part in the affairs of the church were to share in the election.[6] The various brotherhood councils and other agencies of the Confessing church issued pronouncements urging the people to remain faithful to historic Christian values and to the church of their fathers. The congregations awoke to the challenge. Churches were filled to overflowing when prominent Confessing leaders came to speak.[7] Often services had to be repeated to accommodate all who wanted to hear. The newspapers, even the church papers, however, carried little comment, for they were held down by the heavy hand of the censor.

During this period of uncertainty and agitation, Otto Dibelius directed an open letter to Kerrl in which he stated:

> Luther has taught us that we, in accordance with the word of God, are obligated to serve the state with body and soul as long as it remains a state. Likewise the state of Adolf Hitler can count on the support of the Evangelical Christians in Germany. It would be undignified for us again publicly to give this assurance. But as soon as the state assumes itself to be the church and wants to take over the control of the souls of individuals and of the sermons of the church, then we, according to the teachings of Luther, are called upon to offer resistance in God's name. And this we will do![8]

A group of pastors who considered themselves as standing somewhere between the Dahlem group and the Thuringian German Christians formed a League of the Center (*Bund der Mitte*). They issued an appeal calling for a "united Evangelical Reich church, based only and definitely on biblical doctrines and openly and honestly supporting the Reich of Adolf Hitler.''[9] This league hoped to win the support of the so-called neutral group of pastors, but it never prospered or attracted much support.

Regrouping of the German Christians

The various German Christian groups welcomed the new elections. Bishop Martin Sasse of Thuringia was one of the first to issue an election appeal making a bid for Nazi party support. He proclaimed what was actually a one-point program. All the general synod had to do was to pass an ordinance stating: "The regulation and administration of the German Evangelical church will be given over to the safe hands of the German state.''[10] Pastor Wilhelm Rehm, head of the German Christian Reich Movement, issued a manifesto titled "For a Jewish-Free German Evangelical National Church.''

As the German Christians began to expand their campaign, it became evident that their factionalism was a great handicap. They therefore undertook to share burdens and exchange speakers; Bishop Müller was scheduled to speak at many meetings. Out of these common electoral efforts grew a desire for more organizational unity. At the beginning of June, agreement to unite was reached between the Thuringian-centered German Christian Church Movement, the German Christians in Baden, the Folk Church Movement of German Christians in Württemberg, the German Christian Faith Movement in Mecklenburg, and the German Christians in the Rhineland. It actually was a matter of certain small groups joining the Thuringian group, which now changed its name to "German Christians (National Church Movement)'' (*Deutsche Christen* [*Nationalkirchliche Bewegung*]).[11] Pastor Hossenfelder brought the greater part of his group into the new organization and subsequently other small groups joined. The Thuringian-led organization came to have adherents throughout Germany. In the beginning and later under the leadership of Dr. Christian Kinder and Wilhelm Rehm, the German Christians had sought to establish a national church on Lutheran patterns, but the guidelines of the new National Church Movement spoke of a German church where occupation, regional loyalty, or confession played no role. They sought a church embracing all Germans. The movement still mouthed adherence to Christianity; it still had the motto "Germany is our duty, Christ is our strength,'' but it placed the emphasis more and more on Germany and less on Christ.[12]

Yet the radical German Christians made no great headway. In spite of many bids, the Nazi party as a whole did not lend them its support. By this time the party was beyond being interested in churches, even if they were German Christian oriented. The party's attitude is indicated by the restriction (at this precise moment) of the term "movement'' (*Bewegung*) to the National Socialist German Workers party alone, so

that the German Christians (National Church Movement) had to rebap-
tize itself the "German Christians (National Church Union)" (*Einung*).[13]

While the radical Thuringian-led German Christians had achieved
greater strength and unity, the other wing of the German Christians, the
German Christian Reich Movement under Wilhelm Rehm continued to
decline. Cooperation with the church committees had weakened both
the more orthodox groups and the radical Thuringians. Rehm steadfastly
refused to make any agreement with the radicals, even refusing an
electoral alliance. To mark the differences with the Thuringians in July,
1937, Rehm added to the already lengthy title of his group the explanatory phrase "Reformation Reich Church."[14] His refusal to go along with
the National Church Movement cost him support in the Reich church
ministry.

Within the Ministry of Church Affairs itself, since November, 1936,
Dr. Hermann Muhs had been in charge of relations with the German
Christians.[15] He was a radical and withdrew support from Rehm. A
number of district organizations of Rehm's group disintegrated, and finances were short. The financial difficulties of the Confessing church
are often stressed, but the German Christians also had their financial
crises, partly because, after the period of the church committees, the
German Christians under Rehm controlled no Land church, whereas the
National Church Movement controlled the Thuringian church and commanded its finances.[16] Finally, at the end of 1938, Rehm withdrew as
head of his group, now known as "German Christians (Reformation
Reich Church)." The leaders of the various Land groups who remained
in the organization elected Dr. Werner Petersmann of Breslau as his
successor, a man who for years had played a leading role in German
Christian circles. At the same time the name of the organization was
changed to "Luther-Germans (Reformation Reich Church)" (*Luther-
Deutsche* [*Reformatorische Reichskirche*]).[17] The bewildering number of
names which the German Christians had to devise is in itself a manifestation of how disunited and diverse the movement was. In contrast, by
its concentration on historic Christian values and the Reformation confessions, the Confessing church had an inner unity which the German
Christians could never achieve.

New State Administrative Orders

While the churches were busy preparing for the elections, a number of decrees were issued which were designed to handicap them. On
February 18, Minister of the Interior Frick, in consultation with Minister
of Church Affairs Kerrl, forbade any public announcement of the names
of persons who had withdrawn from the churches.[18] It was especially
forbidden to read these names from the pulpit, a common but by no
means universal practice. Violations of the order were to be punished
by no less than a month in prison or a fine of from 150 to 15,000 marks.
A person who withdrew from the church excluded himself from all its

services and from the right to act as a sponsor at baptisms. To announce
the names to other members of the congregation was certainly not out
of line with orderly congregational procedure, but it did publicize a
person's private religious convictions. A short while later, Kerrl issued
an ordinance which placed the day-by-day administration of churches
in the hands of the head of the church chancellery and gave the finance
sections control of all financial matters. This order challenged the legiti-
macy and right to govern of all existing church administrations, and
prompted a statement by the Second Provisional Directory that the
churches would continue to carry on their duties even if their right to do
so was challenged by the state.[19]

On June 9, 1937, the minister of the interior again intervened, and
along with the Ministry of Church Affairs issued a decree restricting the
right of churches to take up any but officially prescribed collections.[20] In
Germany, where most of the finances are raised by church taxes, it was
(and still is) customary to have collections practically every Sunday for
some special purpose. These collections had become one of the main
means of financial support for the Confessing church in the disturbed
church areas. Ministers sent the collections to Confessing church authorities rather than to official church headquarters. Now all this was to
stop, and even taking up collections at special Confessional services
was forbidden. Hundreds of pastors were arrested for violating the decree and usually were imprisoned for a couple of weeks. The number of
arrests was particularly large in East Prussia, and the Bavarian church, as
a gesture of support, sent six young clergy to help to take care of the
congregations. They soon were also subjected to police restrictions. The
custom was inaugurated of placing the collections on the altar and the
police were loath to confiscate from this place of safety. The pastor, the
deacons, or even some unsuspected boy or girl would then take the
collection to safety. Pastor Hugo Linck reports that by the time he had
found his way through the congregation at the end of the service the
pockets of his gown were thrust full of contributions.[21]

Some court decisions did help the pastors. The courts decided that
offerings taken in church services were not a violation of the general
Reich law on collections, although they might be a violation of church
discipline.[22] On November 15, 1937, the superior court of Brandenburg
decided that taking up collections for the Confessing church was not
permissible; four days later the superior court of Naumburg decided that
they were.[23] In some places the collections were confiscated and in
some places they were not, depending on the ardor of officials. The
Confessing church authorities accordingly recommended that pastors
should announce to the congregations if the collections could be safely
forwarded.[24] In order to meet regulations, they should announce officially scheduled collections, but did not have to recommend them. The
congregations would take the hint and place their gifts on the altar or on
rear benches as they left the church, instead of in the official collection
boxes.

The Confessing churches had always to some extent followed the plan of the official church, that is, collecting for foreign missions, for the Gustav-Adolf-Verein, and so forth. Not holding such collections would have upset the whole collection program of the official church, which also had an interest in keeping these mission establishments going. After long and tedious negotiations, the officials sponsored by Minister Kerrl agreed to call for no collections which the Confessing church could not support; the Confessing church agreed to ask its members to contribute, but continued to distribute the funds directly. The Confessing church officials were also able to negotiate some easement of police confiscation of other special collections. Agreements were worked out that varied in different Land churches and which alleviated, if they did not completely abolish, the difficulties over this problem.[25] The government could hamper but simply could not cut off completely the freewill offerings which members chose to make; to the very end the Confessing church maintained its program of collections.

To tighten further the state's financial control over the churches, Kerrl on June 25 issued new regulations regarding the finance sections of the national church administration and of all Land churches.[26] Some of the Land churches earlier had escaped the finance sections, and they continued to do so, largely because the Ministry of Church Affairs was not sufficiently powerful to assert itself over the state governors who in certain states supervised church finances. The governors did not want to permit the finance sections to function in their jurisdictions, and consequently the whole system remained a skeleton one.[27] In addition to the national church administration, only ten Land churches—among them the large churches of the Old Prussian Union and Hanover—received finance sections, while fourteen remained without. No finance sections were imposed on the Catholic church. The 1937 regulations made it possible to appoint men to the finance sections who were not members of the general church administration. This opened the door wider to financial "experts" and good party men from other state offices; even individuals who had withdrawn from the church were appointed.[28] Such practices increased the possibility of disrupting the existing Land church administrations through appointment of "foreigners," a procedure which was energetically followed by Dr. Muhs in the years 1942–45. The provision in the law that the finance sections were to administer all lands and endowments was also very disturbing to the churches.

Meanwhile, the churches continued to be concerned with the upcoming church elections. It was generally expected that, as in 1933, the state would not allow much time between setting the date and the elections themselves. Not to be caught napping, the Brotherhood Council of the Church of the Old Prussian Union issued secret directions to its congregations on June 17. At eight o'clock of election day, the congregation was to assemble in church, and a statement decrying the unconstitutional way the elections were being carried out was to be read. Thereupon the congregation was to boycott the elections.[29] Kerrl had excellent sources of information, but whether he heard of this plan is immaterial. On June 25, he issued further regulations forbidding the use of church buildings for election purposes. All public meetings and

the preparation and dissemination of broadsides for electoral purposes
was forbidden until the day the elections were announced.[30] This was
tantamount to an indefinite postponement, and in fact the elections
were never held. By this time officials in the Ministry for Church Affairs
apparently felt that a defeat of the German Christians, which seemed
certain, would be evaluated abroad as a sign of weakness in the National Socialist movement.[31] Important ecumenical meetings were about
to be held, and it was just as well to forego all the turmoil and reorganization which the election of a new general synod would entail.

Church affairs, however, were far from peaceful. The Brotherhood
Council of the Church of the Old Prussian Union had issued a sharp
attack on the government's decree against publicizing names of people
who withdrew from churches. They declared that this was a legitimate
church procedure, and one that the state had no right to forbid. Confessing synods of the Rhineland and of the Old Prussian Union, meeting at
Halle and Lippstadt, also issued strong statements against the government's actions.[32] As matters now stood, pastors who read the list of
church withdrawals and who conducted unauthorized collections not
only disobeyed the mininster of church affairs, but also the minister of
the interior—and the latter had the police power at his back. A wave of
arrests took place. The arrest of Pastor Paul Schneider of Dickenschied
in the Rhineland aroused particular attention. He supposedly had attacked some members of the congregation by reading the ban which the
presbytery of the congregation had levied against these men. He was an
intrepid soul who could not resist speaking up against the regime even
when in concentration camp, and he was to meet his death there on
July 18, 1939.[33]

The church authorities vigorously protested such police interference at a time when there was supposed to be a free election campaign.
On April 29, 1937, the Second Provisional Directory and the Council of
the German Evangelical church sent a strong letter of protest to all the
Protestant Reich ministers (von Blomberg, Göring, Frick, Rust, Seldte,
von Neurath, Schwerin-Krosigk, Schacht, and Dorpmüller), and also to
Rudolf Hess.[34] The continued arrests led the American churchman
Charles S. Macfarland to send Hitler a personal letter on June 2. He
recalled their interview in the fall of 1933, and then went on to describe
how the church situation in Germany had deteriorated rather than improved since then. He pointedly concluded: "You often praise personal
courage, but you appear to think of this only in a physical sense. If you
want to see the worth of Germans, then look at the pastors who stand
up for the freedom of the Christian gospel, and I include among them
those who are in prison and in concentration camp."[35]

The uproar in the church did not go unnoticed by Hitler. In a
speech to Reich and Gau leaders, he ordered that every individual
initiative in church matters must stop. Hess circulated this directive on
June 20, 1937, and added that it accorded with his own previous order.
In the future, anyone who without express authorization of the Führer

undertook measures in regard to the churches that might harm the prestige of the party and state, could expect to be publicly disavowed by the Führer.[36] Yet on June 23, the secret police raided a meeting of the Reich Brotherhood Council in Berlin and seized eight of its members, hoping to get hold of those who were also members of the Prussian brotherhood council. The police at least had the grace to permit the assembled group to sing a chorale and to permit President Koch to pronounce a blessing before the brethren were led off to jail.[37]

Such a group arrest, along with the disruption of a meeting of one of the most respected groups of German churchmen, caused consternation throughout Germany. Concern was heightened by the arrest of Martin Niemöller on July 1, 1937. The official announcement of his arrest stated:

> that for a long time Niemöller had been making provocative statements from the pulpit and in public addresses; that he had defamed leading personalities of the state and state measures; that he had caused unrest among the populace. Likewise he had urged rebellion against state laws and ordinances. His statements are the steady fare of the hostile foreign press.[38]

The judicial indictment issued on July 28 was more specific, and charged him directly with violating the ordinance of February 2, which forbade the announcement from the pulpit of the names of people who had withdrawn from the church. His trial took place February 7 to March 2, 1938.[39] The court imposed a seven-month sentence and a 2,000 mark fine, 500 marks of which were cancelled as costs. Having already served seven months in jail, Niemöller was a free man.[40] However, the next day, on Hitler's direct orders, Niemöller was again taken into custody by the secret police and placed in the concentration camp at Sachsenhausen and later (July 11, 1941) at Dachau. Many friends and organizations made unavailing efforts to free him.

On March 25, 1938, Kerrl attempted to wash his hands of the whole affair and notified other officials not to forward petitions for Niemöller's release to him, as he had not had anything to do with his imprisonment and his liberation was not in his province.[41] Hitler, however, did not agree that Kerrl did not have jurisdiction.[42] Nevertheless Kerrl, in this as in so many other church matters, had no final authority. He supported the head of the Evangelical Church Council, Dr. Werner, who opposed bringing church disciplinary action against Niemöller, for he thought it could not be successfully carried through. Without such action, Niemöller's salary could not be stopped. Under a new church ordinance, "The Transfer of Clergy for Service Reasons," issued by Werner on March 18, 1939, Niemöller was placed on the waiting list and since it was unlikely that he would be freed he would be eligible for a pension in five years. Meanwhile, he was to receive 80 percent of his salary. Kerrl held as unjustified any actions against Niemöller's family, in particular forcing them to leave their parsonage.[43]

In May, 1938, Dr. Fritz Klinger, head of the Reich Federation of Evangelical Ministerial Associations, in the name of 16,000 Evangelical clergy, petitioned that Niemöller be freed for the dedication of a U-boat memorial near Kiel. All living submarine commanders and crews were supposed to attend. Hitler refused the plea.[44] About a year later, Niemöller's wife asked that her husband be given his liberty on the occasion of Hitler's birthday and their twentieth wedding anniversary. Hitler refused, on the grounds that if Niemöller were freed he would soon be at the head of a group of clergy who through their opposition to national socialism would threaten the unity of the people and could be a danger to the state.[45] On Göring's advice, members of the Niemöller family asked in July 1939 that Martin be given an opportunity to attend the golden wedding celebration of his parents. He had missed the silver wedding because he was with the fleet in Norwegian waters. Lammers forwarded the requests to Himmler, who felt that such a visit (*Urlaub*) would only create new unrest and increase the difficulty of quieting the whole issue. The final decision was put to Hitler, who refused the request.[46] When Niemöller volunteered for service in the fleet at the start of World War II, he was turned down.[47] His brother, the Reverend Wilhelm Niemöller, however, served as an officer in the army throughout the war. The only time Hitler relented one iota was when, at the request of his wife, Martin was permitted to pay a fleeting visit under escort to the deathbed of his father in March, 1941.[48] In June, 1942, Hans Koch, Niemöller's defense counsel, made another plea for the amelioration of Niemöller's confinement. Mrs. Niemöller was hospitalized and their nineteen-year-old son was seriously ill. Would it be possible for Martin to be brought in closer touch with his family so he could help bring up the children? Again the decision went to Hitler and the notation in the archives reads: "The Führer has refused any alleviation of the custody of the Reverend Niemöller."[49]

Niemöller was among the more select group of prisoners at Dachau, and was spared some of the horrors of the concentration camps. He remained there until April 25, 1945, when he and other political prisoners were taken to South Tirol where he was freed by German troops on April 30. On May 3, he and his German liberators were taken into custody by troops of the American Seventh Army.[50]

One of the most important consequences of Niemöller's arrest was that the Pastors' Emergency League lost its leader. Although the league was never dissolved and continued to help pastors in distress, it lost its position as a leading force in the church struggle.[51] The arrests of Niemöller and many others also led to an increase in church services of intercession. The Confessing church authorities regularly circulated lists of persons (*Fürbittenliste*) for whom prayers were asked. The names on these lists varied from Sunday to Sunday, but they constitute one of the best records we have of the state's terroristic action against the church. The lists never contained names of persons arrested for purely political reasons. On June 29, 1937, the names of 45 Pastors and deacons were on the intercessory lists, along with 25 who were temporarily arrested; at the beginning of August the lists numbered 65 imprisonments, 24 denials to speak, and 29 dismissals. In 1937 more than 800 pastors were held in arrest for two days or longer.[52] The police had worked out a gradation of punishments which were to be applied according to local conditions, the personage involved, and the seriousness of the offense. These punishments ranged from (1) warning, (2) posting of bond (3) prohibition to speak, (4) prohibition of stay of residence, (5) prohibition of all activity, (6) short-term arrest, to (7) protective custody. All these could be levied for varying periods of time.[53]

The representatives of the intact churches in the Reich Brotherhood Council had been particularly upset by the police raid on their meeting in Berlin on June 23.[54] Niemöller's arrest heightened their fears, and particularly aroused the ire of Bishop Marahrens. For some time there had been soundings among the different groups of the Confessing church for closer cooperation. Now these came to a climax. At a meeting in Kassel on July 5–6, the Church Leaders' Conference, the Luther Council, and the Second Provisional Directory of the Confessing Church agreed to form an executive committee, the so-called *Kasseler Gremium.*[55] The dire need of the hour had restored a measure of unity and cooperation among the different groups and authorities of the Confessing church. The committee immediately issued an appeal to all congregations to stand fast and support by prayer and help the parishes and pastors subjected to police duress.[56] Indeed, the chief accomplishment of the Kassel Committee was to issue statements on church-state relations; it never contributed much towards working out a new church order.

Increased police interference with the church is evidenced by the action of Himmler, the head of the secret police, who now entered the lists directly. After consultation with the Ministry of Science, Instruction, and Education, and with the Ministry of Church Affairs, he issued a decree at the end of August, 1937, dissolving all the seminaries and ministerial examination committees of the Confessing church.[57] If there was ever a matter which belonged to the inner life of the church, it was the training and ordination of a rising generation of ministers. The Kassel Committee immediately attacked the decree and demanded that it be rescinded. The Confessing Church Synod of the Rhineland also took a strong stand.[58] But the decree was not repealed, and it gave grounds for further arrests when the police wanted to crack down. The seminaries, however, attempted to continue their work. Once closed, a training center soon appeared in a new location and under a new guise. Theological students were also sent from disturbed church areas to Bavaria or Wïttemberg to pass their theological examinations under the supervision of these intact churches. The seminary which was part of the Bethel Institutions also remained available. The disturbed church areas also welcomed pastors from other Land churches, a most uncommon practice. During the war, for example, one-fourth of the candidates and young pastors of the Brandenburg church had come from other church territories.[59]

Himmler's decree was intended to harass rather than to cut off completely the supply of young ministers to the Confessing church. People still demanded that their churches be staffed; they still wanted their children baptized and their dead buried—even if they chose to make an excursion or attend a party rally on Sunday instead of going to hear a sermon. The regime was not yet ready to force the issue by closing down the many churches, and this would have been necessary if the state refused to recognize the ordinations sponsored by the Confessing church. Yet it did have ways of making difficulties and preventing young ministers from entering the church. In Baden, for example, the finance section which had only been established on May 18, 1938, simply delayed approving appointments for young ordained pastors, which led Bishop Julius Kühlewein to seek aid in vain from Kerrl.[60]

Efforts to Deconfessionalize the Party

A policy of deconfessionalizing the National Socialist party and its organizations was undertaken in piecemeal fashion. Under the 1933 concordat with the Catholic church, the papacy was to issue "stipulations which exclud[ed] the clergy and members of orders from membership in political parties, and activity for such parties" and "it [was] understood that similar regulations regarding activity [would] be introduced by the Reich with regard to non-Catholic denominations."[61] Implementing these provisions was difficult and never completely successful, even during the war years.

Clergy who had long been members of the party and its groups could not be summarily dismissed. The attempt to do so started in the SS, and a few of Himmler's ordinances in this field are significant. On September 15, 1934, he strictly forbade to all SS members any interference and tactless behavior in respect to religious services of all confessions. SS men were to show respect for another person's belief, and any violation of his order would bring exclusion from the SS. Moreover, SS leaders were to read this directive every three months at SS roll calls. In October, 1934, in order to prevent controversies within the SS and to bring the organization in line with the provisions of the concordat, he ordered all clerics of whatever confession to resign from the SS. Bishop Ernst Dietrich, head of the official Protestant church in Hesse and a member of the party, protested the measure. Himmler, however, would not change his views, whereupon Dietrich turned in his membership book and pin as a supporting member of the SS (*Förderndes Mitglied des SS*), with the remark that he had always paid his dues willingly and with pleasure. Archbishop Conrad Gröber of Freiburg was also a member of this supporting group, but when he was asked to turn in his membership book and pin in 1937, he twice paid no attention to the request, whereupon he was silently dropped from the organization on Himmler's order.[62]

On September 20, 1935, Himmler forbade all members of the SS to take any leadership part in any confessional organization, including even the German Faith Movement. If they did not want to resign their church offices, they would have to withdraw from the SS. On the other hand, they could continue to be ordinary members of any church, and he again enjoined all SS members to respect religious customs, statues, and pictures, on pain of being dismissed. In an order on April 7, 1936, which shows the trend of events, he stated that any SS member who withdrew from a church should not give "membership in the SS" as the reason for his withdrawal, but rather "because of personal convictions." On August 26, 1936, he forbade SS members either in uniform or in street clothes to participate as musicians in church services. The question of whether an SS man could play in the SS band and also in the customary church brass ensemble was thus answered negatively. On the direction of local leadership on June 26, 1937, an SS leader was degraded to simple SS membership because he had voted for a confessional school, which he knew was contrary to National Socialist policy. (This was, however, not according to Himmler's directive.) On June 28, 1937, Himmler forbade the SS to sponsor any lectures on Christianity or the doctrines and practices of any confession. He further forbade "in the indoctrination courses every attack on Christ as a person, as such attacks, or denunciation of Christ as a Jew, was unworthy of the SS, and certainly historically was not true."[63]

The following July, Himmler dismissed Scharführer Grunow of Elbing from the SS because he had dealt with confessional matters in his speeches and grossly contravened Himmler's long-standing orders. "Men who can't divest themselves of manners of previous centuries, and scoff and sling mud at things which are holy and matters of belief to others, once and for all do not belong in the SS."[64] As religious strife intensified, Himmler, on November 18, 1937, ordered that SS members should not attend church services in uniform. If he did not want a person to be disturbed in his religious feelings by the SS, he also did not want to have an SS man embarrassed by the words of a clergyman who might make unfortunate remarks. Having excluded clerics and theological students from the SS, in February, 1939, Himmler extended this ban to church employees. He was careful to point out that this was not because the two men in question happened to be employed by the Confessing church, but because he did not want "membership in the SS to bring anyone into a conflict of conscience or of faith."[65]

Although the SS became involved in many antichurch police measures, it was never meant to be—nor was it so considered in the Germany of the time—a godless or even a nonchurch institution. In the years 1937–38, when the campaign for church withdrawals was at its height, most of the SS members retained their church affiliation, as two tables prepared on Himmler's orders show.

The compiler of the tables noted that withdrawals were apparently decreasing even more in 1939. He concluded:

> If one adds all these things together, one can say with certainty that the Protestant segment of the populace has more understanding for the struggle and work of the SS, and therefore it is easier to recruit among them than among the Catholics. . . . The confessional resistance is greater from the Catholic side than from the Protestant.[66]

	September 1, 1937		December 1, 1938	
Protestant	110,531	60.0%	122,668	51.4%
Catholic	38,810	21.1%	61,030	25.7%*
God believing	34,369	18.7%	53,937	22.7%
Others	907	0.2%	524	0.2%

*The notable increase of Catholics in 1938 was the result of the annexation of Austria and the addition of a special Danubian division to the SS.

Church Withdrawals by SS Members

	Protestant	Catholic	Others	Totals
1937	11,303	4,506	44	15,853
1938	5,282	1,837	21	7,140

Even as late as December 19, 1942, Himmler wrote the mother of a prospective member of the SS: "I will not tolerate in the SS a man who does not believe in God. . . . What confession the individual belongs to, or if he designates himself as 'God believing' is his own decision."[67] Just a year earlier, Hitler had bragged: "I have six divisions of SS composed of men absolutely indifferent in matters of religion. It doesn't prevent them from going to their deaths with serenity in their souls."[68]

Himmler was a man of many faces, certainly not religiously or church oriented, and a fanatic about keeping the SS racially pure.[69] He was trying to achieve with the SS what increasingly became the goal of the Nazi leadership as a whole—the complete and absolute separation of church and state, with the church exercising no influence whatever on the state. Germany was also to become absolutely free of Jewish influence on the state. These goals led the Nazis to one anti-Jewish measure after the other.[70]

The exclusion of the clergy from the SA came later than from the SS, and was never so complete.[71] On June 11, 1934, the SA were ordered to keep aside from all church controversies and in no way were they to molest a pastor in carrying out his duties. The membership and role of the clergy in the party were also restricted. On February 9, 1937, in order to avoid bringing church differences into the party, it was ordered that clergy and theological students should no longer be accepted. This order was later interpreted to apply also to those who were "strongly tied" to a confession. On July 27, 1938, Martin Bormann ordered that clergy holding party offices should gradually be replaced, and no such new appointments were to be made. The screws were steadily tightened, and on May 10, 1939, the treasurer of the party decreed 'that in the future all party members that entered the clerical profession or turned to theological studies had to resign from the party.'[72]

Although no official general ban on clerical membership in the party was ever issued, in some localities pastors were dropped, which led to protests from them. The issue came to a head in 1940, when

Kerrl sought to find out on what authority these expulsions were being carried out, and Hitler ruled that forced resignations and expulsions of the clergy from the party should be stopped.[73] However, in the summer of 1942, Bormann issued a general order that all party members whose ideological views were not considered dependable should be excluded without formalities. Many clergy could easily have been suspect under this sweeping decree; how rigorously it was applied is not known.[74]

To take the clergy out of the party was one thing, but to take party members out of the churches was another. Officially the party always maintained that no person should incur advantages or disadvantages because of his religious convictions.[75] Party formations ceased to attend services en masse as they had when Hitler first came to power. Restrictions were issued about appearing in party uniform at church functions; participation in honor formations at funerals was the only exception to this order.[76] Many party members withdrew from the churches, and the number of withdrawals reached new heights in 1937–39.[77] The creation of the official designation "gottgläubig," as well as the ban on reading from the pulpit the names of persons who had withdrawn their membership, were designed to further resignations from the churches. But the party was not united on the issue. Hitler himself ordered his chief associates, above all Göring and Goebbels, to retain their church membership, and he too remained a member of the Catholic church until his death.[78] In November, 1938, Rosenberg discovered that an old order of Agricultural Minister Richard Walter Darré forbade Land, district, and local peasant leaders (*Bauernführer*) from withdrawing their memberships. Many Bauernführer were also political leaders and would have preferred to leave the church, but if they did they would lose their positions. Rosenberg wrote to Darré suggesting that he change the policy. Darré, after consultation with his subordinates, insisted that the ban on withdrawal of church membership be retained. Political higher-ups should not at the same time be Bauernführer, and it would be better not to disturb the situation.[79] Darré had no desire to get involved in another quarrel with the churches such as erupted when a peasant almanac which omitted church holidays was issued.

Rosenberg was pushing the problem of party and church membership when another incident came to his attention. The German Christian church authorities in Saxony had consciously nominated men for a synodical meeting who held both party and state offices. This incensed Rosenberg, who felt the party could not permit these men to be involved in church disputes. He sent along to Bormann the draft of a decree which would prevent all party leaders from holding active or honorary church offices, although the rank-and-file members could still do so.[80] The decree was subsequently issued by Hess as deputy of the Führer on January 23, 1939. The efforts of the churches to get leading party men involved in their affairs was to be cut short.

The policy of erecting a wall between church and state, to borrow a figure from the Supreme Court of the United States, is always difficult, if not impossible, to carry out. Each side objected to the other borrowing from its own treasure trove. As the churches objected to party members taking over church hymns, Kerrl forbade setting church songs to party tunes.[81] On August 9, 1938, he circulated an order of Hitler forbidding the naming of any church building after party heroes.[82] The Nazis had long popularized bonfires as solstice celebrations, and when the churches began to have special Easter fires as part of Easter Dawn services, this practice was strictly forbidden.[83] On December 21, 1937, Himmler forbade the use of the cross with the swastika. Bishop Walther Schultz, the German Christian leader of Mecklenburg, protested to the Reich Chancellery that this combination had been the hallmark of the German Christians; the order only meant giving in to Meiser, Wurm, and Marahrens. Secretary Lammers sent the protest to Himmler, who maintained that the order had been issued so as to avoid the appearance that the party and state were behind the German Christians. This was the constant charge of the Confessing church, and one could not give them the opportunity of saying they were correct.[84] In February, 1938, Kerrl ordered that the churches should not use any party symbols, a ruling with which Goebbels concurred.[85] A year later, on February 2, 1939, Bormann issued a special directive that the party should be careful not to take over religious phraseology. It was unwise to say that party and state should serve matters on "this side" (*Diesseits*), while the church prepares for the "other side" (*Jenseits*). This would give the impression that the church knew something about the beyond which the party did not. They were to refer to "church services" (*Kirchendienst*), not to "divine services" (*Gottesdienst*).[86]

The state also threatened to curtail financial ties with the churches. On January 1, 1938, a directive of Hitler of the previous July went into effect which limited state and local authorities in helping to collect church taxes from natural persons (not corporations or businesses) who had declared they were church members at the last census. Church tax exemptions were noticeably curtailed by a land tax ordinance of April, 1938, which restricted freedom from taxation to property which was being used purely for church purposes.[87] Subsidies formerly paid to churches were cut.[88]

On December 10, 1938, it was ordered that the religious services customary in connection with the swearing in of military recruits should be abolished, although the recruits were free to attend services in nearby churches if they wished.[89] In Pomerania, veterans' organizations in the spring of 1939 refused to attend a comrade's funeral services if a pastor were present, but this was not true elsewhere.[90]

As the Nazis tightened their regime, they advanced ever more rapidly towards their goal of completely secularizing the party, the state, and society in general. Sundays were regularly booked with party meetings, rallies, and excursions. As far as the party was concerned, the thing to do was to stay away from church, a fashion many Germans quite easily and willingly accepted.

The regime's hostility towards the churches is not only clearly manifested in the measures enumerated above, but also in the campaign against confessional schools and traditional religious school observances such as opening prayers and group attendance at church services.[91] Religious instruction was not abolished in the schools, but in many places it was neglected or new nonbiblical material introduced. Party members were encouraged to refuse to teach the customary religious classes, and in some places pastors were denied the right to teach religion in the schools.[92]

The educational institutions of the inner mission societies were hard hit. Many of them were closed down, especially the kindergartens and the institutes where kindergarten teachers were trained. Since its inauguration, the regime had attempted to coordinate the various inner mission societies and the deaconess organizations. By establishing the monopolistic Winter Help Organization in 1933–34, the government soon ended one of the great fields of inner mission activity. The rigid restrictions on public collections inaugurated in 1934 made it impossible for the societies to carry on their usual public collection drives, and they were more than ever restricted to the special offerings made on Sundays. To protect their interests, the inner and foreign missionary organizations, in the fall of 1934, formed the Association of Missionary and Deaconess Societies and Organizations of the German Evangelical Church. The inevitable brotherhood council was formed to head it. In spite of continued and increasing harassment, the inner mission societies were able to escape liquidation or even complete Gleichschaltung. Yet the restrictions placed upon them caused their supporters great concern.[93]

In the first years of the regime, religious broadcasts were encouraged and a morning religious hour was a regular part of all network programs. From 1935 on, restrictions were gradually imposed—sometimes speakers were censored, funds were not available, or the program was dropped entirely. Over the protests of church leaders, both Protestant and Catholic hours were ended on April 7, 1939.[94] During the war, even the customary morning orchestral playing of church chorales at the spas was stopped.[95]

Great resentment was created in Munich when the historic Saint Matthew's Church was demolished in 1938 in accordance with Hitler's plan to rebuild the city, and indignation was not lessened when the site was at first converted to a parking lot.[96] In an order on July 28, 1939, Bormann, carrying out Hitler's directive, ordered that no churches should be built in new urban developments, nor should land be reserved for their construction.[97]

Rosenberg, the party leader in matters of Weltanschauung and cultural affairs, again came forward with a pamphlet, *Protestant Pilgrims to Rome (Protestantische Rompilger)*. While not as well known as his *Myth of the Twentieth Century*, it actually was an even more direct attack on

Christianity and the Protestant church in particular. He charged the Protestants with giving up their Reformation heritage and approaching Rome. The Kassel Committee drew up a statement which it sent out to be read as a pulpit declaration on Reformation Sunday, 1937. The people were also to be told that a detailed refutation of Rosenberg's book had been prepared, but it had been confiscated at the printers.[98] The Gestapo forbade reading the declaration, and confiscated such copies as it could get its hands on. Yet the declaration, bearing the signatures of ninety-six prominent churchmen, was widely circulated.[99]

Unmindful of the increasing opposition within the churches, Kerrl, in a decree of December 10, 1937, went ahead with his plans to take the direction of the church out of the hands of the churchmen and place it in the hands of officials in his office, mostly trained lawyers.[100] There was some space for maneuvering, for questions of confessions and observance were not supposed to be affected by the decree, and the existing church governments were to be consulted before further decrees dealing with so-called nondoctrinal outer matters were issued. The inevitable protest by the Kassel Committee followed, pointing out that it was impossible to draw a line between outer and inner church affairs. Their views made no impression, and on March 5, 1938, by a further ordinance, all laws and ordinances, insofar as they did not apply to matters of doctrine or ritual, had to be placed before Dr. Werner in the Ministry of Church Affairs for approval. Through this measure Kerrl was able to increase his control over some of the intact churches.[101]

It cannot be charged that the churchmen did not speak up, or that they took things lying down. Quite the contrary. It is remarkable that so many voices of opposition were raised, considering the system of police terror which prevailed. And it was in connection with this police coercion that a rather famous incident took place.

The Oxford World Conference

The Protestant German churches had long cooperated with the ecumenical movement, and when difficulties arose under the Third Reich, the church leaders were all the more eager to maintain ties with their foreign brethren.[102] In September, 1933, a delegation under the leadership of Dr. Theodor Heckel, soon to be named bishop and head of the Foreign Department of the German Evangelical church, attended the meeting of the executive committee of the Universal Christian Council for Life and Work at Novi Sad, Yugoslavia. Great efforts were made to keep discussions temperate, but nevertheless concern was expressed over the treatment of the Jews in Germany.[103] Heckel again headed the German delegation when the council met at Fanö, Denmark, in August, 1934. This time Karl Koch, president of the Confessing synod, and Dietrich Bonhoeffer, at that time pastor of the German Church in London, had been especially invited by the council to attend the meeting. The discussion on the situation in the German church became acrimonious, and a special delegate was sent from Berlin to uphold the cause. Nevertheless, the council endorsed resolutions which were definitely critical.[104]

The Fänö experience made future ecumenical meetings suspect in the eyes of Berlin officials, and there was always a problem as to who should act as representatives of the German Evangelical church—men from the Confessing church or men from the official church government. Yet no one wanted the German church cut off completely from the other churches of the world. The British, who were to host the meeting of the World Conference on Church, Community, and State at Oxford in 1937, were particularly concerned. Through the efforts of Bishop Bell of Chichester, it was decided to send a German delegation. In September, 1936, it was agreed that one-third of the members of the German delegation would be appointed by the Confessing church, one-third by the Luther Council, and one-third by the Reich Church Committee.[105] Under the direction of an official in the church government office in Berlin, a group of studies was published in preparation for the meeting.[106]

The resignation of the Reich Church Committee early in 1937, and increased harassment of the clergy, changed the situation. Early in 1937, Bishop Wurm proposed sending a letter to Hitler stating that it would be well for the German churches to be represented at Oxford, but that he would not go unless the restrictions on the churches were eased.[107] Instead of being lessened, they were increased. The passports of Niemöller, Dibelius, and some other Confessional church leaders chosen as delegates were seized.[108] The other Confessing church delegates, along with the delegates from the Luther Council, decided as a manifestation of unity that they would not attend if any delegates from the Confessing church were restricted. Knowing full well what he would be up against, Bishop Heckel of the church's foreign office, refused to go unless the heads of the three large Lutheran churches, Bishops Wurm, Meiser, and Marahrens, also went. When they refused, Heckel wrote Bishop Bell on June 9, 1937, that there would be no delegates at the conference from the Land churches, but that delegates from the Free churches were at liberty to attend if they wished. Two did show up at Oxford, June 12–26, 1937: Bishop Otto Melle of the Methodist church, and Paul Schmidt, director of the Federation of German Baptists. Professor R. Keussen, representing the Old Catholics, was also present, as were representatives from German churches in Latvia, Poland, Rumania, Yugoslavia, Austria, and Czechoslovakia, all of whom were in close communication with Bishop Heckel in Berlin.[109]

The Methodist church had long been divided into a Wesleyan congregational group with connections to Great Britain—largely in South Germany—and an Episcopal group with connections to the United States in North Germany. In 1887 the two groups united. The new united church had close ties with the Methodist church in the United States. The Methodists in Germany came to be grouped into five conferences, and were under the jurisdiction of the middle European bishop, regularly an American, with headquarters in Zürich. In 1936, the General Methodist

Conference, recognizing the centralizing and nationalistic designs of the

new Germany, permitted the German Methodists to organize their own Central Conference. Dr. Otto Melle, director of their theological seminary, became the first bishop, with headquarters in Berlin.[110]

The Methodists, like the other Free churches, had been left pretty much to their own devices by the Nazi authorities.[111] They were, after all, a small group, and like most other Germans supported the new order. Some of them felt that because of their foreign connections their patriotism was suspect, and they were often at pains to counter this impression. Bishop Melle took occasion at the Oxford conference to make a statement favorable to the National Socialist state.

The section of the conference dealing with church and state had early decided to send a message to the German Evangelical church, whose delegates, after helping plan the conference, had been prevented by the government from attending. A small committee was appointed to draft the message, and a special messenger was even sent on a hurried visit to Germany to consult with church leaders there. Bishop Melle and Paul Schmidt, who were in Oxford as representatives of the Free churches, were informed of the message and assured that it made no reference to the German government.[112] When the message was presented to the conference on June 19, it was accepted without a dissenting vote. After a reference to "mourn[ing] the absence of their brethren in the German Evangelical Church," the message went on:

> We are greatly moved by the afflictions of many pastors and laymen who have stood firm from the first in the Confessional church for the sovereignty of Christ, and for the freedom of the church of Christ to preach the gospel.
> We note the gravity of the struggle in which not your church alone, but the Roman Catholic Church as well, is engaged, against distortion and suppression of Christian witness, and for training of the young in a living faith in Jesus Christ as Son of God and King of kings and Lord of lords.[113]

The plan was to have the message delivered personally after the conference by a delegation going to Germany. However, Bishop Bell, who had much to do with the formulation of the message, took the precaution, "as a safeguard against any garbled versions which might appear in the press," to send the message to Bishop Heckel, who was in charge of foreign affairs in the official church administration, and to various other German churchmen.[114]

The next day Melle and Schmidt had second thoughts and submitted to the conference business committee a statement critical of the "Message to the German Churches" which the conference had adopted. In discussion with the business committee, they agreed that their statement need not be published provided it was entered in the conference minutes.[115] Nevertheless Melle and Schmidt did make the statement public, and the New York Times carried this excerpt:

> We are convinced that the message which is to be conveyed to the German Evangelical Church will not in its present form, be fitted to render its mediatory ministry. On the contrary, we believe it will tend to aggravate and

accentuate conflicting tendencies, especially as the Roman Catholic Church had been included in this message—a fact that is very baffling to us.

We therefore are compelled, after careful examination of the text, to declare we cannot approve of the message in question. We would ask the members of the conference to continue with us in the prayer that yesterday's message be not considered as the last word of the world conference to the Christians in Germany.[116]

Melle and Schmidt, although they had been informed of the general content of the "Message to the German Churches," had not been consulted in its drafting nor had they seen it before it was presented to the conference and hurriedly adopted. Their later protest may well have been the result of their careful study of the text, as they state, although Bell suspected that it was made as a result of a communication from Heckel's office in Berlin. Not only was Bell correct in regard to Heckel, but pressure was also brought by the German embassy in London.[117]

It was not this statement, but rather an address by Melle to the conference, that aroused attention. On July 21, the conference had "denounced the suppression of national minorities as a sin and a rebellion against God." It went on to declare unequivocally that "the deification of one's own people is a sin against God. . . . Discrimination of race and color can on no possible pretext have a place within [the] life [of the Christian church] if it is true to Christ."[118] It was clear that much of this statement was formulated with Germany in mind, and conditions there also formed the backdrop of Melle's address in which he stated:

> I have often been asked in these past days: what is the attitude of the Free churches towards the National Socialist state? To this question I can only answer that the churches joined together in the Union of Evangelical Free Churches are thankful for the complete freedom they have to preach the gospel of Christ and carry on their work of evangelization, care of souls, care of the needy, and strengthening their congregations. They have viewed the national resurrection of the German people as a manifestation of God's concern, they have directed their congregations in the critical days of change to the directional words of the apostle Paul on the position Christians should take towards the state according to Romans 13, and have sought to encourage loyal intercessory prayer for the government.
>
> With the prayers of intercession we have combined our thanks that God in his wisdom has sent a leader to whom it has been granted to ward off the danger of bolshevism in Germany, to overcome the despair brought by the war, the Treaty of Versailles and its consequences to seventy-seven million Germans, and to give to them a new faith in their mission and their future. I wish to God the churches had not failed, that God had been able to use them to perform a similar service.
>
> In the conflict which broke out in the German Land churches over the problem of how one could unite the twenty-eight Land churches into one national church, we remained neutral, even after the conflict later took another direction. We, however, of course suffered and continue to suffer from the results of this conflict, and along with the brethren of the other churches and all sincere Christians, bow our heads because of the neglect by Christians that could lead to such a judgment.[119]

From the point of view of the Free churches, the statement was neither extreme nor inaccurate, yet it was later blown up and caused much hard feeling. In Württemberg, notably in Stuttgart and Heilbronn, pastors of the Land church had for some time been meeting with Methodists, Baptists, and men from other Free churches for discussion and prayer—the co-called Alliance Meetings (*Allianzversammlungen*).[120] The pastors now asked the church authorities in Stuttgart if their meetings should be continued. The authorities advised against them, the general view being that if discussion and prayer were to be fruitful there must be a common feeling of unity. For Bishop Melle not to mention the wave of current arrests and the persecution the Protestant Land churches had suffered was too much to overlook. Bishop Wurm was absent when the decision was made, but on his return he backed up his administrative officers.[121]

Kerrl took the occasion to send Bishop Wurm a letter charging that "with this declaration the Supreme Church Council of Württemberg, as also the Confessing church, places itself at the side of the outspoken enemies of the German Reich and supports them in the battle against their own fatherland."[122] The letter was broadcast in the press and on the radio, but Wurm did not have great difficulty in refuting the charges that he was defaming a true German patriot; in fact, he had been careful not to attack Melle for his statements. Long letters and memoranda were submitted by various church leaders which found their way to the Foreign Office.[123]

In spite of the assurances of Bishop Melle the situation of the German churches aroused much concern among the churches abroad. The increasing number of arrests, particularly the arrest of Martin Niemöller, for his name was best known, led to many critical articles in the foreign press.

The Oath of Loyalty and the Prayer for Peace

Hitler was at this time not particularly concerned about church affairs.[124] He had begun to make specific plans for the territorial expansion of Germany. In November, 1937, he held a conference with his generals, the proceedings of which were recorded in the so-called Hossbach Protocol. He made clear that he planned to push Germany's frontiers eastward. Shortly thereafter, Foreign Minister von Neurath—a friend of the churches, particularly of his native Württemberg church—was replaced by Joachim von Ribbentrop. Field Marshal Werner Blomberg was replaced at the War Ofice, and Hitler tightened his personal control over military affairs. His first move was the annexation of Austria on March 13, 1938. At this time the Second Provisional Directory drew up a suggested prayer of thanksgiving to be used in the churches.

> Lord, our God, you lead our nation through decisive days of its history. You permit our German brothers in Austria to return to our German Reich. . . . Lord, we praise thy name and pray: lead our Führer and nation according to thy holy will, let thy grace expand over our whole German Evangelical church.[125]

The state-directed central office of the German Evangelical church issued an appeal for all Germans to approve the annexation in the plebiscite to be held on April 10. The Austrian Protestant church now officially became a member of the German Evangelical church, although it kept its special identity. For example, it was not accorded the right to finance itself by church taxes—it had to function as a Free church. Matters relating to the Austrian church were also dealt with separately in the Ministry of Church Afffairs.[126]

The annexation was a popular move, and served as a fillip to Hitler's prestige. The Thuringian church, followed by the Saxon and Mecklenburg churches, ordered all its clergy to take an oath of loyalty to Hitler.[127] Urged on by these churches, Dr. Werner of the national church office decreed on April 20, 1938—Hitler's birthday—that all clergy of the churches of the Old Prussian Union should take a similar oath. The question of a loyalty oath to the Führer had been successfully bypassed by the church in 1933–34, but it had been raised repeatedly since. In 1935, it had come to the fore when all professors were requested to take an oath and Karl Barth had refused to do so. At that time the First Provisional Directory had worked out a reservation which seemed to make it possible for those who had conscientious scruples to take the oath. The question, however, continued to make difficulties. The new requirement that all pastors who taught religion classes in the schools had to take an oath of loyalty to the Führer led to much dispute in Württemberg in 1937.[128] Now, as a present to the Führer, all pastors in the Prussian churches were to take the oath, and similar ordinances were soon issued in most of the Land churches of Germany.

The pastors one and all were on the spot, and most of them did take it—many of them no doubt being aware of the interpretation of the nature of a true oath made by the First Provisional Directory in 1936. Yet many still refused, and several synods occupied themselves with the problem. One of the points raised was whether the state was requiring the oath or whether it was simply a church ordinance.[129] The synods steadfastly maintained that all oaths were limited by the ordination pledge of a minister. It was finally established—or so they thought—that it was a state demand, and that a reservation respecting an ordination pledge was permissible. It seemed to be a compromise road out of a difficult and ticklish situation, and the Confessing Synod of the Old Prussian Union, on July 31, 1938, advised the pastors to take the oath.[130]

By this time the party had reached the decision that an oath was not a vital matter anyway. On June 2, Hess wrote Kerrl that Hitler had not been informed about demanding an oath of loyalty from the pastors, and he placed no value on it. "For an oath not only the will of the man taking it is necessary, but also the will of the man who receives it." As it was a matter of indifference to Hitler, any disciplinary action against anyone who refused to take it was precluded. Hess reminded Kerrl that the Führer was then very desirous that no church quarrels arise and new martyrs be created. He needed the united front of the people more than ever before. For this reason he had also ordered the cessation of trials of the Catholic clergy.[131]

On July 13, Bormann issued a statement to all Gauleiter in line with Hess's letter to Kerrl. The state and party did not care whether pastors took an oath of loyalty to the Führer; this was an internal church affair. He noted that Kerrl had ordered that no disciplinary action should be taken against those pastors who had refused to take it. It did not concern the party, and there must be no discrimination between those pastors who did and those who did not take such an oath. Bormann's directive became public on August 8, when it was published in the party press in Saxony.[132]

With this the tortuous oath problem as it related to pastors was only partially put to rest, for in some places the church authorities still tried to get those who had not taken the oath to do so. Actually, almost all clergy throughout Germany took it in one form or another.[133] To have the party declare that they did not care at all about a pastor's oath of loyalty must have brought chagrin to many a churchman who had spent long hours in exegesis of this difficult problem. The failure to require an oath was generally considered a defeat for the German Christians.

After the collapse of the church committees, no national leadership group recognized by both the Protestant churches and the state had emerged. The German Evangelical church constitution was still in existence, but like Reich Bishop Müller himself, was neglected in practice. The juridically trained officials in the Ministry of Church Affairs gradually extended their influence. Yet they did so with some tact and understanding, and many of the difficulties which arose with church authorities were settled by negotiation. Dr. Werner sympathized with the National Church Union wing of the German Christians and recognized their control of some of the Land churches. On the other hand, within the Ministry of Church Affairs there were officials of more neutral bent, and even one member of the Confessing church, Senior Consistoral Councillor Heinz Brunotte, who with the silent consent of his chief retained close connections with the Luther Council, the Church Leaders' Conference, and the Kassel Committee. He also acted as a regular adviser to Bishop Marahrens.[134] Not everything was a matter of conflict. It would be a truer picture to say that the Confessing churchmen held their position, and the Ministry of Church Affairs held its position—but this stalemate did not prevent talking together or carrying on necessary business.

During 1938, various draft proposals for establishing a new church administration on the basis of the church constitution of 1933 were advanced by people close to the Second Provisional Directory and the Church Leaders' Conference. These suggestions for reform tended towards recognizing two groups, the Confessing church and the German Christians, as two distinct entities, but they never got beyond draft proposals. Minister Kerrl, apparently encouraged by a conversation he had with Hitler, began to elaborate a new plan which would have created a "Spiritual Directory" to act within the Ministry of Church Affairs. But this proposal too was delayed, and was never completely worked out because of the Sudeten crisis of 1938 and a church incident connected with it.[135]

Even the most optimistic commentator would have had to characterize the political climate of Europe as unsettled in the summer of 1938. Clouds darkened, and on September 7, the Second Provisional Directory, as on earlier occasions, suggested an insertion in the general church prayer for the nation and government: "Safeguard us from dissension, insurrection, and war; check the spirit of hate, establish justice among the nations, and graciously bring to fruition all efforts for the preservation of peace."[136] This suggestion aroused no concern, but on September 27, with war seemingly inevitable, the Second Provisional Directory sent out to all Land churches and brotherhood councils an order of worship for a special prayer service to be held Friday, September 30. It consisted of a selection of hymns, scriptural passages, and numerous short prayers, a most effective and well-drafted liturgy. The directory suggested that its use be binding on all pastors. Last minute negotiations at Munich, however, removed the threat of war, and so the liturgy was used only in a few instances.[137] On October 27, a bitter criticism of the prayer liturgy and of the Confessing church appeared in the *Schwarze Korps,* the organ of the SA. The paper was particularly incensed over the opening prayer:

> Let us confess our sins to God and in belief in Jesus Christ our Lord pray for forgiveness:
> Lord our God, we poor sinners confess before thee the sins of our church, its administrations, its congregations and its shepherds. . . . We have tolerated altogether too much a false gospel. . . . We confess before Thee the sins of our people. Your name is derided among them, your word is attacked, your truth has been oppressed. Openly and in secret much injustice has taken place. Parents and people in authority were scorned, the life of the people infringed upon and disturbed, marriage ties broken, property seized and the honor of neighbors trespassed upon. Lord, our God, we lament before Thee our sins and the sins of our people. Forgive us and spare us your punishments. Amen.[138]

The last part of this prayer, which was reminiscent of the Ten Commandments, appeared to some to be an attack on the Third Reich and its leaders in the form of a confession.

Kerrl asked the church leaders to meet with him, and in a dudgeon attacked the liturgy. The distaste for the intercessory service had been heightened by a letter which Karl Barth wrote at the height of the crisis to Professor Josef Hromádka in Prague, and which had since become public. Barth, long a supporter of the Confessing church, wrote:

> I dare to hope that the sons of the Old Hussites will show somnolent old Europe that there are still men about. Every Czech soldier who fights and suffers will do this for us—and I say this without reservation—he will also do this for the Church of Jesus. . . . One thing, however, is certain: every possible human resistance must now be made at the borders of Czechoslovakia.[139]

His statement was too strong even for the members of the Confessing church; it was too reminiscent of a holy crusade. The Second Provisional Directory, in a letter to all church governments and brotherhood councils, disassociated itself and the Confessing church from Barth's statements.

> We know that the freedom of the church of Jesus Christ rests alone in the will of the heavenly Father. Therefore it is forbidden to Christians to summon anyone to arms to defend Christ's church. The church itself has far more the task at such times of calling to prayer—that God will give the gift of earthly peace and permit right and justice to reign among the nations.[140]

There can be no doubt that Barth's statement heightened the crisis over the liturgy. In a meeting on October 29, 1938, Kerrl pressured the church leaders, notably the bishops of the large Lutheran intact churches, to disassociate themselves not only from the liturgy, but also from the circles responsible for drawing it up. The first was not particularly difficult. The bishops had not been consulted about its formulation, and objections could be raised against it on theological grounds if one chose to look for points of disagreement. It did tend to mix religious and political matters, and as Marahrens put it, "You can't pray to God and at the same time give the impression that you are also directing your petitions to an earthly address."[141] However, the bishops refused to sign the formula Kerrl had prepared which would have charged the people who had drawn up the liturgy with treason. To have done so would have placed them in a united front with the Thuringian German Christians. Nevertheless, they knuckled under on the issue itself. They disassociated themselves from the liturgy and from the people who were responsible for it, but not from the Confessing church and those in it working towards a new structuring of the German Evangelical church on a confessional basis.

That the bishops waited to declare their opposition to the liturgy until pressured by Kerrl was generally held against them.[142] On the other hand, the Church-Theological Society within the Württemberg church issued a pronouncement criticizing Wurm's action and upholding the theological appropriateness of the liturgy.[143] Wurm felt called upon to issue an explanatory statement to his churchmen, and writes in his memoirs:

> In pique over the disturbance caused by the action of the Dahlem group, we made a mistake. In spite of the pressure of the minister [Kerrl], we should have left the matter with the explanation that we had no responsibility for this step. But none of us had in this hour the internal fortitude to do and to declare what would have been right. There are such hours, where the powers of darkness are greater than those of light, and we must humble ourselves because of them before God and man.[144]

Although forced by circumstances during the winter of 1938–39 to consult with the Second Provisional Directory and the brotherhood councils on many questions, it was not until nearly two years later (September 11, 1940) that Bishops Wurm and Meiser formally notified the Ministry of Church Affairs that they no longer felt bound by their declaration of October 29, 1938, and would again cooperate on all matters with the members of the Second Provisional Directory.[145] Bishop Marahrens, however, never conceded that he had been in error in the dispute.[146]

During the five-hour meeting with Kerrl in October, 1938, when Meiser remonstrated that they should be given time to consult with the men who had drawn up the liturgy, he was cut short with the remark that there was no longer time, for they were probably at that very moment being arrested. Indeed, all members of the Second Provisional Directory responsible for sending out the prayer liturgy were suspended and their salaries stopped. Superintendent Martin Albertz and Pastor Fritz Müller were actually unfrocked by the official disciplinary authority of the church, but this action did not lessen their standing among their fellow pastors of the Confessing church, and the Second Provisional Directory continued to function. Most of these penalties subsequently were rescinded during the war.[147]

The incidents of the liturgy and of Barth's letter had deep and lasting repercussions, which again brought dissent and recrimination within the ranks of the Confessing church. Kerrl never could grasp the serious religious concern of the men who called for the special prayer service. He and others in the government and party broke what tenuous ties still existed with the so-called Dahlem wing of the Confessing church. He did try to work further with the bishops of the intact churches, but since they insisted that they had broken ties only with certain men, not with the Confessing church as a whole, this cooperation was not very fruitful.

It is no wonder that at this time Göring confessed to Charles A. Lindbergh that he had "told Hitler he would be willing to take on any problem in Germany except the religious problem, but that he did not know how to solve the religious problem."[148] Neither did anyone else, and diverse policies were followed. While Rudolf Hess had his child named in a folk ceremony, Göring had his daughter baptized by Reich Bishop Müller, with Hitler acting as godfather. The followers of Rosenberg and other extremists were dismayed by this display of religiosity, but the ambivalent policy of the party and state towards the churches was to continue.[149]

Further Attempts at a Church-State Settlement

At the end of October, 1938, Kerrl proposed a new plan for reorganizing the church. There were to be three authorities. One was to take care of the juridical administration of the German Evangelical church as a corporation under public law, and would be headed by the church chancellery; the internal affairs of the church were to be left to a synod which would be constituted on the basis of the constitution of July 11, 1933; and a secular administration would be established to supervise disciplinary matters and regulate relations to the National Socialist state and the German folk. In general, Kerrl's proposal was grounded on the conception of separating "secular-juridical" and "spiritual-theological" governmental functions. Men in the church chancellery set about drawing up lists of "internal" (spiritual) affairs, and "external" (administrative) affairs. Since it was impossible to fit everything into these two classifications, they set up a third group; *res mixtae* ("common affairs"). They made a noble attempt at classification, but their proposals would never have found acceptance, for the Confessing church always—and quite correctly—held that the government of the church could not be divided.[150]

The Church Leaders' Conference, to which the proposal was sent, pointed out that the plan—which was drawn up by men of the middle and sought to unite the German Christian controlled churches and the others into one organization—would not lead to a permanent solution. Kerrl rejected their protest.[151] Nevertheless, the church leaders continued to work on a counter-proposal consulting men of other church groups who were not represented in the conference, particularly the Organization of Pastors (*Pfarrerverein*) under the leadership of Church Councillor Dr. Klinger in Nürnberg. On January 11, 1939, this plan was submitted to Kerrl. It was subsequently circulated among all Evangelical pastors by the Pfarrerverein. 10,693 (71 percent of the total number) answered the questionnaire, and of these 10,081 approved.[152] In short, two-thirds of the pastors favored the new proposal, a remarkable expression of support considering the general church situation in Germany. The church leaders insisted that the basic provision of the church constitution that the national church is a federation of churches based on the historic confessions be observed, and that the pastors and laity be given a substantial role in church affairs. But the proposal by the churchmen was unacceptable to Kerrl, and he turned his attention to another scheme.

This scheme was to get all the church administrators to sign a declaration of principles which would manifest their unity and express the relationship of politics and religion, of National Socialist Weltanschauung and Christian belief. The statement was worked out by ministry officials and Thuringian church leaders. It was impregnated by German Christian theology. This Godesberg Declaration of April, 1939, taking its name from the place where it was drawn up, was signed by Dr. Werner for the Evangelical Church of the Old Prussian Union and by representatives of the churches of Saxony, Nassau-Hesse, Schleswig-Holstein, Thuringia, Mecklenburg, Palatinate, Anhalt, Oldenburg, Lübeck, and Austria.[153] If these church administrators ally spoke for all the people within their jurisdictions, it v. ... d ...ve meant that about three-fourths of the Evangelical Christians had adhered to the Godesberg Declaration. This was far from the case. The church governments in these states had remained under the control of German Christians long after the movement lost its significance among the people at large. The Confessing church, which had congregations everywhere, did not accept the declaration. Even Dr. Petersmann, head of the Luther-German wing of the German Christians, expressed his reservations. That Mathilde Ludendorff of the German Faith Movement spoke enthusiastically for the Godesberg Declaration did not help its acceptance in orthodox church circles.

The signers of the Godesberg Declaration immediately issued a sharp denunciation of the archbishop of Canterbury, who had joined with the leaders of the Russian church in a call for common action for the furtherance of peace after the German occupation of Prague on March 15, 1939. That the archbishop would join hands with Bolsheviks in a scarcely veiled action against Germany was scandalous, and called for refutation by a renewed pledge of loyalty to Hitler.[154] A few weeks later, on the Wartburg in Eisenach, a place hallowed by Luther's confinement, they inaugurated the Institute for Research on Jewish Influence on the Life of the German Church.[155] It was to be headed by a director and outfitted with all the trappings customary to German scientific centers. A surprisingly large number of academicians put themselves at the disposal of the institute, which issued numerous thick volumes of proceedings and prepared a revised version of the New Testament (published in an edition of 200,000 copies in early 1941). It omitted terms such as "Jehovah," "Israel," "Zion," and "Jerusalem," which were considered to be Jewish; it seemed to them merely a matter of translating Hebraic words much as Luther had translated Latin![156]

In an effort to get a statement more acceptable to the Church Leaders' Conference, Kerrl recast the Godesberg Declaration into five statements on the reorganization of the church. It was much more moderate in tone, full of references to Luther and the necessity of supporting the state. There was nevertheless a reference to the antagonism between Judaism and Christianity: "an earnest and responsible racial policy for maintaining the integrity of the folk is approved."[157] Kerrl approached Bishop Marahrens as head of the conference, and apparently convinced him of the desirability of getting some sort of statement signed which would appease the party hierarchy. It was to be considered more a political than a theological statement. When Marahrens brought it before the conference, the majority did not see it in this light, and they undertook a reformulation of the five points. Kerrl bluntly refused to accept this new version, and stated he could only undertake the promised reforms in church organization if his original statement were accepted. Apparently convinced that this was a last chance to achieve a settlement, Bishop Marahrens (Hanover-Lutheran), Bishop Helmut Johnsen of Brunswick, and Pastor Karlheinz Happich, chairman of the Land church committee of Electoral Hesse-Waldeck, signed the original statement, adding some minor explanatory commentary. Kerrl threatened Bishop Franz Tügel of the Hamburg church with removal from office if he did not sign, but Tügel refused.[158]

With this action, Marahrens drew a line between himself and Bishops Wurm and Meiser, with whom he had worked closely in the past months. He also destroyed the unity of the Luther Council, although it continued to function. Wurm and Meiser issued a statement explaining why they could not sign Kerrl's statement, and the pastors of the brotherhood council in Hanover criticized their bishop's action. It was a most unfortunate incident, and after the war, although in general he firmly upheld his compromising policies, Marahrens confessed that he had erred in signing Kerrl's proposals.[159]

As was to be expected, the Second Provisional Directory and the
Confessing Synod of the Old Prussian Union denounced both the Godesberg Declaration and the statements subsequently formulated by
Kerrl, and so did the the Reformed Confederation for Germany. The
embryo World Council of Churches showed its concern by a statement
opposing the Godesberg Declaration, which led to a protest from
Bishop Heckel of the Church Foreign Office that the council had over-
stepped its competence. This was but a minor tit for tat, but it indicates
clearly that the position of the German Evangelical church in the ecumenical movement, instead of improving, had steadily declined since
1933.[160]

While these discussions, which were supposed to inaugurate a reorganization of the German churches, were taking place, the day-to-day
life of the church, with its incessant harassment by police and state
authorities, continued. There was no uniform policy. In places the
churches could function fairly freely; salaries were paid regularly by the
official church authorities. But the special funds established by the
Reich Brotherhood Council, by the two Provisional Directories, and by
the Luther Council, were hard pressed to aid pastors whose salaries had
been suspended, to subsidize families of pastors who were in prison,
and to deal with the countless other claims upon them. When the
authorities refused funds, the congregations tried to meet the needs with
freewill offerings.[161] In general the finance sections were extending their
powers, but not everywhere did this lead to great difficulties. In the
summer of 1939, however, a crisis occurred in the Church of the Rhineland. The Reichsleiter, who was in charge of the financial section, made
a determined effort to get all church collections delivered to him. This
had long been the law, but pastors in many instances still sent them in
to the Confessing church authorities. Now, if they continued, their salaries were to be impounded. The Confessing Church Synod of the Rhineland protested indignantly, which, however, brought no immediate relief. An agreement on the collection funds was finally reached during
the war. There were also new difficulties about the examination and
appointment of ministerial candidates. In Württemberg, the conflict over
religious education in the schools again raised its ugly head.[162]

In an effort to bring about more cooperation among all church
groups and ease his administrative tasks, Dr. Werner called a meeting of
the Church Leaders' Conference for August 29. There he asked the
conference to name a special Spiritual Confidential Council (*Geistliche
Vertrauensrat*) of leading men of the church to advise him on matters
regarding the responsibility of the German Evangelical Church to the
Führer, folk, and state. The conference complied, naming Bishop Marahrens of Hanover (Lutheran), Bishop Walter Schultz of Mecklenburg
(German Christian) and Senior Consistorial Councillor Friedrich Hym-
men of the Old Prussian Union; later Otto Weber, representing the
Reformed, joined the council.[163] It never developed into an important
body, but it did perform some useful service during the first years of the
war that Hitler unleashed with his attack on Poland, September 1, 1939.

12.

The Catholic Church
and the Accession
of Hitler

The Bishops' Statement

Eight days after Hitler became chancellor, Ambassador Diego von Bergen at the Vatican reported that it was not to be expected that the pope would take a position in regard to Hitler's assumption of office. The *Osservatore Romano,* which had close relations with the Vatican, restricted itself to mentioning only the course of events and pointing out that all had gone on in constitutional fashion. Bergen, however, remarked that Hitler's appeal to God in his radio address to the nation, his assurances that the government would take Christianity as the basis for the total reconstruction of the nation, his support of the family as the foundation of the folk, and his declaration that he would combat bolshevism had all made a good impression.[1] These statements and the other proreligious manifestations of the government in the first weeks were not without their effect on the Catholic hierarchy in Germany. Yet they kept silence, and continued their active support of the Center and the Bavarian People's parties in the elections of March 5, 1933. The Center even gained three seats in the election, while the Bavarian People's party lost only one; there manifestly was no landslide of Catholics to the National Socialist party. The people had spoken and accepted Hitler, at least for the present, as head of the government, but this did not as yet make them all Nazis.

The church hierarchy was now confronted with a ticklish problem. They had long denounced the Nazi party and its philosophy, but how could they decry a National Socialist government which had won power in what was then generally accepted as constitutional fashion? Upholding legitimate governmental authority was rooted deeply in Catholic faith and doctrine. Cardinal Bertram of Breslau, as head of the Fulda Bishops' Conference, decided to place the concern of the bishops before President Hindenburg. In a letter of March 10, he wrote:

> We as bishops are particularly concerned whether the movement which has achieved power will call a halt before the holiness of the church and before the position of the church in public life. . . . [That the position which the church and its institutions] have attained will be subject to the gravest

dangers during the present disturbed period is the fear which besets wide circles of the Catholic population. The hour has come when we must turn to the head of the state with an urgent plea for the protection of the church and its life and activity. May our call not go unheard.[2]

Hindenburg, in acknowledging the letter, said he not only had forwarded the letter to the chancellor, but also would discuss these issues with him.

Perhaps it was as a result of this initiative that Vice-chancellor von Papen, who as a Catholic was anxious to win the support of the hierarchy, visited Cardinal Bertram on March 18. He asked if the bishops would not revise their position towards national socialism, but was told that the one who should revise his position was the leader of the National Socialists. The local clergy, however, were pressing the hierarchy for some guidelines, and Cardinal Bertram proposed a draft of such directions to his fellow bishops. His letter reiterated the position taken the previous year—that in cases of duress and confusion, adherence to national socialism would not be held against Catholics. Demonstrations by the party or its organizations in churches were still undesirable; the ban on SA or SS participation at services was thus still upheld. The answers of the bishops to this proposal are not available, but at least the cardinals of Trier and Cologne felt the statement was not broad enough. Archbishop Conrad Gröber of Freiburg, Bishop Konrad Preysing of Eichstätt, and Bishop Michael Buchberger of Regensburg had serious reservations and advised further consideration.[3]

The rapid pace of events soon altered the situation. On March 20–22, Hitler held intensive conversations with leaders of the Center party in which he promised not to abolish the states, to respect the state concordats, the confessional schools, and religious instruction, and agreed to other demands, among them that he would mention these points in his opening speech to the Reichstag on March 23. He kept his word, and his statements on that occasion did much to appease both Catholic and Protestant leaders.[4] The same evening, the Center party voted for the Enabling Act which gave Hitler power to enact ordinary legislation by decree. He could also conclude international agreements on matters of Reich jurisdication without submitting them to parliament for approval. There were some safeguards in the law, but they soon became a dead letter.[5]

Cardinal Faulhaber, head of the Munich-Freising Bishops' Conference, on March 24 addressed a letter to the bishops of his conference and to the archbishop of Bamberg, expressing the view that a more positive statement by the bishops for the guidance of the clergy than Cardinal Bertram's was necessary. While in Rome, Faulhaber had attended a consistory on March 13, where the pope, in an obvious reference to Hitler, praised German opposition to bolshevism. Faulhaber had also had a private audience with the pope. What was said there is unknown, but it is highly probable that the pope spoke words favoring accommodation to the new Germany. In any case, Faulhaber wrote to his bishops:

I must, after what I have encountered at the highest places in Rome—which I cannot communicate to you now—reserve to myself, in spite of everything, more toleration towards the new government which today not only is in a position of power—which our formulated principles could not reverse—but which has achieved this power in a legal fashion incomparable with any other revolutionary power. Just consider for a moment the implications of the words of the Holy Father, who in a consistory, without mentioning a name, publicly designated (vor aller Welt) Adolf Hitler as the first statesman, aside from the Holy Father, who raised his voice against bolshevism.[6]

Faulhaber asked them to consider the draft of a public statement which he had drawn up in the light of Hitler's declaration of the previous day.

At the same time, on Faulhaber's suggestion, Cardinal Bertram also sent a draft of a public statement to all German bishops, requesting those of the Munich-Freising conference to report their views to Munich, and those of the Fulda conference to report to Breslau. The Fulda bishops approved Bertram's draft with some minor emendations, and many bishops urged him to wait "no hour more" in issuing it. Under these circumstances, Bertram asked the Bavarians to accept his statement, for it was really impossible to consider any special requests they might have.[7] Haste was the order of the day all over Germany, and the bishops too had became infected with this spirit. The common bishops' statement was published in the various dioceses on March 28–30.

In light of the recent assurances of the Führer in respect to Catholic religious rights and the maintenance of the state concordats, the bishops declared:

> Without revoking the judgment made in our previous declarations in respect to certain religious-ethical errors, the episcopate believes it can cherish the confidence that the designated general prohibitions and warnings need no longer be considered necessary. For Catholic Christians, to whom the voice of the church is sacred, it is not necessary at the present moment to make special admonition to be loyal to the lawful government and to fulfill conscientiously the duties of citizenship, rejecting on principle all illegal or subversive behavior.[8]

The bishops' frequent admonitions to work for peace and support the social welfare of the people, to further religion and the rights of the church, and to support the various Catholic organizations remained in effect. The warning not to turn religious services or manifestations into political demonstrations was renewed.

All in all, it was a rather modest and conservative statement. It lifted the ban against national socialism, but it did not urge people to join the party. It is a statement of toleration and of accommodation, not one of collaboration. It was designed to make it possible for Catholics, overcome with the enthusiasm of the moment, to remain within the church. As Cardinal Bertram in suggesting the announcement pointed out, Catholic SA members, since they were unwelcome in Catholic churches, commanded by their leaders were streaming into Protestant churches.[9] The practice would increase, and something should be done to stop it. The restrictions on administering sacraments to National Socialists, on their attendance at church services in uniform, and on church dedication and display of Nazi flags were gradually set aside. No one in the hierarchy wanted to lay down the gauntlet to the regime and run the danger of loosing a Kulturkampf. It seemed best to try to get along with the legally established authorities, and not to maintain roadblocks in the rush towards German regeneration that was to end the dangers of communism. There was no renunciation of the Center party in the statement, and had the Center party leaders themselves not consented to bow to the dissolution of their party, the hierarchy would no doubt have continued to give it their support.

Negotiation of the Reich Concordat

The bishops' statement was well received by most German Catholics. Now they could cooperate in the stirring events of the day without qualms and shout with all the rest, "Heil Hitler." To win a favorable word from the bishops was no doubt a bright feather in the cap of the Nazi officials, for they were also winning acclaim at this time from Protestant leaders. Vice-chancellor von Papen obtained the consent of the Führer to seek further kudos by concluding a concordat. Hitler apparently was not very optimistic about the prospects of his success, but von Papen was allowed to go ahead.[10] While chancellor (June-November, 1932) he had been kept informed of the negotiations in regard to an exempt army bishop, and the demands of the pope made in return had seemed reasonable to him.[11]

At the beginning of April, 1933, von Papen and Monsignor Ludwig Kaas, head of the Center party, travelled together to Rome, ostensibly for an Easter visit.[12] Before he left, von Papen had been supplied by Councillor Fritz Menshausen of the Foreign Office with a memorandum surveying the discussions since 1920 concerning a concordat, the 1924 draft and 1926 guidelines for a proposed concordat, the papal pro memoria of October 25, 1932, and the two drafts of the proposed reply which had just been considered by experts from various departments. Von Papen confided to Menshausen that one of the chief demands he would make would be "to include a provision contained also in the Italian concordat, to the effect that the clergy are forbidden to register and be active in any political party."[13] Von Papen found the curia—which after all had been carrying on concordat discussions in one form or another with Germany ever since the close of World War I—receptive to his advances. Minister President Göring was also in Rome, and he shared in some of these early discussions.[14]

On April 18, von Papen returned to Berlin, but Kaas stayed in Rome, where he was to become one of the most trusted advisors to the curia until his death in 1952. Long a go-between in the German government's negotiations with the Vatican, he now played a most significant part in concluding the concordat.[15] He had participated in the discussions that von Papen held with Cardinal Pacelli on April 15, when von Papen had outlined the draft of a concordat (based on earlier drafts of the 1920s) which he had brought with him. Suggestions were made for additional provisions in regard to an oath of loyalty, prayers for the state, the removal of clergy from politics, the problem of marriages in case of moral emergencies, protection of minorities, the problem of the chaplaincy in the armed services, and matters regarding diplomatic missions. On the basis of these discussions, Kaas was asked to work out a new draft. He forwarded this to von Papen on April 20.[16]

Hitler also did his part. On April 26, he received Bishop Dr. Wilhelm Berning of Osnabrück and Vicar General Prelate Dr. Johannes Steinmann, adviser to the German embassy in Rome, who came as delegates from a conference of diocesan representatives. They raised four concerns of the Catholic Church: "(1) the freedom of the church, (2) the freedom of the Catholic schools, (3) the independence of Catholic associations, and (4) the dismissal of Catholic officials because of their Catholic ideology or their past activity in and for the Center party."[17] Hitler's assuring statements make strange reading today. The prelates could hardly have expected more favorable answers to any of their questions, or a more fervent adherence to Christianity as the foundation of the state. Hitler emphasized again that he attached the greatest importance to cooperation with the Catholic church and spoke of himself as a Catholic.

> I am absolutely convinced of the great power and the deep significance of the Christian religion, and consequently will not permit any other founders of religion (*Religionsstifter*). Therefore I have turned against Ludendorff and separated myself from him; therefore I reject Rosenberg's book. That book is written by a Protestant. It is not a party book. It is not written by him as a member of the party. The Protestants can settle matters with him.
> My desire is that no confessional conflict arise. I must act correctly to both confessions. I will not tolerate a Kulturkampf. . . . I stand by my word. I will protect the rights and freedom of the church and will not permit them to be touched. You need have no apprehensions concerning the freedom of the church.

In regard to schools, a matter of utmost importance to the Catholic hierarchy, Hitler went on:

> Secular schools can never be tolerated because such a school has no religious instruction and a general moral instruction without a religious foundation is built on air; consequently, all character training and religion must be derived from faith. From our point of view as representatives of the state, we need believing people. A dark cloud threatens from Poland. We have need of soldiers, believing soldiers. Believing soldiers are the most valuable ones. They give their all. Therefore we will maintain the confessional schools in order to train believing people through the schools, but this depends upon having truly believing teachers, not by chance Marxists who do not stand fully by their religious faith, as teachers.[18]

Hitler requested that his remarks be treated confidentially but said that the other bishops might be informed of them. Minister Rust, Minister President Göring, and Vice-chancellor von Papen, with whom Berning also spoke, made similar statements.[19] In much the same vein, Hitler on April 28 wrote a long letter to Cardinal Bertram.[20] It was a reply to letters Bertram had written to various officials, including President Hindenburg and the chancellor himself.

The same day that he granted Berning and Steinmann an interview, Hitler, with von Papen, went over the draft of the concordat submitted by Kaas. Proposed changes, article by article, were then submitted to Kaas, who discussed them with Pacelli and submitted a revised draft to Berlin. This in turn elicited detailed textual changes, Hitler being particularly concerned about the article dealing with the political activity of the clergy. Von Papen had kept Foreign Minister von Neurath informed of what was taking place, but the Foreign Office and Ambassador Bergen in Rome had pretty much stood aside. Von Neurath, while content that von Papen and Kaas should continue to carry out the negotiations, now insisted that Bergen be kept informed. This was henceforth done.[21]

Bergen, however, felt that the negotiations had already reached a point which made it impossible for him to have any significant influence on them. The pressure for a speedy conclusion of the concordat had led the government to make too many concessions. As he wrote privately to von Neurath: "The merit for concluding the concordat and the responsibility for the extent of the agreed-upon concessions *cannot* be charged to our [Foreign Office] account."[22] He did nevertheless submit his views on desirable changes in the draft concordat, and was generally helpful in carrying forward the negotiations.

The officials at the Vatican were particularly occupied toward the end of May with events connected with the Holy Year, and Monsignor Kaas found it difficult to carry on the concordat discussions. The Vatican also wanted to await the outcome of the Fulda Bishops' Conference on May 30, to which the draft of the concordat was submitted for study. The bishops approved the concordat in general, but submitted their own draft for the article dealing with Catholic organizations. They also desired to have a provision inserted which would free the clergy from military duty should universal service be again enforced in Germany. Kaas, in forwarding their wishes to Berlin, saw nothing in the bishops' proposals which would ban final agreement, and suggested the addition of a secret annex to cover the matter of military service. Meanwhile, the Foreign Office also had suggested certain changes in the draft submitted by Monsignor Kaas on May 11.[23] It had been thoroughly gone over, and both sides were well prepared when von Papen returned to Rome for further across-the-table discussions with Pacelli.[24]

Final agreement was reached in four sessions. Ambassador Bergen, on the express wish of von Papen, accompanied him at all discussions with Cardinal Secretary Pacelli; Monsignor Kaas was present at the last three, and Archbishop Gröber of Freiburg, whom Pacelli summoned by telephone, shared in the last two.[25] Bergen, reporting on the negotiations, wrote: "I myself stated a number of times that I was not participating in the negotiations, and intervened in the debate only when general questions came up for discussion and it seemed advisable to second Herr von Papen, in particular in warding off attacks."[26] He had nothing but praise for the "skill and verve" with which the vice-chancellor had carried on the negotiations, and repeatedly called attention to Kaas's loyal cooperation.

On July 3, a special courier took the new concordat draft, which had the approval of the cardinal secretary and the pope, to Berlin. Hitler again had done his bit to help out by making promises. In a report sent along with the draft, von Papen wrote:

> I must not conceal from you, Chancellor, that the reports at hand here at the Vatican regarding the numerous arrests and abusive treatment of clergymen, the confiscation of diocesan property, etc., had brought about a frame of mind which made the conclusion of this concordat very difficult. However, on the basis of your telephoned instruction of yesterday, I informed the Cardinal Secretary of State that you, Chancellor, would be willing after the conclusion of the concordat to arrange for a thorough and full pacification between the Catholic portion of the people and the Reich Government or the Länder governments, and that you would be willing to put a finish to the story of past political developments. I myself am convinced that the conclusion of this concordat must be considered a great success in foreign policy for the government of the National Uprising, precisely because a number of foreign powers have exerted their full influence at the Vatican to keep it from concluding a treaty with the new Germany. I also believe, however, that the conclusion of the treaty will introduce an era of pacification that will in a high degree assist the great work of inner national unification.[27]

No doubt with an eye towards furthering approval of the concordat draft in Berlin, von Papen, late on July 3, informed von Neurath: "In the discussion which I had with Pacelli, Archbishop Gröber, and Kaas this evening, it developed that with the conclusion of the concordat, the dissolution of the Center party is regarded here as certain and is approved."[28] The Center party did actually dissolve itself on July 5.

Von Papen pressed for an early answer so that he could initial the treaty and start home. In this atmosphere of urgency Hitler, Foreign Minister von Neurath, Minister of the Interior Frick, and Finance Minister Schwerin-Krosigk examined in detail the draft of the concordat on July 4 and 5.[29] Hitler had asked Director Rudolf Buttmann of the Ministry of the Interior to study the draft and prepare a memorandum on proposed changes.[30] Numerous textual alterations were made by Hitler and his ministers, and on the afternoon of July 5 Buttmann started for Rome with the revised draft.[31] It was discussed with von Papen the next day, and that evening sent to the cardinal secretary. On July 7, Pacelli, Gröber, von Papen, Kaas, and Buttmann met in the cardinal secretary's large office.[32] Von Papen and Gröber sat on a divan, with Buttmann and Kaas sitting on chairs to the right and left of Pacelli. The latter began by citing new incidents of antichurch manifestations in Germany, and Buttmann put himself out to change the cardinal's state of mind. He stressed the need for careful consideration of the text, so that a true and lasting peace between Germany and the Holy See could be arranged, and added: "The intrigue of the *Temps* and the American Associated Press were the result of the machinations by the Free Masons and the Jews, who wanted to cause difficulties between us, for they see in us both their most dangerous opponent."[33] "That flattered [Pacelli] noticeably," Buttmann noted in his report, "and we could begin."

They then went over the concordat article by article, and hammered out a new final draft. It was typed up that evening, and von

Papen telephoned Berlin for approval of the final text. This was obtained, and on July 8 the concordat was initialed.[34] Few treaties, certainly no concordats, have ever been put together so rapidly.

July 8 was a Saturday, and the Sunday papers brought news of the concordat. On Monday Hitler issued a statement which had been approved by the Vatican. The conclusion of the concordat gave him sufficient guarantee that the Roman Catholic citizens of the Reich would henceforth unreservedly place themselves in the service of the state. He therefore rescinded the dissolution of those Catholic organizations now recognized by the concordat, which, he pointed out, had been dissolved without directives from the Reich government. Moreover, all coercive measures taken against the clergy and other leaders of these organizations were to be cancelled, and any such actions in the future would be punished according to existing laws. The agreement, he felt, would serve the establishment of peace in this era, and he expressed the hope that it would soon be completed by the settlement of pending questions with the Protestants.[35]

Hitler was then at his hideaway near Berchtesgaden, and Buttmann stopped off on July 10 to brief him on the concordat.[36] All went well, and Hitler was well primed to push the concordat through the cabinet meeting scheduled for July 14. Frick, who had reservations about it, proposed some changes. Von Papen argued against them, but in turn proposed a couple of minor textual alterations. Hitler, stressing that "one should see only the great success," refused to permit a debate on the particulars of the concordat. "In the Reich concordat Germany had been given a chance, and an area of confidence had been created which was particularly significant in the urgent fight against the international Jews. Possible shortcomings in the concordat could be rectified later, when the foreign policy situation was better." He saw "three great advantages in the conclusion of the Reich concordat."

1. That the Vatican had negotiated at all, while they operated, especially in Austria, on the assumption that National Socialism was un-Christian and inimical to the Church.

2. That the Vatican could be persuaded to bring about a good relationship with this purely national German state. He, the Reich Chancellor, would not have considered it possible even a short time ago that the Church would be willing to obligate the bishops to this state. The fact that this had now been done was certainly an unreserved recognition of the present regime.

3. That with the concordat, the Church withdrew from activity in associations and parties, e.g., also abandoned the Christian labor unions. This, too, he, the Reich Chancellor, would not have considered possible even a few months ago. Even the dissolution of the Center could be termed final only with the conclusion of the concordat, now that the Vatican had ordered the permanent exclusion of priests from party politics.

That the objective which he, the Reich Chancellor, had always been striving for, namely an agreement with the Curia, had been attained so much faster than he had imagined even on January 30; this was such an indescribable success that all critical misgivings had to be withdrawn in the face of it.[37]

From Hitler's remarks it is clear that Monsignor Kaas was wrong when he told Rev. Alois Eckert on August 13, 1933:

Do you know, Reverend Sir, that originally they [the German government] didn't want a real concordat? They thought of something like a "military chaplaincy treaty" that they then could blow up to a so-called concordat for political purposes. We, however, kept them firmly to a consideration of one article after another. Do you realize that they came to a concordat the way a girl comes to an illegitimate child, in other words accidentally![38]

Pastor Eckert reports that Kaas felt he had brought this about through his diplomatic ability, and in good spirits the two men drank a toast.

The Führer having spoken, agreement was soon reached at the cabinet meeting, and the concordat was approved with only three minor changes in wording. Meanwhile, the Ministry of the Interior, on July 17, had come to an amicable agreement with Archbishop Gröber and Bishop Berning, as representatives of the bishops, on the interpretation of Article 31. Purely religious organizations were to be permitted to regulate themselves; organizations which also served other purposes could, but need not, be coordinated with general state organizations. In either case they should be permitted to retain their Catholic character and their own organizational setup, including the right to use their customary uniforms, insignia, and banners. In all it was an interpretation very friendly to the church, and Pacelli later stated that this had led to the signing of the concordat.[39]

At the last minute a difficulty arose. The pope discovered that a clause on which he placed great weight, one dealing with state property devoted to purposes of the church, had vanished from the concordat. Hurried telephone calls to Berlin from Kaas, from the German embassy in Rome, and even from Pacelli eventually brought a solution. The cabinet had gone on vacation and Hitler was in Obersalzberg. Regulations demanded that the cabinet approve any changes in the text. Buttmann telephoned Hitler, who authorized him to make the desired papal change in the final protocol without a new cabinet meeting. Buttmann recounted the episode in a letter to his wife, and added the laconic comment: "That is no doubt the first time in German legal history that such an adamant regulation has been broken, but what does not go today?"[40] Germany was in the Third Reich.

On July 20 the concordat was formally signed by von Papen and Pacelli. It was well that Buttmann, who was a member of the German party, requested that the text be read before it was signed, for a misplaced line and an omitted word were discovered in the German text. Gifts were exchanged at the time of signature. Pacelli received a Meissen Madonna, Cardinal Giuseppi Pizzardo an oil landscape of the Park at Sanssouci by Franck, and Cardinal Alfredo Ottaviani a silver platter, which he immediately spirited away, all with an inscription by the German government. In addition the embassy made a customary gift of 25,000 lire to the Vatican for charitable purposes. Von Papen received an order, and a similar one was promised to Buttmann, who in the meantime received a picture of the Pope in a silver frame.[41] Ratifications were still to be exchanged.

The same day that the concordat was signed, Hitler, "to his regret," declined the bishop of Trier's invitation to the exhibition of the famous Holy Cloak. Because of cabinet vacations no official representative of the government could attend.[42] Clearly Hitler was not anxious to put the Catholicism of his government on parade.

Terms of the Concordat

The concordat consists of a preamble, thirty-four articles dealing with specific issues, a final protocol carrying explanatory statements to some of the articles, and a secret annex regulating the induction of theological students and regular and secular clergy into the armed services in the event of universal military service.[43] The concordat is not unlike the other concordats of the modern era. There are the usual guarantees of the freedom of religion, the rights of the church to administer its own affairs, and the regulation of diocesan boundaries and appointment of clergy. The concordat contained what is usually referred to as the "political clause," which obligated the church before appointing a bishop to inquire of state authorities if they had any political objection against the individual.[44] This was a customary provision of nineteenth-century concordats, although strictly interpreted it was contrary to a section of Article 137 of the Weimar Constitution: "Every religious association . . . shall fill its own offices without assistance from the state or local authorities." The bishops, before taking possession of their dioceses, were to take an oath of allegiance, swearing and promising to respect and to have their clergy respect "the constitutionally constituted government."[45] Further, "on Sundays and on authorized holidays in all episcopal churches, as well as in parish churches, their associated churches, and in the monastery churches of the German Reich as part of the main service, in accordance with the precepts of the church liturgy, a prayer [was] to be included for the well-being of the German Reich and folk."[46]

The concordats with Bavaria (1924), Prussia (1929), and Baden (1932) are recognized as remaining "in force, and the rights and liberties of the Catholic Church recognized in them remain unchanged within the territories of their respective states." Future concordats with individual states should "be effected only in accord with the Government of the Reich," which was in line with previous practice (Article 2). These provisions in respect to state concordats were at least a partial recognition of the old commitment of November 13, 1920, which the papacy had included among the four requests in the pro memoria of October, 1932, on the matter of granting the Reichswehr an exempt army bishop.[47] The Reichswehr obtained this in the concordat, and the papacy in turn received ample assurances on the other three points: easement of the marriage law, assurances about subsidies, and safeguards for Catholic schools.

The church got essentially what it had been asking for in regard to both the marriage law and the future of church subsidies. Subject to more comprehensive regulation later on, it was "agreed that in the case of a critical illness of a betrothed person admitting of no delay, also in the case of serious moral emergency, the existence of which must be confirmed by the appropriate episcopal authority, the consecration of the marriage by the church may precede the civil wedding" (Article 26). On the question of future subsidies, Article 18 stated: "In case those payments to the Catholic Church by the state which are based on law, treaty, or special legal titles should be commuted, a friendly agreement will be reached in good time between the Holy See and the Reich before the working out of principles to be laid down for the commutation. . . . The commutation must accord to the party entitled to commutation appropriate compensation for the loss of previous government payments." Clearly there would have to be much negotiation before the state could end its subsidies to the church.

It was in the field of education that the Vatican obtained the greatest concessions. In October, 1932, the papacy, in view of the forthcoming school law, had simply asked for "binding promises of the protection of the rights of Catholics in regard to parochial [confessional] schools and instruction in religion."[48] At the very beginning of the concordat negotiations, von Papen had informed Kaas that Hitler "was ready to concede far-reaching measures in regard to the schools because he was convinced that the new ethical basis for the national state could only be laid by the church."[49] Privileges the church had in some of the Catholic regions of Germany were now guaranteed for the whole Reich. "Catholic religious instruction in the primary schools, vocational schools, secondary schools, and higher educational institutions is a regular subject of instruction and it is to be taught in accordance with the principles of the Catholic church" (Article 21). Moreover, ecclesiastical authorities were to be given the opportunity, together with school authorities, "to examine whether the students are receiving religious instruction in accordance with the tenets and requirements of the church." Appointment of Catholic teachers of religion was to be made in accordance with an agreement reached between the bishop and the respective Land governments. Bishops could declare a teacher unsuited for the further teaching of religion and he could no longer be employed for this purpose. These articles constituted a radical change from the regulations existing in many German states.

Perhaps the most controversial educational provision was the one recognizing the right of Catholic parents or guardians to demand Catholic confessional schools—"if, with due regard for local conditions of school organization, the number of pupils allows a regular school operation, in accordance with the standard prescribed by the state, to appear feasible" (Article 23). Such schools could now be established throughout Germany, even in the old nondenominational (Simultan) school lands. The second clause of Article 174 of the German constitution, intended to protect these territories from the confessional school system, was ignored. In the 1920s, the Catholic forces had tried to achieve guarantees for confessional schools in all three of the national school laws which were defeated in the Reichstag. Now they had accomplished by treaty what they had failed to achieve by law. Thanks to the Enabling Act of March 23, the concordat could become the law of the land without ever being presented to parliament.

There were other provisions in regard to Catholic private schools, theological faculties at the universities, and teacher-training institutes established along denominational lines. Von Papen in his *Memoirs* underlines the importance of the school provisions.[50] Yet agreement on them was apparently reached rather easily. The article which did cause difficulty was Article 31, dealing with Catholic organizations.

Hitler was particularly concerned about Article 31, and Berlin officials had requested substantial alterations in its wording as drawn up in the negotiations on July 2. It caused prolonged discussion in the final negotiating session on July 7.[51] An attempt was made to separate organizations into those which were to be permitted to continue as church organizations and those which might be dissolved or absorbed into National Socialist bodies. This proved impossible, and the task was left to future agreement between the German government and the German episcopate. It was a fateful decision, for in spite of much discussion no agreement could ever be reached. The article caused much recrimination between church, party, and state authorities in the following years, no doubt in part because the wording is ambiguous. What are "exclusively religious, purely cultural and charitable purposes," and which organizations are or are not subject to ecclesiastical authorities? The last section on youth and sport organizations was also far from precise.

> Those Catholic organizations and societies which serve exclusively religious, purely cultural and charitable purposes, and as such, are subordinate to the ecclesiastical authorities, will be protected in their establishments and their activity.
> Those Catholic organizations which, in addition to their religious, cultural and charitable purposes, also serve other purposes, such as social or professional interests, will without prejudice to a possible future inclusion in State associations, enjoy the protection of article 31, paragraph 1, provided they guarantee to carry on their activity outside any political party.
> It is reserved to the Government of the Reich and the German Episcopate, to determine by joint agreement which organizations and associations come within the scope of this article.
> In so far as the Reich and Länder have in their charge sports and other youth organizations, care will be taken that the members of the same are enabled regularly to perform their church duties on Sundays and holidays, and that they will not be required to do anything irreconcilable with their religious and moral convictions and obligations.

Hitler had stressed the exclusion of Catholic clergy from politics, and this was the one demand von Papen had set out to obtain in the concordat. He succeeded, but the article was one of the most difficult to draft, and necessitated a long explanatory statement in the supplementary protocol.[52] The Reich was to introduce similar regulations regarding the political activity of non-Catholic denominations, but much undefined ground was left to cause future difficulties. The clergy were not to be members of a party or participate in party activities, but this did "not involve any sort of limitation of the preaching and interpretation of the dogmatic and moral teachings and principles of the church in accordance with their duty" (final protocol, Article 32). The negotiators were no more able than anyone else to draw a clear line between religion and politics.

Germany undertook to permit Catholic minorities the same liberty to use their mother tongue as "individuals of German descent and language [had] within the territory of the foreign state in question" (Article 29). The Vatican in turn promised, when negotiating concordats with other countries, to seek a similar provision protecting the rights of German minorities. Von Papen thought this was a most important provision, and apparently had visions of the papacy crusading for German minority rights.

The secret annex concerning Catholic clergy being called to military service was valuable to him, less "for the content of the regulation than for the fact that here the Holy See is already reaching a treaty agreement with us for the event of general military service."[53] "I hope," he continued to Hitler, "this agreement will therefore be pleasing to you." The papacy knew well that universal military service was denied to Germany by the Treaty of Versailles, but it nevertheless cast an anchor to windward. By the secret annex the concordat met a specific wish of the German episcopate.[54]

Under this secret agreement, students of philosophy and theology preparing for the priesthood in Catholic institutions were exempt from military service except in the event of general mobilization. Should there be a mobilization, "bishops, members of the diocesan courts, principals of seminaries and ecclesiastical hostels, professors in seminaries, the parish priests, curates, rectors, coadjutors, and the clergy who permanently preside over a church of public worship" did not have to report for service. This provision covered almost all secular clergy, but the few others were to be liable for pastoral service under the ecclesiastical jurisdiction of the army bishop, unless they were inducted into the medical service. Clerics *in sacris* or in the orders, and, as far as possible, students for the priesthood who had not yet taken the higher orders, were to be assigned to the medical service. A notable concession to the church, the agreement was honored by the government, at least in the first years of World War II, and this accounts for the fact that proportionally more Protestant than Catholic clergy and theological students were called to service, and when called up were largely spared active combat service.

The negotiators were well aware that unsettled points remained, and the Vatican sought some protection in regard to them. Matters relating to ecclesiastical persons or ecclesiastical affairs not dealt with in the concordat were to "be regulated for the ecclesiastical sphere in accordance with applicable Canon Law" (Article 33), "Ecclesiastical persons" may be definite enough, but "ecclesiastical affairs" and "spheres" are hardly well-defined concepts. Finally, as if to cover the whole concordat with an aura of good feeling and optimism, the negotiators included a statement found also in the state concordats: "Should any difference of opinion occur in future regarding the interpretation or application of a stipulation of this Concordat, the Holy See and the German Reich will effect a friendly solution by mutual agreement" (Article 33). This provision was to be used many times in the next years by church officials in their attempts to obtain redress of their grievances.

Ratification and Evaluation

The signing of the concordat elicited official commentaries in the German press; they were answered by two articles in the *Osservatore Romano,* written by Pacelli but not published under his signature. These led to a counterattack by Buttmann, and a real press polemic seemed likely to develop until agreement was reached on curtailing further press statements.[55] But there were also many enthusiastic expressions of thanks to Hitler, among them a letter from Cardinal Bertram, on behalf of the Fulda Bishops' Conference, and a personal letter from Cardinal Faulhaber. If they seem fulsome today, they did not at the time they were written, for after all, they recognized a singular accomplishment. As Cardinal Faulhaber stated: "This event of worldwide historical significance, which the old parliament and parties had never accomplished in sixty years, your statesmanlike vision has achieved in six months. This handclasp with the papacy, the greatest moral power in world history, signifies an achievement of unmeasurable blessing for Germany's position in the east and west and in the whole world." But the cardinal was not swept away by his joy and gratitude. He also pleaded for Hitler to grant "amnesty to those who, without committing a crime, but only because of their political views, were in prison and who along with their families were undergoing terrible suffering."[56]

These were the very days when the new German Evangelical church constitution was being publicized, and there was much ado about the Protestant church elections. Governmental agreement with both the Catholic and Protestant churches was indeed bringing a new order. While there was no real religious peace in Germany, the signing of the concordat did bring some religious rapprochement. Some Catholic organizations voluntarily took the lure of coordination offered by party and state officials. The Nazi flag could now be displayed by Catholic organizations, and there were no restrictions on the universally used "German greeting." Right hands extended, all could say, "Heil Hitler."[57]

But the actions of the secular authorities against Catholic organizations and institutions continued, in spite of Hitler's promise that they would be stopped. It should, however, always be remembered that antichurch activity was not uniform throughout Germany. It differed from one Land to another, from one government district within a Land to another, and much depended on the energy and views of particular officials. Practices of party and government officials often did not coin-

cide, the latter on the whole being more respectful of established laws
and practices. The clergy, both high and low, also differed in their willingness to cooperate with national socialism. The result was that conditions varied from diocese to diocese, which increased the difficulty of getting bishops to agree on common policies and led to weak pastoral statements.

While the Nazis were restricting both the Protestant and Catholic church press, and trying to coordinate both Protestant and Catholic organizations, their actions were seemingly more severe upon the Catholic church and aroused the most furor. Not only did Catholics have many more church-oriented organizations than did Protestants, but the property and leadership of these organizations were more directly in the hands of church authorities. Then too, Catholics had reason to think that they had now arranged for special governmental guarantees for their organizations in the concordat.

Just as the Protestant church-state conflict was sharpest in predominantly Protestant areas of Germany, the Catholic church conflict was sharpest in the predominantly Catholic areas—above all in Bavaria. Munich had for years been the Nazi party headquarters, and if the Nazis hated the Center party, they detested its counterpart, the Bavarian People's party, even more. Many church organizations had long supported this ultra-Catholic party, and in the eyes of the Nazis they were still suspect even after the party was formally dissolved. At this time two particularly ardent and adept party men, Heinrich Himmler and his deputy Reinhard Heydrich, were in control of the Bavarian political police, and they set themselves to end what they considered to be "political Catholicism" once and for all.

The first national congress of the German Journeymen's Association (*Deutscher Gesellentag*), was scheduled to meet at Munich, June 8–11, 1933.[58] The leaders had taken care to give the program a folk and fatherland orientation, and Hitler had asked von Papen to represent him at the meeting. Suddenly, with overseas guests already en route and all plans made, the Bavarian police, supposedly fearing disturbances, forbade the meeting. While the congress included all journeymen, the Catholic Journeymen's Association was actually the group behind it, and its leaders were successful in persuading von Papen and Faulhaber to use their good offices to have the prohibition lifted.

The congress opened with a religious service, and as the participants streamed from the church, the mounted police intervened—supposedly to preserve order. The Catholic Journeymen wore orange shirts and various special insignia which acted as a "red rag" to the Munich SA and SS troopers. Incidents increased; the police took no protective action. On Saturday night, while the mass meeting was being addressed by von Papen, news arrived that the police had forbidden the Catholic Journeymen to wear their distinctive shirts, and as they left the meeting a real donnybrook developed. The entire Munich SA and SS had been alerted, and they began to tear off the shirts and special insignia. The closing field mass on Sunday, at which Faulhaber was to officiate, had to be cancelled when the police refused to guarantee protection, and the molestation by the SA continued as the delegates found their way to the railway station. An old regimental friend who witnessed the brawl wrote to State Governor Epp that he could not see how this disgraceful action would help the new Germany, to which Epp added the marginal note, "neither do I."[59]

The disturbances aroused much attention in Germany and abroad. Cardinal Faulhaber protested to both the Bavarian and Reich authorities.[60] But the incident gave the Bavarian authorities the desired excuse for further restrictive measures. On June 13, 1933, they issued an order forbidding all public and private gatherings, including outdoor processions.[61] Normal religious services, including baptisms, weddings, and funerals, were exempt from the decree. The measure was supposed to be in the interest of public safety, but apparently nowhere else in Germany was it necessary. In order to hold a meeting in Bavaria, one had to obtain permission from the police, giving them endless opportunities for interference. For example, they could easily stop the visiting of shrines, which they at times did. The situation in Munich was tense, and the same day, June 13, Gauleiter and Bavarian Minister of the Interior Adolf Wagner, in a conference with Cardinal Faulhaber, got his agreement "that in view of the present rage of the SA against Catholic organizations, all manifestations in groups and in uniform would have to be suspended for two to three months."[62]

Meanwhile, the Vatican, the German bishops, and the Ministry of the Interior undertook to draw up a list of Catholic organizations in line with Article 31 of the concordat. It specified which organizations were to be guaranteed their future existence because of their purely religious character and activity, and which might be expected to be coordinated (gleichgeschaltet) into state organizations. Vatican authorities drew up a grouping according to categories, and Archbishop Gröber of Freiburg and Bishop Berning of Osnabrück were designated as the hierarchy's representatives to negotiate with Buttmann of the Ministry of the Interior.[63] They were logical choices, for Gröber had participated in the concordat negotiations, and Berning, who had held a conference with Hitler in April, was known to have good relations with the Berlin authorities and had just been appointed to the Prussian upper chamber (Staatsrat). Cardinal Faulhaber would have liked to have a bishops' conference discuss the list of organizations, but there was no time; the government authorities were pressing for a meeting so that they could proceed with ratification of the concordat.[64]

On July 17, Gröber and Berning met with Buttmann and in a friendly conference worked out a general list of organizations. The bishops were impressed with the results. Only two organizations had really been lost: the Volksverein, which was in financial difficulties anyway, and the Peace League of German Catholics, which was already gone. The next day Gröber and Berning met with the heads of the great Catholic organizations to go over these discussions with Buttmann. The Ministry of the Interior now drew up a detailed list based on the organizations given in the last edition of the *Kirchliches Handbuch für das katholische Deutschland*. It was submitted on July 31 to Cardinal Bertram head of the Fulda conference, for distribution to the rest of the bishops for study and suggestions.[65]

Nevertheless, punitive measures against Catholic organizations continued in Bavaria and elsewhere. In a letter of August 1 to his fellow bishops, Bertram urged them to publicize in their official papers the necessity for holding on to the church organizations. All too often the local clergy thought it the better part of valor to accede to the demands and threats of local government authorities or organs of the SA. They should be told that they must obtain permission before consenting to the dissolution of an organization.[66]

As the number of incidents increased, the curia was uncertain whether it should proceed with the ratification of the concordat or insist on clarification of the unsatisfactory conditions first. Cardinal Secretary Pacelli asked the German bishops for their views and they discussed the question in a meeting at Fulda toward the end of August.[67] A second bishops' conference within three months was unusual, but it was necessary to discuss the increasing restrictions on the church. The bishops were particularly concerned with what was happening to the church organizations and press, and the minutes of the meeting express their fear: "If the persecution and suppression of the Catholic press continues to the same extent as in the past weeks, there will soon be no Catholic press." Yet in spite of everything, the bishops decided for the immediate ratification of the concordat. Bertram, in a letter to Pacelli on behalf of the bishops, argued:

(1) Many voices are being raised against the concordat. Some even are maintaining that the Reich chancellor is seeking only to gain foreign political prestige with the concordat and does not wish to see the full internal developments which it entails.
(2) Wide circles declare the government has gone too far in its concessions; a contrary movement would be desirable. Such voices would become louder if ratification were delayed. This causes concern among the Catholics.
(3) Only with the ratification will we achieve the possibility of proceeding more definitely against the numerous anti-Catholic measures. But if ratification is delayed the position of the episcopacy will be made worse, which will not benefit the Catholic cause.[68]

The bishops, however, felt that it would be highly desirable to demand the end of antichurch measures and a declaration of honorable intentions to carry out the stipulations of the treaty when it was ratified. They mentioned particularly actions against Catholic organizations and press, and the dismissal of Catholics from the civil service. They added the plea: "Would it be possible for the Holy See to say a heartfelt word for those Christians who had converted from Judaism, who themselves or their children or grandchildren, because of non-Aryan descent, were suffering great hardship?"[69]

Gröber and Berning went over the list of organizations as approved by the Fulda conference with Buttmann on September 6. No special difficulties were encountered, and Buttmann promised help in regard to other complaints as soon as the concordat had been ratified. Frick also promised the bishops to think over again the proposed law on sterilization and the law placing cremation on the same basis as Christian burial. The upshot of the conferences, as Gröber reported to the German episcopate, was that the concordat should be ratified as soon as possible.[70]

The cardinal secretary had meanwhile been discussing matters raised by certain articles of the concordat directly with the German government. The views of the German bishops, however, were the determining factor in persuading Pacelli to forego further detailed discussions and to proceed to immediate ratification. He also was apparently impressed by assurances from Berlin that only with ratification would the Reich government be able to use the full weight of its authority against those who were trying to prevent carrying out the concordat in certain states and districts. He did negotiate the text for a joint communiqué, to be released at the time of ratification, in which the German government expressed its willingness to consult on matters needing clarification and settlement.[71] On September 10, the ratifications of the concordat minus the secret annex were exchanged in Rome between Cardinal Pacelli and Counselor Eugen Klee of the German embassy. The secret annex was ratified on November 2, 1933.[72]

At the time of ratification, the cardinal secretary handed Klee a memorandum raising the points made by the German bishops. Klee objected that he had been promised a memorandum on the implementation of the concordat. This statement about "the dismissal of Catholic officials and Catholics of Jewish descent" had nothing to do with the concordat, and he could accept only a memorandum dealing with matters relating to Catholic associations and the press. Pacelli rewrote the memorandum and put the material on civil servants and the Jews in a *pro memoria*. Klee again objected that these were internal German matters, and he would have to insist that the beginning of the *pro memoria* state "that the Holy See had no intentions of interfering in Germany's internal affairs, that the sentence about equal status for Catholics of Jewish descent be deleted, and that there be a toning down in other respects too." The cardinal thereupon decided not to deliver it. Nevertheless, he later submitted a note covering the same topics, and this time the opening sentence stated: "The Holy See [has] no intention of interfering in Germany's internal affairs." However, in the interest of furthering the friendly understanding established with the Reich government, he wished to raise certain requests about the dismissal of Catholic civil servants and Catholic Jews. He wrote: "The Holy See takes this occasion to add a word in behalf of those German Catholics who themselves have gone over from Judaism to the Christian religion or who are descended in the first generation, or more remotely from Jews who adopted the Catholic faith, and who for reasons known to the Reich Government are likewise suffering from social and economic difficulties."[73] Like Protestant leaders at the time, the curia was primarily concerned with Jewish Christians, not with Jews as such. There also was at least an indirect recognition that the broader Jewish question was an internal German problem which was not a matter for discussion on the level of foreign policy. These matters were to cloud the relations between the Catholic church and the state throughout the Nazi era.

The ratification of the concordat was celebrated with a festive thanksgiving service at Saint Hedwig's Cathedral in Berlin, attended by leading government, party, and church officials, and an overflow crowd of the populace. After the service, Prelate Steinmann for the first time read the prayer for the German Reich and the Führer as provided for in the concordat. Nuncio Orsenigo blessed the huge crowd outside the cathedral, which before dispersing sang the first verses of the national anthem and the Horst Wessel song.[74]

This service (there were others, although some bishops refused to authorize them) manifested the general acceptance by German Catholics of the concordat.[75] The German episcopate had certainly approved, and there had been consultation and cooperation between the bishops and the Vatican throughout. To the curia it was the culmination of the modern era of concordat negotiations. The tenacity with which the church authorities have held to the validity of the concordat ever since—and it is still in effect today—testifies to the significance they have always attached to it.[76] As Pacelli anticipated, it was certain to be violated at times by the government but, as he also foresaw, "the Germans would probably not violate all the articles of the concordat at the same time."[77] He was a true prophet, and not all provisions proved to be dead letters.

It is relatively easy to point out German violations of the agreement; it would be a far more difficult and tedious task to enumerate the instances when it was observed. That it often served as a restraining influence on both party and state officials is evident. It always afforded a foundation on which church protests could be based, and while they were not always honored, this does not necessarily mean that they had no effect. Catholic churchmen's recourse to the concordat was similar to the policy of the Protestant leaders when they appealed to the historic confessions of the church, the observance of which was guaranteed by the new church constitution, an agreement accepted by Hitler. Protest, after all, is about the only weapon that can be used against a totalitarian government, and the more solid its legal foundation, the more effective it is likely to be. The Nazis were always legally minded, but particularly in the earlier years. Pacelli, on the eve of his election to the papacy in 1939, stated: "For me the concordat was and remains a fortified trench across all Germany, perhaps through all Europe, from which the faithful can always defend themselves."[78] He retained this view throughout the war, and in 1945 remarked: "Without the legal protection afforded by the concordat, the subsequent persecution of the church might have taken even more violent forms. The basis of Catholic belief and enough of its institutions remained intact to permit their survival and resurgence after the war."[79]

The curia and the German bishops were strengthened by the legal protection provided by the concordat, but their reliance on it also brought weakness. It tended to limit the differences between the Catholic church and the state to a matter of upholding the concordat; the church officials were slow to place their difficulties with the Nazis on the higher and broader plane of maintaining religious and humanitarian values. Like the Protestants, the Catholics were constantly bedeviled by the dilemma of being against certain Nazi practices and doctrines, but not being against the government—the hallowed *Obrigkeit* of German history. It is easy to decry this dilemma today; it was much more difficult to see a way out of it in the Germany of that time.

The curia had negotiated the concordat to protect its interests in Germany, and on the whole it had obtained a very generous settlement. As Pacelli put it: "The German Government had offered him concessions, concessions, it must be admitted, wider than any previous German Government would have agreed to, and he had to choose between an agreement on their lines and the virtual elimination of the Catholic Church in the Reich."[80] Immediately after the war, in an allocution to the Sacred College, he made a similar statement:

> It must, however, be recognized that the concordat in the years that followed, brought some advantages, or at least prevented worse evils. In fact, in spite of all the violations to which it was subjected it gave Catholics a juridical basis for their defense, a stronghold behind which to shield themselves in their opposition—as long as this was possible—to the ever-growing campaign of religious persecution.[81]

To obtain a firm legal foundation for its status and rights by an international treaty was no mean advantage considering the more or less chaotic state of German law at that time, particularly after the passage of the Enabling Act practically threw constitutional safeguards out the window.[82] The demands the curia had raised in October, 1932, were all met. Unfortunately, some of the provisions lacked precision, notably in regard to Catholic associations. That this was left to future friendly agreement was unfortunate both for the church and the state, but it is a common method of settling difficult points in negotiating treaties. That the concordat brought advantages to the state the church knew full well; indeed, the church has always pointed out that a negotiated settlement of church-state relations was advantageous to both parties. Mussolini had urged Germany to negotiate the agreement for the prestige it would give to the new government.[83] Hitler was well aware of the advantages. He also saw it as a way of ending the church's meddling in politics and an important step in the Gleichschaltung of the religious life of Germany. Many in his party, as well as some of the old government officials who had long dealt with church affairs, felt that too many concessions had been made. Within a few months they were already talking about negotiating a new concordat.[84] Hitler, unlike Pius XII, soon came to regard the concordat as a thorn in the flesh, and in the end he held the agreement in contempt.

13.

Interpreting the Concordat

The Background of Discussions

Two days after the ratification of the 1933 Reich concordat, the German government issued a one-sentence law instructing the Minister of the Interior to promulgate the ordinances necessary to give effect to the agreement.[1] As in the past, the Ministry of the Interior would supervise religious affairs. In accord with plans made on the eve of ratification, Director Buttmann inquired in Rome if he might visit Cardinal Pacelli, who had gone for a vacation to Rorschach on Lake Constance. He intended to initiate the discussions foreseen by the communiqué issued when the concordat was ratified. The pope felt that Pacelli deserved a rest, and so the meeting was postponed. Ambassador Bergen, however, thought the decision was motivated by the pope's desire to follow "the course of negotiations from close at hand so that he [could] step in directly at any time."[2] The Germans later tried to foster the idea that if there had been a meeting at Rorschach the settlement of differences would have proceeded more successfully and rapidly.[3] This seems unlikely, for within a few weeks direct negotiations were begun anyway, and as they proceeded it was always the German authorities who resorted to delaying tactics.

Meanwhile, the Bavarian political police, on September 19, 1933, issued a supplementary decree which reviewed and sharpened the decree of July 13 against public meetings.[4] The police maintained that the agreement in regard to purely religious and mixed religious-secular organizations, foreseen in Article 31 of the concordat, had not yet been drawn up; therefore, except for what were clearly church services, all Catholic activities, such as public or closed meetings, theater presentations, excursions, athletic gatherings, and gymnastic exercises, including the formation of new organizations, must cease. Himmler submitted all kinds of "evidence" to the Ministry of the Interior to justify his treatment of Catholic organizations.[5]

In the ministry itself, the permanent officials in charge of religious affairs were genuinely eager for a settlement of concordat matters. They prepared revised lists of those Catholic organizations which were to be considered purely religious and those which were of a mixed religious and secular character. The two types were accorded different safeguards in Article 31. On October 2, the lists were submitted to the various state governments for their comments.[6] Their replies evidenced a clear opposition to the concordat. Again the authorities in Bavaria and Württemberg were the most caustic, repeatedly making annotations such as "without any value for the German folk," "considering the existence of the German Labor Front, no reason for its continued existence," or "wolves in sheep's clothing." With this evidence before them, the men in the ministry considered it futile to enter upon negotiations with the state authorities about classifying the various Catholic organizations.[7]

Bishops are supposed to make periodic visits to Rome, and whether by chance or design, an unusually large number of German bishops now decended on Rome in the autumn of 1933. In their audiences they asked for "energetic redress of grievances," although some, notably Cardinal Bertram, suggested proceeding cautiously.[8] The pope, annoyed by the continued unfriendly German actions, wanted to send a strong note of protest. To ward it off, Ambassador Bergen, after consulting Cardinal Pacelli, advised that Director Buttmann be sent at once to Rome to give binding promises about the effective implementation of the concordat. With Hitler's express permission and instructions, Buttmann set off immediately.[9] Arriving October 22, he was presented with a long pro memoria which Cardinal Pacelli had turned over to the German ambassador.

Without going into detail, since he assumed "that the continuing acts of interference with the Catholic element of the nation are amply known to the Reich Government," Pacelli listed the grievances requiring discussion and settlement. These included: (1) "the curbing and repression of Catholic associations and organizations, carried on by every means, and the prohibition in many localities of their program of activities (one Land even prohibited the sewing circle evenings for the Winter Relief held by the Catholic Women's League) . . . "; (2) the suppression of the Catholic press; (3) the dismissal of Catholic civil servants; (4) the scheduling of party activities on Sunday, which made it impossible for Catholics to fulfill their religious obligations; (5) the obligation of Catholic theological students to engage in military sports and join the Labor Service; (6) the continued sequestration of church property and endowments, the arrest of priests, the dismissal of clerical teachers of religion, and the attempt "to apply to the members of the clergy the so-called Aryan clause, which has not been recognized by the Catholic Church"; (7) the threat to the Catholic confessional schools; (8) the compulsory courses for National Socialist indoctrination, which in some parts of the Reich had to be attended by all civil servants and employees, even by nuns who were engaged in nursing the sick; and (9) the implications of the sterilization law.[10]

Pacelli had indeed prepared a full agenda, and Buttmann was not to be envied. Three long conferences were held on October 23, 25, and 27, in which Pacelli was backed up by Monsignor Kaas and Archbishop Gröber of Freiburg. Kaas offered to assist Buttmann in working out an answer to the Vatican demands, but his offer was rejected. As Buttmann

reported: "The double role that Kaas undertook in the concordat negotiations, in which on the one hand he appeared as adviser to the Reich
and on the other as the intimate friend of Pacelli, must in my estimation
be ended."[11] Gröber had worked out the July 18 agreement with the
Ministry of the Interior on the interpretation of Article 31, and it was
only natural that the implementation of this statement should come up
for discussion. Buttmann was hard pressed. He referred to the provisions
of the agreement as guidelines, but he could not guarantee that they
would be part of the contemplated law on carrying out the concordat.
When Pacelli countered that implementing these provisions had been
one of the conditions for signing the treaty, Buttmann pointed out that
there was nothing official about them, that they had not been referred to
in the concluding protocol or in Vice-chancellor von Papen's note.
Pacelli found his response "very disquieting." When the concordat was
signed, Kaas had given Buttmann a short statement requesting that the
determining factor in classifying organizations should be whether they
belonged to Catholic Action. Since it was the Holy See's prerogative to
determine what organizations belonged to Catholic Action, the interpretation of the article would have been thrown largely into the hands of
the church. Although a reference to association with Catholic Action as
a determining factor had been included in the draft of the concordat as
first agreed upon by the negotiators in Rome, it had been expressly
eliminated by Berlin officials, and Pacelli's new attempt to resurrect it
was rejected.[12] When Buttmann then intimated that it might be necessary to incorporate all youth, sport, and occupational organizations into
broad national groups, Pacelli, enraged, declared such a state monopoly
was a violation of the concordat. Buttmann's reply that this would be
done under a law applicable to all, which was provided for in Article 1,
elicited the rejoinder that "this would be a violation of international law
[and] international law supersedes Reich law."[13]

The conversations, as both sides had expected, were mostly explor-
atory. To sum them up, Cardinal Pacelli submitted three notes to Buttmann before the latter left Rome. In the first two, Pacelli outlined a
proposal for interpreting Article 31 which be based largely on the Ministry of the Interior statement of July 18, 1933. He also mentioned that
double membership in state and church organizations should be permitted, and that church organizations should get in touch with church
authorities at the time of their coordination; he again referred to association with Catholic Action as a guide to classifying organizations. Article
31 was clearly the main topic for future agreement, although other
issues, such as the relation of the state concordats to the matters at hand
and the choice of instructional material for confessional schools, were
also raised. A third note was devoted exclusively to the relation of Reich
law to the concordat. It summarizes very succinctly the view that the
Vatican consistently held.

> In certain political circles the opinion is held that the government, through
> general Reich law, is in the position to declare, for example, the Hitler Youth
> the only youth organization permitted in the state, and that in such a case, as

a consequence of Article 1, this Reich law applicable to all, rescinds concordat law. There can be no doubt that this interpretation of Article 1 contains a fundamental fallacy, and that a continued adherence to this interpretation would be synonymous with cancelling the worth of all concordats. The nature of concordat law is determined by the fact that it is a negotiated law, and that it denies to both partners the unilateral changing by law of the contents of an accepted agreement. If each partner, without consideration of the agreement which had been made, should assume for itself the right to change by law those particular provisions of the agreement it happened to want to change, it would by this action make the singular nature of concordat law illusory.[14]

After his return to Berlin, Buttmann presided on November 3 over a small conference of representatives of various departments which met to discuss the implementation of the sterilization law of July 14, 1933, due to go into effect the following January 1.[15] This was one of the grievances Pacelli had listed. Archbishop Gröber of Freiburg and Bishop Berning of Osnabrück were invited to attend the meeting, and Gröber began by pointing out that while the purpose of the law was acceptable, the method of carrying it out was bad. The church could not accept sterilization as such. If the law was made voluntary, the church might be able to agree, but in this case it should be voluntary for doctors and directors of institutions as well. Berning also expressed his opposition to the law.[16]

The views of the bishops were not incorporated in the implementation ordinance issued on December 5, which went no further toward meeting their objections than to state: "If the authorized doctor holds that sterilization is warranted, he should attempt to get the person or his legal representative to request it. If this request is not forthcoming, then he himself must make the demand for sterilization."[17] In other words, there would still be compulsory sterilization on the advice of medical authorities. There were further ordinances on the implementation of the law, notably in regard to the courts which were to administer it.[18] The church never accepted the sterilization measures, and expressed its opposition on numerous occasions. For example, in the Berlin diocese on January 14, 1934, a set of instructions which Catholics who were to be married were to observe was read in all churches. Among these was the statement that to permit oneself to be sterilized or to request sterilization for someone else was contrary to the teachings of the church.[19]

While Buttmann acted with dispatch in calling the meeting on sterilization, the Reich officials were in no hurry to continue general negotiations with the Vatican in the fall of 1933, for Germany was in the confusion of an election campaign. Hitler had withdrawn Germany from the disarmament conference and from the League of Nations, and had scheduled a referendum on these steps as well as new Reichstag elections for November 12. No one doubted what the results would be, but it seemed wise to help the cause along a bit. On the direct intervention of Hitler, the Bavarian authorities suspended the order of September 19, 1933, which had called for strict enforcement of the law on meetings of various Catholic organizations.[20] Statements were sought by party officials from members of the hierarchy in support of the referendum. Cardinal Bertram undertook to ask the views of the bishops of the Fulda conference, but they were so disparate that he gave up trying to reconcile them and issued his own statement, leaving it up to the other bishops to do the same.[21]

Bertram's statement was a moderate approval of Germany's claim to equality among the powers and the freedom of the people to vote. It made only passing reference to the episcopate's demands on the government. Archbishop Gröber's electoral summons, however, was so warmly worded that he even received a special thank-you note from von Papen.[22] The Bavarian bishops' statement was very different. While urging the Catholic populace out of patriotic and spiritual concern to give its support for peace among nations and for the honor and equality of the German nation, they pointed out that such support did not mean approving all the measures the government had taken in recent months to the discomfort and detriment of the church. They expressed confidence, nevertheless, that the concordat would be observed, and affirmed "their agreement with the far-sighted and vigorous efforts of the Führer to save the German folk from the horrors of war and the abominations of bolshevism, to protect public order and to provide work for the unemployed." As to the election, this being a party matter, in accordance with Article 32, which forbade the clergy to engage in political activity, they left participation in it to "the free discretion and conscience of those qualified to vote."[23]

As if anticipating what might happen, the bishops added that only the full text of their statement could be publicized; excerpts would not be permitted. Furthermore, it was not meant to be read from the pulpit, and clergy should adhere strictly to the provisions of the concordat. The overzealous Bavarian government reacted at once. They broadcast on the radio only the first paragraph, which gave general support to the referendum, and forbade the publication of the whole statement in the church or secular press. The police forbade the dissemination of the pronouncement in the churches. The bishops' statement was certainly not extreme, but it apparently irritated the National Socialists no end.[24] It led to an exchange of notes between Cardinal Pacelli and the Bavarian government which settled nothing, but only further clouded the atmosphere.[25]

The November 12 referendum and election were a great success for the Nazis.[26] The Sportspalast meeting which followed immediately thereafter further disrupted the Protestant churches, including the German Christian wing, and Catholics had good reason to fear mounting radicalism in the government's religious policy.[27] The denunciation of the Old Testament by German Christian representatives gave Cardinal Faulhaber cause to preach his famous Advent sermons in 1933, which were published with the English title *Judaism, Christianity, and Germany* (1934). In these sermons, as well as in his 1933 New Year's Eve sermon, he upheld the Old Testament and decried the current vogue of seeking German salvation in the doctrines of race and blood. The cardinal carefully avoided a direct attack on anti-Semitic sentiment and policies, and, as he stated later, "in the Advent sermons I defended the Old Testament. I did not take a position in regard to the Jewish question of today."[28] Nevertheless, it was the first important statement by a member of the German episcopate criticizing the National Socialist religious policy. The sermons were read throughout Germany by Catholics, Protestants, and Jews alike, in spite of efforts by some local authorities to prevent their distribution.

The Opening Round

In the closing weeks of November and the beginning of December, Pacelli repeatedly inquired why the negotiations, interrupted at the end of October, had not been resumed; the notes he had submitted then had not yet been answered. More concern was aroused at the Vatican when von Papen urged Archbishop Gröber to take the initiative in integrating the Catholic youth groups into the state organizations. In turn the state would guarantee the church authorities its cooperation and adequate time for religious training of the youth. This request was tantamount to asking for the surrender of the youth organizations. Gröber sent von Papen's letter to Rome. Other German bishops who happened to be at the Vatican spoke against accepting the vice-chancellor's proposal, and Pacelli immediately ruled that this was a major matter that could only be settled between Rome and Berlin. It was up to the bishops to confront von Papen "as a solid phalanx."[29] With this decision Pacelli prevented any possibility that the bishops might make separate agreements for their respective dioceses. The Vatican had been taken aback by the diversity of the bishops' statements in regard to the November 12 elections, and it was concerned about preserving a united front. As Kaas put it in a confidential letter to Gröber: "in the state there is the leadership principle; at the Vatican the same holds. If parliamentarianism continues to rule in the episcopate, the church will be the one to suffer."[30]

Ambassador Bergen, fearful that the cup of woe was about to run over, urged that something be done. In Berlin the decision was finally made that Buttmann would pay another visit to Rome for clarifying discussions.[31] On December 18, Pacelli had a long conference with him at which Buttmann was told that the pope was much disturbed, and felt "he would definitely have to speak about Germany in his Christmas allocution. . . . If I could only present something pleasant to His Holiness," continued Pacelli, "I believe the disposition of the Pope would be improved."[32] Pacelli requested a written statement which he could hand to the pope dealing with five points which he enumerated.

The last thing the Germans wanted at this juncture was a sharp public statement by the pope. Buttmann acted with dispatch. He telephoned Berlin, Hitler was consulted, and the next day the cardinal secretary had the desired note: (1) the Reich government promised to enter into oral negotiations in the near future in regard to the interpretation of the concordat; (2) the Prussian government had given up its objections to the appointment of Bishop Dr. Niklaus Bares of Hildesheim as bishop of Berlin; (3) Catholic theological students would be exempted from service in the SA or the Labor Service, and the government was pleased that they would be trained in the Samaritan service; (4) in the interim period of the dissolution of the Länder, the Reich government expressed its willingness "for the duration of the negotiations regarding a new Reich concordat, to continue to fulfill as far as possible the obligations, especially of a financial nature, resulting from the concordats concluded by the Curia with individual Länder, without thereby wanting to assume now final obligations to take over these payments unchanged."[33]

The phrase referring to a new concordat worried Pacelli, and Buttmann had to do a lot of explaining about the contemplated constitutional reform which would do away with the Länder and therefore would require a redrafting of the concordat. The cardinal also spotted the fact that the note did not mention his point in regard to reinstating clerical teachers. This was the point on which Hitler was adamant, and Pacelli had to accept Buttmann's explanation that the government "could not differentiate between officials who were Catholic theologians and other officials."[34] Yet in general the note was acceptable enough, and the promised forthcoming negotiations could be used to straighten out differences. The pope refrained from his contemplated criticism in his Christmas allocution, although he expressed his continued displeasure over the situation in Germany to Ambassador Bergen when the latter was received in the customary holiday audience.[35] The incorporation of Protestant youth organizations into the Hitler Youth just before Christmas added to the curia's concern.[36]

Bergen, who feared that the curia was contemplating publishing a white book on relations with Germany, urged the Foreign Office to take the offensive and submit a reply to the various notes Pacelli had sent. Pacelli, he wrote, liked documents, and would appreciate having a written reply. Von Neurath agreed, and on January 15, 1934, Bergen was able to present the cardinal secretary with a memorandum preparatory to the resumption of oral discussions. A significant part of the memorandum was devoted to complaining about the actions of Catholic clergy, particularly about the Austrian episcopate's Christmas pastoral letter, which was very critical of national socialism. The government intimated that the curia should restrain the Austrians from interfering in German affairs.[37]

It was precisely at this time that events were approaching a crisis in the Protestant church in Germany, and Hitler sought to restore peace by appealing to the German Evangelical church leaders.[38] For the moment he appeared to succeed; if a settlement could also be reached with the Catholics, it would be a second feather in his cap.

Pacelli now had something to work on, and on January 31, 1934, he submitted a twenty-four-page, fourteen-point pro memoria in reply.[39] It actually crossed with another German note which complained anew that many Catholic clergy were not supporting the German government. Pacelli's pro memoria was skillfully drafted and refuted point by point the statements made by the German Foreign Office; the curia did not give way one bit. The positions expressed in the two documents provided a basis for the oral discussions which Buttmann again undertook in Rome, February 6–13, 1934. To ease the situation, on the suggestion of von Papen and Ambassador Bergen, Hitler received Cardinal Karl Joseph Schulte of Cologne. All went well, and the cardinal characterized the meeting as a "good beginning."[40] The German Foreign Office also requested the Bavarian government to apologize to Cardinal Faulhaber for shots fired at his residence on the night of January 27–28. The Bavarian cabinet met and refused to do so. The SA was pressing them for not being aggressive enough against the church, and the head of the Bavarian state chancellery said at the meeting:

> The attacks on Cardinal Faulhaber are objectively justified. The four Advent sermons which he had read were a broadly conceived attack against the folk ideology, based on the premise that the Old Testament as a part of the New was binding as an article of faith on all Catholics. The result was an inevitable conflict of conscience for all Catholics.[41]

It is not surprising that with the general situation as tense as it was, Buttmann and Pacelli were unable to make any progress.[42] Each advanced his complaints, and only mutually observed protocol enabled them to circumvent their difficulties. The result of the conference is indicated by the fact that on the day following (February 14, 1934), the curia announced that Rosenberg's *Myth of the Twentieth Century* had been placed on the Index.[43] Contrary to its usual practice (and this aroused attention) it stated its reasons for doing so. The extreme veneration of race and blood expressed in the volume could only lead to a denial of Christianity. Rosenberg was trying to overthrow Catholic dogma and challenged fundamental Christian beliefs. It was a stinging rebuke to Hitler for having put Rosenberg in charge of the spiritual and ideological education of the National Socialist party and its coordinated organizations. The possibility of Rosenberg being in charge of Catholic organizations which under Article 31 might be secularized only heightened the church's determination to hold on to as many as it could.

Buttmann, who realized the future of Catholic youth organizations was the crux of the problem, got in touch with von Papen after his return to Berlin. The latter immediately consulted von Schirach, who confirmed the results of their discussions in a written statement on February 20. Both the Hitler Youth and the National Socialist party stood on the ground of positive Christianity, and religious education by both confessions was expressly recognized. If the Catholic youth organizations were incorporated into the Hitler Youth, ample time would be set aside for their religious training and for them to meet their Sunday obligations. Once the Catholic youth organizations were restricted to purely religious activities, the Hitler Youth would be willing to urge its members to promote them. The statement had Hitler's personal approval, and actually seemed to make important concessions. Yet there was a hitch in it. Von Papen was asked to refrain from publishing these "basic prerequisites"; there must

first be another discussion.[44] This meant that von Schirach was actually retaining a free hand for future discussions. A few weeks later he revealed his cards when he declared in a speech at Essen: "We will not halt before the groups of Catholic youth organizations. We solemnly declare that confessional groups have no special rights."[45]

At the same time a modest rapprochement was taking place in Bavaria, where relations between the government and the episcopate had been virtually broken. Monsignor Johann Neuhäusler arranged for Minister Adolf Wagner to have a conference with Cardinal Faulhaber on March 7. They talked about the Catholic organizations and their relation to the Hitler Youth. The cardinal pointed out that the youth were not given enough time on Sunday to meet their religious obligations. Wagner, in a conciliatory mood, expressed the opinion that one day during the week should be cleared for their religious activity, an idea which Faulhaber approved. Wagner concluded his account of the interview with the note that Faulhaber, on greeting him and on saying farewell, had used the Hitler greeting in exemplary fashion.[46]

The von Schirach statement to von Papen did provide a new gambit. In conference with Buttmann and Ambassador Bergen on March 29, Hitler agreed that in his forthcoming conversations with Pacelli, "Buttmann should make use of the concessions granted by the Reich youth leader and should express the wish to reach some agreement on them, but that he did not want any other concessions to be made regarding the other Catholic organizations."[47] Bergen, on the same visit to Berlin, was given a "list of Catholic societies and organizations protected by Article 31 of the Reich concordat."[48]

Buttmann thus had something new to work on, when he set out for Rome at the beginning of April, 1934; he made further preparations by stopping off en route to see Cardinal Archbishop Schulte of Cologne and Archbishop Gröber of Freiburg.[49] The conferences in Rome, April 9, 12, and 19, however, were unsuccessful. Pacelli advanced a plan for carrying out the much-disputed Article 31, but Buttmann, bound by instructions, could make no real concessions. The cardinal, on the other hand, refused to limit Catholic youth organizations to being "purely prayer societies." The two negotiators, however, did agree that there should be discussions between the Ministry of the Interior and representatives of the German bishops about Article 31.[50]

The relations between the German government and the Catholic church were such that they involved negotiations on two levels—with the Vatican directly and with the German episcopate, and these two were not completely free agents because they had to consult each other. In fact, there was often a third-level of negotiations going on simultaneously. These involved the state governments—particularly Bavaria, with its special Bavarian concordat, and until June 30, 1934, its own representative at the Vatican. For example, at the beginning of April, when Buttmann was trying to work out a settlement in Rome, a nasty incident occurred in Würzburg.

The Reverend Josef Stöger, a Catholic priest in the suburb of Waldbüttelbrunn, had been arrested in the summer of 1933, and again in January, 1934, because of trouble with the local National Socialists.[51] He had been freed on the promise that he would not return to Waldbüttelbrunn. When the bishop appointed him to a new charge, the government of Lower Franconia delayed and finally refused to approve the appointment. The bishop had meanwhile not appointed a new man to Waldbüttelbrunn because of interference by the laity in matters of episcopal jurisdiction. Since Holy Week was at hand, the bishop of Würzburg sent Stöger, who had no position, back to his former parish to conduct the first communion service. He was promptly arrested again, and notice was sent out that the first communion service could not be held. The people, suddenly very devout and angered by this deprivation, demonstrated before the bishop's palace on April 7. It was an affair led by local party men and participated in by many outsiders. The doors of the palace were battered down and the bishop was hailed as a fit candidate for Dachau. The crowd confronted him and exacted the promise that the first communion service would be held as soon as possible. The bishop was not one to be coerced into rapid action.

Amid charges that the bishop had not kept his word, a second rowdy demonstration took place at the palace on April 28, 1934, supposedly led by the workers of Waldbüttelbrunn demanding a new pastor. The eight policemen sent to the palace were unable to cope with the situation, and again the crowd broke in, only to discover that a new man had already been named. The incident aroused much attention, eliciting a formal protest from Cardinal Faulhaber to the Bavarian government. Finally Minister of the Interior Frick intervened on May 11, 1934, and told his Bavarian counterpart that he would have to stop such demonstrations.[52] It is clear that the officials in Bavaria were at cross-purposes with some of the officials in Berlin.

Negotiations with the German Episcopate

From the exchange of ratifications of the concordat in September, 1933, to April, 1934, the curia had been trying to reach an agreement with the German government on implementing it. It now stepped into the background—but definitely not out of the picture—and on April 20 turned the task over to the German bishops.[53] On May 3, 1934, Minister Frick, in line with the agreement reached by Buttmann, asked Cardinal Faulhaber of the Munich-Freising Bishops' Conference to name representatives to meet with him to discuss questions about carrying out the concordat. The Fulda Bishops' Conference, on June 5–7, 1934, chose Archbishop Gröber of Freiburg, who had shared actively in the final concordat negotiations, Bishop Berning of Osnabrück, and Bishop Bares of Berlin as their delegates.[54] The continuing difficulties between the state and the Protestant churches, along with the widening cleft between the Confessing church group and the German Christians, no doubt also worried the Catholic leaders. Both the Protestants—including even some German Christians—and the Catholics were concerned over the emergence of the radical German Faith groups. They feared what this wave of neopaganism, supported by some party men, might lead to, and the church came increasingly to see its various organizations as valuable safeguards against the new paganism. But Robert Ley, the leader of the Labor Front, on April 27 had forbidden double membership in the Labor Front and any Catholic workers' organization. Since membership in the Labor Front was increasingly becoming a prerequisite for a job, this order virtually sounded the death knell for a large segment of the Catholic lay organizations.[55]

Cardinal Pacelli felt it time to speak frankly and more sharply than in the past. He drew up a long memorandum on May 14 in which he took apart, politely but completely, the German notes, answering each of the government's charges against specific clergy. He had much to say about the antichurch material used by the party in its various schooling courses, and especially in some Hitler Youth groups. That the following bit of doggerel distributed by some Hitler Youth was included in a formal Vatican note to Germany is indicative of the temper of church-state relations at the time.

> We are the happy Hitler Youth;
> We have no need of Christian virtue;
> For Adolf Hitler is our intercessor
> And our redeemer.
> No priest, no evil one
> Can keep us
> From feeling like Hitler's children (sic).
> Not Christ do we follow, but Horst Wessel!
> Away with incense and holy water pots.
> Singing we follow Hitler's banners;
> Only then are we worthy of our ancestors.
> I am no Christian and no Catholic.
> I go with the SA through thick and thin.
> The Church can be stolen from me for all I care.
> The swastika makes me happy here on earth.
> Him will I follow in marching step;
> Baldur von Schirach, take me along.[56]

Well might the church raise the question of whether, in a dictatorial authoritarian state, there was no central body which could keep local officials in check. And if the government constantly proclaimed that Rosenberg's *Myth of the Twentieth Century* was a private study for which it denied all responsibility, why was it being forced on the youth by party and state officials? The note as printed is thirty-four big pages long. Its sharp tone and forthrightness aroused consternation in Berlin. No attempt was made to answer it, but it received careful study. The Foreign Office sent it to the Chancellery along with a summary of its contents, pointing out: "The repeated keynote of the pro memoria was that the causes which gave rise to the complaints of the church should not be permitted, particularly in an authoritatively led state (*Führerstaat*). The Reich government had methods of exerting influence and physical power to a degree that formerly was unknown."[57] The papal document was forwarded to Hitler for his information.

Meanwhile, within Germany, church leaders and organizations arranged special religious services, processions, and pilgrimages, which were designed as manifestations of loyalty to Catholicism and its institutions and showed that others besides the party could arrange demonstrations numbering 30,000 to 60,000 participants. It was clear that the Catholic organizations could not be gleichgeschaltet at once, and the secret police made plans instead for increased restrictions which would bring about their gradual elimination. Such a widespread outburst of religious loyalty as occurred in May–June, 1934, was not to be permitted again.[58] The state officials also continued their efforts to reach a settlement with the church authorities.

An invitation to a conference at the Ministry of the Interior went off on June 19 to the three designated bishops (Gröber, Berning, and Bares), to the head of the SA leadership in Munich, to the head of the party bureau for cultural peace, to ex-Captain von Pfeffer, whom Hitler had recently made his confidant in church affairs, to Robert Ley, the head of the Labor Front, and to Baldur von Schirach, the leader of the Hitler Youth. Conrad, who was then in the Ministry of the Interior, notes that special care was taken to get the chief party and state "sinners" at the conference. The bishops' views were to be heard on the morning of June 25; in the afternoon the party and state officials would decide what position to take, and they would then meet with the bishops again the next morning.[59]

This schedule was followed, with additional meetings with party and state officials and a further meeting of the minister of the interior with the three bishops on June 29. The bishops came prepared, and at the opening session placed four questions before the conference, also explaining why they had been led to ask them.

1.   What is the position of the state towards Christianity and the church? Interpretation of Article 24 of the party program [positive Christianity] and the Führer's statements varied, and unchristian ideology was being disseminated in state organizations, schools, and training courses.
2.   What is the position of the state towards the concordat? It was often being asserted that the concordat either in its entirety or in certain articles had been superseded by changing conditions.
3.   What is the position of the state towards the church's preaching of the Christian message? Often it is maintained that the preaching of doctrines not in harmony with state and party views are hostile to the state and subject to prosecution.
4.   What is the position of the state towards the obligation of the church to oppose attacks on Christianity and its representatives? When this has been done, either in the pulpit, in pastoral letters, on in meetings, it has been labelled as confessional agitation, disturbance of national unity, and political activity.[60]

The party and state officials debated sharply, stopping at times to read aloud pages of the papal pro memoria. They finally produced a friendly but equivocal four-point answer in which they reaffirmed the party's adherence to positive Christianity and its desire to further the moral and ethical values anchored in the two Christian confessions. It accepted the concordat as the basis of relations with the Catholic church, although negotiated changes might be necessary at the proper time. Within the limitations of laws binding on all, the Catholic church had the freedom to regulate its own affairs, and it was free to proclaim its doctrines and teachings.[61]

On June 27, Hitler received the three bishops. They expressed their acceptance of the new state, but also their worries about whether all the provisions of the concordat would be implemented. Hitler reassured them, emphasizing that he wanted the church to cease criticizing the state and the party, and to steer clear of politics. He agreed, on the completion of the negotiations, to issue a public statement stating that "both the government and party were favorably and helpfully disposed toward the activities of the Catholic church in her own sphere, and that neither would have anything to do with the so-called third religion, the German National church and similar movements opposed to Christianity."[62]

It is clear that both the bishops and state officials were resolved to reach some sort of agreement, and this was accomplished on June 29, 1934. A draft agreement on the interpretation of Article 31 was drawn up, as well as a statement in regard to other related issues. A large number of church organizations were recognized as purely religious in character, and it was specifically recognized that Catholic youth organizations could continue to exist as long as they confined their activities to the religious and moral education of their members. Sport and labor organizations did not come under the protection of the article, but these associations, and particularly their funds, could be merged into other organizations of Catholic Action which served purely religious, cultural, or charitable purposes. Physical training was declared to be within the sole province of the state; a weekday was to be set aside for it. Sunday and other religious holidays were to remain free of such activity.[63] On the whole it was a rather favorable settlement for the church, and recognized many points which the church authorities had stressed ever since the ratification of the concordat. The bishops in turn promised that, in the interest of maintaining peace, the Catholic youth organizations during the current summer months would refrain from wearing uniforms and from any camping activity. When the draft agreements had been formally approved, assurances were given by party authorities that the ban against double membership in church and party organizations would be rescinded. This applied particularly to labor and youth organizations.

Papal Rejection of the June Agreement

The bishops, as well they might, expected no difficulties in getting the agreement approved. Bishop Berning took it to Cardinal Bertram with the expectation that it would be sent to the other bishops to solicit their views and their approval. The Reich minister of the interior would then send the text to the Foreign Office for further negotiations with

Rome. Bertram, however, crossed up the well-laid plans by immediately sending the draft agreements to the Vatican as well as to the bishops.[64]

The next move was up to the pope. Shocked by political events in Germany and Austria, he refused to approve the agreements.[65] On the night of June 30, 1934, occurred the notorious Blood Purge in which, among many others, the respected head of Catholic Action, Dr. Erich Klausner, and the leader of the Catholic sports organization, Adalbert Probst, lost their lives.[66] On July 3, the Ministry of the Interior added to the episcopate's consternation by forbidding distribution of the pastoral letter of the last Fulda Bishops' Conference, charging: "The pastoral letter contains statements that are likely to endanger public safety and order and are derogatory to the image of the government and the movement, and the policy it is following."[67] While willing to postpone the reading of the letter, the bishops refused to withdraw it. Shortly thereafter, on July 25, Chancellor Engelbert Dollfuss of Austria was assassinated in a Nazi putsch. He had been attempting to establish a Christian corporative state, drawing much of his inspiration from the papal encyclical *Quadragesimo Anno* (1931). On June 5, 1933, he had concluded a concordat with the Vatican assuring church control over Austrian education and abolishing divorce.[68] The pope could not ignore the murder of such a friend of the church. The death of Hindenburg on August 2, 1934, added to the uncertainty about future developments in Germany. The Vatican had taken to heart the all too rapid conclusion and ratification of the concordat in 1933; it was not going to confirm another written agreement with dispatch.

Meanwhile, Hitler had objected to the first draft of the public pronouncement he was supposed to issue when the agreement was concluded. On July 31, 1934, Minister Frick, in a personal interview with Hitler, was able to come up with a text which Hitler accepted.[69] However, since the Vatican never approved the June 29 arrangements, Hitler's public statement was left in the files.

Having solicited the views of the German episcopate, Cardinal Pacelli, on September 2, submitted the Vatican's rejection of the June agreement as drawn.[70] The concessions made by the German government "in various essential matters [were] below the degree of religious freedom guaranteed by the text of the concordat."[71] The church could not agree to the abandonment of the former Catholic occupational organizations. They could become sections of Catholic Action, and certain of their activities not in line with the religious principles and aims of Catholic Action could be abandoned. Above all, the highest governmental authorities must make commitments in the agreement, not the leaders of party organizations. A number of proposed amendments to the agreement were submitted.

Pacelli's proposals were not well received in the Foreign Office, but further discussions could not well be declined.[72] The three bishops who had negotiated the June agreement were again invited to Berlin, where they held discussions September 14–20. This was just at the time Reich Bishop Müller chose to make his demand for a Rome-free German church.[73] The bishops wanted an agreement before Pacelli left for the

Eucharistic Conference in Buenos Aires on September 23, but it was not obtained because Hitler ordered Buttmann to be dilatory. Urged by his advisers to make a conciliatory gesture by issuing the statement on relations with the Catholic church to which he had earlier agreed, Hitler refused. Relations remained unsatisfactory. Rumors were so persistent that the papacy was considering laying an interdict on Germany that Ambassador Bergen finally made inquiry of the acting state secretary, Monsignor Pizzardo, who laughingly replied that a general interdict had become obsolete in the last two hundred years.[74] Later, when the pope expressed his great concern over the way things were going in Germany, Bergen recommended protracting the discussions until the cardinal-secretary was back in Rome. Bergen considered Pacelli a moderating influence.[75]

In view of the exceptional turmoil in the Protestant church caused by the deposition and arrest of the Protestant bishops of Bavaria and Württemberg, the government was only too willing to lay aside negotiations with the Catholics.[76] Finally, at the beginning of November, Frick not only took new steps to establish peace in the Protestant church, but again invited the three Catholic bishops to Berlin. They were given a revised draft of the June 29 agreement. The Holy See, to which the document was referred, considered that this new text met its wishes only on unimportant points, and that it would be premature for Buttmann to come to Rome to resume direct negotiations. It suggested that Buttmann should first come to some agreement with Nuncio Orsenigo in Berlin over the application of Article 31.[77]

Hitler's Reaction and Sharpening Conflict

The scene of the discussions now shifted to Berlin. Orsenigo stressed that the negotiations must be kept secret, even from the German bishops. He felt that a public statement by Hitler opposing the rampant neopaganism would be a real aid in easing the situation and von Neurath, anxious to bring about a settlement with the Catholic church, requested Hitler to make one. Foreign political problems, particularly those involving the Saar plebiscite and Austria, also seemed to make such a statement advisable. But although he had agreed to make a somewhat similar one the previous summer, Hitler now refused to do so.[78] On January 28, 1935, Buttmann met with Orsenigo and Berning and informed them that "in accordance with the decision which the Führer and Chancellor had reached in the meantime, the Reich government were abiding by the outcome of the negotiations with the representatives of the German Hierarchy which were completed on June 29, 1934, and could make no further concessions on important points."[79] Von Neurath also met with the nuncio, and once more asked Hitler if he would not make a public declaration against neopaganism. Hitler this time asked to have the agreement of June 29 and the text of his proposed statement laid before him again. He now found various points in the draft agreement objectionable, and refused anew to make the desired public statement.[80]

With Hitler's rejection of the June 29 agreement, attempts to reach an understanding on carrying out the concordat were in effect ended, although not definitely broken off. On April 16, 1935, Bergen was instructed to explain the status of negotiations to Pacelli. He claimed that the government had believed they were negotiating with delegates who had been granted full powers in June, 1934, and that final approval would be only a formal matter. It had not expected that the agreement would be submitted to all the bishops for their consideration. Subsequent amendments suggested by the curia were responsible for the failure to reach an agreement.[81] The cardinal secretary demolished these arguments in a sharply worded answering note on June 6.[82] It was now clear that the Vatican had no intention of accepting the June 29 agreement as originally drawn, and the Reich government in turn would not accept any amendments. The interpretation of Article 31 of the concordat and the status of Catholic organizations remained to plague church-state relations to the very end of the Nazi regime.

After the Saar referendum on January 13, 1935, hailed by Catholics as a Catholic victory,[83] the state assumed an even more aggressive policy towards both Protestant and Catholic churches. A number of critical Catholic studies of Rosenberg's *Myth of the Twentieth Century* elicited a heated rejoinder by Rosenberg with the provocative title, *To the Obscurantists of Our Time.*[84] More restrictive measures were taken against the church press, bringing repeated protests from the Vatican.[85] A campaign against confessional schools and against the employment of members of religious orders as teachers was launched. On March 31, 1935, Baldur von Schirach, in a major address, made derogatory references to Catholic youth organizations and charged them with wanting to continue the opposition of the Center party. "But I am of the opinion that if the Center party was as pleasing to God as they always have maintained, then the Almighty would not have permitted that the Center was destroyed." Practically all bishops protested his remarks, foremost among them Archbishop Gröber. On May 12, 1935, there was a particularly nasty demonstration against the archbishop of Paderborn when he visited the city of Hamm to participate in confirmation services.[86] The Catholic authorities had long been asking for a public disavowal of neopaganism, but now Göring, in a much-heralded address in June, 1935, did exactly the opposite. At the Frankentag in Bavaria he hailed the recognition of the old German cults and the practices that went with it.[87] Frick declared, in a widely publicized speech at Münster on July 7, that Germany had to be freed from the divisiveness of confessional differences. His assertion that according to the concordat the Catholic church, under the provision recognizing state laws as binding on all, had to consider the sterilization law as binding on Catholics brought a long sharp protest note from Rome. To recognize Frick's views would be tantamount to letting the state determine the doctrines of the church.[88]

Göring added to the conflict when on July 16 he issued a secret circular letter to Prussian administrative heads blasting political Catholicism.[89] This was followed on July 23 by a decree severely restricting the activity of all confessional youth organizations.[90] The members of such organizations were forbidden: to wear uniforms or insignia; to undertake marches, hikes, camping trips, or marching musical bands; to carry banners, flags, or pennants, except while participating in traditional processions, pilgrimages, or other church activities such as funerals; and to undertake any sport activity. Violations would be punished with imprisonment or fines. It was a severe restrictive measure, but on the other hand, it did not dissolve any particular Catholic or Protestant organizations or confiscate their property. Later decrees extended these restrictions on youth organizations to the whole Reich. There was plenty of room for future dispute as to what was purely religious activity, and what were traditional activities.

In February, Hitler had criticized the way the negotiations in regard to the concordat were being carried on,[91] and a growing estrangement had developed between him and Director Buttmann, who was most directly engaged in them. Frick, in whose province church affairs primarily lay, had lost heart, in part because he had repeatedly failed to win Hitler's direct support.[92] As the churchmen, both Catholic and Protestant, became more obstreperous and determined, Frick gradually shifted from a policy of trying to work with the churches to one of coercion and asserting the authority of the state. By mid-1935, the disruption in both Catholic and Protestant churches was greater than ever as the conflict among party, state, and church authorities intensified. In an effort to bring about the long-sought religious peace in the Reich, Hitler on July 16, 1935, transferred the supervision of religious affairs to a newly created Ministry of Church Affairs under Hanns Kerrl.[93] The new faces were, however, confronted by the same old problems. They had the same state and party superior officers above them, and the same church officials on the other side of the table to deal with. Motivated by the best of intentions and great confidence in his own abilities, Kerrl was, however, not destined to become a worker of miracles. His failure with the Protestant churches has already been traced; it remains to follow his efforts in relation to the Catholic church.

The Catholic Church Conflict, 1935–39

The Bishops and the German Government

As he had in the case of the Protestant churches, Minister Kerrl decided to proceed slowly in his relations with the Catholic church.[1] He had a long friendly conversation with Cardinal Bertram of Breslau,[2] and on September 9, 1935, he invited the bishops to prepare a new list of Catholic organizations to be protected under the concordat. This was done by Bishop Berning of Osnabrück, and after approval by the other bishops, Bertram, as chairman of the Fulda Bishops' Conference, submitted it to Kerrl on October 2. Subsequent negotiations by officials of the Ministry of Church Affairs, the Ministry of the Interior, and representatives of the bishops were unsuccessful.[3] The list of organizations foreseen by church and state officials when the concordat was signed never did appear. It might have clarified, but surely would not have ended, the controversy over the status of Catholic organizations; disputes continued to the end of the regime. The church held tenaciously to its organizations as a bulwark of its position and mission, while the state, bent on establishing its totalitarian power, sought equally tenaciously to nullify if not entirely destroy them.

At the conference in Fulda on August 20, 1935, the bishops had drawn up a long memorandum which they sent directly to Hitler. They pointed out those matters which threatened the peaceful relations between church and state, and how they conflicted with earlier governmental pronouncements and promises. Among their grievances were the neopagan attacks against Christianity and the church, the official toleration and support of these attacks, and the restrictions placed upon the church in combating them. The bishops cited the matter of conscience and the new moral codes; the defamation of the pope, bishops, and everything Catholic; the constant charges by government officials of political Catholicism on the part of the church; the numerous restrictions of confessional organizations, especially youth and workers' groups and the prohibition of dual membership in similar church and party organizations; and finally, the general secularization of all aspects of public life. It was a skillfully drawn document, and ended: "We pray to Almighty God that he take under his protection the life of our Führer and Reich chancellor, and that he grant his blessing to your great statesmanly goals, especially the expansion of employment, the maintenance of European peace, and the consolidation of the internal unity of our national community."[4] Drawn up at the same time, the bishops' pastoral letter was in general an exhortation to Catholics to remain firm in their faith. It had its hard-hitting passages; for example:

> Stand firm in faith when they say to you: religion has nothing to do with politics; therefore political Catholicism must be rooted out. We cannot repeat everything which we have said before against the Marxist principle, "religion is a private matter." The messengers of Christianity are to be "the salt of the earth" and "the light of the world" (Matt. 5: 13–14), and "should let their light shine before the people" (5: 16). The church should be as "a city on the hill" (5: 14), visible afar in the life of the people.[5]

Hitler did not submit a written answer to the bishops' memorandum, but he did reply to it in a proclamation at the party congress in Nürnberg on September 11, 1935:

> The party never had the intention, either formerly or today, to wage any kind of a struggle with Christianity in Germany. The National Socialist state, however, will not under any circumstances tolerate that in any indirect way the "politicization" of the confessions be continued or indeed begun anew. In regard to this, one should not be under any illusion as to the determination of the movement and of the state. We have fought the political clergy once and got them out of the parliaments, and that after a long struggle in which we had no state power and the other side had it all. Today we have the power, however, and we will never fight this battle as a battle against Christianity or even against just one of the confessions. But we will fight it for the sake of keeping our public life free from those priests who have failed their calling, who should have become politicians rather than clergymen.[6]

A few days later, on September 15, the notorious Nürnberg law was issued which limited German citizenship to those of German or kindred blood. The supplementary decrees of November 14 defined exactly who was to be considered a Jew, and limited severely the marriage of even Christian non-Aryans.[7] The state was thereby legislating on a sensitive topic so far as Catholicism was concerned. Yet, as in the case of the Protestants, there was no Catholic protest against the Nürnberg laws. The same policy was followed now as at the time of the first Jewish boycott movement in 1933. At that time Cardinal Bertram had written to the archbishops of the German church provinces, asking their position in regard to intervention. He noted: "My scruples [against intervention] are first of all based on the consideration that this is an economic battle that does not have anything to do with our immediate church interests."[8] At about the same time, Cardinal Faulhaber had written to Cardinal Secretary Pacelli:

> We bishops are being asked why the Catholic church, as so often in its history, does not intervene on behalf of the Jews. This is not possible at this time because the struggle against the Jews would at the same time become a struggle against Catholics, and because the Jews can help themselves, as the sudden end of the boycott shows. It is especially unjust and painful that by this action the Jews, even those who have been baptized for ten and twenty years and are good Catholics, indeed even those whose parents were already

Catholics, are legally still considered as Jews, and as doctors or lawyers are to lose their positions.[9]

Archbishop Gröber had also mentioned, in a letter to Professor Robert Leiber in Rome, that some Germans had lamented the fact that Catholics had not done more for the Jews, and then added: "I immediately intervened on behalf of the converted Jews, but so far have had no response to my action from Karlsruhe. I am afraid that the campaign against Judah will prove costly to us."[10]

These early comments characterize well the church's policy towards the Jews during the Nazi period. With some exceptions, particularly in the later years of the war, the church drew a line between religious Jews and converted Christian Jews. It was the church's duty and obligation to look after the latter; the former could take care of themselves. After the promulgation of the first racial laws of 1933, the authorities of the archdiocese of Cologne suggested to Catholic Jews who wished to emigrate that they get in touch with the Saint Raphael's Society, which would give them advice and aid. For those with no means they noted: "These we can for the time being only advise to consider themselves as members of a guest nation in Germany, and to take those aids which are offered to all those in need."[11] There is not one word of protest in the whole directive against the racial legislation. The party security officials noted this Catholic reluctance to take a public stand against the anti-Jewish measures, but added that "from numerous statements their sympathy for the Jews is clear."[12] When the curia, following the suggestions of the Fulda conference, tried to intervene on behalf of Catholic Jews at the time of the ratification of the concordat, it was made clear to Pacelli that Germany's racial policy was solely an internal governmental matter.[13] Neither the Catholic authorities in Germany nor those in Rome approved of the anti-Jewish policy, but they did nothing drastic for fear of heaping even more troubles on their own heads.

Vatican-Reich Negotiations

While the German bishops were carrying on their negotiations with the German government, the diplomatic relations between the Vatican and Berlin authorities continued on their course of protest and counterprotest at a snail's pace. The Vatican note of July 10, 1935, on nonobservance of the concordat was not answered until September 18, and the broader note of July 26 not until December 16; nothing was settled one way or another.[14] Like the German hierarchy, the Vatican had plenty to protest about, for they had the same concerns. The sterilization law of July 14, 1933, heightened Catholic apprehensions when it was sharpened by further amendments in June and July, 1935, and Frick announced its more rigorous enforcement.[15] The campaign against confessional schools, which the hierarchy had thought were well safeguarded by the national and state concordats, was under way.[16] Catholic organizations and individual clergymen were constantly harassed. Although the heyday of such charges was to come later, in 1935 the Reich began the so-called morality trials, chiefly prosecuting monastic lay brothers indicted for sexual offenses.[17] The trials particularly affected certain teaching orders and orders devoted to caring for the mentally ill. Gestapo reports are filled with this sort of material, for the police were indeed a bunch of busybodies. The government also inaugurated a highly publicized series of trials involving Catholic clergy charged with violating currency regulations. The problem of currency exchange bedeviled most European countries during the depression in the 1930s and, like others, Germany had issued a labyrinthine set of regulations, about sending funds abroad. Many monastic orders had mother houses or supported missions in other lands, or had simply incurred debts abroad. They felt honor bound to meet their financial obligations, and there is no question that at times they did not abide by the currency regulations. Indeed, Cardinal Schulte of Cologne and Cardinal Bertram issued acknowledgments and apologies for the failure to observe the laws, whether it had happened willfully or in ignorance.[18] Nazi propaganda equated currency smuggling with monasticism, although secular clergy were also involved. On December 6, 1935, Ambassador Bergen undertook on his own initiative to inform the Vatican, as a matter of courtesy, of the conviction of Bishop Petrus Legge of Meissen for violation of the currency regulations. His case did not stand alone, for there were some 60 processes under way against regular and secular clergy. The curia was greatly concerned about the bishop's conviction, which the pope considered unjust and a blow at the Catholic church. Bergen reported that the pope and others at the curia accepted the bishop's appeal to God and his declaration of innocence rather than the court's verdict. Curia officials asserted that natural law was superior to state law, and that natural law maintains one must meet one's obligations, which the unjust currency laws prevented. The curia intimated that the laws were being particularly enforced against the church, and objected to the widespread antichurch publicity in connection with the trials. Bergen himself felt that after settling the present extreme tension it would be well to start preparations for a new concordat which would replace both the concordat of 1933 and the state concordats and establish a new modus vivendi.[19]

It never came to that, although there were brief periods of less tension, as during the spring and summer of 1936. For a time attention was focused on the military reoccupation of the Rhineland on March 7, an act supported by the hierarchy along with practically all other Germans. Bishop Clemens August, Count von Galen, of Münster took occasion to send Secretary Meissner a sermon he had given on March 22 and asked that at least certain marked passages be presented to Hitler. Galen thanked the chancellor for what he had done, but then pointedly raised the question of whether Hitler knew how the church was being treated. He was sending him the sermon because the chancellor had repeatedly declared that he wanted to hear the voice of the people.[20]

Germany also played host to the Olympic Games in 1936, and
religious controversy was played down. Even Jewish sport organizations were permitted until after the games were held.[21] Both Catholic and Protestant churches shared in the Olympic activity. Special masses were said in French, English, Italian, Spanish, and Portuguese in the Hedwigs-kirche on the three Sundays of the games. Nuncio Orsenigo and Bishop Preysing said mass in the Olympic village. The Protestant churches named a special Olympic committee and manned a special Olympic tent near the railway station. There was a special Protestant festival service at the Kaiser-Wilhelm-Gedächtniskirche, and special musical services were held on the Sundays of the games.[22]

The foreign exchange and morality trials of Catholic clergy were discontinued in July, although charges continued to be filed.[23] The Spanish civil war, which broke out in July, 1936, revived fear of communism, and this was one issue on which the Catholic church and the German government saw eye to eye. On the very day that Hitler denounced the Bolshevik danger at the party congress in Nürnberg, the pope spoke in a similar vein to a group of Spanish refugees. The hierarchy hailed the coincidence of the two speeches as evidence of the need for the collaboration of church and state against a common enemy.[24] To further this cooperation, Nuncio Orsenigo arranged to have Hitler receive Cardinal Faulhaber at his retreat at Obersalzburg on November 4, 1936.

Hitler was a most gracious host, and in the three-hour conference he made a deep impression on Faulhaber. The danger of bolshevism was the main topic of their congenial discourse, and Hitler asked for another attempt at real cooperation. In his very secret report on the interview Faulhaber noted:

> The Führer commands the diplomatic and social forms better than a born sovereign. . . . Without doubt the Chancellor lives in faith in God (*Der Reichs-kanzler lebt ohne Zweifel in Glauben an Gott*). He recognizes Christianity as the foundation of western culture. . . . Not as clear is his conception of the Catholic church as a God-established institution, with its great historic and cultural position and with its divine independent mission over against the state.[25]

After the interview Faulhaber submitted the draft of an episcopal letter to his fellow bishops. The final text was ready on Christmas Eve, 1936, and it was read in all churches on January 3, 1937. It was a pledge of cooperation of church authorities with the state in the struggle against bolshevism. Nevertheless, the bishops mentioned that their aid would be more effective if the rights of the church under the concordat were upheld.[26]

The Encyclical *Mit brennender Sorge*

While 1936 was a relatively peaceful year in the relations of the Catholic church to the state, none of the controversies had really been settled. They were to break forth with renewed vigor in 1937, which was "for the Catholic church in Germany a year of indescribable bitterness and terrible storms."[27]

On January 12–13, 1937, the bishops of Germany assembled at Fulda for a conference. They had never received an answer to their memorandum of August, 1935, and they determined to try again. This time they drew up their memorandum in the form of seventeen citations of violations of the concordat, starting with the preamble and ending with Article 33.[28] Immediately following the conference, Germany's three cardinals, Bertram, Faulhaber and Schulte, along with Bishops Galen and Preysing, went to Rome. It was a strong delegation and had been invited to Rome by the pope before the Fulda conference. To Cardinal State Secretary Pacelli they repeated a request which the bishops had made at their August, 1936 conference. They sought a public declaration by the pope on the situation of the Catholic church in Germany. Pius XI was still recovering from an illness at that time, and Pacelli requested Faulhaber, who had just engineered the recent German bishops' statement, to prepare a draft of such a papal encyclical. Faulhaber's eleven-page draft, although it was thoroughly revised by Pacelli and the pope himself, remains the heart of the encyclical *Mit brennender Sorge* ("With Deep Anxiety").[29] It dealt with the condition of the Catholic church in the German Reich. The encyclical was sent to Nuncio Orsenigo in Berlin, who arranged for its printing and distribution, and it was read from the Catholic pulpits of Germany on March 21, 1937.[30]

What the authorities had long feared, and had always sought to hinder, had now happened.[31] The pope had publicly stated his grievances and thereby focused the attention of the world on the situation of the church in Germany. Early on the morning of the day that the encyclical was read in the churches Heydrich ordered the police to confiscate any copies of the encyclical found outside of churches or parish buildings. Two days later, the minister for church affairs directed a letter to all German bishops charging:

> [The encyclical] is in flat contradiction to the spirit of the concordat and to its express provisions. The encyclical contains serious attacks against the welfare and interests of the German nation. It attempts to diminish the authority of the Reich Government, to harm the interests of the German nation abroad, and, above all, to endanger the internal peace of the community by means of a direct appeal to the Catholic citizens by a party to the treaty with the Reich Government. For such a hostile attitude the Reich concordat grants no license.[32]

Kerrl held that the statements in the encyclical were contrary to the oath which the bishops took to uphold and honor the government and the Reich, and consequently the bishops and ordinaries "were forbidden to print, reproduce, or disseminate the encyclical in any form."[33] Under the government's interpretation of Article 4 of the concordat, church ordinances, pastoral letters, and official statements could be published in the official gazettes (*Amtsblätter*) and read from the pulpit.

The freedom to publish, however, did not apply to offprints, flyers, church papers, and other publications. If the latter contained criticism of the Führer or party, or other hostile material, they could be confiscated by the police. This interpretation of Article 4 had been called to the attention of all church officials in October, 1936.[34]

The result was that pastoral letters and encyclicals could usually be printed in the official church gazettes and read from the pulpits, but were immediately confiscated when there was an attempt to distribute them outside of the churches. The Gestapo also had a rule, generally observed, that they should halt at the doors of the churches; above all, they should not disrupt a religious service.[35] There were relatively few cases when this rule was violated, but the police naturally did not always follow the same policy in all sections of Germany. Thus State Secretary Hans Georg Hoffmann complained to the Bavarian police that confiscating the bishop's letter of 1934, when it was sold openly in the book trade in many parts of Germany, made little sense to him.[36]

Although the encyclical was drawn up in the usual involved Vatican phraseology and well larded with biblical citations, Pius XI nevertheless clearly laid his grievances on the line. If the concordat had:

> not borne the fruit we desired in the interest of your [German] people, no one in the whole world who has ears to hear can say today that the fault lies with the church and with her Supreme Head. The experience of the past years fixes the responsibility. It discloses intrigue which from the beginning had no other aim than a war of extermination. In the furrows in which we had laboured to sow the seeds of true peace, others—like the enemy in Holy Scripture (Matt. XIII, 25)—sowed the tares of suspicion, discord, hatred, calumny, of secret and open fundamental hostility to Christ and His Church, fed from a thousand different sources and making use of every available means. On them and on them alone and on their silent and vocal protectors rests the responsibility that now on the horizon of Germany there is seen not the rainbow of peace but the threatening storm-clouds of destructive religious wars.[37]

He went on to define "true belief in God," protesting against the recently introduced religious designation of "God believing," and the deification of race, people, state, or constitution. He admonished the bishops to "watch that such pernicious errors which usually bring in their train more pernicious practices find no support among the people" and that "the morality of the human race is grounded on faith in God kept true and pure. . . . The number of such fools who presume to separate morality from religion has today become legion." He called for a recognition of natural law, and, like John Locke, in an earlier period, held: "The believer has an inalienable right to profess his faith and to practice it in the manner suited to him. Laws which suppress or render difficult the profession and practice of this faith are contrary to natural law." Confessional schools and instruction were upheld, and there were words of gratitude for the loyalty and steadfastness not only of the bishops, but of priests, religious orders, youth, and the laity in general.

There were no doubt things which he passed over—notably there was no outright condemnation of anti-Semitism—but the encyclical was and remains a strong and forthright condemnation of the way the church was being treated in Germany. And this is exactly how the German government viewed it. The nuncio was told it was a "call to battle," and the German ambassador at the Vatican was ordered not to participate in Easter ceremonies and to go on leave.[38]

Both Cardinal Bertram, as chairman of the Fulda Bishops' Conference, and Nuncio Orsenigo protested the ban on distributing the encyclical and closing the publishing houses which had printed it.[39] This time at least there were prompt replies. The cardinal received a sharply worded rejection from Minister Kerrl, and the Foreign Office sent a similar one directly to the curia. This in turn was rejected.[40] Hitler publicly took note of the encyclical in his May Day address, stating:

> And from every German I must demand: you must also be able to obey or you will never be worthy or entitled to command. That is the prerequisite. To this end we will educate our people and pass over the obstinacy or stupidity of the individual. Bend or break—one or the other! We can not tolerate that this authority, which is the authority of the German people, is attacked by anybody else.
>
> That holds also for the churches. So long as they concern themselves about religious problems, the state will not concern itself about them. When they attempt by any other means—writings, encyclicals, etc.—to assure themselves rights which belong only to the state, we will push them back into their proper spiritual activity and the care of souls. It is not proper for them to criticize the morals of the state, when they have enough grounds to be concerned about their own morality. For the morals of the state and of the people the German state leadership will concern itself—of that we can assure all those who are worried about it within and without Germany.[41]

The controversy became more involved when Cardinal Mundelein of Chicago, in an address to 500 diocesan priests on May 18, undertook to defend the German clergy against the charges of immorality being levied against them. On April 6 Hitler had personally ordered the resumption of the currency and morality trials which had lain dormant since July, 1936.[42] Mundelein compared the action of the German government to the Allied atrocity propaganda during World War I, to which the Germans had always bitterly objected. He posed a question: "Perhaps you will ask how it is that a nation of 60 million intelligent people will submit in fear and servitude to an alien, an Austrian paper hanger, and a poor one at that, and a few associates like Goebbels and Göring, who dictate every move of the people's lives."[43] To the German government—yes, to the majority of Germans of that day—it was an insulting question. No one has ever found a satisfactory answer, except perhaps the postwar German wit who asked, "Who was the greatest surgeon during the Third Reich?," and then admitted that it was Hitler, for he had removed the brains of sixty million Germans and they did not even notice it!

Minister Goebbels undertook to deal with Cardinal Mundelein in a two-hour address in the *Deutschlandhalle* on May 28, 1937.[44] He maintained it was necessary to expose the sexual crimes of the clergy, and intimated that he was revealing only a tiny bit of the material available

on this subject. It was not long before an open letter to Goebbels,
refuting his extravagant charges and signed "Michael Germanicus," was being passed from hand to hand. The police were soon after the letters, but as late as October 3, 1937, they still came up with fifty-five copies which had been distributed in Eichstätt the night before.[45] Cardinal Mundelein's speech also led to another series of acrimonious diplomatic notes, fueled by the Pope's reception of pilgrims from Chicago, to whom he "was pleased to point out the greatness of their city and—why not say it?—the greatness of their estimable cardinal archbishop, who is so solicitous and zealous in the defense of the rights of God and of the Church and in the salvation of souls."[46]

While the diplomatic tug-of-war between the Vatican and the German government was going on, attempts were being made to come to some basic decisions on the matter of church and state relations. The controversy over Pius XI's *Mit brennender Sorge* coincided with the turmoil in the Protestant churches over Hitler's call for new church elections. In the end the church elections were not held, and the conflict within Protestantism went on as before. Likewise, the government's plans to bring about a basic settlement with the Catholic church never materialized.

Plans for a New Settlement

Minister Kerrl had never had much stature in either governmental or party circles, and the failure of his pacification policy had added nothing to it. Kerrl was actually a man to be pitied, for he never had a free hand, and from 1937 on he was undermined wherever he turned. Hitler had overruled him in regard to the Protestant church elections. While Kerrl had prohibited the printing, reproduction, and distribution of the papal encyclical, the Gestapo and Ministry of Propaganda had ordered more far-reaching police and press measures.[47] Hitler had ordered the resumption of the currency and morality trials, and Goebbels whipped up the publicity about them. Minister of the Interior Frick, who supposedly controlled the police, never removed his hands entirely from church affairs. It was he who issued the controversial ordinance on how people might designate their religious affiliation and instituted the term *Gottgläubig*. The minister of education pushed school reform and the policy of minimizing the influence of the churches over education. Von Schirach went his own way in regard to the Hitler Youth, the minister of labor interfered with the church labor groups, and Rosenberg, in charge of the cultural and educational supervision and training of the Nazi party, constantly stepped over into religious and church affairs. The army command issued orders in regard to the relationship of the churches to the armed services. The finance minister supervised the currency regulations which profoundly affected the churches, particularly in regard to their missionary activity. The minister of justice had the thankless task of supervising judicial proceedings against clergymen and a host of other complicated

problems, notably those involving church property. Above all, the Foreign Office insisted, and doubtless rightly so, on conducting business
with the curia. It is not necessary to look for other officials who also had
their fingers in church matters; it is clear that Kerrl was far from being in a
position to formulate, let alone carry out, a policy.

In 1940 Kerrl was to admit to Bavarian State Secretary Hoffman that
the state and party should not only declare for religious toleration but
should finally carry it out. He had not had the least support in trying to
bring this about, and he feared the consequences—a union of Protestants and Catholics in a battle against the anti-Christian movement represented by state and party. "And so I approach things as a practical
man," he went on to say, "as the man who is responsible in the eyes of
the public, but in spite of this, neither from the state or the party have I
been granted any authority or the possibility to carry out what is necessary and recognized as right."[48] What he wrote of his position in 1940
was essentially true in 1937 as well.

The Ministry for Church Affairs, in consultation with the Foreign
Office, drew up a proposed note to the Vatican in which the concordat
was to be declared invalid. Kerrl discussed this with Hitler, who wanted
the facts which justified the conclusion that certain provisions of the
concordat had become inapplicable more strongly emphasized. Kerrl
was instructed to draw up a new draft. It was "not to be equivalent to a
declaration of the invalidity of the entire concordat, but [was] to declare
four or five particularly important articles intolerable and therefore no
longer binding [on Germany]. For the rest, however, it [would] leave the
concordat in force."[49] Looking ahead, Hitler was considering the preparation of a law concerning the relations between church and state.
When that was completed the concordat would be denounced, and
twenty-four hours later the new Reich law would be published. This
would prevent the creation of an interim with no law in effect, as would
have happened if the concordat were denounced immediately as the
original draft provided. State Secretary Muhs of the Ministry of Church
Affairs and State Secretary Mackensen of the Foreign Office, who discussed the matter with Minister Kerrl, did not like the proposed changes,
and they persuaded Kerrl to prepare two drafts for the Führer, who
would then make the final decision.

Hitler had sensibly curbed Kerrl's desire to take drastic action at
once. In July the Führer again ordered that no more major trials be held
in the immorality proceedings against the Catholic priests.[50] The German Foreign Office also counselled more circumspect measures. "Although I am entirely of the opinion that firm language is advisable in
dealing with the Vatican," von Neurath wrote to Kerrl, "I do not, as you
know, share your opinion regarding the tone to be used. What may be
appropriate for authorities at home is by no means suitable for inter-
course with the outside world, as we have had to discover repeatedly to
our cost."[51] The concordat note was postponed. Certainly the law on
church and state was not ready, and now it also became involved in the
timing of the proclamation of the Reich school law.[52]

Rumors spread that the settlement of religious matters would be taken up at the annual Nürnberg party congress in September, 1937.[53] However, aside from the award of the first National Prize to Rosenberg for his writings, which was a slap in the face of Catholic and Protestant churchmen, church and religious affairs were passed over. By this time Hitler, in agreement with Kerrl, had decided to settle the matter of church and state in a big speech to the Reichstag on Reformation Day. Kerrl reported that Hitler had said his "speech would greatly eclipse Luther's ninety-five theses and that it was to complete the work of the Reformation in the German spirit."[54] The party's adherence to positive Christianity was to be reiterated, and every citizen was to be guaranteed true religious freedom. The note in which the concordat was to be "described as outdated by the course of developments" was to be handed to the Vatican on the day of the speech. In the end Hitler never gave the speech, the famous concordat note was never sent,[55] and the disputes over the breaches of the concordat continued. Hitler, however, had apparently come to some personal decisions. Instead of speaking to the Reichstag on October 31, 1937, he spoke to a group of party propaganda leaders in Berlin, and declared: "After difficult inner struggles I had freed myself of my remaining childhood religious conceptions. I feel as refreshed now as a foal on a meadow."[56] This was not true of the pope, who in his customary Christmas allocution again "vigorously complained of the 'persecution' of the Catholic Church in Germany," and pointedly remarked: "We do not engage in politics; everyone knows this; everyone sees it who wants to see it."[57]

While Hitler, Kerrl, and the Foreign Office were trying to come up with some final definition of church-state relations, the police had worked out a program of their own. On July 1, 1937, Heydrich had issued an order defining the province of the security police of the SS and of the secret police (Gestapo). To the former were allotted, in general, education, folk relations, art, party and state relations, foreign countries, Free Masonry, and organizations; to the latter were allotted Marxism, treason, emigration, churches, sects, pacifism, Jewry, organizations hostile to the state, the economy, and the press.[58] To leave organizations to the security police of the SS and churches and sects to the Gestapo shows that the purpose was not so much to draw a line between jurisdictions as to bring about greater police cooperation. The measure indicated a desire on the part of Heydrich, who headed both police groups, to step up their activity and increase their efficiency.

On July 18, 1937, a long directive was communicated to various security police headquarters.[59] It was considered supersecret, and those who violated the prohibitions against duplications and further distribution of this directive were threatened with severe punishment. The most important task was to gain information about the churches, the leading personalities in them, the activities of their organizations, and so forth. To this end one of the most important tasks was to expand the network of informers (Verbindungsmänner, V-Männer). There could be no action on the national level against church organizations and monastic constitutions at that time; the ground had still to be prepared by further propaganda. As far as Protestantism was concerned, there was no need to hasten the conflict; a restrained defense was for the present the best program. On the other hand, the battle against the small religious sects must be intensified, for they not only operated with Bolshevik methods, but were havens for former Marxists. The sects were dangerous because they helped disrupt the unity of the German people. Harmless sects could for the time being be permitted to continue, and the German Faith groups should be watched but dealt with gingerly.

The detailed directive informed the police heads about the nature of the problem and the procedures to be followed. In general it was to gather information, through informers, by surveillance of church activity of every kind, including reporting on sermons and the reactions of the congregations. When police prohibitions were to be undertaken, they should be extended to as great a territorial area as possible. This was, however, to be a policy of undermining and of piecemeal attrition, rather than a frontal attack on a national basis. In essence this was not a new policy, and it was maintained to the end of the regime. Decrees were issued right and left; sometimes they were carried out strictly, at other times they were winked at, or understanding officials blunted the rigor of the measures. Yet the direction of the drive was maintained—toward the constant restriction of the historic privileges of the churches, the negation of religious values, and the increased secularization of the all-powerful totalitarian state.

Conflict Intensifies

To describe the actual status of the Catholic church in Nazi Germany at any particular time is nearly impossible. To do so would involve recounting the extent of its tribulation, its persecution, and yes, also its moments of glory, and would necessitate detailing innumerable incidents scattered throughout Germany. Even when total figures on, for example, imprisonments in certain dioceses are available, they are likely to be for the whole Hitler period, and it is difficult to discern how events proceeded. The situation always changed; the early years were quite different from the last years of peace and different again from the years of war. Yet the more it changed the more it remained the same.

Basically, of course, there was no difference between the way the Protestant and Catholic churches were treated, although the impact of the measures was at times different. All denominations, including the smallest sects, were subject to the law regulating public collections of November 5, 1934,[60] the law against malicious attacks on state and party of December 20, 1934,[61] and other similar measures. All were subject, under the presidential decree of Feburary 28, 1933,[62] to arbitrary police measures "in combatting communism," and nowhere was the definition of what constituted communism more elastic than in Nazi Germany. Thus, for example, both the Protestant and Catholic press were curtailed; both the Protestant and Catholic organizations had to obtain government permission to hold certain kinds of meetings; both Catholic and Protestant clergy were punished by prohibitions to speak, were exiled from certain areas, or were denied the right to give religious instruction in the schools. Or again, when the minister of the interior, on February 17, 1937, forbade public pronouncement of the names of people who had withdrawn their membership from a church, particularly reading the names from the pulpit, the measure affected both, although the impact was greater on Protestant churches.[63] It is not a question of who was persecuted or suffered the most; the Nazis were not particularly partial. Certainly the small sects, like the Jehovah's Witnesses and the many others that were dissolved and whose property was liquidated, were treated the most severely. They were given short shrift and no one spoke up in their behalf.[64]

It is true that the Catholic church was spared some of the tribulations which struck the Protestants. There was no attempt to restructure or control the government of the Catholic church. There was little conflict over the naming of officials to high ecclesiastical posts, and the authority of the bishops over the church and the faithful was never challenged. The troublesome question of taking an oath of loyalty never became an issue in the Catholic church as it did in the Protestant. The bishops took their oath of loyalty to the regime and nation as provided by the concordat, which was made easier for them because of established Catholic doctrine. In 1934, the Fulda Bishops' Conference included in its pastoral letter the following statement:

> You have heard and read you must take an oath of unconditional followership. We, your bishops, say to you: An oath is a solemn appeal to God; it can therefore never obligate one to commit an act which is contrary to the commandments of God. By an oath, as for example in the case of an official or soldier, you can obligate yourself loyally to carrying out your word or to obedience to the legal government. If, however, an order should demand something that was contrary to God's commands and to your conscience, then that would hold which the Bishops' Conference at Fulda in November, 1919, in a solemn declaration in respect to the Weimar Constitution, stated: As for the oath of loyalty to the constitution, Catholics will of course not be obligated to anything which is contrary to God or church law and thereby is contrary to their conscience.[65]

It is not surprising that the Bavarian police objected to this statement and advanced it as a reason for confiscating the pastoral letter. They argued that if everyone were to test if an act was contrary to his conscience, anarchy could result.[66]

Although the government's currency regulations seemed to hit the Catholic church particularly hard because of its international charities and obligations to transfer funds, there was probably less interference with the total financial system of the Catholic church than with that of the Protestant churches. The state-dominated financial sections which came to supervise the funds of the Protestant Land churches in some areas were never inflicted on the Catholic church. State subsidies were curtailed in later years, but as in the case of the Protestants, they were never completely cancelled. The removal of members of religious orders as teachers from the educational system hit the finances of some monastic orders hard, for state salaries had gone to the orders and not to individuals. Many of the members of the monastic orders undertook to give private instruction in various subjects without pay or for a mere pittance. This instruction was popular, for the teachers were usually very competent. The government tried unsuccessfully to put an end to it.[67] The Catholic church suffered financially from the confiscation of the property of the relatively few monastic establishments which were closed, and likewise by the occasional seizure of property of those religious organizations which were liquidated.[68] The Catholic clergy were also hit by the special "bachelor tax" which the Nazis inaugurated as a supplement to the income tax.[69] Yet in spite of all the harassment, the restrictions on special collections, and the confiscations, the financial structure of the Catholic church remained intact and under the supervision and administration of church authorities.

That the state used the currency and morality trials as coercive and propaganda measures against the Catholic church is clear from the way Hitler ordered that they be suspended or pushed. How effective they were is hard to assess; in the end they probably did much to rally Catholics to more loyal support of their church.[70] The hierarchy never denied that there were some moral delinquencies among the clergy and condemned such individuals, but rightly emphasized that those involved were only a very small minority.[71] The Nazis attempted to prove too much; the people knew that the picture the regime was trying to paint was inaccurate. Sometimes the authorities overreached themselves in their attempts to pin something on the church. In a speech on January 25, 1937, Julius Streicher stated he could name clerics who had one or more children. The babies were put in a nunnery where they soon died, and this was why they were called "angel nunneries" (*Engelklöster*).[72] In September, 1937, Minister of the Interior Wagner asked the Bavarian secret police "to determine what Catholic clergy in Bavaria had fathered children, with whom, and if the priests paid child support. What action had the church taken against these clergy?"[73] The police worked out a somewhat more detailed inquiry and circulated it to all district police offices. It was meant to be a secret and discreet investigation. Instead, some of the police officials confronted the clergy directly. The inquiry came to the hand of Cathedral Prelate Johann Kraus at Eichstätt, a man whom a police official compared in forthrightness to Pastor Martin Niemöller. He had been a major in World War I and then studied theology. Kraus had been ordered to leave the district in April, 1937, but on direct orders of his bishop remained. When he did not go, his right to teach was withdrawn, but again he did not recognize the police order. In a sermon in the beautiful Eichstätt cathedral on October 30, 1937, the eve of the festival of Christ the King, Kraus spoke out:

> Truly, the blush of anger crossed my face as this circular letter came into my hands. Are we Catholic clergymen mangy dogs? Has one forgotten the more than 3,000 Catholic clergy who for four years wore the grey mantle of honor

and carried weapons? Is it a matter of trying to destroy the honor of the clergy, and create a people without clergymen?[74]

Bavarian State Secretary Hoffmann now demanded that the police trace the origin of their directive. They did so, and promised to take disciplinary measures against those police officials who had made the mistake of revealing the order. The Ministry of Church Affairs heard about the matter and the results of Hoffmann's inquiry were submitted to that office.[75] How many reports were ever turned in remains unknown, but the roll of film on which this material was found contains the name of exactly one priest about whom such a report was made.[76] The whole incident is a good example of police activity and of inner party and state differences; it shows that strong and courageous protest did have effect.

Some aspects of the government's program to secularize the school system hit the Catholics particularly hard. The gradual curtailment of school prayers and religious services struck at both Catholic and Protestant practices. So did the general curtailment of religious instruction in the schools. Yet here one of Bormann's remarks is worthy of note. In a major review of the schools sent to Minister Rust on March 20, 1939, he wrote: "The retention of religious instruction in the schools results only out of consideration of the provisions of the concordat. No universal philosophical or pedagogical necessity for its retention exists."[77]

The conversion of confessional schools into interdenominational schools was opposed by both confessions. Yet this latter action was more severe upon the Catholics, for they thought they had safeguarded their confessional schools in the concordats, and that in 1933 they had even won the right to establish such schools throughout Germany. The Catholics had also always maintained that parents should have the right to decide whether their children should attend a confessional or an interdenominational school. Now the tables were turned on them. By coercion and often by fake elections, the government persuaded parents to choose interdenominational schools. This struck at the very heart of Catholic doctrine and practice. Members of religious orders taught in both public and private schools, and when they were denied the right to teach this was a blow which did not affect the Protestants. To a lesser extent this was also true of the virtual elimination of private schools.[78]

The government's attempt to remove all crucifixes from school buildings caused the most anguish in Catholic regions. The campaign was started in Oldenburg in 1936, but had to be rescinded because of Catholic opposition.[79] The same effort was made in other areas, but it was never completely successful. When the confessional schools had legally been ended, schools in purely Catholic regions were still likely to be attended only by Catholic pupils and to be staffed by Catholic teachers. In the Koblenz area it was ordered that crucifixes could remain in such a school, but if it was attended by both Protestants and Catholics they had to be removed.[80] This order naturally brought the one or two Protestant pupils that fate had lodged in those districts into great disfavor. Quite rightly, the local police reported that it would be better to remove crucifixes from all schools than try to do so only in mixed schools. The ostensible purpose of removing crucifixes from nondenominational schools was to bridge the gap between confessions; instead such action increased it.

In Bavaria on April 23, 1941, Minister Adolf Wagner ordered that religious pictures and crucifixes were gradually to be eliminated from schools as, for example, when classrooms were renovated. The order led to a letter of protest by the Bavarian bishops on July 26, 1941, asking him not to make the schools a battle field for Weltanschauung. They pleaded that the cross be kept at a time when the soldiers in the field were fighting bolshevism, so that upon entering a school one would know it was not a Jewish or a pagan school, but a state school of a people that upheld Christian culture.[81] This protest, along with great unrest among the populace, apparently had some effect, for Wagner soon issued a stop decree on the removal of crucifixes, although it was not well publicized. A Gauleiter in Mainfranken, for example, did not proclaim it because he was strongly in favor of the removal of crucifixes.[82] Rosenberg found such measures of dubious value; he felt that the experiment of the removal of crucifixes in Oldenburg should have caused the Bavarian officials to think it over several times before attempting it; besides, it was contrary to Hess's order at the start of the war to refrain from doing anything which would arouse religious controversy.[83]

The Catholics were also harder hit by all the petty restrictions on church organizations, if for no other reason than that they had more such organizations and were determined to hold onto them because they felt they were protected by the concordat. While they suffered great restrictions, the Catholic organizations were not all swept away. With the failure to achieve agreement in 1935 on the status of various Catholic organizations under Article 31 of the concordat, von Schirach planned an extensive campaign to bring all young Germans into the Hitler Youth. He proclaimed 1936 the "year of youth" and his efforts to enroll all ten-year-olds on the eve of Hitler's birthday on April 20 were remarkably successful.[84] He devised plans to make membership in the Hitler Youth compulsory, and these were incorporated in the Law on the Hitler Youth of December 1, 1936.[85] It was recognized that the goal could not be accomplished overnight; for one thing, the leadership was not available. In fact, the implementary decrees were not issued until 1939.

The ban on double membership in the Hitler Youth and other youth organizations still remained in force.[86] The only way out of this cul-de-sac was to dissolve the other organizations, and this policy was soon initiated. On July 27, 1937, on the grounds that the Catholic Young Men's Association (*Jungmännerverband*, JMV) in the diocese of Paderborn had violated the ordinance of July 23, 1935, against confessional youth groups participating in hikes, camping activity, and so forth, the secret police dissolved it and confiscated its property. Since this association was a sort of cover confederation of all the various Catholic youth groups, its dissolution virtually put an end to the existing Catholic youth organizations in the diocese. The police continued

their policy of attrition by dissolving the Young Men's Association in
the diocese of Münster on October 27, 1937, in the diocese of Trier
on November 12, in part of the diocese of Breslau on November 27,
in all of Bavaria on January 20, 1938, and in the diocese of Cologne
and Aachen on February 1, 1938. It was not until February 6, 1939,
that an ordinance extending the dissolution to the whole Reich ended
this piecemeal procedure.[87]

The first dissolutions had confronted the hierarchy with a very practical question—should they voluntarily dissolve their groups and thereby
save their considerable assets from confiscation? The decision was ultimately against doing so, for that would have meant surrendering to the
government's interpretation of Article 31 of the concordat. Instead, the
church authorities set about reorganizing its youth work and conducting
special youth leadership courses for laity and clergy. Some of the property of the youth organizations could be saved by judicious transfer to
diocesan authorities. They were also able to change the emphasis of
some of the organizations and continue them under new names. Thus
the *Sturmschar* became "the Community of Saint Michael," and the *St.
Georg Pfadfinderschaft* became "the Community of Saint George." The
seeming victory of the state in the long controversy over the status of
Catholic youth organizations did not end, but rather stimulated the activity of the Catholic church in respect to its youth and led to a deepen-
ing of religious feeling among members of the groups.[88]

The dissolution of the last youth sodalities and congregations in the
diocese of Münster led Bishop Galen to address a letter of protest to the
Führer. As usual, this dissolution had been based on the presidential
order of February 28, 1933, which was designed to protect Germans
from communism. Galen saw this as charging good Catholics with being communists. Minister Lammers of the Reich Chancellery took up the
issue with Himmler, who explained that the courts had long extended
the decree to include all actions hostile to the state. The police needed
to cite some law to support their actions, and so they used the order of
1933. Galen received only an acknowledgment of his letter. A further
protest of August 30, 1939, against the dissolution of the Association to
Aid the Education of Priests (*Priesterhilfwerk*) because some of the members had allegedly violated the laws regulating collections, also went
unanswered. Bishop Galen, who was a staunch German patriot, was
especially irritated that such an action was undertaken during a period
of crisis when men were being called to the colors.[89]

In January, 1938, the Gestapo also ended the study center (*Hauptarbeitsstelle*) which the German episcopate had established in Düsseldorf. It was under the supervision of the archbishop of Cologne,
who sent off a number of protests to various officials. Bishop Heinrich
Wienken, the special representative of the hierarchy in Berlin, tried to
reverse the decision, but to no avail. The center was held to be conducting activity inimical to the state.[90]

Catholics also suffered more than Protestants from the restrictions
on church processions and pilgrimages. Traditional pilgrimages and pro-

cessions could always be held, although they were thoroughly supervised and regulated.[91] If they were held solely on church property, the
church was able to do what it wished; if they used the streets, it is
surprising how the necessity of keeping traffic moving could prevent the
erection of Corpus Christi Day altars on thoroughfares. In 1936 Hess, in
agreement with Kerrl, ordered that government and party buildings
should not be decorated for Corpus Christi Day, and although officials
could participate as individuals in the processions, the party and its
ancillary organizations should not take part as a group.[92] The point,
however, should be made that even if there was frequent interference,
nevertheless pilgrimages, processions, and the traditional welcoming
ceremonies for clergymen did go on throughout the Nazi era.[93]

Another bit of rowdyism hit Catholics more specifically than others.
This was the destruction and desecration of roadside crosses or religious
statues.[94] The incidents increased to such an extent that in the fall of
1937 the Munich-Freising diocesan office instructed the faithful that
anyone who discovered molestation of a cross should report it immediately to the police and the diocesan authorities. The following Friday or
Sunday there should be a special service of repentance in the local
church, with sermon and service honoring the stations of the cross.
Crosses in churches and homes were to be decorated, and the damaged
crosses restored as soon as possible. The police firmly believed that the
publication of this directive was done to arouse sympathy for the
clergy.[95] On November 16–17, 1940, the cross in the hands of a figure
on the bridge across the quiet Altmühl in Eichstätt was removed. Again
Cathedral Prelate Kraus delivered a ringing sermon, in which he proph-
esied that in spite of the abundance of police in the town (it was a
police training center), the culprit would not be caught. Actually, it was
a drunken higher police officer who had taken the cross, and he did
penance by committing suicide. Kraus was arrested because of his acid
sermon, but after he sat in jail for almost a year, the higher authorities in
Ansbach dropped the charges against him and he was freed on November 5, 1941.[96]

The desecration of crosses and their removal from schools and other
public buildings was only one of many antichurch tactics which the
Nazis at times pursued. The Ministry of Agriculture had long sponsored a
Bauernkalender, the German version of the New England Farmers' Almanac. In 1935 this publication appeared without the Christian church
festivals, which traditionally indicated the special Catholic holidays and
saints' days. Many of the church festivals were now designated as commemorative days for Woden and Thor, the heroes of the Germanic Faith
enthusiasts. Good Friday was transformed into a day of commemoration
for the 4,500 Saxons slain by Charlemagne in his policy of conversion by
the sword.[97] The outcry was tremendous, and Minister Richard Darré did
not need to have his ear to the ground to know that he had better apologize and blame his subordinate in charge of the publication, even if the
introduction did carry his signature. Ambassador Bergen reported that
articles in the Osservatore Romano showed that they were not impressed

by Darré's *démenti* at the Vatican, and that the *Bauernkalender* indicated
how things were going in Germany.[98]

The National Socialist leaders reiterated time and again that an individual should neither be penalized nor gain any advantage from ties he might or might not have with any churches.[99] Although it had been the thing to do to go to church in 1933, this ardor for church attendance on the part of active party members had tapered off. In 1937 the unofficial party campaign for withdrawal from church membership really got under way. Withdrawals reached new heights in that year; there were 108,000 from the Catholic church, and 396,000 from the Protestant.[100]

The problem of whether Catholics could belong to similar church and state organizations was never successfully solved. The Catholic hierarchy forbade the leaders of Catholic organizations to turn over their membership lists, in order to prevent party and state officials from bringing pressure on the members to withdraw.[101] Even when Minister Robert Ley forbade double membership for members of the Labor Front, he left loopholes: "Membership in church organizations and groups that serve solely religious, cultural, or social welfare purposes is of course permitted to members of the German Labor Front, and is not considered to be under the ban of double membership."[102] To have pushed the issue too far would have deprived the Labor Front of virtually all members in some Catholic regions. Whether members of Catholic youth organizations could be members of the Hitler Youth also always remained a problem. The churches had to request permission, but they were able to hold special vacation retreats for their youth. Members of the Hitler Youth and of the girls' organization (*Bund Deutscher Mädel*) could attend these confessional gatherings if they obtained special absence permits from their units. The young people did not always bother to do so, and so the police ordered that if members of the Hitler Youth were in attendance at a confessional retreat without an official excuse, the whole retreat would be closed down.[103]

The party leaders also were notorious for arranging meetings on Sundays and at hours which interfered with religious services. The Catholic Church set aside a special youth dedication Sunday (*Glaubensfeier*), and the party consciously tried to cut the attendance by scheduling competing Nazi-sponsored sport events.[104]

The Catholic church did not take the many restrictions easily. It constantly protested, and not without result. Above all, however, the church worked hard to expand its services.[105] The government suspected, and no doubt correctly, that the church had established a special courier service for the distribution of encyclicals and as a means of keeping church officials in touch with one another.[106] It instituted special missionary services, and traveling preaching padres increased their activity.[107] The latter were closely watched by the police and a number were arrested. The police always paid special attention to the Jesuits, who were considered the root of all evil.[108] The arrest and imprisonment for six months of an especially able Jesuit speaker, Rupert Mayer, who worked with men's groups, created something of a furor in Munich and throughout Bavaria in 1937.[109] Cardinal Faulhaber took occasion to preach a sharp sermon, deriding the National Socialist-sponsored religious designation "God believing."

> "God believing" in present-day religious statistics no longer has the former meaning of the first article of the Creed. "God believing" today means: I just believe in God, as the Turks and Hottentots are God believing; I declare myself free from Christ and his church. He who designates himself "God believing" has betrayed Christ, and declared his departure from the Catholic church. The hour of decision has come. When an individual is asked: Are you God believing or what are you? . . . then every Catholic must declare: . . . "I am Catholic. I believe not only in God, but in Christ and in my church. I am Catholic."[110]

But Faulhaber was a man of many faces, and in his New Year's Eve sermon in 1938 he astonished his hearers by saying: "That is one advantage of our time; in the highest position of the Reich we have the example of a simple and modest alcohol and nicotine-free way of life." Father Mayer, whom the cardinal had so recently defended, was shocked and later noted: "Since that moment something struck my heart and prevented me from ever putting in my appearance again."[111] Faulhaber's statement seems all the more incomprehensible as it was made only a couple of months after the notorious Crystal Night pogrom of November 9, 1938.

There is no question that the Catholic laity rallied to support their church and their clergy. Processions, pilgrimages, and regular church services were well attended, as was noted time and again in police reports. The people went to church but they also sometimes stayed away. Thus the police official in Kochem, in his monthly report to headquarters on May 20, 1939, noted that church attendance had been exceptionally good at the regular services, but at the specially announced masses on Hitler's birthday (April 20) and on May 1, an official holiday, the churches were almost empty.[112]

Both the Protestant and Catholic churches (and for that matter also the state) were careful not to confront the people with an absolute choice between church and state. The churchmen knew that the state had many popular accomplishments to its credit—the lessening of unemployment, the upturn in economic prosperity, the destruction of the shackles imposed by the Treaty of Versailles, the recreation of a German Wehrmacht, and, not least, spectacular public festivals and rallies which gave the people a sense of active participation in the rebuilding of Germany. Instead of excluding active National Socialists and men in uniform from services, which was the pre-1933 Catholic policy, they were now welcomed. The church leaders fought to keep supporters of the government within the churches; they could not do otherwise and still be true to their Christian mission.

The party leaders were well aware of the church efforts to infiltrate the party, and the churches' use of party terminology was resented. Thus in reporting that the Catholic clergy constantly agitated against national socialism, a police official noted in 1934 that the clergy were apt to end their sermons with the summons: "Our highest Führer, Jesus Christ, Heil!," or "Salvation lies alone in Christ, our only Führer!"[113] Göring, in his famous attack on political Catholicism in 1935, charged the church had converted "those abbreviations which have entered into the flesh and blood of all Germans, like H.J. (*Hitler Jugend*) to the Heart of Jesus (*Herz Jesu*), BDM (*Bund Deutscher Mädel*) to Daughters of Mary (*Bund der Marienmädchen*), and applied the German greeting (*Deutscher Gruss*) to Jesus Christ."[114] The security police in the Koblenz district reported on November 22, 1937, that at the feast of Christ the King on October 31, 1936, a new custom had been introduced in local churches which was now used at all high church festivals. There was a church procession with the crucifix carried in the lead, which was then followed by the mass servitors with censers, the lay church authorities in formal attire with high hats, and then the flags of the various church organizations. They proceeded to the altar, then circled the church twice, after which the flags were placed beside the altar where they remained during the service. Such imitation of Nazi party practices was not liked by party officials.[115]

In 1938 Bormann got hold of the report of a meeting of Catholic churchmen at Paderborn. In this paper guidelines were worked out for the clergy in regard to activities of Catholic Action. The clergy were henceforth to attempt to work with party organizations and influence the faithful in line with party directives without permitting a clash of views. Catholics were to be urged to join party organizations, wear party uniforms and designations in church processions, establish close relations with local Wehrmacht leaders, give generously to party collections, and use the German greeting. The police with great secrecy were informed of this program for "undermining the party" and asked to apply close surveillance.[116]

Enough has been said to indicate the general nature of the conflict between the Catholic church and the leaders of Nazi Germany. A summary of what happened to the 1,296 diocesan priests (including 162 monastic priests) of the Munich-Freising archdiocese provides representative quantification data for the whole Nazi period, including the war years. On the part of state authorities there were 1,526 interrogations, 292 house searches, 189 confiscations of documents and other material, 696 official warnings involving 274 priests, 21 denials to speak, 23 denials to preach, 42 restrictions of residence, 17 deportations, 137 prohibitions to teach in schools, 34 forced changes of assignment, 52 forced resignations, 32 refusals of advancement, 26 fines, 39 impositions of bail, 141 police arrests, 84 cases of imprisonment in jail, 48 cases of protective custody, 24 confinements in concentration camps, 131 court inquiries without detention, 46 inquiries with detention, 84 court trials, 78 convictions (for which there were 45 fines, 27 jail terms, 3 penitentiary terms, and 3 death sentences, of which 2 were carried out). In addition there were inquiries, threats, and warnings undertaken by the party, by professional control officials, by the army, and by the armed forces. There were also press and radio attacks.[117]

This makes an imposing list for only part of Germany, and does not cover many restrictions and limitations on the monastic clergy. On the other hand, when one considers that many of the inquiries were not third-degree investigations, that many sentences were short, that a priest who was under denial to speak could still often carry out his parish duties, say mass, and preach in his own parish, and that the figures cover a period of over twelve years, the totals take on a new light. Actually, the Nazis were very careful not to get involved in a bitter drawn-out Kulturkampf. They did not close parish churches, people could regularly attend services, and the sacraments were always available. The Nazis could have done much worse—as was evidenced in their treatment of the occupied territories, above all Poland, during the war. To preserve as much as possible and to prevent even worse things, the church authorities often cooperated with the state, when clearly they did so with misgivings and heavy hearts. They agreed whenever possible, and at times muted their protests, when with the wisdom of hindsight it seems clear that they should have spoken out more forthrightly.

Hitler Moves Toward War

Little changed following the pope's denunciation of the condition of the church in Germany at Christmas, 1937. Minister Kerrl felt that action on the Vatican notes and those of the nuncio "could now no longer be considered," but the Foreign Office took a different position.[118] As long as diplomatic relations had not been broken off, the regular course of business would have to be followed. Discussions were, however, slowed down.[119] A new protest by the Bavarian bishops and by the nuncio regarding measures against Catholic private schools was left unanswered.[120] Then came the annexation of Austria on March 12–13, 1938. No doubt in connection with the annexation, Himmler, as head of the SS and chief of the German police, issued an order on March 15 stating that the Führer and Reich chancellor wanted no German Catholics to attend the Eucharistic Congress scheduled to be held in Budapest May 26–30, 1938. No permits were to be granted to travel bureaus, and no passports were to be issued. This ban now also included Austrian Catholics. Later, films of the Eucharistic Congress were not permitted to be shown in Germany.[121] While the Eucharistic Congress at Budapest was out of bounds to Germans, the Reich Chancellery, at the request of Bishop Berning, actually supplied 7,000 marks, the Foreign Office 14,000 marks, and Chancellor Hitler 3,000 marks, for the support of the German delegation to the Eucharistic Congress in Sydney, Australia, in September, 1938.[122]

The Austrian hierarchy had been very outspoken in their pronouncements against national socialism in the early years of the Nazi era, and at times had jibed at the Catholic hierarchy in Germany.[123] They had also pushed their control over the old German foundation in Rome, S. Maria dell' Anima.[124] The Austrian bishops were happy with their own concordat and the favorable treatment they received from the state. Yet when the annexation took place, the Austrian bishops, headed by Cardinal Theodor Innitzer, issued a solemn declaration welcoming national socialism to Austria and the assurance it brought that the danger of godless bolshevism had been parried.[125] This statement was a bit too enthusiastic for the Vatican authorities, and, after a visit to Rome, Innitzer issued another statement that "the earlier declaration of the Austrian bishops should not be understood as approval of what was incompatible with the laws of God or to be seen as binding in conscience upon the faithful."[126]

The people of Germany and Austria were to be called upon to approve the Austrian annexation in a plebiscite on April 10, 1938. A question now arose: would the bishops issue statements in support of the annexation? Minister Kerrl had ordered that all church bells in Germany and Austria should be rung on the eve of the election, "as an overwhelming expression of confidence of the entire nation in the Führer and his work."[127] The church leaders had always insisted that they should have the final say as to when church bells should be rung, particularly in connection with nonchurch events. Yet it was generally recognized that this was an extraordinary occasion. Cardinal Bertram, for the Fulda Bishops' Conference, and Cardinal Faulhaber, for the Munich-Freising Bishops' Conference, decided the bells could be rung. Public declarations in support of the plebiscite were another matter.[128] A majority of the bishops did issue such statements, and all except Bishop Johann Sproll of Rottenburg went to the polls on April 10, when a new Reichstag was also to be elected. Sproll would have no part in the pseudoballoting, and was immediately under attack for his unpatriotic conduct. He shortly left his diocese, returned unobtrusively, was again forced to leave, and returned once more.[129] This time he issued a pastoral letter on July 28 justifying his conduct. He was not against the annexation of Austria; in fact he greeted it warmly, and had given his approval by ordering the bells of his diocese to be rung. However, it was supposed to be a free secret ballot, and he had chosen to absent himself. "What kept him from participation was the fact that at the same time he would have had to vote and express his confidence in men whose fundamentally hostile position against the Catholic church and all Christendom was becoming clearer year by year."[130] It was a courageous statement, and the Gestapo forced him to leave again, supposedly to forestall public demonstrations. This time he was permanently banned from his diocese and from the state of Württemberg on August 24, 1938.[131] He spent his exile in Bavaria, and it was not until June 12, 1945, that he returned to Rottenburg. Except for the bishop of Meissen, who was briefly held because of his contravention of currency regulations, Sproll was the only German bishop in charge of a diocese against whom the authorities took action.

The German Foreign Office had gone so far as formally to request the Vatican to recall Bishop Sproll. Correspondence over this incident was the chief subject of Vatican-German relations during the summer of

1938. When the pope refused to recall him, it was the Ministry of Church Affairs which insisted upon the bishop's exile, a step which the Foreign Office reluctantly accepted.[132] Meanwhile, at the Foreign Office in Berlin, a list was compiled of complaints brought up by the Vatican or the nuncio which "in accordance with instructions" had been left pending. The list gives a good idea of the run-of-the-mill unanswered questions with which Vatican-German relations were concerned as the crisis over the fate of the Germans—mostly Catholics—in the Sudeten areas of Czechoslovakia developed. Vatican grievances included:

Reduction of Government subsidies to the Catholic Church in Bavaria and Saxony,

Introduction of public [interdenominational] schools in Trier and Cologne,

Violation of the Baden Concordat by the Baden law of January 29, 1934, concerning elementary and advanced schools,

Closing of the Bishop's main office (Canisius House) in Düsseldorf,

Disciplinary punishment of priests because of their sermons,

Abolition of Catholic [private] schools maintained by Orders in Bavaria,

Transformation of denominational [confessional] schools into public [interdenominational] schools in Prussia,

Abolition of Catholic [private] schools in East Prussia,

Prohibition of religious instruction by Catholic priests,

Search of the offices of the Vicars-General of Cologne and Trier,

Start of general negotiations regarding the concordats.[133]

With war threatening it is understandable that the Foreign Office did not center its attention on these problems. The steadily intensifying Sudeten crisis culminated in the Munich Conference at the end of September, 1938. Peace had been preserved, but at a price. The proposed litany for peace caused a furor in the Protestant church, but the Catholic hierarchy behaved more circumspectly.[134] At the request of the other German cardinals, Cardinal Bertram sent an appreciative telegram to Hitler: "The great deed of safeguarding peace among the nations moves the German episcopate, acting in the name of the Catholics of all the German dioceses, respectfully to extend congratulations and thanks, and to order a festive ringing of bells on Sunday."[135] The telegram was published in the *Völkischer Beobachter* on October 2 and won great acclaim. Other bishops added their words of thanks, and Cardinal Bertram issued a special pastoral letter greeting the new citizens of the great German Reich. The bishops' office of Berlin ordered a Te Deum sung in all churches on October 2, and the following statement was to be read from the pulpits:

God has heard the prayers for peace of all Christendom. Through his grace and the untiring efforts of responsible statesmen, the terrible affliction of a war has been turned aside from our fatherland and all Europe. In deepest thankfulness we will therefore now, through prayer and a Te Deum, praise God for his goodness, that he has preserved peace to us, while at the same time assuring the joining of our Sudeten comrades to the German Reich. Because of this occasion the bells will ring from 12:30 to 1 o'clock today, as a token of our thanks and as a greeting to our compatriots who are returning home.[136]

The addition of the Sudeten areas following that of Austria had increased the number of Catholics in the Reich by about 10 percent; they were now close to becoming a majority within the new Germany.

Flushed with the diplomatic successes of the past year, Hitler delivered a major address to the Reichstag on January 30, 1939. He devoted a special section to refuting the charges made by "so-called democrats" that Germany was an antireligious state. No one, he maintained, had been persecuted in Germany because of his religious convictions. Since 1933, the state through the tax system had yearly put large sums at the disposal of the churches—130 million, 170 million, 250 million, 400 million, and 500 million marks from 1933 to 1938. He failed to point out that these funds were special church taxes, only collected by the states, for which they received a percentage fee. He further maintained that the various states had contributed 85 million marks more in subsidies, and municipalities an additional 7 million marks.[137] The churches were also among the greatest property holders and received special tax concessions. How much money had the churches in France, the United States, and other countries received from the public treasury in the same period? If the churches considered their position unbearable, the National Socialist state would be ready at any time to bring about a clear separation of church and state as existed in France or the United States. Furthermore, the National Socialist state had closed no churches nor interfered with their services. He would not tolerate, however, that clergymen disrupt the state by their political agitation. Pederasty and sexual misconduct with children was punished in Germany, no matter who was guilty of the offense. The state, however, was not a prude, and the authorities did not care if clergymen violated their vows of chastity in other ways. He had tried in 1933 to intervene and bring about the unity of the Protestant churches, but the attempt had failed because of the opposition of some church leaders. If certain democratic statesmen interceded on behalf of a few German priests, they remained silent when hundreds of thousands of priests and nuns were cut down in Russia and Spain. These were facts that could not be denied, yet the democratic statesmen remained silent while numerous National Socialist and fascist volunteers had put themselves at the disposal of General Franco to prevent the bloody persecution of bolshevism from overspreading Europe. After going on to recount the achievements of the state, he ended with the pious exhortation: "Let us thank God, the Almighty, that he has blessed our generation and us, and granted us to be a part of this time and this hour."[138]

That Hitler was playing high, wide, and handsome with the true state of affairs is obvious. But there was just enough truth in what he misrepresented as a whole to make it plausible to willing ears. He failed to mention the historical origin and basis for the state grants to the churches, many of them resulting from the confiscation of church property when ecclesiastical states were secularized. The increase in church revenue from church taxes was the natural result of the upturn in the German economy. Yet it was true that the National Socialists had not disrupted or ended the state-based financial structures of the church. Hitler in his speech hinted at the possibility of doing so; it was to be a club over the heads of the churchmen. Instead of finding fault with the government, the churches should be thankful for the great blessings brought by the new Germany. Naturally nothing was said about the real contradiction of the teachings of the church involved in Nazi doctrine and practice, nor of the effort to censor church criticism.

The disruption of Czechoslovakia in March, 1939, through the establishment of a protectorate over Bohemia, the creation of an independent Slovakia, and the annexation of Sub-Carpathian Ruthenia by Hungary, brought spectacular new successes in foreign policy. On March 21, Memel was reincorporated into Germany. Everyone was grateful that war had not broken out. That same month Cardinal Pacelli had become Pope Pius XII, and in the customary notification of his election to Hitler as head of the German state, he had expressed his hope for friendly relations. It was to avoid jeopardizing them that he refrained from joining in the hue and cry of some states, notably France, against the final dismemberment of Czechoslovakia. He gave those around him to understand that he saw "no reason to interfere in historic processes in which from the political point of view, the Church is not interested."[139]

Hitler was to be fifty years old on April 20, 1939. To the Germans, who have a liking for special birthday celebrations, this seemed a proper time to pay homage to the Führer who had achieved the creation of the new great Germany, and had done so peacefully. Goebbels led off with a long adulatory address on the eve of the great day. Protestant and Catholic church bells joined in ringing in the happy anniversary. Cardinal Bertram, in the name of his fellow bishops, sent a congratulatory telegram to Hitler. Votive masses were celebrated in all Catholic churches. Nuncio Orsenigo, as doyen of the diplomatic corps at Berlin, extended the felicitations of his colleagues. The ambassadors of England, France, and the United States were noticeably absent from Berlin on this memorial day, but that did not dampen spirits. The heads of many states sent congratulatory messages and there was one reception after another, along with a grand parade. All in all, it was a glorious celebration.[140]

The annexation of Austria and the Sudeten areas of Czechoslovakia brought a host of problems to the Catholic church. The Austrian diplomatic mission at the Vatican was ended, and the Austrian bishops joined in the Fulda Bishops' Conference.[141] While the Austrian concordat of 1933 was no longer recognized, Hitler refused to consider the German concordat as extending to Austria. It was soon evident that the Nazis intended to revise the basis of church-state relations in the newly acquired lands. Restrictive measures similar to those practiced in Germany were applied.[142]

Within Germany proper, relations between church and state continued on their accustomed lines—constant police surveillance, petty harassments, and constant protests, but no break in relations; church and state continued to function side by side. Hitler meanwhile had his mind on further conquests. The concept of the Third Reich had served its day. On June 26, 1939, Bormann issued a secret circular directive: "The Führer desires that the designation and concept 'Third Reich' should no longer be used. Please bring this to the attention of the leaders in your districts in proper fashion."[143] Agreement with communist Russia, did-memberment of Poland, and reshaping the entire map of Europe with the cooperation, more or less, of Mussolini and Stalin, went far beyond the original concepts of the Third Reich. By launching an attack on Poland on September 1, 1939, Hitler had indeed planned to establish a new Germany. He did, but it was not to be the Reich of his dreams.

15.

The Protestant
Churches and the
Outbreak of War

Official Wartime Policy

The relationship between the German Evangelical church and the National Socialist state which had developed during the six years since 1933 was to follow the same pattern during the war. No significant changes in church administration and organization were made, except in some of the newly conquered territories. The same limited cooperation, the same harassments and persecutions—at times modified, at times intensified by the exigencies of war—continued. The one new development was the growing realization on the part of churchmen, and indeed of the laity as well, of the unbridgeable antagonisms between the National Socialist state and the churches. That there was no way to overcome these differences was also increasingly accepted in party circles. As Reichsleiter Bormann put it in 1941:

> National Socialist and Christian concepts cannot be reconciled. The Christian churches build on the ignorance of people and are anxious so far as possible to preserve this ignorance in as large a part of the populace as possible; only in this way can the Christian churches retain their power. In contrast, national socialism rests on scientific foundations. . . .
> We would repeat the mistakes, which in past centuries were disastrous for the Reich, if, after recognition of the philosophic (weltanschaulich) hostility of the Christian confessions, we should now in any way contribute to strengthening one of the various churches. The interests of the Reich lie not in overcoming, but in maintaining and strengthening this church particularism.[1]

Bormann's views were extreme, but his opinions came to be more and more taken for granted within the party, especially as his influence grew with the Nazi leadership. The official party policy, however, was not to push these matters during the war; they would be left until after victory had been achieved. In fact, on July 24, 1940, the minister of the interior notified all higher administrative officials that Hitler wanted, so far as possible, all measures avoided that might disturb the relationship of state and party to the churches.[2] At about the same time, Kerrl received a direct admonition from Hitler to put aside all church organizational matters. "Everything was to be avoided that could lead to strengthening and union of the Evangelical church. The status quo was to be maintained."[3]

Maintaining the status quo in religious matters also applied to Bishop Müller's position. In April, 1940, Müller asked Minister Lammers to find out if Hitler wanted the office of Reich bishop continued. Müller submitted a long memorandum in which he complained that Kerrl refused to cooperate with him, and that the entire Evangelical chaplaincy was oriented towards the Confessing church. If the Führer wanted him to continue as bishop, he requested a budget large enough to carry out his work. This budget should be supervised by the Reich Chancellery and not by the Ministry of Church Affairs.[4] Müller received no satisfaction, but he continued to hold his anomalous position.

The official policy of not stirring up the churches remained in effect throughout the war, although it was often breached in practice. Hitler made Bormann responsible for informing party authorities about the policy, and Bormann therefore sent a secret order to all Gauleiter on July 30, 1941.[5] With Bormann's consent, Goebbels in August, 1941, informed responsible authorities that no subject or issue was to be raised which might lead to division and quarrels among the people; "among the themes which for the moment cannot be discussed are religious and confessional questions."[6] At a meeting in Berlin in September, 1941, church affairs specialists of the state police were admonished that no major actions against the churches should be undertaken, and that all measures against monasteries were to cease. They were to restrict themselves to seeing that the churches did not win back any lost position. In December, 1941, the appropriate party officials held a conference and issued special instructions on how to counter foreign propaganda in relation to the churches. Religious controversies were not to be mentioned, and the existence of normal church life should be stressed.[7]

The Spiritual Confidential Council

The opening of hostilities gave the Spiritual Confidential Council, which had been named only two days before, its first opportunity to act. Along with Dr. Werner, as director of the church chancellery, the council on September 2 issued a statement to be read in all churches. The statement, as had others issued during similar crises in the past, expressed the support of all Evangelical Christians for the war. It was soon followed by a war prayer to be used in services and by a special prayer for Thanksgiving Day. These contained some patriotic phrases cast in National Socialist verbiage, which was more or less to be expected in the excitement of the times.[8] The Spiritual Confidential Council, after all, had German Christians among its members, and no one man could have his own way entirely if the council were to continue to function.

The Spiritual Confidential Council had no constitutional basis, which was a handicap in the legally bound church system. Werner sought to remedy the situation by a decree on March 28, 1940. He attempted to stake out the council's field of competence, and announced that he would henceforth issue no ordinance without its consent. It was particularly to help clarify the internal relationships between the churches as this became necessary during the war. From this time on a representative of the Reformed church, Professor Dr. Otto Weber of Göttingen, who had already been meeting with the Spiritual Confidential Council, was to become a regular member. The council met every two to three weeks, and soon a real feeling of confidence developed among the four members. Bishop Walther Schultz, a German Christian, was at first viewed with some suspicion by the other members, but he proved to be as anxious as any of them to support the rights of the church against the party and state.[9]

The leading member of the Spiritual Confidential Council was no doubt Bishop Marahrens, who had reluctantly accepted his new appointment out of a sense of duty.[10] His fellow churchmen had made a good choice. Marahrens knew some of the problems of the armed services from his experience as a chaplain in World War I, and he was far from being a pacifist, which helped him with the government. Furthermore, he was an adept compromiser. Most important, he had standing at home and abroad. As head of the Church Leaders' Conference he continued to keep in touch with a great number of important churchmen; as bishop of the Hanoverian Lutheran Church he was a leading member of the Luther Council and knew firsthand the complex problems facing the intact churches. He held to the basic concepts of the Confessing church, but was not sympathetic to the Dahlem wing of the movement, which was pretty much going its own way at this time. With war at hand, no one in state or church wanted to stir up controversy, and the Spiritual Confidential Council sought to act as a mediating group. A moderate, patriotic compromiser suited the temper of the times.

The council sponsored sermon meditations, occasionally congratulated the Führer, and from time to time issued public statements. These activities are sometimes considered to constitute the sum total of its work.[11] But it did more. Because it was an advisory body, much of its work was behind the scenes and is difficult to evaluate. Records are not fully available, but it is known to have submitted memoranda to the political authorities protesting many restrictions placed on the churches. It sought to put an end to the program of euthanasia, to maintain religious instruction in the schools, and to prevent the annihilation of the religious press; it also pleaded for the continuance of the various programs of the inner mission societies. It had a hand in arranging an amnesty for many churchmen on October 9, 1939, which freed some from imprisonment, quashed many pending prosecutions, and voided some punishments. It tried to put limits to the increasing dominance over the churches by the finance sections, and to assure protection of minority groups under the various church administrations. It did much to establish ties with the churches in the territories which were "returned" to the Reich, and provided some church services for the great numbers of the evacuees and new settlers.[12]

These memoranda and protests were not publicized—partly because the Spiritual Confidential Council did not want to lend aid to enemy propaganda efforts, but also because it was felt a frank but secret word might have more effect on party and state authorities, who notoriously did not like to submit to public pressure. In the end the council was unable to bring a turn in church and state relations, but it no doubt acted as a moderating influence and brought some alleviation to the hard-pressed churches. It continued to function right up to the end of the war. Its members worked in the hope that by serving within the established order they might achieve goals unattainable by attack from without.

The Impact of War on the Clergy

With the reintroduction of universal service in 1936, a chaplaincy corps was again established for the army and navy, while the air force assumed a special position. The Protestant chaplains were under the direction of a field bishop assisted by a field general vicar. Field Bishop E. Dohrmann was able to recruit a generally able group of young chaplains, among whom there were few German Christians. Among this group, as in great sections of the officer corps, the traditions of the old imperial army prevailed. Thus when war broke out, Protestant and Catholic chaplains were a regular part of the army and navy. Gradually, however, the chaplaincy too came under pressure from party officials and Nazi officers, and in the later days of the conflict no chaplains were attached to the newly formed divisions.[13]

With the declaration of war, many Evangelical pastors and vicars were immediately mobilized, usually as regular soldiers and officers. By October, 1941, of the approximately 17,000 Evangelical ministers and vicars, 6,800 (40 percent) were mobilized.[14] A year later the number had risen to 42.89 percent. The Spiritual Confidential Council undertook to prepare figures, and in April, 1943, reported that 41.4 percent of the ordained ministers and 78.6 percent of the nonordained vicars and theological candidates were in the service; in October, 1944, the numbers were 45 and 98 percent respectively. The impact of mobilization apparently varied. In the disturbed church areas some of the official church governments, in order to get rid of obstreperous ministers, encouraged their being called up. At a meeting of the Luther Council it was mentioned that 67 percent were called in Mecklenburg, 65 percent in East Prussia, 60 percent in Brunswick, and 52 percent in Württemberg. In 1943, following a protest to the Ministry of the Interior that pointed out the unequal treatment of the two large confessions (no doubt because of the provisions in the concordat which assured certain protections for Catholic clergy in case of mobilization), there was some letup in mobilizing Protestant clergy.[15] Clergy were also exempt from the decree of January 13, 1943, on the mobilization of men and women for the defense of the Reich. Persons who had passed their theological examinations and those who were full-time pastors in the sects were to be considered clergy. Those clergymen remaining at home, mostly elderly ministers, were further exempted in November, 1944, from service in the home reserve (*Volksturm*).[16]

What this mobilization meant to a Land church, both for the war years and the years ahead, can be illustrated by the situation in Württemberg, where fairly exact figures are available.[17] Out of 1,910 ministers and vicars, 759 were mobilized. Of these 184 were killed, 35 were officially reported as missing, and 20 were still missing without any official word as of February 19, 1949. In addition, 130 theological students were killed, and 27 were among the missing. The Provincial Church of Silesia provides another illustration.[18] As of June 30, 1942, out of some 800 clergymen, 424 ordained and 52 nonordained pastors and vicars had been called to service, 20 army chaplains, and 5 others—making a total of 501. Of these, 24 pastors and 26 vicars had fallen, and 3 were missing—a total of 53. In East Prussia, where ministers were in short supply even before the war, 245 out of 437 pastors were called into service, along with most of the theological students.[19] In Brunswick, as of February 11, 1941, 112 out of 232 clerics were called to service, along with 164 church officials and employees.[20] From Germany as a whole (including Austria), between September, 1939 and December, 1943, the Protestant church had lost 22 chaplains, 789 pastors, 460 vicars and candidates, and 1,500 theological students. Of pastors' sons, 1,767 had been killed, and among these were 163 cases of two brothers and 20 cases of three brothers.[21] The start of the war had an immediate impact on theological students. In 1914 there were 3,716 theological students at the universities; in the summer semester of 1933, there were 5,809, in the summer semester of 1939, 1,164, and in the first semester of 1939–40, 380.[22]

The mobilization meant that many pastors undertook to serve additional charges. The burden was especially great in South Germany, where there were many small villages, each with its own church and school that had to be taken care of. As lay teachers gave up their religion classes in the schools or were drawn into the armed services, pastors found their teaching loads increased. Again this was most notable in South Germany, where it was customary for pastors to give religious instruction. In other sections, for example in Hanover, they were forbidden to take over the discontinued classes.[23] Often religion classes had to be combined or otherwise curtailed. In places where they were ended the period of confirmation instruction was extended to two or even three years.[24] In addition, there was all the extra work which war inevitably brings to a pastor. Although he was forbidden by the state to try to maintain contact with soldiers in the field, he nevertheless had duties to families when death notices arrived or wounded were furloughed home.[25] In Lübeck, the night before Palm Sunday (March 29, 1943), Allied bombers destroyed a large part of the city, including the cathedral and several other historic churches. Under the impression of this night of horror, Pastor Karl Friedrich Stellbrink spoke in his Palm Sunday sermon of God's judgment that had come to Lübeck, and expressed his opinion that its citizens would learn again to pray. He was arrested for treasonous remarks and for causing unrest among the people. Three Catholic clergymen, Edward Müller, Johannes Prassek, and Hermann Lange, suffered the same fate. Trials were held, and on November 10, 1943, all four were executed.[26]

In order to alleviate the shortage of clergy, the churches sought the help of retired ministers; the general ministerial amnesty of October 9, 1939, also brought some relief. The aid of pastors' wives, particularly of those men who were called into service and whose families continued to occupy the parsonages, was welcomed.[27] They were encouraged to hold Bible hours and conduct services, so-called *Lesegottesdienste*, where a sermon was read. This was an old established practice, formerly often undertaken by teachers in emergencies. A regular *Lektorendienst* was organized, and these specially trained lectors were authorized to hold services, the pastors appearing only every two or three weeks in many of the smaller parishes.[28] Deaconesses were called on for additional church services, although the state tried to recruit them for the Red Cross and for other duties. Many a church deacon also had new duties thrust upon him. In many ways the situation led to a true awakening among the laity of the church.

In another effort to help meet the crisis, the Eleventh Confessing Synod of the Old Prussian Union in October, 1942, officially provided for the use of theologically trained women (*Vikarin*) in the service of the church.[29] Such women were to be formally installed with laying on of hands and could administer the sacraments, although the prime service was to be directed to children, youth, and the women of the parish. In time of need the ultimate was conceded and they could preach. The synod bolstered this decision with a number of Bible passages and approving statements from Luther and Calvin. As is usually the case, Luther's words are the more direct: "for the sake of order, decorum, and honor, women keep silent when men speak. When, however, no man preaches, then there is the need that women should preach."[30] A beginning was made at training special lay catechists (who were not professional teachers) to undertake religious instruction, but this was actually to be one of the great postwar developments.[31]

While the churches were grossly understaffed and hard put to keep the services going, Bormann was trying to induce men to leave the ministry. He issued detailed regulations about finding jobs and providing adequate compensation for former clergymen. Although his efforts were directed primarily at Catholic clergy, he displayed no partiality and welcomed the Protestants as well.[32]

Growing Party Indifference to the Churches

By 1939, Hitler and other important party leaders had pretty much lost all interest in the problem of church unification.[33] At this time Hitler confided to Rosenberg that he had made a mistake in trying to create a

United Evangelical church as a counterweight to Roman Catholicism.

He was glad his efforts had not succeeded. He was proud that he had
kept party and church separate. The National Socialists never had any
religious services at party meetings, and he had not permitted the presence of clerics at funerals of party comrades. As for himself, "he would
not like to see a cleric within a radius of ten kilometers when he was
buried."[34] Although Hitler felt the days of the churches were numbered,
he believed this historical process would take one or two hundred years.
"He regretted that, like Moses, he would be able to see the Promised
Land only from afar." As a youth he had believed religion was: "Dyna-
mite! Only later had he come to realize that you couldn't break this
over your knee. It would have to rot away like a gangrenous limb.
Sound youth was with us [i.e., the Nazi movement]."[35] During the war
he wanted no unnecessary difficulties. At times he mouthed words of
prayer, but the references to God became fewer as the tide of war went
against him. His remarks to his table companions became increasingly
disparaging, not only of the churches but of religion in general.

It is notable, however, that Hitler never paraded his antichurch
attitudes publicly, and Rosenberg even chided him gently about this.[36]
Many people continued to believe in Hitler's piety. The police in July,
1941, noted: "Since the beginning of the war, as is evident from numerous reports, the rumor is constantly spread that the Führer daily visits a
church or chapel and prays for victory."[37] In November, 1941, in a long
speech commemorating the 1923 putsch, he took time to deride "Roose-
velt's charge" that the Nazis wanted to extinguish all religions in the
world. He was not concerned about how the peoples of the world stood
towards religion. "In Germany—and according to our views—everyone
can go to heaven in the way he pleases." Whereas in the United States
the churches didn't get one red cent from the state, in Germany they
received 900 million marks. Most clergy backed the German state in the
war, for they realized that if it was lost, "religion would fare much
worse under the protectorate of Stalin than under ours."[38] Albert Speer
writes: "Even after 1942 Hitler went on maintaining that he regarded
the church as indispensable in political life. . . . He sharply condemned
the campaign against the church, calling it a crime against the future of
the nation. For it was impossible, he said, to replace the church by any
'party ideology'."[39]

Hitler was content to let others in the party push antichurch measures, for most of the state governors were sharper in these matters than
he.[40] The upper echelons of party leaders also tended to be aggressively
antichurch; Bormann, Himmler, Rosenberg, Ley were among the leaders, supported to lesser degree by Göring, and eventually by Rust and
Frick. Some local Gau leaders were notoriously antichurch; others at
times were willing to close their eyes. Yet the overall party policy was
increasingly antichurch, and during the war the party strengthened its
position in relation to the state. This too worked against the churches,
for while they could assert their legal rights against the state and its
various agencies, they had little recourse against the party. The party

was a law unto itself. It pressured members to withdraw from the churches, and party rowdies disrupted services or threatened pastors. The terror of Nazi police power, heightened now by the easy charges of helping the enemy and disloyalty to the fatherland, cast a shadow of fear and suspicion everywhere. It was under such conditions that churchmen struggled to maintain their rights and preach the verities of the Christian faith.[41] They sought succor and assurance in the biblical injunction: "Be not deceived; God is not mocked: for whatsoever a man soweth, that shall he also reap" (Galatians 6:7).

The Euthanasia Program

One of the first state war measures which aroused the opposition of both Protestant and Catholic churches was the euthanasia program inaugurated in October, 1939, after the end of the Polish campaign. Euthanasia was illegal according to German law, and Hitler despaired of altering the situation immediately because after seizing power he expected church opposition. However, as early as 1935 he had confided to Dr. Gerhard Wagner, the leader of the Doctors' Association, that in case of war he would take up euthanasia and carry it through.[42] In the meantime, he contented himself by setting up a system whereby people could appeal to him to permit mercy killings of the incurably sick. This program was developed especially in relation to babies with birth deformities. After investigation by officials if the "mercy death" was authorized and carried out, those persons responsible were guaranteed exemption by Hitler from prosecution under the law. The same held for abortions when either parent had an hereditary disease. However, a law enacted on June 26, 1935, made abortions legal only if the woman had an hereditary disease and gave her consent.[43]

Since Hitler did not wish to create a furor by enacting a euthanasia law and wanted the program carried out secretly, he had to establish procedures outside the regular governmental structure. The program of "voluntary mercy killings" had been supervised by a division of his "personal chancellery" (*Kanzlei des Führers*), and he quite naturally turned to these officials to carry out the new euthanasia policy. A rescript, postdated to September 1, 1939, the date of the outbreak of war, and signed by Hitler, stated: "Reichsleader Bouhler and Doc. med. Brandt, being responsible, are charged with extending authority to specified doctors that those incurably sick according to human judgment, after critical examination of the state of their health, can be granted a 'mercy death.' "[44] This brief authorization was the program's only legal basis. Hitler always refused later suggestions by the Justice Department and others to enact a law, which would have meant public acknowledgement of the program and the establishment of guidelines for the courts.

Various camouflaged bureaus were established to carry out the program, and since it involved sanitoria, hospitals, and asylums, it was

necessary to involve Division 4 (Health and Care of the Sick) of the
Ministry of the Interior. This division was under the independent supervision of Reich Health Officer Dr. Leonardo Conti, who also held the
position of state secretary, and he had Dr. Linden as ministerial director
for this particular operation. It was Dr. Linden who had to send out
questionnaires to all the inner mission institutions, and it is not surprising that he was at times considered by churchmen as heading the whole
program.[45]

Soon reports began to reach responsible church offices that patients
(the elderly, feebleminded, epileptics, and others) at various sanitoria
and hospitals were being transferred to other institutions without notice
to relatives, supposedly to make room for war wounded. Usually a
second transfer was made in order to disguise further what was going
on. Shortly after their transfer the patients invariably died of grippe,
pneumonia, stroke, heart trouble, or some other sudden ailment. Relatives were notified that because of the danger of spreading infectious
diseases it had been necessary to cremate the body immediately, and
the funeral urn was at their disposal. If they desired to receive it, they
should remit a statement from their local cemetery board approving
burial, and the urn would be delivered without charge. If the request
was not received within fourteen days, other arrangements would be
made.[46] There was a sameness about these death reports that began to
crop up throughout Germany. What was happening could not be suppressed, for many of the institutions of the inner mission societies were
being forced to provide lists of patients in various categories. The Spiritual Confidential Council began to investigate. It consulted with Pastor
Bodelschwingh of the Bethel Institutions and with others. Pastor Paul
Gerhard Braune, director of the Hoffnungstal institutions near Berlin,
and vice-president of the Central Committee for Inner Missions of the
German Evangelical church, began to receive reports from all over Germany about the deaths. He went to Berlin to discuss the problem with
men at the Reich chancellery and the Ministry of Justice. At the security
headquarters of the Wehrmacht supreme command he had a helpful
and sympathetic reception from Hans von Dohnanyi, the brother-in-law
of Dietrich Bonhoeffer. These men, at least officially, knew nothing of
the events, and asked Braune to write up a memorandum with supporting concrete evidence, so that they might have a basis for action. This
Pastor Braune did in May–June, 1940.

Braune consulted with Bodelschwingh, but the euthanasia program had not yet started in Westphalia. The two men visited Minister
Kerrl, who, Braune reports, knew nothing of the program and was
thoroughly frightened. They also visited the Reich Chancellery again,
and Justice Minister Gürtner. The latter was incensed, and characterized the program as "murder on the assembly line."[47] Braune did a
thorough job—after all, the detective work was not very difficult—
which left no doubt that hundreds of invalids were being put to death.
Many were being clinically killed by injections or overdoses of drugs,
but others were being put on such short rations that they soon died.

This report was passed on by the church chancellery to the responsible state authorities.[48]

The church chancellery never received an answer. Pastor Braune, after repeated inquiries, was told by his confidant (Friedrich W. Kritzinger) in the Reich Chancellery that Minister Lammers had discussed the memorandum directly with Hitler. The measures would not be repealed, but they would be carried out in a "decent" (anständig) way. No mention was made of what was considered "anständig," but Braune assumed the victims were not to be tortured. Pastor Braune also sent the memorandum to Field Marshal Göring, by way of his nephew, Dr. M. H. Göring. The field marshal, however, did not concern himself with the matter. On August 14, 1940, Braune was arrested and spent three months in prison, being freed on his promise not "to undertake further actions against measures of the state or the party."[49]

Bishop Wurm meanwhile had also been gathering material on the situation in Württemberg. When he was sure of his facts, he addressed a letter to Minister of the Interior Frick on July 19, 1940. He did not mince words. He pointed out that such procedures were contrary to all Christian principles and that the sight of the transports and the smoke rising from the crematoriums was arousing resentment and disgust among the people.[50] When he received no answer, Wurm wrote another blistering letter to Frick on September 5, 1940, for now the inhabitants of old peoples' homes were also being seized. He ended his letter with a series of questions: "Must the German nation be the first civilized people which in its treatment of the weak returns to the customary practice of primitive peoples? Does the Führer know of this matter? Has he approved it? I plead not to leave me without answer in this extremely serious matter."[51] Finally he received a registered letter, valued at 1,200 marks, in which State Secretary Dr. Conti of the Ministry of the Interior assured him everything was in order. There was a legal basis for the measures which could not be revealed at present.[52]

Bishop Wurm's letter was distributed far and wide, and did much to establish him as one of the foremost spokesmen of the Protestant churches. On August 11, 1940, on behalf of Catholic bishops, Cardinal Bertram sent a letter of protest against euthanasia to the Reich Chancellery, and five days later to the minister of justice. Cardinal Faulhaber on November 6 sent a strong letter to Minister Franz Gürtner, protesting on the basis of the concordat and from his position as bishop, and calling for an answer to Bertram's earlier letter.[53] There was some relaxing of the program, notably as it affected institutions run by the churches. Public institutions were another matter, although, as in most programs under the Nazis, the policy was not administered uniformly. In Hanover two public institutions were able to prevent any of their patients from being delivered to the extermination centers.[54]

The euthanasia program not only aroused the churches, but also ran afoul of individuals within the German judiciary. The courts often had been assigned as guardians to individuals placed in institutions, and they now inquired what had happened to their wards. The disposition of property also caused problems. Dr. Lothar Kreyssig, a Brandenburg judge, was pensioned off when he persisted in refusing to recognize the will of the Führer as a sufficient legal basis for what was happening.[55] Private individuals also brought suit. Bishop Galen, for example, not only publicly denounced the program from his pulpit in a famous sermon of August 3, 1941, but also brought formal charges in court. Under German law, a person who had believable knowledge of an intended crime against a person and did not notify the authorities was subject to punishment.[56] Because the program was top secret, the judges and prosecuting attorneys did not know what to do and applied to the Ministry of Justice for guidance. The situation had reached such an impasse that the minister of justice called a meeting of higher court presidents and higher prosecuting attorneys at Berlin in April, 1941, where they were informed of the euthanasia program and assured that Hitler's rescript of September 1, 1939, gave a legal basis for the mercy deaths. There was no discussion after the various addresses, and the officials were asked to inform their subordinates circumspectly. The courts now resorted to a policy of delaying action and reporting to Berlin, where nothing happened.[57]

Meanwhile there were indications of increasing alarm and opposition among the populace. In places there were demonstrations against the transport caravans which took the victims from one institution to another. Opposition to euthanasia appeared in party reports, and even Heydrich and Himmler disassociated themselves from the way in which the program was carried out. Notice of all these protests and difficulties were channelled to Lammers at the Reich chancellery, and he regularly reported them to Hitler. Finally, after thousands had been put to death, Hitler suspended the program on August 24, 1941, although individual and even group killings by injection and starvation diets—the so-called wild euthanasia—continued spasmodically. The program of mercy deaths for children with birth defects was continued to the collapse of the regime, and the undertaking to exterminate the Jews was in a way only a radical extension of the euthanasia program.[58]

The experience of the great inner mission institution at Bethel, which concentrated its efforts on the care of epileptics, is not only illustrative of the euthanasia program but also of how the Nazi state operated.[59] At times determined opposition did have an effect. In June, 1940, the Ministry of the Interior sent 3,000 forms to Bethel which were to be filled out by August 1.[60] These were needed, as the accompanying letter stated, in order to incorporate properly the hospitals and sanitoria into the planned economy. Pastor Fritz von Bodelschwingh, aware that these forms were to be used to designate patients to be put to death, refused to have them filled out. He wrote a letter to Reich Health Officer Dr. Conti, asking for an interview. Conti refused to see him, but referred him to two specialists in his department. From these men Bodelschwingh obtained an admission that the forms were in effect death warrants. Bodelschwingh informed the local district officials, with whom he stood on good footing and who knew nothing of the program.

His staff, as well as the boards of the institution, were unanimous in support of his position that the forms should not be filled out. Thereupon officials from Berlin came to Bethel and tried to persuade him to conform. At about this time a bomber attack hit one of the buildings at Bethel and killed thirteen patients, giving Goebbels the opportunity to make a play on "Child Murder in Bethel," and the institution was in newspaper headlines. The episode actually strengthened Bodelschwingh's hand, for, as he wrote to the officials: "Shall I condemn the acts of the English and then extend my hand to child murder on a far larger scale? I would consider myself a liar as well as a betrayer of my father, whose name has just again been honored throughout the Reich."[61]

The situation remained precarious, and in January, 1941, Bodelschwingh decided to make an effort to get in touch with the inner circle of authorities. He wrote a letter to Field Marshal Hermann Göring and entrusted it to Göring's nephew for delivery. He may have had some hope for help from this source, for Göring's wife's brother was a patient at Bethel.[62] In reply he was informed that his information "was inaccurate and in great part false." Professor Dr. Karl Brandt would personally get in touch with him and inform him correctly. Brandt was Hitler's personal doctor, and he and Reichsleiter Philipp Bouhler were the final authorities for carrying out the euthanasia program, although this was not known at the time.

Brandt did come to Bethel, and Pastor Bodelschwingh explained to him why it was impossible from a Christian standpoint to accede to the program. Brandt's visit coincided with the presence of a Berlin deputation (February, 1941) which had come to Bethel to register the inmates themselves. The registration was done under protest, but in the presence of institution personnel who had classified the patients into various groups in accordance with the seriousness of their affliction. Bodelschwingh apparently made an impression on Brandt, and the two continued to correspond on the problem. On August 28, 1941, Bodelschwingh wrote a particularly challenging letter to Brandt, pointing out how much unrest and harm the program was causing both at home and abroad; it was a weapon in the hands of the enemy. He also appealed to Brandt's conscience, for he had admitted the whole program weighed heavily upon him. Four days previously Hitler, apparently influenced by the many protests, had ordered Brandt to suspend the program.[63] Since no one was told about this order, officials at Bethel continued to live in dread of the time when transports might appear at their doors.[64] A new batch of forms were received at the end of 1942, but these too were not filled out. Not one patient from Bethel, thanks to Pastor Bodelschwingh's courageous leadership, met death under this euthanasia program.

Unfortunately, this was not true in the case of another program inaugurated at this time. On August 30, 1940, the minister of the interior sent a letter to the government president in Minden, stating it was no longer tolerable that Jews and Germans could be cared for in the same sanatoria or hospitals. A transport would be dispatched on September

25 or 26 to take the Jews to one institution. The authorities in Bethel were informed of this order on September 5. They were able to send three patients home, but an attempt to get the Jewish community in Bielefeld to take over the others failed, largely because that community practically did not exist any more. A Jewish woman was placed in a local home for the aged by a neighboring pastor. But eight patients remained when the transports arrived. One of these could still be rescued by relatives at the last moment. Seven, however, were apparently transported to Poland and relatives shortly received reports of their deaths.[65]

16.

The Protestant
Churches and Wartime
Restrictions

Limitations on Pastoral Work

There had been no protest from the churches when war was declared.[1]
Hitler had done a good job of preparing the people for the conflict, and
the early victories tended to arouse some patriotic fervor. Yet there was
little real enthusiasm, and the responsible church authorities acted cautiously. The Confessing church issued two statements to serve as guidelines for ministers during the war. It is not without interest that they were
issued anonymously. "Looking back on the special problem of wartime
sermons 1914–18 makes us wish," the writer notes, "that this time the
church will be given better understanding than was the case in many
instances at that time."[2] Bishop Meiser expressed the same thought in
"Guidelines for Evangelical Preaching during the War," which he
issued for the Bavarian church on October 30.[3] "There is only one
gospel. Therefore, we have to undertake no preaching different from
that in times of peace. The war also does not change the theological
basis of the sermon. The core and star of the Evangelical message remains at all times Jesus Christ who was crucified and arose from the
dead." Meiser, recognizing there were special war problems, cautioned
against selecting texts which led especially to war commentary and
recommended adhering to the pericopes. "Above all, the soldiers at the
front were often disillusioned when the pastor had nothing to say but
exactly what they heard from their officers. What they were quite
willing to hear from their officers, they did not want to hear again from
their pastors." It was truly a gospel-centered appeal to the clergy, and
one which might well be issued in any country by church authorities
when war breaks out.

The task of the ministers was not easy. As one perceptive Confessing pastor wrote after the war:

> I considered myself lucky because I was no longer an active pastor [he had
> been pensioned off] and did not have to preach during this war period.
> Against the war? That was impossible. For the war? That was even less
> possible. The situation was also religiously entirely different from 1914. What
> a role the moral law of war played at that time. How we wrestled with the
> problem of whether a man of war could die in a state of grace; how the best
> brains troubled themselves over "a moratorium of the Sermon on the

Mount." And now in public there was not a breath of this to be felt—that war and war service had also to be justified before God.[4]

But if pastors might have reservations about the war, they had none about their pastoral duty to keep in touch with servicemen from their parishes.

At the start of the war, the church chancellery, the Evangelical Press Service, and the heads of the chaplaincy corps had made an agreement about distributing religious material to the armed services. The army authorities furnished the addresses of chaplains, the church chancellery paid the costs, and the press agency sent out the material quarterly in quantity shipments.[5] All this material had to pass the censorship of the Ministry of Propaganda, which insisted that literature of the German Christians be included. Individual pastors also began gathering the field addresses of servicemen so that they could be sent congregational papers and other religious literature. In some congregations pastors resorted to mimeographed letters, but soon this practice was stopped. On October 27, 1939, the minister of church affairs, in consultation with the high command, forbade pastors because of security reasons to assemble mailing lists of soldiers.[6] Furthermore, all religious material had to be approved before it could be sent out.

In July, 1940, further restrictive measures were enforced. The religious care of servicemen was to be restricted to service chaplains, and no supplementary religious activity by civilian pastors was to be permitted. The sending of all confessional religious literature, including mimeographed or printed letters, was forbidden. Bibles, and parts of Bibles, but no Bible selections, could still be sent.[7] The contact of pastors with mobilized members of their parishes was thus practically ended. They could, of course, still send individual letters, but without address lists, and given the size of many German parishes and the additional work the war placed on them, pastors simply did not have time to keep in contact in this fashion. In many service units, notably in the air force and SS, there were no chaplains, and so the official position that the service chaplains were adequately meeting religious needs did not satisfy the churches.[8] The exclusion of clergy from what they considered an important part of the ministry to their parishes was a grievance that struck deep.

Not unrelated to these restrictions were decrees which limited pastoral work at public hospitals, nursing homes, and sanitoria. In April, 1941, it was ordered that pastoral visits should take place only at the definite request of patients, and religious services were limited.[9] The government attempted to explain these measures by the desire to protect patients of one confession from being visited by clerics other than their own. When these restrictions were extended to private institutions run by deaconesses and other religious orders, the regulations were largely bypassed.

There had been censorship and restrictions on the church press even before the war. Nevertheless, the big church papers, as well as many district and local papers, had been able to continue. However, on June 1, 1940, the Reich Press Chamber practically ended the entire church press. The suspended periodicals were ordered to publish the following notice in their last numbers: "The war economy necessitates the strongest concentration of strength. Because of this, it is necessary that our periodical cease publication with today's issue, in order to free people and materials for other war purposes."[10] The notice was not adeptly drawn; it might at least have mentioned the supposed paper shortage. No such drastic measure had been taken in World War I. For example, the Sontagsblatt of the Hanoverian church, which still had a circulation of 50,000 and had appeared regularly since 1868, was closed down, as were many other venerable publications. Restrictions soon followed which virtually ended the publication of all religious books, including the Bible. The distribution of religious literature in churches was forbidden; the familiar literature racks stood empty. The activity of the Bible societies ground to a halt.[11]

The churchmen reacted vigorously. The Spiritual Confidential Council had already tried to forestall these restrictions. Bishop Wurm issued a denunciation and raised the pointed question of why the press of the German Faith Movement was freer than the Christian press. In an outspoken letter to Goebbels in 1942, he responded to an article recently published by the Ministry of Propaganda.

> Not only the Christian parish press has been completely suppressed, but the whole of Christian literature has been subjected to severe restrictions. It is even impossible to print the Bible and song books. In contrast, anti-Christian literature can be thrown on the market in great masses and sent to the front. The large Christian part of the nation gladly accepts all necessary restrictions, but it demands justice in the distribution of burdens, which you support in your article, but which we sadly miss to a great extent in your office.[12]

Wurm apparently gave the letter to the Swedish consul in Stuttgart, and in December, 1942, it appeared in a weekly Swedish paper from whence it received worldwide publicity. The letter was considered grounds for arrest, but Hitler personally ruled against taking such action.[13]

The government, however, did not change its policy, and the religious press suffered even sharper curtailments as Germany's military situation deteriorated. The churches resorted to carbon and mimeographed copies to circulate their reports and messages. The collections in the various archives are filled with documents labelled "copy of a copy." The typists are unsung, but nevertheless were important campaigners in the Church Struggle.

Restrictions on Religious Education

By the beginning of the war, the National Socialists had succeeded in establishing the German school system on an interconfessional basis. Interdenominational schools, attended by children and staffed by teachers of both confessions, had replaced confessional schools, attended and staffed by pupils and teachers of one confession. Private schools had largely been done away with, and Catholic teaching orders were denied the right to act as regular teachers. Religious instruction was still a regular part of the curriculum, but in many places it had been restricted or its contents diluted, although in some schools it continued to be given much as always.

The war brought many new restrictions, but not abolition.[14] In the first place, religious education was hampered by an increasing shortage of teachers, and very often the religion hours were the first to be curtailed. Reading, writing, and arithmetic seemed more essential to most Nazi-oriented school officials. Pastors undertook more of the religious instruction in the schools, but they too were overburdened. And if there was a shortage of teachers because of the military draft, this was doubly true of ministers. After 1939, when teaching posts in religion became vacant at teachers' institutes no reappointments were made, and in the teacher-training institutions opened after 1941 there was no opportunity to prepare for teaching religion.

In March, 1940, religious instruction was abolished in the last four years of the secondary schools because of the teacher shortage and the pressure to provide more time for instruction in the sciences. A year later it was ordered that religious instruction should be offered only during the period of compulsory school education, which had been set at eight years in 1938. Efforts were made to replace opening and closing school prayers by more secular ceremonies. A further indication of the declining importance of regular school instruction in religion was the removal of a place for a grade on the regular report cards; if religion was still taught and a child had not withdrawn from instruction, he could receive a mark on a separate form. In the territories newly won from Poland, only interdenominational schools were permitted, and confessional religious instruction was not allowed. Added to these and many other restrictions on traditional religious practices was an increasing emphasis on Nazi ideological and racial instruction.

In November, 1939, the Reich youth leaders instituted a compulsory youth service for fourteen to eighteen-year-old boys, a sort of premilitary training which was to be held four half-Sundays a month. Like the activities of the Hitler Youth, these sessions were regularly held on Sunday mornings, in spite of objections from the churches. In May, 1940, Himmler forbade all church-sponsored youth retreats, summer camps, and similar meetings because time was needed for premilitary training, for gathering in the harvest, and for other war activity. This order finally eliminated most of the newly organized programs which the churches had instituted to keep contact with their youth and further their religious education.[15]

The initiation of Hitler Youth dedication services (*Verpflichtungsfeiern*) was yet another attempt to win over youth to party and state. These were to be national patriotic celebrations of the whole German people. Although the local party officials were warned that they should make no direct or indirect appeal to parents not to have their children confirmed (this would have had bad repercussions among the soldiers in the field), the dedication services were designed to counter the significance of traditional church confirmation. These services were first carried through on a large scale on March 23, 1942, and did necessitate shifting the traditional day for confirmation or first communion in many places. The clergy feared the dedication services might replace confirmation, but this was not the case. The police report on the dedication services in 1942 stated that confirmation services were more extensive than ever. In 1943 the report noted: "the dedication service made little impression on the people. Most of our citizens had no inkling of what the ceremonies were all about." These dedication rites, like all the other services (Lebensfeiern) designed by the party to replace church rites, did not prove popular. A police summary on Lebensfeiern of December 9, 1943, stated that National Socialist services did not constitute 1 percent of such services. Their best showing was in respect to weddings, but even so the couples who were not married in churches usually were content with civil marriages. Figures showed "that above all at the grave the Christian churches triumphed."[16]

In the spring of 1941, the government began to confiscate the kindergartens, most of which were traditionally run by the churches, and to turn them over to the National Socialist Social Care Agency (Versorgungsamt). This action led to sharp protests from both Protestant and Catholic church leaders, and in some places (East Prussia, Berlin, Brandenburg, Westphalia, Nürnberg, Frankfurt/Main, Württemberg, and Saarland) the seizures were stopped.[17]

The churches found these restrictions very hard to take, when at the same time placards were being posted in the occupied parts of Russia saying: "Your children will be baptized again, your marriages blessed. Away with the system which has ravished the churches."[18] The churches resisted, but the tide of opposition to religious instruction as previously given could not be completely turned.

Interference with Church Customs and Holidays

Long before there was any real metal shortage in Germany the authorities in charge of the Four-year Economic Plan in March-April, 1940, ordered all bells made of bronze to be delivered to the government.[19] The order was generally interpreted as a measure against the churches, although it applied to all bells, including those of city halls.[20] The great victories of that spring delayed the deliveries; instead, the state decreed that all bells in Germany had to be rung at noon on June 5 to 7, 1941, in commemoration of the triumphs over Belgium, and on June 25 to July 1, 1941, for the victory over France.[21] The churches were able to effect some changes in the delivery orders. Bells were classified into four groups (A, B, C, D) according to their worth. Class D bells, because of their exceptional worth, were to be spared, and each church was to be left at least one bell. A member of the commission on historic monuments did yeoman service in saving some 5 percent of the bells. Most of the deliveries were made during 1942. Although the government demanded them for the war effort, in 1945 many still remained unused and intact in the cemetery for bells along the Elbe in Hamburg.[22] The surrender of the bells did not come easily, even if many Germans did not heed their summons to church. Special "bell services" were held to mark their surrender, and at times there was opposition and "lack of understanding" by congregations.[23]

On October 31, 1940, the minister of the interior ordered that cemeteries must be open for the burial of all citizens, even if they did not belong to the particular confession which owned the cemetery. People not members of the confession could hold grave side addresses and gravestones did not have to have Christian symbols.[24] In Germany the peal of bells was a valued and stately part of funeral services. On May 5, 1942, the acting minister of church affairs, in a broad-minded gesture, ordered that bells might also be rung for people who had withdrawn from the church.[25] He had overlooked a specific ruling of 1939 that the ringing of church bells was a church matter, and that a person who withdrew from the church had no right to the tolling of bells as he was being taken to the grave.[26] Disputes arose, for it was a question involving historic church rights. Finally the minister of the interior, on April 10, 1943, issued an edict that if the relatives of a man who had withdrawn from the church requested it, those bells which were left must be rung, if need be by the police.[27] There were in fact times when the police did act as bell ringers. The state also passed regulations on behalf of weary sleepers silencing all bells on Sunday until 1 p.m. if there had been an air raid alarm on Saturday night.

In addition to confiscating bells, the government headquarters for iron and steel undertook, in March, 1944, to register all organs preparatory to confiscating their pipes.[28] The war was over before this extreme was reached.

There were certain legal church holidays in Germany: New Year's Day, Good Friday, Easter Monday, Ascension Day, Pentecost Monday, Repentance Day (*Busstag*), Christmas, and the day after Christmas, as well as Reformation Day in Protestant regions and Corpus Christi Day in Catholic areas.[29] There were other church holidays that were not state protected and fell on weekdays, such as Maundy Thursday. As early as 1939 efforts were made to postpone Repentance Day, set for the Wednesday before the last Trinity Sunday by a Reich law of 1934, to the last Trinity Sunday.[30] These attempts failed, but on October 27, 1941, the Reich government issued an ordinance stating that Ascension Day, Reformation Day, and Repentance Day should not be celebrated during the week but on either the previous or the following Sunday.[31] Services could not be held until 7 p.m. on unprotected holidays. The celebration of Ascension Day, forty days after Easter, was a fixed legal church holiday, and most pastors felt that logically it could not be celebrated on any other day. Some tried to hold services at seven in the evening, but the authorities disapproved, since the day had been officially declared a workday and the festival shifted to a Sunday.[32] In 1943, the Bavarian police forbade evening services on Ascension Day. Bishop Meiser protested that the prohibition discriminated against Protestants, for Catholics held devotional services every evening and thus had an opportunity to mention the Ascension. He pointed out that the peasants refused to work on that day anyway.[33]

Although there were rumors at times that Christmas and Good Friday would also be shifted, the government did not attempt this. In the Warthegau (a former Polish territory) they did try in 1942 to restrict services on Good Friday to seven in the evening, but the people simply appeared in their churches at the customary hour and the government had to yield. The police usually enforced these state regulations of church holidays, but at times they closed their eyes, especially to evening services on the customary festival days. Also by law, Sunday religious services could not begin before 10 a.m. on the morning after an air raid alarm, but this decree was finally cancelled on March 5, 1945. By then it was impractical, for the front was so near and the time between alarm and attack so short that service times could not be regulated.[34]

Confiscations of Church Property and Financial Controls

The Nazis had long battened on seizing property held by Jews, communists, and others whom they considered opponents. Now, under the guise of wartime necessity, they also confiscated many church properties. A report of the Tenth Confessioning Synod of the Church of the Old Prussian Union illustrates the situation of the church at the turn of the year 1941–42:

> Church properties of great value were suddenly confiscated: institutions valued at millions of marks, such as Karlshof in East Prussia, Kückenmühle in Stettin, the Christian Periodical Society, the CVJM in Berlin, etc. The Württemberg church lost the famous old monastic schools Maulbronn, Blaubeuren, Schöntal, and Urach. The same thing is happening to the Catholic church.[35]

Many kindergartens, old peoples' homes, and rest homes were also seized. The national government also collected a special war contribution (*Kriegsbeitrag*), set on November 1, 1939, as 1,000,000 marks for the Protestant church and 800,000 marks for the Catholic church for the next three months.[36]

In addition, the state governments cut their church subsidies. Some figures from the Church of Württemberg indicate the trend. On March 1, 1941, the state subsidy was suddenly cut by 1,900,000 marks which meant the total state subsidy had been cut by 4,414,000 marks from 1934 to the end of 1941.[37] In 1931 two-thirds of the revenues of the Württemberg church were received from state subsidies and one-third from church taxes; in 1944 the proportions were exactly reversed. The state subsidies were regarded by the churches, and recognized by the state in the past, as compensation for historic confiscations of church property. The Nazi officials maintained that since church taxes had increased as a result of the improved economy, direct state subsidies could be cut.[38] The increased reliance on church taxes also brought problems during the war because servicemen and their dependents were exempted from paying them.[39]

In April, 1941, the Prussian minister of finance, claiming authority from the Führer, undertook to end all subsidy payments. This led Minister Kerrl to lodge a vigorous protest with Minister Lammers. Eliminating subsidies would mean an overall cut of 37 percent in salary and care funds, and indeed in some Land churches a curtailment of over 50 percent. It would mean a loss of about 24 million marks for the Protestant churches and 9 million for the Catholics, at a time when 44 percent of the Protestant pastors were in the military service, and from East Prussia even 54 percent. He simply could not be responsible for such nonpayment, and he asked that the subsidies be continued.[40] Lammers submitted Kerrl's letter to Hitler, who said the curtailment went back to Hess, who had misinterpreted the directions. Hitler wanted subsidies in the new territories cut when the church financial system in these districts had been fully established. In the Old Reich he did not want the subsidies used for buildings, organs, and so on. Subsidies that were based on legal obligations should be continued, as for example in Prussia and Württemberg. The chief reason for his decision was that if the subsidies were ended, the salaries of the Protestant ministers, many of whom were in the army, would have to be cut. Lammers notified not only Kerrl, but also Finance Minister Count Schwerin von Krosigk, Bormann, and the governor of Württemberg. The latter disagreed and asked for a review of the matter, as taxes and freewill offerings had increased so much that there would be no need to cut salaries. The reduction of subsidies in Württemberg remained in force.[41]

Hitler, however, thought state subsidies were still much too large. He felt more would be gained if the state contributed less, for then the churches would be so fearful that even this smaller amount would be cancelled that they would be more obliging. The money thus saved could be spent to more advantage in establishing peasant-military colonists in the newly acquired territories.[42] Customary state subsidies to churches in these territories were drastically curtailed. In Austria and in the Sudetenland it was not customary to levy special church taxes, and when Kerrl sought to introduce the German system in May, 1939, he was overruled.[43] In general the Nazis aimed at limiting church support in the new territories to unsolicited freewill offerings. Meanwhile, the German government continued the established practice of paying subsidies to German churches in foreign countries, although at a reduced rate.[44]

Hitler had studies made at this time of the value of church property and of the amount of state funds going to the churches. The value of Evangelical property—not including church buildings, parish houses, and seminaries—was 632,770,657 marks, and of Evangelical foundations, 52,230,710 marks.[45] These figures compare to 448,306,134 marks for the Catholic church and 143,239,081 marks for the property of Catholic orders. The total subsidies to the churches from the Reich and the states had decreased from 113,890,000 marks in 1933 to 71,574,782 marks in 1943. Church taxes raised by the Evangelical Land churches rose from 221,500,000 marks in 1938 to 238,892,000 marks in 1940; those of the Catholic church rose from 95,700,000 to 116,049,000 marks in the same period. Hitler in his speeches tended to add to the state subsidies (which were in fact in many cases payment stemming from earlier confiscations) the church taxes (which were in fact church, not state, revenues) and came up with exaggerated figures for state aid.[46] It is nevertheless true that there was a substantial and important financial bond between the state and the churches. Hitler liked to use the threat of sundering these bonds as a means of intimidation from time to time.

In those Land churches where they had been established, finance sections supervised state subsidies, church property, and general church finances; church authorities willy-nilly had to work with them in drawing up budgets and administering the church.[47] The finance sections were not supposed to determine all financial matters; they were rather to "supervise, approve, and consent to financial transactions." But they had the right to decide what were financial matters, and the head of a finance section had practically an open field for the extension of his jurisdiction and power. The heads of the finance sections in Baden and Brunswick were especially aggressive and caused the church officials there many difficulties.[48]

That differences should arise is not surprising, although there was not always conflict. The churches had to be kept running, for no one was as yet ready to close all church doors. Officials knew the people would simply not have tolerated it. Yet it was also clear that the power of the finance sections was constantly growing, and that they increasingly interfered with the legitimate functions of other church offices. For example, they could simply refuse to make salary payments available, which could prevent the official appointment of a young pastor to a parish—and without an appointment he had no right to occupy the pulpit. They at times refused to make salary payments to pastors who they considered had not carried out the laws and ordinances of the state. Eleven pastors in Hanover had their salaries suspended for this reason. In those churches where German Christians were very much in the minority, the finance sections could intervene to see that they received funds, and the finance sections were usually generous patrons of the German Christians. Only in Bremen, where a finance section was instituted in October, 1941, did it work against the German Christians to the benefit of the Confessing church.[49]

Minister Kerrl had tried to restrict somewhat the activity of the finance sections and maintain the financial autonomy of the various Land churches. Ever since 1937, when Hitler had overruled him and called for Protestant church elections, Kerrl felt he no longer could carry out a policy on his own responsibility and initiative. He repeatedly sought interviews with Hitler, and in a personal letter to Lammers on March 3, 1941, lamented that since the end of 1937 he had been unable to see Hitler on official business.[50] He carried on the necessary tasks, but the Ministry of Church Affairs maintained a neutral line, neither for nor against the official church administration. Kerrl never gave up completely his efforts to unite the Protestant church factions, although his attempts were always stymied by Rosenberg, Bormann, Hess, and Goebbels, who found him far too active. In 1939 they succeeded in getting Hitler to stop the publication of Kerrl's book, *Wëltanschauung und Religion,*[51] and they also kept Kerrl and his office from exercising any authority in the new territories. Perhaps Kerrl's most effective step during the war was his intervention in April, 1941, which brought Hitler to cancel the discontinuance of state subsidies to the churches.

When Kerrl died on December 14, 1941, while on a visit to Paris, his office was taken over by State Secretary Hermann Muhs.[52] Muhs, however, was never appointed minister, largely because of the opposition of Bormann and the party chancellery, who considered him too impulsive and imbued with a desire to surprise. Bormann, in consenting to Muhs as administrator of the office, insisted that Muhs should never use his position to establish church policy.[53] Muhs nevertheless stood better with the party than had Kerrl, and he threw his support to a gradual extension of the power of the finance sections. Churchmen had come to realize what dangers lay ahead of them; they were spared a final showdown by the collapse of the Reich. The expansion of the finance sections was, however, one of the greatest irritants and burdens placed upon some of the church administrations during the war.

Racial Policies

The National Socialist emphasis on race and soil did not diminish during the war. One aspect of the state's population policy which hit at traditional Christian concepts was the party's propaganda for honoring the unwed mother, which became prominent in the fall of 1939. Himmler, head of the SS, issued a secret directive stressing the great contribution German women and girls of good blood could make to the fatherland by bearing children.[54] SS soldiers, if they should be killed, need not fear for their legitimate or illegitimate children, for they and their mothers would be cared for by the state. The state built homes where unwed mothers could await their confinements, and it paid them subsidies for their children's care. The churches naturally tried to uphold the sanctity of the marriage bonds. In May, 1944, the Brotherhood Council of the Church of the Old Prussian Union issued a special declaration to its pastors and congregations on the matter.[55]

The war brought new racial problems to the Reich, for it now ruled over more people of different races than ever before. In the Warthegau the state forced a separation of churches on Polish and German lines;

the two races were even to be buried in separate areas of the cemeteries.[56] Yet the greatest problem for the churches was still their relation
to the Jews.

Even before the outbreak of war, the German government began to
prepare further anti-Semitic measures. Immediately after the annexation
of Austria, by a decree of March 28, 1938, Jewish communities were
deprived of their status as public law corporations, which handicapped
them seriously in carrying out their activities. Decrees restricting Jewish
property rights, eliminating Jews from professions, and limiting their
choice of names to a prescribed list followed in rapid succession. On
November 9, 1938, following the murder of Ernst vom Rath, third secretary of the German embassy at Paris, by the son of a Polish-Jewish
deportee, a pogrom was unleashed throughout Germany, the notorious
Crystal Night. Synagogues were put to the torch, Jewish stores were
smashed and looted, and many Jews suffered physical violence and
arrest.[57] As a follow-up, Minister Rust issued a decree on November 15,
1938, excluding all Jews from elementary as well as higher schools. It
did not specifically apply to children of mixed blood, and they were not
always removed from elementary schools. It did, however, apply to the
racial Jews who were Christians, and who thus far had generally been
permitted to attend regular schools.[58] In July–August, 1939, all Jews, as
defined by the 1935 Nürnberg laws, without reference to religion, were
united into the National Organization of Jews (*Reichsvereinigung der
Juden*).[59] Some exceptions, however, were still made in regard to mixed
marriages.

The following description summarizes well the normal situation of
a Jew in wartime Berlin before the policy of transportation was
inaugurated.

> Every time he took a step out of his house he had to put on his yellow star. In
> the house, which likewise had to be designated by a star, he lived in extremely
> cramped quarters. Every tie with the rest of the world, by telephone, radio, or
> personal visits, was denied to him. Groceries could be bought only at certain
> times with secretly marked ration cards. Certain important nutrients, such as
> fish, meat, and other proteins, were denied him entirely. All possibility of
> obtaining a position was closed to him. At the same time there was strict
> compulsory labor. This meant the heaviest bodily work with inadequate nour-
> ishment in special departments of defense factories until the point of collapse.
> During the increasing number of air attacks he had to continue to work with-
> out consideration of danger; if this was technically not possible the missed
> hours had to be made up. The use of public transportation was forbidden.
> Only if the way to work was more than seven kilometers could a special permit
> to use public transportation be obtained. Not only were all public institutions
> such as the theater, cinemas, libraries, parks, museums, etc. closed to him,
> even the benches in public squares and parks bore the inscription: "Forbidden
> to Jews." Baths and barber shops could not be visited. Laundries were not
> permitted to accept Jewish laundry. Shoes could not be soled. Yes, access to
> whole streets and areas was denied to him. After eight o'clock in the evening
> he could not appear on the streets unless he had a special pass to return home
> after the night shift. Children also had to wear the Jewish star; they could not
> associate with other children. Finally the Jewish schools were closed and the

children remained without instruction. Most of the time they had to do the household work while their parents worked in the factories. And so the tortured people, caught in the mouse trap of the marked houses, were constantly subject to the clutches of the Gestapo.[60]

Now that all Jews were excluded from schools, the next step was to exclude baptized racial Jews from the Land churches and force them to live completely to themselves. Because their records were of a semipublic character, the churches were deeply involved in furnishing data about racial origins from the very beginning of the Nazi era. Even Bishop Wurm saw no harm in this, and in 1934 informed his clergy: "The use of the 'hereditary passports' (*Ahnenpässe*) can also be recommended from the standpoint of the church."[61] Furnishing the data became time-consuming and expensive, and the official church Amtsblätter are full of ordinances on this matter.[62]

Some pastors filled out such forms as to their Aryan heritage, particularly in the early years of the regime. But the practice came to be opposed within the Confessing church so far as the clergy were concerned. On May 8, 1936, the Reich Church Committee had requested officials of all Land churches to submit the names of their non-Aryan pastors.[63] At this time both the Reich Brotherhood Council and the Second Provisional Directory advised against doing so. Three years later, on May 13, 1939, Dr. Werner, head of the church chancellery in Berlin, ordered that all Land church administrations should ask their pastors to submit, in accordance with the German law on officials (*Beamtengesetz*) of January 26, 1937, statements in regard to the Aryan descent of themselves and their wives.[64] The Provisional Directory, in consultation with the Conference of Land Brotherhood Councils (*Konferenz der Landesbruderräte, Kodlab*), requested all pastors not to fill out such papers. The Brotherhood Council of the Church of the Old Prussian Union and the Westphalian brotherhood council took similar steps. President Koch in Westphalia refused to send out the forms to pastors in his synod.[65] Yet in some localities officials loyal to the Berlin church administration began to enforce the measure. In Nassau-Hesse, Pastor Max Weber was relieved of his parish because he was a Mischling second grade (two of his grandparents were Jews).[66] In Baden, the head of the finance section, a particularly antichurch character, made the submission of such statements a condition of appointment to a pastorate. Fiancées of young pastors had to submit such forms before their marriages were approved.[67]

In general the churches always distinguished between "the Jews" and "the Jewish Christians." It was the latter who were their particular concern and to whom they felt a special obligation. Hermann Diem quite rightly states: "From the outset differentiation between baptized and not baptized Jews not only lamed the opposition of the church, but it was craftily exploited by the National Socialists, who naturally could not recognize this distinction."[68] The Pastors' Emergency League, from its very conception in 1933, had done much to succor non-Aryan pastors, their families, and numerous other Jewish Christians. The two provincial directories had concerned themselves with problems relating to non-Aryan Christians, and in September of 1936 created the so-called Grüber Bureau in Berlin.[69] By July, 1939, there were thirty-five people working at these headquarters, along with others in centers outside Berlin. The work was divided into five sections dealing with (1) emigration, (2) old peoples' homes, (3) sending children abroad, (4) care of the needy, and (5) schools and spiritual care. Pastor Heinrich Grüber, head of the organization, was arrested at Christmas time, 1940, and others suffered the same fate.[70] Other valiant souls still struggled to carry on the work, but more and more it was driven underground and finally there were practically no more Jews to help. The policy of transporting Jews to the "East" had begun in Stettin in February, 1940, although it did not get into full swing until October, 1941.[71] The venerable Association for Furtherance of Christianity among the Jews, which had also sought to alleviate hardships, was dissolved and forbidden to carry on its work on January 30, 1941.[72]

Another aspect of the renewed wave of anti-Semitism was Hitler's discovery that Gothic letters were really not a German script but were "*Schwabacher Judenlettern.*" On January 3, 1941, he decided that Latin letters (*Antiqua-Schrift*) should be the normal German script. Officials were no longer to use Jewish "Gothic" letters, and newspapers and schools were to convert as soon as possible.[73] This is one Hitlerian reform which was carried over with vigor into postwar Germany, and today as a rule school children no longer read the old German written script. The order was in line with Hitler's modernization policies. On July 13, 1939, he had expressed his desire to end the use of the term "Third Reich," and this was further elaborated in the beginning of 1942. Just as the British had been able to bring about the use of "Empire" for all its possessions, so he was going to establish the use of the term "Das Reich" for Germany and its possessions. In the future in referring to other nations the word "Reich" was not to be used. "There are states and nations, but there is only one Reich and that is Germany."[74]

On September 1, 1941, a national law made it compulsory for all Jews to display the Star of David when they appeared in public.[75] The ordinance increased the problems for the churches, for many Jewish Christians were not known as such in their congregations. Now they were clearly designated and there was the open challenge: "What are you going to do about it?" With the Thuringian church in the lead, the other German Christian dominated churches—Saxony, Nassau-Hesse, Mecklenburg, Schleswig-Holstein, Anhalt, and Lübeck—on December 17 issued a declaration:

> From the crucifixion of Christ to the present day, the Jews have fought Christianity or misused and falsified it in order to reach their own selfish goals. By Christian baptism nothing is altered in regard to a Jew's racial separateness, his national being, and his biological nature. A German Evangelical church has to care for and further the religious life of German fellow countrymen; racial Jewish Christians have no place or rights in it.[76]

Less than a week later, on December 22, 1941, the German Evangelical church chancellery, untouched by any spirit of Advent and with the consent of the Spiritual Confidential Council, asked the authorities of all Land churches to take steps to see that baptized non-Aryans absented themselves from the life of German congregations. These baptized non-Aryans were to be left to make their own arrangements for their religious life; the chancellery promised to seek state approval for their establishments.[77]

The number of Christian non-Aryans was not large. In 1939 there were 233,646 racial Jews in the Old Reich. Of these 19,716 (8.5 percent) were not Jewish by faith, and these were divided as follows: Lutherans, 10,461; Roman Catholics, 3,025; other Christian denominations, 320; deists, 2,859; no religion, 2,712; and no designation, 339. Of the 52,005 Mischlinge of the first degree, only 5,177 (9.9 percent) were Jews by religion; of the 32,669 Mischlinge of the second degree, there were only 392 (1.6 percent). Thus only about 11 percent of the children of mixed marriages were brought up as Jews, the rest being affiliated with Christian churches.[78]

The finance section in the church of Hanover was among the first to comply with the church chancellery edict to segregate non-Aryan Christians. On January 9, 1942, it ordered that no church taxes should henceforth be collected from non-Aryan Christians because Jews could not be considered members of a public corporation such as the Evangelical Lutheran Land church of Hanover.[79] In Schleswig-Holstein, Dr. Christian Kinder, former head of the German Christians but now back in the Land church office, hit upon the plan of gathering the 124 Jewish Christians within the Land church into a separate congregation. He entrusted the group to Pastor Auerbach, a racial Jew who had been forced to resign by his church patron. He had ceased preaching but was still receiving his full salary. Now to his great joy, he was activated and undertook to administer to his scattered congregation as an official pastor of the Schleswig-Holstein church. Dr. Kinder, who reports with considerable pride on this arrangement, never mentions whether or not Pastor Auerbach wore his Star of David on his robe.[80]

The Confessing churches, of course, could not accept the chancellery edict, for it struck at the very foundation of a Christian church, the congregation of baptized members. Bishop Wurm was among the first to react, and on January 2, 1942, the Evangelical Council of the Württemberg church denounced the measure as contrary to the gospels and pleaded with the chancellery to rescind it.[81] Even sharper statements were drawn up by the Second Provisional Directory and the Conference of Land Brotherhood Councils.[82] Whatever the churches did, and the Confessing churches did do their best to protect their Jewish members, the state continued to deport racial Jews regardless of their beliefs.[83] Many of the deportees from Germany, Austria, and Czechoslovakia were sent to Theresienstadt, a city on the Eger River in Bohemia, where the SS erected an entirely Jewish city, an enclave in the Protectorate of Bohemia. Here the non-Aryan Christians under their own lay leadership gradually were able to form both an Evangelical and a Roman Catholic congregation. At first clandestine, they slowly received grudging recognition by the SS commanders. Leavened bread but no wine was provided for communion services, and so tea and sugar were used instead.[84]

On October 24, 1942, the Supreme Command at Hitler's direction issued an order barring any soldier from marrying a woman who had been married to a Jew. In special cases requests for exceptions could be submitted to Hitler for decision. When an appeal was made to him it was denied, for any woman who had lived with a Jew had shown she had no racial consciousness.[85] In the spring of 1943, the government began to take action against mixed marriages in which a "German" was married to a Christian Jew. This rupture of families brought renewed denunciations from Bishop Wurm. He now struck at broader Nazi policies as well, and his statements indicate that news of the extermination camps was circulating in Germany. After calling for an end to the agitation against Christianity and the church, he continued:

> An end must also be made of all the measures through which members of other nations and races, without trial by civil or military courts, are put to death simply because they happen to belong to another nation or race. Such measures have become increasingly known through men on furlough, and they burden all Christian citizens because they contradict God's commandments just like the measures for elimination of the mentally sick, and they could cause terrible revenge on our people.[86]

Or, as he stated in another letter to Minister Lammers on December 20:

> Not out of any particular philosemitic leanings, but rather because of religious and ethical convictions, I must, in agreement with the opinion of all positive Christian circles in Germany, declare that we Christians consider this extermination policy directed against the Jews as a great and disastrous injustice committed by Germany. Killing without justification because of war and without trial is against God's command, even if the government orders it, and as every deliberate violation of God's commandment is avenged, so will this be sooner or later.[87]

Wurm's letters are all the more to be commended, for at this time Bishops Meiser and Marahrens were keeping silent. At Easter, 1943, Bishop Meiser was presented with an anonymous memorandum by members of the church in Munich, which urged him to protest against the persecution of all Jews, not just the Christian Jews. Meiser could not bring himself to act upon the request, although he did send the letter on to Wurm.[88] In June, when Meiser and Marahrens happened to be in Berlin together, an unsuccessful attempt was made to get them to try to stop the increasing persecution.[89] Discussions between Meiser and Wurm did lead, however, to a letter on July 16, 1943, from Wurm to members of the Reich government about the treatment of non-Aryan Christians.[90] But all these belated protests went unheeded.

There never had been a large number of non-Aryan pastors in the Protestant churches. Many of them had been retired or forced to emigrate before the war.[91] More of them were forced out of office during the war, but some retained positions in church organizations and a few were even able to continue as ministers. In Baden, for example, there were three non-Aryan pastors in 1933. One of these was retired in 1935, but with the express statement that the retirement had nothing to do with his being non-Aryan. The other two continued to serve as pastors, although the minister of culture in 1938 withdrew their right to give religious instruction in the schools.[92]

In the end most Christian as well as Jewish non-Aryans in Germany fell victim to Hitler's fury. Neither the Protestant nor Catholic churches covered themselves with glory in trying to stem the anti-Semitic measures taken by the state after 1933.[93] As the *Kirchliches Jahrbuch* summarized it after the war:

> The anti-Semitism of the NSDAP found the Evangelical church unprepared. Indeed, at least the Confessing church resisted the Aryan paragraph in the church and the separation of Jewish Christians out of the Evangelical church of Germany, but against anti-Semitism they uttered no word, and even at the time of the Jewish persecutions and of their extermination it could not bring itself to stand up against these acts of terrorism in the Third Reich. The official church in general approved openly or secretly the Jewish policy and accepted the measures of the National Socialist regime both in and without the church.[94]

The study prepared under the direction of the Ecumenical Council of Churches points out that the church in Germany had long been schooled to preach absolute obedience to the government and to restrict its concern to "inner church affairs." The study goes on: "And so it is no happenstance that even the Confessing church after 1933, while it directly opposed the introduction of the Aryan paragraph in the church, took only very tardily a stand against the anti-Semitic laws and persecution of the Jews in the Reich."[95] The basic cause of this equivocal attitude was the failure of the churches to realize that anti-Semitism was contrary to Christianity and to be judged a sin. Just so have many institutions and people always been able to equate Christianity with slavery and other forms of racial segregation. To many a German, excluding a Jew from a school or church was permissible, just as separating blacks from whites in the schools and churches has been accepted by many in parts of the United States or in South Africa. The German acceptance of Hitler's rabid anti-Semitism is, however, more difficult to comprehend in view of the high position Jews had attained in Germany in the preceding era.

The Protestant Churches and the End of the War

Bishop Wurm and Church Unification

The Spiritual Confidential Council made no significant contribution to the task of uniting and reorganizing the German Evangelical church. It was trying to square a circle consisting of the state, the moderate groups of the Confessing church including the intact churches, and the German Christians. The militant heart of the Confessing church—the Reich Brotherhood Council, the Second Provisional Directory, and the various Confessing church groups in the Old Prussian Union and elsewhere— were all without direct ties with the Spiritual Confidential Council. It was clear that something would have to be done to recreate ties among these groups if there ever was to be a true German Evangelical church. It was Bishop Wurm who undertook this task.

He was seriously ill in 1941, and at this time he concluded that the existence of separate marching groups within the Confessing church was an offense and sin. The serious turn of events inaugurated by the attack on Russia in June, 1941, drove home the realization that a union between the Land churches and the various brotherhood councils must be attempted. He raised this point at the Church Leaders' Conference in October, 1941, where his suggestion was unanimously accepted, and he was asked to try to bring about some form of unification. He immediately got in touch with some of the leaders of the Conference of Land Brotherhood Councils. By this time the Reich Brotherhood Council and the Provisional Directory were hardly functioning, and the Conference of Land Brotherhood Councils had taken over the leadership of the brotherhood wing of the Confessing church. The leaders of the brotherhood-directed churches heartened Wurm by their confidence in him and their eager promise to cooperate.[1]

By this time Wurm had won widespread respect and admiration, not only because of his public statements against party and state policies which directly threatened his Württemberg church, but also because of statements critical of national policies, particularly the euthanasia program. Speaking sometimes as head of the Württemberg church, at other times as the representative of the Luther Council and the Church Leaders' Conference, Wurm was now also to speak as head of the Church Unification Work (*Das kirchliche Einigungswerk*). In one capacity or another, he represented a broad spectrum of the Evangelical church and was rightly considered the spokesman of the whole church.[2]

Bishop Wurm began by addressing a letter to all German pastors in December, 1941, and at various times he repeated this procedure.[3] He also negotiated with various prominent churchmen. He proceeded cautiously and discreetly; he did not create a big organization, although a council of interested men was formed (*Rat der Kirchlichen Einigungswerkes*). In March, 1942, the Brotherhood Council of the Confessing Church of the Old Prussian Union delegated Pastors Otto Dibelius and Heinrich Held to work with him. At this time the government and party were regulating church affairs in the newly annexed territories in a way which caused alarm in all church circles. There was to be a radical separation of church and state; the churches in former sections of Poland were not to be rejoined to their old "mother church," the Church of the Old Prussian Union. On the suggestion of Dibelius, a statement was drawn up which was meant to serve as a bond among the Land churches and as a defense against anticipated further attacks by the party. Preliminary drafts were circulated for discussion, the appeal being directed to all who upheld Article 1 of the church constitution. The result was a carefully formulated thirteen-point statement which paid special attention to the views of the Confessing groups in Prussia. Four of the statements defined the mission of the church, and nine were directed to its needs and obligations. Finally at Easter, 1943, this statement of eighty-six prominent churchmen, including some from the newly "liberated" territories, was circulated to pastors and congregations. The names of the bishops of the South German churches, and leading men of the Confessing church in Prussia and elsewhere were there. No church statement had received such wide support for a long time, and it continued to serve as an orientation statement in the following months.[4]

Bishop Wurm's standing in the Confessing church continued to rise, not only because of his efforts to settle church differences, but also because of his fearless championship of the churches in sermons and other public statements. Wilhelm Niemöller, not always a great admirer of the actions of the leaders of the intact churches, evaluated Wurm's efforts at unification:

> It is difficult to estimate the influence and results of the Church Unification Work. It was a work of emergency and a work of love. It attempted to make a beginning. It saved many from a feeling of isolation. It prepared the Evangelical church in Germany for the expected collapse of the Third Reich.[5]

Bishop Wurm provided a certain leadership for the German churches, and he also maintained secret contacts by courier with the ecumenical church leaders in Geneva. From 1942 he was kept informed of preparations to provide ecumenical help to Germany after the war. To be able to cooperate with these efforts, in February, 1944, Wurm invited leading German Protestant churchmen to a confidential discussion at which it was decided to make ready an Evangelical church aid society (*Hilfswerk*) for the time when the fighting should have stopped.[6]

The Confessing synods, both local and national, had brought the Confessing church into being and remained the great rallying centers. The fourth and last national Confessional synod had met at Oeynhausen in February, 1936. Since then many local synods had met, but in 1943 they too were to come to an end. They all were in essence a reaffirmation of the declaration of faith and purpose of the first national synod at Barmen. Among the various synods, the meetings of the Confessing church of the Old Prussian Union were the most important. Not only did they represent the largest church body, but here also were to be found some of the most important and outspoken leaders of the opposition movement.

The Prussian synod had met in May, 1939, and did not meet again until October, 1940, when it convened in Leipzig to escape the ever-watchful eyes of the Prussian police. The resolutions of the first synods could be freely distributed, and those of later meetings could be printed secretly, but the reports on the last three synods could only be distributed as typewritten carbon copies to the provincial brotherhood councils. Committees prepared their reports well, and much could be accomplished in relatively short sessions of the synod. The acting chairman of the brotherhood council, Pastor Fritz Müller of Dahlem, carried the major burden in preparing the agenda.[7]

Unlike former gatherings, the Leipzig meeting was relatively uneventful. It formulated a "Word to the Congregations" calling them to be faithful to the church and its teachings, and to a renewed study of the Old Testament. A year later the synod again met outside Prussia, this time in Hamburg-Hamm. Here discussion of the nature of the church, above all the nature of its membership, was the order of the day. It was a burning question, for attempts were being made to eliminate baptized non-Aryans from the churches, and in the Warthegau the government sought to limit church membership to adults who requested it. The synod held that all baptized members belonged to the church and the local congregations. It also discussed greater use of laity in order to alleviate the shortage of pastors.[8] This subject was again one of the chief concerns of the eleventh synod, which also met at Hamburg-Hamm on October 17–18, 1942. Here the synod reached a decision on the place of theologically trained women in the church. While it was recognized that the regular Berlin church offices in many ways did attempt to further the life of the church on the basis of scripture and confession, it was, however, true that these offices were still honeycombed with German Christians and in numerous instances furthered their doctrines. This the Confessing church could not condone.[9]

Germany's military situation had greatly deteriorated by the time the Prussian synod met in Breslau on October 16–17, 1943. The synod again sought to rally pastors and congregations to the declarations of Barmen and Dahlem, and cautioned against recognizing the state-favored church bureaucracy as the true church government. It approved Bishop Wurm's statement indicating awareness of the policy of annihilating the Jews:

> [Our German people] has burdened itself with great guilt by the way it has carried on the struggle against other races and nations before the war and in the war. How many personally innocent people have had to suffer for the sins and injustices of their fellow citizens? Can we be surprised if we now also get to feel some of this discrimination? And even if we have not approved of this, we have often remained silent when we should have spoken up. This is how many people feel, especially the Christians in our country, and we do not undertake to quiet their consciences in regard to this matter, but rather say to them: You are right in your feelings, and we bow with you under the burden of this guilt.[10]

The synod drew up a pointed exposition of the Fifth Commandment: "Thou shalt not kill." If the state uses the sword to kill anyone but criminals or wartime enemies, it goes beyond its authority.

> Concepts like "elimination," "liquidation" and "worthless lives" are unknown to God's order. Annihilation of people merely because they are dependents of a criminal, are old, or mentally sick, or because they belong to a foreign race, is not an exercise of the power of the sword which God has given the magistrate.[11]

The synod also approved a remarkably well-phrased pulpit declaration based on the Ten Commandments, which was an open protest against current conditions and practices. It was to be used on the Day of Repentance and Prayer, 1943, and turned out to be the last of the long list of forceful pulpit declarations in which the Confessing church in Prussia bore witness to God's word and proclaimed the truth to the Nazi authorities.[12]

The synod did not expect to be the last. It reconstituted the Council of the Evangelical Church of the Old Prussian Union and the brotherhood council. They paid Martin Niemöller, imprisoned as he was in Dachau, the honor and compliment which he richly deserved by naming him both chairman of the brotherhood council, his old post, and a member of the church council. When the time came to reassemble the synod in 1944, travel conditions made it impossible. Anticipating the end of the war, the synod had chosen "guidelines for an Evangelical church order" as the subject for deliberation. Preliminary studies were handed over to the brotherhood council, which considered them in a meeting on January 10, 1945. This distinguished body of front-line participants in the Church Struggle continued to meet periodically until the very end of the war. The Confessing church in Prussia, as elsewhere, was able to maintain itself; it had not surrendered to Hitler's might; it was on hand to gather up the pieces and build anew in postwar Germany.[13]

The Last Gasps of the German Christians

The attempt to unite and rally the German Christian dominated Land churches by the Godesberg Declaration of April, 1939, bore little fruit.[14] Perhaps the most successful effort of the Godesberg meeting was the establishment of the Institute for Research on Jewish Influence on the Life of the German Church, which continued to function into the war period. With the start of hostilities the German Christians, ever loyal to the beck and call of the government, willingly observed the request that nothing should be done to create dissension or controversy in the nation. The war brought an end to their organizational development and the movement seemed to stagnate. They too suffered from the extinction of their church press, from travel restrictions, and from other wartime measures. Most important, the German Christians also came to recognize the Nazi state's growing hostility to any form of religion. With the failure of the German Christians to achieve the Gleichschaltung of the Evangelical church, Hitler had actually dropped the idea of uniting church and state that had always been one of the chief desires of the German Christians. They wished to place the church at the service of the state. Now, as Hitler made clear that he wanted a radical separation of church and state, their very raison d'être was being demolished. Like other church leaders of "Old Germany" the German Christians did not think that the new regime should be forced upon the churches of the Warthegau by the government. The German Christians wanted to bolster the state, but in turn they expected some aid and comfort. The state, it is true, did not turn against them as it did against the Confessing church, but the German Christians were also often given the cold shoulder and their letters of protest went unanswered.[15] Thus when in June, 1939, the German Christians (National Church Union) sent a letter to all upper circle party leaders (Kreisleiter) offering to make one pastor available in every district to serve party members who had left the church for baptisms, weddings, and funerals, Bormann sternly forbade entering into any such arrangement.[16]

In May, 1939, Bishop Sasse of Saxony and Bishop Schultz of Mecklenburg, both ardent German Christians, drew up a detailed memorandum intended to inform party and state officials of the antichurch and anti-Christian propaganda which threatened the religious liberty assured to Germans in the first days of national socialism by the deputy of the Führer, Rudolf Hess. At the request of an official in the Ministry of Propaganda, Heydrich had the memorandum confiscated in the interest of preserving religious peace and order. The house of Pastor Dung in Weimar, who had prepared the memorandum for Sasse, was searched and seventy to eighty copies seized.[17]

Even Cajus Fabricius, professor of theology at Breslau, who had long been a supporter of national socialism and had received a certain standing in the movement through his pamphlet *Positive Christianity in the Third Reich,* began to criticize some party practices.[18] As early as 1936 he had noticed the rationalistic, materialistic, and antireligious ideas in the educational addresses given to party members. He periodically drew up memoranda on church topics and forwarded them to selected party leaders.[19] For example, in May, 1939, he sent Rosenberg an article on "God, Immortality, and Jesus." He also prepared various drafts of a lecture on positive Christianity and sent them to the authorities. In the autumn of 1939, in line with his accustomed practice, he prepared a substantial study on "Internal Armament."[20] He sent it first to the chief of staff of the armed forces, who expressed interest in his ideas and promised to protect him. He then forwarded it to other high officials; it was never meant for general distribution. It was a forthright indictment of many National Socialist policies towards the churches. While Fabricius did not oppose the dissolution of the Jehovah's Witnesses, he advocated leaving other sects alone, for they constituted a small percent of the population and in general were harmless solid citizens. He wanted measures against the Ludendorff German Faith Movement and certain party officials. He decried the exclusion of churchmen from the party and the measures taken against religious education in the schools, particularly in Württemberg. However, he never attacked or opposed anti-Jewish policies. What he wanted was a positive declaration from the upper party echelons for the church; this would do much to give inner strength and unity to the people. Goebbels said of the memorandum: "He is the Erzberger of our war, and this memorandum is the peace declaration of our time."[21] Rosenberg referred to it as "this impudent, shameless memorandum that teems with narrow-minded arrogance."[22] For his efforts to "tell Hitler the truth," to borrow a phrase from Wilhelm Niemöller, Fabricius was awarded arrest and expulsion from the party. Hitler ordered Fabricius, like Martin Niemöller, placed in a concentration camp, but unlike the leader of the Confessing church he was pardoned because of his advanced blindness. On his release he had to sign a pledge "that he would refrain from every political activity," and it was made clear to him that at the least violation of the pledge he would be put in the concentration camp for life. He could not leave Berlin, and so could not resume teaching at the University of Breslau.[23]

As the radical Nazi antichurch agitation spread, many moderate German Christians formed ties with the Confessing church. Even the official German Christian leaders opposed Nazi toleration of the German Faith Movement. They were also opposed to the euthanasia program and other government measures. At first many German Christians had honestly thought they were modernizing the church and expected a genuine church renewal, but after early popular support it was clear that renewal was not taking place. It was not the devout, the deeply religious people, who had flocked to their camp, but rather those who in many ways had been indifferent to religion. All accounts attest that church attendance in German Christian congregations was poor, that their members succumbed easily to Nazi propaganda against baptism, confirmation, church marriages, and church burials, and tended to heed exhortations to withdraw from church membership.[24]

A general resignation seemed to overwhelm the German Christians. They issued statements and appeals, but the fire was out of the movement, although the German Christian leaders hung on to their posts and churches until the end. Their movement always had a dominantly political aspect, the renewal of Germany through the acceptance of national socialism and the Führer's leadership. These three—the Führer, Nazism, and German Christians—were all ended by the military defeat; but differences in the past and mutual recriminations over failed policies remained a burdensome legacy for the church of postwar Germany.[25]

The Warthegau: Pattern for the Future?

After the conquest of Poland by Germany and Russia in 1939, small portions of the territory acquired by Germany were annexed to the district of Danzig-West Prussia, and to the provinces of East Prussia and Silesia. However, most of the territory that Hitler annexed from Poland was incorporated into a new administrative unit called the Reichsgau Wartheland (usually Warthegau).[26] It contained lands which had been part of Germany up to 1919, but new areas as well. The rest of German-occupied Poland, as distinct from Polish territories annexed by Germany, was incorporated into the Government General of Poland. Many Germans who returned from the Baltic states and from Volhynia were settled in the Warthegau, bringing their own church leaders, church practices, and customs. This added to the complications of reorganizing the Protestant churches in the area.

The Church of the Old Prussian Union had expected returned brethren to be reunited with it. This was a natural assumption, for Posen (Poznan) was the capital of the Warthegau and before 1919 the Posen church was a member of the Prussian church. Even after World War I, the Church of the Old Prussian Union had sought to retain close ties with the Protestant churches of Poland. Now, to the consternation of the church officials in Berlin as well as in the Warthegau, the return to the mother church was forbidden.[27] Even the Ministry of Church Affairs under Kerrl was denied any jurisdiction over the Warthegau churches.[28] For a while the minister of the interior took over, and then Lammers, head of the Reich chancellery, reserved to himself questions regarding church affairs in the Warthegau so that he could refer them directly to the Führer. Lammers's authority was meant to be only a formal supervision and not a real administration.[29] The Ministry of the Interior continued to exercise police control over church questions in the territory, and for a time it was not clear what central Reich office did have jurisdiction.

From the beginning it was officially held that the Warthegau was unlike the other districts in Germany and that it was directly under the Führer.[30] On October 26, 1939, Arthur Greiser of the SS was named Gauleiter and Reichsstatthalter of the Warthegau.[31] He claimed special authorization from Hitler in church matters apart from existing regulations in the old Germany (*Altreich*). His sweeping authority did not go unquestioned, particularly by Secretary Ernst von Weizsäcker at the Foreign Office in matters relating to the validity of the concordat.[32] The church administrations and even the Ministry of Church Affairs at times attempted to intervene.[33] It was not until the summer and autumn of 1942 that the legal position was clarified. By then it was definitely decided that the concordat did not apply to the recently annexed or occupied territories. On November 13, 1942, Lammers notified all governors and heads of conquered territories that the Führer wished the Ministry of Church Affairs to be restricted to the Old Reich. The powers that the minister of church affairs had been exercising in concordat-free territory had not gone to any other Reich minister, but according to the will of the Führer had gone to the governors and other heads of territories.

> For the uniform regulation of political-confessional matters in the concordat-free territories of the Reich, the head of the party chancellery is in charge; he also has responsibility, for the whole territory of the Reich, to determine the party's position in political-confessional matters in relation to overall political exigencies. Therefore, in all important and fundamental questions, the responsible authorities in the above named territories of the Reich should promptly seek the views of the leader of the party chancellery [Bormann, since May 29, 1941].[34]

This final legal clarification was in line with the developments which had taken place. From the start Greiser had the support of Himmler and Bormann, and he was left free to reorganize the churches in the Warthegau as he wished. He was assisted by August Jäger, who had exercised a baneful influence on church affairs under Bishop Müller before he was dismissed from all his church offices in the fall of 1934.[35] Jäger, with his sharp but narrow legalistic mind, must have felt himself in heaven, for he was now free to create and legalize an entirely new church establishment.

The authorities in the new district set about formulating an overall program which they communicated orally to the Warthegau churchmen on July 10, 1940. It was not an ordinance, as it is sometimes called, but rather a thirteen-point platform for the future.[36] It was largely enacted into law, but in practice it could not be carried out entirely, for both clergy and laity circumvented many of the regulations. Legislation enacted in the Warthegau is usually considered a guide to what would have happened in the Reich had the Nazis remained in power after the war, and the thirteen points therefore merit analysis.[37]

(1) Henceforth there were to be no churches as state institutions, only religious associations as private organizations, which meant churches were no longer to be corporations under public law, with all the privileges that status entailed. Churchmen bitterly opposed this change from historic German practice, but to no avail.

(2) The religious associations were not to be administered by publicly recognized authorities, but simply by association representatives.

(3) As a result of the above provisions, there would in the future be no church laws, orders, or edicts, which meant that the churches could not be financed by church taxes, a restriction which was strictly enforced here as it was in Austria and some other annexed territories.

(4) There were to be no connections with groups outside the Gau, notably no legal, financial, or service ties with the Old Reich churches.

Some ties could be maintained with German Protestantism, but in essence the Church of the Warthegau was to be independent. The same provision was to apply to the Catholic church, and ties with the Vatican were to be cut.

(5) Only adults could be church members, and they would have to make a written application. Persons were no longer born into the church; the concept of a Land, folk, or territorial church was ended. Persons from the Old Reich who came to the Warthegau would also have to make written application for membership. This provision in particular raised objections, for it struck at the very conception of the Christian church as a congregation of baptized Christians. Were not chidren also members of the church?

(6) All lesser church groups, such as youth, women's, and men's associations, were dissolved; nothing was to stand in the way of bringing about unity among the German people.

(7) Germans and Poles could no longer attend the same services. This provision simply carried the principle of nationality over into the churches. The Poles had their own designated churches. It was later ordered that churches staffed by German clerics were to display a permanent sign: "Forbidden to Poles." Polish churches could be used for German services with police permission, but would have to display a card: "From ———— o'clock to ———— o'clock only Germans permitted." There were few Protestant Poles, and so the issue was not acute for the Evangelical church. The Poles, of course, also had their own churches. The churches in general did not post the sign, although in some places it could not be avoided. It must have been with a sense of humor and protest that the man who posted the sign on the church at Konstantinou placed it directly under the inscription on the portal: "Come to me all ye."[38] These national-racial rulings, of course, hit the Catholic church very severely, although many Poles had left or been driven out of the annexed territories.[39] One citation will indicate what was going on. "Of the 300 Polish-Catholic churches in the Territory of the Warthegau, there were only 26 open during the [German] occupation; of the 660 Polish Catholic priests, 400 were sent to concentration camps, and 220 lost their lives there."[40]

(8) Henceforth no confirmation instruction was to be given in the schools, a ban which was later extended to all religious instruction. Religious instruction was limited to young people between ten and eighteen, and was to be given only by pastors of state-recognized religious bodies in church buildings, although eventually some schoolrooms were put at their disposal. All religious services, such as Bible study groups, were forbidden in private rooms. Clearly a man's house was not his castle. Deaconesses, pastors' wives, and in fact all lay persons were denied the privilege of giving religious instruction, although this prohibition was frequently ignored. The official theory was that the laity should devote any extra time they had to war work. These restrictions on religious education were a particular cause for grievance.[41]

(9) Gifts by association members were to provide all financial sup-

port; there were to be no other subsidies. Contributions of over 500 marks would be subject to a gift tax. Church collections in services were forbidden, and all alms boxes were sealed. Actually the congregation contributed more generously than before, forming processions to the altar where gifts were placed, or depositing gifts on the rear benches as they left the church. They were permitted to make customary contributions for special services such as baptisms, marriages, confirmations, and burials.[42]

(10) The associations were not to own any property but the church building itself. Cemeteries were to be state-owned, and should not be restricted to a single confession since that disturbed communal unity. Germans and Poles, nevertheless, had to be buried in separate sections. The churches had, of course, long considered cemeteries as integrally part of their cult, and now they were simply confiscated. Since according to German custom the peal of church bells was part of a "suitable and dignified burial service," they were to be rung at the funeral of a fellow German countryman even if he did not adhere to any church.[43]

(11) Churches were not to undertake social welfare work; this was the sole province of the National Socialist party.

(12) All religious foundations and monasteries were to be confiscated since they were not in accordance with German standards of morality or population policy.

(13) The religious associations could appoint only people from the Warthegau to serve them. These were not to be full-time pastors, but should have another profession as well. It is difficult to see how the party officials expected this provision to work, considering the amount of work even they laid out for a pastor. In any case, it was never implemented. The University of Posen was not to have a theological faculty, although the existing theological school in Posen might continue; it could not, however, call itself a university (*Hochschule*).

This lengthy program was not enacted all at once; Paul Gürtler gives the date and details of each ordinance in an excellent monograph on which this summary is largely based. The program, however, had been to a great extent carried out by the fall of 1941. It disturbed German churchmen of all persuasions, but none as much as those of the Warthegau itself. They had not expected such treatment on being gathered into the protecting arms of the fatherland. The letters to Hitler of General Superintendent Paul Blau, the venerable head of the Evangelical Church of Posen, of Senior Consistorial Councillor Kleindienst of Litzmanstadt, of Provost Thomson, the former head of the Evangelical church in Estonia, and others bear witness to shattered hopes and deep despair, to the cries of the homeless in a world of intrigue, ruthless power, and deceit. As Protestant Provost Thomson, having enumerated all that was taking place in the Warthegau, stated in his letter to Hitler in September, 1941:

> We came in expectation of finding a new home in the Reich and being able to safeguard and nurture the heritage of our fathers. My Führer—I say it openly and frankly—we have been deceived in our hopes. From the

experiences—and it is not a matter only of experiences in connection with the life of the church—that we have had, it has been impossible for us to feel at home in the Wartheland. On the basis of our experiences we can place no trust in the government of the Wartheland. That we will do our duty as citizens of the German Reich under all circumstances is not to be questioned. But we have to do it without joy and with the feeling of deepest disappointment.[44]

Hitler did not answer these letters, for he did not believe it necessary, especially when churchmen were involved. As he stated on another occasion: "it was absolutely senseless, as the Ministry of Foreign Affairs believed, that you had to answer every note of the Vatican. By answering, you recognized the right of the Vatican to involve itself in internal German affairs—even if it was in church affairs—and to strike up official discussions with us."[45] The last thing in the world that Hitler wanted was for churchmen to tell him or party leaders how to administer the Warthegau. And so Reichsstatthalter Greiser and August Jäger were left to govern on their own. What they inaugurated in the Warthegau was not a separation of church and state, but a church unsupported yet controlled by the state. What was happening in the Warthegau was not generally known in Germany, but enough was surmised to cause shivers to run down the backs of many who were attached to the historic German church system. Some of the party instructional leaders did begin to enlighten party gatherings about events in the Warthegau and what was probably in store for Germany.[46]

The Churches and the Political Opposition Movement

There were no protests by the church against the war when it started, nor were there any antiwar statements, pacifistic utterances, or support of conscientious objectors in the many church pronouncements during the war.[47] There is no record of pastors refusing to serve when called into the armed services. Yet the churches often did not speak as ardently for the war as the government would have liked, and certainly resistance to Gleichschaltung, criticism of Nazi policies, and other protests by churchmen must have been unwelcome to the authorities.[48]

In 1859 the old Eisenach Conference had caused a prayer of supplication for the whole German fatherland to be inserted into the liturgy. This was before German unification, and when the Franco-Prussian War broke out in 1870, prayers for church and Reich were made part of the liturgy of all Land churches. Such prayers for country and government are usual in all states, and Germany was no exception. When Hitler took over the government he was included in these prayers of intercession, often with words of adulation and thanks.[49] This practice was continued during the war, yet the prayers began to be worded more circumspectly.[50] Pastors were at times arrested because of the vagueness of their petitions; often the petitions were omitted entirely. In Württemberg the officially suggested petition finally became a transitional sentence from the general prayer to the Lord's Prayer: "All that we would yet pray to God for—the prayer for our people and fatherland and those who lead it—we include in the prayer of our Lord."[51] It had always been customary to take special notice of Hitler's birthday, but this practice was apparently stopped, at least in Bavaria and Württemberg in 1942. Such intercessory prayers, when given at the close of service at which the pastor had spoken out sharply against current theories and practices or read a pulpit declaration at the behest of a brotherhood council, seem particularly incongruous today. Churches, however, have always prayed that evil be righted, and few prayers have ever been uttered publicly that a government be overthrown, or that the enemy be victorious. To close a letter to a government bureau with "Heil Hitler" came to be a formality similar to many other ceremonial concluding phrases. Pastors, except while conducting services, were to use the "German greeting" even if they were in their robes.[52]

What governmental actions are unlawful and what position an individual should take against such actions has long been controversial within the Christian church. Hard as these questions are for individuals, they are even more difficult for the church as an organized body, since it is bound by creedal statements and the necessity of following established procedural methods. The churches, Protestant and Catholic, were haunted by the words of Paul in Romans 13:1–7 on the duty of obedience to those in authority and by the summons in 1 Peter 3:17, "Honor the king," as well as by the heritage of the past. During the war years it was impossible to debate the issue as a theological problem; the lack of a church press, censorship, and the police took care of that. But it was an issue which was pounced upon in theological discussions after the war. The result seems to have been a clear and unqualified affirmation of the right to oppose an unjust government, even at times of the right to kill a tyrant.[53] As Bishop Eivind Berggrav of the Norwegian church stated at the Lutheran World Congress in 1952: "When the government with sheer arbitrariness becomes tyrannical, then demoniac conditions prevail, and results in a regime which does not stand under God. Obedience to a devilish power would be nothing less than a sin. . . . Under such conditions there exists in principle the right of insurrection in one form or another."[54] If this is the ethic of the postwar world—clarified and formulated as a result of the experiences of the recent past—it was not the one which prevailed in Hitlerian Germany. There it was an issue which increasingly troubled many a conscience as the war dragged on, but no clear answer was ever formulated.

The Confessing church never made a point of being a political opposition movement.[55] It is true the government charged that it was a religious cloak for all kinds of opposition and treasonable elements who desired to carry on political agitation against the Third Reich. The First Provisional Directory had issued a pulpit declaration refuting the accusation: "We deny this charge before God and man. We have a good conscience in carrying on our struggle and are ready to give account of our acts. We stand by our word. We do not want to become a refuge for political malcontents.''[56] Martin Niemöller always emphasized that the struggle was a Reich-church conflict and attempted to maintain it on a nonpolitical level.[57] No doubt many who opposed the regime politically did lend their support to the Confessing church. In the best sense, some who had strayed were thus brought back into the church. Nevertheless, it seems clear that the motivation and driving force within the Confessing church was religious, a desire to maintain the purity of the gospel message and the universality of Christian fellowship. This commitment lay at the very center of the activity of the Confessing Christian. Although many theological considerations were involved, the two great anchor points were opposition to the Aryan paragraph and opposition to the elimination or downgrading of the Old Testament.

Yet the Bavarian courts quite rightly did consider the Confessing church as an opposition movement (*Widerstandsbewegung*) when it came to denazification proceedings after the war.[58] The church inevitably was forced into this role by the very course of events, for any organization which resists the policies of the totalitarian state is in opposition.[59] There is insight and truth in the comment attributed to Albert Einstein, whether apocryphal or not:

> Having always been an ardent partisan of freedom, I turned to the Universities, as soon as the revolution broke out in Germany, to find the Universities took refuge in silence. I then turned to the editors of powerful newspapers, who, but lately in flowing articles, had claimed to be the faithful champions of liberty. These men, as well as the Universities, were reduced to silence in a few weeks. I then addressed myself to the authors individually, to those who passed themselves off as the intellectual guides of Germany, and among whom many had frequently discussed the question of freedom and its place in modern life. They are in their turn very dumb. Only the Church opposed the fight which Hitler was waging against liberty. Till then I had no interest in the Church, but now I feel great admiration and am truly attracted to the Church which had the persistent courage to fight for spiritual truth and moral freedom. I feel obliged to confess that I now admire what I used to consider of little value.[60]

Even if the actions of the churches were motivated by a desire to promote their own interests and Christian values, in a broad sense their actions surely constituted an opposition movement. And they paid the penalty for their actions. Thousands were imprisoned or suffered other punishments, while the ever-present fear of police action was no slight burden to bear.[61] A memorial volume issued at the request of the brotherhood council of the Evangelical church has essays on eighteen persons who were executed, died in concentration camps, or suffered death as a result of imprisonment.[62] The total number who died because of governmental persecution or by execution, however, has never been satisfactorily compiled. Nor was the list of martyrs confined to the clergy. In February, 1943, Hans Scholl and his sister Sophie, leaders in the student group the White Rose, were executed because they passed out anti-National Socialist flyers at the University of Munich. Both were motivated by evangelical considerations, as was another student, Hans Karl Leipelt, who was executed in January, 1945.[63]

The step from general opposition to conspiratorial action is a very significant one. The intricacies of the various plots, notably the one of July 20, 1944, when the bomb did go off but Hitler survived, cannot be discussed here. Certainly some of the conspirators, both Protestant and Catholic, were influenced by religious considerations.[64] This was particularly true of many of the so-called Kreisau Circle, named after the estate of Count Helmuth James von Moltke, the leader of the group. On the Protestant side the most famous activist was no doubt Dietrich Bonhoeffer. He had long been a part of the opposition movement, and was arrested on April 5, 1943, months before the spectacular assassination attempt was carried out. He was not executed until April 9, 1945, and his brother and two brothers-in-law suffered the same fate. Eugen Gerstenmaier, a member of the church's foreign office and later to become president of the Bundestag, narrowly missed death.[65] They, among others, had carried their religious convictions over into the field of conspiratorial political action. Bishop Wurm had been in touch with these activists, but to his surprise he was never arrested. He did receive a letter from Reich Minister Lammers on March 3, 1944, enumerating his sins of commission against the Reich and warning him severely to mend his ways.[66] Wurm himself held that in his case, as in that of Bishop Galen, the most outspoken member of the Catholic hierarchy, Hitler did not want to involve himself in a "bishop's process." Wurm indeed was not directly involved. He writes: "Over the way the opposition movement hoped to achieve the removal of Hitler I was uninformed. I did not conceive of it as an assassination, but thought of it as a military action, occupation of the highest headquarters and the capture of its members. It is not within my competence to give an opinion why this was not possible."[67]

The Confessing church, and at times even some less radical German Christians, had battled the state in order to maintain the very existence of a church. Their opposition had caused anguish, suffering, and pain. But it had also brought a quickening of spirit and a reassessment of values. The years of opposition had laid a foundation and set the guidelines for the reconstruction of the church in the new Germany.

18.

The Catholic Church during the War

The Unity of the Church

The outbreak of war brought no basic change in the relations of the state to the Catholic church. A Catholic hierarchy that had given thanks and approval to Hitler's major foreign policy moves ever since his assumption of power could hardly be expected to change course when the marching began. There was no time to sit and ponder if the attack on Poland was a just war or not, and whether according to Catholic theology it should be supported or condemned. To expect the bishops to do so is asking too much. They, like all other Germans, rallied to the flag and in time-honored fashion called upon the faithful to do their duty for the fatherland.[1] This duty of course, also involved fighting for the Führer; there was no way out of the dilemma. To fight for Germany and not for Hitler would have meant advocating revolution, which no member of the hierarchy could bring himself to do. Yet as the war ground on to its weary close and the basically un-Christian aims and practices of the Nazi regime became clearer, the Catholic leaders progressively came to make a distinction between fighting for fatherland, home and folk, and fighting for Hitler. As Bishop Galen stated in 1941: "Bravely we continue to fight against the foreign foe; against the enemy in our midst who tortures and strikes us we cannot fight with weapons. There is but one means available to us in this struggle: strong, obstinate, enduring perseverance."[2] "Strong, obstinate, enduring perseverance" indeed had characterized church policy in the prewar years, and it continued during the war itself. As one Gestapo report of November 12, 1939, put it, the attitude of the church had not changed. Church attendance was better; there were many soldiers present, especially men from the Ostmark. The sermons were much the same, except, he noted, for one by an army chaplain who called for support of the Führer.[3] In his New Year's Eve sermon in 1939, the bishop of Eichstätt summoned Catholics to do their duty and stand firmly together in the hard struggle which Germany faced. In the interest of unity he was willing to overlook all the hardships that had been inflicted on the church and its priests. But as the police officer reported, the bishop would not go a step further and pray God to bless the work of the Führer; "They simply can't bring themselves to do this" (*Den Namen des Führers bringt man eben nicht über die Lippen*).[4] Yet the liturgical prayers prescribed by Article 30 of the concordat continued to be read in the Catholic services in Germany. Even Bishop Galen ended his famous sermons on July 13 and 20, 1941, with the prayer "for our German nation and fatherland and its Führer."[5] Such prayers were but the traditional ones "for those in authority" and a plea that they might act according to God's commandments. They were one of the commitments the church had assumed in negotiating the concordat; if the church wished the state to live up to that agreement the church must live up to it as well.

Government leaders had sought to establish a truce with the churches at the start of the war.[6] Nothing was to be done which would disrupt the unity of the people. This policy was never successful. Old differences continued and new ones arose, widening the chasm between church and state. Everything that has been said about wartime restrictions on the Protestant churches applies equally to the Catholic church. The clergy were limited in their contacts with men in the armed services, press and publications suffered new restrictions (partly, to be sure, because of paper shortages), religious education was limited, churches had to surrender their bells, observe the regulations in respect to religious holidays, suffer confiscation of property and a diminution in church grants, and face up to new racial and wartime policies. While the reactions of the two churches were much the same, and while many instances of opposition and protest, as well as compliance, can be cited in both, the impact of the war measures on the churches was not always the same.

While both the Catholic hierarchy and the laity supported the war, there was never a Catholic wing comparable to some Protestant German Christian groups who unreservedly supported Nazi ideology and policies. There were no deep-seated internal conflicts, no questioning of the forms of church government or how the church was to be shaped in the postwar world. The very unity of the church, deriving from the leadership of an internationally respected pope and a strong hierarchy, gave it great power. Outwardly it presented a united front, although it was not as united as it seemed, and unity could be maintained only by agreeing to certain compromises. In a letter to the German episcopate gathered at Fulda in August, 1940, the pope urged them to greater unity. "Never did the believing Germans have more longing and greater need for a united leadership by its episcopal shepherds than in the present moment."[7]

Heydrich, head of the security service, in writing to Rosenberg noted that the Fulda meeting was mainly concerned about the attitude that should be taken towards the National Socialist state. Cardinal Faulhaber of Munich, Archbishop Gröber of Freiburg, Bishop Preysing of Berlin, Bishop Galen of Münster and Bishop Michael Rackl of Eichstätt led a group who felt that national socialism could only be overcome by open conflict. There had been much controversy. Bishop Franz Rudolf of Trier, Bishop Berning of Osnabrück, Cardinal Bertram of Breslau, and Cardinal Schulte of Cologne led the group who believed that national socialism could be overcome only through compromises. Archbishop Gröber had been most active in opposing this viewpoint.[8] Heydrich speculated that the Vatican had also urged compromises, for it wanted an armistice in order to consolidate southwestern Europe. The Vatican hoped to obtain a concordat with France and then form a Catholic-Latin bloc of France, Spain, and Portugal, which Italy might join later. Heydrich believed that as soon as this group was consolidated the Vatican hoped to disrupt the National Socialist state, if this had not been accomplished earlier by the intervention of the United States. In any case, Germany need not expect approaches in the near future from the Vatican.[9]

The letter indicates the interest the Nazis took in the differences among the bishops, and at least Heydrich's opinion as to the basic hostility of the Vatican and the United States to national socialism. Whatever attitude one has toward Pius XII and his wartime policies, it is clear that the Nazi leaders never felt that he was on their side.[10] When Heydrich ordered the Gauleiter to prevent the distribution of the papal letter of April 20, 1941, to Cardinal Secretary Luigi Maglione, he reasoned that the "letter had pacific tendencies and dealt with the horrors of war; it was drafted in the spirit and mentality of our enemies."[11]

The hierarchy spoke for the church, and when Cardinal Bertram in the name of the episcopate congratulated Hitler on his birthday in April, 1940, pledging loyalty and prayers, and Hitler in turn sent a cordial thank-you, pledging the loyalty of the state and government to the church, the exchange helped to give the impression that relations between church and state were far better than they actually were.[12] Although he did not continue to send birthday greetings in the name of the bishops, Cardinal Bertram sent his personal felicitations yearly until 1944.[13] Such greetings, however, did not keep Bertram from seeking to rectify the regime's actions. He was particularly active in protesting the seizure of Catholic kindergartens in 1941.[14]

It is impossible to assess the total effect of the constant round of Vatican and German hierarchical protests in protecting the Catholic church.[15] Hitler avoided receiving the nuncio and foisted him off on Minister Lammers while maintaining that it was unnecessary to answer every Vatican note, for to do so would acknowledge that it had a right to mix in German internal affairs.[16] Yet all indications are that the repeated protests did make an impression, for Hitler was constantly concerned about stirring up public opinion during the war by interference in confessional questions. The police reports indicated an "exceptional uneasiness" among the people in all parts of the Reich as a result of the reading in the churches of the hard-hitting pastoral letter issued by the Fulda Bishops' Conference of June 26, 1941. The letter enumerated the many restrictions placed on the church, particularly on monastic establishments.[17] In July, 1941, the Vatican submitted a private notice to Ambassador Bergen sharply protesting the seizure of monasteries in Germany and in the Ostmark.[18] This was sent on to Secretary Weizsäcker in Berlin, who forwarded it to the responsible authorities. Nuncio Orsenigo also repeatedly raised the issue, and Bishop Galen made his forthright protests against the confiscation of monastic property at this time. The upshot was that Hitler, on July 31 and August 8, ordered the cessation of any further attacks on either female or male monastic foundations.[19] This was followed by another directive on September 3, which stated that it was "absolutely essential that all measures be stopped which could adversely affect the feeling of unity among the populace."[20] Bishop Galen had irritated Hitler, who assured his entourage that he would "take care of him" at the end of the war, and in the settlement not a thing would be forgotten. Galen's actions would give him additional grounds for cancelling the concordat when the fighting was over.[21] The ending of the euthanasia program, a result of Protestant and Catholic denunciations, is perhaps the best example that forthright protests occasionally do have results, even in a dictatorship.[22]

The War and the Concordat

Just as the German Evangelical church constitution of 1933, with its recognition of the historic confessions, gave the Confessing church a certain protection, so the concordat of 1933 supported the Catholic church. In 1935 the German government had recognized that the concordat applied in the Saarland. Not all of its articles were flouted recklessly, and in spite of the fact that he had no use for it, Hitler never abolished it for the Old Reich.[23] On January 6, 1940, Foreign Minister Ribbentrop requested a study of the status of the German and Austrian concordats, which was handed in two days later. It pointed out that the Reich government secretly regarded the concordats as antiquated. Although there had been internal discussions on the validity of the Austrian concordat in 1938, and it was then held to be invalid, a notice to this effect had never been sent to the Vatican.[24] While the papal authorities had submitted many specific violations of the concordat (elimination of confessional and private schools, curtailment of subsidies, etc.), the German government had complained not about specific violations, but about the general attitude of the Catholic church and its "failure to understand the requirements of national socialism."[25]

Nothing was done to clarify the situation at that time. The issues of the validity of the concordats and of Nuncio Orsenigo's right to extend his jurisdiction to the annexed and occupied territories came to a head somewhat later, over the question of whether the Vatican was obliged to submit appointments of all higher church officials in these areas to the German government before final appointments could be made. The German authorities based their right of approval on their general rights of sovereignty over the territories, and for the sake of uniformity they wanted such officials submitted for approval even when appointed in the Old Reich. Their demand lengthened the list beyond that agreed upon in the concordat, which included only those exercising episcopal powers. The German claims were presented to the Vatican on August 29, 1941.[26] The curia repaid the government for its delays and refusals to answer notes by not replying until the following January. To meet the requests would be tantamount to altering the Land and Reich concordats and to recognizing the wartime territorial changes as well, something which was contrary to Vatican policy.[27] When the German government continued to make difficulties over certain appointments, the posts were left unfilled and lesser officials were named to carry on. Another governmental request, to have German bishops or administrators appointed to Polish dioceses, was never met.[28]

The disputes over appointments did nothing to clarify the status of the concordats. The nuncio continued to raise protests about the treatment of the church in the occupied lands.[29] Secretary Lammers discussed the issue with Hitler who had a ready solution—the nuncio could advance his claims, but Germany could refuse to recognize them.[30] On June 2, 1942, Lammers pressed Foreign Minister Ribbentrop to come to a decision.[31] Before Berlin officials got around to it, Hitler, on June 10, 1942, gave Councillor Walter Hewel, the foreign minister's personal representative at the Führer's headquarters, a clear directive.[32] Hitler did not want relations with the Catholic church to be conducted uniformly for the whole Reich. Relations with the Vatican were to be restricted to the Old Reich, that is, to the territory which was part of Germany when the concordat was concluded in 1933. Although the concordat was frequently violated by both sides, officially he considered the agreement valid. Inasmuch as the Vatican had informed the German government that it could not recognize any territorial changes as long as the war continued, it automatically had excluded itself from any official ties with the territories annexed or occupied by Germany since 1939. In addition he declared he wanted the same concordat status established for Austria and the other territories annexed before 1939. Reich protectors or governors were to act for the annexed and occupied territories, while the church could be represented by local church officials, as, for example, bishops or administrators. The jurisdiction of the minister of church affairs was to be limited to the Old Reich.[33] Only the Foreign Office was to maintain contacts with the Vatican, while officials in the conquered territories were to receive instructions in ecclesiastical matters from the head of the party chancellery.

Hitler's directive ended a lot of discussion among officials in the various departments, and Nuncio Orsenigo was immediately informed on June 25, 1942, that his jurisdiction was limited to the territories of the Old Reich as they existed in 1933.[34] The directive was also immediately discussed at a conference in the Foreign Office to which representatives of various ministries, the security police, and the security service were invited. Minister Lammers, however, did not inform top officials in the occupied territories and in the German Länder of the status of the concordats until October 18, 1942.[35]

Hitler had actually simply confirmed a practice which had been followed for some time. About a year earlier, on August 25, 1941, the government had informed the Vatican that it could not extend the concordat of 1933 to the new territories—Austria, the Sudeten German area, the Protectorate of Bohemia and Moravia, the Memel area and other incorporated eastern areas, and Eupen-Malmédy. Nor was the concordat "applicable in Alsace, Lorraine, Luxembourg, and the liberated areas of Styria, Carinthia, and Carniola."[36] Not only did the concordat not apply, but Germany refused to recognize the concordats and agreements which had previously applied to these territories.[37]

According to the German position the Catholic church had no rights guaranteed by a concordat in the new territories, and when the nuncio tried to discuss Catholic affairs in the annexed or occupied regions he was simply told that he had no standing in these areas. Nevertheless, he continued to inquire, protest, and intervene on behalf of the church and of various persecuted groups in the occupied territories.[38] At the Foreign Office he was received sympathetically by State Secretary Ernst von Weizsäcker and, after Weizsäcker became the German ambassador at the Vatican in April, 1943, by his successor, Baron Gustav Adolf Steengracht von Moyland.[39] For example, when the pope in March, 1943, decided to make an extended protest about conditions in the Warthegau, the note was received at the Foreign Office and translated and read by Weizsäcker. It apparently was actually forwarded to Ribbentrop, but the Vatican was officially informed that it had not been sent on to the Foreign Minister since it did not relate to matters in the Old Reich. Papal Secretary of State Cardinal Maglione wrote Ribbentrop that the return of the note was an unfriendly act, but that the Holy See considered that the document had reached its destination. Ribbentrop rejected the cardinal's position, which again was taken by papal authorities as an indication that conditions in the Warthegau had been called to the attention of the Reich government officially.[40]

In other words, communications from the Vatican about the new territories did get through to the German authorities. Officially they produced no results, and German policy was not noticeably changed. However, it is also clear that Weizsäcker and others often did as much as was in their power to alleviate the fate of oppressed Polish clergy and others.[41] At least three times after March, 1943, the Vatican made formal protests about conditions in the occupied and annexed territories.[42]

It is clear that Germany during the war followed a restrictive and hostile policy in regard to its own concordats and those of the states which it conquered. Far greater hardships befell the Catholic church in parts of the "Greater Germany" than in "old Germany," and these hardships had many causes. Yet the concordat of 1933, all things considered, did play a significant role in protecting the position of the Catholic church within the boundaries of the Old Reich, and it always served as a basis of appeal and protest for the church authorities.

The Impact of War on the Clergy

One provision of the concordat which was on the whole observed by the government was the secret annex regarding the induction of Catholic clergy and theological students into the armed services. The

provision had been recognized in the Defense Law of May 21, 1935,
which stated that Roman Catholics consecrated as subdeacons could not be called to military service.[43] A general decree on recruitment and conscription of April 17, 1937, recognized that Catholic theological students could be exempted, and in an annex listed the specific institutions (state universities, episcopal schools, and two papal institutions in Rome) where students would qualify for such an exemption.[44] The Vatican protested that the list of schools had been drawn up without consulting it, excluded the monastic theological schools, and made invidious distinctions among qualified papal institutions in Rome.[45] The notes were not answered. The Vatican indeed was not in a strong position, for to have raised the issue publicly would have meant revealing the secret annex and acknowledging that it had anticipated the reintroduction of compulsory military service in Germany as early as 1933.

In the spring of 1939, the German authorities had a study prepared on the problem of calling up Catholic theological students.[46] It pointed out that in the winter semester of 1938–39, there were 1,440 Protestant theological students at the universities, among whom were 163 beginners—the lowest number since 1911. In contrast there were 4,950 Catholic students, among whom there were 786 beginners, the largest number ever. There was clearly a direct relation between enrollments and draft status, for when the exemption was denied to those attending monastic higher schools, the students all flocked to the state and episcopal institutions. The author of the study advised that nothing need be done about the Protestant students, but something should be done about the number of Catholics. Plans were made to call them up as soon as they had finished their work at the gymnasium. The education ministry had approved the plan, but it still had to be signed by the High Command of the Army and by the minister of church affairs. Differences developed among the ministries, and Lammers, head of the Reich Chancellery, on May 30, 1939, referred the matter back to them for agreement before he would ask Hitler for final approval.[47] No decision had been reached before World War II broke out, and with general mobilization the whole situation changed. By that time the Catholic faculties at Innsbruck, Salzburg, and Munich (with its affiliate Graz) had been closed. The closing of Munich was the result of Cardinal Faulhaber's steadfast refusal to approve a professor of church law selected by the government.[48]

On October 10, 1939, the High Command of the Army issued a directive on the mobilization of Catholic clergy.[49] In line with the concordat, a certain group of the clergy could not be called in at all: "the bishops, the members of the diocesan courts, principals of seminaries and ecclesiastical hostels, professors in seminaries, the parish priests, curates, rectors, coadjutors, and the clergy who permanently preside over a church of public worship."[50] Other Catholic clergy could be called only into the medical service, and only those theological students were to be called to service with weapons who had not yet been consecrated as subdeacons. The directive thus conformed to Article 14 of the Defense Law of May 21, 1935.[51]

These regulations of course meant that Catholics had a certain protection against the depletion of their present staffs and also assurance for a future postwar generation of priests. Their situation was very different from that of the Protestants, whose clergy and students were regularly called in for combat duty. Thus Wilhelm Niemöller, brother of the well-known Martin, along with many others, served throughout the war as a regular officer. The Jesuits were always viewed suspiciously by Hitler, and on May 31, 1941, he ordered that they be discharged at once from the armed services, and that henceforth they should not be summoned.[52] This was done more or less under the guise of permitting them to continue their studies; they were not to be considered unworthy of service under the Defense Law. According to a further army directive of February 18, 1942, Roman Catholic theological students, deacons, and regular clergy should not be appointed reserve officers. Bormann inquired whether this policy should be changed; the replies were mixed.[53]

The result of these directives based on the concordat was that a disproportionate number of Protestant clergy were called up. Recognizing the situation, the High Command of the Army, in October, 1943, ordered an end to the induction of all officiating clergymen. A few months later, Bormann clarified this directive by defining "clergyman": a person who had passed his theological examination, or in the case of sects, a man who was engaged full time as a preacher. If an individual also held another job, however, he should be drafted. Bormann added in another directive: "It was impossible to call Catholic clergy for military service in certain parts of Germany, and equality of treatment made it necessary to treat other confessions the same, especially since a greater percentage had already been called into service."[54]

That mobilization nevertheless did draw many Catholic clergy into the armed forces is shown by the summary of "Contributions to the War Effort" compiled by Archbishop Gröber for his diocese, covering the period September 1, 1939, to December 1, 1940. During that time 170 priests, 238 theological students, 45 youths from seminaries, and 464 monastics—a total of 817—had entered the services. Yet of these only 5 had either died of sickness or in battle.[55] In 1943 Goebbels wanted information on the Catholic church in Germany, and the Ministry of Church Affairs submitted a report including statistics on the number of Catholic clergy in the armed services in 1941. Of the 2,734 mobilized secular clergy, 424 were chaplains, 2,166 in the medical corps, and only 114 were serving "elsewhere;" of the 3,003 monastic clergy mobilized, 5 were chaplains, 2,166 in the medical corps, and 832 were serving "elsewhere."[56] At the beginning of 1944, out of 18,379 Catholic ministerial positions (Seelsorgestellen), 5,953 were vacant; the occupants of 2,246 positions were over sixty-five years old. The police noted that "these figures are the cause of the Catholic church's concern over the future supply of priests."[57] Bishop Wienken, on behalf of the Fulda Bishops' Conference, submitted a report on the number of monastics in the armed services as of May 1, 1944: there were 2,410 monastic clergy, 2,863 monastic theological students and novices, and 4,624 lay brothers. If these numbers are compared to the 1938 membership figures, it appears that 40 percent of the monastic clergy, 54 percent of the students and novices, and 60 percent of the lay brothers were mobilized.[58] In the end, around 1,150 priests were killed or listed as missing.[59] There were more Catholic than Protestant theological students throughout the war, although only four Catholic university faculties were left, at Breslau, Freiburg, Prague, and Vienna.[60]

It is clear that the concordat had accomplished pretty much what Catholic authorities had sought; it kept most of the clergy from serving with arms. With a smaller percentage of clergy mobilized, with fewer engaged in active combat duty, and with more students, the Catholic church in Germany, so far as manpower was concerned, was generally in a better position to face the postwar world than was the Protestant. Both Catholic and Protestant clergy did their duty to the state as they had done in past wars; there were no conscientious objectors.

As in the case of the Protestants, the war brought more work to the Catholic clergy. At times the request for masses for men killed in action and for intercessory masses for soldiers in the field were so numerous that they had to be limited.[61] The clergy sought strenuously to further their ministrations to the faithful, and particularly to extend their contacts and work with youth groups.[62] Pastoral care of the many foreign laborers brought to Germany, most of whom were Catholic, presented additional problems. The government's policy towards these unfortunates was about as restrictive as it could be.

Polish civilian workers in Germany were always treated more severely than others, were paid less, had shorter rations, were not permitted as freely to return home and so on.[63] This discrimination was also extended to their religious care. All German priests were forbidden to instruct Polish children and prepare them for confirmation. German priests were ordered by the governor of Upper Silesia not to administer in any way to Poles. No religious literature could be handed out to them. In June, 1940, the regulations were modified somewhat, and Poles could attend church if mass was said for them alone or if they sat apart from others. Yet this concession was revoked on July 15, 1941. Cardinal Bertram and other bishops protested to no avail.[64] The police often reported that priests befriended the Poles and admired their exemplary piety.[65]

On September 9, 1942, the Ministry of Church Affairs, after consultation with Himmler, issued a new comprehensive directive for the spiritual care of Polish workers. Except for special high festivals, there was to be a service between ten and twelve o'clock on the first Sunday of every month, although it could be shifted to another Sunday. Additional participation in services in neighboring districts was not permitted, although special permission might occasionally be granted. There was to be no use of Polish (in hymns, confessions, prayers, etc.) except in the general absolution, where a few Polish texts could be mentioned. Poles were not to attend German services nor Germans Polish ones.

There were to be no marriages for Polish workers among themselves or with other foreigners in the Old Reich.[66]

The measure led the papal secretary of state to ask Cardinal Bertram on November 18, 1942, to attempt to do something on behalf of Polish workers. Cardinal Bertram replied that he was well aware of the restrictions but that his protests and those of other bishops had been ignored. Bishop Wienken, spokesman for the bishops at Berlin, had supported the protests in a personal interview with authorities.[67] Contemporary police reports indicate that the German laity also differed from the government on these matters. The peasants continued to observe old religious and customary holidays, which under recent legislation were no longer legal holidays. Not only did they not work, they also gave Poles and other eastern workers a holiday. One police officer wanted a new decree to end this waste of manpower.[68] Another officer reported that foreign workers did not preserve proper decorum on railways and streetcars. Germans too did not have the proper attitude, for at times they sided with the workers.[69]

Ukrainian Uniates in the Rhine Province were accorded services by a Uniate priest. If workers came from the Government General of Poland and had to wear a "P," they could not attend regular services. This was also the case of civilian workers from various eastern territories overrun by Germany who were designated "East" (*Ost*). They could attend services only in their camps, and these services were to be held by their own priests.[70] It was reported that these captured priests at times agitated against the German state. They were to be watched and if necessary separated out. For special reasons—not detailed—the priests, however, were not to be stopped entirely from holding services in the camps. German youths were not to be used as altar boys in special services for Poles, although a second priest or church sacristan could be employed. Civilian workers, for example those from France or Belgium who were not forced to wear the designation *Ost,* could attend regular German services. Dutch-speaking German priests were not to hold services for Dutch workers, although the latter were permitted to attend regular German services.[71]

On June 5, 1943, the church ministry relented a bit. German priests could participate in baptisms and burials for Poles working in Germany. The baptisms, however, had to be separate from those of German children; only Latin was to be used; sponsors had to be Poles; no Germans except the sacristan could be present. Last rites and confession for Polish workers were not permitted. There was to be no ringing of bells at burials, and again at the service only Latin was to be used.[72] These extreme regulations were modified once more in August, 1943, when last rites and confession for Polish civil workers were at last allowed.[73] Yet what was extended with the left hand was withdrawn with the right. Confessions were to be received only in German, and no Polish was to be used in church services. Bormann in 1944 discovered that the church was using eastern priests, which required special permission, as did holding services for eastern workers. He asked all Gauleiters to report on this.[74] He also issued a nine-page directive on Orthodox services for workers of that faith. The Orthodox priests should not live in the camps, they did not have to wear the designation *Ost,* and their wives were not to be subjected to compulsory labor, although the children, if of age, had to work. No German was to be used.[75]

In contrast to these restrictions on providing religious services, Bormann issued highly confidential decrees establishing brothels for the eastern workers. At least he was consistent in that no German-blooded girls were to work in these houses and German citizens were not permitted to frequent them.[76]

That the authorities found it necessary to issue such restrictive measures about the spiritual care of the eastern workers is indicative in itself of the church's concern for them. Nevertheless, one would like to be able to cite a strong public denunciation of these policies by the hierarchy similar to the ones Bishop Galen made when monastic property was seized and the euthanasia program was being carried through. Actually, these policies simply carried over into the Old Reich the segregationist religious practices which the government was enforcing in the Warthegau and some other occupied areas.[77]

There was not much that any one, aside from Hitler and those directly in charge, could do about the concentration camps. Yet in 1940 the papacy, through Nuncio Orsenigo and Bishop Wienken, was able to negotiate an arrangement with the secret police which brought some relief to clerical prisoners in concentration camps.[78] The Nazis were not anxious to make martyrs out of the hierarchy and were circumspect about imprisoning bishops or other higher clergy, especially in Germany proper. During the war Bishop Dr. Michal Kozal of Poland, Bishop Gabriel Piquet of France, and Bishop Dr. Johannes Neuhäusler of Munich were sent to Dachau, but they apparently were the only bishops who were ever consigned to concentration camps.[79] Dachau was the best of the camps, but comparing them is like trying to measure temperatures in the abysses of hell. Abbots and other high prelates were also imprisoned. Of the total number of Catholic clergy in concentration camps, 9.78 percent were higher clergy; of these 8.27 percent were from Germany, 17.87 percent from Czechoslovakia, and 18.08 percent from Austria.[80] It was the rank-and-file clergy from Poland who suffered most and constituted the mass of Catholic clerical martyrs to Nazi tyranny. Within a few months after the war began, 214 Polish priests were executed, and by the end of 1939 some 1,000 Polish secular and regular clergy were imprisoned in concentration camps.[81] A summary of the effect of the war on the Polish archdiocese of Posen shows that on September 1, 1939, there were 681 secular clergy and 148 regular clergy in the diocese, making a total of 828. Of these, on October 1, 1941, 34 were active in the spiritual care of Poles and 17 of Germans; 22 priests were without permission to carry out their calling; 17 had died natural deaths; 120 had been shot or died in concentration camps; 57 were in hiding; 24 were outside the boundaries of greater Germany; of 12 there was no knowledge at all; and 451 were in concentration camps. Of the 441 churches functioning in 1939, on October 10, 1941, 30 were being used by Poles and 15 by Germans. All the others had been closed or were being used for other purposes.[82]

Even in Dachau the Polish priests were kept separate and did not enjoy the concessions granted to other clergy. Whereas Dutch, German, and Norwegian clergy were used in garden work in the Heilkräutergarten under a Himmler decree of April, 1942, Polish and Lithuanian priests were to be used in all work details.[83] Of the 2,579 Catholic clergy in Dachau, 1,748 were Polish (68 percent), 411 were German (16 percent), and 420 were of other nationalities (16 percent). Of the 1,034 clergy who died in that camp, 857 were Poles (83 percent), 94 were German (9 percent), and 83 were of other nationalities (8 percent). These figures do not of course include the Polish clergy who were shot in Poland or died in other concentration camps. Most of the Polish secular clergy in Dachau came from the annexed territories (1,044) while 351 came from the other Polish dioceses, and there were in addition 353 priests belonging to orders, among them 70 Jesuits.[84] In Austria under the Nazi regime, 724 priests were imprisoned, of whom 7 died; 110 priests were in concentration camps, of whom 20 died; 15 were sentenced to death and executed.[85]

Monastic Foundations

At the outbreak of the war many monastic foundations, particularly the Dominicans, had put their houses at the disposition of the army for use as hospitals. They avoided seizure and collected some rent; a staff of members could also continue to live there.[86] It was not an unusual procedure, and certainly additional hospitals were soon necessary, but it sometimes had unfortunate results. On October 15, 1940, the Congregation of Franciscan Sisters at the shrine of Vierzehnheiligen in North Bavaria made a contract with the responsible authorities to house Germans who were returning to the Reich from Bessarabia. They rented forty-eight rooms, seven halls, dining rooms, and sitting rooms for 30 pfennig per person per day. The nuns were to pay for the heat and upkeep. By October 1941, unpaid rent amounted to 29,500 marks, and the nuns needed money to pay their bank obligations and taxes. They complained and tried to get their money, but were told that the *Reichsführer* and *Reichskommissar für die Festigung deutschen Volkstums* had not yet made a decision as to just how the churches were to be compensated for property they had put at the disposal of the state.[87]

Not always were there negotiated agreements. In June, 1941, the Reich labor minister issued an order that members of monastic houses could be called up for labor service, although care should be taken that sufficient members were left to till the monastic lands. There was some difficulty in finding suitable positions for those called, and church authorities reacted unfavorably to the measure.[88] At times the government simply moved in, took over the monastic buildings, and put the occupants on the street. On January 13, 1941, Bormann in a notice to all district party leaders stated that the population did not show indignation if confiscated monasteries were devoted to what was generally considered suitable purposes, such as hospitals, convalescent homes, or special schools. He advocated far-reaching use of these alternatives. Bormann had his eye on Klosterneuburg in Austria and on February 22, 1941, this venerable monastery was seized and converted into an Adolf Hitler school.[89]

The city of Münster was heavily bombed on July 6, 1941. On July 12 the secret police seized two Jesuit establishments in Münster and ordered these Jesuits to leave Westphalia and the Rhine Province. The property of the Mission Sisters of the Immaculate Conception was seized the next day and the nuns ordered to leave by 6 p.m. On July 14 Bishop Galen sent protest telegrams to Lammers at the Reich Chancellery, to Göring, and to the ministers of the interior, of church affairs, and justice, and to the supreme commander of the armed forces. Only Lammers replied, saying he had referred the telegram to the minister of the interior. This was most discouraging to Galen and he told Lammers so. He had wanted Lammers to inform Hitler, for the Führer was too busy to attend to everything; he was no god. In the middle of a war, the Gestapo was destroying the inner front by seizing German property.[90]

On July 6, the very day of the attack on Münster, the pastoral letter of the Fulda Bishops' Conference was to be read in all masses.[91] It recounted the numerous restrictions not based on wartime considerations that had been placed on the churches. It lamented particularly the closing of many monasteries and other church institutions, and their conversion to nonchurch uses. Instead of heeding the bishops' protest, the Gestapo had continued seizing church property. Bishop Galen decided to take the cause to the people. In a hard-hitting sermon on July 13 in the Lambertuskirche in Münster, he described the recent events to his congregation. The confiscation of monasteries which had been going on in South Germany, in the Warthegau, Luxemburg, and Lorraine was now touching Westphalia. He mentioned the imprisonment of Martin Niemöller and paid tribute to the courage and actions of this "noble German man." "Justice is the foundation of a state, and if this no longer exists where will the state be?" In a sermon the following Sunday he recounted further confiscations: the provincial house of the Missionaries of the Holy Heart of Jesus in Hiltrup had been seized. From there 161 men had gone forth to serve in the army, 53 in the medical service and 108 as soldiers with arms, many of whom had received decorations. When they returned, their home would be gone. There was no chivalry in driving German women from their homes. "As long as they do not change, as long as they continue to rob the innocent, to drive them out of the land, to imprison them, so long as this continues, I reject any community with them." He compared his hearers to an anvil and summoned them to "Become hard; remain firm; remain steadfast, as the anvil does under the stroke of the hammer." The service ended, nevertheless, with the customary prayer for fatherland and Führer.[92]

In an even sharper sermon the following Sunday, August 3, 1941, he again mentioned the confiscations and then attacked the euthanasia program. "If they start out by killing the insane, it can well be extended to the old, the infirm, sick, seriously crippled soldiers. What do you do to a machine which no longer runs, to an old horse which is incurably lame, a cow which does not give milk? They now want to treat humans the same way." The reference to crippled soldiers aroused a storm. The Gauleiter in Münster maintained that Galen had said they would be killed, although the published texts made it appear that he had only said there was a danger of this happening.[93]

In spite of attempts to prevent it, copies of the sermons were soon spread across Germany.[94] They were indeed the most outspoken and forthright denunciation of government practices that issued from a prominent Catholic leader throughout the war. But it should be noted they were directed at issues (euthanasia and the confiscation of property) which touched the Catholic church directly. There was no denunciation of the government's anti-Semitic policies nor of inhumane practices being inflicted on various conquered peoples.

Galen had spoken out before this series of three sermons, and he was to do so again. Early in 1942 the Gestapo had confiscated the monastery of the Community of Benedictine Nuns of Perpetual Adoration under the Führer's decree of May 29, 1941, regarding the seizure of the property of enemies of the state. Galen again took the pulpit on February 1, 1942. He related that he was reputed to have good nerves and did not lose his temper easily, but when he heard of this seizure he had to pace his study for ten minutes before he got himself under control. How possibly could these sisters who spent their lives in prayer be considered enemies of the state? Besides, the property did not belong to the sisters, but to the diocese, a gift of the king of Prussia in 1821. And so he as bishop of Münster and the people of the diocese were all to be treated as enemies of the state and declared to be such![95]

The Gauleiter of Münster thought Galen would have to be arrested after the 1941 sermons, and Minister Kerrl called for action against him.[96] Walter Tiessler, leader of the Reichsring for National Socialist Propaganda and Popular Enlightenment in the Ministry of Propaganda, proposed to Goebbels and Bormann that Galen be hanged forthwith, a sentence Bormann thought he deserved.[97] Goebbels, however, was calmer, saying it was up to the Führer to decide. Hitler ordered that no action should be taken against the bishop, and, on July 30, 1941, that the seizure of church and monastic property be halted.[98] If urgent circumstances necessitated the use of church property, the Gauleiter should first submit a report to Hitler via Bormann. This order was supposed to be secret, but it soon was generally known. Hitler similarly halted the euthanasia program on August 24.[99] To say that he did this because of Galen's sermon, although that did have a powerful effect, would be going too far, for it seems clear that the program was already on its way out. Protestant leaders had long campaigned to end it, and there had been numerous earlier public and private protests against the practice by members of the Catholic hierarchy.

Following Hitler's two orders, the police inaugurated a kind of détente with the church. On September 22–23, 1941, a conference of church specialists among the secret police was held. Here the speaker summarized the policy to be followed: (1) all sweeping measures and actions against the churches and their establishments were to be avoided; (2) measures, including camouflaged measures, against monasteries and convents were to be suspended; (3) actions against monasteries could still be taken in individual cases, but headquarters was to be informed in each case; (3) above all, care should be taken that the churches did not win back any of their lost ground; and (5) the information service was to be expanded by the recruitment of new informers (*Vertrauensmänner, V-Personen*).[100] Most of the informers against the Catholic church were Catholic clergy, who, however, usually had no direct access to information from diocesan or subordinate headquarters (*Generalvikariate*). Special efforts were to be made to infiltrate the Generalvikariate, for "no fortress is so secure that one cannot achieve entrance by secret ways."[101]

There is no completely accurate list of confiscated and occupied monasteries, but apparently as far as Germany proper is concerned the number was not very large. In 20 of the largest monastic provinces, only 30 houses were confiscated, while 49 were occupied and 9 were forced to rent, making a total of 88 out of 370 foundations. Between 1938 and 1941, the number of monastic foundations dropped from 687 to 629.[102] Since the seizures on Hitler's direct orders were generally, if not completely, stopped after August, 1941, it is unlikely that the numbers declined much more.[103] In Austria there were far more confiscations of monastic foundations, including some famous old ones such as Klosterneuburg and Göttweig.[104]

Racial Policies and the Hierarchy

The papacy and members of the German hierarchy in the pre-war years had at times denounced the cult of racism, of blood and soil. But there were no clarion protests against the anti-Semitic policy of the Nazi rulers then or during the war years. When the government began to treat Christians who were racial Jews in the same way as full Jews, the Catholic church leaders—concerned about safeguarding their own, began to take more notice.[105] In general their reaction was similar to that of the Protestant leaders, but there were some noteworthy Catholic reactions. For example, the decree of September 1, 1941, which required all Jews to wear a Star of David, prompted Cardinal Bertram to send advice to his fellow bishops. Guenther Lewy has summarized it admirably.

> His counsel was to avoid "rash measures that could hurt the feelings of the Jewish Catholics, as the introduction of special Jewish benches, separation when administering the sacraments, introduction of special services in spe-

cific churches or private houses." The segregation of the Catholic non-Aryans would violate Christian principles, and, therefore, should be avoided as long as possible. The priests, Bertram suggested, might however advise the Jewish Catholics to attend the early mass whenever possible. An admonishment to the faithful to exercise brotherly love toward the non-Aryans similarly should be postponed until disturbances resulted. "Only when substantial difficulties result from attendance at church by the non-Aryan Catholics," the Archbishop of Breslau continued, "(like staying away of officials, Party members and others, demonstrative leaving of divine services), should the Catholic non-Aryans be consulted about the holding of special services." In case a reminder to the faithful to treat the Jewish Catholics with love should become necessary, Bertram suggested a statement that included St. Paul's admonishments to the Romans and Galatians not to forget that among those believing in Christ there is neither Jew nor Greek, for all are one in Jesus Christ (Romans 10:12, Galatians 3:28).[106]

Bertram was certainly not recommending a courageous policy but one of servile accommodation: the presence of officials and party members was more desirable than that of a hard-pressed Christian of non-Aryan descent seeking solace and redemption in God's word. In much the same vein, Bishops Berning and Wienken tried to obtain permission for Jewish Catholics not to wear the star when they went to church; apparently they were not very concerned about other times. The Gestapo, as on other occasions, operated with an even hand—even if it was a damnable one—and refused to make any alterations in their general edict. Actually the people in the churches caused no difficulties, although Jewish Christians often did refrain from attending church.[107]

In the end the problem of racial segregation never became acute in the churches, partly because so many Christian Jews were deported. On the other hand, both Catholic and Protestant churches (no doubt unwilling but without strong protest) did succumb to the government's extreme racial segregation measures against the Poles.[108]

In 1942 the government began considering a plan to force the dissolution of racially mixed marriages. This compulsory divorce policy would affect a large number of Catholics and challenged one of the most important doctrines of the church. Cardinal Bertram addressed letters of protest to the ministers of justice, the interior, and ecclesiastical affairs. Bishop Wurm and other Protestant leaders also protested. The compulsory divorce law was never issued, perhaps because of ecclesiastical protest, but perhaps also because some hundreds of Aryan wives demonstrated in Berlin when their non-Aryan husbands were about to be transported "to the East."[109]

The most compelling factor in easing policies towards the churches was the disastrous course of the war. On February 2, 1943, Stalingrad surrendered, the beginning of May brought German defeat in North Africa, July 10 the invasion of Sicily, July 25 the fall of Mussolini, September 3 the invasion of southern Italy, and five days later the announcement of the Italian armistice. On September 10 German troops took over the occupation of Rome. Such sledgehammer blows clearly called for a united home front, and measures were taken to decrease internal tensions.

On January 13, 1943, Hitler had issued an ordinance, "The Employment of Men and Women in Tasks of National Defense."[110] It specifically exempted clergymen and monastic priests, others who were in the service of churches forty-eight hours a week, and nurses or members of monastic orders fully employed in agriculture. On April 26, 1943, Bormann issued a special directive on dealing with political-confessional matters. Nothing was to be done to cause confessional difficulties or unrest among the people. "Every little pinprick policy must be stopped."[111] On May 9, Bormann expressly forbade any agitation against the churches in the Labor Service: "One must carefully avoid injuring true religious conceptions. Such actions simply antagonize the best persons. . . . It is entirely wrong—and therefore fundamentally forbidden in the National Labor Service—to enter upon any polemic against church institutions and dogmas."[112] The Labor Service was not a church but a state service, whose duty it was to unify, not divide, the people.

In February, 1939, Heydrich as head of the security service had prepared a long memorandum on Catholic higher schools for the training of priests in which he proposed cuts in state support. The memorandum was considered again on July 19, 1943, when it was decided that nothing should be done about it.[113]

At this time German cities were being subjected to heavy bombing; Hamburg was virtually destroyed at the end of July, with a death toll estimated at around 40,000.[114] This bombing led the minister of education, with Bormann's approval, to issue a directive on August 25, 1943, concerning confessional religious instruction at schools which had been evacuated. It was most favorable to the traditional demands of the churches. Confessional instruction was to be given to the same extent as before, and teachers were to be moved with the school if possible. If no religion teachers were available, local clergymen were to be asked to give confessional instruction in local church rooms and to issue certificates to pupils. If local regulations permitted, religious instruction could be given in other rooms as well, if they were not more than four kilometers from the place to which the school had been moved. His intention to conciliate the churches is clearly shown in his closing plea: "Please take care that in administering this directive you observe a generous line of action."[115]

Going easy on the churches was on the whole the policy during the rest of the war. As the ring was drawn more tightly around Germany and collapse threatened, the churches also tended to make as few difficulties as possible for the state. It is clear that the hierarchy were aware of the deportation of Jews and what it meant. Yet the German bishops never spoke out as Dutch, Belgian, or French bishops did when Jews were being transported from their countries.[116] The nearest the hierarchy came to a joint protest was the Fulda pastoral letter of September 12, 1943, "Ten Commandments as Laws of Life for Nations." In the introduction the bishops recognized the critical situation the Reich was facing and spoke words of tribute and encouragement to the Catholic faithful. By way of commentary on the individual commandments they could make many pointed statements without directly attacking the government. Cardinal Bertram objected, but it was nevertheless read in Catholic pulpits.[117] It was the last joint pastoral letter issued by the German bishops during the Hitler era. The police summary on the letter lacked the customary sharp denunciations and concluded: "in no other pastoral letter was the span of its possible effects between positive and negative so great as in this case."[118] The bishops clearly had done a remarkable job of tightrope walking.

The statement on the Fifth Commandment, "Thou shall not kill," while it was directed against the gas ovens and the killing of Jews, nevertheless was not worded openly and fearlessly.[119] There was no indication of the magnitude of the Nazi extermination policy, although the hierarchy must have had some knowledge of what was going on. The bishops, as well as the government, were concerned about maintaining "internal unity" during the war. After commenting that no one had the right arbitrarily to interfere with God's power over life and death, the bishops declared:

> Killing is bad in itself, even when it is done in the interest of the common welfare: against innocent and defenseless mentally ill and other sick; against incurable invalids and fatally injured, against those with inherited disabilities and children with serious birth defects, against innocent hostages and disarmed war and other prisoners; against people of alien race and descent. Even the government can and is permitted to punish with the death penalty only those who are truly death deserving-criminals.[120]

Here the bishops made no distinction between Christian Jews and other Jews. However, the former were always their chief concern, as they were when the Vatican came to protesting the deportation of Hungarian Jews in 1944.[121] There were a few who took a broader view. Foremost among them was Provost Bernhard Lichtenberg in Berlin, who spoke up against anti-Semitism and daily said a prayer for all Jews, not only the baptized ones. He was arrested in 1941 and died while being transported to Dachau in 1943.[122] Others sought to protect and help various individual Jews.[123] No one, however, has successfully contradicted Lewy's conclusion: "In sharp contrast to the countries of western Europe, in Germany only a handful of Jews were hidden by the [Catholic] clergy or otherwise helped by them in their hour of distress."[124] The churchmen, as probably most of their congregations (and as 99 percent of all postwar Germans aver), did not approve of the government's rabid policy, but they were inclined to play it safe and not do much about it. The cannonball of anti-Semitism had started rolling down the hill many years in the past, no one bothered to stay its momentum after 1933, and when the war came it dragged Germany with increasing acceleration into a moral abyss.

Catholicism always involves not only the laity and the hierarchy, with its leadership of the local churches, but also the papacy. And papal policy was not very different from that of the German people or the German hierarchy. The pope too played it safe. His very international position forced him into a policy of neutrality and impartiality at the start of the war. He had sought to prevent the hostilities, and then his attention was bent on restoring peace.[125] His was not an enviable position, and the involvement of the Soviet Union and later the United States made it no easier. Whatever he said and did in public would be held against him by one side or another. He naturally fell back on diplomatic procedures, on confidential negotiations with the responsible governments, in which he had long years of practice. He instructed his nuncio to raise constant protests in Germany about wartime policies; he sought to alleviate the suffering caused by the war. In his efforts to achieve peace he even went so far as to offer his good offices (1939–40) to German resistance leaders in their approach to British authorities.[126] He did seek to prevent the deportation of Jews in Italy, Hungary, and other countries.[127] In the realm of diplomacy, in his efforts to achieve things from behind the public scene, the pope did not remain silent or inactive. On the other hand, he was indeed circumspect in his public utterances in his efforts to maintain official impartiality. The history of World War I also showed that it was easy to be misled as to what was propaganda and what was reality. Unfortunately, the war atrocities were true this time, and the pope never issued a solemn public indictment. There were many other things he might have denounced, such as saturation bombing by both sides and the killing of thousands of defenseless men, women, and children. Perhaps such a protest might have been effective, but perhaps Hitler, and other wartime leaders as well, would have raised the same question Stalin was reputed to have asked: "How many divisions does he [the Pope] have?"

That a ringing denunciation of Hitler's policies would have made the situation of the Catholics in general, and of the Catholic church in particular, more difficult in Germany is doubtful, considering the plans Hitler had in mind for the future of the churches anyway. Yet the possibility of evoking immediate harsh retaliatory measures was always taken into consideration at the Vatican.[128] That a public papal plea for the Jews would have led to an effective upsurge of Catholic opposition to the National Socialist regime seems most unlikely. That it would have led to a worldwide crusade against Hitler's tryanny is improbable and in fact inconsequential, for the mass of the available manpower of the world was already enrolled under the banner of the United Nations. What would have happened had the pope spoken out more openly than he did, is speculative; speculation may be interesting, but it is hardly historical. However, some things are historically clear. The pope and the German hierarchy worked closely together in the war years as they had in former periods of German history; the hierarchy did not beseech the pope to speak out during the war as they did in August, 1936, and at the time of the encyclical *Mit brennender Sorge* (1937). Neither hierarchy nor pope ran away, none succumbed, none won crowns of martyrdom; all lived on to fight for their faith another day.

Catholics were, if anything, even more schooled than Protestants to uphold the legitimate government of the state. Tyrannicide was condemned by Saint Thomas Aquinas, and this condemnation had become the accepted doctrine in Catholic theology.[129] Indeed, it was specifically reconfirmed in the Syllabus of Errors of 1864. The same was true of revolution. In 1947, Dr. Simon Hirt, of the bishop's office in Freiburg, in refusing the imprimatur for an article in the *Fährmann* which spoke approvingly of Christoph Probst and his opposition to the Third Reich, wrote: "[Probst] and his friends in their opposition to the so-called Third Reich followed ways which could not be brought into harmony with Christian moral principles. For revolution, even against a government which practices injustices and exemplifies a tyranny, is not permitted."[130] Postwar theologians have criticized this stance, but certainly it was the position of the German bishops and the church as a whole at that time. As Mary Alice Gallin concludes in her excellent study of German resistance to Hitler: "[It is] clear that the German hierarchy at no time, either individually or collectively, publicly or privately, urged revolution against the Nazi government; in fact, there was repeated admonition to German Catholics to avoid violence, demonstrations, conspiracy, and outright revolution."[131] When in the spring of 1942 Göring wrote Bishops Berning and Galen and charged them with violating their oath to the state, both were at pains to deny the charges.[132]

Many did oppose Hitler, and there were many Catholic clergy, the majority from the occupied countries, in the concentration camps.[133] There were Catholics who forfeited their lives, often innocent of the charges against them. This was true of Father Alfred Delp, who belonged to the Kreisau Circle, the group of men centering about Count Helmuth James von Moltke who were concerned with problems of the Third Reich and the postwar world. He was executed for his supposed connection with the July 20, 1944, assassination attempt, although he steadfastly maintained that he knew nothing of it. Considering the hatred and suspicion with which the Nazi leaders always viewed the Jesuits, he no doubt was correct when he wrote friends on the eve of his execution: "The actual reason for my sentence is that I am and remain a Jesuit."[134]

Another man who paid with his life was Dr. Max J. Metzger (Brother Paulus), who wrote a letter to Bishop Eidem of Stockholm asking him to attempt to mediate peace. Metzger was arrested in June, 1943, and beheaded on April 17, 1944. Insult was added to affliction when the nuns of the convent where Metzger had been stationed were billed for his death expenses.[135]

Charge for death penalty	R.M.	300.00
Expenses		
Postal charge		.12
Prison charges June 29, 1943–April 16, 1944, 293 days at R.M. 1.50		439.50
Total charges		739.62
Covered by his own money		368.36
Amount still due	R.M.	371.26

The Nazis did indeed extract heavy penalties from anyone they even suspected of treasonable activities, according to their own definition of what constituted treason.

There were several Catholics among those executed as participants in the July 20, 1944, attempt on Hitler, including August Roesch, the provincial of the Jesuits in Bavaria, Jacob Kaiser, Bernhard Letterhaus, and Count Claus Schenk von Stauffenberg, who placed the bomb, "in whom religious motives and the determination to resist would seem to have developed hand in hand."[136] Considering the number implicated, and that practically all Germans were either Protestant or Catholic, it was inevitable that church members were involved. How much they were influenced by religious convictions is an unanswerable question. There is some evidence that Bishop Preysing of Berlin and Cardinal Faulhaber were in touch with the opposition leaders, much as Bishop Wurm of the Protestant Church of Württemberg was.[137] That they actually knew of the assassination attempt or would have approved of it is highly unlikely. It is hard to conceive, however, that they would have been convulsed with grief had the coup been successful.

The Catholic church in Germany was German to the core, and like the Protestant church upheld the state and its authority.[138] In both churches there was opposition in good measure to certain policies of the totalitarian state; of active political revolutionary resistance there was virtually none, neither in the years of peace, nor, least of all, in the war years when the enemy had to be met on the field of battle.

19.

The Free and Other Traditional Churches

The Position of the Smaller Churches

The policy of Gleichschaltung which Hitler launched immediately after coming to power on January 30, 1933, inevitably raised the problem of what the status of small religious bodies would be in the National Socialist state.[1] Would they in some way or other be absorbed into or attached to the Reich church which was to be built out of the twenty-eight Protestant Land churches? What role were they to have in the new Germany?

On April 22, 1933, the Reverend Paul Schmidt (Baptist) and the Reverend Otto Melle (Methodist), as leaders of the Association of Evangelical Free Churches, asked to be received by Hitler so that they could present their views and wishes to him.[2] The chancellor was too busy to see them.[3] They were passed over and were no party to the negotiations for establishing a new United Protestant Reich church. No doubt they were pleased when Chaplain Ludwig Müller, as Hitler's representative, agreed that the separate identities of the Lutheran, Reformed and so-called Free churches should be maintained.[4] There were rumors that the government would demand the formation of a United Free church to be incorporated into the Reich church and exist as a Free church wing beside the Lutheran and Reformed wings. Some Free church representatives even went so far as to draft a plan for such a union, but the government never demanded its implementation.[5] Yet an air of uncertainty prevailed which was not dispelled when Müller, as Reich bishop, declared in a speech at the synod's meeting in Wittenberg the following September: "In the face of the great tasks confronting the German nation the Reich church has an ardent desire for friendly cooperation with the Free churches of Germany."[6]

For a time the German Christians seemed in the ascendency, and Bishop Hossenfelder, Reichsleiter of the German Christians and recently appointed bishop of Brandenburg, undertook to negotiate with the Free churches. Toward the end of October a semiofficial announcement stated that the Free churches were showing a "wide understanding for the unification of the churches."

> It is expected a final agreement will be reached in the next few weeks and that in some form or other the free churches will become subject to the government of the Reich bishop. As a result the free churches in the future

will be able to work much more intimately with the other evangelical churches and congregations than was possible in the past.[7]

The leaders of the Association of Evangelical Free Churches became uneasy and conferred with both government representatives and Reich church authorities. The day after the Sportspalast affair,[8] when church officials were busy trying to counteract the effects of this outburst of German Christian ardor, Bishop Daniel Schoeffel of the Reich church administration, who was in charge of relations with the Free churches, sent the following statement to the association:

> In response to repeated requests from Free church communicants and after a conference with Reich Bishop Müller, I am in a position to affirm emphatically that no intentions are entertained anywhere in the government or the Reich Evangelical Church, for the forcible integration therein of the Free churches. The confessional of the Reich church as well as its respect for the freedom of conscience would forbid such intentions.[9]

Schoeffel went on to affirm Müller's expression at Wittenberg of an ardent desire for friendly cooperation. Schmidt and Melle gladly made public Schoeffel's letter, "because it not only refuted rumors of the coerced incorporation of the Free churches, but because it seems to us of great significance by virtue of its fraternal spirit and of the vista that it opens for common tasks within the German nation."[10]

The policy enunciated by Bishop Schoeffel actually was followed throughout the Third Reich, although at times the Free church ranks were uneasy. Müller confirmed the policy of freedom for the Free churches to a delegation of the Fifth Baptist World Congress meeting in Berlin August 4–10, 1934. J. H. Rushbrooke, general secretary of the Baptist World Alliance, characterized Müller's declaration that "there is no question of any compulsory incorporation of the Baptist churches in the Reichskirche" as of "cardinal importance," and the verdict of the delegation to whom Müller made the statement was that "it was worth going to Berlin if only to hear that."[11] Müller also expressed his desire to establish a cordial relationship with the Baptist congregations in Germany.

In the spring of 1934, a certain Dr. Gustav Rauter was assigned to the church law division of the Union of National Socialist German Jurists. He was asked to report on the situation of the Free churches. He decided to send out a ten-point questionnaire and also ask the recipients to state any wishes they might have.[12] To what churches he submitted his questionnaire is uncertain, but we do have at least part of his correspondence with the Evangelical Lutheran Free Church of Saxony, one of the more conservative bodies, and one which maintained close relations with the Missouri Synod of the Lutheran church in the United States. Like the Baptists, Methodists, and others, this Lutheran Free church wanted above all to retain its independence and the unfettered opportunity to preach the gospel. Its members stood for equal rights for all churches, and did not want their children to attend religion classes in the public schools. They wanted the religion faculties at the universities dispersed, believing it was the duty of the churches, not the state, to educate their own clergy. Since, like all Free churches, their church received no state support, the members argued that they should be freed from paying church taxes to the Land churches which in practice, in spite of regulations to the contrary, were often collected from them. They also asked that contributions made to their churches be deducted from income taxes, much as the church taxes were deducted in the case of members of the Land churches.[13]

How many replies Dr. Rauter received is not known, but on September 9, 1934, he drew up what he termed the "Demands of the Small German Churches." It was formulated in twenty-one points, almost all concerned with assuring the independence and rights of the Free churches. One of the old demands of the Free churches, that their members be permitted to teach religion classes in the schools, was advanced again, as was their opposition to church taxes. He expressed the view that there would be no mass exodus to the Free churches to escape taxes, for these required large contributions. Rauter was opposed to asking the Free churches to introduce the Aryan paragraph. He proposed that they form an ad hoc confederation (*Zweckverband*) where creeds would not be considered, except for the acceptance that Jesus was the son of God. Groups of like-minded churches could be formed within this confederation. He concluded:

> It is obvious that the Free churches are happy in the New Reich, inasmuch as its program specifically states that the party stands on the ground of positive Christianity. They would like, however, that this program be taken seriously. This also means that the state shall intervene in the internal affairs of the churches only to the extent that public security absolutely requires it.[14]

The Führerprinzip within the churches, Rauter held, was opposed to the very nature of the Free churches, who recognize only Jesus as the leader of the church, and are willing to follow man only from "instance to instance."

Rauter's summary was no doubt a reasonably accurate reflection of the position of the Free churches. It was again sent out to the Free churches for comment, but as might have been expected, the Lutheran Free Church of Saxony did not approve it. Dr. Martin Willkomm was opposed to the confederation and had reservations on many other points. He did agree with the general approval Rauter accorded the Third Reich, stating:

> We welcome and are thankful that in the Third Reich honor and uprightness, decency and discipline, are recognized and cultivated as the foundation of public life. This civic righteousness is of course not Christianity, but it is that which a folk needs if it wants to live and protect its place among the nations.
>
> We especially welcome that the principle of freedom of belief and conscience for all is recognized, and desire that really serious effort be made to carry through these rights in every respect, as is expressly demanded in Point 24 of the program of the NSDAP.[15]

This correspondence between Rauter and Willkomm indicates the general attitudes and problems of the Free churches, particularly those of one of the old Lutheran Free churches. Whether it ever reached governmental or Reich church authorities is uncertain. In 1935, after the division of the Union of National Socialist German Jurists to which he belonged had been dissolved, Rauter got in touch with the Academy for German Law (*Akademie für Deutsches Recht*) and asked if he should present to it his report on "State and Church." It is perhaps indicative of the temper of church-state relations at that time that Rauter was told the Academy would not deal with these questions in the forseeable future.[16] The creation of a church law committee within the academy was raised in 1937, however, and Minister Kerrl warmly supported the project.[17] In July, 1938, Kerrl and Dr. Hans Frank, president of the academy, approached Dr. Karl H. Meyer of the Prussian finance ministry to see if he would head the committee. He accepted, and in due course Catholic and Protestant sections of the new Committee for Church Law were formed.[18]

Meyer's committee received various materials on the Lutheran Free Church of Saxony from Dr. Willkomm, including Rauter's 1934 questionnaire and Willkomm's answers to these communications.[19] Willkomm raised anew the desirability of credit on income tax payments for contributions made to the Free churches.[20] The Committee for Church Law did not move rapidly, and it was not until September 26, 1939, that Dr. Meyer finally thanked Willkomm for his letter and the other material. He had been considering it, and how the small religious bodies could best be related to the work of the Committee for Church Law. However, in view of the war situation he would permit the question to rest for the time being.[21]

And rest it did. In 1940 Hitler was informed by Minister Lammers that a Committee for Church Law had been formed in the Academy for German Law and was even meeting during the war. As well he might, Hitler thought the church situation was so muddled that he could not envision any fruitful action by the committee. The result was that Lammers recommended to the head of the academy that the committee be permitted to exist, but that it should not conduct any work.[22]

The Free churches were particularly concerned to retain their independence, and this the Nazis were, at least for the time being, willing to accord. The government was aware that many of the Free churches had influence among their kindred members in the United Kingdom and the United States, and during the early years of the regime the Nazis were particularly concerned about their relations with these countries.[23] Then too, their German membership was small and insignificant, and their belief in the separation of church and state was highly approved by many Nazi leaders. That the Free churches supported themselves, collected no church taxes, and only now and then received small gifts from the government[24] won them even more approval as the Nazis undertook to cut church subsidies. The Free churches gained favor as the government's relations with the Protestant Land churches deteriorated. Moreover, the Free churches had always favored nondenominational schools, and when the government moved against the confessional schools, the

Free churches approved. They showed no particular sympathy for the

Confessing church movement, and continued as in the past to maintain their contacts with state officials, and such ties as they had with the state-recognized church administrations. In their annual convention in Essen in 1936, the Association of Evangelical Free Churches voted to remain neutral in the church struggle and again stated that their activities had not been disturbed.[25] They issued no denunciations of Nazi racial or other policies that in any way offset their many statements favorable to the government.

Such support was rewarded when the government permitted only representatives of the Free churches and of the Old Catholics to attend the World Conference on Church, Community, and State in Oxford (July 12–25, 1937) and the World Conference on Faith and Order in Edinburgh (August 3–18, 1937). At the Oxford meeting Methodist Bishop Melle and the Reverend Paul Schmidt, a Baptist, made a written protest against the message which the conference sent to the Evangelical church in Germany. Melle went even further and made a speech stressing the freedom permitted the German Free churches and lauding Hitler's achievements.[26] This speech caused tension between the Confessing church and Melle, but earned Hitler's gratitude for the Methodist church. On March 24, 1938, Hitler donated 10,000 marks to the Methodist church in Schneidemühl for the purchase of a new organ. "This was done," as the Reich Chancellery put it, "for propaganda purposes, in recognition of the position Bishop Melle took at the Oxford conference in which he spoke of the freedom enjoyed by the Methodist church."[27]

The Melle-Schmidt protest at Oxford has always received much attention, while a somewhat similar protest made at the Edinburgh conference has gone unnoticed. Dr. Henry Smith Leiper of New York spoke of powerful movements in the world trying to build a totalitarian era. His remarks prompted a formal statement signed by Dr. J. W. Ernst Sommer, head of the Methodist theological seminary in Frankfurt/Main and by Bishop Erwin Kreuzer of the Old Catholic church, the two German delegates.

> We don't believe that the modes of life growing up on the basis of the totalitarian state, which in its actual existence brought to our country and nation new courage, unity, strength, necessarily are opposed to the gospel.
> We believe you ought to be very careful in the use of the word persecution regarding the conflict of the Roman Catholic Church with the state and that of the Confessional Church with other groups within the German Evangelical church. The state has not touched our churches. We do not wish to enter into these questions, but we nevertheless regard it as our duty imposed upon us by our conscience to say that by judging complicated situations too quickly and on the ground of one-sided information, grave injury may be inflicted on the cause of church unity. We would, therefore, ask our brethren to maintain their sympathy for all Christians in Germany, which has been very precious to us, and to believe that with these words we wish to promote union among those who love Christ.[28]

Their statement is no doubt more circumspectly formulated than Melle's remarks at Oxford, but it again stressed the freedom which the

Free churches enjoyed in Germany and played down the whole church conflict.

The Free churches and Old Catholics were simply not affected by many of the Nazi regulations; they were not specifically exempted, but the decrees were not applicable to them. The conflicts between governmental and church authorities over the administration of the Land churches left the Free churches untouched, just as the continual controversy over the interpretation of the concordat bypassed the Old Catholics. Indeed, the Free churches even benefited by some of the new legislation. The establishment of the interdenominational school system pleased them, as did the decree of October 31, 1940, which opened up the cemeteries to all citizens.[29] While the latter measure was designed primarily for those who classed themselves as "God believing" and had withdrawn from the established churches, it did alleviate one of the old grievances of the Free churches.

The Free churches, of course, were subject to the general regulations about collections, giving notice of meetings, curtailment of youth groups in favor of the Hitler Youth, and police surveillance. The neopagan enthusiasts met no more favor with them than with the established churches. They too suffered from the additional restrictions, hardships, and destruction which came with the war. All told, the Free churches were relatively well off only in comparison to other churches. They did not take an active part in the Kirchenkampf and were mainly attentive and nervous spectators.

Various Churches and Groups

A summary of the position of the Free churches during the Kirchenkampf should be completed by individual accounts, for each church had its own particular history. In order to avoid very fragmented accounts of these numerous groups, their postwar activities will also be noted here. There is still much research to be done on these organizations, but some brief remarks may help fill out the picture.

Methodists

The Methodist church very early took steps, in accordance with the policies of the German government, to reorganize its structure and loosen its ties with the church in the United States. In November, 1934, at the annual meeting of the Methodist Board of Foreign Missions in New York, it disclosed plans for a Methodist Episcopal Church of Germany with its own bishop, although the church would still be part of the General Conference of the Methodist Episcopal Church in the United States.[30] These plans were then submitted to the General Conference in 1936, where they were approved. American-born Bishop John Louis Nuelson, who had been in charge of the German and other European Methodist churches, warmly supported the change in governmental structure. Otto Melle, then director of the seminary in Frankfurt/Main, was elected bishop of the German Methodist church and took up his residence in Berlin. The government recognized it as a corporation under public law, a status it had attained in only some of the German states before. Nuelson, who continued to have his headquarters in Zurich, had always got along well with the Nazi regime, and he had spoken favorably of the new Germany while on a speaking tour in the United States in 1935. The *Cincinnatier Freie Presse* reported he had declared that in no other land did the Methodist church have greater freedom than in Germany. The state churches received state aid and could naturally expect some interference. Religious freedom did exist in Germany. On his return to Zurich, a Methodist pastor in Gera, Thuringia, in view of the great service Nuelson had done for Germany by his speeches abroad, asked that Secretary Lammers arrange an interview for him with the Führer. Hitler, however, was unavailable.[31] Nuelson's views were corroborated by Bishop Harry Lester Smith, who reported to the New York Methodist Conference that Methodism in Germany "was alive and awake and seemed thriving throughout the nation."[32]

The Nazi police, of course, did not exempt Methodists from their purview. In the spring of 1935 they reported that in a few cases Methodist pastors had issued hostile statements. One minister in Krefeld had spoken against membership in the Labor Front.[33] The police sought evidence of moral derelictions among the Methodists as well as among the Catholic clergy. In July, 1937, a former Methodist pastor at Schwelbein was sentenced to jail for ten months on charges of immoral practices. He was not in charge of a parish, for he had been removed from his pastorate by the Methodist General Conference when the charges were preferred against him.[34] No doubt numerous other incidents of police interference occurred. In 1939 both Methodists and Baptists were permitted to hold their customary tent missions, but the police ordered that they be kept under surveillance. The missions were to be restricted to preaching "Christian life," and there were to be no political or church-political polemics.[35]

Bishop Melle not only spoke in favor of the German government at Oxford, but also apparently never made any pronouncements against the racial policy of the regime, against euthanasia, or against any other Reich policies.[36] Like other church administrators, he sought to protect the security and future of his church.[37] In this he was successful, and he presided over the church until 1946. No Methodist minister came before the denazification courts for adherence to National Socialist ideas or actions. As Friedrich Wunderlich, a later bishop of the German Methodist church, has written:

> In looking back we have much cause to bow before God in deep repentance for great lack of loyalty, courage, and love. But thanks be to Him that we also undeservedly may glory in His heart-strengthening grace. . . . The Methodist church in Germany survived the storm and emerged newly strengthened, confirmed in faith, quickened by new love of brother and all mankind, in the midst of so much deceit and despair filled with a new hope that is not founded on the visible, the transitory, but on the invisible, that is eternal.[38]

The German Baptists did a remarkably successful job of organizing the Fifth Congress of the Baptist World Alliance which met in Berlin in August, 1934. Within the conference hall the Baptists had absolute freedom of expression, but the participants soon noted that "the only portions of the speeches reported in the German press were those supporting the present government's policy."[39] The chairman of the committee on temperance paid tribute to Chancellor Hitler for the example he set by not using intoxicants or smoking.[40] The congress listened to Dr. Ernst Siedler, a Baptist pastor and father of the mayor of Munich, give an exposition of Hitler's anti-Semitic policy. A reporter writing about the speech noted: "The explanation received the acclaim of Germans in the audience, but appeared to arouse no sympathy in the ranks of delegates from other countries."[41] Two days later the Congress hit the issue of racialism straight on, and passed a formal resolution such as is not to be found in any other contemporary church statements.

> This Congress, representing the world-wide, inter-racial fellowship of Baptists, rejoices to know that despite all differences of race there is in Christ an all-embracing unity, so that in Him it can be claimed with deepest truth there is neither Greek nor Jew, circumcision nor uncircumcision, barbarian, Scythian, bond nor free, but Christ is all!
>
> This Congress deplores and condemns as a violation of the law of God, the Heavenly Father, all racial animosity, and every form of oppression or unfair discrimination toward the Jews, toward colored people, or toward subject races in any part of the world.
>
> This Congress urges the promotion of Christian teaching concerning respect for human personality regardless of race, and as the surest means of advancing the true brotherhood of all people, urges the active propagation of the gospel of Christ throughout the world.[42]

The congress passed equally forthright resolutions on war, church and state, and religious persecution in Russia. The German delegation supported all of them. Not one of these resolutions, however, appeared in the German press.[43] To offset this lack of publicity, the London secretariat of the Baptist World Alliance sent the resolutions on church and state and racialism adopted by the congress to all foreign embassies in London, asking that they communicate them to their governments. The German embassy did so with the pointed yet noncommittal remark, "that the Baptist Alliance brings these resolutions to the attention of all governments is of interest."[44]

The Sixth Baptist World Congress, meeting in Atlanta, Georgia, in 1939, could do no better than reconfirm the resolution on racialism adopted in Berlin. The Reverend Paul Schmidt again represented the German Baptists, and in an address he remarked on the "conspicuous lack of understanding on the part of many of our brethren for the real situation in our native land."

> We must declare emphatically that we most deeply regret the fact that our Baptist brethren seem to put more trust in the reports emanating from a Church (German State Church) that has not always dealt too kindly with us in the past, than in what their own Baptist brethren are able and willing to

report. We might well have given an account of actual conditions in Germany, but no one at this Congress has thus far asked us to do so.[45]

If the Reverend Schmidt was not called on to explain, he was by no means neglected. In the German-speaking sectional meeting, Prof. William A. Mueller of Philadelphia undertook to chide the German Baptists:

> My visits to your land revealed to me a certain spiritual lack. A complacent bourgeois mentality seems to be gripping increasing numbers of your people. Again, German Baptists seem to withdraw more than in the postwar era into their own shell. The burning questions of the day remain unanswered. Thus far, we have not heard of a clear word from our Baptist brethren in Germany concerning the racial problem that is a burning issue in your land as well as in ours. Again, you have from time to time assured your brethren and the world that the Free Churches of Germany may carry on their work without the least interference by the present government. . . . But is it really true that there is no interference? . . . While in Stettin last summer I noticed on the bulletin-board of a Baptist church in that city an ordinance forbidding the distribution of religious pamphlets in nearly 50 strategic streets and public squares of that city. Is that freedom? Again, is it freedom when, according to a recent order, no sub-leaders of the party are henceforth permitted to accept an office in any church?[46]

Mueller's admirable summary points out what should never be forgotten—the Baptists also had to bow to police, party, and governmental regulations. Whether they were enforced as strictly against them as against others, or whether they could adapt themselves more easily, is another matter. They regularly were permitted to carry on their tent missions, but always under the watchful eyes of the police. If attacks were made on the party or state the permits would be cancelled.[47]

Like the Methodists, the Baptists made some organizational changes which met with governmental approval. In 1938 they accepted into their fellowship the *Elimgemeinden,* a group of congregations that had grown out of the Tent Mission, Berlin-Lichterfelde (founded in 1922).[48] The move toward consolidation or elimination of small religious groups was then in full swing. The Gestapo did not like organizations with no responsible head, and in 1937 two small, loosely organized, congregationally based groups, the *Christliche Versammlung* (Darbyist in origin) and the *Offene Brüder,* had united to form the *Bund Freikirchlicher Christen.* In spite of persistent police opposition, this "Union of Free Church Christians" was able to complete a merger with the Baptists in 1941, forming the Union of Evangelical-Free Church Congregations in Germany (*Bund Evangelisch-Freikirchlicher Gemeinden in Deutschland*). The groups had much in common doctrinally and in church practices, especially in their adherence to a congregational form of church government. With the union the Baptists had to surrender, officially at least, their beloved name; the other groups benefited by sharing in the privileges of a public corporation, which the Baptists had and which was accorded to the union. By cooperating in tent missions and other inner mission activity, each group was strengthened.[49] Above all, it helped many scattered small congregations to survive so that they could pick up their work anew at the close of the war. Bombs and artillery play no favorites, and the Baptists like all others suffered damage to their churches and to the lives of their members.

Evangelical Association and Union of Free Evangelical Congregations
Two other organized churches joined with the Methodists and the Baptists in the Association of Evangelical Free Churches. One was the Evangelical Association (*Evangelische Gemeinschaft*), which had a close relationship to the Evangelical church in the United States that traces back to Jacob Albright.[50] The other was the Union of Free Evangelical Congregations (*Bund Freier Evangelischer Gemeinden*), deriving via Switzerland from the work of the Scottish leader Robert Haldane. Both bodies were primarily congregationally oriented.

The Evangelical Association had received corporate rights in various states from 1921 on. Their efforts to achieve corporate status in all Germany were finally successful in 1938, when they were granted the rights of a corporation under public law by the Berlin government,[51] although they never exercised the privilege of levying a church tax. The Union of Free Evangelical Congregations was substantially strengthened when in 1934 it was joined by the *Holstenwallgemeinde* led by Pastor Friedrich Heitmüller, which had seceded from the Hamburg Land church. This was a particularly active congregation in both evangelical and inner mission work.[52]

Lutheran Free Churches
When Hitler took over there were eight Evangelical Lutheran Free Churches in Germany, and all survived the Nazi era.[53] The status of the churches differed according to the corporate rights they enjoyed in the various states, but none of them was controlled by the Land churches, nor did any rely on church taxes. They all zealously guarded their independence, especially in doctrinal matters. There were rumors that they might be coerced into joining the Reich church in the summer of 1933. Gottfried Nagel, for example, wrote a short pamphlet entitled *Can the Evangelical Lutheran Church of Old Prussia Join in the German Evangelical Church?*[54] He gave a resounding no to the question, as of course did the Evangelical Lutheran Free Church in Saxony and Other States.

There was talk at times of a flight to the Free churches, but no one in the government, the administration or the Land churches, or the Confessing church really wanted or advocated it. Whether the Lutheran Free churches gained membership during the Hitler era is uncertain, for there never was an accurate census of church membership. Some of the largest of the Old Lutheran Free churches emerged notably weaker because of the loss to Poland and Russia of territories where many of their strongest congregations were located.

When the Council of the Evangelical Lutheran Church of Germany was established in 1936, it agreed that Lutheran churches that were not members of the German Evangelical church would be permitted to join

the council. This the Evangelical Lutheran Free Church of Old Prussia did the same year, and it participated in the Luther Council until the end of the war.[55] The trials of the war did indeed bring about a cooperative spirit which bore fruit in closer confederation among some of the Lutheran Free churches after the war.

Reformed Free Churches

As among the Lutherans, there were some groups of Reformed
congregations who were considered to be Free churches, as, for example, the Confederation of Reformed Congregations in Lower Saxony
and the Old Reformed Church in the Province of Hanover. Some of the
Old Reformed congregations in East Friesia had ties with the Reformed
church in Holland.[56] These Reformed Free churches had some association with one another in the Confederation of Free Reformed Congregations. They, however, had few contacts with the more important Reformed Confederation of Germany (now usually called *Reformierter
Bund*) founded in 1884 to bring together the various Reformed congregations and synods scattered among the Land churches. Closely tied to
this Reformed Confederation were the Evangelical Reformed Land
Church of the Province of Hanover and the Land Church of Lippe,
whose congregations were largely Reformed. It was this Reformed Confederation and the two Reformed Land churches which carried the
burden for the Reformed constituency in the Kirchenkampf.[57]

When committees or councils were formed in either the official
national church administration or the Confessing churches, there was
always an attempt to give the Reformed church representation on them.
Some of the most intrepid leaders in the Church Struggle were Reformed
pastors, among them the Reverend Wilhelm Niesel, Superintendent
Martin Albertz, the Reverends Paul Humburg, Karl Immer, Hermann
Hesse and his son Helmut Hesse, and Ludwig Steil. Helmut Hesse and
Steil died at Dachau. There were some few in the Reformed congregations who were favorable to the German Christians, and some congregations compromised more with state authorities than did others. There
was no united Reformed front, any more than there was a united Lutheran front, but on the whole the Reformed congregations remained
true to their historic confessional stand and their presbyterian form of
church government. One and all, they disliked bishops and the centralized leadership that the church authorities in Berlin sought to impose.

The so-called Reformed Free churches survived. The *Kirchliches
Jahrbuch* lists five such bodies united in the Confederation of Evangelical Reformed Churches in Germany (*Bund Evangelisch-Reformierter
Kirchen Deutschlands*) after the war.[58] This union, while not a member
of the Evangelical church in Germany, has affiliated with it and has
some ties with the old Reformed Confederation. The latter was reorganized on a more centralized basis in 1946.[59]

New Apostolic Churches

The New Apostolic church was one of the largest of the Free

churches. In the last forty years of the nineteenth century it had been gathered together, many congregations having previously been part of the Catholic-Apostolic movement. In 1907 it was officially designated *Neuapostolische Kirche,* and after World War I had received the rights of a public corporation in Hamburg and Baden.[60] As the National Socialist party grew in strength, the officials of the church sought contacts with it. When in 1932 a member of the SA wished to join a New Apostolic congregation, he was asked to check first with the party to see if there would be any objections. He wrote directly to Hitler, who had one of his subordinates thank the man for his letter and give the following assurance:

> From the position Hitler has taken so far in regard to church-political matters, it is clear and certain that there can be no talk of a prohibition of the New Apostolic congregation by a National Socialist government. This confession will receive, exactly as the other Christian confessions, protection and support in the Third Reich.[61]

In July of 1932, the chief apostle of the New Apostolic church, whose headquarters was in Frankfurt/Main, informed all congregations that National Socialists should be permitted to attend services in uniform. This was one of the moot questions in the established churches. After Hitler came to power, the chief apostle sent out a letter on March 20, 1933, to be read to all congregations enlightening them about the atrocity propaganda against the party. The next day, the same day the Reichstag opened, all congregations were asked to have an evening service based on Ecclesiasticus 10:1–5. These are verses in praise of a wise ruler, and the German version of this text from the Apocrypha is far more pointed than the English translation.[62]

The tenth and last point in the summation of the creed of the New Apostolic church states: "I believe that the government (*Obrigkeit*) is God's servant to our benefit, and who opposes the government, opposes God's order, because it is so ordained by God."[63] The New Apostolic churches lived up to this credo. On April 23, 1933, the congregations were enjoined to check with local party headquarters to be sure applicants for membership had good records and were not hostile to the government. That year they raised a special collection of 57,533.25 marks for the drive to further national employment, and 63,972.55 marks for the Winter Help Organization.[64]

Such loyalty did not go unnoticed, and on April 3, 1935, the Reich finance minister granted to the New Apostolic congregations in all Germany the rights of a public corporation in regard to property and corporation taxes, which meant they were freed from property taxes and most corporation levies.[65] The central office of the church, in a circular letter, called upon all the membership to be sure to vote in the election on March 3, 1936. That May the New Apostolic congregation, jointly with the SA brigade in Grünau contributed 500 marks to the so-called Thank Offering of the Nation.[66]

In spite of these repeated manifestations of support for the regime, the Gestapo had a special study drawn up on the New Apostolic congregations (1936–37).[67] This was not an exceptional procedure; in fact it is rather surprising that it was not done earlier. The study thoroughly covered the group's history, doctrines, and organization, and enumerated all the church districts and leaders. The general conclusion was that "although the sect had until then given the state no cause to intervene, careful surveillance of the New Apostolic congregations was absolutely essential." The church's membership had steadily gone up since the National Socialists' assumption of power, and presumably all these persons did not join the New Apostolic church only out of religious motives. It had to be assumed that many Marxists or other enemies of the state had found refuge there, but basically, the New Apostolic church should be rejected because its ties to the Judaic-Christian international world of ideas could not be reconciled with true national socialism.

The Gestapo recommended planting at least one informer in all Apostolic districts, checking on all members who had joined the church since 1933, and keeping the central headquarters under close observation. Although all churches and organizations at this time were being subjected to such treatment, the New Apostolics remained suspect, for, after all, they were somewhat different. In the middle of the war, when an SS man wanted to marry a member of the group, time was taken to make an inquiry, with the verdict that "membership of SS persons in this sect could not be approved, inasmuch as the New Apostolic congregation, through its teaching and activity, in the last analysis contributes to the ideological division of the German folk."[68] The New Apostolic congregations had trials and tribulations, and certainly they were not free from wartime restrictions and the hardships of the war itself. Yet the church remained intact; it was not dissolved as were so many other lesser religious groups.

Mennonites

Mennonites had long existed in Germany, and their refusal to take an oath, serve with arms, or hold governmental office had often caused difficulties with the state. Yet over the years an accepted relationship had been established. Prussia, for example, from 1866–1915 had accorded them the alternative of serving in the medical or transportation units rather than with a gun. Yet refusal to bear arms was not an absolute command among German Mennonites, and in the Constitution of the Mennonite Congregations of June 11, 1934, the principle of refusal to bear arms was given up completely.[69] In the same year, their headquarters sent out a circular letter dealing with the relationship of the Mennonites to national socialism. It pointed out that there was the community (Gemeinschaft) of the gospel and also the community of the people, and raised the question of which stood higher. The answer was clear: "The gospel stands higher." They did say yes to a racial hygiene program conducted with responsibility, but added: "Race can never be the most important thing for a Christian."[70]

Their refusal to take an oath still caused some difficulties. In the

summer of 1938, when the dispute over an oath to the Führer was at its
height in the Confessing church, the association of German Mennonites
requested a special dispensation in favor of making an affirmation of
loyalty instead of taking an oath. It took Bormann almost six months to
answer. On December 15, 1938, he replied in a secret circular letter to
various authorities. There could be no exceptions to taking the oath,
since the act was both an acknowledgment of national socialism and
the idea of community which it upheld. Until this time few Mennonites
had refused to take the oath, and there was no reason to make an
exception for them. Whether they could join the party would depend on
whether they could accept the party program without reservations and
were personally acceptable as party members. Earlier that year it had
been decided they could not be members of the SS.[71]

It is not certain whether Bormann's order on taking oaths was enforced. The Mennonites were on the whole a quiet, law-abiding people
and got along with the authorities. During the war, groups of Mennonites from the Black Sea region were settled in the Warthegau. Karl
Götz, an SS Sturmbahnführer, wrote a very laudatory pamphlet about
them.[72]

The expulsion of Germans from territories lost to Poland and Russia
after the war meant the dissolution of numerous Mennonite congregations. Many found refuge in Uruguay and Canada; others joined established congregations and even founded some new ones in Germany.
Their numbers have diminished, but the Mennonites still continue as a
Free church in Germany and cooperate with the other churches in the
Working Community of Christian Churches in Germany (*Arbeitsgemeinschaft christlicher Kirchen in Deutschland*).[73]

Friends

The Friends, or Quakers, are somewhat akin to the Mennonites in
being basically pacifist. There were not many in Germany, but they
were organized as the *Religiöse Gesellschaft der Freunde*, with headquarters in Berlin. They were respected and had a good reputation
because of their relief activity after World War I. In investigating the
activity of the Socialist Workers party and the German Socialist party in
1935, the police found that certain members had received money,
shelter, and care from the Friends. As the Friends impartially aided
members of all confessions, even Jews, the Nazis feared they might
become a haven for hostile state elements. Prof. William Hughes of
England, a former member of the Labor party, visited Germany and
dispensed aid, even visiting prisoners in concentration camps. He was
questioned by the police, who suspected that he was collecting atrocity
propaganda against Germany, but he was not, and was released. Nevertheless, the order went out to watch the Friends.[74] Clarence E. Pickett,
the executive secretary of the American Friends Service Committee,
stated in April, 1936: "Now part of the standard equipment of our
workers [in Germany] is the ability to stand confinement in jail and the
pain of the third degree."[75] In May, the Bavarian state police in Bavaria

eased the lot of the Friends somewhat. The police were to report matters relating to them to headquarters, but were not to press action against individuals except for clear violations of the law.[76] Though the Friends suffered restrictions, the police never went so far as to dissolve the minimal organization that they maintained in Germany.

Herrnhuter

The small but long-established group of United Brethren congregations with headquarters at Herrnhut in Saxony had been affiliated with the German Evangelical Church Confederation during the Weimar Republic.[77] It stood aside from the controversy over the revision of that body and the attempt with the advent of Hitler to form a more united Protestant church. The group receives scant notice in the literature of the Kirchenkampf. Its connections with Brethren churches throughout the world must have aroused concern among the suspicious secret police. Yet the Brethren had a tradition of surviving under hostile governments and quietly carrying on their activities. The Brethren were also one of the Free churches which the Nazis tolerated. Today the Brethren again cooperate with the Land churches as an affiliated member of the Evangelical church in West Germany and with the Confederation of Evangelical Churches in the German Democratic Republic.

Seventh Day Adventists

The Seventh Day Adventists were a well-established group when Hitler came to power, numbering some 255,000 members.[78] With the outbreak of World War I, their leaders, on August 4, 1914, had written to the Ministry of War that they would serve in the army even on Saturday.[79] Some members, however, did not agree, which led to the formation of a secessionist group called the Seventh Day Adventists, Reform Movement.[80] In the Third Reich the latter group refused to serve in the military or use the German greeting, and emphasized their international connections, considering all people as their brothers. These beliefs furnished enough cause for police action against them. On April 29, 1936, the Seventh Day Adventists, Reform Movement (*Siebenten-Tags-Adventisten-Reformbewegung*) were forbidden, dissolved, and their property confiscated, because they were likely to arouse confusion among the populace.[81] An offshoot of the reform movement, called the *Reformations-gemeinde der Siebententags-Adventisten, Deutsche Union e. V, Sitz Saarbrücken,* was likewise dissolved on June 19, 1936.[82] On April 19, 1937, the *Siebenten-Tags Adventisten vom III Teil* were forbidden for the whole Reich and dissolved at once.[83] But dissenting groups continued to crop up. On December 18, 1941, the *Missionsvereinigung Siebenten-Tags Adventisten Laubhütten-bewegung* was dissolved effective January 28, 1942.[84] These Adventists would not serve with arms or give the German greeting.

The dissolution of smaller Adventist groups did not affect the main body, and police headquarters noted this in sending out their instructions. The Adventists were not above sending an encouraging word to

Hitler. On March 11, 1936, their mission society sent him an appeal for peace and for a just distribution of colonies. "It is our desire to support your Excellency somewhat in the fulfillment of your great work of reconstruction. May God's providence richly reward your work."[85] On the other hand, at times the refusal of certain Adventists to work on Saturdays caused difficulties. On January 29, 1937, the Ministry of the Interior circularized various ministries, asking for their reaction to a proposed directive that henceforth no Seventh Day Adventist should be excused from Saturday work.[86] If the directive was ever in fact issued, it did not settle matters. In May, 1940, the head of the Adventist Association was informed by the Security Headquarters (*Reichssicherheitshauptamt*) that some Adventists were refusing to work on Saturday. He was urged to prevent this or the police would have to intervene. The head of the association was successful in persuading some to change their attitude, but police were ordered to report on any who still refused to conform.[87] Whatever the results of this police coercion were, it is clear that compulsion to work on the Sabbath was a real restriction on the religious freedom of the Adventists and a burden to their consciences.

Salvation Army

Although the Salvation Army never considered itself a church, the *Kirchliches Jahrbuch* included it in its list of Free churches, with the note that it was "no closed religious association."[88] It was well established in Germany, and maintained numerous shelters, orphanages, and other social service institutions. The Bavarian state police, under the direction of Himmler and Heydrich, were among the most active in curbing religious activities in the early period of national socialism. On February 14, 1934, they ordered that the Salvation Army be restricted as much as possible.[89] There were to be no meetings on public grounds or in establishments open to the general public. Its collections were against the law regulating public collections, and in any case, about 70 percent of the money went to the headquarters in England. However, the police were to be careful, for their actions could lead to foreign policy complications.

Apparently no grave incidents occurred, and on October 19, 1934, General Evangeline Booth sent Hitler the following telegram from New York:

> Please permit me to express my very deep appreciation and sincere gratitude for your conciliatory attitude toward the Salvation Army in Germany. The only purpose for our existence is the alleviation of sorrow and the amelioration of suffering. I want our people to do their full part individually and collectively toward making a better Germany.[90]

The Reich chancellery was surprised by the message and did not know what led to its being sent. It asked the Foreign Office to acknowledge the message with thanks through the German consulate in New York. Heinrich Borchers, the consul in New York, informed Berlin that the message was connected with Evangeline Booth's taking over the supreme command of the Salvation Army. She now was at her headquarters in London, and he advised that Hitler's thanks be conveyed

through the German embassy there, which was done on January 15, 1935.

Whether this gesture on the part of Commander Booth had anything to do with it or not, Hitler spoke favorably of the Salvation Army at this time. On December 8, 1934, the Gestapo in Berlin sent out this message:

> The Führer and Reich Chancellor has recently said that he was not opposed to the activity of the Salvation Army, which had never engaged itself politically, and that also out of considerations of foreign policy he wanted no action to be taken against them.[91]

This policy was usually followed, but incidents did occur. On August 15, 1935, the *Frankfurter Zeitung* reported that the Salvation Army in Ebingen, Württemberg, had been publicly warned by the district leader of the party, because members of the organization had ostentatiously refused to salute the swastika flag.[92] A decree of the minister of the interior on June 19, 1937, forbade the distribution of the Salvation Army paper *Der Kriegsruf* for money except to registered members and subscribers. Army members had a practice of handing out the paper and then presenting a collection box for an offering; this practice was now stopped. The Salvation Army even had to obtain permission for collections in their regular services becaue it was not a corporation under public law and therefore did not enjoy the privilege of taking up collections in services that was accorded to churches.[93]

One of the police objections to the Salvation Army was the difficulty of determining exactly who was a member. In 1938 it was ordered to institute a regular contribution from each member *(feste Mitgliederbeitrag)* and thereby give itself a concrete organizational form.[94] Although the Salvation Army was not specifically forbidden to carry on meetings outdoors, the police did not like it to do so. In a directive of September 16, 1941, these meetings were declared undesirable, and police were asked to report any to headquarters.[95] A year later the minister of the interior stated that the Salvation Army no longer had any grounds for existing in Germany, and that its dissolution was contemplated. The people for whom they cared would have to be cared for by someone else in the future. He asked various local authorities if they could take over the homes and shelters.[96] Some communities did, but they paid no compensation. The Salvation Army lost many other buildings and stations through war damage, but it was never dissolved, and had a corps of workers left to help relieve the distress and misery of the postwar years. As in the case of some of the churches, its international connections proved a boon to the German organization.

The Old Catholics

The Old Catholics have always been adamant in resisting classification as a Free church or confession.[97] Yet it is in order to consider them as one of the smaller independent churches. Among the many congratulatory telegrams that were sent to Hitler in the first months of his chancellorship was one from Bishop Georg Moog of the Old Catholic church. He had supported the national movement and promised Hitler his further support. According to doctrine, cult, and organization Catholic, but at the same time independent, the Old Catholics were supporters of Germanism and were truly a national church. Hitler thanked him for his telegram.[98]

Good relations continued between the Old Catholics and the government. They continued to collect their church taxes and received a state subsidy. Werner Haugg, an official in the Church Ministry of Church Affairs, wrote in 1940: "The Old Catholic church, which expressly desires to be a national church (*Volkskirche*), did not oppose the National Socialist state, wherefore the bishop of Bonn was administered the oath to the Führer on December 17, 1935, by the Reich minister for church affairs."[99] Taking the oath was of course exactly what all the bishops of the Roman Catholic church did under the concordat, but what most of the leaders of the Confessing church refused to do. In 1937, the government permitted representatives of the Old Catholics to attend the world church conferences at Oxford and Edinburgh. At the latter the Old Catholic bishop joined with the Methodist representative in issuing a statement favorable to the German government.[100] The police summary of 1938 on conditions in the churches noted that the Old Catholics did not make gains in membership in spite of their "apparent complete effort for the interests of the state."[101]

Such support did not spare them the usual police restrictions, or the horrors of war. Most of their town churches were destroyed, but not those in the country, and there still were 120 Old Catholic centers in Germany in 1945. In the postwar years the Old Catholics cooperated with the Evangelical Hilfswerk and joined in the work of the Working Community of Christian Churches in Germany.[102]

The Orthodox Church

Like the Old Catholics, the Orthodox church in Germany got along very well with the government. In October, 1935, a constitution for the Orthodox church in Germany was worked out with the aid of the Ministry of Church Affairs. The following March, largely through the efforts of Hermann von Detten in the ministry, the Orthodox church was granted the coveted recognition as a public corporation. This brought a word of thanks from the head of the Orthodox Congregational Board. The ministry also helped substantially in financing the construction of a church building in Berlin. It provided a grant of 15,000 marks and prevailed upon the Labor Front to provide 20,000 marks and the Foreign Office another 3,000. Hitler was asked to grant the additional 12,000 marks needed, but he refused. The church was nevertheless built, and Hitler received a letter of thanks. Since the building was built by public funds, it was considered to be state-owned, and only lent to the church, which led to the enactment in 1938 of a special law on the property rights of the Russian Orthodox church in Germany.[103] The Orthodox church in Germany was connected with the Orthodox church in Yugoslavia, and the German bishop was appointed by the Russian Orthodox Bishops' Council in Belgrade with the approval of the German government.

The Postwar Period

What distinguishes the churches surveyed above is that all of them survived the Hitler period intact. They all enjoyed relative freedom as they stood aside from the struggle between the government and the Protestant Land churches, the Roman Catholic church, and the smaller religious sects to be considered in the next chapter. They were indeed subject to the many regulations which were applicable to all churches and organizations, and to this extent shared in the religious turmoil of the period. Yet protests against the Nazis' racial policies, euthanasia, and other programs, if they ever were made, were not publicized. And after the war there were no public confessions of guilt and repentance commensurate with the Stuttgart Declaration by the Evangelical church in Germany.[104] Perhaps because they asked so little from the government they were left free to carry on with little direct coercion.

These churches, along with all other churches, suffered heavily from war damage; the loss of eastern territories to Poland and Russia also hit some of them particularly hard. However, they had not been dissolved, nor was all their property confiscated. There remained a basis on which to rebuild. Some of them had close connections with churches abroad which sent relief and helped to get them functioning again. The smaller churches rapidly achieved new stature in the postwar period.

The Hitler period and the postwar years have had the effect, however, of bringing about greater willingness to cooperate with other churches. The Association of Evangelical Free Churches is more strongly knit together than ever before. There is more cooperation among the Old Lutheran Free churches than in any time in their history. Today the Evangelical Lutheran (Old Lutheran) Church, and the Evangelical Lutheran Free Church (a union of some former independent Lutheran groups) join in supporting one theological seminary in Oberursel. These two, along with the Independent (*Selbstständige*) Evangelical Lutheran church, have formed a loosely organized federal Cooperative Association of Evangelical Lutheran Free Churches. These Lutheran Free churches have united their foreign missionary efforts.

The relations between the Free churches and the Land churches have become more intimate. As the *Kirchliches Jahrbuch* states:

> We have come closer together in Germany. The chasm between "Land" church and "Free" church has remarkably narrowed. On both sides, one has learned to see in the other a Christian brother, and to respect the ways that he and his forefathers have travelled. One can today as a representative of a Land church dare to meet with brethren from the Free churches, yes, even to speak in their meetings without being charged with unseemly conduct.[105]

This new friendship is partly the result of carrying over the modern ecumenical international spirit to the national scene.

The Lutheran Free churches, it is true, have not sought ties with the World Council of Churches. Other Free churches have done so, and it is these which joined with the Evangelical church in Germany in 1948 to form the Working Community of Christian Churches in Germany.[106] This organization has done much to tear down the barriers between German churches. In 1962 a separate branch of this Community was established in the Democratic Republic, and with the final division of the German Evangelical church into east and west in 1969, the two associations have also become separate. Since 1969 the Roman Catholic church has cooperated with the Community in West Germany but not in East Germany. This separation into eastern and western bodies is indicative of what has generally been taking place in Germany. In the first postwar years the eastern and western Free churches were one. Then gradually they were divided into self-governing branches, one for the Federal Republic and one for the Democratic Republic. In this they parallel the division of the Evangelical church and the de facto, if not yet de jure, division of the administration of the Roman Catholic church.

20.

Sects and Other Societies

Nazi Antisectarian Policies

The word *sect* is of uncertain definition and while it is usually used pejoratively in Germany, no such sense is intended here; in fact, most of the churches or associations discussed in chapter nineteen were at times and often still are described as sects. However, most had achieved the status of a church by being granted the rights of public corporations in some German state. They all had the good fortune to survive the Hitler years. There were other small religions or philosophical groups which did not have those rights, and these, at least in Germany, were always classed as sects. These organizations in particular aroused the ire of the Nazis; many were liquidated, and their property usually, if not always, confiscated.

The National Socialists came to power pledged to uphold positive Christianity and to establish and strengthen the unity of the German folk. In the years of party conflict they had found many things to attack, but there were five chief enemies: parliamentarianism, with its system of political parties; pacifism or internationalism, of which acceptance of the Treaty of Versailles seemed to be a part; communism; Free Masonry; and the Jews. These had to be dealt with if the Nazis were to achieve their goals, and anyone associated with these concepts or groups was suspect in their eyes. No doubt it was often the other way around, and organizations that the Nazis wished to liquidate were charged with harboring Marxists, communists, pacifists, Free Masons, or Jews whether or not they actually did so. Since the legal basis for the dissolution of the sects was always the ordinance of February 28, 1933, for "warding off communist acts of violence against the state," the police at times were careful to include charges of communist activity in order to help legitimate their actions.[1] The police were in many ways tidy souls; they wanted to have everything well catalogued to facilitate keeping order. Many small groups, often with no responsible leaders or exact membership rolls, were an annoyance to them; they claimed such groups brought confusion among the people and were harmful to the unity of the nation.[2]

Some of the actions of the sects were considered to be disparaging to the established churches and therefore a disturbing influence. When the Jehovah's Witnesses were forbidden in Prussia, one of the reasons advanced was that under the guise of being biblical research scholars they were agitating against the Christian church and the state.[3] The Bavarian supreme court, in upholding the ban against them, stated on December 7, 1933, that by their attacks on the recognized Christian churches and the laws protecting them, the Jehovah's Witnesses were in line with the antireligious and antichurch activities of the Communist party, and therefore constituted a danger to the state, and that they furthered communist aims.[4] They were noted for their opposition to the pope and Roman Catholicism in general.[5] When the Revival Mission in Germany was dissolved on May 30, 1936, the police added this statement:

> The meetings of the Revival Mission in Germany cannot be considered religious activities. In the prayer meetings the members, through the fanatical and rousing words of the preachers, are placed in a state of ecstasy and rapture. Such meetings are of a nature to exert a bad influence on the spiritual conceptions of the participants. Through such influences citizens, under the pretext of religious involvement, are materially exploited, their health injured, and their place in the community endangered.[6]

In like manner the Nazis, representing themselves as protectors of the welfare of the people, came to oppose spiritualism and the occult. One of the first of the spiritual groups to be banned was the rather well-established Weissenberg sect.[7] Under the guise of religious meetings, they held séances in which they contacted the great men of Germany's past. With the advent of national socialism they began to bring it into their séances, and even claimed to have contacted Horst Wessel. This was considered a degradation of national socialism and a threat to the unity and safety of the state. The Weissenberg sect was banned by the Gestapo for the whole Reich on January 17, 1935.[8] In forbidding the *Gottesbund Tanatra* on July 10, 1936, the police charged that the ministers worked themselves into a trance and attacked national socialism. "The ceremonies used in their meetings are of a spiritualist and occult character and are no longer to be considered as a religious service."[9]

The police sometimes assumed the right to protect not only the health but the moral standards of the nation. The yearly report of 1938 noted that fewer sects had been dissolved because such groups had become more cautious. Yet six had been forbidden and dissolved on the grounds that their activity had nothing to do with true religious practices. "Faith healing, sexual excesses, deceit, and other matters made it certain that these sects merely served the corrupt instincts of their preachers and leaders."[10] The Nazis always took a dim view of faith healing. They considered it dangerous to the health of the citizenry and that it brought the whole medical profession into disrepute.[11] The healing practice which was part of Christian Science was one of the black marks against that organization.

At first the Nazis made no move against astrologers, for some of them foretold the success of the party by the stars, but after the war began not all of them promised success.[12] The party finally decided that it had to free itself from astrology and all occult groups. In accordance

with a specific directive from Hitler on June 4, 1941, Heydrich, as chief
of the Security Service, issued a sweeping order to all police headquarters, including those in the Ostmark, Alsace, Lorraine, Luxemburg,
and the Protectorate:

> In the present struggle for the fate of the German people, it is necessary
> to maintain not merely the physical but also the spiritual health of the
> people, both individually and collectively.
> The German people can no longer be exposed to occultist teachings,
> which pretend that the actions and missions of the human being are subject
> to mysterious magic forces.[13]

On June 9, 1941, if possible between seven and nine o'clock, measures
were to be taken against astrologers, occultists, spiritualists, followers of
the occult theories of rays, fortune tellers of any type, faith healers,
Christian Scientists, Anthroposophists, Theosophists, and Ariosophists.
The "organizations, clubs, unions, circles, etc." were to be dissolved
and their properties and membership lists confiscated. The police were
admonished to be very strict in carrying out the order, and they took
action against many groups and individuals. Perhaps the most significant result was the final dissolution of the Christian Scientists.[14]

Some of the dissolved "sects," as they were usually referred to by
the police, were no doubt esoteric in nature and hardly to be considered
religious organizations. Here it is not necessary to decide whether this
was religious persecution or simply the denial of freedom to form organizations and groups freely. Certainly there was no protest against the
dissolutions from either Protestants or Catholics; neither church had a
high opinion of the *Sektenwesen* which existed in Germany.[15] The police actions against these groups no doubt involved inquisitions, imprisonments, and hardships. Yet apparently, except for the Jehovah's Witnesses, they did not resist vigorously. Groups often were dissolved one
day only to crop up the next with a new name, or simply to get together
in a new meeting place. One thing is clear—although the Nazis harassed and curtailed, they never ended sectarianism, for it mushroomed
again immediately after the war.

A lecturer on occult organizations in the party's educational training course stated that in the Germany of 1933 there were 320 Judaic-
Christian sects, 170 Free Mason, occult, and spiritual sects, 75 non-
Christian sects, and 35 folk-religious groups.[16] Whether this count of
around 600 sects and organizations is correct or not is of no great
moment; much depends on definition and if local organizations were
counted separately. His figures were probably as accurate as the official
postwar statistics that indicated 926 different religious designations in
Germany.[17] The police probably had a more exact conception of a sect
when they drew up a list in July, 1939, of all sects prohibited between
1933 and December 31, 1938.[18] They numbered 39, but Gestapo headquarters was not certain the list was complete, and asked to be informed
"if further prohibitions during this period have been ordered in individual towns or administrative districts which are not listed." One must
always remember that there were often great variations in policy in

different sections of Nazi Germany. A sect might be banned in one state or district and not in another, and even decrees issued for the whole Reich were enforced unevenly. Even the most persecuted sect of all, the Jehovah's Witnesses, was never completely stamped out.

Individual Sects and Organizations

Jehovah's Witnesses

Just as the Bavarian police took the most severe measures in Germany against Catholic organizations in the spring and summer of 1933, likewise they were the first to proceed against the Jehovah's Witnesses.[19] The Witnesses were particularly active at this time. In a worldwide special campaign April 8–16, 1933, called "The Remnants' Thanksgiving Period," there were 19,268 Witnesses in the field in Germany who distributed 2,271,630 pieces of literature, compared to 20,719 workers in the United States who only distributed 877,194 pieces of literature.[20] On April 13, the Bavarian minister of the interior intervened; he outlawed the Jehovah's Witnesses, ordered their organization dissolved, and prohibited the distribution of their literature.[21] This led the headquarters of the Jehovah's Witnesses on April 26, 1933, to ask Hitler to receive a delegation so that they could explain the movement to him. They were concerned about the Bavarian measures and had heard over the radio that Saxony had taken similar steps. Theirs was a purely religious movement which had been active in Germany since 1904, and they had always observed a politically neutral course. Along with their request they submitted a memorandum describing their organization. As in the case of the representatives of the Association of Evangelical Free Churches, Hitler was too busy to see them.[22]

Without officially banning the Witnesses in Prussia, the police had taken over the headquarters and printing plant of the Watch Tower Bible and Tract Society in Magdeburg. This was an American corporation, organized under the laws of Pennsylvania, and its American headquarters appealed to the U.S. State Department for aid. On April 27, 1933, the American embassy in Berlin was instructed to investigate and lend appropriate assistance.[23] Action was prompt, and on May 2 the consulate general in Berlin could report that through its good offices the premises of the Watch Tower Society had been freed.[24] Meanwhile the governments of Bavaria, Saxony, Thuringia, Lippe, Mecklenburg, Hesse, and Württemberg had interdicted the Society's activities and confiscated its property, valued at 750,000 marks.[25] On May 18, the U.S. consul general in Berlin was again asked to lend appropriate assistance.[26] The German minister of the interior, who held the same office in Prussia, thereupon promised to investigate the activities of the state governments, with the surprising result that on June 24, 1933, he banned the Jehovah's Witnesses throughout Germany and ordered their property, valued at about five million marks, confiscated. Consul Raymond H. Geist immediately visited the ministry and was able to secure a reversal of the decision to confiscate, although the German authorities insisted that the properties be liquidated. The consul general hoped to "be able to obtain a sufficient delay with regard to the disposition of their property so that a minimum loss may be sustained."[27] The German authorities wanted the Witnesses to dismantle their printing plant and move it out of the country, which was the last thing the Witnesses wanted or intended to do.

Judge Joseph Franklin Rutherford of Brooklyn, the head of the Jehovah's Witnesses, was then in Berlin, and he was informed: "That the Consulate General would be unable to make any representation to the German Government regarding the ban that had been put upon their activities and that it could use its good offices only to protect the physical property of the organization excluding pamphlets, booklets and brochures which the police had condemned as being anti-revolutionary and communistic in tendency."[28] In stressing that the consulate and embassy staff felt that it would be useless to go beyond protecting the society's physical property, which it had been successful in doing, the consul general added:

> I have gone into the activities of the Society and of its agents, and have read some of the pamphlets which have been distributed by the Society widely in Germany, and I can see that objection could reasonably be raised to them by the German Government. Although acting as a religious society, the pamphlets contain comment of not a purely religious character. In view of the present situation in Germany, I believe that it would be entirely useless to endeavor to assist the Society to continue its operations and I doubt very much whether our Government, in view of the nature of the activities, would find it possible to assist it. I believe therefore that the only efforts which we can make on behalf of the Society are in connection with the protection of its physical property.[29]

This indeed was pretty much the policy the State Department followed from this time on.

In spite of promising to release the property, the police kept it "as a guarantee that no propaganda will be made by the Society abroad against the German Government." Consul Geist again visited the Ministry of the Interior to protest, and requested a statement "stating precisely the conditions upon which the property will be released." Meanwhile, the consulate requested that the State Department study the facts as stated in their reports and decide whether, under the Treaty of Friendship of 1923, "the property of an American firm, for certain alleged political reasons, can in this way be seized or confiscated."[30]

The police continued to occupy the property in Magdeburg, and ordered M. C. Harbeck, an American citizen and the society's resident manager, to vacate his house. The police acting as custodians of the society's factory, were also reported to be burning "a portion of the Society's property including books."[31] The consulate was again asked for help. The State Department advised that the basis for the protest against the seizure of the property was "the absence of a proper judicial hearing as provided for under Article 12 of the Treaty of 1923." A further protest on the same basis against curtailment of the society's activities was left to the discretion of Ambassador William E. Dodd.[32]

As early as September 12, the embassy reported that the Society's property had been released, although its activities were still prohibited.[33] After further careful study, Ambassador Dodd on September 20 submitted a *note verbale* to the German Foreign Office which raised the whole problem of the banning of the Jehovah's Witnesses.[34] Six days later, September 26, 1933, the governor (*Regierungspräsident*) in Magdeburg was instructed "to rescind the confiscation of the property of the prohibited Society. Furthermore the former personnel of the Society [were to be] permitted to live in its buildings again."[35] On the other hand, teaching and holding meetings continued to be forbidden, and supervision of the buildings was maintained in order to insure that no printed matter of any kind was prepared there. Clearly there were restrictions on its use, but the society did get its property back.[36]

The German answer to the *note verbale* was not submitted until November 13, 1933. It pointed out that the society could seek a legal judgment in the courts in accordance with Article 12 of the 1923 treaty.[37] Harbeck was inclined to do so, but shortly thereafter the consulate was informed that such judicial steps had been taken in the summer of 1933, and the court had decided that actions taken under the presidential decree of February 28, 1933, could not be legally contested.[38] The question now arose: "whether, since local remedies have apparently been exhausted, grounds exist for interposition by the government of the United States." Ambassador Dodd placed the matter before the State Department. The editors of the documents add the footnote, "apparently no further action was taken by the Department."[39]

The Prussian minister of justice took the next step in the tortuous procedure of returning the Jehovah's Witnesses' property. On June 9, 1934, he published in the official organ *Deutsche Justiz* a notice that the Prussian Ministry of the Interior had freed all the property of the *Internationale Bibelforscher-Vereinigung* and its subsidiary organs. The society was still prohibited from publishing, teaching, or holding meetings.[40] Minister Crohne sent the notice to the Watch Tower Society in Magdeburg on June 22, and three days later it directed a letter to all pertinent police headquarters in Germany, asking them to turn over seized property to the bearer of the letter. The police were not in a hurry to do so, especially the Bavarian police, who considered it a Prussian affair.[41]

On July 17, 1934, Consul Raymond H. Geist sent a letter to the Ministry of the Interior inquiring about the restoration of property to the Jehovah's Witnesses. On September 13, the ministry answered:

> In reply to your kind communication of July 17, 1934, I have the honor to inform you that I have directed all state governments to free the property of the International Bible Researchers organization, including its subsidiary organizations, and no longer to forbid the printing and distribution of Bibles and other nonsuspicious writings. Nevertheless, all further activity of the Earnest Bible Researchers, such as teaching and holding of meetings, as well as the preparation and distribution of tracts, flyers, solicitation for members, etc., must remain prohibited.[42]

The same day, the Ministry of the Interior issued a similar directive to all state governments.[43] This decree of September 13, 1934, eased somewhat the lot of the Jehovah's Witnesses. At this very time they were holding an international conference in Basel, which was attended by 3,500 visitors, among them some Germans who were mostly promptly arrested when they returned. At the conference Judge Rutherford denounced the persecution in Germany, and a telegram of protest was sent to Hitler. The Witnesses had attempted a friendly approach but had received no reply. "Therefore we leave judgment with confidence to divine justice."[44] A plan was laid to carry out a common action throughout Germany on October 7, 1934. At nine in the morning on that day, all Jehovah's Witnesses were to gather in a convenient spot in their various places of residence and listen to a letter from Judge Rutherford. Then a telegram was to be sent to the local governments stating that Witnesses followed the admonition of the true apostles and must be obedient to God more than to man, "and that this they would do." They were also to send the following telegram to the Reich government, signing it with the name of their organization and with the name of the city where the congregation had assembled: "Your ill-treatment of the Jehovah's Witnesses shocks all good people of earth and dishonors God's name. Refrain from further persecuting Jehovah's Witnesses; otherwise God will destroy you and your national party."[45] Not only Germans sent the message; Witnesses all over the world met on the same day and rained cables on Berlin.[46] It was not exactly a tactful telegram, and Hitler was far from intimidated. On November 17, 1934, he asked the Reich Chancellery to turn over all its material on the Jehovah's Witnesses for submission to the secret police.[47]

Meanwhile the Witnesses had done nothing to better their position with the police. They had apparently agitated against the important elections of November 12, 1933, which gave Heydrich, still at that time with the Bavarian police, the opportunity to order more vigorous measures against them, including arrest. In February, 1934, he ordered the confiscation of all their mail.[48] In June, 1934, Secretary Hans Pfundtner of the Ministry of the Interior sought the names of all members of the society employed by the state. He admitted they were not communists, but a person who refused to give the German greeting was in truth not worthy of being an official.[49] Many Witnesses lost their jobs and suffered harassment, yet there were relatively few police actions that led to trial and imprisonment in 1933–34.[50] In January, 1935, came the victory in the Saar plebiscite, in March the reintroduction of military service, and that summer brought a more active policy against all churches and organizations. The Jehovah's Witnesses refused to serve in the army, which led to more severe measures against them.

On April 1, 1935, the Ministry of the Interior directed the governor in Magdeburg to dissolve the Watch Tower Bible and Tract Society, which he did on April 27. On July 13, 1935, the minister of the interior requested all other heads of government to take similar action.[51] In this piecemeal fashion the society was finally dissolved and all its property

confiscated. With a circular notice of May 21, 1935, the minister of the
interior cancelled his directive of the previous September. Jehovah's
Witnesses could no longer even distribute Bibles.[52]

In June the minister of the interior and the minister of justice
agreed that the police could place in "protective custody" Jehovah's
Witnesses who had already served their jail sentences. Under this policy Witnesses who had been sentenced to jail only for a number of
months often spent years in prison.[53] Actually the police often did not
know what to do with them. New directions, effective immediately,
were issued by the Bavarian police on September 23, 1935. Those
Jehovah's Witnesses arrested for the first time, if no court order existed,
were to be kept in custody for seven days, given a warning, and freed.
If they were leaders, they could be kept for two months. If they renewed their activity, request had to be made to headquarters to send
them to concentrations camps. A report on their economic and family
conditions had to accompany this request "in order that in deciding on
the length of the incarceration unnecessary hardship be prevented."[54]
The national police headquarters became alarmed at the increasing
number of cases in which both parents were arrested simultaneously,
because their children then became a burden on public charity. In
order to protect the children from severe spiritual and economic hardships, the police were ordered as far as possible to desist from arresting
both parents at the same time.[55] Yet such concern soon became a
mockery. Marriage to a Jehovah's Witness became grounds for a divorce for the non-Witness.[56] In 1937 the courts decreed that children
could be taken away from Jehovah's Witnesses to preserve them from
the influence of their parents.[57]

The moral and spiritual support of their brethren outside Germany
was most important to the Jehovah's Witnesses, but had no alleviating
effect upon their situation. In the 1935 official yearbook, Rutherford
reported on the persecution in Germany and added:

> Without doubt there is no country on the globe where such measures exist as
> have been taken by Hitler. Manifestly the man is under the direct watch of
> the Devil, and is his special representative on earth. While he deceitfully
> maintains to represent Jesus Christ, he persecutes every one who loyally and
> truthfully serves Jesus Christ.[58]

Such passages of course found their way into the police files. The
Witnesses held one of their periodic conventions in Lucerne from September 4–7, where they passed a resolution protesting the persecution
in Germany and Austria and charging that Hitler's government was
supported by the Jesuits. Not only did they send a copy of the resolution to Hitler and the pope, but on the night of December 12–13,
1936, they stuffed the resolution into countless mailboxes and under
doormats. The police made frantic efforts to get their hands on this
forbidden literature.[59]

Such actions show that the members of the organization never gave
up bearing witness according to their concepts.[60] The police summary of
events of 1938 laments that in spite of orders for their dissolution,

Jehovah's Witnesses continued their activity; however, their importation of literature from Switzerland and France had almost been stopped. In that year approximately 700 Witnesses had been taken in custody. Among them were many who did not participate in the election on April 10, 1938, and also openly agitated against the Führer. Many were also arrested because they later refused to respond to mobilization orders and refused military service.[61]

The police kept careful track of those Witnesses who were not under arrest. The Witnesses hold an annual memorial service (instead of frequent communion services) at the time of Passover. In 1939, this service was scheduled for April 4, and the police were ordered to watch the houses of known members and conduct some searches, especially if the members had guests. Guests should be searched, arrested, and reported to headquarters.[62]

With the outbreak of the war, the lot of the Jehovah's Witnesses grew even worse. They were not reticent in proclaiming the war as a punishment sent by God.[63] By February 7, 1940, fifty-five had been sentenced to death for refusal to bear arms, but the police noted that Witness activity continued, especially in the Sudeten areas and in the Ostmark.[64] The number of Witnesses executed for failure to bear arms increased. Hitler, in a remark made at table on June 7, 1942, put the number at 130 and added: "These 130 executions had acted like an atmosphere-clearing storm. Thousands of like-minded individuals, on hearing of these shootings, had lost the courage to attempt dodging war service by reference to one or another Bible passage."[65] In general, however, the record shows that the Witnesses held true to their convictions. No one knows for certain, but it has been estimated that one to five thousand lost their lives in prison and concentration camps.[66] The camps were full of them, and they received a special group classification and wore a violet clothing patch.[67] They never ceased to carry on their missionary work, and their "witnessing" even brought conversions within the camp.[68] They maintained their pacifistic attitudes, and were often sought after as members of labor battalions. The SS guards even trusted Witnesses to shave them, for they knew these people would not cut their throats.[69] Their steadfastness to their convictions, their exemplary personal habits, and their industry even won them a certain admiration from Himmler. He considered settling them after the war in parts of seized Russian territories, where they might convert the inhabitants to their belief in pacifism and nonresistance.[70] He actually gave some Witnesses their freedom and settled them in small colonies on isolated estates.[71]

Free Masonry

In *Mein Kampf* Hitler referred only four times to the Free Masons, and on each occasion they were libelled because of their supposed connections with the Jews.[72] In the period of Nazi struggle for power, the Masons were often condemned because of their internationalism and liberal democratic philosophy. When there was a rumor that Hin-

denburg had joined the lodge *Zum blühenden Tal* in Hanover in September, 1930, the propaganda headquarters of the party was at pains to
deny it. No such lodge existed, and besides, Masons were usually enlisted before they were fifty years old.[73]

With the Nazi assumption of power in 1933, many of the local
lodges voluntarily dissolved themselves.[74] Others changed their constitution, converting themselves into new organizations and calling themselves an "order" (*Orden*). Thus the *Grossloge Deutsche Bruderkette* in
Leipzig became *Bund Christlicher Orden Deutscher Dom*. Membership
was restricted to German Aryan men; Jews and Marxists were specifically excluded. In April, 1933, even the former Prussian *Landes Grossloge, zu den drei Weltkugeln* became the *Nationale Christlicher Orden,
Friedrich der Grosse,* and appealed to the party to accept 20,000 men
who were devoted to the fatherland. This lodge claimed that for two
hundred years they had not taken in Jewish members.[75] The situation in
the spring of 1933 was well summarized in an article in the *Osservatore
Romano* which Ambassador Bergen forwarded to the Foreign Office.
The article explained Hitler's attitude towards Masons, which was not as
well known as that towards the Jews.

> The fact that the chancellor had dissolved all masonic lodges, with the
> exception of the Landes Grossloge, zu den drei Weltkugeln, indicates that
> the battle against Free Masonry was not so much because of fundamental
> views as out of a desire to bring about consolidation in order to make it
> easier for the government to control them. It was to be noted that the
> surviving lodge extended its influence over all Germany and had the largest
> membership, while the dissolved lodges were of more local importance.[76]

Somewhat ironically, the author pointed out that the Free Masons were
now putting on a very nationalistic face and offering their loyal cooperation. Yet the NSDAP was still suspicious, and was exercising strict measures and great care in taking former Masons into membership.

The party's reluctance to accept Masons as members continued
throughout the Nazi era. In October, 1933, Hitler ruled that men who
had dropped their membership in the Free Masons before January 30,
1933, could become rank-and-file members of the party, but could not
become leaders. They had to sign a declaration: "I assure herewith on
my honor and conscience, that through my resignation I feel myself
free from the oath given to the lodge ———— and have given up all
connections with it."[77] Those who had discovered their National Socialist hearts after the Nazi take-over could not join; if a Mason had
somehow got into the party he should be removed. These rulings
aroused some opposition within local party groups where Masons who
were not active in the lodge had even held party offices. The police
summary report of May–June, 1934, states that the Prussian grand
lodges had been able to escape a ban, mainly because many of their
leaders were in the bureaucracy and government, and some were even
in the party.[78] There were also many influential Masons in banking,
industrial, and publishing circles. They no doubt played a part in preventing a clean sweep of the lodges in these early years.[79] Reichsbank

Director Waldhecker sent a report to the government written by a
friend who had gone to the United States to encourage exports.[80] He stated that in America membership in a lodge was a sign of good citizenship, and Americans from the president on down were members of lodges. To agitate against the lodges and churches would turn Americans against Germany. On April 3, 1934, Minister Frick ordered that no further steps should be taken against the so-called Old Prussian lodges and their branches in Saxony and Oldenburg.[81] Yet it was only a brief respite. These lodges too were hit by the party's more aggressive policy after the Saar plebiscite. On July 17, 1935, it was decreed that by the end of July the Orden, the successors of the lodges, were to be dissolved. By the end of August, the Bavarian police at least could report that the Free Masons, except for the Jewish lodges, were totally eliminated (*restlos zerschlagen.*)[82]

Many of the lodges had carried group insurance contracts, and it proved difficult to convert these to individual contracts. Since it could not be permitted to discuss insurance matters in group meetings—for that would be like permitting a lodge meeting—the insured were to designate one man to the police who would continue to receive insurance collections.[83] The property of the lodges was often confiscated, and their libraries sent to a central library. Some other material found its way into the Nürnberg Lodge Museum, which was opened September 2, 1938, in the building where "Free Masons and Jews had held their meetings since 1864."[84]

While the lodges were dissolved as of 1935 and restrictions were imposed on former members, there were no wholesale arrests or persecutions. Unlike the Jehovah's Witnesses, Masons did not refuse to give the German greeting, swear an oath, or serve in the army. In fact, it was the army which for a time excluded them. On May 26, 1934, War Minister Blomberg decreed that Masons could neither serve in nor be employed by the army. In 1936 there was some relaxation for lower degrees, and in 1937 lodge members who had resigned before January 31, 1933, were not to suffer any restrictions in the army except for certain offices.[85] On April 4, 1938, Hitler granted an amnesty, which, however, applied to no one above the third degree. Third degree Masons, even if they had not resigned before January 30, 1933, could now become members of the party. This amnesty caused former holders of higher degrees to hope that there would be an extension to cover them, but this was not to be.[86]

Hitler had a long memory. On May 25, 1939, Bormann issued Hitler's order that no party members were to use the Hotel Excelsior in Berlin. The proprietor was a high Mason and had once refused Hitler a room, saying the hotel was filled up when it was not.[87] In 1941 the question arose of whether former lodge members could be used to represent industrial firms connected with the Wehrmacht. Bormann, consistent with past practice, ruled no if they had more than a third degree or had held leading positions; he also had reservations against employing ordinary (below third degree) lodge members as such representatives.[88]

The Anthroposophical Society in Germany was founded by Rudolf Steiner (1861–1925) just before World War I. He was a most versatile and intellectually stimulating individual, and greatly influenced the organization of the Christian Community (*Christengemeinschaft*) in 1922. His unique educational theories led to the founding of the progressive Waldorf Schools. In Nazi eyes, the Anthroposophists were internationally minded and had close connections with foreign Free Masons, Jews, and pacifists. Steiner's pedagogy was built on an individualism that had nothing to do with the educational concepts of national socialism, and it was considered a threat to the state. The Anthroposophical Society was dissolved on November 1, 1935, and its property confiscated.[89]

The constant equation of Anthroposophists with Free Masons raised the question whether they too should benefit from the amnesty extended to lower degree Masons on April 4, 1938. Many thought so, but Rosenberg wanted them treated on a case-to-case basis.[90] Hitler finally ruled in July, 1939, that members of the Anthroposophy Society should be treated as Masons. He nevertheless thought that they were more subversive than Masons, for they infected more people with their ideas. If a street sweeper was an Anthroposophist, that did not matter, but Hitler did not want any former Anthroposophists in the party or in the Wehrmacht.[91]

After Hitler's ruling, Steiner's anthroposophical and pedagogical works continued to be banned, but his other noncontroversial books, some thirty in number (among them an edition of Goethe's *Naturwissenschaftliche Studien*) reappeared, and were still in book shops in 1941.[92] Furthermore, the banning of the Anthroposophical Society in 1935 did not immediately close the Waldorf schools. These were hit one after the other, the one in Stuttgart being one of the first to be closed in the spring of 1938, while those in Dresden and Hamburg-Wandsbek, both still functioning in February, 1940, were among the last to be closed.[93]

There were rumors that the Anthroposophists influenced Rudolf Hess to make his futile flight to Scotland on May 10, 1941, in order to bring about peace with England. As a police report admitted, there was no connection, but nevertheless the rumors persisted. They contributed to closing the Waldorf school in Dresden, and to the arrest of a number of pastors of the Christengemeinschaft.[94] On June 9, 1941, on direct orders of Hitler, Heydrich instituted his general police sweep against astrologers, occultists, Anthroposophists, and other such persons. As part of that action, the Christengemeinschaft, as a successor society of the Anthroposophy Society, was dissolved and forbidden July 25, 1941. Its property was to be set aside for liquidation.[95] Officially this ended the anthroposophy movement in Germany, but its immediate reemergence with the end of the war shows that it had only been temporarily driven underground.

Christian Science

Like other small religious groups, the Christian Scientists in the spring of 1933 sought an interview with Hitler in order to explain their standpoint and receive assurances from him. Count Helmuth von

Moltke was about to go to the United States, where he planned to explain to the mother church authorities in Boston that Christian Science and the national movement in Germany were thoroughly compatible. Before leaving he wanted an assurance that Christian Science members would not be discriminated against in employment. Hitler was too busy to see him.[96] On the other hand, after some of the Christian Science organizations had been dissolved in South Germany, the mother church asked Lord Astor to intercede, and Hitler received him on September 29, 1933.[97]

The nature and result of Lord Astor's intervention is not clear, but the Christian Scientists had no difficulties until 1935, when they, along with all other religious groups, began to receive more attention from state authorities. A 1935 report stressed the Christian Scientists' increased activity, and that they might become dangerous if their membership grew rapidly as a result of the conflict within the German Evangelical church. They were suspected of sending money to the United States, of practicing faith healing, and of teaching "the God-ordained dependence on America."[98] In view of the many charges against them, the German headquarters of the Christian Scientists sent a memorandum to the governor of Bavaria on September 1, 1936, to inform him about Christian Science. Because of the economic situation in Germany, the mother church was making a gift of all literature sent to the German church. This material was then sold, and the money used to build new churches or for charitable and other purposes. The mother church had ordered the strictest observance of the currency regulations, and in the interest of creating employment had set aside 200,000 marks for building a church in Germany.[99]

Such "enlightenment material" was hardly helpful. The highest party court on November 21, 1936, in considering the case of party member Rolf Hein, declared "the Christian Scientists to be one of the largest and most dangerous international sects, whose headquarters were in Boston, U.S.A." It charged that among the fourteen directors of the mother church, ten were Free Masons, some of high degree, and one was a Jew. Among directors in five German branch churches, five were Free Masons, three were Jews, and one was half Jewish. In the opinion of the court, no party member should be a Christian Scientist. But the court also noted: "Up to now the state has not intervened against this sect because of foreign policy considerations."[100]

The minister of the interior now began to harass the Christian Scientists. In an edict on December 12, 1936, he forbade them to take up collections in their churches and meetings or to sell books and periodicals in their services, lectures, or reading rooms.[101] Since the Christian Scientists were not a recognized religious body, they were not entitled to the privilege granted in the Collection Law which permitted official churches to take up offerings in services. Police were cautioned to enforce the ban.[102] However, international connections again came to their aid. Ambassador Ribbentrop reported that Lord

Halifax, Lord Lothian, Lord Astor, and the editor of the *Times* were all Christian Scientists, and to dissolve the society in Germany would have a bad effect in England.[103] On May 7, 1937, at the request of the directors of the mother church, Lord Lothian spoke with the Führer. He complained about the false charges levied against the Christian Scientists and asked that leading officials receive General Kundinger, head of the public relations bureau of the German Christian Scientists, in order to establish recognition of Christian Science as a Christian religion and church, and to correct false charges about its aims and organization. Hitler agreed to the meeting, and on June 5, 1937, the Ministry of Church Affairs authorized State Secretary Muhs to conduct the conversations.[104]

Whether it was a result of this intervention is not clear, but in November, 1937, Christian Scientists were allotted 20,000 marks monthly for the importation of books and periodicals, and the prohibition of sale of books and periodicals at services and reading rooms was lifted. The ban against taking up collections remained in effect.[105] The Ministry of Church Affairs also agreed to recognize Christian Science as a religion and church, but refused to grant it the rights of a public corporation. These rights were no longer being given, and besides, it was declared, religious freedom existed in the Third Reich.[106]

In March, 1938, Kundinger requested an interview with Hitler and submitted a long memorandum. He protested the continued restrictions in some places on collections and reading rooms, and the derogatory articles that had appeared in the *Völkischer Beobachter* on December 23, 1937, and February 27, 1938.[107] The charges were incorrect and attacked the honor of the church. He requested state protection of Christian Science, and, on the basis of Point 24 (support of positive Christianity) of the party program, the same recognition and the same freedom as were granted to other churches. Another long memorandum was submitted in July as an answer to articles in the German press.[108] Christian Science was a religion which, like national socialism, supported positive Christianity. Both sought to combat evil; one followed the political path, the other the religious.

If the Christian Scientists had achieved a certain recognition as a religion, although not as an official church body, they were nevertheless subject to attack from another quarter. As early as March 11, 1937, the official National Chamber of Doctors had submitted a report to the secret police, the "Practice of Healing through so-called Practitioners of Christian Science."[109] The report pointed out that deaths had occurred following such treatment and that Christian Scientists refused to recognize inherited or communicable diseases. Their objections were picked up in an eleven-page report prepared by the secret police that concluded that Christian Scientists could no longer be tolerated.[110] The police security headquarters on November 7, 1938, proposed to the Führer's deputy that party members be forbidden to belong to the Christian Science church. On February 1, 1939, the deputy promised to make a decision on this matter.[111]

Meanwhile the government got around to enacting a law which had been under consideration since June, 1934. On February 17, 1939, the Healing Practitioner Law was issued, which required all those who wanted to practice healing without being qualified as doctors to obtain special permission. A person who up to then had practiced healing as a profession could obtain permission to continue and would be known as *Heilpratiker*. This had to be done by April 1, 1939.[112]

On March 6, 1939, Hess finally made a ruling as to whether Christian Scientists could be members of the party. He decreed against it because of their strong international connections. Double membership would have to be ended at once, although there were no objections to Christian Scientists continuing as members of affiliated organizations.[113]

The combination of the new Healing Practitioner Law and the exclusion of Christian Scientists from the party led General Kundinger to seek an interview with Hess on March 27, 1939. When he received no answer, he requested an interview with State Secretary Lammers, in order to clear up misconceptions about Christian Science. The Christian Scientists were strongly opposed to registering as healing practitioners and refused to do so. They sought more precise recognition and guarantees as a religion and a church. Even if their churches were not recognized as public law corporations, they desired the right to hold religious services according to the church service book in their own or rented buildings, support the church through freewill offerings of the members and by collections at services, hold free public religious lectures, and pay for Christian Science literature sent from the publishing house in Boston, Massachusetts, instead of receiving it as a gift. Furthermore, they requested voluntary payment to practitioners by those seeking religious help, analogous to payments to pastors and doctors for services performed, and taxation of churches and practitioners according to general Land laws. The Christian Scientists would promise to support the state and not mix in church or political quarrels. Lammers refused to see Kundinger, saying he was sure these matters were in the province of the Ministry of Church Affairs and it would be better to seek an interview there.[114]

Whether Kundinger took his advice is uncertain. He had already talked with Secretary Muhs of the Church Ministry with no significant results. He did take the matter up with the Academy for German Law, and there is a notation from the head of the academy in September, 1939, which says, "the matter through a discussion with General Kundinger is settled for the time being."[115] How it was settled is not known.

The ban on membership in the party caused difficulties. On June 6, 1939, Bormann further ruled that while Christian Scientists could continue to be members of party-related organizations, they could not hold office in them.[116] Cases multiplied of party members who did not want to give up their Christian Science memberships. The party courts were ordered to proceed against them in regular fashion, and difficulties continued.[117] Some party members dropped their memberships in the German churches and supposedly transferred them to the mother church in

Boston, while others dropped their memberships but continued to attend services. In other cases their wives continued their Christian Scientist memberships. Such actions had kept Hess's staff from elaborating on the membership ban, but police were to watch individual party members who maintained their contacts with Christian Science.[118] Finally, on June 19, 1941, the highest party court in Munich ruled "that the ban on double membership included attendance at religious services of the Christian Scientists."[119]

Within a month all Christian Science churches were closed and their property confiscated. The police had already closed all Christian Science branch churches and reading rooms on June 6, 1941, as a result of Heydrich's order against occultists and faith healers.[120] When news of this action reached the German ambassador in Washington, he telegraphed to the German Foreign Office on July 10 that closing down the Christian Scientists right at the time of the Russian campaign would have a bad effect on public opinion in the United States.[121] But the final decision had been made. On July 14, 1941, on the basis of the presidential ordinance of February 28, 1933, against communist activity, the sect of Christian Scientists was dissolved and forbidden for the whole territory of the Reich, and its property confiscated.[122]

A month later, Heydrich drew up a summary exposition on the Christian Scientists and sent it to all state and district leaders. It gave a short history of the Christian Scientists in Germany, advanced reasons why they no longer could be tolerated, although "they had not been forbidden earlier because of foreign policy considerations during a time when the officials were trying to settle differences with England," and stated the measures which had been taken against them. There was a small elite group of Christian Scientists in Germany—among them the family of Count Moltke, chief of staff in 1914. "In this family, as is known, the horses were even cured through prayer." The widow of the poet Rainer Maria Rilke was also a member. The Christian Scientists' rejection of a personal God put them into opposition with other Christian churches; their denial of material existence put them into opposition to the National Socialist Weltanschauung. They had close connections with the United States and the democratic world, had no racial theories or teachings, included many Free Masons among their leaders, had close ties with anthroposophy and other occult circles, and constituted a real danger to the health of the nation. All told, it was a sect dangerous to the welfare of the state and had to be banned.[123] Such a postmortem justification was unusual for the Gestapo, and lends a mark of distinction to what proved to be only the temporary demise of Christian Science in Germany.

Church of Jesus Christ of Latter-Day Saints (Mormons)

The Mormons also had close connections with the United States, but they numbered only 11,306 in Germany in 1930.[124] The U.S. ambassador noted in his diary on July 31, 1934: "Hitler has not dissolved their organizations or expelled their active preachers. There are other than religious aspects to Hitler's let-up on the Mormons."[125] American-born Mormon missionaries' skill at basketball brought them favor in Nazi eyes, and four of them were asked to referee basketball games at the 1936 Olympic Games in Berlin. The Mormon ardor for genealogy also gave them a certain standing with Nazis.[126] In 1938 the editors of the *Völkischer Beobachter* drew a parallel between the ejection of the Mormons from Missouri and Illinois and the Jewish problem in Germany, thinking it might help enlighten opinion in the United States as to what Germany was up against.[127] With the start of the war, the Mormon headquarters in the United States withdrew all its missionaries from Europe. Some of the missionaries in Germany were to leave via Denmark and others via Holland, but when the latter country refused to receive them they all went through Denmark. Thomas E. McKay, European president of the Latter-Day Saints, was among the last of the 697 missionaries to return. On landing in New York in March, 1940, he expressed his regret at leaving Europe and stated: "The Mormons have never been molested in Germany. We could not ask for better treatment. The only way the Nazis have affected our work is that our Boy Scout movement has been curtailed by the Hitler Youth movement."[128] The withdrawal of the missionaries from Europe, however, saved the Mormons from many wartime difficulties. In Germany they were among the few small sects which were not banned and dissolved, being accorded a treatment similar to that enjoyed by the Methodists and Baptists.

The Mormons, like most Germans, supported the war effort, and some of their leaders were strong supporters of the Nazi party. One deacon of Jewish descent was sent to the Theresienstadt concentration camp; other partly Jewish members in Hamburg were left unmolested. Three Mormon youths were arrested for printing and distributing anti-Hitler leaflets during the war. One of them was executed, and the worried Hamburg Mormon church officials excommunicated him after his death. (In 1948 church officials in Salt Lake City posthumously reinstated him.) On the whole, Mormons suffered no special discrimination and persecution; they simply suffered war casualties and property losses as did all other Germans.[129]

After the war, German Mormons received special help from their brethren in the United States and other countries. The lure of sharing in this welfare aid led some Germans to convert to Mormonism, but most of these were later excommunicated when they neglected their church memberships.[130] The Mormons achieved the status of a "registered association" (*Eingetragener Verein*) in December, 1951, and two years later the much sought-after recognition as a corporation under public law.[131] Their church property was thus made exempt from taxation, and they have since enjoyed the benefits accorded to such legally recognized church bodies in Germany. Membership underwent a rapid postwar growth, but began to slow down in the late 1960s. The increase was in no small part due to the numerous missionaries sent from abroad.[132] While before World War II Mormonism was confined almost entirely to the largest cities, its work today has spread to small cities as well. The church has undergone administrative reorganization, and higher church bodies peculiar to the structure of the Church of Jesus Christ of Latter-Day Saints have been established. Today the church in Germany ranks ninth among the Mormon churches in the countries of the world, but still has a membership of only about 25,000.[133]

Germanic-Nordic Religious Groups

In the turmoil and enthusiasm that prevailed in Germany as Hitler took over, the various Germanic religious groups were faced with the problem of what their position would be in the new Reich.[134] Many of those who still had some concern for Christianity found their way into the ranks of the German Christians. They tended to join certain splinter groups as that movement began to disintegrate following the Sportspalast scandal of November, 1933.[135] Those groups which were opposed to Christianity and eager to build a truly Germanic Nordic religion met at Eisenach July 29–30, 1933. Here they formed the Working Association of the German Faith Movement, largely through the efforts of Prof. Jakob Wilhelm Hauer of the University of Tübingen.[136] He had served as a missionary in India, and through his study of Indian religions had become disillusioned with Christianity's absolutist claims. After study at Oxford he turned to teaching religious history, particularly the history of Indian religions. Hauer was elected chairman of the new association and was aided by a directorate of prominent men. Among them was Count Ernst Reventlow, author of numerous historical works, a member of the Reichstag since 1924, and a member of the National Socialist party since 1927.[137]

Hauer was able not only to persuade the various Germanic groups to join the association, but also the League of Free Religious Congregations with its 70,000 members. The latter was a well-established organization of freethinkers dating back to 1859, which had many Marxists among its members and actually had nothing much in common with the Germanic religious groups. They sought a certain protection under Hauer's wings and actually elected him chairman of their own confederation the following September.

The Working Association of the German Faith Movement was an amorphous sort of organization, and at a meeting in May, 1934, at Scharzfeld, an attempt was made to strengthen and centralize it. The name was now changed to "German Faith Movement," the directory was abolished, and Hauer became sole Führer of the new body, with Reventlow as deputy Führer. Not all groups went along with the changes and some withdrew. Among these were most of the freethinkers. They later reconstituted themselves, only to be banned at the end of 1934. They then formed a new organization, but fell back to an old name, calling it the "People's Church" (*Deutsche Volkskirche*). It too was dissolved by the police in 1936. All that was left to the old Freethinkers' Association was freedom to continue their burial insurance program.[138]

The German Faith Movement under Hauer now began to assert

itself. It demanded the introduction of German Faith instruction in the schools, but first books and curricula had to be worked out, which was never accomplished. A large-scale membership and propaganda campaign was launched in February, 1935, after the Saar plebiscite. As many as sixty meetings were scheduled in a week, and on April 26, 1935, a big meeting was held in the Sportspalast in Berlin at which both Hauer and Reventlow spoke. This activity alarmed the churches, which started a counteroffensive against the neopaganism threatening to engulf the nation.[139] In large part, what they wanted to proclaim against Hitler they shouted at Hauer; it was still safe to be against paganism.

The activity of the German Faith Movement no doubt added to the religious turmoil caused by the campaign against confessional schools and the other church measures which the government launched in the summer of 1935. Church peace was needed, and achieving it became the great task of Minister Kerrl and the new Ministry of Church Affairs. On August 15, 1935, the secret police headquarters in Berlin wrote to Hauer, asking him as leader of the German Faith Movement to stop all public propaganda and restrict his activity to closed membership meetings until an expected fundamental regulation was issued by the Ministry of Church Affairs.[140] In November, 1935, the German Faith Movement was permitted to have guests at meetings by written invitation, but open meetings were still forbidden.[141] In the same month, police in Regensburg and Düsseldorf forbade the German Faith Movement to present Walter Knickendorff's choral work, "Trotz der Sünde," because it injured the feelings of many Germans.[142]

The propaganda campaign of 1935 had brought to the fore many new speakers for the German Faith groups. Many of them were more radical than Hauer and gave a different thrust to the movement. They concentrated on attacking Christianity and the churches, while Hauer sought instead to create a real Nordic Germanic faith.[143] Anti-Christian propaganda, however, was easier and more immediately successful, and the result was that Hauer lost control of the German Faith Movement. Heydrich, who favored the tactics of the more radical elements, brought pressure to bear and in 1936 forced both Reventlow and Hauer to resign their leadership.[144] Many defections followed, and the influence of the Faith Movement declined. In 1938 the *Deutsche Glaubensbewegung* changed its name to "Combat Ring for German Faith" (*Kampfring Deutscher Glaube*). In December, 1938, a splinter group established itself as the "National Ring for God-believing Germans" (*Reichsring der gottgläubigen Deutschen*).[145] The force of the movements was spent, although they continued to exist throughout the war. In April, 1941, National Socialist party headquarters specifically ruled that in view of the directive of the Führer's deputy to observe neutrality in all religious questions, the party should not lend its support to the Reichsring der gottgläubigen Deutschen.[146]

Under the guise of general religious toleration, the party and state permitted the German Faith Movement to carry on. Although party and state seemingly encouraged it at times, they never gave it their full support. The ban of 1935 on open meetings remained.[147] As the party more or less dropped the German Christians after the Sportspalast scandal of 1933, so they also dropped the German Faith Movement in 1936 when the term "God believing" was introduced. An individual could be in good standing with the party whether or not he was a member of any church or German-Nordic Faith group. The ban on active participation by party leaders in religious organizations diminished the influence of the folk-religious groups on the party and its organizations. The yearly police report for 1938 noted a remarkable decline in the activity of these religious groups.[148] Hitler did not have a high opinion of the Nordic groups and never lent them his personal support. In 1941 he stated: "It seems to me that nothing would be more foolish than to reestablish the worship of Woden. Our old mythology had ceased to be viable when Christianity implanted itself."[149]

Not all Germanic groups were spared by the Nazis. On May 31, 1937, the German People's Church; Dinter Movement (*Deutsche Volkskirche; Dinterbewegung*) and the *Wartburghaus Gwb H,* Bad Homburg, were dissolved. The police gave no reason for the dissolution, but they did leave the property to the organizations to be liquidated.[150] The Deutsche Volkskirche; Dinterbewegung was a transformation of the Spiritual Christian Religious Association founded by Dr. Arthur Dinter in 1927, which sought to establish Christianity on a Nordic basis. He had, however, fallen into party disgrace and a similar fate was doled out to his movement.

In 1933 the Tannenbergbund of General Ludendorff and his wife Mathilde was dissolved.[151] Yet the Ludendorffs had a publishing company and managed to keep in touch with their followers. In October, 1934, the Bavarian police were ordered to watch their meetings, and a year later meetings of the Ludendorff publishing company (*Verlag*) were forbidden for the time being. On July 27, 1936, the national political police commander forbade former members of the Tannenbergbund or former speakers of the Ludendorff Verlag to address meetings.[152] Early in 1937 the Ludendorffs reorganized their followers into the Union for German Perception of God (*Bund für Deutsche Gotterkenntnis*). The minister of the interior, on April 23, 1937, ordered that this union could have closed meetings like any of the other German religious associations. The ban against certain speakers was lifted, and a long list of authorized speakers was sent out. They were to be permitted to conduct burial services at church and communal cemeteries as long as they did not deride other religious groups.[153] The Ludendorffs were further recognized when on May 8, 1937, the minister of the interior ordered that their followers could officially register their religion as "*Deutsche Gotterkenntnis (Haus Ludendorff)*," which could be shortened to "*Gotterkenntnis (L)*."[154]

At the time of Ludendorff's death on December 20, 1937, his religious organization had achieved official status, and the papers eulogized him as one of Germany's great men.[155] His wife continued her religious activity, and after the war the Ludendorff movement was reor-

ganized, this time as the *Bund für Gotterkenntnis*.[156] It had a small
membership of 5,000–6,000, but on May 25, 1961, the federal government banned the organization and its related publishing company *Hohe
Warte* because of their anti-Semitic, anti-Christian, and authoritarian
doctrines. The government's action, later upheld by the courts, was
under Article 9 of the constitution, which states that associations "which
are directed against the constitutional order and the concept of international understanding are prohibited."[157]

The Postwar Period

It has not been possible to detail the history of all the sects and
similar organizations during the Hitler period. Many questions remain as
to what happened to their members and to confiscated property. With
the exception of the Jehovah's Witnesses, apparently few members of
these small groups were sent to concentration camps. One thing, however, is clear—while many sects were dissolved, they were not ended.
Except for the Nordic groups, which ran into difficulty under the Allied
denazification measures, most soon reappeared in the postwar years.
They prospered as never before. The masses were seeking a new orientation and often the sects promised more than the older religious denominations. Many sought the contacts and fellowship which the
smaller groups offered.

Those groups with foreign connections received help and greatly
needed supplies from their coreligionists abroad. The Mormons and
others resumed active missionary campaigns. The Jehovah's Witnesses,
in spite of restrictions in East Germany, have made rapid gains, and they
were estimated in 1949 to have between 100,000 and 300,000 members.[158] Kurt Hutten, who more than any other person has made the
study of the sects in Germany his special province, writes:

> After the winter numbness of 1933–45, there is to be observed in recent
> years a flowering of the sects. Yes, it is not just a flowering, but a luxuriant
> growth. All the "old" sects are back. Many more have been added, often
> one-man undertakings and temporary foundations which it hardly pays to
> register. But nevertheless they find believers and contribute to increasing the
> religious jumble and undermine the Christian community. Church statistics
> show a growing number of withdrawals to the sects. And also special asso-
> ciations have been formed within the churches that go their own way with-
> out withdrawing from the churches. And so the church from without and
> within is being threatened by a sectarian spirit.[159]

The antifascist and pro-civil rights emphasis in the postwar period
has done much to contribute to the revival and growth of sectarianism,
and the sects are drawing more scholarly attention than formerly. Hutten's volume on the leading sects in Germany, first published in 1950,
has repeatedly been revised and expanded, until the eleventh edition
of 1968 comprises 832 pages.[160] That a book like this would sell
thousands of copies reflects the interest in the subject. The Lutheran

church has also established a commission to edit a handbook on Free churches and sects,[161] and is issuing a looseleaf volume, adding studies as they are completed, which will both give a brief synopsis of their history and beliefs and state the position of the Lutheran church in regard to them. One can only conclude that in spite of Hitler's efforts, or maybe because of them, religious diversity is greater in Germany than ever before.

EPILOGUE

The Protestant Churches in Postwar Germany

The Reestablishment of the Historic Land Churches

The chaos confronting the churches at the end of the war is hard to imagine and impossible to describe. Hundreds of church buildings, parish houses, parsonages, and schools had been destroyed. Congregations were disrupted through evacuation and flight, and hordes of refugees flooded the country. Catholics and Protestants were intermingled to an unprecedented degree; the need to minister to this new diaspora laid heavy burdens on both churches. Catholics were able to hold their services in Protestant churches, and the reverse was also true.[1] A degree of ecumenism had been brought about by common antagonism to Nazi policies, and this was furthered by the overwhelming problems which faced defeated Germany. There were shortages of every kind. For many months no Bibles, catechisms, song books, or prayer books had been printed, and with the loss of much material in the bombing raids it was frequently difficult even to conduct divine services. But in some areas, especially in rural regions, church buildings still stood, pastors were at hand, and the work of the churches could go on as before.

The elimination of a central German government, the partition of the country into four occupation zones, and the very gradual reestablishment of local and state governments naturally affected the churches. State and Land church boundaries were not coterminous, which complicated raising necessary finances. The postal and transportation systems were at first virtually nonexistent, which made it difficult for the churches to establish contact with each other. It was essential to reestablish a functioning church government, for in Germany (much more than in the United States, for example) the local congregations were, as their history shows, closely dependent upon the higher church bodies. This problem was not so acute for Catholics, for as in 1918–19, the hierarchy remained intact, and there had been no disruption of church government. Among the Protestants, however, the old established church administrative bodies had been subverted by the National Socialists. Government-dominated finance sections had in many areas come to exercise church powers, and regular church synods had ceased to be held. During the Kirchenkampf, when in general the churches resisted efforts to create a single government-controlled church, the traditional church governing bodies were disrupted.

Protestants were confronted by three great tasks: (1) the reestablishment of some sort of regional church organization; (2) the formation of a national church body and the renewal of ties with the ecumenical church world; and (3) the reconstitution of church organizations, especially inner and foreign missions. Carrying forward these tasks had to be done simultaneously, for each was dependent on the other; indeed, solving a difficulty on one level helped to advance the solutions on another.

The churches were relatively free of political interference. The German authorities, where they existed, were not inclined to intervene, and the occupying powers also held the reins lightly in the religious field. The churches were not unaffected by occupation regulations, but the resistance they had offered to Hitler's policies was known abroad. Clergy, especially the Catholic clergy, were held to be about the only anti-Nazis in Germany. Nevertheless, the churches did not have a tabula rasa on which to build; their heritage from the past was both an encumbrance and a source of strength. This fact had been brought home in many ways during the Kirchenkampf, when Hitler and his minions had tried to bring about revolutionary changes. The question was how much of the past to hold on to in the troubled years ahead. Opinions differed as to what lessons were to be drawn from the recent struggle and the experiences of the Confessing church. Compromises had to be made. In the end the road to the New Jerusalem, which everyone wanted to construct, was largely built with well-worn paving blocks from the past.

With the total destruction of the state of Prussia and the violation of other former state and provincial boundaries by the creation of occupation zones, it might seemingly have been logical to organize the Protestant churches on a new territorial basis. Napoleon had tried it when he introduced the new departments to France. But the occupation zones were not a final political settlement, and basing church organization on them would have meant a delay of unspecified duration before the churches could put their own houses in order. Then too, the intact churches which had maintained themselves throughout the Hitler period continued to function. To have attempted to reorganize them—which would have been resisted in any case—would only have added to the disorder. The obvious and sensible thing was to attempt to reestablish the old church governments as soon as possible. This was done, although the methods varied from church to church. The men in charge of the old official church offices, many of them German Christians, were generally discredited and gave up their positions without resistance. Thanks to the Confessing church, there were responsible and able men to take over. This is in contrast to the schools, where many teachers were removed by denazification procedures. It was not long before the old established churches, with territorial boundaries going back to 1815, were again functioning.

Constitutional alterations, in some cases extending to the drafting of
an entirely new church constitution, formed a task that went on for
some years. Schleswig-Holstein reinstated its two bishoprics.[2] In Hesse
and Nassau, where the church union created in 1933 had never become stable, negotiations extending into 1949 were necessary before a
constitution was finally adopted. Martin Niemöller had been chosen to
head this church body in 1947, and it was from this position that he
carried out his many activities in the church at large.[3]

In one notable respect the churches profited from the sad experience of 1933, when suffrage in church elections for all adult baptized
members proved disastrous. The day when baptism, payment of church
taxes, and residence were sufficient to give a person the right to vote in
church elections is past. Today it is generally recognized that membership in a church normally results from baptism, and if a person moves
from one place to another he becomes a member of the church in his
new home. Within a year he can declare that he would like to join
another church in his district. Various churches have accepted this standard regulation, which is not without significance in regard to church
taxes.[4] During the Nazi period the churches had found it necessary to
limit voting in church elections to active and participating members.
Now provisions vary in the churches, but usually a person must personally ask to be put on the voting list and declare he wants to help elect
people who have the interests of the church at heart. He must be
twenty-one years of age, pay church taxes, and be permitted to participate in the Lord's Supper. People who refuse to be married in the
church, have their children baptized, or send them to instruction cannot
vote. There are also rather high qualifications of active participation in
church affairs for officers. The number of women elected to church
councils has steadily risen, the average increasing from approximately
5 percent in 1955 to 20 percent in 1973.[5] In practice, however, it is not
so much a matter of electing as of soliciting persons to fill congregational offices.

The Evangelical church has also adopted an easier procedure for
withdrawals from membership. Oral or written requests are to be made
at the registrar's office in one's place of residence, and go into effect a
month later. Within this period the churches have a right to counsel
with the person withdrawing; payment of church taxes is cancelled at
the end of the month in which the withdrawal becomes valid. Withdrawals can likewise be cancelled in a month.[6]

The Church of the Old Prussian Union, the largest of the former
church bodies, was unable to reestablish itself within its old boundaries. With the loss of the territories east of the Oder-Neisse line to
Poland and Russia, the old provincial churches of East Prussia, West
Prussia, and Posen, and a large part of the provincial churches of
Pomerania, Silesia, and Brandenburg, were no longer in Germany. The
Old Prussian Union was left with six member churches. Of these, the
former provincial churches of Westphalia and Rhineland in West Germany constituted themselves as separate Land churches and drew up

new constitutions. The four eastern provincial churches (Berlin-Brandenburg, Pomerania [later Greifswald], Silesia [later Görlitz] and the Province of Saxony) did the same. Although the Church of the Old Prussian Union lost its strong centralized character, it was able to maintain certain ties among its former members. This new relationship was first set forth in an agreement reached at Treysa in August, 1945, by the member churches, and reinforced in a constitution adopted in 1950.[7] In 1953 the venerated name of "*Altpreussiche Union*" had to be abandoned because the USSR as an occupying power insisted that "Prussia" must in no way be recognized. It is now called the "Evangelical Church of the Union" (*Evangelische Kirche der Union*). In 1960 the Land church of Anhalt, one of the historic churches of the Soviet zone, joined the union. The constitution provided for regular synod meetings and a directing council. About half of the Evangelical Church of the Union, as established in 1950, was in East Germany and half in West Germany.[8]

It was the administrators of all these reconstituted Land churches who set the churches functioning again. They were the ones who had to see about finances, paying pensions, reconstructing church buildings and parsonages, taking care of refugees, placing the many clergy who came from the east, finding support for church organizations and social services, and seeing that the multitude of other activities of any large church body were reactivated. Perhaps some of these were peripheral to the main function of the church, that of preaching the gospel, as Hitler liked to put it, "to the saving of souls," but nevertheless they were necessary if the church was to continue to play a significant role in the life of the German people.

There was little to recommend a radical reorganization. Reaching agreement would take time, and the need for church services of all kinds was urgent. There was no time for extended controversy when the need to bind up the wounds of the spirit was so pressing. Some reconstruction was inevitable, especially in view of the physical changes in Germany, but a desire to retrieve what was available from the past was pervasive and compelling.

These Land churches broke no new paths, and it is easy to charge that everything remained as it had been (*Alles blieb beim alten*). But considering the situation, tribute might well be paid to those who put the churches into action again so quickly. They did try to pour new spirit into traditional institutions, and if they did not always succeed it was not entirely their fault. The churches, as in the past, were a part of the total German setting.

It was not only the Land churches and the Catholic church which had to reorganize in the postwar period. It should be repeated that the Free churches and sects revived and have been particularly active in postwar Germany. They found a fertile field in which to carry on their evangelical work among the many displaced persons who sought new church homes.

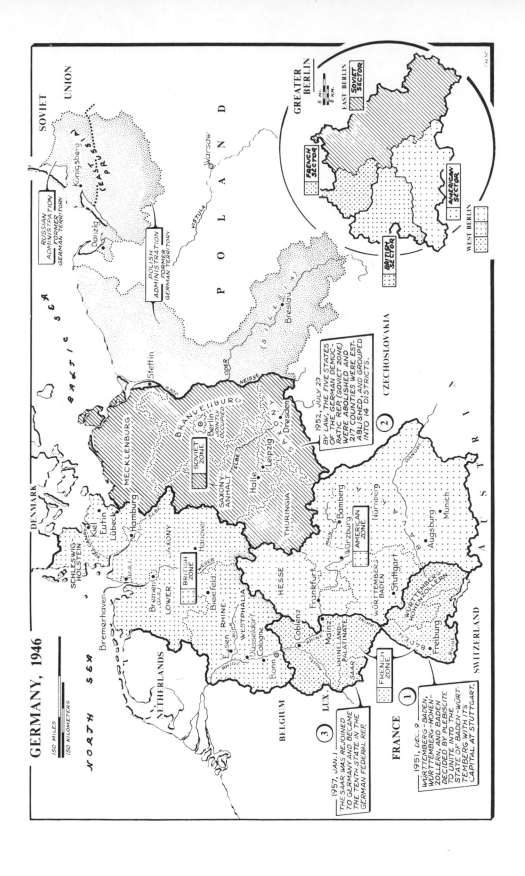

GERMANY, 1946

150 MILES
150 KILOMETERS

NORTH SEA

BALTIC SEA

DENMARK

NETHERLANDS

BELGIUM

LUX.

FRANCE

SWITZERLAND

AUSTRIA

CZECHOSLOVAKIA

POLAND

SOVIET UNION

U.S.S.R.

Königsberg

Danzig

Warsaw

VISTULA

ODER

NEISSE

Breslau

(S I L E S I A)

Stettin

Kiel

Eutin

Lübeck

Hamburg

Bremerhaven

Bremen (U.S.)

Hanover

Bielefeld

Düsseldorf

Cologne

Bonn

Essen

Coblenz

Mainz

Saar

Freiburg

Stuttgart

Frankfurt

Würzburg

Bamberg

Nürnberg

Augsburg

Munich

Leipzig

Halle

Dresden

Berlin JOINTLY OCCUPIED

SCHLESWIG-HOLSTEIN

MECKLENBURG

LOWER-RHINE

WESTPHALIA

HESSE

RHINELAND-PALATINATE

WÜRTTEMBERG-BADEN

WÜRTTEMBERG-HOHENZOLLERN

BADEN

SAXONY

BRANDENBURG

SAXONY-ANHALT

THURINGIA

SAXONY

KIEL CANAL

ELBE

WESER

RHINE

MOSELLE

RHINE

DANUBE

MAIN

RHINE

ELBE

SOVIET ZONE

BRITISH ZONE

AMERICAN ZONE

FRENCH ZONE

RUSSIAN ADMINISTRATION FORMER GERMAN TERRITORY

POLISH ADMINISTRATION FORMER GERMAN TERRITORY

GREATER BERLIN

EAST BERLIN

SOVIET SECTOR

FRENCH SECTOR

BRITISH SECTOR

AMERICAN SECTOR

WEST BERLIN

5 MI.
5 KM.

① 1951, DEC. 9
WÜRTTEMBERG-BADEN, WÜRTTEMBERG-HOHEN-ZOLLERN, AND BADEN DECIDED BY PLEBISCITE TO UNITE INTO THE STATE OF BADEN-WÜRT-TEMBERG WITH ITS CAPITAL AT STUTTGART.

② 1952, JULY 23
BY LAW, THE FIVE STATES OF THE GERMAN DEMOC-RATIC REP. (SOVIET ZONE) WERE ABOLISHED AND 217 COUNTIES WERE EST-ABLISHED, AND GROUPED INTO 14 DISTRICTS.

③ 1957, JAN. 1
THE SAAR WAS REJOINED TO GERMANY AND BECAME THE TENTH STATE IN THE GERMAN FEDERAL REP.

The Provisional Council for the Evangelical Church in Germany

The leaders of the Land churches undertook to establish greater unity among the Protestants within Germany and in the world at large. The desire for a more perfect union was there, but how was it to be implemented? Past differences, not least among them the disputes that had always plagued the Confessing church, remained, but so too did a basic loyalty to the Confessing church and what it had stood for. This loyalty no doubt was sincerely felt by most church leaders and active laity. Yet it must be noted that not to have held to the Confessing church at this time would have indicated a failure to renounce Hitler and all his works. Nothing did more to raise the status of the Confessing church than did the victories of Allied arms. It was not always easy for the men who had carried the burden of the struggle against Hitler's church policies to welcome the former "men of the middle" and even some German Christians into their fold. There was also resentment on the other side against the leadership of the brotherhood councils and their assumption that they spoke for the whole German church. But there was remarkably little inclination on either side to cast stones, and a real willingness to do penance along with the repentant brother.

The desire to bring about more unity and cooperation among German churches was not new. Almost exactly one hundred years before, the territorial churches of Germany had joined in the Eisenach Conference, and again after World War I had established a loose church confederation. The Nazi attempt to establish a more united church in 1933 had brought home to all the dangers of too centralized an institution. To create more unity and at the same time maintain local autonomy and decentralized church administration would not be easy. But the very existence of the Confessing church had shown that it was possible. There had been loyalty to a common central ideal and end in the Confessing church but great diversity of church government, confessional groupings, and practices. This combination of a shared ideal and diverse local practices, along with the statement of Barmen, was an important heritage from the Confessing church, and it was taken over in establishing the new national church organization. The active leaders of the Confessing church were also leaders in this postwar task.

In the last years of the war Bishop Wurm of Württemberg had undertaken to organize a movement to bring about greater unity among the Protestant churches.[9] It was only logical that he, as chairman of the council which had been appointed to further this work, should take the initiative. At the end of June, 1945, after visits to fellow churchmen which took him as far north as the Bethel Institutions in Bielefeld, he issued a call to the heads of the various church governments to meet at the end of August in a conference at Treysa, near Kassel, Here there was an inner mission institution which was still capable of hosting a meeting. This conference was in fact an expanded version of the Church Leaders' Conference established by the Reich Church Committee in 1936.[10]

By this time Martin Niemöller, who had been detained by American forces in Italy following his liberation from Dachau, had returned to Germany. He now was responsible for calling a meeting at Frankfurt/Main of the Reich Brotherhood Council, which had been moribund but still technically had a position of leadership in the Confessing church. With Karl Barth in attendance, the council drew up, a week before the Treysa meeting, a statement to the forthcoming conference in which it upheld the authority of the brotherhood councils and of the theological declaration adopted at Barmen in 1934.[11]

The Reich Brotherhood Council represented one wing of the Confessing church; another was represented by the Council of the Evangelical Lutheran Church of Germany. It met at the call of Bishop Meiser of the Bavarian Land church and also assembled at Treysa on August 25, 1945, just before the meeting called by Bishop Wurm. In their statement the Lutheran churches expressed their willingness to unite in a confederation with the Reformed and United churches, but also affirmed their determination to establish a united Lutheran church of Germany and to assert its position in the confederation. Bishop Wurm was not pleased with this action, and was later to keep his Württemberg church out of the United Lutheran church. When Wurm told the assembled Lutheran leaders that the Reich Brotherhood Council had again come to life, some were inclined to leave.[12] Calmer heads prevailed, but it was clear it would take considerable negotiation to subdue the differences between the Lutheran Land churches and the Reich Brotherhood Council, which found its strongest support in the Reformed and United churches.

On August 27, representatives of the Committee for Church Unity, of the Reich Brotherhood Council and of most of the Land churches finally met at Treysa. Pastor Bodelschwingh held the opening religious services and throughout the conference exerted a moderating influence. Bishop Wurm spoke, as did Martin Niemöller as the representative of the Reich Brotherhood Council. The negotiations were difficult, and Wurm comments that he had never before taken part in a conference where he offered so many silent prayers.[13] In the end the desire for some kind of a church union prevailed, and a suggestion Bishop Wurm made in his opening address was adopted:

> As a result of our conference I envision the establishment of a provisional council, in which, as in the one of November, 1934, the Land churches and the brotherhood councils will be able to work together in order to prepare a new bond (*Zusammenschluss*) among the Land churches in Germany, and until the adoption of a new constitution will take over leadership within Germany and will represent before the outside world the Evangelical Christians of Germany.[14]

The conference named a twelve-member Provisional Council headed by Bishop Wurm, with Martin Niemöller as vice-chairman.[15] It was made up of six men from Lutheran churches, four from United, and two from Reformed. The Reich Brotherhood Council turned over its governing functions to this Provisional Council for the duration of its existence.[16]

The conference adopted few directives. It recognized the impossibility of returning to the constitutions of 1922 or 1933, and adopted a new name. The "Evangelical Church in Germany" (*Evangelische Kirche in Deutschland* [EKD]) replaced the "German Evangelical Church" (DEK). A carefully drawn statement recognized the common efforts made in the Kirchenkampf and managed to pay tribute to various groups.

> The Evangelical Church in Germany (EKD), in defense against the false doctrines of the times and in the struggle against a state-church centralism, was led to a church-based inner unity that extends beyond that of the German Evangelical Church Confederation of 1922. The unity was first manifest in the Confessing synods of Barmen, Dahlem, and Augsburg. It was furthered by the activity of the Church Unification Work and by the Church Leaders' Conference of the Land churches.[17]

A "Word to the Congregations" not only spoke of repentance but also sought to bring comfort and encouragement. "Christ wants to refresh the worried and burdened. He remains our Saviour. No hell is so deep that God's hand does not extend into it."[18]

The conference took another very practical and necessary step. It founded a centrally directed relief organization for all the Evangelical churches (*Hilfswerk der Evangelischen Kirche in Deutschland*).[19] Eugen Gerstenmaier, a trained theologian from Württemberg, was placed in charge. He had gained much administrative experience while serving in the foreign office of the German Evangelical church and in the government. Having been involved in the July, 1944, plot against Hitler, he was imprisoned and narrowly missed being executed. This gave him prestige, and he was able to establish good relations with churches abroad. Relief centers were founded in the various Land churches. The Hilfswerk distributed the tons of food and clothing which the churches abroad—notably in the United States, Switzerland, and Sweden—sent to Germany, and helped to reestablish many churches by the distribution of Bibles, song books, and other materials. It also did much to assist congregations in other ways. This centralized relief activity served as an important precedent for the later unification of the inner mission institutions of the various Land churches.[20]

The tasks confronting the Provisional Council were enormous, and might well have led anyone to despair. Yet there were also moments of encouragement and many acts of support. None meant more than the willingness of the Provisional Committee of the future World Council of Churches to renew contacts with the German churches. The Provisional Council had scheduled its second meeting for October 18–19, at Stuttgart. A delegation from the World Council of Churches made an unexpected visit to Germany and arranged a meeting with the Provisional Council.[21] Not only were old personal friendships renewed, but an understanding was reached on the resumption of ecumenical activity by the German churches. At this meeting the Provisional Council issued statements, not only to the World Council of Churches but also to "The Christians in Other Lands." Each was an acknowledgment of wrongs committed and a public statement of repentance. The following excerpt from the declaration to the World Council of Churches is often reprinted as the "Stuttgart Declaration of Guilt."

> We are all the more thankful for this visit, as we with our people (*Volk*) know ourselves to be not only in a community of suffering, but also in a solidarity of guilt. With great anguish we state: Through us inestimable suffering was inflicted on many peoples and lands. What we have often witnessed before our congregations we now declare in the name of the whole church: Indeed we have fought for long years in the name of Jesus Christ against the spirit that found horrible expression in the National Socialist regime of force, but we charge ourselves for not having borne testimony with greater courage, prayed more conscientiously, believed more joyously, and loved more ardently.[22]

The statement aroused much attention, both abroad and within Germany. It brought the whole question of war guilt to the fore and raised the vexed problem of individual and collective guilt. It was a matter which weighed heavily upon the conscience of many Germans, and the philosopher Karl Jaspers turned his attention to it in special lectures at the University of Heidelberg in the winter semester of 1945–46. He entitled them "The Question of Guilt" (*Die Schuldfrage*), and in them he classified guilt into various categories—criminal, political, moral, and metaphysical guilt growing out of the relationship of one person to another. He held that there was a political responsibility and guilt for the Hitler era which all Germans shared as members of the German state. Moral guilt, however, was always an individual matter, and could not be identified with a collectivity. It was necessary for the individual to free himself from this moral guilt by making restitution wherever possible and doing penance. How he did this was again an individual matter. Jaspers made no direct reference to the Stuttgart Declaration, nor did he refer to acts of commission or omission on the part of either the Protestant or the Catholic churches.[23]

The Stuttgart Declaration was not meant to be a political statement, but rather a religious confession of penance addressed by Christians to other Christians, asking for forgiveness. In the long run, this was how it came to be accepted. If there was to be no repentance and forgiveness, then Christianity and the churches held no hope for the future. The Stuttgart Declaration did not stand alone; there were other statements of repentance by church leaders and by Land churches.[24] From the time of the Stuttgart meeting, the Evangelical Church in Germany was again a part of the ecumenical movement, sharing its burdens but above all strengthened by its help and support.

The Constitution of the Evangelical Church in Germany

While the Reich Brotherhood Council had turned over its governing functions to the Provisional Council, it did not cease its activity. In March, 1946, and again in January, 1947, it issued statements suggesting how the Evangelical church should be organized. The Lutheran

Council set about drawing up a constitution for the United Evangelical Lutheran Church of Germany (Vereinigte Evangelisch-Lutherische Kirche Deutschlands [VELKD]). Behind the attempt to form a distinct Lutheran church entity, was, as in the 1930s, the desire to prevent Niemöller and his circle from dominating the whole German church.[25] The Provisional Council, burdened with its many administrative tasks, did not have much time to spend in drafting constitutions. Nevertheless, on June 24, 1947, it established regulations for a second church conference.[26] With this gathering in the offing, Pastor Asmussen, who had played such a leading role during the Kirchenkampf, called a meeting of those Lutheran churches which did not want to go along with the Lutheran Council's United Evangelical Lutheran church. These were, aside from the Lutheran churches of Württemberg, Oldenburg, and Eutin, mostly predominantly Lutheran provincial churches of the Old Prussian Union. This group came to be called "the Detmold Circle" (*Detmolder Kreis*), and constituted a sort of third force along with the Reich Brotherhood Council and the Lutheran Council.[27]

The second church conference called by the Provisional Council met at Treysa June 5–6, 1947. Here, after difficult negotiations, many basic decisions were made.[28] The Barmen declaration was to be recognized, and the Lutheran Council stated that the United Evangelical Lutheran church wished to work with the other Evangelical churches in a United Evangelical Church in Germany. No solution was reached as to communion fellowship between Lutherans and Reformed. The conference authorized the appointment of a three-member committee to draw up a constitution. Using as a basis a draft submitted by the Reich Brotherhood Council, this committee proceeded to formulate a church constitution.[29] It was submitted to the Provisional Council, and when the Lutherans had reached the point that the conclusion of their constitution was also assured, the council called another church conference to meet at Eisenach in the Russian zone on June 10–13, 1948, to take final action. The introduction of the currency reform in the western zones a few weeks before threatened to postpone the meeting, but the divisive effects of that measure, which soon led to the establishment of the Federal Republic of Germany and the German Democratic Republic, were not yet manifest. In comparison to later years, Germany was still a unit and the delegates could travel freely. At the end of the conference the Russian occupation authorities held a reception in the Wartburg Hotel, at which a Russian general and Bishop Wurm exchanged friendly greetings.[30]

There were moments of difficulty at the conference, but in the end the constitution was approved unanimously. Nothing aroused greater diversity of opinion than the question whether the new body was a "church" or a "church confederation." The German word *Kirche* has all kinds of historic and legalistic connotations. A common confession is usually considered a sine qua non for a church. Obviously the new church body was not a Kirche in this narrow sense, for the Lutheran, Reformed, and United confessions were specifically recognized. Yet at the same time the churches did hold many doctrines and practices in common; enough in the eyes of many to justify calling them collectively a Kirche. Inevitably both views of the issue found expression in the document; the organization is referred to both as "church" and as "confederation," and Germans still are academically divided on the issue.[31] Bishop Wurm reached a practical conclusion and held: "It is a church and will constantly become more so in the future" (*Sie ist Kirche und wird immer mehr Kirche werden*).[32]

All the differences and conflicts of the preceding months were honestly recognized and compromised in the first article, no doubt the most important provision of the document. The preamble had referred to adherence to the historic church confessions, and then Article 1 states:

> The Evangelical Church in Germany is a confederation (*Bund*) of Lutheran, Reformed, and United churches. It honors the confessional basis of the member churches and congregations and gives assurance that they will not be disturbed in doctrine, church life, and administration.
>
> In the Evangelical Church in Germany the existing community of German Evangelical Christians is made manifest. Along with its member churches, the Evangelical Church in Germany confirms the decisions made at the Confessing synod of Barmen. It pledges itself as Confessing church to further the experiences gained in the Kirchenkampf in respect to the nature, commission, and governance of the church. It calls upon the member churches to listen to the witness of the brethren. It will help them, when called upon, in a common defense against church-disrupting false doctrine.[33]

It should be noted that the article refers to "member churches" (*Gliedkirchen*), and not, as was formerly customary, to Land churches. This reference, as well as those to Barmen and to the activity of the Confessing church in the Kirchenkampf, were particularly welcome to the Reich Brotherhood Council circle, while the Lutherans were pleased by the statement about the church being a confederation and by the recognition of the confessional basis of the different churches.

The conference had been unable to come to a meeting of minds on the old controversial question of communion fellowship. It was finally recognized as a problem needing further consideration, and was solved by making a factual statement of existing practices. In some member churches there was full communion fellowship for all Evangelical Christians; in none of them was a person who belonged to another member church denied communion where local circumstances and the care of souls made it expedient. Existing church membership requirements and general church disciplinary procedures were recognized as not being affected by this communion fellowship. On the other hand, baptism and other church rites, such as confirmation and marriage, enacted in one church were recognized by all.

The constitution in many ways preserved the autonomy of the member churches. The national church body, however, represented the member churches in foreign affairs and in the ecumenical movement.[34] It was charged with bringing about greater unity among the member churches. To this end it could make suggestions about undertaking certain tasks, for example regulating inner mission work or the church press. It could also establish guidelines, as, for example, for the education and examination of pastors, for the gathering of statistics, or for such a mundane but practical matter as bookkeeping. Member churches were not required to follow these guidelines, but they usually did. The national church could also adopt church laws in regard to matters which formerly had been regulated uniformly among the German churches or if the member churches requested such action. Such laws required a certain legislative procedure in the synod and a two-thirds vote, but differences did arise about whether they were binding on all member churches. In the process of adopting a church disciplinary law in 1953–54, the interpretation was reached that if all member churches accepted the law, it was binding throughout the Evangelical Church in Germany; if not, it became effective only in those churches which had approved it.[35] This interpretation became important when the national church in 1957 made an agreement with the federal government about a chaplaincy corps in the armed services. The Democratic Republic objected strongly, and since the churches in the east did not specifically approve the law, it was not considered effective in their jurisdictions.

The governing organs of the Evangelical Church in Germany were to be a synod, a church conference, and a council. The synod as originally constituted consisted of 120 members, 100 elected by the synods of the member churches and 20 nominated by the council. It was to be elected for a six-year term and normally meet yearly. The synod was to elect its own head as well as other officers, and was designed to be the most important governing body. The church conference was to be made up of one delegate from each of the member churches, usually the presiding officer. It was to meet two or three times a year, and be presided over by the chairman of the council. It was intended to have largely advisory powers, but in practice it became an important body, for it was here that the various church governments were able to make suggestions to the council and to the synod. The council was to consist of the head of the synod and eleven (increased in 1965 to fourteen) additional members elected by a two-thirds vote in joint session by the synod and church conference, this joint body also electing the chairman of the council.[36] He was to be in fact the top executive officer and head of the Evangelical Church in Germany. The constitution never mentioned the office of bishop, no doubt because of Reformed susceptibilities and the sad experiences of the Kirchenkampf. In electing this collegial executive, although there were no constitutional prescriptions, attention came to be paid to a distributive representation of areas and confessions. Thus there were usually five Lutherans, five United, and two Reformed representatives, and until recently four from the eastern and eight from the western churches.[37] Since the council was to meet only about every six weeks, a church chancellery and church foreign office (a heritage of Nazi times) were established. The officials of these organizations were to be appointed by the council and conduct affairs according to general church regulations and the requests of the council.

Among the many tasks assumed by the council was the issuing of studies and pronouncements on various public issues. Their actions stimulated other church bodies to issue statements as well. These often caused controversy within the churches, and in order to provide some guidelines for such actions, the council appointed a special committee to study the problem. Their long report, "The Exercise and Limitations of Church Pronouncements on Social Questions," was issued in 1970. It pointed out that the practice of issuing statements on political and social questions was closely related to experiences under the Third Reich. "At that time one experienced and learned where insufficient or postponed coresponsibility for matters of this world or uncritical trust in authority led."[38] The report upheld in particular the right and duty of the churches to make such statements, and in accepting it the synod at Stuttgart urged the council and the other church administrations to do more to further the distribution and study of church pronouncements than had been customary in the past. The church in postwar Germany has truly not been a silent church, and has repeatedly borne public witness in regard to contemporary issues. For example, it has spoken out on the Cold War, the rearmament of Germany, the rights of conscientious objectors, the atom bomb, the Berlin Wall, the reunion of East and West Germany, détente with eastern Europe, Vietnam, the treatment of foreign workers in Germany, and combating racism in the world, as well as on issues in numerous electoral campaigns. The *Kirchliches Jahrbuch* now devotes many pages to a chronicle and discussion of these church statements.[39] Public statements by church bodies, however, continue to be an issue within the church. On March 23, 1971, the head of the United Evangelical Lutheran church, on behalf of the bishops' conference of that body, submitted to the Council of the Evangelical Church in Germany a formal request for a discussion of the question: "What significance does the gospel have for the community of the church and the congregation in view of the fact that Christians differ in their views on political and ethical questions?"[40] The question was discussed at subsequent synods without reaching any definite conclusions, although the obligation of the church to take a position on questions of the day was generally upheld. At the meeting of the synod at Coburg in 1973, there was some indication that the newly elected leaders were inclined to emphasize the priority of preaching over the issuance of pronouncements on social policy.[41]

The constitution provided that the existing Land and provincial churches should constitute the original member churches. It was specifically stated that any member church was free to join with others on a confessional or territorial basis, but that it nevertheless would retain its rights of direct communication with the governmental organs of the united church. This made it possible to establish a United Lutheran church and an Evangelical Church of the Union, while the individual churches remained as participating members of the larger body.

More recently, the Land churches of Eutin, Hamburg, Hanover, Lübeck, and Schleswig-Holstein have united to form a North Elbian Evangelical Lutheran Church.[42] The new church body is to have the status of a public corporation, and to what extent it will replace the present administrations of the Land churches remains for future deliberations. Likewise the Evangelical Lutheran Land churches of Hanover, Brunswick, Oldenburg, and Schaumberg-Lippe, and the Evangelical Reformed Church of Northwest Germany have united into the Confederation of Evangelical Churches of Lower Saxony.[43] Whereas the North Elbian church is composed of only Lutheran bodies, this confederation is a union of Lutheran and Reformed churches. Both of these new church unions attest to a desire to bring about greater church unity within the Evangelical Church in Germany.

The Evangelical Church in Germany as originally constituted had twenty-eight member churches, the same number as under the Weimar Republic. Twenty-seven of these can roughly be designated Land churches, although their jurisdictions no longer coincide with present-day political boundaries; the twenty-eighth member is the Evangelical Church of the Union—a recognition of its historic past as the Church of the Old Prussian Union. It sends no representatives to the synod and pays no part of the joint budget, but does send a delegate to the church conference. The United Lutheran church is only a confessional union, and has no special status within the organization of the Evangelical Church in Germany.

The following list, grouped along confessional lines, shows that the size of the member churches varies greatly, as is indicated by the number of congregations in each church body (given in parentheses following the name of the individual church).[44] The Evangelical Church of the Union contains seven individual churches: Berlin-Brandenburg (1,916), Pomerania (328), Silesia (74), Province of Saxony (2,367), Anhalt (221), Westphalia (555), and Rhineland (789). Other United confessional churches are: Hesse and Nassau (1,088), Electoral Hesse-Waldeck (966), Baden (539), Palatinate (449), and Bremen (53). The United Evangelical Lutheran Church of Germany contains eleven individual churches: Saxony (1,229), Hanover (1,629), Bavaria (1,251), Schleswig-Holstein (469), Thuringia (1,406), Mecklenburg (501), Hamburg (70), Brunswick (419), Lübeck (29), and Schaumburg-Lippe (21). Other Lutheran churches are: Württemberg (1,256), Oldenburg (107), and Eutin (17).[45] The Reformed churches are: Lippe (67) and Northwest Germany (128). These figures show the strength of the five basic divisions of the Land churches of the Evangelical Church in Germany, and thus how significant it was when the Lutheran churches of Württemberg, Oldenburg, and Eutin, with their total of 1,380 congregations, joined the Evangelical Church in Germany but refrained from membership in the United Evangelical Lutheran church. The Lutherans are still unable to present a united front. The statistics also reveal that while historical entities have disappeared, they live on in the nomenclature and jurisdictions of various Land churches. The Lutheran churches all told embrace about 20,210,000 individuals, the United churches 21,500,000, and the Reformed 440,000.[46]

According to the ordinance of the Provisional Council which provided for the calling of the Eisenach Conference, the constitution once agreed upon was to be submitted to the various member churches for their approval.[47] This was done. The Reich Brotherhood Council immediately formally surrendered all powers with which it had been vested, and on July 15, 1948, this body which had played such an important role in the history of the Protestant church ever since 1934 ceased to exist.[48] In the course of the autumn all churches except Bremen ratified the constitution, although many also submitted interpreting statements to the Provisional Council. The failure of the Bremen church to ratify threatened to delay putting the constitution into effect. It seemed unreasonable to permit the internal difficulties of the small Bremen church to nullify the arduous achievements of the conference which all other churches approved. With no doubt some specious interpretation of the legal situation, the Provisional Council, on December 3, 1948, decided to declare the constitution in force. With equally liberal interpretation of the law, Bremen finally was welcomed into membership of the Evangelical Church in Germany in 1953.[49] The first synod of the Evangelical Church in Germany met in Bethel on January 9, 1949, elected the necessary officials, and the new church body was under way.

Partnership between Church and State

While the churches had been busy reestablishing themselves and agreeing on a national church constitution, the political reorganization of Germany was also taking place. State constitutions were being drawn up, and finally in 1949 the Federal Republic of Germany and the German Democratic Republic were established. The churches received favorable consideration in all these many constitutions. In West Germany the constitutions by and large took over the articles on church-state relations from the Weimar Constitution, the similarities being closest in predominantly Catholic Lands. Religious liberty was guaranteed and religious instruction in the schools permitted. The churches were accorded the privilege of public corporations with the right to tax their own members, and in general they were to administer their own affairs.[50] In East Germany more restrictions were imposed and there was less cooperation on the part of state authorities than in the west.[51] Yet there was little that could be called outright persecution, and the churches were able to carry on, although they had increasingly to adapt themselves to the Soviet-dominated political, social, and economic order.

The adoption of church and state constitutions and the general recognition of existing state and church laws still left many matters unclear. As always there was the problem of whether church affairs could or should be settled unilaterally by state or church, or by both cooperatively. With the increasing autonomy of the churches, the states in the Federal Republic have come to settle these matters by negotiated agreements rather than by enacting laws. This is in line with the concept of a "partnership between state and church" popularized in the early postwar years.[52] One of the most important factors producing these state-church treaties was that state and church jurisdictions did not coincide.[53] For example, in Rhineland-Palatinate the government has three so-called Land churches to deal with—the Church of the Palatinate, the Church of the Rhineland, and the Church of Hesse and Nassau. Each of these churches controls areas in other political jurisdictions as well. Within the state of Hesse are the churches of Hesse and Nassau, of Electoral Hesse-Waldeck, and of the Rhineland. Lower Saxony has seven churches functioning within its borders: Hanover, Brunswick, Oldenburg, Schaumburg-Lippe, Hamburg, Bremen, and the Evangelical-Reformed Church of Northwest Germany. This recitation of conflicting church and political jurisdictions could be continued and become even more complicated. In some cases the churches, as for example Hanover and Brunswick, have congregations in both West and East Germany. Then too, there are variations in the laws that apply to different churches. It is generally held that the Prussian agreement with the Evangelical church of May 11, 1931, applies to all former Prussian territory, which is now divided among a number of states.[54] Thus in Hesse, the Church of the Rhineland, of Electoral Hesse-Waldeck, and the areas of Nassau and Frankfurt are covered by the old Prussian law, but the other areas are not.

This maze of overlapping and conflicting jurisdictions needed to be simplified, which was even more important because the churches had historic rights to subsidies from the various political jurisdictions. Clearly the best and most amicable way to solve both these financial matters and a host of lesser problems was for a state to negotiate agreements with the church. Such a procedure, of course, was not new; it had been followed at times under the Weimar Republic.[55] An example from one of the recent agreements will serve to illustrate this solution. The Treaty of the Land of Hesse with the Evangelical Land Churches in Hesse of February 18, 1960, provides that the state subsidies to churches shall amount to 7,950,000 marks yearly, of which 1,800,000 marks are to go to the Church of Hesse and Nassau, 5,900,000 to the Church of Electoral Hesse-Waldeck, and 250,000 to the Church of the Rhineland. The text of the treaty covers fourteen pages, and its very length is indicative of the complexity of the issues involved.[56]

The church-state treaties usually have sections concerning church taxes. The right to collect these taxes, however, goes back to legislation under the Empire. After World War II, all church bodies entered into agreements with the Lands under which the governments are to collect this tax for the churches, for which service the state takes a fee of 3 to 4.9 percent.[57] The tax, usually about 8 to 10 percent of the income tax, is deducted from wages and salaries like the income tax and social security charges. This is far from "historical tithing," where the tenth applied to all income. In a certain sense it is a voluntary payment, for by formally withdrawing from church membership before state authorities a person can escape paying.[58]

While there has been much press commentary on church withdrawals and the numbers have grown, actually few Germans do withdraw from the big church bodies.[59] The figures that are quoted in the press need interpretation. Some Protestants withdraw and transfer their memberships to the Catholic church (or Catholics transfer to Protestant churches) where they are again subject to church taxes. Others join the Free churches or sects where they pay no taxes, but where their contributions are likely to be at least as high as the ordinary church tax payments. The motives for church withdrawals are manifold, and while the desire to escape church taxes is no doubt important, it is not the only cause. In general Germans realize that if the church is to be available for baptisms, marriages, and above all for funerals, something ought to be paid for its support.

There has been some agitation both within and outside the churches against the continued collection of church taxes. Some church members feel that the church would have more vitality and independence if it relied entirely on freewill offerings as the Free churches and sects do. However, this view has never won much support in church government circles. Critical articles in the press and general public concern did cause the Evangelical church to take notice. Reports on the income from church taxes are to be a regular feature of the *Kirchliches Jahrbuch*.[60]

State authorities have no objection to the levying of church taxes, for if they were ever discontinued the state almost certainly would be called upon to take over many of the social services now performed by the churches. For example, in Bavaria 80 percent of the kindergartens are run by the churches, and the state has been glad to unload this financial burden on them. The state and local governments help out at times through small building and instruction subsidies, but the main source of revenue for these kindergartens is the church tax.

Cooperation in Church Activities

Increasing prosperity in Germany has meant a corresponding increase in church revenue. Indeed, the churches are popularly considered to have become rich, although that is scarcely the case. Ministerial salaries have been coordinated with those of certain civil service classifications and correspond approximately to those of teachers at the gymnasiums, with scheduled raises and children's allowances. Parsonages are provided, and ministers often still receive traditional perquisites that supplement salary payments. The Land churches have slowly been able to undertake badly needed renovations of church buildings and parsonages. Many new churches have been built, and while there have been striking innovations in church architecture, the buildings evidently were economically constructed.[61] The constant growth of cities, the development of new residential sections, and the need to break up over-expanded church districts has made the founding of new congregations necessary. On the whole the church authorities have been conservative about building new churches, weighing the question raised by skeptics and critics—why build when existing churches always have ample room? There is also the question of how best to use available manpower.

The German churches have always supported a great number of social service institutions—orphanages, old peoples' homes, sanitariums, residential homes for itinerant workers, and kindergartens, and above all they have trained and supported deaconesses and deacons in their varied services. In this area too there was need for change and modernization in the postwar years. The Hilfswerk begun as an Evangelical church project in 1945 proved the value of joint efforts. As the economy recovered and the millions of refugees were integrated into German society, the individual churches merged the emergency relief activity of the Hilfswerk with the functions of established inner mission institutions. Many of these had long been carried on with cooperative support by Land churches. At the meeting of the synod of the Evangelical Church in Germany in 1957, it was decided to unify the social service activities of the various churches. The Inner Mission and Relief Work of the Evangelical Church in Germany was established with headquarters at Stuttgart. It has a directing council of nineteen members and a conference made up of representatives of the Evangelical Church in Germany, of the various inner mission institutions, and of other interested persons. This organization brings together most of the charitable and social service institutions of the Land churches; it was a major step in the long road toward greater church union. The Inner Mission and Relief Work of the Evangelical Church in Germany also entered upon an agreement with the Association of Evangelical Free Churches to coordinate the work of their deacons and deaconesses.[62]

Foreign missions have also been centralized. Through the central church council, an agreement was reached with the German Evangelical Mission Council, which represented the thirty-odd German foreign mission societies. The Evangelical Associates for World Missions (*Evangelische Arbeitsgemeinschaft für Weltmission*) was formed, with its headquarters in Hamburg.[63] The German churches cooperate with churches in other countries in the annual "Christmas ingathering" of "Bread for the World" and similar activities. In 1960 the Committee for Service Overseas (*Dienste Übersee*) was established to recruit and sponsor skilled personnel (teachers, doctors, nurses, agriculturists, etc.) on specific requests from overseas countries for limited periods of service. The German churches, with some help from government agencies, make up the difference between the normal local salary and the income the person had last received in Germany.

If inner and foreign missions were well established and needed only to be reshaped and given new life, there were two quite new church institutions which became prominent after the war. Both were designed to involve the laity in church affairs and to establish new lines of communication. So-called Evangelical Academies were organized.[64] These were nothing more than study and discussion groups, usually constituted by invitation from special professional groups such as doctors or engineers. Topics were carefully selected and able leadership provided. These academies soon became a regular part of the activity of all Land churches.

On a much broader scale was the inauguration of a regular series of Kirchentage. This term has been and at times is still used variously in German church affairs. However, the German Evangelical Kirchentage of today are large church rallies with thousands in attendance. The experiences of the Evangelical Church Weeks of the Kirchenkampf period[65] and the example of the Katholikentage which have long been a feature of Catholic church activity stimulated Reinold von Thadden-Trieglaff to organize an Evangelical Kirchentag to meet in Hanover in 1949. Over 10,000 persons attended, and the meeting was so successful that it was at first decided to hold such assemblies annually, but now they are held every two years, alternately with the Catholic rally. Until 1961 Germans from east and west participated; in fact, the rally held at Leipzig in 1954 drew an attendance of 650,000, the largest ever. The Russian government had put its exposition pavilion at the disposal of the Kirchentag, and important East German federal leaders participated in the proceedings.[66] Since 1961, the year of the construction of the Berlin Wall, East Germans have not been free to attend the general meetings but have at times had Kirchentage of their own.[67]

The rallies offer a rich fare: numerous religious services, public addresses, discussion groups, theatrical and film presentations. All sorts of printed material is prepared in advance and there are reports of the proceedings. All these are available for study and discussion in local congregations. The rallies naturally lead to much press comment both in Germany and throughout the world. There seems to be general agreement that Kirchentage have had great impact, and that the rallies are one of the most successful innovations of the postwar period.

In 1971 the regular Kirchentag was replaced by an ecumenical congress held in conjunction with the Catholic church in Augsburg on June 2–5, where there was lively discussion on such topics as intercommunion and mixed marriages. The desire expressed at the meeting for future joint Protestant and Catholic Kirchentage did not materialize, and the Protestants again held their own rally, in Düsseldorf in 1973, in Frankfurt in 1975, and in West Berlin in 1977. There were 35,000 regular participants with 450 ecumenical participants from different countries at Düsseldorf, and even larger numbers at Frankfurt. Franklin H. Littell, an acute observer of the German churches, wrote in his report on the Düsseldorf meeting: "Despite its critics the Kirchentag remains the most lively and free-wheeling center of lay initiative in the world today, and the astonishing variety of its groups, discussions, and celebrations is proof enough that Christians can still tackle in a spirit of Christian joy the most difficult spiritual, moral, and ethical issues of the times."[68] At the huge Frankfurt meeting the socialist-liberal Protestant group came very much to the fore, as they also did in West Berlin.

There has also been a revival of youth organizations, and of men's and women's groups. The church press flourishes and radio and television programs are constantly expanding. Religion is a regular subject of instruction in the schools of West Germany under conditions which meet very generously the wishes of the churches. Confirmation remains important, although it does not take long for youth thereafter to imitate their elders in very spasmodic church attendance. In this respect the Germans of today follow pretty much the footsteps of previous generations.

A sociologist who recently attempted to measure the interest of Germans in religion and in their churches concludes that if there are proportionally more Catholics than Protestants in an area, both faiths are stronger in their religious practices. Moreover, the religious activity of the Protestants increases parallel to the growing proportion of Catholics, but the same is not true of Catholics. There is also a discrepancy between the frequency of religious practice and the intensity of religious attitudes among Catholics but not among Protestants. He also points out that there is a widespread belief in West Germany that the influence of the church on individuals is diminishing. He attempted to test the idea, and found that there was "some evidence of a trend of diminishing religious orientation, but this trend is quite weak."[69]

The forms of worship have not changed, although in some congregations there have been innovations such as the use of guitars, discussion services, and new liturgical forms for special occasions. In general the use of prescribed gospel or epistle selections as sermon texts still prevails. Agreement has been reached with the Catholics on a common version of the Lord's Prayer and other texts.[70] The church authorities have attempted to improve the training of their pastors.[71] Yet in response to casual inquiry, the almost universal verdict of the laity seems to be that there has been no renaissance in preaching.

Unity and Division

The Evangelical Church in Germany, through its active participation in the ecumenical movement where it speaks for all the member churches, and also through its day-by-day administrative practices, has done much to further unity among the churches.[72] It has also taken steps to lessen confessional differences. In 1948 the Evangelical Church in Germany united with some of the Free churches and the Old Catholics to establish the Working Community of Christian Churches in Germany (*Arbeitsgemeinschaft christlicher Kirchen in Deutschland*). Martin Niemöller was its first chairman, and he did much to get this "ecumenical movement at home" under way. The organization, like the National Council of Churches in the United States, was designed to further ecumenism and to discuss not only problems common to the German churches but also matters of faith and doctrine. From time to time the Working Community has issued statements on issues of the day.[73] There has also been much closer cooperation between the Evangelical church and the Catholic church, particularly since the Second Vatican Council.[74]

The problem of communion fellowship had not been solved when the constitution of the Evangelical Church in Germany was formulated in 1948. Two years later the church council appointed a committee of twenty-two members to study the question. They hastened with considerable deliberation, and only in 1957 submitted a report for consideration by the churches.[75] In 1962 the committee made a final explanatory report to the council,[76] and a year later a second committee was named to evaluate the results of the past fifteen years of theological study. A report from this committee in 1965 recommended that the various churches take action by January, 1967, although it was expected that this terminal date would probably not be observed. When one considers that Reformed and Lutheran theologians had been debating the problem of communion fellowship ever since the Reformation, a few more months or years seem insignificant.

Differences arose over whether the church constitution should be amended in order to state more clearly the various positions of the churches on communion fellowship. Some also wanted to extend the communion fellowship by establishing full pulpit fellowship, which would have meant that Reformed and Lutheran pastors could celebrate communion in each other's churches, a step farther than simply permitting Reformed and Lutherans to stand before the same altar rail. Sixteen member churches voted for communion fellowship without reservation and for the proposal to amend the constitution. Of these sixteen, nine would have liked to see communion fellowship extended to full pulpit fellowship. Ten churches wanted communion fellowship but did not want to amend the constitution. Only the Bavarian church held back. It resolved to continue its practice of turning no one away, except in matters involving church discipline, but did not wish to commit itself further. It rejected the proposed change of the constitution out of church, theological, and legal considerations.[77]

The pros and cons of the theological arguments have not been considered here. Certainly the advances made in this most difficult of questions warrant the conclusion that the Evangelical Church in Germany has in essence achieved communion fellowship. The churches of both West and East Germany participated in the deliberations on communion fellowship, but by the time the discussions were concluded their practical day-by-day association had ended. Appropriately enough, the establishment of communion fellowship, long such a divisive issue among German churches, was one of the last things which churches of East and West Germany were able to achieve together.

Since 1967 representatives of the German churches have cooperated with Lutheran, Reformed, and United churches of other European countries at conferences held first at Schauenberg and then at Leuenberg in Switzerland, where attempts were made to clarify and reconcile differences of doctrine and practice. On September 28, 1971, the Leuenberg conference issued a draft statement on "The Concord of Reformation Churches in Europe." Generally referred to as "the Leuenberger Konkordie," the statement has been submitted to the various cooperating churches in Europe for study and comment. It has aroused much interest, and whatever the final action of the European Reformation churches on the statement will be, it has done much to stimulate the thinking and further the cooperation of Lutheran, Reformed, and United churches in Germany.[78]

While Land churches of both East and West Germany were joined in the Evangelical Church in Germany, in the United Evangelical Lutheran Church of Germany, and in the Evangelical Church of the Union, and to this extent have a common background, the developments in east and west have been quite different. The difference is most striking in regard to religious education in the schools. Not only was the matter left entirely to the churches in the east, but soon the authorities there ruled that such education could not be held in school buildings or during regular school hours.[79] The state also countered with compulsory instruction in Marxism, and confirmation had to compete with secularly oriented communist "Youth Dedication Services" (*Jugendweihe*). A real conflict developed over the confirmation-Jugendweihe issue when the church authorities held it was an either-or matter.[80] The churches found it necessary to give way, and today will confirm even if children have participated in the state-sponsored services.[81] This relaxation of practice has in no way meant church approval of the Jugendweihe and the training that goes with it. The state authorities continue to use participation in the Jugendweihe as a criterion when it comes to admission to secondary and higher education institutions. No exact figures are available, but probably less than fifty percent of the youth are still confirmed in East Germany.[82] In the cities one can no longer speak of a custom of confirmation. Pastors have also had recourse to receiving members into the church, not without instruction but without the customary confirmation classes. Difficulties were placed in the way of this procedure when the state decreed in the early 1970s that even all traditional activities and religious services required advance approval by local authorities. Such activities included not only concerts and similar events in churches or parish houses, but also Bible study courses. The churches steadfastly refused to register such activities and were forced to pay thousands of marks in fines.[83]

The German Democratic Republic has never cut off all church subsidies, but the grants for general purposes (including salaries) and for building have not been as generous as in the west. Government officials have been particularly interested in restoring certain historic churches, such as the cathedrals at Magdeburg, Halberstadt, Merseburg, and Erfurt, the Hofkirche in Dresden, the Klosterkirche in Doberan, and the Thomaskirche in Leipzig. Yet church renovation and reconstruction has lagged far behind that in West Germany. During the war, out of 10,900 churches in East Germany, 310 were completely destroyed and 2,790 seriously damaged. Two-thirds of this total of 3,100 unserviceable buildings had been neither rebuilt nor repaired by 1963. Between 1945 and 1963, only 68 new Evangelical churches, 24 Free churches, 3 synagogues, and 140 Catholic churches and chapels were built in East Germany. Protestants were better supplied from former times, and the influx of Catholics to East Germany from Silesia, Bohemia, and other areas also made it more necessary to erect new Catholic churches.[84]

There are state-supported Protestant theological faculties at the universities of Leipzig, Rostock, Greifswald, Jena, Halle, and Berlin. Here the theological students customarily receive scholarships and can eat at modest prices at the university dining halls.[85] There are also three church-supported higher educational institutions: the Evangelisches Sprachenkonvikt Berlin, the Katechetisches Oberseminar Naumberg, each with approximately 90 students, and the Theologisches Seminar Leipzig with about 150 students.[86] Somewhat over a quarter of the theological students are women. Most of the East German churches ordain women, as do a number of the Land churches in the west, and such women, known as *Pastorin,* can preach and administer the sacraments.[87]

All East German churches have had increasing difficulty in levying church taxes. In 1956 Justice Minister Benjamin ruled that recourse could no longer be had to the courts by "parties, mass organizations, or religious bodies" to enforce payment of dues.[88] This well-publicized edict led many to stop paying church taxes. The government also refused to permit church officials access to tax lists or the address records of local housing authorities, which made it difficult to keep track of church members in the large city congregations. Until 1957–58 the state deducted church taxes from wages and salaries, but since then the churches have had to collect the taxes themselves without any state cooperation.[89] The East German churches have worked out certain taxes, based on total income, which members are supposed to pay. Many members pay regularly, some pay after several reminders, and of course others make no payment at all. At best, the church taxes are hardly more than a rough guideline to what parishioners should be giving, and the churches have become increasingly dependent on other freewill offerings. In recent years the Protestant and Catholic churches as well as the Red Cross have been permitted to collect money in boxes on streets and public places. The money from the spring collection is given to hospitals, kindergartens, homes for aged, and similar institutions; the fall collection goes for religious instruction of children and to support financially needy congregations. These collections have been very successful.[90]

The uneven economic progress in east and west and the growing political estrangement between the two Germanies as a result of the Cold War was bound to affect the relationship between the churches. The resulting differences came to light very pronouncedly when the Evangelical Church in Germany entered upon a treaty with the Federal Republic for the establishment of a chaplaincy corps in February, 1957.[91] It should be noted that the Federal constitution recognizes the right of conscientious objection to service in the armed forces, and this right has been approved by both the Protestant and Catholic churches. The council of the Evangelical church had studied the problem of reli-

gious services for the armed forces long before obligatory military service was introduced in 1956.[92] That year the synod of the Evangelical
Church in Germany discussed the problem of the reintroduction of a
military establishment in both German republics and sent delegations to
each government to convey their concern.[93] There were strong reservations about the reintroduction of compulsory service. The synod expressed its expectation that the council would not make any binding
agreements about religious care for the military services without bringing the matter before the synod again. There were apparently conflicting
views and interpretations among churchmen as to exactly what limitations had been placed on the council. In any case, the council went
ahead and concluded a treaty with the Federal Republic authorities on
February 22, 1957, which it presented to the synod meeting March 3–8
in Berlin for ratification. To be asked to approve or disapprove without
having any real chance to introduce amendments aroused more opposition to the treaty than did the actual terms of the agreement. In the end a
church law putting the treaty into effect was approved by a vote of
ninety to nineteen, with five abstentions.[94] The treaty went into force on
July 30, 1957, with the exchange of ratifications with the West German
government.

The need to offer religious services to the soldiers was generally
recognized. Some wanted such care to be left to local congregations,
but because barracks were often located in remote places, and because
Protestants might be stationed in predominantly Catholic regions, this
did not seem practical. On the other hand, there was great concern
about the establishment of an autonomous military church such as had
existed in the years before 1918; thus the bishop for the armed services
is not appointed by the state but by the council of the Evangelical
church.[95] The West German government does maintain a Church Office
for the Armed Services where there are permanent officials to supervise
affairs in the various army districts. Chaplains, however, remain attached to their Land churches, and after six or eight years of service
return to civil duty. They have no military rank, wear no uniform, and
are free of all army directives in their religious activities. If a local
congregation is able to take over the service to the military, it may do
so. In some cases special military congregations are formed. The government is responsible for all costs, and the soldiers pay church taxes,
part of which goes to the Land churches and part to defray the cost of
the chaplaincy corps. In addition to regular yearly furloughs, members
of the armed forces can obtain a week's leave to attend special religious
retreats or discussion groups. In few countries today is the chaplaincy
corps so free from state control as it is in West Germany.[96]

The government of the German Democratic Republic was informed
that the ratification of the chaplaincy treaty with the Federal Republic
would be discussed at the March, 1957, synod meeting, and that the
church desired to enter upon a similar arrangement with the Democratic
Republic. This message elicited a caustic reply to the effect that the
armed forces in East Germany were completely voluntary, that no one

in the forces had requested religious services, and that the "activity of the Evangelical church in the National People's Army could never be a matter of negotiation."[97] The latter point was the important one, for to have entered upon an agreement with the church would have been a recognition that the state could not legislate unilaterally in this field.

After the synod of the Evangelical Church in Germany approved the chaplaincy treaty with the Federal Republic, the Democratic Republic on March 7, 1957, announced the creation of the State Secretariat for Church Affairs. Werner Eggerath, a former East German minister to Rumania and an ardent Communist, was placed in charge. The Office of Church Relations, which had been understandingly administered by Deputy Prime Minister Otto Nuschke, was now abolished and all relations with the church centered in the new secretariat.[98]

The propaganda campaign by the East German officials against the chaplaincy corps was vigorously maintained. They charged that it constituted recognition by the churches of militarism, of the reestablishment of the Wehrmacht, and of the use of atom bombs. In fact, not only the Evangelical Church in Germany but also many of the Land churches individually had at various times expressed their reservations about the reintroduction of military service and had denounced nuclear warfare.[99] Although synodical representatives from the eastern churches had approved the chaplaincy treaty, in the course of 1958 it was recognized that the agreement did not apply to their jurisdictions, and only the western Land churches specifically approved the treaty.[100] The German Democratic Republic took the conclusion of the chaplaincy treaty as a justification for breaking off relations with the Evangelical Church in Germany as a whole, and insisted on dealing only with representatives of the Evangelical churches within its borders. This intransigence eventually led to the complete separation of the eastern and western churches.

The synod of the Evangelical Church in Germany was scheduled to meet in East Berlin in 1958, and in spite of demonstrations against holding it there, the meeting did take place. The synod instructed its plenipotentiary to the East German government, Pastor Heinrich Grüber, who had headed the Grüber Bureau for relief of Jews in Berlin and since 1945 had acted in many capacities as liaison officer, to discuss the activities of the synod with East German authorities.[101] He sought an interview, but President Otto Grotewohl refused to see him.

> In view of the proceedings of the synod of the Evangelical Church in Germany in April, 1958, in Berlin, and the way it dealt with the military chaplaincy treaty, a representative of the council of the Evangelical Church in Germany can no longer be recognized by the government of the German Democratic Republic. With this decision the duties of the representative of the council of the Evangelical church at the government of the German Democratic government are ended.[102]

Grotewohl did express willingness to receive a delegation of churchmen who were resident in the Democratic Republic or in the Democratic sector of Berlin.[103] Grüber protested, but was informed that there was nothing more to be done. This incident occurred exactly when a crisis threatened to arise in the East German party leadership over the issue of de-Stalinization. The hard-liners won out, which in turn meant that the men who wished to separate the eastern churches and western churches and break the unity of the Evangelical church had the upper hand.[104]

Unofficially the administration of the Evangelical Church in Germany complied with Grotewohl's wish to deal only with men resident in the Democratic Republic or in East Berlin. After October, 1958, the church chancellery was divided into two sections, one in East Berlin and the other in West Berlin. The East German secretary for church affairs, however, did not recognize the East Berlin chancellery since it was a creature of the whole Evangelical church, and he insisted on dealing with each Land church directly.[105]

In spite of increasing harassment and the basic desire of East German authorities to sever the church ties between east and west, synods, with representation from all churches, could still be held.[106] This was later made impossible by the erection of the Berlin Wall in 1961. No attempts were made in 1962 to hold synods of any of the three Evangelical church bodies. A year of observation and waiting was indeed possible, but something had to be done in 1963. The Evangelical Church in Germany called a synod to meet in Bethel, the Lutherans a synod to meet in Nürnberg, and the Evangelical Church of the Union one to meet in East Berlin.[107] Delegates from East German churches were not permitted by their government to attend the first two synods; the delegates from West German churches were not permitted to attend the one held in East Berlin. However, the synod of the Church of the Union was held in simultaneous split sessions—one in East Berlin and one in West Berlin. All three church bodies now amended their operating regulations to make it possible to have such split synod meetings in the future if they were necessary, which proved to be the case.[108] Technically the churches were still united, but they were constantly being forced farther apart. Statistics on the eastern churches were no longer available to the editors of the *Kirchliches Jahrbuch* in 1961, and, from the 1962 issue on, the eastern churches vanished statistically from the yearbook of the Evangelical Church in Germany.

In 1967, the four hundred and fiftieth anniversary of the start of the Reformation was celebrated throughout Germany. There was much talk about Luther and the desire for church union. The synod of the Evangelical Church in Germany did assemble in split sections, the eastern churches in Fürstenwalde, the western churches in West Berlin. Both groups adopted statements expressing their intention to maintain the unity of the Evangelical Church in Germany. The East German statement, however, contained a rather ominous remark: "We will have to free ourselves to the extent that we can fulfill our duties in that part of Germany in which we live."[109]

Within a year the unity so recently acclaimed by both east and west was shattered. In the beginning of 1968 the German Democratic Republic adopted a new constitution. It contained the usual guarantees of individual rights and of religious freedom, and indeed the churches fared rather well, although they were no longer to have the status of public corporations.[110] The constitution stated that the churches had the right to regulate their own affairs in accordance with the provisions of the constitution and the laws of the German Democratic Republic; details could be settled by agreements with state officials.[111] The eastern churches, long under pressure from the government, now undertook to separate from the western churches. In June, 1968, they appointed a committee to study how the churches in the Democratic Republic could intensify their cooperation and their witness. The so-called Structure Commission acted with zeal, and on September 3, 1968, produced a draft constitution for a "Confederation of Evangelical Churches in the German Democratic Republic."[112] It was clear that the eastern Land churches were taking themselves out of the Evangelical Church in Germany. On December 1, 1968, the Lutheran churches of Saxony, Thuringia, and Mecklenburg formed the Evangelical Lutheran Church in the German Democratic Republic, an action which was accepted with sadness but understanding by the United Evangelical Lutheran Church of Germany.[113]

The Evangelical Church of the Union already had so much regional autonomy that it could continue functioning much as it had before. In 1963 the Church of the Union had adopted an arrangement for separate synod meetings of eastern and western member churches under special circumstances. Regionalism was slowly extended, and in 1968 an "Ordinance for the Regional Administration of the Churches of the Union" was adopted.[114] The Synod of the Evangelical Church of the Union, Eastern District, had as its members the Evangelical Land churches of Anhalt, Greifswald, Görlitz, the church province of Saxony, and the eastern synod of the Berlin-Brandenburg church, all being within or attached to the Democratic Republic; the Synod of the Evangelical Church of the Union, Western District, consists of the Evangelical churches of the Rhineland and of Westphalia, and the western synod of the Berlin-Brandenburg church, all being within or attached to the Federal Republic. The two synods, meeting separately in 1970, again confirmed the unity of the Evangelical Church of the Union in spite of its being governed largely by the regional synods.[115]

The ordinance of 1968 establishing the two synods was a formal amendment to the constitution of the Evangelical Church of the Union, and this document has never been cancelled. The ordinance recognized the de facto division of one of its bodies—the Berlin-Brandenburg church—into eastern and western sections. This church had long been administered from separate offices in East and West Berlin, but the bishop residing in West Berlin was at least theoretically the head of the whole church. After the Berlin Wall was built, the bishop was not permitted to visit the eastern areas of his diocese. Both synods of the Berlin-Brandenburg church, however, continued to uphold the nominal unity until the autumn of 1972, when the separation of this historic church into eastern and western sections, each with its own church government presided over by its own bishop, was mutually recognized.

Although the bishop's office is split, it is held that the church is still one, and the two regions can realize "their unity in dialogue, in joint consultation, and in common action."[116]

The Confederation of Evangelical Churches in the German Democratic Republic (*Bund der evangelischen Kirchen in der Deutschen Demokratischen Republik*) officially came into being with the adoption of its constitution on June 10, 1969.[117] The constitution establishes governing bodies and provides for distribution of powers along the lines of other constitutions of the postwar period. An innovation is the provision for the establishment of commissions in various fields which will prepare material for the synod and church officials and advise them. These commissions are expected to be more important than the usual committees. After the governing organs were constituted in September, 1969, the East German members of the council of the Evangelical Church in Germany resigned, and the eight eastern Land Churches also formally withdrew from the Evangelical Church in Germany.[118]

The East German Confederation is "to further and coordinate the work of the member churches in the ecumenical movement."[119] It states in reference to the churches of West Germany:

> The confederation recognizes the special community of interests (*Gemeinschaft*) of all Evangelical Christians in Germany.
> Recognizing the responsibility resulting from this community of interest, the confederation through its governing officials accepts in free partnership the tasks that confront jointly all Evangelical churches in the German Democratic Republic and in the Federal Republic of Germany.[120]

The confederation assumes responsibility for coordinating the missionary and deaconess work of the member churches. For years much of this activity has been carried on jointly by the German churches. Separate headquarters and governing personnel have now been established in both republics, and it remains to be seen how much cooperation and common policy there can be in the future.

The establishment of a self-governing and separate church confederation for the Democratic Republic was hardly more than a practical recognition of existing conditions. The governing authorities had long brought pressure to this end, and now by their compliance the eastern churches have no doubt cut down the areas of conflict with the state. Whether they will have gained strength and be in a better position to carry on their work than if they had retained their tenuous connections with the western churches can only be a matter of speculation at present. One thing is obvious: the churches in the East far more than in the West are losing the status of a Volkskirche, a church embracing all the people. Acting Bishop Albrecht Schönherr of the Berlin-Brandenburg Church (East), in his report to the synod in 1970, stated it well:

> Out of a Volkskirche, into which one was as a matter of course baptized and in which one as a matter of course participated and lived, we are becoming a minority church. Just compare the percentage of the populace being baptized, given Christian instruction, confirmed, and married, with that in the time of our fathers. . . . The church is receiving a new position in society. If it

was formerly one of the supporting pillars, today many regard it as a superflu-
ous ornament or even a useless relic of former times.[121]

However, one should not sound the death knell of the churches in the
Democratic Republic. They often have introduced innovative practices.
New songs are sung, there are scripture readings from modern translations of the Bible, dialogues and discussions of sermons are organized,
more "free" prayers are being used, and radio and television carry
church music, religious news, and occasional sermons. Publishing
houses print Bibles, hymnals, and other religious literature. Protestants
and Catholics are cooperating more, and the East German churches
share in the work of the World Council of Churches.[122] All told, the
Protestant Land churches are still viable institutions, continuing to carry
the gospel to an often indifferent populace and constantly making adjustments with the Communist state.[123]

On September 26, 1969, the Council of the Evangelical Church in
Germany (the name has not been changed) regretfully accepted the
decision of the churches of the Democratic Republic to withdraw from
the united church.[124] The reconstitution of its governing bodies in line
with the existing membership was reserved for later meetings of the
synod. Committees were appointed and proposals made and discussed,
but it was soon evident that the organizational structure of the Evangelical church in the Federal Republic would not be much changed.[125] In
acknowledging the secession of the eastern churches, the council noted:

> The establishment of the Confederation of Evangelical Churches in the Ger-
> man Democratic Republic constitutes a deep rupture with serious conse-
> quences in the hundred-year history of uniting the Evangelical churches in
> Germany. The services that the Evangelical Church in Germany has per-
> formed in furthering the inner and outer unity of the member churches in
> both parts of Germany is to be remembered with gratitude. The outer forms
> of this association are broken. The common interest and responsibility for
> witness and service to the church remain.[126]

If many of the achievements of the past hundred years had gone by the
board, a much longer effort to bring about German political unity had
also been nullified by the political settlement after World War II. The
German churches are still faced with the problem of establishing a more
perfect union, with the issues today less theological than before, but
politically more divisive than ever.

22.

The Catholic Church in Postwar Germany

Immediate Issues Confronting the Church

In confronting the chaos and problems of postwar Germany, the Catholic church had certain advantages over the Protestant churches. It had first and foremost the help and leadership of the pope. Whereas the Protestants had to establish ties with the ecumenical world, the ties which united German Catholics with world Catholicism had not been broken. There was someone to speak for them and a worldwide organization to channel aid from fellow Catholics. The Vatican, however, could not perform miracles, and had many other countries besides defeated Germany to care for. The papal nunciature had at first been transferred from Berlin to Eichstätt, Bavaria, as a result of bombing raids, and then, with the disappearance of a central German government, the nunciature de facto ceased to exist. After the death of Nuncio Orsenigo on March 23, 1946, no nuncio was named, but through special appointees the pope sought to maintain the continuity of the nunciature in Germany.[1] The last German representative to the Vatican, Baron von Weizsäcker, had lost his position and was soon to be tried at Nürnberg for war crimes.[2]

In 1946, the pope appointed Bishop Aloisius Joseph Muench, of Fargo, North Dakota, as apostolic visitor to Germany.[3] He took up residence at Kronberg in Taunus, near Frankfurt/Main. He also was appointed head of the Vatican mission, Catholic liaison consultant for religious affairs to the American military government, and vicar delegate to American Catholics.[4] This combination of positions, which he tactfully and ably filled, gave him a position of great influence in postwar Germany. In 1949 he was made regent of the apostolic nunciature in Germany, and two years later, after Germany had reestablished a foreign office on March 15, 1951, he became nuncio to the Federal Republic and doyen of the diplomatic corps.[5] The Vatican at no time considered the 1933 concordat abrogated or the nunciature ended.

While the papacy had only a tenuous connection with political authority in Germany, it always had direct contact with the hierarchy and could work through and with them. The papacy, as always, reserved for itself the establishment of church jurisdictions, and refused to alter the prewar boundaries of German dioceses. Yet it was necessary to consider existing realities. After the death of Cardinal Bertram of Breslau on August 15, 1945, Polish apostolic administrators were established for the territories which were now under Polish administration. These areas now came de facto under the immediate jurisdiction of the primate of Poland. All Germans, including former church officials and priests, were soon expelled from these districts. In 1951 the administrators became general vicars, with the rank of titular bishops. The new political boundaries left only a small bit of the once large diocese of Breslau within Germany, and this was henceforth administered from Görlitz. It was, however, not until 1972, after the West German treaties with Poland and Russia accepting the Oder-Neisse boundary had been ratified, that the Vatican definitely recognized that the former German territories should be transferred to Polish dioceses. Six new dioceses were created out of the three (Breslau, Ermland, and the free prelature of Schneidemühl) that previously existed east of the Oder-Neisse line. These, to use their former German names, were Breslau, Oppeln, Landsberg, Kolberg, Stettin, and Ermland.[6]

There were other such administrative adjustments as the curtain between East and West Germany became more impregnable. One by one, in the period before 1972, each of the territories in East Germany belonging to predominantly West German dioceses had received its own local administrative official. The effects of the division of Germany can most clearly and easily be shown by the jurisdictional districts of the Catholic church in East Germany: (1) the bishopric of Berlin; (2) the bishopric of Meissen; the eastern sections of the bishoprics (3) of Fulda; (4) of Paderborn; (5) of Osnabrück; (6) of Würzburg; (7) of Hildesheim; and (8) the remainder (*Restteil*) of the bishopric of Breslau.[7]

If some of the bishoprics were spared division in the establishment of the two Germanies, few of them escaped the effects of other territorial changes. Of the twenty-three bishoprics, twelve were crossed by zonal boundaries and seventeen by state boundaries. The bishopric of Osnabrück was soon subject to legislation by five parliaments (Bremen, Hamburg, Lower Saxony, Schleswig-Holstein, and Mecklenburg) and by three occupying powers (the United States, the United Kingdom and the Soviet Union). Three state governments (Berlin, Bremen, and Baden) had only one Catholic bishop to deal with, but Lower Saxony and Rhineland-Palatinate had five, and Bavaria seven. All the Bavarian bishoprics were old and brought no new organizational problems; only Würzburg had territories outside Bavaria.[8]

Four of the bishops (Aachen, Münster, Speyer, and Trier) had jurisdiction over detached territories outside of the occupation zones. There was pressure from France to separate the Saar (not technically in the French occupation zone) from the dioceses of Trier and Speyer, and to establish a separate bishopric with its seat at Saarbrücken. The Vatican refused, as it also had after World War I.[9]

The unity of the church, its established organization, and the availability of officials with authority to act were all sources of strength. The Catholic church was spared the time-consuming efforts

and frustrations which went into the Protestant attempt to establish a
united church. But it also did not benefit from the soul-searching and
regeneration which accrued to the Protestants in the course of their
discussions and conferences.

445 *The Catholic Church in Postwar Germany*

The hierarchy, speaking for the church, made no declaration of
guilt or penance to parallel the Stuttgart Declaration.[10] Perhaps the very
concept of the infallibility of the church would preclude such a statement, for although there is much self-criticism within the church, the
extent to which such criticism may be openly practiced is always carefully circumscribed.[11] Instead of acknowledging its lack of vision, its sins
of commission or omission and need for penance in a public statement
to the world, the church very early began to explain and justify its
policy during the Hitler period. That it had suffered much hardship was
generally known, and now the church began to present evidence of its
persecution. When the pope, on February 18, 1946, elevated three
Germans to the college of cardinals, all noted for their opposition to
Hitler—Archbishop Joseph Frings of Cologne, Bishop Clemens August,
Count von Galen of Münster, and Bishop Konrad, Count von Preysing of
Berlin—he centered world attention on the church's resistance during
the Nazi years.[12] Books on this opposition began to appear. One of the
first document collections was the important volume by Bishop Johannes Neuhäusler, *Kreuz und Hakenkreuz* (Munich, 1946). Until he
was imprisoned during the war, Neuhäusler was in charge of collecting
material on all Nazi antichurch actions at the diocesan headquarters in
Munich. Much of this evidence had been submitted to Rome, whence it
found its way into Nathaniel Micklem's *National Socialism and the
Roman Catholic Church* (London, 1939). This was the first collection to
present detailed documentary evidence of Hitler's harassment of the
Catholic church. After the war Neuhäusler supplemented this collection
and made it available to German readers. This was the beginning of a
whole list of books building up the church as the great opponent of
national socialism. The volumes did not always present a rounded account and historians have been adjusting their lenses ever since so as to
get a more accurate picture. But these early books remain to this day
invaluable sources, and they did contribute significantly to a favorable
image of the Catholic church in postwar Germany, especially abroad
and among western Allied occupation authorities. This was no small aid
to the church in its work of reconstruction. There were a few books on
the Protestant struggle, but Protestant publicity in the early postwar
years did not equal the Catholic. In 1947 Heinrich Schmid published his
*Apokalyptisches Wetterleuchten: Ein Beitrag der evangelischen Kirche
zum Kampf im Dritten Reich,* and the following year the important
*Kirchliches Jahrbuch für die Evangelische Kirche in Deutschland 1933–
1944,* edited by Joachim Beckmann, and Wilhelm Niemöller's *Kampf
und Zeugnis der Bekennenden Kirche* appeared. In 1950 Heinrich Hermelink's *Kirche im Kampf* presented a documentary collection from the
Evangelical church similar to Neuhäusler's volume.

Besides the diocesan and hierarchical organization, many Catholic societies existed to aid in tackling the problems of postwar Germany. The Protestant church had first to establish the Hilfswerk, which took months to organize; the Catholics had one already at hand. In 1897 the German Association of Catholic Charities (*Deutsche Caritasverband*) had been established with headquarters in Freiburg/Breisgau. It came to embrace all the many social and health organizations of the church and was represented by directing agencies in each diocese. In spite of all attempts to restrict Catholic organizations under Hitler, the Caritasverband had maintained itself.[13] As of July 1, 1947, there were 121,000 men and women doing full-time relief work, among them 80,000 nuns and members of orders.[14] To this figure should be added 700,000 part-time associates, and one should not forget the millions who lent their support. No one will ever be able adequately to evaluate what the work of the Caritasverband meant for postwar Germany and for the Catholic church. In 1945–46 in the Munich archdiocese alone, it distributed 6,732 tons of food to the needy and furnished 3,687,442 meals at its kitchens. The Caritasverband was the channel for distributing relief shipments from abroad, such as the 6,000 tons of food donated by the Vatican up to the fall of 1947, and the 5,000 tons of food and 780,000 Care packages sent by the National Catholic Welfare Conference in America. Swiss Catholics also contributed much aid.[15]

But even existing organizations were not equal to the task, and a special Church Aid Center for Refugees from the East (*Kirchliche Hilfstelle für Ostflüchtlinge*) was established in Frankfurt with a branch in Munich.[16] In June, 1946, the papacy placed the bishop of Ermland, Maximilian Kaller, who had lost his diocese to the Russians and Poles, in charge of this center and entrusted him with the care of all refugees from the east. The aid center was concerned with finding housing and homes for children, helping run the large refugee camps, and providing spiritual care to the scattered Catholic refugees. Many specialized agencies were formed, some designed to bring comfort and comradeship to people from various areas, and others to provide work or counselling. These centers are still functioning today, and they make an imposing list in the official handbook.[17]

The church had another valuable and experienced agency at hand to provide spiritual aid to the Catholics of the diaspora. This was the Boniface Association, dating back to the third Katholikentag in 1849. Its purpose was to provide Catholics living in predominantly Protestant or mixed regions of Germany with church services and school support. The organization had a distinguished record, but even it was unable to cope adequately with the needs of the day.[18]

Of some eleven to twelve million German refugees from the east, about six million were Catholics—many of them from Czechoslovakia, Hungary, and Yugoslavia.[19] Perhaps about two million of these were soon settled in regions where there were Catholic churches and priests, leaving roughly four million scattered throughout the rest of Germany, many of them in the overwhelmingly Protestant areas of northern Germany. Schleswig-Holstein, Lower Saxony, and Hesse had a particularly

large influx, while some of the more Catholic areas of the south remained practically unchanged because the French government excluded refugees from its occupation zone. When compared to the 1940
census, that of 1946 shows the following increases in the number of
Catholics in various dioceses: Meissen (176 percent), Fulda (123.5 percent), Hildesheim (122.2 percent), Osnabrück (86.8 percent), Eichstätt
(53.2 percent), Freiburg (10 percent), Berlin (4.6 percent), and Cologne
(0.7 percent).[20]

Both Protestants and Catholics had the problem of a diaspora to
contend with, but it was perhaps greater for the Catholics. The Protestants were always more widely distributed in Germany, partly because
there were more of them. Now the Catholics had to carry on their work
where they had few established churches or congregations. They were
often awarded guest privileges in Protestant churches, especially in the
Russian zone.[21] The president of the Boniface Association reported in
1949 that in the past four years more than 4,000 emergency stations for
worship had been opened. But in the same report he noted that half of
those Catholic refugees who died did not receive extreme unction, and
that half of the number of Catholic children were without regular religious instruction.[22] By 1951 the number of emergency places of worship
had increased to 7,115 as compared to 754 in 1945.[23] To man the many
preaching stations and administer to the scattered faithful, the church
had the aid of many priests who had left or had been driven from their
homes in the east. By far the largest number came from the diocese of
Breslau. In 1950 there were 2,291 such secular priests and 504 priests
who were members of orders serving in Germany, most of them in those
dioceses with the largest influx of refugees.[24]

The problem was naturally greatest in the first postwar years. Since
then there has been readjustment with Catholics tending to settle in
Catholic regions. In the end, if one considers areas larger than particular
districts, the distribution of Catholics and Protestants has not substantially changed. In Germany as a whole, Catholics numbered 32.4 percent of the population in 1924, 33 percent in 1933, and 35.2 percent in
1946.[25] They remain a minority in both West and East Germany, and
their numbers have remained practically constant in the postwar years.
In West Germany, not including Berlin, the census of 1946 showed 45.9
percent of the population was Catholic, that of 1950 showed 45.2 percent, and that of 1961 showed 45.5 percent.[26] In East Germany the
census of 1946 showed 12.2 percent were Catholic, but later censuses
under Soviet influence provide no statistics on religious affiliation.

The traditional strongholds of Catholicism still remain the South
German-Rhineland areas, with four (North Rhine-Westphalia, Rhineland-Palatinate, Saarland, and Bavaria) out of the ten states having Catholic majorities. What overall figures do not show is that within these and
other states there are many predominantly Protestant or Catholic districts which can only be explained by their having been under the
jurisdiction of a Protestant or Catholic prince about the time of the
Peace of Westphalia (1648). Nor do they reveal that Catholics are still

more rural than Protestants. Before 1914, the large cities of Germany were 71 percent Protestant and only 26 percent Catholic, and although these figures have shifted somewhat, Catholics are distinctly a minority among most big city dwellers.[27] This is a factor to be taken into consideration if Catholic-Protestant statistics are compared in regard to size of family, incomes, suicide rate, mixed marriages, church attendance, and so on. Perhaps urban-rural rather than Catholic-Evangelical is the determining factor in such matters. Sociologists have only begun to study this field.

The Shortage of Clergy and the Catholic Educational Deficit

There is no question that the postwar influx of Catholics into Germany and their final settlement brought great problems to the Catholic church. None was more important than establishing new parishes and finding priests to administer them. The Catholic church traditionally has had many small parishes in Germany, which may not always be the most efficient way of running the church as a whole, but does provide strength and loyalty. A priest can much more easily serve a thousand or more souls in a large urban congregation than if they are scattered about in rural villages. In 1964 about half of the parishes in Germany had less than 1,000 souls, and 71.3 percent of all parishes were served by one priest.[28] In comparison with other European countries this no doubt is a favorable distribution of congregations.

The numerous small historic parishes contribute to creating a shortage of priests when the overall needs of the church are considered. Automobiles have made it easier for one man to serve a number of the smaller parishes and some consolidations have also been undertaken. Villagers, however, usually do not want to give up their churches and resident priests. There is also the problem of providing religious instruction in the schools, although busing and the consolidation of schools is simplifying that task. In Germany the ideal goal is one priest to 1,000 souls, although it is accepted that in urban parishes the ratio will be higher.[29] Some dioceses are better supplied than others. In 1967 the ratio of priests to total Catholic population ranged from 1:1,169 in Eichstätt to 1:2,234 in Cologne. Numerically the ratio is best in the German Democratic Republic, but this advantage is more than offset by the greater difficulties the church encounters there.[30]

While it seems warranted to conclude that the Catholic church in Germany is well supplied with priests as compared to many countries, there is no excess number of either secular or regular clergy. With justification the German church—along with others the world over—fears a growing shortage of priests and is greatly concerned about recruiting and training.[31] In spite of the increase in total population, the number of German priests has remained practically constant, hovering around 20,000 to 21,000 ever since the early days of the Weimar Republic. Yet the number of students studying to be secular priests has declined, and the 364 ordinations in 1968 set a new low, the yearly numbers having ranged between 419 and 527 from 1955 to 1967. The total number of ordinations in all dioceses in 1972 was 204. On the other hand, for a time there was an over-all increase in the ordination of priests in the religious orders, the first notable drop occurring in 1968.[32] This has been attributed to the maintenance of traditional classical requirements and high academic standards for secular priests, whereas the orders provide a more practical education with perhaps less exacting standards. Some of the orders have not required graduation from a gymnasium (*Abitur*), which would be unthinkable in the case of a secular priest.[33] The total number of theological students at the universities where there are Catholic faculties and at the church-run Hochschulen has declined only slightly.[34] These statistical totals, however, include many women and men who are simply seeking to educate themselves as lay theologians or teachers of religion. The church will no doubt increasingly use these lay people, but it is clear that if the church is to continue as before, more students must be recruited to go into the priesthood.

Whether the declining number of candidates has any direct relation to the controversy over clerical celibacy and other matters resulting from the Second Vatican Council is impossible to say. So far the number of resignations from the priesthood has not been unduly large. In the years 1964 to 1968, 195 secular priests out of a total of approximately 21,000 (.93 percent) and 85 priests of orders out of a total of 6,780 (1.3 percent) resigned. Approximately half of these were granted dispensation by the Vatican, and no doubt a number of them will continue to serve the church in some fashion.[35]

The religious orders had been able to retain their foundations and membership to a remarkable extent during the Third Reich.[36] After a period of expansion following the end of the war, the supply of priests in religious orders declined and a drop in future ordinations seems inevitable. The number of lay brothers had remained relatively stable, but their ranks have also been somewhat depleted.[37] The number of monastic sisters increased steadily to about 1957, but after some years of relative stability their membership started to decline. In 1950 there were 4,005 novices, but in 1959, 3,284, and in 1966, 1,903.[38] If this trend continues, there may be no alternative to closing a number of institutions which have been staffed by sisters. There has already been a consolidation or closing of establishments of all kinds, including small hospitals, nursing homes, and schools. The number of institutions maintained by sisters declined from 8,114 in 1950 to 7,538 in 1966. The work of sisters might be supplemented by employing more lay help, which would mean an additional financial burden, but one the church could no doubt assume. The laity will also be asked to contribute more for the services which these church institutions provide, and in Germany there is always the possibility of obtaining more public funds. The state often finds it financially advantageous to keep church-run institutions going rather than to undertake the tasks itself. It is, of course, possible that the decline in monastic enrollments will lead to a wiser and better utilization of what forces are available, which may well in the end strengthen the church. A period of adjustment, however, does seem at hand, and it is almost certain to curtail traditional church services and lead to a more secular society.

Not unrelated to the problem of a future supply of clergy (the convenient German term *Priesternachwuchs* is really untranslatable) is the fact that Catholics still do not share in higher education in the same proportion as do Protestants. This is a phenomenon long recognized in Germany, but never satisfactorily explained. Today the number of Catholics attending gymnasiums, the traditional approach to academic life, is about equal to their proportion in the population. However, many do not complete their course. Attendance figures at the universities show an even greater discrepancy between Catholics and Protestants. For example, in 1961, 34.4 percent of university students were Catholic, whereas Catholics numbered 41.1 percent of the population; Protestants accounted for 59.7 percent of the students, while constituting only 51.1 percent of the population. Although the total number of Catholic students has increased with the contemporary rush to the universities, the relative number in comparison to Protestants has steadily declined.[39] Many reasons have been advanced for the discrepancy, ranging from the simple availability of cash to the more rarified sphere of freedom of inquiry and general educational philosophy. A recent sociological study lists some twenty-eight factors or arguments to be considered in explaining why Catholics lag numerically in seeking higher education.[40]

Catholics are often held to have had a minority complex in the Germany of the past, and certainly they did not have their proper share of governmental positions under the empire. Then political Catholicism and the problems of the German government with French minorities in Alsace-Lorraine and Polish minorities in Prussia seemed to be related.[41] Happily this minority complex is virtually nonexistent today, largely because of Catholic achievements in the political field. From 1918–69, except for the Hitler period, Catholic-centered parties have participated in the national cabinets. In the post-World War II years, the Christian Democratic Union (CDU) and its Bavarian counterpart, the Christian Social Union (CSU), drew heavily on Catholic support. However, political-religious ties have tended to grow weaker. In 1973 the Fulda Bishops' Conference passed a resolution which allowed priests as citizens to become members of political parties so long as the party did not pursue anti-Christian aims, but which prohibited them from working publicly for the interests or election of a party.[42] This resolution was in line with Article 32 of the concordat of 1933, which at that time was meant to implement Hitler's determination to take the clergy and the church out of politics. But if Catholics have come to the top politically, and often hold some of the higher appointive positions in the civil service, judiciary, army, education, and industry, Catholics are still in a minority as compared to their numbers in the population.[43]

The end of the war also led to a rapid revival of church organiza-tions. Harassment and Nazi efforts to destroy the church societies seemed to make them all the more valuable. They were soon function-ing in local congregations and the former national headquarters were again at work. The hierarchy gave special attention to youth organiza-tions. In 1947 a Confederation of German Catholic Youth (*Bund der Deutschen Katholischen Jugend*) was established.[44] Each of the member organizations—for example, the Boy Scouts of Saint George, the Cath-olic German Business Youth, and the Land Youth—retained its separate identity but benefited from a general directorship. The girls' organiza-tions had their own president. In general the church in West Germany continued to sponsor organizations that appealed to special regional occupational or age groups, and those that supported missionary activity or special charities. Conditions in East Germany were not so favorable for activity of this kind.[45]

Although there were paper shortages and the occupation powers exercised licensing control, it is surprising how many and how rapidly church papers appeared.[46] Each diocese soon had its diocesan paper, although the customary Sonntagsblätter revived more slowly. Most news-papers and many periodicals claimed to be nonconfessional, yet as early as 1951 the official Catholic handbook gives an imposing eight-page list of Catholic papers and periodicals. Since that date Catholic publications have continued to expand, and a recent handbook lists 547 journals.[47] Many of these are very up-to-date and their quality excellent; the church has even entered the "illustrated" field. In 1968, amid some fanfare, a progressive weekly paper *Publik* was launched and achieved a circula-tion of around 90,000. However, it aroused the opposition of the more conservative bishops, and in November, 1971, when the twenty-two bishops of the Diocesan Association of West Germany refused to grant further subsidies, *Publik* ceased publication. The paper had provided a forum for frank discussion of questions such as clerical celibacy, the infallibility of the pope, birth control, and legalized abortion. The Evan-gelical Press Service lamented: "In the ecumenical dialogue Protestants have been robbed of their partner."[48] Critical articles do continue to appear, but on the whole the press conforms to what might be considered the accepted Catholic point of view. Moreover, if the church is attacked from without the Catholic press tends to unite in defense, as was the case when Rolf Hochhut's play *The Deputy* aroused attention by charging that Pius XII had not done enough to succor Jews during World War II.[49]

Germany has no private radio stations, but the state-run networks allow ample time to the churches. The morning meditations and other religious broadcasts which had been eliminated in the Nazi era have been resumed. A special headquarters to supervise radio and television work has been established in Frankfurt/Main and it works closely with diocesan centers.[50]

One of the most effective means of rallying support and asserting the position of the church has been the Katholikentag. None had been held in the Nazi period, the last one having assembled in Essen in September, 1932. On September 1–5, 1948, the first postwar meeting and the seventy-second in the long series was held. Katholikentage have been held regularly since. The Central Committee of German Catholics, for years under the presidency of Dr. Karl Prinz zu Löwenstein, is in charge of organizing these rallies.[51] They now alternate with the similar Protestant Kirchentage and are a regular feature of present-day German life. Their function as large pep rallies has its value, and more important, they also serve to educate and help to establish lines of communication between the laity and the church authorities.

Another opportunity for lay consultation with the hierarchy was established when the first meeting of the Joint Synod of Bishoprics was held in Würzburg in May, 1972. In addition to the bishops, carefully chosen laymen, priests, and theologians attended. Among the numerous topics on the agenda was that of allowing qualified laymen and women to preach in church services. The German churches have in general furthered the reforms suggested at the Vatican council on greater use of the laity in church services. While the gathering remained a synod of discussion, it was generally held to have been useful in inaugurating more codeliberation in the church.[52]

Simply put, there is a vast complex of Catholic church organizations in Germany. Even the authorities of the Third Reich could never master the set-up or win the upper hand against the church authorities who were fighting to maintain their existence. Through these organizations the church keeps contact with its members and enlists their help; they are all designed to aid in the "salvation of souls," and they bring home the fact that the church today is far more than a Mass-saying, sacrament-dispensing, and preaching institution.

The new liturgical movement in the church which received such impetus in 1962–65 through the decisions of the Second Vatican Council was underway long before that time in Germany.[53] Along with other leaders, Benedictine scholars at their great foundations of Maria Lach and Ottobeuren were particularly active in the movement to bring about more lay participation in the services and administration of the sacraments. The movement to use less Latin and more German in the Mass found widespread support among German Catholics. A Catholic visitor from South America, writing in 1954, observes:

> What a foreign cleric who travels about Germany notices most of all is the special style of German piety. Prayer is slow and dignified; the rosary prayer takes from twenty to thirty minutes (in contrast to the seven or eight minutes I experienced in southern churches); the congregational singing even in the smallest village church has its character; every diocese has its own song and prayer book; one sees many new churches, in rural regions even crucifixes along the roads, and what is most important, the people to a high degree take part in the liturgy.[54]

Like all broad comparisons, this statement must be read with understanding and even with reservations. Yet it does at the same time stress the important fact that Catholicism in Germany has its own particular style. This is not to say that the Germans are "good" Catholics in comparison to others; how great an impact the church has on individual lives no one can tell. Figures on baptisms, church marriages, and burials indicate a general decline in church activity, although not an alarming one. The Catholic church in Germany has not been spared the growing indifference to religion which marks modern times. This was indeed one of the main reasons why Pope John XXII called the Second Vatican Council into being, "to open the windows" and bring new life into the church.

A recent official handbook carries an interesting table covering the years 1915–67 which tabulates "church baptisms," those who received communion, those who had fulfilled their Easter obligation, and church attendance since 1927.[55] It is not clear exactly what territories are covered, for the boundaries of Germany varied considerably during this period, and it is questionable if the figures for various years are equally accurate. The figures on Easter communion, for example, are based on the distribution of small pictures which are given out at Easter confessions and Easter communions, a procedure which might well lead to some duplication. Church attendance may often be more estimate than actual count. Yet this is the best statistical evidence we have, and all things considered does indicate trends. Again a breakdown of the figures would show a more active participation in church life in rural areas than in the big urban centers. Church participation seems to have reached a postwar high about 1951; since then the figures indicate a slow but steady decline. The percentage of all Catholics attending church declined from 54.2 in 1951 to 40.4 in 1967; the percentage of those fulfilling their Easter obligation sank from 54.2 to 47.4. On the other hand, the number of communions rose from 12.9 for every Catholic in Germany to 14.0.

From 1946 to 1949 the Catholic church had slightly more conversions and readmissions than withdrawals. Since then it has uniformly had more losses than gains. The number of withdrawals reached a high of 44,003 in 1958 and has ranged down to about 24,000 in other years, although there are no reports from parts of the East German dioceses for some of the years. The withdrawals are no doubt motivated in part by the desire to avoid payment of church taxes, but also by many other factors. Many join the Evangelical churches and the various sects have also made their share of converts. Yet a net loss by resignation of 2,555 to 22,567, the yearly range between 1951 and 1967, is a slight loss in a church of 29 million, and is more than offset by the normal population increase.[56]

The Catholic church has consistently lost more members than it has gained through mixed marriages, and the number of such marriages has regularly increased. For every 100 civil marriages where both parties were Catholic, there were 64.1 civil mixed marriages in 1951 and 82.3 in 1966; for every 100 of church marriages where both parties were Catholic, there were 25.5 mixed marriages in 1951 and 37.4 in 1966.[57]

This shows that the number of mixed marriages has increased rapidly, both among those who resort only to civil marriage and those who are also married in the church. In Germany by law all couples must have a civil marriage, and a religious ceremony is then optional. In 1966, for example, of the 148,853 purely Catholic couples, 92.5 percent later were married by the church; of the 122,569 mixed couples, only 41.9 percent were married by the Catholic church. In the eyes of the Catholic church, therefore, about 58 percent of the mixed couples had contracted an invalid marriage. If one projects this figure back for a generation, the number of people living in marriages religiously considered invalid and the number of children resulting from them runs into the millions. A Jesuit scholar who has written a provocative article on the Catholic attitude toward mixed marriages concludes that the present regulations cause people to lose respect for the church, and drive them not only out of the Catholic church but often away from all religion into a sort of "religious no man's land;" such measures do not encourage church life. He advocates that the church should recognize state marriages.[58] The church of necessity has had to accommodate itself to the prevailing mores, and its treatment of individuals who have not been married in the church differs considerably in practice from what strict interpretation of church regulations would demand. The German Catholic hierarchy have repeatedly considered the problem, and were strong supporters at the Vatican Council of a change in the church's attitude toward mixed marriages.[59]

The German hierarchy in general constituted a part of the liberal wing at the Vatican Council. This attitude has carried over to affairs in Germany. For example they have left the problem of birth control to the consciences of the individuals concerned. They have also shown more cooperation and a livelier ecumenical spirit than formerly in day-by-day contacts with the Evangelical church.[60] It would not have made much sense to come to an agreement on a common German text of the Lord's Prayer with the Evangelical church if there was no intention of using it. The Catholics cooperate in the Ecumenical Committee for Common Liturgical Texts of the Churches of the German-speaking Territories. This committee, with over forty members from the churches of West and East Germany, Austria, and Switzerland, have worked out common texts (with slight customary Protestant and Catholic variations) for the Gloria, the Nicean and Apostles' Creeds, the Sanctus, and Agnus Dei, and the Praise to the Father. On publishing the texts in May, 1971, President Joachim Beckmann of the Evangelical church in the Rhineland and Catholic Bishop Hermann Volk announced: "The publication of the common texts is a call, not to forsake the common Christian creeds, but to confess the old beliefs with new trust."[61] The new texts are to be put into use gradually, starting with ecumenical services and mixed marriages, and are to be introduced officially later. In 1969 the Catholic church appointed an observer to cooperate in the Working Community of Christian Churches in Germany, the interdenominational body founded in 1948, and in

September, 1973, the German Bishops' Conference decided to apply

for active membership in it.[62] Cardinal Julius Döpfner, as head of the bishops' conference, has joined with Protestant Land Bishop Hermann Dietzfelbinger, as head of the Council of the Evangelical Church of Germany, in issuing public pronouncements, such as the one on "The Law of the State and Social Order" (1970), on pastoral care in cases of mixed marriages (1971), on the condition of the rural population in North Rhine-Westphalia (1971), and on help for Pakistani refugees (1971).[63] In 1973 the Catholic bishopric of Münster and the Evangelical church in Westphalia published a joint study entitled "Ways to One Another for the Churches."[64] It developed the possibilities of practical cooperation and put them forward for further discussion and study. It can also be said that in general there is a wider and more understanding acceptance of the Protestant Reformation and its leaders by German Catholics today than in former periods.[65] Yet all this does not mean that the special position of the Catholic church has in any way diminished.

Closer Catholic cooperation with the Old Catholics has also been furthered. By agreement a member of either church can now ask a priest of the other for the sacraments of Eucharist, atonement, or extreme unction. However, when the bishop of Limburg appointed a priest converted from the Old Catholics, who was married and had two sons, to head the Maria Hilf parish in Frankfurt, the bishop was denounced by the nuncio, who requested the Vatican to remove him. The nuncio's action created a furor among the people, who in general approved the innovations introduced and condoned by the bishop of Limburg.[66]

The Catholic church in Germany extends its activity throughout the world, and this work is largely supported by freewill offerings of the faithful. German orders and priests share in the general worldwide mission work of the church.[67] A permanent secretariat with headquarters in Bonn supervises the care of German-speaking Catholics who have emigrated and maintains churches in many cities of the world for more or less temporary residents.[68] The Association of Catholic Charities (*Caritasverband*) has a special international section which undertakes relief work abroad.[69] In recent years it has had a Near East program and also undertook aid to Nigeria-Biafra. The Caritasverband works closely with another special fund established by the bishops in 1959 to combat hunger and sickness throughout the world. This is known as *Misereor* ("to have compassion"), and is not designed to grant relief to individuals or to support churches or monasteries, but to furnish aid wherever it is needed, without regard to race or religion. Between 1959 and 1968 it supported some 6,404 projects scattered in many countries, furnishing experts, technical aid, and money for agriculture, health, housing, slum clearance, education, and other needs.[70]

Whereas Misereor is nonconfessional and works closely with the World Council of Churches, Bread for the World, the United Nations Food and Agricultural Organization, and other international agencies, German Catholics have also undertaken a most effective support program for the Catholic church in South America. Known as the *Adveniat* (from *Adveniat regnum tuum*—"Thy kingdom come"), it was started in 1961 when the bishops in a pastoral letter asked for a special Christmas offering for the work of the South American church.[71] The main efforts are to train a greater number of native priests and to supply modern aids to make their work more effective. The program has developed rapidly; bishops in other countries have followed the German example in establishing special organizations to aid the Latin American churches. The pope has repeatedly called attention to the great need for such efforts, and these organizations work in close cooperation with the Papal Commission for Work in South America.

The Church and the Lands in the Federal Republic

It has been noted that the new postwar state and federal constitutions dealt favorably with the churches, particularly in West Germany. The Catholic church was greatly concerned about securing safeguards for Catholic religious instruction in the schools, and in general it was successful except in the state of Bremen, which was exempted from the general guarantee that religious instruction should be given in accordance with the teachings of the churches. Bremen was at that time giving instruction in Bible history on an interconfessional basis, and it was permitted to continue this policy.[72] The teachers of religion must have the approval of church authorities (*missa canonica*) which safeguards the orthodoxy of instruction, and the church also sought to have the right to erect confessional schools inserted in all constitutions. It was not very successful in this effort, for while there was little opposition to making religious education a regular subject of instruction—which no teacher was compelled to give and from which any parent could ask that a child be excused—the question of school type was always a controversial issue. Regions which were used to having interdenominational schools were opposed to interspersing confessional schools among them. In the end only interdenominational schools were permitted in Bremen, Hamburg, Schleswig-Holstein, and Hesse; in four others—Lower Saxony, North Rhine-Westphalia, Rhineland-Palatinate, and Bavaria—both confessional and interdenominational schools were permitted.[73] Only interdenominational schools are allowed in Baden and North Württemberg, whereas both types are permitted in the former Württemberg-Hohenzollern region, which is now known as "Governing Circle of Tübingen." In Lower Saxony, the former territory of Oldenburg has only confessional schools, and this is also true in the Saarland. In Berlin, as in all of the Democratic Republic, all schools are organized on an interdenominational basis.[74]

The right to establish confessional schools was anchored in the concordats which the papacy had concluded with Bavaria and Prussia, and most importantly in the concordat of 1933 with the Reich, where the papacy was accorded the right to establish confessional schools throughout Germany. Prussia had disappeared, but it was generally held that the Prussian-Vatican agreement of 1929 still applied to former Prussian territories. The Soviet occupation authorities never recognized this claim, nor did they consider the concordat of 1933 valid; the same holds for the authorities of the Democratic Republic today. In Bavaria the Bavarian concordat was recognized as still in effect. Just what status that Reich concordat of 1933 had was not clear, for although church authorities pressed for its express recognition in the constitution of the Federal Republic, the founding fathers refused. On the other hand, no one in the federal government thought of cancelling it, or for that matter even questioning if it still was a valid treaty. When Baden-Württemberg was drawing up its fundamental law in 1952, the Vatican requested the German federal authorities to exert their influence so that the terms of the new state constitution would be in keeping with the concordat of 1933, especially in regard to the schools. This the federal authorities did, and although the Württemberg-Baden officials did not accept the views emanating from Rome and Bonn, they were able to sidestep a showdown. When Lower Saxony in 1954 was debating a new school law, the Vatican charged that the confessional schools, to which the church had a right according to the concordat, were being jeopardized by the special position accorded the interdenominational schools.

The issue obviously needed clarification, and the Federal government brought charges against Lower Saxony in the constitutional court at Karlsruhe, charging Lower Saxony with violation of its duties and loyalty to the Federal Republic by enacting the school law of 1954. Bremen joined Lower Saxony, arguing that to enforce the concordat in Bremen would be a violation of Article 141 of the constitution whereby Bremen was exempt from giving confessional instruction in the schools. Hesse too joined the case, maintaining that the concordat was invalid because it had not been concluded legally, having been enacted under the Enabling Act of 1933.

The case naturally drew much attention and aroused much debate throughout Germany. Important constitutional questions were at stake. It was not until March, 1957, that the court handed down its verdict. It held that the concordat as a whole was valid, but the school clauses were no longer binding, for under the constitution of 1949 the states were given supreme power over education. Even before the enactment of the federal constitution, the states had enacted both constitutional and other legislation that was contrary to the provisions of the concordat. This was known to the people who had drawn up the federal constitution, and if they had wanted to lay a restriction on the states in the field of education in line with the 1933 concordat, they should have specifically recognized the agreement in the constitution. It was, all told, a practical compromise which, in accordance with traditional German practice, left the regulation of schools to the various German states.[75]

With friendly interpretation and cooperation, the concordat still provided enough mutual benefit to make it a valuable agreement. Thus under the concordat the reestablishment of a Catholic chaplaincy in the army caused no difficulties comparable to those with the Protestant churches. Today there is again a Catholic military bishop for the Bundeswehr, one of the main desiderata which had first led the German government to initiate concordat negotiations in 1932–33.[76] The bishops also continue to take their oath of loyalty to the state, although Bremen refuses to participate in the ceremonies in respect to the bishops of Hildesheim and Osnabrück, whose dioceses include portions of the territory of Bremen. Bremen maintains that such procedure is contrary to the federal constitution. Hesse permits the bishops to take their oath, but disputes the legality of Article 16 of the Reich concordat requiring it.[77]

Since the mid-1950s the church has relaxed its battle for confessional schools, in part because of state-sponsored educational reforms such as the establishment of consolidated schools and the use of school buses. Much public discussion arose in the late 1950s and 1960s over what was generally called the "educational catastrophe." In 1958 the synod of the Evangelical Church in Germany issued a statement calling for a thorough revision of the German educational system which would place less emphasis on confessional differences.[78] No doubt the ecumenical spirit which has developed in Germany and in the world in the wake of the recent Vatican Council has also played a part. Even Bavaria amended its constitution in 1968, striking out the provision that all public elementary schools must be confessional or interdenominational, and established a common school for all children (Gemeinsame Volkschule), "where the pupils are to be instructed and brought up according to the principles of the Christian confessions."[79] There had been much negotiation with church leaders, both Catholic and Protestant, and neither church fought this constitutional change when it came before the people in a referendum. If the schools are no longer confessional, they are still Christian, with opening and closing prayers and a cross in classrooms. To accommodate children who do not adhere to a Christian confession the law refers to a constitutional provision that in all schools the religious susceptibilities of all pupils are to be respected.[80] No child is compelled to attend religion classes, but the Bavarian constitution demands as an alternative "instruction in the generally recognized principles of morality."[81] For years such instruction in ethics was not provided, but in view of the increasing number of pupils who were declining to attend religion classes, the Bavarian Ministry of Education in 1972 drew up syllabi for classes in ethics and began instituting the program.[82]

The new Bavarian school law of 1966, as further amended in 1968, 1969, and 1970, does not mention confessional schools, but the principle is not entirely abandoned. Classes are to be organized according to efficient administrative and pedagogical practices; however, if parents agree, school administrators are to place pupils of the same confession together if a class is divided into two or more parallel sections.[83] This practice had been common in gymnasiums in the past, because of the separate religious instruction each group had to receive, but it had been ended under the National Socialists. The Bavarian law also states that teachers can be assigned without reference to confession, but the religious affiliation of the pupils should be considered. This provision can be traced to the old confessional school requirement that pupils should be taught by teachers of their own confession. It is repeated in the changes which were made in the Bavarian concordat of 1924, and was given additional emphasis: "In classes and instructional groups at primary schools that are made up entirely of Catholic pupils, instruction and education are to be in accord with the special provisions of the Catholic confession."[84] This clause clearly means that Catholic teachers should be employed to teach solidly Catholic classes wherever they may appear.

The persons who teach the regular religion classes, given to pupils of each confession separately, must have the approval of the churches. In the revision of the Bavarian concordat the Catholic church sought to assure, as far as possible, the appointment of at least one Catholic teacher at all schools, so that a Catholic teacher would always be available to give religious instruction to Catholic students. Pedagogical Hochschulen are no longer to be organized on a confessional basis, but in the revision of the concordat as well as in the revision of the agreement with the Evangelical Lutheran church, provision is made for the establishment of special Catholic and Protestant faculties so that teachers can be trained to give religious instruction.[85] Religious orders can be employed in the Bavarian schools if their members are as well qualified as other state teachers, and if two-thirds of the parents request that instruction be given by the orders.[86] Private schools, which at times receive some state help, are permitted.

The interdenominational school, which the National Socialists had imposed on Bavaria with so much pressure and with so much opposition from the Catholic church, by agreement has now become the order of the day. No doubt the official church still prefers the confessional school system, but the issue is no longer a serious one.[87] In this respect the Catholic church has approached the position held by the Protestant churches for some time. The autobahn was not the only modern institution furthered by the Third Reich.

Like the Protestant churches, the Catholic church has negotiated agreements with the various state governments to regulate postwar problems.[88] For example, the agreement of March 4, 1963, which Hesse negotiated with the four bishops whose sees are partially within its boundaries, provides that the state shall pay a yearly subsidy of 1,924,900 marks to the bishopric of Fulda, 507,700 to the bishopric of Limburg, 768,500 to the bishopric of Mainz, and 23,100 to the bishopric of Paderborn. The treaty covered other points, but was largely concerned with financial matters. It was the nuncio to Germany who exchanged ratifications of the agreement, and so the Vatican was also party to the accord.[89]

By far the most formal and detailed of such agreements was the concordat which the Vatican concluded in 1965 with the state of Lower

Saxony, whose school legislation had led to the Supreme Court decision on the validity of the 1933 concordat. The new concordat permitted confessional schools on the request of parents if they were consistent with a well-ordered school system. There were also provisions in regard to religious education in schools, the establishment of a Catholic theological faculty at the University of Göttingen, the collection of church taxes, and many other matters. In scope it compares to the Bavarian, Prussian, and Baden concordats of the Weimar period.[90]

By various constitutional, treaty, and legislative provisions, the Catholic church in West Germany has, like the Evangelical church, been granted the right to collect church taxes from its members on the basis of state tax lists. These taxes are levied on a diocesan level, and then distributed to various parishes and other institutions. They usually amount to 8 to 10 percent of the income tax and are collected by the state for the usual fee of 3 to 4 percent. In some dioceses Kirchgeld, an additional small fee of perhaps 3 to 5 marks, is collected from every parishioner.[91] There are also the usual freewill offerings, especially for missions, and income from property and state subsidies. A brief summary of income and expenditures of the various dioceses in 1968 shows that the church taxes constitute by far the largest source of income. Only in the diocese of Münster is it exceeded by other income.[92]

The numerous agreements which both churches have negotiated with the states are in line with a general German recognition of a new partnership between church and state. The states now settle matters with the churches less by unilateral legislation than by negotiated agreement; the churches are increasingly being recognized as contractual entities in our modern pluralistic society.

The Church in the German Democratic Republic

Although former German territory now held by Poland has been transferred to Polish dioceses, the diocesan boundaries are not as yet (1977) restricted to the territorial boundaries of the German Democratic Republic. Negotiations with the Vatican to achieve this end have been initiated.[93] Through the establishment of special administrative districts, however, the goal of the East German authorities—not to have to deal with other than East Germans—has been achieved. Although the German Catholic church was still considered one, and the East German bishops were held to be members of the Fulda Bishops' Conference, they were not free to attend its meetings after the erection of the Berlin Wall in 1961. Instead they have attended their own meeting (*Berliner Ordinarienkonferenz*).[94] Contact with the church in West Germany is now largely by letter, and gradually the Catholic church in East Germany has been restricted to East German boundaries. In 1961 Suffragan Bishop Dr. Alfred Bengsch, living in East Berlin, was appointed bishop of Berlin with jurisdiction over both parts of the city. He has since been made a cardinal, and continues to reside in the eastern sector of the city, which on the whole has been very advantageous to the church. For years he was permitted to visit West Berlin only three days a month; the church there is actually administered by a general vicar and his staff. Cardinal Bengsch was also chairman of the Berliner Ordinarienkonferenz, and as such had certain supervisory duties over the church in the whole of the Democratic Republic. In October, 1976, the Vatican announced the establishment of an independent East German Berlin Bishops' Conference with the same canonical standing as the Fulda Bishops' Conference in West Germany. Cardinal Bengsch will head the new group and will also remain a member of the Fulda conference. The Berlin conference will have full church jurisdiction for the territory of East Germany.[95]

Neither the Soviet nor the East German governmental authorities recognize the validity of the concordat of 1933, or that the provisions of the Prussian concordat of 1929 still apply to former Prussian territory. Like the Protestant churches, the Catholic church has had to assume the burden of religious education without the aid of school authorities. The state-sponsored Youth Dedication Services, designed to compete with Christian confirmation, met with the same condemnation by Catholic as by Protestant church leaders. As in the case of the Evangelical churches, the state no longer cooperates in the collection of church taxes, but does contribute certain subsidies to supplement salaries and particularly for reconstruction of historic church buildings.[96]

Under the 1968 constitution of the German Democratic Republic, the Catholic church, along with others, lost its position as a public corporation. While its property is not considered "social property," it has the protection accorded to all private property. Churches are given the right to conduct their own business in line with the constitution and laws. The constitution also provides that certain matters may be regulated in agreement between church and state. How far this will lead to settlement of difficulties by negotiation rather than by unilateral legislation remains to be seen. The constitution guarantees each citizen the right to belong to a religious faith and to practice it. In general there has been little interference with holding religious services, administering sacraments, holding pilgrimages or processions, giving religious instruction on church property or in homes, or arranging special church gatherings. The government has never attempted to enforce an active antichurch policy as did the Russian government in the early 1920s. There are three seminaries and a number of preparatory schools for the training of priests in the Democratic Republic. Monastic establishments number about 121, and the Catholic church still maintains hospitals and children's and old people's homes.[97]

It is not direct interference with the activities of the church that has caused the greatest difficulties in East Germany, but rather indirect pressure and the constant upholding of Marxism and what are often considered non-Christian values. The bishops have not remained silent, but their objections are considered as protests of private individuals.[98] The church has never taken on the characteristics of a resistance movement. It has been able to retain its own unity, and there are no special peace priests' groups such as have existed in other eastern bloc countries. Under the burden of a cross, at times quite heavy but always bearable, the Catholic church has been able to continue to carry forward its work in the Democratic Republic.

23.

Survey and Evaluation

This study has dealt primarily with the actual working of church institutions in Germany during the Nazi era, a time of great stress and uncertainty. It is apparent to all that the churches were slow to move, were beset by differences both among the leaders and among the ranks, and cannot be said to have won any glorious battles against Nazi activities and Weltanschauung. On the other hand, if one looks at the history of Nazi Germany, the resistance of the churches and, more especially, the creation of the Confessing church stand out in contrast to the submergence of all other organizations, labor unions, political parties, and even the army to the policies of national socialism. This book traces the slow rise of resistance in both the great divisions of the Christian church, and examines the reservations, the stumbling blocks, and the varying points of view that hampered its development. Finally, in order not to leave the churches stranded amidst the chaos of Germany's collapse in 1945, the main features of the present religious picture in Germany are indicated. Twelve years of national socialism and World War II have left their mark.

To understand the complex relationships and the diversity of institutions in the Protestant church at the time of Hitler it was necessary to go back to the Reformation to see how closely the states and churches were tied together, and how in the course of subsequent centuries and territorial changes many of the states of Germany became religiously mixed, with varied obligations and agreements between each state and the religious groups within its borders. The churches were organized on a Land basis, but while this made them somewhat similar, each church evolved its own rules, regulations, and practices. It was also necessary to trace, if only briefly, the varying fortunes of the Catholic hierarchy in its efforts to maintain its privileges and authority in the German states.

Religious diversity, not uniformity, was characteristic of Germany, and this created problems both for the churches and for the state. This diversity was not manifested only in the division between Protestant and Catholic. Among the Protestants there were differences between Lutheran, Reformed, numerous Free Churches, and diverse sectarian groups; the Protestant churches also experienced such varied developments as pietism, religious socialism, and national-folkish groups. Within the Catholic church there were also differences, although more along administrative than doctrinal lines. There were disputes between lay and ecclesiastical princes in times past, and differences between German and minority Polish and French-speaking Catholics in more recent days. The Fulda and Munich-Freising conferences of bishops did not always coordinate their policies, and after 1870 there was the problem of the Old Catholic movement.

By the time of the Weimar Republic certain trends had become well established. A steady growth of self-government and an increasing desire for greater unity among the Protestant churches had brought many changes and new organizations. When Hitler took over, most of the Protestant churchmen were ready for a more centralized and national church body. In this they were at one with Nazi aspirations, and there was no real objection in the churches to the drawing up of a new church constitution establishing a German Evangelical church. Yet the current of the movement for independence and self-administration within the church did not agree with any restoration of state authority over the churches. While there was the facade of a national church, and there was to be a Reich bishop, the church leaders insisted on retaining the autonomy and confessional basis of the various Land churches. Above all they wanted to keep the churches under their own administration and control. The two movements, one for unity, the other for self-government, which had been developing side by side during the past decades were now on a crash course. The state sought to dominate the church governments, to coordinate the churches for its own ends. The result was the Kirchenkampf of the Nazi period. Deep and new rifts again appeared within the Protestant church, and also within the Confessing church, between the more radical Dahlem wing and the more conservative intact churches. There were also those who sought to remain neutral. Only in this context can the Kirchenkampf be understood.

The Catholic as well as the Protestant churches had in the eighteenth century been turned largely into servants of the state (*Staatskirchentum*). The secularization of the great Catholic ecclesiastical states at the time of Napoleon and the seizure by the princes of much church property tightened the financial ties between the state and the Catholic church. As compensation for the seized property the states guaranteed a set subsidy to the churches. These obligations, written down in legal documents, were honored by Hitler and are still recognized today. The postrevolutionary years brought the growth of ultramontanism and an internal revival within the whole Catholic church. The remnants of Staatskirchentum were gradually swept aside. The church sought to define its relationship to the state in a new era of concordat negotiation. The concordat of 1817 with Bavaria marks its one success in Germany until the period of the Weimar Republic, and the much desired concordat applying to all Germany did not come until the days of Hitler. In Germany as in other predominantly Protestant countries, the Catholic church grew more self-assured and aggressive.

Catholics as well as Protestants benefited by the ideas of religious liberty and individual rights which had been stimulated by the French

Revolution. More than ever before the state came to adopt an impartial attitude toward both Christian confessions. This so-called *Paritätischer Staat* was gradually to develop into the religiously neutral state where all confessions and all sects would receive impartial treatment. Even Jews, whose emancipation became a reality after 1815, were to benefit by this development until they held a position under the Weimar Republic that compared favorably with their status in any other country.

The lessening influence of the churches on the educational system during the Empire and the Weimar Republic foretold the changes and conflicts of the Hitler years. Hitler abolished the confessional schools in favor of interdenominational schools and did away with most of the private schools. Religious instruction in the schools was curtailed but not abolished. With the end of Nazism the confessional schools were restored in most states of West Germany, although they have since lost ground. Private schools were again permitted. Religious instruction re-gained its old position in the curriculum, and churches were even given the right to approve the teachers. In East Germany the interde-nominational schools established by Hitler were retained and gradually religion classes were abolished. They are now left entirely to the churches. In West Germany the state has befriended the churches and their programs, but in East Germany the state has often assumed a hostile attitude.

The ecumenical movement was well under way in the German Protestant churches during the Weimar Republic, and though radically curtailed under Hitler, ecumenical ties were never completely broken off. Since the war, Protestant churches in both West and East Germany have shared in the work of the World Council of Churches and in the Lutheran World Federation. Participation in the international ecumeni-cal movement has carried over a spirit of cooperation to affairs within Germany. The formation of the Working Community of Christian Churches in Germany in 1948 brought formal ties between the Land churches and some of the Free churches and subsequently even with the Catholic church. In general, the Land churches today show greater understanding and toleration of smaller religious groups, although the term "sect" has lost few of its derogatory overtones. The ecumenical spirit, strengthened by common suffering under Hitler, has brought more intimate and better relations between the Protestant and Catholic churches. They talk together and work together more than ever before, although of course areas of disagreement still exist.

If the German Protestant churches and movements have had their share in shaping the Protestant world at large, so too has the German Catholic church within the Roman church. The German church led the opposition to the curtailment of liberalism and the increase of papal powers at the Vatican Council of 1870. So sharp was the feeling that some German churchmen refused to accept the dogma of papal infalli-bility and took the lead in establishing the Old Catholic church. Yet Catholics as a whole in Germany have remained loyal to the papacy.

The Center party helped shape the constitutional framework of the

Weimar Republic and became the leading government party, a role the Christian Democratic Union again played after World War II. Not only did the Catholic parties bring Catholics into the mainstream of German political life, but they also did much to destroy the minority complex which at times seemed to infect German Catholicism. In the nineteenth century, largely through the efforts of Bishop Wilhelm von Ketteler of Mainz, the Catholic church was made aware of the church's social and charitable obligations to the working class. So much did his ideas infect the Catholic church that Leo XIII, in issuing his famous encyclical *Rerum Novarum,* referred to Ketteler as "my great predecessor." The Second Vatican Council again found German Catholic bishops as leaders within the liberal wing. Some of the most challenging books on present-day Catholic doctrines and practices have come from German Catholic theologians. The Reverend Hans Küng, although a German Swiss, teaches at the University of Tübingen, and in his studies and pronouncements has attacked some of the dogmatic teachings of the church, notably that of papal infallibility. He has been censored for his views by the pope, but the German hierarchy has not moved against him.

There have been many studies of German theological thought and writings during the centuries since the Reformation. No country has produced more eminent theological scholars. Their teaching and writings were extremely important in shaping the thinking of the leaders of the German churches, and this has not been overlooked. But no attempt has been made to analyze all the developments in this field; instead the day-to-day problems of keeping the churches functioning and free from state control have been brought to the fore. Nor has an attempt been made at a detailed study of Nazi anti-Jewish policy. That has been done by others. Yet the problem of anti-Semitism could not be avoided. Here emphasis has been placed on the all-too-slow realization of the meaning of Hitler's racial policy for the Christian world. The evidence is overwhelming that church leaders, both Protestant and Catholic, were indeed slow to think of much outside their own bailiwick. At first their concern with Nazi racial policy stemmed from its impact on converted baptized Jews. These were indeed Christians, whatever their race, and the churches tried to protect them. They also sought to uphold the Judaic-Christian heritage, notably against the efforts of the Nazis to revile and do away with the Old Testament. The survival and independence of the churches (and in the Protestant churches combating the doctrines of the German Christians) seemed to be the transcending problem. While this concern continued, gradually the church leaders took more cognizance of the inhuman and un-Christian policies of the Nazis. From merely speaking out against euthanasia and for the Christian Jews, they eventually spoke up for all Jews. This was a much belated and not very effective condemnation of Nazi racial policies. By that time the damage was done; there was no way of stopping the Holocaust.

Hitler had come to power on a platform of restoring German honor and Germany's "rightful place among the nations of the world." The revival of national and patriotic feeling was welcomed by most Germans. Nationalism in modern times, with its chauvinism and pride, has shown itself time and time again to be the strongest force to reckon with in all world problems. It is the force on which dictatorships batten. It is often charged that the churches were too circumspect and too inherently conservative in opposing Hitler's aggressive policies. Yet to oppose Hitler's rebuilding efforts was a daring thing to do, and even in the years before the war was considered treason by the authorities. What made the churches' resistance significant was that they were almost alone in the Germany of that day in criticizing the state, and in doing so they spoke for many who did not venture to raise their voices. How effective they were is impossible to assess, but even Hitler at times stayed the hands of his lieutenants because he wanted no new Kulturkampf. He would have liked to have the party stand impartially above the churches; his was a political, not a religious, movement. Likewise the churches desired to restrict themselves to their own affairs; they would have liked to stand aside from political opposition and controversy. Yet the Nazi party and the churches upheld values and practices that inevitably led to conflict. Neither churches nor state were able to draw an acceptable dividing line between their activities, basically because the churches upheld the Christian as opposed to the Nazi ethic and Weltanschauung. On this foundation they were able to maintain their existence and protest to the very end.

It was not easy for the churches to pick up the pieces and put them together again after the collapse of the Hitler Reich. The Protestant churches, torn apart by the German Christian and the Confessing church movements, were far more disrupted by the years of Nazi dominance than the Catholic church. Yet by forbearance and compromise they were able to get their churches reorganized and functioning again. The old Land churches were retained, although their boundaries in most instances no longer corresponded with the territorial boundaries of the newly drawn states. The new national Evangelical Church in Germany, while a more centralized church body than ever existed before, still remains a federation. Yet the long struggle to arrive at greater unity has continued and has achieved remarkable success in the postwar years, particularly in the field of communion and pulpit fellowship. The division of the church into separate governing bodies in the Federal and the Democratic Republics was the result of political pressure and only reluctantly acceded to by the churches.

The concept of a *Volkskirche*—a "people's church"—has been characteristic of Germany throughout the centuries. Just what the term covers is not always clear, but in general it has seemed to mean that a person is born, reared, and dies within either a Protestant Land church or the Catholic church, as well as within the state. Citizenship and church membership pretty much went together, for the state in great measure supported the church financially. To do away with the Volkskirche would be to convert all churches into bodies made up only of covenanted members who furnish its finances. Germany would become a country of Free churches and sects. There were those in the Confessing church movement who wanted such a radical reorganization in 1945, but they were persuaded that there was still much virtue and vitality in the idea of the Volkskirche. The nature of the Volkskirche has changed under the impact of an increasingly secular society. Church withdrawals have become easier and have increased, yet at no overwhelming rate. The Germans, particularly in West Germany, still are willing to pay a relatively small church tax in order to consider themselves church members, if only to have a church available to baptize their children, to give them a certain amount of religious instruction, perhaps to marry them, and most important, to bury them. Even in the Democratic Republic the concept of a Volkskirche has not been entirely abandoned, although to a great extent only the trappings remain. The concept of building a wall between the church and the state is alien to German history; even the government in East Germany, with its penchant for building walls, has not attempted to construct a wall against religion. East German state subsidies to the churches have not entirely disappeared, although they are much reduced. The government has indeed insisted that the churches be organized independently from those of West Germany, but it has not tried to hinder the East German churches from cooperating with the World Council of Churches.

In this study attention has been centered on the steady growth of church self-government, the increasing desire for unity among the churches, the lessening influence of the churches on the educational system, and the increasing impact of the ecumenical movement. These movements developed in the midst of other historically important events and were influenced by them. There are to be sure no lessons of history, only experiences of history, and even these are seen differently by different individuals. The experience of the Hitler era did not fundamentally change the historical trends of the past; rather it confirmed them. It awakened a determination, more resolute than ever before, that the churches must not be dependent on the state, and that they must not withdraw, having nothing to say about what the state is doing. In post-World War II West Germany there has been an almost pathological determination on the part of the churches to speak up on public issues before it is too late.

A realization on the part of churchmen that the gap between Christian ideals and state actions is in fact the responsibility of the Christian churches may well be the most significant consequence of the churches' resistance to Hitler. Numerous German churchmen, foremost among them Martin Niemöller, have openly owned their failure to recognize early the full significance of Hitler's treatment of the Jews. They admit their narrow vision when at first their concern was only for Christian Jews. They are penitent for their slow realization that inhumanity to man includes all men, and that the church should insist upon Christian practices towards all races and creeds. They consider their early blindness to Nazism a fundamental error for which they carry personal guilt and for which they have sought forgiveness from a forgiving God. Along with their declaration that the churches should admit their failure to uphold Christian standards from the first, stated by the Protestant leaders in the Stuttgart Declaration of Guilt, they have also maintained that individuals should not be hounded by an eternal specter of collective guilt. They recognize that there are degrees of guilt, and while a certain collective guilt cannot be denied, individuals as such find it difficult to accept, if only because of their individual helplessness and often ignorance. There is no answer as yet to this troubling question of collective guilt, but it has become a force in society, not only in Germany but in other countries as well.

The resistance in Germany to Nazi practices is open to the charge of being belated and to some extent half-hearted, but there were those who suffered for it, and the impact of their resistance has been felt far beyond Germany. The names of Bonhoeffer and Martin Niemöller, Galen and Faulhaber, and many others are known internationally. Perhaps the Church Struggle—actually the only real resistance by organized groups in Germany—may have begun a new trend, one away from the comfortable Volkskirche to a church much smaller in numbers but more vital. The future of the churches in the two Germanies cannot be predicted, but it is to be expected that, as in the past, they will be able to make the adjustments that a changing society and government necessitate.

Notes

Abbreviations

ADAP	*Akten zur Deutschen Auswärtigen Politik, 1918–1945*
AK	*Allgemeines Kirchenblatt*
Akad. D. Recht	Akademie für Deutsches Recht
Ausw. A.	Auswärtiges Amt
BA	Bundesarchiv in Koblenz
Berlin, K. Arch.	Archiv für die Geschichte des Kirchenkampfes an der Kirchlichen Hochschule Berlin-Zehlendorf
Besetz. Gebiete	Reichsministerium für die besetzen Ostgebiete
BFSP	*British Foreign and State Papers*
Biel. Arch., Coll. W. Niemöller	Bielefeld Archive, Collection Wilhelm Niemöller. (Officially: Archiv der Evangelischen Kirche in Westfalen; Bestand: Bielefelder Archiv des Kirchenkampfes [Wilhelm Niemöller].)
CH	*Church History*
CHR	*Catholic Historical Review*
DBFP	*Documents on British Foreign Policy, 1919–1939*
DGFP	*Documents on German Foreign Policy, 1918–1945*
EvTh	*Evangelische Theologie*
HZ	*Historische Zeitschrift*
KH	*Kirchliches Handbuch. Amtliches statistisches Jahrbuch der katholischen Kirche Deutschlands*
KJ	*Kirchliches Jahrbuch für die evangelische Kirche in Deutschland*
KZ	*Kirchliche Zeitschrift*
LM	*Lutherische Monatshefte*
Misc. Ger. Rec.	Miscellaneous German records
Nbg. Doc.	Documents presented at the war crimes trials in Nürnberg. Some have been published; the unpublished documents were consulted at the Institut für Zeitgeschichte in Munich.
NSDAP	Nationalsozialistische Deutsche Arbeiterpartei
Nürnberg, LK. Arch.	Landeskirchliches Archiv Nürnberg
RE	*Realenzyklopädie für protestantische Theologie und Kirche*
Reichsführer SS	Reichsführer SS und Chef der Deutschen Polizei
Reichskanzlei	Reich Chancellery documents
RGG	*Religion in Geschichte und Gegenwart*
SA	Sturm-Abteilung (Storm Troops; Brown Shirts)
Schumacher	Schumacher Collection on Church Affairs, Berlin Document Center
SS	Schutzstaffel (elite corps of the NSDAP; Black Shirts)
SZ	*Stimmen der Zeit*
VZ	*Vierteljahreshefte für Zeitgeschichte*
ZevKR	*Zeitschrift für evangelisches Kirchenrecht*

1. *RE*, 10: 752–59; Wilhelm Maurer, "Die Entstehung des Landeskirchentums in der Reformation," in Walther Peter Fuchs, ed., *Staat und Kirche im Wandel der Jahrhunderte*, pp. 70–75.

2. Karl Heussi, *Kompendium der Kirchengeschichte*, p. 308; James M. Estes, "Johannes Brenz and the Institutionalization of the Reformation in Württemberg," *Central European History* 6 (1973): 44–59.

3. R. Rehbein and O. Reincke, *Allgemeines Landrecht für die Preussischen Staaten*, 4: 129–30, pt. 2, sec. 11, pars. 143–46.

4. Rudolf Smend, "Die Konsistorien in Geschichte und heutige Bewertung," *ZevKR* 10 (1963–64): 136–37.

5. *RGG*, 3: 1575–78. At first the term *reformiert* was used to designate all followers of the new doctrines, but after about 1570 the followers of Calvin were designated *reformiert*. They wanted to retain Luther's teaching but carry the new doctrines further in accordance with Calvin's teaching (Heussi, *Kompendium*, p. 350).

6. Always to translate the term *Land* as "state" would at times involve misleading connotations in English. Because of territorial changes the Landeskirche often was no longer coterminous with a state. Therefore it seems best to use the German term. On the historic concept of Landeskirche, see Otto Friedrich, *Einführung in das Kirchenrecht unter besonderer Berücksichtigung des Rechts der Evangelischen Landeskirche in Baden*, pp. 253, 257.

7. *RGG*, 6: 526.

8. For a good historical article on *Patronatsrecht*, see Heinrich J. Wetzer and Benedikt Welte, *Kirchenlexikon*, 9: 1620–30; see also *RGG*, 5: 155–59; Friedrich, *Kirchenrecht*, pp. 294–99.

9. The Saxon delegate to the Corpus Evangelicorum, however, obtained his instructions from the *Geheimratskollegium* in Dresden rather than from the king (Fritz Wolff, *Corpus Evangelicorum und Corpus Catholicorum auf dem Westfälischen Friedenskongress*, pp. 193–94). My brief summary of the Corpus Evangelicorum is based on this excellent study; see particularly pp. 195, 197, 202, 207; see also Horst Stephan and Hans Leube, *Handbuch der Kirchengeschichte*, pt. 4, *Die Neuzeit*, p. 35.

10. See "Synods and Interchurch Cooperation," below.

11. Hans Liermann, "Der Westfälische Frieden," *Jahrbuch des Martin Luther Bundes*, 1949–50, pp. 147–58; F. Dickmann, "Das Problem der Gleichberechtigung der Konfessionen im Reich im 16. und 17. Jahrhundert," *HZ* 201 (1964): 265–305; Emil Friedberg, *Lehrbuch des katholischen und evangelischen Kirchenrechts*, p. 66.

12. Ernst R. Huber, *Deutsche Verfassungsgeschichte seit 1789*, 1: 414; Heussi, *Kompendium*, p. 425.

13. Robert M. Bigler, *The Politics of German Protestantism*, pp. 47–50, 125–37, 155.

14. Friedrich, *Kirchenrecht*, p. 343.

15. Walter Elliger, ed., *Die evangelische Kirche der Union*, pp. 34–48; Hermann Mulert, *Konfessionskunde*, p. 380; Georg Wehrung, *Kirche nach evangelischen Verständnisse*, p. 331.

16. Hermann Lutze, "Das konfessionelle Problem in der Evangelischen Kirche im Rheinland," in *Lutherisches Bekenntnis in der Union*, p. 140.

17. Elliger, *Ev. Kirche der Union*, pp. 48–53; *RE*, 10: 350; Heussi, *Kompendium*, pp. 458–60; see also Hans Herzfeld, ed., *Berlin und die Provinz Brandenburg im 19. und 20. Jahrhundert*, pp. 444–51.

18. As quoted in *RE*, 20: 258–59.

19. For example, in the Evangelical Church of the Rhineland in the 1960s, 5 congregations designated themselves as Evangelical Lutheran and 9 as Evangelical Reformed; 421 congregations used the Lutheran catechism, 177 congregations the Heidelberg catechism, and 173 a combination of the Lutheran and Heidelberg catechisms, while a few used both. It would appear that in the Rhineland church there were 173 United (*Unierte*) congregations that could be designated as having achieved a Consensusunion. Actually the Evangelical Church of the Rhineland should perhaps properly be "designated not as a United church, but as a Church of the Union, where both Lutheran and Reformed congregations live together" (Lutze, in *Lutherisches Bekenntnis*, pp. 142–43).

20. As quoted in *RE*, 12: 2. On the development of the Lutheran Free churches, see Oskar Büttner, *Die evangelischen Freikirchen Deutschlands*, pp. 201–64; Heinrich

Martin, *Der Kampf der deutschen lutherischen Freikirchen im 19. Jahrhundert,* pp. 5–24.

21. Par. 3 of the "Generalkonzession für die von der Gemeinschaft der evangelischen Landeskirche sich getrennt haltenden Lutheraner, vom 23 Juli 1945," in C. F. Koch et al., *Allgemeines Landrecht für die Preussischen Staaten mit Kommentar und Anmerkungen,* 4: 151.

22. The Prussian *Allgemeines Landrecht* distinguished between the privileged corporations (*privilegierter Korporationen*) and others which on application were tolerated (*geduldet*) as religious associations. Between these two groups there was a third, made up of sectarian bodies which were granted corporative status but did not have the full status of a privileged corporation. Among these were: the Moravian Brethren, who received status in Prussia in the mid-sixteenth century; the Mennonites, first tolerated by Frederick William II and given definite corporative status by a law of June 12, 1874; the Herrnhuter, by concessions of Frederick II in 1742–46; the Old Lutherans, July 23, 1845; the Old Catholics, July 4, 1875; and the Baptists, July 7, 1875. Jewish synagogues had the rights of a judicial personage (*die Rechte juristischer Personen*). Article 12 of the Prussian constitution of 1850 did away with the provision that a religious group needed the specific permission of the government to conduct religious services. Henceforth there was to be freedom of religious association, but to achieve corporative rights or the rights of an association (*Verein*), a group had to obtain governmental approval (Justizrat Sachse, "Sind die Mitglieder evangelischen Freikirchen [Sekten] im Gebiet der evangelischen Kirche der altpreussischen Union dieser Kirche steuerpflichtig," *Verwaltungsarchiv* 32 [1927]: 29). See also Koch, *Allgemeines Landrecht,* 4: 154; Rehbein and Reincke, *Allgemeines Landrecht,* 4: 100–2; Joseph Löhr, *Das Preussische Allgemeine Landrecht und die Katholischen Kirchengesellschaften,* p. 14; Hans Liermann, *Sind die preussischen Brudergemeinen Körperschaften des öffentlichen Rechts?* Liermann answers with a definite yes, except for those of Breslau and Hausdorf (p. 48). In Baden the Old Catholics, Mennonites, Herrnhuter, *Neutäufer,* and German-Catholics (a small dissident Catholic group dating from the 1840s) had corporative status, in Württemberg and Saxony the Herrnhuter and German-Catholics, and in Hesse the Old Catholics. In Bavaria the Herrnhuter, Mennonites, Anglicans, and Greek Catholics had the status of private corporations (Adolf Fellmeth, *Das kirchliche Finanzwesen in Deutschland,* pp. 11–12).

23. The Irvingians were a Catholic apostolic group which stressed the outpouring of the Holy Spirit and the imminent return of Christ, a doctrine propagated by Edward Irving of Scotland (1792–1834). On the establishment and development of the various Free churches in Germany, see Büttner, *Evangelischen Freikirchen,* and Ulrich Kunz, ed., *Viele Glieder ein Leib.*

24. Heussi, *Kompendium,* p. 466; Stephan and Leube, *Kirchengeschichte,* pp. 344–45; *RGG,* 4: 359–61; the chapter on "The Friends of Light," in Bigler, *Politics of German Protestantism,* pp. 187–230. In East Prussia Rev. Julius Rupp was a prominent member of the Lichtfreunde and was very influential. On his activity and that of other sectarians, see Walter Hubatsch, *Geschichte der Evangelischen Kirche Ostpreussens,* 1: 297–306; Jörn Brederlow, *"Lichtfreunde" und "Freie Gemeinden."*

25. In 1917 the Templars in Palestine were interned by the British. Following the advice of the German government, the Templars supported the Arab tribes in their revolts in the 1930s. On the eve of World War II Britain again interned the group and sent most of the men to Australia, where they were joined by their families and others in 1948. With Professor Sörensen of the Danish University of Aarhus acting as arbitrator, Israel in 1965 paid forty-five million marks for the property of the Templars; the German Federal Republic distributed the money to the surviving members of the sect in Germany, Australia, and the United States (*Neue Züricher Zeitung,* July 30, 1964; *Die Welt,* December 11, 1965; *Frankfurter Allgemeine,* October 7, 1967).

26. *1974 Yearbook of Jehovah's Witnesses,* pp. 67–84; Stephan and Leube, *Kirchengeschichte,* p. 375. The author of "Sektenwesen in Deutschland," *RE,* 18: 157–66, states that it is impossible to present exact statistics on membership of the various sects. What figures he does give he considers unsatisfactory, but he concludes that it is certain that the membership was slowly but constantly rising; see also Hans G. Haack, *Die evangelische Kirche Deutschlands in der Gegenwart,* pp. 101–14; chaps. 19–20, below.

27. *RE*, 19: 275.
28. *RGG*, 3: 1582; Friedrich, *Kirchenrecht*, pp. 104–7.
29. *KJ*, 1914, pp. 4–5.
30. Horst R. Flachsmeier, *Geschichte der evangelischen Weltmission*, pp. 180–302.
31. C. Werckshagen, ed., *Der Protestantismus in seiner Gesamtgeschichte bis zur Ge-genwart in Wort und Bild*, 1: 555–65; W. Schmidt, *Geschichte des Lutherischen Gotteskastens in Bayern (1860–1930)*, pp. 5–23. The Württemberg church, how-ever, chiefly supported the Gustav-Adolf-Verein (Evangelischer Pfarrverein in Württemberg, eds., *Für Volk und Kirche*, pp. 38, 46).
32. Heussi, *Kompendium*, p. 470; see Erich Beyreuther, *Geschichte der Diakonie und Inneren Mission in der Neuzeit*, pp. 88–125; see also A. Pilger, "Johann Hinrich Wichern," *KZ* 55 (1931): 193–208.
33. Beyreuther, *Geschichte der Diakonie*, pp. 61–78.
34. Ibid., pp. 141–51; Karl Kupisch, *Zwischen Idealismus und Massendemokratie*, pp. 101–2.
35. Haack, *Evangelische Kirche*, pp. 56–61; Erich G. Rüppel, *Die Gemeinschaftsbeweg-ung im Dritten Reich*, pp. 11–26; *RGG*, 2: 1366–73, 1630.
36. See chap. 2, "Church-State Controversies," below.
37. Werckshagen, *Protestantismus*, 1: 554–55; *RGG*, 1: 243; Erwin Fahlbusch, *Tasch-enlexikon*, 1: 24–25.
38. See chap. 2, "Church-State Controversies," below.
39. Werckshagen, *Protestantismus*, 1: 566–72; *RGG*, 2: 790; Heussi, *Kompendium*, p. 480; Haack, *Evangelische Kirche*, p. 54.
40. Alfred Voight, *Kirchenrecht*, p. 239.
41. *RE*, 10: 666–70; ibid., 23: 794; Friedrich, *Kirchenrecht*, pp. 313–14.
42. For a registry of topics discussed, names of reporters, dates of meetings, and officers of the conference, see *Hauptregister zu den Protokollen der Deutschen Evangelisch-en Kirchenkonferenz 1851–1917*.
43. The old provinces of Prussia had three representatives, while the new provinces had two; Saxony, Bavaria, and Württemberg had one each, and the other Land churches had seven (Stephan and Leube, *Kirchengeschichte*, 4: 364; Friedrich, *Kirchenrecht*, p. 314).
44. *RE*, 21: 833.
45. *KH*, 1914–16, p. 353; see also *KJ*, 1914, pp. 485–90.
46. The Prussian legal code made it compulsory to have children baptized, at the latest six weeks after birth (Rehbein and Reincke, *Allgemeines Landrecht*, 4: 159). Com-pulsory baptism was ended with introduction of civil registration of vital statistics.
47. A Prussian law of 1873 made it possible for a person to withdraw from a church and not have to join another (ibid., 104). Other states soon enacted similar legisla-tion (*KJ*, 1931, p. 168; Friedberg, *Kirchenrecht*, pp. 266–68).
48. It is difficult to obtain reliable statistics as to which of the Free churches or sects those who left the Land churches joined. It is clear that many withdrew because they felt lost in the large congregations of the Land churches and sought fellowship and active participation in the life of a congregation by joining the independent churches (*KJ*, 1909, p. 329; 1915, p. 463). Of the 4,703 who left the Land church in Saxony in 1899–1903, 2,029 joined New Apostolic congregations, 879 became Methodists, 190 became Baptists, 236 became Roman Catholics, 661 joined other groups, and only 245 (about 5.2 percent) joined no other church at all (*KJ*, 1951, p. 366).
49. See the tables presented in "Kirchenaustritte aus den deutschen evangelischen Landeskirchen und Übertritte (Eintritte) zu den deutschen evangelischen Landeskir-chen in der Zeit von 1884 bis 1949," *Statistische Beilage Nr. 4 zum Amtsblatt der Evangelischen Kirche in Deutschland*, 1952, pp. 1–16; see also a commentary on these tables by Herbert Reich, "Die Aus- und Übertrittsbewegung, 1884–1949," *KJ*, 1951, pp. 363–85.
50. Based on *KJ*, 1917, pp. 140–41. It should be noted that there are differences between Protestant and Catholic figures on shifts in church membership, in large part because of different conceptions of what constitutes church membership. Yet it is clear that the balance of gain over loss was in favor of the Protestant Land churches (see Reich, *KJ*, 1951, pp. 367, 375–76).
51. *RE*, 1: 97; Friedberg, *Kirchenrecht*, pp. 532–33; Hans Liermann, *Deutsches Evan-gelisches Kirchenrecht*, pp. 90–91; Fellmeth, *Kirchliche Finanzwesen*, pp. 152–70. Fellmeth (pp.. 168–70) presents a table of church revenues raised by taxes in various states in 1907.

52. In some states, notably Württemberg, a person who was a member of another church which had the status of a public corporation did not have to pay taxes to the Land church; in other states, notably Prussia, no one was exempt unless he had withdrawn by formal written procedure from the Land church. Thus in Prussia members of other churches often still remained on the Land church tax rolls (Herbert Wehrbahn, "Zur Kirchensteuerpflicht der Protestanten in Deutschland," *Recht und Staat,* no. 167 [1952], pp. 12–13). See also G. J. Ebers, *Reichs und preussisches Staatskirchenrecht,* pp. 720–24, 753–55; Justizrat Sache, "Sind die Mitglieder evangelischen Freikirchen (Sekten) im Gebiet der Evangelischen Kirche der altpreussischen Union dieser Kirche Steuerpflichtig," *Verwaltungsarchiv* 32 (1927): 25–36.

53. See the statement by Karl Liebknecht quoted in *KJ,* 1914, p. 115.

54. *KJ,* 1914, p. 104; Victor Bredt, *Neues evangelisches Kirchenrecht für Preussen,* 2: 464.

55. *KJ,* 1919, p. 137.

56. *KJ,* 1919, p. 138; 1914, p. 188; Fellmeth, *Kirchliche Finanzwesen,* p. 141.

57. Haack, *Evangelische Kirche,* pp. 16–29.

58. *KJ,* 1914, pp. 108, 521–27.

59. Fellmeth, *Kirchliche Finanzwesen,* p. 50; *KJ,* 1914, pp. 66–67.

60. *KJ,* 1914, pp. 491–512.

61. Fritz Fischer, "Der deutsche Protestantismus und die Politik im 19. Jahrhundert," *HZ* 171 (1951): 510; Karl Kupisch, Christlich-kirchliches Leben in den letzten hundert Jahren," in Herzfeld, ed., *Berlin und Brandenburg,* pp. 488–95.

62. Ernst C. Helmreich, *Religious Education in German Schools,* pp. 103–18.

Chapter Two

1. Heussi, *Kompendium,* pp. 344–45.

2. See chap. 1, "The Land Churches and Smaller Denominations," above. The pope protested against this settlement of the Peace of Westphalia in the bull *Zelo domus dei* (1648). This condemnation, renewed at various times, remained in effect until the Congress of Vienna in 1815 (Konrad Repgen, *Die Römische Kurie und der Westfälische Friede,* vol. 1, *Papst, Kaiser und Reich, 1521–1644,* pp. 5–28).

3. See chap. 1, "The Establishment of State Control," above.

4. Heussi, *Kompendium,* p. 421; Stephan and Leube, *Kirchengeschichte,* p. 160; Ernst Heinen, *Staatliche Macht und Katholizismus in Deutschland,* 1: 1–18, 22–26.

5. Stephan and Leube, *Kirchengeschichte,* p. 178.

6. These territories were not secularized because of certain constitutional considerations connected with the continued existence of the Holy Roman Empire (Hubert Gastgen, *Dalbergs und Napoleons Kirchenpolitik in Deutschland* pp. 13, 271–79; Peter Wende, *Die geistlichen Staaten und ihre Auflösung im Urteil der zeitgenössischen Publizistik,* pp. 47–96).

7. Ludwig A. Veit, *Kirchengeschichte,* 4, pt. 2: 18–20; Heussi, *Kompendium,* p. 425.

8. Hesse in 1802, Baden 1803 and 1807, and Nassau and Württemberg in 1803 (Veit, *Kirchengeschichte,* 4, pt. 2: 22).

9. Some overwhelmingly Protestant North German states, notably Mecklenburg-Schwerin, did not grant Catholics parity until late in the nineteenth century (ibid., p. 55).

10. For the text of the Bavarian concordat see *BFSP,* 3: 1074–81; the important article dealing with the financial settlement is given in Lothar Schöppe, *Konkordate seit 1800,* pp. 43–46; see also Heussi, *Kompendium,* p. 436.

11. Rudolf Lill, *Die Beilegung der Kölner Wirren, 1840–1842,* pp. 16–17; Heinen, *Staatliche Macht,* 1: 20, 42–47.

12. On the Kölner Kirchenstreit and its settlement, see Lill, *Kölner Wirren,* passim; Heussi, *Kompendium,* pp. 439–40; for a critical evaluation of it, see Karl Bachem, *Vorgeschichte, Geschichte, und Politik der Deutschen Zentrumspartei, 1815–1914,* 1: 157–77; Helmut Tiedemann, *Staat und Kirche vom Untergang des alten bis zur Gründung des neuen Reiches, 1806–1871,* pp. 34–37.

13. See chap. 1 at n. 42, above.

14. *RGG,* 2: 112–13; Stephan and Leube, *Kirchengeschichte,* p. 268; see also chap. 1 at n. 24, above.

15. As quoted in Friedrich, *Kirchenrecht,* p. 463.

16. The pertinent articles of the constitution are quoted in Hans Liermann, *Kirchen und Staat,* 1:10–11; see also Friedrich, *Kirchenrecht,* p. 463.
17. Helmreich, *Religious Education,* pp. 43–45.
18. As quoted in Georg Franz, *Kulturkampf,* pp. 222–23; for the causes of Bismarck's hostility to the Center party, see Bachem, *Zentrumspartei,* 3: 184–92.
19. In addition to Franz's *Kulturkampf,* good recent studies are: Erich Schmidt-Volkmar, *Der Kulturkampf in Deutschland;* Adelheid Constabel, ed., *die Vorgeschichte des Kulturkampfes.* A representative Catholic account is to be found in Bachem, *Zentrumspartei,* 3: 193–94; 4: 1–438. He discusses the Kulturkampf in Bavaria, Württemberg, Baden, and Hesse (4: 316–438). For a summary of the Kulturkampf with evaluations of that conflict and further bibliographical references, see Ernst C. Helmreich, *A Free Church in a Free State?,* pp. xiii–xiv, 58–82, 111.
20. Stephan and Leube, *Kirchengeschichte,* p. 266; Heussi, *Kompendium,* p. 450. Tables giving the growth of religious orders 1872–1918 are to be found in Hubert Mohr, *Katholische Orden und Deutscher Imperialismus,* pp. 51–55; on the long fight to repeal the anti-Jesuit law, see pp. 65–67.
21. Helmreich, *Religious Education,* pp. 60, 79–84.
22. Johannes B. Kissling, *Geschichte der deutschen Katholikentage,* 1: 187–227; E. Filthaut, *Deutsche Katholikentage 1848–1952 und soziale Frage,* pp. 9, 375; Hans Maier, "Katholizismus, nationale Bewegung und Demokratie," *Hochland* 57 (1964–65): 320–21; Heinen, *Staatliche Macht,* 1: 97–104, 122–24.
23. *KH,* 1914–16, p. 224.
24. On the founding of the People's Association, see Wilhem Spael, *Das katholische Deutschland im 20. Jahrhundert,* pp. 15–24; see also Sándor Agócs, " 'Germanis Doceat!' The Volksverein, the Model for Italian Catholic Action, 1905–1914," *CHR* 61 (1975): 31–47.
25. For a tabular survey of all the religious charitable organizations with the number of local groups and membership figures, see *KH,* 1914–16, pp. 262–89. On the activity and work of the various Catholic organizations for the years 1890–1918, see Spael, *Das katholische Deutschland,* pp. 15–195; good bibliographies are appended to the chapters. For a summary of the youth organizations, see Barbara Schellenberger, *Katholische Jugend und Drittes Reich,* pp. 1–4.
26. Veit, *Kirchengeschichte,* 4, pt. 2: 276; see also "Tabelle der Kirchenblätter mit Erscheinungszeit," in Rudolf Pesch, *Die kirchlich-politische Presse der Katholiken in der Rheinprovinz vor 1848,* pp. 348–49; Heinen, *Staatliche Macht,* 1: 104–8.
27. These statistics are taken from *KH,* 1914–16.
28. The concordats and circumscription bulls of the period 1817–27 established many of the state subsidies to the Catholic church (Gerhard Anschütz, *Die Verfassung des Deutschen Reichs vom 11. August 1919,* p. 561). The tax laws for the Catholic church were similar to those for the Protestant Land churches; see chap. 1 at n. 51, above. A person under excommunication was not exempt from paying church taxes (F. Thiele et al., *Das Kirchensteuerrecht,* p. 12). Old Catholics had the right to collect their own church taxes (ibid.; Wehrbahn, *Zur Kirchensteuerpflicht,* p. 12).

Chapter Three

1. For a discussion of some of the powers still exercised by the rulers as summi episcopi, see *KJ,* 1919, p. 357.
2. Ibid., pp. 359–64; 1921, pp. 391–415; "Wegfall des Summepiskopats," in Gottfried Mehnert, *Evangelische Kirche und Politik, 1917–1919,* pp. 218–22; Hans Liermann, *Staat und evangelische Landeskirche in Baden während und nach der Staatsumwälzung von 1918,* pp. 10–25.
3. Howard McBain and Lindsay Rogers, *The New Constitutions of Europe,* p. 231; Ebers, *Staatskirchenrecht,* p. 244; Claus Motschmann, *Evangelische Kirche und preussischer Staat in den Anfängen der Weimarer Republik,* pp. 53, 91, 139.
4. *KJ,* 1921, pp. 391–92; 1922, p. 462.
5. Johann Frank, "Geschichte und neure Entwicklung des Rechts der kirchlichen Beamten," *ZevKR* 10 (1963–64): 269–70.
6. *KJ,* 1919, p. 322; 1920, p. 422; Helmreich, *Religious Education,* pp. 105–8; Karl-Wilhelm Dahm, "German Protestantism and Politics, 1918–39," *Journal of Contemporary History* 3 (1968): 33–36.
7. *KJ,* 1919, p. 328.

8. Ibid., pp. 332–33.

9. The changes in the articles on religion in the first, second, and final readings are conveniently arranged in a table in Friedrich Giese, "Staat und Kirche im neuen Deutschland," *Jahrbuch des Öffentlichen Rechts* 13 (1925): 250–56.

10. Ernst R. Huber, *Deutsche Verfassungsgeschichte seit 1789*, 4: 647–48; Ernst R. Huber, *Dokumente zur deutschen Verfassungsgeschichte* 2: 248; Henri Brunschwig, *Enlightenment and Romanticism in Eighteenth-Century Prussia* p. 290.

11. Anschütz, *Kommentar*, p. 540.

12. Liermann, *Ev. Kirchenrecht*, p. 287; *RGG*, 5: 158–59; see also chap. 1, "The Establishment of State Control," above.

13. Anschütz, *Kommentar*, p. 559. Bavaria and Württemberg had church tax laws which taxed juridical personages (Giese, *Jahrbuch des Öffentlichen Rechts* 13 [1925]: 277–80, 306–10).

14. The German text uses the term *abgelöst*, which means these subsidies could be ended only in return for compensation (Anschütz, *Kommentar*, p. 562; McBain and Rogers, *New Constitutions*, pp. 203–4, 211).

15. On the relations of the churches to the schools and on religious education under the Weimar Constitution, see Helmreich, *Religious Education*, pp. 111–50.

16. Wolfgang Schanze, "Der kirchliche Zusammenschluss in Thüringen nach 1918," *Evangelisch-Lutherische Kirchenzeitung* 10 (1956): 245. This strong centralization of church administration made it difficult for any local congregations to break with the state authorities during the church conflict in the Hitler period.

17. The agreement of November 29, 1921, between Prussia and Waldeck-Pyrmont on the union of Pyrmont with Prussia (effective 1922), stated that in Pyrmont the laws of Waldeck in regard to church matters remained in effect, and that church legislation would not be affected (G. J. Ebers, *Evangelisches Kirchenrecht in Preussen*, 3: 563. The Land church of Waldeck-Pyrmont remained a separate entity until 1934, when by negotiated agreement the church in Pyrmont was united to the Evangelical Land Church of Hanover, and the church in Waldeck was united with the Land Church of Hesse-Kassel to form the Land Church of Electoral Hesse-Waldeck. For these latter agreements, see *AK* 83 (1934): 293–98, 346–51; see also chap. 7 at n. 56, chap. 9 at n. 1.

18. *KJ* regularly carried a section on the churches in the lost territories immediately after the statistical material on the Church of the Old Prussian Union. The church in Memel was self-governing, but retained close ties with the Church of the Old Prussian Union (*KJ*, 1925, p. 539). The free city of Danzig remained a church province of the Church of the Old Prussian Union (ibid., pp. 326–27), while the churches in the territories ceded to Poland had no official ties with it (*KJ*, 1929, pp. 537–38).

19. See *KJ*, 1925, pp. 600–665, for summaries of each of the constitutions, the names of the chief governing bodies and administrative officials, and the territorial divisions into which the churches were divided; see also Haack, *Evangelische Kirche*, pp. 43–46. The Land church of Lippe finally adopted a new constitution on February 17, 1931 (*AK* 80 [1931]: 141–60). See also J. R. C. Wright, *'Above Parties,'* pp. 20–28.

20. *RGG*, 5: 1086.

21. Ebers, *Ev. Kirchenrecht*, 1: 1; "Der Streit um die Präambel," *KJ*, 1922, pp. 470–80.

22. Ebers, *Ev. Kirchenrecht*.

23. There was a great profusion of terms for the various church bodies and officials, so many that even Professor Schneider, for many years the guiding genius of *KJ*, admits there was truth in the quip that you had to have a church dictionary at your elbow when you started to read the new constitutions (*KJ*, 1925, p. 517).

24. *KJ*, 1920, pp. 43–44; Liermann, *Ev. Kirchenrecht*, p. 225; Haack, *Evangelische Kirche*, p. 41; Horst Kater, *Die Deutsche Evangelische Kirche in den Jahren 1933 und 1934*, pp. 15–16.

25. "Staatsgesetz betreffend die Kirchenverfassung der evangelischen Landeskirchen vom 8. April 1924," reprinted in Ebers, *Staatskirchenrecht*, pp. 639–48; also in Liermann, *Kirchen und Staat*, 1: 234–38. In Württemberg the state imposed few restrictions on church self-government (see "Württembergisches Gesetz über die Kirchen vom 3. März 1924," reprinted in Liermann, *Kirchen und Staat*, 2: 97–122. Everywhere some state supervision of the churches remained (Friedrich, *Kirchenrecht*, pp. 467–68).

26. *KJ*, 1919, p. 378; 1920, p. 343. The *Konferenz Deutscher Evangelischer Arbeitsor-*

ganisationen, founded in 1916, brought together representatives of the most important church organizations (Stephan and Leube, Kirchengeschichte, p. 438).

27. For the membership of the committee, minutes of the meetings, and results of their deliberations, see AK 68 (1919): 519–57; see also Wright, 'Above Parties,' pp. 28–31.

28. For a list of the members, the minutes of the meetings, and the measures approved, see AK 68 (1919): 475; see also "Der Dresdener Kirchentag," in Mehnert, Evangelische Kirche, pp. 223–34.

29. AK 68 (1919): 568.

30. "Beschluss des Kirchentages, Kirchentag, und Kirchenbund," ibid., pp. 537–39; KJ, 1920, pp. 344–52.

31. KJ, 1922, pp. 442–45; for the minutes of the meetings, membership, the text of the constitution, and reports of committees, see AK 70 (1921): 773–838.

32. Art. 1 of the constitution (ibid., p. 794).

33. AK 73 (1924): 97–105.

Chapter Four

1. Denkschrift über den Umfang der Staatsleistungen der deutschen Länder an die evangelischen Kirchen bis zur Ablösung, pp. 73–82; see also Giese, Jahrbuch des Öffentlichen Rechts 13 (1925): 346–55; Schöppe, Konkordate, pp. 46–51. The agreement of Prussia with the Protestant Land churches paralleled the Prussian concordat of August 13, 1929, wherein the Catholic church was promised a yearly subsidy of 2,800,000 marks. For a summary of these agreements concerning the payment of subsidies see Friedrich Giese, "Staat und Kirchen im neuen Deutschland," Jahrbuch des Öffentlichen Rechts 20 (1932): 120–34.

2. For excerpts and summary of the most important tax legislation for the years 1925–31, see Giese, Jahrbuch des Öffentlichen Rechts 20 (1932): 150–65. Until 1921, Württemberg was the only larger state which had no church tax, all state revenues for the churches coming out of the general budget (Württemberg Ministerium to Reichskanzlei, August 2, 1921, BA, R43 I/2202, p. 49).

3. See Thiele, Kirchensteuerrecht, pp. 29–31; see also Friedrich, Kirchenrecht, pp. 418–21.

4. Thiele, Kirchensteuerrecht, pp. 39–40. For church taxation in post-World War II Germany, including some references to earlier periods, see "Was machen die Kirchen mit den Kirchensteuer?," Der Spiegel, May 27, 1964, pp. 38–61.

5. Helmreich, Religious Education, pp. 122–25.

6. Kurt Klotzbach, Gegen den Nationalsozialismus, pp. 219–20. On the conservatism of the Lutheran clergy, see Hans Tiefel, "The German Lutheran Church and the Rise of National Socialism," CH 41 (1972): 328–30; Wright, 'Above Parties,' pp. 49–65.

7. KJ, 1932, pp. 39, 58; pertinent sections of the Erfurt Program are reprinted in Liermann, Kirchen und Staat, 1: 15.

8. Stephan and Leube, Kirchengeschichte, pp. 435–36; RGG, 5: 959. For mostly critical discussions, see KJ, 1923, pp. 414–18; 1924, pp. 470–74; 1925, pp. 564–66.

9. KJ, 1930, p. 544.

10. For example, see "Die Auseinandersetzung mit dem Marxismus," KJ, 1932, pp. 38–40; see also 1925, pp. 566–67. Paul Tillich was one of the important leaders of the group. See the excellent summary essay "Der Religiöse Sozialismus," Ger van Roon, Neuordnung im Widerstand, pp. 35–40. The author concludes: "Zusammenfassend sei bemerkt, dass der Religiöse Sozialismus ein wichtiger Versuch war, zwei einander entfremdete Gruppen wieder in Kontakt zu bringen und die Kirche auf ihre Pflicht hinzuweisen, zu einer gerechten Lösung der sozialen Frage beizutragen" (p. 40).

11. Hans Buchheim, Glaubenskrise im Dritten Reich, pp. 44–48; RGG, 2: 104; Lexikon für Theologie und Kirche, 3: 308; Wolfgang Tilgner, Volksnomostheologie und Schöpfungsglaube, pp. 71–81. For critical discussions of various national church movements on the Catholic side, see KH, 1914–16, pp. 343–59; on the Protestant side, see KJ, 1924, pp. 467–69; 1925, pp. 556–57.

12. RGG, 2: 104.

13. Friedrich Zipfel, Kirchenkampf in Deutschland, pp. 210–11; BA, Parteikanzlei, NS

6/386; Adjutantur des Führer, NS 10/272, p. 197; Carsten Nicolaisen, ed., *Dokumente zur Kirchenpolitik des Dritten Reiches,* 1: 317.

14. Pastor Knappe had left Bavaria with Leutheuser and Leffler but he soon returned to the fold of the Bavarian church (Erik Wolf, ed., *Zeugnisse der Bekennenden Kirche,* 4, *Der Kampf der Bekennenden Kirche wider das Neuheidentum,* p. 54.

15. As quoted in Wolfgang Schanze, "Der kirchliche Zusammenschluss in Thüringen nach 1918," *Evangelisch-Lutherische Kirchenzeitung* 10 (1956): 244.

16. On the origin and growth of the Thuringian German Christians, see Buchheim, *Glaubenskrise,* pp. 48–62; Kurt Meier, *Die Deutschen Christen,* pp. 2–10.

17. *Lexikon für Theologie und Kirche,* 3: 305–7; see also Walter Künneth and Helmut Schreiner, *Die Nation vor Gott,* particularly pp. 343–92 on the Tannenbergbund; see also Buchheim, *Glaubenskrise,* pp. 168–76.

18. Haack, *Evangelische Kirche,* pp. 92–101; Heussi, *Kompendium,* p. 520; *RGG,* 3: 379–80; *KJ,* 1925, pp. 555–56; Johannes Hessen, *Die Geistesströmungen der Gegenwart,* pp. 164–66. Hansen's theses are reprinted in *KZ* 54 (1930): 302–9.

19. Luther to Duke Albert of Prussia, February 14, 1543, as quoted in Th. Traub, *Lutherworte zum Verständnis evangelischer Wahrheit,* p. 125.

20. Haack, *Evangelische Kirche,* pp. 84–91; Ernst Wolf, *Barmen,* pp. 19–32; Hessen, *Geistesströmungen,* pp. 155–59; Stephan and Leube, *Kirchengeschichte,* pp. 439–40; Heussi, *Kompendium,* pp. 521–24.

21. *KJ,* 1932, p. 39; ibid., pp. 202–72.

22. *Statistische Beilage Nr. 4, Amtsblatt der Evangelischen Kirche in Deutschland,* 1952; *KJ,* 1951, pp. 363–86.

23. *Zeitschrift für Politik* 21 (1931): 344, as quoted in *KJ,* 1932, p. 38.

24. *Beilage Nr. 4, Amtsblatt der EKD,* 1952; *KJ,* 1951, p. 377; *Denkschrift über Staatsleistungen,* pp. 79–80.

25. "Die Zahl der Theologie-Studierenden," *KJ,* 1932, pp. 254–63; see also 1931, pp. 183–90. The number of women studying theology increased from 5 in 1911 to 77 in 1926 to 330 in 1931.

26. See *KJ,* 1932, pp. 322–94.

27. Ibid., pp. 355–61; 1931, pp. 298–312.

28. U.S. Dept. of State, *Papers Relating to the Foreign Relations of the United States, 1919,* 13: 280, 734–35; *KJ,* 1925, pp. 231–33; 1926, p. 245; 1927, p. 91. The activity of the mission societies can be followed in the annual surveys of foreign missions in *KJ.* The Catholic church was very disturbed about the restrictions on German missions imposed by the Treaty of Versailles, since it was felt that they restricted the rights of the pope as head of the church. The papacy protested against these clauses of the treaty (*KH,* 1919–20, pp. 122–50; 1922–23, pp. 56–63; 1924–25, p. 70). Various Catholic orders sought the aid of the German government in reentering certain of their missions fields (BA, R 43 I/2197, pp. 70–125).

29. For the main mission fields of each society, see the table *KJ,* 1932, pp. 480–81.

30. There is, however, no such report in *KJ,* 1931. See the article by D. Weber, "Die Judenmission des neunzehnten Jahrhunderts," in Werchshagen, *Protestantismus,* 1: 551–52; see also "Christlich-jüdische Verständigungsversuche," in the 1920s in Karl H. Rengstorf and Siegfried von Kortzfleisch, *Kirche und Synagoge,* 2: 332–33.

31. *RGG,* 3: 977.

32. *KJ,* 1932, p. 488. The collection had been under attack from Volkish circles (Richard Gutteridge, *The German Evangelical Church and the Jews, 1879–1950,* p. 56). For a word of appreciation of the Jewish mission by a Jewish writer, see Werner E. Mosse and Arnold Paucker, eds., *Entscheidungsjahr 1932,* pp. 257–59.

33. *KJ,* 1925, pp. 370, 372.

34. Haack, *Evangelische Kirche,* pp. 64–65.

35. *Der Spiegel,* May 27, 1964, p. 55.

36. *KJ,* 1932, pp. 283–321, particularly p. 299; see also Haack, *Evangelische Kirche,* pp. 76–83; Howard Becker, *German Youth,* p. 106.

37. *Evangelium im Dritten Reich,* 3, no. 3 (January 1934): 28; see chap. 7 at n. 100, below.

38. Freely translated from Gerhard E. Stoll, *Die evangelische Zeitschriftenpresse im Jahre 1933,* pp. 76–77; see also pp. 50, 56, 71, 73–74.

39. Focko Lüpsen, *Mittler zwischen Kirche und Welt,* pp. 31–44.

40. *AK* 73 (1934): 105–7. The Moravian Brethren achieved the status of a public corporation in Saxony in 1922 and severed their connections with the Land church

of that state (*AK* 72 [1923]: 73; see also *KJ*, 1924, p. 445; Liermann, *Sind die preussischen Brudergemeinen Körperschaften des öffentlichen Rechts?*, passim).

41. *AK* 74 (1925): 273. The admission of various churches can be traced in subsequent issues of this well-indexed gazette. For example, the synod of Rio Grande, Brazil, joined the confederation on January 1, 1929; the synod of Saint Catherine, Parana, and other Brazilian states on January 1, 1933 (*AK* 77 [1928]: 359; *AK* 82 [1933]: 132). For the admission of the Austrian churches, see *AK* 75 (1926): 35–36.

42. *AK* 79 (1930): 205–8; *KJ*, 1930, p. 470.

43. *RGG*, 3: 1416.

44. *KJ*, 1924, pp. 442–50. The reports on inner missions in *KJ* regularly carried summaries of the battles against alcoholism and prostitution.

45. *KJ*, 1927, p. 487. At this meeting Professor Paul Althaus of Erlangen also denounced the attempts to found a "folkish religion," with its emphasis on race (Rengstorf and Kortzfleisch, *Kirche und Synagoge*, 2: 332–33).

46. *KJ*, 1930, pp. 407, 445–47, 467–71, 544–45.

47. *KJ*, 1932, p. 595.

48. *RGG*, 2d ed., 3: 1779, 1786–87.

49. Hermann Sasse, *Die Weltkonferenz für Glauben und Kirchenverfassung*, pp. 598, 610–11; Armin Boyens, *Kirchenkampf und Ökumene 1933–1939*, pp. 18–21.

50. *KJ*, 1927, pp. 534–44; 1930, p. 534; D. Mahling, *Die Weltkonferenz für praktisches Christentum in Stockholm 19.-30. August 1925*.

51. *KJ*, 1925, p. 560; see also *RGG*, 2: 1110–12; 3: 1325–26; 5: 1681–82. For the shifting definition of Free church and sect during the Weimar and post-World War II periods, see Rudolf Mayer, "Kirche, Freikirche, Sekten," *ZevKR* 7 (1959–60): 156–186; Wolfgang Metzger, "Kirche, Freikirche, Sekten in der Perspektive einer Landeskirche gesehen," ibid., pp. 128–56.

52. *KJ*, 1932, pp. 591–93; see also 1929, pp. 386–90; Giese, *Jahrbuch des Öffentlichen Rechts* 20 (1932): 139–40.

53. *KJ*, 1926, p. 679.

54. *KJ*, 1930, p. 98; 1932, p. 245. Churches such as the Methodists and Baptists are included under sects, but not the Old Lutheran and Old Reformed congregations.

55. *KJ*, 1929, p. 390.

56. *KJ*, 1932, p. 246; see also Haack, *Evangelische Kirche*, p. 30.

57. Martin Riemer, *Die neuzeitlichen Sekten und Häresien in ihrem Verhältnis zur evangelischen Kirche in Deutschland*, pp. 45–51.

58. *KJ*, 1922, p. 427; 1925, p. 563; 1929, pp. 388–89.

59. These derived from the Holy Catholic Apostolic church started by Henry Drummond (1786–1860) in England (*Lexikon für Theologie und Kirche*, 6: 73–74; *RGG*, 3: 1196).

60. *KJ*, 1927, p. 636.

61. *RGG*, 3: 430.

62. *KJ*, 1929, p. 388; *1974 Yearbook of Jehovah's Witnesses*, p. 103; on the whole Weimar period, ibid., pp. 84–108.

63. Gilbert Scharffs, *Mormonism in Germany*, pp. 58–65, 79–86.

64. *KJ*, 1928, pp. 34–35; *AK* 77 (1928): 294–99.

65. See the petition of the Vereinigung der Ev. Freikirchen in Deutschland to Chancellor Marx, August 26, 1926, BA, Reichskanzlei, R 43 II/179, p. 54. For historic legal restrictions on burials by Methodists, see Herbert C. Fritz, *Die Methodistenkirche in Deutschland*, pp. 250–59. The "question of burial services by Free churches in Land church cemeteries" was one of the problems dealt with by the *Arbeitsgemeinschaft christlicher Kirchen in Deutschland* after World War II (see the letter of Martin Niemöller, *KJ*, 1949, pp. 55–56).

Chapter Five

1. *KH*, 1918–19, pp. 129–34; 1919–20, p. 96. According to a summary made by *Osservatore Romano*, the papacy had donated 4,100,689.30 lire for aid to destitute German children (Ambassador Bergen to German Foreign Office, January 21, 1921, National Archives of the United States, Microfilm: Ausw. A., Abteilung IIa, Akten betreffend Politische Beziehungen des Päpstlichen Stuhls zu Deutschland, March, 1920–March, 1924, Microcopy no. T120, Roll 55719, Frame K622183). Hereafter the microfilms will be cited by the name of the German department or

office, microcopy number, roll number, and frame number (some rolls lack frame numbers).

2. Fulda Bishops' Conference to President Ebert, October, 1919, BA, R 43 I/2197, pp. 21–23, Ebert's answer, pp. 51–52; Spael, *Das katholische Deutschland,* pp. 250–52; *KH,* 1919–20, pp. 107–20; Helmreich, *Religious Education,* pp. 108–18.

3. *KH,* 1919–20, pp. 107–9; Arts. 10, 137, 138, and 173 of the Weimar Constitution.

4. *KH,* 1919–20, p. 80.

5. *KH,* 1919–20, pp. 80–81, 454; 1920–21, pp. 316–17; 1922–23, pp. 329, 402.

6. *KH,* 1920–21, pp. 189–91. The 1910 census did not ascertain the languages used by a member of a religious confession, but the 1905 census showed that 27.5 percent of Prussian Catholics were "foreign-speaking" or bilingual (p. 191); see also *KJ,* 1919–20, p. 82.

7. Spael, *Das katholische Deutschland,* pp. 264–65; *RGG,* 2d ed., 1: 1895; *KJ,* 1923, p. 432; 1932, p. 119.

8. Fritz von der Heydt, *Die Parität bei der Anstellung der Beamten,* p. 3; see also the sections on "Konfessionelle Unterrichtsstatistik" in *KH,* 1927–28, pp. 283–92; 1930–31, pp. 288–98; Helmreich, *Religious Education,* pp. 66, 138, 241.

9. Heydt, *Anstellung der Beamten,* p. 29.

10. Bergen presented his credentials April 30, 1920, and received a most cordial reception (Ausw. A., T120, R. 5719, K622115).

11. Reichskanzlei, T120, R. 5718, K621420; Ausw. A., T120, R. 5721, K624104.

12. Reichskanzlei, T120, R. 5718, K621551, K621556; Ausw. A., R. 5721, K624104.

13. Ernst Deuerlein, *Das Reichskonkordat,* p. 13; see also pp. 1–15 for a discussion of the establishment of diplomatic relations between Germany and the Holy See.

14. See the long Denkschrift, Reichskanzlei, T120, R. 5718, K621814–18. On the negotiations with Russia and the final settlement, see K621823–25, K621833, K621840–42.

15. Ausw. A., T120, R. 5721, K623972; Deuerlein, *Reichskonkordat,* pp. 2, 75.

16. The Bavarian mission at the Vatican was originally scheduled to be closed on April 30, 1934; it was postponed until May 31 and then until June 30, 1934 (Georg Franz-Willing, *Die Bayerische Vatikangesandtschaft, 1803–1934,* pp. 247–50).

17. The pope refused to get involved in the separatist movement (Ausw. A., T120, R. 5719, K622194–96, K622969).

18. Reichskanzlei, T120, R. 5718, K621526–28; Ausw. A., T120, R. 5721, K624824. Particular care was taken not to publish any documents which touched on papal-Italian relations in the great collection *Die Grosse Politik* (Ausw. A., T120, R. 5719, K622323–26, K622333–35).

19. Bischöfliche Hauptarbeitsstelle Düsseldorf, *Die Katholische Aktion (Das Katholische Laienapostolat) in den deutschen Diözesen,* pp. 19, 34. For an excellent summary of the varied activity and significance of Pius XI's pontificate, see Heinrich Hermelink, *Die Katholische Kirche unter den Pius-Päpsten des 20. Jahrhunderts,* pp. 27–44; see also Heussi, *Kompendium,* pp. 513.

20. Government officials ruled that under Arts. 123 and 135 of the Weimar Constitution it was no longer necessary to get special permission to hold processions in places where they had not been customarily held (*KJ,* 1923, p. 431; Anschütz, *Kommentar,* pp. 503, 539; see also *RGG,* 2d ed., 1: 1894; 3: 667–68; Ausw. A., T120, R. 5721, K624267).

21. *KJ,* 1923, p. 428; 1924, p. 500; 1925, p. 570.

22. Spael, *Das katholische Deutschland,* pp. 229–30; see also his chapters on Catholic poetry (pp. 195–201), art (pp. 202–15), and "Wiederbegegnung von Kirche und Kultur in Deutschland" (pp. 258–67); Heussi, *Kompendium,* pp. 514–15.

23. *RGG,* 2d ed., 1: 1897–98; Stephan and Leube, *Kirchengeschichte,* p. 430; Spael, *Das katholische Deutschland,* p. 275.

24. *KH,* 1919–20, p. 386; 1933–34, p. 222. Territorial losses are taken into consideration in these figures except for Eupen and Malmédy (ceded to Belgium), which are included in the figures for 1920 but not for 1932. For a list of all the monastic establishments and their membership, see *KH,* 1919–20, pp. 288–345; 1933–34, pp. 221–71. Lay brothers included in the membership figures numbered 4,132 in 1920 and 7,294 in 1932.

25. *KH,* 1920–21, p. 344; 1935–36, p. 364.

26. *KH,* 1924–26, p. 420; 1927–28, p. 356; 1937–38, p. 252.

27. *KH,* 1933–34, p. 275.

28. *KH,* 1922–23, p. 405; 1927–28, p. 420; 1935–36, p. 367.

29. In 1924 (1932 figures in parentheses): 97.9 percent (97.69) marriages were solemnized where both parties were Catholic, and 37.1 percent (39.23) mixed marriages; 99.6 percent (99.79) of the children were baptized where both parents were Catholic, 43.4 percent (51.67) of the children of mixed marriages, and 93.1 percent (94.07) of the children of Catholic unmarried mothers; 95.3 percent (96.12) of the Catholics who died received church burial; 11,632,173 Catholics (12,864,610) performed their Easter obligation (*KH,* 1925–26, pp. 458–59; 1935–36, pp. 364–65). These figures do not include the Saar.

30. The Catholic church lost 34,743 members in 1925, 52,594 in 1930, and 54,450 in 1932. By conversions and readmissions it gained 2,959 in 1925, 4,686 in 1930, and 6,497 in 1932 (*KH,* 1926–27, p. 314; 1933–34, p. 281; 1935–36, p. 292).

31. *KH,* 1922–23, p. 301; 1926–27, p. 314; 1933–34, p. 281; *KJ,* 1932, pp. 241–48.

32. *KJ,* 1932, pp. 119, 242; *KH,* 1922–23, p. 305.

33. *KJ,* 1924, pp. 512–13.

34. *KH,* 1930–31, pp. 202–39; pp. 108–201 are devoted to a commentary on these organizations. For a tabular summary of the organizations as they existed at the beginning of the Weimar Republic, see *KH,* 1919–20, pp. 246–67; on Catholic youth organizations in general, see Schellenberger, *Katholische Jugend,* pp. 4–19; on the establishment of *Neudeutschland,* an organization of Catholic students in the gymnasia, see Ronald Warloski, *Neudeutschland,* pp. 1–23.

35. See the article on the Catholic press, *RGG,* 5: 556–68.

36. Friedrich Muckermann, *Der Deutsche Weg,* pp. 28–29; see also Spael, *Das katholische Deutschland,* pp. 282–87.

37. For a list of the concordats and other significant papal agreements with various states 1800–1962, see Schöppe, *Konkordate,* pp. xxxi–xxxvii.

38. See Deuerlein, *Reichskonkordat,* pp. 40–51 for a concise discussion of these negotiations.

39. Ausw. A., T120, R. 5720, K623234–36. This is an excellent chronological Aufzeichnung by R. Mutius of the main steps in concordat negotiations from June, 1920, to December, 1922; this study was the basis for another Aufzeichnung in 1925 (K623513–19, K623540–44).

40. Ausw. A., T120, R. 5720, K623323, K623350.

41. Ausw. A., T120, R. 5720, K623540.

42. This account of these negotiations is based on an Aufzeichnung made by Councillor Dr. Meyer-Rodehüser on March 20, 1928 (Ausw. A., T120, R. 5720, K623789–93), and on another made April 3, 1928 (K623797–98). See also Franz-Willing, *Vatikangesandtschaft,* pp. 183–84; Ludwig Volk, *Das Reichskonkordat vom 20. Juli 1933,* p. 10.

43. Ausw. A., T120, R. 5720, K623792. On July 21, 1921, the Aufzeichnung of November 13, 1920, was sent to the Reich Chancellery (BA, Ausw. A., II Va. 516; RK 6872; L888918 and L88919 are stamped on it).

44. Deuerlein, *Reichskonkordat,* p. 43. Deuerlein mentions a note of November 13, but the contents are not given correctly, and the document is quoted as coming from "Abschrift Nachlass Anton Scharnagl, München" (p. 285, n. 150) and is dated November 23, 1920. Pacelli, however, is obviously referring to the November 13, 1920, commitment.

45. Ausw. A., T120, R. 5720, K623295, K623298, K623301.

46. The representative of the Reich in Munich reported regularly to Berlin on the progress of the concordat through the Bavarian Landtag. These reports can be followed in Ausw. A., T120, R. 5720, K623364–424.

47. Ausw. A., T120, R. 5720, K623816.

48. Ausw. A., T120, R. 5720; various notes K623433–36, K623453–74; BA, R 43 I/2198, pp. 249, 307.

49. For the text of the concordat, see Schöppe, *Konkordate,* pp. 46–51; Liermann, *Kirchen und Staat,* 1: 90–105, gives both the German and Italian texts; an English translation is in *BFSP,* 125 (1926, pt.3): 193–200. Since the agreement was concluded on March 29, 1924, but not ratified until January 24, 1925, it is sometimes referred to as the Bavarian concordat of 1924, sometimes as the concordat of 1925. The parallel agreements reached with the Evangelical Lutheran Church in Bavaria Right of the Rhine, and with the United Protestant Evangelical Christian Church of the Palatinate on November 15, 1924, are reprinted in Liermann, *Kirchen und Staat,* 1: 106–16.

50. Ausw. A., T120, R. 5720, K623321, K623328.

51. Ausw. A., T120, R. 5720, K623322–25, K623331–33, K623517–19, K623513–16, K623540–44.

52. Ausw. A., T120, R. 5720, K623350; Aufzeichnung Meyer-Rodehüser, July 17, 1926, *ADAP*, B, 3: 338.

53. Ausw. A., T120, R. 5721, K623978, K623983.

54. Ausw. A., T120, R. 5720, K623577–78; BA, R 43 I/2202, p. 277; see also the Vermerk of March 23, 1928, BA, R 43 I/2203, p. 108. The curia considered regulation of the school problem a *conditio sine qua non* for the conclusion of a concordat. See Kaas's statement in "Protokoll über die Besprechung btr. Konkordatsfragen, 10 November 1921, in Reichskanzlerhaus," BA, R 43 I/2202, pp. 65–66; see also Aufzeichnung Meyer-Rodehüser, July 17, 1926, *ADAP*, B, 3: 339; Volk, *Reichskonkordat*, pp. 12–13, 19, 31, 212.

55. Ausw. A., T120, R. 5720, K623699–703, K623710; see also R. 5721, K624018–23; "Bemerkung zu den Telegram des Botschafters von Bergen," April 19, 1929, Ausw. A., T120, R. 5721, K624103. The Foreign Office was, however, able to keep itself fairly well informed about the negotiations ("Vertrauliche Mitteilung über den preussische Konkordat," K624112–17). A copy of the concordat was handed to the Foreign Office for personal and confidential information before June (K624140), and was later officially handed by the Prussian government to Reich authorities for their approval, which was given.

56. Ausw. A., T120, R. 5720, K623793; see also Helmreich, *Religious Education*, pp. 123–24.

57. Ausw. A., T120, R. 5720, K623758–59; Günther Grünthal, *Reichsschulgesetz und Zentrumspartei in der Weimarer Republik*, p. 172; Franz-Willing, *Vatikangesandtschaft*, pp. 212–14.

58. Ausw. A., T120, R. 5720, K623790–93.

59. Stresemann favored the interdenominational school (Henry Bernhard et al., *Gustav Stresemann Vermächtniss*, 3: 27–28).

60. Keudell to Foreign Office, January 18, 1928, Ausw. A., T120, R. 5720, K623772.

61. Ausw. A., T120, R. 5720, K623773.

62. Bischöfliche Arbeitsstelle für Schule und Erziehung, *Das Ringen um das sogenannte Reichsschulgesetz*, p. 187; Grünthal, *Reichsschulgesetz*, pp. 237–44.

63. Ausw. A., T120, R. 5720, K623788, K623795.

64. Aufzeichnung Meyer-Rodehüser, April 3, 1928, Ausw. A., T120, R. 5720, K623797–98.

65. Ausw. A., T120, R. 5720, K623800–801.

66. Ausw. A., T120, R. 5721, K629087; Deuerlein, *Reichskonkordat*, p. 76. The agreement is usually referred to as a concordat, but technically it was not, and the Prussian government preferred that it not be referred to as such. The German term was *Vertrag* ("treaty"), and the Italian term *Convenzione* (Alfons Kupper, *Staatliche Akten über die Reichskonkordatsverhandlungen* [Mainz, 1969], p. 491). The text of the agreement can be found in Schöppe, *Konkordate*, pp. 63–70; Liermann, *Kirchen und Staat*, 1: 119–38, gives both the German and Italian texts; English translation in *BFSP*, 130 (1929, pt. 1): 767–76. For the Prussian agreements with the Protestant churches, see Liermann, *Kirchen und Staat*, 1: 139–46.

67. *KJ*, 1929, p. 405; the position taken was based on a "Denkschrift des Evangelischen Oberkirchenrats" of June 19, 1929.

68. Deuerlein, *Reichskonkordat*, pp. 80–82; Ausw. A., T120, R. 5721, K624094; Schöppe, *Konkordate*, pp. 67–68, gives the German text; Liermann, *Kirchen und Staat*, 1: 133–37, gives both the German and Italian texts.

69. Ausw. A., T120, R. 5721, K624340–41, K624414.

70. *KJ*, 1929, pp. 421–22; Buchheim, *Glaubenskrise*, pp. 71–72; Wright, *'Above Parties,'* pp. 42–48.

71. Notation of Legationsrat Klee, November 18, 1930, Ausw. A., T120, R. 5721, K624359. Many subsequent frames on this roll deal with this controversy; for a summary see Minister President Braun's note to Ambassador Bergen, January 19, 1933, K624484–90, and the Anlage to the note, K624491–98.

72. Deuerlein, *Reichskonkordat*, pp. 85–87.

73. For Baden's inquiry about the commitment of November, 1922, see Ausw. A., T120, R. 5720, K623844–45, K623848–49, K623852–53, K623856.

74. Ausw. A., T120, R. 5720, K623837–38; see also *DGFP*, C, 1: 267n.

75. Ausw. A., T120, R. 5720, K623834, K623843. The text of the Baden concordat is in Schöppe, *Konkordate*, pp. 38–43; for the German and Italian texts, see Liermann,

Kirchen und Staat, 1: 147–59; for an English translation, see *BFSP,* 135 (1932): 557–64. For the agreement of Baden with its Protestant Land church, see Liermann, *Kirchen und Staat,* 1: 161–66.

76. On the approval of the concordat by the Landtag of Baden and its ratification, see Ausw. A., T120, R. 5720, K623857–58; R. 5719, K622950–51, K622954–55.

77. Schöppe, *Konkordate,* pp. 36–37; see also the long report on the agreement, Ausw. A., T120, R. 5720, K623871–80. At the time of the negotiation of the Reich concordat in 1933, when it was important to know the terms of the state agreements with the Vatican, Anhalt, at the request of the Foreign Office, submitted (June 20, 1933) the agreements to it, along with the historical explanation which had been presented to the Landtag of Anhalt (ibid.). An official of the Berlin nunciature confirmed that the Anhalt agreement was in the nature of a "little concordat," that it had not been published in the *Acta Apostolicae Sedis,* and that no official notification of the agreement had been submitted to the German Foreign Office. In contrast to Bavaria, Prussia, Baden, and Anhalt, Württemberg as early as March 3, 1924, had unilaterally by law settled matters with the churches (*Regierungsblatt für Württemberg,* no. 13 [March 11, 1924]; see also Ausw. A., T120, R. 5719, K622421, K622425).

78. See n. 54, above. The school provisions of the various concordat drafts are conveniently summarized in Deuerlein, *Reichskonkordat,* pp. 103–5; see also pp. 52–71 for the positions of the various political parties.

79. Ausw. A., T120, R. 5721, K624065; see also Stresemann to Bergen, April 4, 1927, *ADAP,* B, 5: 125.

80. Deuerlein, *Reichskonkordat,* p. 88. Pacelli became a cardinal on December 19, 1929, and cardinal state secretary on February 7, 1930.

81. BA, R 43 I/2197, pp. 137–38; Ausw. A., T120, R. 3312, E581607; Volk, *Reichskonkordat,* pp. 44–45.

82. BA, R 43 I/2203, pp. 76–77; Ausw. A., R. 5720, K623744–45.

83. Ausw. A., T120, R. 5720, K623836.

84. Ausw. A., T120, R. 5721, K624397.

85. Alfons Kupper, "Zur Geschichte des Reichskonkordats," *SZ* 171 (1962–63): 33. For a discussion of the articles of the Weimar Constitution referred to, see chap. 3 at n. 14, above.

86. Reichskanzlei, T120, R. 5718, K621856; Kupper, *SZ* 171 (1962–63): 34–35.

87. BA, R 43 I/2201, pp. 135–36.

88. Kupper, *SZ* 171 (1962–63): 35–41. Schleicher's letter was written July 13, 1932. See also Ausw. A., T120, R. 5720, K623836–39.

89. Archbishop Klein informed the War Office on September 12, 1932 (Kupper, *SZ* 171 [1962–63]: 28).

90. As translated *DGFP,* C, 1: 267n; for the German text, see Ausw. A., T120, R. 5720, K623836–39.

91. Ausw. A., T120, R. 3312, E581587–600; Volk, *Reichskonkordat,* p. 56.

92. Ausw. A., T120, R. 3312, E581601–3; the suggested revised draft is given at E581604–9. Menshausen's marginalia of May 2 state the note was not sent because the situation had changed (E581601).

93. Ausw. A., T120, R. 5719, K622268.

94. See Ernst Deuerlein, *Der deutsche Katholizismus 1933,* pp. 33–60; see also the introduction and documents on the years 1930–33 in Hans Müller, *Katholische Kirche und Nationalsozialismus,* pp. 1–47; Rengstorf and von Kortzfleisch, *Kirche und Synagoge,* 2: 397; Walter Adolph, *Hirtenamt und Hitler-Diktatur,* pp. 26–27. On the increased involvement of various Catholic youth organizations in politics from 1930 on, see Schellenberger, *Katholische Jugend,* pp. 20–30.

95. Deuerlein, *Deutsche Katholizismus,* p. 50.

96. "Die Bischöfe der Kölner Kirchenprovinz zur nationalsozialistischen Bewegung," March 3, 1931, in Wilhelm Corsten, ed., *Kölner Aktenstücke zur Lage der Katholischen Kirche in Deutschland 1933–1945,* pp. 1–2. Reference is also made here to statements by various other bishops.

97. Bergen to Foreign Office, May 11, 1931, Ausw. A., T120, R. 5719, K622889–90.

98. Wilhelm Josef Doetsch, *Württembergs Katholiken unterm Hakenkreuz 1930–1935,* pp. 35–36, 73; Thomas Knapp, "The Red and the Black: Catholic Socialists in the Weimar Republic," *CHR* 61 (1975): 386–408.

99. Ausw. A., T120, R. 5719, K622886–90; Deuerlein, *Deutsche Katholizismus,* pp. 53–54.

100. Walter Conrad, *Der Kampf um die Kanzeln,* p. 32.
101. Corsten, *Kölner Aktenstücke,* p. 3.
102. Müller, *Dokumente,* pp. 13–15; Doetsch, *Württembergs Katholiken,* pp. 56–63; *KJ,* 1932, p. 117; Anthony Rhodes, *The Vatican in the Age of the Dictators, 1922– 1945,* p. 166.

Chapter Six

1. Art. 137, McBain and Rogers, *New Constitutions,* p. 202.
2. Cardinal Faulhaber, head of the Munich-Freising Bishops' Conference, was one of the most pronounced royalists (see Ludwig Volk, "Kardinal Faulhabers Stellung zur Weimarer Republik und zum NS. Staat," *SZ* 177 [1966]: 173–95).
3. See chap. 1 at n. 35 above.
4. Wolfgang Treue, *Deutsche Parteiprogramme 1861–1954,* p. 146; Gottfried Feder, *Hitler's Official Programme and its Fundamental Ideas,* pp. 43, 107–9, 122.
5. When Christian Kinder became head of the German Christians (December, 1933) he changed the name of their journal from *Evangelium im Dritten Reich* to *Positives Christentum.* He tried to convey what the term meant by articles in the journal, partly because many party organs were disgracefully misinterpreting what was meant by "positive Christianity" (Christian Kinder, *Neue Beiträge zur Geschichte der evangelischen Kirche in Schleswig-Holstein und im Reich 1924–1945,* p. 51). Reich Bishop Ludwig Müller undertook to explain the term in his *Was ist positives Christentum?,* but states that he was not commissioned by the party to do so. Although D. Cajus Fabricius is careful to point out that his "book is in no way an official statement," he gives perhaps the best apology for positive Christianity in *Positive Christianity in the Third Reich.*
6. In 1935 Hitler was declared exempt from taxes ("Hitler is Revealed as Master of Ruse in Evading Taxes," *New York Times,* April 8, 1970). On his public image as a supporter of religion, see Zipfel, *Kirchenkampf,* p. 6; Max Domarus, *Hitler Reden und Proklamationen 1932–1945,* 1: 16–19; the note on "The Treatment of Religion by Hitler in *Mein Kampf,*" in Norman H. Baynes, ed., *The Speeches of Adolf Hitler, April 1922–August 1939,* 1: 333–41.
7. Point 4 of the party program also might well have caused churchmen to take note, for it indicated what was in store for non-Aryan Christians. It states: "No one can be a citizen who is not a folk comrade (*Volksgenosse*). Only those of German blood can be a folk comrade without consideration of confession. No Jew can therefore be a folk comrade" (Treue, *Deutsche Parteiprogramme,* p. 144; Feder, *Hitler's Official Programme,* p. 39).
8. Adolf Hitler, *Mein Kampf,* edition by E. Reynal and C. N. Hitchcock (New York, 1940), pp. 365–66. In places the style, if not the accuracy, of this standard edition leaves much to be desired.
9. Ibid., pp. 144–45.
10. Ibid., p. 367.
11. Ibid., pp. 479–80.
12. Ibid., pp. 150–51.
13. Ibid., p. 829. According to Hermann Rauschning, Hitler stated in 1933: "These professors and mystery-men who want to found Nordic religions merely get in my way. Why do I tolerate them? Because they help to disintegrate, which is all we can do at the moment. They cause unrest. And all unrest is creative" (*The Voice of Destruction,* p. 51). In general Rauschning's quotations from Hitler on religion (ibid., pp. 48–56) should be used with caution. They are based on memory and seem more typical of a period later than 1933.
14. Walter Künneth, "Das Judenproblem und die Kirche," in Künneth and Schreiner, *Nation vor Gott,* pp. 90–105, provides a good summary of contemporary opinions; for a discussion of anti-Semitism in Catholic circles, see Karl Thieme, "Deutsche Katholiken," in Mosse and Paucker, *Entscheidungsjahr 1932,* pp. 274–86; Hermann Greive, *Theologie and Ideologie,* pp. 198, 206.
15. See chap. 5 at n. 70 above; BA, 43 I/2196, p. 123.
16. Buchheim, *Glaubenskrise,* p. 73; on this period in general, pp. 68–79; Wright, *'Above Parties,'* pp. 100–109.
17. On Kube's activity and the organization of the Glaubensbewegung Deutsche Christen see Meier, *Die Deutschen Christen,* pp. 10–16. Up to about 1930, the

party observed a tactical indifference in church matters but then began to shift to the position that the state should protect the church and religion against the left. Rosenberg and some other old party stalwarts never accepted this new policy (Kurt Meier, "Die Religionspolitik der NSDAP in der Zeit der Weimarer Republik," in Heinz Brunotte, ed., *Zur Geschichte des Kirchenkampfes*, 2: 16–24). On the church elections, see Wright, *'Above Parties,'* pp. 93–98.

18. Hossenfelder was born in 1899 at Kottbus, entered the army in 1917, and later fought in various *Freikorps* during 1919–21. In 1925 he became pastor in Upper Silesia, some of the members of his congregation residing in Poland. Here he developed a strong feeling of political nationalism and in 1929 he joined the Nazi party. After World War II he again served as a parish minister.

19. Meier, *Die Deutschen Christen,* p. 13; Buchheim, *Glaubenskrise,* p. 17.

20. "Richtlinien der Glaubensbewegung 'Deutsche Christen' vom 26. Mai 1932," *KJ,* 1933–44, pp. 4–7.

21. Otto Langmann, *Deutsche Christenheit in der Zeitenwende,* pp. 34, 77; see also Tilgner, *Volksnomostheologie,* pp. 221–22. Later Minister of Church Affairs Kerrl maintained that "National Socialism and Christianity were identical" (Coetus Reformierter Prediger reporting on an interview with Kerrl on November 27, 1935, Biel. Arch., Coll. W. Niemöller, N-6, Kerrl).

22. Groups could not be organized overnight, and this work continued into 1933. "In general it can be said that by the time of the national meeting in April, 1933, organized district groups (*Gaue*) existed in almost all the Reich" (Meier, *Die Deutschen Christen,* p. 16).

23. On Sunday, July 17, 1932, there was a street fight in Altona which resulted in seventeen deaths. It caused much concern in church circles, and twenty-one local pastors joined in the declaration of January 11, 1933, which had been prepared by Pastors Asmussen, Hasselmann, Knuth, Thomsen, and Tonnesen (Ernst Deuerlein, *Der Aufstieg der NSDAP in Augenzeugenberichten,* pp. 392–94; Wilhelm Niemöller, *Kampf und Zeugnis der Bekennenden Kirche* p. 29; Kinder, *Neue Beiträge,* p. 32).

24. "Das Wort und Bekenntnis Altonaer Pastoren in der Not und Verwirrung des öffentlichen Lebens vom 11. Januar 1933," *KJ,* 1933–44, pp. 8–12; also with short introduction and evaluation in Günter Heidtmann, ed., *Glaube in Ansturm der Zeit,* pp. 11–28.

25. For enthusiastic declarations by various church offices and officials, see Günther van Norden, *Kirche in der Krise,* pp. 46–49, 60. Most of the Protestant church press commented favorably on the Nazi take-over (Stoll, *Ev. Zeitschriftenpresse,* pp. 239–40, 249). "Von der grossen Menge, auch der späteren Führer der Bekennenden Kirche ist Hitler zunächst ebenso freudig begrüsst worden, wie von dem späteren Aufstandsführer Goerdeler" (Kurt D. Schmidt, "Probleme und Ergebnisse der Forschungsarbeit über den Kirchenkampf in Deutschland," *ZevKR* 72 [1961]: 125). "Auf Hitler setzte Wurm seine Hoffnung für den Wiederaufstieg Deutschlands" (Evang. Pfarrverein in Württemberg, eds., *Für Volk und Kirche,* p. 9). See also Tiefel, *CH* 41 (1972): 330–36.

26. Hans Asmussen, *Zur jüngsten Kirchengeschichte,* p. 28. This is the point that Friedrich Baumgärtel also makes in his *Wider die Kirchenkampf-Legenden,* pp. 3–4.

27. February 1, 1933, Domarus, *Hitler Reden,* 1: 192; Baynes, *Hitler's Speeches,* 1: 369–70.

28. Nicolaisen, *Kirchenpolitik,* 1: 8–9; see also excerpts from Hitler's speech at Königsberg on March 6, 1933 (pp. 13–14).

29. Johannes Kübel, "Mensch, und Christ, Theologe, Pfarrer und Kirchenmann. Erinnerungen," MS dated Nürnberg, 1947; in possession of Kübel family.

30. *Gesetzes- und Verordnungsblatt für die Vereinigte evang. prot. Landeskirche Badens,* 1935, p. 83.

31. *Zentralblatt für die gesamte Unterrichts-Verwaltung in Preussen,* 1933, p. 65; Helmreich, *Religious Education,* pp. 105–8, 155.

32. *Amtsblatt für die Evangelisch-Lutherische Landeskirche in Bayern rechts des Rheins,* 1933, p. 33; Karl D. Bracher, Wolfgang Sauer, and Gerhard Schulz, *Die nationalsozialistische Machtergreifung,* p. 328; see chap. 20, below, for an account of the Nazis' treatment of the Jehovah's Witnesses.

33. Karl Heinz Götte, *Die Propaganda der Glaubensbewegung "Deutsche Christen" und ihre Beurteilung in der deutschen Tagespresse,* p. 195.

34. *AK* 82 (1933): 338–40, 349–51; 83 (1934): 98–102, 338–40; 84 (1935): 153–59.

35. BA, Reichskanzlei, 43 II/150, pp. 22–24; Rep. 320, no. 471; Nicolaisen, *Kirchenpolitik,* 1: 11–13.

36. The ordinance is given in Werner Hoche, ed., *Die Gesetzgebung des Kabinetts Hitler,* 1: 236–37; one of the best brief accounts of the Nazi takeover of power is in Bracher, *Machtergreifung,* pp. 75–88.

37. *Evangelium im Dritten Reich,* no. 9 (February 26, 1933), as quoted in Götte, *Deutsche Christen,* p. 232; see also Wilhelm Niemöller, *Die Evangelische Kirche im Dritten Reich. Handbuch des Kirchenkampfes,* pp. 70–75.

38. For an analysis of the vote, see Erich Matthais and Rudolf Morsey, eds., *Das Ende der Parteien 1933,* pp. 790–93.

39. As quoted in Niemöller, *Kampf und Zeugnis,* p. 34.

40. Otto Dibelius, *In the Service of the Lord,* pp. 138–39.

41. Henry Picker, *Hitlers Tischgespräche im Führerhauptquartier 1941–42,* December 13, 1941, p. 349, February 27, 1942, p. 353. Hitler's absence was explained in an official statement on the radio. He had remained away because the bishops had declared some of his statements, as well as those of other National Socialists, derogatory to the church, and therefore he had been excluded from the sacraments. The bishops' declarations had never been withdrawn, and consequently he had not attended the church services. Goebbels was placed on the same plane as Hitler, although Cardinal Faulhaber in reporting to the Vatican noted that Goebbels, although a Catholic, had married a divorced woman in a Protestant church and thereby excluded himself from the Catholic church (Ludwig Volk, *Kirchliche Akten über die Reichskonkordatsverhandlungen, 1933,* p. 6). Hitler's official statement of March 21, 1933, in regard to his absence from the church service is given in Nicolaisen, *Kirchenpolitik,* pp. 22–23.

42. For the address and an account of the events, see Domarus, *Hitler Reden,* 1: 226–28.

43. Baynes, *Hitler's Speeches,* 1: 370–71, italics added. Slight changes have also been made for the sake of clarity in the translation. See also Buchheim, *Glaubenskrise,* pp. 82, 213. The italicized sentence was omitted in the somewhat abbreviated account of the speech given in the *Völkische Beobachter;* it also did not appear in the official text published by the Eherverlag in 1934, in the authorized translation, or in the text given in Domarus, *Hitler Reden,* 1: 229–37. The last sentence in my quotation is not in Baynes's volume, but is taken from the last paragraph of the speech as given in Domarus; it is also part of the selection as given in *KJ,* 1933–44, p. 13. The statement was the result of negotiations with Kaas, the leader of the Center party, and was part of the conditions made by the Center party for voting for the Enabling Act. See the Center party's demands and excerpts from Hitler's speech as given in Matthais and Morsey, *Ende der Parteien,* pp. 429–31.

44. On the negotiations between Hitler and the Center party, see Matthais and Morsey, *Ende der Parteien,* pp. 357–66; for the attitude of the Bavarian People's party, see pp. 492–93, and for that of the Social Democrats, see pp. 166–67; see also Detlef Junker, *Die Deutsche Zentrumspartei und Hitler 1932–33,* pp. 171–89; Volk, *Reichskonkordat,* pp. 82–83.

Chapter Seven

1. *KJ,* 1933–44, p. 14; Niemöller, *Kampf und Zeugnis,* pp. 35–37.

2. The drafting of the constitution is traced in Kater, *Ev. Kirche,* pp. 74–111.

3. Since 1927 there existed an informal "German Lutheran Bishops' Conference," and the Würzburg conference was a continuation of these meetings (Paul Fleisch, "Das Werden der Vereinigten Evangelisch-Lutherischen Kirche Deutschlands und ihre Verfassung," *ZevKR* 1 (1951): 25–26; see also Julius Schieder, *D. Hans Meiser DD. Wächter und Haushalter Gottes,* p. 76.

4. Joachim Gauger, *Gotthard Briefe,* 1: 74.

5. Kinder, *Neue Beiträge,* p. 45; Meier, *Deutsche Christen,* pp. 317–18.

6. Karl Barth maintained that while Müller had to be heard, he should never have been permitted to participate in and influence the deliberations because of his position as Schirmherr of the German Christians and also because of his theological views ("Theologische Existenz heute," reprt. in Walter Fürst, ed., "*Dialektische Theologie*" in Scheidung und Bewährung 1933–1936, p. 66. The Loccumer Mani-

fest is given in *KJ*, 1933–44, pp. 15–16; Kurt D. Schmidt, *Die Bekenntnisse und grundsätzlichen Äusserungen zur Kirchenfrage*, 1: 153–54.

7. Gauger, *Kirchenwirren*, 1: 70.
8. Reichskanzlei, T120, R. 4419, L124324, L124329.
9. Ibid., L124334–36.
10. Rendtorff resigned as bishop of the Church of Mecklenburg-Schwerin on January 6, 1934. In May, 1934, Landeskirchenführer Walther Schultz, Gauleiter der Deutschen Christen, became bishop of the newly formed Mecklenburg Land church (Gauger, *Kirchenwirren*, 1: 72).
11. Point 3 of the ten-point program (ibid., p. 77).
12. Ibid., p. 79; see also Tilgner, *Volksnomostheologie*, pp. 222–32.
13. On the consultations with Bodelschwingh in regard to his acceptance of the office of bishop see Wilhelm Brandt, *Friedrich v. Bodelschwingh 1877–1946*, pp. 119–24; see also Wilhelm Niemöller, *Aus dem Leben eines Bekenntnispfarrers*, p. 104; Niemöller, *Kampf und Zeugnis*, p. 43.
14. Kübel, "Erinnerungen," pp. 156–57.
15. Dibelius, *In the Service of the Lord*, p. 142.
16. Buchheim, *Glaubenskrise*, pp. 101–3. Matthias Simon states that Bishop Meiser joined Rendtorff when the latter asked Bodelschwingh to resign ("Landesbischof Meiser im Kirchenkampf," *Evangelisch-Lutherische Kirchenzeitung* 10 [1956]: 62). On the election of the bishop, see also Wright, *'Above Parties,'* pp. 126–37.
17. Wurm was quoting from a German drinking song. Kübel later wrote him a letter protesting his failure to support Bodelschwingh, but received no answer (Kübel, "Erinnerungen," pp. 161, 165, 345–47).
18. The press carried many enthusiastic articles on Bodelschwingh. There is an extensive collection of clippings, Nürnberg, LK. Arch., Kirchensammlung 0–1.
19. Walter Conrad, Ministerial Councillor for Church Affairs in the Ministry of the Interior, who was friendly to the churches, nevertheless maintains there was no legal basis for Bodelschwingh's election (Conrad, *Kampf um die Kanzeln*, p. 15).
20. Liermann, *Kirchen und Staat*, 1: 140.
21. Nicolaisen, *Kirchenpolitik*, 1: 68–69; Niemöller, *Kampf und Zeugnis*, pp. 47–50; Buchheim, *Glaubenskrise*, p. 107.
22. Dibelius, *In the Service of the Lord*, p. 143. Jäger did not join the party until March 1, 1933; his party card was number 1,490,118. He apparently was frequently unfaithful to his wife Edith, and they were divorced in 1930. See the sworn statement by Edith Jäger, née Grunow, made in Munich on September 25, 1934 (copy in Biel. Arch., Coll. W. Niemöller, N-5, Jäger). Charges against her for defamation of her former husband were dropped in October, 1936 (Guertner Diary, T988, R. 41, B042436).
23. Characterization by Buchheim, *Glaubenskrise*, p. 117; Conrad, *Kampf um die Kanzeln*, p. 14.
24. Reichskanzlei, T120, R. 4419, L124379, L124381; he did grant Bodelschwingh a private interview on November 16, 1933 (Nicolaisen, *Kirchenpolitik*, 1: 172–74).
25. This report was drawn up by Pastor Backhaus at the time. The secret police got hold of it in February, 1934, and it found its way to the Reich Chancellery (Reichskanzlei, T120, R. 4419, L124560–64; reprinted Nicolaisen, *Kirchenpolitik*, 1: 94–98).
26. The request was made by Pastor Sittel (Sittel to Hitler, June 9, 1933, Reichskanzlei, T120, R. 4419, L124358). The letter informing Sittel that Hitler was sending a Bible has this marginal note: "Eintrag in die Bibel: Der Gemeinde Ober Saulheim Gestiftet. Berlin den 22 Juni 1933, gez, Ad. Hitler" (L124359). On a visit to the church in Ober-Saulheim on August 9, 1968, I found that the Bible is still in use, but that the dedicatory page had been cut out by Pastor Bordowsky in 1949 (information furnished by the sexton, Friedrich Vallbracht, who stood beside Brodowsky while he did it).
27. Reichskanzlei to Bormann, November 21, 1938, BA, Reichskanzlei, R 43 II/152, p. 33; a list of congregations receiving gifts from June 8, 1936, to October 16, 1937, is given pp. 31–32. In February, 1935, he made a major gift of 5,000 marks for decorating the Cathedral of Saint Zeno in Bad Reichenhall; in November, 1935, he gave 15,000 marks to help restore six Württemberg churches that had been damaged by an earthquake, and most exceptionally, on March 24, 1938, he gave 10,000 marks to the Methodist church in Schneidemühl for a new organ. This last gift was in recognition of Bishop Melle's references at the Oxford conference to the

freedom of the Methodist church in Germany (see chap. 11 at n. 110 and chap. 19 at n. 26, below). For other references to Hitler's gifts to churches, see BA, Reichskanzlei, R 43 II/175, pp. 299, 303, 471–72, 475–83, 491–93, 665.

28. Nicolaisen, *Kirchenpolitik,* 1: 82.

29. Dibelius, *In the Service of the Lord,* p. 136; for numerous examples of the deification of Hitler, see Götte, *Deutsche Christen,* pp. 184–91.

30. *Friedensglocke* 41, no. 18 (1934); microfilm copy in Ausw. A., T120, R. 4420, L124969–70.

31. Barth, "Theologische Existenz heute," in Fürst, *Dialektische Theologie,* p. 56; Arthur Frey, *Cross and Swastika,* pp. 138–42; Kater, *Ev. Kirche,* pp. 71–73.

32. Niemöller, *Kampf und Zeugnis,* p. 48.

33. Reichskanzlei, T120, R. 4419, L124373, L124376, L124405; Dibelius, *In the Service of the Lord,* pp. 144–45.

34. Niemöller, *Kampf und Zeugnis,* p. 50.

35. Reichskanzlei, T120, R. 4419, L124386; on this whole episode see Oskar Söhngen, "Hindenburgs Eingreifen in den Kirchenkampf 1933," in Kurt D. Schmidt, ed., *Zur Geschichte des Kirchenkampfes,* pp. 30–44.

36. Götte, *Deutsche Christen,* p. 98; Gerhard Niemöller, *Die erste Bekenntnissynode der Deutschen Evangelischen Kirche zu Barmen,* 1: 44–45.

37. Reichskanzlei, T120, R. 4419, L124394; Niemöller, *Handbuch,* p. 105.

38. The cabinet approved the Protestant church constitution at the same meeting (July 14, 1933) where it gave approval to the conclusion of the concordat with the Vatican (Nicolaisen, *Kirchenpolitik,* pp. 107–9; *KJ,* 1933–44, pp. 17, 20).

39. The German text of the constitution is given in *AK* 82 (1933): 225–31; *KJ,* 1933–44, pp. 17–20; five preliminary drafts and the final text are given in Kater, *Ev. Kirche,* pp. 194–213; an English translation is in Charles S. Macfarland, *The New Church and the New Germany,* pp. 181–86.

40. The draft of this article was based on a paragraph of the Württemberg church constitution of June 24, 1920 (see letter of Bishop Wurm of July 30, 1938, Biel. Arch., Coll. W. Niemöller, Präsidium der Bekenntnissynode der DEK, V-8, Kirchensteuerfragen).

41. Niemöller, *Kampf und Zeugnis,* p. 39; Robert Steiner, "Der Weg der reformierten Kirchen und Gemeinden von 1933–1950," *KJ,* 1950, pp. 233–38; Herwart Vorländer, *Kirchenkampf in Elberfeld 1933–1945,* pp. 64–65.

42. The five men were Karl Fezer, Otto Koopmann, Fritz Müller, Simon Schöffel, and Heinrich Schumann. Their period of administration is described in Ernst-Victor Benn, "Die Einstweilige Leitung der Deutschen Evangelischen Kirche (Juli-September 1933)," *ZevKR* 1 (1951): 365–82.

43. Götte, *Deutsche Christen,* p. 106.

44. Gauger, *Kirchenwirren,* 1: 93.

45. Götte, *Deutsche Christen,* p. 114, see also pp. 115–18; Stoll, *Ev. Zeitschriftenpresse,* pp. 183–86, 240–51.

46. Wilhelm Niemöller, *Bekennende Kirche in Westfalen,* p. 61; Vorländer, *Kirchenkampf,* pp. 57–62. On places where single lists prevailed, see Götte, *Deutsche Christen,* p. 121. In Schleswig-Holstein the lists were made up of 87 percent German Christians and 13 percent representatives of the group called *"Evangelium und Kirche"* (Kinder, *Neue Beiträge,* pp. 41, 87).

47. Schmidt, *Bekenntnisse,* 1: 145–48; Kater, *Ev. Kirche,* pp. 65–67.

48. The term *Bekennende Kirche* ("Confessing church") was first used in one of the Young Reformation Movement's election proclamations; see G. Niemöller, *Erste Bekenntnissynode,* 1: 27. Germans usually use *Bekennende Kirche,* less frequently *Bekenntniskirche* ("Confessional church"), *Bekennende Gemeinde* ("Confessing congregation"), or *Bekenntnisgemeinde* ("Confessional congregation"). Each term has a different shade of meaning, and writers using English vary in usage. The term "Confessing church" will be used here, for it most closely describes the nature of the movement; despite emphasis on the historic confessions, it was more a "Confessing" than a "Confessional" church. The Nazis often used the term *Bekenntnisfront* in order to underscore it as an opposition movement (Werner Koch, *Bekennende Kirche gestern und heute,* p. 16). The term was firmly rejected: "Die Bekennende Kirche (die Bezeichnung Bekenntnisfront halten wir nicht für glücklich und gebrauchen sie daher nicht). . . . " (Vorläufige Leitung to Ingenieur v. Mirman, May 21, 1937, Berlin, K. Arch., no. 381a, p. 8).

49. Gauger, *Kirchenwirren,* 1: 93; Niemöller, *Handbuch,* p. 107.

50. Baynes, *Hitler's Speeches,* 1: 377. For the German text as well as for other statements by state officials, see Nicolaisen, *Kirchenpolitik,* pp. 110–22.
51. Gauger, *Kirchenwirren,* 1: 95; Niemöller, *Handbuch,* pp. 108–10.
52. Bishop Meiser, "Vertrauliches Rundschreiben an die sämtlichen Geistlichen der Evang. Luth. Landeskirche Bayerns," August 2, 1933, Nürnberg, LK. Arch., Sammlung 0–1.
53. Hans Liermann, "Das evangelische Bischofsamt in Deutschland seit 1933," *ZevKR* 3 (1953–54): 1–13.
54. *AK* 82 (1933): 374–81; 83 (1934): 115–27, 274–78, 293–98, 346–51.
55. See, for example, the description of the meeting of the Brandenburg synod by a Swedish reporter, as quoted in Zipfel, *Kirchenkampf,* pp. 36–38.
56. See Johann Bielfeldt, *Der Kirchenkampf in Schleswig-Holstein 1933–1945,* pp. 40–46; see also pp. 46–51 on the results of the synod.
57. *Neue Kirche im Neuen Staat,* pp. 6, 11–81.
58. *KJ,* 1933–44, p. 24; translation in Macfarland, *New Church and the New Germany,* pp. 71–72. The church law containing the Aryan paragraph was repealed on November 16, 1933; this repeal was cancelled by the Reich bishop on January 4, 1934, and this cancellation was in turn repealed on April 13, 1934 (Wilhelm Niemöller, "Ist die Judenfrage 'bewältigt'?" *Junge Kirche,* Supp. no. 2 [1968], p. 6). On September 14, 1933, twenty-five pastors from Nürnberg and the surrounding territory issued a statement on the Prussian action: "The Aryan paragraph in this form has no right in the church. It is contrary to its ordinances and its doctrines" (Nürnberg, LK. Arch., Bestand no. 222). When the authorities of the Prussian church asked all its pastors and their wives to submit evidence of their Aryan background, the Westphalian brotherhood council requested all pastors in Westphalia to refuse, and circulated their memorandum on the Aryan question all over Germany (Biel. Arch., Coll. W. Niemöller, D-6, Bekennende Kirche im Weltkrieg).
59. Niemöller, *Kampf und Zeugnis,* pp. 60–62.
60. On the boycott, see Karl A. Schleunes, *The Twisted Road to Auschwitz,* pp. 61–96; Kurt Meier, *Kirche und Judentum,* pp. 11, 25–27; Boyens, *Kirchenkampf und Ökumene, 1933–1939,* p. 293; Gutteridge, *Evangelical Church,* pp. 76–80. Even many Jews considered the party's rabid anti-Semitism political propaganda which would abate as the regime established itself (Ernst Simon, *Aufbau im Untergang,* pp. 20–24).
61. The resolution was introduced by Freiherr von Pechmann of Munich. For Pechmann's reaction to his defeat, see Friedrich W. Kantzenbach, *Widerstand und Solidärität der Christen in Deutschland 1933–1945,* pp. 17, 47, 110, 139, 168, 263, 314–15; for his further opposition to anti-Semitic measures, see also pp. 37, 39, 61, 66, 202, 267, 341. See chap. 14 at n. 9, below, for contemporary statements by Cardinal Faulhaber and Archbishop Gröber.
62. Kapler states the memorandum was prepared by a "church personality," and is dated June 7, 1933 (Reichskanzlei, T120, R. 4419, L124360–72). The memorandum was drawn up by Oberkonsistorialrat Hans Wahl, and was also sent to the Universal Christian Council in Geneva (Boyens, *Kirchenkampf und Ökumene, 1933–1939,* pp. 54, 299–308).
63. For the Marburg statement of September 19, 1933, drawn up by their dean, Dr. Hans von Soden, see Schmidt, *Bekenntnisse,* 1: 178–82; for the Erlangen statement of September 25, 1933, drawn up by Professors Paul Althaus and Werner Elert, ibid., pp. 182–86. A group of New Testament professors from various universities issued a statement, "Neues Testament und Rassenfrage," on September 23, 1933, which also was in opposition to the Aryan paragraph (ibid., pp. 189–91). For an answer to the Erlangen statement, see Rudolf Bultmann, "Der Arier-Paragraph im Raume der Kirche," reprinted in Fürst, *Dialektische Theologie,* pp. 86—101. The Marburg and Erlangen memoranda, along with statements by other groups and individuals, are reprinted in Fürst, *Dialektische Theologie,* pp. 86–101. The Marburg and Erlangen memoranda, along with statements by other groups and individuals, are reprinted in Flüchtlingsdienst des Ökumenischen Rats der Kirche, *Die Evangelische Kirche in Deutschland und die Judenfrage,* pp. 46–113. It should be noted that neither the Marburg nor the Erlangen statement dealt with Jews or anti-Semitism in general, but only with the position of the Jewish Christians in the churches. See also Meier, *Kirche und Judentum,* pp. 17–23.
64. Strathmann's statement, published in *Theologische Blätter,* 12 (1933): 324–27 is reprinted in Schmidt, *Bekenntnisse,* 1: 186–89. Although it was maintained that the

church could not distinguish between Gentile and Jewish Christians and the latter could not be barred from holding church offices, the idea that it might be well to restrict leading positions in the Volkskirche to non-Jewish Christians was advanced in Künneth and Schreiner, *Nation vor Gott*, pp. 97–98, 120–26; see also Gerhard Kittel, *Die Judenfrage*, pp. 103–8. For views of various German churchmen against and in support of the Aryan paragraph, see Gutteridge, *Evangelical Church*, pp. 94–120.

65. Karl Kupisch, "Zur Genesis des Pfarrernotbundes," *Theologische Literaturzeitung* 91 (1966): 721–30. Precedents for the Notbund were the formation of a *"Pfarrerbruderschaft"* in the Rhineland in the summer of 1933 and a meeting of pastors in Essen on September 11, 1933. See also Wilhelm Niemöller, *Texte zur Geschichte des Pfarrernotbundes*, pp. 3–16, 22–23; W. Niemöller, *Junge Kirche*, Supp. no. 2 (1968), p. 14.

66. See the characterization of their mother by Wilhelm Niemöller in his *Leben eines Bekenntnispfarrers*, pp. 37–38; see also Dietmar Schmidt, *Martin Niemöller*, p. 22; Franz Beyer, *Menschen Warten*, p. 38.

67. *KJ*, 1933–44, p. 25; Niemöller, *Geschichte des Pfarrernotbundes*, p. 26; Macfarland, *New Church and the New Germany*, p. 120. See also Martin Niemöller's personal statement of November 2, 1933, "Sätze zur Arierfrage in der Kirche," *Deutsches Pfarrerblatt*, no. 4 (1933), p. 46; copy in Biel. Arch., Coll. W. Niemöller, C-8-11, Judenfrage; Martin Niemöller, *Das Bekenntnis der Väter und die bekennende Gemeinde*, pp. 35–36.

68. "Der Reichsführer SS, Sonderbericht. Die Lage in der prot. Kirche, Feb./März 1935," BA, Reichssicherheitshauptamt, R 58/233, pp. 15–17. On the police supervision of the Pastors' Emergency League, see also Nicolaisen, *Kirchen Politik*, 2: 70–78.

69. The statement had been drafted by Martin Niemöller and Fritz Müller in a boat on the Wannsee on September 24. It was worked over later and did not arrive from the printer until the night before the synod meeting. Niemöller and Müller took it by automobile to Wittenberg where they and others distributed it, posted it on trees, etc. (Martin Niemöller to Wilhelm Niemöller, January 28, 1958, Biel. Arch., Coll. W. Niemöller, D-3, Geschichte des Pfarrernotbundes, II; see also Martin Niemöller's "Vorwort" to W. Niemöller, "Geschichte des Pfarrernotbundes," ibid.; Gauger, *Kirchenwirren*, 1: 105).

70. Bishop Müller informed Hitler all were party members except Schöffel, and he was one in spirit (Reichskanzlei, T120, R. 4419, L124440–41). Müller had also cleared his own election as bishop with Hitler (ibid., L124439).

71. For the archbishop of Sweden's letter, see Ausw. A., T120, R. 4418, L123483; for the Foreign Office letter, L123485; for Müller's awareness of international opposition to the Aryan paragraph, see his letter to the Foreign Office of November 9, 1933, L123536–38; for the protest against the Aryan paragraph by the Executive Committee of the Universal Christian Conference for Life and Work at their meeting in Novi Sad, L123496; see also protests from various individuals and groups, L123487, L123510, L123550.

72. Aufzeichnung by Stieve, September 30, 1933, ibid., L123500.

73. The police in May, 1934, estimated the membership of the league at about 8,000 as compared to 2,000 German Christian pastors. Most pastors were neutral, but the majority of these sympathized with the league ("Lagebericht Mai/Juni 1934," BA, Reichssicherheitshauptamt, R 58/229, p. 42). In spite of the insistence of the Pastors' Emergency League leaders that their organization was nonpolitical and concerned only with the church, the police considered it as being against the regime (p. 43).

74. Of the remaining 29 non-Aryan pastors, 17 were in the Prussian church, and of these 11 had been in service before August 1, 1941, or were front line soldiers. This meant that for the time being only 6 pastors were hit by the Prussian Aryan paragraph (Otto Fischer, "Arische Abstammung und evangelische Pfarrer," *Deutsches Pfarrerblatt*, October 31, 1933, pp. 607–10). Fischer lists the names of 63 non-Aryan pastors who had served in the church during the years 1554–1891; see also Gauger, *Kirchenwirren*, 1: 104. Pastor H. Grüber, who was later entrusted with the care of non-Aryan pastors, estimated their number at about 24 in 1938 when he sought to place them in German congregations abroad. Many of these pastors were at this time in Basel (Grüber to Pastor Hesse, August 19, 1938, Biel. Arch., Coll. W. Niemöller, C-8-11, Judenfrage).

75. BA, R 43 II/150, p. 21; also Schumacher, T580, R. 41 (there are no frame numbers in the Schumacher microfilms). In April, 1937, Rosenberg asked Frick to withdraw this decree or at least expand it to include those converting to "Gottgläubig." The Confessing church had got hold of Frick's decree and were exploiting it (BA, Kanzlei Rosenberg, NS 8/169, pp. 89–90).

76. "Kundgebung für den gesamten Pfarrerstand, October 11, 1933," *KJ*, 1933–44, p. 27.

77. For Hess's order see Gauger, *Kirchenwirren*, 1: 106; on Hess's position as the Führer's deputy, see Buchheim's statement "Der 'Stellverträter des Führers'," in *Gutachten des Instituts für Zeitgeschichte*, pp. 323–25.

78. Reprinted in Nicolaisen, *Kirchenpolitik*, pp. 124–25; see also ibid., pp. 143–45; Gauger, *Kirchenwirren*, 1: 98; Meier, *Die Deutschen Christen*, p. 302. Many Nazi leaders felt that the extralegal actions of the German Christians should not be permitted to burden the party (Kurt Meier, "Kirche und Nationalsozialismus," in Schmidt, *Gesammelte Aufsätze*, p. 16).

79. Götte, *Deutsche Christen*, p. 132.

80. Reichskanzlei, T120, R. 4419, L124295–302; Nicolaisen, *Kirchenpolitik*, pp. 166–69; Macfarland, *New Church and the New Germany*, pp. 51–55, 145–46.

81. Macfarland, *New Church and the New Germany*, pp. 147–48. The book was sent to the German Foreign Office by Ambassador Luther in the spring of 1934. Luther commended it but noted that Macfarland was critical of the treatment of the Jews and of the Confessing church (Ausw. A., T120, R. 4418, L123704–5).

82. As quoted in Baumgärtel, *Wider die Kirchenkampf-Legenden*, p. 4.

83. The German Christians were particularly fond of singing Luther's great hymn, and therefore it was not used so often in many of the Confessing churches (Niemöller, *Leben eines Bekenntnispfarrers*, p. 107).

84. *KJ*, 1933–44, pp. 29–30; translation in part taken from Macfarland, *New Church and the New Germany*, p. 141.

85. Theophil Wurm, *Erinnerungen aus meinem Leben*, p. 90.

86. Gauger, *Kirchenwirren*, 1: 110. The position of the German Christians on the Old Testament was not uniform; most retained it but tended to play down its importance and its significance in relation to the New Testament (Carsten Nicolaisen, "Die Stellung der Deutschen Christen zum Alten Testament," in Brunotte, *Gesammelte Aufsätze*, 2: 197–220; see particularly pp. 216–17, 219–20).

87. BA, Kanzlei Rosenberg, NS 8/257, p. 73; Nicolaisen, *Kirchenpolitik*, pp. 171–72.

88. Wurm, *Erinnerungen*, p. 89. Wurm estimates that there were now 1,100 Württemberg pastors backing him and only 50 supporting the German Christians.

89. Buchheim, *Glaubenskrise*, p. 137; Heinrich Hermelink, *Kirche im Kampf*, pp. 54, 144.

90. Coch had his difficulties with the Freethinkers, who were now also appearing among the Brown Shirts. He denounced them and wrote in his introduction to Walter Grundmann's *Totale Kirche im totalen Staat*: "Wenn wir uns gerade als überzeugte Lutheraner aus innersten Ueberzeugung in dem Kampfe um Volk und Staat bewusst hinter Adolf Hitler gestellt haben, für dem wir unserm Leben gelassen hätten—so lassen wir uns auch jetzt noch und nun erst recht lieber totschlagen, als dass wir uns den Christus nehmen lassen, in dem sich Gott offenbart hat. Es ist in keinem anderen Heil. Das ist positives Christentum" (p. 6).

91. Niemöller, *Kampf und Zeugnis*, p. 81; for the twenty-eight theses, see *KJ*, 1933–44, pp. 30–32; for comment on them, see Hugo Hahn, *Kämpfer wider Willen*, pp. 41–42.

92. Letter of Bishop Meiser, "An die Herren Geistlichen unserer Landeskirche," Nürnberg, LK. Arch., Kirchensammlung, 0–1; Gauger, *Kirchenwirren*, 1: 115–17; Meier, *Die Deutschen Christen*, p. 303.

93. Niemöller, *Kampf und Zeugnis*, p. 81; Gauger, *Kirchenwirren*, 1: 116.

94. Gauger, 1: 116–18; Reichskanzlei, T120, R. 4419, L124480–L124482.

95. Gauger, *Kirchenwirren*, 1: 119.

96. Kinder, *Neue Beiträge*, pp. 41–42; Buchheim, *Glaubenskrise*, p. 146; Schmidt, *Bekenntnisse*, 1: 177.

97. As quoted in Gauger, *Kirchenwirren*, 1: 116; see also Götte, *Deutschen Christen*, pp. 134–36, 153, 157–62. Conrad states that Frau Winifred Wagner had enlightened Hitler on the German Christians (*Kampf um die Kanzeln*, p. 60).

98. Conrad, *Kampf um die Kanzeln*, p. 61. Hitler no doubt had no definite plan in mind. On November 16, 1933, Meissner had told Bodelschwingh that Hitler did

not know what to do about the Protestant church and did not want to concern himself about the matter (Nicolaisen, *Kirchenpolitik*, p. 174).

99. Various directives of the Ministry of Propaganda are given in Nicolaisen, *Kirchenpolitik*, pp. 177–79. On the request for funds, see Reichskanzlei, T120, R. 4419, L124450–58, L124468, L124477–79.

100. Manfred Priepke, *Die evangelische Jugend im Dritten Reich 1933–1936*, pp. 58–74, 186–87. The agreement between Bishop Müller and Reich Youth Leader Baldur von Schirach is also reprinted in Nicolaisen, *Kirchenpolitik*, pp. 183f. See also H. W. Koch, *The Hitler Youth*, pp. 108–10.

101. Müller's statement to Hindenburg, January 12, 1934, Reichskanzlei, T120, R. 4419, L124485–89; *KJ*, 1933–44, pp. 33–35, Nicolaisen, *Kirchenpolitik*, 2: 6–8. Under the agreement purely religious activity of the churches with their youth was permitted. See also Dieter Frhr. von Lersner, *Die evangelischen Jugendverbände Württembergs und die Hitler-Jugend 1933–1934* pp. 26–37, 53–56.

102. Wurm, *Erinnerungen*, p. 91.

103. *Evangelium im Dritten Reich, Kirchenzeitung*, no. 3 (January 23, 1934), p. 28.

104. Bavarian Political Police, November 8, 1935, Besetz. Gebiete, T454, R. 81, 000668.

105. Hermann Kolb, ed., *Aus der Geschichte der Schüler-Bibel-Kreise (BK) in Bayern*, pp. 75–77, 91–93, 97–100; Koch, *Hitler Youth*, pp. 219–20. The Landjugendpfarrer of Bavaria, Württemberg, Baden, Hanover, Hesse-Kassel, and Silesia established an association to further their common efforts. See chap. 14 at n. 85, below, where further state regulations are discussed in relation to Catholic youth organizations; these regulations also applied to Protestants.

106. Conrad, *Kampf um die Kanzeln*, p. 62.

107. *KJ*, 1933–44, pp. 36–37.

108. Ibid., pp. 37–38.

109. Reichskanzlei, T120, R. 4419, L124490–91, Aktennotiz by Buttmann. Bodelschwingh as early as November 16, 1933, had urged Hindenburg in a secret interview to say a word for the freedom of the church to the state and party authorities (Nicolaisen, *Kirchenpolitik*, p. 174).

110. Reichskanzlei, T120, R. 4419, L124483–89; Nicolaisen, *Kirchenpolitik*, 2: 6–10.

111. Gauger, *Kirchenwirren*, 1: 136; see Harvey Fireside, *Icon and Swastika*, pp. 60–64. Hitler often spoke disparagingly of Rosenberg's book (Albert Speer, *Inside the Third Reich*, p. 96).

112. Nicolaisen, *Kirchenpolitik*, 2: 18–19; Wilhelm Niemöller, *Hitler und die evangelischen Kirchenführer (Zum 25. Januar 1934)*, pp. 25–31.

113. This version of the conversation stems from Bishop Coch of Saxony, a German Christian (Niemöller, *Hitler und die evangelischen Kirchen-Führer* p. 38). For a slightly different version, see Wurm, *Erinnerungen*, p. 92, which is essentially the same as Wurm's statement in a letter (written without notes and based simply on his memory) to Hammerschmidt dated April 5, 1939 (Berlin, K. Arch., no. 81, p. 18). The letter, however, does amplify Wurm's account in his memoirs, especially as to Niemöller's reactions. Hugo Hahn relates that the phrase "letzte Ölung" was contributed in a jocular way by Frau Niemöller when her husband was momentarily searching for a way to end his remarks (*Kämpfer wider Willen*, p. 50). Hitler's version of the remarks, dating from April 7, 1942, is: "Dem Alten haben wir die letzte Ölung gegeben. Wir haben ihn so eingeschmiert, dass er den Hurenbock jetzt endgültig raussetzt" (Picker, *Hitlers Tischgespräche*, p. 357). Hitler had previously touched on the interview in a dinner conversation in January, 1940 (Hans-Günther Seraphim, *Das politische Tagebuch Alfred Rosenbergs aus den Jahren 1934/35 und 1939/40*, p. 97).

114. As quoted in Jørgen Glenthøj, "Hindenburg, Göring und die evangelischen Kirchenführer," in Schmidt, *Gesammelte Aufsätze*, pp. 61, 86; also in Wilhelm Niemöller, "Epilog zum Kanzlerempfang," *EvTh* 20 (1960): 107–24.

115. Wurm, *Erinnerungen*, p. 92. On the meeting in general, see Nicolaisen, *Kirchenpolitik*, 2: 20–33; Niemöller, *Hitler und die evangelischen Kirchenführer*, pp. 40–43; Kinder, *Neue Beiträge*, pp. 44–48. Bishop Wurm's wife noted in her diary after her husband had told her of the interview: "Wie wollten sie Hitler alles erklären, und nun standen sie da wie begossen. Vater [Bishop Wurm] sagte es sei die schwerste Stunde seines Lebens gewesen" (Theophil Wurm, ed., *Tagebuchaufzeichnungen aus der Zeit des Kirchenkampfes*, p. 10). Frau Wurm's comment is in line with Hitler's description of the meeting on April 7, 1942: "Die Abgesandten

der evangelischen Kirche seien daraufhin vor Schreck so in sich zusammenge-
rutscht, dass sie fast nicht mehr dagewesen seien" (Picker, *Hitlers Tischgespräche,*
p. 357).

116. Bishop Wurm commented on this: "Es wäre nach unserem Empfinden richtiger
gewesen, wenn er dann in die Reihen zurückgetreten wäre. Stattdessen meldete er
sich immer wider zum Wort, wurde aber geflissentlich übersehn" (Wurm to Hammerschmidt, April 5, 1939, Berlin, K. Arch., no. 81, p. 18).

117. Hitler's handshake with Niemöller led to many rumors and much speculation.
Wurm, who was standing close by, felt Niemöller had held Hitler's hand a long
time, "as if he wanted to emphasize that it meant much to him, that the tie should
not be torn asunder" (Wurm to Hammerschmidt, April 5, 1939, Berlin, K. Archiv.,
no. 81, p. 18). Niemöller himself saw nothing special in the handclasp (see his
statement about the episode in a letter to his brother Wilhelm, quoted in the latter's
Hitler und die evangelischen Kirchenführer, p. 45).

118. On this meeting see Jørgen Glenthøj's account in Schmidt, *Gesammelte Aufsätze,*
p. 66; there is a long mimeographed report on the meeting in Berlin, K. Arch., no.
38, pp. 56–68.

119. Wurm, *Erinnerungen,* p. 93; Niemöller, *Hitler und die evangelischen Kirchenführer,* pp. 52–61.

120. This was out of a total of 18,000 pastors (Niemöller, *Geschichte des Pfarrernotbundes,* p. 10). In September, 1937, there was a significant loss of about 567
members when the Luther Council formed a special *Lutherischer Hilfsverein.* A
revision of the by-laws of the Pastors' Emergency League in 1938 set the monthly
dues at 8 marks for active ministers, 5 for those who had retired, 3 for vicars, and
.50 for theological students (ibid., p. 68).

121. Luth. Landeskirchenamt, Kiel, to Asmussen, January 30, 1934; Asmussen's answer
of February 3, 1934, Biel. Arch., Coll. W. Niemöller, N 11–12, Hans Asmussen.

122. See, for example, Asmussen's pamphlets *Kreuz und Reich; Die Grundlagen der
bekennenden Kirche; Her zu uns wer dem Herrn angehört!; Kurze Auslegung der
zehn Gebote; Sola fide, das ist lutherisch!*

123. Nicolaisen, *Kirchenpolitik,* 2: 65–66. The bureau never played a great role and was
dissolved by Hitler on November 14, 1935, after the establishment of the Ministry
of Church Affairs.

Chapter Eight

1. *KJ,* 1933–44, p. 39.
2. Ibid., p. 40; for a partial list of disciplined ministers in the first quarter of 1934, see
Gauger, *Kirchenwirren,* 1: 143, 145. In the Foreign Office documents there is a
table of the disciplinary actions taken at this time which shows that a large majority
were in the churches of the Old Prussian Union; some Land churches had none. It
also indicates that many of these disciplinary actions were soon rescinded (Ausw.
A., T120, R. 4418, L123880–81).
3. *KJ,* 1933–44, pp. 46–47; Gauger, *Kirchenwirren,* 1: 150–51; on the appointment
of the new Spiritual Ministry, ibid., p. 146.
4. *KJ,* 1933–44, pp. 47–48; Gauger, *Kirchenwirren,* 1: 152.
5. Gauger, *Kirchenwirren,* 1: 144; Ausw. A., T120, R. 4418, L123659, L123684,
L123710.
6. *KJ,* 1933–44, p. 55; Niemöller, *Kampf und Zeugnis,* pp. 10–11; Niemöller, *Kirche
in Westfalen,* pp. 122–23.
7. Wurm, *Erinnerungen,* pp. 93–94; Ausw. A., T120, R. 4420, L125195–96,
L125199. Because Hitler had received Wurm and Meiser, Bishops Coch of Saxony and Sasse of Thuringia, both German Christians, asked for an interview, but
Hitler refused to see them (Reichskanzlei, T120, R. 4419, L124599, L124602–3).
8. Wurm, *Erinnerungen,* p. 94; Hermelink, *Kirche im Kampf,* pp. 75–76; Nicolaisen,
Kirchenpolitik, 2: 79–82.
9. Bell to Dr. Nils Karlström, March 23, 1934, in Ronald C. D. Jasper, *George Bell,
Bishop of Chichester,* pp. 110–12; Boyens, *Kirchenkampf und Ökumene, 1933–
1939,* pp. 323–25.
10. Eino Murtorinne, *Erzbischof Eidem zum Deutschen Kirchenkampf 1933–1934,* pp.
57–77; the "Promemoria an Hitler," is given pp. 113–17. Eidem's account of the
interview is given in Nicolaisen, *Kirchenpolitik,* 2: 126–30.

11. Wurm, *Erinnerungen,* p. 95; Hermelink, *Kirche im Kampf,* pp. 76–79; *Amtsblatt für die Evangelisch-Lutherische Landeskirche in Bayern rechts des Rheins,* 1934, pp. 35–42; Gauger, *Kirchenwirren,* 1: 156.

12. *KJ,* 1933–44, pp. 55–56.

13. Gauger, *Kirchenwirren,* 1: 170; Nicolaisen, *Kirchenpolitik,* 2: 108–10.

14. Gauger, *Kirchenwirren,* 1: pp. 179–80; Ausw. A., T120, R. 4420, 125186.

15. Ausw. A., T120, R. 4420, L125220–85.

16. For the Ulm declaration, see Gauger, *Kirchenwirren,* 1: 181; *KJ,* 1933–44, pp. 59–60.

17. Much of the rest of this chapter was published as Ernst C. Helmreich, "The Nature and Structure of the Confessing Church in Germany under Hitler," *Journal of Church and State* 12 (1970): 405–20.

18. Wilhelm Niemöller, ed., *Lebensbilder aus der Bekennenden Kirche,* p. 67; G. Niemöller, *Erste Bekenntnissynode,* 2: 7–8.

19. Koch was one of the most able administrative officials among German churchmen. Not only president of the Synod of Westphalia, he was also president of the national and the Prussian synods of the Confessing church and chairman of both the Prussian brotherhood council and the Reich Brotherhood Council. He had been a member of the German National People's party, had served in the body which drew up the Prussian constitution, was a member of the Prussian Landtag from 1921–33, and a member of the Reichstag from 1930–32. See Wilhelm Niemöller, *Karl Koch, Präses der Bekenntnissynode,* pp. 52–56, 66; Niemöller, *Kirche in Westfalen,* pp. 98–100; Kurt Klotzbach, *Gegen den Nationalsozialismus,* p. 220; Werner Danielsmeyer, "Präses D. Karl Koch," in Reinhold Hedtke, ed., *Materialen für den Dienst in der Evangelischen Kirche von Westfalen,* ser. A, no. 5, pp. 3–7.

20. Niemöller, *Kirche in Westfalen,* pp. 100–102; Niemöller, *Kampf und Zeugnis,* p. 118.

21. Niemöller, *Kampf und Zeugnis,* p. 98; Niemöller, *Karl Koch,* p. 57; Klotzbach, *Gegen den Nationalsozialismus,* pp. 224–25.

22. G. Niemöller, *Erste Bekenntnissynode,* 2: 10.

23. For the text of the red card, see Niemöller, *Geschichte des Pfarrernotbundes,* p. 34.

24. Wilhelm Niesel, *Um Verkündigung und Ordnung der Kirche,* pp. 7–9; Niemöller, *Kampf und Zeugnis,* pp. 127–28. In the intact churches of Bavaria and Hanover, special "Confessing Associations" were formed which circulated reports among the members. In Bavaria the dues were 50 pfennig a month (Nürnberg, LK. Arch., Kirchenkampfsammlung 0–6). In Württemberg the *Sozietät,* a group of ardent Confessing pastors, performed a similar function.

25. For a list of the delegates with short biographical notes, see G. Niemöller, *Erste Bekenntnissynode,* 2: 11–25.

26. Ibid., pp. 196–202; *KJ,* 1933–44, pp. 63–65; Arthur C. Cochrane, *The Church's Confession under Hitler,* pp. 238–42.

27. Arthur C. Cochrane, "The Message of Barmen for Contemporary Church History," in Franklin H. Littell and Hubert G. Locke, eds., *The German Church Struggle and the Holocaust,* p. 191. Translation of creedal statement as given in Cochrane, *The Church's Confession,* pp. 239, 241; for further evaluation of the Synod of Barmen, see pp. 129–216 and the translation of Asmussen's address on the Barmen theological declaration, pp. 248–63; see also G. Niemöller, *Erste Bekenntnissynode,* 1: 113–258; Ernst Wolf, *Barmen,* pp. 74–166. The Barmen Declaration of Faith has been accepted in varying degrees by the German churches, and in May, 1967, the United Presbyterian Church in the United States added it as one of the creedal statements it accepts (Cochrane, in Littell and Locke, *German Church Struggle,* pp. 185–86).

28. The members were President Koch, Bad Oeynhausen; Bishop Meiser, Munich; Bishop Wurm, Stuttgart; Pastor Beckmann, Düsseldorf; Pastor Bosse, Raddestorf in Hanover; Pastor Karl Immer, Barmen; Pastor Asmussen, Altona; Pastor Hesse, Elberfeld, as moderator of the Reformed Confederation; Dr. Eberhard Fiedler, a lawyer from Leipzig; and William Link, a businessman from Düsseldorf (G. Niemöller, *Erste Bekenntnissynode,* 2: 204–5).

29. Ibid., p. 207.

30. Götte, *Deutsche Christen,* p. 162.

31. A visitation conducted in 1935 by the Confessing church in Berlin revealed the following numbers of red card signers in various parishes (total number of souls in the parish in parentheses): Versöhnung, 372 (19,000); Himmelfahrt, 840 (17,000);

Zion, 145 (30,000); Gethsemane, 474 (25,000); Segen, 179 (21,000); Frieden, 150 (21,000); Golgatha, 433 (25,000); Kapernaum, 380 (70,000). The visitors were asked to fill out long questionnaires, and these reports constitute a telling commentary on the activity of the Confessing church in some of the large city parishes. In many sections of Germany, especially in the smaller parishes, the ratio of red card signers to total membership was much higher. See the reports in Berlin, K. Arch., no. 159.

32. Texts of cards varying slightly in wording in Nürnberg, LK. Arch., Kirchenkampf-sammlung, 0–3.

33. Vorländer, *Kirchenkampf*, p. 567.

34. Kerrl to Dietrich, October 10, 1935, Biel. Arch., Coll. W. Niemöller, N-6, Kerrl.

35. Eberhard Klügel, *Die lutherische Landeskirche Hannovers und ihr Bischof 1933–1945*, pp. 484–85.

36. Kübel, "Erinnerungen," pp. 188–89. For police reports on Pastor Veidt and his transfer to a small parish near Darmstadt, see Reichsführer SS, T175, R. 193, 2732234–38. For conditions in the churches of Hesse at this time, see Wilhelm Lueken, *Kampf, Behauptung und Gestalt der Evangelischen Landeskirche Nassau-Hessen*, pp. 41–55.

37. Heinz Gefaeller, "Die Kirchensteuer seit 1945," *ZevKR* 1 (1950): 81. "Vielfach haben sich eine Reihe von Kirchengemeinden zur gemeinsamen Kirchensteuer-erhebung in besonderen Kirchensteuerämtern zusammengeschlossen. Die Kirchengemeinden wurden dazu gezwungen weil die Finanzämter und kommunalen Kassen während der nationalsozialistischen Herrschaft die weitere Verwaltung der Kirchensteuer ablehnten" (Thiele, *Kirchensteuerrecht*, p. 39).

38. Letter to the Finanzabteilung des Oberkirchenrats in Berlin, January 16, 1937, Biel. Arch., Coll. W. Niemöller, Präsidium der Bekenntnissynode der DEK, V-8, Kirchensteuerfragen.

39. Notiz, Finanzabteilung beim Ev. Konsistorium der Kirchenprovinz Westfalen, March 13, 1937, ibid.

40. See the decision of the court and letter of Bishop Wurm of July 30, 1938, ibid.

41. Asmussen, *Zur jüngsten Kirchengeschichte*, p. 75.

42. One of the first theological seminaries of the Confessing church was in Elberfeld, under the direction of Pastor Hermann Hesse. Others were established in East Prussia under the leadership of Professor Hans Iwand, in Pomerania under the direction of Dietrich Bonhoeffer, in Silesia under Rev. Gerhard Gloege, and in Westphalia under Professor Otto Schmitz. Kirchliche Hochschulen were started in the winter of 1935–36 in Berlin and Elberfeld. By an order of the head of the SS and chief of the German police on August 29, 1937, the seminaries, holding of examinations, and similar activities of the Confessing church were forbidden. See *Archiv für evangelisches Kirchenrecht*, 1937, pp. 390–91; Wilhelm Niemöller, *Kirchenkampf im Dritten Reich*, p. 11; "Theologisch-akademischer Nachwuchs," in W. Jannasch, *Deutsche Kirchendokumente*, pp. 65–69; Herzfeld, ed., *Berlin und Brandenburg*, pp. 504–5; Eberhard Bethge, *Dietrich Bonhoeffer*, pp. 484–560. Often when a seminary was closed it simply opened its doors again in another place (Asmussen, *Zur jüngsten Kirchengeschichte*, pp. 75–76). See also the section on the training and examination of ministerial candidates in Günther Harder, "Die kirchenleitende Tätigkeit des Brandenburgischen Bruderrates," in Schmidt, *Gesammelte Aufsätze*, pp. 190–98. As late as May, 1941, the police arrested ten men and four women in Berlin for participating in illegal theological examinations (BA, Reichskanzlei, R 43 II/156, p. 44). The arrests were made on the basis of the decree of August 29, 1937, and there were similar arrests in the Rhineland (ibid., p. 45).

43. Reichsführer SS, T175, R. 38, 2547765. Himmler on October 10, 1938, asked for an evaluation of Dr. Christian Marhenholz and Pastor Bodelschwingh (ibid., 2547766).

44. Heinz Boberach, ed., *Berichte des SD und der Gestapo über Kirchen und Kirchenvolk in Deutschland 1934–1944*, p. 278.

45. Kurt D. Schmidt, "Fragen zur Struktur der Bekennenden Kirche," *ZevKR* 9 (1962–63): 225; Gottfried Fuss, *Der Wille zur Einheit*, p. 53.

46. See the protest of Bishop Coch of Saxony (July 12, 1934) against the cancellation of the morning Evangelical services on the radio and the favoritism towards broadcasts by a representative of the German Faith Movement (Reichskanzlei, T120, R. 4419, L124654). On October 5, 1934, he submitted a long memorandum to Hitler protesting Rosenberg's speeches, increased government support of

the anti-Christian German Faith Movement, and the party obligations placed on the SA every Sunday. (ibid., L124731–39). The memorandum was shown to Hitler but there was no answer. It was buried by being sent to Hitler's deputy, Hess (ibid., L124740). Coch later drew attention to the fact that he had received no evaluation of his memorandum but this did him no good (ibid., December 8–11, 1934, L124808–9). Coch also asked to be received by Hitler but was refused (ibid., L124765–66).

47. This statement seems justified by the whole history of the church conflict and was the opinion of numerous men with whom I spoke, among them Wilhelm and Martin Niemöller, Karl Lücking, Günther Harder, Hans Liermann, and Walter Künneth. Otto Dibelius takes a contrary position. He writes: "The struggle of the Confessing church was a struggle of theologians, backed by a very small group of courageous laymen. That is how it was, and that is how it continued, more and more. The time simply had not come when such a hopeless struggle of the church against the State could be founded on the congregations" (*In the Service of the Lord*, p. 162). Bishop Hahn writes: "Whereas in other lands the Confessing church remained predominantly a pastor's affair, it was exactly in less Christian oriented Saxony that it was a distinctly congregational movement" (*Kämpfer wider Willen*, p. 46). See also Karl Kupisch in Herzfeld, ed., *Berlin und Brandenburg*, p. 503; the view of Hermann von Detten in Nicolaisen, *Kirchenpolitik*, 2: 289.

48. Hugo Linck, *Der Kirchenkampf in Ostpreussen 1933 bis 1945*, p. 204.

49. Wilhelm Niemöller, who is on the whole critical of the intact churches, writes: "Es war also schon vor Augsburg [June, 1935] evident und ausgesprochen, dass man in der Bekennenden Kirche Pferd und Esel zusammengespannt sah, ungleiche Partner vereinigt." A convoy cannot proceed faster than the slowest ship, and the intact churches kept the Confessing church back ("Zum Verständnis der Bekennenden Kirche. Eine Herausforderung," *EvTh* 29 [1969]: 609).

Chapter Nine

1. Actually the incorporation laws (*Eingliederungsgesetze*) were not legal (Microfilm, Guertner's Diary, Ex 858, 3751-PS, pp. 17, 31). These incorporations at times involved force and coercion. For an account of procedures in various Land churches, see Niemöller, *Kampf und Zeugnis*, pp. 134–46; see also "Aus authentischen Berichten über die Vorgänge bei der Eingliederung der Kurhessischen Landeskirche," Nürnberg, LK. Arch., Kirchenkampf Sammlung 0–6; for procedures in Baden, see Otto Friedrich, "Die kirchen- und staatskirchenrechtliche Entwicklung der Evang. Landeskirche Badens von 1933–1953," *ZevKR* 3 (1953–54): 300–303. Over half of the pastors in Baden rejected this incorporation. The German Christians had long been ensconced in most of the church offices of the Hanoverian church, and Marahrens was far from having an undivided intact church to administer (Heinz Brunotte, "In Kirchenkampf," in W. Ködderitz, ed., *D. August Marahrens*, p. 87). See also Klügel, *Landeskirche Hannovers*, p. 143.

2. Koch to Reichsinnenministerium, July 11, 1934, Biel. Arch., Coll. W. Niemöller, Präsidium der Bek. Syn., III, 1, Reichsregierung; Conrad, *Kampf um die Kanzeln*, p. 105.

3. Reichskanzlei, T120, R. 4419, L124660.

4. *KJ*, 1933–44, pp. 68–69; Günther Harder and Wilhelm Niemöller, *Die Stunde der Versuchung*, p. 22. The Bavarian and Württemberg delegates challenged the legality of the synod and its procedure. The Bavarian Land synod on August 23, 1934, also protested the actions of the national synod. See Christian Stoll, *Dokumente zum Kirchenstreit*, pt. 5, pp. 11–12.

5. *AK*, 1934, pp. 300–301, 306; *KJ*, 1933–44, pp. 70–71; Gauger, *Kirchenwirren*, 2: 278–84.

6. *KJ*, 1933–44, p. 72.

7. Gauger, *Kirchenwirren*, 2: 312–20. Bishops Meiser, Wurm, and Marahrens had sent a letter to Hitler urging him not to permit the installation of Müller (copy of letter sent to President Koch, no date, in Biel. Arch., Coll. W. Niemöller, Präsidium der Bek. Syn., III, 1, Reichsregierung). The folder on Müller in Biel. Arch., Coll. W. Niemöller, N-8, Lud. Müller, contains many clippings and pictures of the installation ceremonies.

8. Much of the material in this section appeared in Ernst C. Helmreich, "The Arrest

and Freeing of the Protestant Bishops of Württemberg and Bavaria, September–October 1934," *Central European History* 2 (1969): 159–69.

9. *Amtsblatt Landeskirche in Bayern,* 1934, p. 127; *Amtsblatt der evangelischen Landeskirche in Württemberg,* 1934, p. 321; Stoll, *Dokumente,* pt. 5, pp. 13–14.

10. *Amtsblatt Landeskirche in Württemberg,* 1934, p. 333.

11. As reported in a confidential letter of Köpke to Bergen, September 24, 1934, Ausw. A., T120, R. 3312, 581235–36; Bergen to Foreign Office, September 28, 1934, Ausw. A., T120, R. 4418, L123966.

12. Bismarck to Foreign Office, September 22, 1934, Ausw. A., T120, R. 4418, L123949. The passage mentioning catastrophic effects is heavily underscored and the document also bears the notation: "Der Herr Reichskanzler hat Kenntnis."

13. "Aufzeichnung des Reichsministers des Auswärtigen Freiherrn von Neurath über seine Unterredung mit dem Herrn Reichsbischof, September 20, 1934," Reichskanzlei, T120, R. 4419, L124716–18; Hitler received the Aufzeichnung (ibid., L124719); Nicolaisen, *Kirchenpolitik,* 2: 174–76. See also Klaus Scholder, "Die evangelische Kirche in der Sicht der Nationalsozialistischen Führung bis zum Kriegsausbruch," *VZ* 16 (1968): 25–26.

14. Von Neurath to Stadtdekan Dr. Lempp in Stuttgart, September 21, 1934, Ausw. A., T120, R. 4420, L125129. Lempp, a friend of World War I days, had sent von Neurath a letter from his brother who was pastor in Stanislau, Galicia, expressing concern over the situation in the German church (ibid., L125130–34).

15. See the "Kirchengesetz zur Änderung der Verfassung der Evangelischen Landeskirche Württembergs von 28. September 1934," *Amtsblatt Landeskirche in Württemberg,* 1934, pp. 342–44; "Kirchengesetz zur Änderung der Verfassung der Evangelisch-Lutherischen Kirche in Bayern rechts des Rheines von 26. Oktober 1934," *KJ,* 1933–44, pp. 75–76.

16. *Amtsblatt Landeskirche in Bayern,* 1934, pp. 177, 189; mimeographed report "Der Eingriff Dr. Jägers in die bayerische Landeskirche am 11. Oktober 1934. Wie es wirklich war. Rundbrief von den Vorgängen in der bayerischen Landeskirche 11 bis 17 Oktober 1934," Nürnberg, LK. Arch., Bestand 221. There is much material on the reaction among the people to Meiser's arrest in the same folder. For a dramatic description of the church service on the evening of October 11, see Heinrich Schmid, *Apokalyptisches Wetterleuchten,* pp. 93–94. The most important documents on the crisis are collected in Stoll, *Dokumente,* pt. 5, pp. 4–42. For a summary of events in Württemberg and Bavaria, see Niemöller, *Kampf und Zeugnis,* pp. 166–78.

17. *KJ,* 1933–44, pp. 74–77; Wilhelm Niemöller, *Die zweite Bekenntnissynode der Deutschen Evangelischen Kirche zu Dahlem,* pp. 37–38. This protest of October 20 reached the Foreign Office on October 22, and Roediger in transmitting it to von Neurath commented that the members of the Confessing church would not be satisfied with Jäger's retirement; they wanted Müller's as well, and a clear-cut change in procedure (Aufzeichnung, Roediger to von Neurath, October 22, 1934, Ausw. A., T120, R. 4420, L124026–28).

18. This statement, sent to the minister president and to the minister of culture in Württemberg as well as to Wurm, was forwarded to von Neurath by a friend, Carl Frhr. von Cotta (Ausw. A., T120, R. 4420, L124957–58).

19. "Mittelfränkische Bauernabordnung bei den Staatsbehörden in München," carbon copy in Nürnberg, LK. Arch., Bestand 221. On October 22, 850 Protestant clergy met in Nürnberg, pledged their loyalty to Meiser, and demanded the recall of the state-appointed commissioners (notice by Klinger, Vereinsführer des bayer. Pfarrervereins, Ausw. A., T120, R. 4420, L125423). See also many other protests printed or reported in Gauger, *Kirchenwirren,* 2: 321–65; Schmid, *Apokalyptisches Wetterleuchten,* pp. 81–110; Nicolaisen, *Kirchenpolitik,* 2: 180–94.

20. Helmut Witetschek, ed., *Die kirchliche Lage in Bayern nach den Regierungspräsidentenberichten 1933–1943,* 1: 31; 2: 35–43.

21. Freifrau Johanna v. Gemmingen to von Neurath, September 19, 1934, Ausw. A., T120, R. 4420, L125138. See also many other protest letters on this roll of film, particularly frames L125087–104, L125146–64.

22. Gauger, *Kirchenwirren,* 2: 361. The unexpected release brought jubilation to Wurm's household. Two friends were summoned, and after singing the chorale "Praise to the Lord," Wurm read Psalm 118. Then they had a little celebration (Wurm, *Tagebuchaufzeichnungen Maria Wurm,* p. 36).

23. Aufzeichnung of an interview with Kinder sent to von Neurath, October 19, 1934,

Ausw. A., T120, R. 4418, L124034–36; Aufzeichnung of an interview by Roediger with Kinder, October 23, 1934, ibid., L124029–30; report on an interview with Kinder by an official of the Reich Chancellery on October 26, 1934, Reichskanzlei, T120, R. 4419, L124758–60. Hitler was informed of this interview. When Kinder saw the announcement in the papers that Jäger had resigned as Reichswalter, he telephoned the Reich chancellery and told them Jäger would also have to be relieved of his other church appointments (ibid., L124761). Hitler was informed of this conversation. Jäger was later relieved of all his church offices (Niemöller, *Kampf und Zeugnis*, pp. 180–81).

24. "Streng vertraulich. Bericht über zwei Tage in München," unsigned, Nürnberg, LK. Arch., Bestand 221. The interview of Gürtner with Hitler took place on October 20, 1934 (Bethge, *Bonhoeffer*, p. 455; Guertner's Diary, Ex. 858, 3751-PS, p. 31).

25. Wurm, *Erinnerungen*, p. 119. "Seit dem Ereignissen im Spätherbst 1934, die mit durch das Eingreifen des Herrn Reichsaussenministers einen günstigen Ausgang gefunden haben, haben wir uns verhältnismässiger Ruhe zu erfreuen gehabt" (Wurm to von Neurath, May 23, 1936, Ausw. A., T120, R. 4420, L124929). A memorandum was drawn up in the Foreign Office on October 15, 1934, stressing that all reports from abroad indicated increasing alarm over the use of force in the German church (Ausw. A., T120, R. 4418, L124001–2). The documents show that the Foreign Office did indeed receive many such reports including some from the United States (see the report of Ambassador Luther to Foreign Office, October 16, 1934, ibid., L124010–12).

26. Bismarck to Foreign Office, October, 1934, ibid., L123998–4000. Bishop Bell, after consultation with the archbishop of Canterbury, had a somewhat similar interview with Ambassador Hoesch on April 31, 1934, during which he objected to the dictatorial actions of Reich Bishop Müller (Hoesch to Foreign Office, May 1, 1934, ibid., L123764). Jasper, in his excellent biography *George Bell*, does not mention the April 31 interview; he makes only scant reference to the October interview and fails to evaluate its importance (p. 201). He does present a good account of Bell's long-time concern over the strife in the German churches.

27. Von Neurath to Foreign Office, October 17, 1934, Reichskanzlei, T120, R. 4419, L124743–46.

28. Hoesch to Foreign Office, October 17, 1934, Ausw. A., T120, R. 4418, L124014–17, L125403–6; see also the notes of Alphons Koechlin, president of the Swiss Evangelical Church Confederation, on a telephone conversation with Bishop Bell on the evening of October 17, 1934, in Andreas Lindt, *George Bell-Alphons Koechlin Briefwechsel 1933–1954*, p. 162.

29. Aufzeichnung, Roediger to von Neurath, October 16, 1934, Ausw. A., T120, R. 4418, L124001–L124002; von Neurath to Lammers, October 17, 1934, Reichskanzlei, T120, R. 4419, L124747–51.

30. Von Neurath to Lammers, ibid., L124747; text of Hoesch's report with underscoring of notice, "Hitler was informed," L124748–51.

31. Graf von Schwerin-Krosigk, *Es geschah in Deutschland*, pp. 313–15.

32. Notiz by Roediger, October 22, 1934, Ausw. A., T120, R. 4418, L124018.

33. Hoesch to Foreign Office, October 22, 1934, ibid., L124024–25; see also Ausw. A., T120, R. 4420, L125415–16; for marginalia to report, see Reichskanzlei, T120, R. 4419, L124756–57.

34. Aufzeichnung of interview by Roediger with Kinder, October 23, 1934, Ausw. A., T120, R. 4418, L124029.

35. Aufzeichnung of interview by Roediger with Marahrens, October 23, 1934, ibid., L124040.

36. As early as October 19, Marahrens had recommended to von Neurath that the taking of the oath be postponed (Marahrens to von Neurath, October 19, 1934, ibid., L124037–39; see also L124040–41, L124043, L124047–48). On drafts of the oath to be taken by Müller, see Reichskanzlei, T120, R. 4419, L124752–54.

37. Personal letter archbishop of Canterbury to Hoesch, October 27, 1934, Ausw. A. T120, R. 4418, L124054.

38. Personal letter archbishop of Canterbury to Hoesch, November 7, 1934, ibid., L124103. The phrases as indicated were underlined by some reader in the Foreign Office.

39. Superintendent Karl Nold of the Protestant church in the Saar had sent Hitler a long Denkschrift on September 17, 1934, on the situation in the Confessing church, which he said jeopardized Germany's position in the Saar and lessened the joy over

the prospective return to the fatherland (Ausw. A., T120, R. 3296, E574794–803). For a similar complaint on the Catholic side by Archbishop Bornewasser of Trier, see his letter to Hitler of August 27, 1934, ibid., E574779–86.

40. Wurm to von Neurath, October 27, 1934, Ausw. A., T120, R. 4420, L124954. Von Neurath had requested Wurm to see him when he reached Berlin (von Neurath to Wurm, October 26, 1934, ibid., L124955–56).

41. Vermerk, October 29, 1934, Reichskanzlei, T120, R. 4419, L124762.

42. Wurm, *Erinnerungen,* p. 120; Klügel, *Landeskirche Hannovers,* p. 144.

43. Wurm, *Erinnerungen,* p. 121. Frau Wurm noted in her diary on November 1: "Reibi [Müller] ist noch am Leben, wird aber wohl doch bald erledigt sein. Frick enttäuscht immer wieder, er ist schuld, dass er nicht gleich wegmusste" (Wurm, *Tagebuchaufzeichnungen Maria Wurm,* pp. 37–38).

44. Wurm, *Erinnerungen,* p. 120. Hitler immediately ordered a memorandum prepared on the effects of the separation of church and state (Nicolaisen, *Kirchenpolitik,* 2: 199–211).

45. Wurm, *Erinnerungen,* p. 120; Gauger, *Kirchenwirren,* 2: 362.

46. Müller retained his title of Reich bishop and a salary equal to that of a Reich minister until the end of World War II. He was captured by the Russians, but managed to conceal his identity as Reich bishop, even convincing them that he had always been a friend of the Jews. He was freed after fourteen days, but soon learned he had been discovered, and, realizing that he faced imprisonment and trial at Nürnberg, committed suicide on July 31, 1945. Müller's wife for years drew a pension from the city of Berlin, for the authorities there did not connect her husband as a former naval chaplain with his later position as Reich bishop. When she moved to Cuxhaven she again made a claim for a pension and this time Müller's identity was revealed. An investigation and the establishment of his suicide followed (Werner Koch to Wilhelm Niemöller, March 8, 1961, Biel. Arch., Coll. W. Niemöller, N-8, Ludwig Müller). Jäger, the other leading character in the episode of the arrest of the bishops, was later to play a dire role in the reorganization of the church in the Warthegau. After the war he was tried by the Poles as a war criminal and executed at the end of 1948 ("Mitteilung aus dem Amtsblatt der Bekennenden Kirche in Nassau-Hessen vom 1/4/1949," Biel. Arch., Coll. W. Niemöller, N-5, Jäger).

47. On November 1, 1934, Meiser and his council were back in their old offices, but Wurm and his officials did not get control of their offices until November 20 (Stoll, *Dokumente,* pt. 4, pp. 37–38; *Amtsblatt Landeskirche in Württemberg,* 1934, p. 365).

48. Reichskanzlei, T120, R. 4419, L124764. Frick's order no doubt implemented the "Entscheidung des Führers und Reichskanzler vom 30/10/34, Zurückżiehung von Staat und Partei aus dem Kirchenstreit," BA, Reichssicherheitshauptamt, R 58/233, Lagebericht Feb./März, 1935, p. 2.

49. Pfarrer Jacobi to Reichskanzlei, November 20, 1934, Reichskanzlei, T120, R. 4419, L124795. Superintendent Diestal of Lichterfelde also requested of Lammers that Dibelius be freed at once (L124798; see also L124795–96). Hitler was kept informed of these events. See also Dibelius, *In the Service of the Lord,* pp. 150–53.

50. Wagner to Hitler, November 14, 1934, Reichskanzlei, T120, R. 4419, L124768–74; for answer of November 20, see L124778. Hitler had made a statement on November 1 to a Reichsstatthalterkonferenz on the policy to be followed in the church struggle (L124800).

51. Ibid., L124776–77; *Gesetzes- und Verordnungsblatt Badens,* 1934, pp. 133–34. Bishop Kühlewein informed his pastors and asked them whether they approved of his action. Three-quarters of them did (Friedrich, *ZevKR* 3 (1953–54): 305. The synod of the Baden church had been dissolved and the church was administered by the bishop and the Supreme Church Council until the collapse in 1945.

52. Gerhard Ehrenfort, *Die schlesische Kirche im Kirchenkampf 1932–1945,* pp. 56–59. Zänker was friendly to the Confessing church but never could bring himself to join it (ibid., p. 58; Hahn, *Kämpfer wider Willen,* p. 291). He stood alone among the Prussian provincial bishops, not only in his cooperation with the Confessing church but also in his limited support of the German Christians. He was finally suspended from his office on May 3, 1939, and pensioned off December 1, 1941. Many efforts, including those by Bishops Marahrens, Meiser, and Wurm, failed to keep him in office (Ehrenfort, *Schlesische Kirche,* pp. 254–55).

53. *KJ,* 1933–44, p. 81.

54. Gauger, *Kirchenwirren,* 3: 146; for a similar speech on December 7, see Nicolaisen, *Kirchenpolitik,* 2: 231–32; for Göring's decree, *ibid.,* pp. 233–34, 269–70.

55. *KJ*, 1933–44, pp. 81–82; Niemöller, *Kampf und Zeugnis,* pp. 198–99; Ausw. A., T120, R. 4418, L124073 and succeeding frames.

56. Hermann Kunst and Siegfried Grundmann, eds., *Evangelisches Staatslexikon,* p. 952. Otto Dibelius felt the synod had gone too far (*In the Service of the Lord,* p. 149); see also *KJ*, 1933–44, p. 82; Klügel, *Landeskirche Hannovers,* p. 173.

57. *KJ*, 1933–44, p. 82; Wurm, *Erinnerungen,* p. 127; Karl Kupisch, *Die deutschen Landeskirchen im 19. und 20. Jahrhundert,* p. 150; Ködderitz, *August Marahrens,* pp. 91, 98. There had been a heated conflict over the election of Marahrens, who was favored by the bishops of the Land churches; the Dahlem circle wanted President Koch (Hahn, *Kämpfer wider Willen,* pp. 94–96). For biographical appreciations of Flor and Humburg, see Niemöller, *Lebensbilder,* pp. 24–27, 54–62; see also Niemöller, *Kampf und Zeugnis,* pp. 191–92. Flor's superior, the Reichsgerichtspräsident, refused him permission to take over the office (Hahn, *Kämpfer wider Willen,* p. 96).

58. For the directions for the organization of the Confessing church, see *KJ*, 1933–44, pp. 77–80; see also p. 83.

59. Niemöller, *Geschichte des Pfarrernotbundes,* p. 62. The income of the Pastors' Emergency League from 1933 to December, 1936, amounted to 432,530.34 marks, a considerable sum (ibid., p. 63).

60. Bismarck to Foreign Office, January 24, 1935, Ausw. A., T120, R. 4418, L124159.

61. Klügel, *Landeskirche Hannovers,* pp. 185–86; "Draft Proposal for Reorganization of the Church," Berlin, K. Arch., no. 238, pp. 1–3. Wurm and Meiser had a conference with Koch of the Provisional Directory in regard to procedure. Their proposals called for the replacement of officials by men loyal to the confessions and the elimination of the Müller regime. The national church was to have the power to pass only normative legislation, doctrinal matters remaining in the province of the Land churches; the finances of the national church were to be part of the budgets of the Land churches ("Ergebnis einer Besprechung Meiser, Wurm einerseits, Oberpräsident Koch anderseits, December 19, 1934," Berlin, K. Arch., no. 35d, p. 494).

62. Gauger, *Kirchenwirren,* 3: 447. The Land churches of Schleswig-Holstein, Brunswick, and the Palatinate separated themselves from the Müller regime, but did not adhere to the Provisional Directory; neither did the Reformed Land churches of Lippe and northwest Germany (Klügel, *Landeskirche Hannovers,* p. 184).

63. "Verordnung über die Vereidigung der kirchlichen Beamten vom 13 September 1934," *AK*, 1934, p. 309. The ordinance stated: "Über die Vereidigung der Geistlichen ergeht besondere Entschliessung."

64. Reichskanzlei, T120, R. 4419, L124811, L124813, L124814; see also Nicolaisen, *Kirchenpolitik,* 2: 240–43.

65. As quoted in Klügel, *Landeskirche Hannovers,* p. 191.

66. Ibid., p. 191n; Karl Kupisch, "Karl Barths Entlassung," Helmut Gollwitzer and Hellmut Traub, eds., *Hören und Handeln,* pp. 265–66.

67. For more details on the German Faith Movement, see chap. 20, below.

68. *KJ*, 1933–44, pp. 84–86. Both statements are also to be found in Flüchtlingsdienst, *Ev. Kirche in Deutschland,* pp. 142–52. Otto Dibelius at this time wrote a series of six brochures on "Christus und die Deutschen." In *Die Grosse Wendung im Kirchenkampf,* he wrote: "The struggle between the German Christians and the Confessing church is, it is true, not ended, but it is decided." Attention now had to be given to the German Faith Movement, which was trying to dechristianize Germany (pp. 24, 27).

69. Reichskanzlei, T120, R. 4419, L124822; see also Nicolaisen, *Kirchenpolitik,* 2: 274–77.

70. Niemöller, *Kampf und Zeugnis,* pp. 218–19.

71. On November 11, 1936, the Reich and Prussian minister of the interior officially decreed that henceforth in all public lists and documents there were to be three designations: (1) members of a religious or Weltanschauung body, (2) "God believing" (*gottgläubig*), and (3) "without belief" (*glaubenslos*) (*Amtsblatt Landeskirche Württemberg,* 1937, p. 34). In the Ministry of the Interior they had considered using the designation "dissident," but it was abandoned because in common parlance it meant "without faith" (*glaubenslos*). There was much correspondence among the ministries on the adoption of "gottgläubig," and it was decided at this time that a Jew, especially if he had left the synagogue, could use the designation (BA, Reichskanzlei, R 43 II/150, pp. 65–92). In an ordinance of May 5, 1937, the minister of the interior decreed that followers of the Ludendorff movement could designate themselves "*Deutsche Gotterkenntnis (Haus Ludendorff)*," which could be shortened to

"*Gotterkenntnis*" (Besetz. Gebiete, T454, R. 88, 000510. In 1939 the number of persons who designated themselves *gottgläubig* averaged 3.5 percent in all Gaue; the number in cities was larger: Graz, 12.8 percent; Brunswick, 11.3 percent; Solingen, 10.6 percent; Berlin, 10.2 percent; Leipzig, 9.9 percent; Hamburg, 7.5 percent; and Vienna 6.4 percent (*Partei-Kanzlei Rundschreiben* [vols. for 1942, 1943, 1944–45; *Anordnungen 1941–1945* in one vol., *Bekanntgaben 1944* in one vol., available at Institut für Zeitgeschichte, Munich], August 15, 1941, 99/41).

72. Heinz Brunotte, "Die Kirchenmitgliederschaft der nichtarischen Christen im Kirchenkampf," *ZevKR* 13 (1967): 161.

73. *Fränkische Zeitung,* June 6, 1935; *Reichsausgabe der Frankfurter Zeitung,* June 6, 1935; Helmut Baier, *Die Deutschen Christen im Rahmen des bayerischen Kirchenkampfes* pp. 233–34.

74. Staatspolizeistelle Köln an Geheime Staatspolizeiamt Berlin, March 3, 1935, Biel. Arch., Coll. W. Niemöller, unclassfied, Otto Voight papers.

75. *KJ,* 1933–44, p. 89; Niemöller, *Kampf und Zeugnis,* pp. 219–28. There had been a special wave of arrests in Nassau and Saxony (Hahn, *Kämpfer wider Willen,* pp. 96–100).

76. Wurm to Rust, April 11, 1935, Berlin, K. Arch., no. 181, p. 212.

77. BA, Adjutantur des Führers, NS 10/30, pp. 170–78; see also the report sent by Reich Bank Director Waldhecker of a friend who had gone to the United States to encourage exports. "The struggle against the Jews had led the church people—Methodists, Baptists, Presbyterians, etc. who have nothing to do with Jews—to join with them in the boycott 'Buy America'." He also stressed the need to settle the Protestant church problem, for it was uniting the Protestants and Catholics in the United States against Germany (ibid., Ns 10/32, pp. 113–18).

78. Protokoll über die Ergebnisse der Besprechungen in Bad Oeynhausen am 17/4/35. Anwesend Präses Koch, Jacobi, Immer, Asmussen, Stratenwerth, Frör, Weber, Kunkel, Thiemme, Biel. Arch., Coll. W. Niemöller, Präsidium, I, 13, Konferenz der zerstörten Kirchen, Mai 1935. This and some of the other documents regarding the Augsburg synod which I first used in the Bielefeld archives have now been published in Wilhelm Niemöller, *Die dritte Bekenntnissynode der Deutschen Evangelischen Kirche zu Augsburg;* here see pp. 17–19.

79. Meiser to Pfarrer Weber and to Oberkirchenrat Breit, April 29, 1935, Biel. Arch., Coll. W. Niemöller, I, 9, Augsburger Synode der DEK.

80. Kirchenrat J. Sammeltreuther to Präses Koch, May 21, 1935, ibid.

81. Niederschrift über die Besprechung in München am 9/5/35 zwischen Herrn Landesbischof D. Meiser und den Vertretern von Herrn Präses D. Koch, ibid.; Protokoll der Konferenz der zerstörten evangelischen Kirchen Deutschlands am 22 und 23 Mai in Golfeld und Bergkirchen, Biel. Arch., Coll. W. Niemöller, Präsidium I, 13, Konferenz der zerstörten Kirchen, Mai 1935. For a touching biographical note on Armin-Lützlow, see Niemöller, *Lebensbilder,* pp. 16–23.

82. Pastor Karl Immer went to see Barth. Barth's statement went back to January, 1935, when a representative of the University of Basel asked him: "Wie stehen Sie zur Landesverteidigung? Darauf antwortete er [Barth]: 'Natürlich bin ich dafür,' und fügte scherzend hinzu: 'Inbesondere für Befestigung der Nordgrenze.' Dieser Scherz war nun in der damaligen Situation durchaus naheliegend, weil in den Tagen über die Forts an der Nordgrenze ein Abstimmung in Bundesrate folgte" (quotation from Immer's statement to the conference, "Protokoll der zerstörten Kirche Deutschlands am 22–23 Mai 1935," Biel. Arch., Coll. W. Niemöller, I, 13, Konferenz der zerstörten Kirche).

83. Meiser to Koch, May 16, 1935, Biel. Arch., Coll. W. Niemöller, I, 9, Augsburger Synode; Niemöller, *Augsburger Bekenntnissynode,* pp. 37–39.

84. Adapted from the "Vorlage für die Konferenz der zerstörten evangelischen Kirchen Deutschlands am 22 und 23 Mai 1935 in Bad Oeynhausen," Biel. Arch., Coll. W. Niemöller, Präsidium I, 13, Konferenz der zerstörten Kirche.

85. "Vorlage aus Sachsen (20/6/35) zur Durchführung der Dahlemer Botschaft von 20/10/34 unter III, 3 in Kirchengemeinden die sich weiterhin hinter DC Landeskirchenregierungen stellen," ibid.,; see also *Bekenntnissynode der deutschen evangelischen Kirche, Dahlem 1934,* pp. 27, 45.

86. See the "Beschlüsse der Arbeitsgemeinschaft der Kirchen mit noch nicht staatlich anerkamtem Kirchenregiment," Augsburg, June 3, 1935, and the protocol of the meeting in Berlin June 20, 1935, Biel. Arch., Coll. W. Niemöller, Präsidium, I, 13, Konferenz der zerstörten Kirche.

87. "Besprechung über die Einberufung der Bekenntnissynode der EDK. Anwesend: Marahrens, Meinzolt, Breit, Meiser, Müller-Dahlem, v. Thadden, Kloppenburg, Fiedler, Koch," Biel. Arch., Coll. W. Niemöller, Präsidium I, 9, Augsburg Synode.

88. "Kirchenführertagung in Würzburg 27/5/35," ibid.

89. KJ, 1933–44, pp. 89–94; Klügel, Landeskirche Hannovers, pp. 179–82; Niemöller, Augsburger Bekenntnissynode, pp. 73–93.

90. Marahrens had played a leading part in getting this amnesty granted (Klügel, Landeskirche Hannovers, p. 190). Twenty-one ministers were freed from concentration camps, and eleven from prison (Niemöller, Kampf und Zeugnis, pp. 235–36). Bishop Hahn attributes the release to Hitler's desire to maintain good relations with England so as not to jeopardize the conclusion of the naval treaty of June 18, 1935. The English bishops were concerned about the situation of the churches in Germany and had ordered prayers for the imprisoned pastors (Hahn, Kämpfer wider Willen, pp. 102–3; see also Nicolaisen, Kirchenpolitik, 2: 315–16). The news of the release was given to the synod at its second session (Lücking to pastors, June 6, 1935, Biel. Arch., Coll. W. Niemöller, Präsidium I, 9, Augsburg Synode). As if in anticipation of the amnesty, Himmler on May 27, 1935, had ordered that no Protestant or Catholic clergyman in Prussia should be arrested without previous permission of the Gestapo headquarters in Berlin (copy of order, Biel. Arch., Coll. W. Niemöller, unclassified, Otto Voight papers). Shortly thereafter all state police officers were asked to report monthly on how many Protestant and how many Catholic clergy suffered various punishments (Geheimes Staatspolizeiamt an alle Staatspolizeistellen, July 26, 1935, ibid.).

91. Klügel, Landeskirche Hannovers, p. 181; Kupisch, "Karl Barths Entlassung," in Gollwitzer and Traub, Hören und Handeln, p. 273.

92. KJ, 1933–44, pp. 94–95.

93. Ibid., pp. 95–96; Nicolaisen, Kirchenpolitik, 2: 277–83.

94. Heinz Brunotte, "Die Entwicklung der staatlichen Finanzaufsicht über die Deutsche Evangelische Kirche von 1935–1945," ZevKR 3 (1953–54): 30–34. Finance sections came to be established in the Church of the Old Prussian Union and its various provincial member churches and in the churches of Saxony, Hanover-Lutheran, Hanover-Reformed, Schleswig-Holstein, Electoral Hesse-Waldeck, Nassau-Hesse, Brunswick, Baden, and Bremen, as well as in the national church office. There were thus finance sections in ten Land churches, while there were none in fourteen Land churches, nor were any ever established in the Catholic church.

95. See Niemöller, Handbuch, pp. 245–60.

96. KJ, 1933–44, pp. 96–97; Nicolaisen, Kirchenpolitik, 2: 323–25; Klügel, Landeskirche Hannovers, p. 194; Niemöller, Kampf und Zeugnis, pp. 481–83.

97. Dateline of dispatch Berlin, March 2; New York Times, March 23, 1935. In May, 1935, Hitler told Christian Kinder, head of the German Christians, that "he intended to appoint a church minister and hoped through his efforts to bring about peace in the church" (Kinder, Neue Beiträge, pp. 49, 165–66).

98. On July 24, 1935, Ambassador Dodd in reporting to the State Department on Kerrl's appointment stated: "It may be recalled that the scheme for a separate Ministry for Church Affairs was mooted as far back as the beginning of this year, and that Herr Kerrl's name was among the candidates for the post. It was then feared that this device would be employed to impose Reichsbishop Müller's administration upon the Confessional opposition in the Evangelical Church." On April 15, 1935, the embassy had submitted certain biographical notes on Kerrl to Washington (U.S. Dept. of State, Foreign Relations of the United States, 1935, 2: 359).

99. KJ, 1933–44, p. 101; Hoche, Gesetzgebung, 14: 51–52; The New York Times, July 19, 1935, p. 1. The comment in the German press was directed to Kerrl's ending the conflict in the Protestant church (see clippings, Biel. Arch., Coll. W. Niemöller, N-6, Kerrl).

100. Schwerin-Krosigk, Es geschah in Deutschland, p. 256.

101. Ibid., p. 255; Conrad, Kampf um die Kanzeln, p. 137.

102. Conrad reports that it can be taken for certain that the growing antagonism between Minister Director Buttmann and Hitler was an important reason for taking church affairs from the Ministry of the Interior (Kampf um die Kanzeln, pp. 133–34).

103. See Helmreich, Religious Education, pp. 162–78.

104. Quoting Angriff, no. 186 (August 12, 1935), on the microfilm Schumacher, T580, R. 40; a slightly different version is given Domarus, Hitler Reden, 1: 520.

105. Besetz. Gebiete, T454, R. 81, 000571–72; on Frick's retention of police powers, see Joachim Fischer, *Die sächsische Landeskirche im Kirchenkampf 1933–1937*, p. 130.
106. Besetz. Gebiete, T454, R. 81, 000562, 000569.
107. Biel. Arch., Coll. W. Niemöller, N-6, Kerrl; *New York Times,* October 30, 1935.
108. Besetz. Gebiete, T454, R. 81, 000714.
109. Ibid., 000562; BA, Reichssicherheitshauptamt, R 58/226; Schumacher, T580, R. 41.
110. Zöllner to Generalmajor Bertram in Stettin, January 28, 1936, Ausw. A., T120, R. 4420, L124832.
111. Wurm to Kerrl, December 30, 1936, ibid., L124917–22; see also L124916.
112. See the Niederschrift of the events at Erfurt sent by Wurm to von Neurath, January 9, 1937 (misdated 1936), ibid., L124912–15.
113. See the extensive ''Denkschrift des Verbots Evangelischer Wochen,'' submitted by the Rat der Evangelisch-Lutherischen Kirche Deutschlands to von Neurath, August 18, 1938, ibid., L124827–38. On the the Evangelical Weeks, see also Heinz Brunotte and Otto Weber, eds. *Evangelisches Kirchenlexikon,* 1: 1209; Biel. Arch., Coll. W. Niemöller, D-7, Deutsche Evangelische Woche; this latter folder contains programs of various meetings and correspondence in regard to them. Although the program was officially halted, a Church Week was held in Nürnberg, January 1–5, 1939. The addresses delivered at this meeting are given in *Kirchliche Woche Nürnberg vom 1. bis 5. Januar 1939;* see also *KJ,* 1945–48, p. 370.

Chapter Ten

1. ''Die kirchliche Lage im Reich. Besprechung zwischen dem Reichskirchenminister und den Vertretern der Länder,'' August 8, 1935, in John Conway, *Die nationalsozialistische Kirchenpolitik 1933–1945,* pp. 356–63. This document is not in the original English edition of Conway's book.
2. See chap. 14, below.
3. See the report on ''Besprechung mit Reichsminister Kerrl in Berlin, 23 August 1935,'' in Kurt D. Schmidt, *Dokumente des Kirchenkampfes II,* 2: 1372–77; see also Hahn, *Kämpfer wider Willen,* pp. 110–12. In his later speeches Kerrl constantly stressed that national socialism was compatible with Christianity; in fact the two were identical. There are reports on many of his speeches in the folder on Kerrl in Biel. Arch., Coll. W. Niemöller, N-6, Kerrl. For a list of the people at the August 21 conference, see Wilhelm Niemöller, ''Zur Geschichte der Kirchenausschüsse,'' in Gollwitzer and Traub, *Hören und Handeln,* p. 312; Meier, *die Deutschen Christen,* pp. 114–15.
4. Hoche, *Gesetzgebung,* 15: 49–54.
5. The Third Confessing Synod of the Evangelical Church of the Old Prussian Union which met in Berlin-Steglitz September 23–26, 1935, did condemn those who would deny baptism to Jews, but there is no reference to the Nürnberg laws (Niesel, *Bekenntnissynoden,* p. 20). A long memorandum, ''Zur Lage der deutschen Nichtarier,'' had been drawn up for presentation to the synod, but no broad statement on policy towards Jews was made. The memorandum had been finished mid-September, 1935 (Biel. Arch., Coll. W. Niemöller, C-8- 11, Judenfrage III; see also Karl Kupisch, *Durch den Zaun der Geschichte,* p. 392; Johan M. Snoek, *The Grey Book,* p. 39. *Der Stürmer,* Julius Streicher's strident paper, in the summer of 1935 had been charging the churches with protecting Jews and decried the idea that baptism changed the nature of a Jew (Biel. Arch., Coll. W. Niemöller, C-8-11, Judenfrage II).
6. Brunotte, *ZevKR* 13 (1967): 150.
7. Conrad, *Kampf um die Kanzeln,* pp. 134–35.
8. For the membership of the two committees, see Schmidt, *Dokumente der Ausschusszeit,* 1: 21.
9. Interview of Kerrl with Lücking et al., October 29, 1935, Biel. Arch., Coll. W. Niemöller, Präsidium, III-15, Kirchenausschüsse.
10. BA, Reichskanzlei, R 43 II/154, p. 26.
11. *KJ,* 1933–44, pp. 104–5.
12. Gollwitzer and Traub, *Hören und Handeln,* p. 307. The pronouncement was actu-

ally in line with Zöllner's basic conceptions (Schmidt, *Dokumente der Ausschusszeit*, 1: 161–64, 343–44, 482–91).

13. Dibelius to Marahrens, December 7, 1935, Schmidt, *Dokumente der Ausschusszeit*, 2: 1381.

14. Anordnung no. 225/35, November 14, 1935, Schumacher, T580, R. 42.

15. Minutes of the meeting of the Provisional Directory, October 23, 1935, Berlin, K. Arch., no. 35b, p. 110.

16. *KJ*, 1933–44, pp. 10–11; Klügel, *Landeskirche Hannovers*, pp. 200–201.

17. Minutes of the meeting of the Provisional Directory, October 30, 1935, Berlin, K. Arch., no. 35b, p. 158.

18. Minutes of November 6, December 11, 1935; January 29, 1936, ibid., pp. 160, 178, 194, 202.

19. *KJ*, 1933–44, pp. 103–4; Klügel, *Landeskirche Hannovers*, pp. 200–201; many reports and letters in the folder in Biel. Arch., Coll. W. Niemöller, Präsidium, III-15, Kirchenausschüsse; Ehrenforth, *Schlesische Kirche*, pp. 74–76; Linck, *Kirchenkampf in Ostpreussen*, pp. 122–29; Fuss, *Der Wille zur Einheit*, pp. 62–63; Johannes Kübel, *Die Bekennende Kirche in Selbstgericht*, pp. 10–15; Kübel, "Erinnerungen," pp. 189–90.

20. "Pastor v. Bodelschwingh und der Beirat der Arbeitsgemeinschaft der missionarischen und diakonischen Werke und Verbünde in der DEK," January 17, 1936, Biel. Arch., Coll. W. Niemöller, Präsidium, III-15, Kirchenausschüsse; see also Bodelschwingh to Präses Koch, December 13, 1935, ibid., III-14, Kirchenfragen.

21. See mimeographed summary "Die beiden Wege," ibid., III-15, Kirchenausschüsse.

22. Kinder, *Neue Beiträge*, pp. 50, 60; Meier, *Die Deutschen Christen*, pp. 44, 106.

23. See chap. 9, n. 46, above. Confessing church leaders had told Kerrl when he took office that if he expected to be successful in his work he would have to put Müller aside (Hahn, *Kämpfer wider Willen*, pp. 110–11). Müller's salary, equal to that of a Reich minister, was paid by the German Evangelical church; instead of a housing subsidy he received a free official dwelling paid for by the Prussian church. Until the fall of 1935, he had a fund of 2,400 marks at his free disposal. See the communication from the Finanzabteilung bei der Deutsch Evangelischen Kirchenkanzlei of May 8, 1936, Biel. Arch., Coll. W. Niemöller, N-8, Ludwig Müller.

24. Statement by Reichskirchenausschuss, October 26, 1935, Biel. Arch., Coll. W. Niemöller, Präsidium III-15, Kirchenausschüsse; letter of Dr. Thom of the Ev. Oberkirchenrat, December 23, 1935, ibid.; letter of Zöllner, December 8, 1935, Berlin, K. Arch., no. 68, p. 42.

25. Fischer, *Sächsische Landeskirche*, pp. 45–47; Hahn, *Kämpfer wider Willen*, pp. 109–56. Hahn in 1948 still spoke of the era of the church committees as "eine gottgesegnete Zeit" (Gottfried Voight, "Der Weg der Evang.-Luth. Landeskirche Sachsens in die VELKD," *Evangelische-Lutherische Kirchenzeitung* 10 [1956]: 65).

26. Meier, *Die Deutschen Christen*, pp. 116–17; Niemöller, *Kampf und Zeugnis*, p. 302.

27. Interview Kerrl with the Provisional Directory, November 27, 1935, Biel Arch., Coll. W. Niemöller, Präsidium III-15, Kirchenausschüsse; also "Auszug aus einem Bericht des Coetus Reformierten Prediger vom 28 Nov. 1935," ibid.

28. *KJ*, 1933–44, p. 106.

29. "Die Staatskirche ist da! Ein Wort zur gegenwärtigen kirchlichen Lage, Januar 1936," Schmidt, *Dokumente der Ausschusszeit*, 1: 165–75; see also Dibelius to Marahrens, December 7, 1935, ibid., 2: 1380–82. In ordering the confiscation of the pamphlet the authorities somehow got the title changed, and police inquired in many parsonages for the brochure "Die Staatskrise ist da!" (Niemöller, *Kampf und Zeugnis*, p. 314).

30. Klügel, *Landeskirche Hannovers*, pp. 204–7; Wilhelm Niemöller, *Die vierte Bekenntnissynode der Deutschen Evangelischen Kirche zu Bad Oeynhausen*, pp. 24–36; Schmidt, *Dokumente der Ausschusszeit*, 1: 188–91, 198, 253.

31. Schmidt, *Dokumente der Ausschusszeit*, 1: 198, 245–46.

32. Niemöller, *Vierte Bekenntnissynode*, pp. 12–13, 36; Niemöller, *Kampf und Zeugnis*, pp. 319–24.

33. Klügel, *Landeskirche Hannovers*, p. 221; see also "Der bayerische Bericht über Oeynhausen (17. bis 22. Februar 1936)," and "Der Bericht Niemöllers über Oeynhausen (24. Februar 1936)," in Hermelink, *Kirche im Kampf*, pp. 315–21.

34. Niemöller, *Vierte Bekenntnissynode*, pp. 112–26; *KJ*, 1933–44, pp. 117–23.

35. Schmidt, *Dokumente der Ausschusszeit*, 1: 492. For a fine appreciation of Fritz

Müller, see Martin Niemöller's biographical sketch in W. Niemöller, *Lebensbilder*, pp. 74–80.

36. The members of the First Provisional Directory maintained that they could not recognize the new directory as its legal successor; they refused to turn over certain funds to it (minutes of the Provisional Directory, Berlin, K. Arch., no. 35, pp. 214, 220–24, 237, 239).

37. "Gründung des Arbeitsausschusses der reformierten Kirche," *KJ*, 1950, pp. 278–84. Membership was drawn primarily from the so-called Reformed intact churches of Hanover and Lippe-Detmold, from the synod of Free Reformed Congregations, and from some Reformed congregations of the Church of the Old Prussian Union. See also Martin Pertiet, *Das Ringen um Wesen und Auftrag der Kirche in der national-sozialistischen Zeit*, pp. 264–67.

38. Gauger, *Kirchenwirren*, 1: 72.

39. *Amtsblatt Landeskirche in Bayern*, 1933, p. 61; Schieder, *Hans Meiser*, pp. 76–77.

40. Niemöller, *Kampf und Zeugnis*, pp. 128–29.

41. Paul Fleisch, "Das Werden der Vereinigten Evangelisch-Lutherischen Kirche Deutschlands und ihrer Verfassung," *ZevKR* 1 (1951): 25–26; Niemöller, *Handbuch*, p. 194.

42. See Theodor Dipper, *Die Evangelische Bekenntnisgemeinschaft in Württemberg 1933–1945*, pp. 17–23.

43. Niemöller, *Handbuch*, p. 212; see also the fine essay by Gustav Bossert, "Die Eigenart der evangelischen Landeskirche Württembergs im Wandel der Zeit," in *Evang. Pfarrverein in Württemberg*, ed., *Für Volk und Kirche*, pp. 33–51.

44. Dipper, *Bekenntnisgemeinschaft in Württemberg*, pp. 30–31, 119–29, 144–47; Niemöller, *Handbuch*, pp. 215–16; *RGG*, 6: 206–8.

45. Schmidt, *Dokumente der Ausschusszeit*, 1: 479, 503–5, 514–21. Not only the Confessing church in Saxony but also the official Land church of Saxony joined the Luther Council in May, 1936 (ibid., 680–95; Hahn, *Kämpfer wider Willen*, pp. 134–35); Klügel, *Landeskirche Hannovers*, p. 221; Hermelink, *Kirche im Kampf*, p. 331. In addition to the Land church of Saxony, the Land churches of Brunswick and Schaumburg-Lippe joined the Luther Council (Hahn, *Kämpfer wider Willen*, p. 146). The changing of names continued, and on November 25–26, 1936, the Land churches of Bavaria Right of the Rhine, Brunswick, Hanover, Saxony, Schaumburg-Lippe, Württemberg, and the Lutheran section of the church of Lippe joined to form the *Bund der Lutherischen Landeskirchen innerhalb der Deutschen Evangelischen Kirche*. The brotherhood councils of the Confessing churches of Lübeck, Mecklenburg, and Thuringia were also associated with it. The so-called Luther Council and the secretariat remained the directing bodies (Schmidt, *Dokumente der Ausschusszeit*, 2: 1167–68, 1282, 1322–24).

46. As quoted in Fleisch, *ZevKR* 1 (1951): 28. The aim of the Luther Council was to establish a Lutheran confederation as a step towards an Evangelical Lutheran church of Germany (ibid., p. 30). The Luther Council was never officially recognized by the Ministry of Church Affairs, yet it remained in existence until the end of the war (ibid., pp. 40–41). In the meeting of the Luther Council at Leipzig on March 18, 1936, there was a long discussion on the necessity and possibility of working with the directing bodies of the Confessing church (Berlin, K. Arch., no. 114, p. 13).

47. *KJ*, 1933–44, pp. 126–29; Schmidt, *Dokumente der Ausschusszeit*, 1: 509–14; for the answer of the Luther Council, see pp. 525–28. Wurm wrote later: "I have never been able to understand the indignation with which Niemöller and his closer friends received this step; it was only the logical result of their actions (*Erinnerungen*, p. 131).

48. Klügel, *Landeskirche Hannovers*, p. 224; "Der Lutherische Rat über sein Verhältnis zum Reichskirchenausschuss (25. Juni 1936)," in Hermelink, *Kirche im Kampf*, pp. 337–38.

49. Hermelink, *Kirche im Kampf*, p. 338; *KJ*, 1933–44, pp. 140–41, 150–53.

50. "Wort an die Gemeinden, 10. Juli 1936," *KJ*, 1933–44, pp. 139–40; see also pp. 141–44; Hermelink, *Kirche im Kampf*, p. 341.

51. BA, Adjutantur des Führers, NS 10/228, pp. 24–35; Schmidt, *Dokumente der Ausschusszeit*, 1: 695–719 includes the 28 *Anlagen* which are missing in the other texts; *KJ*, 1933–44, pp. 130–35; Wilhelm Niemöller, *Die Bekennende Kirche sagt Hitler die Wahrheit*, pp. 9–18; translation of the letter in Cochrane, *The Church's Confession*, pp. 268–79. The letter was signed by F. Müller, Albertz, Böhn, Forch, and Fricke for the Second Provisional Directory, and by Asmussen, Lücking, Middendorf, M.

Niemöller, and von Thaden for the council. On the deification of Hitler, see also Conrad, *Kampf um die Kanzeln,* p. 9; Götte, *Deutsche Christen,* pp. 184–91.

52. Minutes of the Provisional Directory, March 18, 20, May 15, 1936, Berlin, K. Arch., no. 15, pp. 231, 243, 258.

53. Schmidt, *Dokumente der Ausschusszeit,* 2: 917.

54. Niemöller, *Bekennende Kirche sagt Hitler die Wahrheit,* p. 29; Wilhelm Niemöller, "Corrigenda zur neuesten Kirchengeschichte," *EvTh* 28 (1966): 594–605; see also Bethge, *Bonhoeffer,* pp. 602–7; Boyens, *Kirchenkampf und Ökumene, 1933–1934,* pp. 172–74. Tillich and Weissler were arrested on October 6, 1936, and Koch on November 13. All were placed in concentration camps, from which Koch was freed in December, 1938, and Tillich a year later; Weissler died in the Sachsenhausen camp on February 19, 1937. For an appreciation of Weissler, who was racially a Jew but was baptized in childhood, see Bernhard H. Forck, *und folget ihrem Glauben nach,* pp. 11–12.

55. Mayer to Secretary of State, no. 2863, June 4, 1936, National Archives, Washington, D.C.. I obtained this document from the archives; it is referred to but not printed in U.S. Dept. of State, *Foreign Relations of the United States, 1936,* 2: 168.

56. Jasper, *George Bell,* p. 212; Boyens, *Kirchenkampf und Ökumene, 1933–1939,* p. 173.

57. BA, Adjuntantur des Führers, NS 10/228, p. 24. Ernst C. Helmreich, "Die Veröffentlichung der 'Denkschrift der Vorläufigen Leitung der Deutschen Evangelischen Kirche an den Führer und Reichskanzler, 28. Mai 1936'," *ZevKR* 87 (1976): 38–53.

58. *KJ,* 1933–44, pp. 135–39; Niemöller, *Bekennende Kirche sagt Hitler die Wahrheit,* pp. 33–44; Schmidt, *Dokumente der Ausschusszeit,* 2: 984–89. In the Ministry of Church Affairs, officials had considered forbidding the reading of the pulpit declaration, for they did know about it. They did not do so because they feared a repetition of the events that had taken place on the memorial day for veterans in 1934. Had they forbidden the reading of the declaration, they believed they would "surely have had over 1,000 pastors in jail the next day." Instead of forbidding the reading of the declaration, the ministry telegraphed all the Land church governments, asking them to forbid it. (Ministerialdirigent v. Detten to Adjutant des Führers, August 1936, BA, Adjuntantur des Führers, NS 10/109, pp. 103–11). Von Detten was considered by the police to be on the side of the Confessing church (ibid., p. 120) and was pensioned off on April 1, 1937 (ibid., NS 10/272, p. 55).

59. Hermelink, *Kirche im Kampf,* pp. 359–64. The publication of the letter to Hitler caused strained relations between the Luther Council and the Provisional Directory. On November 6, 1936, the Luther Council notified the directory that until they were informed of the details of how the letter became known abroad, relations between the two groups would be in abeyance (Lutherrat to Vorläufige Leitung, November 7, 1936, Berlin, K. Arch., no. 114, p. 45).

60. This practice dates back to the Nazis' assumption of power; see Götte, *Deutsche Christen,* pp. 183–91; also pp. 192–96.

61. "Bericht über ein Schulungslager der NS-Studentenbundes Juli-August 1936," Biel. Arch., Coll. W. Niemöller, C-7, Neuheidentum.

62. Copy of the address, Berlin, K. Arch., no. 81.

63. Meier, *Die Deutschen Christen,* pp. 112, 305.

64. *KJ,* 1933–44, p. 144. The Reich Church Committee had published a study critical of the Thuringian movement because of its attempt to equate church and folk. The Thuringian church published a pamphlet in reply, *Irrlehre? Unsere Antwort an den Reichskirchenausschuss* (Weimar, 1936). The pamphlet is to be found BA, Kirch. Angelegenheiten, R 79/4.

65. BA, Reichskanzlei, R 43 II/154, pp. 26, 29. On November 9, Müller also requested to be received by Hitler but was refused (BA, Adjuntantur des Führers, NS 10/228, pp. 61–62). Hitler shortly before had told Kerrl that in church matters he wanted quiet to prevail and all cause for unrest avoided (Vermerk, August 29, 1936, BA, Reichskanzlei, R 43 II/152, p. 3).

66. See Niemöller, *Kampf und Zeugnis,* pp. 352–65; see also p. 377; Niemöller, *Leben eines Bekenntnispfarrers,* p. 150; Meier, *Die Deutschen Christen,* pp. 135–44, 305–6.

67. *KJ,* 1933–44, pp. 144, 151.

68. Ibid., pp. 144–46.

69. Ibid., pp. 147–51; see also Karl F. Reimers, *Lübeck im Kirchenkampf des Dritten*

Reiches, pp. 288–300. Zöllner's appeal to Hitler on February 5, 1937, to have the restrictions on his visit to Lübeck rescinded brought no results. The telegram was simply referred to the Ministry of Church Affairs (BA, Reichskanzlei, R 43 II/154, pp. 31–32.).

70. The Luther Council undertook to bring about the restoration of the nine pastors in Lübeck to their congregations. Dr. Lilje and Dr. Gauger conducted fruitless negotiations with the Lübeck church authorities. On February 15, 1937, Kerrl issued an ordinance which limited the authority of all church officials. Lübeck also lost its political independence and became an area of the Prussian province of Schlesweg-Holstein on April 1, 1937, which gave Prussian and Reich Gestapo headquarters more authority in Lübeck. In Berlin the Gestapo had been ordered to settle the Lübeck dispute and its representatives were able to work out an agreement. The nine pastors recognized the organizational jurisdiction of the regular church authorities, and the latter agreed not to attempt to exercise spiritual supervision of the pastors. On April 4, 1937, the pastors rejoined their congregations. The loyalty of the parish members to their pastors as well as the support of the Luther Council had been an important influence on the ultimate resolution of the conflict (see Reimers, *Lübeck im Kirchenkampf,* pp. 344–57).

71. BA, Adjutantur des Führers, NS 10/260, pp. 157–59; *KJ,* 1933–44, pp. 151–53; Schmidt, *Dokumente der Ausschusszeit,* 2: 1339–47; see also "Wort des Reichskirchenausschusses an die Gemeinden," *Amtsblatt Landeskirche in Bayern,* 1937, pp. 11–12; Gollwitzer and Traub, *Hören und Handeln,* pp. 316–20; see also Fischer, *Sächsische Landeskirche,* pp. 76–78.

72. Kübel, "Erinnerungen," p. 169.

73. "Die Vorläufige Leitung der DEK an die Vorläufige Leitung der DEK angeschlossenen Kirchenregierungen und Landes Bruderräte," January 14, 1937, Biel Arch., Coll. W. Niemöller, Präsidium, III-15, Kirchenausschüsse.

74. From Rosenberg's diary as cited by Klügel, *Landeskirche Hannovers,* p. 199.

75. Statement as noted by Dibelius in an open letter to Kerrl, *KJ,* 1933–44, pp. 158–59; Wurm, *Erinnerungen,* p. 136; two versions of Kerrl's remarks are given in Schmidt, *Dokumente der Ausschusszeit,* 2: 1347–55.

76. For Dibelius's letter, see *KJ,* 1933–44, pp. 158–61; Schmidt, *Dokumente der Ausschusszeit,* 2: 1358–62; see also Wilhelm Niemöller's article in Gollwitzer and Traub, *Hören und Handeln,* p. 317.

77. Martin Niemöller to Kerrl, February 18, 1937, Schmidt, *Dokumente der Ausschusszeit,* 2: 1382–83.

78. Agreement between the Landeskirchenausschüsse der EK der APU and the Bruderrat der EK der APU of May 4, 1937, Berlin, K. Arch. no. 397, p. 2.

79. Fischer, *Sächsische Kirche,* pp. 82–88; Hahn, *Kämpfer wider Willen,* pp. 146–56.

80. Niemöller, *Kampf und Zeugnis,* pp. 381, 409; *KJ,* 1933–44, pp. 191, 200; Klügel, *Landeskirche Hannovers,* p. 234.

Chapter Eleven

1. Hermelink, *Kirche im Kampf,* p. 380.

2. Hoche, *Gesetzgebung,* 23: 675; *KJ,* 1933–44, p. 162; Wurm *Erinnerungen,* p. 136; Wilhelm Niemöller, *Gotteswort ist nicht gebunden,* p. 117.

3. Klügel, *Landeskirche Hannovers,* pp. 235–36; Hermelink, *Kirche im Kampf,* pp. 280–82; "Wahldienst der Vorläufigen Leitung der DEK, Nr. 7, 6. März 1937," Biel. Arch., Coll. W. Niemöller, B 4–5, Kirchenwahl 1937, II.

4. *KJ,* 1933–44, pp. 167–68.

5. Klügel, *Landeskirche Hannovers,* p. 236.

6. "Die Vorläufige Leitung der Deutschen Evangelischen Kirche 17/2/37; 6 Sätze der Landeskirchenführer zur Frage der Wahl 19/2/37," Biel. Arch., Coll. W. Niemöller, B 4–5, Kirchenwahl 1937, II. The German Christians wanted the payment of church taxes to be a basis for the right to vote; the Confessing church preferred to use regular church attendance and participation in the sacraments as the test. Ministerialdirigent Hermann von Detten, in drawing up a proposal (March 2, 1937) for carrying out the church elections, had found the question of who might vote most difficult to solve (BA, Adjutantur des Führers, NS 10/272, pp. 60–62).

7. Wurm, *Erinnerungen,* p. 136; Niemöller, *Kampf und Zeugnis,* pp. 390–92; Klügel, *Landeskirche Hannovers,* p. 239.

8. Dibelius to Kerrl, February, 1937, Schumacher, T580, R. 41; see also Dibelius, *In the Service of the Lord*, pp. 157–58.

9. Election appeal signed by Probst Bestmann et al., Berlin, K. Arch., Hekt. R.

10. *KJ*, 1933–44, p. 163; "Wahldienst der Vorläufigen Leitung der DEK, Nr. 3, 23/2/37," Biel. Arch., Coll. W. Niemöller, B 4–5, Kirchenwahl, 1937, II.

11. Meier, *Die Deutschen Christen*, p. 220.

12. Ibid., p. 224.

13. Ibid., p. 258; Klügel, *Landeskirche Hannovers*, pp. 239–40; "Gesetz zum Schutze von Bezeichnungen der nationalsozialistischen Deutschen Arbeiterpartei vom 7. April 1937," *Gesetzes- und Verordnungsblatt Badens*, 1937, pp. 56–57.

14. Meier, *Die Deutschen Christen*, p. 258.

15. Ibid., pp. 226, 230. On April 19, 1937, Muhs was advanced to the post of state secretary in the Ministry of Church Affairs and steadily extended his authority over the church, especially over the finance sections (Hermelink, *Kirche im Kampf*, p. 388).

16. Meier, *Die Deutschen Christen*, pp. 227, 230.

17. Ibid., p. 258. In regard to Petersmann, who was a relatively moderate German Christian, see Ehrenforth, *Schlesische Kirche*, pp. 184–99.

18. Hoche, *Gesetzgebung*, 22: 676; Niemöller, *Kampf und Zeugnis*, p. 393. The ban was only on public announcements, and when a pastor informed the parents of an SS member of their son's withdrawal from the church Heydrich could do nothing about it. He proposed forbidding both public and private disclosure of withdrawals (Reichsführer SS, T175, R. 38, 2547860–61). For a police study of church withdrawals, proposals for making withdrawal procedures easier, and the marked decline in withdrawals with the outbreak of World War II, see "Meldungen aus dem Reich," April 22, 1943, Boberach, *Berichte*, pp. 810–19. According to 1922 regulations, withdrawals from the Bavarian church were noted on the baptismal record; withdrawals had to be reported to the Bavarian church where the person had been baptized if it differed from the place of withdrawal. On July 23, 1937, this obligation was extended to report to all Evangelical Land churches where a person's baptism was recorded (*Amtsblatt Landeskirche in Bayern*, 1937, p. 98).

19. *KJ*, 1933–44, pp. 165–67.

20. Ibid., p. 201. On June 18, 1936, Kerrl had requested the Prussian secret police not to undertake any measures in regard to collections of the Confessing church, but to keep him informed about them (BA, Reichssicherheitshauptamt, R 58/266).

21. See Linck, *Kirchenkampf in Ostpreussen*, pp. 204–16; see also pp. 236–41.

22. See Gunther Harder, "Die Kirchenleitende Tätigkeit des Brandenburgischen Bruderrats," in Schmidt, *Gesammelte Aufsätze*, pp. 208–11.

23. Manfred Koschorke, *Materialsammlung vom Kirchenkampf in Ostpreussen September 1934 bis 1939*, p. 116; Linck, *Kirchenkampf in Ostpreussen*, p. 239.

24. "Kollektenanweisung für den 25/9/38," Berlin, K. Arch., no. 240b, p. 122; for the recommendation of a "freewill offering" instead of the regular collection, ibid., no. 93, p. 32. Collections had to be announced but not necessarily recommended. If such announcements were made pastors who had their salaries stopped because of difficulties over church collections would have them restored (Koch to Pfarrer Sachse, 19/6/1940, ibid., no. 224).

25. Asmussen, *Zur jüngsten Kirchengeschichte*, p. 74; Linck, *Kirchenkampf in Ostpreussen*, p. 240; Zipfel, *Kirchenkampf*, p. 125.

26. *KJ*, 1933–44, pp. 188–90.

27. Heinz Brunotte, "Der kirchenpolitische Kurs der Deutschen Evangelischen Kirchenkanzlei von 1937 bis 1945," in Schmidt, *Gesammelte Aufsätze*, pp. 104–5; see also Brunotte, *ZevKR* 3 (1953–54): 34–35, 52–55. Brunotte gives the dates of establishment and personnel of each finance section. There was great concern in Bavaria and Württemberg when a finance section was suddenly imposed on Baden, on May 18, 1938. Studies were made which concluded that such action was illegal, especially in areas where orderly church procedures prevailed (Nürnberg, LK. Arch., Bestand 221).

28. For example, on February 25, 1943, Dr. med. Engelhard, an *Obstkonservenfabrikant*, who was twice divorced and had withdrawn from the church, was appointed chairman of the finance section of Baden (Brunotte, *ZevKR* 3 [1953–54]: 40).

29. *KJ*, 1933–44, pp. 190–91, 194.

30. Ibid., p. 190.

31. Klügel, *Landeskirche Hannovers,* p. 241. In a speech at Fulda on November 24, 1937, Kerrl stated that the churches were responsible for the elections not being held; the state was meanwhile waiting (*B.Z. am Mittag,* November 24, 1937, in Biel. Arch., Coll. W. Niemöller, N-6, Kerrl).

32. For various protest statements, see *KJ,* 1933–44, pp. 174–76, 181–87, 194–95, 202–9, 212–15. On the synod meeting at Halle, May 10–13, 1937, see Gerhard Niemöller, *Die Synode zu Halle 1937,* pp. 436–47.

33. "Paul Schneider zum Gedächtnis," in W. Jannasch, *Deutsche Kirchendokumente,* pp. 97–116; *KJ,* 1933–44, p. 192; Niemöller, *Gotteswort ist nicht gebunden,* p. 134.

34. Berlin, K. Arch., no. 114, p. 60; see also letters signed by Hahn to Hess, Frick, and Kerrl of March 18, 1937, ibid., no. 381, pp. 100–101; there are also other protest letters in these dossiers.

35. Copy of the letter in German in Berlin, K. Arch., no. 256, pp. 24–28.

36. "Hess an die Reichsleiter u. Gauleiter der NSDAP," June 20, 1937, Schumacher, T580, R. 42; also circulated by Chef des SS Hauptamtes, July 15, 1937, ibid.

37. *KJ,* 1933–44, pp. 193–94; Niemöller, *Kampf und Zeugnis,* pp. 400–401. The arrested men were Müller-Dahlem, Böhm, Iwand, Lücking, Beckmann, Rabenau-Schöneberg, Perels, and Rendtorff. They were soon freed.

38. Niemöller, *Kampf und Zeugnis,* p. 401. That Niemöller had been exempted even so long from arrest was probably due to the protection of Justice Minister Franz Gürtner (*KJ,* 1933–44, p. 196; conversation with Martin Niemöller, August, 1968). For a good character sketch of Gürtner which stresses his independence of mind, see Schwerin-Krosigk, *Es geschah in Deutschland,* pp. 317–25.

39. Rosenberg was very much opposed to the prosecution's accusing Niemöller of attacking his theological opponents because this turned the state into a protector of theological views. After seven months of investigation, one of the state attorneys had approached a representative of Rosenberg and pleaded "that he give him material against Niemöller that would stand up in court." Goebbels and Kerrl had not been able to gather good evidence in a year (Rosenberg to Hess, February 14, 1938, BA, Kanzlei Rosenberg, NS 8/179. pp. 138–39). Rosenberg's representative at the trial reported: "This trial belongs to the most shameful and unworthy trials I have ever witnessed." He considered it an attempt by Kerrl to rehabilitate himself ("Aktennotiz des Beobachter des Beauftragten des Fuhrers für Überwachung der gesamten weltanschaulichen und geistigen Schulung und Erziehung der NSDAP," February 10, 1938, BA, Adjutantur des Führers, NS 10/463, pp. 66–76). This report, with an introduction by Hans Bucheim from a copy found among the Nürnberg documents (NG-910) at the Institut für Zeitgeschichte in Munich, is reprinted as "Ein NS-Funktionär zum Niemöller Prozess," *VZ* 4 (1956): 307–15.

40. Wilhelm Niemöller, *Macht geht vor Recht,* pp. 29–98; Hermelink, *Kirche im Kampf,* p. 403.

41. BA, Reichskanzlei, R 43 II/155, p. 160.

42. April 28, 1938, ibid., p. 171.

43. Kerrl to Lammers, July 7, 1939, ibid., pp. 250–52.

44. Ibid., pp. 175–83; Fritz Klinger, ed., *Dokumente zum Abwehrkampf der deutschen evangelischen Pfarrerschaft gegen Verfolgung und Bedrückung 1933–1945,* p. 123.

45. April 18–19, 1939, BA, Reichskanzlei, R 43 II/155, pp. 206–10. At this time Dr. Klinger renewed his plea for the freeing of Martin Niemöller, and a Vermerk on the party affiliation and military record of Martin's brother Wilhelm, as well as of Mrs. Martin Niemöller's brothers, was drawn up and sent to Hitler (ibid., p. 208).

46. Ibid., pp. 219–44.

47. Ibid., p. 261.

48. Ibid., pp. 255–60.

49. July 7, 1942, ibid., p. 264.

50. See Schmidt, *Martin Niemöller,* pp. 165–77.

51. In fact the Pastors' Emergency League paid out the largest sum to pastors whose salaries had been cut off in 1939; the totals for other years rank as follows: 1938, 1940, 1935, 1941, 1937, 1936. Although a certain lull was apparent during the war, the league still distributed 118,000 marks in 1944. The yearly variation in payments is a rough indication of the intensity of the church struggle. Altogether, the league raised 2,224,696.10 marks, and distributed 1,971,563.17 marks to replace terminated salaries, 54,621.54 marks to pay fines, 151,190.50 marks for legal

aid, and 41,320.35 marks to help displaced pastors and their kin (Niemöller, *Geschichte des Pfarrernotbundes*, pp. 11, 14–15).

52. Niemöller, *Kampf und Zeugnis*, pp. 400–412; Hermelink, *Kirche im Kampf*, p. 418; Zipfel, *Kirchenkampf*, p. 124; Bethge, in Littell and Locke, *German Church Struggle*, p. 179.
53. Boberach, *Berichte*, p. 936.
54. *KJ*, 1933–44, p. 193; Klügel, *Landeskirche Hannovers*, p. 244.
55. Klügel, *Landeskirche Hannovers*, p. 245; Hermelink, *Kirche im Kampf*, pp. 409–40.
56. *KJ*, 1933–44, pp. 196–98; Klügel, *Landeskirche Hannovers*, pp. 246–48.
57. *KJ*, 1933–44, p. 209; see chap. 8 at n. 42, above.
58. *KJ*, 1933–44, pp. 209–15.
59. Harder in Schmidt, *Gesammelte Aufsätze*, p. 197.
60. Hermelink, *Kirche im Kampf*, pp. 438–40. The head of the finance section in Baden was particularly zealous and went so far as to appoint a representative with full powers in many congregations (*Gesetzes- und Verordnungsblatt Badens*, 1938, p. IV; 1939, pp. IV–V, 1940, p. IV). Under a national church ordinance of May 13, 1939, each church official had to take an oath of loyalty to Hitler and give evidence that he and his wife were of German or related blood, but the ordinance specifically stated that pastors were not considered church officials (*Gesetzblatt der Deutschen Evangelischen Kirche*, 1939, p. 43). Nevertheless, relying on this national ordinance, the head of the Baden finance section announced on August 11, 1939, that he would not approve the appointment of any pastor who had not submitted statements proving himself, and if applicable his fiancée or wife, to be of German or related blood (ibid., 1939, pp. 162–69, 183–84). On May 28, 1940, he excluded all non-Aryan Protestant church members in Baden from payment of church taxes, although in cases of mixed marriages the Aryan member still had to pay the church tax (ibid., 1940, p. 43).
61. Article 32 and final protocol to it, *DGFP*, C, 1: 676, 678; Schöppe, *Konkordate*, pp. 33–34.
62. This paragraph based on items found in Schumacher, T580, R. 42; see also Nicolaisen, *Kirchenpolitik*, 2: 170, 176–79. On the role of supporting members of the SS, see "Fördernde Mitgliederschaft bei der SS," in *Gutachten des Instituts für Zeitgeschichte*, pp. 350–51.
63. Items from Schumacher, T580, R. 42.
64. Himmler Befehl, July 24, 1937, ibid.
65. Items from Schumacher, T580, R. 42.
66. Der Chef des SS Hauptamts, June 2, 1939, Schumacher, T580, R. 42; see also Zipfel, *Kirchenkampf*, pp. 130–33 on church membership of the SS in units stationed in Berlin and its environs. The percentage of nonchurch members was highest in the SS units, but "Himmler was never able to put over his anti-church program" for the SS (Heinz Höhne, *Der Orden unter dem Totenkopf*, pp. 147–48.
67. Himmler to Frau Schneider, BA, Reichskanzlei, 43 II/151, p. 68. Himmler was hostile to Christianity, especially the Catholic church, but nevertheless insisted on a belief in God (Roger Manvell and Heinrich Fraenkel, *Himmler*, pp. 182–83); Himmler himself confessed to a "belief in God and Providence" (H.R. Trevor-Roper, *The Last Days of Hitler*, p. 33).
68. *Hitler's Secret Conversations 1941–44*, p. 117.
69. All SS men had to show that their ancestry was free of Jewish blood back to the close of the Thirty Years' War, the date set by Himmler; he was a bit more lenient in regard to wives, especially if they were beyond childbearing age (Himmler to Küchlin, April 3, 1940, in Helmut Heiber, *Reichsführer!*, p. 75; see also p. 64). Even as late as August, 1943, Himmler refused an SS man permission to marry a girl because her genealogical chart showed a full Jewish ancestor on her mother's side in 1711 (ibid., p. 231).
70. For a brief account of the piecemeal anti-Jewish policy, see Hans Mommsen, "Der Nationalsozialistische Polizeistaat und die Judenverfolgung vor 1938," *VZ* 10 (1962): 68–87; see also the listing of anti-Jewish measures, mostly after 1938, in Lutz-Eugen Reutter, *Die Hilfstätigkeit katholischer Organisationen und kirchlichen Stellen für die im nationalsozialistischen Deutschland Verfolgten*, pp. 260–67.
71. Zipfel, *Kirchenkampf*, p. 108; see also pp. 104–36; Nicolaisen, *Kirchenpolitik*, 2: 136, 262. How many clergy were members of the SS and SA is not known. In 1935 in Baden, 750 active and retired Protestant pastors answered a questionnaire. Of these 127 were members of the party (56 before 1933), 17 were mem-

bers of the SS, and 96 of the SA (*Gesetzes- und Verordnungsblatt Badens,* 1935, p. 130).

72. Anordnung Nr. 34/39, Schumacher, T580, R. 42. This order was circulated by Bormann on July 14, 1939, BA, Kanzlei Rosenberg, NS 8/182, p. 261. See also Nicolaisen, *Kirchenpolitik,* 2: 176–77.
73. Kerrl to Lammers, April 17, 1940, and Lammers to Hess, April 23, 1940, BA, Reichskanzlei R 43 II/155, pp. 14, 25–27.
74. Zipfel, *Kirchenkampf,* p. 110.
75. See chap. 7, "Crisis Among the German Christians," above; see also Frick to Obersten Reichsbehörden et al., January 3, 1938, Schumacher, T580, R. 42; Bormann's Rundschreiben of March 11, 1938, giving the order of the Reichskriegsminister of June 25, 1937, ibid.; Himmler's order of June 13, 1938, ibid.
76. Bormann's Rundschreiben of March 23, 1937, and of November 11, 1937, ibid.
77. Withdrawals from the Protestant Land churches numbered: 94,031 (1936); 319,708 (1937); 326,513 (1938); 377,721 (1939); 152,591 (1940); 182,310 (1941); 97,148 (1942); 46,125 (1943); 22,459 (1944); 9,493 (1945) (*Amtsblatt der Evangelischen Kirche in Deutschland, Statistische Beilage,* no. 4 [1952], pp. 6–9). Withdrawals from the Catholic church numbered: 46,687 (1936); 108,054 (1937); 88,715 (1938); 88,335 (1939); 51,799 (1940); 52,560 (1941); 38,367 (1942) (Guenter Lewy, *The Catholic Church and Nazi Germany* p. 373, based on the report of the Zentralstelle für kirchliche Statistik, Cologne, 1944). The figures compiled in the Ministry of Church Affairs for the years 1932–40 vary somewhat from the above figures (BA, Reichsministerium für die kirchlichen Angelegenheiten, R 79/19).
78. Speer, *Memoirs,* pp. 95–96. Goebbels had become estranged from the Catholic church during his university years (Helmut Heiber, ed., *Das Tagebuch von Joseph Goebbels 1925/26,* p. 10).
79. Rosenberg to Darré, November 12, 1938; Darré to Rosenberg, November 18, 1938, BA, Kanzlei Rosenberg, NS 8/173, pp. 117–19.
80. BA, Kanzlei Rosenberg, NS 8/180, p. 20; Dietrich Orlow, *The History of the Nazi Party,* 2: 258, 280.
81. Order of Kerrl of August 28, 1936, reprinted in *Anordnungen des Stellvertreters des Führers,* pp. 337–39; order of Bavarian political police, October 8, 1936, Schumacher, T580, R. 40; Bormann's Rundschreiben, October 21, 1936, Schumacher, T580, R. 42.
82. Schumacher, T580, R. 41; see also T580, R. 42.
83. Geheime Staatspolizei, Düsseldorf, April 12, 1938, Reichsführer SS, T175, R. 408, 2931802.
84. BA, Reichskanzlei, R 43 II/150, pp. 94, 97–98, 102–8. The question arose of whether a swastika should be removed from a memorial in a church. Kerrl held it would create too much of a disturbance. On February 1, 1939, Hitler overruled him and supported Hess, who maintained it must be removed (ibid., pp. 112, 121–25).
85. BA, Reichskanzlei, R 43 II/150, pp. 102–8; see also the police report on "Missbrauch nationalsozialistischen Begriffs- und völkischen Sprachguts durch die Kirchen," July 14, 1941, July 6, 1942, Boberach, *Berichte,* pp. 527–34, 689–92.
86. Besetz. Gebiete, T454, R. 82, 000736–000738.
87. BA, Reichskanzlei, R 43 II/150, p. 78; Reichssicherheitshauptamt, R 58/1094, p. 73.
88. See chap. 16, "Confiscations of Church Property and Financial Controls," below.
89. *Verfügungen/ Anordnungen/ Bekanntgaben,* 1: 136–37; see also Bormann to Command of the Armed Forces, January 28, 1939, Nbg. Doc., 117-PS.
90. Berlin, K. Arch., no. 149, p. 36. This was a marked departure from the old rural Pomeranian custom that each family had to send a representative to participate in the funeral procession or pay a fine of a case of beer (Gerhard Gülzow, *Kirchenkampf in Danzig 1934–1945,* p. 17).
91. Helmreich, *Religious Education,* pp. 162–78; Franz Teping, *Der Kampf um die konfessionelle Schule in Oldenburg während der Herrschaft der NS-Regierung,* pp. 14–63; Reinhold Sautter, *Theophil Wurm,* pp. 48–53.
92. On November 11, 1938, the leader of the National Socialist Teachers Organization had issued an order which led teachers to give up teaching religion classes. This led State Minister Freyberg of Anhalt and Bishop Sasse, a German Christian, immediately to protest the order. The matter was brought to the attention of Hitler, who also did not approve of the order, and Secretary Lammers was asked to see that Education Minister Rust righted the matter. On December 2, 1938, Rust, with

Hess's approval, ordered that teachers who had given up their religion classes should reconsider their decision (BA, Reichskanzlei, R 43 II/157, pp. 81–108).

93. See Beyreuther, *Geschichte der Diakonie*, pp. 198–205.

94. Günther Bauer, *Kirchliche Rundfunkarbeit 1924–1939*, pp. 82–100; Klinger, *Dokumente*, p. 24. This prohibition goes back to Bormann's inquiry to all Gauleiter on November 11, 1938, as to whether there were any reasons these broadcasts should not be stopped; he had earlier planned to end them (Walter Adolf, "Unveröffentlichte Bormann Akten über den Kirchenkampf," *Wichman Jahrbuch*, 1953, p. 134).

95. Klügel, *Landeskirche Hannovers*, pp. 435–36.

96. Matthias Simon, *Evangelische Kirchengeschichte Bayerns*, p. 667. For a gripping description of the final services in the church, see Schmid, *Apokalyptisches Wetter-leuchten*, pp. 179–85. On July 7, 1938, Himmler inquired of Speer how he intended to compensate the congregation for the demolition of the church building (Reichsführer SS, T175, R. 38, 2547779). Speer does not mention the destruction of the church in his *Memoirs*.

97. BA, Rep. 320, no. 471, p. 115; Rundschreiben no. 16/39 of July 28, 1939, in *Partei-Kanzlei Rundschreiben*, 63/41; see also Schumacher, T580, R. 42. Speer writes: "Bormann curtly informed me that churches were not to receive building sites" (*Memoirs*, p. 177).

98. Hermelink, *Kirche im Kampf*, pp. 420–21. The study, by Prof. Walter Künneth, was never published (conversation with Künneth, August, 1968), but see his *Evangelische Wahrheit!*, the expansion of an address given in Saint Lorenz Church in Nürnberg. Künneth had previously published *Antwort auf dem Mythus*. He was forbidden to speak throughout the Reich on December 12, 1937 (BA, Geh. Staatspolizei, R 56/266). See also the widely circulated book by Rudolf Homann, *Der Mythus und das Evangelium*.

99. Hermelink, *Kirche im Kampf*, p. 421; Klügel, *Landeskirche Hannovers*, pp. 248–49; *KJ*, 1933–44, pp. 215–23.

100. "Siebzehnte Verordnung zur Durchführung des Gesetzes zur Sicherung der Deutschen Evangelischen Kirche," *KJ*, 1933–44, pp. 224–25. On December 17, 1937, Kerrl sent Hess an eighteenth *Durchführungsverordnung* which he said would give the German Christians the opportunity to work within the Evangelical church denied them by the Confessing bishops. The document was forwarded to Rosenberg who held that it must not be published because it would put the state into church affairs rather than take it out. Kerrl was doing this all for the German Christians and it would put the state behind them. He sent along a study (*Gutachtung*) by an expert (Besetz. Gebiete, T454, R. 63, 000015–17, 000019, 000022–25). Rosenberg was very much opposed to the state's lending support to the German Christians (Nbg. Doc., 005-PS).

101. Klügel, *Landeskirche Hannovers*, pp. 342–46.

102. See Boyens, *Kirchenkampf und Ökumene, 1933–1939*, pp. 15–19.

103. Ausw. A., T120, R. 4418, L123496–97; Jasper, *George Bell*, pp. 102–5; Boyens, *Kirchenkampf und Ökumene, 1933–1939*, pp. 59–66.

104. Jasper, *George Bell*, pp. 114–18; Bethge, *Bonhoeffer*, pp. 431–54; Boyens, *Kirchenkampf und Ökumene, 1933–1939*, pp. 110–12, 119, 330–39. Goebbels was enraged that the Reich Chancellery had permitted the publication of the Fanö resolutions (BA, Rep. 300, no. 57, p. 89).

105. Jasper, *George Bell*, p. 214; on the selection of the German delegation, see also Boyens, *Kirchenkampf und Ökumene, 1933–1939*, pp. 146–56.

106. Eugen Gerstenmaier, ed., *Kirche, Volk und Staat*.

107. Ausw. A., T120, R. 4420, L124905–7. The draft of this letter, which was to be signed by other churchmen as well, was sent to von Neurath on January 17, 1937, for his opinion. He informed Wurm that it was for him to decide if the letter should be sent to Hitler. In any case, the Foreign Office would not be the proper channel; transmittals should be made through the Ministry for Church Affairs (Von Katze, on behalf of von Neurath to Wurm, January 18, 1937, ibid., L124899–900). It is uncertain if the letter was ever sent to Hitler.

108. *New York Times*, July 13, July 23, 1937; NSDAP, T81, R. 184, 0334299.

109. Jasper, *George Bell*, pp. 221–22. On June 3, 1937, the Foreign Office was informed that Hitler that day had decided that no official delegation or private individuals should attend the Oxford meeting (Nbg. Doc., 904-NG). The Ministry of Church Affairs interpreted this directive as applying only to the Evangelical church and not

to the Free churches and the Old Catholics (Boyens, *Kirchenkampf und Ökumene, 1933–1939,* pp. 154–55; see also pp. 158, 162 on the delegates from German churches abroad). See also J. H. Oldham, *The Oxford Conference (Official Report),* pp. 280, 283. Most sources do not mention a delegate of the Old Catholics at the conference, but see the *New York Times,* July 20, 1937, p. 14; see also *Christian Century* 54 (August 18, 1937): 1018; James H. Nichols, *History of Christianity 1650–1950,* p. 389.

110. Gunnar Westin, *Der Weg der freien christlichen Gemeinden durch die Jahrhunderte,* pp. 284–85; Friedrich Wunderlich, *Brückenbauer Gottes,* pp. 154–55; Calwer, *Kirchenlexikon,* 2: 209–10.

111. See chap. 19, below.

112. Jasper, *George Bell,* p. 227.

113. Oldham, *The Oxford Conference,* pp. 259–60.

114. Jasper, *George Bell,* p. 228. On July 26 the archbishop of Canterbury received a letter of thanks for the message signed by Bishop Marahrens as senior bishop of the Evangelical church, by Dr. Fleisch of the Council of the German Evangelical church, and by Pastor Müller of the Provisional Directory of the German Evangelical church (ibid., p. 229). The *New York Times* on July 20, 1937, carried excerpts of the message to the German churches.

115. Jasper, *George Bell,* p. 228; Boyens, *Kirchenkampf und Ökumene, 1933–1939,* pp. 354–55.

116. *New York Times,* July 23, 1937, p. 19.

117. Jasper, *George Bell,* p. 228; Boyens, *Kirchenkampf und Ökumene, 1933–1939,* pp. 167–68, 360–61.

118. *New York Times,* July 22, 1937, p. 17.

119. As quoted in Hermelink, *Kirche im Kampf,* pp. 421–22. The dispatch to the *New York Times,* July 23, 1937, p. 19, referred to the speech as eulogizing Chancellor Adolf Hitler. For a statement issued at the Edinburgh conference in August, 1937, see chap. 19 at nn. 26–28, below.

120. On the Evangelische Allianz, see chap. 1 at n. 37, above.

121. Wurm to Kerrl, October 30, 1937, Ausw. A., T120, R. 4420, L124861–65; this letter was forwarded to von Neurath, L124856–58. Wurm also submitted a letter from Dekan Eytel and Freiherrn von Pechmann on the stand taken by Melle, L124866–69. The Ministry of Church Affairs sought to have charges brought against Pechmann because of his letter to Wurm (Guertner Diary, 978, R. 3, 3757-PS 450).

122. As quoted by Hermelink, *Kirche im Kampf,* p. 422; *New York Times,* October 28, 1937, p. 4.

123. Hermelink, *Kirche im Kampf,* pp. 423–25; Ausw. A., T120, R. 4420, L124856–69. The *Christian Century* in an editorial sided against Melle in the controversy: "We are passionately devoted to the idea of a church free from dependence on the government. But we are on guard against becoming the victims of that sense of superiority which now afflicts German free churches and breaks their fellowship not only with the suffering Confessional Church but with Protestants everywhere" (*Christian Century* 54 [October 20, 1937]: 1288–89).

124. Scholder, *VZ* 16 (1968): 30.

125. The brotherhood council of the Confessing church of Berlin approved this prayer and suggested that it be used on April 3 and 10 (Berlin, K. Arch., no. 240b, p. 70).

126. Werner Haugg, *Das Reichsministerium für die kirchlichen Angelegenheiten* p. 16. The Austrian church might well have been granted more consideration, for a number of its pastors were party members and had been active in furthering its cause (see summary in Fritz Klinger, *Deutscher Pfarrertag Kiel, 26. bis 29. September 1938,* pp. 12–13).

127. Angelika Gerlach-Praetorius, *Die Kirche vor der Eidesfrage,* pp. 95–96.

128. Ibid., pp. 82–89; Wurm, *Erinnerungen,* pp. 138–39; Helmreich, *Religious Education,* pp. 168–69.

129. The Reformed Church of Hanover informed Kerrl it was not issuing instructions to its clergy in regard to the oath since it had not received a state request to do so. The Reformed Church of Lippe also apparently made no attempt to exact an oath (Robert Steiner, "Der Weg der reformierten Kirchen und Gemeinden von 1933–1950," *KJ,* 1950, pp 301–2). Only in Hamburg did the state authorities request that the pastors take the oath to Hitler (Klinger, *Deutscher Pfarrertag Kiel,* p. 5).

130. *KJ,* 1933–45, pp. 256–58, 262; see also the "Beschluss zur Eidesfrage" of the

synod meeting on June 11–13, 1938, pp. 250–53. A group of some 80 pastors in East Prussia met and discussed taking the oath. They placed conditions which were not fulfilled and the oath was not taken (Linck, *Kirchenkampf in Ostpreussen,* pp. 222–24). In Saxony 250 pastors took the oath before civil authorities because the German Christian church officials would permit no reservations (Klinger, *Deutscher Pfarrertag Kiel,* p. 6). In Westphalia most of the clergy took the oath, adding an explanatory statement (Werner Danielsmeyer, "Präses D. Karl Koch," in Reinhold Koch, ed., *Materialien für den Dienst in der Evangelischen Kirche von Westfalen,* pp. 13–15).

131. BA, Reichskanzlei, R 43 II/155a, p. 52. Rosenberg all along had opposed requiring an oath from the pastors because it tended to further state support of the churches (see his letters to Hess of April 26 and May 5, 1938, BA, Kanzlei Rosenberg, NS 8/179, pp. 87–89, 94–97).

132. *KJ,* 1933–44, p. 262; BA, Reichskanzlei, R 43 II/155a, p. 64.

133. For the most thorough discussion of the whole oath problem and the way it was dealt with in various Land churches, see Gerlach-Praetorius, *Eidesfrage,* pp. 72–170; for a theoretical evaluation, see pp. 171–214. In Baden only two or three pastors refused to take the oath even with the customary reservation in respect to their ordination vow (Friedrich, *ZevKR* 3 [1953–54]: 318–19). See also Peter Brunner, "Gutachten über die Eidesfrage," in *Lutherisches Bekenntnis,* pp. 32–38. Brunner concluded that it was impossible on the basis of Holy Writ and confession to take the oath demanded by Dr. Werner (p. 38).

134. Klügel, *Landeskirche Hannovers,* p. 343.

135. Ibid., pp. 334–35, 357–58; Heinz Brunotte, "Der kirchenpolitische Kurs der Deutschen Evangelischen Kirchenkanzlei von 1937 bis 1945," in Schmidt, *Gesammelte Aufsätze,* pp. 107–8.

136. "Vorläufige Leitung der Deutschen Evangelischen Kirche an Landeskirchenregierungen, Landesbruderräte," September 7, 1938, Berlin, K. Arch., no 224, p. 133.

137. The liturgy did indeed have a different tone from the insertion in the general prayer on September 30 recommended by Dr. Werner of the official church administration. The addition gave thanks to God for Hitler's wisdom and patience and for the preservation of peace (Berlin, K. Arch., no. 149, p. 13).

138. The liturgy is printed in *KJ,* 1933–44, pp. 263–65; with slight variations, W. Jannasch, *Kirchendokumente,* pp. 74–79; see also Niemöller, *Kampf und Zeugnis,* pp. 446–52. For the report of the Chefs des Sicherheitshauptamtes des Reichsführers SS, November 8, 1938, on the liturgy, see Boberach, *Berichte,* p. 298

139. As quoted in *KJ,* 1933–44, p. 265.

140. Ibid.

141. Klügel, *Landeskirche Hannovers,* p. 359; see also Marahrens's criticism of the liturgy (no prayer for the government, no prayer for soldiers who might be going to war, etc.) in his letter of November 26, 1938, to Pastor Harnisch in Berlin, Berlin, K. Arch., no. 149, pp. 24–25; see also Hermelink, *Kirche im Kampf,* pp. 455–58. Kerrl complained in a letter of November 9, 1938, to the chief of the security police about not being informed immediately about the prayer liturgy; he heard of it only on October 26. Kerrl's meeting with the bishops was on November 9 (Nbg. Doc., 4966-NG).

142. Meiser had originally thanked the Provisional Directory for sending him the liturgy. The bishops had also met with the Provisional Directory as the Kasseler Gremium and had raised no objection to it (Berlin, K. Arch. no. 240b, p. 83).

143. *KJ,* 1933–44, pp. 269–70, 272; Wurm sent this explanation of his action to Pastor Harnisch in Berlin for his information and use (Berlin, K. Arch., no. 149, pp. 21–22).

144. Wurm, *Erinnerungen,* pp. 145–46; "Wurm und sämtliche Dekanatsämter," November 21, 1938, Berlin, K. Arch., no. 149, p. 2.

145. Hermelink, *Kirche im Kampf,* p. 457.

146. Marahrens to Pastor W. Harnisch, November 26, 1938, Berlin, K. Arch., no. 149, pp. 24–25; Klügel, *Landeskirche Hannovers,* p. 360.

147. Hermelink, *Kirche im Kampf,* p. 458; Niemöller, *Kampf und Zeugnis,* pp. 448–49; *KJ,* 1933–44, pp. 272–73.

148. Charles A. Lindbergh, *Wartime Journals,* p. 103, entry of October 18, 1938.

149. Kurt Meier, "Kirche und Nationalsozialismus," in Schmidt, *Gesammelte Aufsätze,* pp. 24–25; Leon Poliakov and Josef Wulf, eds., *Das Dritte Reich und seine Denker,* pp. 211–17. Himmler was against the SS instituting naming ceremonies for children of SS members (order of June 17, 1937, Schumacher, T580, R. 42).

150. *KJ*, 1933–44, pp. 278–79; Klügel, *Landeskirche Hannovers*, p. 361; Heinz Brunotte, "Der kirchenpolitische Kurs der Deutschen Evangelischen Kirchenkanzlei von 1937 bis 1945," in Schmidt, *Gesammelte Aufsätze*, pp. 110–12.

151. *KJ*, 1933–44, pp. 279–83.

152. Ibid., pp. 283–90; Hermelink, *Kirche im Kampf*, p. 463–74; Klügel, *Landeskirche Hannovers*, p. 362.

153. *KJ*, 1933–44, pp. 293–95; Hermelink, *Kirche im Kampf*, p. 475; Niemöller, *Kampf und Zeugnis*, p. 470; Boberach, *Berichte*, p. 339.

154. *KJ*, 1933–44, pp. 295–96. The archbishop of Canterbury had denounced the occupation of Prague in the House of Lords on March 20, mentioning possible cooperation of Britain with Russia to stop aggression. It had brought denunciations in Germany (Boyens, *Kirchenkampf und Ökumene*, pp. 256–57). The archbishop had written Marahrens suggesting that the German church join in special prayers for peace on Pentecost. Marahrens refused because he felt this was meant as a political action against Germany, which the archbishop denied. The secret police followed the correspondence carefully (BA, Reichskanzlei, R 43 II/156, pp. 27–37; Boberach, *Berichte*, p. 341).

155. *KJ*, 1933–44, pp. 296–97; Meier, *Die Deutschen Christen*, pp. 290–92.

156. Ehrenforth, *Schlesische Kirche*, p. 198. On September 25, 1942, Bormann informed State Secretary Muhs of the Ministry of Church Affairs that the institute was not entitled to recognition or aid from the party and that all references to support from it must cease (BA, Reichskanzlei, R 43 II/151, pp. 44–46).

157. *KJ*, 1933–44, p. 299.

158. Ibid., pp. 301, 306; Heinrich Wilhelmi, *Die Hamburger Kirche in der nationalsozialistischen Zeit 1933–1945*, p. 266.

159. *KJ*, 1933–44, pp. 303–7. Kerrl in an interview with Wurm on August 17, 1939, made one last attempt to get him to sign the statement (Hermelink, *Kirche im Kampf*, pp. 482–84). On Marahrens's position, see Klügel, *Landeskirche Hannovers*, pp. 369–70. Marahrens, however, always insisted that the commentary he submitted with his signature mitigated his actions (Eberhard Klügel, *Die lutherische Landeskirche Hannovers und ihr Bischof 1933–1945. Dokumente*, pp. 212–13).

160. For various protest statements, see *KJ*, 1933–44, pp. 307–17, 331–34; 1950, pp. 305–7.

161. *KJ*, 1933–44, p. 338; Klügel, *Landeskirche Hannovers*, pp. 501–2.

162. On these controversies, see *KJ*, 1933–44, pp. 337–49, 387.

163. Ibid., pp. 472–73; Niemöller, *Kampf und Zeugnis*, pp. 487–88; Hermelink, *Kirche im Kampf*, pp. 487–89.

Chapter Twelve

1. Ausw. A., T120, R. 5719, K622943–44.

2. Müller, *Dokumente*, pp. 71–72; Bernard Stasiewski, *Akten deutscher Bischöfe über die Lage der Kirche 1933–1945*, 1: 7–8; Lewy, *Catholic Church and Nazi Germany*, p. 32.

3. Müller, *Dokumente*, pp. 73–75; Stasiewski, *Akten*, 1: 11–12; Doetsch, *Württembergs Katholiken*, p. 82; Volk, *Reichskonkordat*, pp. 71–80.

4. See chap. 6, "Hitler Becomes Chancellor," above.

5. Ernst-Wolfgang Böckenförde, "Der deutsche Katholizismus im Jahre 1933. Stellungnahme zu einen Diskussion," *Hochland* 54 (February, 1962): 226; for the minutes of the Center party caucus at which it was decided to vote for the Enabling Act, see Erich Matthias, "Die Sitzung der Reichstagsfraktion des Zentrums am 23. März 1933," *VZ* 4 (1956): 306–7; Bracher, *Machtergreifung*, pp. 158–68; Heinrich Brüning, *Memoiren 1918–1934*, pp. 656–59.

6. From the archdiocesan library in Bamberg, as quoted by Deuerlein, *Deutsche Katholizismus*, pp. 113–14; see also Stasiewski, *Akten*, 1: 16–17. Deuerlein argues convincingly for the acceptance of Faulhaber's version of the pope's remarks at the consistory, while Ludwig Volk denies that the pope praised Hitler, and argues that Faulhaber invented that interpretation ("Päpstliche Laudatio auf Hitler," *SZ* 173 [1963–64]: 221–229); Volk, *Reichskonkordat*, p. 65; see also Mary Alice Gallin, "The Cardinal and the State: Faulhaber and the Third Reich," *Journal of Church and State* 12 (1970): 390–91.

7. "Schreiben Kardinal Bertrams vom 27/3/1933," Müller, *Dokumente,* pp. 79–80; Stasiewski, *Akten,* 1: 29; Volk, *Reichskonkordat,* pp. 75–78. Cardinal Pacelli, who heard of the bishops' statement from the press, felt they had acted precipitately (Robert Leiber, "Reichskonkordat und Ende der Zentrumspartei," *SZ* 167 (1960): 217.

8. Müller, *Dokumente,* pp. 76–78; Stasiewski, *Akten,* 1: 30–32. For an enthusiastic approval of the bishops' recognition of the Hitler regime, see the brochure by Joseph Lortz, *Katholischer Zugang zum Nationalsozialismus;* for a critical view, see Brüning, *Memoiren,* p. 664.

9. Müller, *Dokumente,* p. 79.

10. That Hitler was not optimistic is shown by his statement to the cabinet on July 14, 1933, when they met to consider the final text of the concordat (Ausw. A., T120, R. 3312, E581429–30; *DGFP,* C, 1: 653). The details of the concordat negotiations can best be followed in Deuerlein, *Reichskonkordat,* pp. 111–35; Deuerlein, *Deutsche Katholizismus,* pp. 116–68; Volk, *Reichskonkordat,* pp. 90–168; Lewy, *Catholic Church and Nazi Germany,* pp. 53–93.

11. See chap. 5, "The Negotiation of Agreements with the Vatican," above.

12. See Kaas's notation on his conversations with von Papen in Kupper, *Staatliche Akten,* pp. 12–14; Volk, *Reichskonkordat,* pp. 97–99.

13. *DGFP,* C, 1: 266–68; Kupper, *Staatliche Akten,* pp. 9–11, 465–84; for the proposed answer to the pro memoria of October, 1932, see chap. 5, "Towards a Reich Concordat" above.

14. For a day-by-day account of the visits of von Papen and Göring, see Hassell's report to the Foreign Office, April 20, 1933, Kupper, *Staatliche Akten,* pp. 19–23. Papen and Göring made a favorable impression at the Vatican (Stasiewski, *Akten,* 1: 88). This was not the first time Göring was sent to Rome to smooth relations with the Vatican. He had gone there in 1931, when the Catholic bishops spoke out against the National Socialist party. At that time, at the express direction of the pope, he was refused an interview with Cardinal State Secretary Pacelli and was left to express his grievances to Monsignor Pizzardo (Deuerlein, *Der Aufstieg der NSDAP,* pp. 351–52).

15. For Kaas's part in the negotiation of the commitment made by the German Foreign Office to the Vatican in November, 1920, see chap. 5, "The Negotiation of Agreements With the Vatican," above. He was privy to the concordat negotiations in 1922 (Ausw. A., T120, R. 5720, K623082) and later negotiations as well. For his role in the 1933 negotiations, see Karl Otmar Frhr. v. Aretin, "Prälat Kaas, Franz von Papen, und das Reichskonkordat von 1933," *VZ* 14 (1966): 252–79; Volk, *Reichskonkordat,* pp. 37–42; 200–211.

16. Kupper, *Staatliche Akten,* pp. 15, 17–19; Rudolf Morsey, "Briefe zum Reichskonkordat Ludwig Kaas-Franz v. Papen," *SZ* 167 (1960): 11–12.

17. "Aktennotiz betr. Besuch Bernings bei Hitler," April 26, 1933, Kupper, *Staatliche Akten,* pp. 28–30; also in Müller, *Dokumente,* pp. 120–22; Nicolaisen, *Kirchenpolitik,* 1: 45–47; *DGFP,* C, 1: 347–48. For a report by Bishop Berning to the Conference of Diocesan Representatives in session in Berlin April 25–26, 1933, see Müller, *Dokumente,* pp. 104–20; Stasiewski, *Akten,* 1: 98–102, 105, 114, 121.

18. Quoted from Berning's report, Müller, *Dokumente,* pp. 118–19. The government's Aktennotiz (see n. 17) refers to these topics being discussed but does not have the material quoted here.

19. Ibid., pp. 113–16, 120, 122.

20. Ibid., pp. 122–25; *DGFP,* C, 1: 358–61.

21. Von Papen to Kaas, April 27, 1933, Kupper, *Staatliche Akten,* pp. 30–31; Kaas to von Papen, May 2, 1933, ibid., pp. 32–35; Entwurf Kaas II, May 11, 1933, ibid., pp. 40–55; von Papen to Kaas, May 17, 1933, ibid., pp. 57–60; von Neurath to Bergen, May 19, 1933, ibid., p. 62.

22. Bergen to von Neurath, May 26, 1933, ibid., pp. 70–71; on Bergen's objection to the speed of the negotiations, see pp. 86–88, 165.

23. Kaas to von Papen, May 23, 1933, ibid., p. 63; Kaas to von Papen, June 11, 1933, ibid., pp. 83–86; for specific article by article changes desired by the episcopate, see ibid., pp. 120–23. For the minutes of the Fulda Bishops' Conference, see Stasiewski, *Akten,* 1: 196–238, particularly p. 232; see also Volk, *Reichskonkordat,* pp. 112–17.

24. "Bemerkungen Menshausens zum Entwurf Kaas II," June 17, 1933, Kupper, *Staatliche Akten,* pp. 92–113.

25. Ibid., pp. 124, 135–36.

26. Bergen to von Neurath, July 3, 1933, *DGFP*, C, 1: 635; Kupper, *Staatliche Akten*, p. 136.

27. Von Papen to Hitler, July 2, 1933, *DGFP*, C, 1: 624.

28. Bergen on behalf of von Papen to von Neurath, July 3, 1933. ibid., p. 634; Ausw. A., T120, R. 5720, K623892; Kupper, *Staatliche Akten*, p. 134. On the decision of the Center party to dissolve itself, see Matthias and Morsey, *Ende der Parteien*, pp. 377–404; see also pp. 405–11; Junker, *Zentrumspartei und Hitler*, pp. 215, 226–33; Leiber, *SZ* 167 (1960): 220–23; Aretin, *VZ* 14 (1966): 276–79; Brüning, *Memoiren*, p. 673; John Jay Hughes, "The Pope's Pact with Hitler: Betrayal or Self-Defense?," *Journal of Church and State* 17 (1975): 72–73.

29. Kupper, *Staatliche Akten*, p. 163.

30. Ibid., p. 139. Buttmann and Councillor Conrad prepared a suggested annotated revision of the concordat draft, ibid., pp. 142–49.

31. Ibid., p. 164. For the concordat draft resulting from the ministerial conference, ibid., pp. 149–63; *DGFP*, C, 1: 625–33.

32. For Buttmann's account of the meeting, see "Aufzeichnung Buttmanns," Rome, July 8–9, 1933, Kupper, *Staatliche Akten*, pp. 166–75; see also Conrad, *Kampf um die Kanzeln*, pp. 36–45. For Gröber's account, see Gröber to Faulhaber, July 11, 1933, Volk, *Kirchliche Akten*, pp. 140–44, 319–34; see also Volk, *Reichskonkordat*, pp. 146–50.

33. Kupper, *Staatliche Akten*, p. 167.

34. Bergen to Foreign Office, July 8, 1933, *DGFP*, C, 1: 642; for the text as initialed, see Kupper, *Staatliche Akten*, pp. 199–211.

35. Kupper, *Staatliche Akten*, pp. 217–19; there is a long footnote on the drawing up of the public statement. On this see also Conrad, *Kampf um die Kanzeln*, pp. 42–43. The final text is also to be found in Deuerlein, *Reichskonkordat*, pp. 119–20; Lewy, *Catholic Church and Nazi Germany*, p. 77.

36. Buttmann an seine Gattin, July 10, 11, 1933, Kupper, *Staatliche Akten*, pp. 223–24.

37. Extract from the minutes of the Conference of Ministers, July 14, 1933, *DGFP*, C, 1: 651–53; Kupper, *Staatliche Akten*, pp. 234–38 with notes; Ausw. A., T120, R. 3312, E581427–30.

38. Volk, *Kirchliche Akten*, p. 353.

39. Conrad, *Kampf um die Kanzeln*, pp. 44–45, 79; Dieter Albrecht, *Der Notenwechsel zwischen dem Heiligen Stuhl und der Deutschen Reichsregierung*, 1: 14n, 117; Schellenberger, *Katholische Jugend*, pp. 39–40; Kupper, *Staatliche Akten*, p. 248.

40. Buttmann an seine Gattin, July 18, 1933, Kupper, *Staatliche Akten*, p. 248; on the changes in Art. 17 desired by the pope, ibid., p. 244.

41. Ibid., pp. 243, 253–54, 282–83.

42. BA, Reichskanzlei, R 43 II/174, pp. 64–67.

43. Translation of the concordat, except where noted, as in *DGFP*, C, 1: 669–79; for German and Italian texts with notes, see Kupper, *Staatliche Akten*, pp. 256–81; German text also in Schöppe, *Konkordate*, pp. 29–36, with notes as to where various translations can be found.

44. Art. 14 and final protocol to it.

45. Part of the prescribed oath as laid down in Art. 16.

46. Art. 30; I have altered the translation given in *DGFP*, C, 1: 675; see German text, Schöppe, *Konkordate*, p. 33.

47. See chap. 5, "Towards a Reich Concordat," above.

48. *DGFP*, C, 1: 267n; for an evaluation of the school provisions of the concordat, see Helmreich, *Religious Education*, pp. 157–59.

49. Von Papen to Kaas, April 27, 1933, Morsey, *SZ* 167 (1960): 12.

50. Franz von Papen, *Memoirs*, pp. 279–81; see also von Papen's testimony, *Trial of the Major War Criminals before the International Military Tribunal Nuremberg 14 November 1945–1 October 1946*, 16: 281–86; Volk, *Reichskonkordat*, pp. 212–14.

51. Kupper, *Staatliche Akten*, pp. 173–74; Volk, *Kirchliche Akten*, pp. 142–43. On the drafting of this article, see Volk, *Reichskonkordat*, pp. 150–63; Schellenberger, *Katholische Jugend*, pp. 39–42.

52. Kupper, *Staatliche Akten*, p. 182; Deuerlein, *Reichskonkordat*, p. 119; Volk, *Reichskonkordat*, pp. 124–34.

53. Von Papen to Hitler, July 2, 1933, *DGFP*, C, 1: 622–24, see also p. 652. The secret annex is given pp. 678–79. Both the British and the French governments learned about the secret annex in 1933 (Gerhard L. Weinberg, *The Foreign Policy of Hitler's Germany*, p. 54).

54. Kupper, *Staatliche Akten,* p. 86; Volk, *Reichskonkordat,* pp. 197–200.
55. Kupper, *Staatliche Akten,* pp. 283–90, 298–307; the efforts made to cool the press comments can be traced pp. 297–431, particularly pp. 316, 319, 329, 335, 427–28; see also Volk, *Reichskonkordat,* pp. 176–80.
56. Müller, *Dokumente,* pp. 168–71; Stasiewski, *Akten,* 1: 269–72. Faulhaber informed the Freising Bishops' Conference that he did not have the courage to speak in their name and wanted to bear the responsibility alone, particularly for the last sentence quoted. He asked their permission to renew these congratulations when calling on Hitler on the Führer's next visit to Munich. He felt obligated to make the call after the Holy Father had, so to speak, exchanged handshakes with the chancellor (Kupper, *Staatliche Akten,* pp. 293–94). Hitler thanked Faulhaber for his letter on August 2 and told him investigations were under way to see who among the imprisoned could be freed (Ausw. A., T120, R. 3312, E5814287). Bertram's and Faulhaber's letters as well as letters of thanks from the bishop of Aachen and from the Missionaries of the Holy Ghost, are to be found BA, Reichskanzlei, R 43 II/176, pp. 91–121.
57. Müller, *Dokumente,* pp. 53–55; on the accommodation of Neudeutschland to the state, see Warloski, *Neudeutschland,* pp. 146–52.
58. A good account of this incident based on archival material is to be found in Ludwig Volk, *Der Bayerische Episkopat und der Nationalsozialismus 1930–1934,* pp. 92–98; see also Johannes Neuhäusler, *Amboss und Hammer,* pp. 24–29.
59. NSDAP, T81, R. 185, O335187.
60. Faulhaber took occasion to contrast the treatment the French occupation authorities had accorded the meeting of the German Journeymen's Association in Cologne in 1922 with the reception given it in Munich (Stasiewski, *Akten,* 1:249–53).
61. NSDAP, T81, R. 184, 0333845; see also R. 185, 0334956–62; Denkschrift des Erzbischöflichen Ordinariats München-Freising, October 2, 1933, Albrecht, *Notenwechsel,* 1: 2–8. This decree was kept in force in Bavaria during the next years. On September 1, 1938, the secret police in the Nürnberg-Fürth area issued secret directives for carrying out the decree. They listed various organizations in three columns: (1) those that did not come under the ban; (2) those for which permission had to be asked and normally was granted; and (3) those for which permission was not to be granted (NSDAP, T81, R. 184, 0333848–52).
62. Volk, *Bayerische Episkopat,* p. 98.
63. Volk, *Kirchliche Akten,* pp. 132, 151–53.
64. Ibid., pp. 150, 165.
65. Ibid., pp. 173–77, 189–91, 204–7, 209–10, 215. The list went out to all the bishops on August 12, 1933 (*ibid.,* pp. 222–23; Volk, *Reichskonkordat,* pp. 187–92).
66. Brief Kardinal Bertrams an die deutschen Bischöfe, August 1, 1933, Müller, *Dokumente,* pp. 175–76; Volk, *Kirchliche Akten,* pp. 194, 287–88.
67. Kaas conveyed Pacelli's wishes to the archbishop of Freiburg, who raised the question at the Fulda conference (Müller, *Dokumente,* pp. 185–90).
68. Ibid., p. 186; for the minutes of the Fulda meeting, see Stasiewski, *Akten,* 1: 321.
69. Müller, *Dokumente,* p. 190.
70. Volk, *Kirchliche Akten,* pp. 244–49; Stasiewski, *Akten,* 1: 388–91, 394.
71. *DGFP,* C, 1: 782–89; Albrecht, *Notenwechsel,* 1: 390–97; see also Pacelli's pro memoria of October 19, 1933, *DGFP,* C, 2: 24–28; Conrad, *Kampf um die Kanzeln,* p. 74.
72. Editors' note, *DGFP,* C, 1: 790; Kupper, *Staatliche Akten,* pp. 381–84. Some minor textual corrections had been necessary in the concordat as signed on July 20 (ibid., pp. 317, 325–26, 335, 340–41, 349). The text as finally ratified is given on pp. 384–408; on the ratification of the secret annex, see pp. 423, 430–31.
73. On the Pacelli-Klee discussions, see *DGFP,* C, 1: 793–94; Kupper, *Staatliche Akten,* pp. 411–13. At this time Klee submitted a detailed memorandum on the Jewish question in Germany to papal undersecretary Pizzardo. Among other things, he pointed out that the Jesuit order in 1593 had forbidden taking descendants of Jews into their order. In 1608 this exclusion was restricted to Jews of the fifth degree, in 1923 to the fourth degree. This, he pointed out, was even more restrictive than the German laws (ibid., pp. 418–19).
74. See the enthusiastic description of the service in *Katholisches Kirchenblatt für das Bistum Berlin,* September 24, 1933, as reprinted in Müller, *Dokumente,* pp. 202–6.
75. The Berlin party leaders had gone to the nuncio to arrange the celebration because

they felt they could expect nothing from the hierarchy (Gauleitung Gross Berlin to Reich Chancellor, August 23, 1933, BA, Reichskanzlei, R 43 II/174, pp. 84–86). Bertram refused Bishop Berning's suggestion that a general Te Deum be ordered for the whole Reich to mark the conclusion of the concordat. As Bertram put it: 'In das allgemeine Kling-Klang-Gloria einzustimmen, ist heute noch nicht die rechte Zeit. Das ist weder Undank von mir noch Miesmacherei, sondern nur ernste Sorge" (Bertram to Faulhaber, August 10, 1933, Volk, *Kirchliche Akten,* p. 220). As the service in Berlin was conducted by the nuncio, Faulhaber felt it sufficed for the whole Reich and refused to order thanksgiving services in Bavaria (ibid., p. 259). In Bavaria only the archbishop of Bamberg ordered a Te Deum (Stasiewski, *Akten,* 1: 395; Volk, *Reichskondordat,* pp. 186–87).

76. Festellungen zur Auslegung des Artikels 26 des Reichskonkordats, July 16/17, 1956, Schöppe, *Konkordate,* pp. 35–36.
77. Kirkpatrick to Vansittart, *DBFP,* Ser. 2, 5: 525. Even before the concordat was negotiated the officials at the Vatican had no illusions about its being observed, but concluded "es sei besser, das Konkordat zu unterzeichnen da man dann in Zukunft vor aller Welt die zu erwartende Vertragsbrücke als Verstösse gegen geschriebenes und feierlich anerkanntes Recht markieren könne, " (Morsey, *SZ* 167 [1960]: 16).
78. Johann Neuhäusler, *Saat des Bösen,* p. 24.
79. Von Papen, *Memoirs,* p. 282; see also Pius XII's statement on July 19, 1947, to Prelate Natterer, the secretary of the Bavarian organization of clerics, as quoted in Anton Scharnagl, "Das Reichskonkordat und die Länderkonkordate als Konkordats-system," *Historiches Jahrbuch* 74 (1955): 607; statements by von Papen and the pope as quoted in *KJ,* 1951, pp. 296–99; see also David C. Riede, *The Official Attitude of the Roman Catholic Hierarchy in Germany 1933–1945,* pp. 79–80, 609, 636–37.
80. Conversation with I. Kirkpatrick as reported to London, August 19, 1933, *DBFP,* ser. 2, 5: 524.
81. *Nazi Conspiracy and Aggression,* 5: 1039, Doc. 3268–PS; also *Trial of the Major War Criminals,* 16: 284.
82. Councillor Conrad stresses this point (*Kampf um die Kanzeln,* p. 34).
83. Von Papen to Hitler and von Neurath, July 4, 1933, *DGFP,* C, 1: 636; see also 652; Kupper, *Staatliche Akten,* pp. 138, 245.
84. Von Neurath to Bergen, December 12, 1933, *DGFP,* C, 2: 210.

Chapter Thirteen

1. Conrad, *Kampf um die Kanzeln,* p. 71.
2. *DGFP,* C, 1: 928n; See also 782n. Buttmann had fully expected to start negotiations with Pacelli at Rorschach (Volk, *Kirchliche Akten,* pp. 249, 262).
3. Conrad, *Kampf um die Kanzeln,* p. 71.
4. Nuncio Torregrossa to State Minister Esser, October 2, 1933, Albrecht, *Notenwech-sel,* 1: 2–3; see also "Denkschrift zur Durchführung des Reichskonkordats in Bay-ern," pp. 3–8.
5. Conrad, *Kampf um die Kanzeln,* pp. 73–74.
6. Ibid., p. 74; Stasiewski, *Akten,* 1: 422; Kupper, *Staatliche Akten,* p. 418n. Repre-sentatives of the various Catholic organizations had met with Bishops Berning and Gröber in Freiburg on August 24, 1933, and attempted to draw up lists of the Catholic organizations (Volk, *Kirchliche Akten,* p. 346). There had been a similar meeting in Berlin on July 18, 1933 (ibid., pp. 174–77, 222–23).
7. Conrad, *Kampf um die Kanzeln,* p. 83; Stasiewski, *Akten,* 1: 473.
8. Bergen to Foreign Office, October 16, 1933, *DGFP,* C, 2: 4. If, as Bergen reported, Bertram "suggested a temperate procedure," the cardinal nevertheless had great forebodings about the future of the Catholic church in Germany. See his memoran-dum "Gedanken über die Gefahre, die auch nach Abschluss des Reichskonkordats der katholischen Kirche drohen," end of September, 1933, Volk, *Kirchliche Akten,* pp. 263–69.
9. *DGFP,* C, 2: 9n, 24n.
10. Papal Secretary of State to Bergen, October 19, 1933, *DGFP,* C, 2: 23–28.
11. Conrad, *Kampf um die Kanzeln,* p. 78; for a good account of the three-day confer-ence based on Buttmann's report, see pp. 76–82.

12. Text of concordat draft as given *DGFP*, C, 1: 631.

13. Conrad, *Kampf um die Kanzeln,* p. 80.

14. "Persönliches Aide-Mémoire des Kardinalstaatssekretärs Pacelli," October 28, 1933, Albrecht, *Notenwechsel,* 1: 18–19; the three notes are given pp. 14–19.

15. Hoche, *Gesetzgebung,* 5: 633–40.

16. BA, Adjutantur des Führers, NS 10/34, pp. 75–84.

17. Hoche, *Gesetzgebung,* 5: 736–37.

18. Ibid., 6: 334–36, Prussian ordinance of January 29, 1934; 8: 397–98, Reich ordinance of May 29, 1934; 14: 437–43, law of 1935.

19. BA, Reichskanzlei, R 43 II/174, pp. 194, 196–98; for other Catholic protests against sterilization, see Johann Neuhäusler, *Kreuz und Hakenkreuz,* 1: 44, 308; 2: 82, 124, 269, 320; see also the section "Kampf gegen das Sterilisierungsgesetz," in the Lagebericht of May/June, 1934, Boberach, *Berichte,* pp. 8–9.

20. Nicolaisen, *Kirchenpolitik,* 1: 169–70; the police order of September 19, 1933, is given pp. 129–30.

21. Müller, *Dokumente,* pp. 216–18.

22. Stasiewski, *Akten,* 1: 436, 442.

23. Ibid., 1: 440–41; Müller, *Dokumente,* p. 219.

24. On December 18, 1933, Buttmann told Pacelli: "The mood of the Reich Chancellor has been very much depressed by these [electoral manifesto] publications" (*DGFP*, C, 2: 240). On the whole controversy about the bishops' electoral statement, see Volk, *Bayerische Episkopat,* pp. 149–62; excerpts from the Bavarian minister president's critical statement are given in Nicolaisen, *Kirchenpolitik,* 1: 175–77.

25. Albrecht, *Notenwechsel,* 1: 19–23, 29–37.

26. Bergen reported to the Foreign Office on December 1, 1933, that at the Vatican they considered the withdrawal from the League and the Disarmament Conference "ein sehr gewagter Schritt," the result of which could not be easily foreseen. They could not understand the situation in Bavaria where the publication of the Hirtenbrief was forbidden (Reichskanzlei, T120, R. 5718, K621882).

27. See chap. 7, "Crisis Among the German Christians," above; *DGFP*, C, 2: 240.

28. Quoted in Volk, *SZ* 177 (1966): 183. Faulhaber gave the royalty from the printing of his Advent sermons to the National Socialist Winterhilfswerk (ibid., p. 184). See also Volk, *Bayerische Episkopat,* pp. 170–72; Zipfel, *Kirchenkampf,* pp. 278, 294; Gallin, *Journal of Church and State* 12 (1970): 396; Greive, *Theologie und Ideologie,* p. 202. Faulhaber was accused by a Nazi paper in November, 1934, of preaching a sermon against the persecution of the Jews, but "alas, the words put in his mouth were never uttered" (Corsten, *Kölner Aktenstücke,* pp. 45–46; see also Boberach, *Berichte,* pp. 7–8).

29. Stasiewski, *Akten,* 1: 445, 452–55, 463–64, 476–82.

30. Ibid., 1: 482–83.

31. *DGFP*, C, 2: 172, 210, 240; Ausw. A., T120, R. 3312, E581433–40.

32. *DGFP*, C, 2: 240.

33. Ibid, p. 246; see also pp. 244–45, Stasiewski, *Akten,* 1: 441.

34. *DGFP*, C, 2: 245, 247.

35. Bergen to Foreign Office, December 27, 1933, ibid., p. 277.

36. See chap. 7, "Towards a Restoration of Order," above.

37. Bergen to Foreign Office, December 28, 1933, *DGFP*, C, 2: 283–85; see also 339–44; Albrecht, *Notenwechsel,* 1: 37–44, with useful footnotes. On January 31, 1934, Göring sent Hitler a list of political misdemeanors of Catholic clergy which indicated to Göring that there was still a solid bloc of clergymen who were opposed to the goals and ideas of the National Socialist state (BA, Reichskanzlei, R 43 II/174, p. 195).

38. See chap. 7, "Towards a Restoration of Order," above.

39. Albrecht, *Notenwechsel,* 1: 47–71; Neurath to Bergen, January 31, 1934, *DGFP*, C, 2: 440–42; see also pp. 451–52.

40. Lewy, *Catholic Church and Nazi Germany,* p. 120. Cardinal Schulte did tackle Hitler about hs support of Rosenberg, but Hitler sidestepped the issue (Stasiewski, *Akten,* 1: 539–40).

41. NSDAP, T81, R. 185, 0334903. Nicolaisen, *Kirchenpolitik,* 2: 35–38.

42. For Buttmann's report, see Nicolaisen, *Kirchepolitik,* 2: 39–55. Conrad, Buttmann's colleague in the Ministry of the Interior, gives a good account of this conference in *Kampf um die Kanzeln,* pp. 106–8.

43. Gauger, *Kirchenwirren,* 1: 136; Boberach, *Berichte,* p. 5. Ernst Bergmann's *Die Deutsche Nationalkirche* was placed on the Index at the same time (Reichskanzlei, T120, R. 5718, K621895–97, K621909–10).

44. Schirach to von Papen, February 20, 1934, *DGFP,* C, 2: 519; Conrad, *Kampf um die Kanzeln,* p. 108; Lawrence D. Walker, *Hitler Youth and Catholic Youth 1933–1936,* pp. 94–96.

45. As quoted in Conrad, *Kampf um die Kanzeln,* p. 109. At the Ministry of the Interior it was thought inevitable that the Catholic youth would be "sucked up into the Hitler Youth" (Aufzeichnung, March 7, 1934, Ausw. A., T120, R. 3312, K581228). For a list of Catholic youth organizations with notes as to date of their founding, uniforms, officers, etc., see the compilation by the security police of the SS, September, 1935, Boberach, *Berichte,* pp. 118–52. In 1936 there were 27 German Catholic youth organizations with a membership of around 1,500,000. Youths were at times members of several organizations, and so are often counted more than once, but even so it is clear that a large number of young people were involved (Jan C. Ruta and Johannes Straubinger, *Die katholische Kirche in Deutschland und ihre Probleme,* p. 139).

46. NSDAP, T81, R. 185, 0335165.

47. Bergen to von Neurath, March 29, 1934, *DGFP,* C, 2: 693.

48. Ibid., p. 249n.

49. Schulte had submitted a whole series of grievances in February, 1934, which the state claimed were largely misunderstandings. Schulte considered sending a man to Cologne to discuss matters to be the first serious attempt to settle differences (BA, Reichskanzlei, R 43 II/174, pp. 262–96).

50. Buttmann's report in Nicolaisen, *Kirchenpolitik,* 2: 96–108; Conrad, *Kampf um die Kanzeln,* pp. 109–10; Ausw. A., T120, R. 3312, E581487; Walker, *Hitler Youth,* pp. 103–4.

51. On this incident, see especially the report of the Bischöfliches Ordinariat Würzburg, April 10, 1934, and the "Auszug aus dem Halbmonatsbericht des Regierungspräsidenten von Unterfranken und Aschaffenburg," April 19, 1934, NSDAP, T81, R. 185, 0335089–93, 0335126–27; see also 0335090, 0335094–99, 0335116–18; Volk, *Bayerische Episkopat,* pp. 190–95.

52. NSDAP, T81, R. 185, 0335102–3.

53. Albrecht, *Notenwechsel,* 1: 111–17; Stasiewski, *Akten,* 1: 677, 716.

54. No representative of the Bavarian episcopate was included, but Faulhaber was instructed to draw up a letter of protest to Hitler. He did, but the three bishop delegates, in the interest of furthering their negotiations, asked that it not be sent. But the letter as drafted remains a testimonial to the Munich cardinal's forthrightness (draft letter in Stasiewski, *Akten,* 1: 717–25; for the minutes of the Fulda meeting, see pp. 676–704; see also Ausw. A., T120, R. 3312, E581487; Volk, *Bayerische Episkopat,* pp. 198–99).

55. Stasiewski, *Akten,* 1: 665; Lewy, *Catholic Church and Nazi Germany,* p. 121.

56. Albrecht, *Notenwechsel,* 1: 137; for the whole pro memoria see pp. 125–64; priests were arrested for stating this song was sung, Guertner's Dairy, Ex. 858, 3751 PS, pp. 281, 355; for other examples of antichurch literature used in youth groups and Protestant protests, see Kolb, *Schüler-Bibel-Kreise,* pp. 102–3.

57. Ausw. A., T120, R. 3312, E581451–53, E581483.

58. See the excellent account of these religious demonstrations and the planned counteroffensive of the police in Walker, *Hitler Youth,* pp. 101, 107–19; see also Schellenberger, *Katholische Jugend,* pp. 128–29.

59. Conrad, *Kampf um die Kanzeln,* p. 115; Ausw. A., T120, R. 3312, K581485–86.

60. Material on this conference is to be found BA, Reichskanzlei, R 43 II/176a, pp. 86–93; Ausw. A., T120, R. 3312, E581488–89; Stasiewski, *Akten,* 1: 737–38; Schellenberger, *Katholische Jugend,* pp. 48–50.

61. Stasiewski, *Akten,* 1: 738–39; Ausw. A., T120, R. 3312, E581490–91; Conrad, *Kampf um die Kanzeln,* p. 116.

62. Memorandum by Menshausen, June 30, 1934, *DGFP,* C, 3: 109–11; for Berning's account of the interview, see Stasiewski, *Akten,* 1: 731–32. Berning stated to the press that Hitler had given assurances about protecting Christian beliefs and would oppose the neopagan movements (BA, Reichskanzlei, R 43 II/180, p. 2). He again referred to these assurances when he protested against further attacks on Christian beliefs on August 1, 1935 (ibid., R 43 II/150, p. 27).

63. For the terms of the agreements, see Ausw. A., T120, R. 3312, E581493–500;

DGFP, C, 3: 109–11; Stasiewski, *Akten,* 1: 744–46; Conrad, *Kampf um die Kanzeln,* pp. 140–43.

64. Conrad, *Kampf um die Kanzeln,* p. 117; *DGFP,* C, 3: 410–11; Stasiewski, *Akten,* 1: 752–53.

65. Bergen to Foreign Office, July 31, 1934, BA, Reichskanzlei, R 43 II/176a, p. 98.

66. Klausner had no doubt been placed on the death list because as the leader of Catholic Action he was considered a declared enemy of the regime. Furthermore, until 1931 he had been head of the police bureau of the Prussian Ministry of the Interior and was privy to many illegal NSDAP actions which the party must have been anxious to conceal. See the account of his murder in Lothar Gruchmann, "Erlebnisbericht Werner Punders über die Ermordung Klausners am 30. Juni 1934 und ihre Folgen," *VZ* 19 (1971): 405–31. The church authorities made numerous inquiries about Klausner's death. Plans to transfer his remains to the Matthias Friedhof and erect a station of the cross there were given up after direct intervention by the Führer, as was a suit by Klausner's wife for monthly compensation, a suit which would have raised questions about the circumstances of his death and no doubt would have shown that he did not commit suicide as the Nazis maintained (Lammers to Bishop Barres, February 16, 1935, BA, Reichskanzlei, R 43 II/175, pp. 291–92; Adjutantur des Führers, NS 10/162, pp. 181–89). The church authorities had shown from the beginning that they rejected the official version of suicide by giving Klausner a full church burial, which they would not have done for a suicide or for one who had been cremated (Zipfel, *Kirchenkampf,* p. 65).

67. Stasiewski, *Akten,* 1: 760, 776–83.

68. Schöppe, *Konkordate,* pp. 304–12.

69. Ausw. A., T120, R. 3312, E581501–4; Nicolaisen, *Kirchenpolitik,* 2: 145–49.

70. On July 23, 1934, Pacelli submitted the curia's criticisms of the agreement to Bertram, who forwarded them to the bishops on July 31 (Stasiewski, *Akten,* 1: 762–69.

71. *DGFP,* C, 3: 387–90; BA, Reichskanzlei, R 43 II/176a, pp. 103–9; Conrad, *Kampf um die Kanzeln,* p. 129.

72. Köpke to the Embassy to the Holy See, September 21, 1934, *DGFP,* C, 3: 422–23.

73. See chap. 9, "*Gleichschaltung* and Attacks on Church Leaders," above.

74. Nicolaisen, *Kirchenpolitik,* 172–74; Bergen to Foreign Office, September 28, 1934, Ausw. A., T120, R. 3312, E581250; see also E581247, E581252.

75. Bergen to Foreign Office, October 12, 1934, *DGFP,* C, 3: 478.

76. See chap. 9, "*Gleichschaltung* and Attacks on Church Leaders," above. At this time there were also difficulties over the defamation of Cardinal Schulte. A certain druggist named Weber, in a speech to a party gathering, charged that the cardinal had inscribed an erotic book and sent it to a Jewess who was his mistress. The metropolitan chapter at Cologne complained on October 24, 1934, and after prolonged investigation in which Bormann had a hand, it was acknowledged that the statement was false. The metropolitan chapter was informed on February 25, 1935, that the charges were withdrawn on the direction of Hitler (BA, Reichskanzlei, R 43 II/175, pp. 205–21).

77. Nicolaisen, *Kirchenpolitik,* 2: 215; Conrad, *Kampf um die Kanzeln,* p. 130; *DGFP,* C, 3: 646, 672, 686–88; BA, Reichskanzlei, R 43 II/176a, p. 143.

78. Ausw. A., T120, E581507, E581510–11; *DGFP,* C, 3: 687; BA, Reichskanzlei, R 43 II/176a, pp. 154–55; Nicolaisen, *Kirchenpolitik,* 2: 234–36.

79. Köpke to the Embassy to the Holy See, January 31, 1935, *DGFP,* C, 3: 890; Nicolaisen, *Kirchenpolitik,* 2: 247–48.

80. Von Neurath had seen the nuncio on January 26, 1935. His summary of the conversation was sent to Lammers on January 28, who submitted it to Hitler. Von Neurath was informed of Hitler's refusal to make a public declaration on February 2. On February 4 Hitler asked to see again the June 29 agreement and the draft of his proposed public statement. On February 15 he underlined in red the points of the June 29 agreement he now objected to. This underlined document is, however, not on this roll of film, nor in the Reichskanzlei documents in the Bundesarchiv as far as I could discover (see Ausw. A., T120, R. 3312, E581514–16; BA, Reichskanzlei, R 43 II/176a, pp. 163–66). Hitler's objections were communicated orally to Secretary Pfundtner in the Ministry of the Interior by the Reich Chancellery office (notation on back of p. 166, *ibid.*). For the underlined phrases, see Nicolaisen, *Kirchenpolitik,* 2: 261, n. 3. The same day, February 15, 1935, Hitler attended a dinner given by the nuncio in honor of the anniversary of the pope's coronation,

part of the festivities then being staged by Berlin Catholics (Heinz Hürten, ed., Deutsche Briefe 1934–1938, 1: 218).

81. *DGFP*, C, 4: 55–57; Albrecht, *Notenwechsel*, 1: 226–28; BA, Reichskanzlei, R 43 II/176a, pp. 167–70.
82. *DGFP*, C, 4: 286–91; Albrecht, *Notenwechsel*, 1: 246–50.
83. Reichsführer SS, T175, R. 193, 2732249; Müller, *Dokumente*, pp. 330–36; Bernard Vollmer, *Volksopposition im Polizeistaat*, p. 151.
84. Alfred Rosenberg, *An die Dunkelmänner unser Zeit;* Seraphim, *Rosenbergs Tagebuch*, p. 50.
85. See Lewy, *Catholic Church and Nazi Germany*, pp. 133–50.
86. BA, Reichskanzlei, R 43 II/175, pp. 317–87; Guertner's Diary, Ex. 848, 3751-PS, pp. 313, 369.
87. See chap. 9 at n. 73, above.
88. Nicolaisen, *Kirchenpolitik*, 2: 331–32; Pacelli to Bergen, July 10, 1935, BA, Reichskanzlei, R 43 II/176a, pp. 173–79; see also an article in the *Osservatore Romano*, July 10, 1935, pp. 181–86. On the express orders of the pope, the *Osservatore Romano* issued two further articles on the Münster speech (ibid., pp. 195–205). See also Albrecht, *Notenwechsel*, 1: 254–59; for Bergen's answer submitted on September 18, 1935, see pp. 268–70; Lewy, *Catholic Church and Nazi Germany*, p. 128.
89. The Runderlass is published in Albrecht, *Notenwechsel*, 1: 259n–262n. Some press reports about it led to a sharp protest note from Pacelli to Bergen, July 26, 1935, ibid., 1: 259–68.
90. Müller, *Dokumente*, pp. 360–61; see also Walker, *Hitler Youth*, pp. 139–40; Rhodes, *The Vatican*, pp. 189–92.
91. Ausw. A., T120, R. 3312, E581515–16.
92. Conrad, *Kampf um die Kanzeln*, pp. 133–34.
93. See chap. 9, "The Establishment of the Ministry For Church Affairs," above.

Chapter Fourteen

1. See chap. 10, "Kerrl's Appointment of Church Committees," above.
2. Kerrl to Bertram, April 7, 1937, *DGFP*, D, 1: 947.
3. Lewy, *Catholic Church and Nazi Germany*, p. 130; Schellenberger, *Katholische Jugend*, pp. 54–55.
4. Denkschrift der deutschen Bischöfe an Hitler, August 20, 1935, Müller, *Dokumente*, pp. 364–89.
5. Gemeinsamer Hirtenbrief der deutschen Bischöfe, August 28, 1935, ibid., p. 395.
6. Aus der Proklamation des Führers vom 11 September 1935, NSDAP, T81, R. 185, 0335248. Domarus, *Hitler Reden*, 1: 525–26, does not have the first sentence of this quotation.
7. Hoche, *Gesetzgebung*, 15: 49–54; see also "Reich Jews' Status as defined by Frick," *New York Times*, January 19, 1936.
8. As quoted in Greive, *Theologie und Ideologie*, p. 200. On the lack of Catholic protest against anti-Jewish measures during this period, see Nora Levin, *The Holocaust*, pp. 502–6.
9. Faulhaber to Pacelli, April 10, 1933, Volk, *Kirchliche Akten*, p. 11. On April 29, 1933, Faulhaber notified the Bavarian bishops that he had discussed with Reichsstaathalter Epp what could be done for the Christian Jews so that they would not be affected by the anti-Jewish laws. Each bishop was asked to find out how many Christian Jews there were in his diocese, and Faulhaber added: "The matter must naturally be handled very discreetly so that no counteraction may set in before a decision is quietly reached" (Stasiewski, *Akten*, 1: 123); see also Legge's letter to Bertram, May 14, 1933, ibid., p. 141; "Stellungsnahme zum Boykott vom 1. April 1933," in Doetsch, *Württembergs Katholiken*, pp. 137–38. On the failure of the Catholic church to protest against the boycott and the Aryan paragraph in 1933, see Boyens, *Kirchenkampf und Ökumene, 1933–1939*, pp. 82–83.
10. Gröber to Leiber, April 15, 1933, Volk, *Kirchliche Akten*, p. 18. For Gröber's attitude towards racism, see Greiber, *Theologie und Ideologie*, pp. 203–4. Greiber writes: "Von den katholischen Bischöfen ging in der Betonung des Rassischen am weitesten Konrad Gröber."
11. Directive of November 11, 1933, Corsten, *Kölner Aktenstücke*, p. 16.

12. Lagebericht, May/June, 1934, Boberach, *Berichte,* p. 7.
13. Klee to the Foreign Office, September 12, 1933, *DGFP,* C, 1: 793–94.
14. Note of July 10, 1933, Albrecht, *Notenwechsel,* 1: 254–59; note of September 18, 1933, pp. 268–70; note of July 26, 1933, pp. 259–68; note of December 16, 1933, pp. 280–87. Differences between the Ministry of Church Affairs and the Foreign Office in part accounted for the delay in replying; Kerrl had "drawn up the answer personally weighing every word." Von Neurath suggested changes which Kerrl rejected, and von Neurath reluctantly agreed to send the reply in its original form. The Foreign Office was dilatory, and Kerrl complained about the delay of the answer for over six weeks (Ausw. A., T120, R. 3312, E581385–87; for the original note with suggested revisions, see E581295–356).
15. Hoche, *Gesetzgebung,* 3: 633–40; 14: 437–43; Lewy, *Catholic Church and Nazi Germany,* pp. 258–63.
16. Helmreich, *Religious Education,* pp. 172–77.
17. The morality trials began with processes against the Lay Congregation of the Franciscan Brothers of Waltbreitbach in the Rhineland. For the beginning of the trials and the procedures followed, see Hans G. Hockerts, *Die Sittlichkeitsprozesse gegen Katholische Ordensangehörige und Priester 1936/1937,* pp. 4–62; for the numbers involved, see pp. 48–62, 217; see also *The Persecution of the Catholic Church in the Third Reich,* pp. 295–325.
18. Müller, *Dokumente,* pp. 341–42.
19. On the pope's concern, see Guertner's Diary, E. 858, 3751-PS, p. 794, December 2, 1935; Bergen to Foreign Office, December 6, 1935, BA, Reichskanzlei, T120, R. 5718, K622059–72; see also note of January 21, 1936, Ausw. A., T120, R. 3312, E581626–27. On October 8, 1935, Bergen had been instructed to tell the cardinal secretary of state that the action against the bishop of Meissen would be carried on very circumspectly (BA, Reichskanzlei, R 43 II/175, p. 651). The bishop was not convicted for currency violations but was fined for negligence (Walter Adolph, *Kardinal Preysing und zwei Diktaturen,* p. 31).
20. BA, Adjutantur des Führers, NS 10/228, pp. 192–96.
21. Mommsen, *VZ* 10 (1962): 74–75; Meier, *Kirche und Judentum,* p. 7; Eliahu Ben-Elissar, *La diplomatie du IIIe Reich et les juifs (1933–1939),* pp. 163–89.
22. Mitteilungen zur Weltanschaulichen Lage, NSDAP, T81, R. 43, 20503–12.
23. Foreign Office to Embassy at the Holy See, April 7, 1937, *DGFP,* D, 1: 945. "From January 1, 1936, to March 31, 1937, alone, the Ministry of Ecclesiastical Affairs received from the Reich Ministry of Justice 2,877 notices of criminal proceedings being instituted for punishable acts of Catholic clerics" (Kerrl to Bertram, April 7, 1937, ibid., 1: 948).
24. Lewy, *Catholic Church and Nazi Germany,* p. 207.
25. Volk, *SZ* 177 (1960): 187; on the whole interview, see pp. 186–88; see also Gallin, *Journal of Church and State* 12 (1970): 399; Hockerts, *Sittlichkeitsprozesse,* pp. 71–72.
26. Lewy, *Catholic Church and Nazi Germany,* pp. 209–10.
27. Neuhäusler, *Saat des Bösen,* p. 26.
28. Neuhäusler, *Kreuz und Hakenkreuz,* 2: 94–98.
29. Adolph, *Preysing,* pp. 72–73. See the excellent Vorbemerkung containing bibliographical references to Faulhaber's draft and the final version of the encyclical in Albrecht, *Notenwechsel,* 1: 402–3; see also B. Schneider, "Kardinal Faulhaber und die Enzyklika 'Mit brennender Sorge'," *SZ* 175 (1964–65): 226–28. Bergen was wrong when he reported that the encyclical had been prepared by the pope during his stay at Castel Gandolfo in the summer of 1936 (Bergen to Foreign Office, April 1, 1937, *DGFP,* D, 1: 640).
30. The entire encyclical was too long to be read at the March 23 (Palm Sunday) services. In the archdiocese of Cologne specific instructions were issued as to what sections were to be read; the remaining sections were read later at services during Holy Week (Corsten, *Kölner Aktenstücke,* p. 174; the text is given pp. 174–86; English translation in *Persecution of the Catholic Church,* pp. 523–37).
31. Between September 25, 1933, and June 26, 1936, the papacy had prepared three white books containing notes and other documents that had been sent to Germany, and the German Foreign Office was anxious to prevent their publication (Neuhäusler, *Kreuz und Hakenkreuz,* 2: 27; Bergen to Foreign Office, March 23, 1937, *DGFP,* D, 1: 934–35; William M. Harrigan, "Nazi Germany and the Holy See, 1933–1936. The Historical Background of 'Mit brennender Sorge,' " *CHR* 47 [1961]: 193).

32. *DGFP*, D, 1: 935; see also Adolph, *Preysing*, pp. 79–81.
33. *DGFP*, D, 1: 935. The ban was not effective. The encyclical was sold in many churches; in the Munich-Freising diocese there was supposedly an edition of 41,300, and all churches and monasteries received 200 to 1,000 copies; 5,000 copies were sent to Eichstätt, 4,000 to Würzburg, and 2,000 to Regensburg (Witetschek, *Kirchliche Lage in Bayern*, 1: 219; 2: 126).
34. Reich Ministry of Church Affairs, October 1, 1936, Besetz. Gebiete, T454, R. 81, 000541. In Bavaria the police seized the August 29, 1935, diocesan Amtsblatt because it printed the bishops' August 8 letter. On August 31, 1935, a directive from Berlin ordered that the seizure be rescinded and the confiscated numbers returned (NSDAP, T81, R. 184, 0334698–99). On the other hand, in October, 1935, the translation and publication in the church Amtsblätter of articles from the *Osservatore Romano* was forbidden (Besetz. Gebiete, T454, R. 81, 000635).
35. Bayerische Politische Polizei, May 6, 1935, Schumacher, T580, R. 41; Sicherheitspolizei, Munich, July 13, 1939, NSDAP, T81, R. 184, 0333864; Nicolaisen, *Kirchenpolitik*, 2: 188, 233. Practices varied however. It was forbidden to print *Mit brennender Sorge* in some of the Amtsblätter; the police also entered three churches to confiscate it and in one instance stopped the priest from reading it (pro memoria of nuncio, April 5, 1937, *DGFP*, D, 1: 944–45).
36. NSDAP, T81, R. 184, 0334783–84.
37. As translated in *Persecution of the Catholic Church*, p. 524.
38. Von Neurath to Bergen, March 25, 1937, and German Foreign Office to various diplomatic missions, March 26, 1937, *DGFP*, D, 1: 937.
39. Albrecht, *Notenwechsel*, 2: 1n; Corsten, *Kölner Aktenstücke*, p. 189; Bertram to Foreign Office, March 27, 1937, *DGFP*, D, 1: 938–39; pro memoria of nuncio, April 5, 1937, ibid., 1: 943–45.
40. Kerrl to Bertram, April 7, 1937, *DGFP*, D, 1: 945–49; Kerrl to Foreign Office, April 9, 1937, ibid., 950–51; German Foreign Office to various diplomatic missions, April 15, 1937, ibid., 951–56; Pacelli to Bergen, April 30, 1937, ibid., 956–66; see also Albrecht, *Notenwechsel*, 2: 1–15.
41. Domarus, *Hitler Reden*, 1: 690–91.
42. Foreign Office to German Embassy at the Holy See, April 7, 1937, *DGFP*, D, 1: 945; Hockerts, *Sittlichkeitsprozesse*, p. 73.
43. Weizsäcker to German Embassy at the Holy See, *DGFP*, D, 1: 968–69; Albrecht, *Notenwechsel*, 2: 20–21, with extensive notes; Hockerts, *Sittlichkeitsprozesse*, pp. 150–51.
44. Text of the speech in the *Münchner Neueste Nachrichten*, May 29, 1937, to be found NSDAP, T81, R. 184, 0333637–38; the report of the Deutsche Nachrichtenbüro, May 29, 1937, BA, Reichssicherheitshauptamt, R 43 II/155a; for a discussion of Goebbel's speech, see Hockerts, *Sittlichkeitsprozesse*, pp. 112–18; Adolph, *Preysing*, pp. 87–89.
45. Germanicus's letter to Goebbels, n.d., NSDAP, T81, R. 184, 0333663–68; police report on Eichstätt, 0333682–83; for a discussion of the Germanicus letter see Hockerts, *Sittlichkeitsprozesse*, pp. 118–20. Michael Germanicus was the pseudonym used by Dr. Ludwig Winterswyl, a member of the staff of the newspaper *Germania* (Gerhart Binder, *Irrtum und Widerstand*, p. 360).
46. Bergen to Foreign Office, July 20, 1937, quoting from the *Osservatore Romano* of July 19–20, 1937, *DGFP*, D, 1: 989; see also pp. 968–81; 989–98; Albrecht, *Notenwechsel*, 2: 22–30.
47. Kerrl to Foreign Office, April 9, 1937, *DGFP*, D, 1: 950.
48. Kerrl to Hoffmann, February 3, 1940, NSDAP, T81, R. 185, 0335287–89.
49. Memorandum by Mackensen, June 30, 1937, *DGFP*, D, 1: 982–83.
50. Weizsäcker to Bergen, July, 1937, ibid., 995; Hockerts, *Sittlichkeitsprozesse*, p. 74. On May 3, 1937, Mussolini had advised settling differences with the Catholic church (*DGFP*, D, 1: 966). Ciano had advised against resumption of the trials of clerics on June 30, 1937 (Hassel to Foreign Office, June 30, 1937, DZA Potsdam, Nr.23316, reprinted in Mohr, *Katholische Orden*, p. 290).
51. Von Neurath to Kerrl, August 13, 1937, *DGFP*, D, 1: 998.
52. Memorandum by Mackensen, August 26, 1937; memorandum by Bismarck, August 27, 1937, ibid., pp. 1000–1001.
53. Bergen to Foreign Office, August 21, August 22, 1937, ibid., pp. 999–1000.
54. Memorandum by Mackensen, September 29, 1937, of a conversation with Kerrl at a parade at the Nürnberg rally, ibid., pp. 1005–6.

55. Editor's note, ibid., p. 1007.

56. Domarus, *Hitler Reden,* 1: 745; this was in line with Hitler's earlier remark to Rosenberg: "er sei von jeher Heide gewesen" (Seraphim, *Rosenbergs Tagebuch,* p. 32).

57. Bergen to Foreign Office, December 26, 1937, *DGFP,* D, 1: 1013–16.

58. Anordnung des Chefs des Sicherheitshauptamtes und der Sicherheitspolizei, SS-
Gruppenführer Heydrich für den Sicherheitsdienst des Reichsführers SS und die
Geheime Staatspolizei, July 1, 1937, Boberach, *Berichte,* pp. 905–6. The security
police of the SS had long concerned itself with church organizations, and in September, 1935, had prepared a special study listing the various Protestant and Catholic
organizations according to certain categories (ibid., pp. 104–95).

59. Neuhäusler, *Kreuz und Hakenkreuz,* 1: 361–82.

60. Hoche, *Gesetzgebung,* 11: 196–202. The use of restrictions on collections as a
means of harassing the churches is worth a monograph in itself. See the whole
folder on church collections, NSDAP, T81, R. 184, 0334492–668. At times special
collections were permitted and at other times were not, and the law had special
repercussions on the Catholic church. On January 17, 1935, the mendicant orders
were given permission to beg for their own livelihood and for their order (NSDAP,
T81, R. 184, 0334508). On August 20, 1936, the permission was withdrawn (ibid.,
0334563, 0334577, 0334580, 0334584–86). Setting up charity boxes, except in
church buildings or meeting rooms, for example in cemeteries, was forbidden
(ibid., 0334492, 0334640, 0334646). Special offering boxes could be used if they
were given out and returned at the same service; they could not be taken home and
returned later (ibid., 0334601, 0334617, 0334619, 0334650). The Benedictine
missionaries in a small Bavarian village, for example, were denied the privilege of
using a collection box on which there was a Negro figure who bowed his head
when a coin was dropped in the box (police order, Würzburg, September, 13,
1938, Schumacher, T580, R. 41).

61. Hoche, *Gesetzgebung,* 11: 153–56.

62. Ibid., 1: 236–37; see chap. 6, "Hitler Becomes Chancellor," above.

63. Ibid., 12: 676; see chap. 11 at n. 18 above. Unlike the Protestants, the Catholics
did not read from the pulpit the names of those who had withdrawn from the
church.

64. See chap. 20, below. A list of sects prohibited between 1933 and December 31,
1938, is given in J. S. Conway, *The Nazi Persecution of the Churches 1933–45,*
app. 11, pp. 370–74.

65. As given NSDAP, T81, R. 184, 0334780. On the bishops' regularly taking the oath,
see Reichsminister für Kirchliche Angelegenheiten, June 28, 1941, Besetz. Gebiete,
T454, R. 81, 000185. The Protestant churchmen in the end came to the same
doctrinal position on taking an oath to the Führer as the bishops (see chap. 11,
"The Oath of Loyalty and the Prayer for Peace," above).

66. NSDAP, T81, R. 184, 0334783–84, 0334786–88, 0334901.

67. Meldungen aus dem Reich, no. 310, August 20, 1942, Boberach, *Berichte,* pp.
712–15.

68. Mohr, *Katholische Orden,* pp. 137, 152.

69. *Persecution of the Catholic Church,* p. 56.

70. Hockerts, *Sittlichkeitsprozesse,* pp. 218–19; see also pp. 184–216.

71. Erklärung des Erzbishof von Köln zu den Sittlichkeitsprozessen, May 12, 1937, Corsten, *Kölner Aktenstücke,* pp. 200–202. Bishop Preysing of Berlin sent a long protest
to Goebbels on May 27, 1937, about the excessive propaganda concerning the trials.
He pointed out that out of 21,461 secular priests, there were 49 cases, or .23 percent;
out of 4,174 monastic priests, there were 9 cases, or .21 percent (BA, Reichskanzlei,
R 43 II/155, pp. 88–105; Adolph, *Preysing,* pp. 90–100; see also letter to Guertner,
pp. 100–104). See also Hockerts, *Sittlichkeitzprozesse,* pp. 147–83.

72. Nbg. Doc., 1506-PS.

73. Geheime Staatspolizeileitstelle München an Herrn Reichsstaathalter in Bayern, z.
Hd den Herrn Staatssekretärs Hoffmann, November 13, 1937, Besetz. Gebiete,
T454, R. 81, 000474.

74. Ibid., 000061; see also 000073–75, 000464, 000486–87.

75. Ibid., 000472, 000474.

76. Monatsbericht des Regierungspräsidenten von Oberfranken und Mittelfranken von
8 November 1937 für Oktober 1937, ibid., 000482.

77. Besetz. Gebiete, T454, R. 62, 001396.

78. Helmreich, *Religious Education,* pp. 165–69, 176–77. See also the protest notes of

the Vatican on curtailment of religious instruction by clerics (November 26, 1937) and on the closing of private schools (February 6, 1938) in Albrecht, *Notenwechsel,* 2: 66–69, 73–75, with detailed footnotes. The papal notes were not answered.

79. The order was issued on November 4, 1936, and rescinded on November 25, 1936. Bishop Galen had a statement of thanksgiving read in all churches on November 29 (Besetz. Gebiete, T454, R. 63, 001187–88; BA, Kanzlei Rosenberg, NS 8/256, pp. 1–5; for Galen's letter, Kanzlei Rosenberg, NS 8/152, pp. 153–54).

80. Reports from Koblenz police, April–June, 1939, Reichsführer SS, T175, R. 511, 9377644–45; Schumacher, T580, R. 41.

81. Bavarian bishops to Adolf Wagner, July 26, 1941, NSDAP, T81, R. 184, 0334090–92. Steps to remove crosses and religious pictures from schools were also undertaken at this time in other parts of Germany, particularly in the Neisse district in Cardinal Bertram's diocese. Bertram protested sharply to Lammers, October 4, 1941 (Nbg. Doc. 2131-PS).

82. On unrest among the people, see NSDAP, T81, R. 676, 5485155–57; Neuhäusler, *Kreuz und Hakenkreuz,* 1: 119–20; for various reports on the "Stop Erlass," see Schumacher, T580, R. 41.

83. Rosenberg to Bormann, November 28, 1941, Besetz. Gebiete, T454, R. 88, 001111–13. Bormann, who favored removing crucifixes, wrote in 1939 that great care should be taken in doing so; it should not be done by a nationwide order, but by local authorities wherever possible. It was often not worth the turmoil it caused (Bormann to Rust, Besetz. Gebiete, T454, R. 62, 001399; see also BA, Kanzlei Rosenberg, NS 8/121, p. 122). Göring and Goebbels also thought it unwise to remove the crucifixes and give the clergy a chance to stir up the people (Louis P. Lochner, *The Goebbels Diaries, 1942–1943* pp. 141–42). For more detail on the Bavarian crucifix conflict, see Edward N. Peterson, *The Limits of Hitler's Power,* pp. 216–21.

84. Walker, *Hitler Youth,* p. 145.

85. Ibid., pp. 161–62; Hoche, *Gesetzgebung,* 21: 549; Schellenberger, *Katholische Jugend,* pp. 87–90.

86. Corsten, *Kölner Aktenstücke,* pp. 217–18; on the organization of the Jungmännerverband, see Walker, *Hitler Youth,* pp. 26–29.

87. Walker, *Hitler Youth,* pp. 151–56; Schellenberger *Katholische Jugend,* pp. 169–75; Lewy, *Catholic Church and Nazi Germany,* pp. 131–32. In Bavaria the Marianische Jungfrauenkongregationen and the Bund Neudeustchland, a secondary school group, were also dissolved and their property confiscated (Neuhäusler, *Kreuz und Hakenkreuz,* 2: 302; Warloski, *Neudeutschland,* p. 194). For an evaluation of the hierarchy's position in the struggle over youth organizations, see L. D. Walker, "Le Concordat avec le Reich et les organisations de jeunesse," *Revue d'histoire de la deuxième guerre mondiale* 24 (1974): 13–16; Schellenberger, *Katholische Jugend,* pp. 113–15, 140–43, 178–79.

88. Walker, *Hitler Youth,* pp. 152–54; Schellenberger, *Katholische Jugend,* p. 178; Donald D. Wall, "The Reports of the Sicherheitsdienst on the Church and Religious Affairs in Germany, 1939–1944," *CH* 40 (1971): 446.

89. Nbg. Doc., 4975-NG.

90. See pertinent documents in Corsten, *Kölner Aktenstücke,* pp. 322–25.

91. NSDAP, T81, R. 184, 0333793–94, 0333796, 0333822. On September 30, 1938, it was ruled that processions inaugurated after 1931 were not traditional and permits for them were to be denied (Reichsführer SS, T175, R. 511, 9377200).

92. Stellvertreter des Führers, June 6, 1936, Schumacher, T580, R. 42.

93. For example, see the police reports on pilgrimages, Boberach, *Berichte,* pp. 686, 698–701, 881.

94. Neuhäusler, *Kreuz und Hakenkreuz,* 1: 293–94; 2: 281.

95. Monatsbericht der Geheimen Staatspolizei München, November 10, 1937, Besetz. Gebiete, T454, R. 81,000476–77.

96. Ibid., 000040, 000042, 000046, 000049, 000053; Nbg. Doc., 1477-PS.

97. On April 16, 1935, Coch, the German Christian bishop of Saxony, protested to Rust and Hess that the current Nazi publicity about Charlemagne slaying the Saxons was designed to bring Christianity into disrepute. He did not receive a satisfactory answer (Besetz. Gebiete, T454, R. 82, 000826–27, 000828–32).

98. Bergen to Foreign Office, January 3, 1938, March 14, 1935, Reichskanzlei, T120, R. 5718, K622006–7. On the almanac, see Neuhäusler, *Kreuz und Hakenkreuz,* 1: 212; Gauger, *Kirchenwirren,* 3: 460.

99. See Frick's order of January 3, 1938; Bormann's Erlass of March 11, 1938; Hess's Erlass of March 18, 1938, all in Schumacher, T580, R. 42. These orders were usually a reaffirmation of Hess's ordinance of October 13, 1933, establishing a policy of religious neutrality for the party and the state (Gauger, *Kirchenwirren*, 1: 106; see chap. 7, "Crisis Among the German Christians," above).

100. On church withdrawals, see chap. 11, "Efforts to Deconfessionalize the Party," above.

101. Neuhäusler, *Kreuz und Hakenkreuz*, 1: 193. There were certain exceptions to the general prohibition on double membership (Corsten, *Kölner Aktenstücke*, pp. 216–18).

102. Neuhäusler, *Kreuz und Hakenkreuz*, 2: 315.

103. Geheime Staatspolizei Düsseldorf, May 17, 1938, September 25, 1938, Reichsführer SS, T175, R. 408, 2931832, 2931845. If there were difficulties about double membership between the Hitler Youth and church organizations, there were also differences over whether the Hitler Youth could be members of Rosenberg's *Arbeitsgemeinschaft für die gesamte Schulung* and *Die Arbeitsgemeinschaft für deutsche Volkskunde*. Schirach had withdrawn the Hitler Youth from these organizations on October 28, 1938, but Rosenberg said he would have to cancel the withdrawal (Besetz. Gebiete, T454, R. 82, 001350, 001340–44, 001405–10).

104. Meldungen aus dem Reich (Nr.93), June 3, 1940, Boberach, *Berichte*, pp. 435–38; Geheime Staatspolizei Düsseldorf, October 21, 1941, Reichsführer SS, T175, R. 408, 2932089, also 2932191.

105. On protests, see Neuhäusler, *Kreuz und Hakenkreuz*, 2: 399–403. On increased church activity, see, for example, the report of the Leiter der Aussenstelle, Aschaffenburg, of June 21, 1941. He notes that in the district of Aschaffenburg there were 15–20 Catholic meetings a month in 1932, 50 a month in 1935, and 70 a month in 1937. The greater activity was manifest in the amount of electricity used, and 80 percent of the clergy now used automobiles or motorcycles. Pamphlet racks in the churches had increased 100 percent in the last two years, the monasteries were more active, the church press had expanded, membership in Catholic organizations had at least held its own since 1930–32, more altar boys were being trained, etc. (Schumacher, T580, R. 40).

106. Reichsführer SS, T175, R. 511, 9377724. The courier service was established about March, 1938 (9377696–9377731).

107. These travelling padres organized *Volksmissionen*, where a number of services were held in a short time. On surveillance of the padres, see Neuhäusler, *Kreuz und Hakenkreuz*, 1: 48; *Persecution of the Catholic Church*, pp. 65–69. In the monthly report of July, 1935, by party officials on the situation in the churches, these padres were referred to as a plague on the land. The report also stated that Catholic priests who supported the Nazi movement had virtually become museum pieces ("Die 'weisen Raben' nat. soz. gesinnter kath. Geistlichen sind fast zu einer Museumsangelegenkeit geworden," NSDAP, T81, R. 42, 18918).

108. On April 23, 1935, the Bavarian political police ordered that the appearance of a Jesuit in any district as a speaker was to be reported to headquarters at once; on July 25, 1935, orders went out that police should be on the lookout for Jesuits who were dropping "S.J." from their names (Schumacher, T580, R. 40). Friedrich Muckermann, one of the Jesuit padres who was forced into exile, was carefully watched, and his denunciations of the Nazi treatment of the church noted (BA, Reichskanzlei, R 43 II/155a). On the surveillance of the Jesuits, see also Neuhäusler, *Kreuz und Hakenkreuz*, 1: 159–64; Nbg. Doc., 3277-PS.

109. Mayer's arrest led the Vatican to send a protest note to the German government on November 16, 1937; it was never answered (Albrecht, *Notenwechsel*, 2: 61–63, with extensive footnotes). See also Otto Gritschneder, *Pater Rupert Mayer vor dem Sondergericht*. Mayer was later arrested again, placed in a concentration camp, and then "interned" in the monastery at Ettal in August, 1940, under strict Gestapo orders not to undertake any public activity (testimony of Rev. Rupert Mayer, October 13, 1945, *Nazi Conspiracy and Aggression*, 5: 1061–64, Doc. 3272-PS).

110. My translation from Besetz. Gebiete, T454, R. 81, 000129. The sermon was delivered on July 4, 1937, in Saint Michael's Church in Munich, and it is given in English translation in *Persecution of the Catholic Church*, App. 3, pp. 538–43. On March 5, 1937, Cologne diocesan authorities issued a statement to be read in all churches severely criticizing the classification *gottgläubig* and forbidding all Catholics to designate themselves as such (Corsten, *Kölner Aktenstücke*, pp. 172–73).

111. As quoted in Volk, *SZ* 177 (1966): 189.
112. Monatsbericht, Sicherheitsdienst Kochem, April/May 1939, Reichsführer SS, T175, R. 511, 9377642–43.
113. Besetz. Gebiete, T454, R. 82, 00718.
114. *Amtliches Schulblatt für den Regierungsbezirk Wiesbaden*, 1935, pp. 113–14.
115. Reichsführer SS, T175, R. 511, 9337692.
116. Besetz. Gebiete, T454, R. 82, 000755–56; see also chap. 11, "Efforts to Deconfessionalize the Party," above.
117. Neuhäusler, *Saat des Bösen*, pp. 66–67. Neuhäusler also gives a summary for the much smaller diocese of Meissen, p. 68, and statistics on what happened to the Catholic church in Tirol 1938–40, pp. 119–24. See also material from the Potsdam archives as given in Mohr, *Katholische Orden*, pp. 134–37.
118. Memorandum by Schwendemann, February 13, 1938, *DGFP*, D, 1: 1021–22.
119. In the summer of 1938, Pacelli practically stopped exchanging notes with Germany, only to resume after the start of World War II. Vatican notes to Germany: September, 1933–March, 1937, ca. 70; March, 1937–June, 1938, 19; June, 1938–March, 1939, 1; March, 1939–September, 1939, 1. The German notes were far fewer: September, 1933–March, 1937, ca. 30; March, 1937–June, 1938, 6; June, 1938–September, 1939, 0 (Albrecht, *Notenwechsel*, 2: xvii).
120. Memorandum by Haiden, March 9, 1938, *DGFP*, D, 1: 1025.
121. Reichsführer SS, March 14, 1938, NSDAP, T81, R. 184, 0334431; Reichsführer SS, T175, R. 408, 2931562; Neuhäusler, *Saat des Bösen*, p. 96.
122. BA, Reichskanzlei, R 43 II/149, pp. 68, 78.
123. Particularly the Austrian bishops' pastoral letter of December 22, 1933, *DGFP*, C, 2: 277–78; Boberach, *Berichte*, pp. 3–4; Albrecht, *Notenwechsel*, 1: 42–43, 45, 69, 95, 156–57, 159, 316–17; Ausw. A., T120, R. 3312, E581190–92, E581194–209; see also Ludwig Volk, "Die Fuldaer Bischofskonferenz von der Enzyklika 'Mit brennender Sorge' bis zum Ende der NS-Herrschaft," *SZ* 178 (1966): 241–47.
124. Bergen to Foreign Office, February 12, 1924, Ausw. A., T120, R. 3312, E581520–24 gives the history of this foundation; the film also contains much more material on the dispute over control of it. See also Bergen's reports of May 4, 1933, and June 2, 1933, Ausw. A., T120, R. 5720, K623866, K623881.
125. The Austrian Protestant churches were no less eager than the Catholics to welcome Hitler (see the statement issued by the Austrian Evangelical Oberkirchenrat, as quoted in Schwerin-Krosigk, *Es geschah in Deutschland*, p. 257). On July 21, 1938, the Austrian Protestant churches sent a letter of thanks to Hitler for the new marriage law issued on July 8, 1938. They particularly approved that divorce was now possible in Austria. An adulatory poem and paean of praise to Hitler was published in *Der Säemann, Evangelisches Kirchenblatt*, July 15, 1938, p. 90 (BA, Adjutantur des Führers, NS 10/109, pp. 212–13, 217).
126. Lewy, *Catholic Church and Nazi Germany*, p. 215. Cardinal Innitzer's welcoming statement as found in the Potsdam archives is reprinted in Mohr, *Katholische Orden*, p. 293; see also Adolph, *Preysing*, pp. 128–33. When the Vatican radio criticized the Austrian bishops' declaration, the German police were ordered to check whether the criticism was mentioned in church services, and every dissemination of the Vatican statement outside of church buildings was forbidden (Police, Bad Kreuznach to Bereich Birkenfeld, Schumacher T580, R. 41).
127. Lewy, *Catholic Church and Nazi Germany*, p. 213.
128. See the summary of the bishops' actions sent by the Ministry of Church Affairs to the Foreign Office, Mohr, *Katholische Orden*, pp. 292–93; for Bishop Preysing's critical attitude, see Adolph, *Preysing*, pp. 129–33. On April 3, 1938, Suffragan Bishop Eberle of Augsburg had written to all Bavarian bishops urging them to make a declaration on the election; there was never an easier time to invite a "happy yes." Eberle had been received at various times by Hitler and had tried to bring about a reconciliation between the government and the bishops. The Nazis considered him the most loyal to the state of all the bishops (BA, Reichskanzlei, R 43 II/155, pp. 110–31).
129. On July 23, 1938, the party had staged a big demonstration against Sproll, bringing 2,500–3,000 outsiders to Rottenburg; the people of the city did not participate. Archbishop Gröber of Freiburg, who was in the bishop's residence, was mistaken for Sproll and roughly handled. Much damage was done to the residence (Gestapo Berlin to Gestapo headquarters in Nürnberg, July 24, 1938, for immediate delivery by special courier to Villa Wahnfried [Hitler] in Bayreuth (*Nazi Conspiracy and*

Aggression, 3: 613, Doc. 848-PS). See also Paul Kopf and Max Miller, eds., *Die Vertreibung von Bischof Joannes Baptista Sproll von Rottenburg 1938–1945,* pp. 191–203, 265–67.

130. Binder, *Irrtum und Widerstand,* p. 299; see the excellent account of the whole incident, pp. 281–312; Kopf and Miller, *Sproll,* pp. 93–94, 287. Sproll had had previous clashes with the regime. On June 1, 1937, he had submitted such a sharp protest to the minister of education in Württemberg, Christian Mergenthaler, on the measures being taken in regard to religious instruction that the minister refused to receive it. The Vatican considered this action contrary to the provisions of the concordat and asked the Reich government for aid in settling the dispute. The government never answered (Kopf and Miller, *Sproll,* pp. 3, 30–43, Albrecht, *Notenwechsel,* 2: 40–45). On Mergenthaler's policy, see Helmreich, *Religious Education,* pp. 160, 169, 176, 188, 192–93.

131. Archbishop Schulte of Cologne had a protest against Sproll's exile read in all the churches of his archdiocese on September 4, 1938 (Corsten, *Kölner Aktenstücke,* p. 238); there was no united protest by the German hierarchy (Kopf and Miller, *Sproll,* pp. vii, 136–37, 139).

132. For diplomatic exchanges dealing with the Sproll incident, see Kopf and Miller, *Sproll,* pp. 223–30, 255–65; see also *DGFP,* D, 1: 1046–56; *Memoirs of Ernst von Weizsäcker,* p. 282. Kerrl had spoken with Hitler at Bayreuth and received permission to proceed against Sproll as he did (Kerrl to Lammers, August 18, 1938, BA, Reichskanzlei, R 43 II/155a, p. 134; there is a long report on the Sproll incident, pp. 99–164).

133. Memorandum on Matters Pending with the Vatican, drawn up by Counsel of Legation, Dr. Haidlen, June 9, 1938, *DGPF,* D, 1: 1043. There is a footnote to the document stating that the last item on the list was added by an unindentified hand: it was a topic that was certainly never raised by the Vatican.

134. See chap. 11, "The Oath of Loyalty and the Prayer for Peace," above.

135. *Völkischer Beobachter,* October 2, 1938, as reprinted in Mohr, *Katholische Orden,* p. 156; see also Lewy, *Catholic Church and Nazi Germany,* p. 218.

136. Mitteilungen zur Weltanschaulichen Lage, 4 Jahrgang, Nr. 23, October 10, 1938, Schumacher, T580, R. 41. Nevertheless, the security police of the SS were not pleased by the attitude of the church as a whole during the crisis (Boberach, *Berichte,* pp. 297–98, 304–5, 308–9, 356).

137. The amount of money the churches were receiving from the state was a recurrent theme used by state officials at this time. In Bavaria Adolf Wagner, in a speech in June, 1937, justifying the arrest of the Rev. Rupert Mayer, (see n. 109, above) cited the great sums the Bavarian churches were receiving from the state and observed that one might expect that a state which was so generous would not be attacked (*Völkischer Beobachter,* June 10, 1937, Besetz. Gebiete, T454, R. 81, 000496). The speech led to a protest note by the Vatican to the Reich government which received no answer (Albrecht, *Notenwechsel,* 2: 55–57).

138. Domarus, *Hitler Reden,* 2: 1058–60, 1067.

139. Bergen to Foreign Office, March 22, 1939, *DGFP,* D, 6: 74.

140. See the hour-by-hour account, Domarus, *Hitler Reden,* 2: 1144–47.

141. The Bavarian bishops had joined the Fulda conference in the summer of 1933, and the Austrian bishops in August, 1939.

142. On the fate of the Austrian concordat, see chap. 18, "The War and the Concordat," below. For a good brief summary of conditions in the Austrian church under Nazi rule, see Josef Wodka, *Kirche in Österreich,* pp. 380–84; see also Conway, *Nazi Persecution,* pp. 224–28, 393–97; Neuhäusler, *Saat des Bösen,* pp. 119–24.

143. Rundschreiben Nr. 127/39, June 26, 1939, NSDAP, T81, R. 204, 0357267; *Verfügungen/Anordnungen/Bekanntgaben,* 1: 226.

Chapter Fifteen

1. "Verhältnis von Nationalsozialismus und Christentum," *KJ,* 1933–44, pp. 470–72; *Trial of the Major War Criminals,* 35: 7–13, Doc. 075D. Bormann had written the letter in response to a request from a Gauleiter who was somewhat friendly to the church. Impressed by his own effort, Bormann on June 6–7, 1941, sent it to all Gauleiter. It was to be kept secret, but Gauleiter Erich Koch in Königsberg gave it to a friend, a pastor, who copied it and soon it had snowballed throughout

the Reich (Brunotte in Schmidt, *Gesammelte Aufsätze*, pp. 135–36). Bormann's

letter created such a stir that Hitler ordered him to recall and destroy it (*Trial of the Major War Criminals*, 21: 464). This letter was in line with a confidential statement (not to be published) which Bormann had issued on February 2, 1939, in which he cautioned party members not to make use of church vocabulary (copy of the order in Biel Arch., Coll. W. Niemöller, C-7, Neuheidentum I). On Bormann's general antichurch views, see also Walter Adolph, "Unveröffentlichte Bormann Akten über den Kirchenkampf," *Wichmann Jahrbuch*, 1953, pp. 125–30.

2. Hermelink, *Kirche im Kampf*, pp. 494–95. The July 24, 1940, statement is reprinted in Conway, *Nationalsozialistische Kirchenpolitik*, p. 375; it is not given in the English edition. See also statements by Kerrl and Lammers in Boberach, *Berichte*, p. 384n. In May, 1941, the minister of the interior directed that the July 24 statement should not be mentioned; the churches had apparently heard of it and were referring to it. While Hitler maintained his attitude on not disturbing the churches, he had recently approved measures which the churches considered hostile (BA, Reichskanzlei, 43 II/152, pp. 62, 67).

3. Brunotte in Schmidt, *Gesammelte Aufsätze*, p. 129.

4. Besetz. Gebiete, T454, R. 62, 000833–37; see also 000713; for Bormann's opposition to Müller, see 000919–20, 000926; Nbg. Doc., 100-PS.

5. Reprinted in Conway, *Nationalsozialistische Kirchenpolitik*, p. 378; the warning was repeated on April 26, 1943.

6. "An alle Reichsleiter und Gauleiter der NSDAP," August 24, 1941, *KJ*, 1933–44, pp. 467–68. On Goebbel's desire to avoid difficulties with the church during the war, see also Lochner, *Goebbels Diaries*, pp. 120, 142, 285, 374.

7. Boberach, *Berichte*, p. 935; for the minutes of the December meeting, see Boyens, *Kirchenkampf und Ökumene, 1939–1945*, pp. 333–40.

8. *KJ*, 1933–44, pp. 473–75; Klügel, *Landeskirche Hannovers*, p. 403; see also the Spiritual Council's telegram to Hitler pledging loyalty and support in the campaign against Russia, June 30, 1941 (*Gesetzblatt der Ev. Kirche Deutschlands*, 1941, p. 31; "Grusswort zu Beginn des neuen Jahres," ibid., 1942, p. 83). In general the state bypassed the churches at the start of the war. A contemporary statement by Pastor Walter Spitta on "Die Lage der Kirche und unsere Aufgabe, November 1939," pictures the situation correctly. His opening paragraph states: "Als der Krieg ausbrach wurde der evangelischen Kirche von den staatlichen Stellen keinerlei Beachtung geschenkt. Fürbittegottesdienste wurden nicht gewünscht. In dem Daseinskampf, in den unser Volk hineingeraten ist, wurde ihr vom Staat keine Aufgabe zugewiesen. Es scheint so, als hätte die Kirche aufgehört, für den Staat zu existieren. Auf das Volk ist durch die Not des Kreiges ein neues Verlangen, die christliche Botschaft zu hören nicht aufgebrochen" (Biel. Arch., Coll. W. Niemöller, D-6 Bek. Kirche im Kriege). For special prayers to be used in the Baden church, see *Gesetzes- und Verordnungsblatt Badens*, 1939, pp. 173–79; for Bavaria, see *Amtsblatt Landeskirche in Bayern*, 1939, p. 151. On the appointment of the Spiritual Confidential Council, see the last paragraph of chap. 11, above.

9. Brunotte in Schmidt, *Gesammelte Aufsätze*, pp. 123–24; Niemöller, *Kampf und Zeugnis*, pp. 489–90.

10. Klügel, *Landeskirche Hannovers*, p. 375.

11. Hermelink, *Kirche im Kampf*, p. 489; Niemöller, *Kampf und Zeugnis*, pp. 489–90. The Spiritual Confidential Council certainly never developed into a strong administrative body; the government officials under whom it functioned, notably Werner, saw to that. When Werner was called into the armed services in late 1941, Dr. Fürle was placed in charge of the church chancellery, and under him there was more cooperation with the council (Brunotte in Schmidt, *Gesammelte Aufsätze*, p. 131).

12. Brunotte in Schmidt, *Gesammelte Aufsätze*, pp. 125–45, 144–45; Klügel, *Landeskirche Hannovers*, pp. 381–96; for the Spiritual Confidential Council's protests on curtailment of religious instruction in the schools, see BA, Reichskanzlei, R 43 II/157, pp. 135–36, 147, 166–68.

13. Heinz Brunotte, *Die Evangelische Kirche in Deutschland*, p. 114.

14. Hermelink, *Kirche im Kampf*, p. 540; Klügel, *Landeskirche Hannovers*, pp. 410–12. An official summary gives the figures for October 1, 1941, as follows, with the total mobilized up to then in parentheses: Pfarrer und Ordinierten Hilfsgeistliche 6,141 (8,006); Nichtordinierte Hilfsgeistliche, Vikare, Kandidaten 993 (1,259); Kirchen-

beamte und Angestellte 758 (1,034); Kirchengemeindebeamte und Angestellte 3,007 (3,461); total, 10,849 (13,760). Called in as chaplains (*Kriegspfarrer*) October 1, 1941, 293 (total to that date, 351). There were also 1,008 (1,291) called for part-time (*nebenamtlich*) service in hospitals (BA, Reichskanzlei, R 43 II/156, pp. 72–73).

15. Klügel, *Landeskirche Hannovers,* p. 411; see also Schöppe, *Konkordate,* p. 35. Bormann refers to the need for equal treatment of Protestants and Catholics in his circular dispatch of November 2, 1944 (*Partei-Kanzlei Rundschreiben,* 374/44, November 2, 1944).

16. *Partei-Kanzlei Rundschreiben,* 32/43, February 19, 1943; 72/43, May 13, 1943; 374/44, November 2, 1944.

17. Hermelink, *Kirche im Kampf,* p. 602.

18. Ehrenforth, *Schlesische Kirche,* pp. 256–57.

19. Linck, *Kirchenkampf in Ostpreussen,* pp. 247, 256.

20. BA, Reichskanzlei, R 43 II/152, p. 51.

21. Klinger, *Dokumente,* p. 92.

22. From a summary dated February, 1940, Biel. Arch., Coll. W. Niemöller, D-6 Bek. Kirche im Krieg. This was part of a summons to pastors to recruit more ministerial candidates. One of the happier events of the war was that the theological faculties of all the universities agreed to follow the practices of Heidelberg, Jena, Tübingen, and Kiel and give up the degree of *Lizentraten der Theologie* in favor of a doctor of theology (Werner Weber, "Die Umwandlung des Lizentratengrades in den theologischen Doktorgrad," *ZevKR* 2 [1952–53]: 364–74). For slightly different figures on the number of theological students from those cited here, see NSDAP, T81, R. 7, 15448–57; see also the police report of June 15, 1942, Boberach, *Berichte,* pp. 681–84.

23. Helmreich, *Religious Education,* pp. 179–83; Klügel, *Landeskirche Hannovers,* p. 431.

24. Ibid., p. 473.

25. For example, see the directions for holding memorial services issued by the Protestant church in Württemberg, *Amtsblatt Landeskirche in Württemberg,* 1940, pp. 235–36; 1942, 136–38.

26. Reimers, *Lübeck im Kirchenkampf,* pp. 371–74.

27. See, for example, the fine tribute "Bewahrung der Pfarrfrauen" in Ehrenforth, *Schlesische Kirche,* pp. 262–64.

28. "Ausrüstung von Gemeindegliedern zum Dienst am Wort," *KJ,* 1933–44, pp. 393–96; see also the formulas for installation of lectors and deacons as liturgists and readers drawn up at the Tenth Confessing Synod of the Church of the Old Prussian Union (Niesel, *Bekenntnissynoden,* pp. 86–89). The province of Brandenburg alone had 150 *Leseprediger* during the war (Harder, in Schmidt, *Gesammelte Aufsätze,* p. 201); the *Lektoren* were particularly numerous in East Prussia (Linck, *Kirchenkampf in Ostpreussen,* pp. 247–49; on their use in Bavaria and elsewhere, see Boberach, *Berichte,* pp. 897–98).

29. The Tenth Confessing Synod of the Church of the Old Prussian Union in October, 1940, had requested that a study be prepared on the use of Vikarinnen (Niesel, *Bekenntnissynoden,* p. 84; see also decisions of the Tenth Synod, p. 94). The Church of Hamburg on November 8, 1927, had provided for use of theologically trained women. Under Nazi pressure this was cancelled on May 20, 1935 (*AK* 84 [1935]: 176).

30. *KJ,* 1933–44, pp. 390–91; Niesel, *Bekenntnissynoden,* pp. 97–98. The question of giving women voting rights in the church had been considered by the Iowa Synod of the Lutheran Church in the United States during World War I. For an expanded paper presented to the synod which gives many biblical citations on the place of women in the church, see C. L. Ramme, *Soll das Weib Schweigen?*

31. Helmreich, *Religious Education,* pp. 222–24.

32. See Bormann's instructions of May 9, 1939, September 25, 1940, and April 9, 1943, among the Bormann documents published by Adolph, *Wichmann Jahrbuch,* 1953, pp. 138–49.

33. Kerrl held that Hitler in his Reichstag speech of January 30, 1939, had made it impossible to use pressure to achieve a unification of the Protestant churches (Kerrl's letter to Stapel, September 6, 1939, and Rosenberg's reaction to it in Seraphim, *Rosenbergs Tagebuch,* pp. 148–54). On the abandonment of unification, see also Bormann's statement of March 8, 1940, Ngb. Doc., NO. 097; his statement of

July 12, 1940, Besetz. Gebiete, T454, R. 62, 000713; his letter to the Gauleiter on the relation of national socialism and Christianity of June 6 and 7, 1941, *Trial of the Major War Criminals,* 35: 7–13, Doc. 075D; Vermerk of August 16, 1941, referring to the changed situation since 1937: "der Führer hat entschieden dass Bestrebungen zur Schaffung einer Deutschen Ev. Kirche von amtlichen Stellen nicht unterstützt werden sollen" (BA, Reichskanzlei, R 43 II/156, p. 50). When Bormann informed Hitler that Kerrl, in spite of being told that the Führer was opposed, continued to formulate plans for a united Protestant church, Hitler told Bormann, "er wolle sich sofort nach Friedensschluss Herrn Minister Kerrl kommen lassen, um ihm das Notwendige zu sagen" (Bormann to Rosenberg, June 22, 1940, BA, Kanzlei Rosenberg, NS 8/184, p. 177). For Rosenberg's views, see his memorandum "Stellunghahme zu den Uebereinigungsplan der ev. Kirche an Hitler," June 18, 1940, ibid., pp. 178–81. On Kerrl's plans in 1940–41 to create a united church, see Brunotte in Schmidt, *Gesammelte Aufsätze,* pp. 129–31. On August 29, 1942, Hitler stated: "Only once in my life have I been stupid enough to try to unite some twenty different sects under one head; and God to whom be thanks, endowed my twenty Protestant Bishops with such stupidity, that I was saved from my own folly" (*Hitler's Secret Conversations,* p. 545).

34. Seraphim, *Rosenbergs Tagebuch,* p. 97; Picker, *Hitlers Tischgespräche,* pp. 96, 343, 353.

35. Ibid., pp. 348, 353.

36. Seraphim, *Rosenbergs Tagebuch,* p. 97; see also p. 32, where Rosenberg quotes Hitler as saying, "er sei von jeher Heide gewesen," but that these remarks were always kept a strict secret. In the Reichstag handbook of 1943, Hitler and Goebbels still listed themselves as Catholic (Zipfel, *Kirchenkampf,* p. 135n).

37. Meldungen aus dem Reich, no. 202, July 14, 1941, Boberach, *Berichte,* p. 528.

38. Domarus, *Hitler Reden,* 2: 1778–79.

39. Speer, *Memoirs,* p. 95.

40. Picker, *Hitlers Tischgespräche,* p. 372; see also Klügel, *Landeskirche Hannovers,* pp. 424–26; Niemöller, *Kampf und Zeugnis,* p. 495.

41. See Klügel, *Landeskirche Hannovers,* pp. 452–57; see also "Zur Jahreswende 1941/42" *KJ,* 1933–44, pp. 382–88.

42. Lothar Gruchmann, "Euthanasie und Justiz im Dritten Reich," *VZ* 20 (1972): 238; Klaus Dörner, "Nationalsozialismus und Lebensvernichtung," *VZ* 15 (1967): 139. Dörner has a good historical section on the principle of euthanasia in Germany prior to the Nazi period (pp. 121–37). On euthanasia see also Neuhäusler, *Kreuz und Hakenkreuz,* 1: 307–8, 2: 354–56. On the preparation and inauguration of the euthanasia program, see also Helmut Ehrhardt, *Euthanasie und Vernichtung "lebensunwerten" Lebens* pp. 24–25; for a good description of the 1941 proeuthanasia film "Ich klage an," see Adolph, *Preysing,* pp. 167–68. One of the arguments for the euthanasia program was that it would save money and manpower which could be used for better purposes. Gerhard Schmidt, however, has shown convincingly that it was not wartime necessity but National Socialist racial ideology which was in back of the program (*Selektion in der Heilanstalt 1939–1945,* pp. 33–35).

43. Gruchmann, *VZ* 20 (1972): 238–40; Dörner, *VZ* 15 (1967): 140–41; "Gesetz zur Verhütung erbkranken Nachwuchs," June 26, 1933, Hoche, *Gesetzgebung,* 14: 437–43. Hitler in 1928 wrote in favor of euthanasia for defective children (*Hitlers Zweites Buch,* ed. by Gerhard L. Weinberg [Stuttgart, 1961], p. 56).

44. *Trial of the Major War Criminals,* 26: 169, Doc. 630-PS; Hans Christoph von Hase, ed., *Evangelische Dokumente zur Ermordung der "unheilbar Kranken" unter der Nationalsozialistischen Herrschaft in den Jahren 1939–1945,* p. 9; Schmidt, *Selektion,* p. 35; Hans Bucheim, "Das Euthanasieprogramm," in *Gutachten des Instituts für Zeitgeschichte,* pp. 60–61.

45. Gruchmann, *VZ* 20 (1972): 242; a solicited letter of Pastor Braune to Herrn Oberstaatsanwalt bei dem Landgericht, Frankfurt/Main, September 12, 1946, Nbg. Doc. NO-895.

46. For such letters, see Neuhäusler, *Kreuz und Hakenkreuz,* 1: 312–13; Niemöller, *Kampf und Zeugnis,* p. 507.

47. Braune's personal account, NBG. Doc. NO-895. Gürtner until his death kept trying to stop the euthanasia killings (Dörner, *VZ* 15 [1967]: 144).

48. The Denkschrift is given *KJ,* 1933–44, pp. 415–23; Hase, *Evangelische Dokumente,* pp. 14–22. Many of the victims were gassed; others were given large doses of luminal (see Schmidt, *Selektion,* pp. 110–12, 128–45; see also Brunotte in

Schmidt, *Gesammelte Aufsätze,* 1: 125–26; Brunotte in Ködderitz, *August Marah-rens,* p. 93). The killings were carried out largely at Grafeneck in Württemberg, replaced in the spring of 1940 by Hadmar near Limburg; Brandenburg a. d. Havel, replaced in the spring of 1940 by Bernburg in Saxony-Anhalt; Hartheim near Linz; and Sonnenstein near Pirna (Gruchmann, *VZ* 20 [1972]; 243).

49. Braune's personal account, Nbg. Doc. NO-895.
50. Wurm, *Erinnerungen,* pp. 155–56; Gerhard Schäfer, ed., *Landesbischof D. Wurm und der Nationalsozialistische Staat 1940–1945,* pp. 119–24; *Trial of the Major War Criminals,* 38: 195–201, Doc. 152-M; also contained in the material on euthanasia in Nbg. Doc. NG-265. The letter was also sent to Minister Lammers, July 25, 1940, and to Justice Minister Gürtner on August 23, 1940 (Schäfer, *Landes-bischof D. Wurm,* p. 124).
51. Schäfer, *Landesbischof D. Wurm,* pp. 125–26; *Trial of the Major War Criminals,* 38: 202–3, Doc. 152-M. This letter was also sent to Lammers and Gürtner on September 9, 1940. L. Slaich of Stettin, head of an institution for epileptics and the feebleminded, also sent a strong protest against euthanasia to Berlin (Nbg. Doc. NG-265).
52. Wurm, *Erinnerungen,* p. 155.
53. For Bertram's letter of August 11, 1940, Nbg. Doc. 625-PS; Faulhaber's letter of November 6, 1940, Nbg. Doc. 617-PS, NO-846; for protests of August, 1941, by the archbishop of Cologne and by the bishop of Limberg, see Nbg. Doc. 615-PS, 616-PS; for Bishop Preysing's sermon of Nov. 2, 1941, denouncing euthanasia, see Adolph, *Preysing* pp. 169–70. See also Gruchmann, *VZ* 20 (1972): n. 95; Robert A. Graham, "The 'Right to Kill' in the Third Reich. Prelude to Genocide," *CHR* 62 (1976): 60–72.
54. Wurm, *Erinnerungen,* p. 157; Klügel, *Landeskirche Hannovers,* pp. 445–48.
55. Gruchmann, *VZ* 20 (1972): 252–53.
56. Ibid., p. 261; see also chap. 18, "Monastic Foundations," below, where Bishop Galen's protest is considered in more detail.
57. Ibid., pp. 271–76.
58. This paragraph is based on material presented by Gruchmann, ibid., pp. 277–78; Dörner, *VZ* 15 (1967), 144–52; Hermann Weinkauff et al., *Die deutsche Justiz und der Nationalsozialismus,* 1: 144, 168. See also *Trial of the Major War Criminals,* 20: 81–84; 35: 681700, Doc. 906-D. It is estimated that between the autumn of 1939 and the autumn of 1941, 60,000 to 100,000 people were put to death. For various estimates, see Gruchmann, *VZ* 20 (1972): 244; Dörner, *VZ* 15 (1967): 145; Beyreuther, *Geschichte der Diakonie,* p. 202; Ehrhardt, *Euthanasie,* p. 37; Wein-kauff, *Deutsche Justiz,* 1: 198. Exaggerated figures of the number of victims circu-lated in postwar Germany. Rosenberg in his memoirs apparently accepted a figure of over 250,000 (Serge Lang and Ernst von Schenck, *Memoirs of Alfred Rosenberg* pp. 128–29).
59. This account of the experiences at Bethel is taken largely from an article by Eduard Wörmann, "Gefährdung und Bewahrung Bethels in der Zeit der Euthanasie," in Bernhard Gramlich, ed., *Ein Jahrhundert Diakonie in Bethel,* pp. 58–61, and Anne-lise Hochmuth, ed., *Bethel in den Jahren 1939–1943.* See also Brandt, *Bodel-schwingh,* pp. 196–211; Hase, *Evangelische Dokumente,* pp. 121–27. Ernst Wilm, a neighboring pastor, was put in a concentration camp for exposing in his sermons the threat of the euthanasia program to the Bethel Institutions. After the war he was to become president of the Evangelical church in Westphalia. For Wilm's remarks see Hase, *Evangelische Dokumente,* pp. 21–27; Gunther Weisenborn, *Der Lautlose Aufstand,* p. 76.
60. The program had been started in Pomerania, Brandenburg-Berlin, Saxony, Würt-temberg, and Hamburg, and in June, 1940, was extended to most of Germany (Braune's Denkschrift in *KJ,* 1933–44, p. 417).
61. Brandt, *Bodelschwingh,* p. 209.
62. Braune's personal account, Nbg. Doc. NO-895.
63. Ehrhardt, *Euthanasie,* p. 37. At Hans Hefelman's trial for participation in the killings, it was brought out that on August 24, 1941, a group of the inner circle met in his office and were notified that the killings had to be stopped on the Führer's order. Hefelman was a member of the Führer's chancellery, who was supposed to deal with petitions, complaints, etc. He maintained that it was the protest from the churches—there were no protests from any other quarter—which brought those in power to alter their policy (*Die Welt,* March 19, 1964, p. 16). In the fall of 1943,

under the pretext of saving insane persons from bombing attacks, many were evacuated to concentration camps where they met their deaths in the gas chambers (Zipfel, *Kirchenkampf,* p. 225).

64. Bodelschwingh continued discussions with Dr. Brandt about filling out questionnaires until April, 1943, after which no more forms were sent (Hochmuth, *Bethel in den Jahren 1939–1943,* p. 27).

65. Ibid., pp. 34–35; Brandt, *Bodelschwingh,* pp. 186–87, 208. The special program for Jews was carried on throughout Germany; even Jewish and Christian mental patients were not to live or die together. This anti-Jewish program was continued after the euthanasia program against Christians was suspended, and it is estimated that 20,000 Jews died under it (Schmidt, *Selektion,* pp. 67–71; Ehrhardt, *Euthanasie,* pp. 37–38). All Jewish insane were to be isolated at the sanatorium at Bendorf-Sayn near Koblenz and, after that was closed, at the Jewish Hospital, Iranische Strasse, Berlin (decrees of the minister of the interior of December 12, 1940, and November 10, 1942, BA, Inner. Min., R 18/3768, no page references).

Chapter Sixteen

1. Both the Protestant and the Catholic churches failed to protest (see chap. 18, below). Most of the restrictions mentioned in this chapter primarily in relation to the Protestant churches applied equally to the Catholic church and to smaller denominations.

2. *KJ,* 1933–44, pp. 356–57, see also pp. 351–56. For devastating conclusions in regard to sermons during World War I, see Wilhelm Pressel, *Die Kriegspredigt 1914–1918 in der evangelischen Kirche Deutschlands,* pp. 359–60.

3. *Amtsblatt Landeskirche in Bayern,* 1939, pp. 175–80; see also Meiser's "Grusswort" of September 18, 1939, pp. 153–54. He was pleased that his guidelines received the commendation of Pastor Harnisch, and in writing him added this comment on wartime sermons: "Wir wollen mit der Kriegspredigt unserer Zeit nicht unter das gleiche Verdikt fallen wie die Kriegspredigt der Vergangenheit, und sind überzeugt, dass nur eine Predigt die aus reiner Quell schöpft und ihrem göttlichen Auftrag treu bleibt, ausrichten kann, wozu sie gesendet sei (Meiser to Pfarrer W. Harnisch, January 3, 1940, Berlin, K. Arch., no. 149, p. 50).

4. Kübel, "Erinnerungen," p. 298.

5. Brunotte in Schmidt, *Gesammelte Aufsätze,* p. 127. The war brought a great increase in the production of religious literature for soldiers (Boberach, *Berichte,* pp. 358–59).

6. Neuhäusler, *Kreuz und Hakenkreuz,* 1: 84; Hermelink, *Kirche im Kampf,* p. 506; *Amtsblatt Landeskirche in Bayern,* 1939, p. 181.

7. *Amtsblatt Landeskirche in Bayern,* 1940, p. 79; *KJ,* 1933–44, pp. 460–62. For a time the heads of the Chaplaincy Corps continued to distribute material which they had prepared. This was stopped personally by Hitler in April, 1942 (*KJ,* 1933–44, pp. 468–69; see also Focko Lüpsen, "Der Weg der kirchlichen Pressearbeit von 1933 bis 1950," *KJ,* 1949, p. 434).

8. A Protestant brochure led Göring in the autumn of 1939 to eliminate chaplains from the air force (Seraphim, *Rosenbergs Tagebuch,* p. 90). Klügel, *Landeskirche Hannovers,* pp. 384–85; Niemöller, *Kampf und Zeugnis,* pp. 502–3; Albrecht Schübel, *300 Jahre evangelische Soldatenseelsorge,* pp. 103–12. Shortly after the start of the Russian campaign it was forbidden to award an Iron Cross to a chaplain (ibid., p. 112). Chaplains could not write to relatives of dead soldiers until a week had passed, so that relatives would first receive news from local party officials. They were not to express words of Christian comfort until they in turn had received a communication from the relatives. Chaplains did not always follow this directive (Josef Perau, *Priester im Heere Hitlers,* p. 178).

9. Schübel, *Evangelische Soldatenseelsorge,* pp. 138–40; *KJ,* 1933–44, pp. 465–66; Klügel, *Landeskirche Hannovers,* pp. 465–66. In October, 1941, the police complained that the order was not being observed, particularly in Catholic hospitals (Reichsführer SS, T175, R. 261, 2755021–24; Boberach, *Berichte,* pp. 583–85). By March, 1943, according to the police, the restrictions were generally observed in municipal and state institutions (ibid., pp. 778–81).

10. Lüpsen, *KJ,* 1949, p. 434. On March 8, 1940, Bormann called to the attention of Reichsleiter Amann that only 10 percent of the 3,000 Protestant periodicals had

been forced to cease publication because of paper shortages; Bormann wanted tighter restrictions "as confessional writings do not strengthen resistance against the external foe" (*Trial of the Major War Criminals,* 25: 180–81, Doc. 089-PS).

11. Klügel, *Landeskirche Hannovers,* p. 429; Brunotte in Schmidt, *Gesammelte Aufsätze,* pp. 266–67; Hermelink, *Kirche im Kampf,* pp. 635–37.

12. Hermelink, *Kirche im Kampf,* pp. 553–86; *KJ,* 1933–44, p. 431; Schäfer, *Landesbischof D. Wurm,* pp. 296–99. On paper restrictions imposed on the religious press, see also Klügel, *Landeskirche Hannovers,* pp. 386–88; Lüpsen, *KJ,* 1949, pp. 439–40; the letter of Bishop Dietrich to Marahrens complaining about the paper restrictions, December 16, 1940, NSDAP, T81, R. 229, 5011704–6. In his answer to Dietrich of December 21, 1940, Marahrens laments that some church governments give in right away instead of protesting restrictive measures (ibid., 5011243–44).

13. BA, Reichsjustizministerium, R 22/4008, pp. 1–5.

14. On religious education in the war years, see Helmreich, *Religious Education,* pp. 179–95; see also the chap. "Jewish Education in the Third Reich", pp. 196–209; Klara Hunsche, "Der Kampf um die christliche Schule und Erziehung 1933–45," *KJ,* 1949, pp. 508–19; *KJ,* 1933–44, pp. 423–29, 462–64; Klügel, *Landeskirche Hannovers,* pp. 431–35; Hermelink, *Kirche im Kampf,* p. 508; "Religionsunterricht in den Schulen. Schreiben des Stellvertreters des Führers, R. Hess an Ministerpräsident Generalfeldmarschall H. Göring," April 18, 1940, reprinted in Conway, *Kirchenpolitik,* pp. 372–75; the statement by Hess's staff of April 25, 1941, on the abolition of morning religious services in the schools in *Nazi Conspiracy and Aggression,* 3: 118; the police summary on religious instruction of October 26, 1942, Reichsführer SS, T175, R. 264, 2757892–98; also in Boberach, *Berichte,* pp. 743–47.

15. Kolb, *Schüler-Bibel-Kreise,* pp. 108–9.

16. This paragraph is based on *Verfügungen, Anordnungen, Bekanntgaben,* 1: 181; Reichsführer SS, T175, R. 263, 2756638–43; T175, R. 265, 2759125; BA, Stellvertreter des Führers, NS 6/244; Boberach, *Berichte,* pp. 673, 873–76. Rosenberg's office issued guidelines for carrying out National Socialist Lebensfeiern, NSDAP, T81, R. 676, 5485143.

17. For numerous Protestant and Catholic protests, particularly by Cardinal Bertram, see BA, Reichskanzlei, R 43 II/158a, pp. 74–153.

18. Quoted by Bishop Wurm in his letter to Goebbels, April 1, 1942, *KJ,* 1933–44, p. 431.

19. The various decrees are reprinted in *Amtsblatt Landeskirche in Württemberg,* 1942, pp. 165–77. The Organization of Pastors petitioned Göring that a church be allowed to keep at least one bell, a request which at first was refused (Klinger, *Dokumente,* pp. 87–88).

20. *Partei-Kanzlei Rundschreiben,* 143/41, November 9, 1941.

21. Hermelink, *Kirche im Kampf,* p. 507.

22. Klügel, *Landeskirche Hannovers,* p. 450; Bielfeldt, *Kirchenkampf in Schleswig-Holstein,* p. 179. From the provinces of Belgium 3,995 bells with a weight of 3,198,433 kg. were sent to Germany (Nbg. Doc. EC-H12). The prominent Kaiser-Wilhelm-Gedächtniskirche in Berlin surrendered its bells and it took long negotiation and the direct intervention of Lammers and Goebbels before the radio authorities would turn over a recording of the bells which the church wanted (BA, Reichskanzlei, R 43 II/151, pp. 35–41).

23. Boberach, *Berichte,* pp. 434, 614–16, 627, 655, 740–41.

24. Nbg. Doc. 410-PS; *Partei-Kanzlei Rundschreibung,* 66/41, May 22, 1941.

25. This was the personal idea of Dr. Muhs and was opposed by the church chancellery, which led to a dispute between the two jurisdictions (Brunotte in Schmidt, *Gesammelte Aufsätze,* p. 137).

26. Klügel, *Landeskirche Hannovers,* p. 449. This was in line with a decision of the Ministry of the Interior in Baden of July 15, 1931 (*AK* 81 [1932]: 284–85). Officially there were definite regulations on how people who had withdrawn from churches should be treated; among them were that bells should not be rung at their funerals. For example, see the regulations for the Hanover-Lutheran Church and the Church of Schleswig-Holstein (ibid. 81 [1932]: 276–79, 359–60).

27. *Amtsblatt Landeskirche in Württemberg,* 1944, pp. 107–8; Klügel, *Landeskirche Hannovers,* pp. 448–52.

28. *Amtsblatt Landeskirche in Württemberg,* 1944, pp. 98–106.

29. Reich law of February 27, 1934, *AK* 80? (1934): pp. 98–99; *Amtsblatt Landeskirche in Bayern,* 1943, p. 43.
30. *Amtsblatt Landeskirche in Bayern,* 1939, p. 181.
31. The Spiritual Confidential Council immediately protested, to no avail, that the state had no power to change the times of religious festivals. The secret police were put in charge of enforcing the measure (Brunotte, in Schmidt, *Gesammelte Aufsätze,* p. 140).
32. Pastors who held services on Ascension Day were at times prosecuted. Pastor Georg Rothemund in Offenhausen, Bavaria, for example, was fined 500 marks and denied the privilege of teaching religious classes in school for one year (Witetschek, *Kirchliche Lage in Bayern,* 2: p. 425; personal statement to author). See also Linck, *Kirchenkampf in Ostpreussen,* pp. 251–52.
33. Meiser to Minister of the Interior, May 26, 1943, BA, Rep 320, no. 471, p. 139; Hermelink, *Kirche im Kampf,* p. 507.
34. Hermelink, *Kirche im Kampf,* pp. 506–7; Klügel, *Landeskirche Hannovers,* pp. 435–37; *KJ,* 1933–44, pp. 429–30; Brunotte in Schmidt, *Gesammelte Aufsätze,* pp. 140–41; *Partei-Kanzlei Rundschreiben, Anordnungen 1941–5,* no. 112/45.
35. *KJ,* 1933–44, p. 384; see also Klügel, *Landeskirche Hannovers,* pp. 443–45; Hubatsch, *Ev. Kirche Ostpreussens,* 1: 472.
36. Besetz. Gebiete, T454, R. 62, 001081. Bormann thought the contribution was not high enough; see also *Nazi Conspiracy and Aggression,* 3: 158–59, Doc. 099-PS.
37. Hermelink, *Kirche im Kampf,* p. 594; on curtailment of finances in Saxony, see Fischer, *Sächsische Landeskirche,* pp. 72–73.
38. In Bavaria the taxes received by both churches increased from 18 million marks in 1935 to 43.8 million in 1939; in Württemberg the Protestant state and local church taxes amounted to 4,161,000 marks in 1935 and 8,079,000 in 1940; the Catholic church received 2,313,000 marks in 1935 and 4,055,609 in 1940. The churches came up with slightly different figures. See BA, Reichskanzlei, Bormann to Lammers, July 6, 1941, R 43 II/153a, pp. 128–37; see also pp. 149, 156, 162. Bishop Wurm protested the cut in state subsidy, ibid., pp. 36, 40, 166–67; these protests were rejected, p. 159.
39. *Gesetzblatt der D. E. Kirche,* 1940, pp. 3–4. Only those members of the Waffen SS who were subject to the High Command of the Wehrmacht were exempt from church taxes, and then only as long as they were so subject (*Gesetzes- und Verordnungsblatt Badens,* 1941, pp. 28–29). In July, 1942, land owned by the Nazi party and its organizations was specifically withdrawn from church taxes (ibid., 1942, p. 59). In Mecklenburg the state authorities on December 24, 1941, forbade the use of state coercion in the collection of church taxes, but this order was later modified to apply only to taxes up to 20 marks (BA, Reichskanzlei, R 43 II/153, pp. 70–71). However, in places the finance offices and the communal authorities simply refused to collect the church taxes any longer (Thiele, *Kirchensteuerrecht,* p. 39).
40. Kerrl to Lammers, April 12, 1941, BA, Reichskanzlei, R 43 II/153a, pp. 30, 33; Kerrl to Hitler, April 24, 1941, ibid. p. 88.
41. Lammers to Kerrl, May 24, 1941, ibid., p. 107; see also pp. 108–17; *KJ,* 1933–44, p. 384; Haugg, *Reichsministerium,* pp. 15, 37.
42. Picker, *Hitlers Tischgespräche,* April 7, 1942, pp. 355–56; *Hitler's Secret Conversations,* pp. 332–33.
43. BA, Reichskanzlei, R 43 II/152, pp. 36–37; II/150a, p. 3; *Persecution of the Catholic Church,* pp. 54–55; see also chap. 17, "The Warthegau: Pattern for the Future?," below.
44. The Foreign Office reported on June 13, 1941, that the subsidy to churches abroad which had amounted to 700,000 marks annually before 1933 had been cut to 120,000 marks (BA, Stellvertreter des Führers, Parteikanzlei, NS 6/428, p. 15558). For example, in 1941 the Foreign Office doled out the following amounts to churches in various countries: 3,000 marks (Slovakia); 6,300 marks (Yugoslavia); 1,500 marks (Hungary); 12,000 marks (Rumania); 1,500 marks (Turkey); 1,500 marks (the Netherlands); 4,900 marks (Italy); 3,000 marks (Belgium); 3,000 marks (Portugal); 11,800 marks (Brazil); 4,300 marks (Argentina); 1,200 marks (Chile); 1,200 marks (Uruguay); 1,500 marks (Peru); 1,800 marks (Venezuela); 1,500 marks (Guatemala); and 1,200 marks (San Salvador) (ibid., 15552–54). The Reichsverband für das katholische Deutschtum in Ausland received 2,000 marks in 1939, 5,000 in 1940, and 6,000 in 1941 and 1942 (BA, Reichskanzlei, R 43 II/153, pp. 77–81).

45. Figures from a report by the Reichsminister für die Kirchlichen Angelegenheiten to Reichsminister für Volksaufklärung und Propaganda, July 3, 1944, taken from Deutsche Zentralarchiv, Potsdam, and printed in Mohr, *Katholische Orden,* pp. 336–40.

46. See, for example, Hitler's address to the Reichstag, January 30, 1939, Domarus, *Hitler Reden,* 2: 1059.

47. See chap. 11 at n. 26, above.

48. Klügel, *Landeskirche Hannovers,* p. 457; Brunotte, in Schmidt, *Gesammelte Aufsätze,* p. 106. Baden's finance section was imposed over the strong protest of Bishop Kühlewein and became one of the most aggressive of them (Friedrich, *ZevKR* 3 [1953–54]: 320–31).

49. Klügel, *Landeskirche Hannovers,* pp. 316–19, 457–59; Brunotte in Schmidt, *Gesammelte Aufsätze,* pp. 134–35.

50. Kerrl to Lammers, March 3, 1941, BA, Reichskanzlei, R 43 II/153a, pp. 5–7; on requests for interviews, see also R 43 II/150, pp. 156–58. See also Conway, *Kirchenpolitik,* pp. 266–67, 364–65, 376.

51. This correspondence is to be found BA, Kanzlei Rosenberg, NS 8/182, pp. 9, 84–85, 103, 108. See also Scholder, *VZ* 16 (1968): 30–34.

52. On Kerrl's fiftieth birthday on December 14, 1937, Hitler had given him a Spitzweg painting costing 8,200 marks, paid for out of state funds; on Kerrl's death Hitler ordered that his widow be given 15,000 marks to help her through her changed economic situation (BA, Reichskanzlei, R 43 II/139b, no page reference).

53. See statements by Bormann, Kritzinger, and Lammers, December, 1941, Conway, *Kirchenpolitik,* p. 377–78.

54. Neuhäusler, *Kreuz und Hakenkreuz,* 1: 80–81. Hitler approved of stationing SS troops in regions where "the blood was bad" so as to freshen up the population (Picker, *Hitlers Tischgespräche,* p. 301).

55. *KJ,* 1933–44, pp. 404–6; see also Neuhäusler, *Kreuz und Hakenkreuz,* 1: 81–83.

56. See Paul Gürtler, *Nationalsozialismus und evangelische Kirche im Warthegau,* pp. 140–46; note of Cardinal Maglione to Ribbentrop, March 2, 1943, Albrecht, *Notenwechsel,* 2: 135–62, Italian and German texts with good editorial footnotes; English translation in *Trial of the Major War Criminals,* 32: 94–95.

57. Helmreich, *Religious Education,* pp. 204–5. Wilhelm Niemöller writes in relation to the Crystal Night: "Wir haben sehr versagt und allen Zorn verdient" (*Leben eines Bekenntnispfarrers,* p. 239; see also pp. 241, 277). Bonhoeffer's biographer states that all kept silent at the time of the pogrom (Bethge, *Bonhoeffer,* p. 682). Bishop Wurm was one of the few who raised his voice in admonition, but it was a mild statement in comparison to his wartime pronouncements (*Erinnerungen,* pp. 148–49). The Kirchentag at Steglitz, December 10–12, 1938, did draw up a statement condemning the treatment of the Jews, and there were individual denunciations from pulpits. Pastor Julius von Jan of Oberlenningen was imprisoned because of his denunciation of the pogrom (Meier, *Kirche und Judentum,* pp. 32–34, 108–9). See also Heinrich Grüber, *Erinnerungen aus sieben Jahrzehnten,* pp. 108–13; Gutteridge, *Evangelical Church,* pp. 174–92.

58. *Amtsblatt des Reichministerium für Wissenschaft,* 1938, p. 520; Helmreich, *Religious Education,* pp. 205–6.

59. Flüchtlingsdienst, *Ev. Kirche in Deutschland,* p. 165.

60. From Helen Jacob's article in *Unterwegs,* as quoted in *An der Stechbahn,* pp. 55–56. For an account of the situation in East Prussia, see Linck, *Kirchenkampf in Ostpreussen,* pp. 241–47.

61. *Amtsblatt Landeskirche in Württemberg,* 1934, p. 324.

62. See, for example, *AK* 83 (1934): 176–78; 84 (1935); 105–11; 85 (1936): 8–13; *Amtsblatt Landeskirche in Württemberg,* 1934, pp. 314–17, 324; 1935, pp. 37–42, 137–41; 1937, pp. 13–16; 1938, pp. 151–52, 169–73, 253–56; 1940, p. 270; 1941, pp. 1–4; 1943, pp. 51–53; *Kirchliche Gesetz- und Verordnungsblatt für die evangelische-reformierte Landeskirche der Provinz Hannover,* 1934, pp. 399.

63. Niemöller, *Handbuch,* p. 379.

64. Ibid., p. 380; *Gesetzblatt der D. E. Kirche,* 1939, p. 43.

65. Die Vorläufige Leitung der Deutschen Evangelischen Kirche an die bekenntnisgebundenen Kirchenregierungen und Landesbruderräte innerhalb der Deutschen Evangelischen Kirche, June 15, 1939, Biel. Arch., Coll. W. Niemöller, C 8–11, Judenfrage IV; letter of Koch to Pfarrer Dahlkötter, December 11, 1939, ibid.; Der westfälische Bruderrat an die Pfarrer der Bekennenden Kirche in Westfalen, Oc-

tober, 1939, ibid.; Rat der evgl. Kirche der Altp. Union an Dr. Werner, November 4, 1939, ibid., 0–60, Wilhelm Brandes, XII.

66. Der Präsident des Landeskirchenamtes Hessen-Nassau an Pfarrverwalter Max Weber, July, 1939, ibid.; Niemöller, *Kampf und Zeugnis,* pp. 460–61.
67. *Gesetzes- und Verordnungsblatt Badens,* 1939, pp. 162–66.
68. Hermann Diem, "Kirche und Antisemitismus," in Andreas Flitner, ed., *Deutsches Geistesleben und Nationalsozialismus,* p. 10; see also Diem's address published in *Christ und Welt,* January 8, 1965, p. 18.
69. On the founding and work of the Grüber Bureau, see Grüber, *Erinnerungen,* pp. 103–45; Flüchtlingsdienst, *Ev Kirche in Deutschland,* pp. 150–53, 158–59, 180–99, *An der Stechbahn,* passim; Meier, *Kirche und Judentum,* pp. 37–38, 110–13. Herzfeld, ed., *Berlin und Brandenburg,* p. 507; Gutteridge, *Evangelical Church,* 206–12; see pp. 212–18 for other church agencies and individuals who aided the Jews.
70. See Grüber's account of his imprisonment in Sachsenhausen and Dachau 1940–45, *Erinnerungen,* pp. 146–99.
71. Zipfel, *Kirchenkampf,* p. 219; Meier, *Kirche und Judentum,* p. 15. On January 25, 1939, a circular note of the Foreign Office stated: "The ultimate aim of Germany's Jewish policy is the emigration of all Jews living in German territory (*DGFP,* D, 5: 927). On January 24, Göring, as commissioner of the Four-year Plan, had ordered the establishment of a central Reich office for Jewish emigration and placed SS Gruppenführer Heydrich in charge (ibid., pp. 933–34). After the defeat of France the Germans for a time considered sending the Jews to Madagascar, but this proved inadvisable during the war, and, with the Russian campaign providing a new opportunity, the emigration of Jews was forbidden. Instead of "emigration," a policy of "evacuating" the Jews to the east was instituted, with Hitler's direct approval, as Germany's final solution to the Jewish problem (Protokoll der Wannsee-Konferenz, January 20, 1942, *ADAP,* E, 1: 269, 403). On the Madagascar project and the involvement of the SS in the "final solution," see Höhne, *Die Geschichte der SS,* pp. 323–68; see also Lawrence D. Stokes, "The German People and the Destruction of European Jews," *Central European History* 6 (1973): 180–81; Ben-Elissar, *La diplomatie du IIIe Reich,* pp. 399–474; Levin, *Holocaust,* pp. 199–203.
72. Brunotte, *ZevKR* 13 (1967): 163. The police president of Berlin had tried to get this association dissolved in 1936 (Polizeipräsident in Berlin an Die Gesellschaft zur Beförderung des Christentums unter den Juden, April 4, 1936, Berlin, K. Arch., no. 148, p. 7).
73. *Partei-Kanzlei Rundschreibung,* 1941 (January 1, 1941).
74. *Verfügungen/Anordnungen/ Bekanntgaben,* 1: 206. On February 2, 1942, the use of the term *Ostmark* was forbidden. Anyone wanting a collective name for the seven Reichsgaue which were formerly "Reichsgaue der Ostmark" was to use "Alpen- und Donau Reichsgaue" (ibid., p. 207; *Partei-Kanzlei Rundschreiben,* 19/42, February 13, 1942).
75. The proposal to force all Jews to wear the special insignia ("a black-bordered six-cornered star of yellow fabric, the size of the palm of a hand with the black inscription 'Jew' ") was made by Goebbels, who as Gauleiter of Berlin decided to introduce it in his territories in April, 1941. He first inquired if Hitler had reached a decision on extending the practice to the whole Reich (Taubert to Tiessler, April 22, 1941, NSDAP, T81, R. 676, 5485640). In August Goebbels pressed Hitler for a decision, and on September 1, 1941, the police order was issued to go into effect September 19 (Bruno Blau, *Das Ausnahmerecht für die Juden in Deutschland 1933–1945,* 2d ed. (Düsseldorf, 1955), p. 89; Meier, *Kirche und Judentum,* pp. 68–69). On September 9, 1941, the party issued a circular notice that uniform regulations on wearing the star would be issued shortly. It would be beneath the dignity of the party for Gauleiter and other party officials to enforce the measure in individual cases, and there should be no special actions (*Partei-Kanzlei Rundschreiben,* 109/41). Various ministries were officially informed of the measure September 15–22, 1941 (*Trial of the Major War Criminals,* 13: 171–73). By June, 1941, Hitler had concluded that laws in respect to the citizenship of Jews were not important because "he was of the opinion that after the war there would not be any Jews left in Germany anyhow" (Lammers to Bormann, June 7, 1941, ibid., 12: 168).
76. *KJ,* 1933–44, p. 481. Klatsche, of the Saxon church, pressed for the posting of a sign on churches and other church buildings: *Juden haben keinen Zutritt* (Brunotte,

ZevKR 13 [1967]: 164). The plan of separating Christian Jews into special congregations had long been proposed by various German Christian dominated Land churches. In the spring of 1939, the Land churches of Thuringia, Mecklenburg, Anhalt, Saxony, and Lübeck had excluded Jews from their membership; pastors were not obligated to undertake any duties or services to Jews who had formerly been members of their churches, although they were not forbidden to do so. These churches appealed to the national church office to issue such regulations for all Land churches. The office refused to do so at that time, although it was certainly not Judeophile (ibid., pp. 144–51, 157; Niemöller, *Junge Kirche*, Supp. no. 2 [1968], pp. 2–8).

77. *KJ*, 1933–44, p. 482. For an evaluation of the decree, see Brunotte, *ZevKR* 13 (1967): 166–73; Niemöller, *Junge Kirche*, Supp. no. 2 (1968), pp. 18–20. The national church officials did make some half-hearted attempts to organize some services for Christian Jews who were then being arrested en masse; one official had an interview with Obersturmbannführer Eichmann on April 14, 1942, who refused any concessions and maintained "dass die ganze Judenfrage hier im Altreich nur eine Transportfrage sei" (Brunotte, *ZevKR* 13 [1967]: 172). The account of the interview with Eichmann is reprinted in Meier, *Kirche und Judentum*, pp. 120–21.

78. Statistics taken from Bruno Blau, "The Jewish Population of Germany," *Jewish Social Studies* 12 (1950): 162–63; Helmreich, *Religious Education*, p. 200. A study compiled in the Ministry of Church Affairs gives 13,306 as the total number of Jews converting to the Evangelical church from 1900 to 1939; the figures for each year are as follows: 173 (1931), 241 (1932), 933 (1933), not given (1934–35), 323 (1936), 250 (1937), 349 (1938), 233 (1939) (BA, Reichsministerium für die Kirch. Angelegenheiten, R 79/19; for conversions to Catholicism, see chap. 18, n. 105, below).

79. Niemöller, *Handbuch*, p. 380; for a copy of Cölle's order, see Biel, Arch., Coll. W. Niemöller, C 8–11, Judenfrage IV.

80. Kinder, *Neue Beiträge*, pp. 118–25, 191.

81. *KJ*, 1933–44, pp. 483–84. The Spiritual Confidential Council sent a ten-page letter to Bishop Wurm attempting to justify its consent to the December 22 decree (Brunotte, *ZevKR* 13 [1967]: 169; Meier, *Kirche und Judentum*, pp. 118–19).

82. *KJ*, 1933–44, p. 484–85; see also the statement by the Confessing Synod of Brandenburg of September 1942, ibid., p. 391; Harder in Schmidt, *Gesammelte Aufsätze*, pp. 212–13; Gutteridge, *Evangelical Church*, pp. 228–35.

83. When deportation of Jews from the Netherlands began in July, 1942, the Protestant and Catholic churches made a joint protest to the Reichskommissar and announced the protest would also be read from pulpits. The latter informed them if the protest was not read in the churches the Christian Jews could remain. Faced with this dilemma, the Protestants did not read the protest; the Catholics did. The result was that "Catholic Jews" were immediately placed on the deportation lists, only to be followed later by the "Protestant Jews" (Diem in *Christ und Welt*, January 8, 1965, p. 22; Snoek, *Grey Book*, pp. 128–31).

84. See the gripping account by Arthur Goldschmidt, *Geschichte der evangelischen Gemeinde Theresienstadt 1942–1945*, pp. 7–36; on Theresienstadt in general, see Levin, *Holocaust*, pp. 476–93.

85. *Partei-Kanzlei Rundschreiben*, 165/42, 176/42.

86. Wurm to Reichsstatthalter Hier, February 8, 1943, *KJ*, 1933–44, p. 432; see also Wurm's letter to the pastors of Germany of October 1, 1943, ibid., pp. 448–52.

87. Wurm to Minister Lammers, December 20, 1943, Schäfer, *Landesbischof Wurm*, p. 312; Hermelink, *Kirche im Kampf*, p. 657; Nbg, Doc., NG-5874.

88. Hermelink, *Kirche im Kampf*, pp. 650–53; Meier, *Kirche und Judentum*, pp. 40, 124–25; Snoek, *Grey Book*, pp. 108–12.

89. Dr. Bekker to Bishops Marahrens and Meiser, June 2, 1943, Nürnberg, LK. Arch., Bestand 222.

90. Hermelink, *Kirche im Kampf*, pp. 654–56.

91. In the files of the Provisional Directory there are copies of farewell letters to eleven non-Aryan pastors who emigrated in 1938–39 (Arnold, Leo, Benfey, Olsner, Schwannecke, Sussbach, Schweitzer, Ehrenberg, Flatow, Katz, Sunnel), Berlin, K. Arch., no. 124, p. 1. In December, 1938, the Grüber Bureau had obtained from the bishop of Chichester forty-five blank visas for pastors and church workers who were in concentration camps, which enabled a number of them to get to England (*An der Stechbahn*, p. 57).

92. Friedrich, *ZevKR* 3 (1953–54): 318.
93. See chap. 18, "Racial Policies and the Hierarchy," below.
94. *KJ*, 1945–48, p. 222. A condemnation of the lack of protest on the part of the churches is also strongly expressed in Hermann Diem, Paul Schempp, and Kurt Müller, eds., *Kirche und Entnazifizierung*, pp. 34–35, 57–58; see also Meier, *Kirche und Judentum*, pp. 41–44.
95. Flüchtlingsdienst, *Ev. Kirche in Deutschland*, p. 10.

Chapter Seventeen

1. Wurm, *Erinnerungen*, pp. 162–63.
2. Ibid., p. 164; Hermelink, *Kirche im Kampf*, p. 509; see also Schäfer, *Landesbischof D. Wurm*, pp. 269–317.
3. *KJ*, 1933–44, pp. 440–41.
4. Wurm, *Erinnerungen*, p. 165; Schäfer, *Landesbischof D Wurm*, p. 335; Hermelink, *Kirche im Kampf*, p. 704. For the thirteen points and comment on them, see *KJ*, 1933–44, pp. 442–43; Niemöller, *Kampf und Zeugnis*, pp. 514–15; Klügel, *Landeskirche Hannovers*, pp. 399–400.
5. Niemöller, *Kampf und Zeugnis*, p. 516. Klügel writes: "Die eigentliche Frucht dieses Einigungswerkes reifte erst nach dem Zusammenbruch von 1945" (*Landeskirche Hannovers*, p. 400). For some of the most important statements issued in connection with the unification work, see *KJ*, 1933–44, pp. 440–52.
6. Armin Boyens, "Das Stuttgarter Schuldbekenntnis vom 19. Oktober 1945. Entstehung und Bedeutung," *VZ* 19 (1971): 386–87. The Hilfswerk was established in 1945 and was supported by all the Land churches (see chap. 21, "Cooperation in Church Activities," below). See also the fragment of a document "Das Selbsthilfewerk der DEK" of February, 1945, found among Wurm's papers (Schäfer, *Landesbischof D. Wurm* pp. 363–65).
7. Niesel, *Bekenntnissynoden*, p. 5.
8. Ibid., pp. 85–88; Niemöller, *Kampf und Zeugnis*, pp. 499–500.
9. Niemöller, *Kampf und Zeugnis,* p. 518; Niesel, *Bekenntnissynoden*, pp. 95–98.
10. Niesel, *Bekenntnissynoden*, p. 105.
11. Ibid., p. 107; *KJ*, 1933–44, pp. 399–402.
12. *KJ*, 1933–44, pp. 402–4; Niesel, *Bekenntnissynoden*, pp. 109–10; Niemöller, *Kampf und Zeugnis*, pp. 520–21.
13. Niesel, *Bekenntnissynoden*, p. 116; Niemöller, *Handbuch*, p. 156.
14. See chap. 11, "Further Attempts to Achieve a Church-State Settlement," above.
15. See the compilation of letters of protest sent by German Christians to be found in the Reichskanzlei files in the Bundesarchiv in Koblenz as cited by Kurt D. Schmidt, "Der Widerstand der Kirche im Dritten Reich," *LM* 1 (1962); 368; see also Meier, *Die Deutschen Christen*, pp. 308–9; Meier in Schmidt, *Gesammelte Aufsätze*, pp. 9–10; Ehrenforth, *Schlesische Kirche*, p. 195. Asmussen writes that in the later years the German Christians often did more than the Confessing church to right the injustices of the Third Reich. However, they could never make good the evil they had begun (*Zur jüngsten Kirchengeschichte*, p. 35).
16. Schumacher, T580, R. 41; R. 42.
17. Heydrich to Lammers, May 23, 1939; memorandum for Lammers, June 2, 1939, Nbg. Doc., NG-4967.
18. An English edition in 1937 was paid for by the German government and the German embassy in Tokyo subsidized a Japanese edition in 1938 (Rechtsantwalt Gerike to Lammers, January 2, 1940, BA, Reichskanzlei, R 43 II/154, p. 12). Gerike was a personal friend of Lammers and enlisted his support on behalf of Fabricius.
19. On June 1, 1937, Fabricius prepared a study on "Das Reich im Kampf," and between then and January 1, 1938, there were eight further editions; all but the second are to be found ibid., pp. 97–171.
20. Ibid., pp. 174–205; NSDAP, T81, R. 185, 0335501–34.
21. Heydrich to Lammers, January 24, 1940, BA, Reichskanzlei, R 43 II/154, p. 223.
22. Seraphim, *Rosenbergs Tagebuch*, p. 89.
23. Fabricius was arrested November 9, 1939, and freed January 13, 1940; he was put out of the party, which he had joined May 1, 1932, on March 20, 1940 (BA, Reichskskanzlei, R 43 II/154, 210–11, 218, 220, 229, 235, 276. The folio in the Bundesarchiv on Fabricius ends with a letter of Bormann to Lammers of December

12, 1940, saying Fabricius had been arrested on Hitler's direct order (ibid., p. 276). See also BA, Kanzlei Rosenberg, NS 8/169, p. 47. A Denkschrift somewhat similar to that by Fabricius, lamenting the anti-Christian developments in the party and pleading for the party to return to a Christian basis, was submitted by Landrat von Alvensleben on October 31, 1941 (BA, Reichskanzlei, R 43 II/151, pp. 2–13).

24. Klügel, *Landeskirche Hannovers*, pp. 454–56, 483–87.

25. On the general mood of the German Christians, see Meier, *Die Deutschen Christen* pp. 300, 308–11; for German Christian religious appeals to the people, see *KJ*, 1933–44, pp. 489–511; see also the "Aufruf" issued by the Deutsche Christen Nationalkirchliche Einung of May 8, 1941, in which they renewed their call to establish one national church embracing both Catholic and Protestant Germans. They stated: "Der Gott, der sich herrlich zu unserem Volk bekannt und durch Adolf Hitler uns so wunderbar geführt und gesegnet hat, will nicht die Verewigung der religiösen Zerrissenheit" (Biel. Arch., Coll. W. Niemöller, D-6, Bek. Kirche im Kriege).

26. It had a territory of 46,000 sq. km. and a population of 4,600,000, of which 346,000 were Germans (Bernhard Stasiewski, "Die Kirchenpolitik der Nationalsozialisten im Warthegau 1939–1945," *VZ* 7 (1959): 49. See the excellent maps of the territorial division of Poland and of the Polish dioceses in the territories annexed by Germany in the back of pt. 1 of Pierre Blet et al., *Le Saint Siège et la situation religieuse en Pologne et dans les pays Baltes 1939–1945*.

27. Gürtler, *Ev. Kirchen im Warthegau*, pp. 29–43; Arthur Rhode, *Geschichte der evangelischen Kirche im Posener Lande*, p. 237; Martin Broszat, *Nationalsozialistische Polenpolitik 1939–1945*, p. 166.

28. Gürtler, *Ev. Kirchen im Warthegau*, pp. 51–54. Kerrl's jurisdiction over other annexed or occupied countries was also ended. In 1940, when he ordered that the bishops of Austria could appeal directly to him without going through the Austrian Reichsstatthalter, a dispute developed between him and Hess (and Bormann) about his authority over the churches in Austria. Kerrl was forced to rescind the practice of direct appeal to his office and a temporary settlement was arranged by Minister of the Interior Frick (BA, Reichskanzlei, R 43 II/150a, pp. 42–95).

29. Gürtler, *Ev. Kirchen im Warthegau*, pp. 41–42, n. 91.

30. Ibid., pp. 55, 187; Broszat, *Polenpolitik*, pp. 166–69, 171–72. The church leaders in Danzig-West Prussia were able to prevent the measures inaugurated in the Warthegau from being extended to their district (Gülzow, *Kirchenkampf in Danzig*, pp. 34–37).

31. Greiser had previously succeeded Hermann Rauschning as president of the Danzig senate. He had sent his eldest daughter to be confirmed, and when the daughter was asked to consult her parents and select a Bible verse to be used at the confirmation service, Greiser bypassed the Bible and dictated the sentence "Im Glücke Stolz, im Unglück hart wie Ebenholz." The minister refused to use it (Gülzow, *Kirchenkampf in Danzig*, p. 43).

32. *Weizsäcker Process*, closing brief, 4: 455–57; memorandum by Weizsäcker, September 29, 1941, *DGFP*, D 13: 590–91; Weizsäcker to Greiser, January 7, 1942, *ADAP*, E, 1: 192–93, 495. For discussion of the validity of the concordat in the annexed and occupied territories, see chap. 18, "The War and the Concordat," below.

33. Gürtler, *Ev. Kirchen im Warthegau*, pp. 19–54.

34. BA, Reichsjustizministerium, R22/4009, pp. 1012–14. This ordinance was designed to clarify the jurisdiction of the central government agencies. On September 25, 1941, Lammers had notified all the Reichsstatthalter that Hitler had ordered Kerrl's jurisdiction and activity limited to territories where the concordat of July 20, 1933, applied. At that time Lammers cautioned that there should be no publication of the decision or of actions resulting from it (BA, Reichskanzlei, R 43 II/152, pp. 103–4).

35. Biographical notes on Greiser and Jäger, in Gürtler, *Ev. Kirchen im Warthegau*, pp. 20–21.

36. Ibid., pp. 48–50; for a slightly different version where the points are called an ordinance (*Verordnung*), see *KJ*, 1933–44, p. 453. For an excellent summary of events in the Warthegau, particularly as they related to the Berlin church offices, see Brunotte in Schmidt, *Gesammelte Aufsätze*, pp. 132–34; see also Stasiewski, *VZ* 7 (1959): 60–64 for the Protestant church, pp. 64–73 for the Catholic church.

37. Gauschulungsleiter Ruder in a speech on November 10, 1940, in Limburg/Lahn stated: "Zum Beweis dafür dass der Führer es haben will dass die Kirchen verschwinden brauchen wir nur auf die Neuordnung im Warthegau zu sehen" (NSDAP,

T81. R. 185, 0335301, see also 0335304–5, 0335307–8). The Spiritual Confidential Council held that events in the Warthegau presaged what would happen in Germany proper later (Brunotte in Schmidt, *Gesammelte Aufsätze*, p. 134). See also Stasiewski, *VZ* 7 (1959): 73–74; Orlow, *Nazi Party*, 2: 290, 374; Walter Adolph, *Im Schatten des Galgens*, p. 20. In May, 1939, Bormann contemplated introducing into Old Germany the church legislation inaugurated in Austria and the Sudeten areas. This legislation had many similarities to the program in the Warthegau (see Bormann's Rundschreiben of May 9, 1939, in Adolph, *Wichmann Jahrbuch*, 1953, pp. 136–37); see also Broszat, *Polenpolitik*, pp. 168, 175.

38. Gürtler, *Ev. Kirchen im Warthegau*, p. 141.

39. In 1943 the German episcopate estimated that there were 300,000 German Catholics and 3,200,000 Polish Catholics in the Warthegau. By 1944 there were probably about 1,000,000 Germans in the territory, although the majority of the population remained Polish. Of the Catholics, about 10 percent were Germans (Stasiewski, *VZ* 7 [1959]: 49–50, 68). See also the excellent summary of conditions in the Warthegau in the note of Cardinal Maglione to Ribbentrop, March 2, 1943, Albrecht, *Notenwechsel*, 2: 135–62; *Trial of the Major War Criminals*, 32: 94–105; Nbg. Doc., 3264-PS.

40. Gürtler, *Ev. Kirchen im Warthegau*, p. 143, quoting evidence presented in the Polish trial of August Jäger, December 12–21, 1948. A Catholic church report of October 1, 1941, stated that for the archdiocese of Posen, out of the 681 secular priests, 451 were imprisoned, 120 had been evacuated to the area of the General Government in Poland, and 74 had been shot or died. Only 34 priests were available to care for Poles and 17 for Germans. Out of 441 churches, only 30 remained open for Poles, and 15 for Germans (Stasiewski, *VZ* 7 [1959]: 65); see also the summary on Nazi persecution in Poland, including the Warthegau, in *Trial of the Major War Criminals*, 4: 510–19.

41. Stasiewski, *VZ* 7 (1959), 58–59; Gürtler, *Ev. Kirchen im Warthegau*, pp. 123–36.

42. Gürtler, *Ev. Kirchen im Warthegau*, pp. 58–65.

43. Ibid., pp. 136–40. The ordinance on cemeteries in the Warthegau was issued by Greiser on October 3, 1941. On January 26, 1943, the establishment of more German cemeteries was ordered, with the touching word of caution that the water table should be watched so that the water would not be contaminated (NSDAP, T81, R. 286, 2409986).

44. Gürtler, *Ev. Kirchen im Warthegau*, p. 258; for other letters and protests, see the selection of documents pp. 187–354. In 1943 General Superintendent Blau was accused of attacking National Socialist ideology in two of his pastoral letters. He appealed to Minister Lammers to bring the matter to the attention of the Führer. Lammers discussed the matter with Bormann but nothing could be done about it. The citation against Blau was meant simply as a warning to him (Nbg. Doc. 2134-PS). Bishop J. Bursche, head of the Evangelical-Augsburg Church of Poland, was considered pro-Polish and was imprisoned in Germany, where he died February, 1942 (Boyens, *Kirchenkampf und Ökumene*, 1939–1945, pp. 33–39).

45. Picker, *Hitlers Tischgespräche*, July 4, 1942, p. 372.

46. NSDAP, T81, R. 18, 0335301–7.

47. "In den Erlassen, Aufrufen und Synodalerklärungen der BK-Stellen finde ich keine kriegsgegnerischen oder gar pazifistischen Äusserungen" (Bielfeldt, *Kirchenkampf in Schleswig-Holstein*, p. 177). "Ein kirchlicher Protest ist in Deutschland zu Beginn des Krieges nicht laut geworden—auch nicht die Forderung der Kriegsdienstverweigerung" (Klügel, *Landeskirche Hannovers*, p. 402).

48. Seraphim, *Rosenbergs Tagebuch*, pp. 86–88.

49. On October 6, 1934, Reich Bishop Müller ordered that prayers be said for the Chancellor and Führer Adolf Hitler every Sunday in Protestant churches (*Amtsblatt Landeskirche in Württemberg*, 1934, p. 350; *Amtsblatt Landeskirche in Bayern*, 1934, p. 177). Prayers for the government were part of the Confessing church services. When Reverend Albertz, an intrepid Confessional leader, was informed by a young minister that many pastors were omitting the prayer for the Führer, he replied: "Wenn es einige Pfarrer gibt, die diese Fürbitte nicht üben, so tun sie in der Tat Unrecht. Ein inneres Recht, ein evangelisches Wort an die Obrigkeit zu richten, hat nur, wer die Obrigkeit mit der Fürbitte trägt" (Albertz to Prädikant Klapproth, September 11, 1936, Berlin, K. Arch., no. 232, pp. 89, 92).

50. See the Denkschrift prepared in 1946 by Dr. Jonuschat at the request of U.S. members of the Control Commission on "The Struggle of the Confessing Church

against National Socialism," Biel. Arch., Coll. W. Niemöller, D-6, Bek. Kirche im Kriege. Jonuschat writes: "Die Bekennende Kirche gab nunmehr regelmässig liturgische Formulare für die Sonntage der Kriegszeit heraus. In diesen Formularen war eine Bitte um den Sieg der deutschen Waffen peinlich vermieden. Auch die Fürbitte für die deutsche Obrigkeit, die nach den Weisungen des Neuen Testaments nicht fehlen durft, wurde immer vorsichtiger formuliert und beschränkte sich schliesslich ganz darauf, Gott darum zu bitten, dass die deutsche Staatsführung den Willen Gottes tun möchte."

51. Hermelink, *Kirche im Kampf*, p. 663; examples of such prayers used in Bavaria and Württemberg are given pp. 663–65.

52. For regulations issued by the Reich Church Committee, see *Amtsblatt Landeskirche in Württemberg*, 1936, p. 273; *Gesetzes- und Verordnungsblatt Badens*, 1936, p. 76.

53. For a memorandum by Professor Hans-Joachim Iwand on the right of resistance according to Evangelical doctrine, and by Professor Rupert Angermair according to Catholic doctrine, see Hans Royce, ed., *Germans against Hitler, July 20, 1944*, pp. 272–81; see also the letters by Bishop Wurm and the *Gutachten* of the theological faculty of Marburg in Hermelink, *Kirche im Kampf*, pp. 691–700; Schmidt, *LM* 1 (1962): 369; G. Ritter, *Carl Goerdeler und die deutsche Widerstandsbewegung*, p. 463; Walter Künneth, "Die evangelische-lutherische Theologie und das Widerstandsrecht," in Europäischen Publikatione e.V., ed., *Die Vollmacht des Gewissens*, pp. 164–74. Künneth has some reservations about the justification of an individual taking extreme action; see also his *Der Grosse Abfall*, pp. 187–95, and *Das Widerstandsrecht als theologische-ethisches Problem*, pp. 5–18. Heinz Brunotte feels the last word has not been spoken on this issue, and makes reservations about the right of resistance to governmental authority ("Kirchenkampf als Widerstand," in Friedrich W. Kantzenbach and Gerhard Müller, eds., *Reformatio und Confessio*, pp. 320–21). See also Clarence L. Abercrombie, "Barth and Bonhoeffer. Resistance to the Unjust," *Religion in Life* 42 (1973): 344–60.

54. *RGG*, 6:1689. Berggrav was imprisoned in Norway on April 8, 1942, for expressing similar views (Boyens, *Kirchenkampf und Ökumene 1939–1945*, pp. 161–63).

55. Niemöller, *Handbuch*, p. 396. Ernst Wolf writes: "Die Bekennende Kirche wird man immerhin als 'Widerstandsbewegung wider Willen' ansehen dürfen. . . . Die Frage danach, ob der Kirchenkampf zugleich als Widerstandsbewegung im politischen Sinne zu werten sei, tauchte allerdings erst nach 1945 auf" (*Die evangelischen Kirchen und der Staat im Dritten Reich*, p. 36). "Die Bekennende Kirche . . . war in Ansatz eine bewusst ausschliesslich vom Glauben geleitete, das hiess anderseits; eine bewusst unpolitische Opposition" (Klotzbach, *Gegen den Nationalsozialismus*, pp. 230–31). "Wir traten 1933 nicht an, um den nationalsozialistischen Staat zu bekämpfen. Wir wussten aber nicht, dass wir es trotzdem taten. Denn wir durchkreuzten seine Pläne" (Asmussen, *Zur jüngsten Kirchengeschichte*, p. 86). See also Boyens, *Kirchenkampf und Ökumene, 1933–1945*, pp. 166–77; Nicolaisen, *Kirchenpolitik*, 2: 71, 85; Gutteridge, *Evangelical Church*, pp. 129–31.

56. Kanzelabkündigung in allen bekenntniskirchlichen Gottesdiensten, December 16, 1934, Hermelink, *Kirche im Kampf*, p. 232; see also Meier, *Kirche und Judentum*, pp. 43–44.

57. [Martin Niemöller] hat nie einen Zweifel darüber gelassen, dass unser Kampf ein reich-kirchlicher Kampf sei" (Asmussen to Osterloh, August 10, 1938, Biel. Arch., Coll. W. Niemöller, N 11–12, Hans Asmussen); see also summary evaluation of Niemoller's position in Gutteridge, *Evangelical Church*, pp. 287–94.

58. Niemöller, *Handbuch*, p. 396.

59. It is this sort of opposition that Gerhard Ritter writes about in his *Carl Goerdeler*, pp. 101–17; see also Edwin H. Robertson, *Christen gegen Hitler*. Brunotte maintains that it can not be disputed that a good part of the Kirchenkampf was "Widerstand" in the 1930s (in Kantzenbach and Müller, *Festschrift W. Maurer*, p. 315).

60. As quoted in Julius Rieger, *The Silent Church*, p. 90.

61. The church, state, police, and party documents are full of reports of arrests, detentions, and imprisonments. No complete listing has ever been made, nor is it possible to do so. Often ministers were put in prison for a short time, or their punishments lifted or extended. A partial listing of the abundant documentary evidence available includes: a listing of punishments imposed on Protestant pastors as of October 1, 1939 (BA, Reichskanzlei, R 43 II/154, pp. 68–74); a fat folder of arrests, charges, and state proceedings without specific mention of causes (BA, Stellver-

treter des Führers, NS 6/327); a listing of hundreds of police measures against the clergy in the Bavarian Protestant Church right of the Rhine (given in Klinger, *Dokumente,* p. 95; see also for Bavaria Witeschek, *Kirchliche Lage in Bayern*). For a summary of punishments compiled from the notices for intercessory prayers, see Zipfel, *Kirchenkampf,* p. 124. In the Church of East Prussia 142 ministers were arrested, many several times, and one was sent to concentration camp (Hubatsch, *Ev. Kirche Ostpreussens,* 1: 472).

62. Forck, *Gedenkbuch für die Blutzeugen.* Bishop Wurm, in opening the Church Leaders' Conference at Treysa, August 27, 1945, recalled the names of persons who had lost their lives in the Kirchenkampf: "Landgerichtsdirektor Weissler, Pfarrer Schneider-Dickenschied, Pfarrer Sylten, Hildegard Jacobi, Pfarrer Ludwig Steil, Justice Perels, Dietrich und Klaus Bonhoeffer, Rüdiger Sleicher, und Reichsgerichtsrat Dohnanyi" (Paul Kessler, *Kämpfende Kirche,* p. 81); see also Niemöller, *Kampf und Zeugnis,* p. 523.

63. Hermelink, *Kirche im Kampf,* p. 666; Inge Scholl, *Students Against Tyranny.*

64. Hermelink, *Kirche im Kampf,* p. 667; Bethge, *Bonhoeffer,* pp. 882, 889–90, Walter Dress, "Widerstandsrecht und Christenpflicht bei Dietrich Bonhoeffer," *LM* 3 (1964): 198–209; Joachim Kramarz, *Stauffenberg,* pp. 27–28, 122, 147–48, 161, 200; Max Geiger, *Der deutsche Kirchenkampf,* p. 60; Ritter, *Carl Goerdeler,* p. 111; Hans Rothfels, *Die deutsche Opposition gegen Hitler,* pp. 121–26, 146–50; Robertson, *Christen gegen Hitler,* pp. 111–33; Weisenborn, *Der lautlose Aufstand,* pp. 86–91; Klaus Scholder, "Die Kirchen im Dritten Reich," *Beilage zur Wochenzeitung "Das Parlament,"* April 10, 1971, p. 31; Beate Ruhm von Oppen, *Religion and Resistance to Nazism,* pp. 69–74; Ernst Wolf, "Political and Moral Motives behind the Resistance," in Hermann Graml et al., *The German Resistance to Hitler,* pp. 192–224, particularly pp. 199–202, 209–10, 225–33; Hans-Adolph Jacobsen, ed., *July 20, 1944,* pp. 78–103, 105–37, 187–203; Klemens von Klemperer writes: "Almost all the conspirators were religious men" (*Mandate for Resistance,* p. 27; Rudolf Pechel, *Deutscher Widerstand,* p. 121; Victor Conzemius, *Églises chrétiennes et totalitarisme national-socialiste,* pp. 140–47; Eugen Gerstenmaier, "Der Kreisauer Kreis. Zu dem Buch Gerrit van Roons, 'Neuordnung im Widerstand'," *VZ* 15 (1967): 221–46. The best accounts of the Kreisauer circle are in Ger van Roon, *Neuordnung im Widerstand* (about 100 pages of pertinent documents are included in the appendices) and Michael Balfour and Julian Frisby, *Helmuth von Moltke.* On the religious motivation of Widerstand leaders, ibid., pp. 97, 176.

65. Bethge, *Bonhoeffer,* pp. 1038–40; Fabian von Schlabrendorff, *Eugen Gerstenmaier im Dritten Reich,* pp. 33–34.

66. Lammers to Wurm, March 3, 1944, Hermelink, *Kirche im Kampf,* pp. 700–702. On March 17, 1944, Oberkirchenrat Sautter of the Württemberg church wrote Minister Lammers about Wurm's reaction to his letter. Wurm had been deeply hurt by it; state and party leaders did not understand Lammers's motives in writing the letter. Sautter spoke up warmly for Wurm (BA, Reichjustizministerium, R22/4008, no page references).

67. Wurm, *Erinnerungen,* pp. 171–72; see also Schäfer, *Landesbischof D. Wurm,* pp. 339–65; Gerstenmaier, *VZ* 15 (1967): 242–43.

Chapter Eighteen

1. Gordon Z. Zahn, *German Catholics and Hitler's Wars,* pp. 126, 137, 159, 162, 185–93; Lewy, *Catholic Church and Nazi Germany,* pp. 226–27; see also the statement in the Munich diocesan Amtsblatt of September 7, 1939, as quoted in Mary Alice Gallin, *German Resistance to Hitler,* p. 223. The police report of October 16, 1939, as usual was critical of the attitude of the Catholic church (Boberach, *Berichte,* pp. 354–59).

2. Quoted in Zahn, *German Catholics,* p. 87; see also pp. 192–93.

3. Reichsführer SS, T175, R. 511, 9377678–80.

4. NSDAP, T81, R. 184, 0334008–10. The party in general came to hold that the clergy had a defeatist attitude; see, for example, Mitteilungen aus dem Reich, June 24, 1940, Reichsführer SS, T175, R. 259, 2751845–46, 2751928–29; Boberach, *Berichte,* pp. 443–44.

5. Heinrich Portmann, *Bischof Graf von Galen spricht,* pp. 52, 59.

6. See chap. 15, "Official Wartime Policy," above.

7. Burkhart Schneider, Pierre Blet, and Angelo Martini, eds., *Die Briefe Pius' XII. an die Deutschen Bischöfe 1939–1944*, p. 89. This letter was written after differences arose between Bishop Preysing of Berlin and Cardinal Bertram over the latter's congratulatory birthday letter to Hitler in April, 1940 (ibid., p. 74n). In regard to Catholic unity Wilhelm Josef Doetsch writes: "Weder der deutsche Katholizismus, noch der deutsche Episcopat waren ein fest geformter, einheitlicher Block" (*Württembergs Katholiken*, p. 20); see also Klaus Gotto, *Die Wochenzeitung Junge Front/Michael*, pp. 244–45.

8. The bishops were at times greatly dissatisfied with Bertram's leadership. On April 2, 1941, Gröber wrote to Nuncio Orsenigo: "Wenn der deutsche Episkopat führerlos ist, führe ich mich mit Gottes Hilfe selber, und wenn ich deswegen leiden muss" (quoted by Volk, 178 [1966]: 251); see also pp. 250–67.

9. Heydrich to Rosenberg on the Fulda Bishops' Conference, August 21–24, 1940, Besetz. Gebiete, T454, R. 82, 000722–24.

10. Woermann to Bergen, November 30, 1939, Albrecht, *Notenwechsel*, 2: 210–11; Woermann's "Aufzeichnung über den Stand unserer Beziehungen zum Vatikan," January 8, 1941, ibid., pp. 212–15; "Mitteilungen zur weltanschaulichen Lage," October 29, 1939, February 12, 1940, May 31, 1941, NSDAP, T81, R. 42, 19069, 19121, 19138. "Orientierungsbericht," July 15, 1943, in John S. Steward, *Sieg des Glaubens*, pp. 114–18.

11. Heydrich to all Gauleiter, June 6, 1941, Schumacher, T580, R. 42. At least in the Nürnberg-Fürth police district, the police ordered copies of the Amtsblätter which carried the pastoral letter to be confiscated and the printing establishments closed (State Secret Police in Nürnberg-Fürth to the Landrat in Eichstätt, June 24, 1941, NSDAP, T81, R. 184, 0334051; for the Fulda pastoral letter, see frames 0334045–49).

12. Bertram's and Hitler's letters are reprinted in Adolph, *Hirtenamt*, pp. 162–63. Bormann saw fit to circulate Hitler's thanks for Bertram's birthday greetings to party officials (*Partei Kanzlei Rundschreiben*, 72/41, June 4, 1941). That Bertram sent the congratulatory letter in the name of the Fulda Bishops' Conference led to serious differences between him and Bishop Preysing of Berlin, who resigned the special *Pressereferat* with which he had been charged by the conference (see the Preysing-Bertram exchange of letters in Adolph, *Hirtenamt*, pp. 164–71; Adolph, *Preysing*, pp. 159–65). Preysing even thought of resigning his bishopric but the pope requested that he not do so (Pius XII to Preysing, June 12, 1940, Schneider, *Briefe Pius' XII*, pp. 74–75). See also Volk, *SZ* 178 (1966): 247–50.

13. Volk, *SZ* 178 (1966): 249.

14. See chap. 16, "Restrictions on Religious Education," above.

15. See, for example, the nuncio's protests of March 4, July 3, 11, 16, and November 6, 1940, Nbg. Doc. 1737, 1738, 1740, 1757, 1776.

16. Picker, *Hitlers Tischgespräche*, July 4, 1942, pp. 372–73.

17. Meldungen aus dem Reich, no. 204, July 21, 1941, Boberach, *Berichte*, p. 535. The text of the bishop's letter is given pp. 538–43.

18. Privat Notiz aus dem Vatikan für Botschafter Bergen, July, 1941, Albrecht, *Notenwechsel*, 2: 109–12; see especially p. 112, n. 1 giving the letter of Woermann to Menshausen, September 5, 1941, commenting on the papal private notice.

19. NSDAP, T81, R. 185, 0335296, 0335298; Kerrl to Lammers, August 2, 1941, Potsdam archives, as reprinted in Mohr, *Katholische Orden*, p. 328–29; Albrecht, *Notenwechsel*, 2: 109n; Terence Prittie, *Germans Against Hitler*, p. 84.

20. Sent out by Heydrich, September 3, 1941, NSDAP, T81, R. 185, 0335297.

21. Picker, *Hitlers Tischgespräche*, July 4, 1942, p. 374; party officials decreed: "von Galen ist möglichst totzuschweigen" (Boyens, *Kirchenkampf und Ökumene*, 1939–1945, p. 357).

22. See chap. 15, "The Euthanasia Program," above.

23. See the German-Vatican exchanges in 1935 on the Saar (Nicolaisen, *Kirchenpolitik*, 2: 292–97). The government, however, gave the concordats the silent treatment and regarded them as out of date. On August 19, 1938, the Ministry of Church Affairs directed all Land governments to follow the practice of the higher Reich officials and make no reference to the Land or Reich concordats in supporting or opposing any measures (Misc. Ger. Rec., T84, R. 14, 41703; see also the Denkschrift by Woermann of January 8, 1941, Nbg. Doc., 4604).

24. Albrecht, *Notenwechsel*, 2: 81n, 213. On March 22 and 26, 1938, the Ministry of Church Affairs had raised the question of the validity of the Austrian concordat at

the Ministry of the Interior. The minister of the interior then requested the Ministry of Church Affairs, the Foreign Office, the minister of justice, the minister of education, Deputy of the Führer Hess, and Reichsführer SS Heydrich to comment on: (1) whether the Austrian concordat should be declared invalid because it had been concluded in illegal fashion (not approved by parliament), or (2) it simply had ceased to exist through the Anschluss of 1938. The ministers had varying views and in the end it was left for Hitler to decide. On July 12, 1938, he gave his decision: (1) the Austrian concordat had lost its validity through the Anschluss since Austria as an independent state had disappeared; (2) the German concordat of 1933 did not apply to Austria since it had been negotiated in relation to the situation in the Old Reich and was not adaptable to Austrian conditions; and (3) Austria was concordat-free territory (BA, Reichjustizministerium, R22/4009, pp. 1062–1125; Nbg. Doc., 676–PS to 680–PS; Guertner Diary, 978, R. 3, 3757–PS 228, 213, 196, 106). At the first meeting on August 2, 1938, of the Catholic section of the newly created Committee for Church Law of the Academy for German Law, one of the questions proposed for study was the situation in Austria after the cancellation of the Austrian concordat (BA, Akademie für Deutsches Recht, R61/261, pp. 31–32).

25. Woermann's "Aufzeichnung über den Stand unserer Beziehungen zum Vatikan," January 8, 1940, Albrecht, *Notenwechsel,* 2: 212–15; Nbg. Doc., NG 4604.

26. Weizsäcker to Bergen, August 25, 1941, *DGFP,* D, 13: 381–83; BA, Reichskanzlei, 43 II/156, pp. 160–61; Albrecht, *Notenwechsel,* 2:113–15, with detailed footnotes.

27. Verbalnote des Päpstl. Staatssekretariats an die Deutsche Botschaft beim Hl. Stuhl, January 18, 1942, Albrecht, *Notenwechsel,* 2: 116–30. For German analysis and reaction to the papal note, see the "Aufzeichnung des Legationsrat Haidlen," February 5, 1942, *ADAP,* E, 1: 377–79.

28. Albrecht Dieter, "Die Politische Klausel des Reichskonkordats in den deutsch-vatikanischen Beziehungen 1936–1943," in Albrecht Dieter, Andreas Kraus, and Kurt Reindel, eds., *Festschrift für Max Spindler zum 75. Geburtstag,* p. 811.

29. *ADAP,* E, 2: 156, 234, 262–64.

30. Lammers to Ribbentrop, June 2, 1942, ibid., p. 448.

31. Ibid.; Albrecht, *Notenwechsel,* 2: 224–25.

32. "Notiz für Herrn Ges. v. Steengracht," June 11, 1942, Albrecht, *Notenwechsel,* 2: 225–26; see also 230–31; Picker, *Hitlers Tischgespräche,* p. 370; *Hitler's Secret Conversations,* p. 448.

33. Bormann in a Rundschreiben from the Führer's headquarters in September 26, 1941, stated that on February 26, 1941, he had informed the Gauleiter of the new Reichsgaue and of the west territories (Alsace, Lorraine, and Luxemburg) that these areas had been exempted from the jurisdiction of the Ministry of Church Affairs and that church matters had gone over in the new territories to the Reichsstatthalter. Such exemption also applied now to Lower Styria, to the occupied sections of Carinthia and Carniola (the result of the Balkan campaign), and to the Sudeten territories and the parts of Tirol added to Bavaria. This decision was not to be published in the *Reichsgesetzblatt* if it could be avoided (Schumacher, T580, R. 42).

34. Orsenigo to Papal Secretary of State, June 27, 1942, Nbg. Doc., 3262-PS; *ADAP,*E, 3: 40–42, 223.

35. Lammers an Oberste Reichs-, Landes- und Besatzungsbehörden, October 18, 1942, Albrecht, *Notenwechsel,* 2: 233–35; see also 229–32.

36. Weizsäcker to the Embassy at the Holy See, August 25, 1941, *DGFP,* D, 13: 381–82. For the situation in Danzig, see the study by Ministerialrat Roth, "Die Rechtslage der Katholischen Kirche in Danzig," BA, Akademie für Deutsches Recht, R61/262, pp. 16–35.

37. Besides the Austrian concordat there were also the Polish concordat, the modus vivendi with Czechoslovakia, and the Lithuanian concordat. The nunciatures in Vienna, Prague, Warsaw, Brussels (also for Luxemburg), and The Hague were closed at once when Germany occupied these countries. The nuncio in Paris accompanied the French government to Vichy and the portions of occupied France were outside his jurisdiction (Dieter Albrecht, "Deutsch-vatikanische Beziehungen 1936–1943," in Dieter, Kraus, and Reindel, *Festschrift für Max Spindler,* pp. 802, 821).

38. Albrecht, *Notenwechsel,* 2: 131–34, particularly the footnotes; Conway, *Nazi Persecution,* pp. 300–310.

39. Deposition by Herbert Siegfried, Weizsäcker's personal secretary, *Weizsäcker Pro-*

zess, Doc. 339; deposition of Eduard Gehrmann, secretary at the papal nunciature in Berlin. Gehrmann states that Weizsäcker appointed one man in his department to investigate every incident called to the attention of the department and to help as much as was humanly possible (Doc. 138); see also Leonidas E. Hill, *Die Weizsäcker-Papiere,* p. 40.

40. The note dated at the Vatican on March 2 was delivered to Weizsäcker on March 15 (Albrecht, *Notenwechsel,* 2: 135–62). It was returned to the nuncio on March 17. Maglione's protest of April 17 against the rejection of the note was delivered by the nuncio on May 5. Ribbentrop answered May 25, and Maglione replied again on July 20 (ibid., 149n); Ribbentrop to Nuncio Orsenigo, May 25, 1943, ibid., pp. 235–37; on this incident, see also Nbg. Doc. 3264-PS, 3269-PS; Blet, *Le Saint Siège et la guerre mondiale, Nov. 1942–Dec. 1943,* pp. 24–5, 268—70, 277, 304–5, 315–17.

41. See the 241 depositions in favor of Weizsäcker, *Weiszäcker Prozess,* vols. 3 and 4.

42. Albrecht in Dieter, Kraus, and Reindel, *Festschrift für Max Spindler,* p. 826n.

43. Hoche, *Gesetzgebung,* 13: 77.

44. Ibid., 23: 59, par. 25, sec. 10; pp. 89–90, annex 3.

45. Pacelli to Bergen, May 18, 1937, Albrecht, *Notenwechsel,* 2: 16–19, with pertinent footnotes; Pacelli to Bergen, November 25, 1937, ibid., pp. 64–66.

46. Vermerk, March, 1939, prepared by Oberregierungsrat Schwarz, Schumacher, T580, R. 42. Hess had proposed that Catholic theological students be made to serve two years longer in the Labor Service (a total of two-and-a-half years), but this solution of the problem was generally rejected. See also Kerrl to Lammers, March 20, 1939, Potsdam archives, as reprinted in Mohr, *Katholische Orden,* pp. 307–9.

47. Lammers to Kerrl, May 30, 1939, Mohr, *Katholische Orden,* pp. 309–10; for a report on the number of theological students in March, 1941, see Boberach, *Berichte,* pp. 497–99.

48. Neuhäusler, *Kreuz und Hakenkreuz,* 1: 104–5. Innsbruck was closed largely because it was a Jesuit institution (Misc. Ger. Rec., T84, R. 14, 41776–77; see also Wodka, *Kirche in Österreich,* p. 381).

49. Vorlage für Reichsleiter Bormann, Schumacher T580, R. 42.

50. Section b of the annex to the concordat, *DGFP,* C, 1: 678; Schöppe, *Konkordate,* p. 35.

51. Hoche, *Gesetzgebung,* 13: 77.

52. Mohr, *Katholische Orden,* p. 327; *Partei-Kanzlei Rundschreiben,* 11/41g, July 12, 1941.

53. Schumacher, T580, R. 42.

54. This paragraph is based on material in Schumacher T580, R. 42; the directive by Bormann is Rundschreiben 374/44, November 2, 1944; reprinted in Baier, *Die Deutschen Christen,* pp. 562–63.

55. NSDAP, T81, R. 185, 0335417.

56. Potsdam archives as cited by Mohr, *Katholische Orden,* p. 155.

57. Mitteilung des Chefs der Sicherheitspolizei . . . Kaltenbrunner, November 28, 1944, Boberach, *Berichte,* p. 894.

58. Mohr, *Katholische Orden,* p. 155.

59. N. Greinacher and H. T. Risse, eds., *Bilanz des deutschen Katholizismus,* pp. 72–73.

60. Mohr, *Katholische Orden,* p. 155; see also "Die Änderungen in der Rechtslage der staatlicher bzw. philosophisch-theologischen Hochschule seit Kriegsbeginn," BA, Akademie für Deutsches Recht, R61/262.

61. Boberach, *Berichte,* pp. 520–22, 606–9. The police considered the masses to be an important source of revenue for the church.

62. Boberach, *Berichte,* on the increase in memorial services, pp. 589–91, 736–40, 763–65, 774–78; increase in musical services, pp. 747–52, 877–80; increase in youth activities, pp. 785–803, 804–9; see also Steward, *Sieg des Glaubens,* pp. 70–71, 74–84.

63. "Denkschrift Franks über die Behandlung der polnischen Zivilarbeiter im Reich," Nbg. Doc., 908-PS; also in Broszat, *Polenpolitik,* pp. 111–17. Frank argued that the Poles should receive treatment similar to that accorded other foreign workers. See also "Verbot und Strafverfolgung wegen Verkehr Polnischer Zivilarbeiter mit Deutschen Frauen und Mädchen," in *Gutachten des Instituts für Zeitgeschichte,* pp. 387–89; Hans Pfahlmann, *Fremdarbeiter und Kriegsgefangene in der Deutschen Kriegswirtschaft 1939–1945,* pp. 148, 205.

64. Bertram to Maglione, December 7, 1942, *Nazi Conspiracy and Aggression,* 5: 1031–36, Doc. 3266-PS.

65. Boberach, *Berichte,* pp. 370, 373, 381–82, 407, 410, 760–61; Reichsführer SS, T175, R. 258, 2750232.

66. Reichsführer SS, T175, R. 408, 2931728–29.

67. Maglione to Bertram, November 18, 1942, *Nazi Conspiracy and Aggression,* 5: 1029–31, Doc. 3265-PS; Bertram's reply of December 7, 1942, ibid., pp. 1031–36, Doc. 3266-PS.

68. Stimmungsbericht SS, Abschnitt Lemz, December 14, 1942, NSDAP, T81, R. 7, 14419.

69. Reichsführer SS, T175, R. 265, 2759168–72; for reports that civilians were too friendly to Polish workers, see Boberach, *Berichte,* pp. 368, 398, 717, 729–30, 761, 764, 842. Reichsführer SS, T175, R. 264, 2757693–701, 2757776–78, 2758574; R. 263, 2757433.

70. Reichsführer SS, T175, R. 408, 2931726–27; on services for Ukrainians, see Boberach, *Berichte,* pp. 731, 761; for the regulations regarding the wearing of the designations "P" and "Ost," see Pfahlmann, *Fremdarbeiter,* pp. 205–9.

71. Rundschreiben Bormann, 14/43, February 2, 1943, Schumacher, T580, R. 42; Geh. St. Polz., Düsseldorf, April 20, May 6, 1943, Reichsführer SS, T175, R. 408, 2932155, 2932157.

72. Ibid., frame 2932172.

73. Ibid., frame 2932176.

74. Rundschreiben 398/44g, November 14, 1944, Schumacher, T580, R. 42.

75. Rundschreiben 185/44g, Schumacher, T580, R. 42.

76. Institut für Zeitgeschichte, Munich, Fa 506/11, pp. 9–27; *Partei-Kanzlei Rundschreiben,* 126/41. For two such decrees of January 27, 1941, and October 15, 1941, see Conway, *Nazi Persecution,* app. 16, pp. 387–92. Himmler saw to it that the women received additional rations (Heiber, *Briefe an und von Himmler,* p. 135).

77. See chap. 17, "The Warthegau: Pattern for the Future?," above.

78. Reimund Schnabel, *Die Frommen in der Hölle,* p. 154. Protestant Pastor Heinrich Grüber pays warm tribute to Bishop Wienken. He writes: "Ich hatte schon in der NS-Zeit mit ihm zusammengearbeitet und muss sagen, dass ich selten einen Menschen kennengelernt habe der aus christlichen Verantwortung so tapfer den verschiedenen Machthabern die Meinung sagt. Wienken hob sich von den anderen Würdenträgern ab, die in Grundsatzfragen allzuoft faule Kompromisse schlossen (*Erinnerungen,* p. 271).

79. Schnabel, *Frommen in der Hölle,* pp. 99, 154, 281. For an account of Neuhäusler's arrest and imprisonment, see Neuhäusler, *Amboss und Hammer,* pp. 153–203. For a description of the concentration camp, see Johann Neuhäusler, *Wie war das im KZ Dachau.*

80. Schnabel, *Frommen in der Hölle,* p. 78; see also the summary of the number of clergy in Dachau on March 15, 1945, as to nationality, higher officials, and members of orders in Neuhäusler, *Kreuz und Hakenkreuz,* 1: 349.

81. Lewy, *Catholic Church and Nazi Germany,* p. 227.

82. Mimeographed sheet, no statement of origin, Nürnberg, LK. Arch., Bestand 218.

83. *Nazi Conspiracy and Aggression,* 3: 820, Doc. 1164-PS; see also "A short report on the torture of Polish Priests at Dachau," written by Ignacy Walczewski, Prisoner 11059, Nbg. Doc., 1943-PS.

84. Martin Broszat, "Verfolgung polnischer katholischer Geistlichen 1939–1945. Gutachten des Instituts für Zeitgeschichte," p. 83.

85. Wodka, *Kirche in Österreich,* p. 382.

86. Mohr, *Katholische Orden,* p. 151.

87. Besetz. Gebiete, T454, R. 81, 000374–81.

88. "Dienstverplichtung von Ordensangehörigen," Meldungen aus dem Reich, no. 246, December 15, 1941, Boberach, *Berichte,* pp. 605–6.

89. Bormann to all Gauleiter, January 13, 1941, Nbg. Doc., 3927-PS. There were in fact many protests over the seizure of monasteries. In the Bundesarchiv in Koblenz there is a 191 page portfolio of correspondence and protests on the seizure, mostly in connection with Austrian institutions (BA, Reichskanzlei, R 43 II/158; see also R 43 II/158a, pp. 1–56).

90. Galen to Lammers, July 14, 1941; Lammers to Galen, July 17; Galen to Lammers, July 28, NSDAP, T81, R. 185, 0335865–66; Portman, *Bischof Galen,* p. 56. Galen

also wrote a pointed letter to Lammers on July 22, 1941, in which he observed: "Adolf Hitler ist nicht ein göttliches Wesen." He enclosed copies of his sermons of July 13 and July 20 (BA, Reichskanzlei, R 43 II/149, p. 40; also Schumacher, T580, R. 41). Although Kerrl did not reply to Galen, he did send Galen's telegram of July 14, 1941, and another communication from him of July 17 to Lammers on August 2. Kerrl noted that he had written the Reichsführer der SS und Chef der deutschen Polizei on July 11 in regard to the seizure of monastic property. Kerrl could not believe that Hitler approved the way it was being done right in the middle of the war. Up to August 2 Kerrl had received no reply from the head of the police (Kerrl to Lammers, August 2, 1941, Potsdam archives as reprinted in Mohr, *Katholische Orden*, p. 328).

91. The Fulda Hirtenbrief of June 26, 1941 is given NSDAP, T81, R. 184, 0334045–49. Numerous police reports indicated that the people had taken the reading of the letter quietly (ibid., 0334030–44). One report noted that the peasants believed Hitler was overburdened with work; if he knew, he would not tolerate attacks against the Catholic church. After all, at the beginning of the war against Russia he had stated: "Unser Herrgott wolle uns gnädig sein" (ibid., 0334039).

92. The sermons are given in Portman, *Bischof Galen*, pp. 44–61.

93. Ibid., pp. 67–76; for reaction to the sermon, see pp. 98–104.

94. On November 11, 1941, Bishop Galen's sermon of July 13 was confiscated in Belgium, where it was about to be translated into French (Schumacher, T580, R. 41).

95. Portman, *Bischof Galen*, pp. 82–88.

96. Ibid., pp. 98–99. In March, 1941, Kerrl had wanted to cut the state subsidies to Bishop Galen and to Archbishop Gröber, but Hitler ordered that no cut be made (BA, Reichskanzlei, R 43 II/153, pp. 16, 20, 43). In 1938 Kerrl had pressed for charges against Galen because of his remarks on the exile of Bishop Sproll of Rottenburg (Guertner Diary, 978, R. B, 3757-PS289).

97. *Nazi Conspiracy and Aggression*, 6: 405-10, Doc. 3701-PS.

98. Bormann to Gauleiter, July 30, 1941, *DGFP*, D, 13: 536–37; Aufzeichnung Fischer, December 19, 1941, *ADAP*, E, 63–64; Aufzeichnung Woermann, March 28, 1942, ibid., 2: 156, see also 262–64; Adolph, *Preysing*, p. 148.

99. See chap. 15, "The Euthanasia Program," above.

100. Nbg. Doc., 1815-PS; Boberach, *Berichte*, pp. 934–43.

101. Auszug der Staatspolizeistelle Aachen, June 23, 1942, Boberach, *Berichte*, pp. 943–44. On police surveilance of the hierarchy and recruitment of informers, see Heydrich's order of April 19, 1940 (Steward, *Sieg des Glaubens*, pp. 17–19).

102. Mohr, *Katholische Orden*, pp. 137, 150, 152; see also the somewhat larger totals as listed in Neuhäusler, *Kreuz und Hakenkreuz*, 1: 149–55, where Austrian foundations are included. The police reported in September, 1941, that about 100 monasteries had been "secured" in the Reichsgebiet; exactly what territories this included was not defined (Boberach, *Berichte*, p. 938).

103. The Foreign Office was concerned over the continued seizures (Aufzeichnung by Woermann of March 23 and April 21, 1942, *ADAP*, E, 2: 156, 262–64).

104. Wodka, *Kirche in Österreich*, p. 382. There is a list of churches, monasteries, ecclesiastical establishments, associations, youth homes, schools, and institutes, that were seized, closed, and disbanded in the apostolic administration of Innsbruck, Feldkirch, Tirol, and Vorarlberg in *Nazi Conspiracy and Aggression*, 5: 1070–72, Doc. 3278-PS.

105. The number of Jews converting to Catholicism 1900–1939 was 3,546; the number was never above 100 a year until 1933, when it jumped to 304. Totals for the other years are: 234 (1934); 193 (1935); 149 (1936); 95 (1937); 277 (1938); 358 (1939) (BA, Reichsministerium für kirch. Angelegenheiten, R79/19; for Jewish conversions to the Evangelical church, see chap. 16, n. 78, above.

106. Lewy, *Catholic Church and Nazi Germany*, pp. 285–86.

107. Ibid., p. 286.

108. See chap. 17, "The Warthegau: Pattern for the Future?," above, and the material on the ministration of the churches to workers from eastern Europe in this chapter, "The Impact of the War on the Clergy."

109. Lewy, *Catholic Church and Nazi Germany*, p. 289: Manfred Wolfsen, "Der Widerstand gegen Hitler. Soziologische Skizze über Retter (Rescuers) von Juden in Deutschland," *Beilage zur Wochenzeitung "Das Parlament,"* April 10, 1971, p. 35. Wolfsen refers to a demonstration of 200 women. In a protest against the persecu-

tion of alien races, the archbishop of Cologne stated on March 12, 1944: "Die Ehen zwischen Volksangehörigen und Fremdstämmigen, wenn sie mit kirchlicher Gutheisung geschlossen sind und zumal wenn beide Teile getaufte katholische Christen sind, sind unauflöslich, und es ist ein Verbrechen gegen Gottes Recht über die Ehe, durch irgendwelche Machenschaften solche Ehen auseinanderzutreiben," (Corsten, *Kölner Aktenstücke*, p. 310). See also Bishop Preysing's pastoral letter of December 13, 1942. Adolph, *Preysing*, p. 178.

110. Bormann Rundschreiben, 32/43, February 19, 1943, Schumacher, T580, R. 42.

111. Bormann Rundschreiben, 26/43g, Schumacher, T580, R. 42.

112. Bormann Rundschreiben, 76/43, Schumacher, T580, R. 42.

113. Denkschrift über Katholisches Hochschulwesen zur Ausbildung des Priesternachwuches, Schumacher, T580, R. 40.

114. The pope wrote a letter of condolence to Bishop Berning on August 18, 1943, in respect to the bombing (Schneider, *Briefe Pius' XII*, pp. 251–52). Portions of the letter were forwarded by the Gestapo to Bormann (Schumacher, T580, R. 40).

115. Bormann Rundschreiben, 118/43, August 25, 1943, Schumacher, T580, R. 42; see also NSDAP, T81, R. 185, 0335342–43.

116. Lewy, *Catholic Church and Nazi Germany*, pp. 286–93; see chap. 16, n. 83, above.

117. Volk, *SZ* 178 (1966): 260; for the text of the pastoral letter, see Corsten, *Kölner Aktenstücke*, pp. 298–307. The pope read the letter with great satisfaction (Adolph, *Preysing*, p. 194).

118. SD-Bericht zu Inlandsfragen, September 20, 1943, Boberach, *Berichte*, p. 855.

119. See also the veiled protest of the archbishop of Cologne in his Christmas sermon, December 25, 1943: "Und wer mit Absicht nichtkämpfende tötet, sei es aus der Luft oder wie immer, wer ihnen das Leben nimmt, nur weil sie einem fremden Volk, einer fremden Rasse angehören, der sündigt wider Gottes Gebot 'Du sollst nicht töten!' der verstösst wider Christi Hauptgebot, der sagt 'Das ist mein Gebot, dass ihr einander liebt, wie ich euch geliebt habe' " (Corsten, *Kölner Aktenstücke*, p. 310).

120. This passage is printed in dark black print in the excerpt of the letter given in Neuhäusler, *Kreuz und Hakenkreuz*, 2: 70.

121. Jenö Levai, *Geheime Reichssache*, pp. 26–27, 29–31, 40, 49–50.

122. Nbg. Doc., NG-4447; Nuncio Orsenigo sought to intervene on behalf of Lichtenberg on March 10, 1942 (ibid.).

123. In 1933 the baptized Jews, with Catholic aid, had founded a *Reichsverband christlich-deutscher Staatsbürger nichtarischer oder nicht reinarischer Abstammung*. The name was changed to *Paulus-Bund* in 1937; that same year the government forced the dropping of "full" Jews from membership and the society lost all effectiveness. At this time the bishop of Osnabrück established a center to prepare non-Aryan Christians for emigration. The emigration of Catholic Jews was furthered by the St. Raphaelsverein in Hamburg (Zipfel, *Kirchenkampf*, pp. 217–18; Schumacher, T580, R. 48). The most detailed account of Catholic efforts on behalf of Jews is to be found in Reutter, *Hilfstätigkeit katholischen Organisationen*; see pp. 81–256 on Catholic help on emigration, pp. 278–85 on Catholic help to Jews during the war; the Catholics did not have enough funds even to help the Catholic Jews (p. 292); see also Adolph, *Preysing*, pp. 175–79.

124. Lewy, *Catholic Church and Nazi Germany*, pp. 294–95; see also Rhodes, *The Vatican*, p. 297.

125. This was the central theme of his letters to the German bishops during the war (Burkhart Schneider, "Pius XII und die deutschen Bischöfe," *SZ* 177 [1966]: 260–63; Alberto Giovannetti, *Der Vatikan und der Krieg*, pp. 94–97, 102–16; Rhodes, *The Vatican*, pp. 230–33). The seal of Pius XII was dominated by a dove of peace with the motto *Opus justitiae pax* ("The Work of Justice is Peace") (Hermelink, *Die katholische Kirche*, p. 45).

126. Harold C. Deutsch, *The Conspiracy Against Hitler in the Twilight War*, pp. 103–48, 349–52; John S. Conway, "The Vatican, Great Britain, and Relations with Germany, 1938–1940," *Historical Journal* 16 (1973): 157–67; Gallin, *German Resistance to Hitler*, pp. 112–13; Prittie, *Germans Against Hitler*, pp. 90–91; Rhodes, *The Vatican*, pp. 240–42.

127. Leiber, *SZ* 167 (1961): 428–36; Hill, *Die Weizsäcker-Papiere*, pp. 41–42; John S. Conway, "The Silence of Pius XII," *Review of Politics* 27 (1965): 128–29; Saul Friedlander, *Pius XII and the Third Reich*, pp. 198–235; Levai, *Geheime Reichs-*

sache, pp. 126–30; Beate Ruhm von Oppen, "Nazis and Christians," *World Politics* 21 (1969): 392–424; Rhodes, *The Vatican,* pp. 303–6, 317, 331; Joseph L. Lichten, *A Question of Judgment,* pp. 13–31.

128. While the Polish clergy in exile seemed to feel that the pope had forsaken Poland, at least some of the clergy within Poland urged that no protest be made. For the fate of the Polish Catholics, see the citations in Burkhart Schneider, "Der Heilige Stuhl und Polen während der Kriegsjahre," *SZ* 180 (1967): 25–31; Rhodes, *The Vatican,* p. 289; Lichten, *A Question of Judgment,* p. 6; Conzemius, *Églises chrétiennes,* pp. 47–54; Victor Conzemius, "Pius XII and Nazi Germany in Historical Perspective," in J. C. Beckett, ed., *Historical Studies VII.*

129. Binder, *Irrtum und Widerstand,* p. 374.

130. Ibid., p. 375; for the attitude of postwar theologians, see pp. 376–78; Gallin, *German Resistance to Hitler,* pp. 228–29.

131. Gallin, *German Resistance to Hitler,* p. 203; see also Conzemius, *Églises chrétiennes,* pp. 142–44.

132. Nbg. Doc., 1233-PS.

133. The microfilms of police reports give innumerable cases of arrested clerics; actions against many individual clerics are mentioned in the "Meldungen aus dem Reich," October, 1939–November, 1944, Boberach, *Berichte,* pp. 350–898, passim; Lewy, *Catholic Church and Nazi Germany,* p. 318; Prittie, *Germans Against Hitler,* pp. 86–89; Rudolf Pechel, *Deutscher Widerstand,* pp. 58–59; Conway, *Nazi Persecution,* pp. 323–25; for short accounts of Catholic as well as Protestant clergy executed by the Nazis, see Benedicta Maria Kempner, *Priester vor Hitlers Tribunalen.*

134. Gallin, *German Resistance to Hitler,* p. 226; Kempner, *Priester vor Hitlers Tribunalen,* pp. 61–74; on the Kreisau Circle, see chap. 17 at n. 64, above.

135. M. Laros, *Dr. Max J. Metzger (Br. Paulus),* pp. 4–8; Kempner, *Priester vor Hitlers Tribunalen,* pp. 273–89; Spael, *Das katholische Deutschland,* p. 345. For a consideration of what constituted treason in Nazi Germany, see Gallin, *German Resistance to Hitler,* pp. 108–9.

136. Ernst Wolf's essay in Graml et al., *German Resistance,* p. 225.

137. Cardinal Faulhaber was questioned after the assassination attempt and he denounced "das himmelschreiende Verbrechen des 20. Juli" (Volk, *SZ* 177 [1966]: 193); Adolph, *Preysing,* pp. 181–84.

138. Warloski, *Neudeutschland,* pp. 118, 133, 136, 204–5.

Chapter Nineteen

1. The definitions of "church," "Free church," and "sect" have shifted over the decades. Here I have in general followed the listing of Free churches as given in *KJ,* 1926, pp. 673–80.

2. See chap. 4, "Free Churches and Sects," above.

3. Reichskanzlei, T120, R. 4419, L124322–23.

4. *New York Times,* May 7, 1933, p. 1.

5. Methodist Bishop J. L. Nuelson as quoted by Macfarland, *New Church and the New Germany,* p. 58.

6. *New York Times,* November 20, 1933, p. 6.

7. Ibid., October 20, 1933, p. 12.

8. See chap. 7, "Crisis Among the German Christians," above.

9. *New York Times,* November 20, 1933, p. 6.

10. Ibid.

11. J. H. Rushbrooke, ed., *Fifth Baptist World Congress, Berlin, August 4–10, 1934,* pp. v, vi, 19. The German text of Reich Bishop Müller's declaration is given p. 229.

12. Akad. D. Recht, T82, R. 43, folder 168.

13. See the reply of Martin Willkomm, Hochschuldirektor, Theologische Hochschule der Ev. Luth. Freikirche in Sachsen und anderen Staaten, ibid.

14. Ibid.

15. This statement reiterates the thanks expressed to Hitler in a statement drawn up at the fifty-second meeting of the synod in Berlin, May 23–28, 1933 (ibid.; also *Frankfurter Zeitung,* May 26, 1934, clipping in Biel. Arch., Coll. W. Niemöller, K12, Freikirchen).

16. Rauter to Akademie für Deutsches Recht, December 28, 1938, Akd. D. Recht, T82, R. 44.

17. The formation of the Academy for German Law can be followed in the dossier, BA, Akad. D. Recht, R61/261, pp. 5–56.

18. Rauter immediately contacted the committee (Rauter to Akad. D. Recht, December 28, 1938, Akad. D. Recht, T82, R. 44).

19. Willkomm to Meyer, March 22, 1939, Akad. D. Recht, T82, R. 43.

20. Meyer to Kohl, October 6, 1939, forwarding letter of Willkomm, BA, Akad. D. Recht, R61/262, pp. 14a, 14b.

21. Meyer to Willkomm, September 26, 1939, Akad. D. Recht, T82, R. 43.

22. Lammers to Frank, December 23, 1940, BA, Reichskanzlei, 43 II/150a, p. 25.

23. See Ambassador Luther's report on the visit of Methodist Bishop MacDowell and Samuel M. Calvert, general secretary of the Federal Council of Churches of Christ in America, October 16, 1934, Ausw. A., T120, R. 4418, L124010–12.

24. For example, subsidies such as the 600 marks that the Foreign Office gave to Pastor Holschuher and Pastor Melle to attend the meeting of the General Methodist Conference in the United States in 1931. Melle was scheduled to give a declaration against Art. 231 of the Versailles treaty at the conference (BA, Reichskanzlei, 43 II/179, pp. 77–89).

25. *New York Times,* November 12, 1936.

26. The "Melle incident" is discussed in more detail in chap. 11, "The Oxford World Conference," above.

27. Reichskanzlei to Bormann, November 22, 1938, BA, Reichskanzlei, R 43 II/152, pp. 31–33.

28. *New York Times,* August 7, 1937, p. 16.

29. Nbg. Doc., 410-PS; *Partei Kanzlei Rundschreiben* 66/41, May 22, 1941.

30. *New York Times,* November 23, 1934, p. 13.

31. Holzschuher to Lammers, January 7, 1936, BA, Reichskanzlei, 43 II/181, pp. 9–13; clippings from the *Cincinnatier Freie Presse* of October 22 and 23, 1935, were enclosed.

32. *New York Times,* April 18, 1936.

33. "Sonderbericht. Die Lage der protestantischen Kirche und in den verschiedenen Sekten und deren staatsfeindliche Auswirkung," February–March, 1935, BA, Reichssicherheitshauptamt, R58/233, p. 20.

34. *New York Times,* June 15, 1937, p. 7.

35. Reichsführer SS, T175, R. 408, 2931765, 2931767; T175, R. 490, 9351193; Schumacher, T580, R. 48.

36. *Der Evangelist. Organ der Bischöflichen Methodisten Kirche in Deutschland* 84 (June, 1933): 404 upheld the boycott of Jewish business in 1933. "Die Juden sind zurückgedrängt ohne dass ihnen ein Haar gekrummt worden ist . . . von Verfolgung ist absolut keine Rede."

37. Franklin H. Littell says about the bishop's policy: "When Bishop Melle of the German Methodist Episcopal Church achieved peace with the Nazis by reducing the congregations for which he was responsible to pietist conventicles, he betrayed the church" (*The Free Church,* p. 7).

38. Wunderlich, *Brückenbauer Gottes,* pp. 174–75.

39. *New York Times,* August 11, 1934, p. 5.

40. Ibid., August 8, 1934.

41. Ibid., August 9, 1934.

42. Rushbrooke, *Fifth Baptist World Congress,* minute 163, p. 17; see also the notes of the address by the chairman, Rev. C. E. Wilson, in submitting the report on racialism (pp. 65–66).

43. Ibid., p. v; minutes 122, 126, 171, pp. 13, 14, 17; remarks by Dr. Clifton D. Gray, president of Bates College and honorary associate secretary of the congress, J. H. Rushbrooke, ed., *Sixth Baptist World Congress Atlanta, Georgia, U.S.A.,* p. 283.

44. Bismarck to Foreign Office, October 8, 1934, Ausw. A., T120, R. 4418, L124006–9.

45. Rushbrooke, *Sixth Baptist World Congress,* p. 263.

46. Ibid., p. 208.

47. Geh. St. Pol., Berlin, July 7, 1937, Schumacher, T580, R. 48; Geh. St. Pol., Bielefeld, February 27, 1939, Reichsführer SS, T175, R. 490, 9351174.

48. On April 25, 1933, the directory of the Tent Mission (*Zeltmission*) wrote Hitler wishing him God's blessing, thanking him, and pledging their support. They were disturbed, however, by rumors that all missionary organizations aside from the large churches would be dissolved. The minister of the interior, on May 24, 1933,

took a reserved stand and advised that the attitude of the government toward the Tent Mission and other similar missionary organizations would depend on whether it was convinced "that they deepened the religiosity of the German people." This communication was sent to the directors of the Tent Mission on June 2, 1933, and they sent a thank-you letter (BA, Reichskanzlei, R 43 II/150, pp. 1–3, 12–13).

49. Herbert Stahl, "Der Bund Evangelisch-Freikirchlicher Germeinden in Deutschland . . . , " in Kunz, *Viele Glieder ein Leib,* pp. 163–64; Erwin Fahlbusch, ed., *Taschenlexikon Religion und Theologie,* 1: 82.

50. In 1946 in the United States, the Church of the United Brethren and the Evangelical church united to form the Evangelical United Brethren church. The Evangelische Gemeinschaft from then on had relations with this new united church. In 1968 the Evangelical United Brethren church and the Methodist church in the United States merged to form the United Methodist church. So far there has been no merger of the German Methodist church and the Evangelische Gemeinschaft.

51. Reinhold Küchlich, "Die Evangelische Gemeinschaft," in Kunz, *Viele Glieder ein Leib,* p. 326.

52. Wilhelm Wöhrle, ibid., p. 247.

53. These were the: (1) Evangelische-lutherische Kirche in Preussen (Alt Lutheraner), (2) Selbständige evangelisch-lutherische Kirche in Hessen, (3) Hannoverische evangelische-lutherische Freikirche, (4) Die Evangelisch-lutherische Kirche in Baden, (5) Die Ev. luth. Hermannsburg-Hamburger Freikirche, (6) Renitente Kirche ungeänderter Augsburger Konfession in Hessen, (7) Freie evangelische-lutherische Bekenntniskirche zu St. Ansgar, Hamburg, and (8) Die Evangelisch-lutherische Freikirche u. A. K. in Sachsen und anderen Staaten. In 1919 the first seven of these formed a loose association, the Vereinigung Evangelisch-lutherischer Freikirchen in Deutschland. After World War II another church was added: Die Ev. Luth. Flüchtlingsmissionskirche (after 1951 called Die ev. luth. Bekenntnis K. in der Diaspora) which was formerly the Ev. Luth. Freikirche in Polen (*KJ,* 1926, pp. 673–75; 1945–48, p. 473; 1951, p. 446).

54. Gottfried Nagel, *Kann die Evang.-luth. Kirche Altpreussens sich der Deutschen Evang. Kirche eingliedern?*

55. Fleisch, *ZevKR* 1 (1951): 36; Schmidt, *Dokumente der Ausschusszeit,* 2: 1153–54. The superintendent of the Hermannsburg-Hamburger evangelisch-lutherische Freikirche sent a letter of congratulation to the Luther Council but refused to bring his church into it (ibid., 2: 1301–3).

56. *KJ,* 1926, pp. 675–76; Berend H. Lankampf, "Die altreformierte Kirchen in Niedersachsen," in Kunz, *Viele Glieder ein Leib,* pp. 53–54.

57. See the substantive article by Steiner, *KJ,* 1950, pp. 228–333; here p. 228.

58. Members were: (1) Konföderation evangelisch-reformierter Gemeinden in Niedersachsen, (2) Reformierte Gemeinden im Lande Sachsen, (3) Reformierte Gemeinde Hamburg, (4) Niederländische und Wallonische Gemeinden in Hanau, (5) Reformierte Synode in Bayern (*KJ,* 1945–48, p. 473; 1949, p. 615).

59. *RGG,* 5: 894. The Reformed Union again represents primarily the scattered Reformed congregations, the Land church of Lippe, and the Reformed Church of Northwest Germany, the latter being primarily an outgrowth of the former Reformed Church of Hanover.

60. *KJ,* 1926, pp. 269–70; Fahlbusch, *Taschenlexikon Religion und Theologie,* 3: 118.

61. Leitheft über die Neuapostolische Gemeinde e. V. Mai 1937, Reichsführer SS, T175, R. 408, 2932404–47; here Anlage 6, frame 2932440.

62. For example, Ecclesiasticus 10:1 reads according to the authorized version: "A wise judge will instruct his people; and the government of a prudent man is well ordered," while the German version (Sirach 10:1) reads: "Ein weiser Regent ist strenge; und wo eine verständige Obrigkeit ist, da gehet es ordentlich zu." There could have been no more appropriate text to celebrate the new government than verse 4 in the German version: "Das Regiment auf Erden stehet in Gotteshänden, derselbe gibt ihr zu Zeiten einen tüchtigen Regenten." Verse 5 speaks of "einen löblichen Kanzler," while Ecclesiasticus in this same passage refers to a scribe.

63. Leitheft, Reichsführer SS, T175, R. 408, 2932438.

64. Ibid., Anlage 6, 2932440–42.

65. Ibid., 2932414.

66. Ibid., 2932418.

67. The study is not dated, but it must have been drawn up between May, 1936, and May, 1937; the Leitheft is dated May, 1937, and is to be found Reichsführer SS,

T175, R. 408, 2932404–47; see also BA, Reichssicherheitshauptamt, R58/230. The study has an "Übersichtskarte über die Verbreitung der Neuapostolischen Gemeinde," and cited a membership of 242,000 on December 31, 1933, and 245,729 on December 31, 1934. A graph projected a possible membership of 300,000 soon after this date.

68. Chef der Sicherheitsdienst an den Chef des Rasse-und Siedlungshauptamtes, March 8, 1943, Schumacher, T580, R. 48.

69. The Mennonites in 1883 had formed an Association of Mennonite Congregations in Germany which included all congregations except those in Baden, Württemberg, and Bavaria, which at this time had their own organization. The association had its headquarters in Hamburg, where it had been granted the privileges of a public corporation (KJ, 1926, p. 676). In 1938 the head of the association, Pastor Händiges, confirmed again the provision of their church constitution of 1934 about serving in the army (Zur Weltanschaulichen Lage, March, 1938, NSDAP, T81, R. 23, 20199–200).

70. Quoted in "Der Reichsführer SS und der Chef des Rasse-und Siedlungshauptamtes," April 9, 1938, Schumacher T580, R. 48.

71. Ibid.; the letter from the Mennonites was dated June 22, 1938. Bormann's Rundschreiben, no. 2/39 is to be found in Schumacher, T580, R. 48.

72. Das Schwarzmeerdeutschtum. Die Mennoniten (Posen, 1944), to be found Schumacher, T580, R. 48.

73. RGG, 4: 856; KJ, 1951, pp. 444, 466. On the Working Community, see n. 106, below.

74. Geh. St. Pol., June 18, 1935, May 5, 1936, Schumacher, T580, R. 48.

75. New York Times, April 5, 1936.

76. Bavarian political police to various police headquarters, May 5, 1936, Schumacher, T 580, R. 48.

77. KJ, 1926, pp. 670–71; 1950, p. 503. The official name is Die evangelische Brüder-Unität, but they are often referred to as Brüder-Gemeine, Herrnhuter, or Herrnhuter Brüdergemeine.

78. KJ, 1926, p. 680.

79. BA, Reichskanzlei, R 43 II/179, p. 63.

80. Bavarian political police, July 12, 1935, Schumacher, T580, R. 48.

81. BA, Reichssicherheitshauptamt, R58/266; see also the "Verzeichnis der seit 1933 verbotenen Sekten [to December 31, 1938]," which is found here; also reprinted from the Schumacher collection, Berlin Document Center, in Conway, Nazi Persecution, pp. 370–74.

82. BA, Reichssicherheitshauptamt, R58/266; Bavarian political police to various police headquarters, June 30, 1936, Schumacher, T580, R. 48.

83. Geh. St. Pol., Düsseldorf, May 3, 1934, Reichsführer SS, T175, R. 408, 2931882; BA, Reichssicherheitshauptamt, R58/266.

84. Geh. St. Pol., Düsseldorf, August 18, 1942, Reichsführer SS, T175, R. 408, 2931740.

85. BA, Reichskanzlei, R 43 II/181, p. 28.

86. Ibid., p. 6.

87. Geh. St. Pol., Düsseldorf, May 30, 1940, Reichsführer SS, T175, R. 408, 2931752.

88. KJ, 1926, p. 680.

89. Bavarian political police, February 15, 1934, Schumacher, T580, R. 48.

90. BA, Reichskanzlei, R 43 II/179, pp. 259–60, 277–80.

91. BA, Reichssicherheitshauptamt, R58/266; repeated by the Bavarian political police, January 23, 1935, Schumacher, T580, R. 48.

92. Clipping found in Biel. Arch., Coll. W. Niemöller, Col. Präsid., III, 2, NSDAP.

93. Geh. St. Pol., Darmstadt, quoting the Erlass of the minister of the interior of December 17, 1937, Schumacher, T580, R. 48.

94. Jahresbericht 1938, BA, Reichssicherheitshauptamt, R58/1094, p. 75; Zipfel, Kirchenkampf, p. 483.

95. BA, Reichssicherheitshauptamt, R58/266; Geh. St. Pol., Düsseldorf, September 26, 1941, Reichsführer SS, T175, R. 408, 2931742.

96. Minister of the interior to Regierungspräsident in Cologne, November 2, 1942, Nbg. Doc., NG-3441; see also Max Gruner, "Die Heilsarmee," in Kunz, Viele Glieder ein Leib, p. 342.

97. Paul F. Pfister, "Die Alt-Katholische Kirche," in Kunz, Viele Gleider ein Leib, p. 74.

98. BA, Reichskanzlei, R 43 II/179, pp. 117–18.

99. Haugg, *Reichministerium*, p. 24. Haugg reports that the Old Catholics had 100,000 adherents in 200 congregations with 90 priests. It raised 335,000 marks in taxes and received a subsidy of 200,000 marks (p. 23).

100. See "The Position of the Smaller Churches," above.

101. Jahresbericht 1938, BA, Reichssicherheitshauptamt, R58/1094, p. 62.

102. C. B. Moss, *The Old Catholic Movement*, p. 351; Pfister in Kunz, *Viele Glieder ein Leib*, p. 67.

103. This brief account is based on material found in BA, Reichskanzlei, R 43 II/181, pp. 34–53; Haugg, *Reichsministerium*, pp. 25–26. The constitution of the Orthodox church can be found in Schumacher, T580, R. 48.

104. Stewart W. Herman, *The Rebirth of the German Church*, pp. 137–41.

105. *KJ*, 1949, p. 53.

106. The original members were the Evangelical Church in Germany, the Baptists, Methodists, Evangelical Association, Mennonites, and the Old Catholics, who were later joined by the Evangelical Brethren (Moravian Brethren, Herrnhuter). With the exception of the Baptists, all are members of the World Council of Churches. Cooperating with the Working Community are the Union of Free Evangelical Congregations, the Reformed Free churches, and the Salvation Army. In September, 1973, the Catholic Bishops' Conference decided to apply for full membership in the Working Community in West Germany (*KJ*, 1949, pp. 52–58; 1955, pp. 351–81; Wunderlich, *Brückenbauer Gottes*, pp. 190–93; Fahlbusch, *Taschenlexikon Religion und Theologie*, 1: 60; *The German Tribune*, October 25, 1973; see also chap. 21 at n. 73, chap. 22 at n. 83, below.

Chapter Twenty

1. For the ordinance see Hoche, *Gesetzgebung*, 1: 236–37; see also chap. 6, "Hitler Becomes Chancellor," above.

2. The reasons given for forbidding the Gnossis sect on July 10, 1936, were that it had no firm organization and harbored anti-Nazis under the guise of being a religious association (Prussian Sec. Pol., Schumacher, T580, R. 48).

3. *KJ*, 1949, p. 357.

4. Weinkauff, *Deutsche Justiz*, 2: 77.

5. A Jehovah's Witness publication quotes with approval a statement from *The German Way* (May 29, 1938) written by a Catholic priest, who states that the German episcopate asked Hitler to dissolve the Earnest Bible Students, and Hitler complied because they were troublemakers and disturbed the harmonious life of the Germans (*Jehovah's Witnesses in the Divine Purpose*, p. 130). Protestant pastors also submitted anti-Jehovah's Witnesses material to the government (BA, Reichskanzlei, R 43 II/179, pp. 147–201).

6. "Erweckungs-Mission in Deutschland, Sitz Berlin, nebst unterorganisationen Missiongemeinde und Freie Pfingstgemeinde," BA, Reichssicherheitshauptamt, R58/266; also in Schumacher, T580, R. 48.

7. Officially *Die Evangelisch-Johannische Kirche nach der Offenbarung St. Johannis*.

8. BA, Reichssicherheitshauptamt, R58/238, p. 20; R58/266; Bavarian State Police, February 5, 1935, Schumacher, T580, R. 48.

9. Prussian Geh. Pol., July 10, 1936, Schumacher, T580, R. 48.

10. Jahresbericht 1938, BA, Reichssicherheitshauptamt, R58/1994, pp. 75–76; Boberach, *Berichte*, p. 326. The sects listed as dissolved were: Möttlinger Bewegung, Verein religionshygienische Erholungsstudien, Heim der Liebe, Vereinigung von gemeinsamen Leben, Knupfer Gemeinde, Christliche Vereinigung Mutter Berggötz.

11. Reasons for dissolving the sect *Gottgläubiges Deutschtum, Wahrheit* on May 22, 1939, Reichsführer SS, T175, R. 490, 9351230–31; Geh. St. Pol., Bielefeld, BA, Reichssicherheitshauptamt, B58/266.

12. Lagebericht auf dem Gebiet der astrologischen Schriftums, BA, Kanzlei Rosenberg, NS 8/185, pp. 49–72; also a police report of October 23, 1939, remarking on the increased number of "prophets," etc., who were responsible for many political rumors. Most were prophesying that the war would soon end (Reichsführer SS, T175, R. 258, 2750125). See also the police reports on increased belief in miracles, prophecies, protective medallions, and charms in Catholic regions, which was considered a church-inspired attack against state propaganda (Boberach, *Berichte*, March 17, 1941, pp. 488–92, November 13, 1941, pp. 594–96, April 2, 1942, pp. 645–47).

13. German text in Schumacher, T580, R. 48; English translation Nbg. Doc., D-59, reprinted in Conway, *Nazi Persecution,* pp. 378–82. Rudolf Hess, who always was attracted to faith healers and astrologers (Seraphim, *Rosenbergs Tagebuch,* p. 89) had made his flight to Scotland on May 10, 1941, and the way was then clearer for those who wanted more extreme measures against the sects. Heydrich had long advocated firmer action against astrological groups which he considered to be under the influence of England. Their evil prophecies disturbed and alarmed the people. Other sects, such as Christian Science, the Christengemeinschaft, Friends, and Baptists, because of their international ties and pacifist tendences, were helpful to the enemies of Germany (Heydrich to Lammers, October 20, 1939, Poliakov and Wulf, *Dritte Reich,* pp. 194–98).

14. I have not attempted to compile a complete list, but among my notes I have reference to the ending of the following sects after June, 1941: Christengemeinschaft, July 25, 1941 (Reichsführer SS, T175, R. 408, 2931744); a long memorandum on the Oxford Movement which concluded it was "eine gemeinschaftsgefährdende psychopathische Erscheinung," July 31, 1942 (BA, Reichskanzlei, R 43 II/151); Sekte der Evangelisten, auch James Jardine, Christliche Gemeinschaft, oder Namenlose Sekte genannt, September 3, 1942 (Reichsführer SS, T175, R. 408, 2931730).

15. The Protestant and the Catholic churches, as already pointed out, lost many of their ancillary organizations at this time. In May, 1941, the Protestant organizations Christliche Gasthausmission and Deutsche Verband gläubiger Bäcker (Bäckermission), were dissolved because their activity hindered the Labor Front (Reichsführer SS, T175, R. 408, 2931754, 2931756; T175, R. 90, 9351619, 9351627).

16. Amt Lehrwesen des Hauptschulungsamtes der NSDAP, Munich, December 19, 1941, Schumacher T580, R. 48, The census of 1933 supposedly brought 1,000 different religious designations (Zur Weltanschaulichen Lage, October 2, 1936, NSDAP, T81, R. 23, 20481).

17. *KJ,* 1949, p. 362.

18. BA, Reichssicherheitshauptamt, R58/266; Conway, *Nazi Persecution,* app. 11, pp. 370–74.

19. The name "Jehovah's Witnesses" was adopted in 1931. Up to then they had been known under various names, particularly the names of their corporations, "The Watch Tower Bible and Tract Society" and "The International Bible Students' Association." These latter names continued to be used at times (*Jeh. Wit. Divine Purpose,* pp. 125–26). In Germany they were known as *Die Ernsten Bibelforscher, Wachtturm, Bibel und Traktatgesellschaft,* and *Jehovahs Zeugen.* The Bavarian political police sent out a special notice on July 26, 1935, pointing out that they were all one and the same (Schumacher, T580, R. 48).

20. *Jeh. Wit. Divine Purpose,* pp. 128–29. Police action against Jehovah's Witnesses, although not of the radical nature instituted by the Nazis, was nothing new in Germany. In 1931 and 1932 a total of 2,335 legal actions were pending against German Witnesses (ibid., p. 129); *1974 Yearbook Jeh. Wit.,* pp. 103–8.

21. Reichsführer SS, T175, R. 218, 2756268.

22. BA, Reichskanzlei, R 43 II/179, pp. 98–113; another long memorandum was submitted on June 22, 1933, which stressed that the Jehovah's Witnesses had not joined in the anti-German propaganda in the United States, either in 1918 or at present (ibid., pp. 119–40).

23. Hull to Chargé Gordon, April 27, 1933, U.S. Dept. of State, *Foreign Relations of the United States, 1933,* 2: 406.

24. Messersmith to State Department, May 2, 1933, ibid., p. 406. This April seizure is mentioned in *Jeh. Wit. Divine Purpose,* p. 130, where it is stated that the society got its property back on April 28, 1933.

25. Hull to Messersmith, May 18, 1933, U.S. Dept. of State, *Foreign Relations of the United States, 1933,* 2: 406–7. Thuringia banned the Jehovah's Witnesses on April 26, and Baden on May 15 (Zipfel, *Kirchenkampf,* p. 181; Michael H. Kater, "Die Ernsten Bibelforscher im Dritten Reich," *VZ* 17 [1969]: 191). Both Zipfel and Kater have excellent accounts, but only Kater mentions U.S. intervention and he only touches on it (p. 192). Neither has used the material in *Foreign Relations of the United States;* they have differing accounts of the confiscation and freeing of the Witnesses' property. This problem is therefore examined here in some detail.

26. Hull to Messersmith, May 18, 1933, U.S. Dept. of State, *Foreign Relations of the United States, 1933,* 2: 406–7.

27. Messersmith to Hull, July 12, 1933, ibid, p. 409. M. C. Harbeck, the society's superintendent in Central Europe, submitted a long memorandum to the government asking for a repeal of the confiscations, basing his claims chiefly on the fact that the Jehovah's Witnesses were a religious society (BA, Reichskanzlei, 43 II/179, pp. 203–18).
28. Messersmith to State Department, July 12, 1933, U.S. Dept. of State, *Foreign Relations of the United States, 1933,* 2: 408. The Witnesses held a convention in Berlin on June 25, 1933, attended by 7,000 persons. They drew up a letter of protest against their treatment and sent it to numerous high government officials; 2,500,000 copies were distributed publicly (*Jeh. Wit. Divine Purpose,* p. 130).
29. Messersmith to Hull, July 12, 1933, U.S. Dept. of State, *Foreign Relations of the United States, 1933,* 2: 409–10.
30. This paragraph is based on Messersmith to Hull, July 27, 1933, ibid., pp. 410–12.
31. Hull to Messersmith, September 7, 1933, ibid., p. 412.
32. Hull to Dodd, September 9, 1933, ibid., p. 413.
33. Dodd to Hull, September 12, 1933, ibid., pp. 413–14.
34. The U.S. *note verbale* is not printed in the documents but it is referred to in the German answer of November 13, 1933, (ibid., pp. 415–16) and in Dodd's dispatch of December 4, 1933, (ibid., pp. 414–16).
35. *Note verbale* from the German Foreign Office, ibid., pp. 415–16. Two days later, on September 28, 1933, the minister of the interior issued an Erlass which freed the property of the Jehovah's Witnesses again (Bavarian Political Police, June 21, 1935, quoting the Erlass of September 28, 1933, Schumacher, T580, R. 48; see also Weinkauff, *Deutsche Justiz,* 2: 29; Zipfel, *Kirchenkampf,* p. 181). Kater, *VZ* 17 (1969): 192, questions the date of September 28, 1933, for the freeing of the property and correctly says Zipfel does not document this date. Zipfel, however, cites the right date; when Kater puts the freeing in September, 1934, he actually refers to another measure. See also *1974 Yearbook Jeh. Wit.,* p. 112.
36. Statement of Harbeck, December 1, 1933, Dodd to Hull, December 3, 1933, U.S. Dept. of State, *Foreign Relations of the United States, 1933,* 2: 414.
37. Ibid., p. 415.
38. Dodd to State Department, February 1, 1934, ibid., p. 416. The banning of judicial action was not always observed, and in Darmstadt and Schwerin the courts held that the dissolution of the Jehovah's Witnesses was invalid (Weinkauff, *Deutsche Justiz,* 2: 98).
39. U.S. Dept. of State, *Foreign Relations of the United States, 1933,* 2: 417.
40. Schumacher, T580, R. 48; Reichsführer SS, T175, R. 411, 2936368–69.
41. Bavarian Political Police, July 14, 1934, Reichsführer SS, T175, R. 411, 2936366; Bavarian Political Police, June 21, 1935, reviewing past procedure, Schumacher, T580, R. 48.
42. BA, Reichskanzlei, R 43 II/179, p. 273.
43. Bavarian Political Police, October 2, 1934, Schumacher, T580, R. 48; Reichsführer SS, T175, R. 411, 2936364. It was no doubt with reference to this directive of September 13, 1934, that the judicial court at Weimar in 1936, while trying 12 Jehovah's Witnesses, stated that in September, 1934, the state governments were advised to free the property of Bible Researchers and not to hinder the distribution of Bibles or other permissible writings. Thuringia had done this on November 7, 1934 (see p. 3 of the court report of the trial, Schumacher, T580, R. 48; see also Kater, *VZ* 17 [1969]: 192).
44. The Basel conference was held September 15, 1934, BA, Reichskanzlei, R 43 II/179, pp. 253–56.
45. Text as given in *Jeh. Wit. Divine Purpose,* p. 142; German version in *Jahrbuch 1935 der Zeugen Jehovahs,* to be found in Schumacher, T580, R. 48.
46. *Jeh. Wit. Divine Purpose,* p. 142; *1974 Yearbook Jeh. Wit.,* pp. 133, 137, 139.
47. BA, Reichskanzlei, R 43 II/179, pp. 264–66; on Hitler's reaction, see also *1974 Yearbook Jeh. Wit.,* pp. 138–39.
48. Schumacher, T580, R. 48.
49. Reichsführer SS, T175, R. 411, 2936371; see also Schumacher, T580, R. 48.
50. See the tables in Zipfel, *Kirchenkampf,* pp. 181, 188, which show only one court conviction in 1933–34 and very few arrests.
51. Bavarian Political Police, June 21, 1935, July 26, 1935, summarizing measures, Schumacher, T580, R. 48; *1974 Yearbook Jeh. Wit.,* p. 116.
52. Minister of the interior, January 30, 1936, referring to his Erlass of May 21, 1935, Reichsführer SS, T175, R. 411, 2936330.

53. Bavarian Political Police, June 26, 1935, Schumacher, T580, R. 48; Nbg. Doc., D-84; Kater, *VZ* 17 (1969), p. 206. Especially in Baden difficulties arose. On February 4, 1938, Heydrich ordered that Witnesses could be retained in their regular jails about six days after finishing their sentences while the decision was reached whether they should be freed or sent to concentration camp; formerly they had been automatically sent on to concentration camps (Guertner Diary, 878, R. 3, 3757-PS 438).

54. Bavarian Political Police, September 23, 1935, Schumacher, T580, R. 48.

55. Schumacher, T580, R. 48.

56. Landgericht, Rodalstadt, January 11, 1937, Schumacher, T580, R. 48. There were 108 such divorces (*1974 Yearbook Jeh. Wit.*, p. 212).

57. Geh. St. Pol., Munich, July 2, 1937, Schumacher, T580, R. 48; Geh. St. Pol., Bielefeld, Reichsführer SS, T175, R. 490, 9351061; Zur weltanschaulichen Lage, March 21, 1938, NSDAP, T81, R. 23, 20198; Weinkauff, *Deutsche Justiz*, 2: 195. There were 860 children taken from their parents (*1974 Yearbook Jeh. Wit.*, p. 212).

58. Schumacher, T580, R. 48. It should be noted that the society was banned in Italy in 1932, and harassed in the United States and many other countries in this period. As Hitler took over various European countries during World War II the society was banned in them. It was also banned in Japan in 1939, and in Canada and Australia in 1941. See *Jeh. Wit. Divine Purpose*, pp. 128, 154–55, 157, and index, p. 298; Herbert E. Stroup, *The Jehovah's Witnesses*, pp. 146–48; Kurt Hutten, *Seher, Grübler, Enthusiasten*, pp. 114–15.

59. Geh. St. Pol., Würzburg, December 13, 1936, Schumacher, 580, R. 48. About 2,500 German Witnesses were able to attend the Zurich meeting. In Germany 300,000 copies of the resolution were distributed the night of December 12 within a few hours (*Jeh. Wit. Divine Purpose*, p. 164; *1974 Yearbook Jeh. Wit.*, pp. 154–56). Passports were not denied to Jehovah's Witnesses until 1937, when it was charged they were being used to smuggle literature into the country and currency out (Geh. St. Pol., Munich, May 19, 1937, NSDAP, T81, R. 184, 0334296; Geh. St. Pol., Darmstadt, May 7, 1937, Schumacher, T580, R. 48).

60. On the underground activity of the Jehovah's Witnesses, see *Jeh. Wit. Divine Purpose*, pp. 162–65.

61. Jahreslagebericht 1938 des Sicherheitshauptamtes des Reichsführers SS, BA, Reichssicherheitshauptamt, R58/ 1094, pp. 76–77; Boberach, *Berichte*, pp. 326–27; Vierteljahrslagebericht, 1939, ibid., p. 345.

62. Reichsführer SS, T175, R. 490, 9351189; Geh. St. Pol., Würzburg, Schumacher, T580, R. 48. On similar police action in 1935, see *Jeh. Wit. Divine Purpose*, p. 162; on the memorial services in general, ibid., p. 24; Stroup, *Jehovah's Witnesses*, pp. 144–46.

63. Reichsführer SS, T175, R. 258, 2750829.

64. Ibid., 2750769; Boberach, *Berichte*, pp. 388, 393.

65. Picker, *Hitlers Tischgespräche*, p. 249.

66. Kater estimates 4,000 to 5,000 lost their lives, *VZ* 17 [1969]; 181; Zipfel states 5,911 were imprisoned and over 2,000 killed (*Kirchenkampf*, p. 176); Weissenborn says 10,000 were imprisoned, 1,000 executed, and 1,000 killed or died in concentration camps (*Der Lautlose Aufstand*, pp. 77–78); the *1974 Yearbook Jeh. Wit.*, p. 212, states that 6,019 were arrested, 2,000 were placed in concentration camps, 635 died in prison, 253 were sentenced to death, and of these 203 were executed.

67. Eugen Kogen, *Der SS-Staat*, pp. 41–42; Zipfel, *Kirchenkampf*, pp. 192–97; Kater, *VZ* 17 (1969): 207–11; *1974 Yearbook Jeh. Wit.*, pp. 163–208.

68. See *Jeh. Wit. Divine Purpose*, pp. 166–74.

69. Ibid., p. 169.

70. Himmler's letter to Kaltenbrunner, July 21, 1944, Heiber, *Briefe an und von Himmler*, p. 273; also quoted in Zipfel, *Kirchenkampf*, p. 200. Trevor-Roper, relying on testimony from Schellenberg, writes: "Even in April 1945 . . . Himmler was contemplating the colonisation of the Ukraine with a new religious sect recommended by his masseur" (*Last Days of Hitler*, p. 21).

71. Heiber, *Briefe an und von Himmler*, p. 302; Herma Briffault, ed., *The Memoirs of Doctor Felix Kersten*, pp. 113–15, 117; *1974 Yearbook Jeh. Wit.*, pp. 195–202.

72. Hitler, *Mein Kampf*, pp. 433, 443, 699, 927; in his "Table Talk" he apparently referred only twice to Free Masonry, and this in a lighthearted, disparaging manner (*Hitler's Secret Conversations*, pp. 152, 229–30); there are no references to Free

Masons listed in the index of Picker, *Hitlers Tischgespräche,* or in Domarus, *Hitler Reden).* According to the Verein deutscher Freimaurer in 1928, "the Prussian lodges numbered 57,000 members, not one of whom was a Jew; the humanistic lodges had 24,000 members, and of these less than 3,000 were Jews. By 1930 the number of Jews had shrunk even more" (Jacob Katz, *Jews and Freemasons in Europe 1723–1939,* pp. 189–90). On Rosenberg's and Hitler's reactions to Free Masonry, see ibid., pp. 186–88, 228–29. The slogan "Freemasons and Jews" was a product of the 1880s and became current in Germany at the end of World War I (ibid., pp. 224–26). The American editors of Hitler's *Mein Kampf* state there were only 76,360 Masons in Germany in 1931 and refer to Rosenberg's crusade against Free Masonry (Hitler, *Mein Kampf,* p. 433n). See also *Hitlers Zweites Buch,* p. 222.

73. Reichspropaganda Leitung, October 28, 1932, Schumacher, T580, R. 48.

74. NSDAP Ortsgruppe, Leipzig, May 3, 1933, as well as other citations given in Schumacher, T580, R. 48; on dissolutions, see Weinkauff, *Deutsche Justiz,* 2: 22–23.

75. National Christlicher Orden Friedrich der Grosse, April 12, 1933, Schumacher T580, R. 48; a Jew had to convert to Christianity in order to become a member of a Prussian lodge (Katz, *Jews and Freemasons,* p. 191).

76. Bergen to Foreign Office, May 31, 1933, reporting on *Osservatore Romano,* no. 126 (May 29–30, 1933), Ausw. A., T120, R. 5719, K622967.

77. Oberste Parteigericht, Rundschreiben 12, Walter Buch, January 8, 1934, Schumacher, T580, R. 48.

78. Reichführer SS, Lagebericht, May–June, 1934, BA, Reichssicherheitshauptamt, R58/229, pp. 68–69. The Lagebericht was labelled "Geheim; im Panzer aufbewahren; Vernichtung nur durch Verbrennung." The material on the Masons is not in the Lagebericht as reprinted in Zipfel, *Kirchenkampf,* pp. 272–326.

79. The Reichsführer SS compiled a list of 237 publishers (mostly of local papers) who were Masons; another 57-page list gives the names of lodge members who were employees of the federal railways (Schumacher, T580, R. 48).

80. BA, Adjutantur des Führers, NS 10/32, pp. 115–18.

81. Schumacher, T580, R. 48.

82. Bavarian Political Police, July 17, 1935, August 29, 1935, Schumacher, T580, R. 48. The Masons had escaped real prosecution because of the "national orientation of the Old Prussian lodges" (Guertner's Diary, Ex. 858, 3751-PS, p. 409, July 22, 1935).

83. Bavarian Political Police, April 4, 1936, Schumacher, T580, R. 48.

84. *Fränkische Tageszeitung,* September 2, 1938, Schumacher, T580, R. 48.

85. Various decrees affecting Masons in the army are summarized in BA, Reichssicherheitshauptamt, R58/998.

86. Ibid.; see also Jahresbericht 1938, R58/1094, pp. 3–13.

87. NSDAP, T81, R. 204, 0357272.

88. *Parteikanzlei Rundschreiben* 19/41g, September 22, 1941, Schumacher, T580, R. 48.

89. Geh. St. Pol., Prussia, November 1, 1935, Schumacher, T580, R. 48; Geh. St. Pol., Darmstadt, November 15, 1935, Schumacher, T580, R. 48.

90. Besetz. Gebiete, T454, R. 62, 001467; Rosenberg to Hess, November 1, 1938, BA, Kanzlei Rosenberg, NS 8/180, p. 111.

91. Bormann to Kerksich, July 31, 1939, NSDAP, T81, 58008; Gauamtsleiter, Stuttgart, March 11, 1943, quoting Bormann's letter of July, 1939, Schumacher, T580, R. 48.

92. NSDAP, T81, R. 55, 57737, 57849; for the list of books and lectures not to be freed, 58055, 58090.

93. Head of the German Security Police, October 22, 1941, NSDAP, T81, R. 55, 57866, 57869. This roll of film is mostly devoted to Steiner and attempts to keep the Waldorf schools going.

94. Police report, August 6, 1941, NSDAP, T81, R. 55, 58261–62. There was also a rumor that Steiner had influenced Moltke and caused him to lose the Battle of the Marne in 1914. The police held that this was not true either (58264–65). Such rumors were not welcome just at the time Germany was invading Russia.

95. BA, Reichssicherheitshauptamt, R58/266.

96. Battista Radowitz to von Papen, May 27, 1933, BA, Reichskanzlei, R 43 II/179, pp. 115–16. Christian Science is called *Die Christliche Wissenschaft* in German.

97. William E. Dodd, Jr. and Martha Dodd, eds., *Ambassador Dodd's Diary 1933–1938,* pp. 40–41. The U.S. Department of State also requested information from Ambassador Dodd about the treatment of the Christian Scientists.

98. BA, Reichssicherheitshauptamt, R58/233, p. 20.

99. Publicity Office of the Christian Scientists, September 1, 1936, Besetz. Gebiete, T454, R. 81, 000552–61.

100. Reichsführer SS an das Oberste Parteigericht, November 21, 1936, Schumacher, T580, R. 48. On July 20, 1936, the state of Thuringia suppressed the Christian Scientists, but on December 4, 1936, the security police rescinded the ban (*New York Times,* December 5, 1939, p. 4).

101. Geh. St. Pol, Munich, May 19, 1937, Schumacher, T580, R. 48.

102. Geh. St. Pol., Darmstadt, May 10, 1937; Munich, May 19, July 1, 1937, Schumacher, T580, R. 48.

103. Nbg. Doc., NG-5139.

104. BA, Reichskanzlei, R 43 II/181, pp. 79–81.

105. Geh. St. Pol., Düsseldorf, November 4, 1937, Reichsführer SS, T175, R. 408, 2931792; Geh. St. Pol., Darmstadt, November 3, 1937, Munich, January 12, 1938, Schumacher, T580, R. 48.

106. From Kundinger's memorandum of March 7, 1938, BA, Reichskanzlei, R 43 II/181, pp. 84–90.

107. The article of February 27 was drawn up by Wilhelm Bachmann and furnished to the press by the party's official correspondence bulletin (*New York Times,* February 27, 1938); the article is to be found NSDAP, T81, R. 23, 20198.

108. Publicity Office to General Ritter von Epp, July 25, 1938, Besetz. Gebiete, T454, R. 81, 000450–58.

109. Reichsärztekammer, Berlin, March 11, 1937, KK741/37, to Geh. St. Pol., Schumacher T580, R. 48.

110. The report is not dated, but apparently was drawn up in 1938; it is to be found Schumacher T580, R. 48.

111. Reichsführer SS an das Oberste Parteigericht, January 18, 1939; see also letter of February 1, 1939, Schumacher, T580, R. 48.

112. BA, Rep. 320, 575, pp. 7–23, 153–56.

113. The decree was issued for Hess by Bormann; see *Nazi Conspiracy and Aggression,* 3: 605; Nbg. Doc., 838-PS; German text in Schumacher, T580, R. 48.

114. BA, Reichskanzlei, R 43 II/181, pp. 100–107. This letter, as well as another of May 15, 1939, found its way to the Academy for German Law (BA, Akad. D. Recht, R61/263, p. 7); see also Akad. D. Recht, T82, R. 44, ADR 168.

115. Meyer, when sending Kundinger's letters to the academy archives, BA, Akad. D. Recht, R61/263.

116. Rundschreiben 122/39, Schumacher, T580, R. 48.

117. Gaugericht, Hamburg, August 1, 10, 1939, Schumacher, T580, R. 48.

118. Deputy of the Führer's Staff to Highest Party Court, Munich, December 18, 1940, Schumacher, T580, R. 48.

119. Highest Party Court, Munich, to Gaugericht, Württemberg, June 19, 1941, Schumacher T580, R. 48.

120. See n. 13, above.

121. Nbg. Doc., NG-5139.

122. Chief of Security Police, August 11, 1941, NSDAP, T81, R. 185, 0335409; Nbg. Doc., NG-5139; Reichsführer SS, T175, R. 408, 291747.

123. Kurze Zusammenfassende Darstellung der Christlichen Wissenschaft, August 11, 1941, NSDAP, T81, R. 185, 0335382–409; BA, Reichsjustizministerium, R22/4006, pp. 1467–87.

124. Gilbert W. Scharffs, *Mormonism in Germany,* p. xiv; Scharffs gives the membership in Germany as 9,100 (1920), 13,480 (1940), 18,190 (1960), and 21,300 (1967) (ibid., pp. xiv, 221).

125. Dodd and Dodd, *Ambassador Dodd's Diary,* p. 136.

126. Scharffs, *Mormonism in Germany,* pp. 86, 88, 143.

127. *New York Times,* November 21, 1938, p. 4.

128. Ibid., March 5, 1940, p. 6; Joseph F. Smith, *Essentials in Church History,* pp. 647–48. Evacuation was ordered on August 24, 1939. Such evacuation had been ordered during the Munich Crisis in September, 1938, but was not carried out. For an account of the difficulties of carrying out the evacuation in 1939 see Scharffs, *Mormonism in Germany,* pp. 91–100.

129. Scharffs, *Mormonism in Germany,* pp. 100–124, particularly pp. 100–101, 104.

130. Ibid., p. 162.

131. Ibid., p. 174.

132. Missionaries from church headquarters in Salt Lake City were not permitted in Germany until 1949 (ibid., p. 119).
133. Ibid., pp. 155–223.
134. On the Germanic Faith groups, see chap. 4, "Diverse Movements Within the Churches," and chap. 9, "The First Provisional Church Directory," above.
135. See chap. 7, "Crisis Among the German Christians," and chap. 11, "Regrouping of the German Christians," above.
136. On Hauer's career, see Buchheim, *Glaubenskrise,* pp. 157–58; *Neue Deutsche Biographie,* 8: 83–84.
137. One of the best accounts of the association and the organizations which joined it is in Buchheim, *Glaubenskrise,* pp. 164–204; see also "Deutsche Glaubensbewegung," in SS Lagebericht of May–June 1934, Reichsführer SS, T175, R. 408, 2932494–95; Zipfel, *Kirchenkampf,* pp. 324–26.
138. Buchheim, *Glaubenskrise,* p. 188; *KJ,* 1949, p. 404.
139. See chaps. 9, 13, and 14, above.
140. Bavarian Political Police, Munich, September 1, 1935; Security Police, Darmstadt, October 16, 1935, both reports in Schumacher, T580, R. 48. Guests were forbidden at the meetings.
141. Bavarian Political Police, November 15, 1935, Schumacher, T580, R. 48.
142. Police, Regensburg, November 18, 1937, Schumacher, T580, R. 48; Police, Düsseldorf, November 16, 1937, Reichsführer SS, T175, R. 408, 2931915. This was not the first time the Glaubensbewegung got into difficulty because of its vilification of Christianity. On February 11, 1935, the Prussian secret police sent out a notice that Paul Orlowsky, speaker of the Glaubensbewegung, had repeatedly spoken in derogatory terms of Christianity. The police were to give special attention to his addresses and if necessary intervene (BA, Reichssicherheitshauptamt, R58/266).
143. *New York Times,* April 9, 1936; Buchheim, *Glaubenskrise,* pp. 195–98.
144. The Deutsche Glaubensbewegung adopted a new constitution (*Grundsätze*) on October 15, 1936. Point 10 stated: "Die Deutsche Glaubensbewegung verneint das Christentum. Sie lehnt es in jeder Form ab, weil seine Grundforderungen den Lebensgesetzen von Volk und Rasse wiedersprechen und den deutschen Wesen artfremd sind" (Schmidt, *Dokumente der Ausschusszeit,* 2: 1369–70).
145. Buth to Parteigenosse Brennecke, April 8, 1941, NSDAP, T81, R. 45, 47227.
146. Buth to Parteigenosse Brennecke, April 4, 1941, NSDAP, T81, R. 45, 47226.
147. For example, the Düsseldorf police on May 6, 1938, ordered that the Kampfring Deutscher Glaube could have meetings of members with invited guests at a ratio of one to one. The meetings, however, were to be kept under surveillance (Geh. St. Pol., Düsseldorf, Reichsführer SS, T175, R. 408, 2931895). Meetings with guests had been forbidden, (October 5, 1937, ibid., 2931914).
148. Jahresbericht 1938, BA, Reichssicherheitshauptamt, R58/1094; Boberach, *Berichte,* p. 327.
149. *Hitler's Secret Conversations,* p. 51.
150. BA, Stellvertreter des Führers, NS 6/386; Reichsführer SS, T175, R. 408, 2931888; Bavarian Political Police, June 25, 1937, Schumacher, T580, R. 41; Zipfel, *Kirchenkampf,* pp. 210–11.
151. *RGG,* 2: 109.
152. Bavarian Political Police, October 12, 1934, November 22, 1935, July, 1936, Schumacher, T580, R. 48.
153. Geh. St. Pol., May 25, 1937, Schumacher T580, R. 48; Geh. St. Pol., Düsseldorf, Reichsführer SS, T175, R. 408, 2931937. For further lists of authorized speakers, see February 4, 1938, ibid., 2931920–26; April 19, 1938, ibid., 2931897–98.
154. Besetz. Gebiete, T454, R. 81, 000510; BA, Reichskanzlei, R 43 II/181, p. 75.
155. There is a large collection of newspaper clippings on Ludendorff's death in Biel. Arch., Coll. W. Niemöller, N-7, Ludendorff. In spite of the adulation, a police report of January, 1938, stated that a small part of the Ludendorff movement continued in its malicious opposition to the state (Lagebericht, January 1–January 31, 1938, BA, Reichssicherheitshauptamt, R58/999, p. 18).
156. *RGG,* 2: 109; Kurt Hutten, "Sekten und sonstige Sondergemeinschaften," *KJ,* 1949, pp. 406–8.
157. *Keesing's Contemporary Archives,* 1961–62, p. 18122; *New York Times,* May 26 1961, p. 6; *Bielefelder Tageblatt,* May 26, 1961; for the decision of the court, see *Allgemeine Wochenzeitung der Juden in Deutschland,* August 28, 1964.

158. *KJ*, 1949, p. 370; on East German restrictions, see *1974 Yearbook Jeh. Wit.*, pp. 221–32; on growth in West Germany, ibid, pp. 232–53.

159. *KJ*, 1949, p. 359; see also p. 363.

160. Hutten, *Seher, Grübler, Enthusiasten.*

161. *Handbuch zu Freikirchen und Sekten.*

Chapter Twenty-one

1. Statistics on this matter are not carried regularly in the church yearbook, but in 1951, 1,210 Evangelical services were regularly held in churches of other denominations, and 841 in 1961. On the other hand, in 1951, 3,198 services of other denominations were held in Evangelical churches, and 1,463 services in 1961 (*KJ*, 1962, p. 427).

2. The constitutions and other fundamental laws of the individual churches can be found in Friedrich Merzyn, ed., *Das Verfassungsrecht der Evangelischen Kirche in Deutschland und Ihrer Gliedkirchen;* for a summary, see *KJ*, 1945–48, p. 157.

3. Lueken, *Landeskirche Nassau-Hessen,* pp. 88–100; Wilhelm Niemöller, *Neuanfang 1945,* pp. 111–20. Martin Niemöller did not see eye to eye with many of the other church leaders of that time. He favored a more radical revision of church government and greater unity between the Lutheran and Reformed churches. See especially his addresses to the conference at Treysa (ibid, pp. 49–53) and to the council of the Evangelical Church in Germany on December 13, 1945 (ibid., pp. 90–99). His brother Wilhelm writes: "Er [Martin] wurde betitelt als die 'Unruhe in der Uhr der Kirche' oder als der 'streitbare Pastor von Dahlem.' Aber das geschah nicht in freundlichem Ton. Was ihm Not machte, war nicht der Mangel an Anerkennung, sondern der Mangel an Verstehen und Liebe" (ibid., p. 56). On July 6, 1946, Bishop Dibelius wrote to Wilhelm Niemöller: "Die Lage und die Stimmung Ihres Bruders macht mir grosse Sorge. Er fühlt sich enttäuscht und beiseite geschoben— während wir doch versucht haben, ihm alle Möglichkeiten von Stellung und Einfluss offenzuhalten. Voraussetzung war dabei immer, dass er nach Berlin zurück- käme, womit wir als mit einer Selbstverständlichkeit gerechnet hatten. Jetzt ist nun in der Tat alles sehr schwierig geworden. Aber wir wollen tun, was wir können, um ihm aus dieser Situation herauszuhelfen" (Biel. Arch., Coll. W. Niemöller, D-6, Bekennende Kirche im Krieg).

4. *Amtsblatt der EKD* 24 (1970): 2–3. When Axel Springer, the publishing magnate, moved from Hamburg to West Berlin in 1967, he did not notify Berlin church authorities that he did not want to be considered a member. Two years later he withdrew his membership and joined an Old Lutheran congregation. He brought suit to recover from the Berlin-Brandenburg church 4 million marks already paid and to void 2 million marks that were assessed. The court ruled that since he had not given notice of withdrawal on moving to Berlin he was liable for the tax. He was ordered to pay about four-fifths of the 6 million marks under dispute and the church waived claim to the remaining one-fifth as a goodwill gesture (*Christian Century* 88 [1971]: 980–81).

5. See Fahlbusch, *Taschenlexikon, Religion und Theologie,* 4: 240–42; *KJ*, 1973, pp. 502–11.

6. *Amtsblatt der EKD* 24 (1970): 336–38.

7. *KJ*, 1945–48, pp. 119–25.

8. Brunotte, *Ev. Kirch in Deutschland,* pp. 83–84; Elliger, *Ev. Kirch der Union,* pp. 157–66.

9. See chap. 17, "Bishop Wurm and Church Unification," above.

10. See chap. 10, "The End of the Church Committees," above.

11. Bechluss des Reichsbruderrates in Frankfurt am Main zur Kirchenleitung, *KJ*, 1945– 48, pp. 2–4.

12. Wurm, *Erinnerungen,* p. 180.

13. Ibid., pp. 180–81; *KJ*, 1945–48, pp. 8–15; Niemöller, *Neuanfang 1945,* pp. 49– 53.

14. *KJ*, 1945–48, p. 9.

15. The other members of the council were: Bishop Hans Meiser, Munich; Bishop Otto Dibelius, Berlin; Oberkirchenrat Hanns Lilje, Hanover; Superintendent Heinrich Held, Essen-Rüttenscheid, Pastor Wilhelm Niesel, Reelkirchen; Pastor Hans Asmus- sen, Schwäbisch Gmünd; Superindendent Hugo Hahn, Stuttgart; Professor Rudolf

Smend, Göttingen; Rechtsanwalt Dr. Heinemann, Essen; and Oberstudiendirektor Meier, Hamburg-Altona (*KJ*, 1945–48, p. 16).

16. Ibid., pp. 106–7.
17. Ibid., p. 15.
18. Ibid., pp. 18–19.
19. The establishment of such a relief organization had been secretly discussed since 1942 by Bishop Wurm, as head of the Committee on Unification, and leaders of the embryo World Council of Churches (Boyens, *VZ* 19 [1971]: 586–87; Boyens, *Kirchenkampf und Ökumene, 1939–1945*, pp. 237–41; Jasper, *George Bell*, pp. 292–93).
20. *KJ*, 1945–48, pp. 228, 389–413; Brunotte, *Ev. Kirche in Deutschland*, pp. 93–94; Wurm, *Erinnerungen*, pp. 181–82; for the activity of the Hilfswerk in Berlin, see Grüber, *Erinnerungen*, pp. 267–88.
21. Apparently Martin Niemöller was the only one who had been informed that the ecumenical delegation would be at Stuttgart (Hartmut Ludwig, "Karl Barths Dienst der Versöhnung. Zur Geschichte des Stuttgarter Schuldbekenntnisses," in Brunotte, *Gesammelte Aufsätze*, 2: 295n).
22. *KJ*, 1945–48, pp. 26–27; Jasper, *George Bell*, p. 294. On the Stuttgart declaration, see also Frederic Spotts, *The Churches and Politics in Germany*, pp. 11, 93–95.
23. Karl Jaspers, *Die Schuldfrage*, pp. 31–34, 37–40, 56, 62, 89–91, 99–102.
24. *KJ*, 1945–48, pp. 43–66; Herman, *Rebirth of the German Church*, pp. 133, 140–46; Snoek, *Grey Book*, pp. 291–95; Günter Heidtmann, ed., *Hat die Kirche geschwiegen?*, pp. 11–15; Diem, Schempp, and Müller, *Kirche und Entnazifizierung*, pp. 66–73. On the whole, the Stuttgart statement received a critical acceptance in Germany, partly because of the headlines and political connotations which the press gave it. On the background, issuance, and general acceptance of the declaration, see Boyens, *VZ* 19 (1971): 574–97; See also Boyens, *Kirchenkampf und Ökumene, 1939–1945*, pp. 262–63, 271–86; Hartmut Ludwig's article in Brunotte, *Gesammelte Aufsätze*, 2: 265–326, particularly pp. 290–99; see also Niemöller, *Neuanfang 1945*, pp. 59–61; Dibelius, *In the Service of the Lord*, pp. 259–60; Künneth, *Der Grosse Abfall*, pp. 241–45; Friedrich W. Kantzenbach, *Der Weg der evangelischen Kirche vom 19. zum 20. Jahrhundert*, pp. 26–27.
25. Wurm, *Erinnerungen*, p. 192.
26. *KJ*, 1945–48, pp. 8–82.
27. Ibid., pp. 82–84.
28. Heinz Brunotte, *Die Grundordnung der Evangelischen Kirche in Deutschland*, pp. 41–51; Herman, *Rebirth of the German Church*, pp. 146–53.
29. The members of the committee were Oberkirchenrat Ehlers, Oberlandskirchenrat Brunotte, and Professor Erik Wolf. See Brunotte, *Die Grundordnung der Ev. Kirche*, pp. 52–66; see also *KJ*, 1945–48, p. 79.
30. Wurm, *Erinnerungen*, p. 194.
31. Brunotte, *Ev. Kirche in Deutschland*, pp. 68–69; Kunst and Grundmann, *Evangelisches Staatslexikon*, p. 483; *KJ*, 1973, pp. 14–15.
32. Wurm, *Erinnerungen*, p. 192. Asmussen, one of the founding fathers, writes, "Der Kirchenbund der bis 1933 bestand, ist an Festigkeit mit der EKD in nichts zu vergleichen. Es mag uns nicht sehr angenehm sein—den Anstoss zu einer Einung, die bereits vorher reif war, hat uns das unkirchliche Handeln der Deutschen Christen gegeben. Wir selbst haben den Absprung dazu nicht gefunden" (*Zur jüngsten Kirchengeschichte*, p. 101). The desire for greater church unity has steadily grown and it is being pushed with vigor (*KJ*, 1969, pp. 7–24; 1970, pp. 16–18; 1971, pp. 12–32).
33. *KJ*, 1945–48, p. 96.
34. For example, in 1967 it concluded treaties with the Evangelical Lutheran churches in Peru and Columbia for mutual help in ministering to German-speaking Protestants in those countries (*Amtsblatt der EKD* 21 [1967]: 415–17).
35. Brunotte, *Ev. Kirche in Deutschland*, p. 73.
36. Fahlbusch, *Taschenlexikon, Religion und Theologie*, 1: 271.
37. Brunotte, *Ev. Kirche in Deutschland*, pp. 79–80.
38. *KJ*, 1970, p. 118; see also pp. 117–32.
39. For examples see *KJ*, 1969, pp. 67–155; 1970, pp. 117–86; 1971, pp. 110–208, 1972, pp. 115–216; 1973, pp. 70–158; see also Spotts, *Churches and Politics*, pp. 119–30, 237–68, 354.
40. *KJ*, 1971, p. 111.

41. "Evangelical Church Meets in Coburg," *German Tribune,* June 21, 1973; Spotts, *Churches and Politics,* pp. 123, 148.

42. "Die Nordelbische Evangelisch-Lutherische Kirche," *KJ,* 1970, pp. 56–61.

43. "Konföderation evangelischer Kirchen in Niedersachsen," *KJ,* 1970, pp. 61–65.

44. The number of congregations in the eastern churches as of January 1, 1961; the number in the western churches as of January 1, 1964 (Brunotte, *Ev. Kirche in Deutschland,* p. 77).

45. Eutin joined the United Evangelical Lutheran Church of Germany on May 18, 1967, (*Amtsblatt der EKD* 21 [1967]: 324).

46. Brunotte, *Ev. Kirche in Deutschland,* p. 82.

47. Brunotte, *Die Grundordnung der Ev. Kirche,* p. 74.

48. *KJ,* 1945–48, pp. 106–7.

49. See Brunotte, *Die Grundordnung der Ev. Kirche,* pp. 74–88.

50. Konrad Hesse, "Partnerschaft zwischen Kirche und Staat? Zur heutigen Staatskirchenrechtlichen Lage in der Bundesrepublik," in Karl Forster, ed., *Das Verhältnis von Kirche und Staat,* p. 130; E.G. Mahrenholz, *Die Kirchen in der Gesellschaft der Bundesrepublick,* pp. 23–29, 101–6; Hans Maier, ed., *Deutscher Katholizismus nach 1945,* p. 205.

51. There were periods of harassment and relaxation. Up to approximately 1948–50, the relations of the churches with the Soviet regime were surprisingly cordial; there were increased restrictions 1950–53, and then with the "New Course" in Soviet policy a brief period of concessions. A third major crisis arose in 1957 with the dispute over providing chaplains for the army in the Federal Republic. These fluctuations in policy can be followed in Richard W. Solberg, *God and Caesar in East Germany,* especially pp. 28–30, 87–113, 224–45. Since about 1969 there has in general been a relaxation of tension between the state and the churches (see *Christian Century* 88 [1971]: 982–83; 89 [1972]: 1274; 90 [1973]: 242–43; Adolph Schalk, "Post-Conciliar Catholicism: Germany," *Commonweal* 98 [1973]: 287–88).

52. Mahrenholz, *Die Kirchen in der Gesellschaft,* p. 32.

53. Ibid., p. 94; Alexander Hollerbach, *Verträge zwischen Staat und Kirche in der Bundesrepublic Deutschland,* pp. 60–67, 289.

54. Hollerbach, *Verträge zwischen Staat und Kirche,* pp. 65, 289. The constitution of North Rhine-Westphalia specifically recognizes the provisions of the old Prussian church agreements and this is also the case in the postwar treaties between some of the Länder and the Land churches (see Jürgen Schleichert, *Staat und evangelische Kirche seit der Staatsumwälzung 1918,* pp. 32–34).

55. For example, the agreement (*Vertrag*) of Prussia with its Evangelical Land churches of May 11, 1931, and of Baden with its Protestant church of November 14, 1932 (Hermann Weber, *Staatskirchenverträge,* pp. 150–56, 37–42).

56. Ibid., p. 77. Other such church-state treaties are those of Lower Saxony of March 19, 1955, of North Rhine-Westphalia of September 26, 1957, and of May 28, 1958, of Schleswig-Holstein of April 23, 1957, and of Rhineland Palatinate of March 31, 1962 (all reprinted ibid.). These treaties are analyzed and discussed in Schleichert, *Staat und evangelische Kirche,* pp. 35–48.

57. The average in 1970 was 3.5 percent. It has been estimated that if the churches set up their own collection system the cost of collection would be in the neighborhood of 20 percent (*KJ,* 1969, p. 66). In most Land churches taxes are also collected from sources other than income, although the sums derived are comparatively small. In addition most churches collect Kirchgeld, a small set sum, from each individual. See *KJ,* 1969, p. 410; 1970, pp. 374–75; 1971, pp. 367–69 for total sums collected and the cost of collection. There are also regular Sunday offerings and many collections for special purposes to which churchgoers contribute.

58. The churches recognize this step taken before state authorities as withdrawal from the church. It has been argued that in this way the state in fact determines church membership, which is held to be wrong. See Oswald von Nell-Breuning, "Kirchensteuer und Kirchenmitgliederschaft," *SZ* 184 (1969): 309–15; see also 185 (1970): 127–29.

59. See, for example, *Die Welt,* May 16, 1964; *Der Spiegel,* May 27, 1964; *Erlanger Volksblatt,* May 6, 1971; *Time,* European ed., May 10, 1971, p. 60; *KJ,* 1969, pp. 63–67; Greinacher and Risse, *Bilanz des deutschen Katholizismus,* p. 250. Withdrawals from all Land churches in West Germany are as follows: 42,263 (1967); 58,547 (1968); 108,844 (1969); 199,691 (1970); 157,334 (1971); 138,970 (1972).

These are insignificant numbers in a total membership of around 30 million, and against them should be set the number of accessions: 28,939 (1967); 26,154 (1968); 21,409 (1969); 18,994 (1970); 16,347 (1971); 15,997 (1972) (*KJ,* 1968, pp. 492–93; 1969, pp. 435–36; 1970, pp. 398–99; 1971, pp. 393–94; 1972, pp. 465–66; 1973, pp. 500–501; see also the graph showing withdrawals and accessions 1950–69, *KJ,* 1971, p. 398; withdrawals 1900–1973, *KJ,* 1973, p. 524). In 1966, 4 out of 5 persons who withdrew from the Catholic church joined the Evangelical church; 1 out of 5 who withdrew from the Evangelical church joined the Catholic church (*KH,* 1962–68, p. 584).

60. See *KJ,* 1968, pp. 501–3; 1969, pp. 409–11; 1970, pp. 373–75; 1971, pp. 367–69; 1972, pp. 467–69; 1973, pp. 512–13. In the summer of 1973 a commission of the Free Democratic party drew up a fourteen-point document on "A Free Church in a Free State" in which, among other things, it called for an end to church taxes (*German Tribune,* September 27, 1973, p. 5).

61. At the Conference for Evangelical Church Construction in October, 1966, it was announced that there were 11,717 Protestant churches in West Germany as compared to 9,794 in 1938. There were 2,270 destroyed or severely damaged in World War II; subsequently 1,784 were rebuilt and 2,409 new churches were constructed (*New York Times,* October 2, 1966). For statistics on Land churches, see *KJ,* 1970, pp. 402–7.

62. Wunderlich, *Brückenbauer Gottes,* pp. 193–94.

63. Brunotte, *Ev. Kirche in Deutschland,* pp. 134, 139–40.

64. Ibid., pp. 107–10; *KJ,* 1945–58, pp. 368–88; Spotts, *Churches and Politics,* pp. 132–34.

65. See chap. 9, "The Evangelical Weeks," above.

66. Grüber, *Erinnerungen,* pp. 355–59.

67. The expenses of the rallies are mostly met by the churches, with help from the federal, state, and local governments (*The German Tribune,* November 23, 1972). In 1970 there were four Kirchentage held in East Germany sponsored by various Land churches, with attendance running from 5,000 to 15,000. In Saxony they have changed the Kirchentag format into the Kirchentagskongress, a meeting of around 300 specially invited representatives from the different districts of the church. It is designed as a training meeting for lay workers (*KJ,* 1970, pp. 338, 341–42).

68. *Christian Century* 90 (1973): 833; on the Augsburg meeting of 1971, ibid., 88 (1971): 931–32; for criticism of the Kirchentage by conservative theologians, see *KJ,* 1973, pp. 39–41. See also Spotts, *Churches and Politics,* pp. 134–36; on the 1975 Frankfurt meeting, see *Die Zeit,* June 27, 1975; *German Tribune,* July 3, 1975; *Christian Century,* 92(1975); 795–97.

69. Franz-Xaver Kaufmann, "Zur Bestimmung und Messung von Kirchlichkeit in der Bundesrepublik Deutschland," *Internationales Jahrbuch für Religionssoziologie* 4 (1968): 62–100, particularly conclusion, p. 100.

70. See chap. 22, "Church Organizations and Church Life," below.

71. As of 1967 there were Protestant theological faculties at the following universities in the Federal Republic: Bochum, Bonn, Erlangen, Göttingen, Hamburg, Heidelberg, Cologne, Mainz, Marburg (including Frankfurt and Giessen), Münster, Tübingen, and Saarbrücken. In addition there are four Hochschulen supported mostly by the churches: Berlin-Zehlendorff, Bethel, Neuendettelsau, and Wuppertal. Various Land churches also have seminaries for specialized training (*KJ,* 1968, p. 495).

72. The West German churches in 1972 furnished about 30 percent of the support of the World Council of Churches (*Christian Century* 89 [1972]: 1039).

73. *KJ,* 1949, pp. 52–58; 1955, pp. 357–81; Wunderlich, *Brückenbauer Gottes,* pp. 190–93. In 1969 the Roman Catholic church began participating with the Arbeitsgemeinschaft in West Germany through an observer, and the Bishops' Conference in September, 1973, decided to apply for membership in the organization (*The German Tribune,* October 25, 1973, p. 5).

74. For more details on this cooperation, see chap. 22 at n. 60, below.

75. *KJ,* 1958, pp. 134–36. The report consisted of eight theses (*Arnoldshainer Thesen*) named after the place where they were formulated. Since 1967 the so-called Arnoldshainer Conferences consist of representatives of the United churches, the Reformed churches, and the Lutheran churches of Oldenburg and Württemberg. They study problems confronting the German churches (*KJ,* 1967, pp. 45–46).

76. *KJ,* 1962, pp. 9–14.

77. The churches approving without reservation and favoring constitutional amendment were: *Anhalt, Baden, Berlin-Brandenburg,* Bremen, *Görlitz, Hessen-Nassau,* Electoral Hesse-Waldeck, *Lippe,* Northwest Germany Reformed, Oldenburg, *Palatinate,* Greifswald, Rheinland, Church Province Saxony, *Westphalia, Württemberg.* The nine italicized wanted to extend agreement to pulpit fellowship. The following ten approved, but did not want to amend the constitution: Brunswick, Eutin, Hamburg, Hanover, Lübeck, Mecklenburg, Saxony Lutheran, Schaumburg-Lippe, Schleswig-Holstein, Thuringia (*KJ,* 1968, pp. 8–9). For the Bavarian decision of December 2, 1967, see *Amtsblatt der EKD* 22 (1968): 23.

78. *KJ,* 1967, pp. 46–48; 1970, pp. 37–46; the Leuenberg statement is given *KJ,* 1971, pp. 51–56; see also *KJ,* 1972, pp. 46–91 for resolutions of various West German churches on the statement; for East German churches, see pp. 276–77, 299–301, 309–18; *KJ,* 1973, pp. 18–32, 224–42.

79. Helmreich, *Religious Education,* pp. 255–77; Mina J. Moore-Rinvolucri, *Education in Germany,* p. 15.

80. Helmreich, *Religious Education,* pp. 268–70; *KJ,* 1957, pp. 151–57; 1958, pp. 182–99; 1960, pp. 213–20; Solberg, *God and Caesar in East Germany,* pp. 192–201, 271–76. For the new oath taken at Jugendweihe pledging patriotic support of the socialist state, see *KJ,* 1968, pp. 214–16. For statements of church leaders in the German Democratic Republic against the Jugendweihe, see also Heidtmann, *Hat die Kirche geschwiegen?,* pp. 248–52, 280–82.

81. *KJ,* 1969, p. 180; Grüber, *Erinnerungen,* pp. 378–83; for an excellent summary of the Jugenweihe-confirmation conflict, see *KJ,* 1973, pp. 246–55.

82. *KJ,* 1969, p. 180. In the Greifswald church there were 11,139 confirmations in 1955, but only 1,874 in 1960; they increased to over 3,000 yearly 1963–69; in 1969 there were 3,642 confirmed (*KJ,* 1970, p. 335). Special commissions have been established by the East German churches to study baptismal and confirmation doctrines and practices (*KJ,* 1972, pp. 398–413).

83. *New York Times,* May 30, 1972. In an address to the spring session of the Görlitz Synod, Bishop Hans-Joachim Frankel "gave notice to the government that all Evangelical churches in the GDR are united in opposing attempts of the state to require advance notice of church programs and activities" (*Christian Century* 90 [1973], 955).

84. *KJ,* 1965, pp. 198, 201–2; *New York Times,* October 2, 1966; Moore-Rinvolucri, *Education in East Germany,* p. 14.

85. Bé Ruys, *Stimmen aus der Kirche in der DDR,* pp. 121–24. Ruys states that 25–35 new theological students matriculate at each university every year; 90 percent of the theological students receive scholarships of 140–220 marks a month. See also Markus Barth, "Church and Communism in East Germany," *Christian Century* 83 (1966): 1441.

86. *KJ,* 1970, p. 343. These institutions are usually considered Kirchliche Hochschulen, but they actually do not have this status. In addition there are 14 seminars and proseminars for specialized purposes, as well as 13 cathechetical training centers.

87. The Evangelical Church of the Union (largely in East Germany) adopted Pastorin July 3, 1962 (*Amtsblatt der EKD* 20 [1966]: 409). Whether to ordain women or not is a decision left to the individual Land churches. The church of Lübeck, for example, decided to ordain women July, 1966; Brunswick, January, 1968; Hesse-Nassau, December, 1968 (ibid., 22 [1968]: 127; 23 [1969]: 68, 159). In 1975 it was reported that there were 266 women pastors among the approximately 12,900 Lutheran clergy in West Germany; 163 of these had their own parishes (*German Tribune,* Feb. 6, 1975, p. 14).

88. Grüber, *Erinnerungen,* p. 377.

89. Ibid., p. 239; *KJ,* 1970, p. 344; Greinacher and Risse, *Bilanz des deutschen Katholizismus,* p. 262. Bormann had advocated a similar church tax system in December, 1937 (Guertner Diary, 978, R. 3, 3757-PS 590). For a statement by East German churchmen upholding the collection of a "church tax" as a minimal contribution to the church, see *KJ,* 1973, pp. 255–56.

90. *Christian Century* 88 (1971): 983.

91. Weber, *Staatskirchenverträge,* pp. 18–27.

92. See the statement by Martin Niemöller in *KJ,* 1957, pp. 31–34.

93. *KJ,* 1956, p. 21; Brunotte, *Ev. Kirche in Deutschland,* p. 115.

94. *KJ,* 1957, pp. 21–48; Weber, *Staatskirchenverträge,* pp. 18–27.

95. See Kunst and Grundmann, *Evangelisches Staatslexikon,* pp. 1306–7; Dr. Hermens, "Die evangelische Verkündigung im Heer und Marine," in Werckshagen, *Protestantismus,* 2: 717–32.

96. Kunst and Grundmann, *Evangelisches Staatslexikon,* pp. 1307–8; Brunotte, *Ev. Kirche in Deutschland,* pp. 116–17.

97. Stoph to Bishop Dibelius, March 4, 1957, *KJ,* 1957, pp. 47–48.

98. Solberg, *God and Caesar in East Germany,* pp. 226–27.

99. *KJ,* 1956, pp. 20–21, 33–118; 1957, pp. 72–96; 1958, pp. 17–74; Heidtmann, *Hat die Kirche Geschwiegen?,* pp. 101–3, 242, 245–47, 275–76, 296–308, 359.

100. Kunst and Grundmann, *Evangelisches Staatslexikon,* p. 1307.

101. The Evangelical Church of Germany maintained a plenipotentiary (*Bevollmächtigten*) both in Bonn for the Federal Republic and in Berlin for the Democratic Republic (*KJ,* 1958, p. 140; Grüber, *Erinnerungen,* pp. 391–92).

102. *KJ,* 1958, p. 138, Grüber, *Erinnerungen,* p. 400.

103. For some years the East German government had expressed the desire to have only men of the DDR responsible for the affairs of the Evangelical church in the east (Grüber, *Erinnerungen,* p. 372).

104. Ibid., pp. 375, 401.

105. *KJ,* 1958, p. 141.

106. The increasing harassment of the churches is shown by the churches' intercessory lists for imprisoned church officials in East Germany. They had 7 names in January 1957, 13 in August, 1957, 19 in December, 1957, and 22 at the beginning of 1958 (Grüber, *Erinnerungen,* p. 383).

107. *KJ,* 1963, pp. 8–9.

108. *KJ,* 1963, pp. 11–17, 244–48. The Gustav-Adolf-Verein, which had its headquarters in Leipzig as early as 1947, had established a western headquarters at Assenheim, near Friedberg in Hesse. They too were soon unable to hold joint meetings (*KJ,* 1955, pp. 338–43).

109. *KJ,* 1957, p. 29.

110. *KJ,* 1958, pp. 176–99; Klemens Richter, "Katholiken, Kirche, Staat in der DDR," *SZ* 182 (1968): 133–36.

111. Art. 39 of the constitution, as quoted in *KJ,* 1968, p. 191.

112. *KJ,* 1968, pp. 228–34.

113. *KJ,* 1968, pp. 249–53.

114. *KJ,* 1970, pp. 268–69; for the church law of April–May, 1972, on the administrative bodies of the Evangelical Church of the Union, see *KJ,* 1972, pp. 361–63.

115. *KJ,* 1970, pp. 277–79; see also the report on the meeting of the eastern synod in May, 1971, in *Frankfurter Allgemeine Zeitung,* May 13, 1971. For statements of both regional synods of April-May, 1972, see *KJ,* 1972, pp. 363–65.

116. *Christian Century* 90 (1973): 79–80; *German Tribune,* November 23, 1972, p. 4; *New York Times,* November 24, 1972; *KJ,* 1971, pp. 333, 337–38; 1972, pp. 365–83.

117. The constitution is given in *KJ,* 1969, pp. 255–61.

118. *KJ,* 1969, pp. 4, 274–75. Within the East German Confederation the eight Land churches are also grouped into two interchurch groups which have counterparts in the Federal Republic. The three Lutheran Land churches (Saxony, Thuringia, Mecklenburg) have united in the Evangelical Lutheran Church of the Democratic Republic, while the other five Land churches (Anhalt, Greifswald, Görlitz, Church Province Saxony, Berlin-Brandenburg [East]) are members of the Evangelical Church of the Union. By an agreement of October 10, 1969, the Evangelischen Brüder-Unität, District Herrnhut, has joined the "Bund der E. Kirche in der DDR" (*Amtsblatt der EKD* 24 [1970]: 591). In accepting this small body into the confederation its special historic position was recognized, but the conference specifically noted "that individual congregations or enclaves of other Land churches cannot as such be joined to the confederation." This provision would continue the isolation of the few stray congregations along the borders which are still members of western Land churches (*KJ,* 1970, p. 283).

119. Art. 4, Sec. 5, *KJ,* 1969, p. 257. The East German Confederation has become a member of the World Council of Churches.

120. Art. 4, sec. 4, *KJ,* 1969, p. 257.

121. *KJ,* 1970, p. 354. The report of the administration of the Church of Greifswald of November 6, 1970, to the synod on participation in church rites is indicative of the trend of affairs. Baptisms: 11,377 (1955); 6,585 (1960); 4,375 (1965); 2,790

(1969). Confirmations: 11,139 (1955); 1,874 (1960); 3,642 (1969); Church marriages: 4,247 (1955); 2,308 (1960); 1,213 (1965); 798 (1969). Communion: 102,617 (1955); 61,601 (1969). In death the people still seem to desire the services of the church and the figure of around 6,000 church funerals a year has remained constant (*KJ,* 1970, pp. 335–36).

122. *Christian Century* 88 (1971): 346; 90 (1973): 242–43; *KJ,* 1972, pp. 278–79, 318–33; *KJ,* 1973, pp. 206–9.
123. The Land churches still claim an estimated membership of 10,075,000 out of a population of around 17,000,000 and have 4,670 pastors. The Methodists have about 25,000 members and 42 pastors, the Baptists 24,593 members (number of pastors not given), the Evangelical Brüder Unität 3,200 members and 20 pastors, the Confederation of Free Evangelical Churches 1,215 members and 14 pastors (*KJ,* 1970, p. 342).
124. *KJ,* 1969, pp. 5–6, 276.
125. *KJ,* 1970, pp. 16–18; 1971, p. 32; see the whole sections "Der zukünftige Weg der EKD—Strukture und Verfassungsreform," ibid, pp. 12–48; 1972, pp. 7–46; *KJ,* 1973, pp. 3–15.
126. *KJ,* 1969, p. 6; 1970, p. 15; *Amtsblatt der EKD* 24 (1970): 272.

Chapter Twenty-two

1. Colman J. Barry, *American Nuncio Cardinal Aloisius Muench* p. 67.
2. It was not until August 30, 1946, that the last German officials left the German embassy at the Vatican (Hermelink, *Die Katholische Kirche,* p. 52).
3. An apostolic visitor, usually sent to a country for some particular purpose, differs from an apostolic delegate, a permanent representative whom the papacy sends to a country with which it has no diplomatic relations. Muench could not visit the Russian zone of occupation (ibid., p. 52; *KJ,* 1951, p. 290, *KH,* 1944–51, p. 17).
4. On the appointment of Muench to these offices and his activity in Germany in these first years of office, see Barry, *Cardinal Muench,* pp. x–xii, 51–198.
5. Barry writes: "The Vatican wanted it definitely understood that the nuncio was to have the title of apostolic nuncio in Germany. In this way it was clearly stated that the Holy See refused to acknowledge the division of Germany," (ibid., p. 192). On the nuncio being the doyen of the diplomatic corps in Germany, see chap. 5 at n. 14, above.
6. *New York Times,* June 29, 1972; German Press and Information Office, *The Bulletin* 24 (July 12, 1972): 188.
7. Greinacher and Risse, *Bilanz des deutschen Katholizismus,* pp. 149–50; *KH,* 1944–51, pp. 24–35; 1962–68, pp. 43–55; Barry, *Cardinal Muench,* pp. 68–69.
8. See the table "Verteilung der kirchlichen Jurisdiktionsbezirke auf Besatzungzonen und Länder," *KH,* 1944–51, pp. 24–25. Each of the postwar official handbooks carries a detailed account of the territorial makeup of each church jurisdiction; *KH,* 1952–56, 1957–61, and 1962–68 all have good maps showing diocesan boundaries.
9. *KJ,* 1951, pp. 303–6.
10. See chap. 21 at n. 22, above.
11. For example, see the "Hirtenbrief des Kölner Erzbischofs Dr. Joseph Frings zum Kriegsende," May 27, 1945, Corsten, *Kölner Aktenstücke,* pp. 313–14; "Aussprache Pius' XII. an das Kardinals-Kollegium am 2. Juni 1945," ibid., pp. 315–21. The pope definitely rejected the concept of collective guilt (see Oskar Golombek, *Die katholische Kirche und die Völker-Vertreibung,* pp. 49–52; Spotts, *Churches and Politics,* pp. 29–30, 91–93).
12. *KJ,* 1951, p. 316.
13. See the list of 53 Caritasverbände in *KH,* 1944–51, pp. 85–90. The Caritas organizations have continued to expand, and there is a long report on their activity in *KH,* 1962–68, pp. 349–434.
14. *Das Katholische Jahrbuch, 1948–49,* p. 131; on the significance of the work of the Caritas organizations in this period, see Barry, *Cardinal Muench,* pp. 95–96.
15. Barry, *Cardinal Muench,* pp. 89–103; *Das Katholische Jahrbuch, 1948–49,* pp. 132–33.
16. *KJ,* 1951, pp. 319–20; Barry, *Cardinal Muench,* pp. 174–75.
17. *KH,* 1962–68, pp. 134–37.

18. *KJ*, 1951, p. 318; Barry, *Cardinal Muench*, pp. 174–75.
19. Of the 2,800,000 Sudeten Germans in Germany in 1945, some 2,500,000 were Catholics (*KH* 1944–51, p. 209).
20. *KH*, 1944–51, p. 250; Greinacher and Risse, *Bilanz des deutschen Katholizismus*, pp. 22–23.
21. Greinacher and Risse, *Bilanz des deutschen Katholizismus*, p. 149; Barry writes; "2,000 new churches were built in former Protestant ghettos of Germany [and] . . . over 7,000 Protestant churches were used for Catholic services" (*Cardinal Muench*, p. 188).
22. As quoted from the report, *KJ*, 1951, p. 318.
23. Ruta and Straubinger, *Katholische Kirche*, p. 81.
24. There is a table showing the diocese of origin and the diocese where these priests were presently serving in *KH*, 1944–51, p. 208; see also Barry, *Cardinal Muench*, pp. 315–19.
25. *KH*, 1944–51, p. 248.
26. *KH*, 1962–68, pp. 459–60; for the religious affiliation of the populace of the different Länder of West Germany for the years 1939, 1946, and 1950, see the table in Helmreich, *Religious Education*, pp. 228–29.
27. *KH*, 1962–68, p. 504; Greinacher and Risse, *Bilanz des deutschen Katholizismus*, p. 25.
28. These statistics based on *KH*, 1944–51, p. 255, 1962–68, pp. 502–4, 509; Greinacher and Risse, *Bilanz des deutschen Katholizismus*, p. 59.
29. Greinacher and Risse, *Bilanz des deutschen Katholizismus*, p. 74; *KH*, 1962–68, pp. 309–10.
30. *KH*, 1962–68, pp. 506–7, 510, 514–15.
31. Greinacher and Risse, *Bilanz des deutschen Katholizismus*, pp. 71–78. The care of the Catholics among the many foreign workers in Germany has been a particular concern to church authorities. The German Caritasverband has organized some 600 centers for this work. In 1968 there were around 195 priests from foreign countries serving in Germany, among them 78 Italians, 91 Spaniards, 9 Portuguese, 10 Croatians, and 7 Slovenes (*KH*, 1962–68, p. 407). See also, for example, "Catholics Demand Better Conditions for Foreign Workers," *German Tribune*, November 23, 1972, reprinting from the *Frankfurter Allgemeine Zeitung*, October 28, 1972.
32. See the table giving the number of secular and regular priests 1915–62 in Greinancher and Risse, *Bilanz des deutschen Katholizismus*, pp. 81–82; see also *KH*, 1962–68, pp. 299, 516, 528–29; "Fewer Ordinations Reflect Crisis in the Catholic Church," *German Tribune*, January 25, 1973; "Church Publishes Figures on Priest Shortage," *German Tribune*, June 21, 1973. Schalk states: "There has been a fifty percent decline in ordinations over the past five years" (*Commonweal* 98 [1973]: 283).
33. Greinacher and Risse, *Bilanz des deutschen Katholizismus*, pp. 99–100.
34. See figures for the ten-year period 1957–67 in *KH*, 1962–68, p. 304; see also p. 518. There are Catholic theological faculties at the universities of Bochum, Bonn, Freiburg, Mainz, Munich, Münster, Regensburg, Tübingen, and Würzburg, and church-run philosophical-theological Hochschulen at Bamberg, Dillingen, Eichstätt, Freising, Fulda, Frankfurt, Königstein, Paderborn, Passau, and Trier (Greinacher and Risse, *Bilanz des deutschen Katholizismus*, p. 90; *KH*, 1962–68, pp. 80–94).
35. *KH*, 1962–68, p. 516.
36. See comparative figures 1924–50, *KH*, 1944–51, p. 264; see chap. 18 at n. 102, above.
37. *KH*, 1962–68, p. 533; for a listing of German monastic orders, see pp. 56–80.
38. Ibid. p. 537.
39. See *KH*, 1962–68, pp. 274–83, 296–310.
40. See the provocative essay by Wolfgang Zapf, "Angst vor der wissenschaftlichen Frage. Zur Diskussion über das 'katholische Bildungsdefizit': Materialien und Argumente," in Greinacher and Risse, *Bilanz des deutschen Katholizismus*, pp. 504–44.
41. See chap. five at n. 6, above.
42. *German Tribune*, October 25, 1973, quoting an article from *Die Welt* of September 29, 1973; on the clergy and political parties in the postwar era, see Spotts, *Churches and Politics*, pp. 149–57, 291–323, 355.
43. Greinacher and Risse, *Bilanz des deutschen Katholizismus*, p. 410; Maier,

Deutscher Katholizismus nach 1945, p. 44; Spotts, *Churches and Politics,* pp. 220–22.

44. Ruta and Straubinger, Katholische Kirche, p. 157.

45. See the list of organizations as given in *KH,* 1944–51, pp. 69–89; 1962–68, pp. 95–138.

46. *KH,* 1944–51, p. 91; *Das Katholische Jahrbuch,* 1948–49, pp. 97, 245–52. Spotts, *Churches and Politics,* pp. 84–85.

47. *KH,* 1962–68, pp. 138–82; see also Friedhelm Baukloh, "Für und wider das Bistumsblatt. Das Dilemma der katholischen Kirchenpresse," in Greinacher and Risse, *Bilanz des deutschen Katholizismus,* pp. 219–47; Ruta and Straubinger, *Katholische Kirche,* pp. 195–99.

48. *Christian Century* 89 (1972): 232; *New York Times,* November 20, 1971; *German Tribune,* December 9, 1971, reprinting an article in the *Süddeutsche Zeitung* of November 17, 1971.

49. Greinacher and Risse, *Bilanz des deutschen Katholizismus,* p. 233.

50. KH, 1962–68, p. 122.

51. *KH,* 1944–51, p. 83; 1962–68, p. 95. For reports on the first postwar Katholikentag at which Bishop Muench of North Dakota gave the closing address, see Barry, *Cardinal Muench,* pp. 105–12; see also *KJ,* 1951, pp. 290–95.

52. *Christian Century* 80 (1972): 783–84.

53. Greinacher and Risse, *Bilanz des deutschen Katholizismus,* pp. 115–16; "Meldungen aus dem Reich," no. 330, October 29, 1942, in Boberach, *Berichte,* pp. 747–48; Ruta and Straubinger, *Katholische Kirche, pp. 28–40; Hermelink, Die Katholische Kirche,* pp. 132–33; Barry, *Cardinal Muench,* pp. 219–23. For a good short summary of the liturgical movement, see Hermann Schmidt, *Die Konstitution über die heilige Liturgie,* pp. 51–60, particularly p. 54. For a critical discussion, see Carl Amery, *Die Kapitulation oder Deutscher Katholizismus heute,* pp. 78–94.

54. Ruta and Straubinger, *Katholische Kirche,* p. 25.

55. *KH,* 1962–68, pp. 686–93. "According to the prestigious Allensbach Institute only 35 per cent of registered Roman Catholics . . . regularly attend Sunday Mass. Ten per cent do not go at all, and less than 20 per cent attend in cities" (*Commonweal* 98 [1973]: 283). It was reported that in 1950 50.6 percent of the Catholics attended Mass every Sunday; in 1972, 32.4 percent (*German Tribune,* June 13, 1974, p. 15).

56. *KH,* 1962–68, pp. 689, 693; see also pp. 580–84.

57. Ibid., p. 544; see also statistics on pp. 546, 687, 691.

58. Johannes G. Gerhartz, "Mischehen ohne Kirchliche Trauung? Die deutsche Mischehen-Situation und die kirchliche Formvorschrift," *SZ* 181 (1968): 73–77.

59. The Catholic Bishops' Conference in Germany in a statement on September 23, 1970, set very liberal guidelines for mixed marriages in carrying out the pope's moto propio *Matrimonia Mixta.* The Protestant reaction was that the bishops had gone as far as they possibly could in a liberal interpretation of the pope's decision (*KJ,* 1970, pp. 113–17).

60. See, for example, *KJ,* 1970, pp. 109–17; 1971, pp. 92–110; 1972, pp. 104–14; see also 1969, pp. 405–7. The Catholic church has joined in public dialogues with the Protestants, as in the significant June 3–5, 1971, Pentecost meeting in Augsburg, which was arranged by the German Evangelical Kirchentag and the Central Committee of German Catholics (*Süddeutsche Zeitung,* June 4, 1971; *German Tribune,* June 24, 1971). Cardinal Döpfner of Munich said at that time: "If we in brotherly relationship tackle the problem in common, then also there will ripen among us communion in the love of Christ" (*Münchener Katholische Kirchenzeitung für das Erzbistum München und Freising,* June 20, 1971).

61. *Münchener Katholische Kirchenzeitung,* June 20, 1941; all texts are printed here pp. 9–10; see also *KJ,* 1971, pp. 107–10. In the creeds the Protestants, for example, will continue to say "Christliche" or "allgemeinschristliche" Kirche, while the Catholics and Old Catholics will say: "Ich glaube an den Heiligen Geist, die heilige katholische Kirche." More significantly, there is to be no mention of "Auferstehung des Fleisches"; instead "Auferstehung der Toten" will be used.

62. *German Tribune,* October 25, 1973, p. 5; see also chap. 19 at n. 106 and chap. 21 at n. 73, above.

63. *KJ,* 1971, pp. 103–7, 116–26.

64. *Kulturbrief, A German Review,* 1973-E, no. 4, p. 23.

65. See, for example, Cardinal Willebrand's remarks in his address to the Fifth Plenary

Meeting of the Lutheran World Congress at Evian in July, 1970 (*KJ*, 1970, p. 110); see also Hermelink, *Die Katholische Kirche,* pp. 131–33.

66. *German Tribune,* October 25, 1973, p. 5.

67. See the list of German missionary personnel and their financial support in *KH,* 1962–68, pp. 226–38.

68. Ibid., pp. 311–22.

69. Ibid., pp. 359–67.

70. Ibid., pp. 435–42; Greinacher and Risse, *Bilanz des deutschen Katholizismus,* pp. 171–76, 181–94.

71. Ibid., pp. 176–81; *KH,* 1962–68, pp. 442–54.

72. Arts. 7 and 141 of the Constitution of the Federal Republic of May 23, 1949 (reprinted Weber, *Staatskirchenverträge,* pp. 193–94; see also Helmreich, *Religious Education,* pp. 233, 250).

73. The situation in Bavaria has changed; see this chap. at n. 79.

74. In the Federal Republic (not including West Berlin, Hamburg, or Bremen) there were 29,992 primary schools with an attendance of 5,204,684 in 1964. Of these, 17.1 percent were Protestant confessional schools attended by 15.9 percent of the pupils; 39.6 percent were Catholic confessional schools attended by 45.4 percent of the pupils. Catholics clearly are the chief proponents of the confessional schools; the interdenominational schools are steadily increasing in number (*KH,* 1962–68, pp. 250–51).

75. Helmreich, *Religious Education,* pp. 238–40; Spotts, *Churches and Politics,* pp. 218–19; on the general status of the concordat, see pp. 218–33.

76. *KH,* 1962–68, p. 55; see chap. 5, "The Negotiation of Agreements with the Vatican," above.

77. Mahrenholz, *Die Kirchen in der Gesellschaft,* p. 111.

78. "Wort der Synode der Evangelischen Kirche in Deutschland zur Schulfrage," April 30, 1958, in Heidtmann, *Hat die Kirche geschwiegen?* pp. 270–74.

79. Art. 135 of the Bavarian constitution as amended July 22, 1968 (Georg Ziegler and Paul Trempel, *Verwaltungsgesetze des Freistaates Bayerns,* Verfassung, no. 850, p. 25). The revision of the constitution and the changes in the school law necessitated revision of the Bavarian concordat of 1924 and the agreement with the Evangelical Lutheran Church of Bavaria right of the Rhine. These changes were both concluded October 7, 1968 (ibid., Kirchenverträge, no. 372). On the conflict in the late 1960s over establishing interdenominational schools in Baden-Württemberg and North Rhine Westphalia, see Spotts, *Churches and Politics,* pp. 222–27.

80. Art. 7 of the school law and Art. 136 of the Bavarian constitution (Ziegler and Trempel, *Verwaltungsgesetze,* Schulrecht, no. 680, Verfassung, no. 850).

81. Art. 137 of the Bavarian constitution (*Constitutions of the German Länder,* p. 65).

82. *German Tribune,* April 2, 1972, and August 31, 1972, reprinting articles from the *Hannoverische Allgemeine,* March 6, 1972, and the *Frankfurter Allgemeine Zeitung,* August 9, 1972.

83. Art. 2 of the law (Ziegler and Trempel, *Verwaltungsgesetze,* Schulrecht, no. 68, p. 3).

84. Art. 6, sec. 2 (ibid., Kirchenverträge, no. 372, p. 3).

85. Art. 5 of the treaty with the Protestant church as revised October 7, 1968; Art. 5 of the 1924 concordat as revised October 7, 1969 (ibid., Kirchenverträge, no. 372).

86. Art. 21 of the school law, Gustav A. Vischer, *Neuere Rechtsquellen für die Evang-Luth. Kirche in Bayern,* K12.

87. The continued desire for confessional schools is clear from the provision for confessional classes and other matters which were part of the revision of the Bavarian concordat and the Bavarian school laws.

88. See chap. 21 at n. 55, above.

89. Weber, *Staatskirchenverträge,* pp. 71–74; other agreements negotiated by the Catholic church with the Länder are also in this volume.

90. The concordat was concluded February 28, 1965, and after ratification went into effect October 4, 1965 (ibid., pp. 89–104); see also Klaus Obermayer, "Konkordate," in Fuchs, *Staat und Kirche,* p. 179.

91. Greinacher and Risse, *Bilanz des deutschen Katholizismus,* pp. 258, 263. In Bavaria the Kirchgeld is not to exceed 3 marks, and all who have a yearly income of 3,600 marks are liable (Ziegler and Trempel, *Verwaltungsgesetze,* Kirchensteuer, no. 370, p. 7).

92. *KH,* 1962–68, pp. 585–87. This is the first time the official handbook ever carried

figures on the finances of the church (see the comments on the difficulties of furnishing such statistics in *KH,* 1957–61, pp. 509–10). See also the article by Volker Schmitt, "Was macht die Kirche mit dem vielen Geld? Rechtstitel, Herkunft, und Verwendung der finanziellen Mittel," in Greinacher and Risse, *Bilanz des deutschen Katholizismus,* pp. 248–71.

93. *German Tribune,* April 5, 1973; Schalk, *Commonweal* 98 (1973): 288.
94. Richter, *SZ* 182 (1968): 135. The official handbook (*KH*) of the German Catholic church still attempts to give information on the whole German church, but often the statistics are not available from the churches in the Democratic Republic.
95. Herbert Prauss, "Was hat sich in der Religions- und Kirchenpolitischen Situation der Katholischen Kirche in der DDR im letzten Jahrzehnt geändert," *Informationsdienst des Katholischen Arbeitskreises für Zeitgeschichtliche Fragen e.V.,* no. 50 [December, 1970], pp. 9–18, as reprinted in *KJ,* 1970, pp. 199–204; see particularly pp. 203–4; Greinacher and Risse, *Bilanz des deutschen Katholizismus,* pp. 139–40; for Vatican plans for the reorganization of the Catholic church in the DDR, see *New York Times,* March 11, 1973; October 28, 1976.
96. Greinacher and Risse, *Bilanz des deutschen Katholizismus,* pp. 142, 264; *KJ,* 1957, pp. 154–55.
97. There are seminaries at Erfurt, Huysburg, and Neuzelle as well as some preparatory schools (Greisinger and Risse, *Bilanz des deutschen Katholizismus,* pp. 141–42; *KH,* 1962–68, pp. 80–85; Richter, *SZ* 182 (1968): 134–35; Moore-Rinvolucri, *Education in East Germany,* p. 14.
98. Richter, *SZ* 182 (1968): 134–35. The Catholic church has sought on the whole to stay aloof from political involvement; "Protestant church leaders, in contrast to the Roman Catholic hierarchy, have repeatedly made political statements" (*New York Times,* May 30, 1972). For many protests to the East German government, especially in regard to the schools, by Cardinal Preysing in the years 1945–50, see Adolph, *Preysing,* pp. 214–57.

BIBLIOGRAPHY

Microfilms and Archives

I have not listed individually all of the microfilms and archival folders I consulted; they are cited in the notes or in the list of abbreviations. The films of the records of the Reich Chancellery and the Foreign Office, the records of the National Socialist German Workers party, of the Reichsleiter of the SS, of the Ministry for Occupied Territories, and of the Schumacher Collection on Church Affairs proved especially useful. The last is a collection compiled by a certain Herr Schumacher at the Document Center in Berlin from various archival sources. It has now been turned over to the Bundesarchiv in Koblenz to be reclassified and organized. Unfortunately these rolls of film bear no frame numbers. Copies of many films are in my possession, and I consulted others at the Institut für Zeitgeschichte in Munich. The institute has an index, which, if not infallible, is still a most useful guide, and references to religious questions on many rolls of films which deal primarily with other affairs could thus be spotted.

In writing *Religious Education in German Schools,* I consulted various archives and some of the material in them was also helpful in this study. In addition, I worked at various times in the Bundesarchiv at Koblenz, the Archiv der Bayerischen Landeskirche in Nürnberg, the Archiv für die Geschichte des Kirchenkampfes an der Kirchlichen Hochschule Berlin-Zehlendorf, and the Archiv der Evangelischen Kirche in Westfalen in Bielefeld, with its extensive collection on the Kirchenkampf organized by Rev. Wilhelm Niemöller. There are a few folders of documents from the Ministry of Ecclesiastical Affairs, established by Hitler in 1935, available in the Bundesarchiv in Koblenz, but most of them are in the archives at Potsdam. My requests to work in these archives were turned down by East German authorities in 1968 and 1971. However, much material from these archives is available in Hubert Mohr, *Katholischen Orden und deutscher Imperialismus.*

Many other archival collections, both church and state, are available for study. Their holdings are surveyed in the excellent article by John S. Conway, "Staatliche Akten zum Kirchenkampf, Archive und Bestände," in Heinze Brunotte, ed., *Zur Geschichte des Kirchenkampfes,* pp. 25–34. The volumes appearing as *Veröffentlichungen der Kommission für Zeitgeschichte bei der Katholischen Akademie in Bayern* provide abundant material from Catholic archives, particularly on the period of the Kirchenkampf. Much archival material is also reprinted in the various volumes of the *Arbeiten zur Geschichte des Kirchenkampfes* authorized by the Kommission der Evangelischen Kirche in Deutschland für die Geschichte des Kirchenkampfes.

Books and Articles

This study covers such a great span of time that it would be impractical to list all the scattered sources available or even consulted. This is particularly true of the official Amtsblätter and legal collections of each state and church. Official designations and titles, typically lengthy in Germany, vary slightly with administrative shifts in governmental departments or with changes from monarchy to republic, to the Third Reich, and then back to republic. To be accurate one would have to list various titles for what is in reality one file of an official state or church gazette. Official journals are always cited in the notes in sufficient detail to enable a reader to recognize their origin easily, but they are not listed in this bibliography. The periodical and newspaper literature is endless. There are also many significant articles tucked away in Festschriften and other collections. To list them all would be impossible, and if only some of the articles in a Festschrift or collection are noted here, it is not to discount the others.

Abercrombie, Clarence L. "Barth and Bonhoeffer: Resistance to the Unjust." *Religion and Life* 42 (1973): 344–60.

Ackermann, Konrad. *Der Widerstand der Monatsschrift Hochland gegen den Nationalsozialismus.* Munich, 1965.

Adolph, Walter. *Hirtenamt und Hitler-Dikatatur.* Berlin, 1965.

———. *Im Schatten des Galgens. Zum Gedächtnis der Blutzeugen in der nationalsozialistischen Kirchenverfolgung.* Berlin, 1953.

———. *Kardinal Preysing und zwei Diktaturen. Sein Widerstand gegen die totalitäre Macht.* Berlin, 1971.

———. "Unveröffentlichte Bormann Akten über den Kirchenkampf." *Wichmann Jahrbuch,* 1953, pp. 125–51.

Albrecht, Dieter. *Der Notenwechsel zwischen dem Heiligen Stuhl und der deutschen Reichsregierung.* 2 vols. Mainz, 1965, 1969.

———. "Die Politische Klausel des Reichskonkordats in den deutsch-vatikanischen Beziehungen 1936–1943." In *Festschrift für Max Spindler zum 75. Geburtstag,* edited by Dieter Albrecht, Andreas Kraus, and Kurt Reindel, pp. 793–829. Munich, 1969.

———, Kraus, Andreas, and Reindel, Kurt, eds., *Festschrift für Max Spindler zum 75. Geburtstag.* Munich, 1969.

Allgemeines Kirchenblatt für das evangelische Deutschland. 85 vols. Stuttgart, 1852–1936. The journal of the national church organization which printed all important church and state laws, ordinances, announcements, and edicts; a mine of source material. It lost its official character as an Amtsblatt in October, 1933, and much of the material it normally carried afterwards appeared in the *Gesetzblatt der Deutschen Evangelischen Kirche,* published October 7, 1933 to November 18, 1944.

Amery, Carl. *Die Kapitulation oder Deutscher Katholizismus heute.* Hamburg, 1963.

Amtsblatt der Evangelischen Kirche in Deutschland. Hanover, 1946. The successor of the *Allgemeines Kirchenblatt;* gives ordinances and laws of the national church and of the Land churches.

An der Stechbahn. Erlebnisse und Berichte in den Jahren der Verfolgung mit dreiundzwanzig Grussworten zum 60. Geburtstag von Propst D. Grüber am 24. Juni 1951. Berlin, 1951.

An ihren Taten sollt ihr sie erkennen! Gladdach, n.d.

Anordnungen des Stellvertreters des Führers. Zusammenstellung aller bis zum 31. März 1937 erlassenen und noch gültigen. Munich, 1937.

Anschütz, Gerhard. *Die Verfassung des Deutschen Reichs vom 11. August 1919. Ein Kommentar für Wissenschaft und Praxis.* 3d ed. Berlin, 1930.

Archiv für evangelisches Kirchenrecht, 1937–42. Successor to the *Allgemeines Kirchenblatt für das evangelische Deutschland* and the *Preussisches* (after 1934 *Deutsches*) *Pfarrarchiv,* 1909–36.

Archiv für Katholisches Kirchenrecht mit besonderer Rücksicht auf die Länder deutscher Zunge. 1875–.

Aretin, Karl Otmar Frhr. von. "Prälat Kaas, Franz von Papen und Das Reichskonkordat von 1933." *Vierteljahreshefte für Zeitgeschichte* 14 (1966): 252–79.

Asmussen, Hans. *Die Grundlagen der bekennenden Kirche.* Berlin, 1934.

———. *Her zu uns wer dem Herrn angehört! Warum doch Barmen.* Berlin, n.d.

———. *Kreuz und Reich.* Berlin, 1934.

———. *Kurze Auslegung der zehn Gebote.* Munich, 1936.

———. *Sola fide, das ist lutherisch!* Munich, 1937.

———. *Zur jüngsten Kirchengeschichte: Anmerkungen und Folgerungen.* Stuttgart, 1961.

Bachem, Karl. *Vorgeschichte, Geschichte und Politik der deutschen Zentrumspartei. Zugleich ein Beitrag zur Geschichte der katholischen Bewegung, sowie zur allgemeinen Geschichte des neueren und neuesten Deutschlands 1815–1914.* Reprint of 2d ed. (1928). 9 vols. Cologne, 1967.

Baier, Helmut. *Die Deutschen Christen im Rahmen des bayerischen Kirchenkampfes.* Nürnberg, 1968.

———, and Henn, Ernst. *Chronologie des bayerischen Kirchenkampfes 1933–1945.* Nürnberg, 1968.

Balfour, Michael, and Frisby, Julian. *Helmuth von Moltke. A Leader Against Hitler.* London, 1972.

Bammel, Ernst. *Die Reichsgründung und der deutsche Protestantismus.* Erlangen, 1973.

Barry, Colman J. *American Nuncio Cardinal Aloisius Muench*. Collegeville, Minn., 1969.

Barth, Karl. *The German Church Conflict*. Translated by P. T. A. Parker. Richmond, Virginia, 1965.

———. "Theologische Existenz heute." In Walther Fürst, ed. *"Dialektische Theologie" in Scheidung und Bewährung 1933–1936. Aufsätze, Gutachten und Erklärungen,* edited by Walter Fürst, pp. 45–77. Munich, 1966. Also reprinted here: Barth's "Reformation als Entscheidung" (pp. 103–121); "Erklärung über das rechte Verständnis der reformatorischen Bekenntnisse in der Deutschen Evangelischen Kirche der Gegenwart" (pp. 122–27); "Gottes Wille und unsere Wünsche" (pp. 128–41); "Offenbarung, Kirche, Theologie" (pp. 142–68); "Nein. Antwort an Emil Bruner" (pp. 208–58).

Bauer, Günther. *Kirchliche Rundfunkarbeit 1924–1939*. Frankfurt/Main, 1966.

Baumgärtel, Friedrich. *Wider die Kirchenkampf-Legenden*. 2d ed. Neuendettelsau, 1959.

Baumont, Maurice, Fried, John H. E., and Vermeil, Edmond, eds. *The Third Reich*. New York, 1955.

Baynes, Norman H., ed. *The Speeches of Adolph Hitler*. 2 vols. London, 1942.

Becker, Howard. *German Youth: Bond or Free*. New York, 1946.

Beckett, J. C. ed. *Historical Studies VII. Papers read before the Irish Conference of Historians*. London, 1969.

Beckmann, Joachim. *Der Kirchenkampf*. Gladbeck, 1952.

Bekenntnissynode der Deutschen Evangelischen Kirche. Dahlem 1934. Vorträge und Botschaft. Göttingen, 1935.

Bell, G. K. A. *The Church and Humanity (1939–1946)*. London, 1946.

Ben-Elissar, Eliahu. *La diplomatie du IIIe Reich et les juifs (1933–1939)*. Paris, 1969.

Benn, Ernst-Viktor. "Die einstweilige Leitung der Deutschen Evangelischen Kirche (Juli–September 1933)." *Zeitschrift für evangelisches Kirchenrecht* 1 (1951): 365–82.

Bergmann, Ernst. *Die Deutsche Nationalkirche*. Breslau, 1933.

Bernhard, Henry, Goetz, Wolfgang, and Wiegler, Paul, eds. *Gustav Stresemann Vermächtnis. Der Nachlass in Drei Bänden*. 3 vols. Berlin, 1933.

Bethge, Eberhard. *Dietrich Bonhoeffer. Theologe. Christ. Zeitgenosse*. Munich, 1967.

Bewley, Charles. *Hermann Göring and the Third Reich*. London, 1962.

Beyer, Franz. *Menschen Warten. Aus dem politischen Wirken Martin Niemöllers seit 1945*. Siegen, 1952.

Beyer, Hermann Wolfgang. *Im Kampf um Volk und Kirche. Reden und Aufsätze*. Dresden, 1934.

Beyreuther, Erich. *Geschichte der Diakonie und inneren Mission in der Neuzeit*. Berlin, 1962.

———. *Die Geschichte des Kirchenkampfes in Dokumenten 1933/45*. Wuppertal, 1966.

Bielfeldt, Johann. "Die Haltung des Schleswig-Holsteinischen Bruderrates im Kirchenkampf." In *Zur Geschichte des Kirchenkampfes. Gesammelte Aufsätze,* edited by Kurt D. Schmidt, pp. 172–88. Göttingen, 1965.

———. *Der Kirchenkampf in Schleswig-Holstein 1933–1945*. Göttingen, 1964.

Bigler, Robert M. *The Politics of German Protestantism. The Rise of the Protestant Church Elite in Prussia, 1815–1848*. Berkeley, 1972.

Binder, Gerhart. *Irrtum und Widerstand. Die deutschen Katholiken in der Auseinandersetzung mit dem Nationalsozialismus*. Munich, 1968.

Bischöfliche Arbeitsstelle für Schule und Erziehung. *Das Ringen um das sogenannte Reichsschulgesetz*. Cologne, 1956.

Bischöfliche Hauptarbeitsstelle Düsseldorf. *Die katholische Aktion (Das katholische Laienapostolat) in den deutschen Diözesen*. Hildesheim, 1934.

Bischöfliches Ordinariat Berlin. *Dokumente aus dem Kampf der katholischen Kirche im Bistum Berlin gegen den Nationalsozialismus*. Berlin, 1946.

Bizer, Ernst. *Ein Kampf um die Kirche. Der "Fall Schempf" nach den Akten erzählt*. Tübingen, 1965.

Blet, Pierre, et al., eds. *Actes et documents du Saint Siège relatifs à la seconde guerre mondiale. Le Saint Siège et la guerre en Europe, Mars 1939-Août 1940*. Vatican City, 1965.

———. *Lettres de Pie XII aux évêques allemands 1939–1944*. Vatican City, 1966. German ed., *Die Briefe Pius XII. an die deutschen Bischöfe 1939–1944* (Mainz, 1966).

———. *Le Saint Siège et la situation religieuse en Pologne et dans pays Baltes 1939–1945*. 2 parts. Vatican City, 1967.

———. *Le Saint Siège et la guerre en Europe, Juin 1940–Juin 1941*, Vatican City, 1967.

———. *Le Saint Siège et la guerre en Europe, Juillet 1941–Octobre 1942*. Vatican City, 1969.

————. *Le Saint Siège et les victimes de la guerre, Mars 1939–Décembre 1940.* Vatican City, 1972.

————. *Le Saint Siège et la guerre mondiale, Novembre 1942–Décembre 1943.* Vatican City, 1973.

Bloth, Peter C. *Religion in den Schulen Preussens. Der Gegenstand des evangelischen Religionsunterrichts von der Reaktionszeit bis zum Nationalsozialismus.* Heidelberg, 1968.

Boberach, Heinz, ed. *Berichte des SD und der Gestapo über Kirchen und Kirchenvolk in Deutschland 1934–1944.* Mainz, 1971.

Böckenförde, Ernst-Wolfgang. "Der deutsche Katholizismus im Jahre 1933. Stellungnahme zu einer Diskussion." *Hochland,* 54 (1961–62): 217–45.

Bonhoeffer, Dietrich. *Gesammelte Schriften.* Edited by Eberhard Bethge. 4 vols. Munich, 1958–61.

————. *Widerstand und Ergebung. Briefe und Aufzeichnungen aus der Haft.* Edited by Eberhard Bethge. Munich. 1966.

Bossert, Gustav. "Die Eigenart der evangelischen Landeskirche Württembergs im Wandel der Zeit." In *Für Volk und Kirche. Zum 70. Geburtstag von Landesbischof D. Th. Wurm,* pp. 33–51, edited by the Evang. Pfarrverein in Württemberg. Stuttgart, 1938.

Boyens, Armin. *Kirchenkampf und Ökumene 1933–1939. Darstellung und Dokumentation.* Munich, 1969.

————. *Kirchenkampf und Ökumene 1939–1945.* Munich, 1973.

————. "Das Stuttgarter Schuldbekenntnis vom 19. Oktober 1945—Entstehung und Bedeutung." *Vierteljahrshefte für Zeitgeschichte* 19 (1971): 374–97.

Bracher, Karl D. *Nationalsozialistische Machtergreifung und Reichskonkordat. Ein Gutachten.* Wiesbaden, 1956.

————. *Die Auflösung der Weimarer Republik.* 3d ed. Villingen, 1960.

————, Sauer, Wolfgang, and Schulz, Gerhard. *Die nationalsozialistische Machtergreifung: Studien zur Errichtung des totalitären Herrschaftssystems in Deutschland 1933/34.* Cologne, 1960.

Braeunlich, P. *Die Deutschen Katholikentage, auf Grund der amtlichen Berichte dargestellt.* 2 vols. Halle, 1910.

Brandt, Wilhelm. *Friedrich v. Bodelschwingh 1877–1946. Nachfolger und Gestalter.* Bethel, 1967.

Brederlaw, Jörn. *"Lichtfreunde" und "Freie Gemeinden." Religiöser Protest und Freiheitsbewegung im Vormärz und in der Revolution von 1848/49.* Munich, 1976.

Bredt, Joh. Victor. *Neues evangelisches Kirchenrecht für Preussen.* 3 vols. Berlin, 1921–27.

Breuning, Klaus. *Das Vision des Reiches. Deutscher Katholizismus zwischen Demokratie und Diktatur (1929–1934).* Munich, 1969.

Briffault, Herma, ed. *The Memoirs of Doctor Felix Kersten.* New York, 1947.

British Foreign and State Papers. London, 1834– .

Broszat, Martin. "Gutachten des Instituts für Zeitgeschichte. Verfolgung polnisches katholischer Geistlicher." München, 1959. Mimeographed.

————. *Nationalsozialistische Polenpolitik 1939–1945.* Stuttgart, 1961.

Brüning, Heinrich. *Memoiren 1918–1934.* Stuttgart, 1970.

Brunotte, Heinz. "Die Entwicklung der staatlichen Finanzaufsicht über die Deutsche Evangelische Kirche von 1935–1945." *Zeitschrift für evangelisches Kirchenrecht* 3 (1953–54): 29–55.

————. *Die evangelische Kirche in Deutschland. Geschichte, Organisation und Gestalt der EKD.* Gütersloh, 1964. Vol. 1 of *Evangelische Enzyklopädie,* edited by Helmut Thielicke and Hans Thimme.

————. *Die Grundordnung der Evangelischen Kirche in Deutschland. Ihre Entstehung und ihre Probleme.* Berlin, 1954.

————. "Kirchenkampf und Widerstand." In *Reformatio und Confessio. Festschrift für D. Wilhelm Maurer,* edited by F. W. Kantzenbach and G. Müller, pp. 315–24. Berlin, 1965.

————. "Der kirchenpolitische Kurs der Deutschen Evangelischen Kirchenkanzlei von 1937 bis 1945." In *Zur Geschichte des Kirchenkampfes. Gesammelte Aufsätze.* Edited by Kurt D. Schmidt, pp. 90–145. Göttingen, 1965.

————. "Die Kirchenmitgliedschaft der nichtarischen Christen im Kirchenkampf." *Zeitschrift für evangelisches Kirchenrecht* 13 (1967): 140–74.

————, ed. *Zur Geschichte des Kirchenkampfes. Gesammelte Aufsätze.* Vol. 2. Göttingen, 1971.

————, and Weber, Otto, eds. *Evangelisches Kirchenlexikon; Kirchlich-theologisches Handwörterbuch.* 4 vols. Göttingen, 1956–61.

————, Müller, Konrad, and Smend, Rudolf, eds. *Festschrift für Erich Ruffel zum 65. Geburtstag am 25. Januar 1968.* Berlin, 1968.

Brunschwig, Henri. *Enlightenment and Romanticism in Eighteenth-Century Prussia.* Chicago, 1974.

Buchheim, Hans. *Glaubenskrise im Dritten Reich.* Stuttgart, 1953.

————. "Ein NS-Fuktionär zum Niemöller-Prozess." *Vierteljahrshefte für Zeitgeschichte* 4 (1956): 307–15.

Bultmann, Rudolf. "Der Arier-Paragraph im Raume der Kirche." In *"Dialektische Theologie" in Scheidung und Bewährung 1933–1936. Aufsätze, Gutachten und Erklärungen,* edited by Walter Fürst. Munich, 1966.

Bundesministerium für gesamtdeutsche Fragen. *SBZ von A bis Z. Ein Taschen und Nachschlagebuch über die sowjetische Besatzungszone Deutschlands.* Bonn, 1953– . A revised edition of this handbook appears practically every year.

Bunke, Ernst. *Was jedermann von der neuen Kirchenverfassung wissen muss.* 4th ed. Berlin, 1925.

Bussmann, Walter. *Die innere Entwicklung des deutschen Widerstandes gegen Hitler.* Berlin, 1964.

Büttner, Oskar. *Die evangelischen Freikirchen Deutschlands.* Bonn, 1916.

Calwer Kirchenlexikon. Kirchlich-theologisches Handwörterbuch. Edited by Friedrich Keppler. 2 vols. Stuttgart, 1941.

Chandler, Albert R. *Rosenberg's Nazi Myth.* Ithaca, N.Y., 1945.

Chickering, Roger Philip. "The Peace Movement and the Religious Community in Germany, 1900–1914." *Church History* 38 (1969): 300–311.

Clauss, Manfred. "Der Besuch Ribbentrops im Vatikan." *Zeitschrift für Kirchengeschichte* 87 (1976): 54–64.

Cochrane, Arthur C. *The Church's Confession Under Hitler.* Philadelphia, 1962.

Conrad, Walter. *Der Kampf um die Kanzeln. Erinnerungen und Dokumente aus der Hitlerzeit.* Berlin, 1957.

Constabel, Adelheid, ed. *Die Vorgeschichte des Kulturkampfes. Quellenveröffentlichung aus dem Deutschen Zentralarchiv.* 2d ed. Berlin, 1957.

Constitutions of the German Länder. Berlin, 1947.

Conway, John S. "Der Deutsche Kirchenkampf. Tendenzen und Probleme seiner Erforschung an hand neuerer Literatur." *Vierteljahrshefte für Zeitgeschichte* 17 (1969): 423–49.

————. *The Nazi Persecution of the Churches 1933–45.* New York, 1968. The German edition, *Die nationalsozialistische Kirchenpolitik 1933–1945, Ihre Ziele, Widerspruch und Fehlschläge* (Munich, 1969), has been revised slightly, the appendices dropped, and other documents reprinted. The footnotes in the German edition are in much better form than in the English, but there is no bibliography in the German edition.

————. "The Silence of Pope Pius XII." *Review of Politics* 27 (1965): 105–31.

————. "Staatliche Akten zum Kirchenkampf, Archive, und Bestände." In *Zur Geschichte des Kirchenkampfes. Gesammelte Aufsätze,* edited by Heinz Brunotte, 2: 25–34. Göttingen, 1971.

————. "The Vatican, Great Britain, and Relations with Germany, 1938–1940." *Journal of History* 16 (1973): 147–67.

Conzemius, Victor. *Katholizismus ohne Rom. Die Altkatholische Kirchengemeinschaft.* Zurich, 1969.

————. "Pius XII and Nazi Germany in Historical Perspective." In *Historical Studies VII. Papers Read before the Irish Conference of Historians,* edited by J. C. Beckett. London, 1969.

————. *Églises chrétiennes et totalitarisme national-socialiste. Un bilan historiographique.* Louvain, 1969.

Cordier, Leopold. *Evangelische Jugendkunde.* 2 vols. Schwerte i.W., 1925.

Corsten, Wilhelm, ed. *Kölner Aktenstücke zur Lage der katholischen Kirche in Deutschland 1933–1945.* Cologne, 1949.

Crankshaw, Edward. *Gestapo: Instrument of Tyranny.* New York, 1956.

Dahm, Karl-Wilhelm. "German Protestantism and Politics, 1918–1939." *Journal of Contemporary History* 3 (1968): 29–49.

Danielsmeyer, Werner. "Präses D. Karl Koch." In *Materialien für den Dienst in der Evangelischen Kirche von Westfalen,* ser. A, no. 5, edited by Reinhold Hedtke, pp. 1–19. Bielefeld, 1976.

Demokratisierung der Kirche in der Bundesrepublik Deutschland. Ein Memorandum deutscher Katholiken. Herausgegeben vom Bensberger Kreis. Mainz, 1970.

Denkschrift über den Umfang der Staatsleistungen der deutschen Länder an die evangelischen Kirchen bis zur Ablösung. Ausgearbeitet im Deutschen Evangelischen Kirchenbundesamt. Berlin-Charlottenburg, 1928.

Deschner, Karlheinz. *Mit Gott und den Faschisten. Der Vatican im Bunde mit Mussolini, Franco, Hitler und Pavelić.* Stuttgart, 1965.

Deuerlein, Ernst. Der Aufstieg der NSDAP in Augenzeugenberichten. 2d ed. Düsseldorf, 1968.

————. *Der deutsche Katholizismus 1933.* Osnabrück, 1963.

————. *Das Reichskonkordat. Beiträge zu Vorgeschichte, Abschluss und Vollzug des Konkordats zwischen dem Heiligen Stuhl und dem Deutschen Reich vom 20. Juli 1933.* Düsseldorf, 1956.

Deutsch, Harold C. *The Conspiracy Against Hitler in the Twilight War.* Minneapolis, 1968.

Dibelius, Otto. *Christus und die Deutschen.* 6 pamphlets. Berlin, 1935–36. The series includes: *Die Germanisierung des Christentums. Eine Tragödie.* Berlin, 1935. *Die echte Germanisierung der Kirche.* Berlin, 1935. *Der Kampf der Kirche als geschichtliche Tat.* Berlin, 1935. *Die grosse Wendung im Kirchenkampf.* Berlin, 1935. *Die Kraft der Deutschen in Gegensätzen zum Leben.* Berlin, 1936. *Der Galiläer siegt doch!* Berlin, 1936.

————. *In the Service of the Lord: The Autobiography of Otto Dibelius.* Translated by Mary Ilford. New York, 1964. The volume was first published as *Ein Christ ist immer im Dienst* (Stuttgart, 1961).

————, and Niemöller, Martin. *Wir rufen Deutschland zu Gott.* Berlin, 1937.

Dickmann, F. "Das Problem der Gleichberechtigung der Konfessionen im Reich im 16. und 17. Jahrhundert." *Historische Zeitschrift* 201 (1964): 265–305.

Diehm, Otto. *Bibliographie zur Geschichte des Kirchenkampfes 1933–1945.* Göttingen, 1958.

Diem, Hermann. "Kirche und Antisemitismus." In *Deutsches Geistesleben und Nationalsozialismus,* edited by Andreas Flitner, pp. 7–23. Tübingen, 1965.

————. *Sine vi—sed verbo. Aufsätze, Vorträge, Voten. Aus Anlass der Vollendung seines 65. Lebensjahres am 2. Februar 1965.* Edited by Uvo Andreas Wolf. Munich, 1965.

————, Schempp, Paul, and Müller, Kurt, eds. *Kirche und Entnazifizierung. Denkschrift der Kirchlichtheologischen Sozietät in Württemberg.* Stuttgart, 1946.

Dieter, Albrecht, Kraus, Andreas, and Reindel, Kurt, eds. *Festschrift für Max Spindler zum 75. Geburtstag.* Munich, 1969.

Dipper, Theodor. *Die Evangelische Bekenntnisgemeinschaft in Württemberg 1933–1945. Ein Beitrag zur Geschichte des Kirchenkampfes im Dritten Reich.* Göttingen, 1966.

Documents on British Foreign Policy 1919–1939. London, 1949–.

Documents on German Foreign Policy 1918–1945. From the Archives of the German Foreign Ministry. Washington, 1949–66.

Dodd, William E., Jr. and Dodd, Martha, eds. *Ambassador Dodd's Diary 1933–1938.* New York, 1941.

Doetsch, Wilhelm Josef. *Württembergs Katholiken unterm Hakenkreutz 1930–1935.* Stuttgart, 1969.

Domarus, Max. *Hitler Reden und Proklamationen 1932–1945.* 2 vols. Würzburg, 1962–63.

Donohue, James. *Hitler's Conservative Opponents in Bavaria 1930–1945. A Study of Catholic, Monarchist and Separatist Anti-Nazi Activities.* Leiden, 1961.

Dress, Walter. "Wiederstandsrecht und Christenpflicht bei Dietrich Bonhoeffer." *Lutherische Monatshefte* 3(1964): 198–209.

Drummond, Andrew L. *German Protestantism Since Luther.* London, 1951.

Dumrath, Karlheinrich, Eger, Wolfgang, and Steinberg, Hans. *Handbuch des kirchlichen Archivwesens. Vol. 1. Die Zentralen Archive in der evangelischen Kirche.* Neustadt an der Aisch, 1965.

Eberhard, Ernst. "Statistik der kirchlichen Lebensäusserungen." *Kirchliches Jahrbuch* 77 (1950): 425–68. The National Socialist state in 1934 forbade publication of church statistical tables. This article is a résumé of the period 1933–40 and covers baptisms, marriages, burials, etc.

Ebers, Godehard Josef. *Evangelisches Kirchenrecht in Preussen. Sammlung der in den evangelischen Landeskirchen Preussens geltenden kirchlichen Gesetze und Verordnungen.* 3 vols. Munich, 1932.

————. *Reichs- und preussisches Staatskirchenrecht. Sammlung der religions- und kirchenpolitischen Gesetze und Verordnungen des Deutschen Reiches und Preussens nebst den einschlägigen kirchlichen Vorschriften.* Munich, 1932.

Ehrenfort, Gerhard. *Die schlesische Kirche im Kirchenkampf 1932–1945.* Göttingen, 1968.

Ehrhardt, Helmut. *Euthanasie und Vernichtung "lebensunwerten" Lebens.* Stuttgart, 1965.

Elliger, Walter. *Die Evangelische Kirche der Union. Ihre Vorgeschichte und Geschichte.* Witten, 1967.

Europäische Publikation. *Die Vollmacht des Gewissens.* Munich, 1956.

Evangelischer Pfarrverein in Württemberg, eds. *Für Volk und Kirche. Zum 70. Geburtstag von Landesbishof D. Th. Wurm.* Stuttgart, 1938.

Evangelium im Dritten Reich. Kirchenzeitung für Christentum und Nationalsozialismus. Edited by Joachim Hossenfelder. The last issue with Hossenfelder's name on the masthead was vol. 4, no. 25, June 23, 1935. The title then was changed to *Evangelium im Dritten Reich. Die Kirchenzeitung der evangelischen Nationalsozialisten.* Its last issue was vol. 5, no. 11, March 15, 1936.

Evangelium im Dritten Reich. Sonntagsblatt der Deutschen Christen. This publication appeared June, 1932, to December, 1934. On the title page was a cross and swastika with the notation: "*symbolisches Nebeneinanderglauben.*"

Fabricius, Cajus. *Positive Christianity in the Third Reich.* Dresden, 1937.

Fahlbusch, Erwin, ed. *Taschenlexikon: Religion und Theologie.* 4 vols. Göttingen, 1971.

Falconi, Carlo. *The Silence of Pius XII.* Translated by Bernard Wall. Boston, 1970.

Faulhaber, Michael. *Judentum, Christentum, Germanentum. Adventspredigten gehalten in St. Michael zu München.* Munich, 1934.

Feder, Gottfried. *Hitler's Official Programme and its Fundamental Ideas.* New York, 1971. Reprint of the first English ed. (1934).

Fellmeth, Adolf. *Das kirchliche Finanzwesen in Deutschland.* Karlsruhe, 1910.

Fest, Joachim. *Das Gesicht des Dritten Reiches. Profile einer Herrschaft.* Munich, 1964.

Filthault, E. *Deutsche Katholikentage 1848–1958 und soziale Frage.* Essen, 1960.

Fireside, Harvey. *Icon and Swastika. The Russian Orthodox Church under Nazi and Soviet Control.* Cambridge, Mass., 1971.

Fischer, Fritz. "Der deutsche Protestantismus und die Politik im 19. Jahrhundert." *Historische Zeitschrift* 171 (1951): 473–518.

Fischer, Joachim. *Die sächsische Landeskirche im Kirchenkampf 1933–1937.* Göttingen, 1972.

Flachsmeier, Horst R. *Geschichte der evangelischen Weltmission.* Giessen, 1963.

Fleisch, Paul. "Das Werden der Vereinigten Evangelisch-Lutherischen Kirche Deutschlands und ihrer Verfassung." *Zeitschrift für evangelisches Kirchenrecht* 1 (1951): 15–55; 404–18.

Flitner, Andreas, ed. *Deutsches Geistesleben und Nationalsozialismus. Eine Vortragsreihe der Universität Tübingen.* Tübingen, 1965.

Flüchtlingsdienst des ökumenischen Rats der Kirchen. *Die evangelische Kirche in Deutschland und die Judenfrage. Ausgewählte Dokumente aus den Jahren des Kirchenkampfes 1933–1943.* Geneva, 1945.

Forck, Bernard H. *und folget ihrem Glauben nach. Gedenkbuch für die Blutzeugen der Bekennenden Kirche.* Stuttgart, 1949.

Forster, Karl, ed. *Das Verhältnis von Kirche und Staat.* Würzburg, 1965.

Frank, Johann. "Geschichte und neuere Entwicklung des Rechts der kirchlichen Beamten." *Zeitschrift für evangelisches Kirchenrecht* 10 (1963–64): 264–302.

Franz, Georg. *Kulturkampf: Staat und Katholische Kirche in Mitteleuropa von der Säkularisation bis zum Abschluss des Preussischen Kulturkampfes.* Munich, 1954.

Franz, Helmut. *Kurt Gerstein. Aussenseiter des Widerstandes der Kirche gegen Hitler.* Zurich, 1964.

Franz-Willing, Georg. *Die Bayerische Vatikangesandtschaft 1803–1934.* Munich, 1965.

Frey, Arthur. *Cross and Swastika. The Ordeal of the German Church.* Translated by J. Strathearn McNab. London, 1938.

Frick, Robert. "Zur Geschichte des Kirchenkampfes." *Pastoraltheologie Wissenshaft und Praxis* 58 (1968): 130–41.

Friedberg, Emil. *Lehrbuch des katholischen und evangelischen Kirchenrechts.* 5th ed. Leipzig, 1903.

Friedländer, Saul. *Pius XII and The Third Reich. A Documentation.* Translated by C. Fullman. New York, 1966.

Friedrich, Otto. *Einführung in das Kirchenrecht unter besonderer Berücksichtigung des Rechts der Evangelischen Landeskirche in Baden.* Göttingen, 1961.

———. "Die kirchen- und staatskirchenrechtliche Entwicklung in der Evang. Landeskirche Badens von 1933–1953." *Zeitschrift für evangelisches Kirchenrecht* 3 (1953–54): 292–349.

Fritz, Herbert C. *Die Methodistenkirche in Deutschland. Ein Beitrag zum besseren Verständnis der evangelischen Freikirchen in Deutschland.* Wilhelmshaven-Rustersiel, 1959.

Frör, Kurt. *Die babylonische Gefangenschaft der Kirche.* Erlangen, n.d. (ca. 1937).

Fuchs, Walther P., ed. *Staat und Kirche im Wandel der Jahrhunderte.* Stuttgart, 1966.

Fürst, Walther. *"Dialektische Theologie" in Scheidung und Bewährung 1933–1936. Aufsätze, Gutachten und Erklärungen.* Munich, 1966.

Fuss, Gottfried. *Der Wille zur Einheit. Der sächsische Weg im Kirchenkampf des Dritten Reiches.* Berlin, 1964.

Gallin, Mary Alice. "The Cardinal and the State: Faulhaber and the Third Reich." *Journal of Church and State* 12 (1970): 385–404.

————. *German Resistance to Hitler; Ethical and Religious Factors.* Washington, 1961.

Gastgen, Hubert. *Dalbergs und Napoleons Kirchenpolitik in Deutschland.* Paderborn, 1917.

Gauger, Joseph. *Gotthard Briefe. Chronik der Kirchenwirren.* 3 vols. Eberfeld, 1934–35.

Gefaeller, Heinz. "Die Kirchensteuer seit 1945." *Zeitschrift für evangelisches Kirchenrecht* 1 (1951): 80–100, 382–403.

Geiger, Max. *Der deutsche Kirchenkampf 1933–1945.* Zurich, 1965.

Genschel, Helmut, et al. *Die Juden und Wir.* Göttingen, 1960.

Gerhardt, Martin. *Theodor Fliedner.* 2 vols. Düsseldorf, 1933.

————. *Friedrich von Bodelschwingh.* 2 vols. Bethel, 1950.

Gerhartz, Johannes G. "Mischehen ohne kirchliche Trauung? Die deutsche Mischehen-Situation und die kirchliche Formvorschrift." *Stimmen der Zeit* 181 (1968): 73–87.

Gerlach-Praetorius, Angelika. *Die Kirche vor der Eidesfrage. Die Diskussion um den Pfarrereid im Dritten Reich.* Göttingen, 1967.

Gerstenmaier, Eugen. "Der Kreisauer Kreis. Zu dem Buch Gerrit van Roons 'Neuordnung im Widerstand'." *Vierteljahrshefte für Zeitgeschichte* 15 (1967): 221–46.

————, ed. *Kirche, Volk und Staat. Stimmen aus der Deutschen Evangelischen Kirche zur Oxforder Weltkirchenkonferenz.* Berlin, 1937.

Gesetzblatt der Deutschen Evangelischen Kirche. October 7, 1933–November 18, 1944. Successor to *Allgemeines Kirchenblatt.*

Giese, Friedrich. *Deutsches Kirchensteuerrecht.* Stuttgart, 1910; reprinted 1965.

————. "Staat und Kirche im neuen Deutschland. Systematische Übersicht über die quellengeschichtliche Entwicklung des Verhältnisses zwischen Staat und Kirche in Reich und Ländern seit dem Umsturz in November 1918." *Jahrbuch des Öffentlichen Rechts* 13 (1925): 249–357. For the period 1924–31, see vol. 20 (1932): pp. 116–67.

———— and Heydte, Friedrich A. Frhr. v. d. *Der Konkordatsprozess.* 4 vols. Munich, 1959.

Giovannetti, Alberto. *Der Vatikan und der Krieg.* Cologne, 1961.

Glenthøj, Jørgen. "Hindenburg, Göring und die evangelischen Kirchenführer. Ein Beitrag zur Beleuchtung des staatspolitischen Hintergrundes der Kanzleraudienz am 25. Januar 1934." In *Zur Geschichte des Kirchenkampfes. Gesammelte Aufsätze,* edited by Kurt D. Schmidt, pp. 45–91. Göttingen, 1965.

Goebbels, Joseph. *Vom Kaiserhof zur Reichskanzlei.* Berlin, 1934.

Goldschmidt, Arthur. *Geschichte der evangelischen Gemeinde Theresienstadt 1942–1945.* Tübingen, 1948.

Gollert, Friedrich. *Dibelius vor Gericht.* Munich, 1959.

Gollwitzer, Helmut, Kuhn, Käthe, and Schneider, Reinhold, eds. *Du hast mich heimgesucht bei Nacht. Abschiedsbriefe und Aufzeichnungen des Widerstandes 1933–1945.* Munich, 1954.

————, and Traub, Hellmut, eds. *Hören und Handeln. Festschrift für Ernst Wolf zum 60. Geburtstag.* Munich, 1962.

Golombek, Oskar. *Die katholische Kirche und die Völker-Vertreibung.* Cologne, 1966.

Götte, Karl Heinz. *Die Propaganda der Glaubensbewegung "Deutsche Christen" und ihre Beurteilung in der deutschen Tagespresse. Ein Beitrag zur Publizistik im Dritten Reich.* Münster i.W., 1957.

Götten, Josef. *Christoph Monfang. Theologe und Politiker 1817–1890. Eine biographische Darstellung.* Mainz, 1969.

Gotto, Klaus. *Die Wochenzeitung Junge Front/Michael. Eine Studie zum katholischen Selbstverständnis und zum Verhalten der jungen Kirche gegenüber dem Nationalsozialismus.* Mainz, 1970.

Graham, Robert A. "The 'Right to Kill' in the Third Reich. Prelude to Genocide." *Catholic Historical Review* 62 (1976): 56–76.

Graml, Hermann, Mommsen, H., Reichhardt, H., and Wolf, E. *The German Resistance to Hitler.* Berkeley, 1970.

Gramlich, Bernhard, ed. *Ein Jahrhundert Diakonie in Bethel.* Bethel bei Bielefeld, 1967.

Greinacher, Norbert. "Die Entwicklung der Kirchenaustritte und Kirchenübertritte und ihre Ursachen." *Kirchliches Handbuch* 25 (1957–61): 441–52.

———, and Risse, H. T., eds. *Bilanz des deutschen Katholizismus.* Mainz, 1966.

Greive, Hermann. *Theologie und Ideologie. Katholizismus und Judentum in Deutschland und Österreich 1918–1935.* Heidelberg, 1969.

Gritschneder, Otto. *Pater Rupert Mayer vor dem Sondergericht. Dokumente der Verhandlung vor dem Sondergericht in München am 22. und 23. Juli 1937.* Munich, 1965.

Gröber, Conrad. *Kirche, Vaterland und Vaterlandsliebe. Zeitgemässe Erwägungen und Erwiderungen.* Freiburg/Breisgau, 1935.

Grüber, Heinrich. *Erinnerungen aus sieben Jahrzehnten,* Cologne, 1968.

Gruchmann, Lothar. "Erlebnisbericht Werner Pünders über die Ermordung Klauseners am 30.Juni 1934 und ihre Folgen." *Vierteljahrshefte für Zeitgeschichte* 19 (1971): 404–31.

———. "Euthanasie und Justiz im Dritten Reich." *Vierteljahrshefte für Zeitgeschichte* 20 (1972): 235–79.

Gründler, Johannes. *Lexikon der christlichen Kirchen und Sekten unter Berücksichtigung der Missionsgesellschaften und zwischenkirchlichen Organisationen.* 2 vols. Vienna, 1961.

Grundmann, Walter. *Totale Kirche im totalen Staat. Mit einem Geleitwort von Landesbischof F. Coch.* Dresden, 1934.

———. *Christentum und Judentum. Studien zur Erforschung ihres gegenseitigen Verhältnisses.* 3 vols. Leipzig, 1940–43. The last two volumes are titled *Germanentum, Christentum und Judentum.*

Grunow, Richard. *Wichern—Ruf und Antwort.* Gütersloh, 1958.

Grunsky, Karl. *Luthers Bekenntnisse zur Judenfrage.* Stuttgart, 1933.

Grünthal, Günther. *Reichsschulgesetz und Zentrumspartei in der Weimarer Republik.* Düsseldorf, 1968.

Gülzow, Gerhard. *Kirchenkampf in Danzig 1934–1945. Persönliche Erinnerungen.* Leer, Ostfriesland, 1968.

Gürtler, Paul. *Nationalsozialismus und evangelische Kirchen im Warthegau. Trennung von Staat und Kirche im nationalsozialistischen Weltanschauungsstaat.* Göttingen, 1958.

Gutachten des Instituts für Zeitgeschichte. Munich, 1958. Research papers on a great variety of topics dealing with the Nazi era.

Gutteridge, Richard. *The German Evangelical Church and the Jews 1879–1950.* New York, 1976.

Haack, Hans Georg. *Die evangelische Kirche Deutschlands in der Gegenwart.* Berlin, 1924.

Hacker, Rupert. *Die Beziehungen zwischen Bayern und dem Hl. Stuhl in der Regierungszeit Ludwigs I. (1825–1848).* Tübingen, 1967.

Hahn, Hugo. *Kämpfer wider Willen. Erinnerungen des Landesbischofs von Sachsen D. Hugo Hahn aus dem Kirchenkampf 1933–1945.* Edited by Georg Pater. Metzigen, Württemberg, 1969.

Hamann, Andreas. *Das Grundgesetz für die Bundesrepublik Deutschland vom 23. Mai 1949. Ein Kommentar für Wissenschaft und Praxis.* Neuwied-Berlin, 1961.

Hammerstein, Christian Frhr. v. *Mein Leben. Geschrieben für meine Frau und meine Kinder, meine Schwestern und meine Freunde.* Privately printed, n.d. Copy at Institut für Zeitgeschichte in Munich.

Handbuch zu Freikirchen und Sekten. Eine Arbeitshilfe der Vereinigten Evangelisch-Lutherischen Kirche Deutschlands. Lutherisches Kirchenamt, Hanover, 1966– . Looseleaf collection of studies on various Free churches and sects.

Harder, Günther. "Die kirchenleitende Tätigkeit des Brandenburgischen Bruderrates." *Zur Geschichte des Kirchenkampfes. Gesammelte Aufsätze,* edited by Kurt D. Schmidt, pp. 189–216. Göttingen, 1965.

——— and Niemöller, Wilhelm. *Die Stunde der Versuchung. Gemeinden im Kirchenkampf 1933–1945. Selbstzeugnisse.* Munich, 1963.

Harrigan, William M. "Nazi Germany and the Holy See, 1933–1936: The Historical Background of 'Mit brennender Sorge'." *Catholic Historical Review* 47 (1961): 164–98.

Hartmann, Clara. *Christentum und Deutschreligion II.* Paderborn, 1934.

Hase, Hans Christoph von, ed. *Evangelische Dokumente zur Ermordung der "unheilbar Kranken" unter der nationalsozialistischen Herrschaft in den Jahren 1939–1945.* Stuttgart, 1964.

Hauer, Wilhelm, Heim, Karl, and Adam, Karl. *Germany's New Religion: The German Faith Movement.* Translated by T. S. K. Scott-Craig and R. E. Davis. Nashville, Tenn., 1937.

Haugg, Werner. *Das Reichsministerium für die kirchlichen Angelegenheiten.* Berlin, 1940.

Hauptregister zu den Protokollen der Deutschen Evangelischen Kirchenkonferenz 1851–1917. Stuttgart, 1919.

Heckel, Johannes. "Der Vertrag des Freistaates Preussen mit den evangelischen Landeskirchen vom 11. Mai 1931. Zu seiner Ratifikation am 29. Juni 1931." *Theologische Blätter* 11 (July, 1932): 193–204.

Heckel, Martin, Obermayer, Klaus, and Pirson, Dietrich, eds. *Der Jurist und die Kirche. Ausgewählte kirchenrechtliche Aufsätze und Rechtsgutachten von Hans Liermann.* Munich, 1973. Vol. 17 of *Jus Ecclesiasticum.*

Hedtke, Reinhold, ed. *Materialen für den Dienst in der Evangelischen Kirche von Westfalen,* ser. A, no. 5. Bielefeld, 1976.

Heer, Friedrich. *Der Glaube des Adolf Hitler: Anatomie einer politischen Religiosität.* Munich, 1968.

Heiber, Helmut, ed. *Das Tagebuch von Joseph Goebbels 1925/26.* Stuttgart, n.d.

⸻, ed. *Reichsführer! Briefe an und von Himmler.* Stuttgart, 1968.

Heidtmann, Günter, ed. *Kirche im Kampf der Zeit. Die Botschaften, Worte und Erklärungen der evangelischen Kirche in Deutschland und ihrer östlichen Gliedkirchen.* 2d ed. Berlin, 1954.

⸻, ed. *Hat die Kirche geschwiegen? Das öffentliche Wort der evangelischen Kirche aus den Jahren 1945–64.* 3d ed. Berlin, 1964.

⸻, ed. *Glaube im Ansturm der Zeit. Zeugnisse und Manifeste der evangelischen Kirche aus den Jahren 1933–1967.* Hamburg, 1968.

Heine, Ludwig. *Geschichte des Kirchenkampfes in der Grenzmark Posen-Westpreussen 1930–1940.* Göttingen, 1961.

Heinen, Ernst. *Staatliche Macht und Katholizismus in Deutschland.* Vol. 1, Paderborn, 1969.

Helmreich, Ernst C. "The Arrest and Freeing of the Protestant Bishops of Württemberg and Bavaria, September–October 1934," *Central European History* 2 (1969): 159–69.

⸻. "Jewish Education in the Third Reich," *Journal of Central European Affairs* 15 (1955): 134–47.

⸻. "The Nature and Structure of the Confessing Church in Germany under Hitler," in *Journal of Church and State* 12 (1970): pp. 405–19.

⸻. *Religious Education in German Schools: An Historical Approach.* Cambridge, 1959. German ed. *Religionsunterricht in Deutschland von den Klosterschulen bis heute. Mit 54 Bilddokumenten.* Hamburg and Düsseldorf, 1966.

⸻. "Die Veröffentlichung der 'Denkschrift der Vorläufigen Leitung des Deutschen Evangelischen Kirche an den Führer und Reichskanzler, 28. Mai 1938'," *Zeitschrift für Kirchengeschichte* 87 (1976): 39–53.

⸻, ed. *A Free Church in a Free State? The Catholic Church, Italy, Germany, France 1864–1914.* Boston, 1964.

Herman, Stewart W. *The Rebirth of the German Church.* New York, 1946.

Hermann. Gotthilf. *Religionsfreiheit. Amtliche Dokumente. Worte führender Männer.* 5th ed. Zwichau, 1936.

Hermelink, Heinrich. *Die katholische Kirche unter den Pius-Päpsten des 20 Jahrhunderts.* Zurich, 1949.

⸻. *Kirche im Kampf. Dokumente des Widerstands und des Aufbaus in der evangelischen Kirche Deutschlands von 1933 bis 1945.* Tübingen and Stuttgart, 1950.

Herzfeld, Hans, ed. *Berlin und die Provinz Brandenburg im 19. und 20. Jahrhundert.* Berlin, 1968.

Hesse, Konrad. "Partnerschaft zwischen Kirche und Staat? Zur heutigen staatskirchenrechtlichen Lage in der Bundesrepublik." In *Das Verhältnis von Kirche und Staat,* edited by Karl Forster. Würzburg, 1965. No. 30 of *Studien und Berichte der Katholischen Akademie in Bayern.*

Hessen, Johannes. *Die Geistesströmungen der Gegenwart.* Freiburg/Breisgau, 1937.

Heussi, Karl. *Kompendium der Kirchengeschichte.* 12th ed. Tübingen, 1960.

Heydt, Fritz von der. *Die Parität bei der Anstellung der Beamten.* Berlin, 1931.

Hill, Leonidas E. "The Vatican Embassy of Ernst von Weizsächer, 1943–1945." *Journal of Modern History* 39 (1967): 138–59.

⸻. *Die Weizsächer-Papiere 1933–1950.* Frankfurt/Main, 1974.

Hitler, Adolf. *Mein Kampf.* E. Reynal and C. N. Hitchcock ed. New York, 1940. Unabridged, fully annotated.

⸻. *Hitler's Secret Conversations 1941–1944.* Introduction by H. R. Trevor-Roper. New York, 1953.

————. *Hitlers Zweites Buch. Ein Dokument aus dem Jahr 1928.* Edited by Gerhard L. Weinberg. Stuttgart, 1961.

Hoche, Werner, ed. *Die Gesetzgebung des Kabinetts Hitler. Die Gesetze im Reich und Preussen seit dem 30. Januar 1933 in systematischer Ordnung mit Sacherverzeichnis.* 33 vols. Berlin, 1933–39.

Hochmuth, Anneliese. *Bethel in den Jahren 1939–1943. Eine Dokumentation zur Vernichtung lebensunwerten Lebens (Bethel-Arbeitshefte 1).* Bethel bei Bielefeld, 1970.

Hockerts, Hans Günter. *Die Sittlichkeitsprozesse gegen katholische Ordensangehörige und Priester 1936/1937. Eine Studie zur nationalsozialistischen Herrschaftstechnik und zum Kirchenkampf.* Mainz, 1971.

Hoffmann, Peter. *Widerstand. Staatsstreich. Attentat. Der Kampf der Opposition gegen Hitler.* Munich, 1969.

Hofmann, Konrad. *Zeugnis und Kampf des deutschen Episkopats. Gemeinsame Hirtenbriefe und Denkschriften.* Freiburg/Breisgau, 1946.

Höhne, Heinz. *Der Orden unter dem Totenkopf. Die Geschichte der SS.* Gütersloh, 1967.

Hollerbach, Alexander. *Verträge zwischen Staat und Kirche in der Bundesrepublik Deutschland.* Frankfurt/Main, 1965.

Hollos, Franz T. *Die gegenwärtige Rechtsstellung der katholischen Kirche in Deutschland.* Würzburg, 1948.

Homann, Rudolf. *Das Mythus und das Evangelium. Die Abwehr und Angriff gegenüber dem "Mythus des 20. Jahrhunderts" von Alfred Rosenberg.* 4th ed. Witten, 1936.

Hubatsch, Walther. *Geschichte der Evangelischen Kirche Ostpreussens.* 3 vols. Göttingen, 1968.

Huber, Ernst R. *Deutsche Verfassungsgeschichte seit 1789.* 4 vols. Stuttgart, 1957–69.

————. *Dokumente zur deutschen Verfassungsgeschichte.* 3 vols. Stuttgart, 1961–66.

Hughes, John Jay. "The Pope's 'Pact with Hitler': Betrayal or Self-Defense?," *Journal of Church and State* 17 (1975): 63–80.

Hühne, Werner. *Thadden-Triegloff. Ein Leben unter uns.* Stuttgart, 1959.

Hürten, Heinz, ed. *Deutsche Briefe 1934–1938. Ein Blatt der katholischen Emigration.* 2 vols. Mainz, 1969.

Hutten, Kurt. *Die Glaubenswelt des Sektierers.* Hamburg, 1957.

————. *Seher, Grübler, Enthusiasten. Sekten und religiöse Sondergemeinschaften der Gegenwart.* 6th ed. Stuttgart, 1960.

————. "Sekten und sonstige Sondergemeinschaften." *Kirchliches Jahrbuch,* 1949, pp. 357–414.

Jacob, Günther, Kunst, Hermann, and Stählin, Wilhelm, eds. *Die evangelische Christenheit in Deutschland. Gestalt und Auftrag.* Stuttgart, 1958.

Jacobs, Manfred. "Konsequenzen aus dem Kirchenkampf. Kirchengeschichtliche und theologische Aspekte." *Lutherische Monatshefte* 8(1969): 561–67.

Jacobsen, Hans-Adolf, ed. *July 20, 1944. The German Opposition to Hitler as Viewed by Foreign Historians.* Bonn, 1969.

Jannasch, W. *Deutsche Kirchendokumente. Die Haltung der bekennenden Kirche im Dritten Reich.* Kollikon-Zürich, 1946. A reprint of *Hat die Kirche geschwiegen?* (Frankfurt/Main, 1946).

Jasper, Gotthard, ed. *Von Weimar zu Hitler 1930–1933.* Cologne, 1968.

Jasper, Ronald C. D. *George Bell Bishop of Chichester.* London, 1967.

Jaspers, Karl. *Die Schuldfrage.* Heidelberg, 1946.

Jehovah's Witnesses in the Divine Purpose. Brooklyn, N.Y., 1959.

Joffroy, Pierre. *L'espion de Dieu (La Passion de Kurt Gerstein).* Paris, 1969.

Junker, Detlef. *Die Deutsche Zentrumspartei und Hitler 1932–33. Ein Beitrag zur Problematik des politischen Katholizimus in Deutschland.* Stuttgart, 1969.

Kaas, Ludwig. "Der Konkordatstyp des faschistischen Italien." *Zeitschrift für ausländisches öffentliches Recht und Völkerrecht* 3 (1932): 488–522.

Kantzenbach, Friedrich W. *Der Weg der evangelischen Kirche vom 19. zum 20. Jahrhundert.* Gütersloh, 1968. A volume in the paperback *Evangelische Enzyklopädie.*

————, ed. *Widerstand und Solidarität der Christen in Deutschland 1933–1945. Eine Dokumentation zum Kirchenkampf aus den Papiern D. Wilhelm Freiherrn von Pechmann.* Neustadt/Aisch, 1971.

————, and Müller, Gerhard, eds. *Reformatio und Confessio. Festschrift für D. Wilhelm Maurer zum 65. Geburtstag am 7. Mai 1965.* Berlin, 1965.

Kater, Horst. *Die Deutsche Evangelische Kirche in den Jahren 1933 und 1934. Eine rechts-und verfassungsgeschichtliche Untersuchung zu Gründung und Zerfall einer*

Kirche im nationalsozialistischen Staat. Göttingen, 1970. Vol. 24 in the series *Arbeiten zur Geschichte des Kirchenkampfes.*

Kater, Michael H. "Die Ernsten Bibelforscher im Dritten Reich." *Vierteljahrshefte für Zeitgeschichte* 17 (1969): 181–218.

Das Katholische Jahrbuch 1948–49. Heidelberg, 1948. Only one other volume (1951–52) was published. The latter is largely statistical, while the first volume contains survey articles.

Katz, Jacob. *Jews and Freemasons in Europe 1723–1939.* Translated by Leonard Oschry. Cambridge, Mass., 1970.

Kaufmann, Franz-Xaver. "Zur Bestimmung und Messung von Kirchlichkeit in der Bundesrepublik Deutschlands." *Internationales Jahrbuch für Religionssoziologie* 4 (1968): 62–100.

Keesing's Contemporary Archives. Weekly Diary of World Events. Bristol, 1931–.

Kempner, Benedicta Maria. *Priester vor Hitlers Tribunalen.* Munich, 1966.

Kent, George O. "Pope Pius XII and Germany: Some Aspects of German-Vatican Relations, 1933–1943." *American Historical Review,* 70 (1964): 59–78.

Kessler, Paul. *Kämpfende Kirche. Der Weg der evangelischen Kirche in Deutschland seit 1922.* Hamburg, 1949.

Kinder, Christian. *Neue Beiträge zur Geschichte der evangelischen Kirche in Schleswig-Holstein und im Reich 1924–1945.* 2d ed. Flensburg, 1966.

Kinkel, Walter. *Kirche und Nationalsozialismus. Ihre Auseinandersetzung zwischen 1925 und 1945 in Dokumenten dargestellt.* Düsseldorf, 1960.

"Kirchenaustritte aus den deutschen evangelischen Landeskirchen und Übertritte (Eintritte) zu den deutschen evangelischen Landeskirchen in der Zeit von 1884 bis 1949." *Statistische Beilage, Nr. 4. Amtsblatt der Evangelischen Kirche in Deutschland,* 1952, pp. 1–16.

Kirchliche Woche Nürnberg vom 1. bis 5. Januar 1939. Nürnberg, 1939.

Kirchliches Handbuch. Freiburg/Breisgau, later Cologne, 1908– . The subtitle of these volumes varies, but since World War II it has been *Amtliches statistisches Jahrbuch der katholischen Kirche Deutschlands.* It is the counterpart to the Protestant *Kirchliches Jahrbuch* but does not appear yearly.

Kissling, Johannes B. *Geschichte der deutschen Katholikentage.* 2 vols. Münster, 1920, 1923.

Kittel, Gerhard. *Die Judenfrage.* Stuttgart, 1934.

Kleindienst, Alfred. "Die Litzmannstädter ev. Kirche im Wartheland." *Ostforschung* 18 (1969): 447–74.

Klemperer, Klemens von. *Mandate for Resistance. The Case of the German Opposition to Hitler.* Northampton, Mass., 1969.

Klinger, Fritz. *Deutscher Pfarrertag Kiel, 26. bis 29. September 1938. Rückblick und Ausblick.* Essen, 1938.

———, ed. *Dokumente zum Abwehrkampf der deutschen evangelischen Pfarrerschaft gegen Verfolgung und Bedrückung 1933–1945.* Nürnberg, 1946.

Klotzbach, Kurt. *Gegen den Nationalsozialismus. Widerstand und Verfolgung in Dortmund 1930–1945. Eine historisch-politische Studie.* Hanover, 1962.

Klügel, Eberhard. *Die lutherische Landeskirche Hannovers und ihr Bischof 1933–1945.* Hamburg, 1964.

———. *Die lutherische Landeskirche Hannovers und ihr Bischof 1933–1945. Dokumente.* Hamburg, 1965.

Knapp, Thomas. "The Red and the Black: Catholic Socialists in the Weimar Republic." *Catholic Historical Review* 61 (1975): 386–408.

Koch, C. F. et al. *Allgemeines Landrecht für die Preussischen Staaten mit Kommentar und Anmerkungen.* 6th ed. 4 vols. Berlin, 1880.

Koch, H. W. *The Hitler Youth: Origins and Development 1922–45,* New York, 1976.

Koch, Werner. *Bekennende Kirche gestern und heute. Was jedermann von ihr wissen sollte.* Stuttgart, 1946.

Ködderitz, W., ed. *D. August Marahrens. Pastor Pastorum zwischen zwei Weltkriegen.* Hanover, 1952.

Kogon, Eugen. *Der SS-Staat.* Stockholm, 1947.

Köhler, Walther. *Wesen und Recht der Sekte im religiösen Leben Deutschlands.* Giessen, 1930.

Kolb, Hermann, ed. *Aus der Geschichte der Schüler-Bibel-Kreise (BK) in Bayern.* Nürnberg, 1968.

Kopf, Paul and Miller, Max, eds. *Die Vertreibung von Bischof Joannes Baptista Sproll von*

Rottenberg 1938–1945. Dokumente zur Geschichte des kirchlichen Widerstands. Mainz, 1971.

Koschorke, Manfred. *Materialsammlung vom Kirchenkampf in Ostpreussen September 1934 bis 1939.* Privately printed, n.d. (ca. 1964).

Kramarz, Joachim. *Stauffenberg. The Architect of the Famous July 20th Conspiracy to Assassinate Hitler.* Translated by R. H. Barry. New York, 1967.

Kraus, Hans-Joachim. "Die evangelische Kirche." In *Entscheidungsjahr 1932. Zur Judenfrage in der Endphase der Weimarer Republik,* edited by Werner E. Mosse and A. Paucker, pp. 249–70. Tübingen, 1965.

Krausnick, Helmut, Buchheim, H., Broszat, M., and Jacobsen, H. *Anatomy of the SS State.* New York, 1968.

Kubel, Johannes. *Die bekennende Kirche im Selbstgericht.* Gotha, 1936.

———. "Mensch und Christ, Theologe, Pfarrer und Kirchenmann. Erinnerungen." Typed manuscript. Nürnberg, 1947.

———. *Der Vertrag der evangelischen Landeskirchen mit dem Freistaat Preussen.* Berlin, 1931.

Künneth, Walter. *Antwort auf den Mythus. Die Entscheidung zwischen dem nordischen Mythus und dem biblischen Christus.* Berlin, 1935.

———. "Die evangelische-lutherische Theologie und das Widerstandsrecht." In *Die Vollmacht des Gewissens,* edited by Europäische Publikation e.V., pp. 164–74. Munich, 1965.

———. *Evangelische Wahrheit! Ein Wort zu Alfred Rosenbergs Schrift "Protestantische Rompilger".* Berlin, 1937.

———. *Der grosse Abfall. Eine geschichtstheologische Untersuchung der Begegnung zwischen Nationalsozialismus und Christentum.* Hamburg, 1947.

———. *Das Widerstandsrecht als theologisch-ethisches Problem.* Munich, 1954.

——— and Schreiner, Helmuth. *Die Nation vor Gott. Zur Botschaft der Kirche im Dritten Reich.* Berlin, 1933.

Kunst, Hermann, and Grundmann, Siegfried, eds. *Evangelisches Staatslexikon.* Stuttgart, 1966.

Kunz, Ulrich, ed. *Viele Glieder—Ein Leib. Kleinere Kirchen, Freikirchen und ähnliche Gemeinschaften in Selbstdarstellungen.* Stuttgart, 1961.

Kupisch, Karl. *Die Deutschen Landeskirchen im 19. und 20. Jahrhundert.* A part of *Die Kirche in ihrer Geschichte. Ein Handbuch,* edited by Kurt D. Schmidt and Ernst Wolf (Göttingen, 1966).

———. *Durch den Zaun der Geschichte. Beobachtungen und Erkenntnisse.* Berlin, 1964.

———. "Zur Genesis des Pfarrernotbundes." *Theologische Literaturzeitung* 91 (1966): 721–30.

———. "Karl Barths Entlassung" In *Hören und Handeln. Festschrift für Ernst Wolf zum 60. Geburtstag,* edited by Helmut Gollwitzer and Hellmut Traub, pp. 251–75. Munich, 1962.

———. *Zwischen Idealismus und Massendemokratie. Eine Geschichte der evangelischen Kirche in Deutschland von 1815–1945.* 4th ed. Berlin, 1963.

Kupper, Alfons. "Zur Geschichte des Reichskonkordats." *Stimmen der Zeit* 171(1962–63): 25–50.

———. *Staatliche Akten über die Reichskonkordats-verhandlungen 1933.* Mainz, 1969.

Küppers, Werner, Hauptmann, Peter, and Baser, Friedrich. *Symbolik der kleineren Kirchen, Freikirchen und Sekten des Westens.* Stuttgart, 1964.

Kuptsch, J. *Nationalsozialismus und positives Christentum.* Weimar, 1937.

Lamparter, Helmut. *Und ihr Netz zerriss. Buch der Grosskirchen.* Stuttgart, 1961.

Lang, Serge, and von Schenck, Ernst. *Memoirs of Alfred Rosenberg.* New York, 1949.

Langmann, Otto. *Deutsche Christenheit in der Zeitenwende.* Hamburg, 1933.

Laros, M. *Dr. Max J. Metzger (Br. Paulus). Ein Blutzeuge des Friedens der Konfessionen und Völker.* Meitingen bei Augsburg, n.d. (ca. 1946).

Leffler, Siegfried. *Christus im Dritten Reich der Deutschen. Wesen, Weg und Ziel der Kirchenbewegung "Deutsche Christen".* Weimar, 1935.

———. *Kirche, Christentum, Bolschewismus.* Weimar, 1936.

———. *Unser Kampf.* Weimar, 1938.

———. *Unser Weg.* Weimar, 1938.

———. *Weltkirche oder Nationalkirche? Volk. Staat. Kirche.* Weimar, 1936.

Lehmann, Jürgen. *Die kleinen Religionsgesellschaften des öffentlichen Rechts im heutigen Staatskirchenrecht.* Oldenstadt, 1959.

Leiber, Robert "Pius XII und die Juden in Rom 1943–1944." *Stimmen der Zeit* 167 (1960–61): 428–31.

————. "Reichskonkordat und Ende der Zentrumspartei." *Stimmen der Zeit* 167 (1960–61): 213–23.

————. "Der Vatikan und das Dritte Reich." *Politische Studien* 14 (1963): 293–98.

Lersner, Dieter Frhr. von. *Die evangelischen Jugendverbände Württembergs und die Hitlerjugend 1933–1934.* Göttingen, 1958.

Levai, Jenö. *Geheime Reichssache. Papst Pius XII hat nicht geschwiegen.* Cologne, 1966.

Levin, Nora. *The Holocaust. The Destruction of European Jewry, 1933–1945.* New York, 1973.

Lewy, Guenter. *The Catholic Church and Nazi Germany.* New York, 1964.

Lexikon für Theologie und Kirche. 2d ed. 10 vols. Freiburg, 1957–61.

Lichten, Joseph L. *A Question of Judgment. Pius XII and the Jews.* Washington, 1963.

Liermann, Hans, *Deutsches Evangelisches Kirchenrecht.* Stuttgart, 1933.

————. "Das evangelische Bischofsamt in Deutschland seit 1933." *Zeitschrift für evangelisches Kirchenrecht* 3 (1953–54): 1–29.

————. *Kirchen und Staat.* 2 vols. Munich, 1954–55.

————. "Luther ordnet seine Kirche." *Jahrbuch der Luther-Gesellschaft* 31 (1964): 29–46.

————. *Sind die preussischen Brüdergemeinen Körperschaften des öffentlichen Rechts.* Erlangen, 1937.

————. *Staats-und evangelisch-protestantische Landeskirche in Baden während und nach der Staatsumwälzung von 1918.* Lahr in Baden, 1929.

————. "Über die neure Entwicklung des evangelischen Kirchenrechts." In *Festschrift für Erich Ruppel,* edited by Heinz Brunotte, Konrad Müller, and Rudolf Smend, pp. 89–104. Berlin. 1966.

————. "Der Westfälische Frieden." *Jahrbuch des Martin Luther Bundes,* 1949–50, pp. 147–58.

Lilje, Hanns. *Im Finstern Tal.* Nürnberg, 1947.

Lill, Rudolf. *Die Beilegung der Kölner Wirren 1840–1842. Vorwiegend nach Akten des Vatikanischen Geheimarchivs.* Düsseldorf, 1962.

————. *Vatikanische Akten zur Geschichte des deutschen Kulturkampfes. Leo XIII.* Tübingen, 1970.

Linck, Hugo. *Der Kirchenkampf in Ostpreussen 1933 bis 1945. Geschichte und Dokumentation.* Munich, 1968.

Lindbergh, Charles A. *Wartime Journals.* New York, 1970.

Lindt, Andreas. *George Bell—Alphons Koechlin Briefwechsel 1933–1954.* Zurich, 1969.

Littell, Franklin H. *The Free Church.* Boston, 1957.

————. *The German Phoenix. Men and Movements in the Church in Germany.* New York, 1960.

———— and Locke, Hubert G., eds. *The German Church Struggle and the Holocaust.* Detroit, 1974.

Lochner, Louis P., *The Goebbels Diaries, 1942–1943.* New York, 1943.

Löhr, Joseph. *Das Preussische Allgemeine Landrecht und die Katholischen Kirchengesellschaften.* Paderborn, 1917.

Lortz, Joseph. *Katholischer Zugang zum Nationalsozialismus.* 2d ed. Münster, 1934.

Loyzcke, Ernst. "Die restliche Entwicklung in der Evangelischen Kirche der altpreussischen Union von 1937 bis 1945." *Zeitschrift für evangelisches Kirchenrecht* 2 (1952–53): 64–83, 169–85, 270–311.

Luckey, Hans. *Free Churches in Germany.* Bad Nauheim, 1956.

Ludlow, Peter W. "Bischof Berggrav zum deutschen Kirchenkampf." In *Zur Geschichte des Kirchenkampfes. Gesammelte Aufsätze,* edited by Heinz Brunotte, 2: 221–58. Göttingen, 1971.

Ludwig, Hartmut. "Karl Barths Dienst der Versöhnung. Zur Geschichte des Stuttgarter Schuldbekenntnisses." In *Zur Geschichte des Kirchenkampfes. Gesammelte Aufsätze,* edited by Heinz Brunotte, 2: 265–326. Göttingen, 1971.

Lueken, Wilhelm. *Kampf, Behauptung und Gestalt der Evangelischen Landeskirche Nassau-Hessen.* Göttingen, 1963.

Lüpsen, Focko. "Der Weg der kirchlichen Pressearbeit von 1938 bis 1950." *Kirchliches Jahrbuch* 76 (1949): 415–54.

————, et al. *Mittler zwischen Kirche und Welt. Fünfzig Jahre im Dienst der evangelischen Publizistik.* Witten/Ruhr, 1957.

Lutgert, Wilhelm. *Der Kampf der deutschen Christenheit mit den Schwarmgeistern.* Gütersloh, 1936.

Luther, Christian. *Das kirchliche Notrecht, seine Theorie und seine Anwendung im Kirchenkampf 1933–1937.* Göttingen, 1962.

Lutherisches Bekenntnis in der Union. Eine Festgabe für D. Peter Brunner zum 65. Geburtstag am 25. April 1965. Berlin, 1965.

Lutze, Hermann. "Das konfessionelle Problem in der Evangelischen Kirche im Rheinland." In *Lutherisches Bekenntnis in der Union. Eine Festgabe für D. Peter Brunner zum 65. Geburtstag am 25. April 1965.* Berlin, 1965.

McBain, Howard, and Rogers, Lindsay. *The New Constitutions of Europe.* New York, 1923.

Macfarland, Charles S. *The New Church and the New Germany; a Study of Church and State.* New York, 1934.

Mahling, D. *Die Weltkonferenz für praktisches Christentum in Stockholm 19.–30. August 1925, Bericht über ihren Verlauf und ihre Ergebnisse.* Gütersloh, 1926.

Mahrenholz, E. G. *Die Kirchen in der Gesellschaft der Bundesrepublik.* Hanover, 1969.

Maier, Hans. *Deutscher Katholizismus nach 1945. Kirche Gesellschaft Geschichte.* Munich, 1964.

———. "Katholizismus, national Bewegung und Demokratie in Deutschland." *Hochland* 57 (1964–65): 318–33.

———. "Staat und Kirche in Deutschland, von der Fremdheit zur neuen Nähe?" In *Das Verhältnis von Kirche und Staat,* edited by Karl Forster. No. 30 of *Studien und Berichte der Katholischen Akademie in Bayern* (Würzburg, 1965).

Mangolt, Hermann von and Friedrich Klein. *Das Bonner Grundgesetz.* 2d ed. 2 vols. Berlin and Frankfurt a.M., 1957.

Manvell, Roger and Fraenkel, Heinrich. *Himmler.* New York, 1965.

Marré, Heiner. "Die Kirchensteuer. Entstehung, Probematik, und Reform." *Stimmen der Zeit* 180 (1967): 311–25.

Martin, Alfred von. *Die Weltkirchenkonferenz von Lausanne.* Stuttgart, 1928.

Martin, Heinrich. *Der Kampf der deutschen lutherischen Freikirchen im 19. Jahrhundert um Bekenntnis und Freiheit der lutherischen Kirche.* Munich, 1937.

Matthias, Erich, and Morsey, Rudolf, eds. *Das Ende der Parteien 1933.* Düsseldorf, 1960.

Maunz, Theodor, and Dürig, Günther. *Grundgesetz. Kommentar.* 2d ed., 1963.

Maurer, Wilhelm. "Die Entstehung des Landeskirchentum in der Reformation." In *Staat und Kirche im Wandel der Jahrhunderte,* edited by Walther Peter Fuchs, pp. 69–78. Stuttgart, 1966.

Mayer, Rudolf. "Kirche, Freikirche, Sekten." *Zeitschrift für evangelisches Kirchenrecht* 7 (1959–60): 156–86.

Mehnert, Gottfried. *Evangelische Kirche und Politik 1917–1919. Die politischen Strömungen im deutschen Protestantismus von der Julikrise 1917 bis zum Herbst 1919.* Düsseldorf, 1959.

Meier, Kurt. *Die deutschen Christen. Das Bild einer Bewegung im Kirchenkampf des Dritten Reiches.* Göttingen, 1964.

———. *Kirche und Judentum. Die Haltung der evangelischen Kirche zur Judenpolitik des Dritten Reiches.* Göttingen, 1968.

———. "Kirche und Nationalsozialismus. Ein Beitrag zum Problem der nationalsozialistischen Religionspolitik." In *Zur Geschichte des Kirchenkampfes. Gesammelte Aufsätze,* edited by Kurt D. Schmidt, pp. 9–29. Göttingen, 1965.

———. "Der Kirchenkampf im Dritten Reich und seine Erforschung." *Theologische Rundschau* 33 (1968): 120–73, 236–75.

———. "Die Religionspolitik der NSDAP in der Zeit der Weimarer Republik." In *Zur Geschichte des Kirchenkampfes. Gesammelte Aufsätze,* edited by Heinz Brunotte, 2: 9–24. Göttingen, 1971.

Meinecke, Werner. *Die Kirche in der volksdemokratischen Ordnung der Deutschen Demokratischen Republik. Ein Beitrag zur Klärung einiger Grundfragen des Verhältnisses von Staat und Kirche in der DDR.* Berlin, 1962.

Merzyn, Friedrich, ed. *Das Verfassungsrecht der Evangelischen Kirche in Deutschland und Ihrer Gliedkirchen.* 3 vols. Hanover, 1957–. A loose leaf collection sponsored by the chancellery of the Evangelical Church of Germany.

Metzger, Wolfgang. "Kirche, Freikirche und Sekten in der Perspektive einer Landeskirche gesehen." *Zeitschrift für evangelisches Kirchenrecht* 7 (1959–60): 128–56.

Micklem, Nathaniel. *National Socialism and the Roman Catholic Church.* London, 1939.

Middendorf, Friedrich. *Der Kirchenkampf in einer reformierten Kirche (Ev.-reformierte Kirche in Nordwestdeutschland).* Göttingen, 1961.

Mochalski, Herbert, ed. *Der Mann in der Brandung. Ein Bildbuch um Martin Niemöller.* Frankfurt/Main, 1962.

————, and Wolf, E., eds. *Bekennende Kirche. Festschrift für Martin Niemöller zum 60. Geburtstag.* Munich, 1952.

Mohr, Hubert. *Katholische Orden und deutscher Imperialismus.* Berlin, 1965.

Mommsen, Hans. "Der Nationalsozialistische Polizeistaat und die Judenverfolgung vor 1938. Dokumentation." *Vierteljahrshefte für Zeitgeschichte* 10 (1962): 68–87.

Moore-Rinvolucri, Mina J. *Education in East Germany (The German Democratic Republic).* Hamden, Connecticut, 1973.

Mörsdorf, Klaus. *Lehrbuch des Kirchenrechts auf Grund des Codex Juris Cononici.* 7th ed. 3 vols. Paderborn, 1953.

Morsey, Rudolf. "Briefe zum Reichskonkordat, Ludwig Kaas–Franz v. Papen." *Stimmen der Zeit* 167 (1960–61): 11–30.

Moss, C. B. *The Old Catholic Movement. Its Origin and History.* London, 1948.

Mosse, Werner E., and Paucker, Arnold, eds. *Entscheidungsjahr 1932. Zur Judenfrage in der Endphase der Weimarer Republik.* Tübingen, 1965.

Motschmann, Claus. *Evangelische Kirche und preussischer Staat in den Anfängen der Weimarer Republik. Möglichkeiten und Grenzen ihrer Zusammenarbeit.* Lübeck and Hamburg, 1969.

Muckermann, Friedrich. *Der Deutsche Weg. Aus der Widerstandsbewegung der deutschen Katholiken von 1930–1945.* Zürich, 1946.

Mulert, Hermann. *Konfessionskunde. Die christlichen Kirchen und Sekten heute.* 3d ed. Berlin, 1956.

Müller, Hans. *Katholische Kirche und Nationalsozialismus. Dokumente 1930–1935.* Munich, 1963.

Müller, Ludwig. *Deutsche Gottesworte, aus der Bergpredigt, verdeutscht von Reichsbishof Ludwig Müller.* Weimar, 1936.

————. *Für und wider die Deutschen Gottesworte. Dokumente und Tatsachen aus dem Kampf um das deutsche Christentum.* Weimar, 1936.

————. *Was ist positives Christentum?* Stuttgart, 1939.

Murtorinne, Eino. *Erzbischof Eidem zum Deutschen Kirchenkampf 1933–1934.* Helsinki, 1968.

Nagel, Gottfried. *Kann die Evang.-luth. Kirche Altpreussens sich der Deutschen Evang. Kirche eingliedern?* Breslau, 1933.

Nazi Conspiracy and Aggression. 8 vols., 2 supp. Washington, D.C., 1946–48.

Nell-Breuning, Oswald von. "Kirchensteuer und Kirchenmitgliedschaft." *Stimmen der Zeit* 184 (1969): 309–15.

Neue Kirche im neuen Staat. Bekenntnis, Gemeindeaufbau, Kirchenleitung, Nationalsozialistischer Staat, "Deutsche Christen". Gütersloh, 1933.

Neuhäusler, Johann. *Amboss und Hammer. Erlebnisse im Kirchenkampf des Dritten Reiches.* Munich, 1967.

————. *Kreuz und Hakenkreuz. Der Kampf des Nationalsozialismus gegen die katholische Kirche und der kirchliche Widerstand.* Munich, 1946.

————. *Saat des Bösen. Kirchenkampf im Dritten Reich.* Munich, 1964.

————. *Wie war das in KZ Dachau? Ein Versuch der Wahrheit näherzukommen.* Munich, 1960.

Nicolaisen, Carsten. *Die Auseinandersetzungen um das Alte Testament im Kirchenkampf 1933–1945.* Hamburg, 1966.

————. "Die Stellung der 'Deutschen Christen' zum Alten Testament." In *Zur Geschichte des Kirchenkampfes. Gesammelte Aufsätze,* edited by Heinz Brunotte, 2: 197–221. Göttingen, 1971.

————, and Kretschmar, Georg, eds. *Dokumente zur Kirchenpolitik des Dritten Reiches.* Vol. 1. *Das Jahr 1933.* Munich, 1971. Vol. 2. *1934/1935.* Munich, 1975.

Nichols, James H. *History of Christianity 1650–1950. Secularization of the West.* New York, 1956.

Nichols, Peter. *The Politics of the Vatican.* London, 1968. German ed. *Die Politik des Vatikan* (Bergisch Gladbach, 1969).

Niemöller, Gerhard. *Die erste Bekenntnissynode der Deutschen Evangelischen Kirche zu Barmen.* 2 vols. Göttingen, 1959.

————. *Die Synode zu Halle 1937. Die zweite Tagung der vierten Bekenntnissynode der Evangelischen Kirche der altpreussischen Union. Text-Dokumente-Berichte.* Göttingen, 1963.

Niemöller, Martin. *Das Bekenntnis der Väter und die bekennende Gemeinde.* 2d ed. Munich, 1934.

Niemöller, Wilhelm. *Aus dem Leben eines Bekenntnispfarrers.* Bielefeld, 1961.
————. "Aus der Polizeiakte des Bekenntnispfarrers Joachim Beckmann." In *Zur Geschichte des Kirchenkampfes. Gesammelte Aufsätze,* edited by Kurt D. Schmidt, pp. 217–57. Göttingen, 1965.
————. *Bekennende Kirche in Westfalen.* Bielefeld, 1952.
————. *Die Bekennende Kirche sagt Hitler die Wahrheit. Die Geschichte der Denkschrift der vorläufigen Leitung von Mai 1936.* Bielefeld, 1954.
————. "Die Bekennende Kirche sagt Hitler die Wahrheit." *Evangelische Theologie* 18 (1958): 190–92.
————. "Corrigenda zur neuesten Kirchengeschichte." *Evangelische Theologie* 28 (1968): 594–605.
————. *Die dritte Bekenntnissynode der Deutschen Evangelischen Kirche zu Augsburg. Text-Dokumente-Berichte.* Göttingen, 1969.
————. "Epilog zum Kanzlerempfang." *Evangelische Theologie* 20 (1960): 107–24.
————. *Die evangelische Kirche im Dritten Reich. Handbuch des Kirchenkampfes.* Bielefeld, 1956.
————. *Gottes Wort ist nicht gebunden. Ein Tatsachenbericht über den Kirchenkampf.* Bielefeld, 1948.
————. *Hitler und die evangelischen Kirchenführer (Zum 25. Januar 1934).* Bielefeld, 1959.
————. "Ist die Jugendfrage 'bewältigt'?" *Junge Kirche,* supp. 2 (1968).
————. *Kampf und Zeugnis der Bekennenden Kirche.* Bielefeld, 1948.
————. *Karl Koch, Präses der Bekenntnissynode.* Bethel b. Bielefeld, 1956.
————. *Kirchenkampf im Dritten Reich.* Bielefeld, 1946.
————. *Lebensbilder aus der Bekennenden Kirche.* Bielefeld, 1949.
————. *Macht geht vor Recht. Der Prozess Martin Niemöllers.* Munich, 1952.
————. *Martin Niemöller. Ein Lebensbild.* Munich, 1952.
————. *Neuanfang 1945. Zur Biographie Martin Niemöllers nach seinen Tagebuchaufzeichnungen aus dem Jahre 1945.* Frankfurt/Main, 1967.
————. *Die Synode zu Steglitz. Geschichte-Dokumente-Berichte.* Göttingen, 1970.
————. *Texte zur Geschichte des Pfarrernotbundes.* Berlin, 1958.
————. *Die vierte Bekenntnissynode der Deutschen Evangelischen Kirche zu Bad Oeynhausen. Text-Dokumente-Berichte.* Göttingen, 1960.
————. *Westfälishe Kirche im Kampf.* Bielefeld, 1970.
————. "Zur Geschichte der Kirchenausschüsse." In *Hören und Handeln. Festschrift für Ernst Wolf zum 60. Geburtstag,* edited by Helmut Gollwitzer and Hellmut Traub, pp. 301–20. Munich, 1962.
————. "Zur Verständnis der Bekennenden Kirche. Eine Herausforderung." *Evangelische Theologie* 29 (1969): 602–17.
————. *Die zweite Bekenntnissynode der Deutschen Evangelischen Kirche zu Dahlem. Text-Dokumente-Berichte.* Göttingen, 1958.
Niesel, Wilhelm. *Um Verkündigung und Ordnung der Kirche. Die Bekenntnissynoden der Evangelischen Kirche der altpreussischen Union 1934–1943.* Bielefeld, 1949.
————. *Der Weg der Bekennenden Kirche.* Zurich, 1947.
Norden, Günther van. *Kirche in der Krise. Die Stellung der evangelischen Kirche zum nationalsozialistischen Staat im Jahre 1933.* Düsseldorf, 1963.
Obermayer, Klaus. "Die Konkordate und Kirchenverträge im 19. und 20. Jahrhundert." In *Staat und Kirche im Wandel der Jahrhunderte,* edited by Walther Peter Fuchs, pp. 166–83. Stuttgart, 1966.
Oldham, J. H. *The Oxford Conference (Official Report).* New York, 1937.
Orlow, Dietrich. *The History of the Nazi Party.* 2 vols. Pittsburgh, 1969, 1973.
Pannenbecker, Otto. *Geheim! Dokumentarische Tatsachen aus dem Nürnberger Prozess.* Düsseldorff, 1947.
Papen, Franz von. *Memoirs.* London, 1952.
Partei-Kanzlei Rundschreiben. Vols. for 1942, 1943, 1944–5; *Anordnungen* 1941–5 in one vol.; *Bekanntgaben* 1944, in one vol. All are available at the Institut für Zeitgeschichte, Munich.
Pechel, Rudolf. *Deutscher Widerstand.* Zurich, 1947.
Pelke, Else. *Der Lübecker Christenprozess 1943.* Mainz, 1963.
Perau, Josef. "Priester im Heere Hitlers. Erinnerungen 1940–1945." Mimeographed, ca. 1960. Copy in the Institut für Zeitgeschichte, Munich.
The Persecution of the Catholic Church in Germany: Facts and Documents translated from the German. London, 1942. Assembled by Walter Mariaux, S.J.

Pertiet, Martin. *Das Ringen um Wesen und Auftrag der Kirche in der nationalsozialistischen Zeit.* Göttingen, 1968.
Pesch, Rudolf. *Die Kirchliche-Politische Presse der Katholiken in der Rheinprovinz vor 1848.* Mainz, 1966.
Peterson, Edward N. *The Limits of Hitler's Power.* Princeton, N.J., 1969.
Pfahlmann, Hans. *Fremdarbeiter und Kriegsgefangene in der Deutschen Kriegswirtschaft 1939–1945.* Darmstadt, 1968.
Pfliegler, Michael, ed. *Dokumente zur Geschichte der Kirche.* 2d ed. Vienna and Munich, 1957.
Picker, Henry. *Hitlers Tischgespräche im Führerhauptquartier 1941–1942.* Bonn, 1951.
Poliakov, Léon, and Wulf, Josef, eds. *Das Dritte Reich und seine Denker. Dokumente.* Berlin-Grünewald, 1959.
Portmann, Heinrich. *Bischof Graf von Galen spricht. Ein apostolischer Kampf und sein Widerhall. (Das Christliche Deutschland 1933 bis 1945, Katholische Reihe,* Heft 3). Freiburg/Breisgau, 1946.
Pressel, Wilhelm. *Die Kriegspredigt 1914–1918 in der evangelischen Kirche Deutschlands.* Göttingen, 1967.
Preussisches Pfarrarchiv. After 1934, *Deutsches Pfarrarchiv.*
Pribilla, Max. "Der Kampf der Kirche." *Stimmen der Zeit* (July, 1935): 242.
Priepke, Manfred. *Die evangelische Jugend im Dritten Reich 1933–1936.* Frankfurt/Main, 1960.
Prittie, Terence. *Germans against Hitler.* Boston, 1964.
Purdy, W. A. *The Church on the Move. The Character and Policies of Pius XII and John XXIII.* London, 1966. Translated into German as *Die Politik der Katholischen Kirche* (Gütersloh, 1967).
Ramme, Carl L. *Soll das Weib Schweigen?* Chicago, 1919.
Rauschning, Hermann. *The Revolution of Nihilism. Warning to the West.* New York, 1939.
———. *The Voice of Destruction.* New York, 1940.
Realenzyklopädie für protestantische Theologie und Kirche. Edited by D. Albert Hauck. 3d ed. 21 vols., plus 2 vols. of Ergänzungen und Nachträge. Leipzig, 1896–1913.
Rehbein, H., and Reincke, O. *Allgemeines Landrecht für die Preussischen Staaten nebst den ergänzenden und abändernden Bestimmungen der Reichs- und Landesgesetzgebung.* 5th ed. 4 vols. Berlin, 1894.
Reich, Herbert. "Die Aus- und Ubertrittsbewegung 1884–1949." *Kirchliches Jahrbuch* 78 (1951): 363–85.
Reimers, Karl Friedrich. *Lübeck im Kirchenkampf des Dritten Reiches. Nationalsozialistisches Führerprinzip und evangelisch-lutherische Landeskirche von 1933–1945.* Göttingen, 1965.
Die Religion in Geschichte und Gegenwart. Handwörterbuch für Theologie und Religionswissenschaft. 3d ed. 6 vols. Tübingen, 1957–62.
Rengstorf, Karl H., and von Kortzfleisch, Siegfried, eds. *Kirche und Synagoge. Handbuch zur Geschichte von Christen und Juden. Darstellung mit Quellen.* 2 vols. Stuttgart, 1968, 1970.
Renkewitz, Heinz. *Die Kirchen auf dem Wege zur Einheit.* Gütersloh, 1964.
Repgen, Konrad. *Die Römische Kurie und der Westfälische Friede.* Vol. 1. *Papst, Kaiser und Reich 1521–1644.* Tübingen, 1962.
Reutter, Lutz-Eugen. *Die Hilfstätigkeit katholischen Organisationen und kirchlichen Stellen für die im nationalsozialistischen Deutschland Verfolgten.* 2d ed. Hamburg, 1970.
Rhode, Arthur. *Geschichte der evangelischen Kirche im Posener Lande.* Würzburg, 1956.
Rhodes, Anthony. *The Vatican in the Age of the Dictators, 1922–1945.* New York, 1974.
Richter, Klemens. "Katholiken, Kirche, Staat in der DDR." *Stimmen der Zeit* 182 (1968): 133–36.
Riede, David C. "The Official Attitude of the Roman Catholic Hierarchy toward National Socialism, 1933–1945." Ann Arbor, Mich., University Microfilms, 1957.
Rieger, Julius. *The Silent Church. The Problem of the German Confessional Witness.* London, 1944.
Riemer, Martin. *Die neuzeitlichen Sekten und Häresen in ihrem Verhältnis zur evangelischen Kirche in Deutschland.* Gütersloh, 1926.
Ritter, G. *Carl Goerdeler und die deutsche Widerstandsbewegung.* Stuttgart, 1954.
Robertson, Edwin H. *Christians Against Hitler.* London, 1962. German ed. *Christen gegen Hitler* (Gütersloh, 1964).
Roger, Philip C. "The Peace Movement and the Religious Community in Germany." *Church History* 38 (1969): 300–311.

Roon, Ger van. *Neuordnung im Widerstand. Der Kreisauer Kreis innerhalb der deutschen Widerstandsbewegung.* Munich, 1967.

Rosenberg, Alfred. *An die Dunkelmänner unserer Zeit; eine Antwort auf die Angriffe gegen den "Mythus des 20. Jahrhunderts."* Munich, 1935.

——. *Der Mythus des 20. Jahrhunderts; eine Wertung der seelisch-geistigen Gestaltenkämpfe unserer Zeit.* Munich, 1930.

——. *Protestantische Rompilger. Der Verrat an Luther und der "Mythus des 20, Jahrhunderts."* Munich, 1937.

——. *Das Verbrechen der Freimauerei, Judentum, Jesuitismus, Deutsches Christentum.* Munich, 1921.

Ross, Ronald J. *Beleaguered Tower: The Dilemma of Political Catholicism in Wilhelmine Germany.* Notre Dame, Ind., 1976.

Roth, Alfred. *50 Jahre Gnadauer Konferenz in ihrem Zusammenhang mit der Geschichte Gnadaus.* Giessen, 1938.

Rothfels, Hans. *Die deutsche Opposition gegen Hitler. Eine Würdigung.* rev. ed. Frankfurt/Main, 1960. This volume first appeared as *The German Opposition to Hitler* Hinsdale, Ill.: Henry Regnery 1948) and has since appeared in a number of revised German and English editions.

Royce, Hans, Zimmermann, Erich, and Jacobsen, Hans-Adolf. Trans. Allan and Lieselotte Yahraes. *Germans against Hitler, July 20, 1944.* 3 ed. Bonn, 1960.

Ruhbach, Gerhard, ed. *Kirchenunionen im 19. Jahrhundert.* Gütersloh, 1967.

——, ed. *Das Widerstandsrecht Problem der deutschen Protestanten 1523–1546.* Gütersloh, 1969.

Ruhm von Oppen, Beate. "Nazis and Christians." *World Politics* 21 (1969): 392–424.

——. *Religion and Resistance to Nazism.* Princeton, N.J., 1971.

Rüppel, Erich Günther. *Die Gemeinschaftsbewegung im Dritten Reich. Ein Beitrag zur Geschichte des Kirchenkampfes.* Göttingen, 1969.

Rushbrooke, J. H., ed. *Fifth Baptist World Congress. Berlin, August 4–10, 1934. Official Report.* London, 1934.

——, ed. *Sixth Baptist World Congress. Atlanta, Georgia, U.S.A. July 22–28, 1939. Official Report.* Atlanta, 1939.

Ruta, Juan C., and Straubinger, Johannes. *Die Katholische Kirche in Deutschland und ihre Probleme.* Stuttgart, 1954.

Ruys, Bé. *Stimmen aus der Kirche in der DDR.* Zürich, 1967. A translation from the Dutch *Mieuwe Orientatie* (1965).

Sachese, Justizrat. "Sind die Mitglieder evangelischer Freikirchen (Sekten) im Gebiet der evangelischen Kirche der altpreussischen Union dieser Kirche steuerpflichtig?" *Verwaltungsarchiv* 32 (1927): 25–36.

Sammetreuther, Julius. *Die falsche Lehre der "Deutschen Christen".* Munich, 1934.

Sandmann, Fritz. "Die Haltung des Vatikans zum Nationalsozialismus im Spiegel des Osservatore Romano (von 1929) bis zum Kriegsausbruch)." Ph.D. dissertation, Johannes Gutenberg University, 1965.

Sasse, Hermann. *Das Volk nach der Lehre der evangelischen Kirche.* Munich, 1934.

——. *Die Weltkonferenz für Glauben und Kirchenverfassung. Deutscher Amtlicher Bericht über die Weltkirchenkonferenz zu Lausanne 3.–21. August 1927.* Berlin, 1929.

Sasse, Martin, ed. *Der Landeskirchenrat der Thüringer evangelischen Kirche und die Bekenntnisfront. Zum Kampf um die Autorität der Kirche.* Jena, 1935.

Sautter, Reinhold. *Theophil Wurm. Sein Leben und Sein Kampf. Mit einer Auswahl von Zeugnissen aus seinem Wirken.* Stuttgart, 1960.

Schabel, Wilhelm, ed. *Herr in Deine Hände.* Bern and Vienna, 1963.

Schäfer, Gerhard, ed. *Landesbischof D. Wurm und der nationalsozialistische Staat 1940–1945. Eine Dokumentation.* Stuttgart, 1968.

Schalk, Adolph. "Post-Conciliar Catholicism: Germany—A Mixed Picture." *Commonweal* 98 (1973): 283–88.

Schanze, Wolfgang. "Der kirchliche Zusammenschluss in Thüringen nach 1918." *Evangelisch-Lutherische Kirchenzeitung* 10 (1956): 243–45.

Scharffs, Gilbert W. *Mormonism in Germany. A History of the Church of Jesus Christ of Latter-Day Saints in Germany between 1840 and 1970.* Salt Lake City, 1970.

Scharnagl, Anton. "Das Reichskonkordat und die Länderkonkordate als Konkordatssystem." *Historische Zeitschrift* 74 (1955): 601–7.

Schellenberger, Barbara. *Katholische Jugend und Drittes Reich. Eine Geschichte des Katholischen Jungmännerverbandes 1933–1939 unter besonderer Berücksichtigung der Rheinprovinz.* Mainz, 1975.

Scheurlen, Paul. *Die Sekten der Gegenwart und neuere Weltanschauungsgebilde.* 4th ed. Stuttgart, 1930.

Schieder, Julius. *D. Hans Meiser DD. Wächter und Haushalter Gottes.* Munich, 1956.

Schlabrendorff, Fabian von. *Eugen Gerstenmaier im Dritten Reich. Eine Dokumentation.* Stuttgart, 1965.

Schleichert, Jürgen. *Staat und evangelische Kirche seit der Staatsumwälzung 1918 darge-stellt am staatlich-kirchlichen Vertragsrecht.* Cologne University, 1962.

Schleunes, Karl A. *The Twisted Road to Auschwitz. Nazi Policy Toward German Jews 1933–1939.* Urbana, Ill., 1970.

Schlingensiepen, Ferdinand. "Kein Heldenepos. Neuere Literatur über den Kirchen-kampf." *Evangelische Kommentare* 3 (1970): 413–15.

Schmidt, Dietmar. *Martin Niemöller.* Hamburg, 1959.

Schmidt, Fr. W. *Sterilisation und Euthanasie. Ein Beitrag zur angewandten christlichen Ethik.* Gütersloh, 1933.

Schmidt, Gerhard. *Selektion in der Heilanstalt 1939–1945.* Stuttgart, 1965.

Schmid, Heinrich. *Apokalyptisches Wetterleuchten. Ein Beitrag der evangelischen Kirche zum Kampf im Dritten Reich.* Munich, 1947.

Schmidt, Hermann. *Die Konstitution über die Heilige Liturgie. Text Vorgeschichte Kom-mentar.* Freiburg/B, 1965.

Schmidt, Jürgen. *Die Erforschung des Kirchenkampfes. Die Entwicklung der Literatur und der gegenwärtige Stand der Erkenntnis.* Munich, 1968.

Schmidt, Kurt D. *Die Bekenntnisse und grundsätzlichen Äusserungen zur Kirchenfrage des Jahres 1933.* 2 vols. Göttingen, 1934–36.

———. *Dokumente des Kirchenkampfes II. Die Zeit des Reichskirchenausschusses 1935 bis 1937.* 2 vols. Göttingen, 1964–65.

———. "Fragen zur Struktur der Bekennenden Kirche." *Zeitschrift für evangelisches Kir-chenrecht* 9 (1962–63): 200–228.

———. "Probleme und Ergebnisse der Forschungsarbeit über den Kirchenkampf in Deutschland." *Zeitschrift für Kirchengeschichte* 72 (1961): 120–33.

———. "Der Widerstand der Kirche im Dritten Reich." *Lutherische Monatshefte* 1 (1962): 366–70.

———, ed. *Zur Geschichte des Kirchenkampfes. Gesammelte Aufsätze.* Vol. 1. Göttingen, 1965.

Schmidt, W. *Geschichte des Lutherischen Gotteskastens in Bayern (1860–1930).* Neuen-dettelsau, 1930.

Schmidt-Volkmar, Erich. *Der Kulturkampf in Deutschland, 1871–1890.* Göttingen, 1962.

Schnabel, Reimund. *Die Frommen in der Hölle. Geistliche in Dachau.* Frankfurt/Main, 1966. Discussion and data on 2771 clergy of all nationalities who were imprisoned at Dachau.

Schneider, Burkhardt. "Pius XII. an die deutschen Bischöfe." *Stimmen der Zeit* 177 (1966): 252–66.

Scholder, Klaus. "Die evangelische Kirche in der Sicht der nationalsozialistischen Fü-hrung." *Vierteljahrshefte für Zeitgeschichte* 16 (1968): 15–35.

———. "Die Kirchen im Dritten Reich." *Beilage zur Wochenzeitung "Das Parlament,"* April 10, 1971, pp. 3–31.

———. "Zur gegenwärtigen Situation der Erforschung des Kirchenkampfes." *Verkündig-ung und Forschung. Beihefte zu "Evangelische Theologie."* 13 (1968): 110–33. A well organized bibliographical article.

Scholl, Inge. *Die weisse Rose.* Frankfurt/Main, 1952. English ed., *Students Against Tyr-anny. The Resistance of the White Rose, Munich, 1942–1943,* translated by Arthur R. Schultz. (Middletown, Conn. 1970).

Schöppe, Lothar. *Konkordate seit 1800. Originaltext und deutsche Übersetzung der gelten-den Konkordate.* Frankfurt/Main, 1964.

Schreck, Karl. "Aus dem Kampf der Bekennenden Kirche in Lippe 1933–1945." Mimeo-graphed, 1969. Copy in Bibliothek des Landeskirchenamtes, Bielefeld.

Schrey, Heinz Horst. *Die Generation der Entscheidung. Staat und Kirche in Europa und im europäischen Russland 1918 bis 1953.* Munich, 1955.

Schübel, Albrecht. *300 Jahre evangelische Soldatenseelsorge.* Munich, 1964.

Schuldis, A. *Werk aller Werke.* Freiburg, 1955.

Schwaner, Wilhelm. *Germanen-Bibel. Aus heiligen Schriften alter germanischer Völker.* 7th rev. ed. Stuttgart, 1941.

Schwerin-Krosygk, Lutz, Graf von. *Es geschah in Deutschland. Menschenbilder unseres Jahrhunderts.* Tübingen, 1951.

Schwital, Johannes. *Grosskirche und Sekte. Eine Studie zum Selbstverständnis der Sekte.* Hamburg, 1962.

Seraphim, Hans-Günther. *Das politische Tagebuch Alfred Rosenbergs aus den Jahren 1934/35 und 1939/40.* Göttingen, 1956.

Sherman, A. J. *Island Refuge. Britain and Refugees from the Third Reich 1933–1939.* Berkeley, 1973.

Simon, Ernst. *Aufbau und Untergang. Jüdische Erwachsenenbildung im nationalsozialistischen Deutschland als geistiger Widerstand.* Tübingen, 1959.

Simon, Matthias. *Evangelische Kirchengeschichte Bayerns.* 2d ed. Nürnberg, 1952.

———. "Landesbischof Meiser im Kirchenkampf." *Evangelisch-Lutherische Kirchenzeitung* 10 (1956): 61–64.

Smend, Rudolf. "Die Konsistorien in Geschichte und heutiger Bewertung." *Zeitschrift für evangelisches Kirchenrecht* 10 (1963–64): 134–43.

Smith, Joseph Fielding. *Essentials in Church History.* 13th ed. Salt Lake City, 1953.

Snoek, Johan M. *The Grey Book. A Collection of Protests against Anti-Semitism and the Persecution of Jews issued by Non-Roman Catholic Churches and Church Leaders during Hitler's Rule.* Introduction by Uriel Tal. New York, 1970.

Sodeikat, Ernst. "Die Verfolgung und der Widerstand der Evangelischen Kirche in Danzig von 1933–1945." In *Zur Geschichte des Kirchenkampfes. Gesammelte Aufsätze,* edited by Kurt D. Schmidt, pp. 146–72. Göttingen, 1965.

Söhngen, Oscar. "Hindenburgs Eingreifen in den Kirchenkampf 1933." In *Zur Geschichte des Kirchenkampfes. Gesammelte Aufsätze,* edited by Kurt D. Schmidt, pp. 30–44. Göttingen, 1965.

Solberg, Richard W. *God and Caesar in East Germany. The Conflicts of Church and State in East Germany Since 1945.* New York, 1961.

Spael, Wilhelm. *Das katholische Deutschland im 20. Jahrhundert. Seine Pionier- und Krisenzeiten 1890–1945.* Würzburg, 1964.

Speer, Albert. *Inside the Third Reich. Memoirs.* New York, 1970.

Spotts, Frederic. *The Churches and Politics in Germany.* Middletown, Conn., 1973.

Stadelhofer, Manfred. *Der Abbau der Kulturkampfgesetzgebung im Grossherzogtum Baden 1878–1918.* Mainz, 1969.

Stammler, Eberhard. *Churchless Protestants.* Translated by Jack A. Warthington. Philadelphia, 1964.

Stapel, Wilhelm. *Die Kirche Christi und der Staat Hitlers.* Hamburg, 1933.

Stasiewski, Bernard. *Akten deutscher Bischöfe über die Lage der Kirche 1933–1945.* Vol. 1. *1933–1934.* Mainz, 1968.

———. "Die Kirchenpolitik der Nationalsozialisten im Warthegau 1939–1945." *Vierteljahrshefte für Zeitgeschichte* 7 (1959): 46–74.

Steiner, Robert. "Der Weg der reformierten Kirchen und Gemeinden von 1930–1950." *Kirchliches Jahrbuch* 77 (1950): 228–332.

Stephan, Horst, and Leube, Hans. *Handbuch der Kirchengeschichte.* Part 4. *Die Neuzeit.* 2d ed. Tübingen, 1931.

Steward, John S. *Sieg des Glaubens. Authentische Gestapoberichte über den kirchlichen Widerstand in Deutschland.* Zürich, 1946.

Stimmen aus Maria Lach. 1865–1914. In 1914 it was united with *Stimmen der Zeit. Katholische Monatshefte für das Geistesleben der Gegenwart* (1866–).

Stoevesandt, Karl. *Bekennende Gemeinden und deutschgläubige Bischofsdiktatur. Geschichte des Kirchenkampfes in Bremen 1933–1945.* Göttingen, 1961.

Stokes, Lawrence D. "The German People and the Destruction of the Jews." *Central European History* 6 (1973): 167–91.

Stoll, Christian. *Dokumente zum Kirchenstreit.* 5 parts. Munich, 1934–35.

Stoll, Gerhard E. *Die evangelische Zeitschriftenpresse im Jahre 1933.* Witten, 1963.

———, ed. *Kirche an Ruhr und Weser. Das evangelische Westfalen.* Witten, 1964.

Stroup, Herbert H. *The Jehovah's Witnesses.* New York, 1945.

Sucker, Wolfgang. "Der deutsche Katholizismus 1945–1950." *Kirchliches Jahrbuch* 1951, pp. 290–334; 1952, pp. 236–376.

Tal, Uriel. *Christians and Jews in Germany. Religion, Politics, and Ideology in The Second Reich 1870–1914.* Translated by Noah J. Jacobs. Ithaca, New York, 1975.

Teping, Franz. *Der Kampf um die konfessionelle Schule in Oldenburg während der Herrschaft der NS-Regierung.* Münster, 1949.

Thadden-Trieglaff, Reinold. *Auf verlorenem Posten? Ein Laie erlebt den evangelischen Kirchenkampf in Hitlerdeutschland.* Tübingen, 1948.

Thiele, Friedrich, et al. Das Kirchensteuerrecht. Britische Zone mit den Ländern Hamburg, Niedersachsen, Nordrhein-Westfalen und Schleswig-Holstein, sowie Bremen und Saarland nebst Rheinland mit einem Anhang für Baden, Bayern, Hessen und Württemberg. Herne/Westfalen, 1947.

Thieme, Karl. "Deutsche Katholiken." In Entscheidungsjahr 1932. Zur Judenfrage in der Endphase der Weimarer Republik, edited by Werner E. Mosse and Arnold Paucker, pp. 271–88. Tübingen, 1965.

Thurmair, Georg, Sattelmair, Richard, and Lampey, Erich. Weg und Werk: die katholische Kirche in Deutschland. Munich, 1960.

Tiedemann, Helmut. Staat und Kirche vom Untergang des alten bis zur Gründung des neuen Reiches (1806–1871). Berlin, 1936.

Tiefel, Hans. "The German Lutheran Church and the Rise of National Socialism." Church History 41 (1972): 326–36.

Tilgner, Wolfgang. Volksnomostheologie und Schöpfungsglaube. Ein Beitrag zur Geschichte des Kirchenkampfes. Göttingen, 1966.

Till, Klaus. Der Einfluss des Kirchkampfes auf die Grundlagenproblematik des deutschen evangelischen Kirchenrechts, dargestellt insbesondere am kirchlichen Notrecht. Marburg, 1963.

Traub, Th. Lutherworte zum Verständnis evangelischer Wahrheit. Stuttgart, 1925.

Treue, Wolfgang. Deutsche Parteiprogramme 1861–1954. Göttingen, 1954.

Trevor-Roper, H. R. The Last Days of Hitler. New York, 1947.

———, ed. The Bormann Letters. The Private Correspondence between Martin Bormann and his Wife from January 1943 to April 1945. London, 1954.

Trial of the Major War Criminals before the International Military Tribunal Nuremberg 14 November 1945–1 October 1946. 42 vols. Nürnberg, 1947–49.

Trials of War Criminals before the Nuernberg Military Tribunals under Control Council Law No. 10. Nuernberg, October 1946–April 1949. 15 vols. Washington, D.C., 1952.

U.S. Department of State. Foreign Relations of the United States. Washington, D.C., 1861–.

Veit, Ludwig Andreas. Kirchengeschichte. 4 vols. Freiburg/B, 1933.

Verfügungen/ Anordnungen/ Bekanntgaben. Herausgegeben von der Partei. 7 vols. Munich, 1942–44. Considered secret and for internal party use; contains party notices and orders with exception of matters relating to mobilization and religious confessions. Some material relating to churches, especially in regard to racial matters.

Viebahn, Bernd von. Nationalsozialismus und biblisches Christentum. Breslau, 1934.

Vischer, Gustav A. Neuere Rechtsquellen für die Evang.- Luth. Kirche in Bayern. Evangelischer Presseverband für Bayern, 2d ed. Munich, 1959–. A loose leaf collection which gives not only Bavarian measures but also those of the Evangelical Church in Germany.

Voigt, Alfred. Kirchenrecht. Neuwied am Rhein, 1961.

Voigt, Gottfried. "Der Weg der Evang.-Luth. Landeskirche Sachsens in die VELKD." Evangelisch-Lutherisches Kirchenzeitung 10 (1956): 64–67.

Volk, Ludwig. Der bayerische Episkopat und der Nationalsozialismus 1930–1934. Veröffentlichungen der Kommission für Zeitgeschichte, Reihe B. Forschungen Bd. 1. Mainz, 1965.

———. "Die Fuldaer Bischofskonferenz von der Enzyklika 'Mit brennender Sorge' bis zum Ende der NS-Herrschaft" in Stimmen der Zeit 178 (1966): 241–67.

———. "Kardinal Faulhabers Stellung zur Weimarer Republik und zum NS-Staat." Stimmen der Zeit 177 (1966): 173–95.

———. Kirchliche Akten über die Reichskonkordatsverhandlungen, 1933. Mainz, 1969.

———. Das Reichskonkordat vom 20. Juli 1933: Von den Ansätzen in der Weimarer Republik bis zur Ratifizierung am 10. September 1933. Mainz, 1972.

Vollmer, Bernhard. Volksopposition im Polizeistaat. Gestapo- und Regierungsberichte 1934–1936. Stuttgart, 1957.

Vorländer, Herwart. Kirchenkampf in Elberfeld 1933–1945. Ein kritischer Beitrag zur Erforschung des Kirchenkampfes in Deutschland. Göttingen, 1968.

Walker, Lawrence D. "Le Concordat avec le Reich et les organisations de jeunesse." Revue d'histoire de la deuxième guerre mondiale 24 (1974): 3–16.

———. Hitler Youth and Catholic Youth 1933–1936. Washington, D.C., 1970.

Wall, Donald D. "The Reports of the Sicherheitsdienst on the Church and Religious Affairs in Germany, 1933–1944." Church History 40 (1971): 437–56.

Walter, Franz. Die Euthanasie und die Heiligkeit des Lebens. Die Lebensvernichtung im Dienste der Medizin und Eugenik nach christlicher und monistischer Ethik. Munich, 1933.

Warloski, Ronald. *Neudeutschland, German Catholic Students 1919–1939.* The Hague, 1970.

"Was machen die Kirchen mit der Kirchensteuer?" *Der Spiegel* May 27, 1964, pp. 38–61.

Weber, Hermann. *Staatskirchenverträge. Textsammlung.* Munich, 1967.

Weber, Klaus. *Der Moderne Staat und die katholische Kirche.* Essen, 1967.

Weber, Werner. "Die Umwandlung des Lizentiatengrades in den theologischen Doktorgrad." *Zeitschrift für evangelisches Kirchenrecht* 2 (1952–53): 365–74.

Wehrbahn, Herbert. "Zur Kirchensteuerpflicht der Protestanten in Deutschland." *Recht und Staat,* no. 167. Tübingen, 1952.

Wehrung, Georg. *Kirche nach evangelischen Verständnisse.* Gütersloh, 1945.

Weinberg, Gerhard L. *The Foreign Policy of Hitler's Germany. Diplomatic Revolution in Europe 1933–1936.* Chicago, 1970.

Weinkauff, Hermann, et al. *Die deutsche Justiz und der Nationalsozialismus.* 2 vols. Stuttgart, 1968, 1970.

Weisenborn, Günther. *Der lautlose Aufstand. Bericht über die Widerstandsbewegung des deutschen Volkes 1933–1945.* Hamburg, 1953.

Weizsäcker, Ernst von. *Memoirs.* Translated by John Andrews. Chicago, 1951.

––––––. *Prozess.* A collection of documents at the Institut für Zeitgeschichte in Munich.

Weltsch, Robert, ed. *Deutsches Judentum Aufstieg und Krise.* Stuttgart, 1963.

Wende, Peter. *Die geistlichen Staaten und ihre Auflösung im Urteil der zeitgenössischen Publizistik.* Lübeck, 1966.

Wentorf, Rudolf. *Paul Schneider. Der Zeuge von Buchenwald.* Giessen, 1967.

Werckshagen, C., ed., *Der Protestantismus in seine Gesamtgeschichte bis zur Gegenwart in Wort und Bild.* 3d enlarged ed. 2 vols. Bad Nauheim, 1927.

Wesenick, Jürgen. "Die Entstehung des Deutschen Evangelischen Missions-Tages." In *Zur Geschichte des Kirchenkampfes. Gesammelte Aufsätze,* edited by Kurt D. Schmidt, pp. 258–324. Göttingen, 1965.

Westin, Gunnar. *Der Weg der freien christlichen Gemeinden durch die Jahrhunderte. Geschichte des Freikirchentums.* Kassel, 1956.

Wetzer, H. J., and Welte, C. B. *Kirchenlexikon oder Encyclopädie der katholischen Theologie und ihrer Hilfswissenschaften.* 2d ed. 13 vols. Freiburg/Breisgau, 1882–1903.

Wilhelmi, Heinrich. *Die Hamburger Kirche in der nationalsozialistischen Zeit 1933–1945.* Göttingen, 1968.

Wilm, Ernst, *Die Bekennende Gemeinde in Mennighüffen.* Bethel, 1957.

Wischnitzer, Mark. "Die jüdische Wanderung unter der Naziherrschaft 1933–1939." In *Die Juden in Deutschland. Ein Almanach,* edited by Heinz Gunther, pp. 95–136. Hamburg, 1959.

Witetschek, Helmut, ed. *Die kirchliche Lage in Bayern nach den Regierungspräsidentenberichten 1933–1943.* 4 vols. Mainz, 1966–73. Reports from district governors and police presidents. There will eventually be a volume for each of the six Regierungsbezirke.

Wodka, Josef. *Kirche in Österreich. Wegweiser durch ihre geschichte.* Vienna, 1959.

Wolf, Erik. *Ordnung der Kirche. Lehr- und Handbuch des Kirchenrechts auf ökumenischer Basis.* 2 vols. Frankfurt/Main, 1960–61.

––––––, ed. *Gedenket der Lehrer, welche euch das Wort Gottes gesagt haben (Hebr. 13,7). Stimmen aus der Gemeinde für ihre geistlichen Führer.* Tübingen, 1947.

––––––. *Ich bin der Weg, die Wahrheit und das Leben, niemand kommt zum Vater denn durch mich (Johannes, 14,6). Der Kampf der Bekennenden Kirche wider das Neuheidentum.* Tübingen, 1947.

––––––. *Lasset die Kinder zu mir kommen und wehret ihnen nicht. (Matthäus 19,14). Der Kampf der Bekennenden Kirche um die Jugend.* Tübingen, 1948.

––––––. *Im Reiche dieses Königs hat man das Recht lieb. Der Kampf der Bekennenden Kirche um das Recht.* Tübingen, 1946.

––––––. *Suchet der Stadt Bestes (Jeremias, 29,7). Worte der Bekennenden Kirche an den Staat.* Tübingen, 1948.

––––––. *Wir aber sind nicht von denen die da weichen (Hebräer, 10,39). Der Kampf um die Kirche.* Freiburg, B., 1946.

Wolf, Ernst. *Barmen. Kirche zwischen Versuchung und Gnade.* Munich, 1957.

––––––. *Die evangelischen Kirchen und der Staat im Dritten Reich.* (No. 74 of *Theologische Studien*). Zurich, 1963.

Wolff, Fritz. *Corpus Evangelicorum und Corpus Catholicorum auf dem Westfälischen Friedenskongress. Die Einfügung der konfessionellen Ständeverbindungen in die Reichsverfassung.* Münster, 1966.

Wolfson, Manfred. "Der Widerstand gegen Hitler. Soziologische Skizze über Retters (Rescuers) von Juden in Deutschland." *Beilage zur Wochenzeitung "Das Parlament,"* April 10, 1971, pp. 33–39.

Wright, J. R. C. *'Above Parties': The Political Attitudes of the German Protestant Church Leadership 1918–1933.* London, 1974.

Wunderlich, Friedrich. *Brückenbauer Gottes.* Frankfurt/Main, 1963.

Wurm, Theophil. Erinnerungen aus meinem Leben. Stuttgart, 1953.

———, ed. *Tagebuchaufzeichnungen aus der Zeit des Kirchenkampfes. Zur Erinnerung an Frau Marie Wurm.* Stuttgart, 1952.

1974 Yearbook of Jehovah's Witnesses Containing Report for the Year of 1973. Brooklyn, 1973.

Zabel, James A. *Nazism and the Pastors. A Study of the Ideas of Three Deutsche Christen Groups.* Missoula, Montana, 1976.

Zahn, Gordon C. *German Catholics and Hitler's Wars. A Study in Social Control.* New York, 1962.

Zeitschrift der Savigny-Stiftung für Rechtsgeschichte—Kanonistische Abteilung. 1910–.

Zeitschrift für evangelisches Kirchenrecht. 1951–. This journal is a successor to *Archiv für evangelisches Kirchenrecht* (1937–42).

Zeitschrift für Kirchenrecht. 1861–1917. (After 1912, *Deutsche Zeitschrift für Kirchenrecht.*)

Ziegler, Georg and Tremel, Paul. *Verwaltungsgesetze des Freistaates Bayerns.* Munich, 1967–. A loose leaf collection of administrative law in Bavaria.

Zipfel, Friedrich. *Kirchenkampf in Deutschland 1933–1945.* Berlin, 1965.

Index

Ernst Christian Helmreich, Thomas Brackett Reed Professor of History and Political Science Emeritus at Bowdoin College, is a distinguished scholar in the fields of German history, religion, and religious education. The author or editor of several previous books, he has also published extensively in American and European journals.

The manuscript was edited by Sherwyn T. Carr. The book was designed by Richard Kinney. The maps were prepared by Theodore R. Miller. The typeface for the text is Optima, designed by Herman Zapf about 1958; and the display type is Gill Sans, designed by Eric Gill about 1928.

The text was printed on Arbor text paper. The book was bound in Joanna Mills Arrestox cloth over binder's boards. Manufactured in the United States of America.